Information Security Policies Made Easy

A Comprehensive Set of
Information Security Policies

Version 9.0

CHARLES CRESSON WOOD, CISA, CISSP

PentaSafe

PentaSafe Security Technologies, Inc.

Houston

Information Security Policies Made Easy

by Charles Cresson Wood, CISA, CISSP

© 2000-2002 PentaSafe Security Technologies, Inc. All rights reserved.
Printed in the United States of America.

Published by PentaSafe Security Technologies, Inc., 1233 West Loop South #1800, Houston, TX 77027.

Contributing Editor:	Scott Hayden, CISA, CISSP
Technical Editor:	Steven W. Martinson
Copy Editor:	Nadja Pollard
Production Manager:	Liz Carter
Cover Design:	Krista Kirkland
Printing History:	September 2002

ISBN # 1-881585-09-3

*To Andi for her vision
of what could be.*

CONTENTS

Chapter 1: Introduction 1

Chapter 2: Instructions 3

Instructions 3

    Information Security Policies 3

    Importance Of Policies 5

    Policy Development Steps 9

    Policy Development Time Line 18

    Policy Document Length 19

    Policy Usage 25

    Policy Objectives And Scope 26

    Disclaimers 29

Chapter 3: Specific Policies 31

Security Policy 31

    Information Security Policy 31

Organizational Security 35

    Information Security Infrastructure 35

    Security Of Third-Party Access 46

    Outsourcing 56

Asset Classification And Control 61

    Accountability For Assets 61

    Information Classification 65

Personnel 86

    Security In Job Definition And Resourcing 86

    User Training 105

    Responding To Security Incidents And Malfunctions 110

Physical And Environmental Security 124

    Secure Areas 124

    Equipment Security 137

    General Controls 146

Communications And Operations Management 150

    Operational Procedures And Responsibilities 150

    System Planning And Acceptance 163

    Protection Against Malicious Software 168

    Housekeeping 176

    Media Handling and Security 197

    Exchanges Of Information And Software 208

Access Control 270
    Business Requirement For Access Control 270
    User Access Management 280
    User Responsibilities 295
    Network Access Control 302
    Operating System Access Control 314
    Application Access Control 332
    Monitoring System Access And Use 338
    Mobile Computing 349
Systems Development And Maintenance 355
    Security Requirements Of Systems 355
    Security In Application Systems 359
    Cryptographic Controls 367
    Security Of System Files 380
    Security In Development And Support Processes 382
Business Continuity Management 392
    Aspects Of Business Continuity Management 392
Compliance 398
    Compliance With Legal Requirements 398
    Reviews Of Security Policy And Technical Compliance 450
    System Audit Considerations 453

Chapter 4: Sample High-Level Information Security Policy **455**

Chapter 5: Sample Detailed Information Security Policy **463**

Chapter 6: Sample Telecommuting and Mobile Computer Security Policy **475**
Management Issues 475
Access Control 476
Backup And Media Storage 476
Communications Links 477
System Management 478
Travel Considerations 479
Physical Security 479

Chapter 7: Sample External Communications Security Policy **481**

Chapter 8: Sample Personal Computer Security Policy **485**
Document Overview 485
Business Use Only 485
Configuration Control 485
Access Control 486
Viruses 486
Backup 487

Destruction 487

Documentation 488

Networking 488

Physical Security 489

Management 490

Chapter 9: Sample Electronic Mail Policy 491

Chapter 10: Sample Computer Network Security Policy 495

Purpose 495

Scope 495

General Policy 495

Responsibilities 495

System Access Control 496

    End-User Passwords 496

    Password System Set-Up 497

    Logon and Logoff Process 498

    System Privileges 498

    Establishment Of Access Paths 499

Computer Viruses, Worms, And Trojan Horses 500

Data And Program Backup 501

Encryption 501

Portable Computers 502

Remote Printing 502

Privacy 502

Logs And Other Systems Security Tools 503

Handling Network Security Information 503

Physical Security Of Computer And Communications Gear 504

Exceptions 504

Violations 504

Glossary 504

Chapter 11: Sample Internet Security Policy For Users 507

Introduction 507

Information Integrity 507

Information Confidentiality 508

Public Representations 509

Intellectual Property Rights 509

Access Control 510

Personal Use 511

Privacy Expectations 511

Reporting Security Problems 512

Chapter 12: Sample Intranet Security Policy **513**

Chapter 13: Sample Privacy Policy — Stringent **515**

Overview And Applicability 515

Definitions 515

Specific Requirements 516

Information To Be Given To The Individual 517

Individual's Right Of Access To Data 517

Individual's Right To Object 518

Disclosure Of Personal Data To Third Parties 518

Processing Confidentiality And Security 518

Monitoring Of Internal Activities 519

Chapter 14: Sample Privacy Policy — Lenient **521**

Company Intentions and Management Responsibilities 521

Disclosure Of Private Information 521

Appropriate Handling of Private Information 521

Private Information on Computer and Communication Systems 522

Activity Monitoring 523

Handling Personnel Information 523

Private Information from Job Seekers 524

Private Information About Customers 524

Chapter 15: Sample Web Privacy Policy **527**

Chapter 16: Sample Data Classification Policy **529**

Introduction And Overview 529

Access Control 530

Classification Labels 530

Labeling 531

Third-Party Interactions 532

Shipping And Handling 533

Declassification And Downgrading 534

Destruction And Disposal 534

Physical Security 535

Special Considerations For Secret Information 536

Chapter 17: Sample Data Classification Quick Reference Table **539**

Chapter 18: Sample External Party Information Disclosure Policy 543

Determining If Disclosure Is Appropriate 543

Resolving Problems With Disclosure Processes 544

Required Disclosure Records 545

Preparing Information For Disclosure 545

Chapter 19: Sample Information Ownership Policy 547

Chapter 20: Sample Firewall Policy 551

Appendix A: List Of Information Security Policy References 555

Appendix B: List Of Information Security Periodicals 557

Appendix C: List Of Professional Associations And Related Organizations 561

Generic 561

By Industry 563

By Market Segment 564

Appendix D: List Of Suggested Awareness-Raising Methods 565

In Person 565

In Writing 566

On Systems 567

On Other Things 568

Appendix E: External Network Interface Security Policy Harmonization 569

Access Control Considerations 570

Encryption And Public Key Infrastructure Considerations 570

Change Control And Contingency Planning Considerations 571

Network Management Considerations 571

Appendix F: Checklist Of Steps In Policy Development Process 573

Appendix G: Overview Of Policy Development Process Tasks 575

Appendix H: Real World Problem Cases Caused By Missing Policies 577

Government Agency 577

Law Firms 577

Oil Company 577

Local Newspaper 577

Midwest Manufacturing Company 578

West Coast Manufacturing Company 578

Major Online Service Company 578

Appendix I: Suggested Next Steps 579

Appendix J: Agreement To Comply With Information Security Policies **583**

Appendix K: Identify Token Responsibility Statement **585**

Appendix L: Management Risk Acceptance Memo **587**
   When To Use This Form 587

Appendix M: Two-Page Simple Non-Disclosure Agreement **591**

Appendix N: Index Of New Policies **593**

Appendix O: Index Of Policy Title Conversion **603**

About the Author **681**

Index **683**

Chapter 1   INTRODUCTION

Information security policies are a special type of documented business rule. There was no need for them 25 years ago. The explosion of information-handling technologies including cell phones, pagers, and portable computers has prompted this change. Those working in the business environment must have clear and definitive instructions that assist them in securing information in this complex environment. Just as it is unthinkable that millions of automobile drivers would be on the road without laws about the right of way, it is also unthinkable that millions of business people would operate systems without information security policies.

The importance of business rules such as information security policies is becoming appreciated by the top management at many organizations. All around them are projects that critically depend on clearly-articulated business rules. For example, some top managers may remember that when a legacy application was moved from the mainframe to the Internet, one of the important steps permitting this transition was the documentation of business rules. Without clear business rules, those creating a new system cannot be sure they are building something that will perform as management intends. Without information security policies, management cannot be sure that information systems are operated in a secure manner.

Historically, those who have worked in the information security field often were considered to be people who slowed down processes. Some people thought that information security was incompatible with the rapid pace of business required by the new Internet-based economy. This viewpoint quickly changed as people came to appreciate that Internet business was not possible unless an organization had done a good job in the information security area. To offer products or services through the Internet without adequately addressing information security is negligent and an invitation to security incidents that could severely damage an organization's reputation. Information security is coming to be appreciated as an expediter. To the extent that an organization can codify its business rules and internal processes, it can automate or outsource these rules and processes, and enter into new business relationships based on these same rules and processes and move ahead. For all of these projects and many others, information security policies provide clear-cut constraints defining a domain in which an acceptable solution can be found.

The centrality of information security policies to virtually everything that happens in the information security field is increasingly evident. For example, system administrators cannot securely install a firewall unless they have received a set of clear information security policies. These policies will stipulate the type of transmission services that should be permitted, how to authenticate the identities of users, and how to log security-relevant events. An effective information security training and awareness effort cannot be initiated without writing information security policies because policies provide the essential content that can be utilized in training and awareness material.

There are a wide variety of other compelling reasons to have information security policies. For example, policies are important reference documents for internal audits and for the resolution of legal disputes about management's due diligence. Some case law indicates that policy documents can act as a clear statement of management's intent, and thereby reduces management's potential liability. Policy statements can serve as evidence of management's intention to safeguard proprietary information. This is an essential but neglected step in the legal assertion of trade secret protection. Information security policies can serve as evidence of internal quality control processes. In this regard, not only can an information security policy statement give a business partner sufficient confidence to disclose confidential material, but a policy statement can also assist with an ISO 9000 quality control certification process.

While recent information security technological developments like digital certificates are impressive and hold great promise, the state-of-the-art in information security is relatively new. There are many things that cannot be cost-effectively achieved with existing technology. For example, a data classification label cannot be permanently attached to a piece of information so that the label follows the information no matter how the information has been summarized, edited, reformatted, re-transcribed, or merged with other information. Recognizing the limitation of technology is an important step in the process of appreciating the importance of policies. Because so much cannot cost-effectively be done by technological tools, it must be done by humans. Policies provide the most important and most frequently referenced source of instructions detailing how workers should protect both information and information systems.

Some people say information security is a people problem, while others say it is a technology problem. They both are correct. But before anything can be done about information security, management must get involved, allocate sufficient resources for information, and must clearly communicate to all staff members that information security is important. Information security is fundamentally a management problem. A variety of polls indicate that information security practitioners believe the number one key to information security success is the involvement of higher-level management. When writing an information security policy, top management should be engaged in a discussion about the organization's unique needs. It is through this conversation that management's eyes can be opened to the importance and criticality of information security. For more information on using information security policies, see Chapter 2, "Instructions."

Because policies have such a profound impact on all information security efforts, it is important that policies be clear, sufficient, and responsive to the information systems. While this guide can provide a starting point for most any organization, policies will need to be customized to suit the unique circumstances at each organization. Beyond this customization, information security specialists must periodically reexamine information security policies to determine whether the policies need to be modified. This guide is intended to be used a reference to support both the practitioners who are writing policies for the first time and those who are rewriting or expanding existing policies.

Regardless of an organization's size, industry, geographical location, or the extent to which it uses computers, information security is an important matter that should be addressed by explicit policies. Some experts say that the lack of a well-defined corporate information security policy is the single biggest problem with most security efforts. This guide provides concise policy examples that can be quickly tailored to the needs of any organization.

Much as many of us would prefer it to be otherwise, effective information security policies cannot simply be taken off the shelf, written-up, approved by a rubber-stamp process, and issued. Policies must be uniquely tailored to the needs of each organization. This is because the factors that drive information security policies vary considerably from organization to organi-

zation. These factors include business objectives, legal requirements, organizational design, organizational culture, prevailing ethics and morals, the extent of worker education, and the information systems technology deployed.

The ideas behind many information security policies are similar from organization to organization. This guide provides the essential content that should go into policy statements. But to have this content fit a particular organization, it will be necessary for the reader to be familiar with the factors described in the prior paragraph. Perhaps the best way to acquaint oneself with these factors is to conduct a risk assessment. For more information on this topic, see Chapter 2, "Instructions."

This guide includes most every policy now viewed as part of a non-military information security standard of due care. The standard of due care defines the minimum set of information security measures that organizations are expected to have, no matter in what industry the organization belongs. Many additional policies that go beyond this standard of due care because they provide a more rigorous level of security have been included in this material. These additional policies are provided to give the reader a more complete set of options that can be referenced when preparing a draft set of information security policies. Every organization should adopt a combination of policies drawn from the policies considered to be part of the standard of due care and from the additional policies that are provided.

While the notion of a standard of due care is widely acknowledged and supported, a worldwide standard that defines specific information security policies unfortunately does not currently exist. The closest document is International Standards Organization (ISO) document number 17799, which defines an outline and high-level guidance on information security policies. The policies in this guide are organized based on the ISO 17799 outline. Because significant developments in the legal, business, and information systems areas are coming at a rapid rate, there is some question whether a specific set of internationally-standardized policies will ever exist. As the next best thing, this guide and CD-ROM provide the most comprehensive collection of policies currently available anywhere. It is the responsibility of each reader to determine which of these policies are applicable to a specific organization.

Chapter 2 INSTRUCTIONS

INSTRUCTIONS

This section provides an orientation to the information security policy writing process. While it might be tempting to immediately start cutting and pasting policies together, it is very important that these instructions are read first. These instructions will provide background material that will make all subsequent policy writing tasks more efficient and focused.

This section provides guidance on the complex information security policy development process. This process includes writing policies, editing policies, obtaining management approval, communicating policies, and implementing controls to meet policy requirements. The last few subsections within this section contain hints and suggestions on how to best use this guide and the accompanying computer-readable material.

Information Security Policies

Distinct From Guidelines And Standards

Policies are management instructions indicating a predetermined course of action, or a way to handle a problem or situation. Policies are high-level statements that provide guidance to workers who must make present and future decisions. Policies are generalized requirements that must be written down and communicated to certain groups of people inside, and in some cases outside, the organization. Policies also can be considered to be business rules. Although information security policy documents vary from organization to organization, a typical policy document includes a statement of purpose, description of the people affected, history of revisions, a few definitions of special terms, and specific policy instructions from management.

Policies are mandatory and can be thought of as the equivalent of organization-specific law. Special approval is required when a worker wishes to take a course of action that is not in compliance with policy. Because compliance is required, policies use definitive words like "must not" or "you must." The words used to compose policies must convey both certainty and indispensability. For simplicity and consistency, throughout this guide, the word "must" has been employed, but equivalent words are acceptable.

Policies are distinct from, but similar to guidelines, which are optional and recommended. The policies appearing in this guide can be transformed into guidelines by replacing the word "must" with the word "should." As easy as this substitution may be, the transformation of the policies found in this guide into guidelines is not recommended. This is because guidelines violate a basic principle of secure systems design called "universal application" which means controls are significantly weakened if they are not consistently applied. Guidelines are desirable in some cases. For example, when work is to be done by a distributed group of individuals who cannot be compelled to comply with a policy, then a centralized information security function may appropriately issue guidelines as opposed to policies. This approach is commonly found when a centralized information security group issues a guideline for the preparation of departmental contingency plans.

Policies are higher-level requirement statements than standards, although both types of management instructions require compliance. Policies provide general instructions, while standards provide specific technical requirements. Standards cover details such as implementation steps, systems design concepts, software interface specifications, software algorithms, and other specifics. The phrase "information security architecture" is gaining increasing acceptance as a collection of integrated information security standards. Standards would, for example, define the number of secret key bits that are required in an encryption algorithm. Policies, on the other hand, would simply define the need to use an approved encryption process when sensitive information is sent over public networks such as the Internet.

Policies are intended to last for up to five years, while standards are intended to last only a few years. Standards will need to be changed considerably more often than policies because the manual procedures, organizational structures, business processes, and information systems technologies mentioned in standards change so rapidly. For example, a network security standard might specify that all new or substantially modified systems must be in compliance with International Standards Organization (ISO) standard X.509, which involves authentication of a secure communications channel through public key cryptography. This standard is likely to be revised, expanded, or replaced in the next few years.

Policies are generally aimed at a wider audience than standards. For example, a policy requiring the use of computer virus software packages would apply to all personal computer Users, but a standard requiring the use of public key digital certificates could be directed only at staff that conducts organizational business over the Internet.

Distinct From Procedures And Controls

Policies are distinct from and considerably higher-level than procedures. These are sometimes called standard operating procedures or department operating procedures. A policy statement describes only the general means for addressing a specific problem. Procedures are specific operational steps or manual methods that workers must employ to achieve a certain goal. For example, in many information technology departments there are specific procedures for performing backups of server hard drives. In this example, a policy could describe the need for backups, for storage off-site, and for safeguarding the backup media. A standard could define the software to be used to perform backups and how to configure this software. A procedure could describe how to use the backup software, the timing for making backups, and other ways that humans interact with the backup system.

The need to clearly differentiate between policies, standards, and procedures is emphasized by International Standards Organization (ISO) 9000 Quality Standards for the preparation of internal documentation. For example, these ISO standards explicitly state that policies must be separate and distinct from procedures. In some organizations, policies become detailed and lengthy, and in the process of development they become a confused combination of policies and procedures. While a clear demarcation between these document types is useful and highly recommended, nothing in this discussion is meant to imply that these different document types could not coexist in a paper binder or linked within an intranet documentation site.

Even more troublesome is the combination of policies, standards, and procedures in a single document. When it comes time to update such a document, the process is needlessly time consuming and confusing. This is because the three different document types all have different levels of detail and focus on different things. Because these three document types are intended for different audiences, this combination approach also runs a high risk that the material will not be read. People are very pressed for time, and if a document contains a lot of material that is not relevant to them, they will be likely to stop reading. The combination of policies, standards, and procedures in a single document is also not recommended because it can make the location of relevant information much more difficult for the reader. This combination approach is inefficient in terms of distribution because a lot of irrelevant information is sent to people who do not need it. To simplify document maintenance, usage, and cross-referencing, be sure to use separate documents for policies, standards, and procedures.

Policies are different from controls, also known as countermeasures, security measures, and safeguards. A control is a device or mechanism used to regulate or guide the operation of a machine, apparatus, system, or process. An example of a control would be encryption of sensitive data stored on floppy disks. In many cases, policies provide broad objectives that are met with controls. For example, a policy prohibiting actual or apparent conflicts of interest could be partially met through a control requiring employees to sign a statement indicating they have read the code of conduct and agree to comply. Likewise, in many instances, control measures are dictated directly by policy. For example, a requirement to sign a statement of compliance with a code of conduct might itself be a policy.

Importance Of Policies

With all of the attention that information security receives from the news media, one may believe that management understands what an information security policy is and why an information security policy is necessary. Unfortunately, this is often not the case. Before writing a policy document, management should be consulted to ensure that they are all talking about the same thing, and that they understand why a policy development effort is important.

The prior subsection, "Information Security Policies" provides specific words that can go into a memo to clarify work results. The sample policies at the end of this guide also can be submitted to management as rough approximations of the finished products that will be produced. The following section provides specific ideas that can go into a memo detailing the reasons why an information security policy is important. A summary of justifications for the adoption of information security policies is provided in the table labeled Table 1. Some of the more important reasons to have information security policies are described in their own subsections immediately following the next subsection.

Assuring The Implementation Of Controls

With hopes of handling information security expediently, management in many organizations simply purchases one or more information security products. In these cases, management often thinks the new products, such as hardware, software, information content, or services, are all that is needed. Soon after the products are installed, management is often disappointed to learn that the anticipated results have not materialized. In a large number of instances, this disappointment can be traced to the fact that management has failed to establish an adequate organizational infrastructure for information security. And one of the most critical components of an organizational infrastructure for information security is a policy document.

An example should clarify this essential point. Suppose that a large organization has recently acquired a single-sign-on access control package for a multi-user computer system such as a super-server attached to an intranet. Simple installation of the package will do little to improve security. Management must decide which Users should be given access to which information resources, preferably defining the ways to make these decisions in a policy. Management must establish procedures so that the technical staff can configure access controls in a manner consistent with these decisions. Management should define the ways to review system logs and other records generated by the access control package. These and other efforts constitute part of the necessary organizational infrastructure to support security products. Most technology vendors do not provide policies, procedures, and the other things necessary for the immediate usage of their products. The purchasing organization must come up with an organizational infrastructure. In part this is because organizational infrastructure is a function of, and must respond to each organization's unique requirements.

To establish a supporting organizational infrastructure, every organization needs a variety of documents. These include organizational responsibility statements, policies, standards, operational procedures, and enforcement mechanisms. Several management processes also are needed. These include a risk assessment process, a process for coordinating an information security management oversight committee, and an information security budgeting and planning process. Once responsibility for information security has been defined in departmental mission statements and job descriptions, the next step is to perform a risk assessment. Once an initial risk assessment is completed, an initial information security policies document should be prepared. Other documentation such as standards and operational procedures then grow directly from the policy document and subsequent efforts. The timing issues surrounding the preparation of policies are discussed in greater detail below in the subsection entitled "Policy Development Time Line" on page 18.

Guiding The Product Selection And Development Process

Most organizations do not have the resources to design and implement their own controls. They often pick and choose from the set of controls provided by information security product vendors, and they attempt to customize these controls with policies, procedures, standards, and other organization-specific integration efforts. This custom integration process is often performed without sufficient understanding of the security objectives and goals of the organization. As a result, the security products chosen and their implementation may not be responsive to the true needs of the organization. For example, the purchase of devices to bolt computers to desks may have been motivated by a number of thefts. In the absence of guiding policies, management may have selected a product that does not easily permit the secure storage of portable computers.

To avoid these problems, policies stating information security objectives and requirements can provide both the understanding and additional guidance that workers need in order to act as management intends they should. Such policies can be a way to ensure that in-house personnel are appropriately selecting, developing, and implementing information systems. For example, a policy can state that only virus screening software approved by Information Security management may be used on Company X systems. The actual vendor and product name can change from month to month without the need to change the policy. These details could instead be found in a standard.

Demonstrating Management Support

Some people, particularly Users and Information Technology department staff, often say, "When management tells me to, then I'll do something about information security." This attitude is not surprising when one appreciates that most people are unaware of the extent of the information security risks they face, just as they are not inclined to take the time to seriously analyze these risks. Beyond this, because they do not have the expertise, most people are unable to evaluate the need for certain control measures.

Policies are a clear and definitive way for management to demonstrate that information security is important, and workers must pay attention to information security. Policies can compensate for influences that may otherwise cause people to insufficiently protect information resources. One frequently-encountered example involves middle-level managers who repeatedly refuse to allocate money for information security in their budgets. In this case, the other influence is often a bonus plan that rewards them for keeping costs down. But if policies dictating management support have been issued by top management, then middle-level managers will not be able to continue to deny requests for information security funding.

Management at every organization must clarify its intentions with respect to the operation of computers and networks. If management takes the time to prepare an information security policy and other related documented guidance, when the time comes for

disciplinary action, prosecution, or litigation, the organization will not be subject to these same legal problems. Policies are a relatively inexpensive and straightforward way for management to define appropriate behavior.

Avoiding Liability

In addition to explicit statutes, an increasingly compelling body of case law is demonstrating that management and even technical staff may be held liable for inadequately addressing information security matters. The basis for this liability can be negligence, breach of fiduciary duty, failing to use the security measures found in other organizations in the same industry, failing to exercise the due care expected from a computer professional, or failure to act after an actual notice or compromise has occurred. Discussions about liability exposure and the need for policies are often successfully used to gain additional management attention and support for information security efforts. Internal legal counsel should be consulted prior to covering this topic with management.

Policies have been shown to be influential evidence in the eyes of the court that management has been concerned about and done something about information security. If the organization has not yet seriously addressed information security, it is important to promptly start work and to set the direction for future efforts.

Protecting Trade Secrets

Although the laws related to trade secrets vary from jurisdiction to jurisdiction, policies can provide extra protection for sensitive intellectual property. In a court of law, policies can serve as evidence indicating that an organization seriously took steps to protect its sensitive intellectual property, convincing the court that such intellectual property should be deemed a trade secret. If information is deemed a trade secret, an organization has additional legal remedies available that may make a case for larger monetary damages or the issuance of an injunction. Table 2-1 includes many reasons for establishing information security policies within your organization.

Table 2-1: Reasons To Establish Policies

Reason	Result
Expand information security budget and add more personnel.	Policy development process shows management what is needed.
Establish top management communication path.	Participation of management in the development process opens new channels.
Show definitive progress with minor investment.	Only days or weeks are required to generate a credible policy document.
Establish information security effort credibility and visibility.	A policy document should have a chief executive officer's signature on the cover page.
Shift worker attitudes and change perspectives.	The support of all workers who interact with information systems is critical.
Harmonize and coordinate the activities of many workers.	Consistent action is required if security is to be maintained.
Define the boundaries of permissible action.	Workers will clearly understand the boundaries of designated responsibilities.
Control security-relevant events in advance.	Increases chances that things will be done correctly the first time and reduces errors.
Exercise control by exception rather than micro-management.	Every action and decision does not need to be reviewed.
Overcome ambiguity that can lead to information overload.	A policy document will focus worker attention on the essentials.
Permit management to determine if a worker used poor judgment.	No disciplinary action is called for if poor judgment was involved.
Avoid disputes and related internal politics.	The rules to be followed and the boundaries will have been defined in the policy.
Enable rapid development of new systems.	The requirements will have been defined in advance so that they need not be revisited.
Coordinate activities of internal and external groups.	Policies will enable an extranet to be established or outsourcing organization to be used.
Achieve lower costs through control standardization.	The same approach can be used consistently throughout the organization.
Avoid problems because tasks are out of sequence.	On critical issues, staff will not be required to guess how to proceed.

Table 2-1: Reasons To Establish Policies (Continued)

Reason	Result
Prevent all decentralized groups from "reinventing the wheel".	By specifying policies centrally, local groups need not develop them.
Establish a starting point for a process of continuous improvement.	Policies are a baseline that can be referred to and improved upon.
Demonstrate quality control processes.	ISO 9000 compliance requires that business rules be clearly documented.
Establish benchmarks or reference points for future audits.	Internal auditors can determine whether compliance exists.
Guide security product, and service selection and implementation.	Uncoordinated local groups are less likely to go their own way.
Assure consistent implementation of controls.	Each exception weakens a control, and policies can mandate control compliance.
Arrange contractual obligations needed for prosecution.	Use policy compliance agreements and confidentiality agreements.

Adapting To A Dynamic Communications Environment

Workers in organizations are increasingly showing signs of burnout and information overload. The proliferation of new communications technologies such as computers, the Internet, fax machines, photocopying machines, and pagers has destabilized long-standing communications processes. For example, while it used to be polite behavior to return all telephone calls, this is no longer standard procedure if the one requesting a callback is known to be a salesperson. The lack of clear rules dictating appropriate behavior in this dynamic environment has made life more difficult for workers. To effectively manage worker expectations and to effectively guide behaviors, management must dispel this ambiguity by setting clear priorities and defining appropriate actions. The policy messages contained in this guide are intended to do just that for the information security domain.

Achieving Consistent And Complete Security

One of the most serious problems in the information security field involves fragmented and inconsistent efforts. Too often one department will be supportive of information security efforts, while another department within the same organization will be resistant. To the extent that these departments share computing resources, such as an intranet, the resistant department will be likely to jeopardize information security in the supportive department. This could, for example, take place if a hacker were to gain access to an intranet through lax dial-up user authentication processes within a resistant department, and then leverage this penetration to gain additional access that the hacker would not otherwise have been able to obtain. Although it is neither feasible nor desirable to make all persons in an organization familiar with the complexities of information security, it is important that they all subscribe to some minimum level of protection. In high-level terms, policies can be used to define this minimum protection level, sometimes called a baseline.

Coordinating Activities Of Internal And External Groups

Outsourcing and the use of contractors, consultants, and temporary personnel have become business necessities at many organizations. Today's organizations are also establishing close business partnerships with a variety of organizations, and in some cases these organizations are competitors. The large number of participants in business has made system access control, intellectual property protection, and related information security issues more difficult to manage. Because so many different parties are involved, there is a pressing need to consistently coordinate the activities of both internal and external groups. That is where information security policies can help. For example, a policy can address the circumstances where a confidentiality or non-disclosure agreement is necessary, and where it is not. Managers hiring contractors can then read this policy and manage these contractors so that internal information assets are properly protected.

Historically, sensitive information was often concentrated in the hands of middle and top management. These days, information is being pushed down the organizational hierarchy, out to lower-level employee desktops, and even further out to contractors, consultants, and temporaries. As a larger number of individuals get involved in the information management area, and as a larger number of people gain access to sensitive, valuable, or critical information, there is an increase in the need for information security policies.

Direct supervision of all of these people is impractical, and cost-effective technological tools to monitor every action they take are not yet available. Although organizations will rarely admit it, all of these people need to be self-managed, but they need instructions in the form of information security policies in order to do it right. The state-of-the-art in information security involves significant unsupervised reliance on people because sophisticated tools are not yet available. The number one tool for managing the behavior of people in the information security area is a policy document.

Policy Development Steps

Gathering Key Reference Materials

Information security policies should be largely driven by the nature of the information handled by the organization. One should acquaint him- or herself with the nature of the information handled by the organization. A good source for this information, also known as metadata, is a data dictionary. Overviews of internal information systems prepared for top executives, board members, merger and acquisition candidates, and strategic partners, also may be useful background to the policy writing effort. Because information systems change so rapidly, available documentation is likely to be outdated. Knowledgeable workers should be interviewed to accurately identify the nature of the information currently being handled by the organization, including what information is sensitive, what information is valuable, and what information is critical.

When developing a set of information security policies, a recent risk assessment or an information technology audit should be referenced that clearly indicates the organization's current information security needs. A loss history documenting the specifics of recent incidents, may be helpful in terms of identifying areas in need of further attention. Lawsuits, formal written grievances, and other disputes may identify areas that should be addressed in a policy document. To identify further problem areas, meetings with interested parties such as the in-house legal counsel, the director of Physical Security, the chief information officer, the Internal Audit director, and the director of Human Resources are advised.

To identify the policy areas needing further attention, copies of all other relevant and current organizational policy documents should be collected. Relevant policies include application systems development policies, computer operations policies, computer equipment acquisition policies, human resources policies, information system quality control policies, and physical security policies. If obtainable, policies from other organizations in the same industry can provide useful background information. If the organization is a subsidiary or affiliate of another organization, then the parent organization's policies should be obtained and used as reference material. If the organization is a participant in an electronic data interchange, value added network, a multi-organizational Internet commerce arrangement, or any other multi-organizational networks, the policies of these networks should be obtained and reviewed.

Some who are facing significant time or resource constraints will be tempted to skip the above-mentioned data gathering processes. Whenever data gathering is significantly abbreviated, the likelihood that management will reject the resulting document increases. It is through this data gathering process that management's view of information security can be identified, the policies that already exist, the policies that need to be added or changed, how management enforces policies, the unique vulnerabilities that the organization faces, and other essential background information. If serious consideration has not been given to this background information, it is unlikely that a newly written information security policy will be responsive to the true needs of the organization.

Another major reason to do a good deal of background research in preparation for policy writing is to ensure that the requirements defined in the policy document are consistent with management's intentions. One of the fastest ways to lose credibility for an information security policy writing effort is to propose a policy that is clearly inconsistent with existing organizational norms. For example, employees at high-tech company routinely downloaded games from the Internet and played these games on their powerful workstations during breaks and after-hours. Top management knew of and tacitly approved of these activities. At the same time, a published policy indicated that no personal use of the corporation's information systems would be tolerated. This glaring inconsistency caused a large majority of the workers at this company to dismiss the policy document as irrelevant.

Another important reason to spend considerable time on background research is to identify and define the organization's business-related strategic directions. A new or revised policy document needs to be consistent with these strategic directions if top management is going to approve and support the policy. For example, suppose an organization decides it wants to once again centralize its currently decentralized information systems activities. A policy document that stresses many activities to be performed by a group of decentralized information security coordinators would then be inconsistent with management's intentions, and consequently would be unlikely to be approved.

Yet another reason to thoroughly research the current situation before beginning the policy writing process is to identify the internal information systems architecture. An information security policy document should be consistent with and fully support an existing information systems architecture. This is not addressing information security architecture, but an information systems architecture. An information security policy document is typically developed after an information systems architecture is already in place. The development of an information security policy document will permit an information security architecture to be developed. For example, a policy about permissible access through an Internet firewall will enable a security architecture to be specified. It will also enable an appropriate firewall product to be chosen and implemented.

Defining A Framework For Policies

After the above-mentioned reference materials have been collected, a list should be compiled that contains topics to be covered in a new or more comprehensive information security policy document. The first draft of the list should include policies that are intended for immediate adoption and those that are intended for adoption in the future. In most cases, the level of detail in this list will be inconsistent, and at this stage in the process, this should not be cause for concern. For example, the list might include telecommuting and password construction with a minimum of 10 characters. When a high level outline is prepared, the level of detail should be standardized. For more information, see "Preparing A Coverage Matrix."

Next, an attempt should be made to define the ways in which the organization intends to express information security policies. For example, policies may be placed in a standard operating procedures manual. Alternatively, the director of the Information Security department may periodically issue electronic mail memos summarizing policies. It is common for privacy policies to be posted on the Internet. Because workers are bombarded by communications from many people through many different communication channels, it is essential that information security policies be repeated sent through multiple communication channels. For more information about suggested ways to communicate policies, see Appendix D, "List Of Suggested Awareness-Raising Methods." The channels used to express a policy will determine how the policy should be written. For example, if videotape will be used, then an abbreviated colloquial style should be employed. If a policy document will reside on an intranet web server, then a more graphic and hypertext-linked style is appropriate.

The ways that the organization currently uses or intends to use information security policies should be examined. Policies may be used to guide information system acquisition efforts, drive information technology audit plans, and assist Users in securely operating their desktop computers. For additional ideas about potential uses, see Table 2-1 "Reasons To Establish Policies." Defining the uses of policies will identify the audiences to whom policies will be addressed. For more information about identifying audiences, see "Preparing A Coverage Matrix."

Determining the uses for policies will also focuses attention on those areas that most need to be addressed. Other uses soon will be apparent after the policy document has been distributed. This should not be considered poor planning, but should be considered a successful initiative that has unforeseen contributions to the organization. In some instances, the uses of a policy document will be initially unknown, but these uses can be quickly identified through a series of meetings with interested parties.

Study of the style in which existing policies are written, the use of certain words, the conventional format for documenting policies, the system for numbering and naming policies, and the linkages between policies and other management directives like procedures and standards should be completed. For example, existing policies may use the word "must" consistently. To maintain consistency, the information security policies also should use the word "must." Likewise, the existing policies may have a military-style numbering system or something entirely different. The issuance of an information security policy document will be controversial by nature. Do not give critics additional ammunition by failing to be consistent with internal policy style guidelines, whether these guidelines are written or unwritten.

Part of the study of the existing policies and how they are used should entail a review of the level of detail appropriate for the organization's policy statements. The organization may have defined existing policies in very specific terms, in which case many detailed information security policies may be appropriate. Alternatively, the organization may have defined policies in very high-level terms, in which case only a brief overall information security statement may be appropriate. Both of these alternatives may simultaneously exist in that separate policies are provided to different audiences. The level of detail is in part driven by the extent to which management trusts workers to use their judgment, the extent to which specific documentation requirements are being observed, and the extent to which the topics being addressed are new to the involved audiences.

Information about the expression, use, style, and level of detail found in internal policies is rarely documented, but it can be obtained by examining existing policy statements. In very large organizations there may even be a document that provides directions on the policy writing process. In some large organizations, in-house staff in a Policy and Planning group can help with the policy writing effort. Whether explicit written guidance or in-house consulting assistance are available, to ensure their prompt adoption, new and revised information security policies should be written in a manner that resembles and is at least in form indistinguishable from existing policies.

Preparing A Coverage Matrix

After preparing a rough list of the areas needing attention, and after becoming acquainted with the ways in which the organization expresses and uses policies, the policies found in this guide now can be used. At this point the additional topics to be covered should be evaluated. Review the policy titles or the policies themselves, but skip the accompanying commentaries. This task is generally done most rapidly with the hardcopy guide and a marker such as a yellow highlighter.

To obtain additional ideas for the areas to be covered, this guide's Table of Contents can be used. While the Table of Contents is useful and does provide good coverage of the major topics, categories should be developed that uniquely respond to the organization's needs. Alternatively, categories reflecting the areas to be addressed also may be patterned after an internal audit report or an information security guide that management values. Another way to segment the controls would be broad control objectives such as "avoid," "prevent," "deter," "detect," "mitigate," "recover," and "correct."

At this point, a draft high-level outline reflecting the topics to be addressed should be developed. This outline is best if accompanied by a brief explanation with examples of topics to be covered in each section. The explanation can be only a sentence or two and just enough to provide a preview the topics included. At this point, distribution of the high-level outline to interested parties is recommended, and the constructive feedback received should then be integrated with the high-level outline.

At this point, a determination must be made of the proper audiences to which these messages are to be addressed. Often policies will be directed at several significantly different audiences because each audience has distinctly different needs. For example, end users might receive a small booklet containing the most important information security policies that they need to keep in mind. The focus could be on desktop computer information security issues. At the same time, systems developers and other technical staff might receive a considerably longer document that provides much more detail, perhaps focusing on security as part of a standard systems development methodology. Management may get yet another document that deals primarily with the tasks of information Owners.

While separate documents for separate audiences may sound like too much effort, the additional work is not great if a list of the essential messages to be communicated has been made. This list now can be split by audience, and it is this splitting process that is discussed in the next few paragraphs. The development and maintenance of separate documents for separate audiences is much easier if all of these documents are placed on an intranet. Using browser links, those who read the policy can be quickly provided with only the information that is relevant to them. For example, at a large bank, an intranet is used to segment the information security policies by job title. People need to read only those policies that directly apply to their own job. This intranet implementation also provides a key word search mechanism and an index, both of which help readers quickly find policies relevant to their current circumstances. Intranets can also now be used to administer quizzes to ensure that policies were understood.

When more than two audiences will be addressed by separate policy documents, it is recommended that a "coverage matrix" be prepared before actually writing the first draft policy documents. This can be achieved by preparing a separate detailed outline for each of the identified audiences. A coverage matrix is simply an organizational tool to ensure that all the appropriate information security policy messages are presented to all the appropriate audiences. It is a way of looking at the work to be done and can bring order to what otherwise may be a complicated policy writing effort. Once the topics to be communicated have been identified, and organized in a coverage matrix, the preparation of policy documents will be relatively easy and straightforward.

A coverage matrix in its simplest form is a two-dimensional table. It can, for instance, use the primary audiences to which the policies are directed as row identifiers, and policy categories as column headings. These policy categories are the major sections appearing in the above-mentioned high-level outline. The cells in the center of the matrix should be filled with reference numbers, each referring to a policy found in this guide and perhaps elsewhere.

Because there will probably be many columns, but only a few rows, a standard coverage matrix with the row headings filled in for audiences, with blank column headings for policy categories, and with blank cells in the middle for specific policies is recommended. Such a template coverage matrix then can be photocopied many times to save considerable time creating coverage matrices. If seeing only one portion of the coverage matrix at any one moment is acceptable, it is often more time-efficient if a spreadsheet program is used to construct and manipulate a coverage matrix. Use of a spreadsheet program also makes the generation of professional-looking hardcopy easier, just as it makes updates more straightforward.

Often only two or three audiences will be needed. Two possible audiences could be end users and computer-literate technical staff. Using another approach, three possible audiences could be end users, management, and computer support. In almost every instance, there will be a significant amount of overlap in the messages directed to each of these audiences. Make every attempt to minimize the number of audiences at the same time recognizing the needs of different groups to receive different information.

Table 2-2 provides an example of a matrix that can be developed. The policy numbers appearing in this matrix are place holders and are deliberately not the result of an analysis. Each organization will need to prepare its own coverage matrix, inserting policy numbers in the relevant cells to reflect its own unique business and information systems environment.

If the development of this type of a coverage matrix seems too time consuming, a similar table using broad categories such as those found in the Table of Contents to this guide can be prepared.

An alternative approach provides what could be considered a middle ground between a single policy and separate policies for different audiences. In this case, a broad umbrella policy document can apply to all staff, while separate specialized policy documents can be used to address audiences such as information Owners, systems developers, telecommuters, and other target audiences. With this approach there is a basic set of rules that applies to everyone, but then there are also special policies that apply only to selected audiences. At larger organizations with intranets, this approach is increasingly common.

Table 2-2: Sample Coverage Matrix

Audience	Computers	Data Communication	Risk Management	Physical Security
End Users	9.03.01.08 9.03.01.09 9.05.04.13 9.06.01.02	9.02.03.11 9.03.01.09 9.03.01.10 9.03.01.11 9.03.01.12 9.04.03.03 9.05.04.13 9.06.01.02	5.02.01.02 5.02.01.03 8.07.06.31	9.05.04.13 9.05.04.22 9.06.01.02 10.03.02.11
Management	9.04.07.01 9.05.04.13 9.05.04.22 12.01.03.02 12.01.04.23	12.01.04.04 12.01.04.87 12.01.04.88 12.01.04.89 12.01.05.16 12.01.07.03	9.03.01.08 9.03.01.10 9.03.01.11 9.03.01.12 9.02.03.09 9.02.03.10 9.02.03.12 9.04.03.04	8.04.01.15 8.07.05.47 8.07.05.48 9.03.01.07 9.03.01.08 9.04.07.01 9.05.04.22 9.05.05.06 9.05.05.07 9.05.06.01 9.06.01.02 10.04.02.02 12.02.02.01
Information Systems Department	9.04.03.04 9.05.03.03 9.05.04.22	8.03.01.15 10.02.02.02 10.02.02.03	6.03.01.04 8.06.01.01 8.06.03.06	8.01.02.01 8.03.01.19 9.02.01.01 9.05.04.08 9.05.04.13 9.05.04.17 9.07.02.16 10.02.02.05 10.05.01.07 10.05.01.08 10.05.01.09 10.05.01.10 12.01.04.20
Customers	8.03.01.20 8.03.01.21 10.05.01.14	10.01.01.06 10.01.01.07 10.05.01.04	9.05.03.03 9.05.04.22 9.05.04.23 9.05.06.01	9.05.03.03 9.05.04.23 9.05.06.01 9.06.01.02
Business Partners	8.02.02.07 8.02.02.08 8.02.02.09	5.02.02.04 10.01.01.08 10.01.01.09	9.03.01.04 9.03.01.05 9.03.01.06 9.05.04.24	8.07.06.09 9.05.02.01 12.01.04.32 12.01.04.42 12.03.01.01

In an effort to save time, some people often anticipate there will be only one audience. This one-size-fits-all approach may work for the first few policy statements that an organization issues, but the more sophisticated the information security effort, the less applicable this approach will become. It will often save a significant amount of time if the different audiences are targeted from the beginning of a policy writing effort, rather than having to keep modifying a one-size-fits-all policy that was originally intended to meet the needs of multiple audiences. The various audiences will also appreciate the use of separate documents. If separate documents are employed, they will not need to be repeatedly notified about changes that in many cases will not apply to them. The use of separate documents will permit differential treatment without confusion. For example, the rules for third-party access to an organization's information systems can be quite different from the rules for permanent employee access.

Just because there are different audiences for policies does not necessarily imply that there should be different documents. It is possible to have different chapters or sections in an information security manual devoted to different audiences. This approach is attractive because all the policies are then found in one document rather than several. Having all information security policies in a single manual facilitates maintenance and revisions. It is also attractive because individuals often find themselves falling into two or more of the audiences. For example, an individual may be both a general User and a systems developer.

Now the policy numbers should be written directly into the body of the coverage matrix. The process of filling in the body of the coverage matrix often highlights the fact that certain audiences are not being adequately addressed, just as it often indicates that certain areas need additional policies to be truly responsive to the organization's needs. If outlines for policy documents to different audiences were prepared, but no coverage matrix was used, these discrepancies may not have been revealed.

If an area is not adequately addressed, this guide's indexes or Table of Contents can be referenced to obtain additional ideas. The CD-ROM provided with this guide can be searched based on key words. For example, if additional virus policies were needed, a search for the word "virus" would quickly yield results.

After the overall topics to be covered have been clarified through a coverage matrix, a detailed outline of the soon-to-be-prepared policy documents can be compiled. Depending on the management at the organization, there may be a need to get interested parties to review a detailed outline. If no such review is required, then a detailed outline may not be needed. In this case, using the coverage matrix, the first policy documents can begin to be drafted.

Anyone who noticed a great deal of political uncertainty associated with the policy writing process may wish to prepare a detailed outline and subject it to a review process. While this may delay the process, it ensures that the resulting document is on target and truly responsive to the organization's needs. Where only one audience is being addressed, the coverage matrix can be dispensed with, but a detailed outline is needed. Either a coverage matrix or a detailed outline is important. Without one or the other weeks of wasted time writing policies on topics that are not needed or not wanted by management are at risk.

At this point, a decision on the categories to be employed in the policy document must be made. The categories in the coverage matrix or the detailed outline will do, although they will often be modified during the subsequent review process. The use of a large number of subtitles is recommended. This will assist readers in their efforts to quickly locate topics of interest. This will permit readers to skip sections that do not pertain to them.

In those cases where a very large policy document is being developed, or if a significant amount of complexity must be addressed in the policy document, a mind map can be used. Mind maps are graphical representations of the relationships between ideas. They generally use circles to represent ideas and arrows to represent the relationship between ideas. A mind map can be readily converted into a complex outline that can be used to develop a draft policy document. Various guides and software programs are available to assist with the drawing and revision of mind maps.

After the policy writing process is complete, the coverage matrix, outlines, and related working papers should be saved. In a year or two a revised policy document will probably be needed. It will save a lot of time if the person writing revised policies can consult the original working papers. The coverage matrix and related working papers may also serve as important information in a court case, should there ever be any allegations that management did not seriously think about the risks and the policy messages that needed to be communicated.

Similarly, the working papers should be retained for a year or two because internal and external auditors may wish to review them. Having the working papers in an accessible storage location can also be important if a member of the management team claims that his or her comments were not integrated into the final draft policy document.

Making Critical Systems Design Decisions

Before a final version of a policy document can be published, management often needs to make a number of security-related systems design decisions. Examples of these decisions include the:

- Groups of Users that will be given Internet access.

- Frequency that they will need access, whether continuous, regular, or occasional.

- Type of access they will need, whether electronic mail, web surfing, file transfer, remote logon, or chat rooms.

- Type of access they will need, electronic mail, web surfing, file transfer, remote logon, or chat rooms.

- Type of access control, whether dynamic passwords, fixed passwords, or smart cards.

- Types of user activity that will be monitored, whether files transferred, web sites visited, or hours per day of usage.

Identification of these and other systems design decisions is ordinarily indirect. Typically a draft policy document that incorporates a number of suggested options will be prepared. Unfortunately, in an effort to expedite the policy writing process, alternative solutions are not highlighted. As a result, management may approve of a policy document incorporating decisions with far-reaching implications, many of which were unappreciated at the time of the approval. This may lead to excessive costs for information security as the initial approaches described in the policy document soon need to be replaced or revised. It may also mean that the policy document needs to be changed much sooner than it otherwise would be.

If the project schedule and resources permit, the fundamental systems design decisions should be highlighted. If a paper draft of the policy is going to be circulated for comment, this could be accomplished by using footnotes or endnotes that describe the options and the pros and cons of each. Wording reflecting the different design decisions can be incorporated into the body of draft document. Seeing the options in context will often help management make these decisions. If the draft policy is going to be placed on an intranet server with restricted access to selected interested parties, certain words can be highlighted and links can be used to illuminate options and supporting justifications.

In organizations that have been attending to information security for some time, management will have already seriously considered all the necessary fundamental systems design options. In these cases, a policy writing effort will simply involve documenting the decisions already made, and choosing appropriate ways to express these decisions in the form of policies. In these cases, there will be no need for a separate review of the critical systems design issues as discussed above. Instead, the focus can be on the extension of these existing design decisions to new information systems such as extranets, and to new technologies such as new programming languages.

Structuring Review, Approval, And Enforcement Processes

Once the first draft of the information security policy document has been written, a few colleagues should review them. After the changes are made in response to feedback from these colleagues, the policy document should be sent to interested internal parties such as Internal Audit management and the Intellectual Property attorney. After a few critical allies have made changes, it is ready for review by the Information Security management committee. The next release of the draft can involve distribution to a much larger body of interested parties, for example all information Owners and all people employed in Information Systems. This review process is advisable because it builds on support from critical players, pre-selling the document to these critical players, and building support from these same critical players.

Many review cycles, each with more changes to the policy document, are often necessary. This should be viewed as standard procedure, and should in no way be taken as a personal insult. Multiple reviews are in part a reflection of the fact that the information security policy development process is highly political, emotionally-charged, and highly unstructured. Input should be welcomed with an appreciation that this iterative review process makes the policies more clear, concise, and responsive to prevailing conditions. Two appendices to this guide provide additional information on this process. For more information, see Appendix G, "Overview Of Policy Development Process Tasks" and Appendix F, "Checklist Of Steps In Policy Development Process."

The final step in the review process is the signature of the general manager, president, chief executive officer, or chairman of the board. A brief message indicating that compliance is expected as a condition of continued employment should be found on the first page of a policy document, or the opening web page if the policy is posted on an intranet server. This message should be signed by the top executive in a readily visible place so that the reader can have no doubt that the policy document is strongly supported by top management. If there is no realistic chance of getting the chief executive involved, the signature of the chief information officer may suffice. Settling for the approval of a middle-level manager is not recommended. The signature of Information Security management is generally insufficient to show top management adoption and support. While obtaining top management approval may sound like unnecessary marketing, experience has shown that a top management signature and accompanying message about expected compliance is critical to widespread adoption. Before management approves a policy document, it should already have been reviewed and edited several times by various parties within the organization. Perhaps the most desirable review body is an information security management committee.

An information security management committee is generally composed of representatives from departments within the organization who are interested in information security. Participants include members from the Information Security, Internal Audit, Risk Management, Physical Security, Information Systems, Human Resources, Legal, Finance, and Accounting departments, and various user departments. Such a committee typically oversees the work of the Information Security department. This management committee is used to filter and refine proposed policies, procedures, organizational structures, and other information security initiatives so that they will be readily adopted and implemented throughout the organization. In most cases, Information Security management will write a draft version of an information security policy, then submit it to the management committee for review and approval. If the organization does not yet have a management committee, development of an information security policy is an excellent time to propose the formation of such a committee. The committee is generally made up of five to eight individuals who have relevant expertise, who view themselves as influential in the information security area, and who can represent their own department or area of expertise. For more information about such a committee, see *Information*

Security Roles and Responsibilities Made Easy. The policy entitled, "Information Security Management Committee" also can provide guidance.

In some cases, a separate information security policy development committee is formed. Such a committee could be formed regardless of the existence of an information security management committee. This development committee may be a subcommittee of the management committee. If a development committee is created, it should not actually write the policy. Policies written by committees are often a combination of inconsistent ideas and poorly-organized thoughts that never seem to coherently come together into an integrated and understandable document. Instead, the first draft policy should be written by a single technically-competent individual, who has good writing skills, and is familiar with the organization's business activities. If a single individual, who may be on the development committee, will be responsible for writing the first draft policy, a development committee can be most useful. In this case, the development committee can be used for such things as identifying the topics needing to be addressed, preparing a high-level outline, identifying the ways that the policy will be communicated, and to provide editing suggestions.

In the absence of either of the two committees mentioned immediately above, special early review cycles with Internal Audit, Human Resources, and Legal management are highly recommended. These departments are important allies of Information Security and will be called upon to enforce an information security policy. If a draft policy does not have the blessings of these departments, it is unlikely to be taken seriously after it is issued. For this reason, some will meet with senior members of these departments prior to writing a first draft policy, just to ensure that everybody is in agreement about what should go into a policy document. Such meetings can take place even though representatives of these departments are found on one or both of the two committees previously mentioned.

While preparing new information security policies, an adequate enforcement process must exist or soon will exist. If policies cannot be enforced they will, in all probability, not be effective. To have policies that are not enforced may be worse than not having policies at all. This is because the policies may teach workers hypocrisy and tolerance for inappropriate behaviors. Having policies that are not enforced may also lull management into thinking that information security problems have been addressed when the reality is something else.

Management often believes that workers will naturally behave in a manner that is in the best interests of the organization. This is a dangerous and ill-advised assumption. Although policies are unlikely to affect the personal values of workers, management uses policies to give workers the opportunity to conduct themselves in a manner consistent with organizational values. Policies tell workers what is expected of them, that is if they want to continue their employment. Assuming there will always be a variance between personal values and organizational values, policies will be taken seriously only if effective compliance mechanisms are in place.

In advance of the issuance of new policies, ways to achieve compliance should be discussed with the Internal Audit or Information Technology Audit department. These might include compliance-checking tools such as software license management systems. Also consider the difficulty and advisability of conducting periodic manual compliance check efforts. The manner and means for the accomplishment of these compliance checks also should be envisioned in advance. Human Resources policies, such as a disciplinary process and an employee performance evaluation process, will need to be discussed in advance of writing policies.

Compliance in many instances can be assisted when computerized tools are used to assist the User. For example, at some organizations, management-approved non-disclosure agreements (NDAs) can be found on an intranet server accessible to all employees. Whenever an NDA is needed, a User can simply print the relevant form found on this server. The ready availability of tools such as this will help Users translate information security policies into action.

Policy enforcement need not be painful. Consider using special procedures to make a point. For example, if confidential information is left on top of a desk, the information can be taken and a receipt provided indicating how the worker can retrieve it. The second time confidential material is left out, the worker and the worker's manager both must retrieve the information. The third time requires the worker, the worker's manager, and a vice president. A fourth time could be reason to discontinue the worker's employment.

Enforcement actions are often more effective if workers have are aware of what activities would be information security policy violations, and exactly what penalties would be encountered if they were caught. Establishing clear expectations through an information security awareness program is a very important part of an effective and enforceable set of policies. Such awareness programs might, for example, clearly state that business information is the property of Company X, and that it must not to be copied, modified, deleted, or used for unintended purposes without management approval.

Do not attempt to guide workers and positively influence their behavior. It should not be the intent to catch people and discipline the offending worker. While punishment should be used for offenders as necessary, it is not the intent of enforcement mechanisms to generate large numbers of out-of-compliance notices. If a large number of people are out-of-compliance, this is an indication that the policies and related awareness programs have been ineffective. In these situations, the intention behind the policies may need to be communicated more effectively, or the policies may need to be modified to better reflect the organizational culture or prevailing operating circumstances.

Automating Policy Enforcement Through Policy Servers

At many organizations, the complexity of information systems is overwhelming the ability of staff to manage these systems. To deal with this complexity, new expert systems tools are being introduced. For example, some firewalls include an expert system that will tell the person doing the installation whether a configuration inadvertently has created a serious security vulnerability. To deal with this increased complexity, organizations will need to have more centralized network management systems that play an increasing array of information security roles. For example, network management systems can, and in some organizations do, act as a conduit for the relay of intrusion detection information to a network operator on duty.

An interesting new development along these lines is called a policy server. Policy servers take organization-specific policies and code them in a special machine-readable language that then can be accessed by a wide variety of operating systems, access control packages, and network management systems. Examples of these policies or rules include the minimum number of characters in a password, the maximum number of logon attempts before a connection will be severed, and whether attachments to electronic mail files will be passed through firewalls. In many ways a policy server is expected to be like an active data dictionary because it will be called upon to provide definitive instructions from a centralized point. In the near future, suites of products from a single vendor, and suites from a combination of vendors, will start to perform some of the rationalizing and centralizing tasks of a policy server.

To prepare their organizations for these upcoming developments, consideration should be given to how the policies they develop today will be put into the computer models of tomorrow. Attempts should be made to be as logical and straightforward as possible. Not only will this help the readers understand how to behave when it comes to information security, but it will also help tomorrow's programmers in their efforts to create computer-enforced rules. Attempts also should be made to achieve the most cross-organization, cross-network, cross-system, and cross-platform coordination of information security policies. This will also reduce complexity and permit the organization to more readily adopt new policy enforcement tools.

Policy Development Time Line

Before one embarks on an effort to write and obtain management approval for information security policies, it is advisable to clarify who is responsible for issuing and enforcing policies. Only when a clear assignment of responsibility for information security policies exists, should a policy development effort be initiated. Often this means that a centralized information security group mission statement should be prepared and approved before a policy-writing effort gets underway. If responsibility has not yet been clearly assigned, this should be the first step in a policy development effort. If this important step is ignored, be prepared for a barrage of internal politics that is likely to significantly delay the policy writing progress.

Another necessary prerequisite for successfully writing information security policies involves management's perspective. Only after management appreciates that information itself has become a critical factor of production will information security be recognized as a serious matter deserving their attention. This perspective is known by a number of phrases including "information resource management" and "recognizing information as an asset." Management must realize that they are responsible for managing information itself. Historically, management thought information was used only to manage other resources such as people. Management must appreciate that new tools and techniques are needed to manage information itself. In the midst of this discussion, it is appropriate to mention the significant contribution that policies can make. If management does not understand how important information is to their organization, they will be unlikely to support information security policy writing efforts. For more information about this topic, see "Policy Objectives And Scope" on page 26.

Management should acknowledge that there is an information security problem, and that policies are required to address this problem. This must occur before a serious policy writing effort is initiated. While this may appear to be obvious, many good-intentioned policy writing efforts have gone nowhere because the necessary groundwork had not yet been established. This groundwork often includes a brief awareness presentation. Topics at this presentation can include risks that the organization faces, the organization's loss history, incidents suffered by other organizations in the same industry, and generally accepted approaches for dealing with these risks and incidents.

Ideally, a policies development effort should be initiated after the performance of a comprehensive information security risk assessment. The risk assessment should indicate, perhaps only in high-level terms, the value of the information, the risks to which this information is subjected, and the vulnerabilities associated with the current way of handling this information. A risk assessment will provide useful background information that the can be used when selecting appropriate policies from this guide. The general threat types faced by the organization and other general background information from a risk assessment also may be included in an information security policy document introduction or preface.

One of the best times to develop an information security policy is when an information security manual is being prepared. Because a manual is distributed widely throughout an organization, it is an excellent place to put information security policies. Specific written policies also may be prepared just before compiling the material for user training and awareness efforts. These efforts may include a videotape, lectures, posters, or articles in an in-house newspaper. For more information on developing security policies, see Appendix D, "List Of Suggested Awareness-Raising Methods."

Another good time to prepare policies is right after a major information security breach, unfavorable computer-related audit report, security-related lawsuit, or some other type of loss that receives extensive top management attention. This is a good time to move ahead with policy development efforts because management, is especially supportive of and concerned about information security. It is important to work fast at these times because management's level of concern declines rapidly.

To provide direction for the preparation of system development guidelines, access control package implementation memos, computer technical standards, internal control procedural descriptions, and other more specific information security documents, policies should be prepared early in the life cycle of an information security effort. An initial set of policies is typically brief, and is followed by more detailed policy statements addressing specific areas of concern. Examples include telecommuting policies, Internet policies, and user application development policies.

A good objective to keep in mind when writing policies is that they should be written so that they need not be modified for three years. Because things change so often in the information systems field, policies will often be modified only a year or two after issuance. To prevent policies from quickly becoming out dated, policies should be written that are independent of specific commercial products, vendors, and organizational structures. Being independent of these areas does not preclude the insertion of general statements addressing these areas in a policy document. For example, the need for dynamic passwords is often articulated in policy documents, but the vendors and products used to provide dynamic passwords are not generally found in these documents.

Given the lightning-fast pace of changes in the information systems field, attempt to get management to agree in advance that time will be set aside to rewrite the policy document a year or two in the future. In recognition of the need to keep updating information security policies, this guide is also periodically updated. If you are using an older version of this guide, you may wish to contact the publisher to inquire about the availability of a more current version.

Policy Document Length

Determining An Appropriate Number Of Policies

To be effective, information security policies must be tailored to the unique needs of an organization. Some organizations have many policies, while others have only a few. For example, the information security policy manual at one leading telephone company is over 150 pages, at a large aerospace company it is 75 pages, and at a well-known railroad, it is 25 pages. While range in the number of pages across organizations is quite wide, the trend is clearly to have more detailed and therefore longer policy documents.

While industry category is a critical determinant of the number of pages in a policy document, so too is management's view of centralization of the information security function. If local management discretion is valued and encouraged, the policy document generally will be less detailed and therefore shorter. If centralized control is valued and encouraged, then a policy document generally will be more detailed and therefore longer. Most organizations have a combination of these two, where certain information security activities are managed in a decentralized fashion, while others are managed in a centralized fashion. For example, local information security coordinators may handle user ID issuance and password resets at a departmental level, but centralized information security staff may be used for network security matters such as firewall maintenance.

Some management teams will think it is appropriate to be clear about information security matters. In these cases, there may be a need for many policies. Some managers are reluctant to have many policies, preferring to stress reliance on the professional judgement of workers. Other managers want to keep a document brief because they fear that workers will get the impression that they are not trusted. But do not be shy and overly concerned about minimizing the impact on corporate culture. There are some basic information security requirements that must be communicated by policy, and those should be included in a policy document even if they will provoke difficult questions like the appropriate level of trust in workers.

The audiences to be addressed may be highly-literate, such as at a research institute, in which case more written material may be appropriate. The audiences may be marginally literate, such as a manufacturing organization that employs immigrants from countries that speak a different language. An organization may be accustomed to documenting internal business processes, in which case more policies will generally be appropriate. On the other hand, an organization may have deliberately chosen to keep documentation at a minimum, in which case fewer policies will generally be needed.

Although a concise set of policies is more likely to be completely read, there is much to be said for a comprehensive set of information security policies. For example, an employer will find it easier to defend itself in court against employee charges of privacy invasion if policies were very explicit. More importantly, a comprehensive set of policies provides definitive guidance for workers. The definitive guidance in a long policy statement can be quite useful in a court of law where there is need for evidence to show that management has been diligently addressing information security. Longer policy statements are also helpful with disciplinary actions because they explicitly define expected behavior patterns.

Another factor affecting the length of a policy document involves management's expectations for a high-level or a low-level policy document. A high-level document would typically define worker responsibilities and a few major control measures such as dynamic password tokens. A low-level policy would typically get into much more detail, and may make reference to both tasks and procedures. If guidance has not been received from management on this point, be sure to clarify this area before actually preparing a policy document outline.

Internet and intranet technology is also altering the appropriate length of policy documents. In the past, policy documents were sent to workers typically through the delivery of paper. Now policy documents can passively reside on an intranet server, and can be accessed when workers need the information. This means that documents can be more detailed than they were before without imposing any additional burden on workers. Likewise, the hot links that this technology provides facilitate the establishment of interconnections between documents, which permits Users to more quickly locate material of interest.

One overall strategy to minimize the length of a policy document involves mentioning only prohibitions. With this strategy, readers of a policy document will hear primarily about what they should not do, not so much about what they should. There are exceptions to this overall rule. For example, workers should report security incidents to someone who is in a position to take appropriate action. This is something that workers should do, not what they should not do. But in general there is merit to this strategy. With this strategy, document length can be minimized because the set of prohibitions is considerably smaller than the set of actions that workers are supposed to perform. Because it involves only minimal instructions, this strategy can also

provide flexibility as business activities change. Provided that the supporting information systems do not significantly change, such a policy statement can be relevant.

As a general principle of policy writing, it is wise to issue only those policies that are absolutely needed. This is because people are inherently different, as are the groups that they form. To have only those policies that are absolutely needed permits personal initiative, creativity, and an expression to be manifested. Although humans have a tendency to generalize and standardize, this is often taken too far. An example would be an organization that has so many security policies and procedures that they interfere with getting the work done. With this in mind, consider selecting a minimum set of policies that will then be issued on an organization-wide basis, then leave the rest up to departmental, divisional, and other local management.

Rather than starting out with a comprehensive effort, it is best to focus on only the essentials, producing a slim and concise policy statement. Then as circumstances warrant, add additional policies. This approach often takes the form of separate policy statements addressing problem areas such as the Internet and telecommuting. Because it asks for a smaller number of concessions at a particular point, this phased approach is also much more likely to get management approval and user compliance. Both the visibility and the good reputation of an information security effort are more likely to be maintained at high levels with such a phased approach because it forces the obtaining of frequent approval and feedback.

The best way to protect information and information systems will always depend on the circumstances. Factors like the type of Users, the computer equipment configuration, and the sensitivity of the information will dictate what should be done when it comes to information security. Although some people would like it to be otherwise, policies can never define the true and optimal path for all situations at all times. An open mind and a willingness to deal with the circumstances will go a long way toward finding workable information security solutions. An exhaustive set of policies that denies the reality of each situation, and that denies personal responsibility, is bound to inhibit information security, if not generate rebellion and disdain. Try to write policies that provide minimal guidance, yet permit situation-specific responses to the truth of the moment.

Another way to look at the appropriate number of policies involves the intention to make information security as user transparent as possible. The more information security is made user transparent, the more likely it is to be accepted. The more user transparent it is, the less the need for written policies. Policies in large measure address areas where vendors do not yet have user transparent automated solutions. These areas are where we must rely on Users and other workers. When vendors provide sufficiently reliable user transparent cross-platform security solutions, there will be a significantly reduced need for written policies. That ideal world seems many years away, so in the meanwhile a good number of policies will continue to be necessary.

The number of policies to prepare is also a function of the involved audiences. Many organizations prepare several information security policy documents. For example, separate documents might be respectively compiled for users, management, and technical staff. Many of the policies in each of these documents will be the same, although the degree of detail, the technical words used, and the number of examples will generally vary from one document to another. If the audience is composed of end users, the number of policies ideally should be limited to several pages. For a management audience, there will be additional considerations, such as legal matters, and this is likely to expand the number of policies required. A set of policies for technical staff will most often be longer, more technical, and more detailed. To assist with this audience-related segmentation of policies, following the commentary for each policy is an audience designation.

Another factor affecting the number of policies needed is the degree of security required at the organization. As a broad and general indicator, the more information intensive the activities of an organization, the higher the need for security. For example, a bank will have many policies, whereas a chain of coffee shops will have few policies. Involvement in especially sensitive activities such as human life support or national defense will also raise the need for security. An organization with low level security needs, such as a car-wash company, will generally have fewer policies, just as it will have fewer implemented information security measures. An organization with significant security needs, such as an insurance company, will generally have more policies, just as it will have more implemented information security measures.

Although primarily commercial and civilian-government in their orientation, most the policies listed in this guide are applicable to any organization. There are some policies that are relevant only to organizations with certain levels of security. At the end of the commentary section for each policy there is an indication of the environment where this policy would best be used.

Determining Policy Length

Beyond the number of policies, consideration should be given to how long each policy should be. The policies appearing in this document are deliberately kept to a single sentence. This concise statement of policy fosters acceptance by workers because it is both easily read and understood. Keeping policy statements concise also emphasizes that policies provide overall guidance, not the details about handling every conceivable circumstance. The details typically appear in information security standard documents and standard operating procedure manuals.

Another policy length consideration is that they need to be specific enough to be clearly understood and consistently interpreted. At the same time, policies should not be so specific that they eliminate an opportunity for local management to tailor them to local conditions. For example, management may issue a policy that specifies that all users must have passwords that are difficult for unauthorized persons to guess. This policy gives local management the latitude to determine whether they want to use system-generated passwords, or whether they want to permit users to choose their own passwords, perhaps accompanied by a mechanism to ensure that users are doing a good job.

The length of each policy is a reflection of how many options management wants to specify. For example, management can specify that it is sufficient that all connections to an internal network must have a firewall or another approved access control system, or can include what type of a firewall will be used, such as a packet-filtering firewall or an application-filtering firewall. Management also can include what services will be transmitted through the firewall. Generally, it is advisable to keep the policy statements relatively high-level, and to deal with the details, such as those described in the last two questions, in a standard or other supplementary document. Not only will this mean that the policy will be approved more quickly, it will also mean that the policy will not need to keep being modified as the circumstances change.

For those who feel they must produce a policy document with great specificity, the possible options should be identified and evaluated before the policy is written. Reviewing all the options for every policy with management generally results in an extension of the project far into the future. Instead, an expedient way to proceed would be to have the technical decisions made by a small group of employees, perhaps an Information Systems Management Committee. For each controversial policy, the small group can then prepare a list of options, with an indication of the pros and cons. This list can then be taken to management for a brief discussion and pre-approval. This approach can significantly increase the likelihood that the final policy is approved because controversial points have been pre-sold with these supplementary lists and associated discussions.

Some organizations may wish to provide specific examples clarifies policies, although it significantly expands the length of each policy statement. As an illustration of this approach, a policy that prohibits the personal use of Company X information system resources could be followed by examples discussing Internet game playing or the use of the organization's telephones for socializing. Examples make a policy real and tangible rather than abstract. Examples also significantly reduce errors in the interpretation and application of a policy. At the same time, examples may appear to the reader to be demeaning, redundant, and unnecessary. In most cases, examples are not provided with policies except in those circumstances where confusion or disputes are expected.

Another important part of a policy document that may also affect its length, involves explanations of the intentions for policies. If they are going to support information security policies, workers will need to understand why policies are important. The amount of material needed to convey the intention for policies can vary considerably based on the audience involved. As information security is increasingly discussed in the news media, the general public is coming to appreciate what the risks are. This means that the need for words explaining the intention behind a policy document is markedly decreasing. Just in case it is needed, the overall intention for each policy can be found in the commentary section after each policy in this guide. In most organizations, intentions are communicated by in-person training sessions, computer based training software, or some other means besides a written policy.

Other parts of an information security policy document that are not mentioned above, but that may make a significant contribution to the size of a document include a statement of purpose, table of contents, index, glossary, an information-security-related organizational structure chart, statement of information security responsibilities, list of relevant internal documents, risk assessment methodology description, set of information systems security standards, set of information security procedures, history of document revisions, and a case study indicating how the material should be applied. The specific materials to include in a policy document must be determined by the needs of the organization, the organization's sophistication in the information security area, the documents that have been released already, and the responsibilities of the group preparing the policies. An information security policy document that includes all of the above-mentioned supplementary materials can be lengthy, for example 100 pages or more.

Iterative Development Process

If a more comprehensive set of policies is required, a two-step process is recommended. The first step involves obtaining management approval for a generalized set of policies, and the second step involves approval for a more specific set of policies. The generalized set of policies could include only 30-50 policies, and the specific set could include another 50-150 policies. An example of a generalized policy would be the need to positively identify all users prior to giving them access to internal systems. An example of a specific policy would be the need to use identity tokens that generate dynamic passwords whenever a user connects to an internal network from an external location. In order to be able to accommodate both situations, there are both general and specific policies in this guide.

A two-step process is also advisable because it permits the information security group to initially focus on fundamental conceptual models, such as information ownership and data sensitivity classification. After these conceptual models have been emphasized with an initial policy document and communicated through a basic information security awareness program, more detailed requirements can be expressed in a larger policy document. Despite whether this two-step approach is employed, the fundamental conceptual models on which the policies are based should be identified. These conceptual models also should be included in the policy document or other material previously communicated to the relevant audiences.

It is recommended to take an audience-driven approach to policy development. Policies can generally be divided into those for end users and management, and those for programmers, systems designers, and related technical people. The first of these audiences may be addressed in an initial policy development effort, while a subsequent effort could address the second audience.

If the initial set of policies sent to management is too long or severe, management may reject it. As a result, the window to get policies approved may be closed for a certain period. The first set of policies should be kept brief and be relatively easy to comply with. Later, when the first set has been endorsed and implemented throughout the organization, a more comprehensive and more stringent list of policies can be prepared. It is far better to proceed relatively slowly with a series of policy development efforts, in a manner that has credibility and frequent management communication, than it is to prepare a single giant policy document that is then rejected because it was perceived to be too much too fast, and too soon.

It is suggested that policies be written with the classic trial-and-error strategy for dealing with complex problems. After a brief policy has been issued, effects of this policy should be observed, including user reactions and problems with compliance. The undesired effects should be corrected by issuing new or modified policies. The effects of these corrections should be noted, and again corrected for undesired side effects.

Policies should be reviewed periodically, at least annually, to ensure that they are relevant and effective. It is important to eliminate policies that are no longer applicable. Efforts to streamline policies will be appreciated by both management and users. These efforts also improve the credibility of the information security function within the organization. Workers will appreciate that the information security staff is not out to establish a bureaucracy, but is instead focused on establishing the minimum controls needed to protect organizational information assets.

Delays associated with the information security policy approval process are understandably frustrating. Although a respectable job developing policies has been accomplished, management often takes a long time to review and approve them. Even though information security is regularly discussed in daily newspapers and on television, senior management at many organizations does not understand it. While waiting for policies to be approved, newspaper clippings and other evidence of the need for policies can be submitted to management. This will keep the topic alive in the minds of management and also keep reinforcing the need for management attention to information security matters.

Table Of Contents For Typical Policy Document

The actual sections of a policy document will vary considerably from organization to organization. This should be a reflection of many organization-specific factors such as the sensitivity, value, and criticality of the information to be protected. The nature of the systems involved, the business activities performed, the local laws and customs, and other factors also should be considered. In many organizations, there will be several documents, each prepared for a different audience. For more information about creating a policy document, see "Preparing A Coverage Matrix" on page 11.

While duplication should be avoided, no matter what model is chosen as the backbone of a policy document, there will inevitably be some redundancy.

The typical sections in a policy document are a definition of information security, a statement of management's intention to support information security, and a definition of general management and specific organizational responsibilities with respect to information security. Also included will be the specific policies themselves, perhaps with examples or explanations. Some policy documents may include a discussion of the compliance review and disciplinary processes. Mention of the ways to report or otherwise handle out-of-compliance conditions may appear. A list of related in-house documents is also helpful for those who want more information.

Although rare, a table showing the circumstances when certain policies apply is of considerable assistance to readers of a policy document. For example, when a document containing sensitive information is to be sent through traditional mail, policy A would apply, but when it is sent by a trusted third-party courier, policy B would apply. For more information about such a table, see Chapter 17, "Sample Data Classification Quick Reference Table." These tables can be formatted as decision tables. Rather than making reference to specific policies, a decision table could contain numbers that reference sections of the policy document. There are many models that can be used to base information security policy documents. A listing of these can be found in Table 2-3.

Table 2-3: Policy Document Models

Policy Document Model	Document Focus
Information attribute focus	Confidentiality, integrity, and availability
Information ownership and custodianship	Roles and responsibilities
Reader employment status	Employee, contractor, consultant, temporary, business partner, customer
Job title	System administrator, systems developer, user, manager
Data classification	Information sensitivity
Required time to restore scheme	Data criticality
Information valuation	Resource value
Threat types	Legal or business oriented
Equipment types	Mainframes and personal computers
Geographical location	In the office or on the road
Domains of a trust on a network	Different controls within different domains
Decisions people face	How often to backup and how to prevent virus problems

Which Topics To Address First

For an organization just beginning an information security effort, the complexity of the information security field can be overwhelming. To make it easier for Users, management, and other groups who may not be familiar with information security, only a few essential policies should be issued in the beginning. Later, as understanding and support build, additional policies can be issued. For an example of this initial type of information security policy statement, see Chapter 4, "Sample High-Level Information Security Policy."

Rather than copying the policy appearing in Chapter 4, "Sample High-Level Information Security Policy," consideration should be given to which topics most need to be addressed. Different for each organization, these are the topics that should be addressed in the initial policy statement. These topics typically will include, as a minimum, the responsibility for information security,

computer viruses, information backup, contingency planning, system interconnection, user identification, and system access control privileges.

Another way of looking at an initial policy statement is that it should establish the foundation for a successful information security effort. This foundation or organizational infrastructure includes policies, standards, and responsibility statements, and was covered in "Assuring The Implementation Of Controls" on page 5. An initial set of policies can be used to establish or clarify missing parts of an information security organizational infrastructure. For example, if enforcement mechanisms are missing, the initial set of policies can discuss responsibility for compliance checking or penalties for non-compliance.

If an information security policy document already exists, the challenge will be to determine what new and changed policy ideas need to be addressed in a new policy document. One of the fastest ways to make this decision is to use a coverage matrix as described in "Preparing A Coverage Matrix" on page 11. In this case, the existing policy document can be laid out in a coverage matrix, and the reference numbers of those policy ideas that need to change can be underlined or circled. Next the matrix can be populated with additional policies from this guide, and an outline for the new document can be prepared.

Policy Usage

Intended Target Audience

The policies provided in this guide are directed to one who is computer literate and working in a position related to information security. These assumptions permitted the definitions for many common computer and communication system terms like "Internet service provider" to be omitted. To the extent possible, acronyms, and technical computer and communication system terms have been deliberately avoided because policies must be approved by management, who may not have extensive computer backgrounds. General users are often unaware of technical terms.

Policy Customization Specifics

The policies in this guide should be reviewed and compared with the policies in place at the organization. Using any word processing package, the policies that appear relevant may be extracted using cut-and-paste commands, and placed in a separate computer file. This new file can then be modified to reflect the unique circumstances prevailing at the organization.

Throughout this guide, "Company X" is used to refer to a generic organization. This designator is just a placeholder for the organization's name. In spite of the apparent private sector bias, these policies are also relevant to, and have been successfully used by civilian government, military, and non-profit organizations. Use of this designation does not imply that the policies in this guide must be used on an organization-wide basis. It may be appropriate for these policies to be applicable to a subsidiary, a division, or a department. Whenever possible, to keep long-run administrative, enforcement, and related costs down, the widest-possible applicability of the policies should be sought.

The policies in this guide are deliberately written in generalized terms. For example, many policies are equally applicable to diskless workstations, personal computers, super-servers, minicomputers, and mainframes. Rather restricting a policy to only one type of computer, a generalized policy is preferable because it fosters uniform protection of information no matter where it resides, no matter what technology is involved, and no matter what form the information takes. Key word search terms that are general, such as "network," rather than narrow, such as "local area network." The policy effort should be simplified by taking a platform-independent perspective and creating a set of policies that applies to all computing environments. Taking a hardware and software independent view will additionally prevent the need to update a policy document when a computing environment changes.

The policies in this guide generally take a most stringent position with respect to information security. For many environments these policies will be too severe. The policies should be deleted, diluted, or modified to suit the needs of the organization. The strong form was stated throughout this material because it is much easier to soften a strong policy than it is to bolster a weak policy.

Using Key Word Search Facilities

One of the most useful features of this guide and its accompanying CD-ROM is the ability to employ a key word search to locate policies of interest. If the organization is concerned about a certain topic such as viruses, using the CD-ROM search option with the character string "virus" will identify all areas in the material where the word "virus" is found. The CD-ROM contains all of the information found in the hardcopy guide.

When key word searches are performed, be sure to use the most critical characters only. For example, if one is interested in networks, use the singular version of the word "network" rather than the plural. This will locate both the singular and the plural versions and related terms like "networking." An attempt to search with the most significant single words in a phrase rather than all of the words in a phrase is recommended. For example, search using "diligence" when looking for "due diligence."

Key word searches should use synonyms. For example, if searching in information confidentiality matters, use "confidentiality," "secret," "restricted," "internal use only," "private," "proprietary," "access control," and related terms. Search for all the synonyms that describe the area of interest. If the area of interest is unfamiliar, ask someone who knows about it for some key words. In order to make it most likely that relevant material will be found, generally accepted terms used in both technical publications and general business publications are used throughout this guide. To the extent possible, non-technical terms have been used if the essential ideas behind a policy could be concisely communicated.

Another tip for searching the CD-ROM involves the use of truncated rather than full words. For example, by searching for "copy" rather than "copyright," more policies relevant to the topic of interest will be found. If the search includes a verb or a noun that has irregular plural forms, or that has letters at the end of the word that change, it may be appropriate to initiate several searches, each with a different form of the word.

In an effort to be all encompassing, achieve consistent approaches to information security, and simplify the already-too-complicated life of people in the information security field, the policies in this guide have been prepared with general rather than specific terminology. For example, rather than using terms like "local area network," "gateway," and "router," more general terms like "network" have been employed.

Useful policies may be found in other sections of this guide beyond the sections that seem most relevant based on a brief examination of the table of contents. It is important to examine sections in the guide beyond those that seem to directly address the area of interest. For example, if only those policies appearing in the "Physical And Environmental Security" section are read, other important policies may be missed that are also relevant to data confidentiality and are located in other sections.

Policy Organization

The policies in this guide have been organized based on the International Standard for Information Technology—Code of Practice for Information Security Management, generally known as ISO/IEC 17799. This hierarchy is intended to permit easy access to a large number of policies relevant to a topic of interest. This organizational approach also permits quick identification of related policies that may be related to the topic of interest.

Within a section or subsection of the policies part of this guide, policies are organized in no specific sequence. This means that the entire section dealing with the topic of interest should be reviewed when searching for relevant policies. It is important to review the Table of Contents to identify other sections that may be relevant to the topic of interest.

Policy Objectives And Scope

Motivating Objectives

In most organizations, one of the primary assets at risk is information. Recent studies show that, in industrialized economies, from 10% to 95% of an organization's assets are now related to information handling. Information is addressed by the policies found in this guide. Risks to people, equipment, buildings, land, and other assets are most often recognized in other policy documents, not an information security document.

Classical economic theory holds that the assets or resources required to do business are land, labor, and capital. More recent economic theory describes the factors of production as people, money, plant, and materials. As we move further into the information age, we must add information as another factor of production. An introductory paragraph at the beginning of an information security policy should reinforce this fundamental idea.

Another motivating objective involves management's fiduciary duty to conserve and protect assets, and as noted above, information is considered an asset. This perspective can then serve as the foundation for explicit policies dealing with information security. This duty of management should be acknowledged in the introductory paragraph to an information security policy. For more information about using these ideas, see Chapter 4, "Sample High-Level Information Security Policy."

Many policy statements open with a brief overview of what might happen if information security was not adequately addressed. For example, many refer to a number of risks that the policies are intended to address. From a legal perspective, these include sabotage, terrorism, fraud and embezzlement, extortion, industrial espionage, errors and omissions, service interruption, equipment theft, and privacy violation. Another way to view risks is from a business perspective, with reference to business interruption, erroneous management decisions, competitive disadvantage, loss or destruction of assets, improper record keeping, and statutory or regulatory sanctions. It is recommended that all policy statements make reference to a set of motivating risks, however these risks may be characterized.

Operational Objectives

Policies should be tailored to suit the unique operating circumstances found within an organization. This tailoring process can start with policies that are linked to operational objectives. As an example, the following statement of objectives may be used for a set of policies appearing in an information security manual:

> This manual provides a definitive statement of information security policies to which all workers are expected to comply. It is intended to:
>
> — Acquaint workers with information security risks and the expected ways to address these risks.
>
> — Clarify worker responsibilities and duties with respect to the protection of information resources.
>
> — Enable management and other workers to make appropriate decisions about information security.
>
> — Coordinate the efforts of different groups within Company X so that information resources are properly and consistently protected, regardless of their location, form, or supporting technologies.
>
> — Provide guidance for the performance of information system security audits and risk assessments.

Scope

The scope of an information security policy document should be clarified early in the policies development project. Management should, for example, understand that online etiquette or netiquette will not be addressed in this document. A disciplinary process should be found in a Human Resources policy statement, not in an Information Security policy statement. Information quality control and information engineering topics should be outside the scope of an information security policy document. Physical security should be included within the scope of a policy document, but only to the extent that it directly relates to information security. In an information security policy, insurance and legal issues are covered only in high-level terms.

Policy documents should include specific statements about their applicability. A policy statement could, for example, state that the policies are applicable independent of the:

* Way information is represented.
* Technology used to handle the information.
* Location of information.
* Maturity of information within its life cycle.

Policy statements should indicate who must observe the policies and when it may be acceptable for worker actions or activities to be inconsistent with policies. For example, a policy statement could say that policies must be observed by employees, outsourcing organization staff, consultants, contractors, and temporaries, and these workers must observe policies unless they have received specific permission to do otherwise from a vice president or higher-level manager. This approach assumes that a centralized management group has the authority to dictate policy for an entire organization. Another way to look at the applicability of policies to specific individuals would be to require compliance for all system users. By continuing to use Company X systems, users implicitly, and in some cases explicitly through a window at sign-on time, agree to comply with security policies. It is advisable to be very specific about the audiences for whom the policies have been written.

Writing an information security policy document that applies to an entire organization rather than a specific segment is the most efficient and effective way to proceed. This approach achieves consistency and complete application of the rules defined in the policy document. Although this may be the ideal, in some cases this approach may be inconsistent with prevailing decentralized organizational structures. Having a centralized Information Security department that issues policy for the rest of the organization is particularly difficult when subsidiaries and partially owned companies are involved. If a decentralized organizational structure prevails, Information Security may instead issue suggested policies that it can then attempt to sell to the management of the other organizational units. In these cases, the scope of policy statements could make reference to the responsibility of Information Security.

Many information policy statements have in the past applied only to Information Technology. While this approach may have been sufficient 10 years ago, current distributed processing systems require that information security policies apply to all system users within the organization. Some organizations are expanding the scope of an information security policy effort to include suppliers, customers, and other strategic business partners. This very broad definition of the scope of information security policies is warranted by computer systems that include these outside parties as users. Examples of these more-broadly-scoped systems include electronic data interchange, electronic mail, electronic commerce on the Internet, and extranets.

As a matter of principle, each exception weakens security. For example, if an organization adopts a policy stating that all workers must wear photo-ID badges when in the computer center, then permits top management to ignore the policy, security will be noticeably eroded. Not only will this cause other workers to question whether top management supports the policy, but it will permit unauthorized visitors to wander about because authorized workers may assume they are part of the management team. While current organizational structures, organizational politics, and other matters will often prevent it, the scope of information security policies should include as many organizational units, types of workers, and circumstances, as is feasible.

There should be consistency between the scope of responsibility of an information security group that is preparing policies and the scope of the policies themselves. If a group responsible for information security in a subsidiary company attempted to write policy for the parent company without prior management approval, problems may occur. Often the documented scope of responsibility for those preparing information security policies is more narrowly defined than the scope of the soon-to-be-prepared policies. Given that management support for broadly-scoped policies has been obtained, this is an excellent opportunity for Information Security to expand both its influence and its formal responsibility.

It is important that the term "information security" be clearly defined. By its very nature, information security is multi-disciplinary, multi-departmental, and increasingly multi-organizational. Organizations may have trouble determining where in the organization information security should report, just as they have trouble determining the scope of an information security effort. One recommended operational definition of information security is "any activity that protects information and information systems." With this definition,

confidential information might be owned by a third party, and be in the custody of the organization, yet it would be within the scope of an information security effort. This broad definition includes paper-based and voice-based information, not just computer- and network-resident information. It is advisable to augment this broad definition with specific mention of activities performed by certain internal groups such as contingency planning, systems administration, network management, and records management. Other activities should be specifically excluded, such as those performed by the information technology auditing, risk management, legal, and physical security groups.

Another scope-related factor to consider is the time when policies take effect. The policy document should clearly indicate when readers can expect the policies to take effect. Some situation-specific policies go further, indicating when they will expire. For example, if certain security policies were adopted to facilitate business with a third party, those policies may expire at the same time that a contract with the third party expires. In some cases the issuance date for the policy document will precede the effective date by a month or two. This will give management an opportunity to change their systems to be in compliance. Some organizations recognize the fact that frequent changes in their policies are necessary and expected. To this end, organizations may append words to the end of their policy documents indicating that "Company X reserves the right to change these policies at any time without prior notice."

Handling Non-Compliance

According to current research, compliance with information security policies is inconsistent. A recent survey indicated that only 23% of more than 500 respondents said user compliance is complete or near complete. At the other end of the spectrum, 22% said there was little or no compliance. Non-compliance is a serious problem that undermines the usefulness of information security policies. Some time should be spent considering how both compliance and non-compliance are going to be handled.

After policies have been written, workers must be notified that the policies exist and that they are expected to comply. Although outside the scope of this guide, awareness and training efforts are essential to every successful information security policy endeavor. Awareness and training projects should motivate workers to take information security seriously, sell the benefits of controls, and enlist worker participation in efforts to protect the organization's information assets. Studies have shown that if workers are trained shortly after they receive a policy document, they will be more likely to carry on their normal duties in a manner consistent with the newly-issued policy document. For an overview of the various techniques to deliver these and related messages, see Appendix D, "List Of Suggested Awareness-Raising Methods."

Inevitably, some people will think that a policy does not apply to them. If certain managers believe they may be out of compliance, it is important to require them to sign a risk acceptance memo. Such memos typically indicate that a manager believes other control measures compensate for the control indicated by a policy, or is willing to assume the risk of being out of compliance. Because the provision of a signature on such a memo is a relatively intimidating and legally-meaningful prospect, many managers will prefer to comply rather than document the fact that they are out of compliance. The prospect of defending an out-of-compliance situation through the risk acceptance documentation process may

be daunting and a significant intention for management to comply. For a copy of a risk acceptance document, see Appendix L, "Management Risk Acceptance Memo."

Compliance may be fostered by obtaining signatures, either at the time of employment or on a periodic basis. It is recommended that recipients of an information security policy indicate in writing that they have read, understood, and appreciate the implications of the policies. A signature affirming a commitment to comply also may be obtained at the time that a user ID is issued to or renewed by a user. Signatures can emphasize the fact that management takes information security seriously, in addition to providing the organization with specific written evidence justifying disciplinary measures up to and including termination. For an example of a form requiring such a signature, see Appendix J, "Agreement To Comply With Information Security Policies."

Disclaimers

Need For Customization

The policies provided in this guide are in generic form. They should not be used without customization to a specific information systems security environment. For such customization to be properly performed, the following prerequisites must exist:

- A specialist in information security must be involved.

- The specialist must have a broad understanding of the risks faced by the organization.

- The specialist must understand the controls used to handle these risks.

- The specialist must have a good understanding of existing information-security-related policies, guidelines, procedures, standards, and related material.

To meet these prerequisites, certain background work will need to be performed by the organization seeking to compile an information security document. For example, to meet the second prerequisite, a risk assessment such as a scenario analysis, a quantitative risk assessment, or a standard-of-due-care controls review is recommended. To meet the fourth prerequisite, consider completing a series of interviews with involved parties to appreciate not only what the existing policies mean, but

also how well-known the policies are, how well workers have complied with the existing policies, and the costs and benefits the existing policies have engendered.

Balancing Trade-Offs

Because this reference guide contains a comprehensive set of policies, it should not be surprising if a few policies that contradict other policies are found. For example, freedom of information policies may conflict with right to privacy policies. Each organization will need to determine where this and other lines should be drawn. Workers should be informed of these management decisions lest they be left to make these tough decisions on their own, perhaps with catastrophic results.

Like many activities in the information security field, writing policies involves tradeoffs. Frequently encountered tradeoffs include those between cost and security, speed and security, flexibility and security, and ease-of-use and security. There are many conditions and limits in the information security field, and policies must also be designed with these in mind. For example, a policy dealing with the termination of employees for violating certain information security requirements may be incompatible with existing labor union agreements. Other limits include standard industry practices, prevailing corporate culture, societal ethics, laws and regulations, and the structure of third-party relationships.

The intention of this guide is to provide a wide variety of generally-accepted policies. It is not the intention to have the body of this reference guide constitute a logically-consistent set of policies, although several logically-consistent policy statements are provided at the end of this guide. The logical inconsistency between some policies is also a reflection of the fact that there is no standard set of specific policies to which all organizations must subscribe. Instead, a set of policies must be uniquely tailored to the requirements of each organization.

Need For Competent Advice

Many of the policies described in this guide contain specific numbers, time periods, or other information that is technology-, jurisdiction-, or organization-dependent. It is strongly recommended that the services of a computer-literate attorney and an experienced information systems security specialist be retained prior to placing these policies, or policies derived from them, into service. In some instances, such as the establishment of encryption policies, it also may be advisable to get assistance from a specialist in a narrowly-defined subject area. A review by the director of Human Resources is also advisable to ensure that the policies are consistent with an organization's existing policies.

Lastly, the material in this guide is intended to provide guidance and ideas for potential policies. It is not intended to provide a specific course of action or a specific set of words for an organization. Some of the suggestions found in this guide will have little or no bearing on the organization, and in some cases these suggestions may even be illegal in the organization's jurisdiction. The material found in this guide should not be used verbatim, but should instead be customized to the specific circumstances at the organization.

Chapter 3   SPECIFIC POLICIES

3   SECURITY POLICY

3.01 Information Security Policy

3.01.01 Information Security Policy Document

1. Protection Of Information

Policy: Information must be protected in a manner commensurate with its sensitivity, value, and criticality.

Commentary: This policy applies regardless of the media on which information is stored, the locations where the information is stored, the systems technology used to process the information, or the people who handle the information. This policy encourages examining the ways information flows through an organization. The policy also points to the scope of Information Security management's work throughout, and often even outside, an organization. The policy encourages Internal Audit to use integrated techniques such as data flow analysis. The idea behind this policy is important for those preparing a systems security architecture. Integrated access control systems using this idea can include single sign-on to a network of computers, single-point for user registration, centralized access control administration, and centralized access control system auditing. In some cases, specific examples can be provided to clarify this policy.

Related Policies: "Single Sign-On," "Control Implementations Standard," "Information Security Management Committee," and "Computer System Dispersion."

Audience: Technical staff

Security Environments: All

2. Use Of Information

Policy: Company X information must be used only for the business purposes expressly authorized by management.

Commentary: This policy states that all non-approved uses of Company X information are prohibited. For example, an employee may want to use his employer's

database of customers for a charitable mass mailing. The policy may apply across the board, or be written only on the label of storage media containing specific information likely to be abused, such as a customer mailing list. To prevent secondary dissemination problems, marking sensitive information is highly advised. The policy is relevant to all workers coming into contact with Company X information. In this policy, the focus is on use of the information rather than the systems that handle this information.

Related Policies: "Four-Category Data Classification," "Non-Business Use Of Organization Information," and "Sensitive Information Handling."

Audience: All

Security Environments: All

3. Information Handling, Access, And Usage

Policy: Information is a vital asset and all accesses to, uses of, and processing of, Company X information must be consistent with policies and standards.

Commentary: This policy sets the context for a number of other information security policies. Such a statement is frequently incorporated into the first set of policies and summary material oriented toward users and members of the top management team. It is necessary for these people to appreciate how information has become a critical factor of production in business. This policy motivates the need for information security measures and to create a new understanding of the importance of information systems in organizations.

Related Policies: "Non-Business Use Of Organization Information."

Audience: All

Security Environments: All

4. Data And Program Damage Disclaimers

Policy: Company X disclaims any responsibility for loss or damage to data or software that results from its efforts to protect the confidentiality, integrity, and availability of the information handled by computers and communications systems.

Commentary: This policy notifies users that they cannot hold Company X liable for damages associated with management's attempts to secure its system. For example, if a system administrator was performing a routine virus scan of all computers on a local area network, what appears to be a virus may be detected and a virus eradication program may be executed. This action may alter the infected program, rendering it unusable. When the user determines that this program is inoperative, the user cannot hold management responsible for damaging it. This policy is best applied where Company X has facilities used by non-employees, as is the case of a university that has student users.

Related Policies: "Special System Privileges" and "Message Disclaimer."

Audience: End users

Security Environments: All

5. Legal Conflicts

Policy: Company X information security policies were drafted to meet or exceed the protections found in existing laws and regulations, and any Company X information security policy believed to be in conflict with existing laws or regulations must be promptly reported to Information Security management.

Commentary: This policy creates a context for the requirements specified in an information security policy document. Sound policies go beyond laws and regulations, or at least ensure that an organization will meet the requirements specified by laws and regulations. This policy acknowledges support for laws and regulations, and expresses an intention to stay in compliance with existing laws and regulations. The policy is suitable for both internal information security policies and those made available to the public.

Related Policies: "Incident Reporting" and "File And Message Ownership."

Audience: End users

Security Environments: All

6. Exceptions To Policies

Policy: Exceptions to information security policies exist in rare instances where a risk assessment examining the implications of being out of compliance has been performed, where a standard risk acceptance form has been prepared by the data Owner or management, and where this form has been approved by both Information Security management and Internal Audit management.

Commentary: Management will be called upon to approve certain exceptions to policies. This policy clarifies that exceptions will be granted only after a risk acceptance form has been completed, signed, and approved. The form should include a statement where the data Owner or management takes responsibility for any losses occurring from the out-of-compliance situation. The existence of such a form provides an escape value that can be used to address those situations where users insist on being out of compliance with policies. It is desirable to make all out-of-compliance situations both known and documented. This means that if there were to a loss that occurred as a result of the situation, management could demonstrate to a judge or jury that it was aware of the situation, examined the risks, and it decided to waive the relevant policy or standard.

Related Policies: "Consequences Of Non-Compliance," "Privacy Rights Waiver," and "Security Controls Enforceability."

Audience: Management

Security Environments: All

7. Policy Non-Enforcement

Policy: Management's non-enforcement of any policy requirement does not constitute its consent.

Commentary: This policy notifies policy statement readers that they should not expect out-of-compliance conditions to be continued only because management has not yet enforced the policy. This policy eliminates any claim that local management may state that an out-of-compliance condition should remain as it is because the condition has been in existence for a considerable period of time.

Related Policies: "Information System Control Reviews — Internal" and "Network Logon Banner."

Audience: End users

Security Environments: All

8. Violation Of Law

Policy: Company X management must seriously consider prosecution for all known violations of the law.

Commentary: This policy encourages the prosecution of abusive and criminal acts. While a decision to prosecute will be contingent on the specifics of the case, management should not dismiss prosecution without review. This policy may be important in terms of communicating to those would-be perpetrators of abusive or criminal acts. Many computer crimes are not prosecuted and perpetrators often know this, expecting victim organizations to terminate them and suppress the entire affair. A policy like this is, for example, used by a number of telephone companies for those individuals who fraudulently obtain telephone service. Rather than being stated in general terms, this policy could require prosecution for certain crimes that normally happen in the course of the involved business, such as credit card fraud.

Related Policies: "Incident Reporting."

Audience: Management

Security Environments: All

9. Revocation Of Access Privileges

Policy: Company X reserves the right to revoke a user's information technology privileges at any time.

Commentary: This policy notifies users that they jeopardize their status as authorized users if they engage in activities that interfere with the normal and proper operation of Company X information systems, that adversely affect the ability of others to use these information systems, or that are harmful or offensive to others. For example, crashing the system could be expected to be harmful to other users, and would subject the perpetrator to disciplinary action including privilege revocation. The policy attempts to broadly describe an ethic for computing. Rather than specifying all of the adverse things that people could do, such as crashing a system, this policy is discreet and at a high level. This policy may give management latitude when it comes to deciding about privilege revocation.

Related Policies: "Default User Privileges" and "Reauthorization Of User Access Privileges."

Audience: End users

Security Environments: All

10. Industry-Specific Information Security Standards

Policy: Company X information systems must employ industry-specific information security standards.

Commentary: This policy requires systems designers and other technical staff to employ industry-standard controls. For example, in banking, encryption systems should use industry specific systems for key management. Other industry-specific controls are relevant to the medical services industry, the aerospace and defense community, and other industry groups.

Related Policies: "Purchasing Information Security Solutions," "Control Implementations Standard," and "Minimum Information System Controls."

Audience: Technical staff

Security Environments: All

11. Use Of Information Security Policies And Procedures

Policy: All Company X information security documentation including, but not limited to, policies, standards, and procedures, must be classified as "Internal Use Only," unless expressly created for external business processes or partners.

Commentary: This policy prevents workers from disclosing to outsiders the specifics of how Company X secures its information and systems. These details may be used to compromise Company X information and systems. For example, knowledge about an internal process may help industrial spy commit credible social engineering fraud. Because some information security policies are made public, some workers may get the impression that other information security policies may be publicly released with no problem. Information security policies may be revealed to outsiders only when it is required for business reasons or because it is the right thing to do. Not all of the information security policies need to be released in these instances, and a summary statement is not only advisable but is appreciated by the recipients. Each information security policy document should be marked with an appropriate classification in order to emphasize the fact that the policies are not public information.

Related Policies: "Work Agreement" and "Four-Category Data Classification."

Audience: All

Security Environments: All

3.01.02 Review And Evaluation

1. Security Controls Enforceability

Policy: All information systems security controls must be enforceable prior to being adopted as a part of standard operating procedure.

Commentary: Controls that are not enforced have a tendency to become useless. For example, if management has a policy about clean desks by locking up all sensitive materials after work, and it is not enforced, then employees quickly learn to ignore the policy. This policy is intended to require management to review the enforcement of controls, an issue that may not occur before adopting a control. For example, management may adopt a policy about reviewing the access control logs for unauthorized activity, but after adopting the policy, management may find that the policy requires too much staff time. A definition of the word "enforceable" may be advisable in some instances. For a control to be enforceable, it must be possible for management to clearly determine whether staff is in compliance with the control, and whether the control is effectively doing its intended job. The policy is purposefully vague about what constitutes standard operating procedure. This permits the policy to apply to a wide variety of circumstances, despite whether the control is documented, specific to a certain department, or used in an experimental way. In some instances, this policy may require the control designers to add a monitoring mechanism that reports on the status of the control. For example, encryption boxes from some vendors have lights that indicate that they are working as they should.

Related Policies: "Information System Control Reviews — Internal" and "Third-Party Agreements."

Audience: Management and technical staff

Security Environments: All

4   ORGANIZATIONAL SECURITY

4.01 Information Security Infrastructure

4.01.01 Management Information Security Forum

1. Undetected Information Alteration

Policy: Management must establish and maintain sufficient preventive and detective security measures to ensure that Company X information is free from significant risk of undetected alteration.

Commentary: This policy guides systems designers, network specialists, and others to implement adequate control measures to prevent undetected information alteration. The exact nature of these controls will vary considerably from system to system. The policy communicates that it is important to be able to detect all unauthorized modifications, and implies that unauthorized modifications should be prevented whenever possible. The policy also implies that it is important for all changes to information to have an audit trail, such that the reason for the changes and the person initiating the changes can be determined. The controls used to achieve this policy could take many forms, such as digital signatures, message authentication codes, message encryption, and digital certificates. A policy like this is especially important to organizations in the financial services industry because it sets the stage for controls that deal with fraud and embezzlement. Some organizations may modify the policy to restrict it to sensitive, valuable, and critical information. Such a modification to the policy may save money because it can prevent the unnecessary allocation of resources in order to monitor data that is not deemed critical or sensitive.

Related Policies: "Security Requirements Identification."

Audience: Technical staff

Security Environments: All

2. Information Security Management Committee

Policy: An information security management committee composed of senior managers or their delegates from each major Company X division, must meet quarterly to review the current status of information security at Company X, review security incident monitoring processes within the Company, approve and later review information security projects, approve new or modified information security policies, and perform other necessary high-level information security management activities.

Commentary: The objectives of this policy are to provide a mission statement for a middle-level management committee that addresses information security issues, and to describe what the committee is expected to do. Some organizations have a perpetual or standing committee while others have a temporary committee. Temporary committees are often used until an information security effort builds sufficient momentum to sustain itself without the committee's influence. The specific objectives of the committee can be modified to suit organizational needs. Other objectives that could be in the policy include defining specific roles and responsibilities as they relate to information security, approving the use of specific methodologies and processes for information security, ensuring that information security is integrated with other Company X change control and planning processes, coordinating the implementation of specific information security measures, and promoting the visibility of information security within the company. The objectives should not make reference to detailed activities because the work of the management committee should be restricted to oversight, policy, and related higher-level matters. Likewise, detailed activities are likely to change substantially over time, and this policy should be written such that it will be relevant for several years. Committees like this have been shown to be an excellent way to increase management awareness about information security, and also to achieve consistent information security across large organizations with different departmental and divisional organizational cultures and work processes.

Related Policies: "Centralized Information Security" and "Privacy Impact Reviews."

Audience: Management

Security Environments: All

4.01.02 Information Security Coordination

1. Significant Information Security Risks

Policy: For every significant information systems security risk, management must make a specific decision about the degree to which Company X will be self-insured and accept the risk, seek external insurance, or adjust controls to reduce expected losses.

Commentary: This policy requires management, particularly those acting as information Owners, to respond to auditor or other third-party findings that security vulnerabilities exist. Management often ignores the whole situation, becoming self-insured, but not understanding the reasons behind such a decision. To ensure that such choices are made, some organizations may wish to put the words "in writing" into this policy. The policy can be changed to communicate to management that insurance is available to address some of these problems, although the primary decision is either to invest in controls or accept the risk.

Related Policies: "Control Implementations Standard" and "Production System Risk Assessments."

Audience: Management and technical staff

Security Environments: All

2. Insurance Coverage

Policy: Adequate insurance coverage must be obtained and kept in force for every major threat facing the confidentiality, integrity, and availability of information handled by Company X computer and communication systems.

Commentary: This policy requires that management look at the insurance needs of the organization, particularly as they relate to the confidentiality, integrity, and availability of information. The policy requires that insurance coverage be maintained. Management must quantify the financial risk and determine how much insurance is adequate. For many types of coverage, this also means that the insurance company's requirements must be observed by the insured company. The policy communicates that such insurance does exist, which may be news to certain members of the management team. This policy does not require any action with respect to trivial threats. This policy is especially important to all industries where information is, or is becoming, the essence of their business.

Related Policies: "Production System Risk Assessments," "Archival Storage Directory," and "Bonding Workers."

Audience: Management and technical staff

Security Environments: All

4.01.03 Allocation Of Information Security Responsibilities

1. Information Ownership

Policy: The chief Information Security officer or chief information officer must clearly specify in writing the assignment of information ownership responsibilities for databases, master files, and other shared collections of information and designate the individuals who will maintain access rights to these information collections on behalf of the Owners.

Commentary: This policy establishes a clear and documented delegation of information access control-related authority. A definition of delegated authorities is useful when determining access control permissions. This policy clarifies who is responsible for security and related matters for shared information resources such as a database or network file share. Often information security activities are forgotten when several people are potentially responsible but no one has been assigned responsibility. This policy may be helpful within organizations that rely on database management systems and application programs to enforce access controls. Often it is not clear that database administrators and technical systems support personnel are responsible for administering system access controls. The process of designating who is responsible for access control will highlight those situations where no one has been designated as responsible.

Related Policies: "Assigning Information Ownership" and "Custodian Responsibility Transfer."

Audience: Management

Security Environments: All

2. Worker Status Changes

Policy: Every change in the employment status of Company X workers including, but not limited to, consultants, contractors, and temporaries, must be immediately reported by management to Human Resources, who must subsequently notify the involved information system administrators.

Commentary: The intention behind this policy is to foster a connection between the database maintained by Human Resources and the access control database maintained by information system administrators. Companies must remind business unit management that they are responsible for maintaining a clear communication path to Human Resources regarding their personnel status. In many situations, system administrators and sometimes Human Resources are not aware of promotions, transfers, retirements, leaves of absence, and related changes in the status of workers. Administrators do not make necessary changes in the access control privileges of these workers. Not making these changes in a timely manner can result in serious leaks of confidential information or system sabotage. While the policy does not specifically talk about an automated connection, such a connection is desirable in any organization with 100 or more workers. This policy is especially effective if an organization has an enterprise security management system that typically relies on a centralized database of user privileges across all operating systems and specific internal machines. The policy can be implemented on a manual basis, although delays and errors are more likely. If management can hire, fire, or contract with individuals without the involvement of Human Resources, and without notifying Human Resources, then this policy could be changed to require local management to report these changes directly to system administrators.

Related Policies: "Reporting Employee Changes" and "Reauthorization Of User Access Privileges."

Audience: Management and technical staff

Security Environments: All

3. Management Security Approach

Policy: Management must ensure that information security within their departments is treated as a regular business problem to be faced and solved, and they are responsible for promoting security as everyone's business.

Commentary: This policy confronts management about their attitude, to let them know that they must set an example for the workers in their department. In many organizations, management has been hostile toward information security, and has hampered progress. This policy informs management to recognize information security as a business function. The policy highlights the fact that information security is not a project that can be completed, then forgotten. Instead, it is an on-going business activity and must be supported.

Related Policies: "Work Agreement" and "Computer Disaster Recovery Plans."

Audience: Management

Security Environments: All

4. Risk Assessments

Policy: Information security risk assessments must be performed by disinterested third parties.

Commentary: This policy prevents internal staff from reviewing their own work. In the process, internal staff may fail to note serious information security vulnerabilities that later appear when an incident takes place. Because information security is so complex, it should be regularly reviewed by a third party, ideally an expert in the subject area under review. For example, if a network access control risk assessment is to be performed, it should be performed by someone who has experience in this area, not a related area such as computer viruses. With this in mind, the word "expert" could be added to the policy. Independence of the people performing security reviews may be lacking, but management often does not even notice. This is especially true when vendors provide complimentary or low-cost security reviews, then recommend that the organization adopt their solutions to the problems that they found.

Related Policies: "System Risk Assessments" and "New Technology Evaluation."

Audience: Management

Security Environments: All

5. Security Products And Services

Policy: All critical information security functions must be supported with best-of-breed, commercially-available products and services.

Commentary: This policy expresses a secure systems design philosophy and specifies how it should be implemented from a business standpoint. The policy is intended to ensure that all critical information security products and related services are supported with the best currently available commercial solutions. The policy explicitly specifies commercial solutions because non-commercial solutions may not be supported or may not be kept up to date. Information Security personnel would ordinarily determine which functions are critical and determine which should be supported by best-of-breed solutions. This policy requires that internal staff perform additional research to understand what the market currently offers.

Related Policies: "Security Product Maturity" and "Purchasing Information Security Solutions."

Audience: Technical staff

Security Environments: High

6. Information Security Resources

Policy: Management must allocate sufficient resources and staff attention to adequately address information systems security.

Commentary: This policy communicates to lower-level management that information security is important and cannot be ignored. It is particularly appropriate for decentralized organizations, such as a holding company with subsidiaries. This policy also garners the budget money necessary to protect Company X information and systems. The meaning of the word "sufficient" is deliberately vague. The policy implies that a risk assessment must be performed and may be especially helpful to those organizations that employ charge-back systems for computer and telecommunication services. Such charge-back systems often discourage users from using these services to address information security.

Related Policies: "Production System Risk Assessments" and "Minimum Information System Controls."

Audience: Management and technical staff

Security Environments: All

7. Budgeting For Information Security

Policy: Information security products and services are provided through corporate overhead budgets and must not be charged back to each subsidiary company.

Commentary: This policy encourages the allocation of sufficient funds for information security within large organizations that have divisions, subsidiaries, or other types of organizational units. When charge-back systems are used to transfer the costs for information security, unit management often decides to reduce or eliminate information security. This is not a serious problem if each unit has independent and unconnected information systems, but if they are connected through a network, consistency is required to achieve adequate security. By providing a central overhead budget, the compliance with internal information security standards is significantly enhanced. Separate organizational units can go their own way with special approval. This policy ensures that all units have sufficient controls, regardless of their budget or recent financial performance. This policy addresses one of the organizational design issues that often conspires to render information security ineffective or irrelevant.

Related Policies: "Information Security Resources" and "Computer and Communication Service Invoices."

Audience: Management

Security Environments: All

8. Information Systems Change Approval

Policy: Department managers or other members of the management team may not sign contracts, initiate internal projects, or otherwise make promises that obligate Company X to make changes in its computer or communications systems, unless these changes are pre-approved by both the chief information officer and Information Security management.

Commentary: This policy notifies internal management that they must not make promises regarding changes in computer or communication systems without getting the approval of the chief information officer and Information Security management. Without a policy such as this, management may make promises, often to contractors or consultants, that later are shown to introduce serious security problems. While this policy may not be sufficient grounds to legally repudiate a contract, it is intended to get internal management to check with the chief information officer and Information Security management before making promises.

Related Policies: "Hardware And Software Procurement" and "Sales Department Electronic Mail."

Audience: Management

Security Environments: All

9. Centralized Information Security

Policy: Guidance, direction, and authority for information security activities are centralized for the entire organization by Information Security management.

Commentary: This policy clearly communicates to all workers that Information Security management calls the shots when it comes to information security matters. Many organizations have internal arguments about who is ultimately responsible for information security. This area is particularly problematic with local area networks, personal computers, client-server systems, and other small systems that have been largely managed by user departments rather than a centralized Information Systems department. This policy does not imply that all the information security work will be done by Information Security. There should be departmental coordinators, local security administrators, and others specifically charged with information security work. To be effective in the age of integrated networks, information security policies, standards, architectures, and related infrastructure matters must be dictated centrally by an organization-wide information security group.

Related Policies: "Information Security Management Committee," "Systems Development Conventions," "Requests For Organization Information," "Communication Line Changes," "Hardware And Software Procurement," and "Network Central Point Of Failure."

Audience: Management and technical staff

Security Environments: All

10. Information Security Department Responsibilities

Policy: The Information Security department is responsible for establishing and maintaining organization-wide information security policies, standards, guidelines, and procedures.

Commentary: One intention of this policy is to clarify that the Information Security department has organization-wide responsibility. Another intention is to emphasize that Information Security focuses on information, not on computers. Although it may organizationally report to the chief information officer of a large subsidiary or the director of the Information Technology department, Information Security needs to be seen as an authority throughout the organization. This policy communicates to workers what Information Security does. Many workers have the view that Information Security will do everything related to

information security, and that they need not be involved. The tasks outlined in the policy should be modified to reflect the organizational structure and design at Company X. For example, the policy could be expanded to include investigations, compliance review, and other activities. Some organizations would prefer to put the material found in this policy in a mission statement or charter rather than a policy.

Related Policies: "Centralized Information Security," "Information Security Responsibility," "Information Security Department Mission," and "Information Security Department Tasks."

Audience: End users

Security Environments: All

11. Information Security Department Tasks

Policy: Information Security management must provide direction and technical expertise to ensure that Company X information is protected by processes that maintain the confidentiality, integrity, and availability of information and the systems that handle it.

Commentary: This policy provides specific information about the responsibilities of the Information Security department. The department must perform many tasks including, but not limited to, performing risk assessments, preparing action plans, evaluating vendor products, participating on in-house system development projects, assisting with control implementations, investigating information security breaches, and training other staff members. Many workers will be unclear about the duties and the contribution to be made by Information Security. This policy can eliminate uncertainty and focus the work of the department. The policy defines information security in a broad sense so that it includes paper-based, voice-oriented, hand-rendered graphic, product-embodied, and other manifestations of information.

Related Policies: "Information Security Department Responsibilities."

Audience: Management and technical staff

Security Environments: All

12. Information Security Department Mission

Policy: The Information Security department is charged with the prevention of serious loss or compromise of critical, valuable, and sensitive information resources at Company X by coordinating and directing specific actions that will provide a secure and stable information systems environment consistent with Company X goals and objectives.

Commentary: This policy supports Company X goals and objectives. Information Security is often perceived as a hindrance or obstacle to the Company X goals and objectives. This statement or charter tries to minimize statements about negative events. This positive characterization of Information Security fosters a view that the department is a contributor to, rather than an inhibitor of, growth and expansion. The mission statement is also intended to be clearly in support of Company X goals and objectives. Some organizations may wish to be more specific about the ways that the department can support the organization's goals and objectives.

Related Policies: "Information Security Department Responsibilities."

Audience: Management and technical staff

13. Information Security Standards And Procedures

Policy: The Information Security department has the authority to create and periodically modify both technical standards and standard operating procedures that support this information security policy document data that, when approved by appropriate Company X management, will have the same scope and authority as if they were included in this policy document.

Commentary: This policy prevents users and others from contesting the Information Security department's authority to create and modify technical standards and standard operating procedures. This policy is intended to lay the groundwork for the development and adoption of more detailed documents. Each standard or procedure that is intended to become an extension of the policy document must include the words, "This standard or procedure has been created by the authority described in the Company X Information Security Policy, and must be complied with as though it was part of the policy document." The policy permits Information Security to focus on what needs to come next, not on reinventing the wheel in terms of information security-related organizational structure, responsibilities, and management approvals.

Related Policies: "Centralized Information Security" and "Information Asset Control."

Audience: All

Security Environments: All

14. Information Security Plans

Policy: Working in conjunction with the responsible management, the Information Security department must annually prepare plans for the improvement of information security on all major Company X information systems.

Commentary: This policy requires staff from the Information Security department and managers from other departments to annually prepare a formal plan for improving information security. Much of the work in the information security field is handling urgent problems, and Information Security personnel must periodically take another look at what is now being done and what should be done. In other words, this policy requires staff to focus on what is important, not solely on what is urgent. This policy communicates that not only should Information Security personnel perform this review, but management from relevant departments also should participate. The policy indirectly supports the periodic performance of a risk assessment. Without specific knowledge of the current risks and vulnerabilities, an organization cannot prepare information security plans that truly respond to its unique business needs. The term "plans" may be changed to "plan" if needed. The plural was used in the policy because the work to be done will probably show up in several places such as user department budgets, a central Information Security budget, or the Human Resources budget.

Related Policies: "Software And System Classification," "Computer Disaster Recovery Plans," "Computer Emergency Response Plans," "Divisional Plans For Information Security Compliance," "Violation And Problem Analysis," and "Centralized Information Security."

Audience: Management

Security Environments: All

15. Information Security Manual

Policy: The Information Security department must prepare, maintain, and distribute one or more information security manuals that concisely describe Company X information security policies, standards, and procedures.

Commentary: This policy requires Information Security to prepare and maintain a document that describes procedures at Company X. Without instructions on information security, the organization may find it difficult to justify disciplinary actions against employees. Without written instructions, the authority to conduct awareness and training efforts may be problematic. A manual would include how to handle internal mail of various sensitivities, passwords and user IDs, and other end user-oriented topics. The content of the manual should not be mentioned because that will change from year to year. The policy could require subsidiaries, divisions, or other large organizational units to prepare their own manuals. A training department could be responsible. Without indicating which organization is responsible, there will be confusion. The need for this policy comes from the fact that information security is multi-disciplinary, multi-departmental, and increasingly multi-organizational. The word or "instructions" could be used instead of the word "manuals," and the word "manuals" does not imply a paper document. It could be resident on an intranet, a local area network server, an electronic bulletin board, or made available through other electronic means.

Related Policies: "Training And Operating Documentation," "Information Security Training," and "Training Time."

Audience: Management

Security Environments: All

16. Information Security Liaisons

Policy: Every department manager must designate an information security liaison and give this liaison sufficient training, supporting materials, and other resources to properly perform the job.

Commentary: This policy communicates to departmental and other lower-level managers that information security liaisons are important and must be adequately supported. Because information security does not directly contribute to the bottom line, management may erroneously assume that it is not important. The policy is suitable for those organizations that have part-time liaisons. Liaisons often act as both a local contact for information security matters, and as a knowledgeable person regarding information security. Liaisons are frequently local area network administrators or security administrators who take care of access control on systems. This policy is important for departments using personal computers and workstations, local area networks, or client-server systems.

Related Policies: "Designated Security Administrator."

Audience: Management and technical staff

Security Environments: All

17. Assigning Information Ownership

Policy: Executive management must assign ownership responsibility to the single internal individual who makes the greatest use of the information.

Commentary: This policy clarifies how information Owners must be assigned. If the criteria are not specific, an Owner often will not be assigned, and as a consequence, security for the involved information will be lax. With intranets, integrated distributed databases, client-server systems, and other multi-departmental applications, the assignment of ownership can be a non-trivial question. The term "greatest use" is vague because there will be different factors in each decision, most of which will be linked with strategically-important businesses activities. Another way to determine ownership is identify who pays the bill for the storage and other information services associated with the information. Ownership may be determined by identifying the manager responsible for maintenance of the information or related information system.

Related Policies: "Information Ownership."

Audience: Management

Security Environments: All

18. Information Systems Department Ownership Responsibility

Policy: With the exception of operational computer and network information, the Information Systems department must not be the Owner of any information.

Commentary: This policy clarifies that the Information Systems department, which often serves as a Custodian, should not at the same time be an Owner of information. This would create a conflict of interest where security is likely to be inadequately addressed. For example, Information Systems might decide that minimal controls were appropriate for sensitive information because this would speed access and keep costs down. The term "Information Systems" can be replaced with "Information Technology" or other terms used at an organization.

Related Policies: "Information Ownership."

Audience: Management and technical staff

Security Environments: All

19. Default Information Ownership

Policy: If the ownership for a specific type of information resident on a production multi-user computer has not yet been clearly assigned to a specific manager, it will temporarily default to the manager of Computer Operations.

Commentary: This policy clarifies the Owner of production information until the time that an official Owner has been assigned by top management. In the interim, the manager of Computer Operations is typically acting as a Custodian and can make Owner decisions about that same information. There is a need for a temporary Owner in many cases because the manager who should be acting as the information Owner may not yet be aware of the duties, performing these duties, agreed to take on these duties, or may in some way be disputing the assignment of ownership. In the meantime, the production data must be properly protected, updated, and managed so that daily work is completed. It is reasonable that the manager of Computer Operations plays the role of Owner, at least for a short period of time.

Related Policies: "Information Systems Department Ownership Responsibility" and "Information Custodian."

Audience: Technical staff

Security Environments: All

20. Information Custodian

Policy: Each major type of information must have a designated Custodian who will properly protect Company X information in keeping with the designated Owner's access control, data sensitivity, and data criticality instructions.

Commentary: This policy requires that a Custodian be assigned for all significant information types. To determine whether information is significant, an organization may look to see if the information is included in an organization-wide data dictionary. Another objective of the policy is clarify the responsibilities of information Custodians. This policy also implies that Owners should pay Custodians so that they may properly protect the involved information. This idea may be manifested through an internal charge-back system, inter-organizational transfer prices, or other accounting mechanisms. If the Owner does not provide sufficient resources to protect the involved information, the Custodian then must notify the Owner that the information is not being protected in a manner consistent with instructions.

Although Custodians may be either individuals or organizational entities, it is best if they are restricted to individuals as this fosters accountability that is more likely to lead to desired results. Organizations may wish to augment the stated responsibilities of Custodians to include the provision of, and maintenance of, a general security system for information systems.

Related Policies: "Information Asset Control," "Budgeting For Information Security," and "Asset Inventory — Information."

Audience: Management and technical staff

Security Environments: All

21. Information Custodian Responsibilities

Policy: Information Custodians are responsible for defining specific control procedures, administering information access controls, implementing and maintaining cost-effective information control measures, and providing recovery capabilities consistent with the instructions of information Owners.

Commentary: This policy defines what it means to be an information Custodian. For example, the policy clarifies that Custodians do not make all security-related decisions with regard to the information. Custodians instead provide a service in a manner consistent with instructions from Owners. This policy is written with the assumption that Information Security organizationally reports to Information Systems. If this is not the case, the reference to administering access controls may need to be removed from this policy. Ideally, responsibilities should be assigned such that Information Security is not a Custodian for any production information.

Related Policies: "Information Custodian."

Audience: Management and technical staff

Security Environments: All

22. Information User Responsibilities

Policy: All users of Company X information must comply with the control requirements specified by the information's Owner or Custodian.

Commentary: This policy notifies users that they can use this information with the understanding that they must properly protect it. Some organizations make this policy more specific by requiring users to sign a statement that they agree to abide by information security policies and procedures. A signature on a form with this statement, and perhaps a summary of the policies and procedures, can be required before a user is given a user ID and a password. It should be emphasized that the users do not own or control the information to which they have been granted access, and that they should not be making security-related decisions about this information. Without a specific written statement to this effect, users may decide that they can share the information with anyone who requests. As more and more information is distributed to intranets, local area networks, personal computers, and client-server systems, there is a pressing need for policies like this to clarify user security responsibilities.

Related Policies: "Information Ownership" and "Information Security Problem Resolution."

Audience: All

Security Environments: All

23. Information Ownership Delegation

Policy: An information Owner's responsibility for the specification of appropriate information controls may not be delegated to service providers outside Company X.

Commentary: This policy ensures that insiders, who generally have a better understanding of the business and its needs than outsiders, make decisions about the security of information. Outsiders may be committed to maximizing profit and minimizing their own staff's time involvement with this customer, and as a result security may be significantly eroded. Fundamental security decisions must be made by the management of an organization. The actual implementation of the security decisions may be completed by outsiders. This policy may be incorporated into outsourcing agreements, facilities management agreements, or consulting requests for proposals.

Related Policies: "Information Ownership" and "Information Security Problem Resolution."

Audience: Management and technical staff

Security Environments: All

24. Information Access Policies

Policy: Information access policies must be developed that specify that the designated information Owners are responsible for establishing and updating specific written policies regarding the categories of people who will be granted permission to access the information for which they are responsible.

Commentary: This policy notifies information Owners that they must take the time to specify who will, and who will not be able to gain access to the information for which they have been designated the Owner. The rationale for these decisions will be expressed in an access rights policy. A specification of these access rights is a necessary precursor to implementing either a password-based access control package or the native access control facilities found in many operating systems. If an access control package implementation is attempted without having decided what the rules will be, confusion may result. This policy informs management and technical staff that such policies about information access must not only be specified, but also be in writing. If these policies are in writing, they will then also be auditable. This policy is effectively a high-level policy that sets the stage for more specific access control policies. Unlike many other information security policies, only the general structure is dictated centrally by Information Security management, while the specific access control policies come from other designated managers.

Related Policies: "Information Ownership" and "Granting System Privileges."

Audience: Management and technical staff

Security Environments: All

4.01.04 Authorization Process For Information Processing

1. New Technology Control

Policy: In every instance where new technology is used in a Company X production information system, the operations and security controls associated with that new technology must be particularly stringent until the new technology has been shown to be reliable, readily controllable, and truly supportive of business activities.

Commentary: This conservative policy reflects a wise practice when it comes to new technology. Essentially it says that until the new technology has proven itself, extra controls will be necessary. But even after a new technology has proven itself, the removal or loosening of related controls should require approval by Information Security management. This policy reflects the fact that it is much easier to loosen controls than it is to tighten them. Users will welcome the former but complain bitterly about the latter. Workers will generally go along with these additional controls because this is seen as the way they will get the new capabilities that the new technology provides.

Related Policies: "Disabling Critical Security Components" and "Security Requirements Identification."

Audience: Technical staff

Security Environments: All

2. Disabling Critical Security Components

Policy: Critical components of Company X information security infrastructure must not be disabled, bypassed, turned off, or disconnected without prior approval from Information Security management.

4.01.05 Specialist Information Security Advice

1. Production System Risk Assessments

Policy: All production computer information systems must be periodically evaluated by Information Security management to determine the minimum set of controls required to reduce and maintain risk at an acceptable level.

Commentary: The process described in the policy is a risk assessment, also referred to as a risk assessment. This policy requires a risk assessment for all production information systems to ensure that critical business systems have received at least a rudimentary level of security attention. Some readers may wish to put a time period into the policy, although simply using the term "periodic" is recommended. The way the policy is written now, production systems can be prioritized by risk, and those that present a greater risk can be examined more frequently and in greater detail. Instead

Commentary: This policy is motivated by the natural tendency of system administrators to respond quickly to complaints from users. The policy informs administrators and other workers that they must not remove a critical control without obtaining the proper approval. This policy strikes the proper balance between information security and other business objectives. In this instance the competing objective is getting the work done. The policy deliberately avoids a definition for a critical component, thereby encouraging the policy reader with a question to seek management interpretation and guidance. Explicit definition of a critical component in the policy is also not advised because this set of controls will change significantly over time.

Related Policies: "Unnecessary Software" and "Password Attempts."

Audience: Technical staff

Security Environments: All

of the Information Security department, these evaluations could be performed by Internal Audit or Information Technology Audit. It is advisable to specify which group is responsible for performing risk assessments, either through this policy or through a separate policy dealing with overall responsibilities. A risk assessment provides background information on which information security management decisions such as budgets, staffing plans, and project plans can be based.

Related Policies: "Significant Information Security Risks," "Information Security Department Tasks," "Information Security Plans," and "Minimum Information System Controls."

Audience: Management

Security Environments: All

4.01.06 Cooperation Between Organizations

1. Information Security Products Disclosure

Policy: The product names, involved vendors, and configurations associated with installed information security systems at Company X must not be publicly disclosed at any time unless the advance permission of Information Security management has been obtained.

Commentary: This policy prevents staff from mentioning to outsiders the technologies used to protect information at Company X. Staff may not think that such a disclosure is anything for them to be worried about, when this information may in fact be instrumental in the compromise of Company X systems. This policy denies control information from those who do not have a need for such information. This is not security by obscurity, but concealment of material information that might be useful to an adversary. As a side benefit, the policy also prevents workers from endorsing any information security product.

Related Policies: "Public Releases Of Vulnerability Information" and "Public Communications."

Audience: End users

Security Environments: Medium and high

2. Public Disclosure Of Business Information

Policy: Company X must not publicly disclose any information related to a business deal or transaction that could reasonably be expected to be materially damaging to a customer or another third party.

Commentary: This policy maintains good working relationships with customers, business partners, and others. In many organizations the Marketing department is quick to publicly announce a major business deal or a major transaction before it considers the damage that such an announcement might create. The policy is deliberately vague when it comes to the words "materially damaged." Management will need to determine what constitutes material damage on a case-by-case basis. This policy is a business version of what the military calls traffic analysis. In other words, if the enemy can discover who is sending messages to whom or who is doing business with whom, a great deal of intelligence can be gleaned even if the contents of these messages or the nature of these deals is unknown.

Related Policies: "Public Releases Of Vulnerability Information" and "Internet Representations Including Affiliation."

Audience: Management

Security Environments: All

4.01.07 Independent Review Of Information Security

1. Use Of Investigators

Policy: Using investigators posing as other persons in order to test customer service and security policies, or investigate alleged wrongdoing must be authorized by the senior manager responsible for physical security.

Commentary: This policy notifies employees that there may be moles or spies within the organization, who are posing as regular employees or other authorized personnel, but who are actually investigators. These investigators may employ techniques like pretext calling where they use the telephone to masquerade as though they are someone else, in order to obtain certain information, or in order to determine a worker's response to certain questions. Having a policy like this shows management's attempt to be aboveboard and straightforward about a controversial topic, and a policy

such as this may prevent future allegations about being entrapped or mislead. The policy may encourage employees to be on their best behavior. The policy is considered to be a restriction of privacy rights because the workers do not know whom they are dealing with over the phone, over the electronic mail system, or through some other communications channel. Taking that uncertainty seriously is the same attitude that many organizations seek to foster in order to prevent social engineering or spoofing from leading to serious losses.

Related Policies: "Sender Contact Information" and "Identity Validation Of External Parties."

Audience: End users

Security Environments: Medium and high

2. Information System Control Reviews — Independent

Policy: An independent and externally-provided review of information systems must be periodically obtained to determine both the adequacy of and compliance with controls.

Commentary: This policy requires management to periodically seek outside feedback about information system controls. Many organizations assume they are adequately secure, when in fact they are not aware of the significant vulnerabilities they face. This problem is particularly severe in organizations where Information Systems management has been employed by the same organization for many years. In these cases, staff often becomes complacent and does not keep up with either the technology or the new risks that this technology introduces. An outsider's review may be a useful way to overcome internal loyalties and conflicts-of-interest that have conspired to keep vulnerabilities hidden. It is also useful for an independent outsider to come in and provide a reality check, particularly to assure that "standard of due care" controls are being employed. External auditors are required to look at computer-based internal controls during financial audits. They examine controls to determine the degree to which they can rely on the results of the systems employing these controls. However, during a financial audit, external auditors generally do not investigate information system controls in sufficient depth to notice other vulnerabilities besides those directly associated with financial information systems. This is why additional external review, provided by an outside technical consultant or a specialist may be appropriate.

Related Policies: "Minimum Information System Controls."

Audience: Management

Security Environments: All

4.02 Security Of Third-Party Access

4.02.01 Identification Of Risks From Third-Party Access

1. Third-Party User IDs

Policy: Individuals who are not employees, contractors, or consultants must not be granted a user ID or be given privileges to use Company X computers or communications systems unless the written approval of a department head has been obtained.

Commentary: The intention behind this policy is to ensure that unauthorized outsiders are not using Company X resources without specific management knowledge and permission. This policy is also intended to ensure that outsiders like customers and utility service providers are kept off Company X systems unless specific management permission is obtained. Rather than approval of a department head, the approval could be granted by the manager of Information Security or another manager with responsibility for organization-wide systems. Some organizations use a slight variation of this policy where a manager must sponsor an outsider prior to the issuance of any user ID. The word "temporary" does not appear in the policy along with the words "employees, contractors, or consultants." This is because temporaries are often hired with a negligible amount of background checking.

Related Policies: "Computer-Connected Network Access," "Unique User ID And Password Required," "User ID Forms," and "Reauthorization Of User Access Privileges."

Audience: Management and technical staff

Security Environments: All

2. Temporary Worker Privileges

Policy: Temporary workers must not be given any privileges on Company X information systems unless the relevant information Owner has agreed in writing.

Commentary: This policy restricts information system privileges to those who have gone through background checks and who have shown themselves over time to be trustworthy. Temporary employees typically have done neither of these things. Temporary employees generally work in their jobs with a specific organization for a few months at most, and management has very little incentive to invest in them, including the performance of background checks or the provision of training. Seen from the other side, temporary employees have very little loyalty to any specific employer. The recent increased concern about industrial espionage and terrorism has many organizations looking at temporaries as untrusted parties. This policy assumes that the responsibilities of information Owners have been defined in another policy.

Related Policies: "Third-Party User IDs," "Non-Employee Background Checks," and "Temporary Worker And Consultant Access."

Audience: Management and technical staff

Security Environments: Medium and high

3. Third-Party Remote Access

Policy: Inbound dial-up, inbound Internet, or virtual private network privileges must not be granted to third-party vendors unless the relevant system manager determines that these vendors have a legitimate business need for such access provided that these privileges are enabled for specific individuals and only for the time period required to accomplish approved tasks.

Commentary: Inbound dial-up, inbound Internet, and virtual private network privileges have been used by a number of system attackers to gain unauthorized access to systems. It is ill-advised to leave these ports, such as those used by vendors for remote maintenance, open and available if they are not currently being used. This policy keeps maintenance ports turned off, and keeps third parties off the system unless they have obtained approval from Company X management. Having a formal approval process will also discourage, if not prevent, others from attempting to masquerade as though they are a vendor representative. To narrow the coverage of this policy, change the word "privileges" to "maintenance privileges." This policy could be expanded to apply to private branch exchanges, network switching nodes, and other communication systems, and general purpose computer systems like minicomputers and mainframes. The use of the word "inbound" in the policy provides an exemption for sophisticated maintenance systems that automatically dial the vendor's system when they detect a problem.

Related Policies: "Conference Bridge Activation" and "Dial-Up Connections."

Audience: Technical staff

Security Environments: All

4. Consultant Note Taking

Policy: Company X consultants must not take notes regarding their confidential sessions with clients.

Commentary: This policy assures clients that written information about their private affairs will not fall into the hands of unauthorized or unintended parties. The policy is adapted from a statement issued by a psychologist's office, and it reflects his concern that information about his patients will be revealed through a lawsuit or perhaps through a burglary. The psychologist relies on his memory to service his clients and therefore does not worry about his confidential files being examined by other parties. The policy could easily be adapted to fit other lines of work. This policy assumes that the work can be performed without note taking. In some lines of work this is simply not possible because the tasks are too complex to efficiently accomplish without notes of some kind as in the information systems area.

Related Policies: "Disclosure Of Customer Information" and "Private Information Links."

Audience: End users

Security Environments: High

5. Machine Repair Staff Confidentiality Agreements

Policy: Prior to beginning their work, all external office equipment repair staff must have signed a Company X confidentiality agreement.

Commentary: This policy prevents industrial or military espionage. Recent models of ordinary office equipment such as copiers and fax machines now have up to five megabytes of recent information stored in them. If a repairperson were to swap the chip that contains this information, he or she could walk away with significant intellectual property without detection. If there is a paper jam, some sensitive information may have been printed on that paper but it may not have been removed from the machine. The policy is written with a broad scope, and that general purpose computers, including handhelds, would be included within its purview. Some organizations refer to confidentiality agreements as non-disclosure agreements.

Related Policies: "Confidentiality Agreements," "Third-Party Access Terms And Conditions," and "Sensitive Information Storage Media."

Audience: End users

Security Environments: Medium and high

6. Information Dissemination

Policy: Third-party access to any Company X internal information must be granted only when a demonstrable need to know exists, and when such a disclosure has been expressly authorized by Company X management.

Commentary: This policy notifies workers that, in the absence of further instructions, they should restrict the dissemination of internal Company X information. This is a good general policy on which more explicit subsequent policy statements can rely, or it can suffice for those organizations that do not have a great deal of confidential information. This policy is most applicable to those organizations that do not yet have a formal data classification system. No mention of data classification labels is made in this policy. Labels can save time and money and standardize the handling of sensitive information. This policy is especially relevant to those organizations with connections to the Internet or other public computer networks. Recent cases have shown that employees often distribute internal information on electronic bulletin boards, in Internet chat sessions, and in other public forums unless specifically instructed not to do so. Restricting the flow of internal information onto external networks is also possible with certain firewall controls, such as those that examine the content of the data sent. The policy does not make use of formal non-disclosure agreements.

Related Policies: "Four-Category Data Classification" and "Malfunctioning Access Control."

Audience: All

Security Environments: All

7. Non-Disclosure Agreements — Third Party

Policy: Prior to sending any secret, confidential, or private information to a third party for copying, printing, formatting, or other handling, the third party must sign a Company X non-disclosure agreement.

Commentary: This policy defines a clear boundary for the movement of sensitive information. Assuming that all Company X workers already have signed confidentiality agreements, the referenced types of information may be passed around inside the organization without further controls. But outsiders generally have not signed confidentiality agreements. These agreements will be required before sensitive internal information is provided to outsiders. As an example, consider printers who are working on a public company's annual report. These printers must sign confidentiality agreements to prevent them from using the information contained in the report to execute insider stock trades. This policy is relevant to computer data storage media, electronic mail, and old-fashioned hardcopy paper. As a result, the policy does not make specific mention of the technology that may be employed, although accompanying explanatory comments may do this. The policy shown here could be rewritten so that the words "secret, confidential, or private" are replaced with specific data classification labels used within the organization.

Related Policies: "Four-Category Data Classification" and "Non-Disclosure Agreements — Organization."

Audience: All

Security Environments: All

8. Confidentiality Agreements

Policy: All disclosures of secret, confidential, or private Company X information to third parties must be accomplished through a signed confidentiality agreement that includes restrictions on the subsequent dissemination and usage of the information.

Commentary: This policy prevents unauthorized uses of Company X information including secondary dissemination. Specific directions about usage should prohibit additional distribution without the information Owner's consent. This policy could be expanded to delineate the specific requirements that must be stated as part of a confidentiality agreement. These could include return of the information, how the information will be safeguarded, what the information will be used for, and who will be given access to the information.

Related Policies: "Secondary Dissemination Of Secret Information," "Sensitive Information Handling," and "Compliance Agreement."

Audience: All

Security Environments: All

9. Temporary Worker And Consultant Access

Policy: Activities requiring access to sensitive Company X information must only be performed by full-time permanent employees unless the requisite knowledge or skills are not possessed by a full-time permanent employee, an emergency or disaster requires the use of additional workers, or permission of the director of Human Resources and the information Owner has been obtained.

Commentary: This policy restricts access to sensitive information to the most-trusted individuals. Full-time, permanent employees are generally more loyal than temporary employees, contractors, or consultants, and are therefore more trustworthy. Once the employment relationship has ended, Company X has little control over the activities of temporary employees, contractors, or consultants, but it maintains some control over former full-time employees. The risks of using people other than full-time permanent employees can be partially mitigated through confidentiality agreements, and agreements not to compete. Entities that are virtual corporations, that use outsourcing extensively, or that have other decentralized or networked organization structures may have trouble with this policy because it's based on an assumption that a core group of employees runs the organization.

Related Policies: "Non-Disclosure Agreements — Organization," "Four-Category Data Classification," and "Privilege Restriction — Need To Know."

Audience: Management

Security Environments: All

10. Telephone Books

Policy: Internal telephone books must not be distributed to third parties other than contractors, consultants, temporary workers, and other third-parties working for Company X without the specific authorization of a department manager.

Commentary: This policy changes the way people have been thinking about the information contained in an internal telephone book. As a reflection of this, many organizations have now added the words "confidential" or "restricted" to each page in their telephone books or on the cover. Telephone books may be used by recruiters to locate potential candidates. In a similar manner, industrial spies could use a telephone book to identify workers they wanted to bribe, pressure, dupe, or otherwise exploit. Hackers could also use telephone books to identify modem numbers and other system-related numbers. Industrial spies could additionally use telephone books as a way to figure out which people they could best masquerade as when attempting social engineering. This policy can be taken one step further by restricting the dissemination of information contained in the phone book. For example, if someone

was to call Company X asking for the phone number and name of the director of the Information Systems department, a telephone operator would be forbidden from releasing this information. A consequence of designating an internal phone book as confidential is that it needs to be disposed of properly. Some companies place words on the cover saying, "After New Book Is Issued, Return This Book To The Security Department For Secure Disposal."

Related Policies: "Computer-Related Access Numbers."

Audience: End users and technical staff

Security Environments: All

11. Third-Party Access To Internal Systems

Policy: Third-party access to any Company X internal computer systems that are not clearly public must be approved in advance by a designated information security coordinator.

Commentary: This policy prevents system administrators and others from readily granting third parties access to internal machines or systems. Extranets are becoming popular and in the rush to exploit these new systems, management is granting access to third parties without going through established access control approval processes. The involvement of an information security coordinator is indicated because these distributed representatives of a centralized information security infrastructure know the established rules for approving access control privileges. In the policy, the information security coordinator could be replaced by information security management or others who are part of the existing centralized information security infrastructure. As information systems become increasingly distributed and decentralized, end users are taking on many of the traditional roles of system administrators, and are often in a position where they can grant access to third parties. This policy covers a wide variety of access types such as electronic mail accounts, Internet access user IDs, inventory checking applications.

Related Policies: "Privilege Restriction — Need To Know."

Audience: End users

Security Environments: All

12. Third-Party Security Responsibilities

Policy: Before any third-party users can contact Company X systems through real-time computer connections, specific written approval of Information Security management is required that specifies the security-related responsibilities of Company X, the security-related responsibilities of the common carrier, and the security-related responsibilities of all other involved third parties.

Commentary: This policy prevents real-time connections of Company X systems with third parties unless these have been shown to be adequately secure. This policy would, for example, prevent salespeople from opening up the order entry system to customers unless security issues had previously been examined, and approved controls had been properly implemented. Only after clearly specifying security responsibilities can Company X determine whether they want to accept the risks that the connection presents. The policy would permit internal users to employ out-bound dial-up systems to access third-party electronic mail services and online database retrieval services without the need for a security evaluation and approval process. This policy would permit Internet electronic mail connections because these are not real-time connections. This policy would, however, prevent a department from establishing their own Internet firewall.

Related Policies: "System Interconnection," "Communication Line Changes," and "Internet Connections."

Audience: Management and technical staff

Security Environments: All

13. Critical Vendor Financial Review

Policy: The chief information officer (CIO) or an individual designated by the CIO must review the financial condition of vendors providing or supporting critical Company X production information systems annually.

Commentary: This policy requires those responsible for information systems management to periodically consider the financial condition of essential vendors. With mergers, acquisitions, bankruptcies, initial public offerings, and other major events taking place with increasing frequency in the information systems industry, relationships with the vendors on which a business depends may change quite rapidly. An increasing number of information systems products and services are delivered by outside vendors, and purchasing organizations are much more dependent on these vendors. If management knows that there is some question about a vendor being a financially-viable business, it can take remedial measures such as arranging software escrow, establishing back-up contracts with other vendors, and investigating the ways that production data can be converted in order to run with other vendors' software. This policy is written in a general way so that it includes both services and products. In their contracts, many organizations require privately-held vendors to disclose annual financial statements in order to perform the task described in this policy. For vendors who are particularly unstable or risky, quarterly or even monthly financial status reviews may be appropriate.

Related Policies: "Vendor-Provided Systems Software Installation" and "Software Integrity Statements."

Audience: Management

Security Environments: All

4.02.02 Security Requirements In Third-Party Contracts

1. Third-Party Access Terms And Conditions

Policy: Before any third party is given access to Company X systems, a contract defining the terms and conditions of such access must have been signed by a responsible manager at the third-party organization and be approved by Company X Information Security management and the Legal department vice president.

Commentary: In many organizations, outsourcing organizations, consultants, contractors, and other third parties are given access to internal systems as if they were trusted insiders. This can lead to serious breaches of security, especially if the third-party systems are inadequately protected. This policy is intended to notify all internal staff that third-party access is a serious security issue, and that in all instances, it must be supported by a written and approved contract. After the internal managers who must approve such contracts have gone through this process several times, they will develop a checklist of criteria that must go along with each such contract. This checklist can be used to develop a contract that can be used with all outsiders seeking access to internal information systems. The contract ordinarily would cover things such as: a non-disclosure agreement, a description of the specific control measures that must be used for Company X data, clarification of the responses that must be taken after a breach of security, and assignment of liability for any problems that occur.

Related Policies: "Revocation Of Access Privileges" and "Reauthorization Of User Access Privileges."

Audience: Management and technical staff

Security Environments: All

2. Information Transfer To Third Parties

Policy: Company X software, documentation, and all other types of internal information must not be sold or otherwise transferred to any non-Company X party for any purposes other than those expressly authorized by management.

Commentary: Workers have been known to sell mailing lists and other in-house data. Similarly, at software organizations, employees have been known to post pre-release copies of software on the Internet. This policy notifies workers that such information must remain in-house. The existence of such a notice can form the basis for disciplinary actions or prosecutions. In many instances transfer of information to a third party is in good faith, such as when an employee makes a copy of security documentation to show to colleagues at an information security professional association. In this case, disclosure of internal information may help outsiders to compromise the security of the organization involved. Some employees will be relieved to have a policy such as this because it permits them to decline to participate in research surveys, marketing research telephone interviews, and other interactions that they'd just as soon avoid.

Related Policies: "Software And Data Exchange Agreements."

Audience: All

Security Environments: All

3. Third-Party Use Of Organization Name

Policy: No third-party organization may use the Company X name in its advertising or marketing materials unless the permission of corporate legal counsel has been obtained.

Commentary: This policy prevents third-party activities from sullying the good name of a particular organization. For example, if an entrepreneur were to use the name of a large and prestigious company, saying that this company was endorsing his or her activities, this claim would bring great credibility. But if the claim were false, and he or she ended up defrauding customers, the good name of the large company might be degraded even though there was no conscious fault of the large company. In a worst-case situation, some people may even hold the large company responsible for their fraud losses claiming an implied endorsement. To prevent such problems, this policy says that no usage is permissible unless it has been approved by corporate legal counsel. Some companies are now enforcing this trademark protection policy by scanning the Internet through search engines, looking for all instances in which their company name appears. If any unauthorized appearance is found, the responsible parties are contacted and told to cease and desist.

Related Policies: "Intellectual Property" and "Unofficial Web Pages."

Audience: End users

Security Environments: All

4. Information Handling At Contract Termination

Policy: If Company X terminates its contract with any third-party organization that is handling Company X private information, this same third-party organization must immediately thereafter destroy or return all of the Company X private data in its possession.

Commentary: The purpose of this policy is to specify the ways that private data will be handled when it does come time to end a relationship with a third party who has had custody of private data. For example, a hospital might provide medical information to a third-party billing organization so that invoices could be generated and mailed to patients. If the hospital changed billing organizations, then the old billing organization should be required to destroy or return all the involved information. By destroying or returning information, subsequent unauthorized use is prevented. This requirement will need to be written into third-party confidentiality agreements, non-disclosure agreements or third-party consulting contracts because a third party will not be legally bound by an internal policy. In this sense, an internal policy reminds management and technical staff to include this requirement in all arrangements with third parties where private information is handled.

Related Policies: "Chain Of Trust Agreements" and "Certificate Of Destruction Of Storage Media."

Audience: Management

Security Environments: Medium and high

5. Circumventing Privacy Policy With Third Parties

Policy: If a privacy policy prevents Company X from performing a certain act or taking a certain course of action, it must not hire one or more third parties to perform this action.

Commentary: Unlike most information security policies, this policy is intended for public consumption. This policy assures prospects and customers that Company X is not going to use a legal maneuver or a loophole in its privacy policy as a way to get around the requirements of a privacy policy. This policy is in part motivated by certain government agencies who have been buying data from private sector data aggregators. These aggregators bring together information from many different sources such as motor vehicle driver's records, liens and deeds for real estate, telephone number listings, and voter registration records. These government agencies are using aggregators to perform criminal investigations and to compile surveillance information that they may otherwise be prohibited from compiling. The policy assures prospects and customers that the words in the privacy policy mean something, that the issuing organization is not going to turn around and out source the activity so that it can say "we did not do that."

Related Policies: "Security Measures At Third-Party Organizations" and "Transfer Of Customer Information."

Audience: End users

Security Environments: All

6. Chain Of Trust Agreements

Policy: Private or sensitive information in the custody of Company X must not be disclosed to third parties unless these third parties have signed an explicit chain of trust agreement approved by Information Security management.

Commentary: This policy ensures that private or sensitive information is not disclosed to any third party unless this third party has agreed to protect the information in a prescribed manner. Chain of trust agreements typically state that the recipient will return all the information when the project is completed, will destroy all copies of the information, and will refrain from using the information for purposes other than those expressly stated in the agreement. Other stipulations may be included. For example, the recipient may be required to keep the nature and existence of the information provided by the disclosing organization confidential. A chain of trust agreement may be incorporated in standardized contracts, such as a standard consulting services boilerplate contract, or it may be a standalone agreement. With chain of trust agreements, organizations can use outsourcing organizations and other affiliated businesses with the assurance that the information security policies observed internally are also being observed at the recipient organization. Chain of trust agreements are a quick way to overcome the difficult inconsistencies and incompatibilities in information security policies found at two or more organizations. For this reason they are popular with extranets and other Internet trading partner systems. Chain of trust agreements are also legally binding and they clearly identify who is responsible for what information security activities, which is an important but often neglected area.

Related Policies: "User ID Forms" and "Secondary Dissemination Of Secret Information."

Audience: All

Security Environments: All

7. Vendor Relationship Disclosure

Policy: When placing orders for products or services, or when establishing any new or modified business relationship, Company X staff must notify third-party vendors that they must not publicly reveal either the nature of, or the very existence of a relationship with Company X without written approval from a Company X corporate officer.

Commentary: This policy ensures that vendors do not reveal information that could damage Company X or its interests. Vendors may wish to tout the new business they get in order to attract further business, but this can damage Company X by indirectly revealing its strategic initiatives, its long range plans, its resource allocation decisions, or its current activities. The policy prevents the Company X name from being used in ways that it did not approve or intend, and thereby prevent allegations of implied endorsement for a certain product or service. A policy like this can be incorporated into contracts with third-party vendors. It is also wise if internal staff is instructed to verbally remind third-party vendors about the existence of this contractual provision.

Related Policies: "Public Disclosure Of Business Information" and "Internet Representations Including Affiliation."

Audience: Management

Security Environments: Medium and high

8. Third-Party Collection Of Pricing Information

Policy: In an effort to prevent competitors from obtaining proprietary internal information, third parties must not gather a significant number of prices for Company X products and services.

Commentary: This policy deliberately creates an artificial barrier to free information flow. For example, software agents working in the background on the Internet may visit multiple vendor web sites selling audio recordings, then determine which vendor has the lowest prices. This policy instructs systems designers to install mechanisms that will block agents from performing such price comparison tasks. While it may sound like a cut-throat competitive tactic, this practice is already well-established in the physical goods business environment. For example, grocery stores will routinely bar employees from other stores from walking the isles collecting a significant amount of information about prices. In some instances it may be desirable to generalize this policy so that it limits any external information-gathering activity that might then convey a competitive advantage to the third party. The word "significant" in the policy is deliberately vague, permitting information systems to evolve in response to changing conditions. This policy is most useful within an organization that offers many different products or services with different prices.

Related Policies: "Information Collection Restrictions."

Audience: Technical staff

Security Environments: All

9. Sensitive Information Handling

Policy: All disclosures of secret, confidential, or private Company X information to third parties must be accompanied by an explicit statement describing exactly what information is restricted and how this information may and may not be used.

Commentary: This policy can be used to address secondary dissemination issues, unauthorized use, and related abuses of restricted information after it has left Company X. An explicit statement may be part of a non-disclosure agreement signed by a third party receiving the information, or simply given in narrative or verbal form at the time of disclosure. Some organizations will want to add the word "written" to the policy between the words "explicit statement." Simple verbal instructions may be sufficient if the recipient already has a signed confidentiality agreement with Company X or if the recipient has a trusted on-going business relationship with Company X. The intention of this policy is primarily to require those who disclose sensitive information to provide specific instructions on its proper handling. The policy assumes that the terms "secret, confidential, or private" have already been defined.

Related Policies: "Four-Category Data Classification" and "Secondary Dissemination Of Secret Information."

Audience: All

Security Environments: All

10. Receiving Third-Party Information

Policy: If an agent, employee, consultant, or contractor is to receive secret or confidential information from a third party on behalf of Company X, this disclosure must be preceded by the third-party signature of a release form approved by the Legal department.

Commentary: This policy prevents Company X from being obliged to pay royalties or other compensation to third parties if, subsequent to this disclosure, Company X releases a product or service that is related to the ideas disclosed by the third party. A release form should make it clear that Company X is under no obligation to pay any such royalties or other compensation, and that receipt of the information does not imply any contractual arrangement whatsoever. This may be a particularly difficult issue if Company X has been secretly developing similar information. In this case, Company X may determine the nature of the information to be received, then deliberately choose not to accept the information lest some dispute ensue. Some organizations, such as venture capital organizations, are so concerned about this, that without exception they refuse to sign other people's confidentiality agreements. Consultation with the Legal department within Company X will be necessary prior to the release of a policy such as this.

Related Policies: "Delivery Of Secret Information."

Audience: All

Security Environments: All

11. Network-Connected Third-Party Systems

Policy: To gain access to the Company X computer network, every third party must secure its own connected systems in a manner consistent with Company X requirements including, but not limited to, the right to audit the security measures on these connected systems without prior warning and the right to immediately terminate network connections with all third-party systems.

Commentary: This policy notifies third parties who have access to the Company X network that they must maintain the security of their own systems in order to continue to do business over the Company X network. The ability to immediately terminate a connection that has shown to be exploited by a hacker is important as hackers often use a number of different systems to hide their tracks. This policy is an attempt to resolve what has become an increasingly difficult-to-manage problem, namely the reconciliation of differing security policies on separate networks. The policy gives third parties a relatively easy way to achieve consistent security: when connected to the Company X network, a stand-alone system observes Company X security requirements, but after this connection is terminated, the same machine can be connected to another organization's network and use a different set of controls. Some organizations may wish to specify examples of the third parties.

Related Policies: "System Interconnection," "Connecting Third-Party Networks," and "Network Connections with Outside Organizations."

Audience: Technical staff

Security Environments: All

12. Third-Party Agreements

Policy: All agreements dealing with the handling of Company X information by third parties must include a clause granting permission to Company X for the periodic auditing of the controls used for these information handling activities, and specifying the ways in which Company X information will be protected.

Commentary: This policy prevents Company X employees from inadvertently giving away responsibility for the security of Company X information. This might happen when an outsourcing organization takes over data processing operations. While Company X may elect to have contractors or other organizations handle information security activities, it should always retain the right to specify information protection requirements and the right to ensure that the third party is living up to these requirements. The policy is worded such that the auditing could be done by humans or through automated auditing tools.

Related Policies: "Third-Party Information Security Responsibilities," "Outsourcing Contract Approvals," and "Third-Party Access Terms And Conditions."

Audience: Management and technical staff

Security Environments: All

13. Security Measures At Third-Party Organizations

Policy: Before a user ID can be issued to a third party, documentary evidence of an information security system or process must be provided to, and approved by, Company X Information Security management and the third party must agree in writing to maintain this system or process to prevent unauthorized and improper use of Company X systems.

Commentary: This policy recognizes and deals with the risks associated with third-party access to Company X internal systems. Specifically, unless these third parties have and maintain reliable information security measures, then two problems may occur. Unauthorized parties may thereby gain access to Company X internal systems, and second, authorized third parties may use their granted access for improper purposes. This policy insists that documentary proof that a system of information security measures exists be provided before a user ID is issued. The policy also specifies that the information security measures must be consistently observed, and that this requirement must be in writing. The policy additionally gives internal management at Company X written evidence that they performed some due diligence checking of the third party, and this can later be used in court if ever there should be a security problem involving the third party. The policy is intended for organizations rather than individuals. In those cases where the third party is an individual, the individual can be given a list of minimum security requirements to agree in writing to abide by these same requirements. This policy is similar to a practice that requires that before proprietary internal information is released to third parties, these same third parties must provide documentary evidence that they can and will protect the information about to be disclosed.

Related Policies: "Personal User IDs — Responsibility."

Audience: Management and technical staff

Security Environments: All

14. Third-Party Security Policy

Policy: Before any proprietary Company X information is disclosed to a third party, this third party must sign a Company X confidentiality agreement and submit a copy of its information security policy for approval by Company X Information Security management.

Commentary: This policy ensures that proprietary information is not disclosed to a third party who is not able to properly protect it. While requiring a confidentiality or non-disclosure agreement is a standard practice, this policy requires that the third party disclose its information security policy, and that this policy must meet with the approval of Information Security management. In this case, Information Security should be looking to see whether the third party has a system of internal controls that realistically could be expected to adequately protect Company X proprietary information. If Information Security is not satisfied with the policy document, then the request for proprietary information should be denied. For government agencies, the word "proprietary" could be replaced with the word "secret." This policy is intended for third-party organizations rather than individuals. If an individual is being considered for the receipt of proprietary information, Company X can prepare a list of minimum security measures, and this individual can agree in writing to abide by these minimum requirements.

Related Policies: "Security Measures At Third-Party Organizations."

Audience: Management and technical staff

Security Environments: Medium and high

15. Externally-Gathered Information

Policy: Every contract with an outsourcing organization, a contract programmer, or any other external organization that handles Company X information systems or communication systems must stipulate that all information gathered about Company X will be provided on demand to Company X at no additional charge.

Commentary: The intention behind this policy is a variety of recent attempts by third-party vendors to lock-in paying customers. For example, an organization that maintains information systems equipment for a company may keep detailed records, but later refuse to provide these same records to the company. This refusal will make it much more difficult for the company to bring this activity back in-house, just as it will make it more difficult for the company to switch outsourcing organizations. The third party makes switching providers prohibitively expensive or time-consuming. This policy follows the general practice of telephone companies, where they provide a list of numbers called, calling patterns to different parts of the world, and similar information to the company who pays the bill. In many ways this policy is a way to protect the company against exploitation by third parties based on denied access to their own information. This policy could be enhanced by requiring that the information be delivered in computer-readable form using widely-accepted file conventions. This enhancement will prevent a third party from providing the information in a form that is unusable.

Related Policies: "Customer Access To Personal Information" and "Access To Personal Information."

Audience: Management and technical staff

Security Environments: All

16. Third-Party Information Security Responsibilities

Policy: All Company X business partners, suppliers, customers, and other business associates must be made aware of their information security responsibilities through specific language appearing in contracts that define their relationship with Company X.

Commentary: This policy clearly states that management must consider the assignment of information security responsibility when they strike deals with third parties. Not only must these topics be considered, but also specific details about the way these things are going to get handled must be included in contracts. A good example of this is outsourcing facilities management deals, where a third party takes over the information technology operations of an organization. Companies often forget or ignore information security when it comes to these negotiations. As a result, information security suffers. When the organization that outsourced its operations complains, the outsourcing organization will point to the contract saying that they are not required to provide security, and that the organization must pay extra if it wants extra service. This example assumes that some major problem has not already taken place. The policy equally applies to other environments such as the use of a third-party, value-added network service. Internal legal counsel should be consulted on this important topic.

Related Policies: "Third-Party Agreements," "Third-Party Software Agreements," "Information Security Compliance," "Network Message Protection Services," "Network-Connected Third-Party Systems," and "Cross Training."

Audience: Management and technical staff

Security Environments: All

17. Information Return By Contract Personnel

Policy: Upon the termination or expiration of their contract, all contractors, consultants, and temporaries must give their project manager all copies of Company X information received or created during the execution of the contract.

Commentary: This policy clarifies that contractors, consultants, and temporaries must return all information they received in order to complete a contract. Ownership of the information created during execution of the contract may be an issue unless this topic was specified in the contract. In the absence of a formal written agreement, legal issues, such as whether the

work generated was a "work for hire," may control actual ownership. The word "ownership," refers to legal ownership, not to the role of information Owners.

Related Policies: "Property Rights."

Audience: All

Security Environments: All

18. Information Security Compliance

Policy: Outside consultants, contractors, and temporaries must be subject to the same information security requirements, and have the same information security responsibilities, as Company X employees.

Commentary: This policy clearly states who must comply with information security requirements such as policies, standards, and procedures. This policy informs lower-level managers that they need to provide consultants, contractors, and temporaries at least some information about how things are done at the organization. The policy also notifies management that they should not use consultants, contractors, and temporaries as a way to get around security requirements that apply to employees. This policy is another way to express the notion of universal application that holds that controls should apply to all people across all computing environments. For example, every person should be wearing a badge when inside a secured building. Many people consider it wise to reserve certain privileged or highly-trusted activities, such as systems security administration, for employees only.

Related Policies: "Bonding Workers" and "Third-Party Information Security Responsibilities."

Audience: Management

Security Environments: All

4.03 Outsourcing

4.03.01 Security Requirements In Outsourcing Contracts

1. Independent Control Reports

Policy: All agreements with information systems outsourcing organizations must stipulate that Company X will annually receive a report expressing an independent opinion about the adequacy of the controls in use at the outsourcing organization.

Commentary: This policy prevents internal management from entering into any outsourcing organization agreement unless they have included language in the contract that requires the outsourcing organization to provide annual independent control review reports. This is an independent review of the policies, procedures, and other controls with an eye toward whether these are in keeping with the standard of due care. Often provided by accounting organizations, but possibly provided by other consulting organizations, these reports give customer organizations some confidence that an outsourcing organization is doing a good job when it comes to security. These audits are not financial audits, they are internal controls audits. Often customer organizations will not have sufficient expertise in-house to be able to audit an outsourcing organization, even if the outsourcing organization were to permit each customer to conduct such an audit. It is far more efficient for the outsourcing organization to sponsor and arrange such an audit with a third-party consulting organization, perform the audit once, and distribute the results to its customer organizations, than it is for each customer organization to send auditors to the outsourcing organization to perform their own unique audit. This approach additionally saves money for customer organizations.

Related Policies: "Outsourcing Organization Financial Statements" and "Outsourcing Contract Approvals."

Audience: Management and technical staff

Security Environments: Medium and high

2. Application Service Provider Software

Policy: Every application service provider handling Company X production information must license the software to Company X, periodically deposit the most recent version of the source code in an approved software escrow facility, and provide current detailed procedural documentation.

Commentary: This policy ensures that Company X could continue to support an outsourced application even if an application service provider (ASP) were to go bankrupt, or were to otherwise be unwilling or unable to deliver on its contractual promises. The policy is intended to influence the negotiation of new contracts or the renegotiation of existing contracts. This policy pertains only to application systems that typically contain unique business logic and hard-to-recreate routines. The same considerations do not generally apply to systems software, such as firewall software, because one vendor's package can often be used to replace another vendor's package. The scope of the policy could, however, be expanded to include unique systems software. It is not enough to have the code, and to be licensed to use it. An organization also needs to

have the operational documentation and procedures. In an ideal scenario, an ASP will train customer staff in the use of the application software because the documentation may not be comprehensible. The contract with the ASP should be written to give the organization adopting this policy the right to bring the use of the application in-house if for some reason the ASP is unsatisfactory. A conversion plan and a contingency plan will also be needed.

Related Policies: "Computer Disaster Recovery Plans."

Audience: Management and technical staff

Security Environments: All

3. Alternate Processing Provider

Policy: In every case where critical Company X production information systems processing is handled by an outsourcing organization, an alternate provider must be ready to immediately take-over these activities if the outsourcing organization is no longer be able or willing to deliver on its promises.

Commentary: This policy reduces the vulnerability that comes with the retention of an outsourcing organization to handle critical information systems activities. This policy is quite strict in that it requires that an immediate cut-over to a secondary provider be available and ready to go. In this respect, the policy is a contingency planning policy. The policy is motivated by a number of instances where outsourcing organizations have gone out of business abruptly with very little or no advance notice, and without any conversion assistance to the customers who are stranded and scrambling to arrange an alternate provider. The alternate provider could involve bringing the processing in-house. Nothing in the policy as it is written prevents this. This policy covers not just those situations where the provider is unable to meet it contractual commitments, but also can be used in the event of a dispute, in which case the primary provider may stop providing the promised services. This policy assumes that the word "critical" has been formally defined in another policy. Usually there are various levels of application system criticality.

Related Policies: "Computer Emergency Response Plans."

Audience: Management and technical staff

Security Environments: Medium and high

4. Service Provider Contingency Plans

Policy: All contracts with web site hosting organizations, application service providers, managed systems security providers, and other information systems outsourcing organizations must include both a documented backup plan and a periodic third-party testing schedule.

Commentary: This policy establishes a minimum control measure or backup plan that often does not get written into contracts. If this requirement is incorporated into a contract and if the hosting organization does not deliver, then there is legal recourse and a subscribing organization may be able to recover damages. Whatever the words in a contract, due diligence dictates that backup plans must be periodically tested to show that they are working correctly. A subscriber to a hosting organization's service may wish to retain a consultant to perform these tests. Small organizations may not have the leverage to change the contractual terms with a hosting organization. Just because a hosting organization is big does not mean that it is going to do a good job when it comes to a backup strategy, process, or plan. In more general terms, every subscriber should also establish and periodically update a contingency plan that uses these backups to test their viability, such as setting up an Internet business using another hosting organization.

Related Policies: "Chain Of Trust Agreements" and "Third-Party Agreements."

Audience: Management

Security Environments: All

5. Outsourced Production Systems Back-Out Plans

Policy: An effective and regularly-tested back-out plan, that permits Company X to revert to internal processing and has been approved by Information Security management, must be prepared and tested before any production information system processing may be transferred to an outsourcing organization.

Commentary: This policy ensures that Company X can bring outsourced production processing back in-house when necessary. A back-out plan will typically cover issues such as reformatting data, obtaining a current version of the software used for processing, and recruiting necessary expertise to help with computer operations. Many organizations that have outsourced information systems activities find that they no longer have competent staff who could manage the activities associated with in-house production processing. They are at the outsourcing organization's mercy and must therefore accept price increases, undesirable contractual terms when a contract comes up for renewal, and other things that they may otherwise refuse to tolerate. Having a current back-out plan puts Company X in a position where it could realistically revert to internal processing. This policy assumes that Company X will negotiate contracts that permit it to bring production processing back in-house for significant cause, such as when an outsourcing organization fails to meet its service level agreements.

Related Policies: "Software Conversion Contingency Plans" and "Reversion To Manual Procedures."

Audience: Management

Security Environments: All

6. Shared Outsourcer Firewalls And Servers

Policy: Company X does not permit its internal information to be resident on or processed by any firewall, server, or other computer that is shared with another organization at an outsourcing facility.

Commentary: This policy prevents situations where a shared computer with another organization leads to information security or public relations problems. If a computer is shared, staff from another organization may be able to access Company X information resident thereon using disk repair utility programs, even if these staff members do not officially have access privileges that enable them to view Company X information. Organizations have received bad publicity when it was revealed that they shared computers with less-reputable companies. Although these organizations had no idea with whom they were sharing the outsourcing computers, they were nonetheless perceived as guilty by association. This policy is a specific implementation of the secure systems design principle of isolation that states, "To the extent that various components can be isolated, generally their security will be enhanced."

Related Policies: "Excessive Resource Consumption" and "Critical Application Servers."

Audience: Technical staff

Security Environments: All

7. Accessibility To Outsourced Information

Policy: In every case where Company X uses an outsourcing organization to process or otherwise manage its production information, the contract with the outsourcing organization must clearly stipulate either for the daily delivery to Company X of a complete and computer-readable copy of its information, or that Company X has the right to immediately obtain a computer-readable copy of its information at any time and without limitation.

Commentary: This policy confronts and prevents a tactic used by a number of application service providers and other outsourcing organizations that involves holding customer production data hostage until a customer pays its bill or otherwise resolves a dispute in a manner agreeable to the management at the outsourcing organization. While such a dispute remains unresolved, an outsourcing organization's customer may be severely inconvenienced or even threatened with bankruptcy because it cannot perform its normal business activities. This policy is therefore intended to prevent Company X from entering into any outsourcing arrangement where it could not obtain the most recent version of its production information. Not just any copy of the information is sufficient. It needs to be in computer-readable format. In fact, it must be in a format usable by computers inside Company X or at another outsourcing organization. This latter fact may be stipulated in the policy, but it is implied by the words "computer-readable." This policy assumes that the term "production" has been defined as data used in support of regular and recurring business activity.

Related Policies: "Service Provider Contingency Plans."

Audience: Management and technical staff

Security Environments: All

8. Access Control Decisions

Policy: Decisions about who will be granted access to both Company X information and Company X information systems must be made by Company X management and never by outsourcing organization personnel.

Commentary: This policy prevents internal management from delegating a responsibility that they alone must retain. At many organizations, management opts to give everything related to information systems management to one or more outsourcing organizations. While security administration, network intrusion detection monitoring, and other information security tasks may be appropriately delegated to an outsourcing organization, organizations must not delegate decisions about who can access which systems and what information. To do so would be to delegate critical and essential management decision-making which by law, in some jurisdictions, must be retained by internal management. Nothing in this policy prevents management from using outsourcing organizations or consulting organizations to obtain recommendations about how to define access privileges.

Related Policies: "Information Ownership" and "Information Ownership Delegation."

Audience: Management

Security Environments: All

9. Outsourcing Contract Approvals

Policy: All information-systems-related outsourcing contracts must be reviewed and approved by Information Security management who is responsible for ensuring that these contracts sufficiently define information security responsibilities, how to respond to a variety of potential security problems and the right to terminate the contract for cause if it can be shown that the outsourcing organization does not abide by the information security terms of the contract.

Commentary: This policy clearly assigns responsibility for examining outsourcing contracts to ensure that contracts are sufficiently explicit and clear in the area of information security. In many cases, the organization that hired an outsourcing organization overlooked defining explicit security responsibilities and problem resolution procedures. As a result, when a security problem occurs, the outsourcing organization may relax its effort because it is not rewarded or punished based on information security. This policy changes this reaction, giving the organization explicit legal mechanisms such as contract termination that can be used to get the outsourcing organization to take security seriously. The policy is intended to prevent situations where the Information Security department never sees outsourcing agreements until there is a problem. Contract review is often the ultimate responsibility of the Legal department and the policy may be designed to include such a reference.

Related Policies: "Information Ownership Delegation," "Third-Party Agreements," and "Information Security Problem Resolution."

Audience: Management

Security Environments: Medium and high

10. Outsourcing Organization Financial Statements

Policy: All information systems outsourcing organizations contracted to handle production Company X information must provide Company X with quarterly financial statements.

Commentary: This policy affects the negotiation of new contracts, or the renegotiation of existing contracts, with information systems outsourcing organizations. If an outsourcing organization is unwilling to reveal financial information, this is generally a bad sign that it may be in danger of soon going out of business. An unannounced and unanticipated cessation of service could have serious or even fatal repercussions for an outsourcing organization's customers. The information systems industry is notoriously volatile and several outsourcing organizations have gone out of business overnight without prior warning. This policy is a way for management of outsourcing customers to have some early warning. Just receiving financial statements is not going to be enough. That is why this policy must be accompanied by additional policies.

Related Policies: "Critical Vendor Financial Review" and "Computer Disaster Recovery Plans."

Audience: Management and technical staff

Security Environments: All

11. Production Processing Outsourced To Foreign Companies

Policy: Company X management must not outsource any aspect of production information systems management including, but not limited to, systems design, development, testing, operation, and maintenance to an organization that is based in a foreign country or owned by a foreign company.

Commentary: This policy ensures that problems with outsourcing organizations will be minimized. Use of foreign outsourcing organizations, while less expensive, can be problematic. This can impact system reliability, security, and data integrity. Beyond language barriers, Company X staff may not be able to inspect foreign outsourcing organization facilities, may not be able to sue in domestic courts if there are disputes, and may not be able rely upon the fact that the outsourcing organization is subject to the same laws to which Company X is subject. Outsourcing is often fraught with communication problems and these can be made worse by cultural differences. Foreign companies may also withdraw from the marketplace with less public warning than, or according to business criteria different from those used by domestic companies. As a result, Company X may have a more difficult time anticipating when foreign outsourcing organization services will no longer be available.

Related Policies: "Software Escrow" and "Chain Of Trust Agreements."

Audience: Management

Security Environments: All

5   ASSET CLASSIFICATION AND CONTROL

5.01 Accountability For Assets

5.01.01 Inventory Of Assets

1. Software And System Classification

Policy: Information Security must annually prepare a list of software and systems developed in-house and that may provide Company X with a competitive advantage.

Commentary: This policy requires Information Security management or local information security coordinators to periodically examine the importance of software and systems developed in-house. The existence of such a list should then be used as a mechanism to ensure that the software and systems information are properly classified according to an internal data classification scheme. Likewise, the list should be used to determine whether the associated controls are adequate. In this manner, the policy ensures organizations that their most precious information resources are properly protected. This policy is most relevant for those organizations that have developed unique software, expert systems, knowledge management systems, and other materials that give them a distinct competitive advantage. The policy also may be used as a way to provide management with a report reflecting how information systems are being used to achieve competitive advantage. In this respect, it may be appropriate for Information Security to work with the Strategic Planning department or the Systems Architecture group within the Information Systems department. In some organizations, the identification of materials that provide competitive advantage can be done by a data management or data warehousing group.

Related Policies: "Information Security Plans."

Audience: Management and technical staff

Security Environments: All

2. Asset Inventory — Technology

Policy: Information Systems management must prepare an annual inventory of production information systems detailing all existing production hardware, software, and communications links.

Commentary: This policy requires management to prepare an annual inventory of production information systems hardware, software, and communications links.

Only by knowing what system components exist can an organization properly plan for disasters. The information systems at many organizations change so rapidly that a current inventory will be a valuable management tool for other purposes, not just for contingency planning. For example, a current inventory would be useful to management negotiating a volume purchase agreement with a software vendor. Likewise, the inventory will be helpful for information security activities, such as determining which personal computers are protected by virus screening software. Because local area networks and other distributed computing systems are often insufficiently documented, this policy is particularly useful for local area networks, client-server systems, and office automation systems. Software products can perform an inventory of personal computer hardware and software inventory when these machines are connected to a local area network. If a comprehensive production system inventory is unavailable, then an inventory of equipment for critical applications would be helpful for contingency planning purposes. This policy involves what is known as a periodic inventory as opposed to a perpetual inventory.

Related Policies: "Controlling Inventory" and "Key Technical Jobs."

Audience: Management and technical staff

Security Environments: All

3. Controlling Inventory

Policy: Company X equipment Custodians must maintain perpetual inventory control, a record of the new location and new Custodian of all equipment issued to others, and physical security over the equipment in their possession.

Commentary: As information systems equipment becomes increasingly distributed, there is a need to rely on rank-and-file staff to protect and account for this equipment. One common way to do this is through the use of designated equipment Custodians, not to be confused with information Custodians. Equipment Custodians keep track of equipment in their own office, at their home office, or in a computer lab. If an organization designates equipment Custodians, and has written records to back up this designation, it will have less trouble with disputes about equipment ownership at the time of workers terminate their employment. Having Custodians will also help in efforts to identify and control stolen and lost equipment. The existence of equipment inventories will also help with contingency planning efforts, equipment upgrade efforts, and missing equipment insurance reimbursement efforts. The words "perpetual inventory" can be contrasted with "periodic inventory," both of which are standard accounting terms that in some instances will need to be explicitly defined to equipment Custodians. This policy could be modified to require equipment Custodians to safeguard their inventory records against unauthorized alteration that may attempt to hide a theft.

Related Policies: "Information Custodian Responsibilities," "Asset Inventory — Information," and "Asset Inventory — Technology."

Audience: Technical staff

Security Environments: All

4. Corporate Data Dictionary

Policy: All new types of Company X information that are created and used for day-to-day business operations must be promptly reflected in the corporate data dictionary.

Commentary: This policy is intended to notify all workers that the corporate data dictionary must reflect all types of information used in day-to-day production operations. Through a corporate data dictionary, management can become aware of all the major types of operational information within an organization. They can promptly censor information where needed, and apply additional controls to those types of information that warrant these controls. Rather than an overt censorship approach, this policy takes a more information-management-oriented perspective. This assumes that if management knows all the major types of information available within the organization, then it will be able to more readily control this information. If management does not know what kind of information exists it will find it very difficult to properly manage this information.

Related Policies: "Private Information Collection Approval" and "Secret Systems."

Audience: All

Security Environments: All

5. Hardware And Software Procurement

Policy: All hardware and software must be procured through the Purchasing department according to company IT compatibility standards.

Commentary: Users often thwart standard purchasing channels to get their software or hardware more quickly, or to avoid having to comply with internal technical standards. This practice may permit them to purchase hardware and software that inadvertently compromises network or computer system security. For example, they may purchase desktop computers that have a floppy disk drive when diskless workstations are standard equipment. Permitting users purchasing independence also creates chaotic computing environments where systems are not readily supportable, interoperable, or network compatible. This policy requires that all such purchases go through a single organizational unit, that can then monitor the requests for compliance with in-house technical standards. Whenever there is a question about compliance, the Purchasing department can forward requests for information security related hardware and software to the Information Security department for approval. The policy could also be rewritten such that all purchases go through the Information Technology department.

Related Policies: "Purchasing Information Security Solutions," "Centralized Information Security," "Personally-Owned Computer Systems," and "Used Component Release."

Audience: End users and technical staff

Security Environments: All

6. Information Ownership

Policy: All production information possessed by or used by a particular organizational unit must have a designated Owner who is responsible for determining appropriate sensitivity classifications and criticality ratings, making decisions about who can access the information, and ensuring that appropriate controls are utilized in the storage, handling, distribution, and regular usage of information.

Commentary: This policy ensures that all production information has a designated Owner, and that the Owner knows what he or she must do when it comes to information security. While the Owner does not specify how to protect information with a certain sensitivity classification, he or she will designate the classification and the appropriate controls will follow directly. Likewise, the Owner does not specify how to backup or otherwise provide for the continued availability of critical information. The degree of criticality the Owner assigns will imply the availability-related controls that are needed. The access control decisions to be made by the Owner include rights to create, modify, delete, view, and use information. The Owner specifies which people, or which groups of people, will be given what access privileges. Practically speaking, Owners are too busy, and generally not technically-inclined, to get involved with technical security implementation issues. However, they are a critical connection between business management and information systems management, and as such their view should dictate what type of security will be applied. Owners are typically user department, middle-level managers. Some organizations may wish to mention this in the policy itself. On a different point, it is difficult to designate Owners if information inventory has not been completed. This may involve the compilation of an organization-wide data dictionary or a data directory. This policy assumes that both sensitivity classifications and also criticality ratings have been adopted by the organization.

Related Policies: "Four-Category Data Classification," "Five-Category Application Criticality Classification Scheme," "Information Ownership Delegation," and "Asset Inventory — Information."

Audience: Management and technical staff

Security Environments: All

7. Information Asset Control

Policy: Management must specifically assign responsibility for the control measures protecting every major information asset.

Commentary: This policy ensures that responsibility for the controls protecting major information assets such as a customer contact information database has been assigned. Some people differentiate between responsibility and accountability, but this policy does not make that distinction. The policy assumes the major information assets have been identified, for example in a corporation-wide data dictionary. Identification of the major information assets of an organization can also take place when risk assessments are performed and when contingency plans are prepared. Unlike policies dealing with information ownership, this policy refers to assignment of responsibility for the controls, not the information itself. In many instances, the responsibility is assigned to those with job titles like business analyst,

data center computer operator, security administrator, and network administrator. Whoever is responsible, it is important that the responsibility for controls be clear. When such responsibility is not definitively assigned, there are often control lapses. The words "information assets" also may be referred to as "information resources".

Related Policies: "Asset Inventory — Information," "Asset Inventory — Technology," "Database Indexes Containing Private Information," "Nature And Location Of Organization Information," and "Information Custodian."

Audience: Management and technical staff

Security Environments: All

8. Designated Security Administrator

Policy: Every Company X multi-user computer system must have a designated security administrator to define user privileges, monitor access control logs, and perform similar activities.

Commentary: This policy ensures that a specific person is designated as the one responsible for security. When it is not clear who is responsible for security, often security tasks get neglected, and as a result the organization is unduly exposed to various problems. All multi-user systems, including workstations used by more than one person, that handle sensitive, critical, or valuable information should be protected by an access control system. Most often this will involve fixed passwords, but other technologies such as smart cards, identity tokens, and fingerprint recognition also may be used. For purposes of this policy, all computer networks are multi-user systems, and as such should have one or more designated security administrators. There is no requirement that security administrators do their job full-time. Part-time administrators are often used in smaller organizations or for those systems that are managed by departments or other decentralized organizational units. On a different point, this policy is increasingly important as information systems are distributed, as is the case with local area networks, personal computers, and client-server systems.

Related Policies: "Business Production Information Updates" and "Information Security Liaisons."

Audience: Management and technical staff

Security Environments: All

9. Back-Up Security Administrators

Policy: Every multi-user Company X system with an access control system must have a designated employee who is a trained backup security administrator who can substitute in the event the primary security administrator is unavailable.

Commentary: This policy is intended to prevent awkward situations where a security administrator does not have a designated or trained backup person, in which case business activity may be impaired or interrupted. If a backup administrator is ready to fill-in for a regular administrator, then it is unlikely that security systems will need to be compromised in order to continue necessary business activity. Both the regular and the backup persons should be employees. This is because employees are generally more loyal and most often have a longer tenure with Company X than contractors, consultants, or temporaries. Furthermore, this policy can be used to obtain both necessary staffing and training resources. This policy assumes that the words "access control system" have been defined elsewhere. Generally, these words mean a fixed password user identification system with associated user access privilege controls, but many other options such as dynamic password tokens are also available.

Related Policies: "Designated Security Administrator."

Audience: Technical staff

Security Environments: All

10. Asset Inventory — Information

Policy: Information Systems management must compile and annually update a corporate-wide data dictionary and other high-level descriptions of the major Company X information assets.

Commentary: This policy requires Information Systems to organize and document information about information. Most often in the form of a data dictionary or data directory, this information is invaluable when it comes to planning future application development projects, migrating applications from mainframes to client-server systems, and designing an executive information system. It is also helpful when conducting risk assessments and preparing information systems contingency plans. A data dictionary can be used by information technology auditors to determine whether controls have been consistently applied to information across applications and across systems. A data dictionary is essential if the notion of Owners, Custodians, and users is to be successfully applied within a particular organization. These distinctions rely on the ability to define, locate, control, and manage information, as can only be done through a data dictionary or similar tool. This policy is a complexity management policy, helping organizations come to terms with the complexity of their information systems. The policy is most relevant to large organizations, although many middle-sized organizations will also find the policy appropriate. Also, it should not be forgotten that access controls for a data dictionary are essential as not everyone will need to know everything contained in the data dictionary.

Related Policies: "Information Asset Control," "Information Custodian," "Personal Information For Business Functioning," "Secret Systems," "Database Indexes Containing Private Information," and "Nature And Location Of Organization Information."

Audience: Management and technical staff

Security Environments: All

11. Equipment Tracking

Policy: All Company X computer and communications equipment must have a unique computer-readable identifier attached to it such that physical inventories can be efficiently conducted.

Commentary: Many information systems departments do not know exactly what equipment they own, lease, rent, or otherwise control. A current inventory of equipment is an important management tool for making decisions such as whether equipment has been stolen, what equipment needs to be upgraded, and planning network reconfigurations. Such inventories are especially useful when an employee is terminated. In this case, there is often a dispute about what equipment the employee had in his or her possession and which of these pieces of equipment belong to the employer. The "unique identifier" mentioned in the policy can be a bar code, an optical character recognition mark, or some other computer-sensed marking. Ideally, the mark is invisible to the naked eye, making its removal particularly difficult. If it is not feasible to have a computerized inventory system, some type of physical and trackable tag should be used. This policy is relevant to inventories of personal computers, workstations, fax machines, and other small office equipment.

Related Policies: "Change Control Procedure" and "Software Licensing Agreement Reviews."

Audience: Technical staff

Security Environments: All

12. Equipment Identification Codes

Policy: All Company X computer and communications equipment must have an identification number permanently etched onto the equipment that can be used to assist police in their attempts to return stolen property.

Commentary: The theft and illegal resale of computer and communications equipment has become a very large problem. Much of the lost and stolen equipment that has been recovered is never returned because law enforcement officials do not know to whom it belongs. New technologies for the marking of equipment with a social security number, a tax-related employer identification number, a telephone number, or some other unique number are now available. Many of these markings are invisible to the naked eye, so thieves are unlikely to make attempts to obscure the markings. These markings can also be used in the future as input data for databases describing stolen equipment. This policy is especially important for portables, laptops, and other mobile personal computers. The policy may be useful at the time of employee terminations, when it comes to determining the rightful Owner of a piece of equipment.

Related Policies: "Equipment Tracking."

Audience: Technical staff

Security Environments: All

5.02 Information Classification

5.02.01 Classification Guidelines

1. File And Message Ownership

Policy: Company X has legal ownership of the contents of all files and messages stored or transmitted on its computer and network systems, and reserves the right to access this information without prior notice whenever there is a genuine business need.

Commentary: This policy clarifies the ownership of information resident on Company X systems. It can facilitate the examination of electronic mail files and personal computer file directories that users may otherwise consider to be confidential and private. The policy can also act as a deterrent, discouraging users from using Company X systems for personal purposes. Indirectly, the policy may resolve disputes about the ownership of software written by employees, contractors, or consultants. User organizations may expand the scope to include telephone systems such as voice mail. Some organizations may wish to add a sentence acknowledging that Company X does not have legal ownership of information held in custody for a third party, or for software and other copyrighted, patented, or otherwise protected intellectual property obtained from third parties.

Related Policies: "Personal Use Of Computer And Communications Systems" and "Systems Monitoring Tools."

Audience: End users

Security Environments: All

2. Four-Category Data Classification

Policy: All Company X data must be broken into the following four sensitivity classifications: SECRET, CONFIDENTIAL, PRIVATE, and UNCLASSIFIED. Distinct handling, labeling, and review procedures must be established for each classification.

Commentary: This standard data classification system must be used throughout Company X to assign sensitivity classifications with separate handling requirements based on Table 3-1. This policy provides all types of workers with information to guide their security-related handling of Company X sensitive information. This set of classification designations is appropriate for a medium-to-large organization that does not deal with especially sensitive information, such as national defense information. Organizations with many types of sensitive data will want to add additional categories to fine-tune sensitive information handling procedures. Beyond the four above-mentioned categories, a category for "public" information is often in order. This would apply to information that has been approved by management for public release. Disclosure of public information is consistent with policy, and will not adversely impact Company X, its employees, its stockholders, its business partners, or its customers. The default category to be used in the absence of further information, and the most prevalent category, is "unclassified." This policy also may be compressed so that only three or even two categories are involved. Most data classification policies include specific examples to help employees distinguish between the categories. Salary data for employees would be considered "private." Some organizations may wish to add to the policy words that indicate that draft versions of information should be classified and handled in the same matter as final versions. The policy presented here could be made more explicit. This may involve replacement of the words about "adverse impact" with words about financial loss, gains to competitors, significant embarrassment to Company X, sizable loss of confidence in Company X, or notable reduction of the Company X standing in the community.

Table 3-1: Four-Category Data Classification

SECRET
Applies to the most sensitive business information that is intended strictly for use within Company X. Its unauthorized disclosure could seriously and adversely impact Company X, its stockholders, its business partners, or its customers.

CONFIDENTIAL
Applies to less-sensitive business information that is nonetheless intended for use within Company X. Its unauthorized disclosure could adversely impact Company X, its stockholders, its business partners, or its customers.

PRIVATE
Applies to personal information that is intended for use within Company X. Its unauthorized disclosure could seriously and adversely impact Company X and its employees.

UNCLASSIFIED
Applies to all other information that does not clearly fit into any of the above three classifications. While its unauthorized disclosure is against policy, it is not expected to seriously or adversely impact Company X, its employees, its stockholders, its business partners, and its customers.

Related Policies: "Declassification Date," "Annual Declassification Review," "Five-Category Application Criticality Classification Scheme," and "Multiple Sensitivity Classifications Computer Systems."

Audience: All

Security Environments: Medium and high

3. Three-Category Data Classification

Policy: All Company X information and information entrusted to Company X from third parties falls into one of three sensitivity classifications.

Commentary: This standard data classification system must be used throughout Company X to assign sensitivity classifications with separate handling requirements based on Table 3-2. This policy establishes a data classification scheme suitable for a small- or medium-sized organization that does not deal with national defense information. The policy is simple and concise in an effort to minimize costs. The intention of the policy is to create some basic distinctions on which other policies and operational rules can be built. This policy combines two basic philosophies of access control. For the most sensitive information it uses the need to know principle, and for less-sensitive information it uses the need to withhold principle. Caution is in order because once a data classification system has been adopted, it is very expensive and difficult to change to another system. An organization must carefully examine the needs of the organization before adopting a policy like this. Classification systems are also used for data criticality. This policy assumes that the term "information Owner" has been defined elsewhere.

Table 3-2: Three-Category Data Classification

CONFIDENTIAL
Access to this information must be tightly restricted based on the concept of need to know. Disclosure requires the information Owner's approval and, in the case of third parties, also a signed confidentiality agreement. Examples include employee performance reviews and new product development plans.

INTERNAL USE ONLY
This information must be disclosed to third parties only if a confidentiality agreement has been signed. Disclosure is not expected to cause serious harm to Company X, and access is provided freely to all internal workers through the organization's intranet. Examples include the organizational telephone book and staff automated calendars. This is the default classification for any information not specifically designated.

PUBLIC
This information has been explicitly approved by the Marketing or Public Relations department as suitable for public dissemination. Examples include marketing brochures and press releases.

Related Policies: "Five-Category Application Criticality Classification Scheme," "Four-Category Data Classification," and "Information Ownership."

Audience: All

Security Environments: Low and medium

4. Closed Two-Category Data Classification

Policy: All Company X information that has not been specifically marked as "approved for public release" or is not regularly or repeatedly shared with outside parties is confidential and must not be shared with external parties unless permission of the information Owner is obtained.

Commentary: This policy makes data classification easy, inexpensive, and straightforward. The policy dictates two specific sensitivity categories for information, and it also specifies which of these two categories applies when there is no marking evident on the information. This policy is actually quite common in small businesses because it is both expedient and also effective. The policy assumes that information Owners have been assigned. If the organization adopting this policy does not have, or does not want to adopt information Owners, the policy can be modified to make reference to a designated executive, for example the Public Relations director, or the Legal director. This policy assumes that the adopting organization is not a government agency, because a civilian government agency may be expected to share a great deal of information with the public. This may make the policy cumbersome and expensive to administer.

Related Policies: "Open Two-Category Data Classification," "Malfunctioning Access Control," "Default File Permissions," and "Privilege Restriction — Need To Withhold."

Audience: All

Security Environments: Low and medium

5. Open Two-Category Data Classification

Policy: All Company X information that has not been specifically marked as "confidential" is approved for public release and may be shared with external parties without specific management permission with the exception of information that is customarily restricted by laws and regulations.

Commentary: This policy is intended to make life easy for workers who may wonder what information they may share with outside parties. This policy would generally be suitable for a civilian government agency, such as one that compiles economic statistics about labor and business. There is a major problem with this policy, and that involves the removal of a label. If an employee intent on sabotaging the organization adopting this policy were to remove a label saying that information is confidential, the information then becomes suitable for dissemination without further consultation with management. This is an unusual policy, and is unlikely to work for many organizations and is not generally recommended.

Related Policies: "Incorrect Data Classification Labels," "Information System Privilege Usage," and "Privilege Restriction — Need To Know."

Audience: All

Security Environments: Low

6. Data Classification Category Prefixes

Policy: Prefixes such as "medical" and "financial" must be used in front of approved data classification categories.

Commentary: This policy provides greater granularity than standard data classifications provide. If specific information has to do with employee physical examinations, the information might be labeled "Medical—Private." This will designate that only persons dealing with employee medical matters should be given access to this information. In the absence of further access information, to simply label the information "Private" does not sufficiently restrict access. These prefixes do not confer any additional protection than the data classification markings themselves provide. In other words, private information should be handled a certain way, regardless of the prefix. Ideally specific prefixes are defined in this or a similar policy. As an alternative, prefixes may be chosen by the involved information Owners. The second of these two options runs the risk of confusing people, especially when synonymous and overlapping terms are used.

Related Policies: "Data Classification Labeling" and "Storage Media Data Classifications."

Audience: Management and technical staff

Security Environments: All

7. Declaration Of A Trade Secret

Policy: The Company X chief legal counsel is the only person authorized to designate any Company X information to be a trade secret.

Commentary: This policy clarifies that a trade secret designation can be applied to certain information only after the chief legal counsel has done a proper analysis of the circumstances. It is recommended that trade secrets and proprietary information be closely held, that it is not generally known throughout the organization. Trade secrets must also have proven commercial value, specifically the organization must be able to show that it's exclusive knowledge of a trade secret permits it to make a profit. While in general terms these ideas can readily be understood by any lay person, they have a number of legal nuances associated with them that should be left to the attorneys. The designation of certain information as a trade secret does not in any way interfere with the application of a data classification label such as secret. This policy does not prevent an information Owner from designating a data classification label, although trade secrets should generally get the highest classification except in military and diplomatic environments. A data classification designation is separate and distinct from a trade secret designation. Each designation implies different actions to protect the applicable data. The policy prevents others within the organization from declaring information to be a trade secret when it in fact does not qualify.

Related Policies: "Trade Secret Disclosure" and "Critical Business Logic."

Audience: End users

Security Environments: Medium and high

8. Incorrect Data Classification Labels

Policy: If the recipient of Company X internal information believes that the data classification label accompanying this information is incorrect, the recipient must protect the information in a manner consistent with the more stringent of the two possible classification labels and confirm with the information Owner that the label currently applied to the information is in fact correct.

Commentary: The guidance found in this policy is often lacking in data classification policy statements, but should be added to guide information recipients. This policy requires one to check with the information Owner before making any decision on the proper handling of any information with a suspect label. The

policy only applies to internal information in order to keep costs down and to restrict the scope of the policy. It could, conceivably, be expanded to include externally-provided information now in the possession of Company X. The resolution process makes reference to the more stringent of the two possible labels. If a recipient believes information should be "confidential," but in reality it is marked "internal use only," then the recipient should treat it as confidential until he or she has received information Owner instructions to the contrary. Likewise, if a recipient believes information should be labeled "internal use only," but in reality it is marked "confidential," he or she must treat it as confidential until he or she receives information Owner instructions to the contrary. This classification resolution process is sometimes called "system high," reflecting the fact that the highest security label prevails when information of various classifications is combined. This policy assumes a formal data classification system has already been adopted.

Related Policies: "Unknown Sensitivity Label" and "Multiple Classification Labeling."

Audience: End users

Security Environments: Medium and high

9. Assigning Data Classification Labels

Policy: For all existing production information types, the information Owner is responsible for choosing an appropriate data classification label to be used by all workers who create, compile, alter, or procure production information.

Commentary: This policy specifies who must choose and apply a data classification label, also known as a marking. The responsibility assignment made in this policy is by no means the only option. Other parties who could be designated as decision-makers include an information originator's manager and a third party who provided the information. The important objective here is to be clear about who makes the decision and later to ensure these same people have adequate training to make a justified choice. This policy is appropriate for a research and development lab or other organizations where the staff has significant latitude to make their own decisions. Those organizations not wishing to give staff this much latitude may insist that data classification decisions be made by Owners or managers. For cost-effectiveness reasons, the policy is deliberately limited to production information, but it could be broadened to include all types of information defined in a corporate data dictionary. Various types of relatively low sensitivity information may become more sensitive when combined.

Related Policies: "Information Collection Restrictions" and "Information Life Cycle Labeling."

Audience: All

Security Environments: Medium and high

10. Multiple Classification Labeling

Policy: When information of various sensitivity classifications is combined, the resulting collection of information must be classified at the most restricted level found anywhere in the sources.

Commentary: This policy guides users in the proper labeling of files, databases, floppy disks, CD-ROMs, and other collections of information. Often information with various sensitivities is combined, and users are confused about the label they should apply to the resulting product. This policy uses the military concept of "system high" that states that the resulting collection of information should adopt the highest and most stringent requirements found within the information. This policy assumes that a classification system is already in place, and that the notion of sensitivity classifications has been communicated to the users.

Related Policies: "Information Collection Restrictions" and "Multiple Sensitivity Classifications Computer Systems."

Audience: End users

Security Environments: Medium and high

11. Media Exposure To Secret Data

Policy: Any writable computer storage media that can be modified such as floppy disk, magnetic tape, or CD-RW, that has been exposed to secret data or applications must be reclassified at the secret level.

Commentary: This policy instructs users how to label computer storage media with an appropriate data classification after exposure to a secret application or secret data. Rather than "secret," another term can be used. The policy is necessary in high security environments because writable computer storage media can have temporary files, scratch files, and other work files stored on them, entirely without a user's knowledge. The system may not erase these files, or it may only delete the

directory listing for the files, in which case the underlying data is retrievable from the storage media. This policy makes reference to "exposure" to secret data or secret applications. In this context, "exposure" simply means used on a computer when either secret data or secret applications are active. A non-secret application may be working on secret data, in which case some of the secret data may be recorded on the computer storage media. Likewise, a secret application may store some temporary information on computer media. Even when applications are well-designed, this policy is applicable because there could be a power outage, a user-initiated interrupt, an operating systems error, or some other problem that prevents the intended erasure from taking place as originally designed. Reclassification at a secret level means that special disposal processes for storage media are required.

Related Policies: "Multiple Sensitivity Classifications Computer Systems" and "Multiple Classification Labeling."

Audience: End users

Security Environments: High

12. User-Generated Classification Labels

Policy: Classification labels assigned by any individual other than the designated information Owner do not in any way restrict the Company X right to access or otherwise use this information.

Commentary: This policy notifies users that it does not matter if they put the word "private" or some other label on an electronic mail message, or in a file directory name. This material can be accessed by Company X staff if, for any reason, they deem it necessary. This means that users have no computer-based private domain when they use Company X information systems. The policy encourages users to take care of personal matters on computers they have at home or at other locations. This policy discourages personal use of Company X information systems. The policy also makes it clear that only an Owner can assign a sensitivity label, and that all other sensitivity labels can be ignored without penalty.

Related Policies: "Personal Use Of Computer And Communications Systems" and "Information Ownership."

Audience: End users

Security Environments: Medium and high

13. Multiple Sensitivity Classifications Computer Systems

Policy: If a computer system contains information with varying sensitivity classifications, the controls used must reflect the most sensitive information on the system.

Commentary: This policy ensures that sensitive information is not improperly disclosed because it is on the same system as less sensitive information. Although it is an expensive systems design objective, this policy states that information must be protected in accordance with the "highest" classification presently on the system. In the military, this is known as a "system high" policy. Security related costs can often be significantly lowered if the most sensitive information is moved to another system. Likewise, segmenting data by sensitivity onto different disk drives and other system components may lower security-related costs. Various segmented system components containing similarly classified data may be accessible only when processing on the system is at a certain security level. For example, if confidential processing is being done on a system, then secret disks will be inaccessible. This policy would for example indicate that the operating system's access control mechanisms must be strong enough to protect the most sensitive information on the system. This means that all the other types of information must bear the overhead of this most sensitive type of information. This policy is most readily applied to a stand-alone system, and gets quite complex when networks are introduced. Taken to its logical conclusion, all systems connected to the network must have the same type of controls, consistent with the most sensitive data to be handled.

Related Policies: "Four-Category Data Classification" and "Media Exposure To Secret Data."

Audience: Technical staff

Security Environments: Medium and high

14. Storage Media Data Classifications

Policy: If information recorded on computer storage media with a higher sensitivity classification is moved to media with a lower sensitivity classification, then the media with the lower sensitivity classification must be upgraded so that its classification reflects the higher sensitivity classification.

Commentary: This policy provides specific guidance for end users and others who handle data storage media such as CD-ROMs, floppy disks, DAT tapes, and nine track tapes. It tells them how they should proceed when files or other collections of data have different data classifications. For example, if a hard drive has secret information on it, and information from the hard drive is written to a floppy disk that has confidential information on it, then the floppy disk must be reclassified as secret. Rather than commingle information with different classifications, some organizations will chose to employ separate data storage media for each classification, for example, floppy disks can have colored labels indicating the classification of the information stored thereon. Other controls also can be used to expediently deal with multiple data classifications stored on the same media. For example, secret data can be encrypted, while unclassified data can be left unencrypted.

Related Policies: "Multiple Sensitivity Classifications Computer Systems" and "Storing Mixed Classified Information."

Audience: End users and technical staff

Security Environments: All

15. Declassification Date

Policy: If known, the date that secret, confidential, or private information will no longer be sensitive must be indicated as part of the classification information.

Commentary: This policy ensures that information will be declassified or downgraded to a lower classification when necessary. For example, if information about a merger and acquisition is secret, it will become public as of a certain date such as the announcement date. Rather than a specific date, the Owner could specify a particular event such as a merger. Over time, there is a natural tendency for information to get progressively more classified or at least remain over-classified. This policy fights these tendencies, and will keep security costs down because access control costs will be reduced. The date for declassification or downgrading, also known as an expiry date or expiration date, may identify the time for disposal of the information, reducing storage costs. The clear specification of a declassification or downgrading date also facilitates orderly handling of the information by different people who may not be in direct communication with the others involved. This policy assumes the existence of a policy that defines the terms "secret, confidential, or private."

Related Policies: "Sensitive Information Retention" and "Four-Category Data Classification."

Audience: All

Security Environments: All

16. Accelerated Information Declassification

Policy: The designated information Owner may, at any time, declassify or downgrade the sensitivity classification applied to information by changing the classification label appearing on the original document, notifying all known recipients, and notifying the Company X archives Custodian.

Commentary: This policy clarifies exactly what has to happen to declassify or downgrade the classification for information. Declassification involves the removal of a sensitivity label, while downgrading involves only movement to a less sensitive level. The policy implicitly acknowledges that not all copies of the information will be located and either declassified or downgraded. The problems introduced by the incomplete location of recipients are acceptable because any resulting errors will provide more rather than less security. Some organizations will want to change the words "original document" to make a more specific reference to computerized versions of the original. This policy should be distributed only to information Owners or those with the authority to declassify or downgrade information. In some cases, management will want Owners to document the reason for the declassification or downgrading that also can be mentioned in the policy. Instead of an "archives Custodian," a data warehouse manager, a data dictionary administrator, or similar job title could be used. This typically would be someone who keeps track of the information about information.

Related Policies: "Declassification Extension" and "Write Access Sensitive Information."

Audience: Management

Security Environments: All

17. Declassification Extension

Policy: The designated information Owner may, at any time prior to scheduled declassification or downgrading, extend the period that information is to remain at a certain classification level by changing the declassification or downgrading date appearing on the original document, notifying all known recipients, initiating a cost-effective search for additional recipients, and notifying the Company X archives Custodian.

Commentary: This policy clarifies exactly what has to happen to extend the declassification or downgrading date for information. The location of additional recipients of the information is essential if the information is to be protected adequately. Without a search, recipients who did not hear about the extension could in good conscience release the information to unauthorized parties unless another policy required them to check with the Owner before releasing this information. Such a search can be time-consuming and expensive unless detailed logs of recipients have been kept. To avoid the need to extend an expiration date, some organizations routinely add a month or a similar period of time to the expected declassification or downgrading date. Some organizations will want to change the words "original document" to make more specific reference to computerized versions of the original. This policy should be distributed only to information Owners or those with the authority to declassify or downgrade information. In some cases, management will want Owners to document the reason for the date extension. This also can be mentioned in the policy.

Related Policies: "Accelerated Information Declassification" and "Write Access Sensitive Information."

Audience: Management

Security Environments: All

18. Declassification Schedule

Policy: The sensitivity classification of all Company X documents must be routinely downgraded according to Table 3-3 with exception of when a document type has been exempted or when the information Owner has provided other instructions for declassification or downgrading.

Table 3-3: Declassification Schedule

Existing	New	After X Years
Secret	Confidential	10
Confidential	Internal Use Only	15
Internal Use Only	Public	20

Commentary: The intent of this policy is to require an automatic declassification or downgrading of sensitive information. Many documents are left at their original classification level for excessive periods of time. This means that workers will have trouble locating and gaining access to information that would otherwise be available to them. This results in information security costs being higher than necessary. Another reason for automatic declassification and downgrading is to support the open discussion of politics and history, and to learn form this information but not to unduly hamper current management. The automatic declassification of documents ensures that the information Owner's declassification and downgrading job will be performed even when the Owner has not gotten around to dealing with these matters. An automatic declassification system also means that some of the subjectivity surrounding the declassification and downgrading process will be eliminated. The number of years before an automatic downgrading takes place will vary by organization. Likewise, some organizations will prefer never to make information public. This policy assumes that only three levels of data classification, not including "public" information, are used at Company X. Because this automatic declassification process can get a bit complex, it is best applied with a document management system or similar computerized tools. On another point, exempted documents not subject to automatic downgrading can include medical reports, personnel files, internal grievance and dispute resolution files, attorney-client files, and related types of information. Also, some organizations may wish to expand the policy for privacy reasons to specify that information involving an outside organization must not be downgraded without the outside organization's prior consent. This policy would generally be distributed only to information Owners and others who make information classification decisions.

Related Policies: "Declassification Date" and "Information Released To The Public — Authorization."

Audience: Management

Security Environments: Medium and high

19. Annual Declassification Review

Policy: At least once per year, information Owners must review the sensitivity classifications assigned to information for which they are responsible.

Commentary: Sensitive information tends to get over classified over time. Steps to declassify or downgrade it are therefore necessary if costs for information security are to be kept to a minimum. Declassification of information also keeps government and corporations accountable to citizens and stockholders. This policy formalizes a step to declassify and downgrade information and to require Owners to participate in the process.

Typically a status report showing the type of information and its classification will be prepared for review by information Owners. The Owners would then simply check off the items that should be declassified, downgraded, or remain classified as they are. The annual review might be replaced with a periodic review or another time period. This policy assumes that the term "Owner" has been defined elsewhere. In most instances, this policy needs an accompanying policy that defines the term "sensitive."

Related Policies: "Declassification Date" and "Four-Category Data Classification"

Audience: All

Security Environments: Medium and high

20. Declassification Of Sensitive Information

Policy: From the standpoint of sensitivity, information must be declassified or downgraded as soon as practical.

Commentary: To keep information at an excessive sensitivity classification also keeps costs for information security high. It additionally can be inappropriately used as a mechanism to prevent certain authorized people from viewing the information. When this comes to light, it often looks bad for management, implying that they had something to hide. This policy counters the tendency of information to become classified at excessive levels over time. This policy requires that the term "sensitivity" be defined in another policy. Declassification also may be appropriate for information that was critical but is less critical now, and information that was valuable but is no longer as valuable as it once was. Most organizations do not have classification schemes focusing on criticality or value, but the same approach could be adopted. Some organizations will prefer alternative wording for this policy such as: "information Owners are responsible for ensuring that documents are classified at the lowest level consistent with the Company X business needs."

Related Policies: "Four-Category Data Classification," "Five-Category Application Criticality Classification Scheme," and "Annual Declassification Review."

Audience: All

Security Environments: Medium and high

21. Declassification Of Secret Archives

Policy: Secret Company X archives must be made public after 30 years have elapsed from the time when the events described therein took place.

Commentary: This policy assists historians, reporters, book writers, educators, students, and others with the understanding of history. The policy assists with the democratic process in those countries where free and open discussion of historical events takes place. The policy typically would be adopted only by a governmental agency or high-profile non-profit agency. With this policy, after 30 years, military or diplomatic information that at one time was considered to be secret can be made public. This information should be reviewed prior to release to ensure that no information essential to the national security would be disclosed, that no information sources such as undercover spies, would be identified, and that no confidential intelligence gathering and analysis methods in use would be revealed. The major risk of a policy such as this is that the disclosed information will challenge the myths or propaganda that the current administration has sought to perpetuate. There is nothing special about the 30-year period mentioned in the policy. This could just have easily been some other period of time.

Related Policies: "Accelerated Information Declassification" and "Transaction Log Destruction."

Audience: Management

Security Environments: Medium and high

22. Essential Information And Software

Policy: The assigned information Owner must determine whether the information and related software under his or her control is essential such as information that is necessary to represent the accurate current status of Company X business, to complete a business transaction, or to meet legal or regulatory requirements.

Commentary: This policy requires that the information Owner determine whether information is essential. This distinction is useful when determining what information needs to be backed-up, what information needs to be stored off-site or available at an alternative data processing site, what information needs additional integrity controls such as check digits on account numbers, and what information needs to be considered within the scope of a contingency plan.

Related Policies: "Five-Category Application Criticality Classification Scheme," "Data Backups," and "Information Resource Classification."

Audience: Management

Security Environments: Medium and high

23. Data Warehouse Input Labels

Policy: All information included in the Company X data warehouse must be accompanied by information about its origin, its sensitivity classification, its reliability, and the date of its most recent revision.

Commentary: This policy establishes a basic rule for populating a data warehouse or any other large database. The input to the data warehouse should contain background information that will permit management to determine the underlying information's integrity, the extent to which the underlying information is reliable, and the underlying information's relevance for specific decision-making purposes. Without this background information, management may be only guessing about the integrity, reliability, and relevance of the information. This background information also may be important when doing a post-mortem for a failed decision-making process. Management may want to know what went wrong or what input data was erroneous. This background information can also be useful when investigating frauds or misrepresentations.

Related Policies: "Software Copyright Notices" and "Information Attribution."

Audience: Technical staff

Security Environments: All

5.02.02 Information Labeling And Handling

1. File Grouping Data Retention

Policy: Users must save their files on shared servers in directories reflecting four groupings, financial, human resources, research and development, and other, and these groupings imply both access control and data retention requirements.

Commentary: This policy gets users to categorize their files according to type. Once this categorization has been done, then a variety of information security activities can automatically follow from the categorization. For example, research and development information may be a trade secret, or at the very least may be highly proprietary, and should be closely guarded. This data might therefore be automatically encrypted when stored on hard disk. As another example, financial data might be kept for a certain period of time because local laws dictate such a data retention schedule. The categories are going to change from organization to organization. Those shown here are strictly placeholders. The user designation of an information type is in some sense an inferior replacement for a data classification scheme. It is inferior because it uses broad categories that will require many types of less sensitive information to be protected in accordance with the more sensitive information found in that same category. This approach may cost more in the long run, but it may be attractive in the short run because it requires less training and organizational infrastructure than a data classification system.

Related Policies: "Application Transaction Data Retention" and "Four-Category Data Classification."

Audience: End users

Security Environments: Low

2. Naming Conventions

Policy: To achieve consistent access control across different types of computer systems, standard user ID codes, production program names, production file names, system names, and other naming conventions must be supported.

Commentary: This naming convention policy makes administration significantly easier for multi-platform user access control systems, logs, and audit trails. This policy is for example useful when establishing a single sign-on system. It is also helpful for systems designers putting together integrated application systems. Without such conventions, it is very difficult to perform certain security tasks. Examples of these tasks include tracing a user's activity on various systems, and revoking privileges for all user IDs related to a specific individual after that individual has been terminated. Some organizations may wish to change a few words in this policy to reflect additional intentions.

Related Policies: "Employee Contact Information" and "File Naming Convention."

Audience: Management and technical staff

Security Environments: All

3. Computer System Names

Policy: The function performed by a computer or the software that it runs must not be used in any part of the computer's name, if that name is visible from the Company X internal network or occurs in any computer-readable file.

Commentary: This policy makes life more difficult for hackers, industrial spies, former employees bent on revenge, and others with less than exemplary motives. These people may break-into Company X systems or networks and be looking around, trying to figure out what they should do next. If servers or other machines are named in a helpful way, then these intruders will be significantly assisted in their efforts. For example, a revealing name like "PAYSERVER" will tell intruders where they should focus their efforts. On the other hand, if the computer names are something entirely unrelated, for example, the names of planets in the solar system, then intruders will not be aided by this information. System administrators and others may find that this policy makes their job a bit more difficult, but because they know the names for machines they work on, it should not be a significant problem. Just as information about the system reached should not be disclosed to users before they properly log on, so too the name of the system that they have reached should not reveal this information.

Related Policies: "Computer And Communications Center Signs" and "File Naming Convention."

Audience: Technical staff

Security Environments: Medium and high

4. File Naming Convention

Policy: A file naming convention must be employed to clearly distinguish between those files used for production purposes and those files used for testing or training purposes.

Commentary: A file-naming convention that distinguishes production files from other files assists with backups, log analysis, problem diagnosis, and system administration. Such a convention also assists efforts to purge test and training files from a new application, after testing and training efforts have been completed. This policy permits automated handling of files based on file name. For example, a local area network backup program may be instructed to only backup those files on each connected personal computer with the suffix ".dat." Without such conventions, scripted processes, such as searching backup tapes for a certain file, will be much more difficult. File naming conventions like this are especially important in those environments, such as client-server and Internet communications, where different operating systems are involved. Such file naming conventions are also very useful if data replication is being used across multiple machines.

Related Policies: "Naming Conventions."

Audience: Technical staff

Security Environments: All

5. Non-Production Business Transactions

Policy: Transactions used for auditing, testing, training or other non-production purposes must be labeled or otherwise separated from transactions used for production processing.

Commentary: This policy clearly separates auditing, testing, training, and non-production transactions from legitimate business transactions. If this separation is achieved, it will avoid both confusion and improper updates of computerized records. Use of the information technology auditing technique known as a "test deck" for example involves the submission of fictitious transactions to the system to determine whether they are handled correctly. Test deck analysis can show whether controls are working properly and whether transactions were posted to the proper accounts. One way to label these transactions is with a special transaction serial number, perhaps made up of letters rather than numbers. In other words, a special field devoted exclusively to a production designation need not be used. This information could be incorporated into other fields.

Related Policies: "Production Input Transactions," and "Production Change Reconstructability."

Audience: Technical staff

Security Environments: All

6. Trade Secret Disclosure

Policy: Workers must diligently protect from unauthorized disclosure all Company X information specifically identified as trade secrets. Trade secrets must be identified as such prior to being disclosed to any workers.

Commentary: This policy communicates to workers that Company X has certain types of information that it considers to be trade secrets, and that it expects all workers to diligently protect this information. From a legal standpoint, the policy is also intended to ensure that workers who come in contact with certain highly-sensitive information know that such information is considered to be a trade secret. Because most organizations do not have a separate category in their data classification system for trade secrets, the policy defines where trade secrets fit in with respect to a data classification system. Some organizations go one step further by requiring all new employees to sign a non-disclosure agreement that specifies the types of information considered to be a trade secret. This policy only addresses workers such as employees, consultants, and contractors. Different arrangements will be required for strategic business partners and other third parties.

Related Policies: "Internet Trade Secret Releases."

Audience: End users

Security Environments: Medium and high

7. Data Classification Labeling

Policy: All secret, confidential, and private information must be labeled according to standards issued by the Information Security department, while information not falling into one or more of these categories need not be labeled.

Commentary: This policy states what types of information require a sensitivity label. A label is simply one or a few words indicating the relative sensitivity of data. "Secret," "in confidence," and "for internal use only" are typical labels. Separate specifics about how to label information will also be required, although this information can be provided in procedure or standard documents. For example, where to put a label on a computer display, on a floppy disk, on hardcopy, and other places could be specified in a related standard. The movement of information from one operating system to another can prove problematic because sensitivity label information may be stripped off along with file formatting and other operating system-specific information. An organization may wish to additionally adopt standards for representing sensitivity labels inside files, for example in the first line of text files. This policy presumes the existence of another policy that defines the terms "secret, confidential, and private." These terms may be readily replaced with the labels used within the organization.

Related Policies: "Four-Category Data Classification" and "Comprehensive Classification Labeling."

Audience: All

Security Environments: Medium and high

8. Unknown Sensitivity Label

Policy: If information was obtained from Company X facilities that house secret information, and if no sensitivity label for this information can be determined, the information must be treated as though it is secret.

Commentary: This policy clarifies how to handle information with an unknown or unspecified data classification label. The policy provides a high security approach for dealing with an ambiguous data classification label. Most data classification systems default to "internal use only" or a relatively low level of sensitivity. Unlike these data classification systems, to err on the safe side, this policy defaults to the highest category in a data classification scheme. Without this policy, if a worker were to remove or obfuscate a secret label, then the information would be automatically declassified to an "internal use only" status. This would be likely to result in disclosure to persons who should not have had access to the information. This policy will impose additional costs associated with handling information with an unknown classification, but it will also reduce the number of disclosure mistakes that workers make. The policy is appropriate for a research lab, a military unit, a diplomatic government agency, or some similarly highly-secure organization.

Related Policies: "Data Classification Labeling" and "Four-Category Data Classification."

Audience: End users

Security Environments: High

9. Department-Specific Classification Labels

Policy: Department-specific data classification labels must be consistent with and supplemental to the Company X data classification system.

Commentary: This policy attempts to clarify the circumstances under which it is permissible to employ departmental data classification labels. For example, at a hospital there may be an organization-wide label indicating that information is "private." But within the Archiving department, additional labels like "private—psychological" and "private—financial" may be necessary. The use of the supplemental labels in this case would be consistent with the organization-wide labels, and would be acceptable. This policy attempts to prevent departments from creating conflicting or confusing terms that will interfere with the proper handling of the information. In this case, if the Archiving department were to designate private records as "confidential—psychological" and "confidential—financial," this would be a problem and a violation of the policy. Ideally, there would be no supplemental labels necessary, and all workers throughout the organization would use the same data classification labels.

Related Policies: "Vital Record Identification."

Audience: Management and technical staff

Security Environments: Medium and high

10. Externally-Provided Information Labeling

Policy: With the exception of general business correspondence and copyrighted software, all externally-provided information that is not clearly in the public domain must be assigned a Company X data classification system label by the individual receiving the information.

Commentary: This policy specifies who must label externally-supplied information that is not in the public domain. The policy goes further, specifying that the labels provided by the external party must not be modified or deleted. The policy could also specify that the Company X recipient is the initial Owner of the information, and that over time, the role of information Owner may migrate to another person. The policy attempts to clarify an area fraught with confusion and ambiguity. In many cases, sensitive externally-supplied information is not adequately protected by the recipient organization because responsibility for assigning a data classification system label has not been clearly assigned. This means that people who subsequently come in contact with the information may not handle it properly.

Related Policies: "Assigning Data Classification Labels."

Audience: End users and technical staff

Security Environments: Medium and high

11. Classification Labels For New Information

Policy: Any user who creates computer-files or messages must select one of the approved data classification labels at the time that these files and messages are saved or sent.

Commentary: This policy gets data classification labels on new files and messages from the time that they were created, and keeps these same labels attached to the associated information throughout the information's life cycle or until the classification is changed. If a label is attached at the time that information is created, it is much more likely to follow the information as it changes form and location. For example, if an electronic mail message was labeled as confidential when it was prepared, when the recipient viewed this information he or she would be alerted to the fact that it was confidential. When this same recipient talks to someone else about the information over the phone, the label can and should be propagated with the information. This policy is consistent with the notion that information should be protected according to its sensitivity, criticality, and value no matter what technology is used to process it, no matter what form it takes, no matter who comes in contact with it, and no matter where it goes. This policy is inconsistent with other data classification policies that rely on information Owners to assign the appropriate classification label. This policy takes the position that new information is being created by people throughout the organization on a continuous basis, and these creators do not have the time or inclination to repeatedly go back to the information Owners to get the proper classification. Some software packages can prompt the user to assign a classification label at the time a new file or message is created.

Related Policies: "Comprehensive Classification Labeling" and "Unknown Sensitivity Label."

Audience: End users

Security Environments: Medium and high

12. Comprehensive Classification Labeling

Policy: All tape reels, floppy disks, and other computer storage media containing secret, confidential, or private information must be externally labeled with the appropriate sensitivity classification.

Commentary: This policy provides guidance for all workers on the need for sensitivity labels. Sensitivity labels will be required all of the time. This policy would typically be used by an organization very concerned about the handling of sensitive information. Other organizations will find it difficult and too expensive. Before using this policy, management should determine that the additional costs associated with comprehensive labeling are warranted given the risk of mistakes when information is not labeled. This policy presumes the existence of a policy that defines the terms "secret, confidential, and private." These terms may be readily replaced with the labels used within the organization.

Related Policies: "Four-Category Data Classification" and "Data Classification Labeling."

Audience: All

Security Environments: Medium and high

13. Hardcopy Sensitivity Labels

Policy: All printed, handwritten, or other human-readable manifestations of secret, confidential, or private information must have an appropriate sensitivity label on the upper-right corner of each page.

Commentary: This policy gives guidance on the proper location of sensitivity labels. Some organizations may add words about the placement of sensitivity labels on floppy disk labels and other computer storage media, in which case the scope and title of the policy would need to be changed. The last two words in the policy require a label on each page. This prevents sensitive information from being mistakenly disclosed when it is copied or excerpted from a larger document. Some organizations will be less restrictive, requiring a classification label on every page only for the most sensitive types of information. This policy presumes the existence of a policy that defines the terms "secret, confidential, and private." These terms may be readily replaced with the labels used within the organization.

Related Policies: "Four-Category Data Classification."

Audience: End users and technical staff

Security Environments: Medium and high

14. Labeling Bound Hardcopy Material

Policy: When in hardcopy bound form, all printed, handwritten, or other tangible manifestations of secret, confidential, or private information must have an appropriate sensitivity label on the front cover, the title page, and the rear cover.

Commentary: This policy provides specific guidance on the proper placement of sensitivity-related data classification labels. A label on the title page is required, beyond labels on the front and rear covers, because the cover might be damaged or missing. Some organizations may state that a label is needed on every page but this is typically done for the most sensitive information. The policy could be modified to reflect an organization's standard hardcopy policy for securely handling information. This policy presumes the existence of a policy that defines the terms "secret, confidential, and private." These terms may be readily replaced with the labels used within the organization.

Related Policies: "Four-Category Data Classification" and "Labeling Hazardous Products And Services."

Audience: End users and technical staff

Security Environments: Medium and high

15. Presentation Of Sensitive Information

Policy: If information is either secret, confidential, or private, all instances in which it is displayed on a screen or otherwise presented to a computer user must involve an indication of the information's sensitivity.

Commentary: This policy provides system developers with guidance about the display of data classification sensitivity labels. This policy may be accompanied by diagrams and examples showing the specific wording to appear and exact screen location. At some organizations, additional information such as instructions about downloading or copying the sensitive data also may be provided in these examples. This policy presumes the existence of a policy that defines the terms "secret, confidential, and private." These terms may be readily replaced with the labels used within the organization.

Related Policies: "Four-Category Data Classification," "Comprehensive Classification Labeling," "Covering Sensitive Information," "Password Display And Printing," and "Software Copyright Notices."

Audience: Technical staff

Security Environments: Medium and high

16. Information Life Cycle Labeling

Policy: From the time when information is created until it is destroyed or declassified, it must be labeled with a sensitivity designation if it is either secret, confidential, or private.

Commentary: This policy indicates that labels must be attached to sensitive information wherever the information goes, whatever form it takes, whoever handles it, and whatever technology is used to process it. If information previously resident on a departmental server was downloaded to a personal computer, the sensitivity label should move with the information. Likewise, access controls should be consistent as the information's form, location, and presentation changes. The absence of proper labels will often prevent sensitive information from being handled appropriately. If "secret" information is apparently "unclassified" because it is not labeled, it will not be given the security-related handling it warrants. Removing a label can then be an effective way for an unauthorized person to declassify and gain access to sensitive information. This policy presumes the existence of a policy that defines the terms "secret, confidential, and private." These terms may be readily replaced with the labels used within the organization.

Related Policies: "Four-Category Data Classification" and "Comprehensive Classification Labeling."

Audience: All

Security Environments: Medium and high

17. Maintaining Classification Labels

Policy: Workers in the possession of any information containing a Company X data classification sensitivity label must maintain, propagate, and if need be reestablish this same label whenever the information changes form, format, or handling technology.

Commentary: This policy tells users that they must be diligent when they change the form, format, or technology used to handle sensitive information. For example, assume that information labeled as "confidential" was sent by fax to a remote location. The recipient could then extract certain details from the fax and include these details in an electronic mail message. This policy would require that the "confidential" label be included in the electronic mail message. Because users are in control of many of the changes in form, format, and handling technology that occur, they must be the ones to ensure that a label continues to be attached to sensitive information. This policy could be expanded to include labels and restrictions provided by third parties such as copyright notices.

Related Policies: "Data Classification Labeling" and "Classification Labels For New Information."

Audience: End users

Security Environments: Medium and high

18. Copying Sensitive Information

Policy: Making additional copies of, or printing of extra copies of secret, confidential, or private information must not take place without the advance permission of the information Owner.

Commentary: The intention of this strict policy is to notify all those who come in contact with sensitive information that making unauthorized copies is against policy. Another way to do this would involve the Owner as the only one who may make copies of sensitive materials. However, the Owner can, and in most instances will, delegate this activity. An effective way to implement this policy is with paper copies of sensitive information that cannot be copied in an ordinary copy machine. These copies are usually blue or some other color besides white. The policy shown here is especially important in those cases where sensitive materials must be tracked in a log. The policy shown here also presumes the existence of a policy that defines the terms "secret, confidential, and private." These terms may be readily replaced with the labels used within the organization.

Related Policies: "Preventing Copies Of Sensitive Documents," "Logging Movement Of Secret Documents," "Four-Category Data Classification," and "Tracking Sensitive Information."

Audience: All

Security Environments: All

19. Tracking Sensitive Information

Policy: Whenever additional copies of sensitive information are made, the number of copies and recipients of these copies must be recorded in a log and each of the recipients must be informed that either further distribution or additional copying may take place only after the information Owner's permission has been obtained.

Commentary: This policy ensures that all copies of sensitive information can be tracked. This will help with investigations of leaks or other unauthorized disclosures. Maintaining such records also fosters responsible behavior when it comes to releasing the sensitive information to unauthorized parties, making further copies, or destroying the information. The log mentioned in the policy may be kept by the Owner or an individual who the Owner has designated as an authorized distribution point. The reference to a log in the policy is deliberately vague, because it could be implemented in various ways. For example, the entire address of each recipient can be made a part of the document itself, or each of the copies can be numbered and a separate record of the recipients can be maintained. In many cases the words "sensitive information" should be replaced with the words "secret information" or some other indicator of the most sensitive type of information in use at the organization.

Related Policies: "Copying Sensitive Information" and "Logging Movement Of Secret Documents."

Audience: All

Security Environments: All

20. Intermediate Products Containing Sensitive Information

Policy: If a copy machine jams or malfunctions when workers are making copies of secret information, they must not leave the machine until all copies of the information are removed from the machine or destroyed beyond recognition.

Commentary: This policy ensures that bits and pieces of sensitive information are not inadvertently disclosed due to machine malfunction or related problems. This might happen when paper containing sensitive information is left in a jammed copy machine and later revealed to unauthorized persons. While the policy refers to copy machines, it can be broadened to include printing presses, fax machines, and other machines that might handle sensitive information. The scope of this policy may be restricted to the handling of very sensitive information related to internal controls, such as encryption keys. The policy shown here presumes the existence of a policy that defines the term "secret." This term may be readily replaced with the label used within the organization. A related policy requires that an authorized person be present whenever sensitive information is being transmitted over a fax machine or printed at a printer.

Related Policies: "Four-Category Data Classification," "Faxing Sensitive Information — Notification," and "Printing Sensitive Information."

Audience: All

Security Environments: Medium and high

21. Waste Copies Of Sensitive Information

Policy: All waste copies of secret information that are generated in the course of copying, printing, or otherwise handling such information must be destroyed according to approved procedures.

Commentary: This policy notifies employees that intermediate products of their work, in this case unacceptable copies or printouts, should be destroyed according to approved procedures. Unless otherwise notified, some workers may simply put these waste copies in a recycle bin. This policy may be restricted so that it only applies to the handling of sensitive information related to internal controls, such as the handling of encryption keys. The policy shown here presumes the existence of a policy that defines the term "secret." This term may be readily replaced with the label used within the organization. A related policy involves having an authorized person present whenever sensitive information is being transmitted over a fax machine or printed at a printer.

Related Policies: "Four-Category Data Classification," "Faxing Sensitive Information — Notification," and "Printing Sensitive Information."

Audience: All

Security Environments: Medium and high

22. Printing Sensitive Information

Policy: Printers must be attended by persons authorized to examine the information being printed if sensitive information is being printed or will soon be printed, unless physical access controls are used to prevent unauthorized persons from entering the area around the printer and viewing the material being printed.

Commentary: This policy ensures that no unauthorized person examines sensitive printed materials. This is a particular concern when printers are shared among many people, or when the printer is physically located some distance away from the person who originated a printing request. While the policy is intended primarily for use with local area networks, it is also relevant to other computing environments including departmental servers, mainframes, and commercial print shops and manufacturing operations. Some organizations will want to augment the policy shown here with words requiring the person initiating the print commands to be responsible for the proper handling of the printed material. The policy shown here could be rewritten so that the word "sensitive" is replaced with the specific data classification labels used within the organization.

Related Policies: "Four-Category Data Classification" and "Faxing Sensitive Information — Notification."

Audience: All

Security Environments: All

23. Accountability for Sensitive Information

Policy: All sensitive Company X information manifested in paper form must indicate both the current and the last page on each page of the document, such as "Page X of Y."

Commentary: This policy ensures that none of the sensitive information has gone astray. It also makes sure that readers of this information know they have read the whole document. This approach also assists those working in a copy shop or printing department properly account for all pages. The policy is not required for less sensitive types of information because accountability for hardcopy versions of less sensitive information is of less concern to management and is likely to not be worth the trouble. The procedure described is also extendable to less sensitive documents. This is an information integrity policy in that it ensures completeness of the information. The policy shown here could be rewritten so the word "sensitive" is replaced with specific data classification labels used within the organization.

Related Policies: "Four-Category Data Classification" and "Tracking Sensitive Information."

Audience: All

Security Environments: All

24. Preventing Copies Of Sensitive Documents

Policy: When private, confidential, or secret Company X information in hardcopy form must be released to third parties, it must always be distributed exclusively on special paper that cannot be copied using ordinary photocopy machines.

Commentary: This policy prevents the receiving parties from making unauthorized copies that could lead to unauthorized secondary dissemination. Secondary dissemination involves the uncontrolled release of the information to other unknown parties. For example, in the early stages of a lawsuit, the opposing side may use discovery proceedings to gain access to certain sensitive internal information. The use of special paper, that cannot be copied, will help ensure, but not guarantee, that the receiving third party has one and only one copy of the information, that can later be returned to the information Owner. The use of special paper ensures that the copy returned is the copy originally distributed. There is nothing preventing the third party from reading the information, then re-entering it into a computer, from taking a photograph of it, or in some other way creating another version of the original material, that can be copied. This policy does, however, prevent the use of optical character recognition technology, not just photocopy technology. The policy is intended to make it considerably more difficult for unauthorized copies to be made. Given the choice of the representation for certain information such as floppy disk, CD-ROM, or hardcopy paper, some organizations may wish to distribute information only on paper like this because it is so easy for unauthorized copies to be made with other common data storage media. The policy could be expanded to apply to all hardcopy paper containing sensitive information, whether or not third parties are given copies. One drawback to this wider applicability is that such paper is often somewhat difficult to read as it may have a colored background. The reference to the "information Owner" could be changed to refer to Information Security management, Industrial Security management, or the chief information officer. This policy works best when accompanied by another policy requiring the tracking of all copies containing sensitive information.

Related Policies: "Tracking Sensitive Information" and "Archival Storage Media."

Audience: All

Security Environments: Medium and high

25. Printing Secret Information

Policy: Secret company X information may be printed only on paper that will clearly show whether it is an original or a copy by employing colored borders, watermarks, or other technology approved for use by the Information Security department.

Commentary: This policy keeps all printed secret information on special paper that indicates it is an authorized original. The copying of secret information is often forbidden except when made with the permission of the Owner. Distribution should be tracked through logs and other mechanisms like acknowledgements of receipt. Because only the Owner or delegate should have a computerized version of the secret information, only these authorized parties should be able to generate a copy on special paper. All others, even if they have access to the paper original, will be able to only make paper copies. This control limits unauthorized distribution of secret information to approved channels. Anyone who obtains a paper copy of secret information will know whether it is an unauthorized copy, and if it is, the recipient should report the situation to the Owner. Words to this effect can be placed in the document. The technology used to support this policy is basically the same technology used to prevent copying of currency, travelers checks, and regular checks. On a separate point, sufficient inventory of this special paper will need to be on hand if this policy is going to be practical and access to paper stock will need to be restricted with physical access controls.

Related Policies: "Logging Movement Of Secret Documents" and "Preventing Copies Of Sensitive Documents."

Audience: All

Security Environments: Medium and high

26. Delivering Sensitive Computer Output

Policy: Private, confidential, or secret computer system output must be personally delivered to the designated recipients and never delivered to an unattended desk, or left out in the open in an unoccupied office.

Commentary: This policy specifically instructs workers not to leave sensitive computer output in places where unauthorized people could examine or steal it. This is especially relevant to environments where there are a lot of people who have access to computer output such as output from the printers attached to a mainframe. The policy does not prohibit computer operators, data control staff, and other people in a position of trust from handling the output in the normal course of their duties. The special handling for sensitive information required by this policy relies on the existence of appropriate labels printed on the computer output. The policy shown here presumes the existence of a policy that defines the terms "private, confidential, or secret."

Related Policies: "Information Life Cycle Labeling" and "Four-Category Data Classification"

Audience: Technical staff

Security Environments: All

27. Using Couriers

Policy: Private, Confidential, or Secret information in hardcopy form that is sent through commercial courier must always be tracked with a weigh bill number and must always be marked recipient "signature required."

Commentary: This policy acknowledges the reality of business and the reliance on third-party shippers. Knowing how frequently these couriers are used, this policy specifies how sensitive material must be shipped. The weigh bill number permits the sender to discover where the package is and who received it, and if it has been received. The signature required designation means that delivery will not be made unless a signature of an authorized person is obtained. In other words, it will not be left in a mailbox or on a doorstep where it could be stolen. Some organizations may wish to take this signature required step a little further insisting that only the designated addressee sign for the package. This policy does not address storage media such as floppy disks sent through courier, because they can be encrypted, thereby significantly lowering the risk of unauthorized disclosure. This policy does not address how to label sensitive information inside a courier's envelope.

Related Policies: "Comprehensive Classification Labeling."

Audience: End users

Security Environments: All

28. Delivery Of Secret Information

Policy: All deliveries of secret information must be conducted such that the recipient formally acknowledges the information has been received.

Commentary: This policy ensures that secret information is delivered to the designated recipient. This process is sometimes called "positive acknowledgement of receipt." The recipient could telephone the sender, could send electronic mail, or sign a statement. In strict high-security environments, the recipient must sign something before receiving it at all. A specific method for acknowledging receipt could be incorporated into the policy, although this diminishes its general applicability. The policy is also intended to prevent people from subsequently repudiating receipt of the information, thereby denying responsibility for the information's whereabouts. Specific time requirements for acknowledging receipt also may be mentioned in the policy. This policy presumes the existence of a policy that defines the term "secret." This term may be readily replaced with the label used within the organization.

Related Policies: "Logging Movement Of Secret Documents," "Four-Category Data Classification," "Receipt Of Secret Information," and "Receiving Third-Party Information."

Audience: All

Security Environments: Medium and high

29. Receipt Of Secret Information

Policy: Recipients of secret Company X information must provide formal written acknowledgement of receipt at the time they take possession of the information.

Commentary: This policy ensures that secret information is delivered to the designated recipient and the movement of the information is accurately tracked with current records. One common example of this policy in action is the delivery of a legal notice. Delivery can take place only to the person named on the document. The written receipt is especially important as a mechanism to stop recipients from later repudiating receipt, perhaps disclaiming responsibility for the information involved. Sending sensitive information through intermediaries may be acceptable as long as it is encrypted or otherwise in some inaccessible form. This policy is most appropriate for, and may be limited to photographs, hardcopy paper, and other human-readable forms of information. The policy presumes the existence of a policy that defines the term "secret." This term may be readily replaced with the label used within the organization.

Related Policies: "Logging Movement Of Secret Documents," "Four-Category Data Classification," and "Delivery Of Secret Information."

Audience: All

Security Environments: Medium and high

30. Logging Movement Of Secret Documents

Policy: When secret information is involved, a log must be maintained as long as such information retains a secret sensitivity classification that reflects the number of copies made, the location of copies, the names of recipients, the addresses of recipients, and any persons viewing the copies.

Commentary: This policy requires that a log be kept for the most sensitive documents. The log can be instrumental in determining that all copies have been recovered or destroyed. The existence of a log has a deterrent effect, reminding would-be policy violators that their actions are tracked. The policy could be expanded to require all copies to be sequentially numbered, but this is not necessary. This policy is intended for hardcopy documents, but could be expanded to be applicable to the definition of "document," or a computer file that can include audio, formatting, executables, and other types of information.

Related Policies: "Four-Category Data Classification," "Copying Sensitive Information," "Receipt Of Secret Information," "Delivery Of Secret Information," "Secret Document Sequence Numbers," and "Tracking Sensitive Information."

Audience: All

Security Environments: Medium and high

31. Secret Document Sequence Numbers

Policy: All copies of secret documents must be individually numbered with a sequence number to ensure that the persons responsible for the documents and the location of the documents can both be readily tracked.

Commentary: This policy ensures that all secret documents can be readily accounted for. By requiring a sequence number, all secret documents are reflected in a log or described in a disposition report. If two copies with the same number appear, unauthorized copying has occurred. When this happens, the person who should have prevented the copying can be identified. Fraud involving secret documents will be made more difficult if sequence numbers are tracked. If secret

information falls into the wrong hands, a sequence number will indicate who's copy it was that was not properly protected.

Related Policies: "Logging Movement Of Secret Documents."

Audience: All

Security Environments: Medium and high

32. Securing Sensitive Information

Policy: Workers in custody of Company X sensitive information such as Confidential or Secret, must take appropriate steps to ensure that these materials are not available to unauthorized persons.

Commentary: This policy states that those who have custody of sensitive materials have a duty to restrict access to these materials. Materials without a label are often by default defined as "for internal use only." Special access restrictions for internal staff are generally unnecessary for these materials. The presence of a classification label can be used to indicate those cases where information is sensitive. On another point, the policy is deliberately vague about the ways to restrict access because these will vary by situation.

Related Policies: "Information Custodian Responsibilities" and "Removing Hardcopy Sensitive Information."

Audience: End users

Security Environments: All

33. Releasing Declassified Information

Policy: Sensitive information that has apparently been declassified or downgraded because a specified expiration date has been reached must not be released to other persons until the actual declassification or downgrading has been confirmed with the designed information Owner.

Commentary: This policy prevents people in possession of sensitive data from releasing it to others, and basing their decision solely on the fact that a designated expiration date has come and gone. The person possessing this information must confirm that the information was downgraded or declassified, and only then can it be released to others. This policy is warranted because the expiration date may have been postponed, but the person possessing a copy may not have received that notice. Without a confirmation process as described in the policy, the person possessing the information could then prematurely release the sensitive information with potentially serious consequences. The words "designated information Owner" could be replaced with the words "designated information Owner or their delegate."

Related Policies: "Declassification Extension."

Audience: All

Security Environments: All

34. Sensitive Information Storage Media

Policy: Before any computer storage media is sent to a vendor for trade-in, servicing, or disposal, all Company X sensitive information must be destroyed or concealed according to methods approved by the Information Security department.

Commentary: This policy ensures that sensitive information is not disclosed to unauthorized persons working for vendors and other third parties. For example, if a hard disk drive crashed, it might be sent for repair. The service company could examine the data on the drive, perhaps leading to unauthorized disclosure of sensitive information. To counter this risk, the drive could be degaussed prior to being sent to the service vendor. The data held on the drive will be lost, which is a disadvantage of the policy. Such sensitive information destruction makes sense only if the information has been properly backed up or if the consequences of disclosure are significant. This policy needs to be accompanied by information backup policies. A more practical alternative would be to require that all hard drives storing sensitive data employ encryption, in which case there is no problem about sending the drive to an outside vendor. This is why the word "concealed" is included in the policy in addition to the word "destroyed." Another approach is to require confidentiality agreements from all third parties. The policy does not apply to CD-ROMs and other storage media that cannot be modified, nor does it apply to media that does not contain sensitive information. This policy assumes the term "sensitive" has been defined in another policy.

Related Policies: "Data Backups," "Four-Category Data Classification," "Transfer Of Sensitive Information," and "Used Component Release."

Audience: All

Security Environments: Medium and high

35. Labeling Hazardous Products And Services

Policy: All Company X products and services that may present a hazard to consumers, workers, or other involved parties must have labels identifying the nature of the hazard, ways to avoid the hazard, and steps to take in the event that the hazard causes a loss.

Commentary: This policy prevents trouble, such as lawsuits, union grievances, and worker accident related health insurance claims. It is better to notify people than to be required to defend oneself against lawsuits alleging that people hurt themselves or others because they did not know about hazards. This policy also applies to services. For example, a telephone service might have an initial outgoing message that warns callers about the nature of the service, and gives them an opportunity to hang up without being charged for the call. This policy requires extensive discussion with internal legal counsel.

Related Policies: "System Logon Banner."

Audience: Management

Security Environments: All

36. Labeling Management Decision Data

Policy: All data used for management decisions involving amounts over $100,000 must be labeled with both its origin and corresponding date.

Commentary: This policy requires special explanatory information whenever a substantial management decision is to be made. Having a cut-off reduces the overall cost of collecting or generating special explanatory information. A similar policy may be appropriate for all data downloaded from a multi-user machine to a smaller machine. If management is not aware of the movement of data from machine to machine, decisions can be made assuming the information is current or correct when in fact is not. This policy addresses a widespread misconception that if information is from a computer, then it must be both current and correct.

Related Policies: "Intellectual Property Labeling."

Audience: Management and technical staff

Security Environments: All

37. Incomplete Or Obsolete Information

Policy: All incomplete or obsolete information must be suppressed and not distributed to users, unless it is accompanied by an explanation that describes the status of the information.

Commentary: This policy ensures that information consumers are aware of the nature of the information they receive. If consumers are not aware that certain information is incomplete or obsolete, they may make erroneous decisions. This policy gives the information provider the option to either suppress the information or to explain its deficiencies. The policy-writer may wish to embellish on this policy, adding definitions for the terms "obsolete" or "incomplete." Another change could require that if there is a doubt as to the incompleteness or obsolescence of information, then the information provider must provide an explanation.

Related Policies: "Information Integrity Attributes" and "Organization Representations."

Audience: Technical staff

Security Environments: All

38. Official Manually-Prepared Documents

Policy: All Company X official documents prepared by hand must use non-erasable ink and if an entry requires correction, the entry must be lined-out, initialed by the originator, and dated.

Commentary: This policy prevents unauthorized or undetected modifications made to paper documents. The policy applies whether or not the paper documents are later used as computer input source documents. The policy could be expanded to say that it is relevant if the documents are prepared in any way by hand. Therefore the policy covers the application of a signature to an otherwise typed or printed document. This policy establishes which document is an original and which is a copy. This is an important distinction from a legal standpoint.

Related Policies: "Preventing Copies Of Sensitive Documents" and "Business Source Document Retention."

Audience: End users

Security Environments: All

39. Altered Photographs

Policy: Any photograph that has been altered must be labeled with an indication that changes have been made.

Commentary: The sophistication of computer enhanced photographic processes makes it very difficult, if not impossible, to visually determine whether a photograph has been modified. This has lead to a number of abuses by the news media, some of which have resulted in lawsuits. The policy could be restated to say "Do not modify photos unless you make your modification obvious or notify people." Photos deserve special mention because it is so easy for laypersons to make these modifications, and because photos have historically been used as a way to prove reality. The policy is relevant to all advertisements and other public representations, not just to those of the news media.

Related Policies: "Disclosure Of Information Modifications" and "Production Change Reconstructability."

Audience: End users and technical staff

Security Environments: All

40. Disposal Of Payment Information

Policy: The disposal of all paper documents that contain payment information such as bank account numbers or credit card numbers, must involve shredding or other approved destruction methods.

Commentary: This policy prevents payment information from falling into the wrong hands, then being used to commit a fraud. Perhaps the most pervasive example of this involves credit card charge receipts, which are often retrieved from trash bins, then used to place telephone orders. Many businesses discard such payment information without shredding it. If shredding is not used, the information unearthed from a fraud investigation could be embarrassing to explain to customers. It might also become a public relations or legal problem. This policy could complement existing policies requiring shredding of sensitive information. This policy also prevents identity fraud, where an unauthorized person poses as another person in order to obtain credit cards, loans, or other benefits using the good reputation of that other person.

Related Policies: "Waste Copies Of Sensitive Information," "Business Source Document Retention Period," and "Personal Information Access."

Audience: End users

Security Environments: All

6 PERSONNEL

6.01 Security In Job Definition And Resourcing

6.01.01 Including Security In Job Responsibilities

1. Job Descriptions

Policy: Specific information security responsibilities must be incorporated into all worker job descriptions if such workers have access to sensitive, valuable, or critical information.

Commentary: This policy requires management to acknowledge information security responsibilities in job descriptions for those positions that handle sensitive, valuable, or critical information. If job descriptions contain these statements and workers see that promotions and salary increases are related to information security, they are more likely to take these responsibilities seriously. The words "access to sensitive, valuable, or critical information" can be changed to "manage or use Company X information systems." This policy assumes the existence of a data classification system. In some organizations, it may be appropriate to delete the words "valuable, or critical" because only a sensitivity ranking scheme, such as a data classification policy, is available.

Related Policies: "Four-Category Data Classification" and "Performance Evaluations."

Audience: Management

Security Environments: All

2. Performance Evaluations

Policy: Compliance with information security policies and procedures must be considered in all employee performance evaluations.

Commentary: This policy requires management, at the time they write performance evaluations, to decide whether the employee should be concerned about information security, and if the answer is yes, then to determine whether the employee has acted in compliance with policies and procedures. The policy provided here makes direct reference to the management activity of evaluating employees, and only indirectly to a rank-and-file employee activity of complying with policies and procedures. Nonetheless, it implies that both are expected by management. The words "information security policies and procedures" could be changed to "information security requirements" or other generic terms used at the organization.

Related Policies: "Information Security Responsibility."

Audience: Management

Security Environments: All

6.01.02 Personnel Screening And Policy

1. Prospective Employee Information

Policy: Personal information about a prospective employee may not be gathered unless it is necessary to make an employment decision and relevant to the job.

Commentary: This policy maintains the privacy of prospective employees, and keeps personnel records orderly. This policy prevents claims of illegal discrimination. If an organization did not collect certain information, then it is unlikely that it could have used this information to make employment decisions. This policy cannot be used to help defend against claims of discrimination based on race or sex, or other attributes that are readily observable and for which additional information gathering is not required. Indirectly, the policy fosters the identification of information relevant to an employment decision. This is desirable because it documents the criteria used for making employment decisions. Because this policy is dependent on local laws and regulations, be sure to consult an attorney before issuing such a policy. The policy could be expanded to state the types of information that must not be collected. This policy permits the collection of current performance information in those cases where an employee is seeking a transfer. This policy also prevents employees from gaining unwarranted power because they have information that might be used to damage the reputation of the involved individual. Some organizations may wish to prohibit the retention of such information if the decision to which it applied has been made, although certain legal considerations such as statute of limitations should be worked out with internal legal counsel. Policies such as this may bolster employee morale, indicating that an employer does care about employee welfare. The policy may also help limit an employer's exposure to accusations that the privacy of certain individuals has been invaded.

Related Policies: "Electronic Performance Monitoring Notification" and "Honesty And Emotional Stability Tests."

Audience: Management

Security Environments: All

2. Prospective Employee Credit Checks

Policy: All prospective employees must be notified if their credit report will be examined or if a background check will be performed as part of the recruiting and selection process, and must be given an opportunity to withdraw their application if they choose not to disclose such personal information to Company X.

Commentary: This policy gives prospective employees an opportunity to decide whether they want to disclose certain personal information to their future employer. By declining to disclose this information they effectively take themselves out of the competition for the job. Another objective served by this policy is that prospective employees know what information is used in reaching a decision about them. This permits the prospective employees to investigate if they believe that erroneous information led to an unfavorable decision. This policy is in keeping with the notion that individuals should ultimately be the ones who control the flow of personal information about them. This policy could be broadened to include customers and other external third parties, in which case all personal data about these third parties that have been used in reaching a decision about them must be revealed to them. A medical insurance company, when deciding whether to issue a policy to an applicant, might use this wider approach. Banks increasingly use this disclosure-of-sources approach when deciding to make a loan such as a home mortgage.

Related Policies: "Personnel Record Distributions" and "Fingerprinting Employees."

Audience: Management and technical staff

Security Environments: All

3. Prospective Employee Lifestyle Information

Policy: Candidates for a job with Company X must not be subjected to any tests that may illuminate the candidates' lifestyle, political associations, or religious preferences unless this information is clearly needed to determine a candidate's suitability for a certain position.

Commentary: This policy prevents an organization from using tests to determine information about candidates for a job that the candidates did not willfully disclose. The policy protects the privacy of the individuals applying for a position and potentially prevents Company X from being subjected to lawsuits or unfavorable publicity. The policy restricts the use of tests to those tests that are clearly job related. Of particular concern to many employers are psychological tests that provide an indication of an employee's inclination to steal. These tests are consistent with the policy as written because honesty could be considered to be a requirement for certain jobs, such as cashiers.

Related Policies: "Computer-Related Positions Of Trust."

Audience: Management

Security Environments: All

4. Revealing Information To Prospective Employees

Policy: Information systems technical details, such as network addresses, network diagrams, and security software employed, must not be revealed to job applicants until they have signed a confidentiality agreement and also have been hired or retained.

Commentary: This policy prevents a new type of attack that involves posing as an applicant for a technical information systems job. The attacker would ask a variety of technical questions about the computing environment, to determine whether the applicant had the right skills for a job. In the process, the attacker would obtain useful information that could be used for social engineering and mounting a narrowly-focused attack. This policy treats job applicants as untrusted outsiders.

Related Policies: "Systems Documentation Release" and "Software And Data Exchange Agreements."

Audience: All

Security Environments: All

5. Rehiring Involuntarily Terminated Workers

Policy: Former employees, consultants, and contractors who were involuntarily terminated must not be re-hired or retained without the written permission of a senior vice president.

Commentary: Among other things, this policy prevents terminated employees from becoming consultants or contractors to Company X. Because these individuals may harbor ill feelings toward the organization, it is wise to avoid placing them in a position of trust where they could do serious damage. Another intention for this policy is strictly economic. Technical computer specialists who know they are indispensable have been known to quit, requiring their former employer to retain them as consultants or /s at a considerably higher rate of pay. This policy discourages these manipulative ploys. Some organizations take this policy one step further, indicating that all people who are terminated for any reason must not be re-hired or retained. In small towns and other areas with a severely limited number of technical persons, this more stringent version of the policy may unduly prevent Company X from utilizing local talent. In some industries, such as academia, it is customary for staff to leave for a few years and later come back, which makes this policy inappropriate for these industries.

Related Policies: "Probationary Period For New Workers."

Audience: Management

Security Environments: All

6. Probationary Period For New Workers

Policy: All new workers and workers who have been re-hired or retained after a poor performance evaluation, must be placed on a six-month probationary period, during which management to whom they report must actively monitor the performance and attitude of these workers for the purpose of making a decision to retain or release them.

Commentary: This policy gives management a significant period of time to evaluate the performance of employees, and permits them to terminate the employees based on poor performance, refusal to follow internal controls, or in any other way are deemed unsuitable. The policy notifies management that they are to scrutinize the work of these workers to ensure that they are suitable members of the organization. Often management does not get to know the people who directly report to them. This can often lead to security problems. For example, if an employee has a gambling problem and they must get money quickly in order to pay a past due debt, they may commit a computer fraud. If management knew about the problem, it could refer the employee to confidential psychological counseling or suggest other remedial measures. A policy like this also gives management additional flexibility when it terminates an employee within the six-month period that may discourage litigation or complaints. The length of the probationary period can vary by organization.

Related Policies: "Rehiring Involuntarily Terminated Workers."

Audience: Management

Security Environments: All

7. Bonding Workers

Policy: All workers in particularly sensitive computer related positions of trust must be surety bonded for a minimum of $1,000,000.

Commentary: Bonding is a type of insurance policy against various acts such as fraud, embezzlement, and industrial espionage. Bonds are sometimes called "fidelity bonds" or "fidelity insurance." The process of getting a bond for persons in a significant position of trust ordinarily involves a background check. This can be an illuminating process through which management gets an idea of the person's history. Using information from the background check, management will be much better able to make decisions about the degree of trust that should be placed in the individual. Even if a background check reveals nothing indicating there might be a problem, getting a bond against loss defrays the costs of any problems that may be encountered. Such a background check also impresses management with the extent to which certain people hold the keys to the organization's future. Knowing that a background check will be performed is likely to discourage certain inappropriate people from even applying for those jobs that involve significant trust. Some insurance coverage underwriting processes require a company to obtain bonds for certain types of employees.

Related Policies: "Sensitive Information On Small Computers," "Prospective Employee Lifestyle Information," "Background Checks," and "Computer-Related Positions Of Trust."

Audience: Management

Security Environments: All

8. Working On Sensitive Projects

Policy: Only employees with good to excellent performance reviews and tenure at Company X of at least two years may work on new product development and other highly sensitive Company X projects.

Commentary: This policy limits the people who work with the most sensitive information to those who are least likely to succumb to bribes, to be manipulated by an industrial spy, or to exploit their position to obtain information, then sell it outside Company X. The two-year waiting period makes it more difficult for industrial spies to take a job at Company X simply to gain access to information. The policy is also intended to prevent people who are under duress, perhaps from financial pressure, from working on projects where they would have access to the most sensitive information. The policy also justifies another background check before an employee is assigned to a project that involves handling the most sensitive information. The policy makes it an honor to work on these projects, and this may encourage further loyalty and additionally insulate Company X against social engineering attacks such as those mentioned above. There will be occasions when specialized external expertise is needed in order to complete a project. In those instances an approved departure from this policy may be obtained. This policy is only appropriate for well-established and relatively large organizations.

Related Policies: "Third-Party User IDs" and "Prospective Employee Credit Checks."

Audience: Management

Security Environments: Medium and high

9. Convicted Felons

Policy: Job offers must not be extended to individuals who have been convicted of crimes involving violence that, if repeated, would pose a physical danger to Company X employees or property.

Commentary: This policy ensures that the workforce is made up of law-abiding and safe employees. The policy ensures that workers are not unduly exposed to workplace violence. If management knowingly hires such a person, then the person hurts other employees, management may be held liable. Safe employees are also less likely to damage computer and communications systems in a fit of rage. For example, one user shot a display screen with a gun and another took a sledgehammer to his workstation. This policy can be extended to include contractors, consultants, temporaries, and others in addition to Company X employees.

Related Policies: "Computer-Related Positions Of Trust."

Audience: Management

Security Environments: All

10. Computer-Related Positions Of Trust

Policy: Persons who have been convicted of a felony must not be hired into, retained for, promoted into, or maintained in computer-related positions of trust.

Commentary: This policy ensures that the people who Company X depends on are worthy of the trust that has been extended. While some people may object, saying that this policy does not give convicted felons a chance to become reintegrated with the rest of society, the policy takes a strong stand in terms of not hiring those who have shown themselves to be untrustworthy. If written broadly as it stands, this policy can be restricted to felonies that have a bearing on the job that the person will do. For example, banks would not hire a teller who had been convicted of a felony such as fraud or embezzlement, but they may hire somebody who had been convicted of a felony involving driving a vehicle while under the influence of alcohol. Alternatively, the policy can be restricted by making reference to convictions that show dishonesty or breach of trust. For example, one large computer company hired an individual who had been convicted of white-collar fraud to be in Information Security management. This would clearly be a violation of the policy. Another variation on this policy involves restricting it to workers who will have access to sensitive, critical, or valuable information. The policy shown here implies that a background check will be performed to determine whether the individual has a criminal record.

Related Policies: "Convicted Felons," "Background Checks," "Bonding Workers," and "Prospective Employee Lifestyle Information."

Audience: Management

Security Environments: All

11. Background Checks

Policy: All workers to be placed in computer-related positions of trust must pass a background check that includes examination of criminal conviction records, lawsuit records, credit bureau records, driver's license records, and verification of previous employment.

Commentary: This policy informs management that they must know who they are hiring or retaining. For example, if a background check reveals that an individual has a history of bank robbery, management may want to reconsider a hiring decision. Often, computer criminals are not prosecuted and they go on to perpetrate a similar crime with a new employer. While privacy laws often restrict what a previous employer can say about a former employee, those doing background checks can often pick-up significant reservations about the individual. Often the answer of whether the previous employer would re-hire this individual is sufficient to give a clear overall picture of the former worker's status. Even without the details behind the reservations, this is often enough to disqualify a candidate or cause for further research. This process is often called obtaining a character reference, and this too could be added to the policy as it is now written. Other things that could be added to the list of tasks that must be performed are: verification of the completeness and accuracy of the worker's resume, confirmation of academic and professional qualifications, verification that the applicant is a citizen or legal alien, and verification of the applicant's identity through passport or driver's license. Some organizations may want to eliminate mention of the types of background checks to be performed, instead saying only that "a background check must be performed according to standard in-house procedures." In this case, a separate memo from the Human Resources department then can delineate the types of background checks required for different job titles. This approach gives management additional flexibility in its determination of the background checks, which will be performed for each open position.

Related Policies: "Computer-Related Positions Of Trust," "Reporting Status Changes," and "Bonding Workers."

Audience: Management

Security Environments: All

12. Polygraph Tests

Policy: All Company X workers who will be placed into a computer-related position of trust must pass a polygraph test before beginning work in their new position.

Commentary: This policy ensures that system administrators, network administrators, and security administrators pass a lie detector test before they are given access to powerful system privileges. The policy could apply to those who simply have access to highly-restricted information, not just those who work on information technology positions. The policy is deliberately written in a general way, so that both types of workers are covered. People can fail a lie detector test and not be lying. The machines are 85-95% effective for specific issue testing. If an organization adopts this very strict policy, it will need to have a procedure to resolve those cases where people fail the test, but claim that they are telling the truth. Lastly, the policy involves tests only when staff members are hired. It could be broadened to include periodic testing, although this is expensive.

Related Policies: "Bonding Workers" and "Prospective Employee Credit Checks."

Audience: End users

Security Environments: High

13. Accessing Private Information

Policy: Staff members must pass a background check prior to being granted access to private information.

Commentary: This policy requires a background check, above and beyond a pre-employment background check, for each and every worker who will have access to private or personal information. This policy states that only a restricted group of staff members should be able to access private information. A temporary employee or volunteer should not be given access to private data unless he or she has passed this additional background check. The policy assumes that the organization has already defined what data is and is not private. The policy is deliberately silent about the components of the background check but these components should be documented in a separate procedure. This policy is appropriate for a hospital, a medical doctor's clinic, a medical insurance company, or any other organization that acts as a Custodian of private data above and beyond employment records. If the words "private information" were changed to "proprietary information," then the policy would be appropriate to a wide variety of commercial organizations such as high-tech computer companies, pharmaceutical companies, and oil exploration companies.

Related Policies: "Background Checks" and "Personal Record Integrity."

Audience: Management

Security Environments: All

14. Sensitive Product Information

Policy: All workers who will have access to sensitive product information such as marketing plans, engineering specifications, or manufacturing procedures, must pass a standardized background check performed by the Human Resources department.

Commentary: This policy segregates trade secrets or other information of a proprietary nature, and gives only those workers who have passed a background check access to this sensitive information. While a background check is not foolproof, it can help to eliminate certain individuals from consideration who are clearly not good risks. For example, a background check could unearth the fact that an applicant for a job recently worked for a competitor. This may disturb management enough to prevent the individual from gaining access to sensitive product information. This policy is intended for use at private sector organizations that offer a product. The policy could be expanded to include all information that has a designated sensitivity, perhaps "secret." If it were so altered, it would mimic a standard policy found in many military organizations. If the policy were expanded to be linked to a data classification label, then another policy describing the data classification system will also be necessary. The policy applies equally to contractors, consultants, temporaries, interns, and volunteers, just as it applies to employees. The word "product information," as used here, refers to not just new and unreleased products, but also to information about existing products.

Related Policies: "Non-Disclosure Agreements — Organization" and "Third-Party User IDs."

Audience: Management

Security Environments: Medium and high

15. Fingerprinting Employees

Policy: Prospective employees who will have access to sensitive information must be fingerprinted before they begin work, which will be used to determine whether the prospective employees have a criminal record.

Commentary: This policy obtains specific identification data about individuals that can then be run against government databases of known criminals. This policy requires a nationwide background check, while local criminal record background checks may be restricted to regional databases. In some cases, an international background check is necessary. This policy could be broadened to include consultants, contractors, temporaries, and others who are not regular employees. The words "sensitive information" also may be expanded to "sensitive, critical, or valuable information." Likewise, the policy can be expanded to include those who are being promoted or transferred into such a position rather than only new-hires. Significant explanation may be required to ensure this policy does not cause problems with workers.

Related Policies: "Bonding Workers," "Prospective Employee Credit Checks," and "Computer Transaction Initiations."

Audience: Management

Security Environments: Medium and high

16. Honesty And Emotional Stability Tests

Policy: All workers to be placed in computer-related positions of trust must pass honesty and emotional stability tests that have been approved by the Human Resources department.

Commentary: This policy ensures that lower-level management administers tests to ensure that workers who are placed in computer-related positions of trust are worthy of that trust. These tests can be written tests, question and answer interviews, situation case studies, or other types of tests. Statistical studies have shown such tests to be an effective and fair way of determining views on honesty. The tests are increasingly being used as a means to ensure that a prospective worker will perform as intended, particularly when working under pressure or adverse circumstances. Such tests permit an employer to retain workers who are less likely to commit computer fraud, to engage in revenge where data is destroyed. Such tests are sometimes euphemistically called attitude tests.

Related Policies: "Prospective Employee Information" and "Fingerprinting Employees."

Audience: Management

Security Environments: All

17. Non-Employee Background Checks

Policy: Temporaries, consultants, contractors, and outsourcing organization staff must not be given access to sensitive information, or access critical information systems, unless they have gone through a background check commensurate with the background checks given to regular employees.

Commentary: This policy ensures that departmental managers and project managers do not circumvent the background checking process that is required for all employees. In an effort to expedite the work and to lower costs, many organizations' middle management has outsourced a variety of activities, and these activities often involve powerful system privileges or access to sensitive information. Perhaps of gravest concern has been the recent outsourcing of computer programming work for critical applications. This outsourcing is often sent to foreign countries where workers of unknown loyalties and intentions work on the code. This issue should be a serious concern now that terrorism has become a worldwide problem. This policy brings some additional caution to the tendency to outsource virtually every activity except those that are core competencies. In some cases, the organization adopting this policy can rely on background checks performed by a third party, such as a third-party recruiting organization.

Related Policies: "Third-Party User IDs" and "Temporary Worker Privileges."

Audience: Management

Security Environments: All

18. Foreign Nationals

Policy: Foreign nationals must not work on Company X information systems.

Commentary: This policy ensures that the people who are working on internal information systems are trustworthy. A number of high-profile, real-life cases have shown that some foreign nationals take on information systems jobs so that they can engage in industrial espionage or information warfare. This policy should not be construed as a condemnation of all foreign nationals, citizens or those who are in the process of becoming a citizen. If workers permanently reside in the country where they work, they will at least be subject to the laws of that country. However, if the workers will soon leave, they may feel less inclined to follow the laws, policies, and other rules of their temporary country. This policy acknowledges that information systems have become critical to organizations and that not just anybody should work on these information systems. This policy is consistent with military security clearance process criteria, but it is also applicable to the private sector. Care should also be taken to ensure that this policy is not illegal under anti-discrimination laws in the jurisdiction.

Related Policies: "International Transport Of Secret Information — Security" and "Background Checks."

Audience: Management

Security Environments: Medium and high

19. Former Hackers And Reformed Criminals

Policy: Former hackers and reformed criminals must not be hired at Company X to perform information security or forensics work.

Commentary: This policy provides clear and unequivocal hiring guidance to management. Hiring former hackers or reformed criminals assumes a big risk that these people will not once again betray the trust given to them. In no way does this policy prevent management from hiring a consultant to do a penetration attack. This type of risk assessment is now a legitimate approach to the discovery of vulnerabilities. This policy only limits the type of person who could perform such a service. Sometimes the term "white hat hacker" is used for a professional who performs legitimate penetration attack services, while the term "black hat hacker" is used for an underground hacker with a questionable background.

Related Policies: "Information Security Investigation Teams" and "Conflicts of Interest."

Audience: Management

Security Environments: All

20. Significant Increases In Wealth

Policy: If any Company X worker shows unexplained significant increases in wealth, management has a duty to discreetly investigate the source of this new wealth.

Commentary: This policy informs local management that significant unexplained increases in wealth may be an indication of internal fraud. If such a change in wealth is noted, management should interview the involved employee and also investigate the individual's computer privileges and access to organizational funds. While there should be respect for the involved individual's privacy, this change in wealth is often a valid indicator that something is seriously amiss.

Related Policies: "Workers As Customers" and "Computer Crime Investigation."

Audience: Management

Security Environments: All

6.01.03 Confidentiality Agreements

1. Property Rights

Policy: Without specific written exceptions, all programs and documentation generated by, or provided by any worker for the benefit of Company X are the property of Company X and all workers providing such programs or documentation must sign a statement to this effect prior to the provision of these materials.

Commentary: Disputes about ownership of programs and documentation are frequently encountered. Programmers claim that they have the right to take their creations to their next employer or to external consulting clients. Employers claim that such materials are works for hire and as such are the property of the employer. This policy clarifies this area, and gives Company X influence in any related dispute, whether internal or a matter adjudicated in a court of law. This policy notifies programmers and related workers about property rights. In this case, the first half of the policy statement may be sufficient. Those organizations particularly concerned about this matter may wish to include the second half of this policy statement, which is intended to require that management get words to this effect incorporated in employment agreements, and consulting agreements. This policy is not a formal agreement with a programmer. It only requires that an agreement be involved whenever programming and documentation are prepared. The reader should speak with internal legal counsel about the development of both an agreement and a policy like this because there will be jurisdiction-specific considerations.

Related Policies: "Non-Compete Agreements," "Intellectual Property Rights," "Documentation Confidentiality," and "Recovery Of Organization Property."

Audience: Technical staff

Security Environments: All

2. Non-Disclosure Agreements — Organization

Policy: All workers must personally sign a Company X non-disclosure agreement before work begins, or if a worker has been working without a non-disclosure agreement, a signature must be provided as a condition of continued employment.

Commentary: This policy is intended to prevent the disclosure of sensitive information to anybody unless they have previously signed a non-disclosure agreement (NDA). Organizations whose business depends on the continued protection of certain information, such as research labs, high-technology companies, and military organizations, will find this policy a necessity. Each organization's actual confidentiality agreement is often drafted or refined by its Legal department. A draft NDA is included as an appendix to this book. This policy requires that each individual sign the NDA and that they must not sign for a whole organization. This requirement prevents individuals from saying that they did not receive notice that the information was sensitive, and that they did not take appropriate precautions. Personal modifications to the NDA made by workers should not be acceptable. To underscore the importance of confidentiality, in some organizations, workers are required to provide periodic signatures on NDAs, although this is generally considered to be excessively strict. This policy assumes that NDAs are stand-alone contracts, but they could easily be integrated into employment contracts, consulting contracts, or related documents.

Related Policies: "Background Checks," "Compliance Agreement," "Confidentiality Agreements," and "Non-Disclosure Agreements — Third Party."

Audience: All

Security Environments: All

3. Changes In Employment

Policy: Whenever there are changes in employment status or changes in the work status of a third-party worker such as a contractor, consultant, or temporary, the actual words appearing in the Company X confidentiality agreement must be reviewed with the involved individual's manager.

Commentary: This policy is intended to remind workers that they signed a confidentiality agreement, and that Company X intends to hold them to these terms and conditions. Customarily part of an exit interview, this review of the terms and conditions in a confidentiality agreement need not be a time-consuming process. The policy, as written, is deliberately vague about the exact words to be said by the manager, leaving it up to the circumstances and personal preference. In some cases, the reminder may come from a member of the Human Resources staff, rather than from the individual's manager. In either case, the job title of person to do the review should be stated in the policy. The existence and enforcement of this policy may help organizations in their legal efforts to demonstrate that they diligently attempted to protect trade secrets, and that they should therefore be eligible to receive some legal assistance against alleged wrongs of a worker.

Related Policies: "Non-Disclosure Agreements — Organization."

Audience: All

Security Environments: All

4. Confidentiality Agreements At Previous Employers

Policy: Employees who formerly worked at competing organizations are encouraged to abide by the confidentiality agreements they signed with those organizations and every other worker must not pressure these employees to disclose information that might be beneficial to Company X.

Commentary: This policy is intended to make it clear that Company X has no intention of pressuring new recruits from competing organizations to disclose proprietary information from former employers. The policy also indicates that hiring staff from competing organizations is not part of a strategy for indirectly conducting industrial espionage. This policy is most relevant to organizations where turnover is high. Some knowledge will inadvertently be transferred from one organization to another whenever such a staff recruitment situation occurs. Although the specifics of the case involved will dominate any legal action that ensues, a policy like this may be helpful because it shows that management does not support indirect industrial espionage.

Related Policies: "Conflicts of Interest" and "Requests For Organization Information."

Audience: End users

Security Environments: All

5. Non-Compete Agreements

Policy: At the time they join Company X, all employees must sign an agreement not to compete for six months after their separation from Company X.

Commentary: Agreements not to compete essentially prevent former employees from going into business in direct competition with their former employer. They are often constrained by time and constrained by geography. For example, setting up shop across town is unacceptable but in another state may be. Former employees may be a significant competitive challenge to their former employer if they steal proprietary information. Agreements not to compete may be quite useful in court if ever there is a dispute about the actions of former employees. Although theft of information may not be something that a former employer can prove in court, going into business in competition with this employer is relatively easy to prove. This policy requires the signing of an agreement not to compete. Internal legal counsel should be consulted about the agreement and its use in conjunction with a policy like this. This policy requires management to get employees to sign such an agreement. It is best to get employees to sign when they take a job because they will at that time be the most willing to enter into such an agreement.

Related Policies: "Intellectual Property Rights."

Audience: Management

Security Environments: All

6.01.04 Terms And Conditions Of Employment

1. Intellectual Property Rights

Policy: While employees of Company X, all staff members must grant to Company X exclusive rights to patents, copyrights, inventions, or other intellectual property they originate or develop.

Commentary: This common policy assigns the rights to all intellectual property generated by employees to their employer. Some consulting and contracting agreements also contain provisions to this effect. Although generally not done, the policy could be restricted to material that, in one way or another, is related to Company X business. A more general approach is used instead to ensure that Company X retains the option to exploit such intellectual property. On another point, the policy could make reference to both working and non-working hours. Given the current proliferation of outsourcing, it is especially important to clarify the rights to the work generated by outsiders. Without a policy like this, programmers in many instances will claim that code they developed is their own property. To be sure there is no misunderstanding, many organizations get employees to sign agreements that include words similar to those found in the policy. Whether an agreement or policy is used, readers should consult with internal legal counsel on this matter because there are jurisdiction-specific considerations. Furthermore, this policy may be an impediment to the hiring of certain creative people who wish to retain intellectual property rights to their work. The notion behind the policy may be objectionable to some employees. They may believe that the policy reflects an attitude that Company X owns them and everything they create. This notion may be relevant to labor union negotiations and corporate culture redefinition efforts.

Related Policies: "Non-Compete Agreements," "Intellectual Property Developed Off-Site," "Property Rights," and "Public Communications."

Audience: End users

Security Environments: All

2. Recovery Of Organization Property

Policy: Employees, temporaries, contractors, and consultants must not receive their final paycheck unless they have returned all hardware, software, working materials, confidential information, and other property belonging to Company X.

Commentary: This policy ensures that confidential information, personal computers, and other property of Company X gets returned. This policy gives Company X some leverage to ensure these materials are returned. If a worker has already left, and if the worker has already been paid his or her last paycheck, there is very little incentive for the materials to be returned. The company should also keep accurate records of hardware, software, and other materials provided to workers so that these items can be recovered. Written acknowledgments of property ownership signed by the worker are also useful when it comes time to recover these materials. Withholding a paycheck that has been earned may be illegal in some jurisdictions, so be sure to check with internal legal counsel. As layoffs, reductions in force, terminations, and other separations become more common, there is an increasing need to specifically address the information systems issues associated with these changes in status.

Related Policies: "Property Rights," "Intellectual Property Rights," and "Removal Of Sensitive Information."

Audience: Management

Security Environments: All

3. Employees Traveling Together

Policy: Employees must not take the same airplane flight if it would mean that three or more officers, five or more employees, or two or more engineers from the same department, would be on the same flight.

Commentary: This policy implicitly recognizes that one of the most important assets of an organization is the knowledge of its employees. The policy's intention is to ensure that a plane crash will not severely damage the ability of the organization to achieve its goals. The policy could be expanded to include other modes of transport such as auto travel, but airplane crashes are one of the most sudden and catastrophic events where several employees could be lost. Although unusual, the policy could also be broadened to include life-endangering activities such as hang-gliding and motorcycle racing. There is nothing special about the numbers included in the policy. The number of engineers from the same department, for example, could have been three. One assumption behind the policy as written is that engineers are the organization's important type of employee. If this is not the case, then appropriate substitutions such as, "information systems specialists," should be made. This policy assumes that Company X is a relatively large organization.

Related Policies: "Cross Training" and "Contact Information."

Audience: All

Security Environments: All

4. Internal Informants

Policy: From time to time, Company X uses informants who may be placed in various internal positions, and who may appear to be the same as any other worker without notifying other workers about the presence of, or nature of the work performed by, such informants.

Commentary: This policy deters workers from committing crimes, abuses, and other acts that may be against organizational policy or local laws. The use of informants can be a valuable way for management to gain information about the activities taking place inside the organization. While this policy is not limited to the information security area, it can provide significant benefit for that same area. An informant can, for example, tell management that users are sharing passwords, using organizational computer resources for personal purposes, or otherwise doing things that they should not be doing. An auditor or an external consultant who comes in may be unable to obtain this information because workers know that an auditor or an external consultant is going to be preparing a report for management's consumption. One downside to this policy is that it may foster a paranoid corporate culture. This policy is best used in those organizations that place a great deal of reliance on the honesty and loyalty of staff members, and that have relatively few mechanisms to detect fraud, embezzlement, and other abuses.

Related Policies: "Use Of Investigators."

Audience: End users

Security Environments: Medium and high

5. Competitive Intelligence

Policy: When gathering information of a competitive or market intelligence nature, Company X staff, or anybody instructed to gather such information on behalf of Company X staff, must never lie or misrepresent their identity.

Commentary: This policy prevents some questionable practices where people pose as though they are legitimately eligible to receive certain information, when in fact they are not. This policy can prevent the bad publicity that might come from public disclosure of questionable practices. In some instances these data gathering tactics could be considered to be fraudulent, and therefore they may be illegal. This policy addresses those types of behavior, but it also covers behavior that may not strictly-speaking be illegal. The policy takes a stand in favor of telling the truth and being straightforward in business dealings. The policy is a restriction on the actions of internal staff and their designees, including private investigators, such that the privacy rights of competitors are maintained. In reality, there is a tremendous amount of information in the public domain, that if analyzed intelligently, can reveal a great deal about competitors.

Related Policies: "Third-Party Collection Of Pricing Information" and "Identity Misrepresentation."

Audience: End users and management

Security Environments: Medium and high

6. Personnel Record Distributions

Policy: To permit each employee an opportunity to acquaint him or herself with the information, and to ensure that it contains no errors, every employee must be given a copy of his or her personnel file once a year.

Commentary: The provision of a free copy of one's record is a way to reduce complaints about inaccurate reports, and a way to ensure that the information is current and accurate. The policy could be modified to state that "Each employee must be given an opportunity to receive a copy," considerably reducing the paperwork and expense associated with this information-integrity-related policy.

Related Policies: "Access To Personal Information" and "Prospective Employee Credit Checks."

Audience: End users and management

Security Environments: All

7. Health And Safety Information

Policy: Management must fully disclose to the involved workers the results of toxic substance tests and other information relating to the health and safety of workers.

Commentary: This policy is related to the "worker right to know" policy about dangers in the workplace. The policy avoids lawsuits. For example, a lawsuit could allege that a worker would have quit or protected him or herself differently if this information had been known. Beyond forcing management to disclose such information, this policy is also intended to build worker confidence that management genuinely cares about worker welfare.

Related Policies: "Workplace Hazards."

Audience: End users and management

Security Environments: All

8. Workplace Hazards

Policy: Management must inform workers about the existence of workplace hazards, provide safeguards to lessen the risk to workers, and train workers in the proper use of these safeguards.

Commentary: This policy is intended to be used to require management to disclose all hazards. The policy avoids lawsuits and other disputes, and foster worker confidence that management does care about the workers' welfare. For example, if a workplace is noisy, this policy requires that management inform workers of the danger to their hearing, provide ear protectors, and train workers in the proper use of these ear protectors.

Related Policies: "Health And Safety Information" and "External Information Requests."

Audience: All

Security Environments: All

9. Employee Stock Transactions

Policy: Employees must not buy or sell Company X stock or bonds between the end of the fiscal quarter and the time that financial results are publicly announced.

Commentary: This policy prevents employees who may have access to confidential information that is soon to be made public from exploiting their knowledge of this information in the stock market. The time frame given is the time period in which this manipulative exploitation could take place. After the public knows of the information, there is less of a special advantage for those who have insider knowledge. The policy is relevant only to companies that have stocks or bonds on public exchanges. It could be adapted to research institutes or government agencies that collect and analyze information such as the growth rate of the economy, the release of which alters the prices of stocks and bonds. The policy applies to all employees, not just those who are working in the Accounting department or who may otherwise know what the financial results were. The policy may be expanded to include instructing others such as relatives, friends, or attorneys to buy or sell Company X stock on an employee's behalf or for their own benefit. A definition of insider trading also may be an appropriate adjunct to the policy, but review your local laws and regulations. Discussions with internal legal counsel will be needed on this policy.

Related Policies: "Conflicts of Interest."

Audience: All

Security Environments: All

10. Sexual, Ethnic, And Racial Harassment

Policy: Workers must not harass others based on sex, ethnicity, or race.

Commentary: This policy notifies workers that harassing communications are not appropriate at work, and particularly not on Company X computer and communication systems. The reader's organization may already have a policy about harassment, but that policy may say nothing about using Company X systems for harassment. Laws about such behavior vary widely from jurisdiction to jurisdiction, so consultation with internal legal counsel is advisable. Also needed will be a definition of harassment. It is not enough just to have a policy. There must be enforcement of the policy and communication of the policy to workers. The scope of this policy could be expanded to include harassment based on national origin, age, sexual orientation, disability, and religious or political beliefs.

Related Policies: "Employee Off-the-Job Behavior" and "Telemarketing Records."

Audience: End users

Security Environments: All

11. Intellectual Property Developed Off-Site

Policy: Intellectual property including, but not limited to, patent, copyright, trademark, and all other intellectual property rights as manifested in memos, plans, strategies, products, computer programs, documentation, and other materials developed or conceived of while an employee is working at alternative work sites is the exclusive property of Company X.

Commentary: This policy notifies telecommuters and others working off-site that their intellectual property work is Company X property, even if it was developed at another location. Some organizations may restrict this policy such that it only makes reference to materials developed during working hours or that it references intellectual property related to Company X business. The policy has the broadest possible applicability, and so will tend to protect Company X more than the employee. Detailed discussions with internal legal counsel about this topic are advisable.

Related Policies: "Intellectual Property Rights" and "Property Rights."

Audience: End users and technical staff

Security Environments: All

12. Corporate Code Of Conduct

Policy: All workers must read, understand, and behave in accordance with the corporate code of conduct.

Commentary: This policy notifies workers that compliance with the corporate code of conduct is mandatory. A code of conduct includes mention of matters like accepting gifts and conflicts of interest. In many cases it also involves information security matters such as disclosure of sensitive information. Rather than being a good place for information security policies, a corporate code of conduct is intended to be a guide to doing business the Company X way. Honesty and other higher-level considerations are typically addressed in a code of conduct, while information security policies as they might appear in an information security manual or some other document generally are more detailed.

Related Policies: "CodeOfConductAcknowledgement."

Audience: End users

Security Environments: All

13. Code Of Conduct Acknowledgement

Policy: All workers must indicate their understanding of the code of conduct by annually signing a form acknowledging that they agree to subscribe to the code.

Commentary: This policy reminds employees that they must abide by the organization's code of conduct. It is desirable to have employees acknowledge in writing that they understand that a code of conduct is a required part of their job. If they are subsequently terminated due to code of conduct related problems, there is no doubt that the employee understood what was required of him or her. This policy therefore reduces the probability of a wrongful termination lawsuit.

Related Policies: "Corporate Code Of Conduct."

Audience: End users

Security Environments: All

14. Conflicts of Interest

Policy: All workers must avoid the actual or apparent conflict of interest in their business-related dealings with Company X.

Commentary: This policy notifies workers that it is insufficient to have no conflict of interest. There must be no appearance of a conflict of interest. For example, a manager may own a significant block of stock in a competing company through a trust. Although the manager may not be able to exercise any influence over the competing company, and may not have any special relationship with or access to information at the competing company, the manager's ownership implies a conflict of interest. If this ownership information were to get into the newspapers, or if major customers were to become aware of it, it may damage the company's reputation, not just the manager. Many organizations will want to supplement this policy with examples, such as having a close relative who works for a competitor. More than any other policy in this book, this policy is likely to be integrated into a Code of Conduct.

Related Policies: "Employee Stock Transactions."

Audience: End users

Security Environments: All

15. Personal Relationships With Competition

Policy: Company X workers must not have any romantic partners or immediate family working at competing organizations.

Commentary: This policy prevents the unintentional disclosure of confidential information. Even an informal comment might convey information that would be of use to a competitor. The policy is also a safeguard against industrial or military espionage where a romantic partner also happens to be a spy. The policy's scope could be restricted to those working in the Research and Development department, or some other particularly sensitive activity.

Related Policies: "Sharing Marketing Information" and "Confidentiality Agreements At Previous Employers."

Audience: End users

Security Environments: Medium and high

16. Employees Leaving For A Competitor

Policy: All workers intending to work for a competitor must immediately notify Company X management at the time they accept an offer to work for a competitor at which time the worker, while accompanied by an escort, must immediately gather their personal belongings, be shown to the door, and have all Company X rights, privileges, and accesses revoked.

Commentary: This policy is intended to make it clear that every employee who will soon go to work for a competitor should not remain on the premises, and should not remain an authorized user of information systems. This is true no matter what the type of separation such as termination for cause, resignation, or retirement. Access to any system provides a tempting opportunity for departing employees to take customer mailing lists and other information that might be of use to a new employer. One of the most effective things an organization can do to handle these situations is to establish a policy expelling all workers who announce they will be going to work for a competitor. This policy also sends a message to all remaining staff that the former employee is no longer a member of the trusted group. The existence of a policy like this makes it diplomatically and socially acceptable to deal decisively with this type of departing employee. This policy is a special manifestation of the notion of a conflict of interest. The policy is most suitable for those organizations with a high staff turnover, such as high-tech organizations.

Related Policies: "Custodian Responsibility Transfer" and "Deletion Of Terminated Worker Files."

Audience: End users and management

Security Environments: All

17. Notification Of Worker Terminations

Policy: All employees must be immediately notified as soon as a worker has been terminated and the Human Resources department must regularly remind employees that departed workers must not be on Company X property, use Company X resources, or be affiliated with Company X in any way.

Commentary: This policy enlists the support and participation of all remaining employees to tighten the fence separating insiders from outsiders. If remaining employees are going to act as an early-warning system, they must be informed that certain terminated workers must not be inside Company X buildings, on Company X computers, and connected to Company X in any way. This policy goes well with a challenge policy that requires remaining employees to challenge all people currently inside restricted areas who are not conspicuously wearing a valid identity badge with a picture. This policy is a broader scope notification than the notification performed by many organizations, where only system administrators and others who are responsible for updating computer access controls receive such a notice. This policy deliberately makes no distinction between involuntary and voluntary terminations, although the scope of the policy could be narrowed to include only involuntary terminations. Such notification can easily be performed with electronic mail, and if there are pictures of workers on an intranet, this policy is made more effective because the individual can be more readily recognized.

Related Policies: "Escorting Involuntarily Terminated Workers" and "Reporting Employee Changes."

Audience: End users

Security Environments: Medium and high

18. Notification To Third Parties Of Worker Terminations

Policy: If a terminated worker had authority to direct contractors, consultants, or temporaries, or if this same worker had the authority to bind Company X in a purchase or another transaction, then the Human Resources department must promptly notify all relevant third parties that the terminated worker is no longer employed by Company X.

Commentary: This policy prevents a terminated worker from directing third parties in any way. A terminated worker may be in a vengeful spirit and may obligate Company X to purchase certain goods, or may bind Company X to another transaction or contract. A former worker also can embarrass his or her past employer by acting in an unprofessional manner, perhaps offering to sell certain confidential information. If third parties think that the former worker is employed at Company X he or she will have more credibility. This is one reason to collect business cards, credit cards, and other evidence of affiliation at the time of termination. A former worker may also use the implied trust that goes along with employment to engage in social engineering to get passwords and other system access codes that could be used to break-into a former employer's computers. This policy clarifies the distinction between current workers and former workers. The act of notifying third parties can also bring to light certain irregularities that may not have been officially noticed before. For example, if a special and unauthorized discount was being given to a distributor, this distributor may ask whether the discount will be available. Some organizations accomplish the same result when a replacement worker contacts each relevant contractor, consultant, temporary, or vendor, to inform them that the former worker is no longer responsible for certain activities.

Related Policies: "Physical Access Of Terminated Workers" and "Worker Termination Responsibility."

Audience: Management

Security Environments: All

19. Involuntary Terminations

Policy: In all cases where information technology support workers are involuntarily terminated, they must be immediately relieved of all of their duties, required to return all Company X equipment and information, and escorted while they pack their belongings and walk out of Company X facilities.

Commentary: Because information technology workers can do considerable damage, it is wise to immediately eliminate the possibility that they might strike back at their former employer in revenge. This policy singles out information technology support workers for special handling because they are most often in a significant position of trust. Notice that the policy mentions only those who have special privileges to affect what end users do. In this respect, a distinction is made between information technology support workers and information technology workers. Additional words dealing with the immediate revocation of system privileges are also a possible expansion of the policy.

Related Policies: "Immediate Terminations."

Audience: Management and technical staff

Security Environments: All

20. Escorting Involuntarily Terminated Workers

Policy: In every case where workers are involuntarily terminated by Company X, the termination must take place in the presence of a security guard after which they must immediately pack their personal belongings in the presence of the guard, be shown to the door and be informed that they must not reenter the building unless invited to do so by management.

Commentary: This policy prevents vengeful acts, especially damage to computerized information. After workers are involuntarily terminated, they must not log on or gain access to Company X computerized records. If workers have personal information resident on Company X information systems, and if there is a policy against personal use, then the information can be abandoned because it is evidence of a policy violation. If no personal use policy exists, a supervisor can retrieve the personal information and send it to the employee on a floppy disk or similar data storage media. The involved worker's system access privileges should be revoked prior to formal notification that he or she has been terminated. This policy assumes that there is another process for collecting phone cards, credit cards, cell phones, office building keys, identity badges, and similar items. The policy also assumes that the organization has security guards.

Related Policies: "Immediate Terminations" and "Worker Termination Responsibility."

Audience: Management

Security Environments: All

21. Information Retention At Employment Termination

Policy: Upon termination of employment, all Company X information in the custody of the departing worker, other than personal copies of information disseminated to the public and personal copies of correspondence directly related to the terms and conditions of their employment, must be provided to the worker's immediate supervisor at the time of departure.

Commentary: This policy makes it clear that internal Company X information must not be removed when a worker departs from Company X. Often workers walk away with all sorts of information thinking it may help them with their subsequent jobs. The policy implies that workers must not try to negotiate about the provision of information to their supervisor when they depart. The words "in readable form" could be added to make it very clear that all information turned over to the worker's immediate supervisor must be accessible and not encrypted. Ideally this policy is used in conjunction with a policy stating that Company X owns all information created by workers during the course of their employment, except where written agreements provide for alternative arrangements. Some organizations may wish to generalize the policy to include contractors, consultants, temporaries, and other types of workers besides formal employees.

Related Policies: "Custodian Responsibility Transfer."

Audience: All

Security Environments: All

22. Return Of Property At Employment Termination

Policy: At the time that every employee, consultant, and contractor terminates his or her relationship with Company X, all Company X property including, but not limited to, portable computers, library books, documentation, building keys, magnetic access cards, credit cards, and outstanding loans, must be returned.

Commentary: This policy collects all Company X property before the individual leaves Company X and, ideally, before they are paid their final paycheck. If Company X property is not collected at that time, it may be quite difficult to collect it later. Special problems are encountered when Company X property is located at the worker's home, in the worker's car, or in other places not under the direct control of Company X. In these cases, on the worker's last day, Company X should obtain from the worker a written acknowledgement of possession of the property accompanied by a promise to return it. If a computer is to be kept by a former employee, then representatives from Company X should examine its hard disk to ensure it contains no Company X sensitive information. This policy provides only a suggested list of property to be returned. Each organization would ordinarily come up with their own list depending on the nature of the business and the tools of the trade employed. This list is ordinarily not specified in the policy but on a separate terminations checklist for management, and it is better to have the policy reference the checklist than to use the policy as it now stands.

Related Policies: "Worker Termination Responsibility" and "Physical Access Of Terminated Workers."

Audience: Management

Security Environments: All

23. Consecutive Vacation Days

Policy: Management must ensure that workers take a vacation of at least five consecutive days once each year.

Commentary: This policy prevents workers from concealing a fraud or other illegal or abusive acts. If workers come to work every business day, they are much more likely to be able to conceal these activities. A vacation of five business days is long enough that some other worker must get involved with the activities done by the person on vacation. When someone else gets involved, it is likely that this other person will spot improprieties and irregularities. When some additional person does a certain task, then a certain amount of cross-training takes place. This policy also serves as a significant deterrent to on-going internal fraud and related abuses. Another benefit of the policy is that it requires employees to take vacation time. This may prevent significant build-ups of vacation time that would then be a major liability on the organization's balance sheet. The policy may also help stressed-out workaholic employees take a significant vacation when they would not be inclined to otherwise do so. This policy may be an appropriate adjunct to a policy that requires employees to take their vacation time or lose it.

Related Policies: "Cross Training."

Audience: Management

Security Environments: All

24. Second Jobs

Policy: Workers must not work a second job if it may in any way jeopardize or compromise a worker's objectivity when performing duties on behalf of Company X or if the other employer is in any way in competition with Company X.

Commentary: Many people feel the economic pressure to take on a second job. This policy is intended to ensure that these second jobs do not lead to information security problems with Company X. For example, if a purchasing agent took a second job with a vendor to Company X, this would compromise his or her ability to objectively perform purchasing duties, and would therefore be grounds for termination. This type of second job may also involve off-the-books payments to the Company X employee for steering business toward the vendor. These payments may be undetectable without a policy such as this and some monitoring of employee second jobs. Likewise, if a worker took a job with a competitor, there may be some pressure to steal proprietary information from the first employer. The policy could be augmented with words that say that "if there is any question about the interpretation of these words, consult your manager or the Human Resources department." On another point, the policy should apply to consulting engagements, contractor assignments, and temporary positions, not just to traditional full-time permanent jobs.

Related Policies: "Disclosure Of Second Jobs," "Conflicts of Interest," and "Consecutive Vacation Days."

Audience: End users

Security Environments: All

25. Disclosure Of Second Jobs

Policy: Workers must inform their immediate manager that they have a second or more jobs at the time when they are interviewed for a position with Company X or, if already employed at Company X, at the time they take on these other jobs.

Commentary: This policy ensures that management is informed about second and third jobs that Company X staff currently perform. This will help management understand variances in worker performance, perhaps because they are not getting enough sleep. It will more importantly help management determine whether a conflict of interest exists, or whether the other job may in some way compromise a worker's objectivity when performing duties on behalf of Company X. The policy can additionally help to spot potential public relations or legal problems such as interlocking directors of large and influential companies. The information provided through this policy can furthermore be useful when investigating potential frauds or other problems that involve multiple organizations. The policy is a mechanism to ensure that management has a good idea of the intentions driving worker behavior.

Related Policies: "Second Jobs," "Employees Leaving For A Competitor," and "Consecutive Vacation Days."

Audience: End users

Security Environments: All

26. Workers As Customers

Policy: Workers currently in a computer-related position of trust at Company X must not also be customers of Company X.

Commentary: This policy avoids temptation and prevents a variety of abuses that might be encouraged because workers have privileged access to Company X information systems. For example, if a wire transfer clerk at a commercial bank were to have an account at the same bank, this might facilitate fraudulent wire transfers. This policy reduces the suspicion of workers in computer-related positions of trust. The policy is intended primarily for those organizations that are dealing with valuable types of information, especially those dealing with computerized money. For example, a chain of grocery stores probably would not adopt a policy such as this. The policy also may be useful in those circumstances where separation of duties is inadequate. The criteria for determining whether a position is a computer-related position of trust will need to be defined if this policy is adopted. These criteria could include the ability to readily cause computer-related damage to Company X of over $100,000, the ability to modify production system files so that computer-based fraudulent activity could be readily concealed, or the ability to alter customer records anonymously.

Related Policies: "Bonding Workers" and "Working On Sensitive Projects."

Audience: Management

Security Environments: High

27. Reporting Status Changes

Policy: Employees must report to their immediate manager all changes in their personal status that might affect their eligibility to maintain their current position or they subject themselves to disciplinary action up to and including termination.

Commentary: This policy extends the time when employees must disclose information about their personal status beyond the point in time when an employment decision is made. In most organizations, there is usually no mandatory post-employment disclosure policy. Changes in employee status affect the degree to which management can trust them with access to sensitive information and access to other assets such as cash. Computer workers are in a powerful position of trust that can be exploited to an employer's detriment. This policy prevents such difficult situations.

Related Policies: "Background Checks."

Audience: End users

Security Environments: Medium and high

28. Worker Transfers

Policy: Workers who have given notice of their intention to leave the employment of Company X, and those who are aware of an impending involuntary employment termination, and any disgruntled employees must be transferred to positions where they can do minimal damage to Company X assets.

Commentary: This policy prevents disgruntled or upset employees from being kept in positions where they could cause serious damage to organizational property, including the information handled by computer and communications systems. For example, to keep a systems programmer on the job after he or she had received notice of being laid off would invite problems. The policy does not make specific reference to computers and communications related workers, because this policy should apply to all types of workers. For example, a building entrance security guard who has given notice could be, according to this policy, removed from his or her job. The policy has deliberately been written in a manner that requires management to use its discretion. In some organizations a security guard may be in a position to do serious harm to organizational assets, while in other organizations a security guard would not be able to do much of consequence.

Related Policies: "Physical Access Of Terminated Workers" and "Internal Investigations Information Confidentiality."

Audience: Management

Security Environments: All

29. Grievance Resolution

Policy: Management must establish and provide adequate staff for procedures that promptly address each and every written worker grievance.

Commentary: This policy communicates to lower-level management a requirement for the prompt resolution of all worker grievances. Notice the policy does not require that the grievances be resolved in a manner that is satisfactory to the workers, only that each and every one be promptly addressed. Having an effective grievance resolution process also builds employee morale, communicating that management does care what employees have to say. This policy is also consistent with a commitment to having quality be a part of all business processes. Some grievances may relate to control deficiencies, and so the complaints may provide valuable information for improving internal control. The prompt resolution of grievances also lessens the risk of a computer crime or other abuse because a worker felt the need to seek revenge or otherwise make a statement. In some organizations, an internal ombudsman is established as an impartial judge to whom unresolved grievances can be taken.

Related Policies: "Refusal To Provide Unnecessary Information."

Audience: Management

Security Environments: All

30. Confidential Counseling

Policy: All workers with serious personal problems must be given free and confidential counseling services.

Commentary: This policy assists workers with the resolution of personal problems so that these problems do not unduly interfere with the workers' ability to perform their jobs. For example, if a worker were a drug addict, this could affect his or her reasoning ability, which may lead to a problem for the employer. If a worker were under severe financial pressures, he or she might be tempted to sell confidential information to competitors. Many organizations provide some counseling services as a part of a medical insurance plan.

The duration of the counseling and the nature of the specific services in some cases may best be left out of the policy. This gives management the ability to change the services offered as health insurance and related fringe benefits are modified. Although rare, the policy may also set a limit on the number of visits to a counselor, the total cost, or the time-period when free services will be provided. Co-payment arrangements, where the worker pays part of the cost, are also common, although stated elsewhere. For similar reasons, organizations would be well advised to consider interest-free loans for those employees who find themselves in desperate need of extra money.

Related Policies: "Drugs And Alcohol" and "Grievance Resolution."

Audience: Management

Security Environments: All

31. Drugs And Alcohol

Policy: With the exception of prescriptions ordered by licensed health care professionals, workers must not use or be under the influence of either drugs or alcohol when in the workplace.

Commentary: This policy encourages workers to be sober when working for their employer. Sober employees are more likely to make rational decisions in keeping with the organization's objectives. Some organizations may wish to have a written policy giving them a rule that may be pointed to in the event that they discipline or terminate a worker for the use of drugs or alcohol when at work. With telecommuting, including salespeople working out of their cars, the location of the workplace is no longer as clear as it used to be. In the virtual organization, the workplace is wherever people do their work. This policy may cause a problem with some employees who drink during lunch periods, particularly if entertaining prospective customers. Exercising good judgment on these rare occasions would be sufficient, which would eliminate the need for specific mention of these occasions in the policy. To enforce a policy like this, a small but increasing number of organizations are using computer-based sobriety tests, which are video games that test worker reflexes to ensure that workers are sober before they begin work.

Related Policies: "Confidential Counseling."

Audience: All

Security Environments: All

32. Removing Identification Badges

Policy: Immediately after workers leave Company X facilities, they must remove their identification badges and store them in a safe and convenient place away from public view.

Commentary: This policy prevents workers from leaving the work site with their badges on, in the process indirectly notifying everybody that they work for Company X. Keeping a badge on in public may attract corporate spies or hackers intent on obtaining information from the involved worker. This policy is especially important for those organizations that wish to have their personnel remain anonymous. This policy additionally fosters awareness about the correct placement of a badge and how its placement corresponds to the physical location of a worker.

Related Policies: "Third-Party Physical Access" and "Escorting Involuntarily Terminated Workers."

Audience: End users

Security Environments: High

33. Securing Identification Badges

Policy: When off Company X premises, workers must protect their identification badges with the same level of protection as their wallets and credit cards.

Commentary: This policy emphasizes that Company X identification badges are valuable, that badges need protection comparable to a wallet, and that workers are expected to protect their badges from theft or unauthorized use. In many situations, workers leave their badges in unlocked cars or in other locations where the badges are visible and could easily be stolen. An intruder intent on gaining access to Company X facilities wants to get a badge and analyze its components in order to determine how to make a counterfeit. If the intruder cannot put his or her hands on an existing badge, this counterfeit making process will be that much harder. If the badge technology being used is not sophisticated, an intruder may be able to remove the existing picture and insert his or her own image into the card. This policy is deliberately technology neutral. The policy does not even require that a photo ID badge system be used at the organization.

Related Policies: "Individuals Without Identification Badges" and "Third-Party Physical Access."

Audience: End users

Security Environments: Medium and high

6.02 User Training

6.02.01 Information Security Education And Training

1. Policy Quiz

Policy: Users must not be given access to Company X information systems unless they have read the Information Security Policy and taken a quiz that clearly shows that they understand the material described therein.

Commentary: One of the major problems with all information security policies revolves around management not knowing whether users have read and understood the policies. If users have not read the policies, they may ignorantly do things that cause security problems, for example, opening a file sent as an electronic mail attachment without scanning the file with a virus detection package. If users have read the policies, but not sufficiently understood them, they may do things that cause security problems. The true test of understanding would be observation in real-world working environments, but that is too expensive for nearly every organization. As the next best thing, users can be tested to determine that they understood the policy, and if they pass a quiz, then access privileges may be granted. For example, a worker who wanted to telecommute could read the telecommuting security policy, take a quiz, and get a passing score, at which point a security administrator would authorize the user to come into the organization's internal network over the Internet using a virtual private network. In sophisticated organizations, such privileges may be opened up automatically based on a quiz delivered through an intranet computer-based training system or software.

Related Policies: "User ID Forms."

Audience: Technical staff

Security Environments: All

2. Privacy-Related Policies and Procedures

Policy: With exception of those related to the handling of private data about individuals, information security policies and procedures must be revealed only to Company X workers and selected outsiders such as auditors, who have a legitimate business need for this information.

Commentary: This policy addresses the seemingly contradictory policy that information about security should be restricted to insiders only, but can be revealed to outsiders. Some organizations may wish to go one step further, adding a sentence at the end of the policy indicating that Company X recognizes that people have a vested interest in information about themselves. This policy is quite progressive and reflects the privacy policies in use at a number of telephone companies and government agencies. Common practices at commercial concerns throughout the world will vary. The policy is deliberately vague about the specific information to be revealed, leaving that decision up to management. A data classification scheme should be used to designate information that is public.

Related Policies: "Customer Anonymity" and "External Violation Reporting."

Audience: Management and technical staff

Security Environments: All

3. Remote Access Training

Policy: Company X workers must complete an approved remote systems access training course prior to being granted privileges to use dial-up, Internet telnet, or any other remote access data communications system.

Commentary: Recognizing the potentially serious security problems associated with telecommuting and other types of remote system access, this policy insists that all users of Company X remote access facilities be adequately trained. The training course mentioned in this policy would typically include security issues such as protecting remotely-located equipment from theft, encryption of sensitive files stored on a remote machine hard disk, shredding of sensitive hardcopy prior to disposal, locking sensitive hardcopy in cabinets or similarly secure containers, and security-related steps required to establish a data communications system connection.

Related Policies: "Security Requirements For Telecommuters" and "Telecommuter Information Security Procedures."

Audience: End users

Security Environments: All

4. Internet Training

Policy: Workers may access the Internet through Company X facilities only if they have received department management approval and have completed an Internet policies and practices training course.

Commentary: This policy prevents unrestricted usage of the Internet by Company X workers. Because Internet usage presents a number of serious potential security problems, a separate training course is appropriate. Ideally the training course would be delivered by computer-based training, which would permit users to complete the training at their convenience. The policy does not inhibit departmental management from establishing additional requirements for granting permission to access the Internet. These requirements might include a business need for such access.

Related Policies: "Information Security Training" and "Training Time."

Audience: End users and technical staff

Security Environments: Medium and high

5. Information Security Policy Pamphlet

Policy: On or before their first day of work, all new Company X workers must receive a copy of the information security policy pamphlet and be made aware that they must comply with the requirements described in that pamphlet.

Commentary: This policy ensures that all new workers know the information security rules, have read these rules, and understand that they must abide by these rules. Many organizations do not distribute a full information security manual these days, preferring instead to provide a brief pamphlet that contains the most important points. These pamphlets typically contain an intranet address where all information security policies, standards, procedures, and responsibilities are located for review. This approach permits the information security requirements to be updated quickly and automatically without the need to distribute new hardcopy manuals to all workers. Instead, an electronic mail notice can be sent to all people who must abide by these requirements. Giving new workers a pamphlet with their new hire package of material emphasizes management's commitment to information security and brings information security to their attention at the very beginning of the employment relationship.

Related Policies: "Code Of Conduct Acknowledgement" and "Information Security Training."

Audience: Management

Security Environments: All

6. Information Security Training

Policy: All workers must be provided with sufficient training and supporting reference material to permit them to properly protect Company X information resources.

Commentary: This policy requires that sufficient information security training and documentation be delivered to those workers who handle Company X information. The specific material to be delivered to workers will vary based on the nature of the jobs that these workers perform. For example, telephone order-takers should generally receive different training than computer programmers. In many organizations, nearly every worker accesses Company X information in order to do their job. Nonetheless, many workers need only rudimentary training. The policy communicates from top management to lower level management requirements for training and documentation, which could be online rather than in hardcopy form. This policy relies on local management to decide what constitutes sufficient information security training. Some organizations may prefer to say that the Information Security department determines what constitutes sufficient training.

Related Policies: "Training Time," "Information Security Manual," "Information User Responsibilities," and "Technical Training And Continuing Education."

Audience: Management

Security Environments: All

7. Basic Training

Policy: Workers must have successfully completed all other basic training needed in order to perform their new jobs before they receive information security training.

Commentary: This policy prevents people from going through information security training if they are not going to pass other training courses. The delay in training mentioned by this policy will also give many organizations additional time for new hire background checks to be completed, if they have not already been completed. The policy will prevent unsuitable people from gaining access to information that might be used to compromise information security at Company X. Consider standard practice at many banks. Tellers are not given security training until they have passed other training and until they have shown that they can handle whatever the job requires. In a sense, this policy restricts information about security to those who have a need for it, and in that respect it is a manifestation of the general concept known as the need to know. Nothing in this policy is meant to imply that new workers should be placed on the job before they receive information security training.

Related Policies: "Remote Access Training" and "System Capabilities And Commands."

Audience: End users and management

Security Environments: Medium and high

8. Information Security Policy Changes

Policy: All Company X workers must receive prompt notice of changes in the Company X information security policy, including how these changes may affect them, and how to obtain additional information.

Commentary: This policy ensures that all workers know about the latest version of the information security policy. Without a policy such as this, there may be legal problems associated with discipline and termination actions that were based on an information security policy that had not been communicated to the involved workers. These workers may say that they cannot reasonably be held to a standard of behavior defined in a policy about which they have not been informed. This policy clearly states management's intention to inform all affected workers, although it does not specify how to inform them. This will vary by recipient group and available information systems. Electronic mail is one of the most economical approaches, and electronic mail can contain an intranet address where all details can be found. Also effective is a notice inserted into paycheck and automatic deposit stub envelopes.

Related Policies: "Privacy Policy Change Notification" and "Code Of Conduct Acknowledgement."

Audience: Management

Security Environments: All

9. Training Responsibility

Policy: The Information Security department must provide refresher courses and such other materials to regularly remind workers about their obligations with respect to information security.

Commentary: This policy clarifies responsibility for the provision of information security training, documentation, and related materials. This responsibility may not be adequately assigned, and important information security work does not get done. Instead of, or in addition to, an Information Security department, some other departments might have been referred to in the policy. Another objective of the policy is to underline the fact that training and awareness is not a one-time effort. Such work needs to be done periodically. Written between the lines of this policy is an acknowledgement that departmental and other lower level management must give their workers sufficient time to attend refresher courses, run computer-based instruction software, read documentation, and more. The policy mentions "workers" with the intent to cover all persons who may be in a position where they would need to know the proper protection of Company X information resources.

Related Policies: "Training Time" and "Information Security Department Tasks."

Audience: Management and technical staff

Security Environments: All

10. Training Time

Policy: Management must allocate sufficient on-the-job time for workers to acquaint themselves with Company X security policies, procedures, and related ways of doing business.

Commentary: It is unrealistic to expect employees to read information security materials during their own time. Not only is such training required, but management must give their employees enough time to acquaint themselves with the materials. Some managers do not consider information security to be a worthwhile use of a worker's time because it does not directly contribute to the bottom line.

Related Policies: "Production Systems Training" and "Training Responsibility."

Audience: Management

Security Environments: All

11. Work Agreement

Policy: Every worker must understand the Company X policies and procedures about information security, and must agree in writing to perform his or her work according to these same policies and procedures.

Commentary: This policy requires every worker not only to familiarize themselves with information security policies and procedures, but also to sign a statement acknowledging the fact that he or she understands and agrees to be bound by these policies and procedures. From a legal standpoint, it is desirable to have employees acknowledge in writing that they understand information security is a part of their job. If they are subsequently terminated due to an information security violation or related problems, there will be no doubt that such employees understood what was required of them. This policy therefore reduces the probability of a wrongful termination lawsuit. Obtaining something in writing also lends a new credibility that many people may not have previously brought to matters involving information security. Some organizations that are serious about security require that this signed statement be provided annually. Understanding can now be confirmed through software that tests workers on the policies that they have read.

Related Policies: "Policy Quiz" and "Information Security Class."

Audience: Management

Security Environments: All

12. Information Security Class

Policy: Within three months of the date when they began employment with Company X, every worker must attend an information security awareness class and sign an attendance statement that attests that they have attended the class, understood the material, and had an opportunity to ask questions.

Commentary: This policy requires every new worker to attend an in-house class discussing information security. For existing employees, a modification of this policy could state they must attend within six months of the date when such courses become available. To ensure that people actually attend a class, they are asked to sign a statement acknowledging the fact that they understood the material presented. From a legal standpoint, it is desirable to have employees acknowledge in writing that they understand information security is a required part of their job. If they are subsequently terminated due to an information security violation or related problems,

there is no doubt that the employee understood what was required of him or her. This policy therefore reduces the probability of a wrongful termination lawsuit. If the classes are scheduled for working hours, then another intention of this policy is to notify lower level management that they must provide working hours time for their employees to attend information security training events. There is nothing special about the time periods mentioned in the policy. These can be changed to suit organizational needs and resources. The long period of time reflects the fact that classes will probably be offered every so often, perhaps monthly, but not continuously. Ideally information security material is included in new employee orientation, in which case, the three-month requirement will be met.

Related Policies: "Work Agreement."

Audience: End users and management

Security Environments: All

13. Computer Access Training

Policy: All Company X workers must complete an approved information security training class before they are granted access to any Company X computer systems.

Commentary: This policy informs all parties involved that new workers must not be given any production information system access privileges until they have completed an information security training class. The training class is not just any old training class, it must be approved, if not written, by the Information Security department. This policy ensures that every worker knows the rules for information security, so they are then able to sign a form in good conscience that says that they agree to abide by these rules whenever they use Company X information systems. In some organizations, workers are expected to sign such a form but they have not yet gone through a training class, so they do not know to what they are agreeing. This policy is easily implemented through computer-based training (CBT) systems that are set up in a library, a conference room, training center, or some other unrestricted area. New recruits can be sent to this location and at their convenience take a pre-recorded course. An attractive aspect of a CBT system is that it can also be used to give users tests to gauge their understanding of the material. A separate stand-alone training machine or a separate training network is advisable rather than providing CBT over an intranet or production local area network because the individuals receiving the training have not, at that point, received any legitimate system access privileges.

Related Policies: "Temporary Worker And Consultant Access" and "Information Security Training."

Audience: End users and management

Security Environments: All

14. Production Systems Training

Policy: Company X workers must not use any software for production business processes unless they have completed approved training for such software.

Commentary: This policy requires that workers complete an approved training effort prior to running software that affects production business operations. The policy is additionally aimed at assuring that users have sufficient training before changing to a new or significantly enhanced software system takes place. Nothing in the policy prevents workers from running the software in a test environment so that they may familiarize themselves with the software. The policy prevents workers from being in a position where they could adversely affect business records by errors, omissions, and frauds unless they have completed approved training. Beyond the system interruptions and delays, other risks of inadequately-trained users involve poor customer service and adverse public relations. This policy avoids embarrassment for users who may be too proud to admit that they do not know how to use the software or are too afraid to ask. Training also should include familiarization with controls and related security matters. The word "approved" in the policy is deliberately vague, permitting management considerable flexibility when it comes to choosing the type of training that each system requires. Hardware or networks were not mentioned explicitly in this policy because, by implication, new hardware and networks have accompanying new or different software. Some organizations may wish to add the words "hardware and networks" to the policy.

Related Policies: "Training Time."

Audience: Management

Security Environments: All

15. Compliance Agreement

Policy: As a condition of continued employment, employees, consultants, and contractors must annually sign an information security compliance agreement.

Commentary: The intention of this agreement is to require all workers to sign a compliance statement each year, thereby forcing them to acknowledge without a doubt that compliance with security policies and procedures is part of their job. These agreements typically say the individual agrees to comply with information security policies and procedures, has read the security manual, understands the manual, and furthermore understands that violations are cause for disciplinary action up to and including termination. The act of signing something not only provides employers with legally-admissible evidence that workers were notified about information security, but also changes the way that workers view information security.

Related Policies: "Non-Disclosure Agreements — Organization" and "Confidentiality Agreements."

Audience: Management

Security Environments: All

16. Technical Training And Continuing Education

Policy: All technical information systems staff must have sufficient initial training and continuing education in all critical aspects of their jobs including security, quality assurance, and customer relations.

Commentary: This policy ensures that technical information systems staff get the training and education they need in order to do their jobs properly, including doing their jobs with adequate security. A wide variety of problems occur because staff do not know what they are doing. The resolution of security problems should not be left to inadequately trained staff who are guessing what to do. This policy also may foster worker loyalty that should encourage workers to stay with their employer. This policy insists that employers pay for training, at least for information systems staff. This policy addresses different subject matter than that which would ordinarily be delivered by an information security awareness effort.

Related Policies: "Vulnerability Advisories" and "Information Security Training."

Audience: Management and technical staff

Security Environments: All

17. Information Security Responsibility

Policy: Responsibility for information security on a day-to-day basis must be every worker's duty and not solely vested in the Information Security department.

Commentary: The purpose of this policy is to clarify the fact that information security is multi-disciplinary, multi-departmental, and multi-organizational in nature. This means that a single department within Company X cannot possibly adequately address information security. Every worker must do their part in order to achieve appropriate levels of information security. After all, information can be found nearly everywhere in the organization and nearly every worker utilizes information in order to do his or her job. It is only natural that every worker should be specifically charged with responsibility for information security. Some organizations go one step further than this policy, incorporating a question into performance review forms, such as whether the employee observes information security policies in the course of his or her work. To be truly effective, this policy must be supplemented with additional instructions, telling workers exactly what is expected of them. This would ordinarily appear in awareness material although it is recommended that this would also appear in job descriptions. This policy is typically followed by specific user-oriented instructions dealing with choosing strong passwords, not disclosing passwords to other people. This policy is increasingly important as distributed systems are used for production information processing activities because the reliance on users is increased.

Related Policies: "Performance Evaluations" and "Information Security Department Tasks."

Audience: All

Security Environments: All

6.03 Responding To Security Incidents And Malfunctions

6.03.01 Reporting Security Incidents

1. Loss Or Disclosure Of Sensitive Information

Policy: If sensitive information is lost, disclosed to unauthorized parties, or suspected of being lost or disclosed to unauthorized parties, its Owner and the appropriate Information Security personnel must be notified immediately.

Commentary: Prompt notification of sensitive information loss or disclosure is a necessary. For example, if information about a new, but unreleased product has been mistakenly disclosed to a reporter, then the date for the official announcement of the product may need to be changed. The intention of the policy is therefore to require that all workers report all losses or disclosures of sensitive information. This policy works best when the word "sensitive" has been explicitly defined within the organization through a data classification system. Likewise, the term "information Owner" should be defined elsewhere.

Related Policies: "Four-Category Data Classification," "Information Ownership," and "Integrity Controls Failure Notification."

Audience: All

Security Environments: All

2. Disclosure Of Information System Vulnerabilities

Policy: Specific information about information system vulnerabilities, such as the details of a recent system break-in, must not be distributed to persons who do not have a demonstrable need to know.

Commentary: This policy lets those few people who have access to information about information system vulnerabilities, know that disclosure of this information should be strictly controlled. If vulnerability information were to fall into the hands of unauthorized parties, these people could use it to compromise the organization's systems. These unauthorized parties could also use it to extort or publicly embarrass the organization. Such information also may be of interest and useful for internal political battles. The vulnerability information may also erode the confidence that users and management have in the Information Systems department, and for this reason should also be restricted. Some organizations may go further than this policy. For example, they may require that systems vulnerability information be labeled with special restricted access words. Similar to data classification labels such as "secret," these warning labels could get quite specific, forbidding distribution on electronic bulletin boards and similar publicly-accessible systems. Other organizations may keep logs of to whom this information was distributed and when it was returned.

Related Policies: "System Penetration Software Source Code" and "Presentation Of Public Image."

Audience: Management and technical staff

Security Environments: All

3. Public Releases Of Vulnerability Information

Policy: Press releases or other public statements issued by Company X containing information systems vulnerability information must be free of explicit details.

Commentary: This policy prevents Company X representatives from causing trouble because they have released explicit details about information security vulnerabilities. If explicit details are provided, this may enable hackers and others to launch attacks against other sites, and Company X may be held responsible for the damage done thereby. Refraining from disclosing these details may be frustrating for the news media, but it will also help ensure that the attack method is not again used against Company X systems. Public disclosure of these explicit details may additionally inform the perpetrators that certain information about them is known, and this may cause them to destroy evidence that could otherwise be accessible to investigators, and could perhaps be useful in a prosecution. Public disclosure of computer crime details could also encourage perpetrators to flee so as to avoid arrest when they otherwise would have been readily apprehended. This policy will furthermore help to keep Company X representatives from speculating about exactly how attacks were carried out, and this may prevent charges of libel and slander. Disclosure to relevant vendors and to government agencies tracking computer break-ins are not covered by this policy and so are permissible.

Related Policies: "Presentation Of Public Image" and "System Penetration Software Source Code."

Audience: All

Security Environments: All

4. System Vulnerability Exploitation And Victim Data

Policy: Company X staff must not disclose information about individuals, organizations, specific methods used to exploit, or specific systems that have been damaged by computer crimes and computer abuses.

Commentary: This policy is appropriate for vendors of information system products and services. For example, a workstation vendor may release information about the existence of a security problem and how to install a patch to overcome the problem. The customers who were victimized and the specific ways that the attacks were perpetrated should be kept confidential. This policy ensures that unauthorized parties do not use the information to mount further attacks against the victims because they do not know who the victims are, which systems were involved, or the details of the attacks. It also makes it more difficult for unauthorized parties to exploit the vulnerability because they must figure out the specific attack method.

Related Policies: "External Information Requests" and "Disclosure Of Information System Vulnerabilities."

Audience: End users and technical staff

Security Environments: All

5. Production System Problems

Policy: All significant errors, incomplete processing and improper processing of production applications must be promptly reported to the Help Desk.

Commentary: This policy alerts technical staff that something is amiss on production applications. These problems may be more serious than a programming error. They may for example be an indication of a hacker attack in process, or of corrupted data, or of system unreliability. Requiring the reporting of all significant problems also prevents users from rationalizing that a problem is already known by the technical staff, or that others may already have reported it. This policy also provides a new and different set of criteria for determining whether applications ran successfully to completion, and this is desirable because the user has a business perspective that most people in the Information Technology department do not.

Related Policies: "Disruptive Conditions" and "Off-Site Systems Damage And Loss."

Audience: End users

Security Environments: All

6. Information Security Pranks

Policy: Workers must not play practical jokes, engage in pranks, or otherwise humorously make it look like a security incident is taking place, will take place, or has taken place when this is not true.

Commentary: This policy is similar to a policy adopted by airports worldwide in which it is a serious crime to joke about carrying a knife, a gun, or some other weapon. What happens when people do this is that they create a false alarm and this can not only waste resources and cause people to get needlessly upset, but also perhaps serve as a diversion for real attacks. This policy prevents miscommunications and misinterpretations.

Related Policies: "Unofficial Web Pages" and "Pretext Personal Data Collection."

Audience: End users and technical staff

Security Environments: All

7. Offensive Electronic Mail Messages

Policy: Workers must respond directly to the originator of offensive electronic mail messages, telephone calls, and other communications, and if the offensive messages do not cease, workers must report the communications to their manager and the Human Resources department.

Commentary: This policy is meant to encourage workers to initially deal directly with the originator of material that they consider being offensive. Only when the originator fails to take action based on the feedback, should workers escalate the matter to their manager and the Human Resources department. In many instances, the originator does not appreciate that certain material is offensive, and a simple complaint sent to the originator will be sufficient to stop the communications. An originator might be an individual who simply forwards material obtained from another source. The existence of this policy is an indication that an organization takes legal issues such as sexual harassment and a hostile work environment seriously. The policy shows that management is so serious about these matters that they established a process for their resolution.

Related Policies: "Removing Offensive Material" and "Sexual, Ethnic, And Racial Harassment."

Audience: End users

Security Environments: All

8. Off-Site Systems Damage And Loss

Policy: Workers must promptly report to their manager any damage to or loss of Company X computer hardware, software, or information that has been entrusted to their care.

Commentary: This policy ensures that telecommuting workers, and those workers with mobile computers, report all damages or losses promptly. This will permit remedial measures, such as the replacement of a portable computer, to take place expediently so as to minimize the impact on business activity. This also will permit prompt notification of the information Owner if the loss of sensitive information was involved. The policy could be augmented with another sentence requiring department managers to report these damages or losses to the Physical Security department, which generally keeps loss history records. Alternately, users could be told to report all such damage or loss to the help desk, which would report it to the appropriate internal groups, including an insurance department, which may then collect insurance for stolen portable computers. In many cases, the user reporting a loss will need to fill out a loss report, but this is a procedure, so would not typically be detailed, only mentioned, in a policy. This policy requires the reporting of information loss or damage. This may be a particularly important issue for organizations concerned about industrial espionage and portable computer theft. This policy is deliberately written so that it could apply to all locations, not just off-site systems.

Related Policies: "Incident Reporting" and "Violation And Problem Reporting."

Audience: End users

Security Environments: All

9. Incident Reporting

Policy: All suspected information security incidents must be reported as quickly as possible through the approved Company X internal channels.

Commentary: This policy is intended to require that all problems and violations be promptly brought to the attention of those who can actually do something about them. If problems and violations go unreported, they may lead to much greater losses for the organization than would have been incurred, had the problems been reported right away. A good example of this involves computer viruses that, if unreported and uncontained, will continue to spread. Some organizations go further by requiring that reporting take place within a certain time frame, for example 24 hours. Other organizations add specific penalties for not reporting problems. The implementation of this policy could involve a toll-free telephone number to prevent the caller from having to pay toll charges. To encourage reporting, anonymity can partially be achieved by turning off any automatic caller-ID features available with the receiving telephone. Likewise, the Information Security department may wish to publicize the fact that reports can be made anonymously. It may also encourage people to call if they know they will always get an answering machine, never a person on the receiving end of the line. Reference is made to the "approved channels" to encourage people to go to Information Security or other people who are recognized as responsible for investigations. The words "approved channels" also encourage the establishment of such channels for information flow if they are not already clearly defined.

Related Policies: "Off-Site Systems Damage And Loss," "Violation And Problem Reporting," "Information Security Alert System," "Extended Investigations," and "Violation Of Law."

Audience: End users

Security Environments: All

10. Incident Reporting Severity

Policy: Unless it reasonably may be expected to lead to further losses, an information security incident that caused less than $100 in damage, and that has been resolved by the involved parties, need not be reported to the Information Security department.

Commentary: This policy establishes a financial threshold for the reporting of information security incidents. The use of such a threshold permits the Information Security department to focus on those matters that are most important to the organization. A major deficiency in this policy is that the decision about whether to report or not is made by people who generally have very little expertise in the information security area. This might lead to a situation where the person, who otherwise would report an incident, does not report the incident because he or she did not understand the seriousness of the problem or the extent of the losses. For this reason, the policy is not recommended. It is generally preferable to have the staff within Information Security determine which incidents warrant further attention. This policy is best used by Information Security management who is seeking to expand his or her staff. The manager in such a situation could claim that the policy is needed because the present

staff is overwhelmed with the incidents that are currently being reported, and that some sort of triage is necessary. When management engages in a discussion of this proposal, the undesirable side effects that come with this policy can be stressed. Top management should then opt to increase staff to adequately investigate all reported incidents. It is important in another policy or in some other documentation to define what constitutes an incident. There is nothing special about the $100 threshold, it might just as easily have been $1000.

Related Policies: "Incident Reporting" and "Violation And Problem Reporting."

Audience: All

Security Environments: All

11. Violation And Problem Reporting

Policy: Company X workers have a duty to report all information security violations and problems to the Information Security department on a timely basis so that prompt remedial action may be taken.

Commentary: This policy requires workers to promptly report information security violations and problems. For example, immediate reporting is absolutely essential to limit losses from unauthorized system penetrations and other potentially serious security problems. Delays in reporting can mean massive additional losses for the organization. This policy acknowledges that the people who use systems are often the ones to spot problems. This policy requires that problems be reported to someone who can do something about it. The reporting process here is to a central group as opposed to line management or a service provider. The reporting process could also go through line management, although this takes longer and is likely to unduly delay corrective actions. The policy could be expanded to state that workers must not, under any circumstances, attempt to prove the existence of these weaknesses unless they have been specifically charged with this work by top management. This caveat could be added to discourage hacking and other system intrusions that might be interpreted as system misuse. The policy here could be expanded to require a written report following the initial oral report. The scope of this policy could be expanded to include "suspected problems," not just "problems and violations." The word "weaknesses" also may be used instead of "problems." While internal reporting is to be encouraged and required, external reporting is fraught with significant dangers.

Related Policies: "External Violation Reporting," "Computer Emergency Response Team," and "Reporting A Suspected Virus."

Audience: End users

Security Environments: All

12. Violation And Problem Reporting Alternatives

Policy: Company X workers must immediately report all suspected information security problems, vulnerabilities, and incidents to either their immediate manager or to Information Security management.

Commentary: This policy gives workers multiple routes for the reporting of information security problems, vulnerabilities, and incidents. If, for example, the problem involved the Information Security department, then reporting it to Information Security would be problematic. Likewise, if the matter involved the worker's manager, then reporting it to that same manager would be ill advised. This two-path approach ensures that all significant information is communicated, and not withheld because the person reporting it is fearful about political repercussions or some other potential problem. Use of this policy requires that additional communications pathways be established to permit managers to expediently pass information along to the Information Security department, the Help Desk, the Computer Emergency Response Team, or some other worker or group who is in a position to take immediate action. This policy works best if at least one of the reporting pathways is anonymous.

Related Policies: "Incident Reporting" and "User Status Changes."

Audience: End users

Security Environments: All

13. Violation And Problem Reporting Interference

Policy: Workers must never attempt to interfere with, prevent, obstruct, or dissuade a staff member in their efforts to report a suspected information security problem or violation, or retaliate against an individual reporting or investigating information security problems or violations.

Commentary: This policy encourages workers who wish to report an information security problem or violation, yet are concerned that they may find it difficult. These whistle blowers often are concerned that their own immediate management will penalize them for reporting problems or violations. This policy attempts to foster a perspective that is in the best interest of the organization, rather than the internal political interests of certain management.

Related Policies: "Problem Reporting."

Audience: All

Security Environments: All

14. Violation And Problem Reporting Protection

Policy: Company X must protect workers who report in good faith what they believe to be a violation of laws or regulations, or conditions that could jeopardize the health or safety of other workers.

Commentary: This policy assures workers who are considering reporting problems that the organization will protect them. This should encourage workers to make reports when they may otherwise have been deterred by the potential adverse consequences. Beyond that, the policy is also intended to instruct workers to report problems internally rather than externally, thereby reducing adverse publicity and loss of customer confidence. This policy does not prohibit external reporting. It only states that the problem should be internally reported and the worker should give Company X some time to remedy the situation. Nothing in this policy prevents Company X from firing the worker for other reasons, such as poor performance in other areas. The policy is deliberately defined in a broad manner so that it includes information security problems. It also includes physical security problems and worker safety problems.

Related Policies: "External Violation Reporting."

Audience: End users and management

Security Environments: All

15. Violation And Problem Reporting Identity

Policy: Workers who report to the Security department a security problem, vulnerability, or an unethical condition within Company X may, at their sole discretion, have their identity held in strict confidence.

Commentary: This policy encourages whistle blowers to come forward and reveal irregularities, control problems, and other security issues. In many cases whistle blowers do not say anything because they are afraid that they will, as a consequence of the report, lose their job or suffer some other career setback. This policy seems to limit if not eliminate the possibility that the whistle blower will suffer this fate. While suggestion boxes, anonymous telephone answering machines, and other anonymous reporting mechanisms may be made available, without a policy such as this, potential whistle blowers may not come forward because they fear that their identity will come to light during an investigation. By disclosing their identities to Information Security, whistle blowers may also get some favorable treatment if it comes to light that they played some role in the problem. The policy could be augmented to include words that state that the whistle blower will be kept informed of the investigation as it proceeds. This will further encourage people to come forward because if they think that nothing will be done, then they will be further discouraged from coming forward with a revelation.

Related Policies: "Violation And Problem Reporting Protection" and "Centralized Problem Reporting."

Audience: End users

Security Environments: Medium and high

16. External Violation Reporting

Policy: Unless required by law or regulation to report information security violations to external authorities, management, in conjunction with representatives from the Legal department, the Information Security department, the Physical Security department, and Internal Audit, must weigh the pros and cons of external disclosure before reporting these violations.

Commentary: Many organizations refrain from reporting computer crimes because the public embarrassment, cost, and diversion of staff resources appear to outweigh the benefits. Benefits include setting an example to discourage other violations, giving employees the impression that management believes in the criminal justice system, and obtaining restitution. It is often desirable that management be given the ability to choose to report violations on case-by-case basis. This policy requires management to look at the pros and cons of each case before actually making an external report, provided local law gives management such flexibility. Although it is rare, some organizations may wish to establish a committee that will evaluate the merits of external reporting on a case-by-case basis. Law enforcement and criminological researchers rally for public reporting because they need statistics to better understand the nature of crime. As it stands, a significant number of computer crimes go unreported, and a significant number go undetected. Required external reporting is restricted to violations of laws and regulations, while required internal reporting could include violations of policies and other abuses that are not necessarily illegal. The policy provided here is narrowly-scoped in that it deals with information security violations. The policy could be broadened to focus on all security-related violations.

Related Policies: "Security Violation And Problem Information Retention," "Violation And Problem Reporting," and "Problem Reporting."

Audience: Management

Security Environments: All

17. Violation And Problem Reporting To Authorities

Policy: Any potentially material event must be reported by Information Security management to the vice president of the Legal department and the vice president of the Finance department who must decide whether public disclosure is necessary and appropriate.

Commentary: Under a country's securities laws, significant negative events must be promptly disclosed. These events are typically characterized as any important information that may affect an investor's decision process. The test here is whether the investor would consider the information to affect their decision-making. If the investors' decision-making would be affected, then the event must be disclosed. Otherwise the details of the event may be retained internally. Most organizations are quiet about bad news for fear that it may impact their image, customer confidence, supplier confidence, employee morale, and other factors. But a number of companies have been recently hit with lawsuits from shareholders who allege delayed or insufficient reporting of adverse events. This policy requires management to consider disclosures, pay attention to the relevant disclosure laws, and establish a formal process for handling these disclosures. By acting promptly and properly, management may curb or avoid shareholder class action lawsuits. By using this policy, management may also avoid a severe drop in the stock price caused by a loss of investor confidence prompted by the revelation of more details about the problem in the midst of a scandal brought on because the information was initially suppressed. Other organizational structures will be required for reporting other types of material events, such as a staff layoff. This policy applies primarily to publicly-listed companies, but it could also be reformulated for other organizations to take into consideration things that a local community should know.

Related Policies: "External Violation Reporting."

Audience: Management

Security Environments: All

18. Disclosure Of Computer System Attacks

Policy: Unless compelled by law to disclose attacks against its computer systems or networks, Company X must not report these incidents to the public or any government agencies.

Commentary: This policy keeps organizations out of the newspapers if they are to be shown in an uncomplimentary light. This keeps customer confidence high and keep stock prices from being affected. For organizations in regulated industries, such as utilities and transportation, this policy is also intended to keep the organization out of trouble with regulators. The policy furthermore acknowledges that most governments do not have a trusted and secure mechanism to protect information about attacks. Sharing attack information with a government agency could actually be irresponsible because it could lead to the unauthorized exploitation of this information. Many organizations are keeping a low profile and not disclosing attack information. This policy is often unwritten, but in many situations it may be advisable to put it in writing to keep workers from publicly disclosing such information. Another good reason to put this policy in writing is to show that it is a legitimate and justified approach, not a decision rule that must be concealed. The policy deliberately does not distinguish between a successful attack and an unsuccessful attack, both of which may include sensitive information.

Related Policies: "External Violation Reporting."

Audience: End users

Security Environments: All

19. Reporting Security Breaches To Third Parties

Policy: Any computer security breach at Company X that causes private or proprietary third-party information to be exposed must be communicated to the affected third party immediately.

Commentary: This policy gives internal Company X management instructions about when they must report computer security intrusions to outside parties. If, for example, a web merchant's credit card database has been exposed because hackers entered the merchant's Internet commerce site, then the merchant has a duty to inform not only the involved customers, but the issuers of the credit cards as well. Organizations should plan how they will handle a security breach in advance, and this policy is one consideration in that planning process. The policy applies to a wide variety of threats including identity theft and expropriation of proprietary information.

Related Policies: "Violation And Problem Reporting To Authorities" and "External Violation Reporting."

Audience: Management

Security Environments: All

20. Reporting Unauthorized Activity

Policy: Users of Company X information systems must immediately report to Information Security management any unauthorized activity including, but not limited to, loss of, or changes to computerized production data and questionable usage of files, databases, or communications networks.

Commentary: This policy provides users with specific examples of the types of events that should be reported to Information Security management. The policy enlists the participation of users on an information security team, and utilize them to detect unusual events that may be indicative of sabotage, fraud, system malfunction, and other information-security-relevant events. The policy may need additional explanation when delivered to the end user community.

Related Policies: "Reporting Of Software Malfunctions," "Violation And Problem Reporting," and "Centralized Problem Reporting."

Audience: End users

Security Environments: All

21. Reporting Questionable Events

Policy: Users of Company X information systems must immediately report to the Information Security department any unusual and suspicious information security-related events including, but not limited to, unusual requests for Company X information coming from an external party, and atypical system behavior.

Commentary: This policy informs users and technical staff that they should report unusual events. One example would be a welcoming logon message indicating that the involved user ID was last in use at a specific date and time, when the involved user knows that he or she was not using the system then. Such a discrepancy may be an indication that the computer's internal clock needs to be reset, or an indication that an unauthorized party has been using the user ID. This policy is particularly important when it comes to requests for inside information, whether the request is placed through electronic mail, over the phone, casually at a professional society meeting, or otherwise, because these same requests may be indicative of attempted social engineering. When the Information Security department has this type of information at its disposal, it will be able to determine whether a genuine threat is present, and whether remedial action is required. This remedial action might include a memo issued to all staff informing them of the social engineering attacks that have been encountered.

Related Policies: "Law Enforcement Inquiries" and "Requests For Organization Information."

Audience: End users and technical staff

Security Environments: All

22. Reporting Design Problems

Policy: All potentially serious problems associated with information systems being designed or developed, that are not being adequately addressed by planned or existing projects, must be promptly reported to Information Security management.

Commentary: This policy gives workers a reporting channel other than the standard management hierarchy with which they normally operate. Standard reporting channels are often not sufficient for the reporting of major problems because management does not like bad news, does not want to look bad, does not want to spend money now when they can spend it later, or does not have the technical expertise to understand the problem. This policy makes it officially required for technical staff

members to bring problems to the attention of Information Security management. As an alternative, the Internal Audit manager could be used. The nature of the problems was not defined. By leaving this word ambiguous, a very broad scope of possible problems is covered by the policy. This policy establishes that all people throughout an organization are responsible for information security, not just the members of the Information Security department. This reporting process could proceed anonymously, for example through a hot line that is never answered by a person but that connects to an answering machine without caller-ID.

Related Policies: "Designing Information Security Controls" and "Exceptions To Policies."

Audience: End users

Security Environments: All

23. Contacting Law Enforcement

Policy: Every decision involving or contacting law enforcement regarding information security incidents or problems must be made by a Company X corporate officer.

Commentary: This policy prevents serious disruption to the business adopting this policy by well-meaning technical staff or users. When law enforcement gets involved in an investigation they can do a number of things that can bring the business to a halt, or at least cause it to incur significant additional costs. For example, law enforcement may impound the computers involved as evidence, and this can mean that the machines are not available to perform regular business activities. When law enforcement is brought in, the victim organization will lose control of the case. For example, it will no longer be able to decide whether the case goes to court. Likewise, the legal process of assisting law enforcement with the investigation and prosecution may be more time consuming and expensive than internal management desires. Another reason to be wary about bringing in law enforcement is that they may be subject to certain privacy laws that internal investigators may not be constrained by.

Related Policies: "Problem Reporting" and "Information Security Responsibility."

Audience: End users and technical staff

Security Environments: All

24. Computer Crime Investigation

Policy: Whenever evidence clearly shows that Company X has been victimized by a computer or communications crime, a thorough investigation must be performed that provides sufficient information so that management can take steps to ensure that such incidents will not be likely to take place again, and effective security measures have been reestablished.

Commentary: This policy is intended to ensure that management takes appropriate action in response to computer or communications system crimes. Too often management is inclined to do nothing because they do not know what to do. To prevent management from trying to suppress information about vulnerabilities, often because of perceived negative ramifications, this policy requires that they initiate an investigation. In most instances, department and other local management will not have the expertise to carry out such a sophisticated investigation. The policy indirectly requires these managers to contact the Information Security department, Internal Audit, or some other group with the requisite expertise. The policy also guards against lawsuits alleging that management did not take care of problems even though they were notified that security problems existed. Examples of computer and communications crimes that may be suitably included in an accompanying explanation include theft of computer-resident trade secrets and public branch exchange toll fraud. Some organizations may wish to take this policy one step further by requiring investigations if such acts are only suspected. Another variation on the policy is to require that an investigation be performed after an abuse has been noted, even if this abuse is not legally a crime. This approach requires that the term "abuse" be defined. An example of a computer abuse that is not a computer crime in many jurisdictions is privacy violation. Reporting of such incidents to the audit committee on the board of directors may be required in the policy.

Related Policies: "Internal Investigations Information Confidentiality."

Audience: Management and technical staff

Security Environments: All

25. Extended Investigations

Policy: Extended investigations of security breaches must be performed while the suspected worker is given leave without pay and the reason for a suspect's leave without pay must not be disclosed to co-workers without the express permission of the director of Security.

Commentary: This policy provides management with time to gather the information it needs to determine if an employee was the perpetrator of an alleged crime or abuse. Because brief investigations need not involve time off with pay, the word "extended" was used in the policy. Because the policy is deliberately vague, management may decide which investigations will be extended on a case-by-case basis. Having the suspected employee off site prevents important evidence from being concealed, modified, or destroyed. The policy also prevents early judgments about the guilt or innocence of the involved employee. Avoiding preliminary judgments about guilt are also desirable because it prevents defamation of character lawsuits. The confidentiality requirement further prevents defamation of character lawsuits. A recommended alternative is to give leave with pay rather than leave without pay. If the employee ends up being guilty of nothing, there will be few, if any, hard feelings.

Related Policies: "Incident Management Responsibilities" and "Incident Reporting."

Audience: Management

Security Environments: All

26. Missing Access Devices

Policy: Any access device including, but not limited to, identification badges, physical access cards, smart cards with dynamic passwords and telephone credit cards that are missing or cannot be located, must be reported immediately to the Physical Security department.

Commentary: This policy requires all workers to notify the Physical Security department about any badges or tokens that may have been lost or stolen. Physical Security then can take steps to immediately block the privileges associated with these badges or tokens. In this way, losses occasioned by lost or stolen badges or tokens can be minimized. The words "Physical Security department" could easily be "Information Security department" or other words reflecting another organizational unit.

Related Policies: "Use Of Credit Cards" and "Portable Identification Credentials."

Audience: End users

Security Environments: All

6.03.02 Reporting Security Weaknesses

1. Reporting System Vulnerabilities

Policy: Users must promptly report all information security alerts, warnings, suspected vulnerabilities, to the Information Systems Help Desk and must not share such information with internal or external parties.

Commentary: This policy prevents well-meaning users from needlessly causing concern and upset in the user community. This policy has recently become a necessity for many organizations because there have been so many hoaxes reported. The policy indicates that the help desk will act as a filter for such information, screening out hoaxes, inaccurately reported problems, and old problems that have already been resolved. The help desk is also in a much better position to contact the parties who need to know than is an ordinary end user. To make this policy work best, the help desk, which is often on duty 24 hours a day and seven days a week should be able to instantly mobilize a computer emergency response team. Help desks can additionally check digital signatures and valid electronic mail return addresses from official incident response teams to verify the validity of reported problems. This policy prevents a well-meaning user from making false or potentially-libelous representations about systems security to outside parties.

Related Policies: "Computer Emergency Response Team."

Audience: End users

Security Environments: All

2. Disruptive Conditions

Policy: Workers must promptly notify management of all conditions that could lead to a disruption of business activities.

Commentary: This policy requires that workers be vigilant, promptly bringing any condition that could disrupt work to management's attention, so that remedial action may soon follow. Examples of topics that should be reported include: unexplained errors when writing to a hard disk drive, missing files on a personal computer, stolen computer equipment, fire extinguishers that are not charged, and other potential hazards. This policy requests that workers act respon-sibly at least when it comes to noticing problems. It is preferable to have many rather than a few sets of eyes to notice these things.

Related Policies: "Business Restoration Employee Expectations" and "Information Security Alert System."

Audience: End users

Security Environments: All

3. Centralized Problem Reporting

Policy: All known vulnerabilities and suspected or known violations must be communicated in an expedi-tious and confidential manner to the Information Security department and unauthorized disclosures of Company X information must additionally be reported to the appropriate information Owners.

Commentary: This policy is intended to establish a centralized Information Security department as the focal point for all reports of vulnerabilities and violations. In many organizations, these reports go only to lower-level managers, and never find their way back to a centralized group. Unless there is centralized reporting, it will be likely that no loss history will be compiled, no loss analysis will be conducted, and no related organiza-tion-wide decision-making will be performed. Centralized reporting is also useful for the mobilization of a computer emergency response team, an organiza-tion-wide contingency plan, and other important defensive resources. The policy is also helpful because it alleviates the reporting party's concerns about short-circuiting the chain of command. Without a policy like this, local management may get upset because problem reports make them look bad and they did not get a chance to stop the reporting process from reaching top management. The policy is also helpful because it indicates what needs to be communicated and to whom. This policy assumes that a separate policy defining information Owners is already in place.

Related Policies: "Off-Site Systems Damage And Loss" and "Legal Conflicts."

Audience: End users

Security Environments: All

4. Security Weaknesses And Vulnerability Discussion

Policy: Workers who discover a weakness or vulnerability in the information security measures used by Company X must not discuss these matters with anyone other than Information Security management, Internal Audit management, or trained investigators designated by one of these two managers.

Commentary: This policy prevents rumors about weaknesses and vulnerabilities associated with the information security measures used by the organization adopting this policy. Those who discover weaknesses or vulnerabilities often want to share their observations to get some recognition. This policy explicitly forbids that tendency because it runs a high risk of encouraging other people to exploit the weakness or vulnerability that has been discovered. Widespread discussion of these matters may also erode worker confidence in the organization's ability to maintain control of its internal operations. Widespread discussion also increases the risk that this information will be passed to outside parties such as news reporters, competitors, and disgruntled former employees.

Related Policies: "Reporting Security Breaches To Third Parties."

Audience: End users

Security Environments: All

5. Reporting Security Vulnerabilities

Policy: When a new and serious information systems security vulnerability associated with a particular vendor's hardware or software is discovered, it must be immediately reported to appropriate public forums for public dissemination.

Commentary: The policy is based on the theory that if the problem is quietly and confidentially communicated to vendors, then there is little intention for these organizations to promptly fix the problem. Those adopting this policy believe that it is through public embarrassment that some prompt action will take place. Those adopting this policy also believe that system administrators and others need the details about a new problem so they can understand how best to protect their systems. Unfortunately, many system administrators have neither the time nor the training to come up with custom fixes for vulnerabilities that have been publicly announced, that could be used until such time as the vendor releases their own fix for the vulnerability. One big problem with this policy is that it may tip-off the underground hacker community and this may soon thereafter lead to publicly-available programs that automate the attack. In support of this policy, some argue that the hacker community probably already knows about it, and that keeping it quiet only permits the hacker community to continue to abuse the vulnerability in relative secrecy.

Related Policies: "Vulnerability Disclosure" and "External Violation Reporting."

Audience: All

Security Environments: All

6.03.03 Reporting Software Malfunctions

1. Integrity Controls Failure Notification

Policy: If controls that assure the integrity of information fail, if such controls are suspected of failing, or if such controls are not available, management must be notified of these facts each time they are presented with the involved information.

Commentary: The intention of this is to achieve full disclosure about the nature of information used for decision-making. If certain information is suspect or if it may be suspect, management must be notified. This policy requires that management be notified, rather than having the information be suppressed in the hopes that nobody will notice. This policy requires that bad news be delivered, rather than tacitly permitting bad news to be suppressed. Particularly in large organizations, there is a tendency for bad news to be suppressed as information moves up the management hierarchy.

Related Policies: "Information Security Responsibility."

Audience: Management and technical staff

Security Environments: All

2. Vulnerability Disclosure

Policy: Workers must give the vendor a reasonable period of time to fix any serious system vulnerability discovered at Company X before they publicly release any information about that same problem.

Commentary: This policy prevents unfortunate situations where companies, and sometimes individuals, announce the fact that they have found a serious vulnerability, but there is no fix for the problem. To act in this manner permits hackers, industrial spies, disgruntled former employees, and others to exploit this information as they wish. To give the vendor time to come up with a fix, and to announce the availability of the fix, is the responsible thing to do. Nonetheless, pressures to look like an expert, and pressures to get marketing attention before anybody else discovers the same problem, have caused many organizations to announce vulnerabilities before the vendor is ready to provide a fix. This policy deliberately does not state a time period because that will vary based on the nature of the problem. The threat of public disclosure can be used by Company X workers to get the involved vendor to promptly come up with a fix. If the vendor does not do so on a timely basis, the workers may announce it.

Related Policies: "Centralized Problem Reporting" and "Security Weaknesses And Vulnerability Discussion."

Audience: Technical staff

Security Environments: All

3. Reporting A Suspected Virus

Policy: Workers who report a suspected computer virus infestation to the Information Security department immediately after it is discovered, must not be disciplined unless the worker knowingly caused a computer virus to be introduced into Company X systems.

Commentary: This policy is intended to encourage quick reporting of viruses, which is essential if their growth is to be limited and consequential losses are to be contained. A notable aspect of the policy is that disciplinary action will be taken if there is a delay in reporting a problem. Because even minutes can make a great difference when it comes to the propagation of computer viruses, the word "immediately" was used in the policy. If a worker has written a virus and let it loose on Company X computers, then this should be cause for disciplinary action, even if the employee did call the Information Security department promptly after it got out of hand. The policy could be expanded to include worms, Trojan horses, and other unauthorized programs that pose a risk to Company X systems.

Related Policies: "Software Scanning," "Violation And Problem Reporting," and "Eradicating Computer Viruses."

Audience: End users

Security Environments: All

4. Reporting Of Software Malfunctions

Policy: All apparent software malfunctions must be immediately reported to line management or the information system service provider.

Commentary: This policy requires users to note and report any software that appears to be functioning in a manner that differs from documentation. This will help to uncover Trojan horses, viruses, out-of-balance accounting problems, frauds, and other problems. The policy will also indirectly encourage the maintenance of current documentation. This policy could be expanded to instruct users to stop using the computer and to disconnect it from any attached networks. These actions help isolate the problem to minimize further damage. Likewise, in a policy like this, users could be instructed not to attempt a recovery. In these instances, experts should perform the actual recovery effort. This policy could be changed to require reporting to the Information Security department. As organizations expand the connectivity of their networks such as hook-ups with the Internet, this policy is increasingly important because such interconnectivity can provide new pathways for the transmission of viruses, worms, Trojan horses, and other unauthorized software.

Related Policies: "Reporting A Suspected Virus."

Audience: End users

Security Environments: All

6.03.04 Learning From Incidents

1. Violation And Problem Analysis

Policy: An annual analysis of reported information security problems and violations must be prepared by the Information Security department.

Commentary: This policy requires the Information Security department to prepare a status report of actual losses and problems encountered. Such a loss history analysis is helpful when performing risk assessments, when preparing job performance evaluations, and also when preparing budgets and project plans for the coming year. This policy can help establish and maintain a regular communication path with top management. Notice that the methodology for performing such analyses is not mentioned so as to give Information Security the flexibility to change its approach as it becomes more sophisticated. The policy could be expanded to include mention of submitting a written report to the chief information officer, the chief executive officer, or the audit committee on the board of directors.

Related Policies: "Computer Crime Investigation" and "Security Violation And Problem Information Retention."

Audience: Management and technical staff

Security Environments: All

6.03.05 Disciplinary Process

1. Consequences Of Non-Compliance

Policy: Non-compliance with information security policies, standards, or procedures is grounds for disciplinary actions up to and including termination.

Commentary: This policy emphasizes that information security is important, and that significant disciplinary action may result if a worker is not in compliance. The policy is also intended to provide justification for management actions if a worker were to complain that a disciplinary measure is unwarranted or unfair. Some organizations may wish to specify some of the possible disciplinary actions, for example, suspension without pay, demotion, or transfer to another less sensitive job. In the majority of cases, however, this specification will be unnecessary because human resources policies will address possible management actions in accordance with a standardized disciplinary process.

Related Policies: "Consequences Of Violations."

Audience: End users

Security Environments: All

2. Consequences Of Violations

Policy: Assuming the action is inadvertent or accidental, first violations of information security policies or procedures must result in a warning, second violations involving the same matter must result in a letter being placed in the involved worker's personnel file, third violations involving the same matter must result in a five-day suspension without pay, fourth violations involving the same must result in dismissal, and willful or intentional violations, regardless of the number of violations, must result in disciplinary action up to and including immediate dismissal.

Commentary: The laws in many jurisdictions require that a worker be notified before receiving severe disciplinary action or termination. This policy is intended to provide an increasingly severe set of disciplinary actions reflecting information security violations. In many organizations it will be unnecessary to specify such steps because a more general human resources policy will already have covered these matters. The specifics are provided in this book for those organizations that do not have a documented progression of increasingly severe disciplinary measures. The specific disciplinary measures mentioned here could be replaced with others that may be more common in the other organizations, industries, or countries.

Related Policies: "Consequences Of Non-Compliance."

Audience: End users and management

Security Environments: All

3. Loss Of Stock Options

Policy: If the recipient of stock options discloses internal Company X information to unauthorized parties, these options must be revoked.

Commentary: This policy sends a message about the need to keep confidential information under wraps. Sometimes, management ignores information security, thinking that all is fine. This policy is especially relevant to companies that are about to, or have recently gone public with an initial public offering. The policy is more potent the greater the percentage of an employee's income that comes from stock options. Top management would generally pay a great deal of attention to this policy because they often derive a large percentage of their income from stock options. The policy could be modified to include other information security violations, not just unauthorized disclosures.

Related Policies: "Consequences Of Non-Compliance" and "Immediate Terminations."

Audience: End users and management

Security Environments: Medium and high

4. Immediate Terminations

Policy: Unless the special permission of a senior vice president is obtained, all workers who have stolen Company X property, acted with insubordination, or been convicted of a felony, must be terminated immediately, escorted while collecting and removing their personal effects and escorted off Company X premises.

Commentary: This policy requires management to terminate workers who have shown themselves to be an unwarranted threat to the security of the organization or the safety of its workers. For example, if an employee has been convicted of murder while employed by Company X, his or her continued presence in the office may constitute an unwarranted risk. This policy gives management significant flexibility in terms of determining options besides termination, such as suspension without pay if there was an intention to bring the employee back. Lesser responses to these serious problems can always be decided on and approved by a senior vice president. Because keeping these individuals around poses special risks, particularly if they are in a computer-related position of trust, top

management consideration is required before their continued presence is permitted. The specific circumstances leading to instant terminations can be changed to suit Company X management preferences. Documenting these actions in a policy will reduce the likelihood that a terminated worker could claim in court that the termination was unfair or wrongful.

Related Policies: "Consequences Of Violations."

Audience: Management

Security Environments: All

5. Duress Terminations

Policy: The personal computers used by a worker terminated under duress must be immediately isolated from both the Internet and the internal Company X network, have the hard drives reformatted, and have the appropriate systems software reinstalled.

Commentary: This policy prevents workers who have been dismissed in less than ideal circumstances from being able to vengefully do harm to their former employer. Beyond the customary termination of their access privileges, this policy says that their computers must be isolated. This isolation will prevent software that the departed workers wrote, and stored on their computers, from doing damage to Company X systems. The execution of this software may not require the privileges that the departed worker had in order to do serious damage. The reason why the hard drives are reformatted is that this software could be waiting until such time that it is reconnected to a network. Reformatting the hard drive and reinstalling all systems software should be sufficient. The procedure outlined in this policy will also help prevent unauthorized trap doors from permitting the departed worker to once again gain system access. Although this policy may be restricted to technical staff, there are many sophisticated end users who are quite capable of writing the software discussed in this policy.

Related Policies: "Centralized Access Control Database" and "Involuntary Terminations."

Audience: Technical staff

Security Environments: Medium and high

7 PHYSICAL AND ENVIRONMENTAL SECURITY

7.01 Secure Areas

7.01.01 Physical Security Perimeter

1. Third-Party Physical Access

Policy: Visitor or other third-party access to Company X offices, computer facilities, and other work areas containing sensitive information must be controlled by guards, receptionists, or other staff.

Commentary: This policy requires that an authorized staff person get involved in the process of determining whether visitors or other third parties may come into areas containing sensitive information. Unchecked access to such areas may otherwise lead to industrial espionage, fraud, equipment theft, and other problems. This policy defines a way to implement the strategy known as "control the perimeter," a classic approach used since the days of medieval castles. To implement this policy, employee entrances can have man-traps, turnstiles, and other mechanisms to ensure that only authorized workers using a badge or some other access control mechanism may progress through that door. The scope of the policy can be expanded to include valuable, or critical information.

Related Policies: "Four-Category Data Classification," "Five-Category Application Criticality Classification Scheme," and "Physical Access Control To Sensitive Information."

Audience: Management

Security Environments: All

2. Physical Security Plan

Policy: Every Company X data center must have a physical security plan that is reviewed and updated annually by the senior manager in charge of the facility.

Commentary: This policy explicitly assigns responsibility for the development and updating of data center physical security plans. This policy makes it clear that physical security is a line management responsibility, not a staff department responsibility. This means that physical security must be dealt with in the course of ordinary data center operations, not exclusively by a special group. A special technical group, ordinarily called the Physical Security department, is generally available for consulting and assistance. In most cases the senior manager in charge of the data center would not actually prepare the plan. Somebody else who reports to the senior manager will typically do this. Some organizations may wish to include words in the policy indicating that this plan will be subject to periodic review by Internal Audit. This statement can be omitted from the policy as it has been here. Good physical security must be in place if good information security is going to be achieved. For example, if anybody off the street can walk into a data center and reboot a machine, then load their own version of the operating system, much if not all of the good work in the information security area will be null and void.

Related Policies: "Critical Business Logic" and "Computer Emergency Response Plans."

Audience: Management

Security Environments: All

3. Computer And Communications Facility Location

Policy: Multi-user computers and communications facilities must be located above the first floor in buildings, away from kitchens, and in a location separated from the building's exterior wall by an additional internal wall in a room without windows.

Commentary: This policy provides guidance for those responsible for the location of a multi-user computer facility within a building. Many of the managers responsible for locating computer centers do not consider these matters, and problems are encountered after the installation is complete. At least the awareness of these problems will help management install other controls that would reduce or eliminate losses, even if the location of a computer center did not change.

Related Policies: "Positioning Computer Display Screens" and "Computer Center Locations."

Audience: Management and technical staff

Security Environments: All

4. Computer Facility Fire Resistance

Policy: Fire walls surrounding computer facilities and must be non-combustible and resistant to fire for at least one hour, and all openings to these walls such as doors and ventilation ducts, must be self-closing and resistant to fire for at least one hour.

Commentary: This policy clearly specifies a minimum acceptable fire resistance construction for computer centers. The same could apply to communications facilities, such as a network control center. Openings such as ventilation ducts can be self-closing, and doors can have automatic release latches that close the door if a fire alarm is initiated. Fire is the most common cause of a major disaster at computer centers, and often a fire starts in adjacent areas, then spreading to the computer center. If adequate fire resistance is built into the premises, the likelihood that a fire is put out before major damage is caused will be increased.

Related Policies: "Smoking, Eating, And Drinking."

Audience: Management and technical staff

Security Environments: All

5. Computer Facility Door Strength

Policy: Computer facility rooms must be equipped with riot doors, fire doors, and other doors resistant to forcible entry.

Commentary: The intent of this policy is to ensure that the doors to a computer room provide adequate protection for the expensive equipment contained therein. In many offices, there is no locked door to computer facilities, particularly where small systems like local area network servers are located. The policy can be expanded to include the requirement that such doors automatically unlock whenever there is a fire alarm, or whenever there is an emergency need for someone on the inside to get out. The policy could be expanded to include communications facilities, such as network management centers.

Related Policies: "Computer Facility Fire Resistance" and "Computer Facility Door Closing."

Audience: Management

Security Environments: All

6. Computer Facility Door Closing

Policy: Computer facility rooms must be equipped with doors that automatically close immediately after they have been opened, and that set off an audible alarm when they have been kept open beyond a certain period of time.

Commentary: The requirements embodied in this policy prevent people from propping open doors so that others can enter. Such doors help to ensure that the physical access control that management intended is actually being used while worker entrances and exits are being recorded in a log. These doors have been shown to be very effective when it comes to forcing people to use a physical access control system. The policy could be expanded to include communications facilities, such as network management centers. If workers are propping open doors, their reasons should be investigated. For example, an air conditioning system may not be able to handle the heat in the summer and require the door to be propped open.

Related Policies: "Computer Facility Fire Resistance" and "Computer Facility Door Strength."

Audience: Management

Security Environments: All

7. Secondary Computer Center Doors

Policy: All secondary computer center doors must be equipped with crash bars and alarms that activate when the doors are opened.

Commentary: This policy specifies construction standards for computer centers including network operations centers. It states that all doors in addition to the main entrance must have crash bars. The crash bars will signal an audible alarm, even if the power to the computer center is out. In this way the crash bars can alert staff on duty that a door has been opened and that an unauthorized person may be gaining access to restricted areas. The alarm also can warn others remaining in the building that there may be a fire or some other problem in need of their immediate attention.

Related Policies: "Physical Access Control To Sensitive Information" and "Unattended Rooms."

Audience: Technical staff

Security Environments: Medium and high

7.01.02 Physical Entry Controls

1. Physical Access Control To Sensitive Information

Policy: Access to every office, computer room, and work area containing sensitive information must be physically restricted to limit access to those with a need to know.

Commentary: This policy requires that local management restrict who has access to areas where sensitive information may be found. The specific technology required to handle this information is deliberately not stated. The information could be on hardcopy computer output, discussed over the phone, or on building construction blueprints. Local management should consult internal security specialists to determine what type of access control technology should be used. Circumstances often vary so much from work area to work area that it may not be expedient to require all offices to use a certain access control technology, particularly in multinational companies that face widely-differing local customs and requirements. From a cost-containment standpoint, standardization of certain physical access control technology like magnetic cards may be preferred. This policy is particularly relevant to computing environments containing personal computers, local area networks, workstations, and client-server systems because the logical access controls on such systems are often lax or missing. The scope of the policy could be expanded to include "valuable, or critical" information.

Related Policies: "Four-Category Data Classification," "Five-Category Application Criticality Classification Scheme," and "Physical Access Of Terminated Workers."

Audience: Management

Security Environments: All

2. Locking Personal Offices

Policy: All workers with separate personal offices must lock the doors when these offices are not in use.

Commentary: This policy gets workers to employ the office door locks that in many instances are standard equipment in office buildings. Often this basic control measure is ignored, and unauthorized disclosure of sensitive information takes place after hours or when an area is unattended. The policy should be accompanied by a strong physical key management system that permits management and perhaps secretaries to gain access to locked offices when circumstances require. This policy assumes that separate offices are fully enclosed. This policy is not appropriate if all workers have cubicles or other only partially enclosed offices. While this policy may seem basic, obvious, and perhaps not even worth mentioning in an information security policy document, it is important to clarify these instructions in writing if consistent compliance is going to be achieved.

Related Policies: "Physical Access Control To Sensitive Information."

Audience: All

Security Environments: All

3. Identification Badges

Policy: Whenever in Company X secure buildings or facilities, all persons must wear an identification badge on their outer garments so that both the picture and information on the badge are clearly visible.

Commentary: The purpose of this policy is to notify all workers that they must wear their badges in a conspicuous place. This will permit guards and other workers to determine whether a worker may enter a certain area. The policy will permit workers to readily notice if someone is using a stolen or borrowed badge. This policy assumes badges with pictures are used, but reference to pictures can be deleted if this is not the case. This policy works well with a policy dealing with challenges of unauthorized persons in restricted areas. If only certain areas are restricted through badges, the policy can refer to restricted areas rather than stating that it deals with all Company X buildings or facilities. Some workers do not like the picture on their badges They may, for example, think it is not flattering. These people may seek to conceal their badges. This behavior is not acceptable according to this policy. Those individuals should be invited to sit for another picture and to then get a new badge that they will feel more comfortable wearing.

Related Policies: "Individuals Without Identification Badges."

Audience: End users

Security Environments: All

4. Temporary Badges

Policy: Workers who have forgotten their identification badge must obtain a one-day temporary badge by providing a driver's license or another piece of picture identification.

Commentary: The purpose of this policy is to emphasize that everyone must have an identification badge, even if they forgot their regular badge. If workers habitually forget their badges, the Security department records showing temporary badges issued will readily note this. If the number of temporary badges for a specific individual is excessive, this may be cause for a notice to the individual's manager. Temporary badges should expire at the end of the day in case visitors forget to bring them back and also as an inducement to regular workers to bring in their regular badge the next day. To make expiration readily apparent, some types of temporary badges will discolor after a certain period from the time of issuance has elapsed. Identification should be required to prove that a worker is who they say they are. This will help prevent third parties from gaining access to restricted areas by alleging they are authorized workers who forgot their badges. A temporary badge system implies that worker access privileges and photos are resident in a computer database, and that these privileges can be readily recorded on a new badge. If this is not the case, this policy and the procedures it implies may be impractical. The policy applies to all workers.

Related Policies: "Computer Transaction Initiations" and "Identification Badge Reports."

Audience: End users

Security Environments: All

5. Badge-Controlled Access

Policy: Each person must present his or her badge to the badge reader before entering every controlled door within Company X premises.

Commentary: This policy is intended to ensure that the physical access control log reflects the individuals who were actually in an area at a specific time. Often a group will enter a controlled door, and only the first person is actually logged as having entered. This practice can be exploited by industrial spies, competing organization staff, and others seeking to gain unauthorized access to areas containing sensitive information. The specifics of how this policy is implemented will vary based on the physical access control technology involved. Turnstiles are ideal because piggy-backing or

tail-gating is very difficult if not impossible. The policy refers to "persons" rather than "workers" because some persons in the area will be visitors or vendors. This policy may cause a backlog just before work is scheduled to begin as many people all converge on controlled doors at much the same time.

Related Policies: "Badge Access Sharing."

Audience: All

Security Environments: All

6. Badge Access Sharing

Policy: Workers must not permit unknown or unauthorized persons to pass through doors, gates, and other entrances to restricted areas at the same time when authorized persons go through these entrances.

Commentary: This policy is intended to prevent unauthorized persons from following authorized persons into restricted areas, for example, by using the authorized person's key or card to open the door. This also is referred to as piggybacking or tailgating. If turnstiles or mantraps are used, then this policy is less important. The policy could be expanded to require authorized workers to refer all unknown or unauthorized persons to a receptionist or guard station. In the policy statement, the term "restricted areas" can be replaced by specific areas such as "the computer center."

Related Policies: "Individuals Without Identification Badges" and "Badge-Controlled Access."

Audience: End users

Security Environments: All

7. Man-Trap Entrances

Policy: Pedestrian traffic entrances to all Company X data centers must include man-trap mechanisms.

Commentary: This policy prevents people from holding the door open for others, and in the process permitting unauthorized people into a data center. By requiring that people go through a controlled door one by one, an organization prevents what is known as piggybacking or tailgating. Although a turnstile can be used to achieve this purpose, a man trap provides an additional measure of control whereby an intruder can be locked in the man trap until security arrives. A man trap also can be configured to require persons to exit the room area individually. Outsourcing organization facilities also may be considered Company X data centers and covered by this policy. The word "pedestrian" was included in the policy to distinguish these entrances from loading docks that realistically cannot be controlled through man traps.

Related Policies: "Third-Party Physical Access" and "Shoplifting Tags."

Audience: Technical staff

Security Environments: Medium and high

8. Unauthorized Physical Access Attempts

Policy: Workers must not attempt to enter restricted areas in Company X buildings for which they have not received access authorization.

Commentary: This policy notifies workers that they are not to attempt to defeat physical access controls. If workers need access to a certain area, they must go through the proper authorization channels rather than taking matters into their own hands. There may be emergencies and disasters where this policy does not apply. In these circumstances, workers will do what they need to do, and explain the situation later. Access control systems will log repeated attempts to gain access to areas that an individual does not have permission to enter. This policy establishes the basis for disciplinary action whenever there have been repeated attempts to gain access to an off-limits area.

Related Policies: "Testing Information System Controls."

Audience: End users

Security Environments: All

9. Bag Inspection

Policy: All briefcases, suitcases, handbags, and other luggage must be opened for Company X building guards to check when people leave the premises.

Commentary: The objective of this conservative policy is to discourage people from walking out with sensitive or valuable information. The policy is a gesture and a deterrent, not a foolproof method to prevent the theft of sensitive or valuable information. This policy suffers from a serious flaw in that guards are unlikely to spot sensitive or valuable information. For example, generally a security guard is not going to take the time to check the information resident on a floppy disk contained in a briefcase. While sensitive or valuable information can be printed on special colored paper that stands out, or can be tagged with magnetic markers that set off alarms when removed from a building, these and related approaches are relatively ineffective against a determined thief. This policy is more effective in its intent to discourage and occasionally apprehend theft of computer equipment and supplies.

Related Policies: "Property Passes" and "Secret Information Leaving Offices."

Audience: End users

Security Environments: High

10. Access Control System Records

Policy: The Security department must maintain records of the persons currently and previously inside Company X buildings and securely retain this information for at least three months.

Commentary: The purpose of this policy is to require the recording of information about who comes and goes through a building containing sensitive, valuable, or critical information. This information may be especially important when physical access control systems are combined with computer access control systems. For example, if a user ID was used to commit a fraud from a location within the controlled-access building, but the individual who is authorized to use the user ID was not in the building at the time, this might show that an unauthorized person was using the user ID. Knowing who is in a building is very important if there is a fire, a bomb threat, or some other emergency or disaster. If records are kept of entrances and exits, this may also serve as a deterrent to various unauthorized acts such as stealing computers. Such records also may be important for showing that certain time cards are fraudulent. Maintenance of such records may also help with the enforcement of policies about permitting only those with a need to know to have access to certain areas.

Related Policies: "Retention Period Of Logs" and "Identification Badge Reports."

Audience: Management and technical staff

Security Environments: All

11. Physical Access Of Terminated Workers

Policy: When a worker terminates a working relationship with Company X, all physical security access codes known by or available to the worker must be deactivated or changed.

Commentary: This policy is intended to limit further access by terminated workers. The policy is written in a general way so that it includes shared codes like combination lock numbers for the front door, and individual codes such as the identification numbers recorded on a magnetic stripe on a badge. This policy prevents confusion about the identity of the person who is using an access code. The policy may also prevent a terminated worker from using a copy of the access mechanism to gain unauthorized entry to Company X work areas. This last objective is particularly important if the worker is disgruntled. The policy makes mention of "access codes known by the worker," but could be changed to "access codes known by or available to the worker." This change would be called for if the codes were embedded in a smart card, but strictly speaking, unknown to the worker. Distribution of this policy ordinarily would be restricted to Information Security and Physical Security department staff.

Related Policies: "Separation Of Activities And Data," "Return Of Property At Employment Termination," "Worker Transfers," and "Reporting Employee Changes."

Audience: Technical staff

Security Environments: All

12. Terminated Worker Access To Restricted Areas

Policy: Whenever a worker terminates his or her working relationship with Company X, all access rights to Company X restricted areas must be immediately revoked.

Commentary: This policy ensures that workers who have terminated their working relationship with an organization can no longer enter the offices or other controlled areas such as a manufacturing plant's floor. Human Resource department policies should address when the access rights should be revoked. This policy supports information security because if an organization cannot control who is inside restricted areas, it is going to have a great deal of trouble restricting who can gain access to restricted information. This policy is written for management, who often must handle the termination process.

Related Policies: "Physical Access Of Terminated Workers" and "Privilege Restriction — Need To Know."

Audience: Management

Security Environments: All

13. Physical Access Grantor List

Policy: A list of managers who are authorized to grant access to Company X premises must be kept up to date and also be periodically reviewed by the higher-level managers who delegated authority to the manager on the list.

Commentary: This policy establishes a clear hierarchy showing the delegation of authority regarding granting of physical access. The managers mentioned in the first sentence are the ones who, on a day-to-day basis, actually authorize certain workers to gain access to restricted areas. The "higher-level managers" mentioned in the second sentence are the ones who decided which managers would make the day-to-day decisions. The existence of a clear and current delegation of authority will prevent demoted, transferred, terminated, or otherwise no-longer-authorized managers from misusing their authority. Likewise, the existence of this hierarchy will focus attention on the appropriate rights to grant various managers, thereby helping to ensure that the rights actually granted are commensurate with business needs.

Related Policies: "Granting System Privileges," "Production Transaction Authorization," and "Identification Badge Reports."

Audience: Management

Security Environments: All

14. Identification Badge Reports

Policy: A monthly listing of all persons in each department who currently have authorized identification badges must be sent to department heads for review and the initiation of any corrective action.

Commentary: This policy requires the issuance and review of a report reflecting currently authorized badges. This will identify and eliminate expired badges that have not yet had the associated privileges revoked. If unauthorized persons gain access to Company X premises, then the security of the information found in these premises will be unduly at risk. The process of generating and reviewing a report can also be effectively used with computer user IDs, telephone credit cards, and other access mechanisms. This report must pertain to all workers.

Related Policies: "Physical Access Grantor List," "Reauthorization Of User Access Privileges," and "Secret Information Access."

Audience: Management

Security Environments: All

15. Visitor Identification

Policy: All visitors to Company X must show picture identification and sign a log prior to gaining access to restricted areas.

Commentary: This policy requires that all visitors, including employees from different locations, show definitive identification proving who they are before they enter restricted areas. This will discourage unauthorized persons from masquerading as though they are authorized. It will also help ensure that a log showing who entered and exited the restricted area is accurate and reflects the actual identity of the individuals involved. If the organization considers the display of picture identification to be too intrusive, it may scale the policy back, requiring only the sign-in process. If only the sign-in process is used for most people, then access can be restricted to those who had appointments. All others may be required to show identification. The policy could be modified to require both sign-in and sign-out with a time and date for both. The advantage of requiring a sign-out is that if there is an emergency such as a fire, management will be able to readily determine who was, or who is in the building. Another objective of this policy is that it discourages employees from bringing their family and friends into the office.

Related Policies: "Escorting Visitors," "Badge Access Sharing," and "Positive Identification For System Usage."

Audience: End users

Security Environments: All

16. Escorting Visitors

Policy: Visitors to Company X offices including, but not limited to, customers, former employees, worker family members, equipment repair contractors, package delivery company staff, and police officers, must be escorted at all times by an authorized worker.

Commentary: This policy prevents unauthorized persons from gaining access to confidential, proprietary, or private information while inside a controlled area such as an office. They may read a memo that happens to be sitting on a worker's desk. If visitors are escorted, their actions can be supervised and such unauthorized disclosures prevented. This policy also prevents theft of office property like modems and personal property like handbags. This policy works best if restroom facilities are located right off of the reception area. If visitors must go through controlled doors to reach the restroom facility, then they may be able to thwart the escort policy because a receptionist or guard cannot leave the post.

Related Policies: "Badge Access Sharing," "Third-Party Supervision," and "Visitor Identification."

Audience: End users and management

Security Environments: Medium and high

17. Escorts Required For All After-Hour Visitors

Policy: Visitors must be escorted by an employee authorized by a department manager whenever they are in Company X offices or facilities outside of normal business hours.

Commentary: This policy prevents visitors from roaming around offices and facilities outside of normal business hours, and perhaps obtaining confidential information, stealing valuable items, placing wiretaps, or otherwise engaging in unauthorized activities. Outside normal business hours there will be fewer people to notice that a visitor is doing something unauthorized. This policy also permits only an authorized employee to be an escort, preventing contractors, consultants, and temporaries from being an escort. This policy does not prevent deliveries at a shipping dock, building remodeling or reconstruction, and similar activities. It only dictates that these activities be performed in the presence of an authorized employee. The policy does permit visitors to move unimpeded within certain areas during normal business hours, and keeps worker productivity high because no escort is required during those hours. In high-security organizations, automatic electronic tracking of visitor movements with proximity badges could be used in place of an escort.

Related Policies: "Immediate Terminations" and "Unescorted Visitors."

Audience: End users and management

Security Environments: All

18. Third-Party Supervision

Policy: Individuals who are neither Company X employees, nor authorized contractors, nor authorized consultants, must be supervised whenever they are in restricted areas containing sensitive information.

Commentary: This policy ensures that third parties, whose intentions are largely unknown, cannot roam unescorted in areas containing sensitive information. If these people have unsupervised access, industrial espionage, equipment theft, and other problems may occur. For example, a technician installing a digital subscriber line connection should, under this policy, be escorted at all times when in restricted areas. This policy could be expanded to include valuable, or critical information, not just sensitive information.

Related Policies: "Escorting Visitors" and "Individuals Without Identification Badges."

Audience: End users and management

Security Environments: Medium and high

19. Individuals Without Identification Badges

Policy: Individuals without a proper Company X identification badge in a clearly visible place must be immediately questioned about their badge and if they cannot promptly produce a valid badge, they must be escorted to the receptionist desk.

Commentary: The purpose of this policy is to ensure that everyone wears a badge at all times when inside a restricted area. All authorized people must wear badges when inside restricted areas. If they do not, there is no way to readily determine who is authorized and who is not. Physical security is an essential component of information security. If an organization cannot control who is inside restricted areas, then controlling information security is going to be very difficult, if not impossible. Some organizations will want to add another sentence to the policy that says if someone is concerned about their physical safety after a challenge, an acceptable alternative is to immediately call the Physical Security department.

Related Policies: "Unescorted Visitors" and "Temporary Badges."

Audience: End users

Security Environments: Medium and high

20. Unescorted Visitors

Policy: Whenever a worker notices an unescorted visitor inside Company X restricted areas, the visitor must be questioned about the purpose for being in restricted areas, then be accompanied to a reception desk, a guard station, or the person they came to see.

Commentary: This policy prevents unauthorized people from roaming around controlled areas where sensitive, proprietary, or private information is handled. It ensures that only authorized persons are in restricted areas. The policy is applicable to those environments where badges are required, and smaller office environments without badges where everybody knows everyone else. If this policy is too harsh, it can instead require workers to ask third parties if they can help them find a location. If workers are in potential physical danger, they can alternatively call the Physical Security department rather than directly confronting a strange or menacing person in the area.

Related Policies: "Badge Access Sharing," "Escorting Visitors," and "Identification Badges."

Audience: End users and management

Security Environments: Medium and high

21. Data Center And Information Systems Department Visitors

Policy: Visitors who do not need to perform maintenance on Company X equipment, or who do not absolutely need to be inside the Data Center or Information Systems department, must not enter these areas.

Commentary: This policy prevents visitors from learning trade secrets, stealing manuals that could be used to break into information systems, sabotaging equipment, placing bombs, and otherwise engaging in harmful activities. In order to perform these acts, access is often required. The policy acknowledges that certain visitors, for example, computer vendor maintenance personnel, must have physical access, and for these people a perpetual escort can be employed. All other visitors can use a window that opens to an internal hallway to get a rough idea of what is going on. This policy can be impressive to visitors because it shows that management is concerned about security.

Related Policies: "Unescorted Visitors" and "Escorts Required For All After-Hour Visitors."

Audience: All

Security Environments: High

22. Access To Computers and Communications Systems

Policy: Buildings that house Company X computers or communications systems must be protected with physical security measures that prevent unauthorized persons from gaining access.

Commentary: This policy ensures that physical security measures are used to protect computers and communications systems. This will prevent equipment theft, unauthorized use, and other information security-related problems. This policy is relevant to personal computers, workstations, local area networks, and client-server systems, although it applies to all types of information systems. The policy is important because smaller computers and office equipment are often protected only by physical security measures. The policy could be restricted to those computer systems handling critical or sensitive information.

Related Policies: "Third-Party Physical Access" and "Security Of Sensitive Information."

Audience: Management and technical staff

Security Environments: All

23. Securing Critical Or Sensitive Information Handling Activities

Policy: All critical or sensitive Company X information handling activities must take place in areas that are physically secured and protected against unauthorized access, interference, and damage.

Commentary: This policy ensures that management has suitable physical access controls for computer centers, telephone call centers, archival file vaults, and other locations where critical or sensitive information is handled. The technologies to be used are not stated in the policy because management should make this decision. The physical security technologies should be a function of the criticality, value, or sensitivity of the information, and the location of the site.

Related Policies: "Access To Computers and Communications Systems" and "Secret Information Leaving Offices."

Audience: Management and technical staff

Security Environments: All

24. Computer Center Access

Policy: Programmers, users, and others without a business need for such access must not access computer machine rooms.

Commentary: This policy enforces separation of duties between computer operators and programmers, and users. The policy also reduces congestion and confusion in the machine room. The policy also indirectly prohibits visitors from taking tours. The policy could be rewritten so the words "computer centers" are replaced by "computer centers containing personal computers, mainframes, or network control systems." This policy is not generally applied to departmental systems, client-server systems, or local area network servers, although it could be.

Related Policies: "Privilege Restriction — Need To Know," "Separation Of Duties," "Production Changes," and "Access To Media Libraries."

Audience: Management and technical staff

Security Environments: All

25. Computer Center Staff Access

Policy: A list of authorized staff members that may access the computer center must be maintained, reviewed, and updated by the Computer Operations manager quarterly.

Commentary: This policy establishes a mechanism whereby management will periodically review the list of authorized people who may enter the computer center. In many computer shops, management does not know who has access to the computer center. A quarterly review will identify workers who no longer need to be in the computer center and the access can be eliminated. While many organizations pay a lot of attention to who gets into the building, fewer organizations scrutinize who can get into the data center and the reasons why data center access should be granted.

Related Policies: "Computer Center Access" and "Access To Computers and Communications Systems."

Audience: Technical staff

Security Environments: Medium and high

26. Access To Media Libraries

Policy: Magnetic tape, disk, and documentation libraries must be restricted to workers whose job responsibilities require their presence in these areas.

Commentary: This policy restricts access to areas containing sensitive, valuable, or critical information and reduces the chance that such information will be disclosed, manipulated, deleted or otherwise handled in a manner that is not in keeping with management intentions. This policy is a specific manifestation of the separation of duties principle. Reference to the "computer center" could be changed to "computer centers containing personal computers, mainframes, or network control systems" or some other organization-specific descriptions.

Related Policies: "Separation Of Duties" and "Computer Center Access."

Audience: Management and technical staff

Security Environments: Medium and high

27. Computer Facility Tours

Policy: Public tours of major computer and communications facilities must never be conducted.

Commentary: This policy eliminates public tours that can be a covert means for industrial spies, hackers, disgruntled employees, and others intent on doing harm to gain access to restricted areas. Individuals such as these have been known to pick up information while on a tour, which was then instrumental in subsequent compromises of system access controls. Other individuals have used their proximity to computer and communications equipment while on a tour to sabotage systems. The policy does not prevent private tours, such as those for employees, consultants, or contractors who have a business need to know about the facilities. Likewise, this policy does not prevent tours for top management, investors, stockholders, and important customers. However, educational tours and tours for tourists are prohibited.

Related Policies: "Privilege Restriction — Need To Know," "Computer And Communications Center Signs" and "Identification Badges."

Audience: All

Security Environments: All

7.01.03 Securing Offices, Rooms, And Facilities

1. Periodic Sweeps For Surveillance Equipment

Policy: The Telecommunications department manager must initiate and supervise periodic sweeps for unauthorized bugging, interception, and recording equipment in all Company X offices and facilities where secret information is discussed, stored, or handled.

Commentary: This policy clarifies that sweeps for bugging and interception devices must be performed on a regular basis. The policy defines who must initiate and oversee this effort. While historically completed in military establishments, these sweeps are now increasingly common in commercial organizations. The industrial espionage business is expanding and it is now relatively easy to plant very small transmitting devices in telephones, under conference room tables, and in other inconspicuous places. Such sweeps also look for recording equipment in telephone closets. In most cases, an external consultant with specialized equipment will be needed, because most organizations do not have sufficiently trained personnel on staff.

Related Policies: "Telephone Discussions Of Sensitive Information" and "Password Encryption."

Audience: Technical staff

Security Environments: Medium and high

2. Securing Computer Or Communications Systems

Policy: All multi-user computer and communications equipment must be located in locked rooms.

Commentary: No matter how sophisticated the software access controls may be, if physical access to servers and similar equipment can be obtained, then software access controls can be overcome. For example, on many local area network servers, a simple reboot process will permit an unauthorized person to completely control the machine and its data. The policy alerts technical management at remote sites that all multi-user systems must be located behind locked doors. Typical recipients of the policy include system administrators, network managers, and others responsible for remotely-located equipment. The policy requires that switches, private branch exchanges, hubs, routers, firewalls, and other network equipment must be located in a locked room. This policy indirectly encourages the location of servers and similar equipment in raised floor computer rooms.

Related Policies: "Lockable Metal Furniture" and "Equipment Isolation."

Audience: Technical staff

Security Environments: All

3. Securing Propped-Open Computer Center Doors

Policy: Whenever doors to the computer center are propped-open, the entrance must be continuously monitored by an employee or a contract guard from the Physical Security department.

Commentary: This policy ensures that equipment and information are not improperly removed because doors to the computer center are not sufficiently controlled. The policy can also be used to ensure that the movers do not make off with materials that they did not come for, whether intentionally or accidentally. This policy is necessary because many shops do not strictly enforce physical access controls, and the computer center is perhaps the most central repository of important organizational information. The operational implementation of the policy need not be difficult. The computer operator on duty need only call and ask the Physical Security department to then send a guard.

Related Policies: "Property Passes" and "Computer Center Access."

Audience: Technical staff

Security Environments: All

4. Equipment In Secret Information Areas

Policy: All printers, copiers, and fax machines must not be located in the physically isolated zones within Company X offices that contain secret information.

Commentary: This policy prevents people from making paper copies, from printing computer resident information, and from otherwise removing hardcopy versions of secret information. If the devices to perform this process are not provided within a secured area no one will be able to make unauthorized copies of the information contained therein. All other avenues through which secret information could flow must also be blocked. For example, an isolated local area network could be used to prevent users from sending the secret information out over the Internet as part of an electronic mail message. The very high security approach reflected in this policy works best if the movement of paper-resident secret information is strictly controlled, perhaps with sensors that detect that it has been removed from an isolated area. This policy also creates a paperless office that, when deployed in high security areas, has the potential to be more secure than any paper-based office could ever be.

Related Policies: "Diskless Workstations" and "Telecommuting Data Entry Operators."

Audience: Management and technical staff

Security Environments: High

5. Computer And Communications Center Signs

Policy: There must be no signs indicating the location of computer or communications centers.

Commentary: This policy means that organization name signs, communications center signs, computer room signs, Information Systems department signs, and technical support group signs should not be visible from public areas. The policy is intended to prevent terrorist attack or sabotage. Besides preventing physical attack, the absence of signs may also help prevent attacks on data such as wiretapping. A problem with this approach is that employees and others will often be confused and will need to ask for directions or be escorted. Receptionists, guards, and others must not be so polite that the intent of the policy is entirely undone. The amount of directional information these insiders should disclose to a stranger without determining that the stranger has a genuine reason to be there should be quite limited.

Related Policies: "Computer Facility Tours."

Audience: Management

Security Environments: All

7.01.04 Working In Secure Areas

1. Computer Center Staffing

Policy: The main computer center must be staffed at all times by technically-competent staff 24 hours a day, seven days a week, 365 days a year.

Commentary: This policy ensures that downtime is minimized and customer service remains at a high level. The policy also ensures that someone is on duty to respond to an intruder's attack as it is happening. For international networks, such as telephone networks, such continuous staffing is an absolute necessity. Likewise, this policy is often found at Internet service providers, Internet hosting organizations, and large volume Internet merchants. The policy is applicable to large organizations that have the resources to support continuous coverage. Smaller organizations can change the policy to refer to continuously on-call staff, in which case a pager or cellular phone would facilitate communication. The policy can also be changed to remove the central site reference. Some organizations have support staffs in different parts of the world who work when other people in contiguous time zones are working. Having staff on duty continuously enables them to notice things that could not be readily determined by electronic systems. For example, perhaps the water level for the river behind the computer center is rising because there has been extended heavy rain, and a flood is imminent. In some cases, having continuous staff on duty will lower insurance rates. The policy is deliberately silent when it comes to defining "technically competent," leaving this decision up to information systems management staff.

Related Policies: "Unauthorized Access Problems."

Audience: Technical staff

Security Environments: Medium and high

2. Cellular Telephone Usage

Policy: Cellular phones must not be used anywhere within the Company X computer machine room.

Commentary: This policy ensures that computer and communications systems resident in a data center are up and running as much as possible. There have been confirmed reports of cellular phones used near production servers and this usage causing crashes and hard disk corruption. Apparently the strong signals emitted by cellular phones interfere with the sensitive circuitry inside computers and communication systems. This phenomenon may seem unlikely, but major airlines now forbid their passengers from using cellular phones during takeoff and landing. If cellular phones can affect the computers on airplanes, they can affect the computers inside a data center. This policy could be expanded to include two-way pagers.

Related Policies: "Cordless Or Cellular Telephones" and "Property Passes."

Audience: End users

Security Environments: All

3. Working In Restricted Areas

Policy: Workers must never work alone in restricted areas containing sensitive information.

Commentary: This policy prevents workers from taking advantage of the fact that they are the only person in an area containing sensitive information. For example, one worker might look at the private personnel file of another worker, something they would not do if other workers were nearby. Depending on the other policies in force, this policy can be expanded to include mention of valuable, or critical information. To make the policy more restrictive, the word "sensitive" could be changed to "secret." This policy ensures that a separation of duty policy is effective.

Related Policies: "Separation Of Duties" and "Restricted Area Working Hours."

Audience: End users

Security Environments: Medium and high

4. Restricted Area Working Hours

Policy: Authorized workers must not access restricted Company X facilities where sensitive, critical, or valuable information is handled at any time other than authorized access hours.

Commentary: If employees stay late or come in early, they may be unsupervised, and may therefore be able to engage in computer abuse, such as using another employee's computer to view confidential data. If workers are restricted to normal hours, they may not engage in abusive acts because they would not risk being caught or because other people would prevent them from performing these acts. This policy is a background policy that ensures that separation of duties policies are effective. In the policy, the word "official" may be replaced by "authorized" to give management additional flexibility in setting working hours.

Related Policies: "Separation Of Duties" and "Working In Restricted Areas."

Audience: End users

Security Environments: High

5. Vacated Equipment Areas

Policy: All information systems equipment areas that are vacated must be locked and periodically checked by either remote monitoring systems or a security guard.

Commentary: This policy is partially motivated by insurance requirements, which are a reflection of good information systems management. Locking the premises will prevent industrial spies, disgruntled former employees, and curious neighbors from gaining entrance. Checking the premises ordinarily involves confirming that all doors are locked and that everything appears to be secured. This policy does not apply only to data centers. It is equally applicable to offices that have personal computers. Adoption of and implementation of this policy may permit an organization to lower its insurance premiums.

Related Policies: "Computer Center Access."

Audience: Management and technical staff

Security Environments: Medium and high

6. Communications Equipment Areas

Policy: Telephone closets, network router and hub rooms, voice mail system rooms, and similar areas containing communications equipment must be kept locked at all times and not accessed by visitors without an authorized technical staff escort to monitor all work being performed.

Commentary: This policy prevents third parties from placing wiretaps in Company X communications areas. The policy is also intended to prevent unauthorized persons from damaging or interfering with critical equipment needed to perform business activities.

Disgruntled employees will find it more difficult to damage or interfere with these highly complicated systems if the areas are off-limits. The use of an escort will further deter unauthorized activity because every action will be monitored. While the use of an escort may seem to be a waste of valuable technical staff time, it is important that internal staff knows what was done, why it was done, and how to reverse any changes that were made. While accompanying a visitor, the escort can fill out change control paperwork at the same time that a visiting technician is doing the work.

Related Policies: "Network Ports In Vacant Offices" and "Computer Room Deliveries."

Audience: Technical staff

Security Environments: High

7. Audio Or Video Recording Equipment

Policy: Personally-owned cameras, audio recording equipment, or video recording equipment must not be accessible or used within the controlled perimeters of Company X offices.

Commentary: This policy is intended to prevent any audio or video recording equipment, from being used to capture confidential information. Confidential information may include the physical shape of a new product, or even the building layout for a data processing facility. Prohibiting such equipment reduces the chances that it will be used to capture confidential information on black boards or white boards, exchanged in a conversation, or expressed in a memo laying on a staff member's desk. Some organizations will wish to post a sign at the guard's desk to this effect. If a camera, or audio or video recording equipment has been used in violation of this policy, the physical security department could remove the film or confiscate the film and have it developed, later returning the materials that are not specific to Company X.

Related Policies: "Preventing Copies Of Sensitive Documents" and "Positioning Computer Display Screens."

Audience: All

Security Environments: High

7.01.05 Isolated Delivery And Loading Areas

1. Computer Room Deliveries

Policy: A secured intermediate holding area must be used for computer supplies, equipment, and other deliveries.

Commentary: This policy protects computer rooms from unauthorized access, such as from delivery service personnel. For example, loading dock doors should not open directly to the computer room. By restricting the movement of materials, this policy also bolsters access controls to a computer room. The policy keeps the risk of fire down by requiring that paper and other supplies be stored elsewhere than in the computer room. Keeping these materials out of the computer room also reduces the exposure of systems to paper dust, cleaning fluids, and other potentially dangerous substances. This policy also supports a separate Receiving department, that will inspect and account for shipments received. Receiving then will transport the goods to the locations in need of these goods. This policy stops the practice where high-value goods are stored in a computer machine room because that is one of the few physically-secured places available.

Related Policies: "Malfunctioning Access Control."

Audience: Management and technical staff

Security Environments: All

7.02 Equipment Security

7.02.01 Equipment Siting And Protection

1. Smoking, Eating, And Drinking

Policy: Workers and visitors must not smoke, eat, or drink in the raised floor area in the computer machine room.

Commentary: While it may seem to be an inconvenience to those people who do not want to leave the machine room when they work, this policy protects both equipment and information against damage. The policy also may be applied to workstations, personal computers, local area network servers, and other systems not resident in a computer machine room. Another example would be the private branch exchange phone system. Both the equipment and the data storage media on these systems are susceptible to damage from the above-mentioned substances. Volatile chemicals such as glue and solvents may additionally damage magnetic storage media, and can be mentioned in the policy. For fire prevention reasons, it is also wise to keep such chemicals out of a computer machine room.

Related Policies: "Physical Access Control To Sensitive Information" and "Computer Facility Fire Resistance."

Audience: All

Security Environments: All

2. Production Computer System Location

Policy: All production computer systems including, but not limited to, servers, firewalls, hubs, routers, and voice mail systems must be physically located within a secure data center.

Commentary: This policy prevents departments and other distributed organizational units from placing production computer equipment in closets and in other unprotected places where it would be subject to sabotage, power outages, and fire. If a computer system is a production system used for regular and recurring business activities, then it should be protected by housing it in a machine room with protective items such as fire suppression equipment, redundant power, physical access controls, and off-site backup couriers.

Related Policies: "Securing Critical Or Sensitive Information Handling Activities" and "Computer Center Locations."

Audience: End users

Security Environments: All

3. Computer Center Address

Policy: The physical address of every Company X computer center is confidential and must not be disclosed to those without a demonstrable need to know.

Commentary: This policy ensures that terrorists, saboteurs, industrial spies, hackers, and competitors are not able to easily locate Company X data processing facilities. For correspondence, a post office box is recommended. Vendors, consultants, and other third parties who are doing work for Company X will need to know the actual address if they need to go to that location. Phone company directories should similarly not list a physical location for these facilities. There should be no sign at the street level indicating that the facility is the Company X data processing center. This policy could be expanded to include network control centers, record archive sites, and other major facilities for the handling or storage of information. Although reference is made to a computer center, which often implies mainframes and larger systems, this policy is equally applicable to small systems such as those using personal computers, workstations, and client-server systems.

Related Policies: "Nature And Location Of Organization Information."

Audience: All

Security Environments: All

4. Computer Center Environmental Controls

Policy: Local management must provide and adequately maintain fire detection and suppression, power conditioning, air conditioning, humidity control, and other computing environment protection systems in every Company X computer center.

Commentary: These environmental support systems can be essential to continuous computer and communications support. This policy requires local management to provide the systems needed for computers handling critical production applications. This policy can be employed by end users to compel departmental and other local managers to comply with the requirements defined by a centralized information technology management group. For example, the users of personal computers running a critical application might need, but not have uninterruptible power supply (UPS) systems, and these users might be fighting with local management to buy such equipment. The policy could

then be used to compel management to get a UPS system. The distribution or decentralization of information systems has meant that local management now makes decisions previously made by the Information Technology department. To ensure that local management makes the right decisions, a policy such as this is required. Smaller and more advanced computer systems do not have the same environmental requirements as larger and older systems, like the need for air conditioning. This policy is deliberately vague about exactly which environmental systems are required because these are determined by factors such as geographical location, systems technology employed, and business needs. The policy assumes the word "critical" has been defined in another policy.

Related Policies: "Four-Category Data Classification" and "Power Conditioning Equipment."

Audience: Management and technical staff

Security Environments: All

5. Static Electricity Protection

Policy: If weather and building conditions pose a significant risk of static electricity discharge, all personal computers and workstations must be outfitted with static protection equipment that has been approved by the Information Systems department.

Commentary: This policy ensures that computer equipment is properly configured so as to prevent unwarranted loss of data, damage to systems, and related downtime. Often found in colder climates with forced air heating, static electricity can be a significant problem. Specifically, microprocessor chips can burn out and information held in memory can be inadvertently erased. Specific control measures, such as static electricity floor mats, static electricity absorbing touch bars, and proper grounding for equipment, also may be mentioned in the policy. The specific control measures were not included in this policy because they are likely to change over time. This policy could easily be extended to include communications systems and computers. If the organization uses more traditional computing technology, it may wish to add the word "terminals" to the policy right next to reference to "workstations."

Related Policies: "Power Conditioning Equipment."

Audience: Technical staff

Security Environments: All

6. Computer System Dispersion

Policy: Computer and communications systems must be geographically dispersed whenever possible, as long as this does not unduly hinder operational performance, unduly jeopardize security, or unduly increase costs.

Commentary: This policy highlights the contingency planning-related benefits of distributed computing. The mention of ways to jeopardize security in a policy may seem counter-productive because it may give people ideas, but this policy remains at a general level and gives no specific instructions on how to cause Company X specific harm. Instead it expresses a design intention that is fully consistent with systems evolution, particularly client-server systems. Many of the smaller systems, such as client-server systems, often have inadequate security measures, so a trade-off must be struck. In other words, the expanded contingency-planning security to be achieved by decentralization is in part traded off against reduced access-control security.

Related Policies: "Protection Of Information" and "Emergency And Disaster Support Requirements."

Audience: Technical staff

Security Environments: All

7. Backup Data Center Infrastructure

Policy: Company X must segment its data processing centers into three distinct and physically isolated facilities, each able to handle all critical production information systems services, and must not share the same local electric company substation or the same telephone company central office.

Commentary: This data center location policy is increasingly being adopted by large organizations as a strategic alternative to the use of third-party commercial backup services. The policy permits an adopting organization to dynamically reassign critical production processing activities to another data center if one of its data centers should for any reason become unavailable. The policy is intended to direct information systems staff so that they may reorganize information systems internally to provide a greater degree of resiliency against threats such as natural disasters and terrorist attacks. The policy could be expanded to include other separate and isolated infrastructure elements, such as different transportation systems or different local governments. For greater system availability, the words "electric company substation" could be changed to "electric company grid," and the words "telephone company central office" could be changed to "telephone

company." The word "three" in the policy could be changed to "two," but that some flexibility in the reallocation of production processing may be lost in the process.

Related Policies: "Multiple Carriers" and "Network Central Point Of Failure."

Audience: Technical staff

Security Environments: Medium and high

8. Personally-Owned Computer Systems

Policy: Workers must not bring their own computers, computer peripherals, or computer software into Company X facilities without prior authorization from their department head.

Commentary: This policy prevents the propagation of viruses, disputes about ownership of hardware and software, and improper removal of hardware, software, or data at the time when a worker's employment is terminated. The policy is also desirable because it ensures that everyone uses the same type of software. This policy is particularly relevant to personal computers (PCs) and workstations, and client-server systems, for which the ownership status is often unclear. This policy can be supported by another policy requiring all computer and communications equipment to have a pass before it can be removed from Company X premises.

Related Policies: "Property Passes" and "Hardware And Software Procurement."

Audience: End users and technical staff

Security Environments: All

9. Workstation Key Locks

Policy: All Company X desktop workstations must employ a metal key lock to control access to authorized persons, with a copy of this key provided to the department manager.

Commentary: This somewhat dated policy may nonetheless be used as an adjunct to software-based access controls such as a boot protection mechanism that employs fixed passwords. This policy prevents unauthorized parties from gaining access to workstations, which may have sensitive information stored thereon. The trouble with this approach is that users will lose or forget their metal keys, in which case they may be prevented from using their workstations. This is why a backup key is provided to the department manager. The word "desktop" was used in the policy to exempt portable computers such as handhelds. Because they did not usually come with a key from the manufacturer, in order to implement this policy, some computers may need separate security products that use a metal key and that cover the keyboard, floppy drive slot, or other components. Depending on the configuration of the locking mechanism, some keys can also be used to prevent unauthorized people from opening the computer's case, thereby preventing theft of components such as modems and memory.

Related Policies: "Locking File Cabinets" and "Password-Based Boot Protection."

Audience: End users

Security Environments: All

10. Equipment Rack Doors

Policy: All doors on computer and communications equipment racks located in the computer center must be kept locked unless an authorized technician is actively engaged in repair, maintenance, or reconfiguration activities.

Commentary: This policy establishes another layer of physical access control over computer equipment located within a secure computer data center. In many organizations, a large number of people may access a data center. These include programmers, computer operators, and performance analysts. While it is desirable to keep the number of people in a computer room to a minimum to reduce opportunities for sabotage and other types of abuse, sometimes that is not practical or it is not politically expedient. As an alternative, consider adding additional walls or locking metal cages to segment the computer room into different zones each with their own security level. Also consider locking the cabinets that house production equipment. This policy speaks to the latter option. A policy about locking metal cage doors or regular wall doors inside the data center could be written in much the same format as this policy.

Related Policies: "Locking File Cabinets" and "Security Requirements For Telecommuters."

Audience: Technical staff

Security Environments: Medium and high

11. Internet Commerce and Financial Systems

Policy: All Internet commerce servers and equipment, and systems that process or facilitate processing of wire transfers and other financial activities, must be physically isolated and secured.

Commentary: This policy segregates and separately protects the computers that handle digitized money, in an effort to reduce the possibility of fraud. If computer operators are able to reboot a server, they are likely to be able to change the access controls, change the operating system parameters, or in some other way compromise the security of the system. Permitting physical access to these systems may also permit unauthorized parties to steal backup tapes that may contain credit card numbers, checking account numbers, or other information that could be used to commit fraud. This policy acknowledges that some level of physical security is necessary before real information security can be achieved. This policy assumes that a computer center is locked and that only a restricted number of people are given access to that area. This policy provides a further level of physical access control beyond the door to the computer center. The policy is fully consistent with Internet hosting service standard computer center design specifications, which typically employ locked metal cages to separate the machines of various subscribers. But even if an organization does its own hosting, the Internet commerce and related financial servers should be placed in a separate secured room, or in some other way physically isolated from the rest of the machines in the computer center.

Related Policies: "Equipment Isolation" and "Securing Critical Or Sensitive Information Handling Activities."

Audience: Technical staff

Security Environments: Medium and high

12. Equipment Isolation

Policy: Computer and communications equipment managed by Company X staff must be physically isolated from equipment managed by third parties.

Commentary: This policy prevents third parties from gaining unnecessary access to Company X computer and communications equipment. Physical access can permit unauthorized persons to reboot the operating system, which could then permit them to take over the access control system, steal magnetic media such as backup tapes, and to sabotage equipment. If equipment is commingled in a data center, then third parties must be in the same room where Company X managed equipment is located. But if separate rooms are used, then physical access controls can be utilized. Separate rooms need not be employed. A metal locking cage can be used, or glass partitions to an existing room can be added. This policy is relevant, for example, where Company X has equipment resident in an Internet commerce hosting organization's data center. Physical access controls for Company X managed equipment may be a prerequisite to using remote network management tools and to establishing lights-out operations.

Related Policies: "Access To Computers and Communications Systems," "Backup Media Fire Zone," and "Securing Computer Or Communications Systems."

Audience: Technical staff

Security Environments: All

13. Computer Center Locations

Policy: All new Company X computer or communications centers must be located in an area unlikely to experience natural disasters, serious man-made accidents, riots, and related problems.

Commentary: This policy requires management to consider the consequences in advance of locating a computer or communications center in a dangerous area. Often a decision is made to locate a facility and only later are the serious risks appreciated. In effect, this policy requires management to prepare a security impact statement. Although it could be clarified, the phrase "computer or communications centers" is deliberately kept vague, giving the policy a general applicability that may extend to departmental systems, local area network servers, client-server systems, and other smaller systems.

Related Policies: "Redundant Utility Suppliers" and "Computer And Communications Facility Location."

Audience: Management and technical staff

Security Environments: All

14. Computer Center Construction

Policy: New and remodeled Company X computer or communications centers must be constructed so that they are protected against fire, water damage, vandalism, and other threats known to occur, or that are likely to occur at the involved locations.

Commentary: This policy requires those responsible for building new and remodeled computer or communications centers to consider local security risks in advance of construction. The policy is a specific construction-oriented version of the standard of due care.

Related Policies: "Control Implementations Standard" and "Computer Center Locations."

Audience: Management and technical staff

Security Environments: All

15. Water Damage Precautions

Policy: All Company X locations that house computer and communications equipment must meet minimum water damage prevention requirements and minimum water damage alarm precautions established by the Information Security department, being above ground level and above flood levels of nearby rivers and sewers, having adequate drainage, and not being situated immediately below water tanks or water pipes.

Commentary: This policy establishes some minimum standards for computer and communications equipment protection against water damage. Because this is electrical equipment, there is a danger of electrocution in addition to severe damage to equipment if it gets wet while power is applied. Even if the power is off, many types of computer equipment are so finely calibrated that any significant amount of dirt, dust, or rust that gets into the equipment through water would cause it to malfunction, even if the equipment has been dried out completely. These are some of the reasons why many installations use chemical fire suppression systems rather than water sprinklers. The policy was does not mention sprinklers, permitting an Information Security department to make a decision as it deems appropriate.

Related Policies: "Computer Center Staffing" and "Computer Center Alarms."

Audience: Technical staff

Security Environments: All

16. Computer Center Alarms

Policy: All Company X computer centers must be equipped with fire, water, and physical intrusion alarm systems that automatically alert those who can take immediate action.

Commentary: This policy ensures that adequate alarm systems are included in all computer centers. The scope could be changed to also include network operations centers. With the price of computers declining rapidly, production hardware is increasingly being stuck in closets or in regular offices that are not adequately protected by alarms. As the technology becomes more rugged, the protective enclosures and related environmental systems that surround mainframes are not being used for smaller machines. In terms of those who can take immediate action, the fire department could be called by a fire alarm. Likewise, a private guard service could be called if water was detected, and the police could be called if there were a physical intrusion. The building code specifications of these alarms are deliberately missing from the policy. The policy only says that these things must be in place. If the policy seems a bit expensive, it can be restricted so that it instead requires these alarms only for computer centers containing equipment that supports critical business activities, such as Internet commerce. Fire, water, and physical intrusion alarms can be tied into a network management system.

Related Policies: "Property Passes" and "Intrusion Detection Systems."

Audience: Technical staff

Security Environments: All

7.02.02 Power Supplies

1. Power Conditioning Equipment

Policy: All personal computers and workstations must be outfitted with either uninterruptible power supply systems, electrical power filters, or surge suppressors that have been approved by the Information Systems department.

Commentary: A high percentage of computer problems are attributable to dirty electrical power such as surges, spikes, dips, and brownouts. This policy is also relevant to minicomputers, super-minicomputers, and other systems. In most cases, however, larger multi-user systems already have sufficient power protection measures. The intent of this policy is to require systems under local or departmental management to be outfitted with appropriate electrical power conditioning equipment. The specific type of power protection equipment needed is a function of the criticality of the system, and is not specified in the policy.

Related Policies: "Static Electricity Protection."

Audience: All

Security Environments: All

2. Redundant Utility Suppliers

Policy: All new Company X computer or communications centers must be located such that they have ready access to two electrical power substations and two telephone central offices.

Commentary: This policy is intended to establish a minimum design objective for the individuals who are designing new computer or communications centers. The policy specifies that redundant sources of supply for public utilities must be employed. Water could be included in this policy, but it is rarely required to support computer and communications systems except for legacy mainframe systems that use it for cooling. Water can be stockpiled much more easily and inexpensively than electrical power. The policy could be enhanced to incorporate an additional provision that states that the lines for electricity and telephone services must run on separate poles or through separate conduits. Without this separate routing requirement, a backhoe or a crane could cut both supply lines.

Related Policies: "Computer Center Locations."

Audience: Management and technical staff

Security Environments: All

7.02.03 Cabling Security

1. Power And Telecommunications Cables

Policy: The installation and maintenance of power cables and telecommunication lines must be completed by a registered communications distribution designer who follows current industry security standards.

Commentary: This policy ensures that all required computer system cables are properly installed and maintained to prevent any unauthorized interception of transmitted data or damage to the systems. Data can be easily intercepted during transmission if access to the telecommunication line is not secured. There are numerous standards that govern the proper installation of these lines that are followed by trained professionals to ensure that telecommunications cannot be compromised. Power cables must be similarly secured to prevent any damage or service interruption to the computer systems.

Related Policies: "Communication Line Changes" and "Modem Line Registry."

Audience: All

Security Environments: All

7.02.04 Equipment Maintenance

1. Information Systems Products

Policy: All hardware and software products must be registered with the appropriate vendors immediately after Company X staff takes delivery of new or upgraded information systems products, or soon after it has been determined that such products are not yet registered.

Commentary: This policy ensures that all hardware and software is properly registered with vendors. This will indirectly ensure that all these products are legitimately paid for, cutting down on unauthorized software copies and stolen equipment. Proper registration will also mean that users will receive notices of bugs, upgrades, and other relevant offers. Proper registration will permit the user organization to get telephone and other types of technical support. Proper registration may mean that the vendor will be helpful in the event of an emergency or disaster. Under these circumstances, replacement copies might be obtained for free or at least at minimal cost if the product was previously registered. This policy also may be helpful in a court of law or during a software audit. It shows that management genuinely attempted to ensure that all in-use copies of software were authorized copies.

Related Policies: "Software Duplication" and "Making Copies Of Software."

Audience: End users and technical staff

Security Environments: All

2. Preventive Maintenance

Policy: Preventive maintenance must be regularly performed on all computer and communications systems.

Commentary: The policy is deliberately vague in defining preventive maintenance. Middle management must determine what preventive maintenance is appropriate. Preventive maintenance can include replacing old magnetic tapes with new ones, cleaning and oiling disk drives, and cleaning dust under raised floors. Statistics show that preventive maintenance can reduce computer system down time. The policy is fully consistent with dial-out preventive maintenance systems that periodically notify the vendor of a system's internal status, automatically requesting certain remedial actions such as the replacement of a circuit board on which excessive faults have been detected. If the scope of this policy seems too broad, the policy can be restricted to "production systems." Preventive maintenance is relevant to personal computers, local area networks, client-server systems, Internet commerce systems, and other small systems just as it is to mainframes and large systems. The words "computer and communications systems" can refer to software and information collections, and to hardware.

Related Policies: "Business Interruption Support Levels" and "Equipment Maintenance."

Audience: Technical staff

Security Environments: All

3. Equipment Maintenance

Policy: All information systems equipment used for production processing must be maintained in accordance with the supplier's recommended service intervals and specifications, with any repairs and servicing performed only by qualified and authorized maintenance personnel.

Commentary: This policy ensures that information systems equipment continues to operate as it should, supporting the organization in achieving its mission. Equipment downtime can be a serious problem bringing many information systems activities to a halt. This policy does not state anything about the size of the system. It applies to personal computers and the above-mentioned larger systems. This policy can be used to inform end users that they must not try to repair their own personal computer equipment. Instead, they must call the Help Desk or some other authorized staff in the Information Systems department.

Related Policies: "Preventive Maintenance."

Audience: End users and technical staff

Security Environments: All

4. Retaining Hardware and Software

Policy: Hardware and software that is required to read data storage media held in the Company X archives must be kept on-hand, properly configured, and maintained in operational condition.

Commentary: This policy requires that antiquated hardware and software is maintained so that all archived data can be accessed. For example, many organizations have nine track tape reels and other older data storage media, but they no longer use these for production purposes. They may have disposed of the hardware needed to read nine track tape reels, but they keep the reels for legal, historical, and other purposes. This policy would prohibit such disposal because delays would be encountered if information on the nine-track tape reels needed to be recovered. Nothing in this policy prevents

an organization from moving data stored in these formats onto updated storage media. This is advisable to ensure that all data is readable and that a minimum number of hardware devices need to be kept on-hand.

Related Policies: "Archival Storage Media Testing" and "Digital Signature And File Encryption Software Versions."

Audience: Technical staff

Security Environments: All

5. Computer Modifications

Policy: Computer equipment provided by Company X must not be altered or added to in any way without departmental management knowledge and authorization.

Commentary: This policy ensures that users know that they must not tamper with Company X-provided equipment. Such tampering could inadvertently cause any of various security measures to malfunction. For example, a boot protection system that requires a password when the system is turned on could lock a user out of a computer altogether. Tampering could also be used to deliberately circumvent security measures. In an indirect way, the policy prohibits theft of internal components like memory chips. The policy ensures that the equipment issued to a user is the equipment that will be delivered when the user leaves the employ of Company X. This policy is unnecessary if users only employ desktop machines in the office. When the computers are taken off-site the need for this policy increases dramatically. Although generally less of a concern, stand-alone communications equipment such as external modems could also be included within the scope of this policy.

Related Policies: "Telecommuting Equipment" and "Transportable Computers With Sensitive Information."

Audience: End users

Security Environments: All

7.02.05 Security of Equipment Off-Premises

1. Off-Site Equipment Usage Approval

Policy: Management must authorize the use of any Company X equipment outside of company premises.

Commentary: This policy is intended to ensure that management is aware and approves of any equipment that is taken away from any Company X location. Management must determine the need for this equipment to be removed and ensure that the appropriate security measure will be followed while the equipment is at the off-site location. This includes many of the same controls that apply when the equipment is on Company X property. For example, the equipment should not be left unattended and adequate insurance should be in effect. When in doubt, management should apply the identical security controls as they would for local equipment.

Related Policies: "Removal Of Sensitive Information" and "Security Requirements For Telecommuters."

Audience: All

Security Environments: All

7.02.06 Secure Disposal or Re-Use of Equipment

1. Used Component Release

Policy: Information Security must validate that all sensitive information has been removed from any information systems component used for Company X business before releasing components to a third party.

Commentary: This policy prevents the release of sensitive information to third parties. Thinking that they are recycling obsolete equipment, many local managers donate or sell old personal computers to charities, schools, or used equipment brokers. These managers may not have taken appropriate precautions to remove all sensitive information from hard disk drives, non-volatile memory locations, and accompanying storage media. This policy transfers responsibility for removing data from local managers to the Information Security department, and ensures that no donated or sold equipment or storage media is leaking information. This transfer of responsibility is appropriate because local managers do not often have the expertise to adequately determine that all sensitive information has been removed. The transfer is also advisable because it permits the Information Security department staff to perform situation-specific risk assessments to determine whether equipment or media can be adequately desensitized, or whether destruction is necessary. This policy also prevents embarrassing publicity from leaks and assures that the Information Security department knows which third parties are receiving equipment and media. Some may want to exclude from this policy certain equipment such as telephone handsets, fax machines, or copiers that have no data storage capabilities. This policy compliments policies that dictate centralized purchasing of information systems equipment.

Related Policies: "Hardware And Software Procurement" and "Transfer Of Sensitive Information."

Audience: Management and technical staff

Security Environments: Medium and high

2. Information And Equipment Disposal

Policy: Department managers are responsible for the disposal of surplus property no longer needed for business activities in accordance with procedures established by the Information Systems Security department, including the irreversible removal of information and software.

Commentary: Simple file deletion is generally not sufficient. The files must be expunged or repeatedly overwritten by a separate systems utility to be truly irretrievable. This process can be complex, so separate procedures are often issued by the Information Security department. The way the policy is written, the procedures can be changed as the technology changes, without the need to change this policy. While the focus of this policy often is on equipment, the real concern is the information stored on the equipment. This policy also prevents inadvertent violation of the license terms for copyrighted software.

Related Policies: "Transfer Of Sensitive Information" and "Sensitive Information Destruction Procedures."

Audience: Management

Security Environments: Medium and high

7.03 General Controls

7.03.01 Clear Desks And Clear Screen Policy

1. Clean Desks — Non-Working Hours

Policy: Outside of regular working hours, all workers must clean their desks and working areas such that all sensitive or valuable data is properly secured.

Commentary: This policy is a modified clean desk policy. The traditional clean desk policy requires all information to be secured, lest an individual's judgment about the relative sensitivity of information be in error. The revised policy presented here is designed for personal computer and workstation users who often leave floppy disks and printouts out on their desks. This policy prevents people who happen to be in the building after hours from gaining access to sensitive information. The ways to properly secure information may be specified in another policy or in accompanying explanations. This policy has a positive side effect in that desks and work areas will be more neatly maintained. Another positive side effect is that materials that are left out are more likely to be damaged or destroyed in a fire, explosion, or other disaster. In some cases the term "sensitive" could be replaced with specific mention of the sensitive data classifications found at the organization. The policy could be expanded to include mention of internal mail receptacles, unattended fax machines, black boards in conference rooms, and other places where sensitive information might be kept in the open. Although obvious to some, a few organizations specifically include mention in a clean desk policy that the policy is not meant to discourage workers from working outside normal working hours.

Related Policies: "Four-Category Data Classification" and "Clean Desks — Active Use."

Audience: All

Security Environments: All

2. Clean Desks — Active Use

Policy: Unless information is in active use by authorized personnel, desks must be absolutely clear and clean during non-working hours with all information locked away.

Commentary: This clean desk policy intends to prevent inadvertent disclosure of sensitive information. The policy reflects a management attitude where workers are not trusted to decide what needs to be locked-up and what does not. The policy assumes that workers come in and do their job at regular times, for example working from 9:00 AM to 5:00 PM. Many organizations are moving to flexible schedules, so this policy may need to be modified so as to better define non-working hours. A positive side effect of this policy involves the requirement of a neat environment where physical appearance is valued. The policy assumes that the organization has the physical space and the financial resources to provide staff with the needed locking file cabinets, safes, and other secure containers.

Related Policies: "Clean Desks — Non-Working Hours."

Audience: All

Security Environments: Medium and high

3. Information Handling On Off Shifts

Policy: Sensitive information must always be locked in approved containers for sensitive information and must not be left unattended in any unsecured location during the second or third shifts.

Commentary: This policy ensures that sensitive information is not left in a location where some unauthorized person could view or steal it without it being noticed. This is especially likely to happen on second and third shifts, because it is during the second and third shifts that fewer people are around to notice that something is amiss. This policy makes a new distinction between those hours when many people are around and those hours when fewer people are around. The policy assumes that the adopting organization has no non-working hours, only certain shifts when there are fewer people working. The policy assumes the word "sensitive" is defined elsewhere.

Related Policies: "Clean Desks — Non-Working Hours."

Audience: End users

Security Environments: Medium and high

4. Unattended Rooms

Policy: When not in use, sensitive information left in an unattended room must be locked away in appropriate containers.

Commentary: This policy clarifies when it is appropriate to leave sensitive information on a desk. The policy clearly states that this should only take place if the room is unattended. Another possible exception also may be permissible: if the information is left in an area where all persons are authorized to view the sensitive information. This additional exception could be added to the policy. The policy could also be expanded to indicate that the last person to leave an area that contains sensitive information must ensure that all sensitive information is properly secured. This policy assumes the word "sensitive" has been defined in other policy-related materials.

Related Policies: "Four-Category Data Classification" and "Covering Sensitive Information."

Audience: All

Security Environments: All

5. Sensitive Information Storage

Policy: When not being used by authorized workers, or when not clearly visible in an area where authorized persons are working, all hardcopy sensitive information and all computer media containing sensitive information must be locked in file cabinets, desks, safes, or other furniture.

Commentary: This policy is intended to provide specific guidance to end users and others about the proper storage-related handling of sensitive information. It particularly applies to personal computer and workstation users who often leave floppy disks and hardcopy printouts out on their desk. Periodic audits involving a night time check of desks can be used to enforce this policy. In the title, the word "sensitive" may be replaced with specific mention of the sensitive data classifications found at the organization.

Related Policies: "Four-Category Data Classification" and "Sensitive Information On Personal Computers."

Audience: All

Security Environments: All

6. Powering Down Computers

Policy: All computers, except standalone computers located in areas with strict physical access controls, that have been used for processing secret information must be powered-down at the end of the day, at a lunch break, or at the termination of a session.

Commentary: This policy is intended to make users aware that sensitive information may be scavenged from a computer's memory. Because most computers have volatile memory, this information will be erased when power is switched off. In some cases, depending on the types of chips employed, the memory is non-volatile. In these cases, the information will not be erased, and some other actions are necessary to remove the residual information. In recognition of the existence of non-volatile memory, the policy could say, "check the manufacturer's documentation." A turned-off computer is much more difficult to manipulate remotely. If equipment is off it is less likely to be used for a break-in. The policy is particularly relevant to stand-alone departmental servers, and personal computers and workstations located in an open office environment. The policy assumes that other policies instruct users not to store information on systems with inadequate access controls. This policy additionally assumes that the term "secret" has been defined in another policy.

Related Policies: "Storage Media Data Classifications" and "Four-Category Data Classification."

Audience: All

Security Environments: High

7. Covering Sensitive Information

Policy: All workers who handle Company X secret, confidential, or private information must adequately conceal this information from unauthorized disclosure to nearby non-authorized parties.

Commentary: This policy instructs users that they must conceal sensitive information when interrupted in their office or workplace. If they act as prescribed in this policy, workers will prevent the information from being disclosed to unauthorized persons, even though these interrupting parties are most often employees. One positive side effect of this policy will be complaints from those people who find it difficult to work this way. For example, a receptionist will find it difficult to properly handle sensitive information and to handle visitors. Rather than indicating a deficiency in the policy, this complaint indicates that the individual's work on sensitive information is incompatible with her visitor reception duties. As a solution, the individual may do this work on a computer system located in a private office when not performing receptionist duties. This policy assumes that the terms "secret, confidential, or private" has been defined in another policy.

Related Policies: "Four-Category Data Classification," "Unattended Rooms," "Potentially-Offensive Communications," and "Unattended Active Sessions."

Audience: All

Security Environments: High

8. Locking File Cabinets

Policy: All office workers must be provided with locking file cabinets where all sensitive material will be secured when workers are away from their desk, and a copy of the file cabinets' keys must be given to their department manager.

7.03.02 Removal Of Property

1. Property Passes

Policy: Typewriters, cellular telephones, portable computers, modems, and related information systems equipment must not leave Company X premises unless accompanied by an approved property pass.

Commentary: This policy ensures that workers are not stealing equipment and the information stored inside such equipment. Guards at exit points can check property passes to ensure they are current, approved by management, and apply to the equipment. This policy is particularly relevant to personal computers and workstations. A property pass is required for both personally-owned and Company X-owned property. New technology will set off alarms at controlled building entrance/exit points if tagged equipment is being removed. The property pass process can be a method to prevent these alarms from being triggered. This policy could be expanded by prohibiting visitors, temporary staff, and employee family members from removing any equipment from Company X premises.

Related Policies: "Third-Party Physical Access" and "Moving Office Computer Equipment."

Audience: End users

Security Environments: All

Commentary: This policy ensures that workers are given one of the basic tools for preserving data confidentiality. The policy also notifies local management that they must provide this type of furniture to all office workers. The policy additionally requires that employees use the locking file cabinets for sensitive material. The word "sensitive" will need to be defined elsewhere, perhaps in a data classification policy. If the workers lose or forget their keys, a backup key is available from the department manager. In some cases backup keys will also need to be deposited with the physical security manager.

Related Policies: "Workstation Key Locks," "Clean Desks — Active Use," and "Security Requirements For Telecommuters."

Audience: End users

Security Environments: All

2. Shoplifting Tags

Policy: Sensitive Company X information must not be stored or loaded onto any portable computing devices unless the devices have an approved electronic security tag.

Commentary: This policy discourages workers from storing or loading sensitive information onto portable computing devices. If users must store or load sensitive information onto portable devices, not only should they use encryption and rigorous access control, but each of these devices must be tagged so that its removal from the building will be detected by a guard, and hopefully the effort to remove the device will be prevented. This policy will be more effective if the building has a mantrap or turnstiles through which all people must pass as they exit the building. The policy makes use of the same technology used by retail shops to detect the theft of clothing and other goods. The policy acknowledges that there are legitimate uses for portable computers that may contain sensitive information. The use of property passes can be used for the legitimate removal of such portable devices from controlled buildings.

Related Policies: "Traveling With Secret Information" and "Removing Hardcopy Sensitive Information."

Audience: End users

Security Environments: High

3. Media Removal

Policy: All computer storage media leaving Company X offices must be accompanied by a properly authorized pass and must be logged at the building's front desk.

Commentary: This policy ensures that workers are not walking off with sensitive or valuable information. The primary risks that this policy attempts to counteract are industrial espionage, privacy violation, intellectual property theft, and sabotage. The policy may be difficult for organizations that have a large contingent of telecommuting staff, many of which may customarily carry storage media into and out of an office building. Portable computer hard disks are also computer storage media, and they too should have passes. This policy is appropriate for high security environments, such as a diplomatic embassy, a bank data processing center, or a military command post.

Related Policies: "Property Passes" and "Bag Inspection"

Audience: End users

Security Environments: High

8 COMMUNICATIONS AND OPERATIONS MANAGEMENT

8.01 Operational Procedures And Responsibilities

8.01.01 Documented Operating Procedures

1. User Processes, Sessions, And Files

Policy: Company X systems administration staff may, at any time and without notice, alter the priority of, or terminate the execution of, any user process that it believes is consuming excessive system resources or is significantly degrading system response time, terminate user sessions or connections if this usage is deemed to be in violation of security policies or consuming excessive system resources, or remove or compress user disk files if it believes these files consume excessive disk space.

Commentary: This policy notifies users of what system administrators may be doing and prevents some complaints. The policy also notifies users that the systems administration staff has great latitude to immediately deal with anything that they believe might jeopardize system availability, system integrity, or system security. The policy acts as a deterrent to abusive acts such as playing games with Company X systems, especially multi-user games that may consume a great deal of network bandwidth.

Related Policies: "Program Resource Consumption."

Audience: End users

Security Environments: All

2. Critical Application Logs

Policy: All critical business applications must be supported by logs that permit system activities to be resumed within 15 minutes.

Commentary: This policy notifies Information Systems management and user organizations that manage their own systems that critical applications must be recovered within a certain time frame, and that extensive logs play an important part of the restoration process. Specification of a certain time frame for recovery makes it relatively easy for people to determine whether they are in compliance with the policy. The time frame will vary by organization, and ideally should be based on a business impact analysis. The time frame will also be a function of the criticality of the informa-tion handled by the involved application. The logs used for recovery may take the form of replicated databases, database checkpoints, file snapshots, disk shadowing, or disk mirroring. Reference to these types of logs can appear in the explanatory remarks accompanying this policy, although in most instances it is best to keep such technical detail out of the policy itself. The specific time frame also may be stated elsewhere besides a policy because it is likely to change over time.

Related Policies: "Four-Category Data Classification" and "Multi-User Application Criticality Rating."

Audience: Management and technical staff

Security Environments: Medium and high

3. Production Application Documentation

Policy: Documentation for every production applica-tion, which includes a list of system resources required to execute, a list of files employed and affected, a list of security features included, a description of the ways that the job stream or processing will be monitored and managed, and a description of the ways that output will be handled, must have been prepared for, and approved by, the relevant information Owner before the applica-tion can be moved into production.

Commentary: This policy prevents applications developed in-house from being moved into production without adequate computer operations documentation. The policy could be abbreviated when a list detailing the types of documentation required can be found in another document. This policy should not be confused by a similar policy that addresses end user programming documentation. This policy deals with applications that will be managed by an Information Technology department.

Related Policies: "Systems Development Conventions" and "Information Security Training."

Audience: Technical staff

Security Environments: All

4. System Availability

Policy: Users must be able to access all shared computer systems at least 95% of normal working hours, as computed on a monthly basis.

Commentary: The intention of such a policy is to get top management to evaluate what type of system availability is needed at the organization. While the number is likely to change over time, there is considerable merit to defining it as a requirement. Specific contingency planning efforts and systems design decisions can be derived from such a policy. The exact number specified will be a function of an organization's unique needs. The number given here may be acceptable for a manufacturing company, but it may not be acceptable for a telephone company. A policy of this type also may be useful for outsourcing deals, requests for proposals, and other interactions with outside parties. The policy is one form of a service-level agreement.

Related Policies: "Information Security Plans."

Audience: Management and technical staff

Security Environments: All

5. Computer Disaster Recovery Plans

Policy: Management must prepare, periodically update, and regularly test a disaster recovery plan that will permit all critical computer and communication systems to be available in the event of a major loss such as may be caused by a flood, earthquake, or tornado.

Commentary: This policy requires management to financially support and diligently attend to disaster contingency planning efforts. Because disasters happen so rarely, technical management often ignores the disaster recovery planning process. These managers are increasingly changing their attitude about disaster recovery plans, in large measure because they are appreciating that having a good contingency plan is becoming a matter of competitive advantage. Management is coming to appreciate that job performance will increasingly be based on having tended to these matters. The focus of this policy is on disasters, although it is also advisable to have a policy that deals with other types of interruptions. This policy assumes that the term "critical" has been defined elsewhere. The specific natural disasters mentioned in this policy can be adapted to local conditions. This policy is not limited to natural disasters, but applies to any event that results in extended loss of system availability.

Related Policies: "Computer Emergency Response Plans," "Preparation And Maintenance Of Business Contingency Plans," "Five-Category Application Criticality Classification Scheme," and "Information Security Plans."

Audience: Management and technical staff

Security Environments: All

6. Key Technical Jobs

Policy: Management must annually prepare an inventory of key Company X technical jobs and the names of the individuals who currently fill these jobs.

Commentary: This policy highlights the danger in relying on certain people and encourages cross training, job rotation, the development of expert systems, and other ways of providing some redundancy for key people. In large corporations, a similar inventory that considers key members of the top management team is often performed by a risk management department. Succession and new roles in the event that top managers are no longer able to fill their designated roles is a frequent topic of discussion in business circles. This same approach can and should be applied to critical technical personnel, such as the senior individuals who program telephone switches at a telephone company. As a result of preparing an inventory, management in many cases will conclude that they do not have sufficient backup technical staff. The process of identifying critical applications in some cases may help to focus attention on key technical staff resources.

Related Policies: "Cross Training," "Five-Category Application Criticality Classification Scheme," and "Asset Inventory — Technology."

Audience: Management

Security Environments: All

7. Cross Training

Policy: At all times, at least two staff members should be able to provide any given essential technical service for information systems critical to Company X business.

Commentary: This policy ensures that if a technical person who provides essential technical services were to be unavailable, then critical business systems would not soon come to a halt. The methods management can use to remedy the problem are numerous. Therefore, management can be creative when it comes to reducing the reliance on a single individual. This policy also applies to those situations where management wishes to alleviate the exposures it faces but no person on staff can provide essential technical services. For example, management may decide that it wishes to keep certain operational documentation up to date. The actions dictated by this policy can be avoided if management declares certain technical services as non-essential. If management were to declare technical services non-essential even when they were considered by many workers to be essential, at least management will have seriously considered the matter. This policy assumes that certain information systems have already been designated as critical. The policy presented here also assumes that Company X is an organization with a sufficient number of people where some staff redundancy can be achieved. Smaller organizations will need to get more creative, perhaps putting a technical consultant on-call for a small retainer.

Related Policies: "Four-Category Data Classification," "Key Technical Jobs," "Systems Expertise," "Employees Traveling Together," and "Production Systems Documentation."

Audience: Management and technical staff

Security Environments: All

8. Contact Information

Policy: All members of the Information Systems department who travel out of town must wear a pager and provide both their manager and their group secretary with telephone numbers where they can be reached at any time after normal business hours and when they are traveling.

Commentary: This policy acknowledges the significant reliance that is placed on information systems staff. The policy is intended to maintain the ability to quickly reach all technical people who might be needed for disaster or emergency recovery. The policy can be expanded to include members of user departments who are involved in technical computer and communications matters, and contractors on which the organization relies. The policy applies to many workers including those on vacation and attending conventions. The policy also applies to holidays and other non-working hours. Some organizations may not need such an all-encompassing policy. It may be sufficient to ensure that systems programmers, application programmers, and computer network specialists be on call through pagers. Unfortunately, technical staff sometimes travels to locations where pagers do not function. It is this situation that makes it necessary to give other telephone numbers to a manager and a secretary. Organizations that must immediately be in contact with critical technical staff members will want to replace the word "pager" in the policy with the words "cellular phone."

Related Policies: "Computer Emergency Response Team" and "Employees Traveling Together."

Audience: Technical staff

Security Environments: All

9. Production Changes

Policy: Company X production data and production computer programs must be changed only by authorized people according to established procedures.

Commentary: This policy ensures that special controls are used to protect the integrity of production computer data and programs. Because this data and these programs are used for critical business activities, special attention to security is warranted. Generally, the number of authorized people will be small, and authorization will be granted only when such people have a need for these privileges. A formal change control system or a change management system may be used to automate and track the changes and associated authorizations. Authorization may be implemented through passwords, smart cards, digital signatures, digital certificates, encryption, manually-rendered signatures, and other methods. Computer programs can be considered a special type of computer data. For a computing environment to be secure, both need change controls.

Related Policies: "Change Control Procedure" and "Record Change Orders."

Audience: All

Security Environments: All

10. Production Transaction Authorization

Policy: Transactions that update business records must only be processed if Company X management has authorized them.

Commentary: This policy ensures that only properly-authorized transactions update production records despite whether the records are computer-based. The policy can go on to specify what is meant by authorization. This is generally a clear delegation of decision-making power plus management approval to perform certain actions. Password-based computer access controls are the most frequently used means for checking that someone is authorized to submit a transaction. Nonetheless, this policy is written in a general way such that the authorization process might also involve a manual signature on a paper document.

Related Policies: "Production System Input Transaction Authorization" and "Business Production Information Updates."

Audience: Technical staff

Security Environments: All

11. Correcting Business Records

Policy: Any Company X business records shown to be in error must be promptly corrected using standard control procedures.

Commentary: This policy requires that standard control procedures be used to affect all error-correction-related changes to Company X business records. These control procedures might involve getting management approval before a change is made, or making changes through some sort of separation of duties with another worker. It is important to restrict who can make corrective changes to business records, lest people abuse these powers to commit fraud, sabotage, and other unauthorized acts. It is not enough to know that records are in error. The records must be continuously corrected to maintain information integrity. This policy also implies that a separate set of books that does not describe the actual business circumstances must not be maintained. For example, a deceptive set of books could be kept for investor relations purposes, while a realistic set of books can be kept for insiders. This policy does

not prevent or discourage an organization from keeping different sets of books for different purposes if these books are in keeping with standard procedures. This might, for example, involve one set of books for tax purposes and another for financial accounting purposes.

Related Policies: "Error Investigation," "Control Implementations Standard," and "Separation Of Duties."

Audience: Management and technical staff

Security Environments: All

12. Systems Expertise

Policy: Critical computer and communications expertise must be possessed by at least two available persons.

Commentary: This policy prevents an organization from finding itself in an awkward spot where there are no available people to assist with technical matters. For example, this might happen when an earthquake damages a data processing center and kills a critical client-server systems programmer. Because nobody else knows what he or she knew, the recovery of production systems at an off-site location could be significantly delayed. The policy does not indicate that the people with the important expertise must be employees. They could be contractors or consultants. The important word in the policy in this regard is "available." The policy supports the development and maintenance of a database containing information about the skills possessed by employees and others working at an organization. The policy indirectly requires management to consider which areas are important. This fosters an awareness of risks particularly those related to contingency planning. Some organizations may wish to use the word "critical" rather than "important." Likewise, either of the terms "mission-critical" or "strategic" could be used instead of "important."

Related Policies: "Cross Training" and "Independent Security Systems."

Audience: Management and technical staff

Security Environments: All

13. Computer and Communication Service Invoices

Policy: Computer users must promptly review the details of their computer and communications bills including internal charge-back statements to ensure that the charges are appropriate, that no significant mistakes have been made, and that no significant unauthorized usage has occurred.

Commentary: This policy requires user department managers to review their statements to promptly determine unauthorized usage and other errors that may be related to information security. The statements referred to in the policy may be computer service bureau invoices, phone system long distance call detail accounting reports, or internal accounting charge-back reports. The policy does not differentiate between in-house or external computing or communications service providers. The policy is particularly important for private branch exchange telephone switches, where a large bill for unauthorized toll calls can be quickly accumulated. Some organizations may wish to extend the policy's scope to credit card statements as well.

Related Policies: "Budgeting For Information Security" and "Direct Inward System Access Implementation."

Audience: Management

Security Environments: All

8.01.02 Operational Change Control

1. Vendor-Supplied Privileged User IDs

Policy: Before any multi-user computer operating system is installed at Company X, technical staff must disable or rename all privileged user IDs such as those named "administrator," "auditor," or "installer."

Commentary: Vendor-supplied privileged user IDs are the target of many attacks such as password guessing attempts. By deleting or renaming them, Company X technical staff prevents them from being the targets of these hackers. While the policy as it stands will be effective against some automated attacks, to make the renaming process more effective, the policy can be changed to stipulate that new user ID names must bear no resemblance to the prior names. For example, the "auditor" user ID must not be renamed "EDPauditor." For increased security, the words "multi-user" could be dropped from the policy, which would make the policy apply to desktop personal computers.

Related Policies: "Computer System Access Controls."

Audience: Technical staff

Security Environments: All

2. Removal Of Software

Policy: Every operating system module or utility that will clearly not be used, and that is not necessary for the operation of other essential systems software, must be removed or otherwise disabled prior to being used with production information.

Commentary: This policy prevents hackers and others from utilizing systems software routines that are not needed for business activity in order to gain unauthorized entry to a system. The fewer the number of utilities found on a particular system, the fewer the avenues of attack for a hacker or other adversary. Many vendors have recently loaded their systems software with extra features that are not needed by the vast majority of user organizations. These same features may be exploited by an intruder. This policy also indirectly states that all unnecessary systems software should be removed from production systems. This policy may be difficult to implement because many vendors do not want user technical staff altering the applications or operating system, and do not provide instructions for the safe removal or disablement of unnecessary modules or utilities. Reducing the number of systems software packages on a production system also potentially reduces the maintenance required. This policy's approach is used widely on firewalls and Internet commerce servers, both of which are known to use this approach to building systems software. Nothing in this policy prevents the removed software from being reinstalled, if and when necessary. The policy does not state how to determine whether certain software packages will be required and some investigation will be necessary. Some organizations may specify this information and who makes the final decision in the policy.

Related Policies: "Storage Of Systems Utilities" and "Systems Software Utility Usage."

Audience: Technical staff

Security Environments: All

3. Production Operating System Changes

Policy: Extensions, modifications, or replacements to production operating system software must be made only if the written approval of the manager of the Information Security department has been received in advance.

Commentary: This policy discourages and rigidly controls modifications to production computer operating systems. As a general rule, it is wise to keep a standard, vendor-provided operating system. This is because changes to operating systems software can inadvertently introduce vulnerabilities. Maintaining modified operating systems can be exceedingly time consuming and expensive. Customized or simply incompatible operating systems can also seriously interfere with attempts to connect computers to networks. If operating system changes have been extensive, then the organization may be prevented from rapidly moving to new releases of an operating system or application programs. This may also mean that new security fixes incorporated into a recent version of an operating system or special security patches cannot be used by the organization. In technically-sophisticated organizations, this policy may be appropriately distributed to end users.

Related Policies: "Operating System Versions" and "Systems Software Utility Usage."

Audience: End users and technical staff

Security Environments: All

4. Production Operating System Change Reviews

Policy: Periodic reviews or vulnerability assessments of production computer operating systems must be conducted.

Commentary: Because many access control functions are implemented at the operating system level, or at the access control package level, it is important to ensure that only authorized changes to the operating system have been made. Operating systems play an absolutely critical security role that should be periodically validated through a review, perhaps through a file compare program or perhaps through digital signatures. This policy mandates such a review. A policy specifying the need for such review is important because often organizations do not have in-house technical expertise to perform such a review. Increasingly these reviews are being done by software packages. In personal computer, client-server, and local area network environments, license management software containing check sums and periodic use of virus detection software could be used to implement this policy. The reader may wish to include "networked server operating systems" and "firewall operating systems" as a part of the policy.

Related Policies: "Production Operating System Changes."

Audience: Technical staff

Security Environments: All

5. Software Versions

Policy: All Company X production operating systems, database management systems, firewalls, and related systems software, and all production business applications software, must be kept at the most recent stable release level.

Commentary: This policy instructs computer operations staff about upgrading software resident on production systems. Operating systems, firewalls, database management systems, all have an important role to play in the security area. Likewise, application software often includes its own security mechanisms like passwords or privilege restrictions. The most recent software vendor release includes corrections for known security vulnerabilities, and provides the user organization with a higher level of security than can be achieved with older versions. The word "stable" is included in the policy to prevent the user organization from being a test site when it did not intend to be acting in this capacity. Release levels are different than patches and fixes.

Related Policies: "Security Fixes," "Systems Interfacing External Networks," and "Operating System Versions."

Audience: Technical staff

Security Environments: All

6. Back-Off Procedures

Policy: Adequate back-off procedures, which permit information processing activities to quickly and expediently revert to conditions in effect prior to the most recent change in software, must be developed for all changes to production systems software and production application software.

Commentary: Given the complex interconnected nature of computer systems, to require a conversion to a new system without having clear back off procedures is to unduly tempt fate. In the interest of keeping production systems up and running as much of the time as possible, This policy ensures that business processing will be completed with a trusted and stable version of production software. This policy is particularly important in client-server and other complex computing environments where applications span multiple operating systems, multiple locations, and multiple sizes of computer. In these circumstances, it may not be sufficient to simply roll back to a prior version of an application, because many other things also may have changed.

Related Policies: "Software Conversion Contingency Plans."

Audience: Technical staff

Security Environments: All

7. Operating System Versions

Policy: Company X must use the most recent version of all multi-user computer operating systems once the software is proven stable.

Commentary: When it comes to installing the latest release of an operating system, a delay is often called for unless the organization is willing to discover and deal with bugs found in new versions. This policy ensures that the organization has implemented the most recent versions of operating systems because these most recent versions include various security fixes. By using the most current versions of operating systems, the best operating system security is achieved. The policy could be expanded to include network operating systems. Good operating system security is fundamental for both good database management system security and good application security. A security deficiency in the operating system's security could undermine sophisticated controls found at either the database or application level.

Related Policies: "Production Operating System Changes," "Security Product Maturity," "Mature Development Tools And Techniques," and "Security Fixes."

Audience: Technical staff

Security Environments: All

8.01.03 Incident Management Procedures

1. Security Fixes

Policy: All security problem fix software and command scripts provided by operating system vendors, official computer emergency response teams, and other trusted third parties must be promptly installed.

Commentary: This policy is meant to instruct systems managers that they must promptly install security fixes. Often vendors wait until a problem can no longer be ignored before they issue a security fix. This means that user organizations need to promptly implement the fix if they are going to prevent losses. While the policy is meant to apply only to operating systems, it could be expanded to include applications, systems utilities, and other types of software. The policy could also be expanded to include mention of other trusted organizations such as user groups, in addition to trusted computer emergency response teams. This policy also supports systems managers' attempts to keep up with the latest release of operating systems software. The implementation of this policy can be through automatic software distribution over a network, particularly for client-server systems, local area networks, personal computers, and traditional software distribution media like magnetic tape and CD-ROMs.

Related Policies: "Operating System Versions" and "Incident Management Responsibilities."

Audience: Technical staff

Security Environments: All

2. Computer Emergency Response Plans

Policy: For computer and communications systems, management must prepare, periodically update, and regularly test emergency response plans that provide for the continued operation of critical systems in the event of an interruption or degradation of service.

Commentary: This policy requires that management prepare, update, and test emergency response plans in addition to disaster response plans. The reference to "degradation of service" may be omitted without serious damage to the policy. In some organizations such as civilian government agencies and other non-competitive environments, degradation of service may not be particularly important. For this policy to be most effective, the term "critical" needs to have been previously defined.

Related Policies: "Five-Category Application Criticality Classification Scheme" and "Information Security Plans."

Audience: Management and technical staff

Security Environments: All

3. Computer Emergency Response Team

Policy: Management must organize and maintain an in-house computer emergency response team that will provide accelerated problem notification, damage control, and problem correction services in the event of computer related emergencies such as virus infestations and hacker break-ins.

Commentary: External, trusted computer emergency response teams (CERTs) assist users of the Internet, while other CERTs coordinate investigations and problem eradication efforts on an international basis. Beyond these multi-organizational CERTs, there is a need for an in-house CERT to deal with in-house problems. By formally defining an in-house CERT, an organization becomes better prepared to deal with security-related contingencies. Use of an in-house CERT also reduces the probability that problems will become public knowledge. This policy requires that management within the Information Technology department set-up and support a CERT.

Related Policies: "Presentation Of Public Image," "Violation And Problem Reporting," "Incident Management Responsibilities," "Business Restoration Employee Expectations," and "Information Security Alert System."

Audience: Management and technical staff

Security Environments: All

4. Testing the Computer Emergency Response Team

Policy: At least once every three months, the Information Security department must utilize simulated incidents to mobilize and test the adequacy of the Company X Computer Emergency Response Team.

Commentary: This policy requires a certain frequency for exercises to test an internal Computer Emergency Response Team (CERT). If management specifies a certain minimum frequency for these tests, it ensures that these tests will not be ignored in the interests of other pressing business activities. The policy ensures that an internal CERT is operating efficiently and effectively. If the CERT is not operating in this manner, then this situation will be clearly illustrated by a failed simulation test. The policy could be augmented to include the requirement of a one-page report about the test results to be delivered to the chief information officer or some other middle-level executive. This policy assumes that a CERT already exists and has been adequately staffed.

Related Policies: "Security Fixes" and "Computer Emergency Response Team."

Audience: Technical staff

Security Environments: All

5. Suspected System Intrusions

Policy: Whenever a system is suspected of compromise, the involved computer must be immediately removed from all networks, and procedures followed to ensure that the system is free of compromise before reconnecting it to the network.

Commentary: This policy ensures that the compromised computer cannot be exploited to affect any other computer on the network and to ensure that a predefined set of procedures is followed to return the system to a trusted state prior to reconnecting it to the network. Included in these procedures should be running of file comparison software to identify any recent changes, execution of any forensic investigation procedures, restoring system software from trusted backup copies, re-initialization of the access control system, and copying the current system log to separate storage media that is locked away. System administrators often receive pressure from user management not to disconnect from an internal network, not to check to see which files have changed, and not to take the time to reestablish a reliable access control system. This policy overrides user management wishes, requiring these essential steps to be performed. A procedure that might be added is the use of a hash total or digital signature applied to the system log that is stored in an off-line container. This could later be used in court to indicate the integrity of the evidence recorded in the log. This policy ensures that the intruders are no longer logged-in. If a machine does not go off the network, the intruders may be watching and interfering with recovery actions.

Related Policies: "Password Changes After System Compromise," "Powering Down Computers," and "Retention Period Of Logs."

Audience: Technical staff

Security Environments: All

6. Intrusion Response Procedures

Policy: All computer operations staff must have a current documented procedure that clearly specifies how information security incidents will be handled.

Commentary: This policy is motivated by the situation where computer operations staff notice that an attack is underway, but they do not know what to do, or who to contact. As a result, the hacker proceeds, and causes serious damage when he could have been stopped, logged, traced, discouraged, and otherwise dealt with in an expedient manner. While this policy is directed toward those who manage commerce servers, web servers, database servers, and other multi-user machines, it could also be applied to individuals who are not recognized as members of the Information Systems department Computer Operations group. Technical staff in user departments who look after production systems could be considered computer operations staff if the organization chose to define "computer operations staff" in a broad and inclusive manner. This documented procedure would typically specify the types of incidents that are covered by the document, who should be notified and when they should be notified, what should be done after an incident takes place, how to protect evidence such as logs, how to immediately limit the damage, how to prevent future problems of this nature, how to reestablish a trusted information systems environment, and how to document the actions that were taken in response to the incident.

Related Policies: "System Log Review," "Intrusion Detection Systems," and "System Integrity Checking."

Audience: Technical staff

Security Environments: All

7. Vulnerability Advisories

Policy: On a weekly or more frequent basis, systems administration staff must review all information security vulnerability advisories issued by trusted organizations for items affecting Company X systems.

Commentary: This policy ensures that systems administration staff, or another designated group such as information security staff, are regularly reading the advisories about information security. If these people know what is happening they can then request resources from management to upgrade or change their systems so that they will not be unduly vulnerable to attackers like hackers and industrial spies. Information systems technology, particularly Internet technology, changes so fast that it is imperative that staff be regularly monitoring these advisories. By the time that vendors notify customers of a fix, significant periods of time may have elapsed. This policy permits staff to close existing security holes much more quickly. The policy deliberately did not say exactly which sources must be consulted, and it deliberately did not say what technology should be used to gather this information. Some vendors are now filtering these advisories so that customers see only the information they need to see.

Related Policies: "Computer Emergency Response Plans," "Security Fixes," and "System Vulnerability Exploitation And Victim Data."

Audience: Technical staff

Security Environments: All

8. Information Security Alert System

Policy: Information Systems department management must establish, maintain, and periodically test a communications system permitting workers to promptly notify appropriate staff about suspected information security problems.

Commentary: This policy ensures that management establishes and supports an appropriate communications system for the prompt notification of information security staff. This is different from an organizational structure for the prompt mobilization of information security staff, for example a Computer Emergency Response Team. Some organizations may wish to expand the scope of this policy to include efforts to notify in-house staff that this communications system exists and when it should be employed. Without such a communications system, attacks often are ignored, permitting attackers to continue to try other methods. Unless such problems are promptly communicated, there is a serious danger that total losses will be much greater than they need to be. This can be clearly seen with virus infestations on a computer network, where each minute of delay can mean further business interruptions and additional data destruction. The notification process can involve pagers, telephone number calling trees, and other methods. The designated department responsible for the communications system could be the Information Security department, the Institutional Security department, or some other group. It is, however, important that responsibility be specifically assigned.

Related Policies: "Computer Emergency Response Team," "Incident Management Responsibilities," and "Incident Reporting."

Audience: Technical staff

Security Environments: All

9. Unauthorized Access Problems

Policy: Whenever unauthorized system access is suspected or known to be occurring, Company X personnel must take immediate action to terminate the access or request assistance from the Corporate Information Systems Help Desk.

Commentary: This policy informs technical staff and users that they must take immediate action to suppress unauthorized system access. The policy informs workers that they must immediately seek expert technical assistance through the help desk if they are not able to completely stop the unauthorized access. In many organizations, the help desk would contact information security technical specialists. Rather than having the policy get overly complicated with various responses to a variety of problems, it simply directs all such problems to the help desk. Procedures to deal with a variety of contingencies can then be developed by the help desk staff in conjunction with in-house attorneys, physical security specialists, and information security specialists.

Related Policies: "Incident Reporting."

Audience: All

Security Environments: All

10. Messages To Attackers

Policy: A stern cease and desist message must be sent to the source of all attacks mounted against Company X computers whenever the source or intermediate relay points can be identified.

Commentary: This policy sends a message to attackers that their activities have been noticed and that they should stop immediately. Such a message may, in some instances, be enough to discourage an attacker from further efforts. If an attacker is using a shield such as a relay site, then the message can be sent to the relay site's administrator. Even if the attacker does not get the cease and desist message, someone who manages that site can take action. This policy could also be supported by new software that is just starting to hit the market that will trace the source of attacks. This policy applies to a wide variety of networks, not just the Internet. For example, it could apply to dial-up connections and an intranet.

Related Policies: "Information Security Responsibility" and "Production System Problems."

Audience: Technical staff

Security Environments: All

11. Information Security Problem Resolution

Policy: All information security problems must be handled with the involvement and cooperation of in-house information security staff or by external consultants, computer security response teams, or other outsiders that have been approved by the Company X Information Security department.

Commentary: This policy keeps security problems inside the organization, lessening the probability that unauthorized parties like the press will know them. The policy also fosters the use of the in-house information security group rather than alternative suppliers of information security services. It keeps costs down and also assures that in-house policies, standards, and methods, will be consistently applied. Just as end user departments have gone off on their own when it comes to personal computers, local area networks, and client-server systems, they are increasingly also going off on their own in the information security area. Although this policy does not require that all work be done by a central in-house information security group, it does require the group's approval. Outsourcing is therefore an option, particularly when there are not enough in-house staff members to handle a certain project.

Related Policies: "Outsourcing Contract Approvals," "Third-Party Information Security Responsibilities," and "Information Ownership Delegation."

Audience: All

Security Environments: All

12. Incident Management Responsibilities

Policy: The individuals responsible for handling information systems security incidents must be clearly defined and given the authority to define the procedures for handling incidents.

Commentary: Management often is surprised when a security incident takes place. Typically, people will not know to whom to turn, nor will they know what should be done next. The purpose of this policy is to require that specific individuals be defined as responsible for handling such incidents and that these people know that they are responsible for developing and maintaining procedures for handling incidents. The word "incidents" as used here could be construed in its widest sense to include emergencies and disasters. In addition to normal contingency plans, the procedures that these individuals develop can include ways to document an investigation, ways to determine how to prevent the problem's recurrence, ways to report the incident to management and third parties, and ways to protect logs and audit trails should they be needed for disciplinary or prosecution purposes.

Related Policies: "Extended Investigations," "Computer Emergency Response Team," "Information Security Alert System," and "Security Fixes."

Audience: Management

Security Environments: All

8.01.04 Segregation Of Duties

1. Job Rotation

Policy: All computer-related workers in significant positions of trust must be rotated to another position every 18 months.

Commentary: This policy identifies any improprieties or abuses that a worker in a computer-related position of trust may commit. A secondary intention is to cross-train staff so that several people are able to perform in critical positions. After a certain period of time in that position, they are moved to some other position. In some cases, by keeping staff in certain positions for a limited period of time, the chance that they will notice and exploit weaknesses in the system of internal controls is diminished. There is nothing special about the 18-month period. It could just as easily be 12 months or some other reasonable time period. Rotation is also consistent with efforts to expand the skill-sets of workers, also known as professional development. Such rotation is consistent with management training programs that attempt to acquaint workers with a variety of jobs within the organization.

Related Policies: "Off-Site Personnel Rotation" and "Systems Expertise."

Audience: Management and technical staff

Security Environments: All

2. Separation Of Duties

Policy: Whenever a Company X computer-based process involves sensitive, valuable, or critical information, the system must include controls involving a separation of duties or other compensating control measures that ensure that no one individual has exclusive control over these types of information assets.

Commentary: This policy prevents fraud, embezzlement, and other abuses that take advantage of an individual's access to Company X information or the systems that handle such information. For example, a bank teller who checked her own work and reports, may be able to illegally remove bank money without causing suspicion. Getting another person involved in a process ensures that the entire process was performed in accordance with management intentions. Because only a data classification scheme may be in place, at some organizations, it may be advisable to drop the words "valuable, or critical" from this policy. This policy is important in those organizations where small distributed systems are used for production processing. This is because the flexibility and power of these small systems permit downsizing, and often a single person is left doing the jobs of several former employees.

Related Policies: "Separation Of Activities And Data," "Errors And Record Manipulations," "Separation Of Duty Instructions," "Computer Center Access," "Working In Restricted Areas," and "Computer Transaction Initiations."

Audience: Management and technical staff

Security Environments: All

3. Separation Of Duty Instructions

Policy: Whenever practical, every task involving sensitive, valuable, or critical information, must require at least two people to coordinate their information-handling activities, including completing a task from beginning to end and approving the results of the work project.

Commentary: This policy specifically delineates what the separation of duties means within a certain organization. It is intended to provide specific guidance for business process re-engineering specialists, computer systems designers, new application programmers, maintenance programmers, and related personnel. The nature of the business performed by each organization will dictate the specifics to be covered in a policy such as this. Industry-specific laws and regulations may likewise point to the specifics to be mentioned here. In some organizations, it may be appropriate to delete the words "valuable, or critical" particularly if no policies relating to these considerations exist.

Related Policies: "Separation Of Duties."

Audience: Management and technical staff

Security Environments: All

4. Computer Analyses Review

Policy: Company X business decisions that involve over $1,000,000 and that have been researched by one individual working alone with a spreadsheet or another computer application, must be reviewed in detail by at least one manager before any action is taken.

Commentary: This policy is particularly relevant to personal computers, workstations, and other small computers such as client-server systems. The notable aspect of this policy is that it requires another person to review the work of an individual working alone. This can bring to light errors in data entry, errors in logic and incomplete information. This policy prevents an individual from arriving at a conclusion, upon which significant action is then taken, when this conclusion was incorrect or insufficiently researched. The policy imposes a sort of separation of duties in that major decisions must be made by at least two people. While the policy is primarily intended to catch errors, it also prevents fraud and other intentional acts that might be perpetrated if an individual were able to perform certain things alone. Most importantly, it prevents management from unilaterally making incorrect decisions.

Related Policies: "Separation Of Duties," "Control Validation," and "Information Cross-Validation,"

Audience: All

Security Environments: All

8.01.05 Separation Of Development And Operational Duties

1. Production And Development Separation

Policy: Business application software in development must be kept strictly separate from production application software through physically separate computer systems or separate directories or libraries with strictly enforced access controls.

Commentary: The separation between production and systems development is one of the most important aspects of a secure computing environment. If developers, users, and other can make changes to production software, then a wide variety of security exposures are introduced. These exposures include Trojan horse programs, logic bombs, and network worms that could be used to commit fraud, embezzlement, and industrial espionage. This policy supports a variety of separation of duties controls and the restriction of production access privileges to a small number of people. Some organizations may wish to specify separate storage media volumes for production and development files. Although in some instances more difficult to achieve in the client-server, local area network, personal computer, and related small systems environments, this policy is not meant to be restricted to large-scale systems. The words in the policy "business application software in development" refer to both new software and also old software being modified. The policy could be further supported by having separate individuals work in development areas and production areas, just as it could be supported by having a physical separation of development and production equipment.

Related Policies: "Privilege Restriction — Need To Know," "Separation Of Programming And Testing," and "Separation Of Duties."

Audience: Technical staff

Security Environments: All

2. Separation Of Information Technology Duties

Policy: Separate people must perform production application source code development and maintenance, production application staging and operation, and production application data manipulation.

Commentary: This policy gives lower level management instructions that will permit them to establish appropriate separation of duties surrounding applications in production operation. The first of the three categories mentioned deals with a programmer's tasks, the second deals with a computer operator's tasks, and the third deals with a user's tasks. Because different skills are involved in each of these three areas, it will be difficult for a person working in any one area to know what to do in the other areas. Documentation for each of these three groups should ideally be kept separate to further bolster this difficulty. The term "staging" refers to the steps that an application program must go through prior to being used in a production setting. These steps include testing applications, getting the sponsoring Owner's approval, cutting-over to production operation, and submitting jobs. The process of "data manipulation" as described here includes inputting new data, changing data that is already in the computer, and deleting data already in the computer. An organization adopting this policy could enjoy reduced chances of fraud, increased reliability of its systems, and reduced chances of errors and omissions.

Related Policies: "Technical Staff Privileges" and "Change Control Documentation."

Audience: Management

Security Environments: All

3. Separation Of Programming And Testing

Policy: Production business application software in development must be kept strictly separate from this same type of software in testing through physically separate computer systems or separate directories or libraries with strictly enforced access controls.

Commentary: This policy is intended to add security to the separation of production and development environments. This policy is intended to prevent unauthorized modification of software after tests have been performed, which could lead to a situation where the software is placed in a production environment, then used to commit fraud, embezzlement, sabotage, or industrial espionage. The policy could be further supported by having separate individuals work in the development area and the test area, just as it could be supported by having a physical separation of development and production equipment.

Related Policies: "Privilege Restriction — Need To Know" and "Production And Development Separation."

Audience: Technical staff

Security Environments: Medium and high

4. Software Testing

Policy: Workers who have been involved in the development of specific business application software must not be involved in the formal testing or day-to-day production operation of such software.

Commentary: Developers should test their programs as they build them. This policy does not address the informal testing that normally accompanies programming and development work. Using the words "formal testing," this policy refers to a process through which user management and systems management satisfies themselves that a system performs according to specifications. If a programmer or another developer were to perform formal testing of his or her own work, there would be a great temptation to choose only those test cases that show that certain control measures work properly and to ignore certain potentially troubling test cases. Even when there is no intention to be lazy, developers may not consider all of the real-world circumstances the application will be called on to handle. Another review is needed to validate that the application works properly. Although more difficult to achieve in the client-server, local area network, personal computer, and related small systems environments, this policy is not restricted to large scale systems. This policy is a manifestation of the principle of separation of duties.

Related Policies: "Separation Of Duties" and "Developer Access To Production Business Information."

Audience: Management and technical staff

Security Environments: All

8.01.06 External Facilities Management

1. Contractor Risks And Expectations

Policy: When using an external contractor to manage information processing facilities, all risks must be identified in advance, mitigating controls must be established, and all contractor expectations must be incorporated into the contract for these services.

Commentary: This policy ensures that appropriate and effective measures are taken to ensure that Company X facilities are properly controlled and secured when the responsibility for the management of the facilities is the responsibility of a third party. Organizations are outsourcing more and more aspects of their business including facilities management. Without a clear understanding of the risks, controls, and expectations of the outsourcing provider of this service, Company X could be subject to a number of threats, including theft of services and fraud. It is imperative that any arrangement for this type of service be carefully scrutinized and reviewed prior to signing the final agreement.

Related Policies: "Outsourcing Contract Approvals," "Computer And Communications Facility Location," "Backup Data Center Infrastructure," and "Computer Disaster Recovery Plans."

Audience: All

Security Environments: All

8.02 System Planning And Acceptance

8.02.01 Capacity Planning

1. Implementing Multi-User Systems

Policy: Workers must not establish intranet servers, electronic bulletin boards, local area networks, modem connections to existing internal networks, or other multi-user systems for communicating information without the specific approval of the director of the Information Security department.

Commentary: This policy ensures that users are not implementing communication systems that may inadvertently compromise an organization's systems and information. The policy is particularly important for the personal computer and workstation environment including client-server systems, where users often ignore in-house standards or Information Systems department instructions. Unless there is a centralized approval process, supported by an audit and enforcement process, some users may create major information security vulnerabilities without the knowledge of the Information Security department, the Telecommunications department, or the Information Systems department. The approving authority may easily be shifted to another relevant manager and away from the director of the Information Security department. The emphasis on multi-user systems in this policy is a reflection that multi-user systems typically have more information than single-user systems, and as such generally pose greater risks.

Related Policies: "Communication Line Changes" and "Production Application Acceptance."

Audience: End users and technical staff

Security Environments: All

2. System Interconnection

Policy: Real-time connections between two or more in-house computer systems must not be established unless the Information Security department has determined that such connections will not jeopardize information security.

Commentary: This policy keeps certain information within certain areas in the organization, and thereby control its dissemination. This basic design objective involves isolation to achieve security. For example, salary information about employees could be kept only in Human Resources department computers. Establishing a connection with the in-house local area network may open up a pathway for unauthorized dissemination of this private information. This policy does not preclude the movement of tapes, disks, CD-ROMs, and other storage media between systems. Generally non-real-time movements of data are easier to control. A real-time connection often permits unauthorized persons to access information quickly with little or no audit trail. A recommended variation of this policy would broaden its scope such that any connection with an in-house system would need prior approval. Taking this policy one step further would have its scope expanded to include connections between internal and external systems. This is by no means the sole approach. For example, routers and firewalls can be used to create isolated subnets within an organization's internal network.

8.02.02 System Acceptance

1. System Configuration

Policy: All Company X servers, hosts, firewalls, and other multi-user computers must be configured according to security requirements published by the Information Security department.

Commentary: This policy prevents system administrators, network administrators, computer operators, and other technical staff members from configuring multi-user computers in a less-than-secure manner. Technical staff members may have different ideas about how to configure systems, and this inconsistency can lead to unnecessary break-ins, crashes, and support. Consistency is essential if an organization is going to achieve a reasonable level of information security. This policy achieves consistency by specifying that these technical staff must work according to Information Security requirements. Such a policy is not the blueprint with which these systems must be configured. Instead, it specifies that there is such a blueprint and that all multi-user systems must use this blueprint. Many organizations will not want that blueprint to be in the form of a policy because it will change so often.

Related Policies: "Systems Configuration Templates" and "Firewall Configuration."

Audience: Technical staff

Security Environments: All

2. Production Systems Documentation

Policy: Every user who develops or implements any software or hardware to be used for Company X production business activities must clearly document the system in advance of its deployment.

Commentary: If the type of documentation described in this policy is not prepared and kept current, the sudden unavailability of a key person may mean that the production data processing they supervised comes to an abrupt halt. This policy is particularly relevant to small systems such as those with personal computers, workstations, local area networks, client-server systems, and departmental systems. End-user programming of production business systems can lead to serious losses if proper documentation is not prepared. This might, for example, happen if the person who developed the system leaves the organization but nobody else knows how to run the system. Such documentation is also likely to be critical for contingency planning purposes. Words covering the need to update the documentation on a periodic basis, or whenever major changes are made, could also be included in the policy.

Related Policies: "Production Application Documentation" and "Training And Operating Documentation."

Audience: All

Security Environments: All

3. New Technology Evaluation

Policy: Before any new technology is used with a Company X production application software or hardware system or network, the new technology must be evaluated and approved by Information Security management.

Commentary: This policy ensures that a user department or Information Systems does not install new technology without taking the time to evaluate its security implications. Because user department management and Information Systems department management are often in a hurry to get new technology into production, they would prefer to skip the security review. This policy says that a security review must be a part of the change control process if new technology is involved. New technology warrants special consideration because it's security problems are often not immediately appreciated. Often it is deployed and only later shown to be deficient from a security standpoint. This policy reflects the increasingly important technical consulting role played by the Information Security

Related Policies: "Communication Line Changes," "Secret Information System Isolation," and "Intranet Server Approval."

Audience: End users and technical staff

Security Environments: Medium and high

department. Examples of the new technology to which the policy references include personal digital assistants, virtual private networks, and wireless networks.

Related Policies: "Software Migration" and "Security In The Systems Development Life Cycle."

Audience: Technical staff

Security Environments: All

4. Production System Controls

Policy: Before being used for production processing, new or substantially changed business application systems must have received written approval from the manager of the Information Security department.

Commentary: This policy requires that the Information Security department review major in-house software development efforts to ensure that adequate controls have been provided. This policy prevents applications from being moved into production if they do not have adequate controls built into them. Instead of the Information Security department, the policy could make reference to the Information Technology Audit department. In an indirect way, this policy will foster the use of systems development teams that include people knowledgeable about security. Some organizations may believe that this policy gives too much power to the Information Security department. Distribution of this policy to end users and management is recommended to let these audiences know that they must not modify production systems without going through the proper channels. Taking this one step further, some organizations are now requiring user department management to specifically sign-off on the controls found in productions application systems. This process assists user department managers with learning to take security more seriously.

Related Policies: "Business Application Change Control Process," "End-User System Development," and "Projects Involving Human Safety Issues."

Audience: All

Security Environments: All

5. Production Application Acceptance

Policy: The acceptance and sign-off of Computer Operations, the involved user department, and Information Technology Audit must be obtained before a program will be granted production status on a multi-user computer.

Commentary: This policy ensures that multi-user machines run only those applications that have been appropriately approved by the right management representatives. The Information Security department could be added to the policy. The reference to "Information Technology Audit" could be replaced with reference to "Information Security," depending on the mission statements of the groups at the organization. Local area network servers, mail servers, servers in client-server networks, and other small system machines are definitely within the scope of this policy. This policy deals with approval by a number of different groups who have objectives above and beyond the inclusion of controls. The focus of this policy is multi-user systems, which typically have the greatest concentration of sensitive, valuable, and critical information. Multi-user machines are also networked in most instances, again indicating that such machines are deserving of special attention. The policy could be modified to include mention of substantial changes through the program maintenance process.

Related Policies: "Production System Controls" and "Implementing Multi-User Systems."

Audience: Technical staff

Security Environments: All

6. End-User System Development

Policy: All software that handles sensitive, critical, or valuable information, and that has been developed by end users, must have its controls approved by the Information Security department prior to being used for production processing.

Commentary: Development efforts by end users are particularly of concern because users often set-up production processing environments in their own offices without the involvement of the Information Systems department or the Information Security department. This often leads to client-server systems, local area networks, and personal computers that handle important business activities without the requisite controls. This policy defines a process to ensure that needed controls are integrated into these systems. In many organizations, separate change control process policies will be needed for the end-user community and the technical community. Beyond what is described in this policy, additional approval by the Information Systems department may be advisable to ensure that corporate networking standards, documentation standards, and other matters have been properly addressed. The words "Information Security department" in this policy could be replaced with the words "Information Technology Auditing department."

Related Policies: "Production System Controls."

Audience: End users and management

Security Environments: Medium and high

7. Software Conversion Contingency Plans

Policy: Whenever the implementation of new or significantly modified production software introduces potential problems that could cause a loss to Company X of over $1,000,000, management must prepare a conversion-related contingency plan that reflects ways to insure continued service to potentially-affected users.

Commentary: This policy ensures that management prepares specific procedures to deal with problems related to major conversions. There is nothing special about the figure used in the policy. The actual number used should be a reflection of the needs of the organization. The use of a cut-off figure is useful from a security standpoint because it gets management to do a risk assessment, in effect asking themselves whether they could lose $1,000,000 or more through a conversion effort. Some people may wish to specify what a loss of this nature involves, for example, lost revenue, extra public relations efforts, extra consulting assistance, and extra computer service or bureau usage. Rather than just relating to the software aspects of a conversion, this policy implicitly addresses hardware, networking, customer relations and other factors.

Related Policies: "Back-Off Procedures" and "Security Impact Statements."

Audience: Management and technical staff

Security Environments: All

8. Information Security Impact Analysis

Policy: Whenever sensitive information is to be placed in computers or whenever sensitive information is to be used in new or substantially different ways, a risk assessment of the potential security-related impacts must be performed.

Commentary: Acknowledging that security can readily be defeated on many systems, some organizations prohibit the placement of their most sensitive data on any computers. For example, a large bank may never store staff performance evaluations on any computer or network. The data could be kept on floppy disks and locked-up when not in use. Although this approach is overly cautious for most organizations, the underlying concern is valid. Some organizations may wish to restrict the policy only to network-connected computers. The policy could be rewritten to refer to all major system changes involving sensitive information. Similarly, to expand its scope, the policy could be rewritten to refer to "sensitive, valuable, and critical" information rather than just "sensitive" information. This change is recommended although the cost of implementing the policy increases substantially. The policy assumes the organization has already adopted a data classification policy defining the word "sensitive."

Related Policies: "Specifications For Software Developed In-House" and "Security Impact Statements."

Audience: Management and technical staff

Security Environments: All

9. Security Impact Statements

Policy: Prior to being placed into production use, each new or significantly modified or enhanced business application system must include a brief security impact statement that has been prepared according to standard procedures.

Commentary: A security impact statement should discuss how security on the supporting system would change as a result of the new or modified application system. This policy deals with changes to business applications rather than changes to the way in which certain information is handled. This policy also may be expanded to include an overview of the components of a security impact statement, for example, ethical standards and risks to be considered. This policy also may be modified to state when in the systems development life cycle an impact statement must be prepared. This is most effective when completed early in the process. The policy may additionally be expanded to require that the security impact statement be reviewed by Information Technology Audit management or Information Security management.

Related Policies: "Information Security Impact Analysis."

Audience: Management and technical staff

Security Environments: All

10. Privacy Impact Reviews

Policy: Every major systems development or enhancement project that could materially affect the privacy of individuals must be reviewed in advance by an independent committee, which must determine whether individuals will be placed at risk or at a disadvantage as a result of the project, recommend remedial measures, if necessary, and recommend the cancellation of the project, if necessary.

Commentary: This policy requires systems developers to consider the privacy implications of the new systems they build. A privacy committee could be made up of internal or both internal and external people. Some organizations may wish to specify the number of committee members and its composition. Such a committee is generally warranted only in those industries, such as financial services and health care, where privacy is a major concern. Nothing in the policy gives the committee any rights to cancel the project, delay it, or otherwise usurp management prerogatives. Nonetheless, the existence of a report by the committee may notify management that certain actions should be taken. If management does not take these actions they may be derelict in their fiduciary duty to protect organizational assets.

Related Policies: "Information Security Management Committee."

Audience: Management and technical staff

Security Environments: All

11. User Acceptance Of Information Security Measures

Policy: All information security controls must be both accepted and supported by the people who are monitored by and work with the controls.

Commentary: Acceptance by users is essential to the success of all controls. These individuals should be involved in the control-related decision-making process. For example, employee union representatives could be involved in discussions about using computer systems to monitor the work of employees. This policy implicitly requires management to explain and justify controls to employees. Such communications go a long way toward motivating employees to comply with security measures. If employees understand the reasons for security measures, they may be able to achieve the same objectives even when these security measures fail. The policy could be changed to incorporate some indication of when acceptance and support must be obtained.

Related Policies: "Minimum Information System Controls" and "Computer System Access Controls."

Audience: Technical staff

Security Environments: All

12. Systems Configuration Templates

Policy: Every general-purpose computer at Company X must be configured and customized according to one of three security templates issued by the Information Security department.

Commentary: This policy is intended to establish the existence of a three tier computer classification scheme and require all general purpose computers to be customized and configured according to the computer classification requirements. This scheme recognizes that each of the three types of computers have different security requirements. For example, a desktop system will typically have minimal or non-existent logging, while an infrastructure server, such as a mail server, will have heavy-duty logging, and a border server, such as a firewall, will have the maximum logging available. These classifications require security only where needed, and, as a result, reduce the overall cost of security. The existence of a three-tier scheme reestablishes centralized control over the configuration and customization of computers. In many organizations, end users have assumed local computer operations, and a wide variety of configuration and customization approaches are used within the same organization. By standardizing these computer classifications, an organization can help restore operational order and security across all departments. Use of templates also makes the addition of centralized information security services, like a network management system or a centralized intrusion detection system easier to implement. A configuration decision example involves specification of the minimum number of characters in a password. A customization decision example involves specification of the virus detection software package that must be installed and enabled on all machines within a template class. A computer cannot be a member of more than one of these three categories.

Related Policies: "Intranet Style Guide," "Security Configuration," and "Computer System Access Controls."

Audience: End users and technical staff

Security Environments: All

8.03 Protection Against Malicious Software

8.03.01 Controls Against Malicious Software

1. Systems Network Access

Policy: Systems without the required software patches or systems that are virus-infested must be disconnected from the Company X network.

Commentary: This policy acknowledges the fact that one system on a network that is infected with a virus places other systems on that same network at significant risk. The policy is intended to notify users that they will temporarily lose their network connection, and all that goes along with that connection, if they do not diligently post software patches and the latest version of anti-virus software. The policy provides a mechanism to require users to pay attention to security when they have traditionally ignored security, often thinking that it is a matter that computer technicians should handle. The policy may be implemented through vulnerability identification software that can examine the software installed on remote computers, and virus screening software installed at a mail server or a firewall. After a user is barred from using the network, these software-testing mechanisms can be run again to determine whether the user has taken the required actions. A connection with the remote user's machine will need to be enabled in order for these testing mechanisms to execute. Although the policy is written for an internal network, it could easily be altered to apply to an organization that offered services over the Internet, in which case the word "users" will become "customers."

Related Policies: "Internet Connections" and "Internet Connection Approval."

Audience: End users

Security Environments: All

2. Eradicating Computer Viruses

Policy: Any user who suspects infection by a virus must immediately shut-down the involved computer, disconnect from all networks, call the corporate help desk, and make no attempt to eradicate the virus.

Commentary: This policy prevents users from attempting to eradicate computer viruses from their systems. If users try to eradicate viruses on their own, these efforts may result in the virus being spread further or there may be destruction of data or programs. For example, users may try to see whether a malfunctioning program resident on floppy disk works in a coworker's computer, and inadvertently spread a virus. Instead, experts on staff in the Information Security department, on the Help Desk, or at an external consulting organization should be called in. Some organizations may wish to expand the policy to instruct the users to refrain from using diskettes or other data storage media that have been used on the infected computer.

Related Policies: "Reporting A Suspected Virus."

Audience: End users

Security Environments: All

3. Virus Eradication By System Administrators

Policy: Users must not attempt to eradicate a computer virus from their system unless they do so while in communication with a system administrator.

Commentary: This policy prevents users from innocently spreading a computer virus in an effort to isolate and understand a problem. The policy assumes that a virus detection system is installed in all in-house small-scale systems susceptible to viruses, and that users will be alerted to suspected virus infections. The policy instructs users to immediately get technical assistance rather than try to do this complex task themselves. This approach means that only system administrators need to be trained in the use of eradication tools, not the general user population. This approach will also ensure that infections are centrally reported so that statistical tabulations can be prepared. Another important aspect of this approach is the enabling of log software associated with some virus detection packages. The resulting logs indicate the actions taken to eradicate the virus. These logs are often essential references for restoring the computing environment that was in place prior to an infection. These logs can also capture the virus itself so that the virus detection software vendor can subsequently update its package to detect new viruses and mutated versions of old viruses.

Related Policies: "Eradicating Computer Viruses."

Audience: End users and technical staff

Security Environments: All

4. Downloading Software

Policy: Workers must not download software from any other systems outside Company X.

Commentary: This policy significantly reduces the opportunities for infection from computer viruses, worms, and Trojan horses. Unauthorized externally-provided software may additionally cause software incompatibilities, disk space shortages, and reduction of worker productivity. This policy does not prohibit downloading data from third-party systems, only software. Some organizations may wish to add words to clarify this distinction. This is because viruses in most cases attach themselves to software, not data. A macro-virus does attach itself to data such as spread-sheet files. The only sure way to prevent these new viruses is to only download ASCII plain text, RTF data, or permit no attachments to electronic mail messages. The policy as written here encourages use of standard software packages rather than loosely permitting users to employ whatever software they choose. This creates a more-easily-managed and controlled computing environment. Organizations that are very concerned about viruses could adopt a strict policy such as this, although requiring all such third-party software to be scanned with a virus-screening software package prior to use may achieve much the same end. Another option is to require permission from a local information security coordinator prior to downloading software. Software license management software can also be used to prevent the execution of externally-supplied software that has not been approved by management. Some firewalls can be used to enforce this policy. Because viruses and related malicious code historically have been a problem only on small systems, this policy can apply primarily to workstations, personal computers, local area networks, and client-server systems. This policy also becomes increasingly important as organizations connect to the Internet.

Related Policies: "Software Scanning," "Telecommuting Data Entry Operators," and "Downloading Internet Mirror Site Software."

Audience: All

Security Environments: Medium and high

5. Software Scanning

Policy: Workers must not use any externally-provided software from a person or organization other than a known and trusted supplier unless the software has been scanned for malicious code and approved by the Information Security department or a local information security coordinator.

Commentary: This policy keeps all software used on Company X systems free from viruses, worms, Trojan horses, and other unauthorized programs. The policy is not restricted to production systems. These unauthorized programs propagate rapidly and make no distinction between production and non-production systems. The policy requires only a negligible amount of extra work associated with the handling of externally-provided software. Normally, users would employ only that software that has been approved for internal use and that is in keeping with existing licenses with vendors. This policy restricts the software routines that users may run. The policy also discourages unauthorized copying of software for which Company X does not have a license. Although it does not need to be placed in the policy, the testing performed should always be done on a machine isolated from a network. Some organizations may want to specify what constitutes a known and trusted supplier. Some other organizations may wish to expand the policy to require that all such testing of externally-supplied software be documented. Organizations may wish to change the policy such that it requires all specific copies of software provided by non-trusted parties to be tested rather than one copy, which is then alleged to be the same as other copies provided by the organization. This policy does not prohibit users from downloading software from third-party systems. It just prohibits them from executing it until it has been properly tested. This can be enforced by license management software or desktop change control software.

Related Policies: "Downloading Software," "Loading External Programs," "Downloaded Information," "Software Licensing Agreement Reviews," and "Reporting A Suspected Virus."

Audience: End users and technical staff

Security Environments: All

6. Virus Test System

Policy: Whenever software or files are received from any external entity, this material must be tested for unauthorized software on a stand-alone non-production machine before it is used on Company X information systems.

Commentary: This policy maintains strict boundaries surrounding an organization's network and internal information systems. This policy states that software provided by vendors, files provided by associates at professional organizations, and all other externally-provided material must be tested prior to being used on Company X information systems. Viruses can now be embedded in data files like spreadsheet macros, not just in programs. This policy may be too strict for many organizations because maintaining a separate machine for testing externally-provided material may be seen as excessively costly or inconvenient. Screening of externally-provided material through programs that are invoked whenever a disk is inserted into a floppy drive may make the need for a separate non-production machine unnecessary. Likewise, some firewalls can scan data files and electronic mail attachments, and executables. One benefit of this policy is that a log of all screening activity can be kept on the separate non-production machine. This log may provide essential information for the tracking and eradication of a virus. The need to employ a stand-alone machine discourages users from introducing non-standard software, which will assure that standard software will be consistently used throughout the organization. This policy will be superseded by personal computer license management software that will stop users from invoking unlicensed and unscreened software. The Company X definition of production is critical to this policy. If personal computers are not considered to be production machines, the policy is easily implemented through resident screening programs. If personal computers are connected to an intranet, then a separate machine or some intranet disconnection process will be required.

Related Policies: "Downloaded Information."

Audience: End users

Security Environments: All

7. Outbound Software And Executables

Policy: All files containing software or executable statements must be certified as virus free prior to being sent to any third party.

Commentary: This policy ensures that Company X does not spread any virus when providing software or executable files to a third party. The policy addresses the outbound transmission of files that is often unrestricted while the inbound transmission of files is often closely monitored. This policy assumes that each user has the most recent virus screening utility on his or her computer, and has been trained in the ways to properly use this utility. Such screening is not necessary if an outbound file is in text format or rich text format because no executable statements are included in such files. The policy deliberately refrains from talking about a transmission path because the policy applies to any transmission.

Related Policies: "Downloading Software" and "Scanning Downloaded Software."

Audience: End users and technical staff

Security Environments: All

8. Virus Software Installation

Policy: Virus screening software must be installed and enabled on all Company X firewalls, FTP servers, mail servers, intranet servers, and desktop machines.

Commentary: This policy requires virus-screening software to be resident and enabled on many distinct locations in an internal network. The policy does not say how often scanning should take place. Because files may be encrypted or decrypted at any of these three spots, a virus screening package used at another location may miss a virus that has been part of transmission. The same could be said for data compression techniques, although many virus-screening packages can adjust to data compression. Because a virus could be introduced at any of these three locations, and the sooner it is detected and eradicated the less it can spread, it is advisable to be checking for viruses at all of the specified locations.

Related Policies: "Multiple Virus-Screening Packages."

Audience: Technical staff

Security Environments: All

9. Multiple Virus-Screening Packages

Policy: At least two virus-screening software packages must be used at each point where electronic mail and other files enter the Company X network.

Commentary: It is increasingly difficult for virus screening software packages to detect all of them, even if the latest updates are promptly and faithfully applied. To reduce the level of risk, some organizations run several of these virus scanning systems on mail servers, firewalls, and other machines that accept incoming files including electronic mail messages. This policy may have a negative performance impact that may be unacceptable to the organization.

Related Policies: "Electronic Offers And Acceptances."

Audience: Technical staff

Security Environments: Medium and high

10. Virus Certification Decal

Policy: Externally-supplied floppy disks may not be used on any Company X personal computer or local area network server unless these disks have been checked for viruses by an authorized person, and received a decal certifying that no viruses were found.

Commentary: This policy provides a clear audit trail to ensure that all externally-supplied floppy disks are screened for viruses. The policy also discourages users from bringing floppy disks to work for use on desktop systems. This policy removes reliance on end users, assuming that they will not be qualified when it comes to checking for and responding to the presence of a virus. The policy assumes that one authorized person in each location or department will be the designated person to perform virus screening. This person would be the one to place decals on each externally-supplied floppy disk. The decals should include the person's initials and the date when the virus checking took place. As long as the Purchasing department consistently buys one color and brand of floppy disks, internal auditors can visually determine which floppy disks are externally-supplied. Auditors can also visually determine whether these disks were checked for viruses and when. Beyond floppy disks, the scope of this policy could be expanded to include other small system storage media such as CD-ROMs, magneto-optical cartridges, and DAT tapes. Some organizations take this policy one step further by putting bar codes on their floppy disks. These organizations can then create a database indicating the origin, name, sensitivity classification, and contents of each floppy disk. The physical movement and present Custodian of each floppy disk can be automatically tracked, and periodic physical inventories can be used to reconcile this database with the disks on hand.

Related Policies: "Storage Media Data Classifications" and "Data Classification Labeling."

Audience: End users

Security Environments: All

11. Scanning Downloaded Software

Policy: Before software downloaded from non-Company X sources is decompressed, it must be screened with an approved virus detection package after the user has logged off from all servers and terminated all other network connections.

Commentary: This policy instructs users how to protect themselves against viruses contained in software downloaded from the Internet. This policy eliminates the need for the Information Technology department to get involved on a day-to-day basis. The policy assumes that users know when they are downloading software from the Internet, and it assumes that users are somewhat knowledgeable about viruses and how they behave. A new process on the Internet, a "server push" moves client software to an Internet-connected workstation without the involved user knowing that this transfer has taken place. While server-push mechanisms permit a new client-server functionality level to be achieved, they also presents a significant threat of virus propagation. A policy such as this is expected to become obsolete in a few years as virus screening software automatically performs all the steps defined in the policy.

Related Policies: "Downloading Software" and "Transferring Downloaded Files."

Audience: End users

Security Environments: All

12. System Integrity Checking

Policy: All Company X personal computers and servers must run continuously, or at least on a daily basis, integrity checking software that detects changes in configuration files, system software files, application software files, and other system resources.

Commentary: The increasing number of new computer viruses means that traditional virus scanners are no longer as effective as they used to be when it comes to detecting virus infections. There are now so many different viruses in circulation, and the number of new viruses is growing at such an alarming rate, that a lot of work is required to keep such scanners up to date. Recent developments seriously jeopardize the effectiveness of virus scanning software that searches for bit sequences to detect viruses. More sophisticated virus detection tools are now required. These include algorithmic methods and heuristic scanning methods. Integrity-checking software detects unexpected changes to software, and configuration files, then prevents these changes or at least gives the user an opportunity to stop the virus infection process. This policy instructs local department management to use virus integrity checking software on a regular basis in order to protect Company X information and information systems. To make administration and eradication efforts easier, a particular vendor's virus integrity checking package can be made an in-house standard. Some organizations may wish to expand this policy to include mention of virus behavior detection and blocking facilities. This policy is additionally useful because it detects intrusions where an attacker has modified files. To be effective, integrity checking software must also be accompanied by a policy that requires that all problems be promptly reported.

Related Policies: "Violation And Problem Reporting" and "Reporting A Suspected Virus."

Audience: All

Security Environments: All

13. Virus-Checking Programs

Policy: Virus checking programs approved by the Information Security department must be continuously enabled on all local area network servers and networked personal computers.

Commentary: This policy does not make distinctions between integrity checkers, virus screening packages, and virus behavior detection packages. Instead, it relies on the internal Information Security department to identify one or more standard virus detection software packages. The policy's emphasis on networked machines is justified because a virus or similar malicious program can propagate much faster in a networked environment than it can in a stand-alone computing environment.

Computers that are only intermittently networked such as those that connect through dial-up are networked for the purpose of this policy. The policy focuses on small systems because these are the computers that are most often hit by virus infections, not mainframes and other large-scale systems. The words "continuously enabled" are used to indicate that simply having the software on a hard disk drive is not sufficient. It must be executing for protection to be provided. Many firewalls incorporate virus screening facilities. In those environments where the firewalls can support it, the policy should be expanded to include firewalls.

Related Policies: "Virus Software Installation," "Virus Test System," and "Reporting A Suspected Virus."

Audience: End users

Security Environments: All

14. Current Virus Software

Policy: Every Company X worker who examines, processes, or stores Company X information using a computer that he or she owns must install and regularly run the most current version of a virus detection software package approved by the Information Security department.

Commentary: This policy ensures that workers do not lose critical data due to malicious viruses, which among other things can erase the entire contents of a hard drive or insert spurious words into word processing documents. This requirement is not difficult for Company X workers because, if they are managing their systems well, they will already have the most recent virus detection software package on their machines anyway. The policy becomes a service to the user community if Company X actually provides the software to these same workers. In order to maintain multi-location standardization and also to make remote technical support easier, this type of a software gift to workers is recommended. The cost of virus detection software is especially low when volume purchase agreements are arranged with vendors.

Related Policies: "Multiple Virus-Screening Packages" and "Downloaded Information."

Audience: End users

Security Environments: All

15. Decrypting Files For Virus Checking

Policy: All externally-supplied computer-readable files must be decrypted prior to being subjected to an approved virus checking process.

Commentary: Many users do not understand that viruses may remain undetected in an encrypted file. This can lead to serious problems where viruses are propagated when users believed they had been conscientious and had checked for viruses. The policy also makes reference to an approved virus checking process that may change over time as the sophistication of viruses accelerates. The policy could be expanded to include compressed files, which many virus checking programs cannot adequately scan. Viruses can now be found in certain types of data files and other computer-readable materials besides software. This is why the general term "files" is used in the policy.

Related Policies: "Eradicating Computer Viruses."

Audience: End users

Security Environments: All

16. Software Write Protection

Policy: Aside from when it is being installed, when it is being reconfigured, or when it must modify itself in order to properly execute, all software running on personal computers and workstations must be write-protected such that an error will be generated if a computer virus tries to modify the software.

Commentary: This policy sets personal computer and workstation system parameters such that software cannot be modified unless specifically authorized by the user. For example, if a virus were to attempt to infect a word processing package, the user would get an error message saying that the requested write operation cannot be performed. This would be an indication that a virus or some other unauthorized software had infected the system. Because many viruses do not inflict immediate damage, but lurk behind the scenes, this can be an important detective measure. The attractive aspect of this policy is that it is easy to implement and often is effective in detecting viruses and related programs. Mechanisms such as write-protect tabs on floppy disks, can be used to meet the requirements of this policy. Some software packages will require that they be able to modify themselves at set-up time or reconfiguration time, but after that they will not need to modify themselves. After the initial system set-up, write-protection flags can be enabled. If the system parameters need to be changed later, the write-protection flags can be

disabled, the system parameters changed, then the write-protection flags once again enabled. For some software, using write protection will be problematic. This policy could be expanded to include more discussion along these lines. It is generally accepted that this approach is not a sufficient defense against viruses. A separate virus detection system is needed.

Related Policies: "Reporting A Suspected Virus."

Audience: End users and technical staff

Security Environments: All

17. Scanning Backup Files For Viruses

Policy: Before any files are restored to a production Company X computer system from backup storage media, these files must have been scanned with the latest version of virus screening software.

Commentary: This policy ensures that production systems do not suffer from the reintroduction of a computer virus. In some situations, technical staff can work hard to eradicate a virus from a particular system, only to see that this virus has been reintroduced onto the same system through backup storage media. This can happen easily because when backups were made, system administrators may be unaware that files were infected because the current version of virus screening software may not have detected the presence of viruses. Subsequent versions of the virus screening software are more likely to include the ability to detect these viruses.

Related Policies: "File Restoration Access Control" and "Decrypting Files For Virus Checking."

Audience: End users and technical staff

Security Environments: All

18. Involvement With Computer Viruses

Policy: Users must not intentionally write, generate, compile, copy, collect, propagate, execute, or attempt to introduce any computer code designed to self-replicate, damage, or otherwise hinder the performance of any Company X computer or network.

Commentary: This policy clearly prohibits all involvement with viruses. Most appropriate in the university environment where users consider these activities to be of academic interest, this policy makes it clear that all involvement with viruses is off-limits. Because viruses are difficult to contain and isolate, the safest approach is to prohibit users from getting involved with them in any way. The policy also eliminates any possible claims that the organization encouraged a user to refine their computer skills and that these efforts were to learn computer programming. The word "generate" may seem superfluous, but it is actually different than "write." There are a number of freely-available programs that will permit users to construct their own viruses using pre-written virus building software.

Related Policies: "Reporting A Suspected Virus."

Audience: End users and technical staff

Security Environments: All

19. User Installation Of Software

Policy: Users must not install software on their personal computers, network servers, or other machines without receiving advance authorization to do so from a local information security coordinator.

Commentary: Internet access has made many new programs available to the general user population. If users install such programs, or permit an installation process performed by an automatic installation routine, viruses could be propagated, system crashes initiated, and other problems created. This policy explicitly prohibiting users from installing any software unless previously approved by the information security coordinator. New personal computer software packages are available that will prevent personal computer users from running any software besides the software specifically approved by management. By implication, this policy prohibits the use of Java and ActiveX applets, but some users may not make the connection.

Related Policies: "Disabling Java."

Audience: End users

Security Environments: All

20. Loading External Programs

Policy: Users may not place any computer program developed outside of Company X on personal computers, workstations, network servers, or computers connected to the network unless this program has been approved by the Information Systems department.

Commentary: The policy defines a software change control requirement for distributed networked systems. This policy ensures that no software is placed on network-connected computers without having been examined for viruses, worms, and other unauthorized

code. This policy can also be used to prohibit use of unauthorized software when organizational standard software has been adopted. Having consistent software throughout the network permits a help desk to provide better support and also permits the network to be more effectively managed. Some organizations may wish to enforce a policy like this using inventory software. These packages automatically identify all software and hardware components in all personal computers or workstations connected to a local area network.

Related Policies: "Software Scanning."

Audience: End users and technical staff

Security Environments: All

21. Background Push Software Updates

Policy: Automatic updating of software on Company X computers through background push technology must not be executed unless the involved software has been tested by an authorized member of the Information Systems department.

Commentary: A number of vendors are distributing updates to their software products entirely without human intervention through the Internet. This push technology holds great promise, especially for the distribution of updates to virus screening software. Yet it also holds great risks, for example in an office where all the computers are unworkable because an incompatibility in newly-pushed software conflicts with existing software. While push software updating systems can save a lot of time for Information Systems departments, the software testing processes performed by vendors may not be adequate substitutes for the software testing processes performed by user organizations. This policy maintains the stability of existing user systems by requiring that all software sent from vendors be tested before it is used within a user organization. In the future, when vendor-testing processes are shown to be adequate, and when reliable vendor quality control measures exist, exceptions to this policy can be made on a vendor-by-vendor basis. Current exceptions to the policy may need to be made for virus software, because this type of software changes so rapidly. Exceptions also may be needed for intrusion detection software that likewise requires frequent updates.

Related Policies: "Change Control Procedure."

Audience: Technical staff

Security Environments: All

22. Downloading Internet Mirror Site Software

Policy: Software resident on Internet mirror sites must not be downloaded to any Company X computer unless it is received directly from a known and trusted source and software verification tools like digital signatures are employed.

Commentary: This policy directs technical staff on the safe way to download software over the Internet. Many popular information security tool sites are mirrored throughout the Internet. Because the integrity of the software resident on mirror sites is questionable, those people performing downloads should use only well-known sites and digital signature technology to ensure that the code has not been changed. While downloading software updates through the Internet is riskier than getting a CD-ROM directly from a vendor, it is much faster and often less costly. This policy assumes that no prohibition against downloading software exists for technical staff, but such a prohibition could nonetheless exist for other types of users.

Related Policies: "Downloading Software" and "Software Development Source."

Audience: Technical staff

Security Environments: All

23. Downloading Software Using The Internet

Policy: End users must not download software from the Internet under any circumstances.

Commentary: This policy brings some order to what is often a very chaotic software update environment on end-user personal computers and workstations. End users in many organizations are taking the software update process into their own hands, and in the process they often create problems for the Help Desk and others working in the information systems area. This policy assumes that the organization has a process in place to distribute software and related upgrades. The policy works much better if its implementation includes workstation access control packages that prevent end users from updating software themselves. Also useful in the implementation of this policy would be an automated software license management package, that could periodically take an automated census to determine what software is installed on each machine. This policy assumes that all end-user machines are

connected to a local area network, a wide area network, an intranet or some other network through which software updates may be pushed. The delay associated with testing software before it is installed across an organization is often desirable because this delay will permit serious bugs to be reported to public forums. Those performing software testing can install patched versions that have corrected these problems.

Related Policies: "Downloading Internet Mirror Site Software."

Audience: End users and technical staff

Security Environments: All

24. Downloaded Information

Policy: All software and files downloaded from non-Company X sources through the Internet or any other public network must be screened with virus detection software prior to the software being executed or the files being examined through another program.

Commentary: This policy defines the process that users follow before they execute software or open data files that have been down loaded from public networks. While viruses, Trojan horses, and worms used to be threats only with software, they are now increasingly being included with data files. Therefore, the screening of both programs and data files is necessary. To contain the spread of these unauthorized programs, the screening must take place before any other program is used. The most cost-effective place to deal with viruses or similar unauthorized programs is at the point where they enter an organization, as addressed in this policy. Dealing with these unauthorized programs after they have started to spread throughout an organization is considerably more expensive. This policy reduces the negative side effects created by viruses and related programs. These include system downtime, unauthorized erasure of data files, and subtle unnoticeable modification of data files. This policy will be considerably easier to implement if each user has a current virus-detection program on his or her workstation.

Related Policies: "Downloading Software," "Downloading Sensitive Information," and "Software Scanning."

Audience: All

Security Environments: All

8.04 Housekeeping

8.04.01 Information Backup

1. Master Copies Of Software

Policy: All personal computer software must be copied prior to its initial usage, these master copies must be stored in a safe and secure location, and these master copies must not be used for ordinary business activities.

Commentary: This policy ensures that all users have master backup copies of the software they employ. Making backup copies of software should always be in keeping with the software vendor license agreements. Many licenses permit backup copies, provided that the backup copies are not used at the same time that another copy is being used. If a centralized technical support group distributes, updates, and manages personal computer software, then there will be no need for a policy such as this to be distributed to end users. This policy could be expanded to include other types of systems besides personal computers (PCs), but the procedures on these larger systems are ordinarily more organized. Some organizations may also want to specify that initial copies of all production software be stored nearby and off-site rather than simply in a safe and secure location.

Related Policies: "Making Copies Of Software."

Audience: All

Security Environments: All

2. Data Backups

Policy: All critical business information and critical software resident on Company X computer systems must be periodically backed-up on a monthly basis.

Commentary: This policy specifies a minimum acceptable backup time frame and what type of data needs to be backed-up. Certain types of data will need to be backed up more frequently than monthly, but these decisions must be made based on the organization and data type. These decisions will generally be covered in a contingency plan. This policy is relevant to personal computers, local area networks, and client-server systems and larger machines. Users on smaller systems sometimes forget or ignore backups. This propensity of end users to forget about or ignore backups, in the long run, is best handled by automatic backup systems, such as those that operate in a user-transparent fashion at night. This policy assumes the word "critical" has been defined elsewhere.

Related Policies: "Four-Category Data Classification," "Five-Category Application Criticality Classification Scheme," and "Backup Process."

Audience: All

Security Environments: All

3. Backup Media

Policy: Users must provide their own data storage media, make their own backup of important files and never use hard drives and other data storage devices attached to Company X desktop public access computers for backup purposes.

Commentary: This policy informs users that they should not store important files on public machines, such as a computer lab at a university or a testing facility at a computer company. Because the involved computers do not have access controls, there is no practical way that Company X can prevent users from modifying or deleting files saved by other users on these machines. Establishing user expectations about the backup that is or is not performed is also highly desirable. The policy also notifies users that system administrators may at any time delete all user-provided files in order to free-up available disk space.

Related Policies: "Automatic Backups" and "File Restoration Access Control."

Audience: End users

Security Environments: All

4. Backup Media Encryption

Policy: All sensitive, valuable, or critical information recorded on backup computer media and stored outside Company X offices must be encrypted.

Commentary: Physical access controls at commercial backup sites are often inferior to those at an organization's primary site. For example, a padlock on a locker containing data storage media may be all that protects an organization's backup data. Backup sites are frequently unattended and accessible by a variety of subscribing organization personnel. This policy ensures that some access control remains over sensitive, valuable, or critical information stored off-site. For more security, some organizations may want to require encryption for all backups, no matter where these backups are stored. This more stringent approach may be appropriate for telecommuters, and those with portable computers and other systems removed from Company X premises. Keep in mind that encryption of backup data will often slow if not prevent the recovery of the information involved. For example, keys for the decryption of backup media may be unavailable when there is an urgent need to recover data. This policy assumes the terms "sensitive, valuable, or critical" have been defined elsewhere.

Related Policies: "Four-Category Data Classification," "Five-Category Application Criticality Classification Scheme," "Secret Information On Transportable Computers," and "Secret Information Encryption."

Audience: All

Security Environments: Medium and high

5. On-Site Backup Files

Policy: At least one generation of backup files must be maintained on off-line data storage media wherever production computers are located.

Commentary: This policy facilitates rapid recovery of production system files that are erroneously deleted, damaged by a disk head crash, or otherwise corrupted. The ready availability of the last backup gives computer operators the ability to immediately restore the involved files, although some transactions or updates made since the last backup may be lost. This policy additionally provides a way to protect the information in these on-site backups from the effects of hackers, saboteurs, disgruntled employees, worms, viruses, and other threats. If it is stored off-line, it is not immediately accessible to these potential attackers. The damaging effects of these influences may be mitigated because a recent backup was available and immediately accessible.

Related Policies: "Backup Media Encryption" and "Backup Media Storage."

Audience: Technical staff

Security Environments: All

6. Multiple Backup Copies

Policy: At least two recent and complete backups made on different dates containing critical Company X records must always be stored off-site.

Commentary: This policy ensures that a sufficient number of backup copies are always available for restoration after an emergency or disaster. If only one copy were used, that copy might be damaged during a restore operation or in transit to the recovery center. Another objective of this policy is to dictate a backup media rotation process that involves at least two off-site copies. The word "recent" is deliberately vague, forcing management to interpret the word based on information. An incremental copy only provides the changes since the last backup, and would be of limited value unless the prior complete backup was also available.

Related Policies: "Copies Of Sensitive, Critical, Or Valuable Information."

Audience: Technical staff

Security Environments: All

7. Backup Process

Policy: Incremental backups for all end-user files must be performed by the on-duty administrator starting at 6:00 PM each business day with exception of Friday when a full backup of all files must be performed.

Commentary: This policy communicates when both incremental backups and full backups must take place. Local area network administrators and others responsible for making backups cannot claim that they did not know what should be done. Although executing a backup at 6:00 PM may be problematic for some backup software packages because certain files are in use, many packages simply flag in-use files for subsequent retries. These packages will make multiple attempts to backup the in-use file, and if they fail with all attempts, will generate a command script that may be later run by a local area network administrator or the other person taking care of the backup process. The important part is the regularity of the process, not the exact time of day. This policy could be changed to incorporate a courier who picks up backup disks and tapes at a certain time, then transports them to an off-site storage location.

Related Policies: "Automatic Backups."

Audience: Technical staff

Security Environments: All

8. Automatic Backups

Policy: All users with local area network connections must leave their computers turned on at night for the execution of automatic backups.

Commentary: This policy ensures that end users leave their machines, workstations, personal computers, or other computers with local storage, turned on when they go home at night. An automatic backup program will copy their files to a central storage server for backup purposes. There are ecological considerations associated with this policy. The words in the policy "for the execution of automatic backups" imply that workstation access controls should be set-up to permit a backup to proceed without human intervention. If a workstation is unattended, password-based workstation access control may not permit server-based backup software to read the contents of a hard disk drive unless some additional work is performed. Although automatic backup to a local area network server using timer-driven software is desirable, it may be necessary to run access control software on workstations that are left connected to the network and unattended. If the local area network has external communication links, such as Internet firewalls or dial-up modem pools, such access control measures are absolutely essential. The words "local area network" could be replaced with the word "intranet."

Related Policies: "Network Computer Access Control."

Audience: End users and technical staff

Security Environments: All

9. Backup Information Review

Policy: All files and messages stored on Company X systems are routinely copied to tape, disk, and other storage media and must be recoverable for potential examination at a later date by system administrators and others designated by management.

Commentary: This privacy-related policy notifies users that their information may be examined by system administrators, security investigators, and others authorized by management. This policy could be expanded to mention electronic mail messages, Internet file transfer protocol activities, dial-up database searches, and other actions that could be logged and backed-up. In an indirect way, the policy also suggests that users consider not placing certain very sensitive information on Company X systems. While this policy may seem obvious to technically-sophisticated people, the idea behind the policy is not obvious to many users who are new to computers. Backup systems may provide incriminating evidence that users thought they destroyed. This policy could be accompanied by a related policy indicating when data should be encrypted.

Related Policies: "Secret Data Transmission," "Privacy Expectations And Information Stored On Organization Systems," and "Electronic Mail Message Handling."

Audience: End users

Security Environments: All

10. Critical Backup Files

Policy: Critical data that has been backed up must not be used for data restoration purposes unless another backup copy of the same data exists on different computer storage media.

Commentary: This policy ensures that the only current copy of critical data is not damaged or deleted in the process of being restored. In this policy, users are admonished to make another copy of such data prior to doing restoration work, provided an additional copy has not previously been made. This multiple computer approach to making backup copies is advisable because the system to which data is to be restored may be infected by a virus, worm, Trojan horse or some other malicious software. In the process of restoring a file, the backup data storage media itself may be altered, scrambled, or otherwise changed in an unauthorized manner. Likewise, the act of making another copy of the data on different data storage media, if done on the machine to which the data is to be restored, may trigger such malicious software. Having a spare copy of a backup is additionally advisable because the technical staff person performing a restore operation may make a mistake, and may thereby inadvertently delete or corrupt the backup media. As a preferred alternative to making an additional copy before restoration is performed, two copies can be generated when the original backup is made. This policy assumes that the word "critical" has been defined elsewhere.

Related Policies: "Copies Of Sensitive, Critical, Or Valuable Information" and "Five-Category Application Criticality Classification Scheme."

Audience: All

Security Environments: Medium and high

11. Pre-Processing Backup

Policy: Production batch processes must not begin unless a pre-processing backup of all involved master files and master databases has been completed.

Commentary: This policy prevents the organization from being in an awkward position when it comes time to open for business the following day. Without a control such as the one described in this policy, if a batch process failed during the night, and if there was no computer operator on duty to restart the process properly, when workers arrive at the office the next morning they may not be able to access customer records and other production data. This may be because the records have been partially modified and are not suitable for use until the batch process completes. In some organizations, it may be appropriate for these workers to access a version of these files and databases that has not been updated with batch transactions. The policy is also intended to ensure that the organization adopting it will have a usable backup copy of critical production files and databases, should the batch process damage these files or databases beyond repair. Because a batch process may run for several hours, and because it often consumes considerable processing resources, it is important to backup critical data before the process begins. This pre-processing backup should be in addition to a regular nightly backup that could be performed after batch processes and all other production processes have been completed for the day.

Related Policies: "Data Backups" and "Input Data Validation And Rejected Item Handling."

Audience: Technical staff

Security Environments: All

12. Backup Media Storage

Policy: Essential business information and software backups must be stored in an environmentally protected and access-controlled site that is a sufficient distance away from the originating facility.

Commentary: This policy ensures that backups of critical information are not destroyed by a local disaster such as an airplane crash, bomb blast, or chemical spill. Rather than specifying a certain distance from the originating facility, this policy leaves it up to local management to decide how far away the copies should be. This remote location can be 5-100 miles away. Other organizations will find that it is sufficient to have current backup copies stored on-site at a primary location and off-site a few city blocks away. Local considerations, such as earthquake faults, may also affect the distance involved. Some organizations may wish to specify a certain minimum distance to increase the likelihood that the storage location will not be affected by the problem affecting the original site. The farther away the storage location, the more time and expense involved in retrieving the backups. This last trade off can be eliminated with the use of electronic vaulting, where real-time backups are transmitted to a remote location through the Internet.

Related Policies: "Secret Information Encryption."

Audience: Technical staff

Security Environments: All

13. Backup Media Fire Zone

Policy: Computer and network backup storage media must be stored in a separate fire zones from the machine producing the backup.

Commentary: This policy distances backup storage media from the machine that was used to produce the backup. Rather than requiring that the media be stored off-site, or even a certain number of miles away, this policy looks to isolated fire zones that are unlikely to be involved in the same fire. Different buildings on the same corporate campus can be in different fire zones. Different parts of the same large building may be different fire zones. Because the specifics of a certain building will always differ, this policy mandates only the use of the notion of a fire zone, leaving the rest up to the Physical Security department. For greater protection, a backup media rotation system could move media through several fire zones. Some organizations will wish to augment this policy by requiring that a periodic archival copy be stored far away from the machine used to make the backup.

Related Policies: "Backup Media Storage" and "Backup Media Encryption."

Audience: End users and technical staff

Security Environments: All

14. Backup Media Storage Units

Policy: Unless they have an closing mechanism that is triggered by a fire alarm, all areas where backup media is stored including, but not limited to, fireproof computer backup storage rooms, vaults, and cabinets must be kept fully closed when not in active use.

Commentary: This policy ensures that fireproof technology will work as designed. If computer operations staff leaves open a fireproof file cabinet containing the weekly backup and a fire occurs, the file cabinet cannot provide any protection for the backup media. This policy is focused on ensuring that fireproof systems are able to do their job. If there happens to be security such as a lock on fireproof vaults and cabinets, then there may be some access control benefits as well.

Related Policies: "Computer Facility Fire Resistance" and "Unattended Rooms."

Audience: Technical staff

Security Environments: All

15. Web And Commerce Site File Archives

Policy: Every version of Internet web site and commerce site files must be securely archived in two physically-separated locations.

Commentary: This policy creates a redundant archive of every version of Internet web and commerce sites. Such an archive can be very important for legal purposes. For example, if there was a legal dispute about an offer posted to a web site, and if data integrity and access controls are part of the archiving process, then these records could be used to definitively prove what information was posted on the site. A bank may use an archive like this to help resolve a dispute about the rate offered on a particular type of savings account or certificate of deposit. Such an archive can also be useful for contingency planning purposes if, for example, a hosting organization destroys all copies of the site. Because so many organizations use outsourced hosting organizations, it is important that the organization take care of its own archival backup process. In some jurisdictions there also may be legal reasons to keep copies of Internet sites.

Related Policies: "Data Backups" and "Electronic Mail Message Handling."

Audience: Technical staff

Security Environments: All

16. Critical Information Backups

Policy: Critical business information and critical software must be backed-up at least quarterly onto archival storage media and kept for at least one year.

Commentary: This policy acknowledges that viruses or Trojan horses can alter files and that these alterations may not be detected for a long period of time. This means that several generations of backups may contain virus-infected or otherwise altered files, and that the responsible parties may not be aware of the problem before all the rotating backups have been corrupted or overwritten. When facing one of these unfortunate situations, the original installation storage media may be the only hope for software, aside from going back to the vendor or software escrow agent. For critical business information, fraudulent modifications may have been made, and these modifications may be concealed for an extended period of time. Likewise, unless a policy like this is adopted, all the backups may contain fraudulent information. Recovery of the original and unmodified information may be very difficult if not impossible if the process described in this policy is not adopted. The cost of this policy is minor when backup operations are automated. The policy can be augmented with a policy specifying when and how these archival backups should be destroyed. Corporate legal counsel should be consulted about discovery and related legal issues.

Related Policies: "Multiple Backup Copies" and "Data Backups."

Audience: Technical staff

Security Environments: All

17. Archival Storage Directory

Policy: All archival backup data stored off-site must be reflected in a current directory that shows the date when the information was most recently modified and the nature of the information.

Commentary: This policy facilitates the determination of whether certain information is held in archival storage and, if so, its specific location. In some file storage management systems, files are automatically moved between magnetic tapes, disk drives, and other media based on the last date they were accessed. A directory of the files and their locations is automatically generated as a by-product of the system's activity. These directories also may be maintained manually, although both the level of effort and the propensity to make errors is much higher than when they are handled automatically. Such a directory may be useful when there is a business or legal dispute. A directory like this also can be used by the opposing side of a legal case to identify documents that might help the opponent's arguments. A directory like this can also be useful for contingency planning purposes and for insurance claim preparation purposes. This directory will be instrumental in carrying out a purging process.

Related Policies: "Destruction Of Information."

Audience: Technical staff

Security Environments: All

18. Archival Storage Media

Policy: All media on which sensitive, valuable, or critical information is stored for periods longer than six months must not be subject to rapid degradation.

Commentary: This policy specifies the storage media on which important records may be archived. Ideally, the same storage media is used widely throughout an organization, for example, a certain size of magnetic tape cartridge for personal computer backups. If media of different sizes, formats, and types are used, recovery of the information stored thereon may be difficult or even impossible. Examples of acceptable storage media, such as CD-ROM and non-acidic paper for books, may be provided as part of the policy. This policy may be unnecessary when organizations use only the storage media that are suitable for archival purposes. This policy assumes the words "sensitive, valuable, or critical" have already been defined in other documents.

Related Policies: "Four-Category Data Classification," "Five-Category Application Criticality Classification Scheme," "Bag Inspection," and "Preventing Copies Of Sensitive Documents."

Audience: All

Security Environments: All

19. Archival Storage Media Testing

Policy: Critical business information and critical software archived on computer storage media for a prolonged period of time must be tested at least annually.

Commentary: This policy ensures that archival data will be readily recoverable if and when it is needed. If trouble is encountered, then efforts to move the data to more reliable data media should be promptly undertaken. An example of this problem involves information stored on magnetic tapes that tends to create errors over time. This data might be moved to CD-ROM that is likely to be readable years into the future. This policy also may be instrumental in discovering problems associated with an archival storage site, related procedures, and related software. For example, there may be excessive dust in the storage area, and this may be interfering with the recovery of certain data stored on computer-readable magnetic tapes. If management has not noticed these problems, the policy may bring these to light.

Related Policies: "Archival Storage Media Quality."

Audience: Technical staff

Security Environments: All

20. Archival Storage Media Quality

Policy: The computer data media used for storing sensitive, critical, or valuable information must be high quality and must be periodically tested for reliability.

Commentary: This policy requires that only reliable data storage media be used for backup purposes. Old and worn storage media cannot be relied upon to accurately preserve information. Many larger organizations have their own special-purpose machines that test the media on which information is stored. If these machines indicate that the media has an excessive number of errors, then the media should be removed from the backup. While end users do not generally have the equipment to make thorough tests of data media, they are in a position to notice disk read and write errors and other indications that certain storage media is no longer reliable. This policy assumes the words "sensitive, critical, or valuable" have already been defined in other documents.

Related Policies: "Four-Category Data Classification," "Five-Category Application Criticality Classification Scheme," and "Archival Storage Media Testing."

Audience: All

Security Environments: All

21. Archival Storage Preservation

Policy: Computer media storage procedures must assure that sensitive, critical, or valuable information stored for prolonged periods of time is not lost due to deterioration.

Commentary: This policy requires that management take steps to preserve important data held in archival storage. This policy requires that actions be taken if there is reason to believe that data is deteriorating or will soon deteriorate. This policy may be expanded to include transferring data to current data media. For example, to increase accessibility and preservation, data kept on punched cards may be transferred to magnetic tapes. Data stored on paper that is deteriorating may be moved to more reliable storage media. This policy assumes the words "sensitive, critical, or valuable" have already been defined in other documents.

Related Policies: "Four-Category Data Classification," "Five-Category Application Criticality Classification Scheme," "Archival Storage Media," and "Archival Storage Media Testing."

Audience: Management and technical staff

Security Environments: All

22. Paper Forms Stored Off Site

Policy: Paper forms stored off-site must be tested at least every three months for compatibility with Company X printers, fax machines, and other equipment.

Commentary: This policy ensures that the paper forms that are stored off-site are not forgotten until an emergency or disaster takes place, at which point it may be too late to replace them with forms that will work with the equipment involved. Printed forms are much more difficult to procure than standard printer paper or fax paper. This delay in the procurement process means that special attention is required to forms management. The policy acknowledges that paper forms are perishable, and requires that forms be periodically tested. A visual inspection is not sufficient according to this policy, that actual testing of the forms is required.

Related Policies: "Archival Storage Media Quality" and "Archival Storage Media Quality."

Audience: Technical staff

Security Environments: All

8.04.02 Operator Logs

1. Computer Operator Logs

Policy: All Company X multi-user production systems must have computer operator logs that show production application start and stop times, system boot and restart times, system configuration changes, system errors and corrective actions taken, and confirmation that files and output were handled correctly.

Commentary: This policy ensures that all multi-user production systems have an operator log that can be examined to assist with problem resolution efforts. Logs can also be instrumental with investigations should there be a fraud, embezzlement, sabotage, industrial espionage or related incidents. Logs can additionally provide management with assurance that operators are properly following instructions. This assurance is important because operators often have the power to do some damage. The details included in an operations log could be dropped from the policy and replaced with the words "operational details specified by the manager of Computer Operations." The latter approach permits these details to be changed without the need to modify the policy. This approach permits different logging requirements for different operating systems. Turning a log on or off could be considered a reconfiguration of the system, and so was not specifically mentioned in the policy. This policy is relevant to local area network servers, Internet commerce servers, intranet servers, and other multi-user production systems.

Related Policies: "Business Production Information Updates."

Audience: Technical staff

Security Environments: Medium and high

2. Computer Operator Log Review

Policy: All Company X multi-user production systems logs must be regularly reviewed by the Computer Operations manager or another technical specialist designated by the Information Systems manager.

Commentary: This policy is intended to ensure that operators are following documented procedures and that they are held accountable for their actions with production systems. If the logs are recorded, but never reviewed, they will be much less effective as a deterrent against abusive behavior by operators. Likewise, without regular reviews, some problems will come to management's attention only when they become so severe that they demand immediate responses. The reviewer of the logs should not also be a computer operator. The need to designate someone to review the logs becomes apparent in the distributed computing environment. In this environment, there may be no Computer Operations

manager, and without a designated reviewer of the logs, this job may be ignored. A policy is often needed because this task is frequently abandoned in favor of more pressing work.

Related Policies: "System Log Review" and "Computer Operator Logs."

Audience: Management and technical staff

Security Environments: Medium and high

8.04.03 Fault Logging

1. Problem Reporting

Policy: A formal problem management process must be in place to record the problems, reduce their incidence, and to prevent their recurrence.

Commentary: This policy requires that users be able to determine the effects that certain problems have on their data and the quality of service they receive. Only with a good understanding of these problems can users properly appreciate the value of the service they receive and the integrity of the data they use for decision-making. Another intention of this policy is to

require that a problem management system be established and operational. Problem management systems can be important tools in the reporting and resolution of information security problems such as virus infestations and unauthorized system use.

Related Policies: "External Violation Reporting," "Violation And Problem Reporting," and "Preventive Maintenance."

Audience: All

Security Environments: All

8.05.01 Network Controls

1. Trusted Host Relationships

Policy: Unless Information Security management has approved in writing, Company X staff must not enable any trusted host relationships between computers connected to the Company X internal network.

Commentary: This policy notifies system and security administrators that they must not use trusted host relationships between computers connected to the Company X internal network. These systems permit a user to log into one machine, then access the files remotely stored on another. If a hacker were to compromise one of two machines that had this enabled, the hacker would be able to sabotage or use both of those machines without any additional effort. It is more secure to have users log into each of these systems separately.

Related Policies: "Shared Directory Systems" and "Malfunctioning Access Control."

Audience: Technical staff

Security Environments: All

2. Security Configuration

Policy: Configurations and set-up parameters on all hosts attached to the Company X network must comply with in-house security policies and standards.

Commentary: This policy states that all security, system, and network administrators, and any other workers charged with administering systems security must abide by internal security management policies and standards. Often these administrators do things their own way, perhaps inadvertently opening an unauthorized access pathway to connected machines. This policy may seem unnecessary, but there is merit to stating this idea in writing, perhaps giving management something to use when attempting to get administrators to abide by Company X policies and standards.

Related Policies: "Systems Development Conventions" and "Corporate Code Of Conduct."

Audience: Technical staff

Security Environments: All

3. External Network Interfaces

Policy: Company X systems designers and developers must restrict their usage of external network interfaces and protocols to those that have been expressly approved by Information Security management.

Commentary: This policy prevents system designers and developers from writing software that employs new interfaces and protocols for which the security has not yet been proven to be robust, reliable, and operationally manageable. The policy also stops these people from using questionable interfaces and protocols that are employed by packaged software that the organization has purchased, rented, or leased. Use of new interfaces or protocols, or even old interfaces or protocols that are obscure and infrequently encountered, subjects the organization to a variety of unknown vulnerabilities. The more common interfaces and protocols have at least been closely examined, subjected to determined attacks, fixed and patched, and widely tested. This policy minimizes the number of interfaces and protocols only to reliable and generally-accepted alternatives. A side effect of this policy is the promotion of internal network interface and protocol standardization, which facilitates the establishment of centralized network management systems. The policy deliberately refrains from saying anything about the Internet, so it is equally applicable to other types of external networks such as the public switched dial network.

Related Policies: "Systems Interfacing External Networks" and "Operating System User Authentication."

Audience: Technical staff

Security Environments: All

4. Scanning Remote Connections

Policy: Company X must routinely scan the personal computers connected to its networks for viruses while using approved and licensed software while monitoring the activity generated from these systems.

Commentary: This policy notifies remote users that Company X has and uses remote scanning and monitoring software. Many users are not aware that such software exists or that their employer is using such software to monitor the computer they are using at a remote location. This policy alerts users to this possibility and warns them that Company X staff will be examining the contents of, and configuration of, their systems. In an indirect way, the policy discourages personal use, or use for any purpose that might be frowned upon by Company X management. This policy permits examination of browser cache files, the browser history file showing web sites visited, and files stored on a hard drive. This policy assumes that only computers issued by Company X may connect to its internal network. If another approach prevails at the environment, then the policy may be modified.

Related Policies: "Electronic Mail Content Monitoring" and "Sales Department Electronic Mail."

Audience: End users

Security Environments: Medium and high

5. Internet Traffic Control

Policy: Company X must monitor Internet traffic without blocking or filtering web sites visited by workers or censoring transmissions sent or received.

Commentary: This policy notifies users that their Internet traffic is being monitored. Legally, notice such as this is required in a number of jurisdictions if management is going to use logging information for disciplinary purposes. The policy does not require any particular software package to monitor Internet traffic, nor does it require any additional staff to do this work. The policy only says that management will monitor traffic. In that respect, the policy is a deterrent more than anything else. Users are free to surf to any site they wish on the Internet, but abusive conduct will be dealt with through disciplinary measures. This policy, if used without details of what constitutes abusive conduct, probably could not be used as the sole justification for terminating someone. The policy is more suitably used as the first step with efforts to train users to attend to their work, and to not be distracted by non-work web sites, special-interest news groups, music radio stations, and other services available on the Internet.

Related Policies: "Monitoring Internet Activity" and "Internet Content Labels."

Audience: End users

Security Environments: All

6. Cookies And Web Bugs

Policy: Before cookies or web bugs are used on any Company X Internet web or commerce site, a compelling need to gather private data must be presented to and approved by the Information Security management committee.

Commentary: This policy prevents privacy invasions that are not intended by management. In some organizations, technical staff establish web-based systems that perform functions that management does not understand, and never expressly authorized. This policy ensures that cookies and web bugs, both of which have a bad reputation in the privacy advocate community, will only be used if absolutely necessary. The organization should also disclose the use of these technologies if it is going to use them. Both cookies and web bugs can be invisible to users, although more recent browsers can be configured to ask users whether they will accept a cookie from a particular site. Many sites place cookies on user machines or display web bugs on behalf of third-party marketing organizations, and these cookies or web bugs can be used to trace and later report on user activities.

Related Policies: "Internet Cookies And Web Bugs" and "Cookies For Automatic Log On."

Audience: Technical staff

Security Environments: All

7. Concealing Information Transmission

Policy: Information that is sensitive, may be used by adversaries, and is readily available in readable form over public channels must be slightly modified to conceal its true high-integrity nature.

Commentary: This policy delineates the mechanism to provide information that is useful to the public and others, but not of such a high quality that it could be used by adversaries. Consider satellite-provided clock and global positioning system broadcasts as an example. Military satellites may have so precisely defined these signals that a foreign power could use this information to guide nuclear missiles. So the encrypted version of these signals can be made available only to military systems probably with encrypted padding so as to disguise the important information from extraneous information. Yet the public may need access to this information, for example to guide boats and airplanes.

The solution is a slightly modified version that can be made available in a readable form for these public constituencies. Although this policy is most relevant to military and government systems, the notion also may be applicable to commercial interests. Commercial organizations may consider this approach when trying to come to a workable solution for those circumstances where information must be kept confidential, but must also be disclosed. It may be appropriate in some instances to make available only summaries of such sensitive information.

Related Policies: "Information Collection Restrictions," "Encrypted Message Protection," and "Internet Information Reliability."

Audience: Technical staff

Security Environments: Medium and high

8. Network Central Point Of Failure

Policy: Management must design Company X communications networks so that no single point of failure could cause network services to be unavailable.

Commentary: This policy guides systems designers, network technicians, and others so that they may build the types of systems desired by management. Recent high-publicity failures of the phone system have highlighted the dependence of organizations on their networks. This policy implies that the internal department dealing with telecommunications should look into the use of two long distance carriers, temporary microwave links to be employed if land lines are down, and any other redundant telecommunications alternative. While not immediately realizable in many organizations, this policy serves as an objective to which the organization aspires. The term "unavailable" was used in the policy rather than "disrupted." If part of an internal network goes down, one can expect some temporary performance problems, but for most businesses, the real issue is unavailability, not performance degradation. The results of a recent risk assessment may indicate otherwise, in which case a change in wording would be appropriate.

Related Policies: "Multiple Carriers."

Audience: Technical staff

Security Environments: All

9. Multiple Carriers

Policy: Management must design Company X communications systems so that critical communications may immediately be sent through multiple long distance carriers over physically diverse routes.

Commentary: Several major failures of long distance carrier phone lines have demonstrated that, for many organizations, it is wise to have two long distance carriers. This policy provides definitive management guidance to those responsible for communication system management. The policy covers both voice and data networks, and that it only applies to critical communications. The policy assumes the existence of another policy that defines the word "critical."

Related Policies: "Four-Category Data Classification" and "Network Central Point Of Failure."

Audience: Technical staff

Security Environments: All

10. Internet Domain Name Registration

Policy: Payments and paperwork for Internet domain name registrations for all of Company X official sites must be handled in a timely manner and promptly confirmed by the Telecommunications manager.

Commentary: This policy prevents unnecessary interruptions in Internet web site and commerce site activity. A number of large and well-known organizations have recently had their sites go down for significant periods of time because they have not paid their bills in a timely manner. Many companies apparently do not believe that a registration authority will terminate the network router listings for their web and commerce sites just because payment is late, but this is now happening.

Related Policies: "Equipment Maintenance," "Internet Domain Name," and "Preventive Maintenance."

Audience: Technical staff

Security Environments: All

11. Integrity Assessment Tools

Policy: All Internet-connected systems used for production purposes must employ integrity assessment tools that compare hashes or digital signatures from critical files to hashes or digital signatures maintained on an off-line system on a daily basis.

Commentary: This policy requires Internet-connected systems to have a file integrity assessment system that detects changes in critical files. The policy assumes that hackers, disgruntled former employees, competitors, and other intruders will get through a firewall and other security measures. This next line of defense can detect file changes and trigger an investigation, not just the restoration of the approved versions of various files. This approach will not work for files that change a great deal. It works only for files that are relatively static, such as system configuration files. The use of an off-line system prevents intruders from changing the hashes and digital signatures held in the reference machines. An integrity assessment system can be used to detect those occasions when systems developers or technical support staff has made changes without proper authorization to do so.

Related Policies: "Removal Of Logs From Internet-Accessible Computers" and "System Integrity Checking."

Audience: Technical staff

Security Environments: All

12. Network Message Protection Services

Policy: When providing computer-networking services, Company X must not provide message protection services.

Commentary: This policy is for subscribers who use the Company X network and other external parties with which Company X communicates over its network. In some instances, this policy or a derivative thereof may be relevant to those organizations supporting an Internet host that forwards mail or provides services to the larger Internet community. The policy limits Company X responsibilities and liabilities for providing security measures. While the implementation of appropriate security measures would be desirable, this policy is at least better than permitting users to hold onto their erroneous notions that some sort of security or privacy is provided. However, if encryption or other security facilities are provided on the network, the policy will need to be embellished to reflect that fact. A statement that it is the user's responsibility to provide encryption or other protection measures if the nature of the information involved so warrants may follow the policy.

Related Policies: "Protection Of Information" and "Third-Party Information Security Responsibilities."

Audience: End users

Security Environments: All

13. Internal Network Addresses

Policy: The internal system addresses, configurations, and related system design information for Company X networked computer systems must be restricted such that both systems and users outside the Company X internal network cannot access this information.

Commentary: This policy prevents hackers and other unauthorized parties from obtaining information about the Company X internal network and connected systems. The focus of this restriction is that attacks will be made significantly more difficult if this information is not readily obtainable. The more that an attacker knows about internal configurations the greater the chances that he or she will be able to obtain unauthorized entry. With many Internet firewalls, internal electronic mail address information is shared with machines outside the network, inadvertently revealing a target for future attacks. A number of firewalls provide network address translation as a way to increase security. When these translation services are used, the electronic mail address shared with outsiders is different than the address used on internal networks. This firewall feature supports the policy. This policy also requires that system administrators responsible for firewalls establish access control restrictions such that commands like PING cannot be used by external parties to gather information on machines connected to the internal network. This policy makes an assumption that Company X employs external network connections.

Related Policies: "Systems Documentation Release" and "Release Of Organization Information."

Audience: Technical staff

Security Environments: All

14. Network Domains

Policy: All large networks crossing national or organizational boundaries must have separately-defined logical domains, each protected with suitable security perimeters and access control mechanisms.

Commentary: This policy requires network management staff to review access controls on large networks such as wide area networks. While each logical domain need not include a separate access control mechanism, management needs to justify this decision. Large networks often permit users to roam all over the network without encountering any barriers whatsoever.

Many network system designers adopt the no-restrictions approach because it is easier to establish and maintain a network such as this. The logical domains referred to in the policy might be organizational units, activities, or locations. The barriers may be implemented with communications front-ends, routers, gateways, firewalls, modem pools with dynamic passwords, and other network components that include access controls. The most common method used to restrict access to parts of a network is passwords, although other mechanisms like encryption can also be employed.

Related Policies: "Dial-Up Connections," "Information Dissemination," and "Positive Identification For System Usage."

Audience: Technical staff

Security Environments: All

15. Intrusion Detection Systems

Policy: All Internet-connected multi-user computers must be running an intrusion detection system approved by the Information Security department.

Commentary: This policy ensures that those systems that are reachable through the Internet are protected with automated tools to immediately detect attacks, whether these attacks are successful or not. An intrusion detection system (IDS) monitors user activity and matches this activity against a database of known attack methods. If there is a match, an IDS will immediately notify system administrators. This permits immediate response, such as isolating a system from an internal network and disabling certain user IDs. There are less expensive alternatives that do not provide immediate notification, but indicate what has been modified by an attacker. It is up to the Information Security department to determine which of these tools will be suitable for the organization adopting the policy. The scope of the policy could be widened if the words "multi-user" were deleted, in which case personal computers and workstations would be within the scope of the policy.

Related Policies: "System Log Review" and "Override Facility Logs."

Audience: Technical staff

Security Environments: All

16. Host-Based Intrusion Detection Systems

Policy: A host-based intrusion detection system approved by the Information Security department must be continuously running on all Company X mail servers, web servers, application servers, database servers, and firewalls that are connected to any outside network.

Commentary: This policy specifies which types of machines must have intrusion detection systems (IDS). The IDS must be approved by Information Security management. This policy references host-based IDS, although there is another type called a network-based IDS. A network-based IDS is a dedicated computer positioned next to a firewall, but the positioning and deployment decisions for network-based IDS are left to Information Security working in conjunction with Information Technology network specialists. This policy communicates to system administrators that their systems are vulnerable to attack, and that it is essential that an IDS runs on their systems.

Related Policies: "Remotely-Mirrored Logs" and "System Log Review."

Audience: Technical staff

Security Environments: All

17. Personal Computer and Workstation Firewalls

Policy: All personal computers and workstations that connect to the Internet through dial-up, digital subscriber line, integrated services digital network, cable modem, or similar connections must have their own approved firewalls installed and continuously enabled.

Commentary: This policy protects personal computers that directly connect to an Internet service provider rather than going through a company firewall. While firewalls were not previously thought to be necessary on individually-managed computers, this now is a recommended practice. Hackers, industrial spies, criminals, and others use vulnerability identification software to scan the Internet to identify machines that could be broken into. If an individually-managed computer is not protected with a firewall, it may be directly accessible by other persons on the Internet.

Related Policies: "Internet Access Without Firewalls" and "Dial-Up Connections."

Audience: End users and technical staff

Security Environments: All

18. Internet Firewall Administrator Access

Policy: All Company X Internet-connected firewalls must have back channel access that will permit an authorized administrator to establish a connection in the midst of a distributed denial of service attack.

Commentary: This policy ensures that administrators can gain privileged access to firewalls in the midst of a denial of service attack. If they have only Internet access privileges, the attack may keep them from establishing a connection. If they are locked out, they will have a great deal more difficulty dealing with the attack then underway. This can be especially problematic if these administrators are remotely located from the firewall, or those who need to make a connection at night from home or some other non-work location. If dial-up lines are used for this back channel access, it is important that some extended user authentication technology, for example, dynamic passwords or biometrics, be employed rather than just traditional fixed passwords.

Related Policies: "Web Server Firewalls" and "Disabling Critical Security Components."

Audience: Technical staff

Security Environments: All

19. Internet Commerce Server Firewalls

Policy: All Internet commerce servers including payment servers, database servers, and web servers must be protected by firewalls in a demilitarized zone.

Commentary: This policy protects Internet commerce servers from both users on the Internet and users on an internal network. Multiple firewalls are typically used for this task, and the architecture is generally called a demilitarized zone (DMZ). Firewalls can be used to limit the interactions with the commerce servers to only certain applications such as web surfing. This reduces the chances that hackers and other unauthorized persons are able to compromise these Internet commerce servers. The use of a DMZ does not preclude the authorized transmission of information through a DMZ. This policy uses the concept of isolation to help protect information systems.

Related Policies: "Web Server Firewalls."

Audience: Technical staff

Security Environments: All

20. Public Internet Servers

Policy: Public Internet servers must be placed on subnets separate from internal Company X networks and to which public traffic is restricted by routers or firewalls.

Commentary: This policy ensures that systems installers and administrators do not place public Internet servers on the same network as intranets. If a separate subnet with flow controls is not employed, then the general public may be able to access internal computers, and the likelihood that unauthorized people may gain access to sensitive information is significantly increased. This policy may be suitable for an organization that has several web sites of varying sensitivities. Some of these web sites may require firewalls.

Related Policies: "Internet Commerce Server Firewalls" and "Web And Commerce Server Storage."

Audience: Technical staff

Security Environments: All

21. Dial-Up Connections

Policy: All inbound dial-up lines connected to Company X internal networks or computer systems must pass through an additional access control point that has been approved by the Information Security department.

Commentary: This policy restricts dial-in connections from parties such as customers, salespersons, traveling executives, and technicians working from home. It is highly undesirable for these dial-up users to directly connect with desktop systems in the office, and perhaps gaining access to internal networks. This policy requires that all calls travel through a central access point that the Information Security department has determined is sufficiently secure. At this point, as an alternative to requiring two levels of passwords, some organizations may implement extended user authentication systems. The advantage to using extended user authentication technologies is that users would not be required to log on twice. This approach is consistent with the notion of single sign-on. A sentence explaining this option could be added to the policy provided here. Firewalls are a popular way to keep hackers and other intruders out of an organization's systems. In part this policy is an acknowledgement that traditional fixed password systems do not provide adequate security. The scope of this policy could be restricted to multi-user machines that would exclude desktop systems. this change is not recommended, but may be necessary in some environ-

ments. The policy can be rewritten to require all directly connected dial-up systems to be isolated so that no connections to internal networks or other multi-user machines will be permitted. This type of connection could be permitted for testing and other purposes, but only if other systems were not exposed thereby. While this policy includes all types of dial-up connections, the wording could be changed to narrow the scope to only dial-in connections. While the major vulnerability of dial-up connections would be addressed, this narrower scope would be less of a burden on users.

Related Policies: "Systems Accepting In-Coming Dial-Up Calls," "Third-Party Remote Access," "Direct Dial Connections," "Workstation Modems," and "Secret Information System Isolation."

Audience: Technical staff

Security Environments: Medium and high

22. Real-Time External Network Connections

Policy: All in-bound real-time external connections to Company X internal networks or multi-user computer systems must pass through an additional access control point.

Commentary: This policy is intended to ensure that the periphery of an internal network always has strong access control mechanisms. If the boundaries to a network cannot be protected, then the controls inside the network may be superfluous. A firewall is a dedicated-purpose machine that does not run business applications. Its sole purpose is to act as a gatekeeper. This permits unnecessary systems software to be deleted from the system. The absence of these routines means the system is less likely to be compromised. This policy requires all external real-time connections to have a firewall or comparable security system. Because they are not real-time, electronic mail, news feeds, and other store-and-forward network services do not require a firewall. Use of separate machines as firewalls means that security-related systems administration staff can make errors in the access control systems for internal computers without permitting the world to get onto the organization's network. This policy has a broader scope than the Internet. For example, it also applies to value added networks and dial-up lines.

Related Policies: "Positive Identification For System Usage" and "Network Computer Access Control."

Audience: Technical staff

Security Environments: All

23. Firewall Configuration

Policy: All Company X firewalls connecting to the Internet must be configured so that every Internet service is disabled by default, with only those services enabled that have been specifically approved in writing by Information Security management.

Commentary: This policy prevents system administrators from providing responsive customer service that compromises security. Administrators or whoever is managing firewalls, must obtain permission for any proposed new service. Certain services generally are deemed too risky unless additional control measures are adopted. If an organization were to permit all services through a firewall by default, this would be likely to create a chaotic computing environment that would be difficult to secure. This policy does not apply to intranet firewalls.

Related Policies: "Malfunctioning Access Control" and "Information Dissemination."

Audience: Technical staff

Security Environments: All

24. Firewall Computers

Policy: All firewalls used to protect the Company X internal network must run on separate dedicated computers that serve no other purpose.

Commentary: This policy enhances the security of deployed firewalls by reducing the chances that hackers will compromise them. This policy uses the notion of simplicity to help ensure that firewalls will not be defeated through other applications that run on the same machine. If firewalls serve other purposes, other avenues of attack will exist that could be exploited by intruders. For example, if a firewall acted as a mail server, it may be compromised through a mail software bug. The use of a dedicated firewall is also desirable because firewalls have different design objectives than other machines. Having a dedicated purpose machine ensures that unnecessary software like compilers can be removed without jeopardizing the functionality of the firewall. The relatively low cost of hardware makes this policy both feasible and a good practice.

Related Policies: "Removal Of Software."

Audience: Technical staff

Security Environments: All

25. Firewall Configuration Changes

Policy: Firewall configuration rules and permissible service rules must not be changed unless the permission of the Information Security department has been obtained.

Commentary: This policy prevents unauthorized modifications of firewall rules that could jeopardize the security of an organization's internal network. For example, a system administrator may be responding to a user's complaint and may open up a new service through the firewall. In the process he or she may also open up the internal network to hacker intrusions. This policy establishes firewall configuration rules and service rules as relatively fixed, not something that a single administrator can change at their own discretion. Because firewalls are the point of entry to an internal network, it is imperative that their configuration and permissible services be strictly controlled. Because the Information Security department in many organizations does not directly administer firewalls, this policy keeps some control with the Information Security department instead of turning it over to system administrators.

Related Policies: "Firewall Computers" and "Internet Access."

Audience: Technical staff

Security Environments: All

26. Internet Connections

Policy: All connections between Company X internal networks and the Internet or any other publicly-accessible computer network must include an approved firewall and related access controls.

Commentary: This policy is intended to prevent departments, divisions, and other organizational units from establishing their own connections to the Internet or any other external computer network. Some organizations lack a central authority to coordinate network security across the organization. As a result, it is common for separate organizational units to establish their own connections to the Internet. This policy mandates a standard way to make connections between internal networks and external networks. Consistency in network access controls is absolutely essential if effective security is going to be achieved. These connections may later be exploited by outsiders to gain unauthorized access to internal networks. This policy can be supplemented with a clarifying sentence indicating that dial-up connections from a stand-alone personal computer are permissible.

Related Policies: "In-Bound Internet Access," "Third-Party Remote Access," "Network Domains," "Single Sign-On," "Workstation Modems," and "Secret Information System Isolation."

Audience: Technical staff

Security Environments: All

27. Shared Directory Systems

Policy: The use of shared directory systems on any Company X computer that is Internet connected or directly reachable through the Internet must be approved by Information Security management.

Commentary: This policy limits the damage that hackers and other intruders can do if they compromise the security of one computer that is accessible through the Internet. If a shared directory system were used, then the work of these intruders would be made significantly easier. Without a shared directory system, intruders must break-into each system individually. This policy assumes that fixed passwords or other access controls differ from one machine to another. If they are all the same, then this policy only makes work for system administrators. The policy pertains to general-purpose user IDs, not to anonymous users and automatic forms that strictly limit what a user can do through the Internet. This policy limits the places in a network where single sign-on systems may be deployed, even though users like them because they save time and effort.

Related Policies: "Internet Connection Approval" and "Trusted Host Relationships."

Audience: Technical staff

Security Environments: All

28. Network Connections with Outside Organizations

Policy: The establishment of a direct connection between Company X systems and computers at external organizations, through the Internet or any other public network must be approved by the manager of Information Security.

Commentary: Firewalls connected to the Internet have the ability to define a protected channel that permits individuals in one organization to go through the Internet and securely access computers in another organization. While this may be useful in certain circumstances, such as a joint-venture project, it also introduces additional security risks. This policy requires that users obtain approval of Information Security management or some other person responsible for information security before they establish such connections. Before approving such connections, the manager of Information Security must determine who will be able to access Company X systems, what information on Company X systems will be available, what logging systems will track the activity, what the business need is for this connection. Information Security also can include if there is another way that the desired productivity can be achieved without introducing additional information security vulnerabilities.

Related Policies: "Third-Party Remote Access," "Network Domains," "Single Sign-On," "Workstation Modems," and "Secret Information System Isolation."

Audience: End users and technical staff

Security Environments: All

29. Communication Line Changes

Policy: Workers and vendors must not make arrangements for, or actually complete the installation of voice or data lines with any carrier, if they have not obtained approval from the director of the Telecommunications department.

Commentary: This policy ensures that only previously approved changes in communication lines are actually installed. Establishing unauthorized communication paths can significantly compromise the security of Company X systems. Unauthorized lines can provide hackers with avenues of attack that are not properly secured. The policy ensures that all lines are in compliance with existing access control requirements. This policy is relevant to personal computers and workstations, many of which have unauthorized modems attached to them. If there is no additional security for these systems, anyone may be able to dial-up into these systems using the public switched telephone network. This may permit an intruder to access a connected internal network. Some organizations may wish to expand the policy to make specific mention of such modems. Like some other aspects of computer and communication security, there are a number of things that should be done on a centralized basis, for example, establishing communication paths and developing security policies. The words in this policy referencing approval by the Telecommunications department could be replaced by approval by the Information Security department.

Related Policies: "Implementing Multi-User Systems," "System Interconnection," and "Workstation Modems."

Audience: End users and technical staff

Security Environments: All

30. Network Connection Configuration

Policy: All internal networks must be configured such that they can prevent or detect attempts to connect unauthorized computers.

Commentary: This policy prevents intruders from connecting unauthorized computers to an internal network. Even if an intruder is not immediately able to gain access to an authorized internal computer, the fact that an unauthorized machine is on the internal network may permit it to engage in various attacks. These attacks include masquerading through Internet protocol spoofing and clear text password interception through packet sniffing. This policy dictates the use of secure hubs, encrypted intranet communications, or similar technologies that can be used to block all unauthorized machines from the network, or at least detect their presence. The detection of an unauthorized computer on an internal network can then be fed into an intrusion detection system, network or problem management system, and get a response form technical staff, such as a computer emergency response team. The use of a policy like this also ensures that a desktop computer standard is adhered to faithfully. Only after a new desktop computer has shown to be consistent with in-house standards will network operations assign an internal address to that machine and permit it to access the internal network.

Related Policies: "Network Ports In Vacant Offices" and "Walk-Up Network Connections."

Audience: Technical staff

Security Environments: Medium and high

31. Intranet Connection Security Criteria

Policy: All computer systems and network segments must meet the security criteria established by Information Security management including, but not limited to, having an acceptable firewall, an acceptable user-authentication system, an acceptable user privilege control system, an established change control process, a clearly-written definition of system management responsibilities, and adequate operational documentation, before it can be connected to the Company X intranet.

Commentary: This policy establishes management's intention to prevent locally-managed systems from connecting to an intranet without the presence of adequate security controls. Permitting unrestricted intranet server or network segment connections could jeopardize the security of other machines on the intranet. Being connected to the intranet is desirable from a corporate perspective, and this policy leverages that desirability to bring remotely managed systems into compliance with some basic security measures. The policy specifies a few of those basic security measures, but others should be added based on specific organizational needs. The policy is a subtle way to help reestablish centralized organization-wide control over information security.

Related Policies: "Connecting Third-Party Networks" and "Internet Connection Approval."

Audience: Technical staff

Security Environments: All

32. External Network Connection Inventory

Policy: The Information Security department must maintain a current inventory of all connections to external networks including, but not limited to, telephone networks, EDI networks, extranets, and the Internet.

Commentary: This policy gives the Information Security department a complete list of the access points to internal networks. Because hackers most often come in over networks, it is essential that the Information Security department be aware of all of the external access points. The staff in the Information Security department can focus their attention on these access points, ensuring that controls such as firewalls and routers are properly established and operational. Special attention should be paid to business partner access to an organization's network, as this too would be within the scope of this policy. In a more general sense, this policy requires the Information Security department to focus on a certain area. Many organizations are not aware of all the entry points into their networks. When an intrusion occurs, they experience difficulties isolating the entry point used by hackers, industrial spies, or other intruders.

Related Policies: "Asset Inventory — Technology" and "Asset Inventory — Information."

Audience: Technical staff

Security Environments: All

33. Providing Public Network Services

Policy: Prior to utilizing public networks to provide network services to subscribers, Company X legal counsel must assess the extent and nature of the liabilities involved, and top management must expressly accept these risks.

Commentary: Involvement as a message forwarding node on the Internet, as certificate authority, as an encryption key notarization center, as an encryption key distribution point, or some other provider of information services may open Company X up to risks that they had not previously considered. Company X could be liable if a fraud was perpetrated using Company X systems or if Company X systems are used by criminals to store stolen credit card data. This policy prevents Company X personnel from volunteering Company X facilities until the risks and other responsibilities have been fully identified and accepted by top management.

Related Policies: "Message Disclaimer."

Audience: End users and technical staff

Security Environments: All

34. Computer-Related Access Numbers

Policy: Information regarding access to Company X computer and communication systems, such as dial-up modem phone numbers, is considered confidential and must not be posted on the Internet, listed in telephone directories, placed on business cards, or otherwise made available to third parties without the advance written permission of the Information Systems department director.

Commentary: This policy prevents system access information from falling into the hands of unauthorized parties, who may then use it to break into Company X systems. Hackers can discover such information using publicly-available sources. Organizations should make this difficult by withholding this information. Security-conscious organizations may wish to extend this policy to include user IDs and similar contact information, although this will make inter-organizational communications more difficult. For these organizations, it may be sufficient to prohibit the printing of this information on business cards, at the same time permitting the involved persons to disclose it to specific outsiders on a case-by-case basis. For most organizations, however, documented exceptions are necessary.

Related Policies: "Telephone Books," "Disclosure Of Information System Controls," "Bank Account Numbers," and "Logon Banner Information."

Audience: End users and technical staff

Security Environments: All

35. Dial-Up Number Changes

Policy: Company X dial-up computer communications telephone numbers must be changed at least annually.

Commentary: This policy is intended to make it more difficult for hackers and other unauthorized parties to locate Company X computer communication numbers. Hackers frequently trade such information, which means that over time an increasing number of individuals will know the particulars about access to an organization's systems. Changing dial-up numbers periodically can be considered much like changing passwords and encryption keys. At the very least, it will stop many types of unauthorized access that had up to that point in time gone unnoticed. Beyond hackers and industrial spies, in many instances covert unnoticed usage also can be carried out by former employees. The time frame mentioned in the policy can be changed without significantly altering the impact of the policy. Many organizations may find this policy disruptive to normal operations, and therefore a clear assessment of the time and effort required to make adjustments to the new telephone numbers should be performed before the policy is adopted. Some organizations consider the impact of changed phone numbers to be too damaging to user and customer relations, and so this policy is unacceptable to them. There are other ways to compensate for not changing the dial-up number, for example, use of dynamic passwords.

Related Policies: "Production Systems Change Documentation" and "Required Password Changes."

Audience: Technical staff

Security Environments: High

36. Dial-Out Connections

Policy: All users establishing dial-out connections from Company X offices must have their identities authenticated prior to establishing outbound calls and must utilize the dedicated outbound modem pool.

Commentary: This policy prevents hackers and other unauthorized parties from establishing connections through multiple computers on different networks in an effort to thwart attempts to trace the call or log its activity. Hackers, industrial spies, and other unauthorized users are utilizing this technique to conceal their activities. This policy ensures that hackers cannot dial out if they have already broken into the systems at Company X. This policy permits the organization to define who it will authorize to establish outbound dial-up computer connections. Without an access control mechanism on a modem pool, any process to restrict such access will be ineffective. Restrictions on who can dial out can be used to reduce the chances that internal workers would send confidential or proprietary information though a dial-up connection, assuming they do not have Internet access. The policy supports the use of a charge back system that allocates the costs of placing long-distance calls to specific departments, individuals, or projects. The standard practice is to authenticate only inbound dial-up users, but that this policy goes beyond that to provide another layer of protection. An exception to this policy may be made for conference rooms or reception areas, where visitors with portable computers can make outbound connections or where analog public switched dial network ports may be provided. This exception will not in any way compromise the security provided by the policy because these portable computers are not connected to internal networks the way desktop units of employees typically are. This policy is deliberately vague about the ways to definitively authenticate user identities, which often requires the Information Security department to define exactly what these words mean. The technology to support definitive authentication may in fact change over time without the need to rewrite this policy.

Related Policies: "Third-Party Remote Access" and "Dial-Up User Authentication."

Audience: Technical staff

Security Environments: All

37. Cable Modems

Policy: Cable modems must not be used for any Company X business communications unless a firewall and a virtual private network are employed on the involved computers.

Commentary: Cable modems provide a fast alternative to dial-up lines, but also have a security deficiency that permits others in the local subnet to examine the activities of the involved user. This can result in the disclosure of data flowing over the cable modem connection. Speed advantages available with cable modems can be achieved if a firewall and a virtual private network (VPN) are used. No similar problems have been discovered for Digital Subscriber Line or Integrated Services Digital Network, although requiring a firewall and a VPN circuit is advisable for these technologies as well. These technologies may be useful for telecommuters when they make connection to a computer through the Internet.

Related Policies: "Personal Computer and Workstation Firewalls" and "Dial-Up User Authentication."

Audience: End users and technical staff

Security Environments: All

38. Dial-Up Calls Modem Configuration

Policy: All Company X dial-up modems must not answer in-coming calls until the fourth ring.

Commentary: This policy prevents the disclosure of the modem telephone numbers to people who may wish to gain unauthorized access. This policy imposes a slight delay on dial-in callers, yet also is likely to keep these lines off modem line lists circulated in the underground computer hacker community. Automated dialing programs search for telephone numbers with connected computer modems. They often move on to the next number if no answer is provided after a few rings.

Related Policies: "Password Structure" and "Dial-Up Password Attempts."

Audience: Technical staff

Security Environments: All

39. Telnet Connection Passwords

Policy: Users must not establish Telnet connections using traditional fixed passwords over the Internet on Company X computers unless these connections are established using dynamic passwords or some other approved extended user authentication technology.

Commentary: This policy prevents fixed passwords from being intercepted over the Internet and replayed later to gain unauthorized access to Company X systems. With appropriate surveillance devices readily available, it is straightforward for intruders to automatically capture passwords moving over the Internet. These attacks can be thwarted with dynamic password systems, and other extended user authentication technologies like voiceprints and user typing patterns. This policy is also intended to notify technical staff about the privileges that should be permitted through a firewall or other Internet connection devices.

Related Policies: "In-Bound Internet Access" and "Dial-Up User Authentication."

Audience: End users and technical staff

Security Environments: All

40. Active Content Screening

Policy: All inbound applets containing active content must be automatically removed by a firewall.

Commentary: This policy prevents damage to users' computers and information. The types of damage include hard disk erasure and other events that one would customarily see when a malicious virus contaminated a system. Active content programs on the Internet are increasingly being used to circumvent existing access controls and to cause serious damage. To prevent such problems, some organizations are prohibiting all inbound active content even though it may be used on their intranet. This approach, involving screening inbound content at the firewall level eliminates user choices, and achieves an overall higher level of security than any approach that depends on user actions. Organizations may consider this policy to be too strict.

Related Policies: "Java Program Execution" and "Disabling Java."

Audience: Technical staff

Security Environments: All

41. Internet Access

Policy: All Internet access using computers in Company X offices must be routed through a firewall.

Commentary: This policy prevents users from deliberately or unwittingly circumventing the controls supported by a firewall. These controls include the ability to screen downloaded files for viruses, scan outbound files for keywords indicating sensitivity, bar the connection with certain web sites, log the user's activity, and block the downloading of active content. If users wish to access the Internet through an Internet service provider, they may do so but not with Company X equipment. The policy is restricted to computers in Company X offices because telecommuters and mobile computer users cannot practically abide by the requirements of this policy.

Related Policies: "Internet Access Without Firewalls."

Audience: End users and technical staff

Security Environments: All

42. Direct Internet Connections

Policy: In-house production information systems must not be directly connected to the Internet, but instead must connect with a commerce server, a database server, or some other intermediate computer that is dedicated to Internet business activity.

Commentary: This policy limits the damage that a hacker can do if he or she breaks into a Company X computer accessible through the Internet. Some organizations these days are directly connecting their production systems to the Internet. This practice is not recommended because if the machine were compromised, all the production data on that machine would be at risk. If a hacker damaged that production machine, then all production activity normally processed by that system would be stopped. This policy reflects good practice for Internet commerce, and given the low cost of computers, it does not impose a heavy financial penalty on the organization adopting it. To be more effective, the policy could state that the intermediate computer must have another operating system or another access control mechanism than the attached production computer.

Related Policies: "Network Connections with Outside Organizations" and "Internet Business Arrangements."

Audience: Technical staff

Security Environments: Medium and high

43. Publicly-Modifiable Directories

Policy: All publicly-modifiable directories on Company X Internet-connected computers must be reviewed and cleared each evening.

Commentary: This policy prevents Company X computers from being used as a free staging-point for the exchange of illegal, immoral, abusive, or personal information. There are a number of cases where hackers have used publicly-modifiable directories on Internet-connected machines to store the types of information mentioned in this policy. This policy is also desirable because it prevents Company X from unwittingly being named as an accomplice to a crime, or the provider of a controversial and high-visibility computer system. The procedures to support this policy can be automated through command scripts, so the policy's implementation need not be expensive.

Related Policies: "Non-Business Use Of Organization Information."

Audience: Technical staff

Security Environments: All

44. Wireless Networks

Policy: Wireless networks used for Company X transmissions must always be configured to employ encryption.

Commentary: This policy prevents hackers, industrial spies, disgruntled former employees, and other adversaries from being able to intercept the wireless transmissions of Company X. Without encryption, these adversaries would be able to passively wiretap and perhaps obtain fixed passwords, machine addresses, and other information that would be used to attack Company X systems. Wireless networks permit adversaries to attack Company X systems remotely. This policy dictates that encryption be involved for high-speed microwave transmissions, that in many cases have not traditionally been encrypted.

Related Policies: "Cordless Or Cellular Telephones" and "Wireless Transmissions Of Secret Information."

Audience: Technical staff

Security Environments: All

45. Wireless Network Gateways

Policy: Company X wireless network gateways must always be configured so that they employ firewalls to filter communications with remote devices.

Commentary: This policy counters an attack known as address resolution protocol poisoning. This attack permits a hacker or some other intruder to masquerade as though he or she is running an authorized device connected to a particular wireless network. This attack permits an intruder to route all traffic through an unauthorized machine. In order to prevent related attacks it is advised that all wireless network gateways employ firewalls.

Related Policies: "Cable Modems" and "Active Content Screening."

Audience: Technical staff

Security Environments: All

46. Systems Interfacing External Networks

Policy: All Company X systems interfacing external networks must be running the latest version of the vendor-supplied operating software.

Commentary: This policy reduces the success that hackers and other third-party attackers have when attempting to use the latest penetration attack method. Some system administrators may postpone upgrading the software on firewalls and other systems that have external interfaces. This is a dangerous approach to security, and will be prevented with this policy. The vendors involved do not always release patches and fixes in sufficient time to prevent major problems, but if an attack method is serious enough the vendors will release patches shortly after vulnerabilities are discovered in order to limit their own liability. The presence of vulnerability identification software on the Internet makes this policy especially important. Such software permits attackers to determine the version of software a particular system is running and the associated vulnerabilities.

Related Policies: "Operating System Versions."

Audience: Technical staff

Security Environments: All

47. Network Security Measures

Policy: Network security measures on Company X production systems must not be backward compatible.

Commentary: This policy prevents a version rollback attack, that can lead to the compromise of the involved control. While backward compatibility is user friendly and desirable from an interconnectivity and interoperability standpoint, it is dangerous from a network security standpoint. If an attacker can get a new version of a control to roll back to a prior version's protocol, then the attacker may be able to take advantage of a prior version's vulnerabilities, even though these same vulnerabilities may have been fixed in the new version. It is exceedingly hard to design a control that is backward compatible just enough to be functional, but at the same time prevent attackers from exploiting vulnerabilities in the prior version. This policy recognizes that difficulty and opts for the more secure approach prohibiting backward compatibility.

Related Policies: "Operating System Versions" and "Systems Interfacing External Networks."

Audience: Technical staff

Security Environments: High

48. Critical Voice and Data Networking Devices

Policy: All business-critical devices supporting the Company X telephone system, intranet, local area networks, and the wide area network must be centralized in dedicated rooms with physical access controls, closed-circuit TV, environmental monitoring systems, and other measures specified by Information Security.

Commentary: This policy denies unauthorized people physical access to voice and data networking devices such as private branch exchanges, hubs, and routers. This will make it significantly more difficult to configure wiretapping devices or sabotage these systems. Because so many people use networking systems, they are a favorite target for saboteurs. The policy also counters the tendency to place these devices throughout an office, subjecting them to a variety of risks including disruptions due to accidental incidents. This policy may increase cabling costs. The policy's scope could be expanded to include all servers or multi-user computers. The policy assumes the word "critical" has been formally defined during contingency planning.

Related Policies: "Securing Computer Or Communications Systems" and "Physical Access Control To Sensitive Information."

Audience: Technical staff

Security Environments: All

8.06 Media Handling and Security

8.06.01 Management of Removable Computer Media

1. Floppy Disks

Policy: All floppy disks used at Company X must be authorized, formatted, and issued only by the Information Technology department.

Commentary: This policy prevents workers from storing sensitive information on floppy disks which is the most portable and most easily-removed data storage media. At most organizations, sensitive information stored on a floppy disk by a work computer will probably be readable on another computer outside of work. This policy makes use of custom encryption software that has been integrated with the floppy disk input and output drivers, such that each time a write-to or read-from floppy disk command is executed, the relevant encryption process is automatically invoked.

These same disks are therefore unreadable by computers outside the organization. If a user wanted to send information to an outside party through floppy disk, the intervention of the Information Technology department would be required. Software could be entirely loaded from the Internet or from CD-ROM because the capacity of floppies is too small for major software packages. Other complimentary controls like outbound electronic mail content filters are recommended if this approach is adopted.

Related Policies: "Media Removal" and "Preventing Copies Of Sensitive Documents."

Audience: End users

Security Environments: High

2. Storing Mixed Classified Information

Policy: Company X workers must not store confidential or secret information with non-sensitive information on floppy diskettes or other removable data storage media.

Commentary: This policy prevents confusion about the proper handling of removable data media such as floppy disks. Because handling procedures differ based on data classification, to commingle different classifications of data would require a disk or other storage media to be handled with the most stringent procedures, which may be needlessly expensive and inconvenient. Another objective of this policy is to minimize costs associated with security. This policy was designed for users of personal computers and workstations, although it is applicable to mainframe computer operators and others who handle data media. This policy assumes that the word "sensitive" has been defined in another policy.

Related Policies: "Multiple Sensitivity Classifications Computer Systems," "Storage Media Data Classifications," and "Four-Category Data Classification."

Audience: End users and technical staff

Security Environments: All

3. Erasure of Sensitive Information

Policy: When sensitive Company X information is erased from a disk, tape, or other reusable data storage media, it must be followed by a repeated overwrite operation to obliterate the sensitive information.

Commentary: With most operating systems, standard disk file delete and erase commands delete the entry in a file allocation table or directory. A notable aspect of using this overwriting process to obliterate sensitive information is that it can be programmed to happen automatically. A command file can be written to scrub data storage media each time that a sensitive file or other object is erased. Some operating systems do this automatically. The user need not be aware of this process. In the absence of an automated approach, users can invoke an approved software utility to handle this process whenever sensitive data is involved. This policy prevents unauthorized disclosure of sensitive information from computer media scavenging, whether the process is handled automatically or by the end users. The automated approach is recommended because users cannot be counted on to consistently complete this task. Commercial packages are available to perform the overwriting process. This technology will not be relevant to WORM storage media, which by its very nature is not reusable. This policy assumes that the term "sensitive" was defined in another policy.

Related Policies: "Four-Category Data Classification," "Customer Log Information," "Private And Identification Information Linkage," and "Transfer Of Sensitive Information."

Audience: All

Security Environments: Medium and high

8.06.02 Disposal of Media

1. Sensitive Information Destruction

Policy: Destruction of sensitive information captured on computer storage media must only be performed with approved destruction methods including shredders or other equipment approved by the Information Security department.

Commentary: This policy provides guidance on the approved methods for destroying sensitive information resident on computer storage media. The best destruction methods are burning, shredding, or some other approach that renders the media unusable. Another technique is a degaussing method that uses electro-magnetic fields to erase data. Degaussing in not relevant to CD-ROMs, magneto-optical cartridges, and other storage media that do not use traditional magnetic recording approaches. Overwriting programs will write repeated sequences of ones and zeros over the information, reducing the chances that it can be recovered. Technical assistance may be needed because overwriting may or may not be acceptable for certain storage media. In organizations with less pressing security needs, one of the less definitive destruction methods may be acceptable. This policy is written for military, diplomatic, and other organizations with very high security needs. The methods mentioned in this commentary that do not destroy the storage media will permit media recycling, saving money and reducing environmental waste. This policy assumes the existence of another policy that defines the term "sensitive information."

Related Policies: "Four-Category Data Classification," "Erasure of Sensitive Information," "Password Generation Materials," "Key Generation Materials," and "Disk Storage Encryption."

Audience: All

Security Environments: Medium and high

2. Hardcopy Disposal

Policy: When disposed of, all secret, confidential, or private information in hardcopy form must be either shredded or incinerated.

Commentary: This policy prevents the scavenging of information by reviewing documents placed in the trash. Scavenging information from the trash is a favorite tactic of hackers, private investigators, industrial spies, military spies, and the police. In many jurisdictions it is both legal and a successful method for gaining important information. In a related standard, many organizations specify the type of shredding required. This policy assumes the existence of a policy that defines the terms "secret, confidential, or private."

Related Policies: "Four-Category Data Classification," "Sensitive Information Retention For Destruction," "Key Generation Material Destruction," and "Sensitive Information Materials."

Audience: All

Security Environments: All

3. Strip Shredders

Policy: Strip shredders must not be used in any Company X facilities.

Commentary: This policy ensures that users are not shredding paper documents and establishing a sense of false security. Although widespread, strip paper shredders can easily be overcome by a determined adversary who has the time to reconstruct original documents. Their widespread use continues in part because they are inexpensive. Instead of strip shredders, organizations should use shredders that produce confetti or some similarly small particles or shreds of paper.

Related Policies: "Sensitive Information Destruction" and "Electronic Mail Message Handling."

Audience: All

Security Environments: Medium and high

4. Secure Information Containers

Policy: Secret information must be immediately destroyed and sensitive information that is to be destroyed must be placed in a designated locked destruction container within Company X offices and never placed in trash bins, recycle bins, or other publicly-accessible locations.

Commentary: This policy guides staff members in the proper disposal and destruction of sensitive materials. Secret information, because it is so sensitive, must be immediately destroyed. This will lessen the risk that someone could break into a locked destruction container, or even steal the container and at another location break into it. The policy assumes that the words "sensitive" and "secret" have been defined in other policies such as a data classification policy. The policy also assumes that approved methods for destruction of secret material have been published.

Related Policies: "Disposal Of Payment Information," "Waste Copies Of Sensitive Information," and "Sensitive Information Retention For Destruction."

Audience: End users

Security Environments: Medium and high

5. Information Destruction Instructions

Policy: All materials in the destruction container must be destroyed according to approved procedures regardless of recycling implications.

Commentary: The security staff members responsible for destroying information contained in destruction containers may be concerned about ecology. They may pick through the trash thinking that certain items need not be destroyed, and that these items can be recycled without harm to Company X. This policy prohibits them from making these decisions. This policy ensures that all information intended for destruction is destroyed. It eliminates a reason why security staff members responsible for destruction might examine information for which they are not authorized to access. This policy would generally only be distributed to security staff members.

Related Policies: "Waste Copies Of Sensitive Information."

Audience: End users

Security Environments: All

6. Sensitive Information Destruction Procedures

Policy: After it becomes no longer needed, all sensitive or valuable Company X information must be securely destroyed using procedures approved by the Information Security department.

Commentary: This policy requires all persons who handle Company X sensitive information to dispose of it in a secure manner. The specific procedures to be used could be specified in a standard or a guideline rather than a policy. This policy assumes the existence of a policy that defines the terms "sensitive or valuable."

Related Policies: "Hardcopy Disposal," "Four-Category Data Classification" and "Key Generation Material Destruction."

Audience: All

Security Environments: All

7. Information Destruction Personnel

Policy: The destruction of sensitive information must be carried out by Company X personnel or a bonded destruction service.

Commentary: This policy ensures that a trusted individual or organization is used for all sensitive information destruction efforts. There have been cases where destruction services did not shred sensitive data, and instead dumped it into a landfill. Others then discovered this sensitive information. To prevent such problems, this policy requires an employee or a destruction service that has gone through a background check and has received insurance. This policy would need to be used in conjunction with other policies stating how the destruction is to be performed.

Related Policies: "Hardcopy Disposal."

Audience: All

Security Environments: All

8. Sensitive Information Destruction Boxes

Policy: All secret, confidential, and private information in any form that is no longer being used or is no longer needed must be placed in designated locked metal boxes until authorized Company X personnel or a bonded destruction service picks it up.

Commentary: This policy ensures that sensitive information will not fall into unauthorized hands on the way to being destroyed. Collections of information waiting for destruction otherwise present an attractive target for industrial spies, nosy employees, and others. The boxes mentioned in the policy look like public mailboxes, and are heavy enough and big enough so that the whole box cannot readily be stolen. To prevent theft of the box, in some cases boxes are chained, bolted, or otherwise secured to the floor or other furniture. This policy assumes that people responsible for disposal will sort the material based on recycling considerations. In some cases it may be advisable to have separate containers for different sensitive materials to be recycled. This policy would ordinarily be used with other policies specifying how information should be destroyed.

Related Policies: "Hardcopy Disposal."

Audience: All

Security Environments: All

9. Sensitive Information Materials

Policy: All materials used in the handling of sensitive information that includes, but is not limited to, carbon paper, photographic negatives, thermal fax transfer films, aborted computer hardcopy output, and unacceptable photocopies, that could be analyzed for sensitive information, must be destroyed in a manner similar to that required for sensitive information.

Commentary: This policy prevents unauthorized persons from gaining access to sensitive information by examining the by-products of sensitive information handling activities. Disposal of these materials in the trash may permit scavenging to recover the information. Many people are not aware that sensitive information could be disclosed in these ways, so a specific notice to look after these by-products is advisable. The list of by-products found in the policy can be expanded to include materials related to the technologies in use at Company X. This policy assumes that the word "sensitive" has been defined in another policy.

Related Policies: "Key Generation Material Destruction," "Hardcopy Disposal," and "Four-Category Data Classification."

Audience: All

Security Environments: Medium and high

8.06.03 Information Handling Procedures

1. Access To Forms

Policy: Access to Company X letterhead stationary, blank checks, and other forms must be available only to those persons with a demonstrable need for such forms.

Commentary: This policy notifies staff that Company X forms can be used to commit fraud and otherwise engage in unauthorized acts. For example, many cases of fraudulent letters of credit have been perpetrated through the use of letterhead stationary. Distinctions about the types of forms that will be restricted may be incorporated into this policy. In addition to a policy such as this, some forms, like printed check stock, should be locked up when not in use.

Related Policies: "User ID Forms."

Audience: Management

Security Environments: All

2. Distribution Of Marketing Materials

Policy: Workers must not use facsimile machines, electronic mail, auto-dialer robot voice systems, or any other electronic communications systems for the distribution of unsolicited advertising material.

Commentary: This policy prevents internal staff from using information distribution technologies for marketing purposes when the recipient has not indicated an interest in Company X products or service. Such cold call solicitations are increasingly met with resistance and anger. In some jurisdictions, these unrequested solicitations could be illegal. This policy preserves the privacy of the public and is a potential image enhancer assuming the policy or information about the existence of the policy is made public. The policy could be extended to the telephone, in which case unrequested calls would be against internal policy. The mail system has been left out of the policy to permit mass mail because it is a commonly-accepted practice.

Related Policies: "Blocking Private Data Usage."

Audience: Management and technical staff

Security Environments: All

3. Disclosure Of Information System Controls

Policy: Workers must not disclose to any persons outside Company X either the information system controls that are in use or the way in which these controls are implemented without the permission of Information Security management.

Commentary: If information about controls is disclosed, outsiders could use this information to reduce the work required to compromise information security systems. Efforts to obtain such information often involve social engineering. In these cases, system attackers often pose as government officials, employees of the same organization, or other authorized persons so as to be credible. Without a policy such as this, users may attempt to be helpful, and thereby unwittingly compromise security. This policy could be expanded with examples of the types of information not to disclose. Some organizations may wish to expand this policy to include physical security matters as well. The policy could additionally be enhanced by adding an exception for external auditors who have been authorized to receive this information by a vice president or another high-ranking manager. This policy is relevant to technical discussions on Internet chat rooms, on Internet discussion groups, on dial-up electronic bulletin boards, and in other public forums. These forums might, for example, cover the details of how to set up a network firewall. It is possible, and often is desirable, for employees to engage in such technical discussions without providing detailed control information about their employer's systems. Department managers may need to instruct users who engage in these types of discussions so that detailed control information is not inadvertently disclosed.

Related Policies: "Public Communications," "Disclosure Of Information System Vulnerabilities," and "Computer-Related Access Numbers."

Audience: End users and technical staff

Security Environments: All

4. Removal Of Sensitive Information

Policy: Sensitive Company X information must not be removed from Company X premises unless there has been prior approval from the information Owner.

Commentary: This policy prevents sensitive information from being removed from Company X locations, which would increase its risk to unauthorized disclosure. The more information stays in one place, the easier it is to track and control. This policy may restrict the activities of telecommuters and employees who wish to take work home with them. If such sensitive information routinely travels over geographically dispersed computer networks, it may be difficult to identify its location at any particular time. If telecommuters are involved, or if information is already frequently exchanged by geographically-dispersed networks, this policy will be difficult to implement and also may be inappropriate. This policy assumes that a data classification system has already been adopted. The word "sensitive" could be replaced by one or several data classification terms used by the organization.

Related Policies: "Information Ownership," "Four-Category Data Classification," "Sensitive Information Removal Log," "Lockable Metal Furniture," and "Recovery Of Organization Property."

Audience: All

Security Environments: Medium and high

5. Secret Information Leaving Offices

Policy: Secret Company X information, no matter what form it happens to take, must not leave Company X offices unless the approval of Information Security management has been obtained.

Commentary: This policy ensures that workers do not take secret information home to work on it, do not carry it with them when they travel on business, or in any other way subject it to unauthorized disclosure away from Company X premises. This is a strict policy that requires the intervention of Information Security management before such transportation takes place. Under this policy, this manager could grant certain exceptions to the policy if the individual uses adequate security measures. These security measures are deliberately not specified in the policy so that they can change over time without the need to change the policy. This policy also provides an opportunity to respond to the risks of each type of secret information with a different set of controls. If the organization is participating in extranets or similar multi-organizational networks, then this policy may be impractical and could be replaced with a policy specifying the ways to protect secret information when it is away from Company X premises.

Related Policies: "Removing Hardcopy Sensitive Information," "Unattended Rooms," and "Bag Inspection."

Audience: End users

Security Environments: High

6. Sensitive Information Removal Log

Policy: All sensitive information removed from Company X premises must be logged with a record of the date, the information involved, and the persons possessing the information.

Commentary: This policy keeps track of all sensitive information that has been taken from Company X premises. Such records will assist with investigations following an unauthorized disclosure. Logging may discourage theft or unnecessary removal of sensitive information by employees. The policy could be changed to specify who is to maintain these records and whether information Owners are to be notified whenever sensitive information leaves Company X premises. The policy deliberately does not make a distinction between hardcopy and other ways to represent the information. To make the policy apply to a smaller proportion of the information at an organization, the word "sensitive" could be replaced with the word "secret." This policy assumes that the information involved has been properly labeled with a sensitivity designation. The policy also assumes that another policy defining the word "sensitive" has been issued.

Related Policies: "Four-Category Data Classification," "Secret Information On Transportable Computers," and "Removal Of Sensitive Information."

Audience: End users and management

Security Environments: All

7. Release Of Computer Storage Media

Policy: Computer storage media that has been used to record secret information must not leave controlled channels until it has been degaussed or overwritten according to the standards published by the Information Security department.

Commentary: This policy establishes the notion of a controlled channel for the custody of secret information. The word "secret" can be replaced with another term indicating the most sensitive type of information. A controlled channel in this context is a conduit for the handling of information that preserves its security. This conduit may involve several people or only one person. Degaussing involves subjecting magnetic storage media such as floppy disks to a strong magnetic field that will then erase the information stored thereon. Overwriting the storage media with repeated sequences of zeros and ones will obliterate the data. The policy fosters thought about confidentiality agreements and encryption.

Related Policies: "Transfer Of Sensitive Information" and "Sensitive Information Destruction."

Audience: End users

Security Environments: Medium and high

8. Areas Containing Sensitive Information

Policy: All Company X offices and other areas where sensitive information is handled must have operational shredders.

Commentary: This policy ensures that the right tools for information destruction are provided to the people who need to use them. Workers are sometimes trained that they must destroy certain sensitive data using specified procedures, but the tools are not provided. Not only does this policy state that shredders must be present, it states that they must be in good working order. The policy counters the massive disclosures that occur when the organization's trash receptacles are searched. This policy is intended to counter industrial espionage and the efforts of other unauthorized parties.

Related Policies: "Waste Copies Of Sensitive Information," "Security Requirements For Telecommuters," and "Disposal Of Payment Information."

Audience: End users

Security Environments: Medium and high

9. Master Copy Of Critical Production Data

Policy: The master copy of critical production data must be stored on one or more production servers and not on desktop machines.

Commentary: This policy ensures that the master copy of critical production data is not stored on desktop machines where it has a high likelihood of not being properly backed-up, protected from unauthorized alteration, and protected from unauthorized disclosure. With such a large part of the business activity in organizations being handled by desktop machines or personal computers, these smaller machines also maintain the master copy of critical information. Production servers will generally have better physical security, more professional systems management, better intrusion detection systems, and other examples of more rigorous security systems. The policy assumes that the organization has taken the time to distinguish critical data from non-critical data, which is a very important activity that should precede all contingency planning efforts.

Related Policies: "Critical Application Servers" and "Production Computer System Location."

Audience: Technical staff

Security Environments: All

10. Disclosure Of Information Modifications

Policy: If information issued by Company X has been modified in any way, the recipients must be notified about the nature of the modification prior to recipient decisions based on such information.

Commentary: This policy ensures that the recipients of information do not make inappropriate decisions about modified information because they did not understand or were unaware of modifications. The policy requires that Information Systems notify users about changes made to information appearing in reports it generates. The policy can be interpreted to apply to internal and external information consumers. The information consumer is in the best position to determine whether certain modifications are material in nature and whether these modifications could affect a decision.

Related Policies: "Labeling Management Decision Data" and "Altered Photographs."

Audience: Management and technical staff

Security Environments: All

11. Employee Contact Information

Policy: All workers must choose a single way to represent their name, address, and other personal information, and must use this consistently for all Company X related matters.

Commentary: This policy prevents improper matching of files that belong to a single employee. For example, one database might have a "S. M. Smith" while another has a "Samuel M. Smith," but the software may not be able to detect the fact that these names pertain to the same person. Improper matching could for example lead to inaccurate reporting. In some respects eliminating the need for this policy, some new software packages are able to detect possible duplicates in mailing lists and similar files. The explanation accompanying the policy should state that it is permissible for workers to change their name and other personal information. Workers just need to consistently represent themselves with new contact information whenever any change occurs.

Related Policies: "Naming Conventions," "Personal Record Integrity," and "Information Integrity Attributes."

Audience: All

Security Environments: All

12. Secret Data Transmission

Policy: All Company X secret data transmitted over any communication network must be encrypted.

Commentary: This policy forbids the transmission of unencrypted secret data over a network where it could be wiretapped. Encryption, also known as encoding or scrambling, conceals data such that unauthorized parties cannot read it. Encryption can also be used to provide an indication that a certain party sent a message and that the message was not modified in transit, most often through digital signatures, which are rendered through encryption. This policy may be supported with an application-level encryption program or a network level encryption facility. The policy does not specify an encryption algorithm, although some organizations choose to put mention of an algorithm in such a policy. This policy is important for small systems such as personal computers, local area networks, client-server systems, and intranets because users are often unaware of the protection that secret data requires. Unless they are notified with a policy such as this, chances are that they will needlessly expose secret data. This policy assumes that a data classification system has already been implemented.

Related Policies: "Four-Category Data Classification," "Standard Encryption Algorithm And Implementation," and "Faxing Sensitive Information — Unencrypted."

Audience: End users and technical staff

Security Environments: Medium and high

13. Transportation Of Secret Data

Policy: All secret data transported in computer-readable storage media must be encrypted.

Commentary: This policy prohibits workers from transporting secret data in computer-readable storage media when this secret data has not been encrypted. Encryption of such media not only conceals the data, it can be used to detect system errors and tampering. When computer storage media goes through airport x-ray machines and is subjected to other magnetic fields en route, there is a chance that certain parts of the data will be erased or altered. If the data is encrypted erasures and alterations can be made immediately evident, depending on the encryption algorithm employed. This policy assumes that a data classification system has already been implemented.

Related Policies: "Four-Category Data Classification" and "Traveling With Secret Information."

Audience: End users and technical staff

Security Environments: Medium and high

14. Secret Information Encryption

Policy: All computerized secret information must be encrypted when not in active use.

Commentary: This policy prevents secret information from being inadvertently disclosed to unauthorized persons. If encrypted data was stored in unencrypted form, it may end up on backup tapes that then might be viewed by unauthorized persons. In this way, standard access controls could be circumvented. For example, personal computers and workstations can employ commercially-available background encryption software packages that are user-transparent. With these packages, all the data on a hard drive is encrypted, but it is automatically decrypted when needed so that applications can use it. After the data is modified or otherwise used by an authorized application program, it is written back to the hard drive in encrypted form. The user's only involvement is the provision of an encryption key at the time the system is booted. This policy assumes that a data classification system has already been implemented.

Related Policies: "Four-Category Data Classification" and "Backup Media Encryption."

Audience: End users and technical staff

Security Environments: Medium and high

15. Disk Storage Encryption

Policy: All data stored on hard disks must be encrypted through user-transparent processes.

Commentary: This policy prevents unauthorized persons from gaining access to Company X confidential or proprietary data. This policy does not require that users or others distinguish between secret and non-secret data. Removing users from the decision-making process can increase security because the chances of an inappropriate decision are decreased. At the same time, encrypting all data will tax computer system resources more than selectively encrypting data, thereby reducing system response time. Because it defines the most effective way to protect data in a distributed computing environment, this policy is particularly relevant for personal computers, workstations, local area networks, intranets, and client-server systems. An alternative to this policy is the use of a degausser to erase sensitive information stored on a computer hard disk before the computer is sent outside an organization for repair.

Related Policies: "Secret Information Encryption," "Storage Of Sensitive Information," "Transfer Of Sensitive Information," and "Sensitive Information Destruction."

Audience: End users and technical staff

Security Environments: Medium and high

16. Downloading Sensitive Information

Policy: Before any Company X secret, confidential, or private information may be transferred from one computer to another, the worker making the transfer must ensure that access controls on the destination computer are commensurate with access controls on the originating computer.

Commentary: This policy requires users to consider the security implications of downloading sensitive information. Downloading of information has been a significant security problem because controls on destination systems can be less stringent than those on the originating system. Downloading can also be a problem because, in many instances, data sensitivity labels are not propagated from one operating system to another. Another intention of the policy is to prohibit the downloading of sensitive information that cannot be adequately protected. In this respect, the policy is a manifestation of the notion that information should be protected in a manner commensurate with its sensitivity, value, and criticality, no matter where the information resides, no matter who handles it, and no matter what form it takes. Downloading can take place over the Internet, through dial-up line, through online service bureau, and by other methods. Although it would imply significant changes in wording, this policy could be expanded to include controls over alphanumeric papers and other forms that the information may take after it is taken off a computer system with access controls. This policy is likely to generate calls to the Information Security department because users will have questions about what the word "commensurate" means at Company X. One way to reduce these inquiries is to employ control categories such as low-, medium-, and high-security systems with a definition of the controls that accompany each category. This policy assumes the words "secret, confidential, or private" have been defined elsewhere.

Related Policies: "Four-Category Data Classification" and "Protection Of Information."

Audience: End users and technical staff

Security Environments: All

17. Downloading Sensitive Information Approval

Policy: Sensitive Company X information must not be downloaded from a multi-user system to a personal computer or a workstation unless a clear business need exists and advance permission from the information Owner has been obtained.

Commentary: Any information that a user of a mainframe, minicomputer, or departmental server can display at the same time can often be captured on a hard drive or floppy disk on a personal computer or a workstation. In the absence of viable generally-available technical controls to take care of this problem, this policy defines acceptable behavior. The intention of the policy is to clearly delineate the circumstances under which workers must not download data. By implication, all other downloading operations are permissible. This policy assumes that the important word "sensitive" has been defined.

Related Policies: "Four-Category Data Classification," "Information Ownership," "Downloading Sensitive Information," and "Downloading Software."

Audience: End users and technical staff

Security Environments: All

18. Returning Long-Distance Calls

Policy: Company X workers must not return regular phone calls or respond to pager phone calls where charges beyond those for normal telephone calls can be assessed, or where the charges will be reversed.

Commentary: Workers should be sensitive to schemes to perpetuate fraud that lure the receiver of a call or a page to return a call resulting in steep per-minute charges. This policy instructs them not to return these calls. The policy could be expanded to include mention of hanging up as soon as they hear that they will be assessed additional charges.

Related Policies: "Collect And Third-Party Bill-To Calls."

Audience: End users and technical staff

Security Environments: All

19. Unusual Phone Operation Requests

Policy: Unusual telephone operation requests, such as a caller asking for an outside line, must be consistently but politely denied and details of the request must be immediately reported to the Telecommunications department manager.

Commentary: This policy prevents outside parties from taking advantage of sophisticated phone system features to get a free outside line. The requests will vary by location and the phone system in use. These connections are useful for hackers who may want to conceal their tracks and have other people pay the bill for their calls. If the Telecommunications manager receives reports about a number of calls with an unusual request, he or she may choose to issue a memo to all staff reminding them about this policy. This policy prevents staff members from being victims of social engineering ploys where the caller at the other end of a phone line impersonates an authorized party.

Related Policies: "Reporting Unauthorized Activity."

Audience: End users

Security Environments: All

20. Personal Telephone Usage

Policy: Company X telephones must not be used for personal purposes, unless the calls cannot be made during off-business hours, in which case, the personal calls must be kept to a reasonable length.

Commentary: This policy clarifies what is acceptable behavior regarding the use of the telephone system for personal purposes. This policy is a practical position reflecting a mix of the strict position that telephones must never be used for personal purposes, and the acknowledgement that workers will need to make necessary personal calls. A more stringent approach would involve prohibition of all personal use unless it relates to personal arrangements. This more stringent policy is focused on reducing telephone expenses, while both versions help increase worker productivity.

Related Policies: "Personal Use Of Computer And Communications Systems," "Personal Use Of Internet," and "Electronic Mail System Usages."

Audience: End users and technical staff

Security Environments: All

21. Long-Distance Personal Telephone Calls

Policy: Company X telephones must not be used to place personal long-distance calls unless the calls are kept to a reasonable length, reported to management, and reimbursed to the company.

Commentary: This policy clarifies the use of Company X telephones for personal purposes, especially for long distance calls. Emphasis on long distance is appropriate because this is where the major expense for personal calls will be found. This policy implicitly permits local personal calls without the need to report or reimburse them. Some organizations may wish to add an additional sentence requiring that employees use a special accounting code to flag personal calls. In this case, a listing of personal calls can later be presented to employees for payment or automatically deducted from their paycheck. Without such an accounting code entered at the time that a call is placed, it will be difficult in many situations to determine which calls were personal and which were business related. The words "reasonable length" are used in the policy to keep the productivity impact of such calls to a minimum.

Related Policies: "Personal Telephone Usage."

Audience: End users

Security Environments: All

22. Internet Information Exchange

Policy: Company X software, documentation, and all other types of internal information must not be sold or otherwise transferred to any non-Company X party for any purposes other than the business purposes expressly authorized by management.

Commentary: This policy is expressly intended to prohibit the unauthorized exchange of inside information through the Internet. Organizations are sometimes surprised to find that their workers have been releasing information that management considered to be confidential. The issuance of a policy about the release of customer information assists management in discovering that customer information may be sold to outsiders by certain employees.

Related Policies: "Software And Data Exchange Agreements," "Internet Posting Of Material," and "Information Security Responsibility."

Audience: End users

Security Environments: All

23. Bank Account Numbers

Policy: Company X disbursement bank account numbers are confidential and must not be disclosed to third parties in any form.

Commentary: Frauds may be easily committed by unauthorized individuals who enter publicly-available bank account numbers on automatic debit request forms. This policy assumes that the organization adopting the policy has both receiving bank accounts or credit accounts that can be placed on forms, such as wire transfer instructions to customers, and disbursement or debit bank accounts. When a policy like this is adopted, organizations should make arrangements to reject all debits to accounts reserved for incoming funds or credit accounts.

Related Policies: "Computer-Related Access Numbers."

Audience: Technical staff

Security Environments: All

24. Security Of Sensitive Information

Policy: All information storage media containing unencrypted sensitive information must be physically secured when not in use.

Commentary: This policy requires all local managers to implement physical security measures or encryption for sensitive information. This policy is particularly relevant to portable, laptop, handhelds and other small personal computers. Because physical security cannot be assured when these systems are moved from building to building, encryption is required. This policy prevents theft of personal computers containing sensitive information. This policy may be expanded to include valuable or critical information.

Related Policies: "Access To Computers and Communications Systems," "Disk Storage Encryption," and "Secret Information In Electronic Mail."

Audience: End users and technical staff

Security Environments: Medium and high

8.06.04 Security Of System Documentation

1. Systems Documentation Release

Policy: Prior to being released to third parties, all documentation that describes Company X information systems or systems procedures must be reviewed by Information Security management.

Commentary: It is important to communicate to workers that documentation, not just business records, may warrant restricted dissemination procedures. This policy informs staff members that they must not release internal systems documentation without approval. This policy is also necessary because many system hackers use social engineering to obtain information about internal systems, which permits them to break into these systems. If employees are notified that such information is not to be distributed to outsiders without prior permission, it is less likely that they will fall for such ploys. The prevalence of electronic mail systems connected to the Internet also makes the unauthorized transmission of internal documentation to outsiders considerably easier.

Related Policies: "Release Of Organization Information" and "Internal Network Addresses."

Audience: All

Security Environments: All

2. Documentation Confidentiality

Policy: All Company X computer related documentation is confidential, and must not be taken elsewhere when a worker leaves the employ of Company X.

Commentary: This policy prevents anyone who has written Company X material from taking the documentation with them when they leave Company X. The policy reminds end users, Information Systems department staff, and others that computer-related documentation is confidential and should not be disclosed to third parties without management permission. Because this has been such a difficult area, both in terms of communication between the people involved and also in terms of ambiguous laws, it is important to specify the arrangement in a policy, in contracts and other applicable documents. If such documentation were to fall into the wrong hands, it could be used to break the controls found on the systems of the organization. The scope of this policy can be easily expanded to include communications systems, such as private branch exchanges and local area networks.

Related Policies: "Property Rights."

Audience: All

Security Environments: All

8.07 Exchanges Of Information And Software

8.07.01 Information And Software Exchange Agreements

1. Software Distributed To Third Parties

Policy: All software developed by Company X for use by prospects, customers, business partners, and others must be distributed in object code form only.

Commentary: Distribution in source code form would permit other parties to readily use the software in ways that are perhaps different from those originally intended by Company X. For example, purchasers may end up incorporating the code in a product that they sell. Likewise, purchasers may make unauthorized modifications that may cause the software to perform slowly or incorrectly. This policy does not rule out the possibility of a reverse compiler used to derive source code from object code. While not preventing reverse engineering, distribution in object form makes these types of unauthorized use much more difficult. It also is recommended to use other anti-copying and anti-reverse-engineering control measures, such as encryption and dependence on certain software-readable parameters such as computer serial number. This policy may help in court if Company X is attempting to prove that they maintained sufficient controls to keep the software a trade secret.

Related Policies: "Software Escrow" and "Third-Party Software Agreements."

Audience: Technical staff

Security Environments: All

2. Third-Party Software Agreements

Policy: All software developed by Company X for use by prospects, customers, business partners, and others, must be distributed only after the recipients have signed an agreement stating they will not disassemble, reverse engineer, modify, or otherwise use the programs except as agreed with Company X.

Commentary: This policy gets written agreements about the approved usage of software developed by Company X prior to the distribution of the software. This will prevent Company X intellectual property from being stolen or used in ways that Company X does not intend. The policy is for organizations that do not sell or develop software as their main business. Those that do will have a much more formal and legalistic agreement. Some organizations may wish to add another sentence to this policy dealing with exceptions. An example would be a simple dial-up program that permits customers to call up a Company X computer and check the status of an order. Disassembly is much the same as reverse compilation, the difference being the type of computer programming language used. Reverse engineering is deducing the internal operation of a product based on its observable functionality.

Related Policies: "Software Distributed To Third Parties" and "Third-Party Information Security Responsibilities."

Audience: Technical staff

Security Environments: All

3. Software And Data Exchange Agreements

Policy: Exchanges of in-house software or internal information between Company X and any third party must be accompanied by a written agreement that specifies the terms of the exchange, and the manner in which the software or information is to be handled and protected.

Commentary: This policy prevents misunderstandings about the use of and protection of Company X proprietary or sensitive information. For example, if two companies exchange in-house mailing lists, it could be specified in writing that the lists are to be used one time only. Having a written contract also provides some assurance that controls will be used to prevent the information from being further disclosed to some unauthorized third parties and from being used for purposes other than those originally intended. Because it encourages some restraint associated with the dissemination of information, this policy is relevant to electronic mail, electronic bulletin boards, and the Internet. A special exception could be recognized in the policy. Government requests for data, such as through a court order, do not need agreements. Some organizations may want to incorporate in the policy specific words about the topics that need to be addressed in an agreement. These could include security responsibilities of each involved party, procedures for protecting the software or information, and assignment of copyrights and other intellectual property rights. This policy could be restricted such that it refers to confidential and proprietary information.

Related Policies: "Binding Contracts By Electronic Systems" and "Internet Information Exchange."

Audience: Management and technical staff

Security Environments: All

4. Certificate Of Destruction Of Storage Media

Policy: Whenever an external entity providing Company X with information on computer media requests that this media be returned, Company X staff must provide the external entity with written assurance that all copies of the information have been destroyed.

Commentary: This policy prevents Company X information from being unintentionally released to outside organizations. The computer media received might inadvertently have been used for temporary storage of sensitive information, and this sensitive information may not have been deleted before the media was returned. In a manner transparent to the user, the operating system might also have used the media to store files containing sensitive information. The media might also contain a program that gathers information about Company X, in effect doing some automatic industrial espionage, perhaps under the guise of a demo disk. The only reliable method to prevent these types of Company X sensitive information releases is to keep the media. Software vendors or other information providers are most often willing to accept a written statement about the destruction of the material involved in lieu of return of the computer media. The policy could be toned-down by requiring such destruction rather than return only if data storage media can be modified. The policy could be modified such that Company X staff is required to disclose the policy prior to receiving computer media from external entities. Because the non-return of submissions is relatively common in some industries such as the publishing industry, such prior notice is generally unnecessary. This policy is relevant only to those organizations with very stringent security needs.

Related Policies: "Transfer Of Sensitive Information."

Audience: End users and technical staff

Security Environments: High

5. Online Contracts By Exchange Of Paper And Signatures

Policy: Whenever third parties accept an online offer made by Company X, they must provide paper-based, hand-rendered signatures by regular mail or courier.

Commentary: This policy ensures that there will be no legal problems associated with forming a contract through computer networks. In some jurisdictions, digital signatures or logs indicating that a customer clicked an "OK" button are not sufficient evidence to show that the customer intended to enter into a contract. Even with the common use of technology, the hand-rendered signature is considered the conservative and safe way to form contracts. This approach does not slow down the speed of computer-enhanced business and ensures that the necessary legal paperwork is being prepared. This will be very important if ever there should be a dispute. At that point, Company X can point to both an electronic equivalent of a signature and a hand-rendered signature as evidence of the customer's intention to enter into a contract. The policy is deliberately vague about third parties, because these could be parties other than customers. The policy could be made more general by changing the words about third-party acceptances to pertain to both offers and acceptances.

Related Policies: "Vital Record Storage" and "Signatures In Electronic Mail."

Audience: Management and technical staff

Security Environments: All

6. Identity Validation Of External Parties

Policy: Before workers release any internal Company X information, enter into any contracts, or order any products through public networks, the identity of the individuals and organizations contacted must be confirmed through digital certificates, letters of credit, third-party references, or telephone conversations.

Commentary: This policy notifies workers that they need to perform a due diligence check before they rely on the alleged identity of those with whom they correspond over public networks. Identity confirmation is not built into the Internet, and must be achieved through controls added by user organizations. One way to confirm the identity of other users is through digital certificates. Digital certificates are the equivalent of an Internet passport, providing that a third party has vouched for a certain individual's identity or organization's identity. Digital certificates permit digital signatures to be rendered. Digital signatures indicate that a message was not modified in transit, and that it definitively came from the designated originating individual or organization. Use of encryption systems that incorporate source authentication features provide another way to confirm the identity of a correspondent over the Internet.

Related Policies: "In-Person Password Authentication," "Internet Disclosure Of Contact Information," and "Dial-Up User Authentication."

Audience: End users

Security Environments: All

8.07.02 Security Of Media In Transit

1. Third-Party Delivery Of Secret Information

Policy: Unencrypted secret information must not be sent through any third parties including, but not limited to, couriers, postal services, telephone companies, and Internet service providers.

Commentary: This policy ensures that secret information does not fall into the hands of unauthorized parties. The policy encourages trusted insiders to transport the information themselves or to render it unreadable using encryption. The policy is restricted to secret information. Less sensitive information can be transmitted through third parties when it is in readable form.

Related Policies: "Transmitting Secret Hardcopy Information" and "Using Couriers."

Audience: End users

Security Environments: Medium and high

2. Traveling With Secret Information

Policy: Workers must not travel on public transportation when in the possession of secret Company X information unless specific management approval has been obtained.

Commentary: This policy prevents secret information from falling into the wrong hands when traveling on public transportation vehicles. Public transportation includes planes, trains, trolleys, busses, and subway systems. Reducing the movement of secret information lessens the probability that it will be viewed by an unauthorized party. The flexibility of working times and locations may be indirectly restricted as a result of this policy. Telecommuters and employees who wish to work at home may have a problem with this policy. This does not mean that all work outside the office must be brought to a halt. The solution can be to remove from the office only that information that is not secret. Another option would be to encrypt all secret information when outside the office or other physically protected areas. The word "secret" could be replaced by "sensitive" or a set of data classification terms used by the organization. The policy assumes that the term "secret" has already been defined.

Related Policies: "Four-Category Data Classification," "Transportable Computers On Airplanes," "Transportation Of Secret Data," and "Removal Of Sensitive Information."

Audience: End users and technical staff

Security Environments: Medium and high

3. International Transport Of Secret Information — Security

Policy: Whenever secret information is carried by a Company X worker into a foreign country, the information must either be stored in some inaccessible form or must remain in the worker's possession at all times.

Commentary: This policy prevents intelligence agents from obtaining secret information. It is not advisable for such information to be left in hotel rooms unless it is in encrypted form. Encryption should be provided for all secret information stored on a computer. Storage of secret information on paper is less desirable because it can easily be photocopied, photographed, or scanned with an optical character recognition wand. The word "secret" could be replaced by "sensitive" or a set of data classifications used by the organization. The policy assumes that the term "secret" has already been defined.

Related Policies: "Four-Category Data Classification" and "Removing Hardcopy Sensitive Information."

Audience: End users and management

Security Environments: Medium and high

4. International Transport Of Secret Information — Authorization

Policy: Company X workers must not take secret Company X information into another country unless permission has been obtained from the Industrial Security manager.

Commentary: The purpose of this policy is to prohibit the unauthorized transportation of secret information into another country. A change of country brings a new set of laws under which industrial espionage may be legal or at least tolerated. Organizations may also face troubles in their attempts to assert legal rights in another country. This policy attempts to prevent these types of problems. The word "secret" can be replaced by the comparable words in use at any organization. The reference to "Industrial Security management" could be changed to Information Security management, or another manager who would know the relevant laws and risks. The policy is absolute in that it does not mention the form that the information takes. A significant problem for many companies, particularly high-tech companies, has been the hiring of workers of foreign nationality who sometimes return to their countries with secret or proprietary Company X information. While this policy cannot prevent this activity, it can make it clear that such information is not to be removed from the country where it is now found without special

permission. This policy may be difficult to implement for multinational companies that move secret information around the world in the normal course of business.

Related Policies: "International Transport Of Secret Information — Security," "Removing Hardcopy Sensitive Information," and "Foreign Nationals."

Audience: End users

Security Environments: Medium and high

5. Removing Hardcopy Sensitive Information

Policy: Whenever a hardcopy version of sensitive information is removed from Company X premises, it must be carried in a locked briefcase or container when not in use and it must not be left in an unattended motor vehicle, hotel room, office, or some other location, even if the vehicle or room is locked.

Commentary: This policy notifies Custodians of sensitive information that they must handle the hardcopy versions of this information securely. The steps outlined in this policy help prevent the sensitive information from falling into the hands of hackers, industrial spies, competitors, and others who might have interests contrary to those of Company X. This policy can be expanded to include unencrypted floppy disks and other computer storage media.

Related Policies: "Secret Information On Transportable Computers," "Sensitive Information Removal Log," and "International Transport Of Secret Information — Security."

Audience: End users and management

Security Environments: Medium and high

6. Transfer Of Sensitive Information

Policy: All computer storage media sent from Company X to a third party must have never before been previously used, or if used, must have been degaussed or repeatedly overwritten prior to recording the information intended to be transferred.

Commentary: This policy ensures that residual information, which may have been erased, is not left on the storage media, and therefore recoverable by a third party. This policy would for example apply not only to sending demo disks out to potential customers, but also to those cases where old used computer hard drives are sent to a charity. Information that has been deleted from a floppy disk is readily recoverable using various commercially available utility packages. Likewise, even though it has been overwritten, some information stored on magnetic storage media can be recovered using special equipment. Degaussing is one of the most secure mechanisms because it subjects the media to very strong electro-magnetic fields and definitively erases information previously stored on the media. Repeated writings of zeros and ones obliterates the information previously stored on the media. In very high security environments, repeated overwriting of the media may not provide enough protection. This policy may be restricted to those circumstances where sensitive information was previously recorded on the media.

Related Policies: "Certificate Of Destruction Of Storage Media," "Sensitive Information Storage Media," and "Used Component Release."

Audience: All

Security Environments: High

8.07.03 Electronic Commerce Security

1. Interrogation Of Cookie Files

Policy: Company X must not interrogate the cookies placed on any hard drive by other organizations in an attempt to learn where users have been on the Internet.

Commentary: This policy assures users that the systems placed on the Internet by Company X do not surreptitiously examine the contents of customer computers to reveal their web surfing habits. It is possible to examine the cookies placed by other vendors, or simply to determine which cookies exist, in order to get a profile revealing the sites that a customer has visited. Gathering this information without previously obtaining customer permission may be a violation of privacy. The policy assures customers that Company X does not engage in these practices. To post a policy such as this on the Internet does not constrain Company X, because at some future date if it wished to gather this information, it should at the very least inform users.

Related Policies: "Internet Cookies And Web Bugs" and "Cookies For Automatic Log On."

Audience: End users

Security Environments: All

2. Content Rating And Privacy Protection

Policy: Company X must adopt and support all generally-accepted standards for web content rating, web site privacy protection, and Internet commerce security.

Commentary: This policy assures customers that they can safely and securely place their order for products or services through the Internet or other online systems. The policy is written so that it can be posted on a web site as part of a formal privacy statement. A content rating scheme can be utilized that involves defining the nature of the content on a web site with tags that can be automatically read by remote user organization software that screens sites for unacceptable material.

Related Policies: "Cookies And Web Bugs."

Audience: End users

Security Environments: All

3. Marketing Communication Opt-Out Provision

Policy: All written marketing communications with prospects or customers found in the Company X contact database must include words that clearly indicate how the recipients can stop further communications, mailings, or messages.

Commentary: This policy ensures that direct mail, junk electronic mail, and all other unrequested written marketing communications include a mechanism to permit recipients to opt-out of further communications. With respect to electronic mail, this is generally provided at the end of the message, and recipients can simply reply to the sending address. This policy prevents complaints from people who do not want to be bothered with additional solicitations and who want to be left alone, which is an important aspect of privacy. This policy does not apply to rented mailing lists and other third-party databases because Company X generally has little control over updates to those lists. The policy could be modified to describe requests to be removed before being forwarded to the involved third parties.

Related Policies: "Private Data System Opt Out" and "New Or Enhanced Service."

Audience: Technical staff

Security Environments: All

4. Placing Prospects and Customers On Mailing Lists

Policy: Company X must receive a request from an interested third party and confirm that interest prior to placing them on any company mailing list.

Commentary: This policy takes a pro-consumer and pro-privacy perspective that ultimately is likely to be good for business, because it shows that the organization adopting this policy is genuinely concerned about respecting people's rights. The policy also shows the adopting organization to be concerned about data integrity, specifically making sure that its internal records are correct. The policy follows the lead of a number of organizations who have built a business around the development of vetted lists, where the recipients genuinely want to receive information about certain topics. The policy is applicable to a wide variety of organizations, not just those who are building mailing lists. This policy also prevents someone from signing-up someone else to receive unwanted communications.

Related Policies: "Private Data System Approval" and "Electronic Mail Distributions."

Audience: End users

Security Environments: All

5. Web And Commerce Server Storage

Policy: Web and commerce servers must not be used to store any critical Company X business information.

Commentary: This policy prevents damage to critical information. Organizations should not put critical information on the periphery of their networks where it could be damaged or modified by unauthorized parties. Critical information, such as a customer database, should be stored on internal machines that are behind additional firewalls or other security barriers. Web and commerce servers may process critical information. This policy assumes web and commerce servers could be damaged by a hacker without major adverse impact to the organization. It is wise to store critical collections of information on the most secure machines that are behind several layers of access controls.

Related Policies: "Web Server Firewalls" and "Internet Commerce Server Firewalls."

Audience: Technical staff

Security Environments: All

6. Account Calculation Verification

Policy: All customers, employees, and other recipients of calculations performed on their account by Company X must be provided with sufficient information to independently verify that the calculations are correct.

Commentary: This policy attempts to give individuals sufficient information so that they can verify that calculations were executed correctly. This is desirable because it uses an outside party to help identify fraud and errors. For example, a bank customer should be able to calculate the interest due him, and if there is an error, he will bring it to management's attention. This policy is additionally desirable because it reduces the demands on customer service staff. If customers have the information they need to verify calculations, then they do not need to contact the customer service department. This policy is additionally desirable because it will help foster customer goodwill and trust. The policy does not apply to organizations such as a business partner. Accounting standards define the preparation of financial statements and are the governing source of disclosures in the accounting domain. Nonetheless, it is desirable to apply this same concept to organizations to avoid disputes and to enable third-party checking mechanisms. These third-party checking mechanisms can be very useful when it comes to identifying fraud, errors, misunderstandings in contract terms, and other problems.

Related Policies: "Integrity Controls Failure Notification."

Audience: Technical staff

Security Environments: All

7. Confirming Customer-Initiated Changes

Policy: Every customer initiated change to the relationship with Company X must be immediately acknowledged with an electronic mail message, a letter, or some other written confirmation that such a change was made.

Commentary: This policy deters and prevents fraud, or at least to quickly detect it, and thereby minimize losses. If the involved customer did not authorize this change, after receiving the acknowledgement, he or she is expected to quickly contact Company X. The change in the relationship that the policy references could take many forms such as buying products, closing an account, transferring money from one account to another, or changing an address. In order to keep operational costs down, management may decide that acknowledgements are not necessary in certain situations because the risk of fraud is low. For example, if a customer called Company X and provided a new credit card number so that his or her service could be continued, then management could decide that no confirmation to the customer was required. The address for the acknowledgement discussed in this policy should not be exclusively based on the new information provided in the change. For example, a new electronic mail address specified by an Internet browser should not be confirmed to the new address, but sent instead to both the old and new addresses.

Related Policies: "Changes To Sensitive, Critical, Or Valuable Information" and "Address Change Confirmation."

Audience: Management and technical staff

Security Environments: All

8. Error Investigation

Policy: Errors identified by customers in Company X records must promptly be investigated, corrected or resolved, and within two weeks, followed up with a letter specifying that a change was made as requested, no change was made and the reasons why, or the date when a decision about the change will be made.

Commentary: This policy builds customer loyalty and keeps Company X records current. The policy defines a response time for getting back to the customer and communicating to Company X workers that it is important that responses be generated promptly. Even if no definitive decision about a change is made, a response should be sent to inform the customer that Company X is looking into it. This policy could be extended to include errors noticed by any third party or all errors. The emphasis on customers is warranted not only because accurate records containing personal data are a concern of the public, but because customer relations are critical to the success of any business.

Related Policies: "Employee Explanatory Statement," "Errors And Record Manipulations," "Double-Keying Large Transactions," and "Personal Record Integrity."

Audience: All

Security Environments: All

9. Internet Commerce Server Security

Policy: All Company X Internet commerce servers, except servers supporting communications with customers, prospects, or other members of the public, must employ unique digital certificates and must use encryption to transfer information within these servers.

Commentary: This policy creates a very high level of security for communications between Internet commerce servers and any other internal machines that might communicate with these servers. Digital certificates are used to uniquely identify each machine and communications encryption is used to protect information in transit. With this architecture, hackers will not be able to exploit Company X servers, view the traffic sent between these servers, or modify the traffic sent between these servers. The exceptions are necessary because outside communications, such as ordinary web surfing, do not typically involve either digital certificates or communications encryption.

Related Policies: "Web Server Firewalls" and "Virus Software Installation."

Audience: Technical staff

Security Environments: Medium and high

10. New Or Enhanced Service

Policy: Customers receiving computer or communications services from Company X must explicitly agree to receive new or enhanced services before these new or enhanced services are provided.

Commentary: This policy maintains good customer relations and ensures that customer computer and communication systems will continue to be compatible with Company X systems. The policy requires support of previously-available services. This does not preclude Company X from also offering new or enhanced services. The policy is relevant to security because it ensures that previously effective controls will continue to be effective. This policy prevents service providers from forcing a new service on customers before the customers are prepared to receive the service. This includes understanding the security implications of the new service. The policy also supports contingency planning efforts because it requires prior services to continue to be supported. If new or enhanced services introduce a major problem, Company X can always revert to the prior services. This policy may be perceived by some Data Processing managers as too restrictive and can be written to include customers, suppliers, and other third parties, but not internal systems users. The policy can be expanded to include an exception clause in which previous services do not need to be offered if Company X top management agreement is obtained. This will prevent Company X from having to offer obsolete and costly services. In some respects, this policy is similar to the opt-in and opt-out process used for systems handling private data.

Related Policies: "Private Data System Opt Out" and "Production Software Package Change Approvals."

Audience: Management and technical staff

Security Environments: All

11. Binding Contracts By Electronic Systems

Policy: All contracts that implement electronic data interchange and other electronic business systems with third parties must be formed by paper documents prior to exchanging, purchasing, or selling transactions.

Commentary: Contracts formed by electronic messages may not be enforceable from a legal standpoint. Some laws require a document, a writing, or a signature in order to be enforceable. This policy ensures that all contract-related electronic data interchange or electronic mail messages sent between organizations are legally binding. The organization's attorney should review this policy prior to implementation. The policy could be expanded to include words that require all third-party agreements to be approved by the Legal department.

Related Policies: "Trading Partner Network Agreement," "Software And Data Exchange Agreements," and "Binding Signatures."

Audience: Management and technical staff

Security Environments: All

12. International Internet Business Transactions

Policy: Company X workers must not purchase goods or services through the Internet from a foreign organization unless approved by the Purchasing department.

Commentary: This policy prevents fraud, especially fraud with a remote probability of restitution or criminal prosecution. Not all Internet fraud is local, and if the fraud is perpetrated by a foreign business, then it is likely to be expensive and time consuming. If the organization is within the same country, legal dispute resolution remedies will be more available and cost effective. This policy is not to prevent business with foreign organizations over the Internet. If one wishes to proceed, the Purchasing department may wish to complete a background check and special legal structures may be established. Foreign purchases are to be approached cautiously because legal systems between countries can differ significantly. This policy could be modified so that it applies only to transactions over a certain amount.

Related Policies: "Hardware And Software Procurement" and "Electronic Mail Contracts."

Audience: End users

Security Environments: All

13. Trading Partner Network Agreement

Policy: A trading partner agreement, fixing the terms and conditions of use, must be negotiated and approved by Company X legal counsel before Company X computer systems are used in any computerized business network.

Commentary: A trading agreement specifies who is liable if a message is lost, if the system goes down, if fraud occurs, or if other problems are encountered. This policy prevents user department management from entering into an arrangement with an electronic business network without getting the terms and conditions properly worked out. This policy is intended to ensure that centralized control over business network arrangements is maintained. This centralized control over business network set-ups may also provide an opportunity to review the control measures on the system prior to use. Legal counsel should be consulted the specifics of trading partner agreements. A policy is also useful when defining the meaning of digital signatures and message authentication codes used for business network messages and other transactions handled through multi-organizational systems. This policy is deliberately written in a general way so that it applies to the formation of contracts to conduct business over the Internet with a single supplier, customer, or business partner.

Related Policies: "Binding Contracts By Electronic Systems."

Audience: All

Security Environments: All

14. Electronic Mail Contracts

Policy: All workers must include a notice at the end of each electronic mail message indicating that the message does not bind Company X to any contract, position, or course of action unless the worker is specifically authorized to enter into contracts on behalf of Company X, or otherwise authorized to legally represent Company X.

Commentary: This policy strictly defines who can and cannot commit an organization to a certain course of action, contract, or position. Without a policy like this, correspondents may allege that a worker acted as though they were authorized to bind the organization, and that they had no reason to believe that the worker was not authorized. Correspondents may say that they relied on electronic mail, that they took action that put them at a detriment, and that now Company X must follow through on what it said it would do. This policy avoids such disputes and misunderstandings. The policy does not restrict normal business activity. For example, sales staff can negotiate price and delivery terms and the purchasing group can bind the organization for certain goods and services.

Related Policies: "Binding Contracts By Electronic Systems" and "Internet Business Arrangements."

Audience: End users

Security Environments: All

15. Accepting Computerized Transactions

Policy: A transaction sent to be processed automatically must not be accepted or acted on unless the message has been shown to match a trading profile for the initiating organization, or after additional steps have been taken to verify the accuracy and authenticity of any message deviating from a trading profile.

Commentary: This policy ensures that unusual messages are not automatically processed without further investigation. If an active wiretapper were to enter an electronic data interchange (EDI) system and impersonate one of the participants, then the other participants might blindly follow the instructions received. This type of problem is prevented with the general procedure defined in this policy. The verification of the message's accuracy might involve separate communication with the alleged sender through a method other than the EDI system that handled the original message. The words "trading profile" means the typical way that the other party interacts with Company X. This might refer to the networks that the other party typically uses, the way the other party's messages are structured or the frequency of the other party's messages. The whole notion of a customer profile is increasingly incorporated into intrusion detection software. This policy is written for inter-organizational networks, but it could also apply to intra-organizational systems.

Related Policies: "Production Application System Log Contents," "Electronic Offers And Acceptances," "Record Change Orders," and "Production System Input Transaction Authorization."

Audience: Management and technical staff

Security Environments: All

16. Electronic Offers And Acceptances

Policy: All contracts formed through electronic offer and acceptance messages must be formalized and confirmed through paper documents within two weeks of acceptance.

Commentary: Confirmation by a different communication channel identifies fraud and also makes agreements legally enforceable. This policy requires that users always employ multiple communication channels for each contract. As digital signatures and message authentication codes become more pervasive, this policy may become unnecessary. This is because controls built into computerized systems will provide an increased level of assurance that the contract is legitimate, comes from the party who is alleged to have sent it, and has not been modified in transit. This policy is general business practice in the purchasing area, where an order may be initially placed over the phone, then a paper purchase order is sent by mail or fax.

Related Policies: "Accepting Computerized Transactions" and "Operating System User Authentication."

Audience: Management and technical staff

Security Environments: All

17. Telemarketing Records

Policy: Company X sales representatives must maintain records keeping track of prospects who have informed the company they do not wish to receive sales-related telephone calls.

Commentary: This policy is intended to prevent certain potential customers from receiving telemarketing calls from Company X if the potential customers have previously indicated that they do not want to receive such calls. The policy will indirectly prevent public relations problems by preventing calls that could lead to embarrassing lawsuits, newspaper editorials or consumer boycotts. The policy is also relevant to automated calling systems that handle calls through pre-recorded messages.

Related Policies: "Sexual, Ethnic, And Racial Harassment" and "Potentially-Offensive Communications."

Audience: Management and technical staff

Security Environments: All

18. Payment Information Encryption

Policy: All payment information, such as checking account numbers and credit card numbers, must be encrypted when stored on any Company X Internet-accessible computer.

Commentary: This policy ensures that payment information will not be disclosed to hackers, industrial spies, disgruntled former employees and other unauthorized parties if these same parties were able to defeat the access control systems of Internet-accessible computers. Disclosure is an issue with respect to these payment parameters because they are equivalent to a fixed password. Access to the parameters permits unauthorized persons to obtain money. This policy provides a second level of security, which would be effective even if firewalls and password-based access controls had been compromised. The policy avoids making reference to the type of file in which the payment information resides in order to apply to all such files. This policy is a standard recommendation coming from the major credit card companies, but many Internet merchants do not follow this rule. This policy makes reference to "Internet-accessible computers" not just "Internet-connected computers." This means that the policy applies to all machines that an intruder might reach through the Internet, not just the computers on the periphery directly interfacing with the Internet.

Related Policies: "Personal Information Access," "Removal Of Logs From Internet-Accessible Computers," and "Disposal Of Payment Information."

Audience: Technical staff

Security Environments: All

19. Payment Information Confirmation

Policy: When customers are confirming the use of a particular credit card number, checking account number, or other payment information on file with Company X, Company X representatives must share only the last few digits of this information.

Commentary: This policy prevents fraud. If somebody contact customer support and confirm a credit card number stored in the information systems managed by the organization, the customer support representatives should provide only the last four digits. In an Internet commerce application, if the customer needs to confirm the use of a particular credit card, only the last four digits will be displayed. Because the full set of numbers is not revealed, impersonators cannot obtain this payment information and use it for unauthorized purposes. The authorized user will have enough information in order to confirm that he or she wants to use that particular payment method. The least significant digits of the payment information are used because they are the most likely to change from customer to customer and from account to account. If an impersonator were to determine that an individual had a relationship with a certain credit card company, the first four numbers would be predetermined because they apply to all customers, and they would be inadequate when it comes to uniquely identifying a credit card number. This policy applies to those situations where payment information is changing such as when a credit card expiration date has passed.

Related Policies: "Concealing Information Transmission," "Record Change Orders," and "Internet Information Exchange."

Audience: Technical staff

Security Environments: All

20. Payment Data Encryption

Policy: Payment information, such as credit card numbers or bank checking account numbers, must be encrypted when computer-resident and also not in active use for authorized business purposes, when transmitted over a public network, and when held in storage on computer disk or tape.

Commentary: This policy prevents credit card numbers and bank checking account numbers from falling into the wrong hands. For both types of numbers, simple possession of the number may be enough to initiate a fraudulent funds transfer. This is because the numbers are basically fixed passwords authorizing funds transfers. Encryption will prevent the readable versions of these parameters from being accessible to unauthorized individuals. For example, if these parameters are encrypted when stored on a backup tape, they will be unavailable for fraud, even though the tape may be stored at a remote location without strong physical access controls. This policy is consistent with the regulations of major credit card issuing and processing organizations, and is especially important for those organizations that have Internet commerce operations.

Related Policies: "Electronic Mail Encryption" and "Personal Identifiers On Publicly-Accessible Locations."

Audience: Technical staff

Security Environments: All

21. Dormant Credit Card Numbers

Policy: Credit card numbers that have not been used for more than a year must be promptly removed from all Internet commerce systems.

Commentary: This policy ensures that a break-in to an Internet commerce merchant's system does not reveal credit card numbers for those customers who are no longer doing business with that same merchant. This policy works best if combined with other policies such as those that require that credit card numbers be encrypted when held in storage on Internet commerce systems, and perhaps overwriting routines to ensure that these deleted numbers cannot be retrieved with disk repair utilities. The policy does not compromise convenience for current active customers, only those customers who have not purchased anything for more than a year.

Related Policies: "Removal Of Logs From Internet-Accessible Computers" and "Personal Information Access."

Audience: Technical staff

Security Environments: All

22. Accounts Involved With Fraud

Policy: Any financial account with Company X that has demonstrated fraud must be closed immediately.

Commentary: This policy prevents additional fraud if some fraud has already been shown to exist. The policy is suitable for adoption by any organization that maintains financial accounts with various organizations including banks, loan companies, and credit card companies. The policy is also appropriately adopted by organizations that offer such financial accounts, such as an Internet-only bank. If there has already been fraud on an account, then the perpetrator is familiar with the account number and all other details necessary to complete the fraud. If the perpetrator did it once, he or she is likely to do it again, especially if it appears as though the fraud was not detected. By closing an account, the organization adopting this policy prevents the same type of fraud using the same account.

Related Policies: "Payment Information Confirmation" and "Bank Account Numbers."

Audience: End users

Security Environments: All

23. Confirmation Channel

Policy: All transactions initiated through the Internet, the telephone, or any other electronic system must be promptly confirmed by an alternative communications channel.

Commentary: Because orders can be placed using stolen credit card numbers, stolen checking account numbers, stolen driver's licenses, and stolen user IDs, it is advisable for merchants and other service providers to always confirm each transaction. In this context, a transaction could include a change of address and more traditional transactions such as a purchase of goods. For an address change, many banks will send a confirmation to the old address. If the address change was part of a fraud, it will then be detected by the customer, and the customer will notify the involved bank. Likewise, when orders are sent through Internet commerce, electronic mail is used to confirm that an order was placed. The confirmation should be sent through a channel other than the channel used to place the order because if it is sent through the same channel it will simply go back to the potential perpetrator of fraud.

Related Policies: "Electronic Offers And Acceptances" and "Identity Validation Of External Parties."

Audience: Technical staff

Security Environments: All

24. Account Balancing And Reconciliation

Policy: Accounting records reflecting activity on Internet commerce payment systems must be balanced and reconciled daily.

Commentary: This policy requires accounting records to be current and accurate, and be useful for the prompt detection of errors and frauds. Because everything moves so fast in the Internet commerce area, it is essential to perform these activities daily, if not more often. These activities permit management to perform other tests of the accounting records such as balance analysis and ratio analysis. These activities can be automated.

Related Policies: "Privileged System Command Accountability And Traceability."

Audience: Management

Security Environments: All

25. Payment Token Activation

Policy: Payment tokens such as credit cards must be activated only after the intended recipient has indicated receipt through the provision of some information that only that recipient could reasonably be expected to provide.

Commentary: This policy prevents fraud with a payment mechanism such as a smart card, a debit card, or a credit card. Because these payment mechanisms are often sent through regular mail, there often needs to be a mechanism by which the authorized recipient communicates to the issuing organization that he or she has received the payment mechanism. With credit cards this is often done with a toll-free telephone call, where the authorized recipient provides the last four digits of their social security number or some other information generally known only to that individual. After a certain period of time has elapsed, if the intended recipient has not provided confirmation of receipt, it can be assumed that the token was lost or stolen, at which point the previously-issued token can be disabled and a new token can be issued.

Related Policies: "Dynamic Password Tokens" and "Confirmation Channel."

Audience: Technical staff

Security Environments: Medium and high

8.07.04 Security Of Electronic Mail

1. Third-Party Electronic Mail Message Review

Policy: Messages sent over Company X electronic mail systems that permit access by third parties must be read by Company X workers only if either the sender or the recipient has given permission.

Commentary: It is important to specify when electronic mail messages may be read. This becomes a special problem when an organization has third parties on its network, and comes closer to being a common carrier. Common carriers have certain obligations not applicable to private networks. Users of common carrier systems may have certain legal rights that are not available to users of private networks. This policy clarifies when it is permissible for Company X employees to examine electronic mail messages that may contain proprietary, confidential, or personal data relating to third parties. The policy addresses the secondary dissemination problem, whereby one recipient passes a message along to another person, then this person passes it to a third person who the original recipient never intended to have access. Access rights may differ if a network provides public access versus if a network provides access only to third parties involved in business activities. Consultation with internal legal counsel is advisable on policies such as this.

Related Policies: "Electronic Mail Privacy" and "Electronic Mail Message Monitoring."

Audience: All

Security Environments: All

2. Secret Information In Electronic Mail

Policy: Unencrypted secret information must not be sent by electronic mail unless a vice president specifically authorizes each occurrence.

Commentary: This policy's objective is to communicate to users that electronic mail systems are not to be trusted with secret information. Unencrypted electronic mail messages are easily intercepted by unauthorized parties. The policy does not permit a blanket approval from a vice president. If a user needs to send secret electronic mail messages on a regular basis, encryption facilities or other transmission media should be employed. This policy is especially relevant to the Internet, external electronic mail services and external value-added networks.

Related Policies: "Electronic Mail Encryption," "Delivery Of Secret Information," "Faxing Secret Information — Encryption," "Security Of Sensitive Information," and "Standard Encryption Algorithm And Implementation."

Audience: All

Security Environments: Medium and high

3. Electronic Mail Addresses

Policy: Workers must not employ any electronic mail addresses other than official Company X electronic mail addresses for all company business matters.

Commentary: This policy prevents workers from using other free electronic mail services and personal Internet service provider accounts for company business. Some employees may use these outside services because they can circumvent the controls that the organization has implemented for official company electronic mail. Use of an external address may permit virus-infected attachments to electronic mail messages to enter an internal network. This policy presents a professional and organized image to customers and other third parties. Another intention for this policy involves prevention of confusion about personal use of company information systems. If workers are sending business messages on their personal accounts, and sending personal messages on their business accounts, it will be difficult to sort out whether the worker was using excessive amounts of business information system resources for personal purposes. At certain organizations, this policy may need to have a caveat added that would permit such outside addresses to be used in the event of an emergency or a disaster.

Related Policies: "Unique Electronic Mail Accounts" and "Forwarding Electronic Mail Externally."

Audience: End users

Security Environments: All

4. Sender Contact Information

Policy: All electronic mail sent using Company X information systems must contain the sender's first and last name, job title, organizational unit, and telephone number.

Commentary: This policy requires all who use Company X information systems to include a standard set of sender contact details in all electronic mail. This policy prevents confusion in those cases where messages have been forwarded or where excerpts are included in other messages. The policy also is useful because it requires all senders of electronic mail to identify themselves, even if the electronic mail passes through a remailer that strips off the sender's identity. This policy also makes anonymous electronic mail, which might be harassing or derogatory in nature, against policy. Some organizations can expand this policy to include legal disclaimer notices or notices of message monitoring and archival storage.

Related Policies: "Anonymous User IDs" and "Unique Electronic Mail Accounts."

Audience: End users

Security Environments: All

5. Electronic Marketing Material Source

Policy: All marketing materials sent through electronic mail must include an accurate return address and must provide clear and explicit instructions permitting recipients to quickly be removed from the distribution list.

Commentary: This policy prohibits workers at Company X from deliberately sending marketing-oriented electronic mail messages with inaccurate return addresses so they are not bothered by recipients who object to receiving them. This policy indicates that Company X will always indicate the process associated with removal from a list. The policy also implies that Company X staff will delete names and related contact particulars from an electronic mail distribution list, even if this list is owned by third parties and rented or leased to Company X. This policy will assist Company X in its efforts to comply with privacy policies in certain countries.

Related Policies: "Database Removal Of Individuals" and "Information Attribution."

Audience: Technical staff

Security Environments: All

6. Forwarding Electronic Mail Externally

Policy: Unless the information Owner or originator agrees in advance, or unless the information is clearly public in nature, workers must not forward electronic mail to any address outside of the Company X network.

Commentary: This policy ensures that confidential information is not forwarded to unauthorized parties. This could take place when an internal memo is innocently forwarded to an associate at an outside organization. The worker might not think about it at the time, but confidential information could be disclosed in the process. While these automated forwarding mechanisms may provide an expedient way for an employee to stay in touch with personal contacts and associates, such arrangements risk the inadvertent disclosure of confidential information.

Related Policies: "Involuntary Terminations" and "Third-Party Electronic Mail Message Review."

Audience: End users and technical staff

Security Environments: All

7. Inappropriate Electronic Mail Messages

Policy: Workers must not create and send, or forward externally-provided electronic mail messages that may be considered to be harassment or that may contribute to a hostile work environment.

Commentary: This policy notifies workers that they must not create or forward any material that could cause a hostile working environment. Although the policy may result in resistance from users, it is an important step in the direction of avoiding liability for employment discrimination, sexual harassment, and other problems.

Related Policies: "Electronic Mail Archival."

Audience: End users

Security Environments: All

8. Electronic Mail Message Handling

Policy: Company X system administrators must establish and maintain a systematic process for the recording, retention, and destruction of electronic mail messages and accompanying logs.

Commentary: Electronic mail provides an effective way to chronicle the communications within an organization, and even between organizations. Electronic mail messages and logs are often sought as part of discovery proceedings accompanying a legal action. This policy requires that a standard process for handling messages and logs be established. In some instances, electronic mail messages and logs should be kept beyond their normal retention periods. Although rarely expanded in scope, the policy is equally applicable to voice mail.

Related Policies: "Archival Storage Retention Schedule" and "Backup Information Review."

Audience: Technical staff

Security Environments: Medium and high

9. Retention Of Electronic Mail Messages

Policy: An electronic mail message must be retained for future reference if it contains information relevant to the completion of a business transaction, contains potentially important reference information, or has value as evidence of a Company X management decision.

Commentary: This policy prevents the improper destruction of valuable information. Many users are uncertain which electronic mail messages should be retained and which should be erased after receipt. This policy provides explicit instructions about the types of information that should be retained. Many organizations may want to modify the description of the types of messages that should be retained. An explicit definition of a "business transaction" may also assist readers of this policy.

Related Policies: "Electronic Mail Message Handling."

Audience: End users

Security Environments: All

10. Electronic Mail Message Storage

Policy: Users must regularly move important information from electronic mail message files to word processing documents, databases, and other files.

Commentary: This policy addresses what has become a bad habit for many users. Overwhelmed by the volume of communications they receive, users simply elect to save certain electronic mail messages. Unfortunately they assume that a saved message will be there when they go back for it later. Many electronic mail systems were not designed as databases, and they do not have adequate mechanisms to protect important information. A problem with hard disk data corruption could cause the entire electronic mail in-box to be lost. This policy attempts to preserve important information, especially that which is sent as a file attachment in an electronic message. As is the case with backing-up personal data, users take this matter seriously only after they have lost important material.

Related Policies: "Electronic Mail Message Handling."

Audience: End users

Security Environments: All

11. Electronic Mail Message Destruction

Policy: All multi-user electronic mail logs must be destroyed one year after being archived.

Commentary: This policy is intended to minimize the volume of archived electronic mail messages, which will conserve disk space and simplify information management activities. From a legal standpoint, the policy is additionally intended to prevent an organization from being caught in a difficult place where management thought it had deleted all records pertaining to a certain matter, when in fact archived electronic mail was available. A number of lawyers are using electronic mail as a favorite new source of information that comes to light during discovery. When a policy like this exists, there will be no legitimate charges that the involved organization deliberately deleted incriminating evidence because such deletion has been made into an ordinary business procedure. An accompanying explanation, informing end users what information types to retain and for what periods of time is also advisable. Although this policy applies to file servers and other multi-user systems, it could be extended to personal computers. The time period could be shortened from one year to three months.

Related Policies: "Sensitive Information Destruction" and "Data Destruction Moratorium."

Audience: End users and technical staff

Security Environments: All

12. Electronic Mail Privacy

Policy: Electronic mail is private information and must be handled as a private and direct communication between a sender and a recipient.

Commentary: This policy clearly specifies what type of privacy workers should expect when it comes to electronic mail. A clear understanding of the privacy they can expect will enable users to make appropriate decisions about the types of information to send through electronic mail. This policy is purposely vague about matters such as looking at messages in order to support the administration of an electronic mail system. Such message examination would be fully in keeping with this policy as long as the intention was to maintain and administer the system, and not to violate another's privacy. If management wishes to use electronic mail systems to monitor worker performance, discover misconduct, and ensure proper use of the system, the policy can be expanded to include words such as, "Electronic mail may be routinely monitored to discover misconduct." This policy can also be expanded to include specific actions like, "Electronic mail must not be monitored, viewed, reproduced, or otherwise used by anyone other than the sender and the recipient." This policy also may be expanded to apply to voice mail messages.

Related Policies: "Personal File Privacy," "Electronic Mail Message Monitoring," and "Third-Party Electronic Mail Message Review."

Audience: All

Security Environments: All

13. Customer Electronic Mail Encryption

Policy: All electronic mail messages that contain information about one or more specific customers must be encrypted.

Commentary: This policy preserves the privacy of customers who are concerned about an unauthorized interception of their electronic mail. The policy also prevents fraud such as identity theft by preventing unauthorized persons from gaining access to private information. The scope of the policy could be expanded to include prospects in addition to customers, but prospects may not yet have the software required to support encrypted communications. This policy is implemented in some web sites through a special function for sending a message to the vendor or merchant, and this special function typically transmits a message in encrypted form. The policy is also implemented through encrypted software and the encryption facilities built into certain electronic mail systems. The policy is bi-directional in the sense that it applies to communications from a customer to Company X, and from Company X to a customer.

Related Policies: "Secret Information In Electronic Mail" and "Electronic Mail Privacy."

Audience: End users

Security Environments: Medium and high

14. Electronic Mail Encryption

Policy: All sensitive information including, but not limited to, credit card numbers, passwords, and research and development information must be encrypted when transmitted through electronic mail.

Commentary: This policy discloses to users that their electronic mail communications are not protected the way an ordinary letter going through the postal service is. The policy notifies users that sensitive information should not be sent over the Internet unless it is encrypted. It is common for network analyzers to be used to capturing and storing information traveling over Internet links. This policy could be modified to make reference to "Internet and other external electronic mail systems" rather than simply "electronic mail." This would permit internal electronic mail systems to handle sensitive information, whereas workers must not use external electronic mail systems for sensitive information. The policy assumes that the word "sensitive" already has been defined.

Related Policies: "Secret Information In Electronic Mail," "Four-Category Data Classification," "Password Encryption," and "Faxing Secret Information — Encryption."

Audience: End users

Security Environments: All

15. Electronic Mail Message Monitoring Approval

Policy: Workers must not monitor electronic mail systems for internal policy compliance, suspected criminal activity, and other systems management reasons unless electronic mail monitoring tasks have been specifically delegated and approved by the directors of Information Services and Human Resources.

Commentary: This policy clarifies who can read electronic mail messages, and the approved circumstances when messages can be examined. The policy implicitly notifies workers that their electronic mail may be monitored, which is an important step in establishing user expectations. It is advisable to check local laws about monitoring electronic mail messages to get additional input when writing a policy. Some organizations may wish to replace the words in the policy "other systems management reasons" with words like "supervision, control, and efficient operation of the workplace."

Related Policies: "Electronic Mail Message Monitoring."

Audience: All

Security Environments: All

16. Electronic Mail Modification

Policy: Workers must not modify, forge, or remove any information appearing anywhere in an electronic mail message including the body of the message or the header.

Commentary: This policy notifies users that they must not play games with the electronic mail system, that it is to be used for business activities only, and always in a businesslike manner. The policy is necessary because it is actually quite easy to modify an electronic mail message without the modification being detected by the recipient unless the sender uses encryption or a digital signature.

Related Policies: "Internet Web And Commerce Sites" and "Unique Electronic Mail Accounts."

Audience: End users and technical staff

Security Environments: All

17. Electronic Mail Message Contents

Policy: Workers must not use profanity, obscenities, or derogatory remarks in electronic mail messages discussing employees, customers, or competitors.

Commentary: Many users consider electronic mail to be more informal than traditional paper letters. This can lead to the inclusion of obscenities or derogatory comments that would not have been included in a normal letter. This policy is intended to notify workers that they are responsible for the content of their messages, and that inappropriate content may be a legal problem for their employer. The policy also indirectly discourages the practice of venting negative emotions through electronic mail. Some organizations may wish to expand the policy and mention harassing, embarrassing, indecent, intimidating or other unethical, immoral or unlawful material.

Related Policies: "Personal Internet Message Disclaimers."

Audience: End users

Security Environments: All

18. Message Content Restrictions

Policy: Workers must not send or forward any messages through Company X information systems that may be considered defamatory, harassing, or explicitly sexual, or would likely offend someone on the basis of race, gender, national origin, sexual orientation, religion, political beliefs, or disability.

Commentary: This policy protects Company X against a variety of legal problems including defamation of character, libel, sexual harassment, and the creation of a hostile work environment. The policy notifies workers that Company X information systems are not to be used for the exercise of rights to free speech. A policy like this should be accompanied by another policy restricting the use of Company X information systems to business activities.

Related Policies: "Message Disclaimer" and "Personal Use Of Computer And Communications Systems."

Audience: End users

Security Environments: All

19. Electronic Mail Content Monitoring

Policy: Workers must restrict their communications to business matters in recognition that Company X routinely employs automatic electronic mail content scanning tools to identify selected keywords, file types, and other information.

Commentary: The purpose of this policy is to notify users that their electronic mail messages will be automatically scanned for certain keywords and file types. The policy is deliberately vague about the exact nature of the scanning, which permits these facilities to be upgraded without further notice to the user community. The vague nature of the policy is also desirable because it creates some doubt in the mind of users, potentially acting as a deterrent against electronic mail transmissions that are illegal or against policy. Legal counsel should be consulted about all matters dealing with employee monitoring. The monitoring mentioned here is often implemented at the firewall level, or at the mail server level, so that it can detect and perhaps block the outbound flow of sensitive information.

Related Policies: "Content Monitoring Responsibility" and "Message Disclaimer."

Audience: End users

Security Environments: All

20. Unsolicited Personal Electronic Mail Messages

Policy: Workers using Company X information systems must immediately stop sending unsolicited personal electronic mail messages to any recipient if the recipient requests that such messages stop.

Commentary: This policy prevents legal problems such as allegations of sexual harassment or a hostile working environment. Is also prevents workers from bothering prospects or customers who have requested that they no longer be contacted. In a serious case of such electronic mail harassment, the recipient also may be able to claim that his or her privacy has been violated. As a general business matter, it is wise to promptly respond to the requests of external parties for no further contact.

Related Policies: "Sexual, Ethnic, And Racial Harassment" and "Electronic Mail Message Contents."

Audience: End users

Security Environments: All

21. Bulk Electronic Mail

Policy: Workers must not use Company X computer systems for the transmission of any type of unsolicited bulk electronic mail advertisements or commercial messages that are likely to trigger complaints from the recipients.

Commentary: This policy prevents users from abusing the network connectivity that electronic mail systems provide to reach a very large number of people at a very low cost. The policy reduces customer complaints, and the costs that would otherwise be incurred dealing with these complaints. The policy makes it clear that Company X does not permit or employ bulk electronic mail, and that if it was sent, then it was strictly an individual's decision to do so. The policy also permits an organization to terminate a worker who sent bulk electronic mail with its computer facilities. The policy could include a provision forbidding the collection of responses from unsolicited bulk electronic mail transmissions.

Related Policies: "Database Removal Of Individuals" and "Electronic Marketing Material Source."

Audience: End users

Security Environments: All

22. Responding To Unsolicited Electronic Mail

Policy: When workers receive unwanted and unsolicited electronic mail, they must forward the message to the electronic mail administrator and not respond directly to the sender.

Commentary: This policy ensures that internal electronic mail systems are used exclusively for business purposes only by authorized workers. Unwanted and unsolicited electronic mail creates an erosion of worker productivity and a degradation in system availability by clogging networks and incoming electronic mail boxes. This policy tells workers not to respond. Instead, forwarding to an administrator permits the administrator to establish filters at the firewall level or at the electronic mail server level to prevent these messages from reaching inbound mailboxes. Administrators can also report this activity to various blacklists on the Internet that are then used to block electronic mail messages. Administrators can also contact the Internet service provider from which the message originated and complain that the account should be revoked.

Related Policies: "Electronic Mail And Voice Mail Broadcasts" and "Inappropriate Electronic Mail Messages."

Audience: End users

Security Environments: All

23. Sending Unsolicited Electronic Mail

Policy: Users must not send large quantities of unsolicited electronic mail to any address on any network.

Commentary: This policy informs users that it is unacceptable to send large quantities of electronic mail to anyone. Not only does this practice consume computer and network resources unnecessarily, a great deal of time on the recipient's part is required to sort through all the unwanted messages. As a result of this type of attack, the mail server at the recipient's end may also have a disk full condition requiring operator intervention. While some electronic mail programs are able to filter and drop messages from selected addresses, this policy tries to stop the practice at its origination point.

Related Policies: "Program Resource Consumption" and "Retention Of Electronic Mail Messages."

Audience: End users and technical staff

Security Environments: All

24. Electronic Mail Scanning And Footers

Policy: All Company X mail servers must scan every inbound electronic mail message for viruses and personal message content, with a footer appended to each message stating that it has been scanned.

Commentary: This policy informs System Administrators, System Designers, and others who configure and manage electronic mail systems about the requirement not only for virus and content scanning, but also the addition of notices that describe this same virus and content scanning. The provision of a notice also alerts users to the fact that material is being scanned, and is therefore not private. The footer encourages users to restrict their interactions through the electronic mail system to those matters that are clearly of a business nature. The exact nature of the content filtering taking place is not specified in order to encourage users to be cautious when examining messages. Scanning software that supports a policy like this is provided by a number of vendors. Virus scanning also should be implemented and active on desktop machines.

Related Policies: "Responding To Unsolicited Electronic Mail" and "Outbound Internet Communications."

Audience: Technical staff

Security Environments: All

25. Outbound Electronic Mail Footers

Policy: A footer prepared by the Legal department that indicates that the message may contain confidential information, is for the use of the named recipients only, has been logged for archival purposes, may be reviewed by parties at Company X other than those named in the message header, and does not necessarily constitute an official representation of Company X, must be automatically appended to all outbound electronic mail originating from Company X computers.

Commentary: This policy ensures that recipients of electronic mail originating from within Company X are notified of the legal nature of the message they have received. The policy is intended for technical staff that configures and manages electronic mail systems. The policy describes an outbound electronic mail footer that is like the legal words often added to a fax cover sheet. Typically this footer language includes statements like: "This message is intended for the named recipients only and if it is being viewed by other parties, these other parties are hereby notified that the material may be confidential in nature and must not be used by anyone other than the named recipients." Other words found in a footer include: "The statements made in this message are those of the originator and do not necessarily constitute the official policy of Company X." The specific language may change from jurisdiction to jurisdiction.

Related Policies: "Electronic Mail Scanning And Footers" and "Fax Cover Sheet Notice."

Audience: Technical staff

Security Environments: All

26. Electronic Mail Message Monitoring

Policy: Company X must notify every user that electronic mail systems are to be used only for business purposes, all messages sent by electronic mail are Company X records, Company X reserves the right to access and disclose all messages for any purpose without prior notice to anyone and supervisors may review the electronic mail communications of workers they supervise to determine whether they have breached security, violated Company policy, or taken other unauthorized actions.

Commentary: This policy places more importance on the ability to monitor electronic mail than on the rights of workers to communicate privately. The policy will ensure that workers are notified that their communications can be monitored without prior consent. This notice is intended to eliminate disputes about the propriety of management actions to monitor electronic mail traffic. The procedures that go along with this policy could be defeated through encryption. For this policy to be totally effective, an additional policy prohibiting encryption will be necessary.

Related Policies: "Encryption Process Approval — Systems," "Electronic Monitoring Areas," "Systems Monitoring Tools," "Electronic Mail Message Monitoring," and "Third-Party Electronic Mail Message Review."

Audience: End users

Security Environments: All

27. Electronic Mail Archival And Review

Policy: All electronic mail sent through the Company X mail server must be archived and subject to review by someone other than the recipient and sender.

Commentary: This policy ensures that all electronic mail sent through a particular organization is being archived. The senders and recipients are notified that their communications are not private. This policy is also required by some government agencies that are concerned about misrepresentations made to customers. This policy is often appended to electronic mail so that all external correspondents know that their messages will be archived and reviewed.

Related Policies: "Electronic Mail Message Destruction" and "Electronic Mail Message Handling."

Audience: End users

Security Environments: All

28. Sales Department Electronic Mail

Policy: Salespersons must not send electronic mail messages to customers or prospects unless these messages are reviewed and approved by a supervisor.

Commentary: This policy prevents salespersons from making representations that may damage the reputation of their employer, require their employer to honor an agreement that was not intended, or cause their employer to be held liable for any misrepresentations. If, for example, a stockbroker were to use the words "a sure winner" regarding the purchase of a certain company's stock, those words can be detected by a content filter software, then subjected to additional human scrutiny. This policy can be implemented by sending all outbound electronic mail from the Sales department through one or more supervisors who look at certain messages, and spend considerable time examining those messages that a filter flagged as potentially difficult. The need for this policy stems from the tendency of salespersons to go to great lengths to get a commission, and in the process to say things that may compromise information security. This policy prohibits salespersons from using a free electronic mail service to circumvent the outbound electronic mail review procedures built into an in-house electronic mail system. This policy encourages the development of scripted responses for standard inquiries.

Related Policies: "Electronic Mail Archival And Review" and "Electronic Mail Content Monitoring."

Audience: End users

Security Environments: All

29. Electronic Mail Archival

Policy: All official Company X electronic mail messages including, but not limited to, those containing a formal management approval, authorization, delegation, or handing over of responsibility, or similar transaction, must be copied to the Archival Records department.

Commentary: This policy acknowledges the changing nature of the archival records function in many organizations. Rather than being a paper-handling group, it is increasingly an electronic records management group. The copying of such electronic mail messages provides evidence and accountability, should there be disputes, disciplinary actions, or legal proceedings. The process of storing an official copy of correspondence is an announced Internet electronic mail service provided by various organizations. However, they can set up their own in-house group to do this with digital signatures and other technology. If the message contents are sensitive, then the message should be encrypted. This introduces the need to manage the encryption keys. In some cases it may be sufficient for a message hash, digital signature, or extract to be stored rather than the actual message. This would permit the verification of a specific trade, by certain parties, for certain amounts, at a certain time and date, but would not permit the original message to be reconstructed.

Related Policies: "Electronic Mail Message Handling."

Audience: All

Security Environments: All

30. Electronic Mail System Usages

Policy: Workers must use Company X electronic mail systems primarily for business purposes, and any personal use must not interfere with normal business activities, must not involve solicitation, must not be associated with any for-profit outside business activity, and must not potentially embarrass Company X.

Commentary: This policy specifies what type of personal use of a company electronic mail system is permissible. This policy will ensure that the personal use is kept within certain limits. At some organizations, the term "outside business activity" will need to be defined.

Related Policies: "Personal Use Of Computer And Communications Systems," "Unacceptable Use Of Computer And Communication Systems," "Personal Telephone Usage," and "Non-Business Use Of Organization Information."

Audience: All

Security Environments: All

31. Electronic Mail Distributions

Policy: Company X must receive a positive confirmation through an opt-in process for anyone who is placed on an electronic mail distribution list.

Commentary: This policy prevents complaints and bad publicity associated with unwanted or unsolicited electronic mail. In some jurisdictions, it may also prevent legal issues. With this policy, organizations would ask potential customers and others whether they wish to receive a certain type of information, then only if the recipients respond affirmatively, would they be placed on an a specific electronic mail distribution list.

Marketers may object to this policy saying that it unduly constrains their sales activities, without consideration for the preservation of the individuals' privacy.

Related Policies: "New Or Enhanced Service" and "Private Data System Approval."

Audience: End users

Security Environments: All

32. Signatures In Electronic Mail

Policy: Workers must not employ scanned versions of hand-rendered signatures to give the impression that an electronic mail message or other electronic communications was signed by the sender.

Commentary: This policy restricts the dissemination of hand-rendered signatures in digitized form. If these scanned signatures fall into the wrong hands, they could be used to forge checks, fraudulently authorize credit card transactions, and improperly obtain identification cards. Attempts to replicate manual controls in an automated environment are not recommended because the results can be disastrous. There are other much more reliable controls to authenticate the identity of electronic mail message originators. These include digital signatures, digital certificates, encryption, and dynamic password systems.

Related Policies: "Transaction Originator" and "Identity Validation Of External Parties."

Audience: End users

Security Environments: All

33. Electronic Mail Attachments

Policy: Workers must not open electronic mail attachments unless they were expected from a known and trusted sender, and unless these attachments have been scanned by an approved anti-virus software package.

Commentary: This policy prevents virus infections on desktop computers. Executable attachments are a common way for viruses to enter an internal network, and the resulting disruption can be significant and costly. Many of these viruses will look at the address book found in the electronic mail application, then automatically send the virus to all addresses contained therein. These transmissions will be from a known sender, but the attachment will not be expected, so hopefully the recipient will not open the attachment. Certain attachments, such as those in rich text format

will be innocuous because they do not contain any executable statements. The policy could be modified to permit the opening of text attachments, but users cannot be relied upon to definitively know the format of the attached files they receive. This policy will not keep viruses out of internal networks, but it may help. Policy wording that also may be considered is "Opening an attachment is permissible if the explanation accompanying the attachment makes sense given your current business activities, and if the attachment was sent by a known and trusted party."

Related Policies: "Downloading Software" and "Electronic Mail Addresses."

Audience: End users

Security Environments: All

34. In-bound Electronic Mail Attachments

Policy: Workers who need to receive a formatted file, an executable program, or some other non-text message from an external source must use a method other than electronic mail.

Commentary: This policy prevents macro viruses from inadvertently being transmitted to Company X machines through Internet electronic mail attachments. Macro viruses attach themselves to data rather than executable programs. It also partially protects an organization against dynamic content, which is an increasingly dangerous risk that all Internet users face. The policy requires users to put word processing documents, spreadsheets, and other files in simple text format, and embedded in the body of an electronic mail message. This policy acknowledges that, aside from diskettes, electronic mail attachments have become the primary mechanism used to spread macro viruses. This policy also reduces the transmission of executables, which is likely to reduce infections from ordinary viruses attaching themselves to executables. Assuming that it is better to automatically enforce a policy, rather than rely on users, this policy assumes that special code has been written for electronic mail handling programs. Many firewalls now have the capabilities to do this type of filtering, but the filtering may be incomplete or unreliable. This policy may be too restrictive for many organizations.

Related Policies: "Data Censoring."

Audience: End users and technical staff

Security Environments: High

35. Unexpected Electronic Mail Attachments

Policy: Users who receive an unexpected attachment to an electronic mail message that does not have a credible business-related explanation must not open the attachment until they obtain an explanation from the sender.

Commentary: This policy prevents users from inadvertently infecting their computers with viruses, worms, and other destructive items. Opening an attachment is may infect a personal computer with a virus. This policy does not prohibit a user from opening attachments, and it does not block them at the firewall. Attachments are useful and frequently used, but they at the same time can automatically invoke scripting languages that perform undesirable and damaging activities without the involved user's knowledge or permission. Deletion of the attachment is recommended to prevent it from being innocently opened at a later time. This policy is not a replacement for a current virus detection program running on each user's computer.

Related Policies: "Electronic Mail Attachments" and "Mobile Code Execution."

Audience: End users

Security Environments: All

36. Public Electronic Forums

Policy: Workers must not use Company X information systems to participate in Internet discussion groups, chat rooms, or other public electronic forums unless this participation is expressly authorized by the Public Relations department.

Commentary: This policy prevents embarrassment to Company X, and perhaps legal issues. This policy limits who is representing the organization on the Internet. The policy is necessary because so many people take an informal attitude toward posting material on the Internet. The words "public electronic forums" could include online teleconferences and other arrangements. The words are deliberately vague in order to be able to embrace new technologies without having to change the policy.

Related Policies: "Public Representation Approval," "Internet Trade Secret Releases," and "Right To Free Speech."

Audience: End users

Security Environments: All

8.07.05 Security Of Electronic Office Systems

1. Fax Logs

Policy: Logs reflecting the involved phone numbers and the number of pages for all inbound and outbound fax transmissions must be retained for one year.

Commentary: This policy provides a legal record of the faxes that were sent and received. This is important in business environments where contracts, purchase orders, invoices, and other legally-binding promises are handled by fax. The maintenance and retention of a fax log can help resolve day-to-day operational problems. Such fax logs may additionally be useful for the preparation of expense reports and internal charge-back system reports. Many new personal computer software packages that support faxing come with their own logs, which according to this policy, should be turned on. Fax servers also support extensive logging.

Related Policies: "Faxing Sensitive Information — Unencrypted."

Audience: All

Security Environments: Medium and high

2. Personal Computer Software Upgrades

Policy: Users must not install new or upgraded programs on their workstations or personal computers and instead rely on system administrators through automatic network downloads for this maintenance.

Commentary: This policy establishes a consistent set of applications running on all workstations within an organization. This can be achieved with automatic software distribution software packages. Compliance with this policy can be checked by automatic license management software packages. A consistent set of applications is desirable because it is considerably easier to support, less expensive to acquire, and likely to be more secure. Newer software is increasingly customizable and modular. This means that certain features can be turned off or removed before the software is distributed.

Related Policies: "User Installation Of Software."

Audience: End users

Security Environments: All

3. End-User Application Programs

Policy: All small systems must use approved software license management software that is configured to detect unauthorized copies of third-party software and new or modified application programs developed by end users.

Commentary: This policy supports a relaxed computing environment in which end users are permitted to perform their own application system programming as long as these systems are not used as production applications. The policy requires that license management software be used to police this activity. With license management software, all new applications will be flagged, and if later shown to be production applications, the involved users can be required to document the applications and to add supplemental controls. In some environments, a custom-developed screen can be shown to the developer in the end-user department, asking him or her to indicate whether the software is used for production purposes. If it is production software, then compliance with certain development and documentation standards will be required. This policy supports prototyping and related evolutionary systems development approaches. The Information Systems department does not lose control with this approach, because they can prevent the use of any software through the license management system. This step might be appropriate when such systems were missing proper testing or sufficient documentation. With license management software, Information Systems can also monitor all new or changed software on networked systems.

Related Policies: "Systems Development Conventions" and "Higher-Level Programming Languages."

Audience: Technical staff

Security Environments: All

4. Critical Business Logic

Policy: Production applications containing critical business logic must run on multi-user servers that have physical access controls, logical access controls, change controls, and contingency plans.

Commentary: This policy prevents critical business logic from falling into the hands of unauthorized persons if they were to steal a desktop or portable computer. From a different perspective, keeping critical business logic only on larger multi-user machines with physical access controls prevents copies of this logic from being dispersed, and in that respect controls access

to trade secrets, unique business practices, and other sensitive ideas. Desktop and portable systems most often lack change controls, and are susceptible to viruses, worms, and other problems that multi-user systems with access controls do not generally encounter. Desktop and portable systems also often lack passwords, encryption, and other logical access controls to prevent the disclosure of data handled by these critical applications. Desktop and portable systems also may be undesirable for production applications because it may be easy for users to make changes to an application, but not document the changes, because no change control process is enforced. This policy assumes that the word "critical" has been defined in contingency planning documentation.

Related Policies: "Multi-User Production Applications" and "End-User Application Programs."

Audience: End users

Security Environments: All

5. Sending Private And Confidential Information

Policy: Private and confidential information must be shipped or sent through internal or external mails in a sealed opaque envelope marked "To Be Opened by Addressee Only."

Commentary: This policy gives all types of Company X workers specific instructions on the proper way to mark private and confidential information sent by various types of mail except electronic mail. The policy is intended to be used for sensitive information, but not for the most sensitive type of information. An opaque envelope prevents unauthorized people from viewing the contents through the envelope. The use of the word "sealed" to indicate that reusable envelopes are not appropriate for this type of material. It is important that the recipient know if an unauthorized person has examined the involved material as it traveled en route. The policy shown here presumes the existence of a policy that defines the terms "private and confidential." These terms may be readily replaced with comparable label used within the organization.

Related Policies: "Sending Secret Information" and "Four-Category Data Classification"

Audience: All

Security Environments: All

6. Faxing Sensitive Information — Notification

Policy: If secret information is to be sent by fax, the recipient must have been notified of the time when it will be transmitted, and also have agreed that an authorized person will be present at the destination machine when the material is sent unless the fax machine is restricted such that persons who are not authorized to see the material being faxed may not enter.

Commentary: One scenario for inadvertent disclosure involves sensitive materials that have been sent by fax but not yet picked up by the intended recipient. This policy ensures that no unauthorized person examines sensitive faxed materials. If the recipient knows the fax is coming, he or she will be concerned if it does not arrive when scheduled. The policy presumes the existence of a policy that defines the term "secret." This term may be readily replaced with the label used within the organization.

Related Policies: "Faxing Sensitive Information — Human Presence," "Faxing Sensitive Information — Physical Security," "Faxing Sensitive Information — Unencrypted," and "Fax Logs."

Audience: End users

Security Environments: All

7. Faxing Sensitive Information — Human Presence

Policy: Sensitive materials must not be faxed unless an authorized staff member is on hand to properly handle the materials or a password protected fax mailbox is used to restrict unauthorized release of the materials.

Commentary: One scenario for inadvertent disclosure involves sensitive materials that have been sent by fax, but not yet picked up by the intended recipient. This policy requires a human presence or a password protected fax mailbox be used. With respect to the first option, the policy could be modified to require the sending party to confirm the presence of an authorized staff member by telephone in advance of transmission. A more strict approach would be to prohibit the faxing of sensitive information unless both the sending and receiving machine employ encryption.

Related Policies: "Faxing Sensitive Information — Notification."

Audience: End users

Security Environments: All

8. Faxing Sensitive Information — Intermediaries

Policy: Sensitive Company X information must not be faxed through untrusted intermediaries including, but not limited to, hotel staff and rented mailbox store staff.

Commentary: Workers may be traveling for business, pressed for time, and not thinking about the people who may be exposed to sensitive information. The policy could be expanded to include preferred methods for sending the information, for example by courier. The use of encryption is irrelevant here because intermediaries can examine the information in hardcopy form.

Related Policies: "Faxing Sensitive Information — Notification" and "Faxing Sensitive Information — Human Presence."

Audience: End users

Security Environments: All

9. Faxing Sensitive Information — Cover Sheet

Policy: When sensitive information must be faxed, a cover sheet must be sent and acknowledged by the recipient, after which the sensitive information may be sent through a second call.

Commentary: This policy ensures that sensitive information is being faxed to the correct fax machine. The policy prevents unauthorized call forwarding from interfering with the intended fax communication path. With so many fax machines in use these days, the chance that a wrong number would make connection with another fax machine is quite high. Another intention of this policy is to ensure that an authorized party is on-hand and actually watching the destination fax machine. This prevents unauthorized parties from viewing the sensitive faxed material. Confirming that an authorized recipient is on-hand is also desirable in case the second call is unsuccessful. This policy could be augmented with another sentence requiring the recipient to confirm receipt of the second transmission. The policy does not specify how the destination party acknowledges receipt. This could occur on a separate line or by other means such as a pager.

Related Policies: "Faxing Sensitive Information — Unencrypted" and "Faxing Sensitive Information — Human Presence."

Audience: End users

Security Environments: All

10. Faxing Sensitive Information — Unencrypted

Policy: Sensitive information may be faxed over unencrypted lines only when time is of the essence, no alternative and higher-security transmission methods are available, and voice contact with the receiving party is established immediately prior to transmission.

Commentary: This policy notifies staff that sensitive information should not be faxed over unencrypted lines on a regular basis. If there is a need for regular transmission of sensitive information, then workers should request encrypting fax machines. Some international export restrictions may apply to encryption technology. The policy shown here may also include words requiring confirmation of receipt of a fax that includes sensitive information. Transmission to an attended stand-alone fax machine may be preferable to transmission to a fax server, if that server does not have adequate access controls and if it may be readily-accessed by a number of people. This distinction may be stated explicitly in the policy.

Related Policies: "Faxing Sensitive Information — Notification."

Audience: End users

Security Environments: Medium and high

11. Faxing Sensitive Information — Physical Security

Policy: Secret or confidential information must not be sent to an unattended fax machine unless the destination machine is in a locked room for which the keys are possessed only by people authorized to receive the information.

Commentary: This policy ensures that no unauthorized person examines sensitive faxed materials. By physically restricting access, unauthorized persons are prevented from seeing secret or confidential faxes. This policy says nothing about notification of the recipient. The policy presumes the existence of a policy that defines the terms "secret" and "confidential."

Related Policies: "Faxing Sensitive Information — Notification," "Four-Category Data Classification," and "Printing Sensitive Information."

Audience: End users

Security Environments: All

12. Faxing Secret Information — Encryption

Policy: Secret information must not be sent by fax unless the transmission is encrypted using methods approved by the Company X Information Security department.

Commentary: Encryption prevents sensitive information from being revealed to wiretappers and others who may have access to it as it travels by common carriers. At the destination, the information can be decrypted, or recovered by reversing the encryption process. Even though the transmission is encrypted, the information coming out of a destination fax machine will be readable to any person who happens to be present when the fax is received. To prevent this, other controls such as a password to print a fax will be required. This policy thwarts fax transmission wiretapping. It is relatively easy to place a wiretap, record a fax transmission, and later play it back into another fax machine to generate readable hardcopy. If this were done, neither the sender nor the recipient would be aware that a wiretap has taken place. This comment is equally true of the new faxing services that use the Internet rather than dial-up lines. The policy presumes the existence of a policy that defines the term "secret."

Related Policies: "Faxing Sensitive Information — Physical Security," "Four-Category Data Classification," "Secret Information In Electronic Mail," and "Electronic Mail Encryption."

Audience: End users

Security Environments: High

13. Faxing Confidential Information — Speed Dial

Policy: When confidential information is sent by fax, the operator must not use preset destination telephone numbers, but must instead manually enter the destination number.

Commentary: This policy prevents the misdirection of faxes because of a mistaken keypunch. These types of errors can result in embarrassing situations where, for example, one important customer sees that another important customer has a different price for the same product they bought yesterday. One other case involved the misdirection of a confidential merger contract to a business newspaper. If fax operators manually key in the phone number, they may make an error, but the error is likely to be a single digit. This will often cause the fax not to go through because a voice line or a modem line will be reached instead of another fax line. There is, however, no such automatic safety net when preset fax numbers are employed.

Related Policies: "Faxing Secret Information — Encryption" and "Fax Logs."

Audience: End users

Security Environments: All

14. Faxing Secret Information — Passwords

Policy: Secret information must not be sent by fax unless the receiving machine, prior to the initiation of a transmission, successfully provides a password.

Commentary: This policy ensures that the correct fax machine has been reached. There have been reported cases where sensitive faxes were sent to the wrong machine. Two compatible machines, each supporting passwords, are likely to be required. This will reduce the number of machines to which secret faxes can be sent. Other passwords for printing faxes also may be required. The policy presumes the existence of a policy that defines the term "secret."

Related Policies: "Faxing Sensitive Information — Physical Security," "Four-Category Data Classification," "Fax Cover Sheet Notice," and "Fax Logs."

Audience: End users

Security Environments: Medium and high

15. Fax Cover Sheet Notice

Policy: All outgoing Company X faxes must include a cover sheet that includes wording approved by the Legal department.

Commentary: This policy is intended to be responsive to the significant number of faxes that are mistakenly sent to the wrong number. Not only can this involve entering the wrong telephone number on the fax machine, it may also involve telephone system malfunctions, internal mail systems that incorrectly deliver faxes, or monitoring by telephone company technicians. A standard cover sheet will ensure that certain legal words precede all outbound faxes. Typically such a cover sheet includes a notice that the transmission is for use only by the intended individual or entity. This notice may also state that if the reader of the fax is not the intended recipient, then the reader must not use, disseminate,

distribute, or copy the information. The notice may request that the sender be notified if the fax has been sent elsewhere besides the intended destination. The notice can be supplemented with words requesting the destruction of a misdirected fax and that no action be taken relying on the information contained in the fax itself. The policy shown above gives the greatest flexibility in that the words on the cover can be changed without the need to change the policy itself. Changes in the words on the cover will be necessary as the legal and business status of faxes evolves over time.

Related Policies: "Faxing Secret Information — Passwords" and "Potentially-Offensive Communications."

Audience: End users

Security Environments: Medium and high

16. Secret Information On Speaker Phones

Policy: Secret information must not be discussed on speakerphones unless all participating parties acknowledge that no unauthorized persons are in close proximity such that they might overhear the conversation.

Commentary: This policy prevents the unauthorized disclosure of secret information when using speakerphones. Speakerphones often are used in open offices, lobbies, or in other locations where passers-by can overhear the conversation. This scope of this policy may be expanded to apply to teleconferences and speakerphone conversations. Encryption of the phone lines is also advisable in many circumstances where secret information is being discussed. To be in compliance with this policy, at the beginning of a conversation, the parties to a conversation involving secret information can affirm that their location does not have unauthorized persons nearby. Alternatively, if a regular phone conversation is initiated, and later in this conversation it becomes necessary to discuss secret information, then the affirmation mentioned above can take place at that time. The policy presumes the existence of another policy that defines the term "secret."

Related Policies: "Four-Category Data Classification" and "Sensitive Information On Answering Machines."

Audience: End users

Security Environments: Medium and high

17. Diskless Workstations

Policy: All workers in the Research and Development department must use diskless workstations connected to an isolated departmental network when working on new product development projects and tasks.

Commentary: This policy prevents workers from walking away with new product designs and similar highly restricted material. It could be used in other high-security environments such as a Strategic Planning department, a mergers and acquisitions department, or a military battle strategy planning department. Because diskless workstations are used, workers cannot store information onto a floppy disk or other data media, then remove it. Because the network is isolated, workers cannot attach this information to an electronic mail message to send a copy to an address outside of the company. This policy achieves a degree of isolation not found in most offices, and as such it provides a markedly higher degree of security. When these workers are using electronic mail or the Internet, they will need to use other computers that are not connected to the workstations. In those cases where outside information needs to be posted to or removed from the isolated network server, a system administrator can handle this task.

Related Policies: "Telecommuting Data Entry Operators" and "Equipment In Secret Information Areas."

Audience: Technical staff

Security Environments: High

18. Time-Sensitive Information

Policy: The most confidential time-sensitive information must not be handled by electronic mail, voice mail, telephone calls, or other computerized systems until the specifics have been announced publicly.

Commentary: This policy recognizes that information is subject to change and as a result is often unreliable. The policy informs management not to use computerized systems for such information until the information is publicly disclosed. While encryption programs and other automated controls have the potential to more securely protect information, these controls can be used incorrectly, resulting in unintended disclosures. This policy may be best if adopted on a project-by-project basis, rather than being a standing policy appearing in a policies manual. The policy should not be used unless the words "most confidential" have been previously defined. Other words such as "top secret" may be used

instead. Another benefit of this policy is that there is no electronic trail of events or other information that could be discovered in the course of legal proceedings.

Related Policies: "Destruction Of Information" and "Secret Systems."

Audience: Management

Security Environments: Medium and high

19. Storage Of Sensitive Information

Policy: Company X workers must not store private, confidential, or secret information on personal computer or workstation hard disk drives unless Information Security management has determined that adequate information security measures are employed.

Commentary: Because personal computers (PCs) and workstations do not generally provide the same level of security as departmental servers or mainframes, some organizations prohibit sensitive information from being stored on them unless adequate controls are deployed. This policy requires the use of adequate controls, such as a PC password-based access control package. The intention is not to prohibit sensitive information from being stored on hard-disk drives. Special attention to hard-disk drives is warranted because they cannot easily be locked-up at the end of the day. Special attention is also called for when a PC or workstation is connected to a local area network, in which case other users may be able to examine the contents of another's hard-disk drive. The policy deliberately is vague about what control measures are adequate, because it is expected this will change over time.

Related Policies: "Disk Storage Encryption."

Audience: All

Security Environments: All

20. Recording Sensitive Information

Policy: Workers must not record sensitive information with any type of recording device unless the proper sensitivity classification is specified at the beginning and end of each segment of sensitive information, the recording media is labeled with the most stringent data classification found on the media, the media is protected in accordance with the most stringent classification found on the media and the media is erased as soon as possible.

Commentary: This policy discourages the use of audio recording devices for sensitive information. If the use of these systems cannot be avoided, then the precautions specified in the policy should be taken. These precautions are not necessary if the media has been encrypted or scrambled. Tape spools, cassette tapes, and other recording media are easily stolen or copied, and expose sensitive information to unwarranted risks of unauthorized disclosure. For greater security, the requirement in the policy to erase the media as soon as possible can be replaced with words instructing the user to destroy the media according to approved methods.

Related Policies: "Sensitive Information On Answering Machines."

Audience: All

Security Environments: Medium and high

21. Excessive Resource Consumption

Policy: The activities of non-privileged users of shared computer systems must not cause these systems to unduly delay or interrupt the provision of service to other users.

Commentary: While this policy has to do with proper settings for access controls, it also deals with the actions end users are able to initiate. For example, a single mainframe user should not be able to consume all the system's resources such that all other users are prevented from obtaining processing services. This policy is therefore intended to direct the ways in which access controls are established, the ways system resources are allocated, and the ways in which application systems are designed. Computer worms, viruses, Trojan horses, and other unauthorized programs will often consume excessive system resources, leading to the denial of service for users. If the system has been configured to prevent this type of denial of service, then the system manager is more readily informed that a problem has been encountered.

Related Policies: "Privilege Restriction — Need To Know" and "Program Resource Consumption."

Audience: Technical staff

Security Environments: All

22. Portable Computer Backups

Policy: Workers who use portable computers must make backups of all critical information prior to taking out-of-town trips, storing the backups somewhere other than the portable computer's carrying case.

Commentary: This policy ensures that critical information stored on the hard disk drive of a portable machine is not lost forever when a portable computer is lost or stolen. This could happen if the event took place some time since the last periodic backup of a hard drive. This policy also guards against police or customs agent confiscation of a portable computer, in which case the information stored thereon would be unavailable for business purposes. The policy uses out-of-town trips as a trigger for a supplementary backup process. This trigger may not be suitable for traveling sales staff or other workers who go out-of-town nearly every working day. For these people, an out-of-state or out-of-country trip may be the trigger.

Related Policies: "Transportable Computers On Airplanes."

Audience: All

Security Environments: All

23. Copies Of Sensitive, Critical, Or Valuable Information

Policy: Unless other backup arrangements are known to be operational, all end users are responsible for making at least two current backup copies of critical files each time that a significant number of changes are saved.

Commentary: This policy permits end users to handle much of their own data reconstruction work because they have two or more copies of sensitive, critical, or valuable files. The policy also acts as a safety-net for modifications to the important files that have not yet been backed up to a local server or backed-up to a tape drive located at the personal computer (PC) or workstation. To be effective, the policy will also require some user training about backups. The requirements specified in this policy are not difficult. For example, PC or workstation users can store one copy on their hard drive and another on a local area network server, or they can store one copy on a floppy disk and one copy on their hard drive. It is now cost-effective for many end users to employ two or more hard drives. This policy is relevant in those cases where an automatic backup is performed over a local area network or wide area network without user involvement. This policy assumes that the word "critical" has been defined elsewhere.

Related Policies: "Critical Backup Files," "Four-Category Data Classification," and "Five-Category Application Criticality Classification Scheme."

Audience: All

Security Environments: All

24. Backup Review

Policy: Department managers or their delegates must ensure that proper backups of sensitive, critical and valuable data are being made if such data is resident on personal computers, workstations, or other small systems.

Commentary: Unless end users are reminded or required to make regular backups, they may neglect to make backups. End users often do not understand the need for backing-up files until they have had a major data loss. This policy will avoid major data losses and the resulting consequences. The policy is appropriately accompanied by user training dealing with backups. Some systems can automatically backup changes that users make, storing the newest file copies on a server at the end of a business day. If the automatic approach is being employed, this policy requires management to ensure that the process is effective. The policy assumes the word "critical" has been defined elsewhere.

Related Policies: "Five-Category Application Criticality Classification Scheme," "Automatic Backups," and "Data Backups."

Audience: Management and technical staff

Security Environments: All

25. Address Change Confirmation

Policy: Customer requests to change a mailing address must be effective one month after the change has been entered into the system, and requests to change an electronic mail address will take place two business days after the change has been entered into the system, with both being confirmed by sending a notice to the previous address.

Commentary: This policy ensures that unauthorized persons do not successfully request a change of address. Fictitious change of address requests often play a critical part in frauds, such as the fraudulent application for a credit card. This policy gives the authorized decision-maker on the account an opportunity to correct any errors or irregularities before the change

goes into effect. An acknowledgement of the change of address should be sent immediately. A delay on a change of regular mail addresses will ordinarily not be problem because mail forwarding will be in effect. There may be a few returned communications as a result of this policy, but these can be quickly resolved because the relevant new address will be contained in a Company X customer database.

Related Policies: "Confirmation Channel" and "Identity Validation Of External Parties."

Audience: Technical staff

Security Environments: All

26. Critical Message Line Numbering

Policy: In free-form text messages that deal with critical or particularly important business matters, each line must be numbered.

Commentary: Line numbering for free form or unformatted text has long been used in legal documents to ensure that all changes are clearly evident. Some systems are using this approach as a part of the message itself. If line numbers are not automatically generated, users can add numbers to the left of each line using word processors, text editors, and similar programs. Some important multi-organizational networks, such as electronic data interchange systems, may wish to include line numbering for all free-form text messages. Some legal documents also use numbering to clarify changes and make cross-referencing easier.

Related Policies: "Double-Keying Large Transactions," "Error Investigation," and "Errors And Record Manipulations."

Audience: Technical staff

Security Environments: All

27. Right To Free Speech

Policy: Company X computer and communications systems must not be used for the exercise of the users' right to free speech.

Commentary: This policy notifies system participants that they should not expect management to support them in their rights to speak freely when using Company X systems. This policy instead permits Company X to edit or censor electronic mail, electronic bulletin board entries, intranet sites, and voice mail broadcasts. The policy eliminates questions about legal problems associated with the infringement of free speech. Another situation where this policy would be applicable involves sending objectionable or inappropriate messages on the Internet. The policy discourages users from speaking freely if they are using Company X systems, which may be a prudent policy if Company X wishes to avoid legal issues.

Related Policies: "Data Censoring" and "Freedom Of Speech Information."

Audience: End users

Security Environments: All

28. Data Censoring

Policy: Management must not provide Company X computers or networks as public forums for their end users and reserves the right to censor any data posted to them.

Commentary: The intention behind the policy is that organizational systems not turn into mechanisms to damage the company. This could happen whenever members of a labor union, a group of dissatisfied customers, a minority stockholder faction, or another group of individuals disenchanted with the current management gets together online. Another intention is to be able to stop certain uses of the system if they are contrary to Company X policy or contrary to law. For example, if a system is being used to exchange stolen credit card numbers, management will want to censor messages dealing with this activity.

Related Policies: "Right To Free Speech," "Inappropriate Public Postings," and "Message Disclaimer."

Audience: End users

Security Environments: All

29. Removing Offensive Material

Policy: Company X must retain the right to remove from its information systems any material it views as offensive or potentially illegal.

Commentary: This policy is intended to notify users that management has no obligation to retain information stored on its systems if it considers this information to be either offensive, illegal, or otherwise questionable. This policy does not indicate that the system operator will exercise editorial control, that the operator will

review material to determine whether it meets community standards, or whether the operator will subscribe to any particular standard of decency. It simply gives the organization the right to remove material as it sees fit. In most instances this will be in response to a complaint or a tip from another user. The policy deliberately says nothing about giving the involved user advance or concurrent notice of the removal process. This policy is particularly relevant to those organizations running electronic bulletin boards, online chat rooms, Internet pages with user feedback areas, and other systems that make information available to a wide audience.

Related Policies: "Privacy Expectations And Information Stored On Organization Systems," "Unauthorized Copyrighted Information And Software," and "Potentially-Offensive Communications."

Audience: End users

Security Environments: All

30. Content Monitoring Responsibility

Policy: Company X must not ever be obligated to monitor the information content resident on or flowing through its information systems but must retain the right to remove any message, file, database, graphic, or other material from its information systems.

Commentary: This policy is intended to give management the maximum flexibility in promptly removing material from its information systems. At the same time, the statement of this right to remove material should not lead the reader to believe that all content will be monitored to meet certain standards. This policy acknowledges that community standards, a legal term associated with censorship, and business standards will evolve over time. This policy need not change as these standards change. The legal position that this policy attempts to establish is one of a common carrier like a telephone company. The telephone company is not responsible for illegal or unethical use of its facilities. In that respect, this policy is appropriate for an Internet service provider, a value added network, an electronic bulletin board operator, or a similar organization.

Related Policies: "Standards Of Common Carriers" and "Inappropriate Public Postings."

Audience: End users

Security Environments: All

31. Device Synchronization

Policy: Systems that automatically exchange data between devices, such as a personal digital assistant and a personal computer, must not be enabled unless the systems have been evaluated and approved by the Information Security department.

Commentary: This policy prevents the inadvertent release of sensitive information to unauthorized parties, and to prevent operational problems that could have otherwise been avoided. The policy is prompted by the recent development of a wide variety of devices that automatically synchronize files between various devices including handheld computers. While these systems employ useful and attractive technologies, they may also inadvertently release information to unauthorized persons. For example if a radio frequency broadcast is autonomously initiated between two devices, and if this transmission is not encrypted, the information sent might be intercepted by and used by third parties. Likewise, unless certain device IDs are employed, the information may be transferred to the wrong device, overwriting important files, destroying important data, and potentially causing operational problems. Evaluation by the Information Security department ensures that these systems incorporate the necessary controls to be consistent with existing information security measures at the organization. This policy does not prohibit the use of devices that have these features, it simply informs users not to utilize these features without advance permission.

Related Policies: "Clock Synchronization" and "Wireless Transmissions Of Secret Information."

Audience: End users

Security Environments: High

32. Collect And Third-Party Bill-To Calls

Policy: Administrators in charge of Company X voice mail systems must make arrangements with the involved telephone company so that both collect and third-party bill-to calls are unavailable on voice mail telephone lines.

Commentary: When hackers break into a voice mail system, they often create their own mailboxes, then record outgoing messages that accept collect and third-party, bill-to calls. Beyond requiring long passwords for all regular user accounts and the system administrator's account, the system administrator should contact the telephone company to prohibit the calls mentioned in this policy. Many telephone companies will do this at no extra charge. Some will do it only if there have been some abuses in the past. There is no business need to permit collect or third-party bill-to calls coming into a voice mail system, so the limits imposed by this policy only close a back-door security vulnerability that could be exploited. In some cases this prohibition could be applied to regular telephone numbers.

Related Policies: "Sensitive Information On Answering Machines."

Audience: Technical staff

Security Environments: All

33. Information Service Calls

Policy: Administrators in charge of Company X private branch exchange systems must program PBX systems so that all calls to information services numbers are not connected.

Commentary: This policy prevents Company X from being charged for unauthorized information service calls. In the process of prohibiting these calls, Company X may inadvertently make it difficult for employees to obtain some information that they legitimately need to complete their work. This is, however, a rare occurrence, and these calls can be made using other phones such as a pay telephone along with a Company X telephone credit card. This policy could be broadened to include a prohibition on international calls originating from certain telephone stations. Cellular phones billed to Company X could have international calls blocked.

Related Policies: "Credit Card Calls."

Audience: Technical staff

Security Environments: All

34. Calling Areas

Policy: The numbers reachable through Company X private branch exchanges must be restricted to only those needed for ordinary business purposes.

Commentary: This policy prevents telephone toll fraud. A good deal of the fraud now encountered involves calls to certain less industrialized countries from businesses in more industrialized countries. As long as business activities would not be unduly hampered, organizations can prevent fraud if they block calls to these less industrialized countries. In some instances, such as for cellular phones, it is appropriate to block all international calls. In other instances, such as a shared factory floor phone, all long-distance domestic calls can be blocked. In certain business situations such as retail stores, only emergency out-bound calls and incoming calls will be permitted. Phone users can go through operators if they need to reach an area that has been blocked. Certain area codes that assess additional charges also can be blocked.

Related Policies: "Returning Long-Distance Calls" and "Privilege Restriction — Need To Know."

Audience: Technical staff

Security Environments: All

35. Voice Mail Message Storage

Policy: Users must check their voice mail at least once every business day as all voice mail messages that are one month old will be deleted.

Commentary: This policy gets voice mail users to promptly remove their messages from the system, and refrains from using the system as a database. This approach will foster prompt response to requests from customers, prospects, vendors and others. This approach also will minimize the sensitive information that is available through the voice mail system at any particular time, that will lower the chances of unauthorized disclosures. This policy also will lower the disk space requirements for a voice mail system, which often runs on a personal computer.

Related Policies: "Removal Of Logs From Internet-Accessible Computers," "Personal Information Retention," and "Electronic Mail Message Destruction."

Audience: End users

Security Environments: All

36. Credit Card Calls

Policy: Workers must not place direct dial telephone credit card calls though an external private branch exchange system and instead use a public telephone or another direct line.

Commentary: This policy prevents telephone credit card numbers and accompanying personal identification numbers (PIN) from being recorded in call detail records. This will prevent these records from being used as a source of credit card numbers that can facilitate fraudulent toll calls. When using a private branch

exchange system (PBX), workers could provide their credit card number and PIN to a telephone company operator verbally, but this runs the risk of someone overhearing the numbers. For this reason, verbal handling of numbers was not mentioned in the policy. This is a relatively burdensome policy because it inconveniences telephone users to minimize fraud. Rather than using this policy, it may be sufficient for many organizations to have detailed and periodic monitoring of credit card bills. Depending on the recipient audience for this policy, the term "PBX" may need to be defined more specifically.

Related Policies: "Information Service Calls."

Audience: All

Security Environments: All

37. Direct Inward System Access Implementation

Policy: Company X sites must not enable the direct inward system access features on private branch exchange telephone systems unless they are accompanied by a fraud detection and limitation system approved by the manager of the Telecommunications department.

Commentary: This policy prevents the use of DISA facilities unless they are accompanied by special fraud detection and caller privilege disabling systems. Many telecommunications experts instruct phone system administrators to simply disable the DISA feature. DISA can actually save an organization a significant amount of money if implemented securely. This policy is based on the assumption that user organizations will, at least for the near term, continue to be responsible for toll fraud losses. Laws may be passed to shift liability for fraudulent telephone use to carriers and PBX manufacturers, which would alter the need for this policy because these carriers and manufacturers will be likely to build adequate security into their systems, rather than offer it as an option. In addition, recent toll fraud insurance coverage provided by some carriers will lessen the need for a policy like this.

Related Policies: "Use Of Credit Cards" and "Computer Crime Investigation."

Audience: Technical staff

Security Environments: All

38. Record Change Orders

Policy: Orders to change any internal Company X records that are placed over the phone must not be honored unless the identity of the caller has been verified by approved procedures.

Commentary: This policy is intended to define the circumstances under which telephone representations will be given credibility and be used as input for the update of internal records. The process by which a caller's identity is verified can be as simple as providing a social security number or a telephone number, although neither of these are totally effective because this information is available publicly. It is better to call the involved party back at a predetermined number, then to verbally confirm that the transaction should proceed. But even this can be defeated by call forwarding. To provide a higher level of security, a predetermined transfer code or special-use password is recommended. This process is generally employed for bank funds transfer orders placed by phone. The scope of this policy could be expanded to include faxed orders and electronic mail orders. The notion of confirming the identity of callers can also be applied to those circumstances where callers request internal-use-only and more sensitive information.

Related Policies: "Production Change Reconstructability" and "Production Changes."

Audience: End users and technical staff

Security Environments: Medium and high

39. Conference Bridge Activation

Policy: Conference bridges must be specifically activated only when needed and not be left in an activated state when not in use.

Commentary: This policy prevents unauthorized toll fraud. A favorite scam taking place these days involves a conference bridge left in an enabled state. Hackers will sit on the bridge and accept third-party collect calls for other hackers. They may then place additional unauthorized outgoing calls through the bridge that will be charged to the organization. A conference bridge may be used to conceal the work of a hacker because he has traversed so many different systems and networks. These people may also take over a conference bridge and use it for their own purposes, such as exchanging stolen credit card numbers. To thwart these antics, conference bridges can be controlled with passwords or other security mechanisms.

Related Policies: "Third-Party Remote Access" and "Unattended Active Sessions."

Audience: Technical staff

Security Environments: All

40. Personal Internet Service Provider Accounts

Policy: Workers who wish to make a statement in a public Internet forum about any topic that does not involve Company X business, or Company X business interests, must use their own personal Internet service provider accounts and related electronic mail accounts to submit such statements.

Commentary: This policy prevents people who read public Internet forum statements made by Company X workers from believing that such statements were either the policies of Company X or official statements issued by Company X. The use of a Company X electronic mail account to make personal statements implies that the organization supports what an individual says, although there may be no such official support. This policy also reduces the likelihood of alleged libel and defamation of character lawsuits against the organization. The policy also supports the right to freedom of speech, but makes it clear that all such free speech statements must be distanced from Company X. This policy should be accompanied by a policy that makes it clear that all uses of the Company X name need to be approved in advance.

Related Policies: "Use Of Organization Name" and "Release Of Organization Information."

Audience: End users

Security Environments: All

41. Electronic Mail And Voice Mail Broadcasts

Policy: Broadcast facilities found in electronic mail systems and voice mail systems must be used only by top management or with top management approval.

Commentary: This policy is intended to reduce junk mail. The productivity of many workers is adversely impacted by low priority announcements. For some organizations, this policy may too severely restrict the use of broadcast facilities. They may wish to add words permitting use of the facilities in the event of an emergency or disaster. Organizations may wish to establish a formal review and approval procedure for the issuance of broadcast messages. They may wish to grant to both system administrators and members of the security department some blanket permission to issue broadcasts without advance top management approval. In some cases, organizations may wish to restrict end-user system privileges permitting them to issue such broadcasts. The scope of this policy could be extended to include public address facilities such as audio speakers throughout a building.

Related Policies: "Right To Free Speech" and "Unacceptable Use Of Computer And Communication Systems."

Audience: End users

Security Environments: All

42. Voice Mail To Groups

Policy: Electronic mail or voice mail messages that will be sent to groups with more than 10 recipients must be approved by a department manager.

Commentary: This policy prevents workers from sending inaccurate, embarrassing, or inappropriate material to a large number of people through electronic mail or voice mail systems. With this policy, department managers are put in the position of interpreting and applying electronic mail and voice mail policies for workers who may not understand them. This policy also imposes a certain formality to these communications that causes workers to think hard before they prepare a message and seek department manager approval. If the message is not important, then workers probably will not go to the trouble of seeking management approval, and the potential recipients will then not be bothered by yet another piece of irrelevant material. This policy indirectly prevents the use of broadcast facilities, but the policy is broader in scope and includes things like private electronic mail lists. The policy applies to both internal and external recipients of the messages.

Related Policies: "Public Electronic Forums" and "Public Representation Approval."

Audience: End users

Security Environments: All

43. Mobile Code Execution

Policy: Workers must not enter into Internet processes that involve the use of mobile code, permit mobile code to execute on their machines, or permit the placement of mobile code on their machines.

Commentary: This policy addresses two types of mobile code, where the user requests the code and where the user or user-directed software sends a request to the network seeking a response. In both cases, the user at some point either requested the operation of mobile code or at least permitted the operation of this type of code. In many cases, the user may not know that it is mobile code, and may be unable to make choice. Mobile code may reach a user's machine through a variety of pathways. For example, mobile code may come through a file transfer protocol session or as a mail attachment. This policy prohibits all mobile code. Such a conservative position is justified because mobile code may be hostile, containing viruses or worms. Most organizations are not prepared to deal with the complexities of mobile code. This policy may prevent certain types of Internet commerce dialogs. Screening for mobile code at the firewall and mail server is recommended, and should be used in addition to this end user-oriented policy.

Related Policies: "Java Program Execution" and "Active Content On Intranet Sites."

Audience: End users

Security Environments: All

44. Intranet Postings

Policy: Before any information is posted to the Company X intranet, the department manager in charge of the relevant intranet page and the Owner of the involved information must approve.

Commentary: This policy prevents employees from posting information that should not be available over an intranet. The approval processes described in the policy give management an opportunity to review whether the information belongs on the proposed intranet page, whether the information should be disclosed on an intranet, and what if any supplementary access controls will be necessary. Besides preventing inappropriate disclosure of sensitive information, this policy will keep intranet postings organized and consistent with business purposes. A separate set of guidelines for selecting information to post to an intranet is recommended. This set of guidelines can be distributed to the department managers with intranet web pages so that they can better perform their duties as described in this policy.

Related Policies: "Inappropriate Public Postings" and "Internet Posting Of Material."

Audience: All

Security Environments: All

45. Intranet Content Ownership

Policy: Unless approved in advance by the director of the Information Services department, and explicitly noted on the intranet web page, all content posted to the Company X intranet is the property of Company X.

Commentary: The policy eliminates disputes about who owns content posted to intranet web pages. It is advisable for an organization to maintain ownership of the content so that it can censor this content when necessary. While there will be no argument about copyright infringement or libel issues, there may be a dispute about content that is in poor taste, poor judgment, or may reflect badly on Company X. If Company X owns intranet web pages, it also may be liable for the content. This implies that there should be a review process prior to posting material to the intranet.

Related Policies: "Personal Use Of Computer And Communications Systems."

Audience: End users

Security Environments: All

46. Intranet Information Validation

Policy: Before posting material to the intranet, workers must ensure that the information and programs do not contain malicious code, confirm the information's accuracy, timeliness, and relevance to Company X business and resolve all related information legal issues.

Commentary: This policy defines the quality control steps that users must take before they post something to an intranet. The policy assumes that users may post things to an intranet without going through a review committee or some other approval process. While it is not recommended that all users be given permission to post whatever they want to an intranet, this policy can be used by organizations that employ that approach. Standard tools that can be used to check for malicious code also could be provided, and perhaps mentioned in the policy. The policy assumes that personal information is kept off the intranet. If this is not the case, the words "relevance to Company X business" could be deleted.

Related Policies: "Intellectual Property" and "Intranet Postings."

Audience: End users

Security Environments: All

47. Intranet Content Review And Testing

Policy: All new or changed content to be posted to the Company X intranet must pass through a staging area where authorized personnel will review the content and test its operation, unless written approval of Information Security management has been obtained.

Commentary: This policy notifies workers that the intranet is a production system that deserves formal change control procedures. This policy restricts intranet content, so that only high-quality material is ever posted. The policy supports the posting of only content that has been screened and shown to be accurate, relevant, current, and in violation of no internal security policies. Although not stated in the policy, access to the staging area should be restricted with mechanisms like password-controlled file directories. The words in the policy "where authorized personnel will review" imply this but do not require it.

Related Policies: "Production Changes" and "Computer Room Deliveries."

Audience: End users

Security Environments: All

48. Internet Content Moved To Intranet

Policy: All content downloaded from the Internet must go through a structured and documented cleansing process before being posted to the Company X intranet.

Commentary: This policy ensures that content downloaded from the Internet does not include viruses, worms, and other malicious items that could be propagated across desktop systems within Company X. While the cleansing process should include use of virus screening software packages, it should also involve stripping-off, or at least testing, of dynamic content. These dynamic content applets could conceal malicious code that would do damage to Company X systems. The cleansing process additionally should include visual examination of the downloaded content to ensure that it can be reposted internally without restriction.

Related Policies: "Virus Test System" and "Software Testing Information."

Audience: Technical staff

Security Environments: All

49. Active Content On Intranet Sites

Policy: Only those active content applets that have been tested and approved by the Information Systems department may be used on sites connected to the Company X intranet.

Commentary: This policy ensures that developers working for a department or some other decentralized organizational unit do not incorporate active content applets into an intranet site and in the process propagate a virus, worm, or some other malicious software program. The policy assumes that intranet content is provided by a variety of decentralized units, and that there is no central screening process for this same content. If a central screening process is employed, then this policy is unnecessary. The policy supports a repository of tested, approved, and documented programs that can be reused repeatedly. This repository need not be limited to active content, but ideally includes a wide variety of programs including encryption routines and access control system extensions to support extended user authentication.

Related Policies: "Disabling Java" and "Java Program Execution."

Audience: Technical staff

Security Environments: All

50. Intranet Web Page Review

Policy: All user-developed web pages must be tested for security and operational problems according to an approved process issued by the Information Security department before they are posted to the Company X intranet.

Commentary: This policy is intended to prevent vulnerabilities with user-developed intranet web pages that can introduce security problems. Other vulnerabilities that can be detected by a review include the presence of viruses, non-compliance with organizational format conventions, use of unauthorized software, and broken hyper-links. The policy deliberately avoids mentioning these tests because they are rapidly evolving over time. The approved testing process can be changed regularly to reflect these new developments, while the policy remains the same.

Related Policies: "Intranet Style Guide."

Audience: End users and technical staff

Security Environments: All

51. Intranet Information Owner

Policy: All information posted to the Company X intranet must have a designated Owner and the contact information for this Owner must be clearly indicated on the page where the information appears.

Commentary: This policy insists that all information posted to an intranet have a designated Owner. If such an Owner is indicated, then errors can be reported back to this same person who can approve corrective action. This Owner makes decisions about dissemination to users other than those who can currently access the information. Decisions about the use of this information in other contexts, for example the establishment of hot-links to it, also can be made by this Owner. This Owner often makes final decisions about the design of the intranet page. This policy fosters efforts to designate Owners for all types of important internal information. This policy ordinarily would be distributed only to those responsible for maintaining intranet web pages.

Related Policies: "Assigning Information Ownership."

Audience: Technical staff

Security Environments: All

52. Information Owner Digital Signatures

Policy: All information Owners who post the information for which they are responsible on the Company X intranet must generate digital signatures indicating their approval of the final versions of the applicable pages and post these same digital signatures along with the pages.

Commentary: This policy readily detects unauthorized modification to intranet pages. If digital signatures are posted along with the related pages, an intrusion detection system or some other software can be used to automatically determine whether any unauthorized changes have taken place. The existence of a valid digital signature can be part of the process that all pages must go through before they are posted to an intranet. This policy assumes that a public key infrastructure (PKI) encryption system is implemented. PKI permits some flexibility to this control, including having the signature of more than one Owner on a single page, if more than one Owner is involved. Nothing in this policy prevents the automated update to an intranet page. Because an Owner can sign sections of a page rather than the whole page, the automatically updated part of a page could be left unsigned. To recognize this dynamically changing content, an additional sentence describing the Owner's approval of an update process could be added to this policy.

Related Policies: "Java Program Execution" and "System Log Protection."

Audience: Technical staff

Security Environments: Medium and high

53. Intranet Data Review

Policy: The Information Security department must review all postings to the Company X intranet quarterly to confirm that none of these postings contain confidential or secret information.

Commentary: This policy establishes a mechanism to ensure that intranet users are not posting information with a more sensitive classification than "for internal use only". This policy assumes that no central approval authority exists for placing information on the intranet. If there is a central approval authority, this policy is unnecessary because screening will have already been performed. An information security professional is recommended because they are experienced in this process and can easily identify inappropriate postings or policy violations. This policy assumes that the organization has implemented a data classification system.

Related Policies: "Three-Category Data Classification" and "Trade Secrets On Intranet."

Audience: Management

Security Environments: Medium and high

54. Intranet Server Approval

Policy: All Company X intranet servers must be authorized by the network services manager in the Information Systems department before they are connected to the internal network.

Commentary: This policy controls what is often a random process whereby various departments will establish their own intranet servers. Some network management systems can generate alarms indicating the presence of unauthorized machines on a network. Approval of the network services manager is advisable because it provides an opportunity to ensure that only standard software and hardware are used, that a proper network address for the server has been assigned, and that other similar set-up tasks have been performed.

Related Policies: "System Interconnection."

Audience: Management

Security Environments: All

55. Access To Production Systems By Intranet

Policy: The intranet must not be used to provide real-time connections to any Company X production information system that has extended user authentication access controls, unless the approval of Information Security management has been obtained.

Commentary: This policy is intended to prevent users and others from employing the intranet as a new and less burdensome pathway to access internal Company X information systems. For example, one production accounting system might have a dynamic password access control system. If the intranet were used to access this system, the dynamic password access control system may be circumvented, lowering the hurdles that users must clear in order to gain access. The rapid speed with which intranet systems are deployed can mean that management is not able to keep up with all new connections. This policy prevents these connections from circumventing an important type of access control. To make this policy more rigorous, the reference to extended user authentication systems could be dropped. Instead, reference could be simply made to any access control system.

Related Policies: "Real-Time External Network Connections" and "System Interconnection."

Audience: End users and technical staff

Security Environments: All

56. Forwarding Intranet Information

Policy: Workers must not forward information appearing on the intranet to third parties without obtaining approval from appropriate Company X management.

Commentary: Although Internet tools such as browsers are used to access an intranet, the open and free exchange of information found on the Internet does not apply to an intranet. This policy notifies workers that they must not permit unauthorized third parties to gain access to the intranet, and that they must not forward intranet information to third parties without the proper authorization. A policy such as this prevents the release of sensitive information, incomplete information, and information that may be taken out of context. Nothing in this policy prevents an organization from turning an intranet into an extranet, where authorized third parties gain access to an intranet.

Related Policies: "Secondary Dissemination Of Secret Information."

Audience: End users

Security Environments: All

57. Transfer To Internet From Intranet

Policy: Company X intranet users must not be transferred directly to an Internet site without being presented with a notice indicating that the users are about to be transferred to the Internet and a requirement that they confirm their understanding of this network transfer.

Commentary: This policy clarifies when users are on an intranet and when they are on an Internet. It is easy for users to get confused because both intranets and the Internet are accessed through web browsers. Users may accidentally release confidential Company X information on the Internet, then later discover that they were not, as they thought, on the intranet. The notice referred to in this policy would generally include words that remind users about the dangers of communications on the Internet. The intention behind the confirmation process is to require users to understand the notice.

Related Policies: "Internet Hot-Link Establishments" and "Direct Internet Connections."

Audience: Technical staff

Security Environments: All

58. Intranet Style Guide

Policy: All workers developing intranet sites must observe the intranet style guide and use the resources found in the intranet implementation repository.

Commentary: This policy requires all intranet developers observe the intranet style guide that defines legal disclaimers, ways to handle hot-links to other pages, page layout templates, standard graphics, and other standard formatting and content requirements. These people should use the approved utilities found in the intranet implementation repository. These resources typically include, but are not limited to, tools for establishing interfaces to in-house applications, creating custom graphics, and editing pages. Without the consistent use of these tools and requirements, an intranet may become disorderly, difficult to navigate and inadequately secured. This policy prevents the use of unapproved externally-supplied software, which may include serious undocumented bugs or malicious code.

Related Policies: "Corporate Data Dictionary."

Audience: Technical staff

Security Environments: All

59. Moving Office Computer Equipment

Policy: Office computer equipment must not be moved or relocated without the prior approval of the involved department manager.

Commentary: This policy prevents employees from stealing computer equipment, claiming they are using the equipment to perform business activities, when in fact they are not. It also maintains change control in the small systems environment. It gives local management rather than a centralized Information Technology department the ultimate approval regarding the location and uses of small systems equipment. Unauthorized movement of equipment may cause unanticipated problems such as network addressing problems, electrical wiring problems, fire hazards, and ventilation problems.

Related Policies: "Equipment Identification Codes" and "Property Passes."

Audience: End users

Security Environments: All

60. Positioning Computer Display Screens

Policy: The display screens for all personal computers, workstations, and computer terminals used to handle sensitive or valuable data must be positioned such that they cannot be readily viewed through a window, by persons walking in a hallway, or by persons in any public areas.

Commentary: This policy reduces the chance that unauthorized people will be able to view sensitive information displayed on a computer screen. A number of industrial espionage cases involved use of high-power telescopes to read material displayed on a screen through a window. Many people gain access to sensitive or valuable information simply by being in the vicinity of a computer displaying this information. Some organizations may wish to extend this policy to include keyboards and keypads. If unauthorized persons can view typing at a keyboard or keypad they can recover the information that has been entered. Recently, organized criminals have been using binoculars and video cameras at airports to steal telephone credit card numbers. To prevent these abuses, workers can be instructed to cover the keypad with one hand while the other hand types in the numbers. The idea is nonetheless the same. A positive side effect of this policy is likely to be increased concern about unauthorized viewing on the part of those people who work on portable computers. This policy assumes the terms "sensitive and valuable" have been defined.

Related Policies: "Four-Category Data Classification" and "Traveling With Secret Information."

Audience: All

Security Environments: All

61. Electromagnetic Radiation Protection

Policy: Company X systems containing secret information must employ hardware that meets military standards for electromagnetic radiation control and be located inside locked rooms encased with wire mesh or other electromagnetic radiation blocking materials as specified by military standards.

Commentary: This policy addresses a problem largely unknown in the non-military and non-diplomatic world. Electromagnetic radiation generated by computer and network equipment can be detected at significant distances, then converted into readable signals. For example, the information appearing on a computer monitor can be picked up at 1,000 feet using relatively inexpensive equipment, even though there exists no line of sight connection with the involved monitor. The relevant military standards are country-specific, so they are not included in the policy provided here. This policy should apply only to the most sensitive types of information. To this end, rather than referring to "systems containing secret information," the policy could be rewritten to refer to "systems containing collections of security parameters" which may include encryption keys, passwords, and random number generator seeds. For example, a credit card transaction processing company might apply this policy to the computers that store personal identification numbers for credit cards and debit cards.

Related Policies: "Encryption Process Hardware Modules" and "Encryption Key Disclosure — Controls."

Audience: Technical staff

Security Environments: High

8.07.06 Publicly Available Systems

1. Use Of Organization Name

Policy: Every public written use of the Company X name in published material requires the advance approval of a vice president or the Public Relations department.

Commentary: This policy prevents staff members from using the name of Company X for unauthorized purposes. Workers may seek to use the organization's name as a way to obtain additional credibility for other endeavors. Unauthorized usage of the organization's name can lead to a variety of problems including liability for damages sustained by third parties who relied on an implied endorsement by the organization. This policy also prohibits the use of broadcast electronic mail, contributions to Internet chat rooms, and other broadcast communications if the organization's name is mentioned. Staff members may participate in such forums if they do not mention that they work for Company X. This policy is a conservative approach that reflects great concern about the preservation of the goodwill now held by Company X.

Related Policies: "Third-Party Use Of Organization Name" and "Personal Internet Message Disclaimers."

Audience: End users

Security Environments: Medium and high

2. Internet Advertising

Policy: Company X must not enter into any Internet advertising, referral, or lead generation relationship with other organizations if these organizations have failed to post on the Internet a privacy policy that is consistent with or more stringent than the policy adopted by Company X.

Commentary: This policy clarifies that people in the Sales, Marketing, and Public Relations departments must place advertisements only with, or otherwise enter into marketing arrangements with, those organizations that value privacy on the Internet. The policy, which could itself be made public, sends a clear message that Company X does not do business with organizations that do not value the privacy of personal information.

This is important because some third-party organizations are often gathering personal information, and forwarding this information on to Company X. These third-party organizations are representatives or agents of Company X on the Internet, and if Company X has adopted a privacy policy, then those organizations that represent it on the Internet also should have a privacy policy. Ideally the privacy policies of both organizations should be substantially similar. If this is not the case, special care must be taken to assure that personal information gathered by the third party is not inadvertently merged with the Company X main sales and marketing database. The merging of personal information gathered under different privacy policies will make adherence to the relevant policy difficult, or else raise costs unduly because the most stringent privacy policy must apply to all information. For those organizations that do not wish to make a decision about whether privacy policies are consistent, the last part of the policy could be altered to refer only to the existence of a posted privacy policy. This option is notably weaker and not recommended. Similarly, the scope of the policy could be restricted to include only advertising and not referrals or lead generation efforts. In an indirect way this policy may prevent the policy-issuing organization from sending unsolicited electronic mail because third-party organizations that send this type of material often conceal their identities and do not post privacy policies.

Related Policies: "Help Wanted Advertising," "Trading Partner Network Agreement," and "Distribution Of Marketing Materials."

Audience: End users

Security Environments: All

3. Internet Cookies And Web Bugs

Policy: All visitors to Company X Internet web sites and commerce sites must receive a clear notice indicating both the source of and purpose for all cookies and web bugs used by these sites.

Commentary: This policy requires that internal staff inform remote users about existing data gathering mechanisms that employ cookies or web bugs. Cookies are small text files with unique user identifiers, while web bugs are tiny graphics embedded in hypertext markup language code that permit the exchange of user information. Both cookies and web bugs can be invisible to users, although more recent browsers can be configured to ask users whether they will accept a cookie from a particular site. Many sites place cookies on user machines or display web bugs on behalf of third-party

marketing organizations, and these cookies or web bugs can be used to trace and later report on user activities. When users know what type of cookies are being employed, and who issues these cookies, then they can decide whether they want to accept the cookies. Some sites provide an alternative way to interact with the site that does not require the acceptance of cookies. Users cannot intelligently opt for this type of interaction unless they know the nature of and source of the cookies employed. When users know the nature and source of web bugs employed, they can intelligently decide whether they want to interact with the site. This policy is an indication that the sponsor of a site is not in any way wishing to conceal its use of cookies or web bugs, that it is helping users to make intelligent decisions about their relationships with the site, and that it wants to conduct Internet business in a forthright and honest manner. Requiring that all visitors be informed how they may delete or deactivate cookies and web bugs could further enhance the policy.

Related Policies: "Cookies For Automatic Log On" and "Embedded Personal Information."

Audience: Technical staff

Security Environments: All

4. Presentation Of Public Image

Policy: Company X must at all times present a low-profile and secure image to both the public and third parties with any information about the existence and nature of significant assets accessible only to those persons with a demonstrable need to know.

Commentary: This policy reduces potential losses and fosters confidence on the part of the public and third parties. For example, an organization should not have its data processing center on the ground floor of an inner city block and have large picture windows without curtains so that people passing by can look in. To do this would be to invite saboteurs and industrial spies. Although it may seem inconsistent with this policy, certain events, like a fire in an office building, should be made public knowledge because the public could be affected. In some jurisdictions and industries, laws or regulations require reporting security incidents. Although a security-relevant event can be acknowledged, the control measures used to prevent future problems should be kept confidential. This policy and accompanying explanations may be particularly useful background for the Public Relations department when putting together press releases describing certain loss events. A trade-off decision is that it is assumed that a good secure image is a superior objective to deterring others from using the same techniques.

Related Policies: "Public Releases Of Vulnerability Information" and "Disclosure Of Information System Vulnerabilities."

Audience: Management and technical staff

Security Environments: All

5. Trade Secrets On Intranet

Policy: All Company X trade secrets are designated by the chief legal counsel and must be identified and very briefly described on the intranet.

Commentary: This policy notifies workers that Company X information designated as trade secrets must get special protection. Before workers can be expected to treat certain information as worthy of special security precautions, they must know what information is in need of these precautions. One way to do this is with an intranet page that makes a list of trade secrets without providing their details. The preparation and the regular updating of a list of trade secrets can also be an indication that management takes the protection of these types of information seriously, and that a court of law should extend the special protections related to trade secrets to this information in the event of a dispute. Access to the intranet should be strictly controlled to prevent this list from being accessed by an unauthorized party for the identification of interesting target information. A data classification label should also be used for trade secrets. Designations like "top secret" would be appropriate. Posting a list of trade secrets to an intranet does not eliminate the need for labels. Legal counsel should be consulted before adopting a policy such as this.

Related Policies: "Internet Trade Secret Releases" and "Software Distributed To Third Parties."

Audience: Management

Security Environments: Medium and high

6. Internet Telephone Facilities

Policy: Internet telephone facilities must not be used for the unencrypted transmission of secret Company X information.

Commentary: This policy encourages users employing Internet phone services to consider the nature of the information being transmitted, and if needed, to transmit secret information through other more secure channels. Internet phone services are becoming quite popular in large measure because they are inexpensive. At the same time, conversations that travel this way are sent through unknown machines managed by people who may or may not be monitoring transmissions. These transmissions could be recorded and later reviewed if the correspondent identities or other circumstances seem interesting. This policy assumes that the word "secret" has been clearly defined elsewhere, generally in a data classification policy.

Related Policies: "Telephone Discussions Of Sensitive Information" and "Monitoring Or Recording Telephone Conversations."

Audience: End users and technical staff

Security Environments: Medium and high

7. Public Access Workstations

Policy: All user-supplied files and all temporary files created by workstation-resident software must be automatically deleted nightly.

Commentary: This policy prevents the files placed on a public access workstation from being inadvertently revealed to users other than the users who placed these files on a workstation. The policy also prevents users from being infected by viruses and worms that may have been embedded in files that another user placed on these public access workstations. It is always possible for a user to employ a disk utility program to recover deleted files of other users to circumvent the intention of this policy. If the files are particularly sensitive, then the involved user should not place these files on a public access workstation.

Related Policies: "Publicly-Modifiable Directories" and "Backup Information Review."

Audience: End users

Security Environments: Low

8. Identity Misrepresentation

Policy: Workers must not misrepresent, obscure, suppress, or replace their identity on any electronic communications.

Commentary: This policy notifies users that they may not misrepresent their identity on electronic communication systems, for any reason. The scope of the policy is deliberately broad so that it includes telephone systems and electronic mail systems. One example of an act that is prohibited by this policy is the extraction of certain text from an electronic mail message that is then incorporated into another electronic mail message without giving credit to the originator. This policy does not require all the routing information on an electronic mail message to be maintained, only the originator's identity. Under this policy, the use of another person's user ID is a policy violation. This policy assumes that no group user IDs have been assigned, requiring each user to have a personal user ID.

Related Policies: "Organization Representations," "Information Attribution," and "Internet Representations Including Affiliation."

Audience: End users

Security Environments: All

9. Information Cross-Validation

Policy: Important information on which management depends must be periodically compared with external sources or otherwise cross-validated to ensure that it conveys an accurate representation of reality.

Commentary: This policy checks important information to ensure that it is a reflection of reality. Data integrity is meaningful only if one periodically compares the data to the independent or external sources. An example involves inventory figures kept in a computer. If these figures are not periodically reconciled to the actual figure counts, their integrity degrades. The frequency of cross-validation will vary based on the type of information involved. If it is stock prices, then periodically may mean every business day. If it is the medical condition of staff in a position of significant trust, then periodically may mean annually.

Related Policies: "Computer Analyses Review" and "Control Validation."

Audience: Management and technical staff

Security Environments: All

10. Message Disclaimer

Policy: A disclaimer must be placed on all web sites where Company X is acting as a common carrier indicating that Company X does not control the content of messages on the site, does not verify the correctness, accuracy, or validity of the information appearing on the site and is not responsible or liable for the contents of any message appearing on the site.

Commentary: Historically, there have been many legal disputes dealing with bulletin board system (BBS) system operator responsibility for illegal activities taking place on their dial-up BBS. These same considerations apply to Internet web sites or any other electronic forum where third parties interact. This policy places Company X in a position where it is not responsible for these activities much like the way the telephone company is not responsible for the illegal acts that others perform using the telephone system. With this policy, the system operator can censor or delete messages. Although certain other legal doctrines will make an organization responsible for the acts of its employees, this policy reduces Company X exposure for messages posted on its systems. It is important to review this policy with in-house legal counsel. The word "site" in the policy implies that this disclaimer is presented to people when they log on to the site.

Related Policies: "Public Comments On Electronic Systems," "Personal Internet Message Disclaimers," "Data And Program Damage Disclaimers," and "Standards Of Common Carriers."

Audience: End users

Security Environments: All

11. Messages From Criminals Or Terrorists

Policy: Messages issued by criminals or terrorists must not be broadcasted on any public channels using Company X information systems.

Commentary: This policy prevents criminals and terrorists from using public broadcasting channels as a way to further their cause. Passing along such a message would be to permit the enemy to use a broadcasting system as a covert channel. This policy will conflict with the objectives of certain marketing people who believe that passing such a message along will in one way or another increase profits. This policy is a public safety policy combined with an information security policy. A concise summary or analysis of the message could conceivably be broadcasted after management approval was obtained. So that the criminal or terrorist does not obtain more personal fame or notoriety, it is also desirable that no pictures of the individual, and no footage directly involving this individual, be broadcasted.

Related Policies: "Right To Free Speech" and "Electronic Mail And Voice Mail Broadcasts."

Audience: Management and technical staff

Security Environments: Medium and high

12. Public Comments On Electronic Systems

Policy: Unofficial comments that workers post to an electronic mail system, an electronic bulletin board system, or other electronic systems must not be represented as formal statements of, or the official position of Company X.

Commentary: This policy notifies users that they should not immediately assume what they read or otherwise observe on Company X systems is necessarily Company X policy. They should instead look for an indication that the material is a policy statement. Another intention of this policy is to notify users that what they read or observe may soon be deleted. The policy notifies users that the organization does not intend to be bound by these statements, nor does it make any guarantees that they are correct or authorized. Given the ease with which most electronic mail messages can now be mimicked, this position is warranted. Although the policy is intended for data-oriented systems like the Internet and electronic bulletin boards, voice mail and other communications systems could be added. Specific mention of the types of systems could be deleted from the policy, making reference instead to electronic communications systems. This policy is the equivalent of the statement provided by many TV and radio stations that notes "the opinions expressed are not necessarily those of the station or the station management."

Related Policies: "Message Disclaimer."

Audience: End users

Security Environments: All

13. Internet Content Labels

Policy: All information posted to the Company X commerce and web sites must be accompanied by standard content labels.

Commentary: This policy helps the organization that posts content to the Internet avoid bad publicity, complaints, and other problems. Users may employ content screening software to prevent the viewing of specific material. Employers use content filtering software such as that implemented in firewalls to limit employee access to specific material. Content labeling will assist both users and employers in their efforts to limit access to or the display of unwanted information. While it is desirable for the organization posting material to do the labeling, these organizations should be aware that third parties also do their own independent categorization.

Related Policies: "Data Censoring" and "Potentially-Offensive Communications."

Audience: Technical staff

Security Environments: All

14. Internet Discussion Groups

Policy: Users must not post to controversial discussion groups on the Internet or to any other controversial online public forums when using their Company X user IDs.

Commentary: This policy prevents Company X from unwittingly becoming a target of any group that might be offended by a posting in a public forum. Those offended may launch some type of attack to retaliate that would be counterproductive to the organization's operations. This policy does not restrict users' freedom of online expression. It only stipulates that any personal postings must not be initiated with their Company X user ID.

Related Policies: "Discussions Using Computer and Communication Facilities" and "Right To Free Speech."

Audience: End users

Security Environments: All

15. Outbound Internet Communications

Policy: All outbound Internet communications must reflect well on the Company X reputation and public image.

Commentary: This policy is intended to avoid legal complications and also to ensure that workers do not inadvertently embarrass an organization on the Internet. The policy dictates a certain standard of professionalism and a certain decorum that workers need to consistently follow. The policy provides the basis for disciplining or even terminating a worker who made the organization look bad in a public forum.

Related Policies: "Removing Offensive Material" and "Inappropriate Public Postings."

Audience: End users

Security Environments: All

16. Internet Terms And Conditions

Policy: All customers using the Internet to place orders must be presented with a summary of Company X terms and conditions, and in order to complete their orders, they must specifically indicate that they agree to be bound by these terms and conditions.

Commentary: The purpose of this policy to make it very clear exactly how an arrangement or sale between two parties is executed on the Internet. Motivating the need for policy is the fact that the Internet traverses many different jurisdictions with different laws about business contracts. In these cases, the relevant jurisdiction, and the relevant set of laws is unclear. The policy requires that a customer employ a mouse to click on a button that says "I agree," or that the customer type the words "I agree," or that some comparable mechanism be used to clearly show that the customer knew of and agreed to the Company X terms and conditions. Such indications on the part of the customer can be considered to be the equivalent of a hand-rendered signature. In many jurisdictions, the legal basis of this electronic agreement is largely undetermined.

Related Policies: "Binding Contracts By Electronic Systems" and "Trading Partner Network Agreement."

Audience: Technical staff

Security Environments: All

17. Browser Electronic Mail Capabilities

Policy: The electronic mail capabilities found in Internet browsers must not be used for any business communications.

Commentary: This policy prevents users from employing browser electronic mail facilities, and in the process circumventing the controls embedded in an internal electronic mail system. If users employ a browser for electronic mail, especially if they connect with their personal Internet service provider through a dial-up line, they could download an attachment that contains a virus. If this electronic mail attachment instead went through the organization's standard electronic mail server, it could have been filtered and deleted, preventing any damage. Use of a browser for electronic mail could circumvent electronic mail header logging systems and content filtering systems. This policy also discourages workers from giving customers and prospects personal electronic mail addresses because they consider an internal electronic mail system to be too slow or burdensome.

Related Policies: "Electronic Mail Message Monitoring" and "Retention Of Electronic Mail Messages."

Audience: End users

Security Environments: All

18. Internet News Sources

Policy: News feeds, electronic mail mailing lists, push data updates, and other mechanisms for receiving information over the Internet must be restricted to material that is clearly related to Company X business and the duties of the receiving workers.

Commentary: The purpose of this policy is to inform system administrators that they should screen news feeds from the Internet such that only business-oriented material is passed through to company workers. This policy also implicitly gives management the right to examine electronic mail and push data updates to determine that the material is not only business related but related to the duties of the receiving worker. In some cases, the policy can also be issued to users, in effect acting as a response to their requests for certain news feeds and other information services. The policy will prevent news feed discussions about non-business topics from distracting internal staff. The policy will also help conserve disk space and other system resources such as network bandwidth. The policy assumes users are not dialing-out to reach the Internet, but that they go through an internal firewall, an internal mail server, and related systems. If users are dialing-out, then decisions about news feeds will be made by an Internet access provider and the involved users.

Related Policies: "Real-Time External Network Connections" and "Personal Use Of Organization Internet Facilities."

Audience: End users and technical staff

Security Environments: All

19. Internet Information Modifications

Policy: Users connecting to Company X systems through the Internet must not directly modify any Company X information.

Commentary: This policy reflects the evolving security facilities for the Internet and the concerns that many managers have about inadequate security. The policy maintains the integrity of internal records through a filtering process. Internet-connected users can, according to this policy, submit requests for internal record updates, but these requests must be reviewed by either a person or an automated process before being posted to any Company X production information stores such as databases, data dictionaries, master files, and web pages. Using strong user authentication mechanisms such as dynamic password tokens and strong encryption systems, the modification of internal records through the Internet can be secure. This policy, if adopted, may need to be modified in a few years as Internet-based electronic commerce facilities are installed. For example, a definition of "directly modify" may be a "real-time update based on user-provided information without reasonableness checks."

Related Policies: "Business Production Information Updates" and "Production Transaction Authorization."

Audience: Technical staff

Security Environments: All

20. Personal Internet Message Disclaimers

Policy: Whenever a worker posts a message to an Internet discussion group, an electronic bulletin board, or another public information system, without prior approval from the Public Relations department, this message must be accompanied by words clearly indicating that the comments do not necessarily represent the position of Company X.

Commentary: This policy shields Company X against libel claims, copyright infringement claims, unauthorized release of trade secrets, or other problems that arise when one of its workers makes a posting to a public information system. Such disclaimers are needed even if the name of the organization does not appear in the message text. A number of different pieces of information could reveal the involved organization. These include the nature of the comments made, the electronic mail address involved, or the individual's name.

Related Policies: "Message Disclaimer," "Outbound Electronic Mail Footers," and "Public Comments On Electronic Systems."

Audience: End users

Security Environments: All

21. Internet Representations Including Affiliation

Policy: When engaged in discussion groups, chat rooms, and other Internet offerings, only those individuals authorized by management to provide official support for Company X products and services may indicate their affiliation with Company X.

Commentary: This policy limits the number of official representations on the Internet coming from Company X. This will reduce the chances of libel, defamation, misrepresentation, and similar legal problems. Organizations adopting this policy may additionally require that those workers representing them on the Internet complete a public relations training class. An area that may need additional clarification involves official pronouncements such as press releases. In most cases, however, words like "unless they have received instructions to the contrary" will cover these cases.

Related Policies: "Personal Internet Message Disclaimers" and "Public Comments On Electronic Systems."

Audience: End users

Security Environments: All

22. Internet Product And Service Representations

Policy: Workers must not advertise, promote, present, or otherwise make statements about Company X products and services in Internet forums such as mailing lists, news groups, or chat sessions without the prior approval of the Public Relations or Marketing departments.

Commentary: This policy controls what workers say about Company X products and services. This policy ensures that public representations are consistent and a reflection of management's intentions. The communications facilities provided by the Internet are far reaching and these communications need to be carefully controlled to prevent legal problems such as libel and defamation of character. In many instances, workers are well-meaning, hoping to help their employer, but the overall effect may be quite different. This policy permits the organization to train designated people who regularly monitor these forums, and respond as the discussion thread warrants.

Related Policies: "Public Electronic Forums," "Public Communications," and "Release Of Organization Information."

Audience: End users

Security Environments: All

23. Internet Disclosure Of Contact Information

Policy: Children and adults must not disclose their real names, addresses, or telephone numbers on electronic bulletin boards, chat rooms, or other public forums reached by the Internet.

Commentary: This policy is intended to prevent children and adults who are concerned about stalking, harassment, or other invasions of their privacy from being needlessly bothered. Intended to be offered as a public service for personal use on the Internet, the policy is impractical for most Internet business activities because the parties involved will need to exchange money or physical items, in which case contact information must be provided. The policy notifies people that they can conceal their identity and that they need not disclose such information when online. The policy is most relevant to off-hours use of the Internet. Organiza-

tions giving this policy to their users or customers may also want to include instructions that include children need not respond to messages they consider suggestive, belligerent, or that in some other way makes them feel uncomfortable and children must not arrange face-to-face meetings with another computer user without prior parental consent. Parents also may be advised to look into software that can monitor the content of Internet sessions and other software that can block access to certain Internet sites that contain what the parents consider to be inappropriate material. Organizations taking a proactive approach to these potential problems with the children of employees will help reduce personal problems that may interfere with employee work performance.

Related Policies: "Electronic Mail Privacy" and "Identity Validation Of External Parties."

Audience: End users

Security Environments: All

24. Political Advocacy And Product Or Service Endorsements

Policy: Workers must not make any political advocacy statements or product or service endorsements when indicating affiliation with Company X unless the permission of the Public Relations department has been obtained.

Commentary: Chat rooms, news groups, and electronic mail give Internet users a tremendous and unprecedented opportunity to reach others. This policy ensures that such communication is used in a manner that furthers an organization's interests, and that does not create legal or public relations issues. This policy in no way prevents Internet users from making the prohibited statements as an individual without any affiliation to Company X, using a personal electronic mail address and other non-Company X facilities. Some organizations may want the Legal department to approve rather than the Public Relations department.

Related Policies: "Internet Representations Including Affiliation."

Audience: End users

Security Environments: All

25. Internet Trade Secret Releases

Policy: Participation in discussion groups, chat rooms, and other public Internet forums related to Company X business must be restricted to designated workers who have been briefed about the release of trade secrets.

Commentary: This policy prevents inadvertent release of trade secrets in public forums such as Internet discussion groups. Often well-meaning employees will be participating in discussions and only later realize that they have said something that could be confidential or proprietary. This policy deliberately says nothing about participation in public forums on topics that are not related to Company X business. The policy's scope could be expanded to include chat rooms on the Internet.

Related Policies: "Internet Representations Including Affiliation," "Message Disclaimer," and "Trade Secret Disclosure."

Audience: End users

Security Environments: All

26. Internet Computer Security Queries

Policy: Queries about securing computers or networks must not be posted to Internet news groups or any other public forums.

Commentary: This policy maintains a low profile about the security problems being experienced within Company X. To divulge current system vulnerabilities at Company X invites third-party criticism, if not attacks that exploit the vulnerabilities. In many cases, well-meaning technical staff is at a loss about the ways to address various information security problems, and they often search the Internet for answers. This policy permits the searching for answers on the Internet, but does not permit posting anything about the current state of Company X systems. The policy encourages technical staff to consult the Information Security department or an external information security consultant. The policy could be modified to permit anonymous postings, in which case the identity of Company X may not be discernible, but this policy is much simpler, avoiding the steps that one must go through in order to obtain true anonymity on the Internet.

Related Policies: "Disclosure Of Computer System Attacks" and "Internet Disclosure Of Contact Information."

Audience: Technical staff

Security Environments: All

27. Internet Transmission Of Sensitive Information

Policy: Unencrypted Company X secret, proprietary, or private information must not be sent over the Internet.

Commentary: This policy informs users that the Internet does not, by default, provide information protection. This policy ensures that encryption is being used for all sensitive information sent over the Internet. Ultimately, encryption facilities will be incorporated by default into many networks, but until these facilities are provided, it will be necessary to get users involved in the encryption process. Source code is especially proprietary and needs to be acknowledged as such by many organizations. This policy is most suitable for organizations like telephone companies and software houses, which generate their own source code.

Related Policies: "Electronic Mail Encryption," "Security Of Sensitive Information," "Automated Encryption Key Management," and "Faxing Secret Information — Encryption."

Audience: End users

Security Environments: All

28. Inappropriate Public Postings

Policy: Electronic mail sent by Company X workers to Internet discussion groups, electronic bulletin boards, or other public forums must be removed if determined to be inconsistent with Company X business interests or existing Company policy by Information Security management or Human Resources management.

Commentary: The intention for this policy is to notify employees that their public postings may be censored if these postings are later determined to be inconsistent with Company X business interests or policies. This policy is intended to make employees more thoughtful about their postings. The policy is also intended to give Company X the right to quickly delete inappropriate postings without a formal decision process and without the need to consider objections. Some organizations may wish to change the policy slightly to make it clear that if individuals in no way state or imply their affiliation with Company X, including implied affiliations through an electronic mail address, then Company X will have no right to censor their messages. One advisable exception to this restriction involves messages that deal with Company X business activities. For example, if a Company X customer service representative made a personal statement on a pubic Internet forum that painted Company X in a bad light, and if the individual's affiliation was in no way linked to the Company, then the Company could delete that message. The ability to delete messages sent by others will become increasingly difficult if digital signatures, encryption routines, and access controls are employed. In many of these instances, all an employer will be able to do is request deletion from the system manager or service provider. The existence of a policy like this can facilitate message deletion arrangements between Company X management and the involved system operator. The legal rights of Company X suppressing an individual's right to free speech is an issue here, and should be discussed with internal legal counsel.

Related Policies: "Data Censoring," "Message Disclaimer," and "Standards Of Common Carriers."

Audience: End users and technical staff

Security Environments: All

29. Web Sites With Similar Names

Policy: Company X Legal department staff must periodically employ web search engines to determine whether any web sites with similar names are masquerading as Company X authorized or sponsored sites.

Commentary: This policy ensures that an internal staff member, typically in the Legal department, is using search engines to identify potentially confusing sites that may be using a similar name. This policy informs internal staff that they must search for such spoof sites and notify the appropriate internal party, typically the general counsel, when one is detected. This policy would generally only be used by Internet commerce sites that were concerned about fraud, or other sites that were concerned about their good name being tarnished by an unauthorized web site.

Related Policies: "Internet Monitoring For Information Use" and "Unofficial Web Pages."

Audience: End users

Security Environments: High

30. Internet Posting Of Material

Policy: Users must not place Company X material including, but not limited to, software, internal memos, and press releases, on any publicly-accessible Internet computer system unless the posting has been approved by Public Relations management.

Commentary: This policy notifies workers that they are not permitted to release information to outsiders through the Internet unless it has been approved by Public Relations. A policy like this would, for example, provide a software development organization with sufficient justification for terminating an employee who posted copies of new software to the Internet a few days before the software was officially released. Many users of the Internet have the belief that information should be shared. This policy explicitly notifies them not to act using that philosophy. This policy could be expanded to include other examples, such as business prospects, product performance information and union negotiation information. To motivate compliance, an accompanying explanation could make reference to possible libel and defamation problems, and fluctuations in Company X stock price.

Related Policies: "Inappropriate Public Postings," "Public Representation Approval," "Unofficial Web Pages," "Organization Representations," and "Public Communications."

Audience: End users

Security Environments: All

31. Internet Business Arrangements

Policy: Workers must not use Internet connections to establish new or different business channels, unless the director of Information Technology and the chief legal counsel have both approved in advance.

Commentary: This policy stops in-house initiatives to conduct business through the Internet until security can be assured. Because standard security measures for such arrangements are largely undefined, it is critical that in-house staff examine the security of such arrangements before Company X goes live with production systems. Although certain specialty trade associations for doing business on the Internet have recently been developed, most organizations have not yet defined the essential controls that must accompany Internet business transactions. A document containing these essential control ideas is generally known as a security architecture. Advance approval by the managers identified in the policy is required.

Related Policies: "Binding Contracts By Electronic Systems" and "Trading Partner Network Agreement."

Audience: End users and technical staff

Security Environments: All

32. Public Network Postings

Policy: Workers must properly structure comments and questions posted to electronic bulletin boards, electronic mailing lists, online news groups, and other public forums, avoiding the release of any information that might reveal knowledge about secret projects, unannounced software products, research and development projects, or related confidential Company X matters.

Commentary: This policy is intended to sensitize Company X workers about postings on public electronic systems. The policy may seem to be a restatement of common sense. However, an explicit notification to workers by Company X is recommended for disciplinary and legal purposes. The Internet and other public forums may be new to some users and they may not draw a clear line between internal and external networks. This policy is intended to remind them about the importance of this distinction.

Related Policies: "Confidentiality Agreements" and "Information Security Responsibility."

Audience: End users

Security Environments: All

33. Transferring Downloaded Files

Policy: Computers that are not connected to the Company X network must be used when downloading any files from the Internet, and these files must be checked with an authorized virus detection package prior to being moved to any other computer.

Commentary: This policy is intended to prevent viruses, Trojan horses, worms, and other malicious code from being propagated across internal computer networks. It permits Internet access, but only from personal computers that are isolated from other internal machines. In some instances specific instructions about how to isolate a personal computer will be necessary. This policy requires that all downloaded files be checked for viruses prior to being transferred to any other machine. The policy is not limited to software that acknowledges the existence of macroviruses. The policy also emphasizes the role that networks and interconnectivity plays in the propagation of viruses.

Related Policies: "Scanning Downloaded Software."

Audience: End users

Security Environments: High

34. Internet Information Reliability

Policy: All information available from the Internet should be considered suspect until confirmed by another source.

Commentary: This policy informs workers that much of the information on the Internet is not reliable. Workers believe that what they read on the Internet is trustworthy. The Internet is unregulated and unsupervised. This policy defines proper expectations regarding the quality of Internet-provided information. A positive side effect of this policy is that it causes staff to think more deeply about the quality of the information they use for decision-making. The policy could be expanded to include a prohibition against updating or modifying Company X records until the Internet information has been confirmed by another source.

Related Policies: "Concealing Information Transmission" and "Archival Storage Media Quality."

Audience: End users

Security Environments: All

35. Uploading Software

Policy: Users must not upload software that has been licensed from a third party, or software that has been developed by Company X, to any computer through the Internet unless authorization from the user's manager has been obtained.

Commentary: Unauthorized distribution of copyrighted software through the Internet violates the protection of intellectual property belonging to other organizations. This policy informs users that uploading any software is forbidden unless a manager approves. Because this is a user-related information management issue rather than a technical issue, approving management is departmental rather than Information Security management. The policy goes beyond licensed software, including software that has been developed in-house. The policy could include software that had been entrusted to Company X and perhaps not licensed. The policy prevents unauthorized distribution of software that may be a trade secret or simply critical to Company X. Because the Internet makes it so easy for users to transfer files, explicit policies preventing uploading activities are necessary. An extension to this policy prohibits the transfer of software from one computer to another, no matter what communications system is involved.

Related Policies: "Downloading Software" and "Downloaded Information."

Audience: End users

Security Environments: All

36. Unsolicited Internet Information

Policy: Any mechanism that receives comments or suggestions is provided on Company X Internet web sites must be accompanied by the following disclaimer: "The receipt of unsolicited ideas by Company X does not obligate the company to keep these ideas confidential, nor does it obligate the company to pay the person who submits them."

Commentary: This policy establishes the expectations of external parties when they send unsolicited ideas to Company X. The typical mechanism to receive such ideas is through electronic mail, but the ideas could also be received through other mechanisms. While the policy's scope could be expanded to include other communications mechanisms besides Internet web pages, generally only web pages permit a notice to be posted in a conspicuous spot. For example, it would be difficult to ask staff to say these words when people use the telephone to contact the organization. Some organizations may wish to go one step further, specifying that externally supplied ideas be funneled through a designated internal person who is not in the operational side of the business. If the designated person was in the operational side of the business, he or she might be tempted to use the idea to improve operations. This designated person may then follow-up with the submitter of the idea, asking them to sign a release form. If the submitter refuses to sign, then the designated person can destroy all copies except for one copy placed in a sealed and dated envelope, which could be used for evidence. This process permits the designated person to say that he or she was the only one, aside perhaps from the initial recipient, within Company X who saw the submission. The notice in this policy could be expanded to include words indicating that all material received becomes the property of Company X.

Related Policies: "Third-Party Confidentiality Agreements."

Audience: Technical staff

Security Environments: All

37. Internet Information In Production Systems

Policy: With the exception of information provided by prospects, customers, suppliers, business partners, or government agencies, Company X information systems must not depend on free information obtained through the Internet.

Commentary: This policy ensures that production information systems are resilient, reliable, and dependable. Reliance on free information provided by a third party is not advised because the third party can change or withdraw such information at will, and the dependent organization then has no influence over these changes or withdrawals. The policy does not prohibit usage of information obtained over the Internet if there is payment. It would be acceptable for a company to rely on Internet-supplied information from a market research organization through subscription. Some organizations may wish to delete the words "government agencies" from the policy because they do not consider this information reliable or timely. These words were included primarily for the financial industry, which obtains information about interest rates and other macroeconomic data through the Internet. Other organizations may wish to modify the policy so that it does not place reliance on free Internet information alone. Reliance in this case would be acceptable if the information was independently corroborated.

Related Policies: "Internet Information Reliability" and "Scanning Downloaded Software."

Audience: Technical staff

Security Environments: All

38. Unofficial Web Pages

Policy: The sponsor of any unofficial web pages dealing with Company X products or services must have a contract signed by the director of Public Relations.

Commentary: Organizations that do not closely monitor and police these unofficial web pages could find themselves in legal trouble including misrepresentation, trademark infringement, and copyright violation. This policy is intended to take a strong stand against such unofficial web pages unless the operator has agreed to be bound by terms that the director of Public Relations finds acceptable. One of these terms should be that Company X can, at any time and for any reason, require the operator to remove any or all references to Company X products and services. Another advisable term would be that the word "unofficial" must appear in these web pages, along with other words clearly showing that Company X is not sponsoring or taking any responsibility for the page. Some organizations may consider such unofficial web pages to be good advertising. Nonetheless, if such unofficial home pages are permitted, the affected organization should keep a tight reign on them through a legally-binding contract. Discussions with an in-house attorney are appropriate because certain legal rights may be lost if they are not asserted. For example, if an organization permits others to use its trademark without authorization, it risks the loss of its rights. This policy prohibits insiders from constructing web pages without the prior written consent of the director of Public Relations.

Related Policies: "Personal Internet Message Disclaimers" and "Web Sites With Similar Names."

Audience: End users and technical staff

Security Environments: All

39. Personal Web Pages

Policy: Every worker who uses Company X provided systems must sign a statement acknowledging that they are responsible for all content posted on that site before their site will be enabled and that Company X reserves the right to remove access to anyone at any time.

Commentary: This policy provides workers with a free mechanism to create and publish their own personal web pages. An increasing number of organizations now offer this feature. Typically users post pictures or a summary of their background and current responsibilities at Company X. This policy clarifies responsibility for the page, even though Company X provides the computers and other facilities to support it. One danger of Internet-accessible personal web pages is that recruiters are more easily able to find and lure away top technical talent because personal information is readily accessible. One desirable aspect of adopting the approach described in this policy is that Company X can easily determine what its workers are posting on the Internet, and has some control over the content and it can revoke the connection if it does not approve.

Related Policies: "Personal Internet Message Disclaimers" and "Unofficial Web Pages."

Audience: End users

Security Environments: All

40. Internet Web Page Management Committee

Policy: Prior to being posted, all changes to the Company X corporate Internet web page must be approved by a special committee established by the Public Relations department that will ensure that all posted material has a consistent and polished appearance, is aligned with business goals, and is protected by adequate security measures.

Commentary: This policy reflects a practical solution whereby decisions about material posted to a web site are delegated to the committee. These decisions may also require higher management approval. The committee typically includes a few web system administrators, an information security specialist, an intellectual property attorney, a marketing expert, and a public relations expert. This policy would ordinarily only be distributed to information systems technical staff because only they typically have the access privileges to make changes.

Related Policies: "Public Representation Approval" and "Removing Offensive Material."

Audience: Technical staff

Security Environments: All

41. Internet Web Page Design

Policy: All Company X Internet web pages must conform to layout standards, navigation standards, legal wording standards, and similar requirements specified by the Internet web page management committee.

Commentary: This policy makes it clear that all Internet web pages must conform to a standard set of requirements. Rather than explicitly describing these requirements in the policy, the policy only states that they exist and that all web pages must conform. This is because the requirements may change. Typical items to include on the requirements list are:

- Make transfers of a user's session from the Company X web site to another organization's web page very clear.

- Make a transfer from the Internet to an intranet very clear.

- Put the Company X name on all pages to prevent other sites from linking to these pages and indirectly representing that the material is their own.

• Include a disclaimer on hot-link pages indicating that Company X is not responsible for the material found on the referenced sites.

Related Policies: "Public Representation Approval."

Audience: Technical staff

Security Environments: All

42. Internet Hot-Link Establishments

Policy: All hot-links that transfer a user's Internet session from a Company X web site to the web site of any outside entity must be approved of by the Internet web page management committee.

Commentary: This policy prevents web site designers, web site administrators, and others managing internal web sites from establishing hot-links to other sites that could embarrass Company X. Because each hot-link implies Company X endorsement, all hot-link proposals should be screened by a committee, or approved in advance by a designated executive. In some cases specific criteria should be established, and outside entities must meet these criteria before any hot-link can be established. The criteria might include a stellar business reputation, not in competition with Company X, likely to be of interest to those who visit the Company X web site, and the willingness to establish a reciprocal hot-link.

Related Policies: "Intranet Style Guide" and "Internet Hot-Link Disclaimer."

Audience: Technical staff

Security Environments: All

43. Internet Hot-Link Disclaimer

Policy: All hot-links that transfer a user's Internet connection from a Company X web site to a web site associated with a third party must be accompanied by a clearly-displayed disclaimer that has been from approved by the Legal department.

Commentary: This policy prevents customers, prospects, and others from claiming that Company X is legally responsible for third-party staff behavior, products, or services. A party who believes that he or she is wronged will sue all associated parties in an attempt to obtain money or some other benefit. A wronged party may claim that the existence of a link was Company X implied endorsement of a third-party site, their products, or services. This policy requires a disclaimer that should expressly disavow all such implied endorsements. The disclaimer wording will change over time as Internet law changes, and for this reason, the disclaimer wording is not included in the policy itself.

Related Policies: "Internet Web Page Management Committee" and "Internet Hot-Link Establishments."

Audience: Technical staff

Security Environments: All

44. Internet Web Page Review

Policy: A staff member from the Marketing department must check the Company X web page daily to confirm that the page is up-and-running, that no unauthorized changes have been made, and that no unauthorized links have been established.

Commentary: This policy detects the fact that the Company X web page has been defaced. Hackers often change web pages to promote a cause or to embarrass the organization that posted the material. They may also add links to sites that are likely to embarrass the organization. This policy ensures that modified web pages or links will not last long, and that they will be promptly changed. Customers often bring these types of attacks to the organization's attention. But just in case customers or other third parties have not reported such changes, this policy requires a staff member to review the web page. The policy is an approach for organizations that do not want to spend money on an intrusion detection system. For those organizations that have available funds, a better alternative would be to employ a software package that automatically detects modifications to a web page, and will notify technical staff or feeds directly into a network management system.

Related Policies: "Modification Of Production Business Information" and "Log Deactivation, Modification, Or Deletion."

Audience: End users

Security Environments: All

45. Internet Web Site Content Changes

Policy: All Company X web sites must be designed and implemented in such a manner that every unauthorized change to the content of the site will be immediately and automatically detected and corrected.

Commentary: This policy requires Company X technical staff to use one of a variety of products that will immediately detect unauthorized changes to the content files for a web site, and will then automatically reestablish the approved content. While this functionality is rare, it is not all that difficult to program using digital signatures. Products can also be used to immediately detect changes, then a programmed script can reload approved content from a CD-ROM or another type of write-once-read-many-times data storage media. This policy addresses one of the most difficult areas in the web page management area. Hackers and political activists have repeatedly gained unauthorized access to web pages, then changed the content to embarrass the organization managing the web page.

Related Policies: "Internet Web Page Management Committee" and "Web And Commerce Site File Archives."

Audience: Technical staff

Security Environments: All

46. Web Page Defacement

Policy: Before returning a web server that has been defaced back to service, all web pages, systems software, and system configuration files must be checked for changes.

Commentary: This policy prevents web server administrators from restoring a web page to its original status, then putting the web server back on the Internet after a defacement attack. The problems may be much more profound, and hackers may control the machine. It is for this reason that all system software and configuration files must be checked. It is not reasonable to do this checking manually, not only because it is prone to error, but because it takes too long to perform this task.

Related Policies: "Internet Web Site Content Changes" and "Internet Web Page Review."

Audience: Technical staff

Security Environments: All

47. Customer Financial Information Storage

Policy: Company X must not store any customer financial information on its web servers, Internet commerce servers, Internet database servers, or other systems that are directly connected to the Internet.

Commentary: This policy prevents customer financial information from being revealed to hackers or other unauthorized parties. The intention of the policy is to move all financial information off web servers and other systems directly accessible through the Internet and put them behind several layers of firewalls. This type of information can be recorded and stored, just not stored on Internet-connected systems. One alternative to this policy would be to encrypt the financial information.

Related Policies: "Financial Information Disclosure."

Audience: Technical staff

Security Environments: All

48. Internet Domain Name

Policy: The Company X Internet domain name must be registered only with a registrar that provides appropriate security and change control procedures.

Commentary: This policy ensures that no unauthorized party changes the Internet registrar's records regarding the Company X domain name. This can happen if an organization uses the lowest security user authentication mechanisms for making changes. More secure methods to authenticate the identity of a person initiating a change in a domain name include requiring letterhead paper transactions, encrypted passwords, and digital signatures.

Related Policies: "Internet Domain Name Registration."

Audience: Technical staff

Security Environments: All

49. Internet Server Command Response

Policy: Internet servers must be modified so the verbose response to certain commands does not reveal information about the server software installed.

Commentary: This policy ensures that the organization is not revealing unintended information regarding its systems or software. Vendors of server software often ship their software with a default that provides verbose responses to certain commands. This permits them to determine what organizations are using their software. These verbose responses can reveal information that may significantly assist intruders. An abbreviated answer in most cases is equivalent to a verbose answer.

Related Policies: "Internet Hot-Link Establishments" and "Sharing Marketing Information."

Audience: Technical staff

Security Environments: All

50. Web Site HTML

Policy: All HyperText Markup Language code used on Company X web sites must be run through a scrubber or obfuscation routine before being run on any production Internet-connected server.

Commentary: This policy overcomes one of the characteristics of HyperText Markup Language (HTML), which permits any outsider to read not only the code itself, but also all embedded comments as well. The policy tells HTML programmers or web masters that they must remove comments, project names, developer names, and other information that could be used by hackers, industrial spies, disgruntled former employees, and others. Such information might be used for password guessing purposes, or perhaps in a social engineering attack. Passing HTML through a scrubber also optimizes it, which results in faster run times. The policy could be expanded to include a Java script scrubber or obfuscator, which make Java script run faster because they too remove comments and white space. A Java script scrubber or obfuscator also makes reverse engineering more costly and time consuming.

Related Policies: "System Logon Banner" and "Incorrect Logon Feedback."

Audience: Technical staff

Security Environments: All

51. Secret Information On Web

Policy: Company X secret information must not be resident on either Internet or intranet servers.

Commentary: This policy acknowledges that when one uses Internet or intranet technology, one takes on additional risk. To prevent unauthorized disclosure of the most sensitive type of information, it should be handled by more traditional means including face-to-face meetings and personal telephone calls. The most sensitive type of information in this policy is designated as secret, but the label could change based on the internal data classification system in use.

Related Policies: "Secret Information System Isolation."

Audience: Technical staff

Security Environments: All

52. Secret Information On Intranet

Policy: Access to applications on the intranet that handle secret information must be provided only when a virtual private network is employed.

Commentary: This policy ensures that secret data traveling over an intranet is not intercepted by unauthorized parties who may have placed a wiretap. To be concerned about such a wiretap is quite rational because most security incidents are caused by insiders, who in many cases have the knowledge, skills, and access to cause serious damage. A virtual private network (VPN) will prevent wiretapping on an intranet because it encrypts all transmissions. Many VPNs also provide some additional user authentication beyond the user ID and fixed password that may be required by the destination computer. This additional layer of user authentication can further help to restrict access to secret information.

Related Policies: "Network Connections with Outside Organizations" and "Cable Modems."

Audience: Technical staff

Security Environments: Medium and high

53. Security Contact Information

Policy: The opening pages of all Company X web sites must include contact information for the Information Security department.

Commentary: This policy ensures that outsiders who notice there is a problem can promptly report their observations to the correct person. The policy solicits outsiders to assist with information security. Often customers and prospects are the first to notice there is a problem, although intrusion detection systems should notify relevant personnel. The inclusion of such contact information on web pages also permits outsiders to report problems that are not of a security nature such as slow response time or erroneous results to a calculation. Some words that go along with the contact information could be "Please report any suspected security violations or problems to." The scope of the policy could be broadened to include all intranet sites.

Related Policies: "External Violation Reporting" and "Incident Reporting."

Audience: End users

Security Environments: All

54. Public Research

Policy: Whenever Company X performs polls, analytical studies, or other research that is intended for public consumption, the participants in the research must mention in their report both the sponsor and all potential conflicts of interest.

Commentary: This policy restores integrity to the news gathering, drug research, market research, and related fields that have been stung by recent allegations of conflicts of interest. If a researcher, perhaps a university professor, also happens to be doing consulting on the side for a pharmaceutical company to evaluate a new drug, this fact should be disclosed. The fact that the pharmaceutical company is paying a professor to do the drug evaluation should also be revealed in the published findings. Not revealing such information may be considered deceptive. While use of this policy in various organizations may require rewording or adjustment, the idea is fundamentally useful in order to promote a business climate characterized by integrity and fair play. Possible adjustments in wording include requiring the disclosure of any restrictions on the research results specified before the project got underway. This policy is only relevant if Company X publicly publishes newsletters, research reports, or similar material.

Related Policies: "Second Jobs" and "Confidentiality Agreements At Previous Employers."

Audience: End users

Security Environments: All

8.07.07 Other Forms Of Information Exchange

1. Recording Of Internet Communications

Policy: End users must not record any of their interactions with remote parties through the Internet unless these same remote parties are aware that transmissions are being recorded.

Commentary: This policy prevents a breakdown in trust relationships, accusations of privacy violation, and bad publicity. Many people will be surprised that Internet relay chat and instant messaging interactions can be easily recorded. In an indirect way, this policy warns internal users that third parties may record their interactions. One of the major dangers associated with these services is that they generally are used to convey very informal messages that are expected to disappear when the interaction is done. Participants may more readily make embarrassing comments, or even libel other parties. Both services have recently added an archive feature, which makes these interactions potentially as permanent as archived electronic mail. The policy says nothing about logging performed by the organization providing the computers and networks. The policy only deals with end users.

Related Policies: "Surreptitious Collection Of Private Information" and "Use Of Telephone Conference Or Recording Technology."

Audience: End users

Security Environments: All

2. Information Disclosure By Telephone

Policy: Requested customer information must not be disclosed by phone, unless the caller is able to positively identify themselves through a shared secret or through other caller identification measures approved by Company X management.

Commentary: This policy prevents internal workers from improperly disclosing personal or private information, if a caller at the end of a telephone line has not adequately identified himself or herself. This policy prevents help desk staff from being duped by hackers using social engineering techniques. While marketing specialists may consider this policy to be an impediment to speedy and efficient business, it is a necessity if an organization is going to provide telephone disclosures. This policy may give customers additional confidence that their money and information are properly protected. Much the same approach could be used for telephone transactions. If the policy included transactions, a telephone company staff member would refuse to turn-on call forwarding for a business number based simply on a telephone request. They would instead call the customer back at a known number, or in some other way establish positive identification.

Related Policies: "Record Change Orders."

Audience: Technical staff

Security Environments: Medium and high

3. Discussions In Public Places

Policy: All workers must refrain from discussing customer private information in public places such as in building lobbies or on public transportation, unless a customer's explicit permission is obtained.

Commentary: Many organizations such as hospitals critically depend on customers to reveal private information. If customers withhold private information because they are concerned that unauthorized parties will obtain it, then the quality of the product or service that the organization provides will be severely compromised. For example, if a patient worries that a doctor will discuss his case in the lobby in front of other patients, he may not mention a certain type of medication that he is taking. This may lead to a dangerous situation where newly prescribed drugs interact with the secret medication to cause a serious reaction that could have been avoided. This policy emphasizes the importance of maintaining private information in restricted places, such as inside a doctor's office. The policy prohibits all discussion in public places. It does not matter if the identity of the customer is concealed. This position is necessary because workers may be inattentive, and reveal other information from which the customer's identity may be discovered. Nothing in this policy prevents workers from talking about research results in a general sense, perhaps including statistical conclusions, but avoiding mention of specific cases. If it is necessary to talk about specific cases, for example in a presentation given at a conference, advance permission of the individuals can be obtained.

Related Policies: "Customer Record Statistical Information."

Audience: All

Security Environments: All

4. Customers Opt-Out Of Direct Mail

Policy: Company X customers must be given an opportunity to inform Company X that they do not wish to be contacted through unsolicited direct mail promotions.

Commentary: This policy permits customers to tell Company X that they do not wish to receive promotional mass mail. The customers should be notified that they may contact the company if they do not wish to receive solicitations by mail. This notice could be inserted into or printed on billing statements. The policy prohibits Company X from selling these customer contact particulars to third parties who would then use it for mass mail. If a customer asks for information by mail, even if this customer has previously expressed a desire not to receive direct mail, this policy would permit the information to be sent. The policy could be expanded to include fax solicitations, telemarketer solicitations, and electronic mail solicitations, particularly because these communication systems are also increasingly being used to send the equivalent of junk mail. If its scope is expanded, this policy will prevent violations of various laws and regulations.

Related Policies: "Telemarketing Records" and "Private Data System Opt Out."

Audience: End users and management

Security Environments: All

5. Financial Information Disclosure

Policy: Every disclosure of information about the financial condition of Company X, anticipated changes in financial position, and business developments that could reasonably be expected to materially alter the way investors view the company must be cleared in advance with the Public Relations department or a vice president, and made publicly available to all investors and interested parties at the same time.

Commentary: This policy prevents any workers from making selected disclosures to certain securities analysts, who then use this information to formulate buy, sell, or hold recommendations regarding the stock of Company X. This traditional approach permits the people with such restricted information to profit in the stock market while the general public cannot trade on the information. From an information security standpoint, it is desirable to be very careful about all disclosures to the public, especially in the litigious business environment. This policy brings a greater awareness and concern about what is being said publicly and a modicum of fairness to the disclosure process. This policy is relevant only to companies listed on stock exchanges.

Related Policies: "Information Transfer To Third Parties" and "Private Information Disclosure Records — Details."

Audience: Management

Security Environments: All

6. Sending Secret Information

Policy: Secret information must be shipped or sent through internal or external mails in a sealed opaque envelope marked "To Be Opened By Addressee Only," which is enclosed in a plain outer envelope that does not indicate the sensitivity of the contents.

Commentary: This policy gives all Company X workers specific instructions on the proper way to mark secret information sent by various types of physical mail. The policy is intended to be used for the most sensitive type of information, but does not apply to less sensitive types of information. Private and confidential information may be handled by a separate policy. An opaque envelope prevents unauthorized people from holding the envelope up to a bright light to read the contents. The plain outer envelope is intended to present a low-profile approach that is unlikely to draw the attention of those seeking such information. The words "To Be Opened By Addressee Only" are also a low-profile measure intended to subtly indicate that the contents might be sensitive. Some organizations may wish to drop this part of the policy. There is no indication anywhere on either of the two envelopes of the sensitivity of the contents. The use of the word "sealed" to indicate that reusable envelopes are not appropriate for this type of material. It is important that the recipient know if an unauthorized person has examined the involved material as it traveled en route. This policy presumes the existence of another policy that defines the term "secret." This term may be readily replaced with the label used within the organization.

Related Policies: "Presentation Of Public Image," "Sending Private And Confidential Information," "Four-Category Data Classification," and "Sending Sensitive Information."

Audience: All

Security Environments: All

7. Sending Sensitive Information

Policy: If private, confidential, or secret information is sent through internal mail, external mail, or by courier, it must be enclosed in two envelopes or containers with the outside envelope or container providing no indication of the sensitivity of the information contained therein and the inside sealed and opaque envelope or container labeled "Private," "Confidential," or "Secret."

Commentary: This policy gives all Company X workers specific instructions on the proper way to mark private, confidential, or secret information sent by various types of mail. The policy can be used for all sensitive types of information, as opposed to having separate policies for different classifications of sensitive information. An opaque envelope prevents unauthorized people from holding the envelope up to a light to read the contents. The plain outer envelope is intended to present a low-profile approach that is unlikely to draw the attention of those seeking such information. This policy presumes the existence of a policy that defines the terms "private, confidential, or secret."

Related Policies: "Presentation Of Public Image," "Four-Category Data Classification" and "Sending Secret Information."

Audience: All

Security Environments: All

8. Transmitting Secret Hardcopy Information

Policy: Secret information in hardcopy form must be sent by trusted courier or registered mail.

Commentary: This policy informs workers that they must use the most secure transportation methods for secret hardcopy information. Special trusted transportation is warranted for the highest classification of sensitive information. The policy does not address information held in computer data storage media because that could be encrypted and sent by any means without worry of unauthorized disclosure. This policy does not cover the proper containers for hardcopy secret information. This policy presumes the existence of a policy that defines the term "secret."

Related Policies: "Sending Sensitive Information" and "Four-Category Data Classification."

Audience: All

Security Environments: All

9. Binding Signatures

Policy: All signatures on contracts, purchase orders, and other important legally-binding documents provided by third parties must be in paper form.

Commentary: This policy ensures that Company X is able to provide adequate evidence to demonstrate the existence of legally-binding agreements such as purchase orders. If agreements are only in fax form, some judges will claim this is insufficient evidence. Nothing in this policy prevents workers from obtaining a fax with signatures as a preliminary document, to be followed soon thereafter by signatures in traditional paper form. This two-phase approach permits work to get underway immediately, with the paper documents being only a legal formality. This policy is by implication also relevant to electronic mail and other forms of business communication. Some jurisdictions are increasingly recognizing digital signatures and digital certificates as legally binding.

Related Policies: "Online Contracts By Exchange Of Paper And Signatures" and "Binding Contracts By Electronic Systems."

Audience: End users

Security Environments: All

10. Telephone Discussions Of Sensitive Information

Policy: Workers must avoid discussing sensitive information when on the telephone.

Commentary: This policy informs employees that the phones may be tapped or intercepted, and to caution them not to discuss sensitive information. In this context, tricks like the use of code words or nicknames can also be mentioned. The policy could be expanded to include mention of video conferencing facilities, which are often unencrypted and likewise subject to interception. This policy assumes that an organization has already defined the term "sensitive" in a policy.

Related Policies: "Four-Category Data Classification."

Audience: End users

Security Environments: Medium and high

11. Cordless Or Cellular Telephones

Policy: Secret Company X information must never be discussed on unencrypted cordless or cellular telephones.

Commentary: This policy prevents the unauthorized disclosure of sensitive information. A number of highly publicized cases make it clear that it is easy and inexpensive to intercept such conversations sent over the airwaves. This is a particularly important policy to communicate to top management, whom often have such phones, often do not understand the technology involved, and often discuss secret matters. The scope of this policy can be expanded to incorporate other wireless networks such as personal communications services, personal digital assistants with wireless capabilities, alphanumeric pagers, wireless local area networks, specialized mobile radio systems, ham radio networks, wireless packet networks, and satellite networks.

Related Policies: "Four-Category Data Classification" and "Sensitive Information On Answering Machines."

Audience: End users

Security Environments: Medium and high

12. Wireless Transmissions Of Secret Information

Policy: Wireless technology must never be used for the transmission of unencrypted secret information.

Commentary: Interception of radio transmissions is quite easy and many useful details, including telephone numbers, user IDs, and passwords, can be obtained. This policy notifies users that they must not use wireless technology, unless they know the transmissions are encrypted. Unfortunately, encryption is unavailable for a number of these systems such as lavaliere microphones used by public speakers, so prohibition against the use of these systems for secret information is the only option. This policy assumes the word "secret" has been clearly defined elsewhere.

Related Policies: "Electromagnetic Radiation Protection" and "Cordless Or Cellular Telephones."

Audience: End users and technical staff

Security Environments: Medium and high

13. Public Exposure Of Sensitive Information

Policy: Secret, confidential, or private Company X information must not be read, discussed, or otherwise exposed on airplanes, restaurants, elevators, public transportation, or in other public places.

Commentary: This policy prevents the unauthorized disclosure of sensitive information. It is not uncommon for employees to work while on a bus, airplane, or other public place. Often they work with sensitive information. The policy will prevent other travelers from looking over their shoulder on an airplane, read the material while using the same table at a restaurant, or in some other way being exposed to the material. The policy does not address those circumstances where the information is misplaced or stolen. The word "sensitive" might be used instead of "secret, confidential, or private." The policy assumes that a data classification policy explaining these terms has been issued.

Related Policies: "Traveling With Secret Information," "Four-Category Data Classification," and "Positioning Computer Display Screens."

Audience: All

Security Environments: All

14. Discussions In Administrative Areas

Policy: Company X workers must not discuss secret information in administrative areas including, but not limited to, corridors, cafeterias, visitor reception areas, and restrooms, because these areas are likely to include persons who have not been expressly authorized to receive this information.

Commentary: This policy clarifies where secret information may be discussed within Company X facilities. Workers may think that once they are on Company X premises, they can discuss anything, no matter how sensitive the information. The policy emphasizes the distinction between those people who are authorized to receive secret information and those who are not. The policy should be used in conjunction with a data classification system, which can be employed to restrict worker access to information based on a label.

Related Policies: "Public Exposure Of Sensitive Information," "Discussions In Public Places," and "Cordless Or Cellular Telephones."

Audience: End users

Security Environments: High

15. Meeting Attendees

Policy: Persons other than those specifically invited or pre-authorized by management must not attend meetings where secret information will be discussed.

Commentary: This policy instructs workers that uninvited people may not attend meetings where secret information is discussed. To permit this attendance would alter the set of people who have been authorized to access the information. This policy applies to in-person meetings, teleconferences, and virtual meetings where participants meet each other online. The term "secret" can be replaced with the most sensitive data classification label used by Company X. This policy assumes the term "secret" has been defined.

Related Policies: "Four-Category Data Classification" and "Confidential Information In Meetings."

Audience: End users and management

Security Environments: Medium and high

16. Meetings With Third Parties

Policy: If workers in the immediate vicinity of a conference room are handling sensitive information, all meetings with third-party visitors who are not authorized to have access to such sensitive information must take place in fully-enclosed conference rooms.

Commentary: This policy prevents third parties from being exposed to sensitive information. To reduce the chances of this happening, conference rooms must have walls on all sides to the ceiling, and a door that closes. Many offices are open and do not have complete walls or doors, and as a result, sounds from the surrounding area can be overheard by visitors. From a construction standpoint, visitors should not need to go through areas containing sensitive information in order to reach either a conference room or toilet facilities. This is one reason why conference rooms are often situated in a public area, that is an area outside access control points.

Related Policies: "Clean Desks — Non-Working Hours."

Audience: End users and management

Security Environments: Medium and high

17. Confidential Information In Meetings

Policy: If confidential information is discussed verbally in a meeting, seminar, lecture, or related presentation, the speaker must clearly communicate the sensitivity of the information and remind the audience to use discretion when disclosing it to others.

Commentary: This policy ensures that people who hear confidential information at a meeting treat it appropriately. Unless specific steps to remind people about the proper handling of spoken information are taken, they may inadvertently disclose it to unauthorized parties. This policy implies that all workers who are giving presentations should clearly determine whether the information they will deliver is confidential. The policy assumes that a data sensitivity classification scheme has already been adopted.

Related Policies: "Four-Category Data Classification" and "Information Released To The Public — Authorization."

Audience: End users and management

Security Environments: Medium and high

18. Erasable Surfaces

Policy: After each meeting is over, all erasable surfaces in conference rooms including, but not limited to, black boards, white boards, and windows must be erased.

Commentary: This policy ensures that any potentially sensitive information that is recorded on any erasable surface is not inadvertently disclosed to unintended parties. Conference rooms are typically freely accessible. Anyone in the building can enter them and review all the remaining information. Locks on the door and the personal presence of an occupant can, in some instances, protect erasable surfaces in personal offices. This policy is also courteous to the next users of the meeting room who may need to use the surfaces. This policy makes no reference to the methods to erase the information.

Related Policies: "Erasure Of Erasable Surfaces" and "Audio Or Video Recording Equipment."

Audience: All

Security Environments: All

19. Erasure Of Erasable Surfaces

Policy: Sensitive information recorded on erasable surfaces including, but not limited to, black boards, white boards, and windows, must be definitively erased with water or special cleaning fluids before the authorized recipients of this information leave the area.

Commentary: This policy prevents the inadvertent disclosure of sensitive information to unauthorized parties. If sensitive information were left on an erasable surface, then the next people to enter the area could immediately obtain this information. The policy is silent about the location of the black board or white board. In some military organizations, this policy is a standard operating procedure. It also may be appropriate for commercial organizations.

Related Policies: "Meeting Attendees" and "Erasable Surfaces."

Audience: All

Security Environments: Medium and high

20. Organization Representations

Policy: All business-related representations made by Company X workers including, but not limited to, those made in advertisements, in union negotiations, on product labels, and in government reports, must be truthful at all times.

Commentary: This policy informs workers that lying or bending the truth is prohibited. In general, the policy is intended to keep Company X and its workers out of trouble. This policy can be important if there are accusations that management systematically encouraged employees to misrepresent information. The policy also may be helpful in any lawsuits involving fraud or misleading advertising. This policy may also help prevent or defend Company X from employee allegations that they were lied to during an employment interview process. The policy also may be useful in the prevention of practical jokes and clever humor that may ultimately cause problems.

Related Policies: "Incomplete Or Obsolete Information."

Audience: All

Security Environments: All

21. Public Representation Approval

Policy: All public representations including, but not limited to, media advertisements, Internet home pages, electronic bulletin board postings, and voice mail broadcast messages, must be issued or approved by the Public Relations department.

Commentary: This policy prevents separate departments from independently initiating public representations about Company X. One of the major problems that organizations face is that different departments create their own Internet web pages without an internal review or approval. Unless a policy like this exists, there is a danger that such independent efforts will publicly embarrass the organization, confuse customers, or create other unwanted issues. This policy establishes a single point of contact for interactions with the public. Current communications technology permits many people to be reached easily, inexpensively, and quickly. This capability should be tempered by controls so that problems are not inadvertently created. In a conglomerate that owns autonomous companies, and in a large government entity, the Public Relations department of each subsidiary would be involved rather than a centralized Public Relations department.

Related Policies: "Unofficial Web Pages," "Organization Representations," "Public Electronic Forums," and "Public Communications."

Audience: End users and technical staff

Security Environments: All

22. Potentially-Offensive Communications

Policy: Any Company X communications including, but not limited to, phone message recordings, voice mail messages, and letters, that may offend or upset certain segments of the expected recipient population, must contain an appropriate warning on the cover, in the introduction, or in some other place such that the recipient may opt not to receive the information.

Commentary: This policy is intended to reduce the number of complaints about Company X advertising and communications. It is also intended to inform the recipients about the nature of the information, giving them a chance not to proceed. Organizations sending potentially offensive direct mail or mass mail material enclose their solicitations in an inner envelope that clearly indicates that the material may offend some people. The recipient may then open it or discard it. Although the policy could apply to internal communications, it is primarily intended to be used for external communications.

Related Policies: "Fax Cover Sheet Notice" and "Covering Sensitive Information."

Audience: Technical staff

Security Environments: All

23. Sensitive Information On Answering Machines

Policy: Workers must not record messages containing sensitive information on answering machines or voice mail systems.

Commentary: The purpose of this policy is to notify workers that the person picking up messages on a message machine may not be authorized to receive sensitive information. Workers should simply ask the intended recipient of the information to call them back. Not only can the person receiving the message be other than the intended recipient, but also hackers can pick up messages off answering machines without ever having to physically access the answering machine. This policy can be expanded to include prohibition on the use of remote access facilities that permit people to pick up messages from a different location. However, this may be burdensome and unpopular with the user community. The policy could also be expanded to include mention of recording sensitive information on alphanumeric pagers.

Related Policies: "Secret Information On Speaker Phones," "Recording Sensitive Information," "Collect And Third-Party Bill-To Calls," and "Cordless Or Cellular Telephones."

Audience: End users and technical staff

Security Environments: All

24. Use Of Credit Cards

Policy: While using public pay phones, whenever circumstances permit, workers must swipe telephone or other credit cards rather than using the keypad or telephone mouthpiece to relay the billing information.

Commentary: This policy prevents bill-to numbers from falling into the hands of unauthorized parties who may use these numbers to place fraudulent calls. It is increasingly common for these people to listen to, watch, or video tape other people entering their billing information into a keypad at a public phone. The video tape scam is perhaps the easiest because the tape can later be replayed to ascertain the numbers entered. Likewise, if the bill-to information is spoken into the telephone mouthpiece, other people can overhear the information. The safest way to prevent these and related abuses is to swipe a credit card through the readers found in many pay phones. Some public phones will not have readers. This is one reason why the words "whenever circumstances permit" were used in the policy. Another reason is that Company X workers may not have a phone or credit card with them. However, not carrying a telephone credit card may reduce the chances of fraud occasioned by the loss or theft of the card. Another reason to use bank credit cards is that the liability of the user for fraudulent charges is limited, and in many instances is waived entirely.

Related Policies: "Positioning Computer Display Screens" and "Missing Access Devices."

Audience: End users

Security Environments: All

25. Use Of Telephone Conference Or Recording Technology

Policy: When using a telephone, workers must not use speakerphones, microphones, loudspeakers, tape recorders, or similar technologies unless they have obtained the consent of both the originator and recipient of the call.

Commentary: This policy ensures that both parties know that other people are listening or could subsequently listen to the conversation. The originator or the recipient of the call are likely to speak differently when they know about the other people who might hear the conversation. If only one party to a conversation, perhaps the originator, knows about the use of such equipment, this may violate federal or local of wiretap statutes.

Related Policies: "Performance Monitoring Information" and "Electronic Monitoring Areas."

Audience: End users and management

Security Environments: All

26. Recording Video Conferences

Policy: Company X video conferencing sessions must not be recorded unless this recording is approved in advance by the manager of information security and communicated in advance to all video conference participants.

Commentary: This policy prevents future legal liability. If video conferencing sessions are not recorded, they cannot be obtained during discovery proceedings or other legal maneuvers. In some ways similar to a policy at many organizations requiring the routine destruction of outdated electronic mail messages, this policy prevents sensitive internal information from being used in unintended and detrimental ways. This policy also limits the amount of information that organizations must manage.

Related Policies: "Monitoring Or Recording Telephone Conversations."

Audience: Technical staff

Security Environments: All

9   ACCESS CONTROL

9.01 Business Requirement For Access Control

9.01.01 Access Control Policy

1. Hacking Activities

Policy: Workers must not use Company X information systems to engage in hacking activities that include, but are not limited to, gaining unauthorized access to any other information systems damaging, altering, or disrupting the operations of any other information systems and capturing or otherwise obtaining passwords, encryption keys, or any other access control mechanism that could permit unauthorized access.

Commentary: This policy establishes management's position forbidding hacking activities through Company X information systems. This policy is desirable in those jurisdictions where hacking is not clearly illegal. The policy is also needed in academia, where hacking is often seen as justifiable in the name of performing computer research or teaching computer science. The policy is written in such a way that it applies to both internal and external information systems. The policy embraces a wide variety of hacker techniques, including social engineering, and password grabbers. The words "access control mechanism" are deliberately vague. This would include smart cards, dynamic password tokens, and other extended authentication mechanisms. This policy can be used to discipline, and perhaps terminate, a worker who was hacking through Company X information systems. This is desirable if the organization wishes to avoid revealing this activity to the public.

Related Policies: "Testing Information System Controls" and "Computer Crime Or Abuse Evidence."

Audience: End users and technical staff

Security Environments: All

2.   Regulating Software

Policy: All software installed on Company X multi-user systems must be regulated by an approved access control system that will control a user's session prior to passing control to separate application software.

Commentary: This policy prevents the installation of software that cannot be regulated by an access control system. The access control system software does not need to be an operating system. It can be a layered access control package or even a front-end or firewall that performs access control. This policy is less necessary with operating systems where all requests for service are automatically mediated through the operating system's access control mechanisms. Some older operating systems are in need of a policy such as this. The policy is not operating-system specific. This policy indirectly prohibits programmers from installing trap doors and other software that could circumvent an access control system. This policy would ordinarily be delivered only to systems programmers, system administrators, and related technical support staff.

Related Policies: "Malfunctioning Access Control" and "Operating System User Authentication."

Audience: Technical staff

Security Environments: All

3.   Password-Based Access Control

Policy: Any small system that handles either critical or sensitive information must utilize a properly-maintained version of an approved password-based access control system.

Commentary: This policy provides managers of small systems with specific guidance on whether they should employ a password-based access control system. Those systems that do not contain either critical or confidential information are, by default, not required to have access control systems. The words "properly maintained" were included in the policy to signify that the simple installation of a package is not sufficient. In some cases, the package may be installed, but it may not be used to protect either confidential or critical files. This policy assumes that the words "sensitive" and "critical" have been formally defined. The word "valuable" may be added to this policy.

Related Policies: "Four-Category Data Classification," "Network Computer Access Control," and "Physical Access Control To Sensitive Information."

Audience: Management and technical staff

Security Environments: All

4. Read Access Sensitive Information

Policy: Workers who have been authorized to view information classified at a certain sensitivity level must be permitted to access only the information at this level and at less sensitive levels.

Commentary: This policy instructs system administrators and others who set access control privileges to prevent users from gaining unauthorized access to information. For example, a person who has been authorized to view Secret information also may view Confidential and Public information because these are less sensitive than secret information. This person, however, may not view top-secret information unless specific authorization has been granted. This approach is sometimes called "read down" or "no read up" because the user is given permission to read at only his or her classification level and those levels down, progressively getting less sensitive. This policy applies to all levels of data, no matter how many levels are in a classification system. For example, if a user has permission to read only "unclassified" data or the least sensitive level, then the user could not access any other levels. Conversely, if an individual had access to the highest level of data then this individual could access all other levels. This policy is most often seen in military and diplomatic organizations, while commercial organizations often use less complex models. Unfortunately, a large number of commercial operating systems do not support this policy. Additional software is required for policy implementation.

Related Policies: "Four-Category Data Classification."

Audience: All

Security Environments: High

5. Write Access Sensitive Information

Policy: Workers must not move information classified at a certain sensitivity level to a less sensitive level unless this action is a formal part of an approved declassification process.

Commentary: This policy prohibits users from moving data from one classification level to another in order to be able to gain unauthorized access to it. For example, if an individual could copy "top secret" information, then write it to a "confidential," less sensitive file, the individual may be able to give access to another who is not otherwise authorized to view the information. The process of writing information down to a less sensitive classification level can be considered to be effectively declassifying the information so that unauthorized parties then may access it. Some organizations may wish to add words to this policy describing the ways that users will know that a declassification process is approved. This policy is often seen in systems for military and diplomatic organizations rather than in commercial organizations. The policy can be enforced automatically, although most commercial operating systems do not support it. Additional software is required for implementation.

Related Policies: "Four-Category Data Classification."

Audience: All

Security Environments: High

6. Default File Permissions

Policy: File access control permissions for all Company X networked systems must be set to a default that blocks access by unauthorized users.

Commentary: This policy provides both users and system administrators with guidance in the establishment of appropriate access controls for networked systems. Computer systems that are not networked generally need fewer logical access controls because they can rely on physical security measures such as a locked office door. This policy is written so that it applies only to networked systems. Staff members often decide on their own that logical access controls are too time consuming and resource intensive. This policy prohibits staff from making decisions that may not be in the organization's best long-term interests. The policy also may be helpful in cases where local management does not want to spend the money to define access controls. The policy requires them to support technical staff who perform these tasks.

Related Policies: "Default User Privileges," "Malfunctioning Access Control," and "Privilege Restriction — Need To Know."

Audience: End users and technical staff

Security Environments: Medium and high

7. Malfunctioning Access Control

Policy: If a computer or network access control system is not functioning properly, it must default to denial of privileges to end users.

Commentary: Rather than permit open and uncontrolled access, This policy prevents access until the access control system can be repaired. For example, if a password-based access control system on a web server were to malfunction, no end-user access to the system should be permitted. Technical staff would need access in order to fix the problem. Some organizations may wish to add specific exclusions to the policy in order to keep essential business processes operational, such as continuing to clear checks at a bank. All such exclusions should be carefully considered before they are incorporated into the policy, lest they become the areas exploited by industrial spies, embezzlers, and others engaged in information system abuses. In general, if it accurately reflects the environment, it is desirable to keep a policy like this simple and straightforward. Exceptions should be made on a case-by-case basis.

Related Policies: "User Access Capabilities" and "Privilege Restriction — Need To Know."

Audience: Management and technical staff

Security Environments: All

8. Centralized Access Control Database

Policy: Unambiguous, organized, and current records of all production information system access privileges must be maintained in a centralized database maintained by Information Security management.

Commentary: This policy ensures that the Information Security department is aware of all changes in the privileges of users who have access to production systems at Company X. The changes may be performed by system administrators in other departments, or even by outsourcing organization staff, but Information Security management will at least be immediately informed of these changes. A centralized access control database permits all privileges of a departing worker to be turned-off immediately. This is especially important in duress terminations, where somebody is escorted to the door in less than desirable circumstances. For example, they may have been caught defrauding the organization. In these cases revenge is likely, and it is absolutely essential that all privileges available to the departing worker be immediately and conclusively terminated. It is unlikely that this objective will be reliably met if there is no centralized database of

privileges. The centralized database can be used to run certain software that can identify conflicts of interest, excessive system privileges, and other problems that may not have come to the attention of the system administrators who are assigning privileges. Software systems that support a centralized database are sometimes called Enterprise Security Management systems.

Related Policies: "Worker Status Changes."

Audience: Technical staff

Security Environments: All

9. Command Line Interpreter Software

Policy: All command line interpreter software must be removed from those production machines that do not need such software in order to conduct normal processing.

Commentary: This policy instructs staff working in the systems programming area to remove software that could respond to a command entered at a keyboard, as opposed to a command that could be indicated through a mouse clicking on a button in a browser-style screen, or through a mouse selecting from predetermined options listed on a menu. Command line privileges permit systems to be stopped, access control privileges to be changed, logs to be turned-off, and other actions to be taken that could have a material impact on the security of a production system. If command line interpreter software is unavailable, intruders will be significantly impeded in their efforts to gain the most privileged status on a system. The policy does not imply that staff members working in the computer operations area need to be hindered or inconvenienced in any way. The policy does, however, assume that computer operations have been scripted to a certain extent so that all normal actions can be accomplished without the need for a command line. This policy can be used to reduce errors and omissions caused by computer operations staff. If certain commands are not available to them, the risk that these staff members will cause damage with these commands is minimized. Before adopting this policy, the organization should ensure that its emergency response and disaster recovery procedures will not need a command line interpreter.

Related Policies: "Unnecessary Software" and "Firewall Computers."

Audience: Technical staff

Security Environments: Medium and high

10. Circumventing Access Controls

Policy: Programmers and other technically-oriented staff must refrain from installing any code that circumvents the authorized access control mechanisms found in operating systems or access control packages.

Commentary: Trap doors are special code segments that secretly permit a systems programmer, technical support staff member, or someone else to bypass standard access controls. These hidden pieces of code are invoked with special undocumented commands known only to the person who wrote them. Ironically, most trap doors are installed with good intentions such as being able to install system maintenance code without rebooting the machine, being able to issue privileged systems programming commands from ordinary user workstations, or being able to bypass the access control system should the system crash. This policy requires all accesses to go through standard access control mechanisms, which will achieve uniformity, auditability, and a more secure operating environment. If trap doors exist, they could be used by unauthorized parties to damage the system. Likewise, if the person who installed a trap door leaves the organization under less than friendly terms, the former worker could do serious damage through the trap door. This policy could be modified to apply to application system access controls or database management system access controls, and the access controls found in operating systems and access control packages.

Related Policies: "Operating System User Authentication" and "Access Paths In Production Software."

Audience: Technical staff

Security Environments: All

11. Compromising Security Mechanisms For Customers

Policy: Customer requests that Company X security mechanisms be compromised must not be satisfied unless an executive vice president approves it in writing or Company X is compelled to comply by law.

Commentary: This policy addresses the trade off between customer service and security. For example, a software company that makes word processing software with an encryption feature may receive a request from a customer to break the encryption process so that the only available copy of a file may be decrypted. This policy states that the software company must not do this unless one or both of the conditions in the policy are met. If the software company often compromised the encryption process as a customer service, word might get out that the company can and will do this. Consequently, the company would be requested to do it regularly. The company would also need to determine whether the requester had the proper authority to make the request. The policy does not address the compromise of controls on systems external to Company X. Some organizations may wish to expand the scope of this policy to include external systems as well. This would, for example, prevent an information broker from compromising controls on an external system to obtain certain sought-after information.

Related Policies: "System Penetration Software Source Code," "Access Paths In Production Software," "Software Integrity Statements," and "Testing Information System Controls."

Audience: Management and technical staff

Security Environments: All

12. Information Collection Restrictions

Policy: If Company X sensitive information is resident on a computer system, and if users are permitted to request all or part of this information through online facilities, special access controls must be in force to protect the information so that a series of permissible requests for information will not collectively reveal information that is otherwise restricted.

Commentary: This policy gives those responsible for security some guidance in the establishment of access control systems. For example, a network administrator in the process of setting-up an access control system could benefit from a policy such as this. Likewise, a programmer creating a database query facility to be placed on a server accessible through the Internet should keep this policy in mind. This policy suggests that access control privileges should be defined in broad categories, such as job titles, rather than detailed categories, such as data about individuals. The word "sensitive" may be replaced with a designation such as "secret" that is in keeping with an internal data classification policy.

Related Policies: "Four-Category Data Classification," "Customer Record Statistical Information," "Assigning Data Classification Labels," and "Multiple Classification Labeling."

Audience: Technical staff

Security Environments: Medium and high

13. Disclosure Of Third-Party Information

Policy: Company X workers must not disclose sensitive information that has been entrusted to it by third parties to other third parties unless the originator of the information has provided advance approval of the disclosure and the receiving party has signed an approved non-disclosure agreement.

Commentary: With business partnerships so prevalent today, there is often significant cross-organizational sharing of confidential information. Before this sharing of information can take place, originating organizations must feel confident that their information is not going to be disclosed to unknown third parties. To help generate this confidence, this policy makes it clear that Company X is going to require both a non-disclosure agreement and advance approval before any third party is going to get information that has been entrusted to Company X. To make this policy truly effective, it will be necessary to label information so that the originator is readily identifiable, or else provide other facilities, such as a corporate data dictionary, that will identify the originator.

Related Policies: "Third-Party Private Information Disclosure," "Confidentiality Agreements," and "External Information Requests."

Audience: End users and technical staff

Security Environments: All

14. Requests For Organization Information

Policy: Unless authorized by top management, all requests for information about Company X and its business activities including, but not limited to, questionnaires, surveys, and newspaper interviews, must be referred to the Public Relations department.

Commentary: This policy prevents workers, regardless of their intentions, from disclosing sensitive information to the press, market researchers, competitors, industrial spies, system hackers, and others. This policy authorizes only the Public Relations department or designated spokespersons who are often subject matter experts to disclose information about Company X and its business activities. By funneling disclosures through Public Relations, an organization is also able to present a coordinated and orderly image to the public. This also will reduce the chances that industrial spies will use social engineering to obtain information from unwitting employees. This policy is important after a disaster or some other publicly-disclosed problem. Under these circumstances, the press will seek out employees for interviews. When this occurs, if disclosures are not carefully managed, an organization can appear poorly managed and confused. This policy may be a part of contingency planning efforts addressing what to do in the event of bomb blasts, earthquakes, and other disasters and emergencies. Many employees will be relieved to have a simple approach to politely get rid of the people requesting information. In some organizations, the Public Relations department may have designated spokespersons who can speak about certain topics. For example, if an information security problem has taken place, the director of Information Security may be authorized to speak with the public. To be clear, some organizations may wish to add the words "and information systems" after "business activities."

Related Policies: "Release Of Organization Information," "Centralized Information Security," and "Presentation Of Public Image."

Audience: All

Security Environments: All

15. Disclosing Customer Business Information

Policy: Company X workers must not disclose to anyone outside Company X the nature of customer projects, customer business strategies, or customer business relationships.

Commentary: This policy cautions organizations when disclosing information about customers. It would, for example, be relevant to a consulting organization that did fraud investigations. The policy is strict in that it does not permit any disclosure, even if the customer's identity is concealed. The policy's scope could be expanded to include how it is to work with a particular customer. Comments made to reporters like "they're very hard to work with" can damage ongoing relationships, even if they are not, strictly speaking, a disclosure of sensitive information.

Related Policies: "Sharing Marketing Information" and "Public Communications."

Audience: End users

Security Environments: All

16. Sharing Marketing Information

Policy: Marketing information including, but not limited to, prices, sales policies, strategies, plans, market share status, and other marketing information must never be disclosed to competitors.

Commentary: This policy clarifies what is often a confusing point for people working in sales and marketing. On one hand, certain information such as prices and sales policies are discussed with just about any prospect or customer. On the other hand, this information is of great value to the competition. Granted, third parties working for the competition could gather this information on behalf of the competition, but this policy requires the competition to engage in a borderline unethical activity. Just because it is questionable does not mean that the competition will not use third parties to gather competitive intelligence information. This policy will make it harder for them. The policy assumes that people working in sales and marketing know who the competition is. In some industries there are so many competitors, it is not feasible to have a current list of them all. Each organization may wish to explicitly specify the types of information that it wishes to withhold from the competition.

Related Policies: "Confidentiality Agreements At Previous Employers" and "Employees Leaving For A Competitor."

Audience: End users

Security Environments: All

17. Information Released To The Public — Contact Name

Policy: Information generated by Company X and released to the public must be accompanied by the name of a designated staff member acting as the single recognized official source and point-of-contact.

Commentary: This policy provides an organized approach to releasing information to the public. This policy ensures a consistent position with respect to the information and a mechanism to control the different forms in which the information my be presented. It relies on designated sources rather than the Public Relations department to bring some order to this process. The policy could be changed to state that only the designated Owner of the information can release it to the public. With computers on nearly every desk, all workers are potential publishers. Some organizations may want to specify a few exceptions to the policy, such as marketing brochures.

Related Policies: "Public Representation Approval" and "External Information Requests."

Audience: End users

Security Environments: All

18. Legal Action Information

Policy: All third-party requests for information related to a current legal case must not be granted unless the request is made by an authorized government agency.

Commentary: This policy prevents Company X staff from inadvertently commenting on, or providing information related to, matters now in court, and some way prejudicing the case. This could for example take place if a Company X staff member were to provide some background information, but the opposing party did not know this same background information. If this same information were to come to light in a newspaper article, the opposing party's attorney could use this. The policy does permit staff members to respond to discovery proceedings, subpoenas, and other legitimate requests for information regarding a matter now being litigated. Nothing in this policy prevents management from selectively disclosing to the news media certain information that it believes will help it win public support for a legal matter now underway.

Related Policies: "Information Released To The Public — Contact Name," "Use Of Organization Name," and "Requests For Organization Information."

Audience: End users

Security Environments: All

19. Release Of Organization Information

Policy: Permission to disclose any internal Company X information to the news media or to other third parties must be obtained from Company X senior management prior to release.

Commentary: This policy prevents workers from disclosing sensitive information to the press, market researchers, competitors, system hackers, and others. Without explicit approval, disclosure is forbidden. Because the word "internal" is used, certain public information is not covered by the policy. The word "internal" could be replaced by "sensitive" or "classified." This policy does not require that all information flow through a central clearing point. This approach runs the risk of presenting a disorganized and poorly managed image to the public. One option that may be added to this policy would involve getting management's permission in writing prior to each release.

Related Policies: "Requests For Organization Information," "Presentation Of Public Image," and "Systems Documentation Release."

Audience: All

Security Environments: All

20. Future Earnings Or Products

Policy: Workers must not make any public representations about Company X future earnings or the prospects for new products.

Commentary: The rash of recent class-action lawsuits has made senior management at many organizations worry about the repercussions of making any future projections. This policy prohibits any public statement along these lines. Not only will the policy help stop investor lawsuits, it will also help dampen fluctuations in stock prices caused by actual financial results that do not meet management's publicly-released financial projections. This policy is relevant only to publicly-traded companies Those companies without publicly-held stock need not have a policy such as this. This policy pertains to verbal representations made to reporters, and written representation made in stock offering prospectuses, annual reports, and related documents. Some organizations may consider this policy to be too stringent, and they may wish to add the words "with the exception of the CEO" after the word "workers."

Related Policies: "Requests For Organization Information" and "Public Communications."

Audience: End users and management

Security Environments: All

21. External Information Requests

Policy: All requests from a third party for internal information that is not of a sales, marketing, or public relations nature must be approved by the information Owner and the corporate counsel who must each be given five business days to evaluate the merits of the request.

Commentary: This policy defines the ways to handle external requests for internal information that may be of a sensitive nature. The information might invade the privacy of a certain party, be national defense-related information, be needed by law enforcement for an investigation in process, or for some other reason might not be appropriate to disclose. The possibility that it might be sensitive warrants the five-day review period. The policy could be used by commercial organizations if it was restricted to certain information that the public had a right to receive. For example, at an electric utility, information about the systems used to generate electricity might be readily disclosed to the public in the absence of an objection from the parties named in the policy. When used in a governmental agency, the policy's reference to the parties able to veto the request could be changed to middle-level managers in charge of the systems and the related information.

Related Policies: "Requests For Organization Information."

Audience: Management and technical staff

Security Environments: All

22. Controversial Sensitive Information

Policy: Controversial and sensitive Company X information must be released to the public in installments.

Commentary: This policy assures that a Company X-intended explanation accompanies each release of controversial information. This minimizes damage to the reputation of Company X and helps assure that the information is used for intended purposes. This policy's process for the release of controversial information may be in conflict with court orders. In this case, the court orders would prevail. But if Company X were voluntarily releasing information for the public benefit, or in order to assist a non-profit group, then this policy would be applicable. This approach provides time for the organization to research its internal records and to determine all the information that will be released. This approach permits Company X to release the least controversial parts of a sensitive information collection first, and to gradually provide more controversial material.

Related Policies: "Presentation Of Public Image" and "Requests For Organization Information."

Audience: Management

Security Environments: Medium and high

23. Help Wanted Advertising

Policy: All public help wanted advertising or announcements must be approved in advance by Human Resources management prior to being posted.

Commentary: This policy prevents competitive intelligence analysts from using help wanted advertisements to determine what other organizations are doing, and what new products they will release. Help wanted ads can release management's priorities and internal problems, and can indicate an organization's strategic direction. It is advisable not to mention company name anywhere in an ad. Some organizations may take it further, insisting on rotating the contact information such as telephone or fax number. Employment recruiters customarily withhold the name of their clients until they know they have a good candidate, because others might use this information for unknown and unauthorized purposes.

Related Policies: "Public Communications" and "External Information Requests."

Audience: End users

Security Environments: Medium and high

24. Information Released To The Public — Authorization

Policy: All information to be released to the public must have been reviewed by management according to an established and documented process.

Commentary: This policy requires management to establish and observe a formal procedure for the review of information before it is released to the public. Beyond requiring such a procedure be used, this policy also requires the procedure to be documented. The policy could be expanded to require that documentation reflecting each request also be generated. Perhaps the most important part of the latter type of documentation is the specific approvals provided. The existence of documentation is likely to result in well-reasoned decisions. Although appropriate for those organizations with highly developed data classification schemes, this policy can also exist in the absence of a formal data classification scheme.

Related Policies: "Four-Category Data Classification" and "Release Of Organization Information."

Audience: All

Security Environments: All

25. Public Communications

Policy: Every speech, presentation, technical paper, book, or other communication to be delivered to the public must have been approved for release by the involved employee's immediate manager.

Commentary: This policy requires that employees always obtain approval from their managers prior to delivering a speech, presentation, paper, or other communication. It prevents unauthorized disclosure of sensitive information. If an employee discussed the general state of the industry in which Company X offered products or services, this too would need to be approved. This policy could include the phrase "workers should disclose no more Company X-related information than is needed to achieve the desired purpose." Of particular concern is the public disclosure of patentable material. If this information is published prior to the filing of a patent, then the patent can be invalidated. Patent laws vary from country to country.

Related Policies: "Public Representation Approval" and "Release Of Organization Information."

Audience: All

Security Environments: All

26. Information Disclosure Approval

Policy: Disclosure of any file stored on, and every message sent through its network to outside parties must be preceded by the review and approval of the Legal department director.

Commentary: This policy informs users that they should not have any expectations about privacy when using the organization's information systems. This policy ensures that such information is never shared with outside parties unless the disclosure meets with the Legal department director's approval. This intention will help avoid civil liability issues. The involved person might, for example, claim that the disclosure was unflattering and that his or her reputation had been damaged. Or this person might claim that the facts were wrong, and that he or she had been slandered or libeled. To avoid or reduce exposure to these problems, it is good practice to get a legal expert to review the disclosure.

Related Policies: "Information Released To The Public — Authorization" and "Non-Disclosure Agreements — Organization."

Audience: End users and technical staff

Security Environments: All

27. Nature And Location Of Organization Information

Policy: Information about the nature and location of Company X information, such as that found in a data dictionary, is confidential and must only be disclosed to those with a demonstrable need to know.

Commentary: This policy notifies workers that information about information, also known as metadata, is confidential. The distinction here is between restricting access to information based on the need to know, and restricting access to information about information based on the need to know. Metadata is of great use to system hackers, industrial spies, saboteurs, and others intent on doing harm to Company X. In many cases, metadata is more valuable than the information to which it refers. This is because metadata can include a data classification label, a description of relevant control measures, the systems on which the information is resident, and persons who have legitimate access rights to the information. From a commercial perspective, information about the existence of a soon-to-be-released product or service may be more important than the actual specifications for the product. While data dictionaries can be important management tools, access to the information contained therein must be restricted based on the need to know. Document management systems also contain metadata that should be restricted in accordance with this policy.

Related Policies: "Privilege Restriction — Need To Know," "Information Integrity Attributes," and "Asset Inventory — Information."

Audience: All

Security Environments: All

28. Browsing Systems

Policy: Workers must not browse through Company X computer systems or networks.

Commentary: This policy prohibits hacking activities. In many instances, perpetrators of computer abuse are curious rather than deliberately malicious. Often these people take advantage of the information they discover. When caught, these people often claim that they were only looking around, and that they had no malicious, fraudulent, or other bad intentions. To counteract such claims, this policy makes it clear that browsing information systems is not acceptable. If workers browse the Company X network, this policy gives management a tool with which to discipline or terminate these workers. The policy is particularly relevant to personal computers, workstations, client-server systems, and local area networks because these small systems often have inadequate access controls. This policy is not an acceptable replacement for a real access control system. The policy could be expanded to mention intranet surfing, which is permissible and is not considered browsing.

Related Policies: "Errors And Record Manipulations."

Audience: All

Security Environments: All

29. Security Product Maturity

Policy: Information systems security products on the market less than a year must not be used as an integral component of any critical Company X production information system.

Commentary: This policy prevents systems designers and others from using very new information security products for production systems. Nothing in the policy prevents Company X from acting as a beta site, or from testing these new products. It does, however, prevent Company X from relying on these products. The major concern here is discovery of security deficiencies that later embarrass the organization, cause it to discontinue the production systems involved, or permit crimes like fraud to be perpetrated. By waiting a year, Company X relies on the marketplace to identify major security problems. Although rare, this policy or a derivative policy with a smaller time frame could also apply to major releases of existing information systems security products. For the most conservative organizations, the policy could apply to all information systems products, not just information systems security products. If this policy seems too restrictive as written, a special approval process can be provided to deal with exceptions.

Related Policies: "Operating System Versions," "Mature Development Tools And Techniques," and "Security Fixes."

Audience: Technical staff

Security Environments: Medium and high

30. Creating Security Tools

Policy: Internal Company X systems developers and designers must not create new security protocols, compose new security schemes, develop new encryption algorithms, or otherwise be inventive when it comes to information security.

Commentary: This policy addresses a serious problem in the systems development community. Many programmers, systems designers, and others who develop their own security schemes, protocols, and methods do not have the requisite expertise to do this. Because they do not understand the associated risks associated they often create problems for their organizations. This policy is intended to prevent developers from using new applications or new systems as their own personal project. Instead, this policy reinforces that security is serious, and that they must utilize leading practices and methods.

Related Policies: "Publicly-Evaluated Encryption Algorithms" and "Standard Encryption Algorithm And Implementation."

Audience: Technical staff

Security Environments: All

31. Security Control Usability

Policy: All computer and communications security measures must be simple and easy to use, administer, and to audit.

Commentary: This policy requires that all computer and communications controls be practical and sustainable. If security measures are too complex they are likely to be misunderstood, misinterpreted, or misapplied. Whenever controls are awkward, cumbersome, or otherwise poorly designed, users will bypass or resist them. This policy acknowledges reality in that, to be successful, controls must have a balance between security objectives and practical concerns, for example cost and ease of use. The term "user-friendly" may be used in this policy, but it has been used so much that it has lost much of its meaning. To make the policy cleaner, some readers may wish to eliminate two of the three instances of the words "simple and easy." The policy is intended for systems designers, systems integrators, and others who set up information systems. Nothing in this policy prevents systems designers from building complex systems. This policy only requires that the complexity be hidden from the users and others who must interact with the system.

Related Policies: "Minimum Information System Controls" and "User Acceptance Of Information Security Measures."

Audience: Technical staff

Security Environments: All

32. Information System Privilege Usage

Policy: Information system privileges must not be employed for any Company X business purpose until they have been approved in writing by Information Security management.

Commentary: This policy is an expression of what is called restrictive design. It is intended to prevent privileges that have been enabled but not sufficiently examined from being used by intruders and other unauthorized individuals. For example, according to the configuration of a firewall, certain Internet services will be permitted and certain services will be forbidden. Vendors often ship products with many, if not all, services permitted to enable customers to get the systems up and running quickly. Likewise, the Internet is designed with a permissive design approach that says everything that is not specifically forbidden is permitted. This policy imposes a certain degree of inflexibility because privilege changes must be approved in advance, but it assures that services that have not been adequately investigated are not going to be used against the organization. This policy suggests that Information Security management makes decisions about new types of privileges. Some organizations may wish to employ information Owners instead. In an indirect way, this policy also informs users that they should not attempt to discover privileges that they have not been expressly authorized to utilize.

Related Policies: "Privilege Restriction — Need To Know" and "Reliance On Common Mechanisms For Controls."

Audience: Technical staff

Security Environments: All

33. Independent Security Systems

Policy: The security of a computer system must never be entirely dependent on the security of another computer system.

Commentary: In a well-secured network of systems, each system can maintain its own security in a decentralized manner. This approach provides greater resilience to a variety of attacks. For example, if a small system was entirely dependent on another system on a network, then a successful compromise of the security on the other system would leave both systems vulnerable. This might be the case if single sign-on systems were employed because the same password could permit access to a variety of systems. This policy requires designers and other technical staff to consider whether a system is in fact dependent on another system. The policy encourages control measures that compensate for deficiencies or failures of other controls. An example of would be an active logging system that might shut down a certain user ID because activity on the user ID was very different from the authorized user's profile.

Related Policies: "Systems Expertise," "Operating System User Authentication," and "Reliance On Common Mechanisms For Controls."

Audience: Technical staff

Security Environments: All

34. Granting Access To Organization Information

Policy: Access to Company X information must always be authorized by a designated Owner of such information, and must be limited on a need-to-know basis to a reasonably restricted number of people.

Commentary: This policy states who makes decisions about access to certain information. The policy permits Owners to create categories of users, such as accounts payable clerks, to which a predetermined set of privileges may then be granted. This permits Custodians to grant basic privileges to an individual based on their job title, eliminating the need for the Owner to consider the circumstances of each individual. The policy also reminds all who read it that access to information is not granted simply because access was requested. The need to know must also be present. A small minority of organizations is replacing the traditional notion of need to know with the notion of need to withhold.

Related Policies: "Privilege Restriction — Need To Know," "Network Computer Access Control," and "Malfunctioning Access Control."

Audience: Management and technical staff

Security Environments: All

9.02 User Access Management

9.02.01 User Registration

1. Anonymous User IDs

Policy: User IDs must be assigned in a sequential numeric fashion so there is no obvious correlation between a user ID and the name of the involved user.

Commentary: This policy prevents unauthorized persons from being able to employ user IDs to break into systems, deduce confidential information, or to otherwise compromise system security. This might, for example, take place if an industrial spy were going through the trash and was able to recover a phone book and also a system activity console log. If user IDs were equivalent to last names, the spy would be able to determine what activities certain users performed on the system. He may then be able to gather personal information about them, using this information to guess their password. He may be able to use this information to decide whom to bribe to perform certain actions on his behalf. This policy prevents unauthorized persons from guessing user IDs, but unfortunately makes electronic mail and certain other system activities more difficult and less user-friendly. The system may provide a conversion utility that permits users to address electronic mail to a specific name rather than a user ID. The "sequential numeric" approach to assigning user IDs reflected in this policy need not be used if some other way to conceal the actual identity of users is employed. This policy is designed for high security environments.

Related Policies: "Minimum Password Length" and "User ID Naming Standard."

Audience: Technical staff

Security Environments: High

2. Non-Anonymous User IDs

Policy: All user IDs on Company X computers and networks must be constructed according to the Company X user ID construction standard, must clearly indicate the responsible individual's name, and under no circumstances are such user IDs permitted to be generic, descriptive of an organizational title or role, descriptive of a project, or anonymous.

Commentary: This policy requires system administrators, security administrators, and others who assign user IDs to comply with a standard user ID construction format. This policy also prevents users from employing pen names, screen names, and other pseudonyms. Such anonymous user IDs can help conceal the identity of computer crime perpetrators, or at least make tracing abusive or illegal activities back to a specific person considerably more difficult.

Related Policies: "Identity Of Private Information Collector" and "Internet Identity."

Audience: Technical staff

Security Environments: All

3. Unique User ID And Password Required

Policy: Every user must have a single unique user ID and a personal secret password for access to Company X multi-user computers and computer networks.

Commentary: This policy facilitates security administration activities. With the ever-increasing number of computers and networks found in organizations, use of various user IDs for the same person is getting to be too complex. This policy simplifies that for both users and system administrators. Another intention of the policy is to ensure that all multi-user systems and networks have access control software that can uniquely identify and restrict the privileges of each user. These access control facilities also permit special logging and monitoring software to be used. To further limit computer usage by unauthorized parties, some organizations may prohibit users from employing the same fixed password on every machine, although the same user ID may be employed. The use of the same user ID on all computers and networks across an organization is additionally desirable because it makes analysis of activity logs considerably easier. Before issuing a policy such as this, the organization may wish to investigate new security administration packages, often called enterprise security management

tools. These tools provide a consistent platform-independent administrative interface for access control systems. Use of the term "multi-user computer" in the policy effectively exempts workstations, personal computers and other small systems. In many organizations, these small systems are increasingly taking on production and mission-critical functions. If this is true in the organization, then there is merit to dropping the word "multi-user" from the policy. The policy described here also prohibits group user IDs. Some organizations may wish to replace the word "password" in the policy with a more general term such as "positive user authentication." This would permit for smart cards, dynamic password tokens, biometrics and other technologies.

Related Policies: "Secret Information Access," "Anonymous User IDs," "Unique User IDs," "System Access Control Passwords," and "Passwords On Different Systems."

Audience: Technical staff

Security Environments: All

4. Non-Employee User ID Expiration

Policy: Every user ID established for a non-employee must have a specified expiration date, with a default expiration of 30 days where the actual expiration is unknown.

Commentary: This policy ensures that user IDs employed by outsiders do not continue to be activated long after these individuals have ceased employment at Company X. Without an expiration date, many of these user IDs will remain enabled for a long period of time, especially at those organizations where the notification process about third-party worker departures is informal or non-existent. By terminating these user IDs promptly, the risk of unauthorized use, industrial espionage, sabotage, and other abuses is reduced. This policy will also help keep system response time high and disk space requirements low. There is nothing special about the 30-day period mentioned in the policy. This could just have easily been some other period of time.

Related Policies: "Dormant User ID Privileges" and "Involuntary Terminations."

Audience: Technical staff

Security Environments: All

5. Access Privileges Termination

Policy: All Company X information systems privileges must be promptly terminated at the time that a worker ceases to provide services to Company X.

Commentary: This policy instructs system administrators, network managers, and others in similar positions that they must promptly revoke the privileges of workers who are no longer employed by Company X. Often these administrative matters are ignored in favor of more immediate concerns. In some cases, system privileges are maintained as a courtesy to a worker who may not have access to electronic mail or Internet facilities. Whatever the reason, if privileges are not promptly terminated, former workers may be permitted to commit sabotage, industrial espionage, and other undesirable acts. Some organizations may wish to qualify this policy, permitting the forwarding of electronic mail for a certain time after a worker stops work for Company X. This policy encourages the development of an in-house system to communicate changes in worker employment status to the system administrators and others who must alter system privileges.

Related Policies: "Reporting Employee Changes."

Audience: Technical staff

Security Environments: All

6. User ID Expiration

Policy: Expiration dates must be set for all user IDs on multi-user systems at Company X after which the user IDs will be disabled and the related files retained for a two-week period thereafter beyond expiration.

Commentary: This policy defines an organization's approach to authorizing and granting system privileges. This approach is particularly relevant to a university or any other organization with people who have relatively uniform time periods for a relationship with the organization. Other organizations can use the policy even if they do not employ relationship time periods that are so concretely defined. The policy automatically revokes privileges associated with dormant user IDs, so that these user IDs cannot be used by hackers or other unauthorized persons. The policy also requires management to periodically examine the privileges that each user has, and to determine whether these same privileges should be renewed, or perhaps renewed but changed. The policy is written in such a way that system adminis-

trators can define different time periods for different classes of users. The notice about a two-week file retention period informs users that they need to make their own backups to preserve their data after their relationship with the organization has terminated. The two-week clause additionally conserves valuable disk space.

Related Policies: "User ID Expiration" and "Reauthorization Of User Access Privileges."

Audience: End users

Security Environments: All

7. Unique User IDs

Policy: Each computer and communication system user ID must uniquely identify only one user and shared or group user IDs must not be created or used.

Commentary: This policy establishes a definitive link between a user ID and an individual. Without unique user IDs that point to only one person, process, or system, logs would be ambiguous and considerably less useful during investigations and problem resolution efforts. Such ambiguity may prevent an organization from taking disciplinary actions or entering into prosecutions for computer abuse. It may also prevent the provision of needed remedial training. Without unique user IDs, privileges cannot be restricted on a user-by-user basis. If privileges cannot be restricted by user, then it will be very difficult to implement separation of duties, dual control, access to information based on the need to know, and other generally accepted security measures. This is a fundamental policy that underlies many access control policies and procedures. Some organizations will want to expand the words "uniquely identify only one user" to include software processes and computer systems. Nothing in this policy prevents the deployment of systems that make the specific computers involved user-transparent. For example, users may sign-into a network-based application and not a specific computer system.

Related Policies: "Unique User ID And Password Required" and "Privileged System Command Accountability And Traceability."

Audience: Technical staff

Security Environments: All

8. Generic User IDs

Policy: User IDs must uniquely identify specific individuals and generic user IDs based on job function must not be created or used.

Commentary: This policy prevents system administrators and other technical staff from creating generic user IDs based on job titles. This is a short cut that many technical staff members employ to reduce the overhead associated with changes in worker employment status. With this short cut, when someone leaves the organization, the password associated the user ID can simply be changed. The new person who plays the role would employ the new password, while the person who departed would know only the old password. While this approach may sound appealing in theory, there can be difficulties associated with reading system logs. For example, if system clocks have been altered, it may be difficult to determine which individual was using a certain generic user ID. Of greater concern is the practice where generic user IDs are assigned and shared passwords are employed. This may be necessitated by circumstances where several individuals have the same job title. Individual user accountability through logs is very difficult if not impossible to achieve in this environment. Another reason why the generic user ID approach may be chosen has to do with database management systems, and the delegation of privileges. The same idea applies to privileges that may be incorporated into objects or special programs. In either instance, the concept of privilege inheritance is used, which means that dropping a user may cause downstream problems with other users or processes. Before this policy is adopted, the organization should investigate the implications with in-house programmers and other technical staff. The use of generic user IDs is furthermore ill-advised because it does not permit the files in a departed worker's directories to simply exist without modification until they are claimed by others, archived, or deleted. The policy is written such that group user IDs cannot be assigned for contracting organizations, outsourcing organizations, or other third parties.

Related Policies: "Unique User ID And Password Required" and "System Access Control Passwords."

Audience: Technical staff

Security Environments: Medium and high

9. Re-Use Of User IDs

Policy: Each Company X computer and communication system user ID must be unique, connected solely with the user to whom it was assigned, and must not be reassigned after a worker or customer terminates their relationship with Company X.

Commentary: This policy eliminates confusion about the true identify of a user in those cases where one or more users have received a user ID that had been previously assigned to another. With this policy, system logs will be more authoritative and forensic investigations easier to conduct. If this policy sounds too difficult to implement in a certain organization, a helpful step in this direction would be the imposition of a long waiting period, for example one year, before previously used user IDs can be reassigned to other users. This policy makes it easy to accommodate workers who leave, then later are rehired. User IDs may be called other things such as accounts, user names, or screen names, but the idea behind the policy is the same.

Related Policies: "Dormant User ID Privileges" and "Anonymous User IDs."

Audience: Technical staff

Security Environments: All

10. User ID Naming Standard

Policy: Company X worker user IDs must be the same on every computer system and comply with the user ID naming standards specified by the Information Technology department.

Commentary: This policy simplifies both administrative and security work for networked computer systems. In many organizations, a significant number of different user IDs for a single individual can lead to great confusion. This confusion is particularly undesirable at the time that a worker leaves the organization, in which case staff may scramble to determine which user IDs need to be deactivated. The policy simplifies these activities, and forensic activities like log analysis associated with computer crime investigation. A consistent approach to user ID construction may, in some instances, be impossible if the technology does not permit it. Therefore, it is imperative that the naming convention adopted by the organization be flexible enough to satisfy the various limitations of each different platform's operating system or security subsystem. The policy takes a strong stand in favor of centralized user ID naming standards. In some computing environments this may be politically difficult to achieve. This policy may furthermore be costly to implement, especially if a significant number of computer systems are already in operation with non-standard user IDs. The organization should perform a brief benefit analysis before adopting this policy. This policy will facilitate the establishment and administration of a single sign-on system.

Related Policies: "Single Sign-On," "Unique User ID And Password Required," "Master User ID Database," and "Anonymous User IDs."

Audience: Technical staff

Security Environments: All

11. Multiple User IDs

Policy: All Company X workers must employ at least two different sets of user IDs and passwords for two distinctly different classes of computers, those that are directly Internet-connected, and those that are internal network-connected.

Commentary: This policy prevents hackers and other intruders from exploiting a common time-saving practice that many users adopt. This practice involves choosing the same user ID and password across a variety of computers. If users employ this time-saving approach, and if hackers break-into one of these user's accounts, then the hackers will find it easier to penetrate other machines to which these same users have been granted access. The policy makes life slightly more difficult for users, but it is easily justified. Stand-alone machines are to be treated as an internal network-connected system. This policy is particularly suited for those organizations with very strong fortifications between an internal network and the Internet.

Related Policies: "User ID Naming Standard" and "Unique User ID And Password Required."

Audience: End users

Security Environments: All

12. System Access Request Authorization

Policy: All requests for additional privileges on Company X multi-user systems or networks must be submitted on a completed system access request form that is authorized by the user's immediate manager.

Commentary: This policy ensures that there is a paper trail of all changes to user privileges. Such a paper trail will be useful to auditors when determining whether

system privileges were granted in accordance with management's instructions. Such a paper trail can also be important when showing that the user signed a statement indicating that these privileges were required in order to conduct his or her job. This statement can be useful in disciplinary actions or prosecution proceedings. In terms of implementation, it is desirable to give management instructions about the approval process so that they do not just sign every request without determining whether the requested privileges are necessary. Implementation might also include checking the manager's signature with a signature on file. Single-user systems are exempt from this policy because they are most often under the exclusive control of a single user. This policy could easily be modified so that it could be implemented using electronic forms along with digital signatures and digital certificates.

Related Policies: "User ID Forms" and "Granting Access To Organization Information."

Audience: Management and technical staff

Security Environments: All

13. Dormant User ID Privileges

Policy: All user IDs must automatically have the associated privileges revoked after a 30-day period of inactivity.

Commentary: Dormant user IDs or accounts have been used by many to commit fraud and sabotage. Unauthorized users find dormant user IDs attractive because the authorized users are unlikely to notice unauthorized activity. This policy eliminates the opportunity for unauthorized users to employ dormant user IDs for unauthorized purposes. The policy also clarifies access control records so that they reflect only privileges relevant to active users. There is nothing special about the 30-day period mentioned in the policy. This could just have easily been some other period of time. If an authorized user goes on vacation or leave-without-pay for an extended period, this policy will result in their user ID being revoked. When the user returns, he or she can make a request that the security administrator reinstate privileges. The administrator would then check the individual's status with management, and follow-through with the request if it is consistent with management's intentions. The involved user ID can continue to be defined while the associated privileges have been revoked. Likewise, the files in a user's workspace can continue to reside on disk even though the user's privileges have been revoked. Because system administrators are often quite overworked, they may not get around to revoking privileges of users in a timely manner. An automated version of this policy acts as a safety net to reduce vulnerabilities brought on by the lack of timely attention to this matter on the part of an administrator. Another reason why user IDs should be temporarily revoked but defined is that it gives relevant management an opportunity to review the files associated with the user ID, and later to dispose of or transfer responsibility for these files as necessary. This policy applies to voice mail and other systems besides multi-user general purpose computer systems. Some organizations revoke the privileges of outsiders such as contractors, consultants, temporaries, and customers, after a brief period of time without any activity, but provide a longer period of time for employees.

Related Policies: "Last Logon Time And Date."

Audience: Management and technical staff

Security Environments: All

14. User ID Forms

Policy: Users must sign both a confidentiality agreement and an information system security agreement prior to being issued a user ID permitting access to Company X systems.

Commentary: Users should be informed about security policies and their security-related responsibilities before they obtain access to any Company X system. The basic idea behind this policy is to withhold a user ID until users have agreed in writing to respect the basic rules governing system usage. If users do not sign these agreements when they get their user ID, it may be difficult to get them to sign them later. These signed agreements also may be important for prosecutions and disciplinary actions. The paperwork for the issuance of a user ID can include the agreements mentioned in the policy or other agreements, depending on the needs of the organization.

Related Policies: "Compliance Agreement."

Audience: End users

Security Environments: All

15. Reporting Employee Changes

Policy: Management must promptly report all significant changes in end-user duties and employment status to the system security administrators handling the user IDs of the affected persons.

Commentary: End-user privileges must promptly be turned off if an individual has been terminated, transferred, promoted, put on leave without pay, or otherwise is no longer in the same position. Systems security administrators do not generally know about these changes unless they receive notification from the involved management or from the Human Resources department. A separate but related policy requiring that all such status-change information be kept in strict confidence is advisable because a terminated employee may bring a defamation of character lawsuit. This policy may be useful when it is necessary to establish standard procedures for notifying administrators about worker status changes. In the most sophisticated of organizations, an automatic electronic mail notification of all changes in status is transmitted from the Human Resources database to security administrators.

Related Policies: "Physical Access Of Terminated Workers" and "Custodian Responsibility Transfer."

Audience: Management and technical staff

Security Environments: All

16. User Status Changes

Policy: Every user must notify the Systems Administration Unit about changes in their status with Company X.

Commentary: This policy informs users that they must inform Company X system administrators about changes in their status. This policy does not prevent system administrators from at the same time obtaining user status change notices from the Human Resources department, or user managers. Some changes, such as involuntary terminations are not likely to be reported by the users themselves, and must instead come from other sources. Multiple information feeds coming into the systems administration unit are also desirable because sometimes these sources fail to deliver information. Multiple sources of status change information also permit system administrators to corroborate unusual requests before acting upon them. The policy also provides system administrators with the information needed to immediately contact users and ask them whether abusive activity was initiated by them or by an intruder using these same users' accounts.

Related Policies: "Worker Status Changes" and "Reporting Employee Changes."

Audience: End users

Security Environments: All

17. Custodian Responsibility Transfer

Policy: When a worker leaves any position with Company X, both computer-resident files and paper files must be promptly reviewed by his or her immediate manager to reassign the worker's duties and specifically delegate responsibility for the files formerly in the worker's possession.

Commentary: The intention behind this policy is to clearly and expediently transfer Custodian responsibilities, and thereby to ensure that security measures are maintained in minimally acceptable ways. The reassignment of duties process is especially important if the files contain sensitive, critical, or valuable information. This policy also informs employees that others will examine their files after they leave the organization. With this policy, management is notified of the responsibility for the proper handling of a departed worker's information. The policy avoids fraud, sabotage, and other abuses, which frequently take place when no specific person has responsibility for a certain area.

Related Policies: "Physical Access Of Terminated Workers" and "Information Ownership."

Audience: All

Security Environments: All

18. Deletion Of Terminated Worker Files

Policy: Unless Computer Operations has received instructions to the contrary, four weeks after a worker has permanently left Company X, all files held in that user's directories must be purged.

Commentary: This policy establishes a date for the automatic deletion of files held in user-specific directories stored online. A specific deadline will encourage the management responsible for departed workers to examine such files and reassign them to other workers. In those environments with significant user turnover, such as a large multi-user computer for university students, this policy can also be used to notify users about the need to backup their own data. The words "permanently left" are used to prevent deletion of files when a worker is on a leave of absence, a sabbatical, a maternity leave, or some other extended but temporary absence. This policy will help conserve disk space. If accompanied by a script to automatically carry out its objectives, the policy can additionally be used to reduce the need for manual systems administration work. As a safety net, the files can be restored from backup tape, at least until such time as they are overwritten by new backup information. This policy assumes that a refined process for communicating worker departures to the people who manage systems already exists. The policy also assumes that the people who manage systems are able to readily identify the systems on which departed workers had user IDs. It is advisable for Computer Operations to notify management that departed worker files will be deleted as of a certain date to get them to take this policy seriously. The words "Computer Operations" could be "Systems Administration" or some other functional group designator.

Related Policies: "Master User ID Database" and "Custodian Responsibility Transfer."

Audience: Management

Security Environments: All

19. User ID Expiration

Policy: User IDs on Internet-accessible computers must be set to expire six months from the time they are established and renewable in six-month intervals.

Commentary: This policy discourages and limits the use of user IDs on Internet-accessible computers. Intruders can exploit these user IDs, so it is best to keep them to an absolute minimum. The periodic renewal of such user IDs is a minor inconvenience to the users involved. Most importantly, if a user ID is no longer active, the requirement described in this policy eliminates a possible pathway to compromise the involved system. Most Internet activity can be performed from machines behind a firewall. Likewise, in some instances, users will need to be informed that they do not need a user ID on an Internet accessible machine in order to send Internet electronic mail. Typically any mail server on an internal network will also be able to send and receive Internet electronic mail. Some organizations give users a hard time, challenging their need for a user ID on an Internet accessible machine. Users may request these user IDs because they provide an easier way to perform a variety of tasks that are also achievable with better-protected internal systems. There is nothing special about the six-month interval. It could just as easily be three months.

Related Policies: "Initial Passwords" and "User ID Expiration."

Audience: Technical staff

Security Environments: All

20. New Account Authentication

Policy: Whenever Company X opens a new account with a customer, it must authenticate the identity of this customer in a definitive manner.

Commentary: This policy prevents perpetrators of fraud or identity theft from using the anonymity of the Internet, the telephone, and other remote communications systems as an excuse preventing them from providing definitive identification. Obtaining robust identification is not difficult, and it can be accomplished through the provision of a voided check. This approach is widely used in the banking industry to authorize automated clearinghouse payments. This policy is deliberately vague when it comes to opening accounts remotely or in-person.

Related Policies: "Personal Information Access" and "Identity Validation Of External Parties."

Audience: End users

Security Environments: Medium and high

9.02.02 Privilege Management

1. Privilege Restriction — Need To Know

Policy: The computer and communications system privileges of all users, systems, and programs must be restricted based on the need to know.

Commentary: This policy prevents the granting of excessive privileges to users. Excessive privileges often permit users to perform abusive and unauthorized acts, such as viewing private information belonging to other users. Excessive privileges may also permit users to commit errors that have serious consequences, such as bringing a communications server down during business hours. The approach defined in this policy is significantly enhanced through a data classification scheme. This policy could be rewritten to focus on information itself rather than systems. Access to information would be granted only where a need to know exists. Likewise the term "need to know" could be replaced with similar but more general terminology such as "legitimate business need" or "demonstrable business need."

Related Policies: "Four-Category Data Classification," "Special System Privileges," "Granting Access To Organization Information," "Nature And Location Of Organization Information," "Privilege Restriction — Need To Withhold," and "Sensitive Or Valuable Information Access."

Audience: Management and technical staff

Security Environments: All

2. Privilege Restriction — Need To Withhold

Policy: Access to Company X computer and communications systems must be granted by default to all employees unless the management controlling a specific system has specifically defined access control rules.

Commentary: This policy grants access to internal system resources to all employees, which should encourage and motivate employees to better perform their jobs. Rather than calling it a need to withhold approach to access control, these experts often call it open book management. This approach has been heralded as a way to facilitate faster and more efficient information flows within an organization, and has been adopted by some progressive companies. With the need to withhold approach, responsibility is shifted from users who must demonstrate a need for access, as is the case with the traditional need-to-know approach, to management who must demonstrate a need to restrict access. As a compromise, some information security experts advocate use of need to know for sensitive information, but need to withhold for non-sensitive information. The need-to-withhold approach is less expensive than the need-to-know approach because it can be implemented with fewer decisions about access permissions. As attractive as it may seem, the need-to-withhold approach may place internal information systems in a vulnerable and dangerously open state. Contractors, temporaries, and consultants are not mentioned in the policy.

Related Policies: "Privilege Restriction — Need To Know," "Nature And Location Of Organization Information," and "Sensitive Or Valuable Information Access."

Audience: Management and technical staff

Security Environments: All

3. Special Privileged Users

Policy: All multi-user computer and network systems must support a special type of user ID that has broadly-defined system privileges, that will enable authorized individuals to change the security state of the system.

Commentary: This policy requires that management set up a special type of user ID that has greater privileges than the average user ID. This more privileged user ID would for example be able to make backups of all data on a system disk, bring the system down, or terminate another user's session. Changing the security state of the system also takes place when new users are assigned a user ID and when a new version of the operating system is installed. By having a separate type of privileged user for these special tasks, management avoids giving all users super-user privileges. It is not only possible, but desirable for staff backup reasons, that there be more than one privileged user for each system.

Related Policies: "Default User Privileges."

Audience: Management and technical staff

Security Environments: All

4. Special System Privileges

Policy: Special system privileges, such as the ability to examine the files of other users, must be restricted to those directly responsible for system management or security, and granted only to those who have attended an approved system administrator training class.

Commentary: This policy restricts special system privileges, such as the ability to reboot a local area network server, to those individuals who genuinely need these privileges to perform their jobs. The organization may wish to replace the words "system management or security" with the titles used by these individuals in his or her organization.

Related Policies: "Number Of Privileged User IDs" and "Privilege Restriction — Need To Know."

Audience: Management and technical staff

Security Environments: All

5. Number Of Privileged User IDs

Policy: The number of privileged user IDs must be strictly limited to those individuals who absolutely must have such privileges for authorized business purposes.

Commentary: The intent of this policy is to provide system administrators and security administrators with instructions on the assignment of privileged user IDs to the general population of users. If a significant number of users have privileged user IDs, it will be very difficult, if not impossible, to maintain adequate security. This policy implies an approval process for the granting of privileged user IDs. Some organizations may wish to make this management approval process more specific. Some organizations limit the number of privileged user IDs to a specific number. This approach is not generally recommended because it may unduly interfere with the performance of normal business activities. The policy assumes that the words "privileged user ID" have been defined elsewhere. Generally these user IDs permit users to examine the files of other users, change systems software, shut down the system, and otherwise run powerful system commands.

Related Policies: "Special System Privileges" and "Operating System Command Access."

Audience: Technical staff

Security Environments: All

6. System Administrator User IDs

Policy: System administrators managing computer systems with more than one user must have at least two user IDs, one that provides privileged access and is logged, and the other that provides the privileges of a normal user for day-to-day work.

Commentary: This policy is intended to separate the work of system administrators into two distinct categories, each of which has different access control privilege needs. By segmenting the work of system administrators, this policy grants access based on the need to know. No more privileges are used than is necessary to accomplish a specific business objective. Because system administrators know their activities are logged and reviewed when they use privileged user IDs, they will be encouraged to employ these user IDs judiciously and with moderation. Without a policy like this, system administrators may employ their privileged user IDs to perform activities that they would otherwise be prevented from performing, had they been restricted to the privileges of a normal user. System administrators may not notice these restrictions unless two or more user IDs are actually employed. This policy also makes log analysis and review easier because a great deal of irrelevant information is not included in the detailed logs of privileged user ID activities. This policy is particularly relevant to workers who are system administrators on a part-time basis.

Related Policies: "Privilege Restriction — Need To Know."

Audience: Technical staff

Security Environments: All

7. User ID And Privilege Approval

Policy: User IDs, business application system privileges and system privileges beyond the capabilities routinely granted to general users must be approved in advance by the user's immediate supervisor, the information Owner, and the manager of Technical Support, respectively.

Commentary: This policy is intended to clarify who must approve the issuance of a user ID, and who must approve the granting of application and system privileges. The policy assumes that a system administrator or systems security specialist will perform the user ID and privilege granting process. As written, the policy does not mention permissible methods for communicating such approvals. These typically include electronic mail, internal paper mail, and telephone conversations. Some organizations may require communication methods that create a definitive audit trail. Others may want communication methods that cannot easily be spoofed. In some cases management authorization for system privileges must be in writing. The policy assumes the term "information Owner" is defined elsewhere.

Related Policies: "Information Ownership" and "Default User Privileges."

Audience: Technical staff

Security Environments: All

8. Operating System Command Access

Policy: End users must not be permitted to invoke operating system level commands by restricting them to menus that display only those functions for which they have been authorized to execute.

Commentary: This policy significantly restricts user access to powerful system commands. By preventing users from running operating system level commands, such as reformat a hard disk on a local area network server, the security of the system is improved. Offering only menus is often more user-friendly than permitting the users to issue operating system commands. The menus should only show the options that specific users have been authorized to run. Users should also be prevented from exiting from these menus with the break character, escape, control-C, and related commands. When users wish to exit the menu system, they should be logged off. Software to implement this policy comes with some operating systems, while on other operating systems a separate software package is required.

Related Policies: "Privileged System Command Accountability And Traceability" and "Number Of Privileged User IDs."

Audience: Technical staff

Security Environments: Medium and high

9. Business Production Information Updates

Policy: System privileges must be defined so that non-production staff including, but not limited to, internal auditors, information security administrators, programmers, and computer operators are not permitted to update production business information.

Commentary: Updates should only be completed through the normal channels. For example, updates to the human resources database should only be permitted if initiated by authorized staff in the Human Resources department. To permit other people to make updates invites abuses. The technical support staff should be able to examine the production business information, to detect errors and inconsistencies in this information, and to perform similar activities, but they should not be able to update the information itself. Particularly for small systems users, this policy may require an accompanying definition of the word "production."

Related Policies: "Production Transaction Authorization," "Designated Security Administrator," and "Internet Information Modifications."

Audience: Management and technical staff

Security Environments: All

10. Master User ID Database

Policy: Current records reflecting all the computer systems on which users have user IDs must be maintained.

Commentary: This policy ensures that all user IDs assigned to a worker can be readily identified and the associated privileges quickly revoked. This will, for example, be useful when an employee has been terminated for cause, in which case all user IDs should be deactivated immediately. Even when less dramatic changes in user status take place, such a database can be very helpful in determining which systems security administrators should be notified. Some organizations even keep a centralized database that is connected to the human resources database. In this case, changes in the Human Resources database automatically trigger the generation of electronic mail messages that are sent to those people maintaining the centralized database. The messages could be sent to systems security administrators or a script could be sent directly to the access control systems on which the involved employee had a user ID.

Related Policies: "Custodian Responsibility Transfer" and "User ID Naming Standard."

Audience: Management and technical staff

Security Environments: All

11. Granting System Privileges

Policy: Computer and communication system privileges must be granted only by a clear chain of authority delegation.

Commentary: This policy clarifies which managers can grant system privileges and the specific privileges they can grant. If a clear chain of delegation does not exist, a manager does not have the authority to grant access to other people. This notion is particularly important when departmental management and other end-user management is involved in system privilege granting activities. For example, in a mainframe database environment, access privileges can be granted to another person. When a user's privileges are revoked, the ability to delegate privileges to others is also automatically revoked. The software can automatically implement this policy. This policy also supports inheritance, that will be increasingly important in object oriented programming (OOP). In OOP, programs have certain privileges that can be given to other programs, but these privileges must follow a clear line of access control delegation.

Related Policies: "Privilege Restriction — Need To Know," "Sensitive Or Valuable Information Access," "Identification Badge Reports," and "Physical Access Grantor List."

Audience: Management and technical staff

Security Environments: All

9.02.03 User Password Management

1. Initial Passwords

Policy: Passwords issued by a security administrator must be expired, forcing the user to choose another password before the logon process is completed.

Commentary: The intent of this policy is to ensure that only an involved end user knows his or her own password. This will permit system activity logged with a corresponding personal user ID to be uniquely attributable to a certain user. The type of initial password in the policy is sometimes called a temporary password in that it is valid for only one online session. Some vendors are now extending this idea to the default passwords that come with their computer or communications products. Both administrators and end users are required to change default or initial passwords before they do any work on the system. This policy assumes group user IDs are not employed and also that users are permitted to choose their own passwords.

Related Policies: "Password Structure," "Vendor Default Passwords," "Required Password Changes," and "Computer Support Identification Codes."

Audience: Technical staff

Security Environments: All

2. Initial Password Transmission

Policy: The initial password for a new remote user must be sent through a communications channel other than the channel used to log on to Company X systems including, but not limited to, courier service requiring a signature, and in-person appearance at a trusted intermediary's office along with the provision of picture identification.

Commentary: This policy distributes an initial fixed password, an identity token, or any other user identity authentication mechanism in a secure fashion. The main focus in this case is preventing interception by an unauthorized party. Even if a courier service worker were to obtain a fixed password, he or she would be missing a user ID and other connection information, and would be precluded from making unauthorized use of the service. The idea behind this policy is to split the information needed to log in across multiple communications channels, making it considerably more difficult for an intruder to intercept them all. Password resets can be handled remotely by phone, assuming that some other secret information that could be used to identify a remote user has been previously exchanged. This policy is particularly relevant to remote telecommuters or customers using a high-risk Internet service, such as stock trading service.

Related Policies: "Data And Encryption Key Transmission" and "Sending Sensitive Information."

Audience: Technical staff

Security Environments: All

3. Fixed Password Change Confirmation

Policy: All fixed password resets or changes must be promptly confirmed by regular mail so that the authorized user can readily detect and report any fraudulent or abusive behavior.

Commentary: This policy is intended to utilize the user as a part of a security team to identify fraud and abuse. Many organizations supporting Internet commerce use fixed passwords and secure socket layer encryption. The problem with this approach is that another person can, using the telephone, provide certain personal details and thereby masquerade as the authorized user and request a password reset or change. To reduce the damage that can be done by a masquerader, this policy notifies the authorized user that the password was changed. If the system is not a high-security system, then the mail notification can also include the new password. This policy is also relevant to telephone bill payment and other telephone automatic response systems. In either case, if the user did not initiate the change of password process, he or she should contact the system provider and inform them of suspected foul play. The same policy can be used for the establishment of a new online service, such as wire transfer redemption of stock sale proceeds held with a mutual fund company. In this case, the mail notice would indicate that the new system capabilities were established, and ask the customer to contact the system provider if in fact they did not initiate this. For new services, telephone companies in many jurisdictions use this mail confirmation approach without a password. Another reason for sending such notifications is to reduce the number of calls to customer service asking for the newly-issued but forgotten password.

Related Policies: "Initial Passwords."

Audience: Technical staff

Security Environments: Low and medium

4. Sending Passwords By Mail

Policy: If sent by regular mail or similar physical distribution systems, passwords must be sent separately from user IDs, have no markings indicating the nature of the enclosure and be concealed inside an opaque envelope that will readily reveal tampering.

Commentary: This policy makes it more difficult for an unauthorized person to obtain both a user ID and a password that would permit this person to gain system access. By sending these materials in separate envelopes, preferably at different times, the risk is reduced. If only one of the two is intercepted, then unauthorized system access cannot readily be achieved. Multiple communications systems can be used. For example, a user ID may be given over the phone, but the password may be sent by mail. The absence of markings on an envelope reduces the chance that unauthorized parties will notice these security-related materials. The last sentence in the policy reflects the fact that only the intended recipient should know a password, and that if it has been disclosed as it travels through the mail the user should report this to the security administrator. An opaque envelope is also important so that people who handle the mail cannot hold the envelope up to the light to discover the password. High security environments may want to take this notion of segmenting user ID from password one step further in that they may break the password into components that are each sent separately. In this case, only when the full password is reconstructed by the user, and combined with a proper user ID, will system access be possible. This approach involving components of secret parameters is also used in certain manual encryption key management activities.

Related Policies: "Encryption Key Management Systems."

Audience: Technical staff

Security Environments: All

5. Forgetting Fixed Passwords

Policy: All users who forget or misplace their passwords must once again register and receive both new user IDs and new passwords.

Commentary: This policy prevents an unauthorized user from masquerading as an authorized user, using the telephone to request a password reset or change, then using the privileges of the authorized user. For organizations that do not want to incur the costs associated with the issuance of a special password or secret code that the user may forget, this policy provides a practical approach. Used extensively in the Internet commerce area, this policy might for example be appropriate for an information provider such as a subscription service. Reregistration would involve once again providing a credit card number, name, address, and other important user details, perhaps including the creation of a customer profile. This policy eliminates one of the most difficult areas for help desks, namely the resetting and changing of passwords. The policy is also desirable because it can be completely automated. If a customer has never had any face-to-face or voice-to-voice interaction with the system provider, this policy can permit the customers to continue to use the product or service all on their own. The policy works well when users get to choose their own user IDs, but requires the issuance of a new user ID rather than re-use of a previously assigned user ID. This policy is best for customers, and less desirable for internal users such as employees who must have user IDs that conform to a naming standard. The word "users" in the policy could be replaced with "customers". With digital certificates there is no need for a policy like this because the identity of the user can be automatically validated without reissuing the user ID and password. This policy increases security at the expense of user friendliness and ease-of-use.

Related Policies: "Fixed Password Change Confirmation" and "Password Attempts."

Audience: Technical staff

Security Environments: Low and medium

6. Password Reset After Lockout

Policy: All Company X computer systems that employ fixed passwords at log on must be configured to permit only three attempts to enter a correct password, after which the user ID is deactivated and can only be reset by the Help Desk staff after authenticating the user's identity.

Commentary: This policy prevents unauthorized system access by password guessing. The approach described in the policy prevents a large number of passwords from being guessed. The latter unfortunate situation could occur, for example, if a UNIX system have been erroneously configured to permit outsiders to make a copy of the password file. The policy makes it clear to authorized users that somebody has been attempting to gain unauthorized access to their user IDs because the user IDs will be deactivated. This important control goes hand-in-hand with those policies that require that users to construct difficult-to-guess passwords. The password reset manual work could be handled by people other than those in the Help Desk group or in a password self-reset management tool. It could for example be performed by local system administrators or by Information Security department staff. Computer privileges generally are not revoked if the incorrect password entries took place over a longer time period. Although this opens up an opportunity for a coworker to occasionally attempt one or two undetected guesses of another user's password, this small risk is considered acceptable by most organizations.

Related Policies: "Initial Password Transmission" and "Fixed Password Change Confirmation."

Audience: Technical staff

Security Environments: All

7. Passwords Into Software

Policy: Passwords must never be hard-coded into software developed by or modified by Company X workers.

Commentary: To incorporate a password into software means that the password cannot readily be changed. This leads to inflexible security mechanisms that cannot be readily adapted to new circumstances. If users do not enter passwords, it is better to use system tables or some other non-software location to store passwords. Encryption of the passwords is also required. This policy is also applicable to other security parameters besides fixed passwords, such as encryption keys, pseudo-random number generator seed parameters, personal identification numbers and initialization vectors.

Related Policies: "Suspected Password Disclosure."

Audience: Technical staff

Security Environments: All

8. Password Changes After System Compromise

Policy: If a multi-user computer system employs fixed passwords as its primary access control mechanism, all passwords on that system must be changed immediately after evidence of system compromise has been discovered, and all users must change their fixed passwords on other machines, if the passwords on the compromised machine are also used on these other machines.

Commentary: This policy may at appear to be obvious to those people who have been working in the information security field for a long time. However, it is not obvious to newly-appointed system administrators, network managers, and other technical staff. While the changing of all fixed passwords may not eradicate the source of the compromise, it is a necessary step in the direction of reestablishing a trusted computing environment. This policy also stresses that the passwords on other machines must be changed. Some technical people do not appreciate that users often employ the same password across a variety of machines. Unless these other passwords are changed, the other machines are at significant risk of compromise as well.

Related Policies: "Suspected System Intrusions."

Audience: Technical staff

Security Environments: All

9. Password Changes After Privileged User ID Compromise

Policy: If a privileged account has been compromised by an intruder or another type of unauthorized user, all passwords on that system must be immediately changed.

Commentary: This policy informs system administrators and others who are managing information systems that all passwords are potentially compromised if a privileged user ID has been compromised. This is because privileged user IDs can be used to establish and modify privileges of any other user ID on the affected system. The passwords for all user IDs must immediately be changed in order to prevent an unauthorized user from once again gaining system access. This policy is a quick fix, and it may not be able to keep an unauthorized user out of the affected system if operating system software has been modified. Separate control mechanisms can be used to detect changes in the operating system.

Related Policies: "Password Changes After System Compromise" and "Security Changes After System Compromise."

Audience: Technical staff

Security Environments: All

10. In-Person Password Authentication

Policy: A user must be authenticated in person to obtain a new or changed password.

Commentary: This policy ensures that passwords are not disclosed to unauthorized parties. Many people have used social engineering to fool others into disclosing passwords over the phone. To prevent improper disclosure of passwords, some organizations require proof of identity. As an alternative, users may be sent passwords in secure mailers. With this approach, passwords are automatically typed by impact printers using no ribbons into pre-sealed envelopes with embedded carbon paper, which prevents unauthorized persons from viewing the passwords. If a user must get a password in an emergency, some organizations require that the caller prove their identity by providing difficult-to-obtain information that an impostor would be unlikely to know. Some organizations require a combination of personal information such as mother's maiden name, employee number, and automobile license plate number.

Related Policies: "Sending Passwords By Mail," "Password Sharing," "Initial Passwords," and "Computer Support Identification Codes."

Audience: End users and technical staff

Security Environments: All

11. Disclosure Of Passwords

Policy: Security administrators must disclose passwords to a user providing two pieces of definitive evidence substantiating his or her identity only if a new user ID is being assigned, if the involved user has forgotten or misplaced a password, or if the involved user is otherwise locked out of his or her user ID.

Commentary: This policy is intended to make it clear when and how security administrators may disclose a password. There are many cases where social engineering is used to get security administrators to reveal a password over the phone. This policy does permit a security administrator to reveal a password over the phone as long as adequate evidence of identity is provided. This over-the-phone process is expedient, although it is less secure than requiring the user to show up in person. In some cases a fixed password or personal identification number may be needed to activate a token that generates dynamic passwords. To be truly effective, the policy needs to be accompanied by several related policies, such as one requiring that newly assigned passwords be changed during the first session when they are used. The policy assumes the term "security administrator" has been defined within an organization.

Related Policies: "Suspected Password Disclosure" and "Password Sharing."

Audience: Technical staff

Security Environments: All

12. Positive Identification For System Usage

Policy: All users must be positively identified prior to being able to use any multi-user computer or communications system resources.

Commentary: Positive identification ordinarily involves user IDs and fixed passwords, but may also include biometrics, callback systems, dynamic password tokens, or digital certificates. The exact definition of positive identification can also vary based on platform or technology. For example, accessing computers behind an Internet firewall may require dynamic passwords in addition to a fixed password, while using a telephone credit card may only require a fixed password. The exact definition of positive identification may be deliberately omitted from the policy so that the technology may change over time without the need to make corresponding changes to the policy. Some organizations may wish to add words to the policy making it clear that the Information Security department will be the decision maker when it comes to a precise definition of "positive identification." Longevity of the policy is traded-off against making the policy clear and unambiguous. This policy ensures that no unauthorized persons access organizational computers or communication systems. As organizations adopt more interconnected systems, this policy becomes increasingly important. A stand-alone departmental local area network poses a limited vulnerability, but when such a local area network is connected to a wide area network, the need for all users to be positively identified is increased. As small systems are increasingly used to run production applications, this policy likewise becomes more important. In the small systems environment, this policy may require certain network operating systems or workstation operating systems to be upgraded to support strong access controls.

Related Policies: "Single Sign-On" and "Visitor Identification."

Audience: All

Security Environments: All

9.02.04 Review Of User Access Rights

1. Reauthorization Of User Access Privileges

Policy: The system privileges granted to every user must be reevaluated by the user's immediate manager every three months to determine whether currently-enabled system privileges are needed to perform the user's current job duties.

Commentary: As user job duties change, so should their associated system privileges. But in many cases, users change jobs, and the Information Security department or others, such as system administrators, responsible for changing privileges are not notified about these changes. This policy keeps privileges current and restricted to current job requirements. Periodic reviews to restrict privileges are required. In order to implement this policy, many organizations issue a report of privileges by user. This electronic mail message or paper memo goes to the user's manager, and the manager has a certain period of time in which to respond. If no response is received, telephone calls are made, or other follow-up actions are performed to ensure that the manager actually did review the privilege list. In very high security environments, if the manager does not respond in a timely manner, user privileges may be revoked temporarily until the manager reauthorizes them. There is nothing special about three months. The period could be six months in a low security environment, but generally should not be any longer. In some cases, organizations will want to add the words "All privileges that are no longer needed will be revoked" to the end of the policy.

Related Policies: "Privilege Restriction — Need To Know," "User ID Expiration," and "Identification Badge Reports."

Audience: Management and technical staff

Security Environments: All

9.03 User Responsibilities

9.03.01 Password Use

1. Password Structure

Policy: All workers must not employ any password structure or characteristic that results in a password that is predictable or easily guessed including, but not limited to, words in a dictionary, derivatives of user IDs, common character sequences, personal details, or any part of speech.

Commentary: The most frequently-encountered problem with security systems is human error, and choosing an easily-guessed fixed password is one of the most common security-related mistakes. This policy informs users that they must choose passwords that are difficult for unauthorized parties to guess. Ideally, this policy should be enforced automatically by the system managing password changes, and the enforcement software should be invoked at the time users choose new passwords. Other specifics about what constitutes an easily-guessed password may be added to this policy. For example, technical and medical terms may be prohibited. This policy and the related control measures are particularly important if users are employing the same password on multiple systems. This policy may be expanded to provide additional suggestions for constructing a difficult-to-guess yet easy-to-remember password. For example, the policy may suggest that users employ methods such as:

- String several words together also known as a pass phrase.

- Shift a word up, down, left or right one row on the keyboard.

- Bump characters in a word a certain number of letters up or down the alphabet.

- Transform a regular word according to a specific method, such as making every other letter a number reflecting its position in the word.

- Combine punctuation or numbers with a regular word.

- Create acronyms from words in a song, a poem, or another known sequence of words.

- Deliberately misspell a word but do not use a common misspelling.

- Combine a number of personal facts like birth dates and favorite colors.

This policy is intended for distribution to end users. The use of difficult-to-guess passwords reduces the chances that other parties will guess them, reduces the chances that other parties will notice them when they are typed-in, and reduces the chances that users will disclose them to others.

Related Policies: "Password Characters," "Cyclical Passwords," "Dial-Up Calls Modem Configuration," and "Suspected Password Disclosure."

Audience: End users

Security Environments: All

2. Cyclical Passwords

Policy: Users must not construct fixed passwords that combine a set of characters that do not change, with a set of characters that predictably change.

Commentary: Users are often annoyed by password systems that require them to change their passwords often. In an effort to more easily cope with these password systems, users will often employ passwords that change only partially. One technique they use is called cyclical passwords, which permit users to continue to employ the same basic password, varying only a part of the password to satisfy an automated process that compares the old and new passwords to ensure that previous passwords are not reused. This approach is particularly prevalent among users who must log in to many different machines. This policy prohibits users from using this approach. While single sign-on systems may make the logon process easier for users, the security of the network and connected systems will be markedly reduced if users employ cyclical passwords.

Related Policies: "Password History," "Password Reuse," and "Password Structure."

Audience: All

Security Environments: All

3. Storage Of Passwords In Readable Form

Policy: Fixed passwords must not be stored in readable form in batch files, automatic logon scripts, software macros, terminal function keys, in computers without access control, or in other locations where unauthorized persons might discover or use them.

Commentary: This policy prevents readable passwords from falling into the hands of unauthorized persons. Some users store their passwords in various computer-readable locations. While these practices may help save time, it unduly exposes the involved system to unauthorized access. People breaking into systems typically check terminal function keys, logon scripts, and similar locations for passwords. This approach is very often effective. This policy is also applicable to other security parameters besides passwords, such as encryption keys, pseudo-random number generator seed parameters, personal identification numbers, and initialization vectors. Security parameters are the character strings that control a security process, such as those employed when logging-into a local area network server. Because it covers an area where end users can do considerable unintentional damage, this policy particularly applies to end users employing personal computers, workstations, and client-server systems. This policy suggests a practice that is inconsistent with features found in several communications software packages. These systems permit users to store passwords in logon scripts. In order for this policy to be effective, users must be trained how to use such software packages without storing their passwords in logon scripts.

Related Policies: "Public Password Disclosure," "Writing Down Passwords," and "Passwords In Readable Form."

Audience: All

Security Environments: All

4. Passwords On Different Systems

Policy: Computer users must employ different passwords on each of the systems to which they have been granted access.

Commentary: This policy prevents the users from using a single password and exposing all of their user IDs to unauthorized persons attempting to gain access. If a hacker were to discover a fixed password through guessing, or perhaps recover a fixed password through a wiretap, then all the systems to which the individual with the same password had access would be compromised. Because many users now have many different passwords, this policy encourages users to write down their passwords. A policy like this may also cause significant user resistance, because users are trying to simplify their life by using the same password in multiple places. This policy is appropriate only in high-security environments. A more friendly approach is to use a front-end, also referred to as a single sign-on system, which requires people to log on only once.

Related Policies: "Single Sign-On," "Public Password Disclosure," and "Passwords On Different Systems — Permission."

Audience: All

Security Environments: High

5. Passwords On Different Systems — Permission

Policy: Users must not use the same password on multiple computer systems unless they have been informed by the Information Security department that doing so will not unduly compromise security.

Commentary: Instead of a prohibition against the use of the same password, this policy requires the user to get permission. There are some users, who have relatively minor system privileges, for whom it would not be a serious security vulnerability if they were to use the same password on multiple systems. This policy should be reserved for high security environments.

Related Policies: "Passwords On Different Systems" and "Single Sign-On."

Audience: All

Security Environments: High

6. Suspected Password Disclosure

Policy: Each user must immediately change his or her password if the password is suspected of being disclosed, or known to have been disclosed to an unauthorized party.

Commentary: The basic secure systems design principle behind this policy is that only the user should know his or her password. This policy assumes that all users have their own unique user IDs. If the password has been disclosed to some other party, or if this is only suspected, then the password must be immediately changed. This policy implies that users are able to change their password at any time. If this is not possible for technical or administrative reasons, a security administrator could reset the involved user's password. If the latter option is used, ensure that the resulting password is known only by the user. A system administrator can issue a new password that must be changed by the user the next time he or she logs onto the system.

Related Policies: "Initial Passwords," "Security Changes After System Compromise," "Required Password Changes," and "Password Change Interval Synchronization."

Audience: All

Security Environments: All

7. Public Password Disclosure

Policy: Passwords must not be written down and left in a place where unauthorized persons might discover them.

Commentary: Discovering passwords written down and left in the top drawer, taped to a computer monitor, or in some other conspicuous spot is a surprisingly common way for penetration attackers to break into computers. Many users do not think about these risks unless management alerts them to the problems. This policy does not indicate that users must not write down their passwords. They must not be left in a spot where others could recover them. This policy could be modified to become a stricter policy that absolutely prohibits users from writing their passwords down, but in many environments users will do it anyway. The policy recognizes the reality of common practices regarding writing down passwords.

Related Policies: "System-Generated Passwords," "Writing Down Passwords," and "Passwords On Different Systems."

Audience: All

Security Environments: All

8. Password Proximity To Access Devices

Policy: Users must never write down or otherwise record a readable password and store it near the access device to which it pertains.

Commentary: This policy informs users that they must not store a password near the access device to which it pertains. This happens often with portable computers, and users who record passwords and telephone access numbers inside their portable computers. To gain unauthorized access to remote computers, a thief only

needs to examine these files. Likewise, personal identification numbers needed to initialize dynamic password tokens or smart cards should not be recorded on the devices themselves. This policy supports "two-factor authentication" or the use of two techniques to authenticate a user's identity. If the password is combined with the device, what was two-factor authentication becomes only one-factor authentication.

Related Policies: "Portable Identification Credentials" and "Writing Down Passwords."

Audience: All

Security Environments: All

9. Passwords In Communications Software

Policy: Users must not store fixed passwords in dial-up communications programs, Internet browsers, or related data communications software at any time.

Commentary: This policy prevents users from employing the user-friendly feature found in many communications programs. This feature permits fixed passwords to be stored for future reference. Although these passwords are typically stored in encrypted form, and are masked when typed on the screen so that unauthorized parties cannot view them, they can be used by unauthorized persons who have access to the computer on which this communications software resides. In this manner, although the passwords are not revealed, they can nonetheless be used to gain unauthorized system access. This policy is especially important for portable computers or any other computers that do not consistently have the benefit of physical access controls to protect them. Ideally communications software would be modified to prevent users from employing this feature, but in most organizations this type of modification is not practical. The only alternative is to prohibit users from employing a feature that they would otherwise consider to be convenient and desirable. From a secure systems design perspective, if users store their fixed passwords in a computer, then possession of that computer may be all that is needed to gain access to a remote machine, but if users keep these fixed passwords in their heads, then remote system access can be achieved only with such possession accompanied by the provision of a secret password.

Related Policies: "Storage Of Passwords In Readable Form" and "Password Retrieval."

Audience: End users

Security Environments: All

10. Cookies For Automatic Log On

Policy: Company X computer users must refuse all offers by software to place a cookie on their computer so that they can automatically log on the next time that they visit a particular Internet site.

Commentary: This policy prevents users from accepting logon cookies that could later be used by unauthorized parties to gain system access, order products, or obtain restricted information. A cookie is a small file that contains user-specific information that is placed on a user's hard drive, and can be used to uniquely identify that user. The use of logon cookies simplifies and replaces the traditional logon process. Many Internet merchants think they are doing users a great service when they offer to place this type of cookie on user machines. The use of logon cookies reduces security because it replaces information that the user knows with simple physical proximity to a remote machine. Many users only think of the time it would save them or how it reduces the need to remember a password. They do not consider how other people could masquerade as them, and perhaps commit computer crimes. These users additionally do not generally think about the other things that such logon cookies could do, for example create a detailed trail of their Internet activities. If user machines have very strong access controls, such as encrypted hard drives and a boot password, then the restriction described in this policy may not be necessary.

Related Policies: "Embedded Personal Information" and "Passwords In Communications Software."

Audience: End users

Security Environments: Medium and high

11. Dynamic Password Tokens

Policy: Dynamic password tokens must not be stored in the same briefcase or suitcase as portable computers used to remotely access Company X networks.

Commentary: This policy prevents convenience from reducing security. Without instructions to the contrary, users will keep dynamic password tokens in the same carrying case as the computer to which it pertains. In some cases these tokens do not have enabling fixed passwords. This will mean that possession of both the token and the computer will be sufficient to gain unauthorized system access. Even if a fixed password is required to enable a token, the resources required to compromise system security will be notably reduced when tokens are stored with portable computers to which they pertain. This policy advances the cause of multi-factor user authentication, which indicates that several different things will be required before system access is obtained. This includes something the user knows, something the user has, something the user can do, or something the user is. Users do not generally appreciate this notion, but once they understand it, users will more readily comply with policies such as this. With thefts of portable computers on the rise, this policy becomes more important. The dynamic password system mentioned in the policy could pertain to both the portable machine and to a remote computer, or just to the latter.

Related Policies: "Missing Access Devices" and "Positive Identification For System Usage."

Audience: End users

Security Environments: Medium and high

12. Personal Identification Numbers

Policy: All personal identification numbers must be constructed with the same rules that apply to fixed passwords.

Commentary: This policy informs both end users and system administrators that they should not let their guard down when picking or constructing personal identification numbers, also known as PINs. Because PINs are often a part of a multi-factor user authentication scheme, where both a PIN and something else is required for system access, many people think that their PINs do not need to be difficult to guess. This misconception about the role of a PIN, and the resulting choice of an easily guessed PIN makes it easier for an attacker to gain unauthorized system access. The need for difficult to guess PINs is imperative because PINs are often only four characters and this means that there are not many possible combinations. This makes PINs subject to brute force attacks where all combinations are attempted, and makes it particularly important to have a lockout mechanism after a certain number of incorrect logon attempts. Because PINs include only numbers, certain password construction rules are irrelevant, but the same intention, to have them be difficult to guess, applies to PINs.

Related Policies: "Dial-Up User Authentication" and "Dial-Up Password Attempts."

Audience: End users and technical staff

Security Environments: All

13. Writing Down Passwords

Policy: Users must not write their passwords down unless they have effectively concealed such passwords in seemingly unrelated characters or they have used a coding system to conceal the password.

Commentary: This policy gives specific guidance about the appropriate ways to write down passwords, with the expectation that users will write down their passwords. With the recent explosion in the number of passwords that users must remember, coupled with the need to periodically change some of these passwords, users often feel as though they have no choice but to write down their passwords. At the same time, writing down passwords can be an easy way for unauthorized persons to gain system access. This policy proposes a practical compromise to resolve these conflicting objectives. The coding practices that could be mentioned include a method where passwords may be taped in a conspicuous spot because they have been altered using some standard approach.

Related Policies: "Public Password Disclosure" and "Passwords In Readable Form."

Audience: All

Security Environments: All

14. Password Sharing

Policy: Passwords must never be shared or revealed to anyone other than the authorized user.

Commentary: Whenever users disclose their passwords to any other person, they inadvertently compromise system access controls and make logs of user activity less useful. It is important that users keep their passwords exclusively to themselves, and This policy reminds them to do just that. The policy could be expanded to mention that the way a user prevents him- or herself from being improperly held accountable for the actions of another is to keep his or her password secret. At many organizations, in the small systems environment a casual attitude toward security has traditionally prevailed. A policy like this counteracts this attitude.

Related Policies: "In-Person Password Authentication," "Daily Logon Limitation," and "System Access Control Passwords."

Audience: End users and technical staff

Security Environments: All

15. Third-Party Password Usage

Policy: Users must not provide their user IDs and passwords to any third parties including, but not limited to, data aggregators and data summarization/formatting services.

Commentary: This policy discourages users from using a new breed of third-party services called data aggregation service providers. Data aggregators automatically gather information from various organizations through the Internet, then present it to a user in summarized form. Some data aggregators, for example, will combine information from a stock brokerage account, a bank account, and a pension plan account, all managed by different organizations, then present a current consolidated statement to the user. While these services are convenient and do provide a genuine service, in order to work properly, the involved customer must disclose his or her user ID and password to the data aggregator so that information from various sources can be updated and combined. The release of any user identity authentication information to a third party is a dangerous practice, opening up a variety of risks that otherwise may not need to be considered. Other methods, such as unusual formatting of account information on the screen, can be used to make the data collection routines of aggregators more difficult or impossible. These tactics unfortunately may make it more difficult for authorized users to automatically gather their own information and load it into bookkeeping programs. Use of more sophisticated user authentication technologies, such as dynamic passwords, is perhaps the best way to ensure that data aggregators are not being used.

Related Policies: "Circumventing Privacy Policy With Third Parties" and "Bank Account Numbers."

Audience: End users

Security Environments: Medium and high

16. Personal User IDs — Responsibility

Policy: Users must be responsible for all activity performed with their personal user IDs and must not permit others to perform any activity with their user IDs or perform any activity with IDs belonging to other users.

Commentary: This policy clarifies that sharing user IDs and associated passwords is prohibited. If users share user IDs and passwords, logs will not reflect the true identity of the users, and will be less useful for disciplinary actions, prosecutions, and investigations.

User-specific privilege controls mean little when users are sharing user IDs and passwords. This policy also forbids the hacking of external systems with the aid of the Company X systems. In some computing environments, individualized user IDs are called accounts or sometimes UIDs. This policy is not intended for those organizations like some schools that employ group user IDs.

Related Policies: "Unique Electronic Mail Accounts."

Audience: End users

Security Environments: All

17. Access Code Sharing

Policy: Company X computer accounts, user IDs, network passwords, voice mail box personal identification numbers, credit card numbers, and other access codes must not be used by anyone other than the person to whom they were originally issued.

Commentary: This policy states that the information system access codes must not be shared under any circumstances. This policy is different from related policies because it talks about all access codes, not just user IDs and passwords. It is therefore applicable to new technologies that an organization deploys in the future, and need not be changed when these new technologies are introduced. This policy makes system logs and other computerized records like telephone bills more reliable because the entries are more likely to be attributable to authorized persons. The policy reinforces the concept of personal accountability.

Related Policies: "Personal User IDs — Responsibility" and "Unique Electronic Mail Accounts."

Audience: End users

Security Environments: All

18. Testing Information System Controls

Policy: Workers must not test, or attempt to compromise internal controls unless specifically approved in advance and in writing by Information Security management.

Commentary: This policy eliminates an often-invoked excuse for computer crimes, as the perpetrators may indicate that they were merely testing the control system so as to be able to improve it. Internal auditors already have this approval in their departmental mission statement, and they should continue to test controls. While there is merit to regularly testing controls to illuminate weaknesses, this activity needs to be strictly controlled and performed in a confidential manner. In general, this policy applies to the execution of public domain and commercial software packages used to break system controls. This policy will prevent users from running hacking software unless they have management approval. This policy also prohibits penetration attacks unless approved in advance by management.

Related Policies: "Compromising Security Mechanisms For Customers," "Unauthorized Physical Access Attempts," "Hacking Activities," and "Computer Crime Or Abuse Evidence."

Audience: End users and technical staff

Security Environments: All

19. Exploiting Systems Security Vulnerabilities

Policy: Users must not exploit vulnerabilities or deficiencies in information systems security to damage systems or information, to obtain resources beyond those they have been authorized to obtain, to take resources away from other users, or to gain access to other systems for which proper authorization has not been granted.

Commentary: This policy clarifies that users must not take advantage of information security vulnerabilities and deficiencies, even if they are aware of such problems. One example of such a problem involves having knowledge of a special password that permits a user to do things he or she would otherwise not be able to perform. In a broad sense, this policy is saying that users are given only the privileges explicitly granted to them. If they can do something else due to security problems, they are not authorized to take advantage of these problems. As written, the policy includes errors made by system administrators, for example if a user was given additional privileges. While this example may not involve a control vulnerability, it is decidedly a deficiency associated with the deployment of controls.

Related Policies: "Incident Reporting" and "Diagnostic Hardware And Software."

Audience: End users and technical staff

Security Environments: All

20. Voice Mail Password Construction

Policy: Voice mail passwords must not be required to comply with Company X password construction standards yet users must select a password that is different from their phone extension, their office number, their employee number, or any other number that could be easily guessed.

Commentary: This policy clarifies why the minimum number of characters in voice mail passwords is typically fewer than the minimum for computer passwords. Some users have complained that their organization is not following its own standards by not requiring the voice mail system to comply with a password construction standard. This policy explains that such compliance is not necessary, but at the same time reinforces the need to choose a strong, difficult-to-guess password. Stating the minimum number of digits in a voice mail password could augment this policy. This type of password is a personal identification number because only a limited number of digits are available. Because the number of possibilities for a voice mail password with certain number of digits is quite limited, it is recommended that voice mail passwords be at least eight digits long.

Related Policies: "Exceptions To Policies," "Password Structure," and "Sensitive Information On Answering Machines."

Audience: End users

Security Environments: All

21. Unique Electronic Mail Accounts

Policy: Workers must not use an electronic mail account assigned to another individual to either send or receive messages.

Commentary: This policy is intended to reinforce the premise that each user should have their own electronic mail user ID, and that users should not share these user IDs under any circumstances. The policy implicitly prohibits group accounts, one favorite way for some organizations to save system administration overhead costs. Although specific to electronic mail, the idea behind the policy is applicable to other types of user IDs. The policy maintains the accuracy and efficacy of electronic mail system logs, while reducing the confusion that might come about when someone uses another's account. The policy additionally supports the enforcement of privilege restrictions that may be associated with specific accounts. A written policy such as this also establishes electronic mail masquerading as a prohibited act, making termination and less severe forms of punishment justifiable responses. This policy also prohibits a favorite tactic of those who send unsolicited bulk commercial electronic mail in order to avoid tracing messages back to the true originator.

Related Policies: "Unique User ID And Password Required," "Secret Information In Electronic Mail," "Electronic Mail Message Monitoring," "Third-Party Electronic Mail Message Review," and "System Access Control Passwords."

Audience: End users and technical staff

Security Environments: All

9.03.02 Unattended User Equipment

1. Unattended Active Sessions

Policy: If the computer system to which they are connected or which they are using contains sensitive information, users must not leave their personal computer, workstation, or terminal unattended without logging out or invoking a protected screen saver.

Commentary: This policy prevents unauthorized disclosure of information and unauthorized use. Instead of mandating a period of no activity beyond which jobs will be automatically terminated, this policy puts the onus of responsibility on the user. This approach is generally less effective than the automatic termination of an idle session, but it does emphasize that users are responsible for the security of information in their possession. Organizations should not use both of these approaches. In this policy, there is no acceptable period during which systems with sensitive information may be left unattended. A word or two indicating a time frame, such as 15 minutes, could be provided in the policy, but this is not advised because it require the synchronization of system settings across machines. The reference to "logging out" could be expanded to include password-based access control packages.

Related Policies: "Automatic Log Off" and "Unattended Network Systems."

Audience: All

Security Environments: All

2. Unattended Network Systems

Policy: If personal computers are connected to a network, when unattended they must always be logged off.

Commentary: This policy ensures that users log off when they leave their personal computers (PC), provided the PC is connected to a network. The single word "network" was used instead of local area network, wide area network, dial-up telephone network, or other more restrictive terms. This policy is particularly important in those cases where PCs have modems but no access control systems, in which case anyone dialing-up these systems can gain access to the PCs. The task mentioned in the policy would not be left exclusively up to the user. The system would automatically log-off after a certain period of inactivity. Even with automatic log off facilities, users should log off when they leave their PCs. This policy assumes that some access control software is in use on the personal computers.

Related Policies: "Unattended Active Sessions," "Workstation Modems," "Network Computer Access Control," and "Automatic Log Off."

Audience: All

Security Environments: All

9.04 Network Access Control

9.04.01 Policy On Use Of Network Services

1. Discontinuing Service

Policy: Company X must reserve the right to block, conceal, deny, or discontinue its service at any time without advance notice.

Commentary: This policy prevents third parties from holding Company X responsible because it no longer provides an information service, or it no longer provides an information service with certain characteristics. The policy notifies users that the issuing organization may discontinue or change its service at any time without advance notice in order to advance or maintain its own business and security interests. The policy does not hold Company X responsible for any dependent downstream uses of its service that was not expressly agreed to in writing. This policy would generally be used by an organization offering a service, such as a time reference, to the public. This policy permits the issuing organization to discontinue its service without advance notice if a hacker has compromised the supporting systems. Such discontinuance would be warranted in order to reestablish a trusted computing environment.

Related Policies: "Payment Information Confirmation" and "Concealing Information Transmission."

Audience: End users

Security Environments: High

2. Network Computer Access Control

Policy: If workers leave the power for their computers turned on during non-business hours, and if such computers are connected to a network, the computers must be protected by an access control system approved by Information Security management.

Commentary: This policy ensures that unauthorized persons do not gain access to Company X systems during non-business hours. Many hackers and other system attackers are most active during this time. The scope of this policy could be narrowed to say that if computers are connected to a network with external connections, there must be an access control package on each computer so connected. This policy also could apply to all networks, such as an intranet, an extranet, and a dial-up telephone network. The organization may wish to provide examples of the different types of networks in the body of the policy itself. The policy may also discourage the connection to networks unless suitable controls have been arranged in advance. This policy is directly responsive to the frequently-occurring problem where end users keep their computers on over night, and at the same time have a connected modem that is also on. While this permits the end users to connect with their office computers from home or some other location, it also permits unauthorized parties to access the same machine. The vulnerability that this practice presents is particularly serious when the computer is connected to an internal network such as a local area network, wide area network, or client-server system.

Related Policies: "Workstation Modems" and "Automatic Backups."

Audience: All

Security Environments: All

3. Internet Connection Approval

Policy: Workers must not establish any external network connections that could permit non-Company X users to gain access to Company X systems and information, unless prior approval of Information Systems management has been obtained.

Commentary: This policy addresses connections through the Internet and other external networks. This policy is meant to regulate the establishment of connections to the Internet. Without such a policy, users may establish their own web site, or establish their own Internet file transfer protocol site, and in either instance potentially embarrass the organization. There is a need to have all such connections conform to standard security measures and the content and format conventions dictated by Marketing or Public Relations management. This policy alerts users that they may create security problems when they make connections to outside machines.

Related Policies: "System Interconnection," "Third-Party Security Responsibilities," "Internet Connections," and "Network Connections with Outside Organizations."

Audience: End users and technical staff

Security Environments: All

4. Standards Of Common Carriers

Policy: The networking services provided by Company X must be provided on a contractual carrier basis and not those of a common carrier.

Commentary: This policy avoids the need to provide equitable access to the network and other requirements of common carriers, some of which include security. Although Company X may have security superior to that found on common carrier systems, this policy gives Company X management more flexibility to decide just how they want to configure and maintain their network.

Because this policy is legalistic in nature, it is especially important that the organization's Legal department approve it. This policy is more general than most and is best used as an introductory comment appearing before more specific policies. Another intention of the policy is to establish realistic user expectations about the type of service and security that will be delivered.

Related Policies: "Network Message Protection Services" and "Message Disclaimer."

Audience: End users

Security Environments: All

5. Internal Network Access

Policy: Only Company X provided computers must be able to access the Company X internal network.

Commentary: This policy locks down all personal computers that access the Company X internal network. This means that all personal computers have operating-system-based change control mechanisms that permit a remote system administrator to update software and configurations. However, the workers using these machines will not be able to make any updates of either software or configurations. Typically this remote management of machines can be performed automatically through automated software distribution software. In addition to conserving technical staff time, such an approach prevents virus infestations, trouble with worms, incompatibilities due to unauthorized software, and violations of vendor software license terms. This approach also permits extended user authentication software to be added to each authorized personal computer and perhaps virtual private network software. This authentication software could involve challenge/response routines, dynamic password routines, biometrics, or a ticket-based fixed password encryption process. These specialized security software routines can be used to lock out all unauthorized computers, even if the involved user is correctly providing a user ID and fixed password.

Related Policies: "Floppy Disks" and "Telecommuting Equipment."

Audience: End users

Security Environments: All

6. Internet Access Privileges

Policy: All types of Internet access, except electronic mail, must be approved in advance in writing by the relevant department manager who assures that the user has a demonstrable business need for such access.

Commentary: Many organizations are providing full access to the Internet to all office employees without considering the security ramifications of the access. In the process, they are creating problems including reduced productivity and release of confidential and proprietary information. This policy is in opposition to the prevailing attitudes held by many employees, that Internet access is a fringe benefit. This policy will probably not be acceptable in a high-technology organization, where access to the latest technology is considered a perk. Operationally, this policy could be implemented by providing all office workers with a standard suite of applications including a word processing package, a spreadsheet package, and an electronic mail program. Generally-available Internet access can be provided in a corporate library or in other common areas, making it much more difficult for users to waste time surfing the Internet.

Related Policies: "Privilege Restriction — Need To Know."

Audience: Technical staff

Security Environments: Medium and high

7. Internet Access Restriction

Policy: Internet access must be granted only to Company X workers who perform research as a regular part of their job.

Commentary: This policy limits access to the Internet's web features, and in the process to limit a variety of security problems. Such a limitation will, for example, reduce the risk of virus infestation due to dynamic content. Similarly, this limitation will prevent workers from wasting time surfing the net while they are at work. This policy reduces the need for content screening software at a firewall, although it may be desirable to screen electronic mail messages and attachments.

Related Policies: "Internet Access Privileges" and "Internet News Sources."

Audience: End users and technical staff

Security Environments: Medium and high

8. Non-Business Web Sites

Policy: Company X information systems must routinely prevent users from connecting to certain non-business web sites.

Commentary: This policy prevents problems, such as those resulting from accessing inappropriate web sites. These activities might be construed as creating a hostile working environment, which could expose an organization to lawsuits. The policy also recognizes a new breed of products that screen web activity, keeping it within certain limits. Because so many sites are being added to the Internet so rapidly, it is not currently possible for these programs to prevent users from visiting all sites that are off limits according to existing policy. In response to this reality, users must move on, and not continue to pursue things at a particular off-limits site.

Related Policies: "Personal Use Of Computer And Communications Systems," "Message Content Restrictions," and "Internet News Sources."

Audience: End users

Security Environments: All

9. Blocking Access To Non-Business Sites

Policy: Company X must routinely use software that blocks users from visiting any Internet sites that management considers to be objectionable or clearly personal in nature.

Commentary: This policy communicates to all Internet-connected users, telling them that they should have no expectation of reaching any web site that may be considered objectionable or personal in nature. Although the policy does not specifically mention whether management is logging the web sites visited by users, it is often a good idea to state this explicitly in conjunction with a policy such as this. Management will want to update the list of prohibited web sites based on a log indicating where users are going on the Internet. If certain personal or objectionable web sites are frequently found in this log, they should be added to the list of blocked sites. A policy such as this can be used as a shield protecting system administrators from complaints that users may make, specifically complaints about not being able to reach certain web sites such as a news web site.

Related Policies: "Internet Traffic Control" and "User Access To Internet."

Audience: End users

Security Environments: All

10. Large Internet Downloads

Policy: Internet users must not use video streaming facilities, audio streaming facilities, or download large graphics files unless these transmissions are approved in advance by the user's immediate supervisor.

Commentary: The intention of this policy is primarily to encourage productivity among those workers with Internet connections. Having a high-speed Internet connection can be very tempting for many workers. This policy prevents workers from watching movies online, playing online games, listening to the radio while at work, or downloading large, non-work graphics. This policy statement could go into a policy document that is sometimes called an acceptable use policy. This policy does not require any technology such as monitoring software, although such software is often advisable.

Related Policies: "Personal Telephone Usage" and "Internet Usage Logs."

Audience: End users

Security Environments: All

11. Internet Identity

Policy: When using Company X information systems, or when conducting Company X business, workers must not deliberately conceal or misrepresent their identity.

Commentary: This policy is intended to prevent workers from employing Company X systems for questionable activities through the Internet. Without valid user identity information, logs will be considerably less useful. Likewise, the absence of an identifier may encourage people to do things that they would not otherwise do. A fundamental principle of secure systems design is that positive user identification must be obtained before access controls can be applied. If the identity of a user has not been established, then the effectiveness of access controls is diminished. If workers

wish to conceal their identity, perhaps for a special interest discussion group, they can always do so with a personal user ID obtained from an Internet service provider. This policy forbids the use of electronic mail re-mailers, which have allegedly been used to commit crimes and conduct questionable activities.

Related Policies: "In-Bound Internet Access."

Audience: End users and technical staff

Security Environments: All

12. Intellectual Property

Policy: When accessing the Internet using Company X systems, workers must repost or reproduce material only after obtaining permission from the source, quote material from other sources only if these other sources are identified, and reveal internal Company X information on the Internet only if the information has been officially approved for public release.

Commentary: This policy is intended to remind users that the informal environment found on the Internet does not mean that they can ignore intellectual property laws. The informality surrounding the Internet has already sparked a number of libel cases, which conceivably could have been avoided if this policy were stressed. While the policy may seem obvious, there is a great deal of confusion about these matters in the user community. It is necessary to clearly set user expectations, and if necessary, be able to discipline the offending user. Some organizations will want to expand the policy to make reference to libel, slander, defamation of character, and related legal issues.

Related Policies: "Intranet Information Validation" and "Intellectual Property Rights."

Audience: End users

Security Environments: All

9.04.02 Enforced Path

1. Network-Connected Computers Access Control

Policy: All Company X computers that can be reached by third-party networks must be protected by a privilege access control system approved by Information Security management.

Commentary: This policy is intended to clarify which systems must have a password-based access control system. The type of access control system is deliberately not included in the policy because this is expected to change over time. Different access control packages may be required for different computer platforms. The policy will also prevent well-meaning workers from establishing network connections that may jeopardize the security of internal networks and connected machines. For example, this might take place if a user left work for the day and deliberately kept his modem turned-on with a communications package enabled inside his desktop office computer. While this may permit him to work from home, it may also permit others to readily gain access to the organization's systems. This policy is basically a statement about network security architecture, expressed in a manner to prevent users from claiming that they were unaware of the requirement.

Related Policies: "System Interconnection" and "Network Computer Access Control."

Audience: End users and technical staff

Security Environments: All

2. Connecting Third-Party Networks

Policy: Company X computers or networks must be connected only to third-party computers or networks after Information Security management has determined that the combined system is in compliance with Company X security requirements.

Commentary: Many organizations have trouble with systems interconnection issues related to decentralized systems management. For example, without examining the security implications, Marketing department management may connect an internal Company X local area network to a consulting organization's internal network. To avoid the exposures that such actions introduce, a minimum amount of centralization is necessary. The policy informs internal staff that Information Security management does have requirements for connections with third-party networks and systems, and that these requirements must be met before any connection will be permitted. The specific requirements are deliberately left out of the policy, but generally would include extended user authentication, user privilege access controls, and user activity logging. The specific requirements are expected to change over time, whereas the policy need not change with each change in these requirements.

Related Policies: "Network-Connected Third-Party Systems" and "System Interconnection."

Audience: Technical staff

Security Environments: All

3. Workstation Modems

Policy: Workers must not connect dial-up modems to workstations, personal computers, or local area network clients that are simultaneously connected to a local area network or another internal communication network.

Commentary: The purpose of this policy is to prohibit users from establishing a weak link in a system of network access controls. In order to work at home, work while on a business trip, and to permit others to work in real-time with them, users often establish dial-up modem connections to their workstations, personal computers, or local area network clients. Unfortunately, if a workstation is also connected to an internal network, such a modem connection can permit unauthorized parties onto the internal network. This can occasionally happen without a password or other access controls. This can permit the unauthorized parties to access intranet servers, connected mainframes, and other systems. While the policy may seem a bit strict, it does permit users to disconnect from an internal network whenever they are using a dial-up modem. This policy can be expanded to include Internet connections rather than just dial-up connections. In this case, users would not be permitted to be simultaneously connected to the Internet and also an internal network unless they go through an approved firewall system. Firewall software can enforce a policy such as this. The policy also may be expanded to include both analog and digital dial-up communications, in which case the word "modem" should be avoided.

Related Policies: "Dial-Up User Authentication," "Dial-Up Connections," "Communication Line Changes," and "Unattended Network Systems."

Audience: End users and technical staff

Security Environments: All

4. Direct Dial Connections

Policy: All dial-up connections with Company X systems and networks must be routed through a modem pool that includes an approved extended user authentication security system.

Commentary: This policy eliminates a security vulnerability created by dial-up connections that directly enter personal computers. To prevent these types of connections, some organizations will give users a standard computer hardware configuration that does not include a modem. In this policy, the words "extended user authentication" refer to smart card tokens and challenge/response dynamic password systems. These authentication systems are necessary to definitively authenticate the identity of users prior to granting them inbound dial-up communications privileges. If the identity of users has not been reliably established, then privilege controls cannot effectively be enforced. Outbound restrictions in many cases are appropriate because proprietary or confidential information may be easily communicated through dial-up lines. Less security-conscious organizations may wish to modify the policy so that it restricts only inbound connections. One of the best ways to enforce this policy is to physically remove modems from desktop hardware. This is because users may be able to enable previously-disabled inbound connections by simply changing the modem set-up parameters.

Related Policies: "Workstation Modems" and "Dial-Up Connections."

Audience: End users and technical staff

Security Environments: Medium and high

5. Modem Line Registry

Policy: Workers must not install or contract for the installation of modem lines that connect to Company X computers or networks, unless these lines have been approved by Telecommunications department management and entered into the organization-wide modem line registry.

Commentary: This policy prohibits users and others from calling the telephone company and installing modem lines that then connect to internal computers and networks. The policy informs users that they must obtain approval and enter this line in a modem line registry. Information security staff, when conducting penetration attacks or other types of risk assessment, can use this registry. The policy can be used as the basis for disciplinary actions, such as an instance where a worker set-up a modem connection but did not get proper authorization. Telecommunications department management should not approve all requests without determining whether the new modem line would jeopardize internal information systems security. They may require the use of extended user authentication systems to further secure the dial-up connection. Management also should check telephone bills and maintain the registry so that it is current. The registry may additionally be useful when investigating a computer crime because it shows possible avenues of network entry. This policy works best if an organization has a digital phone system, in which case regular analog modems will not work on the lines connected to each office.

Related Policies: "Direct Dial Connections" and "Systems Accepting In-Coming Dial-Up Calls."

Audience: End users and technical staff

Security Environments: All

6. Auto-Answer Modems

Policy: Users must not leave modems connected to personal computers in auto answer mode, such that they are able to receive in-coming dial-up calls.

Commentary: The purpose of this policy is to ensure that users do not go home or leave their desks when their modems are turned on. If users do this, they expose the organization to unauthorized visitors. While the exposure might be serious if the personal computer (PC) was used for production purposes, this problem is particularly serious if the PC is connected to an internal network. Rather than prohibiting the use of modems, or even requiring the use of dynamic password systems, this low-security policy simply relies on users to turn their modems off, exit their communications software, or shut down their computers.

Related Policies: "Dial-Up Connections" and "Dial-Up User Authentication."

Audience: End users

Security Environments: Low and medium

9.04.03 User Authentication For External Connections

1. Remote Access Passwords

Policy: User IDs with blank or null passwords must not be permitted to gain remote access to any Company X computer or network.

Commentary: This policy clarifies that a non-blank or non-null user-chosen fixed password is required for all remote access. This will prevent people who simply know the user ID from gaining unauthorized access. This is a very basic policy that should be in place in every organization, at least fixed passwords are employed for remote access user identity authentication. When considering remote access, fixed passwords should be replaced with stronger technologies such as dynamic passwords.

Related Policies: "Password Structure" and "Minimum Password Length."

Audience: Technical staff

Security Environments: All

2. Two-Factor User Authentication

Policy: All in-bound access through a public network to every Company X computer must employ two-factor user authentication with at least one of the factors not subject to replay.

Commentary: This policy requires systems designers to implement two-factor user authentication into communication systems that connect to public networks. The policy is notable because it addresses replay issues, which are largely ignored in the information security field. Even an encrypted password sent over an Internet connection can be replayed if it can be separated from other information. Certain types of encryption will not provide the sought after level of security. This policy requires some randomizing component, or a certain implementation of encryption where the encrypted text changes each time the same readable text is sent. Only when such a randomizing component is in place will a logon process be immune from interception and subsequent replay threats. Session encryption, such as the encryption provided by a virtual private network (VPN), will provide a randomizing component. Most VPN products on the market will include both session encryption and a fixed password, and that too could be considered to be two-factor authentication.

Related Policies: "Passwords In Readable Form" and "In-Bound Internet Access."

Audience: Technical staff

Security Environments: Medium and high

3. Remote System Access Controls

Policy: All computers that have remote real-time dialogs with Company X production systems must run an access control package approved by Information Security management.

Commentary: This policy defines the computers that must have special access control packages. The policy acknowledges that the distributed processing associated with computer systems brings with it the need to secure all end-points that might be used to enter information into a production system. These end points might be a mobile computer, a personal digital assistant, or a smart phone. To achieve an appropriate level of security for production systems, this policy requires that a remote system with access to a production system must have an approved access mechanism. The exact definition of a remote system is deliberately not included in the policy so that it can cover a wide variety of systems. Batch transmissions are in general more secure, and are not within the scope of this policy. To increase the coverage of this policy, batch systems could be included and real-time systems. One advantage of this policy is that production system users' remote machines can be locked-down with a change control tool, which goes along with an access control system, and that prevents users from changing the configuration of internal software. In an indirect way, the policy also addresses downloading of data. It establishes access control packages on all the remote systems that might store production information.

Related Policies: "Computer System Access Controls" and "Telecommuter Information Security Procedures."

Audience: End users and technical staff

Security Environments: All

4. Computer-Connected Network Access

Policy: All users must have their identity verified with a user ID and a secret password or by other means that provide equal or greater security prior to being permitted to use Company X computers connected to a network.

Commentary: The intent of this policy is to ensure that only authorized users can gain access to organizational networks. This policy implies that a password and user ID could be shared by a group of people, although this practice must be discouraged because it does not provide individual accountability. The policy also permits the organization to move to extended user authentication through biometrics, callback systems, dynamic password identity tokens or digital certificates. The policy could be written so that it applies to multi-user systems rather than computers connected to a network. This would mean that it does not apply to personal computers and workstations. It also may be necessary to define what is meant by a network in this context.

Related Policies: "Computer Support Identification Codes" and "Third-Party User IDs."

Audience: Technical staff

Security Environments: All

5. Remote Administration

Policy: Remote administration of Internet-connected computers must employ one-time passwords over encrypted links.

Commentary: The purpose of this policy is to ensure that intruders do not take advantage of remote administration capabilities enabled on Company X Internet-connected machines. Because administration capabilities often have extensive privileges, these capabilities are an attractive target of intruders. The use of dynamic, one-time passwords and encrypted links goes a long way to restricting this access to authorized persons.

Related Policies: "Real-Time External Network Connections," "Operating System User Authentication," and "Internal Network Device Passwords."

Audience: Technical staff

Security Environments: All

6. Inter-Processor Commands

Policy: All user-initiated commands received from external locations must not be fulfilled unless a user has logged on.

Commentary: One of the ways to gain unauthorized system access to systems connected to the Internet network is to use the finger command. This command provides information about users that can then be used to guess user IDs and passwords. Often no logon is required to execute this command. This policy expresses a systems design objective to be used when establishing system access controls and to be used when defining multi-processor security architectures. The idea is that outsiders should not be permitted to have any information about a system until they have properly identified themselves. The policy does not restrict the use of remote procedure calls initiated by a system outside of Company X.

Related Policies: "Logon Banner Information," "Dial-Up User Authentication," and "Operating System User Authentication."

Audience: Technical staff

Security Environments: All

7. Dial-Up User Authentication

Policy: All inbound dial-up connections with the Company X internal computer data network must employ extended user authentication.

Commentary: This policy requires additional system access controls for every inbound connection with the public switched telephone network. The scope of this policy can be expanded to include all external network connections including in-bound Internet connections. Because these interface points have historically been vulnerable spots, extra access controls are warranted. Extended user authentication systems are most often used in conjunction with user IDs and passwords, although they may also replace user IDs or passwords. Extended user authentication systems are often more expensive, less user-friendly, and more difficult to administer, so this policy can be modified so that it applies only to computer systems that contain particularly sensitive data. Organizations with extensively interconnected systems will find that a limitation of this policy to those machines with particularly sensitive data is relatively meaningless. Depending on flow controls in the internal network, once a user has gained access to a network, he or she may be able to establish connections with a wide variety of machines.

Related Policies: "Workstation Modems," "Changes To Sensitive, Critical, Or Valuable Information," "Identity Validation Of External Parties," "In-Bound Internet Access," and "Operating System User Authentication."

Audience: Technical staff

Security Environments: All

8. Dial-Up Password Attempts

Policy: All dial-up lines must be configured to immediately terminate a connection by a user who has not provided a correct password after three consecutive attempts.

Commentary: This policy prevents password-guessing programs from cracking passwords used for dial-up access. Dial-up lines are frequently the avenue by which unauthorized users gain access to systems. This approach, however, is not without its drawbacks. For example, attackers can immediately call back, but the password guessing process will take much longer and be much more expensive than it would be in the absence of this approach. Another approach, used by organizations with custom-programmed access control systems, involves the progressive elongation of the time period between each attempt. In this case, the delay between the prompt for a user ID and a password for the logon attempt employing a certain user ID might be one second and between the second and third attempt might be two seconds. This approach makes it infeasible to successfully use password-guessing programs to try a large number of possibilities. This policy may be expanded to include Internet connections, in which case all in-bound Internet users would have the logon process aborted if they failed to provide a correct password after a certain number of attempts. A delay between logon attempts using the same user ID may then be imposed.

9.04.04 Node Authentication

1. Systems Accepting In-Coming Dial-Up Calls

Policy: Company X workers must not establish any communications systems that accept in-coming dial-up calls unless these systems have been approved by Information Security management.

Commentary: This policy prevents inadvertent release of Company X information to outsiders, and to prevent workers from establishing unauthorized and insuffi-

This policy has historically been used for fixed password access control systems, but is also applicable to dynamic password systems.

Related Policies: "Dial-Up Calls Modem Configuration" and "Password Attempts."

Audience: Technical staff

Security Environments: All

9. In-Bound Internet Access

Policy: All users establishing a connection with Company X computers on its internal network through the Internet must authenticate themselves at a firewall that employs an extended user authentication process approved by Information Systems management.

Commentary: This policy describes one of the major functions that should be performed by an effective Internet firewall. Firewalls permit unimpeded out-bound connections, but will stop or provide significant hurdles to those who wish to establish an in-bound connection through the firewall. This policy deliberately avoids discussing the technology that will be employed, in large measure because it is expected to change rapidly in the years ahead. Most often dynamic password systems are used at the firewall to authenticate the identity of in-bound users. Besides these smart-card based systems, other dynamic password technology like user-transparent challenge/response systems can be used. Full session encryption can also be used as an alternative to dynamic passwords.

Related Policies: "Internet Connections," "Passwords In Readable Form," and "Dial-Up User Authentication."

Audience: Technical staff

Security Environments: All

ciently-secured pathways to access Company X networks. Because dial-up facilities are so widely available, it is relatively easy for even end users to establish a server or desktop computer with some in-bound dial-up capabilities. To prevent this, there is a need to inform users that they must obtain approval for all such systems accessible over dial-up systems. Even temporary overnight dial-up access, for example established by plugging a modem into an analog voice line, is prohibited by this policy. A special and permissible exception may be added to the policy for stand-alone single-application systems such as interactive voice response units. Other exceptions may be added, such as the testing of new systems that are not connected to any internal networks or the authorized use of vendor remote maintenance ports. While these exceptions could be mentioned in the policy, it is better to handle them through a known and approved exception process. Many network managers do not know all of the access points to their network. This policy keeps the access points to a known and manageable number. The policy can be expanded to include Internet connections. This would mean that it would prohibit the establishment of any in-bound Internet connections unless management approval was obtained. The approval process ideally would include a requirement that the connection use an approved access control system.

Related Policies: "Dial-Up Connections" and "Communication Line Changes."

Audience: End users and technical staff

Security Environments: All

9.04.05 Remote Diagnostic Port Protection

1. Diagnostic Port Access

Policy: Access to all diagnostic ports must be securely controlled with the use of a key lock and effective procedures.

Commentary: This policy ensures that any entry point designed for remote diagnostic purposes by system maintenance engineers is not exploited by any unauthorized parties. Many computer and communication systems are designed with a port dedicated for dialing into the system. If left open or unprotected, these ports can be used for unauthorized access to the system.

Related Policies: "Diagnostic Hardware And Software."

Audience: Management and technical staff

Security Environments: All

9.04.06 Segregation In Networks

1. Walk-Up Network Connections

Policy: All walk-up network access for visitors to connect back to their home networks must employ a separate subnet that has no connection to the Company X internal network.

Commentary: This policy prevents unauthorized parties from gaining access to internal network-connected computers, and the information resources resident thereon. If an organization provides walk-up connections, which permit users to readily connect a portable computer to an organization's internal network, it significantly increases the risks of attacks. To isolate walk-up connections, but to provide this useful connection service, a separate subnet can be used. Although it is not mentioned in this policy, physical security over all these network access points should also be provided. For example, reception areas and conference rooms that have these access points should be locked when the involved organization is closed for business.

Related Policies: "System Interconnection" and "Public Internet Servers."

Audience: Technical staff

Security Environments: Medium and high

2. High-Security And High-Reliability Computers And Networks

Policy: Every high-security and high-reliability system managed by or owned by Company X must have its own dedicated computers and networks, unless approved in advance by Information Security management.

Commentary: The purpose of this policy is to clearly define an essential requirement for every high-security and high-reliability system that Company X owns or manages. When dedicated computers and networks are used, there is considerably less complexity associated with a system. This simplicity will make it much easier to make the system secure and reliable. Dedicated systems also reduce the number of people and organizations associated with the system, and reduces the chances for errors and omissions, and will also permit Company X to make modifications more quickly. Examples of systems that are dedicated include automated teller machine networks. This policy has implications for systems outsourcing arrangements and systems managed in-house.

9.04.07 Network Connection Control

1. Internal Network Device Passwords

Policy: All Company X internal network devices including, but not limited to, routers, firewalls, and access control servers, must have unique passwords or other access control mechanisms.

Commentary: In an effort to expedite administration, technical staff will often use the same fixed password for multiple devices of the same type, or even for a variety of different devices. This policy is intended to prevent the discovery or unauthorized disclosure of a network device fixed password from leading to extensive damage. If unique fixed passwords are used for each device, then the damage should be restricted to that device only. If the same fixed password is used in multiple places, it will also be more difficult to get rid of a hacker. Likewise, the use of a single password for multiple network devices restricts management's ability to establish separation of duties and to restrict access based on job duties. This policy is additionally essential if defensive depth is to be obtained in a network. Defensive depth refers to the establishment of multiple hurdles through which users must go if they are to reach a certain destination. These hurdles might be firewalls, routers, or other internal network machines. Defensive depth is used, for example, when firewalls are used to establish a demilitarized zone on an internal network. While lockwords or shared fixed passwords are to be discouraged whenever the technology supports use of other methods, the reality at many businesses is that shared fixed passwords must be employed. This policy addresses the conflict between ease-of-use and security, coming down clearly on the side of the latter.

Related Policies: "Unique User ID And Password Required" and "Initial Passwords."

Audience: Technical staff

Security Environments: All

Related Policies: "Internet Commerce and Financial Systems" and "Secret Information System Isolation."

Audience: Technical staff

Security Environments: Medium and high

2. Internet Access Without Firewalls

Policy: All Internet access without the use of a firewall must be accomplished from a stand-alone computer that is not connected to any Company X internal network.

Commentary: This policy is intended to control the ways that users connect to the Internet until such time as a proper firewall can be installed and cutover to production operation. This policy permits users to access the Internet for research, electronic mail, and other purposes. The quick-and-easy way to do this is to establish accounts with Internet service providers, which can provide such services and set up a web site isolated from an organization's internal network. Although this policy may be appropriate for brief period of time, for example when an organization is establishing its network connections, it should soon be supplanted with another policy that requires firewalls for all machines that are connected to the Internet, even if they are used for only dial-up connections.

Related Policies: "Real-Time External Network Connections" and "Internet Connections."

Audience: End users

Security Environments: All

3. Public Access To Active Network Ports

Policy: Unattended active network ports that connect to the Company X internal computer network must not be placed in public areas including, but not limited to, building lobbies, company cafeterias, and conference rooms.

Commentary: This policy prevents network designers, network cable installers, and others from placing active data ports in places where unauthorized parties could employ these same ports to gain unauthorized entry to Company X internal information systems. The problem with active ports in public areas is that these ports are available to anybody and could be used to launch a password guessing attack, to place a computer virus on

Company X systems, to passively wiretap and record information flowing over the network, or to perpetrate some other abusive act. According to this policy, it is acceptable for these ports to be installed in public places. They must, however, not be turned on or active. Fixed passwords or other access control mechanisms should be employed.

Related Policies: "Walk-Up Network Connections" and "Network Connection Configuration."

Audience: Technical staff

Security Environments: Medium and high

4. Network Ports In Vacant Offices

Policy: All network ports in vacant offices and other areas that are not customarily in use must be promptly disconnected at the wiring closet or at another centralized location.

Commentary: The intention for this policy comes from an understanding of a common attack method used by industrial spies and computer system intruders. This approach involves use of network ports found in vacant offices, conference rooms, or other unmonitored facilities. Intruders may use these ports to gain access to an internal network, and from there launch an attack against either internal Company X machines or perhaps external machines. This policy informs network technicians and others who manage the physical infrastructure for an internal network that all unused network ports need to be disabled at a central location. It is not sufficient to disable the port at the remote location because an intruder could easily reestablish the connec-

9.04.08 Network Routing Control

1. Network Security Zones

Policy: All Company X internal data networks must be divided into security zones.

Commentary: This policy adopts a zone model for network security. This approach has been implemented at many organizations including large multi-national companies and various military organizations. In most cases the definitions are somewhat like the following description. Red Zone machines are exposed to external networks like the Internet, and no machine should be in this zone unless there is a compelling reason to place it there. A firewall or router protects Yellow Zone machines so that only the required services are exposed

tion with readily available tools like a screwdriver. This policy assumes that telephone closets and other centralized wiring locations are physically protected or locked.

Related Policies: "Walk-Up Network Connections" and "Workstation Modems."

Audience: Technical staff

Security Environments: Medium and high

5. Disabling Java

Policy: All Internet users must disable Java programs by changing the default configuration of their Internet browser software.

Commentary: Although many of the threats from unauthorized Java applets have been generated in research labs rather than experienced in the real world, there exists a significant risk that Java programming language could be used to circumvent existing access control mechanisms. The resulting damage would be very much like a computer virus. While some firewalls can screen out Java applets, in many organizations such firewalls have not yet been installed. This policy is likely to generate significant resistance from users because the capabilities that the Java language provides are powerful and for many users quite useful. The policy could be modified to make reference to other active content products

Related Policies: "Downloading Software."

Audience: End users and technical staff

Security Environments: All

to an external network. Green Zone machines are accessible to Yellow or Blue machines, but not Red. Green Zone machines contain only data required to support the business processes and applications that may not safely be located in the Blue Zone. Blue Zone machines are within the domain of a Company X security architecture and all information sent from other zones must be verified and filtered before being used.

Related Policies: "Equipment Isolation" and "Backup Media Fire Zone."

Audience: Technical staff

Security Environments: Medium and high

9.04.09 Security Of Network Services

1. Web Server Firewalls

Policy: All web servers accessible through the Internet must be protected by a router or firewall approved by the Information Security department.

Commentary: Positioning a web server inside a firewall significantly increases the protection against hacker damage. Common scenarios include the posting of embarrassing or offensive material, denial of service attacks, or using the server to break into other systems. A web server installed behind a firewall reduces the pathways that hackers can use to penetrate the system. A web server inside a firewall also makes maintenance easier. There should be other firewalls between the web server and any production machines on an internal network.

Related Policies: "Internal Network Device Passwords" and "Internet Access Without Firewalls."

Audience: Technical staff

Security Environments: All

9.05 Operating System Access Control

9.05.01 Automatic Terminal Identification

1. Physical Terminal Security

Policy: When terminal identification is used to authenticate a terminal connection to a specific location, the physical access to the terminal must be restricted to those workers with a need to know.

Commentary: This policy is intended to establish controls over the use of terminals that automatically logon to a computer system when the system is initiated or when the terminal is powered on to an active system. These terminals are often found in environments where multiple users must access a single terminal and access to information contained on the system is necessary to ensure an uninterrupted flow of product or services. For example, these terminals can be found in an assembly line function in a manufacturing facility. They key to the usage of this type of terminal is the restriction of physical access to the device. This is critical not only to ensure that the information is not compromised but also to maintain human safety in certain areas. The use of these terminals will sacrifice the accountability of input and consideration should be given to establishing compensating controls, perhaps in the accessed applications, to ensure that the user's identity is captured for all data input operations.

Related Policies: "Automatic Log Off."

Audience: Management and technical staff

Security Environments: All

9.05.02 Terminal Logon Procedures

1. Password Attempts

Policy: After three unsuccessful attempts to enter a password, the involved user ID must be suspended until reset by a system administrator, temporarily disabled for no less than three minutes, or disconnected if dial-up or other external network connections are involved.

Commentary: One of the most frequently successful attack methods for gaining system access is password guessing. Besides context-sensitive guessing, attackers can use password cracker programs to exhaustively go through words in the dictionary. Whether it is a determined manual attack or an automated password guessing attack, this policy will help to ensure that the attack is unsuccessful. Some organizations may wish to put a time frame into the policy, so that the words that "after three unsuccessful attempts" become "after three unsuccessful attempts within five minutes." A similar result may be achieved by qualifying this same phrase with the words "during a single online session." With this approach, some legitimate users would be locked out of their user IDs if they are poor typists, if they are learning how to use the system, or if they are having trouble remembering their password. These users will contact the security administrator for a new expired password. The contact with the security administrator also provides an opportunity for the security administrator to give the involved user the information needed to properly log on the next time they use the system. There is nothing special about the number three here. To support a less secure environment, this number could have just as easily been five or 10. This is one of a number of policies intended for system administrators in that it instructs them on how they should configure the systems they administer.

Related Policies: "Suspected Password Disclosure," "Initial Passwords," "Password Structure," and "Dial-Up Password Attempts."

Audience: Technical staff

Security Environments: All

2. Password-Based Boot Protection

Policy: All workstations including, but not limited to, personal computers, portable computers, transportable computers, and handhelds, must employ an access control system approved by Information Security management.

Commentary: This policy is intended to prevent unauthorized persons from gaining access to workstations and the sensitive information that might be stored thereon. Because each of these computers generally includes storage mechanisms such as a hard drive, they can also store sensitive information. By protecting every machine, Information Security management eliminates squabbles about who should be using workstation access control systems. Some screen saver-based access control packages can be readily circumvented. The approval by Information Security management required in the policy means that only strong screen saver products will be employed. Distributed information on the desktop means that distributed access control is also necessary. It may be necessary to issue a standard about the number of minutes before a screen saver is invoked, which also can be specified in a policy.

Related Policies: "General Purpose Encryption Systems" and "Unattended Active Sessions."

Audience: End users

Security Environments: All

3. Logon Information

Policy: When logging into a Company X computer or data communications system, if any part of the logon sequence is incorrect, the user must be given only feedback that the entire logon process was incorrect.

Commentary: Persons attempting to break into systems can use specific feedback messages to determine what they are doing right. This increases the likelihood that their system attacks will be successful. For example, if a message said "password incorrect," this may be helpful to an attacker because he or she would now know that the user ID was acceptable. To prevent such attacks from being successful, this policy prohibits the provision of detailed feedback information to users. This is slightly user-unfriendly, but the security advantage to be obtained more than compensates for the user-unfriendliness in most environments. To give specific feedback only after all the input has been entered by the user means that the timing of the feedback message cannot be used to deduce what part of the logon was incorrect. This policy can be changed such that users will not be given any feedback by changing the word "specific" to "any."

Related Policies: "Incorrect Logon Feedback."

Audience: Technical staff

Security Environments: All

4. Incorrect Logon Feedback

Policy: When logging on to a Company X computer or data communications system, if any part of the logon sequence is incorrect, the system must terminate the session or wait for the correct logon information.

Commentary: This policy provides absolutely no information that might be used by persons attempting to gain unauthorized system access. In some circumstances, the fact that a logon sequence was expected may itself be a disclosure that would assist attackers. This is a user-unfriendly policy, and is typically found only in high-security environments such as the military. This policy naturally accompanies a similar policy prohibiting any logon banner information that might be used to identify a system, an organization, or otherwise provide information of use to a system attacker.

Related Policies: "Logon Information" and "Logon Banner Information."

Audience: Technical staff

Security Environments: High

5. System Logon Banner

Policy: Every logon screen for multi-user computers must include a special notice that must state that the system may only be accessed by authorized users, users who logon represent that they are authorized to do so, unauthorized system usage or abuse is subject to criminal prosecution, and system usage will be monitored and logged.

Commentary: For legal reasons, in many jurisdictions, it is wise to notify all users that the involved system may be used only for authorized purposes. In the event of a prosecution against those who entered a system unlawfully, one of the most successful defending claims is that there was no notice saying they could not enter. Hackers may cite logon banners that include the word "welcome." Recent court cases have highlighted the need for organizations to inform unauthorized users that their systems are off-limits. As a result, a system logon banner, which is displayed on each user logon screen, should provide the electronic equivalent of a no-trespassing sign. Some organizations go further than the policy indicated above, indicating this is a private rather than a public system, and that they intend to prosecute unauthorized usage. The policy lets users know that management is serious about security and privacy. A policy such as this is desirable for all multi-user computers, especially those systems with external network connections. The same type of banner can be used for selected data communication networks, not just computers.

Related Policies: "Logon Banner Information."

Audience: Technical staff

Security Environments: All

6. Logon Banner Information

Policy: All logon banners on network-connected Company X computer systems must direct the user to log on, and must not provide any identifying information about the organization, operating system, system configuration, or other internal matters until the user's identity has been successfully authenticated.

Commentary: The lack of specific information, such as the name of the organization, will not inform unauthorized persons as to the system that they have reached. This may make the system less interesting to them, but it will give them less information on which to base a password guessing attack or a social engineering attack. Lack of information about the computer operating system will also prevent the users from employing knowledge of specialized weaknesses in these operating systems. This banner disclosure policy is based on the need to know. The policy is vague about the steps necessary to prove one's identity so that when an organization moves from user IDs and fixed passwords to a more sophisticated technology, no change in the policy will be necessary. This policy may be restricted to network systems accessible from external networks, such as the Internet and dial-up lines.

Related Policies: "Password Structure," "Inter-Processor Commands," and "Incorrect Logon Feedback."

Audience: Technical staff

Security Environments: All

7. Network Logon Banner

Policy: The standard warning banner developed by Information Technology management and approved by the Legal department must be used when users connect to the Company X internal computer networks.

Commentary: This policy informs technical systems staff that specific text must be used in all computer network logon banners. An example of a logon banner is, "This system is for the use of authorized users only. Individuals using this computer system without authority, or in excess of their authority, are subject to having all of their activities on this system monitored and recorded by systems personnel. In the course of monitoring individuals improperly using this system, or in the course of system maintenance, the activities of authorized users also may be monitored. Anyone using this system expressly consents to such monitoring and is advised that if such monitoring reveals possible criminal activity, system personnel may provide the evidence of such monitoring to law enforcement officials." This policy is appropriate to dial-up connections, connections through value-added networks, and Internet connections. Individual organizations can modify the wording to fit the policies in place. It is possible that banner content will need to be reviewed by departments other than Information Technology and Legal.

Related Policies: "System Logon Banner," "Logon Banner Information," "Systems Monitoring Tools," and "Dial-Up Connections."

Audience: Technical staff

Security Environments: All

8. Last Logon Time And Date

Policy: At logon time, every user must be given information reflecting the last logon time and date.

Commentary: This policy provides the end user with the information needed to determine whether an unauthorized party has used his or her user ID. Although this policy has been written for technical staff, the policy could be easily expanded to be applicable to end users. If this were done, words would be added requiring the user to recall the last time he or she used the system, then requiring the user to determine whether there has been unauthorized activity. Certain operating systems provide capabilities such as this. On other platforms, additional software may be needed to support this functionality. This policy works best if accompanied by a policy requiring reporting of suspected information security problems and violations.

Related Policies: "Incident Reporting" and "Dormant User ID Privileges."

Audience: Technical staff

Security Environments: Medium and high

9. Daily Logon Limitation

Policy: Users must not be permitted to log on more than 10 times a day.

Commentary: This policy detects, and to some extent prevents, unauthorized system usage. If more than 10 logons with a particular user ID occur in a single day, this situation may indicate that there is unauthorized password sharing. There is nothing special about the number 10 referenced in the policy. This could just as easily be five or some other number high enough to prevent authorized users from ordinarily encountering it. The intention is to limit the number of logons and to generate some sort of a report of excessive logons so that they can be investigated. This control is generally applicable to customers rather than internal users such as employees. When the number of logons exceeds a certain threshold, then an entry in a log can be made.

Related Policies: "Password Sharing," "Last Logon Time And Date," and "Multiple Simultaneous Sessions."

Audience: Technical staff

Security Environments: Low and medium

9.05.03 User Identification And Authentication

1. Single Sign-On

Policy: Users must be asked for only one user ID and password combination at the time they reach the network or destination computer system, after which all user identity related information must then be passed to other computers, firewalls, database management systems, application systems and other information system components.

Commentary: As a systems design objective, some organizations are attempting to minimize the number of times that users are required to enter user IDs and passwords to identify themselves. In organizations with many computers this logon process can be quite complex and time consuming. In response to user demands for simpler interfaces, this policy states that users will identify themselves only once. The process will then automatically convey the user's identity to the destination computer. An exception may need to be made to the single sign-on approach if an involved user has access to special privileges or multiple user IDs. In this case, multiple passwords may be needed to control access privileges and to log the activity. This single sign-on approach is being incorporated into security front-ends that serve as gateways through which all users must pass. This approach is also potentially much more economical because stringent user identification processes, such as those involving smart cards, need be applied only to the front-end machine. The policy could be expanded to include the notion that the suspension or revocation of a user ID is immediately and automatically performed on multiple computers over the network. The policy also may be a part of an in-house systems security architecture.

Related Policies: "Protection Of Information" and "Dial-Up Connections."

Audience: Technical staff

Security Environments: All

2. Portable Identification Credentials

Policy: Portable identification credentials that include or work with computers including, but not limited to, smart cards, identity tokens, and photo badges with magnetic stripes, must require the provision of a password to operate each time they are used, and be automatically disabled if they have experienced three consecutive incorrect attempts to enter that same password.

Commentary: This policy specifies a system design requirement so that information systems staff designing or integrating any type of credential system will consistently select only those vendors who offer especially secure technology. If a password was not required to enable a credential, then anybody who were to steal a credential or even find a lost credential would be able to use it to commit identity fraud, to gain access to confidential information, or to damage the involved information systems. The limit on incorrect attempts to enter the password prevents unauthorized people from being able to use a lost or stolen credential, even if the authorized user has not yet noticed that the credential is missing or has not notified a system administrator that the credential should be disabled. The policy supports two-factor authentication, specifically something that a user knows, the password, and something that a user possesses, a portable credential. The policy does not apply to photo badges that cannot be read automatically, traditional paper passports, and other credentials that do not include some computer interface.

Related Policies: "Password Proximity To Access Devices" and "Missing Access Devices."

Audience: Technical staff

Security Environments: High

3. Operating System User Authentication

Policy: Company X application systems developers must consistently rely on the access controls provided by operating systems, commercially-available access control systems that enhance operating systems, gateways or firewalls, and must not construct other mechanisms to collect access control information, or construct or install other mechanisms to identify or authenticate the identity of users without the advance permission of Information Security management.

Commentary: This policy achieves consistent access controls across application systems. Generally speaking, operating systems, related access control packages, gateways, and firewalls have the strongest access control mechanisms of any type of software. These four systems also generally provide facilities that permit them to be called by applications, database management systems, and other types of software. Not only will this policy make application systems design easier and less expensive, but it will also make it more consistent across

the organization and therefore easier to manage. The policy furthermore eliminates duplicate security administration activities. The policy is fully consistent with the newest generation of enterprise security management packages that integrate all access control administration activities. This policy becomes essential when an organization attempts to establish a consistent user interface and consistent application programming interfaces across platforms within the organization. The policy is fully consistent with single sign-on systems, which will pass user authentication information along to destination machines or other software. To keep application developers away from the development or maintenance of access control systems is a good idea because it limits Trojan horses and unauthorized access paths that they can establish. It also means that the access control system does not have to be re-verified each time changes are made to application code. This policy is also particularly relevant to small systems environments where end users are designing their own application systems.

Related Policies: "Single Sign-On," "Regulating Software," and "Circumventing Access Controls."

Audience: Technical staff

Security Environments: All

4. Multiple Simultaneous Sessions

Policy: Computer systems must not permit any user to conduct multiple simultaneous online sessions unless Information Systems management has granted special permission.

Commentary: Only a very small percentage of users require multiple simultaneous online sessions. Multiple simultaneous sessions are often indicative of unauthorized usage, such as a bunch of hackers all using the same user ID. System activity logging and access control software can alert computer operations or computer security staff to the existence of such sessions. If users are prohibited from having multiple simultaneous sessions, then this software will be able to do its job without inappropriately notifying computer operators, security administrators, and users. In some instances, the need for multiple simultaneous sessions is a reflection of inappropriately assigned privileges. This policy can require a reevaluation of privileges where appropriate.

Related Policies: "Special System Privileges."

Audience: Technical staff

Security Environments: All

5. Computer Transaction Initiations

Policy: The ability to execute business transactions on behalf of Company X must be restricted by both individual user IDs and positive identification of the involved people using these user IDs.

Commentary: This policy prevents unauthorized persons from being able to initiate binding business transactions on behalf of Company X. An example of such a business transaction involves a bank instruction to initiate a wire transfer that has been prepared using Company X systems. To achieve this end, it is customary to require that authorized users provide both their user ID and a secret password. The policy is written in a general way such that passwords are not the only way to achieve positive identification. The same objective could for example be achieved with smart cards, identity tokens, fingerprint readers or digital certificates. Positive identification of users is imperative if separation of duties is to be enforced in a computerized environment. To be effective, it is likely that a definition of a "business transaction" will need to accompany this policy. The notion of "production business systems" may be a helpful idea when preparing this definition.

Related Policies: "Separation Of Duties."

Audience: All

Security Environments: All

6. Computer Support Identification Codes

Policy: Unless the voice of a calling party is definitively recognized, the identity of persons placing telephone calls requesting computer support must be authenti-cated through a special identification code, different from a computer password, and disclosed only to authorized internal staff.

Commentary: This policy thwarts social engineering or the masquerading of an authorized person. Industrial spies, systems hackers, and others frequently use social engineering in an effort to obtain employee numbers, telephone numbers, addresses, passwords, and other information that may be useful for accessing computers and networks. Because passwords should be known only by the person to whom they relate, computer passwords are not an appropriate way for staff to authenticate their identity to computer support staff. Likewise, employee numbers, social security numbers, or other readily-obtainable numbers specific to each worker are not definitive ways to authenticate the identity of internal staff. Computer support identification codes should only be available to those staff that have a justifi-able need to know. In some organizations, use of these identification codes may be expanded to include release of sensitive information like salary and benefits informa-tion over the phone. Organizational culture may need to be changed so that these codes are regularly used, lest the party who has been reached refrain from requesting a code in an effort to appear polite.

Related Policies: "System Access Control Passwords" and "Record Change Orders."

Audience: Technical staff

Security Environments: Medium and high

9.05.04 Password Management System

1. Minimum Password Length

Policy: All passwords must have at least 10 characters and this length must always be checked automatically at the time that users construct or select their password.

Commentary: In many systems, fixed passwords are the only line of defense. Guessing fixed passwords remains an often successful attack method by which unauthorized persons gain system access. Password guessing is most often performed with automated tools like dictionary attack programs. Passwords with only a few characters are much easier to guess than passwords with at least 10 characters. Ten is generally considered by experts to be a good minimum password length for commercial systems. This policy may be expanded with additional requirements, such as a prohibition against repeating characters in a password. The policy is applicable to user-chosen passwords and system-generated passwords. This is why the words "construct or select" were used in the policy. On most platforms, operating systems software or linked access control security software can be used to automatically enforce this policy. The policy can be restricted to system and network access control passwords, to permit database management systems, application programs, and voice mail systems to use fewer characters in a password.

Related Policies: "Anonymous User IDs," "Password Attempts," "Dial-Up Password Attempts," "Logon Banner Information," and "Passwords On Different Systems."

Audience: Technical staff

Security Environments: All

2. Minimum Password Length Constraint

Policy: User-chosen fixed passwords must be at least 10 characters long, or the maximum length permitted by the system.

Commentary: Perhaps the best-known computer control mechanism, fixed passwords are widely-used even though they have been shown to be susceptible to interception when transmitted, and to guessing by parties who know something about the user. The maximum number of characters in a password on some systems may be limited to six, seven, or eight, in which case a policy that specifies a minimum password length of 10 is not feasible. This policy recognizes this constraint, but requires every system that can support a 10-character password to be set at that length. The long password requirement is a way to compensate for the deficiencies of fixed passwords. The longer a password is, the harder it is to guess, and the less likely it will succumb to a variety of automated attacks such as a dictionary attack.

Related Policies: "Minimum Password Length" and "In-Bound Internet Access."

Audience: Technical staff

Security Environments: All

3. Network-Connected Computer Passwords

Policy: All Company X network-connected computers must employ fixed passwords made up of at least 10 characters and all computers that are not network-connected must employ fixed passwords made up of at least six characters.

Commentary: This policy ensures that network-connected computers are protected with a higher standard than those computers that are not network-connected. Network-connected machines need a higher level of security because unauthorized parties can more readily access them. Fixed passwords for network-connected computers often do not provide sufficient security. Dynamic passwords, challenge/response dialogs, biometrics, or other extended user authentication technologies may be needed. This policy diverges from traditional minimum length for fixed password policies in that it recognizes the fact that network-connected machines need significantly more security. Traditional fixed password length policies make no such distinction. Internet-connected machines need more security than machines that are connected to internal networks. This is because the number of unknown and untrusted parties is much greater on the Internet than it is on an internal network.

Related Policies: "Logon Banner Information" and "Multiple User IDs."

Audience: Technical staff

Security Environments: All

4. Role-Based Password Length

Policy: The minimum length for fixed passwords must be set to six for voice mail boxes and handheld computers, eight for all network-connected computers and 10 for administrator and other privileged user IDs.

Commentary: This policy creates different groups of fixed passwords, each having their own minimum length requirements. The requirements specified in a policy such as this guide system administrator efforts to configure both computers and networks. Products now on the market automatically convert policies such as this into enforceable access control rules. There is nothing special about the use of three categories. The organization might just as easily have chosen five categories if required. Likewise, there is nothing special about the use of the six, eight, and 10-character minimums. These might just as easily have been five, 10, and 15. The idea behind the relative lengths is to use more stringent controls only where stringent controls are necessary. This policy reflects an evolution in thinking about fixed password length requirements. No longer must a single length requirement apply to all systems throughout an organization. The policy assumes that users have been given instructions not to handle sensitive information through voice mail or handheld computers.

Related Policies: "Portable Identification Credentials" and "System-Generated Passwords."

Audience: End users and technical staff

Security Environments: All

5. Password Reuse

Policy: Users must not construct passwords that are identical or substantially similar to passwords that they had previously employed.

Commentary: This policy prevents users from recycling passwords that they had previously employed. For example, some operating systems will prevent users from employing any of the last fifteen passwords. A user can then have a list of 16 passwords, generated by a rule of thumb, and repeatedly go through these same passwords. In other operating systems, only one previous password is recorded, so the user can then alternate between two passwords. Reuse of passwords increases the chances that a password will be divulged to unauthorized parties and that these unauthorized parties will then take advantage of this knowledge. Reuse also increases the chances that passwords will be guessed because they will be in use for considerably longer periods of time than other passwords. A less stringent version of this policy would omit the words "or substantially similar."

Related Policies: "Cyclical Passwords" and "Password History."

Audience: All

Security Environments: All

6. Password Characters

Policy: All user-chosen passwords must contain at least one alphabetic and one non-alphabetic character.

Commentary: This policy informs users that they must take specific steps to make their passwords difficult for unauthorized parties and automated system penetration software to guess. There are a number of specific steps that users can be told to perform. These include use of upper and lower case in the same password. Be sure to check systems documentation before writing this policy because some systems have rigid restrictions about the type of characters permitted. Personal identification numbers (PINs), which are a type of password, are generally generated by a security system, and so would not fall within the purview of this policy. Such PINs may for example be used to activate smart cards or dynamic password tokens. If these PINs are user-chosen, however, the number of possible characters may be severely restricted. The combination of alphabetic with non-alphabetic characters may not be possible. Consideration should be given to all of the possible systems on

which user-chosen passwords are used, and the available keyboards, then strive to have the policy consistently apply to as many of these as possible.

Related Policies: "Password Structure" and "Password Case."

Audience: All

Security Environments: All

7. Password Case

Policy: All user-chosen passwords must contain at least one lower case and one upper case alphabetic character.

Commentary: This policy informs users that they must take specific steps to make their passwords difficult to guess. There are a number of specific steps that users can be told to perform. These include the use of alphabetic and non-alphabetic characters in the same password. From a mathematical standpoint, the idea behind the use of both upper and lower case characters is to spread the actual passwords employed more evenly over the total possible values for passwords, thereby making password guessing more difficult and expensive. The organization should be sure to check systems documentation before adopting this policy because some systems have rigid restrictions about the type of characters permitted.

Related Policies: "Password Structure" and "Password Characters."

Audience: All

Security Environments: All

8. Password History

Policy: On all multi-user machines, system software or locally-developed software must be used to maintain an encrypted history of previous fixed passwords that contains the previous 13 passwords for each user ID.

Commentary: The security provided by required password changes is much less effective if users repeat the same passwords. A history file prevents users from alternating between two passwords or following some other rotation scheme with a small number of passwords. Some operating systems provide this security mechanism. It is important to establish a cross-platform policy for password management, especially if the organization currently uses or intends to implement single sign-on systems. One part of a cross-platform policy for password management is provided in this policy. Some organizations may want to additionally specify that the password encryption process must be one-way, so that stored passwords cannot be decrypted. Although historical passwords are no longer being used, it is desirable to keep them absolutely unavailable to unauthorized parties so that knowledge of them cannot be used to predict future passwords. Some organizations may want to increase the minimum number of passwords kept in the history file beyond 13.

Related Policies: "Required Password Changes" and "Cyclical Passwords."

Audience: Technical staff

Security Environments: All

9.   Seed For System-Generated Passwords

Policy: If system-generated passwords are used, they must be generated using the low order bits of system clock time or some other frequently-changing unpredictable source.

Commentary: Because fixed passwords are often the only defense protecting a system, they must be constructed with care if they are to withstand various types of attack. System-generated passwords can be readily circumvented if an attacker gains access to the algorithm used to generate passwords and if the attacker has access to a predictable source for the inputs to this algorithm. Because the on-going secrecy of a password-generation algorithm is doubtful, especially when it is part of an operating system or some other widely-disseminated software, it is critical that the inputs to the algorithm be unpredictable. For example, a number of system-generated password algorithms are readily obtained from hacker bulletin boards or in the public domain. The starting point for these computations should be very difficult to predict by unauthorized parties. Ideally, truly random seeds should be used. But in the real world, frequently-changing seed parameters, or better yet, a combination of frequently changing seed parameters, will suffice. The words "frequently-changing" in the policy are also important. If the current date or other predictable character strings that change infrequently are used to generate passwords, the resulting passwords may be easily guessed. This same policy can be used for encryption key generation processes.

Related Policies: "Encryption Key Generation."

Audience: Technical staff

Security Environments: Medium and high

10. System-Generated Passwords

Policy: All system-generated passwords for end users must be pronounceable.

Commentary: A system-generated password such as "IDTP2EAW9" begs to be written down because it is hard for a user to remember. On the other hand, a system-generated password such as "eatgreenhair" will be more easily remembered, and less likely to be written down. While system-generated passwords do not need to be constructed by stringing together actual words from the dictionary, it does help to construct them with pronounceable components, usually syllables. While the approach described in this policy makes system generated passwords more easily remembered, it also severely restricts the domain of total possible passwords, and therefore reduces the security that system-generated passwords provide. One way to compensate for this is to increase the minimum number of characters in system-generated passwords, perhaps to 15 characters. Another approach is to permit users to pick from a list of 10 or more possible system-generated passwords. This list of possible passwords would be generated differently for each user. Some system-generated passwords are employed for end user-transparent encryption key management, digital signatures, message authentication codes, and other security-related processes.

Related Policies: "Encryption Key Generation."

Audience: Technical staff

Security Environments: Medium and high

11. System-Generated Password Issuance And Storage

Policy: If passwords or personal identification numbers are generated by a computer system, they must always be issued immediately after they are generated and must never be stored on the involved computer systems.

Commentary: This policy ensures that generated but unissued passwords do not fall into the wrong hands. To store system-generated passwords on a computer system, even in encrypted form, is ill advised. The only time when passwords should be stored on a system is when they are encrypted with a one-way function. This prevents them from being decrypted, even by authorized parties. If passwords were to be stored using a one-way function, they could not be reconstructed into readable form. If they cannot be reconstructed into readable form, then they cannot be reissued. Passwords should be issued at the time they are generated. The policy also may be used as a justification for the restriction of both probes that test the workings of a password generation routine, and calls to a system-generated password routine by unauthorized programs. This policy permits passwords and personal identification numbers to be generated at user request in real-time or on a batch basis. If done at user request, typically the user is presented with a few passwords and asked to choose one. The selected password is then stored, using a one-way function, in a password file. If done on a batch basis, the passwords would then be used to program smart cards, encode magnetic stripes for automated teller machine plastic cards, print secure mailers, or perform other security related activities. This same policy can also be used for the construction of encryption keys.

Related Policies: "Password Retrieval."

Audience: Technical staff

Security Environments: Medium and high

12. Password Generation Materials

Policy: All computer storage media and computer memory areas used in the construction, assignment, distribution, or encryption of passwords or personal identification numbers, must be repeatedly overwritten with a series of ones and zeros immediately after use.

Commentary: Overwriting with a series of ones and zeros is necessary because magnetic computer media can provide a weaker signal reflecting prior values of the data rather than the current value. One-time overwriting of data in high security environments will be insufficient. Without multiple overwriting processes, persons knowledgeable about magnetic media can reconstruct the data several generations back. This technique prevents utility programs and unauthorized applications from accessing memory areas that contain passwords, personal identification numbers, or the data used to construct these security parameters. In some very-high-security environments, such as within military units, magnetic media containing sensitive information must be destroyed by burning, shredding, or some related mechanism because overwriting does not provide sufficient security. In these cases, the security provided by the approach described in this policy is not sufficient. This same policy can be used for the construction of encryption keys.

Related Policies: "Password Generation Algorithms."

Audience: Technical staff

Security Environments: Medium and high

13. Password Generation Algorithms

Policy: All software and files containing formulas, algorithms, and other specifics of the process used to generate passwords or personal identification numbers must be controlled with the most stringent security measures supported by the involved computer system.

Commentary: This policy is information about the process by which system-generated passwords are constructed should be given the most stringent protection. If specifics about this critical security process are disclosed to unauthorized parties, then the entire system may be compromised. This is why the password generation mechanism is part of the kernel, most protected portion of some operating systems. Some organizations may wish to include documentation, scratch paperwork, and other materials used to generate passwords within the scope of the policy.

Related Policies: "Password Generation Materials," "Password Encryption," and "Encryption Key Management Systems."

Audience: Technical staff

Security Environments: Medium and high

14. Password Display And Printing

Policy: The display and printing of passwords must be masked, suppressed, or otherwise obscured so that unauthorized parties will not be able to observe or subsequently recover them.

Commentary: This policy prevents passwords from falling into the hands of unauthorized parties. Whenever a user types a password into a system, the password should not be displayed on a monitor or printed on a hardcopy terminal. If a password were to be displayed, persons nearby could look over the user to obtain the password. Persons going through the trash could recover passwords printed on a hardcopy terminal. For a display screen, the mechanism used most often is simple echo-off at the time a password is entered. For hardcopy terminals, over striking the password multiple times is sometimes used. Sometimes it is possible to recover passwords from temporary files or scratch memory locations.

Related Policies: "Password Generation Materials," "Positioning Computer Display Screens," and "Initial Passwords."

Audience: Technical staff

Security Environments: All

15. Masking Password Changes

Policy: Whenever user-chosen passwords or encryption keys are specified, they must be entered twice and masked.

Commentary: This policy prevents unknown typing errors from causing problems. Because masking prevents users from seeing what they enter, without entering parameters twice, users have no idea when they have made a typing mistake. Confirmation of a password or encryption key, also known as double entry of these parameters, will often but not always reveal this problem. For those rare situations where this approach does not detect a typing error because the same error was made twice, there are other control mechanisms. The policy references the time when a user specifies a password, for example when a password is being changed. Likewise, the policy deals with encryption keys that may be entered when a file is about to be encrypted. The policy need not apply to those times when the user later attempts to access a system using a previously-specified password, because the system will inform the user that a mistyped password is incorrect and will then invite the user to try again. Likewise, if an incorrect encryption key is provided at the time of file decryption, the program will either provide unintelligible results or provide an error notice.

Related Policies: "Storage Of Passwords In Readable Form" and "Concealing Customer Account Numbers."

Audience: Technical staff

Security Environments: All

16. Required Password Changes

Policy: All users must be automatically required to change their passwords at least once every 90 days.

Commentary: This policy requires users to change their passwords on a periodic basis. There is nothing special about the 90-day period mentioned in the policy. This could just have easily been some other period of time. If the need for security is great, the interval should be shorter. In fact, some organizations have a tiered approach where different time intervals are used for different user populations, based on the nature of the privileges available to these users. For example, systems programmers may be required to change their password every two weeks, while regular users may be required to change their password once every month. If a password has fallen into the hands of an unauthorized party, then unauthorized system use could continue for some time in the absence of a required password change process.

This policy limits the time period in which this unauthorized use could continue. Likewise, if combined with a dormant user ID privilege revocation process, this policy acts as a safety net if system administrators forget to disable privileges when users change jobs or leave an organization. This policy limits the period of time that such a co-worker can masquerade as another user by sharing their password. Two undesirable side effects associated with frequent password changes are that users write their passwords down or the users develop simple-minded algorithms for generating passwords that can be guessed by unauthorized parties. Unless a high security environment is involved, the organization should refrain from setting the frequency to a period of time less than 60 days. This policy works well when combined with a policy requiring passwords to be changed if there has been a compromise or a suspected compromise of a password security system.

Related Policies: "Suspected Password Disclosure," "Password Structure," "Password Change Interval Synchronization," and "Dial-Up Number Changes."

Audience: Technical staff

Security Environments: All

17. Password Change Interval Synchronization

Policy: The fixed password change interval must be synchronized across all computer and network platforms at Company X.

Commentary: This policy lays the groundwork for single logon systems, whereby users can logon only once, but within a single online session they can use multiple systems. This policy is also helpful in terms of preparing for the use of security servers, through which administration of multiple platforms can take place. The policy is also user-friendly because it permits users to simplify their password management activities, using a single fixed password across multiple systems. Some security experts complain that this is a risky approach, but in the real world users are overburdened with the complexity of information security systems, and they welcome any move in the direction of simplification. If fixed passwords are being used in a high security environment, and these fixed passwords are being transmitted without encryption, then this approach is risky. But if a low security computing environment exists, or if fixed passwords are encrypted as they are sent and stored, then the password synchronization mentioned in this policy makes sense and is advisable. This policy assumes that users are able to change their passwords whenever they wish. The existence of this ability will enable them to change all of their passwords on all systems on a certain date.

Related Policies: "Required Password Changes" and "Security Changes After System Compromise."

Audience: Technical staff

Security Environments: All

18. Passwords In Readable Form

Policy: Fixed passwords must never be in readable form outside a personal computer or workstation.

Commentary: This policy provides direction for the construction, integration, and management of password-based access control systems. Although dynamic passwords are more desirable, many organizations are using fixed passwords. This policy permits fixed passwords to continue to be employed by the end user. Because fixed passwords in readable form can be easily captured as they travel over a network, it is critical that they be encrypted when on a network or other readily-accessible places. Simple encryption is not enough. The encryption must be implemented such that passwords appear differently each time they travel over a network. If the passwords do not appear differently each time they are used, attackers could use replay methods to cause fraud, sabotage, and other abuses. This policy is consistent with commercial products that permit passwords to be stored in logon scripts. In general, such password storage is a dangerous practice because unauthorized people can use these passwords. This policy is particularly well-suited for client-server systems, local area networks, and other small systems.

Related Policies: "Storage Of Passwords In Readable Form" and "Computer-Connected Network Access."

Audience: Technical staff

Security Environments: All

19. Access Control Information In Cookies

Policy: Company X information systems must never store any access control information in cookies deposited on, or stored on, end-user computers.

Commentary: This policy prevents unauthorized access to Company X information systems. Cookies are small files that are deposited on remote computers connected through the Internet. Cookies can be stored permanently on a hard drive or they may be erased when the Internet session is complete or when the user exits the browser. This policy is written so that it addresses both types of cookie files. Popular with a number of web merchants, this approach has serious security drawbacks. It is popular because users do not need to remember a user ID or a fixed password, and in that respect they can be automatically logged on. However, if an unauthorized person were to sit down at an authorized user's computer, and were to direct the browser to the site of one of these same web merchants, then the unauthorized person would be automatically logged on. While this may seem like a remote possibility, it is not if the unauthorized user is visiting the sites that the authorized user stored as favorites in the browser. This unintended log on might permit the unauthorized person to buy products in the name of the authorized person, to discover private information belonging to the authorized person, or to impersonate the authorized person in electronic mail or other communications. This policy is deliberately written in a general way so that it prohibits developers from storing access control privileges in cookies.

Related Policies: "Cookies For Automatic Log On" and "Cookies And Web Bugs."

Audience: Technical staff

Security Environments: All

20. Password Encryption

Policy: Passwords must always be encrypted when held in storage for any significant period of time or when transmitted over networks.

Commentary: Encryption provides one of the few effective ways to safeguard fixed passwords, encryption keys, pseudo-random number generator seeds, and other security parameters. Without encryption, these parameters may be inadvertently disclosed to persons who have access to telecommunication system buffers or temporary working memory inside a computer. Special scavenger computer programs also may be able to record unencrypted security parameters for subsequent retrieval by unauthorized persons. This policy ensures that systems designers always use encryption to protect security parameters such as passwords. Ideally, the type of encryption would ensure that the encrypted quantity differs over time, even though the unencrypted quantity does not. The term "held in storage for any significant period of time" is used to exempt internal memory locations within a system that might temporarily contain an unencrypted password. This policy is particularly relevant to, and may be written so that it is restricted only to Internet communications. Many password collection programs have been used to compromise Internet security.

Related Policies: "Password Generation Materials."

Audience: Technical staff

Security Environments: Medium and high

21. Password Retrieval

Policy: Computer and communication systems must be designed, tested, and controlled to prevent both the retrieval of, and unauthorized use of stored passwords, whether the passwords appear in encrypted or unencrypted form.

Commentary: This policy prevents unauthorized persons from obtaining access to passwords that might then be used to give them unauthorized system access. When a user enters a password, it should be encrypted using a one-way function, and this new encrypted string should then be compared to the relevant encrypted string in the destination machine's password file. Encrypted strings appearing in the password file should never be retrievable by users as this permits a dictionary attack to be mounted. A dictionary attack involves encryption of entries in a computer-readable dictionary, then the comparison of these quantities to the entries in a password file. If a match occurs, then an unencrypted version of a password has been discovered. This clear text password can then be used to compromise the security of the involved system. Even if one-way encryption functions are used, the dictionary attack can be mounted. To avoid such attacks, this policy employs access controls such that all retrieval of passwords is prevented. The same concept can be extended to encryption keys, pseudo-random number generator seeds, and other security parameters. There are other controls that meet the objectives specified in this policy, but these additional controls need to be identified and implemented by local management based on the requirements of the information system.

Related Policies: "System-Generated Password Issuance And Storage."

Audience: Technical staff

Security Environments: All

22. System Access Control Passwords

Policy: Computer and communication system access control must be achieved through passwords that are unique to each individual user.

Commentary: This policy prevents system administrators from establishing access control privileges with a scheme that leads to problems, such as using lockwords rather than passwords. Lockwords, which are often used to control access to a file, can be easily passed along to another user. The file Owner who originally granted access can quickly lose control over who has access and who is changing the file. This defeats the principle of accountability, which attempts to attribute all system events to specific individuals. Use of an individualized password and a user ID, along with specific access control privileges, will prevent secondary dissemination of passwords because passwords must remain the exclusive knowledge of the involved users. This policy is consistent with the use of hand-held identity tokens or extended user authentication systems. Nothing in this policy states that these systems cannot be used in addition to fixed password systems. The policy additionally prohibits the sharing of user IDs, with group accounts. This policy is relevant to telephone systems, local area networks, client-server systems, and other communication systems in addition to traditional mainframe-style access control packages.

Related Policies: "Password Sharing," "Unique User ID And Password Required," and "Unique User IDs."

Audience: Technical staff

Security Environments: All

23. Vendor Default Passwords

Policy: All vendor-supplied default passwords must be changed before any computer or communications system is used for Company X business.

Commentary: One of the oldest, yet most successful ways to break into systems is to employ default vendor passwords. Often the vendor-supplied default passwords are known by both the technical people with experience on this platform and the hacker community. Some organizations forget to change these passwords before they place their systems into production mode. This policy notifies technical staff that they must change all vendor default passwords in order to achieve the most basic level of security. To restrict the scope of this policy, the word "production" could be added to the policy, perhaps accompanied by a definition if the audience is not familiar with the notion of production systems. This policy is particularly important in Internet-connected, client-server, local area network, and small systems computing environments where system administrators may not be trained extensively in data processing. Some vulnerability identification packages can be used to monitor compliance with this policy.

Related Policies: "Initial Passwords."

Audience: Technical staff

Security Environments: All

24. Security Changes After System Compromise

Policy: Whenever a system has been compromised or suspected of compromise by an unauthorized party, system managers must immediately reload a trusted version of the operating system and all security-related software, and all recent changes to user and system privileges must be reviewed for unauthorized modifications.

Commentary: The purpose of this policy is to re-establish a secure operating system and associated password-based access controls following a break-in or some related compromise of the security measures. Immediate response is required because the longer the unauthorized parties are on the system the more the opportunity for them to establish unauthorized user IDs, unauthorized privileges for existing user IDs over which they have control, and trapdoors that would permit future system access. Reloading the operating system and scanning the logs for unauthorized changes that need to be undone will help to eliminate further unauthorized activity. Besides being relevant to Information Systems department computer operators, this policy applies to local area network server administrators, departmental computer system managers, and similar persons who may be organizationally positioned outside the Information Systems department. This policy is particularly important for those in charge of small systems such as client-server systems and local area networks.

Related Policies: "Suspected Password Disclosure."

Audience: Technical staff

Security Environments: All

9.05.05 Use Of System Utilities

1. Security Tool Screening

Policy: Before distributing vulnerability identification software or other tools that could be used to compromise the security of information systems, Company X staff must research and validate the recipient's need for such tools.

Commentary: This policy is intended to restrict the distribution of tools that could be used to compromise the security of information systems. This policy can be augmented to include sensitive security information that could be used to compromise the security of systems. While intended primarily to be used by software developers and other organizations that issue or distribute such tools, the concept described in the policy is generally-applicable to all organizations. The policy is intended to prevent the distributing organization from being held responsible for damage done with their tool. Text accompanying this policy could specify how the staff is supposed to validate the recipients' need for the tool.

Related Policies: "Testing Information System Controls," "System Security Status Tools," "Powerful Information Systems Tools," and "Computer Crime Or Abuse Evidence."

Audience: Technical staff

Security Environments: Medium and high

2. Vulnerability Identification Software

Policy: When vulnerability identification software is not being actively used, it must be removed from the system on which it has been run.

Commentary: The purpose of this policy is to ensure that unauthorized parties do not use vulnerability identification software to break into Company X systems. If this software is not removed, it is possible that an intruder could use it to his or her advantage. While the use of vulnerability identification software is widespread, technical specialists sometimes do not think about how these tools are dangerous when in the wrong hands. Likewise, they do not think about how this software could be used to attack systems managed by other organizations, and how their employer might be held liable for those intrusions. This policy applies to situations where the software runs on a centralized system that probes remote systems, and situations where the software runs on distributed systems, then reports back to a centralized system.

Related Policies: "Vulnerability Identification" and "Computer Crime Or Abuse Evidence."

Audience: Technical staff

Security Environments: All

3. Powerful Information Systems Tools

Policy: If built or distributed by Company X, all powerful information systems tools that could be used to cause significant damage must be automatically restricted, so that they can only be used for their intended purpose.

Commentary: This policy is intended to guide developers in the selection of appropriate functionality. The specific mechanisms to be used are deliberately not specified in the policy, lest this unduly constrains the developers. The policy instructs staff to help limit the liability of the developer or distributor. This policy is applicable to a wide variety of products such as floppy disk utilities, not just information security tools.

Related Policies: "Testing Information System Controls," "System Security Status Tools," "Powerful Information Systems Tools," and "Computer Crime Or Abuse Evidence."

Audience: Technical staff

Security Environments: Medium and high

4. System Security Status Tools

Policy: Every multi-user system must include sufficient automated tools to assist the security administrator in verifying the security status of the computer and must include mechanisms for the correction of security problems.

Commentary: This policy is intended to be used in the acquisition process for new and enhanced computer systems. It also may be helpful in the acquisition of tools assisting administrators in the maintenance of an adequate level of systems security. This policy requires that each multi-user system have sufficient tools to determine whether the security is adequate and whether the security mechanisms are working as they should be. These tools could include a software package to check the logical consistency of assigned user privileges, automatically review systems logs, or automatically check whether security system set-up parameters match organizational policy. Personal computers were deliberately not included within the scope of this policy because such tools are rare on these systems.

Related Policies: "Computer Crime Or Abuse Evidence."

Audience: Management and technical staff

Security Environments: All

5. Diagnostic Hardware And Software

Policy: Access to diagnostic test hardware and software must be strictly controlled and must be used only by authorized personnel for testing, trouble-shooting, and development purposes.

Commentary: Diagnostic test hardware and software can be used to insert unauthorized messages on a communications line so that a fraud may be perpetrated. The tools may also permit people to read communications line traffic that they would otherwise not be able to examine. These wiretapping tools have, for example, been used to capture readable passwords and user IDs that are later used to gain unauthorized system access. This policy restricts the use of such powerful tools to troubleshooting and other authorized business activities. The policy gives local management significant flexibility in determining the ways in which they secure these hardware and software tools. For example, some managers will require that line monitor devices be locked in a closet, while others will be satisfied with the use of a metal key to activate and deactivate the device. There is a greater need for this policy in those environments using fixed passwords for system access control. This is because communications line monitors can be used to intercept fixed passwords. Likewise, this policy is not needed, or at least much less needed, in those environments where all network traffic is encrypted.

Related Policies: "Malfunctioning Access Control."

Audience: Technical staff

Security Environments: All

6. Storage Of Systems Utilities

Policy: Disks and other online storage facilities used on production computer systems must not contain compilers, assemblers, text editors, word processors, or other general purpose utilities that may be used to compromise the security of the system.

Commentary: In spite of the strong position taken in this policy, emergency use of these utilities will be required from time to time. As a practical matter, to meet these exceptional needs, the utilities may be kept on a tape or disk that is locked in a file cabinet in the computer machine room. After they are used, the utilities can be deleted from the system, and the tape or disk can be once again locked in the file cabinet. This policy is equally important for smaller systems such as client-server systems, local area network servers, and personal computer systems, although it is more difficult to control. In these environments, software license management software may be used to identify these utilities. This policy prevents these utilities from being readily accessible to users, thereby reducing the chances that the utilities will be used to circumvent controls. Some of the utilities mentioned in the policy will be needed in certain environments. These may be deleted from the list of utilities found in this policy.

Related Policies: "Systems Software Utility Usage" and "Removal Of Software."

Audience: Technical staff

Security Environments: All

7. Systems Software Utility Usage

Policy: Access to systems software utilities must be restricted to a small number of trusted and authorized users, and whenever these utilities are executed, the resulting activity must be securely logged, and reviewed by the Computer Operations manager.

Commentary: Most multi-user computer systems have one or more utilities that can be used to override either system access controls or application access controls. Examples include a database troubleshooting tool and a disk repair utility. These tools may permit a user to directly alter the payroll database, the accounts receivable check printing spool file, and other computer-resident collections of information, without going through the normal channels and the associated controls. This policy prevents dangerous utilities from being used by unauthorized persons. In those circum-

stances where these utilities must be used to get the work done, This policy ensures that their usage is consistent with management's intentions. With the words "securely logged," the policy also requires facilities to quickly identify unauthorized systems utility use. This policy assumes that the systems have access controls such as those based on passwords and profiles of user privileges. If many people on a multi-user system are able to use such systems utilities, then the associated access controls are ineffective. The phrase "securely logged" means recorded in a manner that is not readily modifiable by users employing the involved system utility. Although it is rarely done, some organizations may wish to go further than the words shown in this policy. They may want to specifically authorize each and every use of a systems utility.

Related Policies: "Storage Of Systems Utilities," "Production Operating System Changes," and "Logging Security-Relevant Events."

Audience: Technical staff

Security Environments: All

8. Control Override Facilities

Policy: Management must establish and restrict the usage override facilities to be used in those exceptional circumstances where controls must be compromised to maintain on-going business operations.

Commentary: This policy informs systems designers, application programmers, and other technical staff about the need for override facilities. The policy is also intended to describe management's intentions regarding the use of these override facilities, and indicate how access controls for these facilities should be defined. Some organizations may also wish to add words to the policy requiring all override facility usage to be logged. If override facilities are used on a regular basis, they can render the controls ineffective. This is why the facilities must be used only when absolutely necessary.

Related Policies: "Privilege Restriction — Need To Know," "Control Override Usage," and "Override Facility Logs."

Audience: Technical staff

Security Environments: All

9. Control Override Usage

Policy: Management must clearly define the specific circumstances and the authorization procedures followed when system controls may be overridden.

Commentary: This policy specifies the circumstances in which system control override facilities may be used. Referencing these instructions, staff can use override facilities without obtaining specific management approval. This is useful, for example, if the system crashes during off hours, the problem has been encountered before, and the solution is well known and already scripted. In a case like this, it is unnecessary to get specific management approval for the use of override facilities. This policy is also applicable to small systems such as local area networks, client-server systems, and multi-user workstations. Some organizations may also wish to add words to this policy, stating that logging is required for all override facility usage. If override facilities are used on a regular basis, they can render the controls ineffective.

Related Policies: "Privilege Restriction — Need To Know," "Control Override Facilities," and "Override Facility Logs."

Audience: Management and technical staff

Security Environments: All

10. File Restoration Access Control

Policy: If end users are given the ability to restore their own files, they must not be given privileges to restore other users' files or to see which files other users have backed-up.

Commentary: This policy ensures that users do not employ a backup system as a way to circumvent an access control system. For example, on a local area network, one user might be able to restore personnel performance evaluation files saved by his or her supervisor, and thereby defeat the access controls normally applicable to these files. Only the local area network administrator or security administrator for other environments should have multiple-user access to file backups. One way to enforce this policy is to encrypt the backed-up files using one or more unique keys for each user. Local area network or security administrators may also want to periodically check logs indicating which users restored which files to determine whether abusive activity has taken place. Some Internet firewall systems are now monitoring outbound traffic volume to determine whether excessive information flows are taking place. Other commercially-available firewalls are limiting the outbound volume of information that can be sent. These same data volume throttle approaches could be used to control backup information to which users have direct access.

Related Policies: "Malfunctioning Access Control," "Backup Media Encryption," and "Backup Media Storage."

Audience: Technical staff

Security Environments: All

9.05.06 Duress Alarm To Safeguard Users

1. Duress Passwords

Policy: Whenever system access to particularly valuable or sensitive data is given to a user, duress passwords must be employed to covertly signal the system that this user is being pressured to log-on.

Commentary: Duress passwords may limit user privileges, turn on supplementary logs, signal a remote alarm, or automatically initiate some other security-related action. Duress passwords are generally different from a regular password, both of which will let the individual onto the system. Because a duress password may be employed when an individual user's safety is endangered, it is advisable to continue to provide some system access. The duress password is a convenient way for the user to tip-off the system operators on duty or other people that something serious is happening. For normal business activities, duress passwords are not necessary.

Related Policies: "System Interruption For Safety" and "Projects Involving Human Safety Issues."

Audience: Technical staff

Security Environments: High

9.05.07 Terminal Time-Out

1. Automatic Log Off

Policy: If there has been no activity on a computer terminal, workstation, or personal computer for 10 minutes, the system must automatically blank the screen, suspend the session, and require a password for the re-establishment of the session.

Commentary: This policy prevents unauthorized disclosure of information and unauthorized system usage resulting from authorized workers walking away from their desks without logging off. Particularly in open offices where there are no walls, many people leave their computers on and available for anyone who happens to walk by. Although most effective when it applies to all workstations, this policy could be restricted to systems containing or accessing sensitive, critical, or valuable information. In many instances, because automatic log-off functionality is not a part of the operating system, for personal computers and workstations a software security package will be needed to implement this policy. Larger multi-user computer systems often provide a feature such as this as part of the operating system. Nothing in this policy requires that a user lose his or her work in progress. After the correct password has been provided, the work can resume. The number of minutes can be adjusted depending on the security level of the system. Where no automatic log-off software is available, organizations can adopt a policy requiring users to log-off when they leave their workstations.

Related Policies: "Unattended Active Sessions."

Audience: Technical staff

Security Environments: All

9.05.08 Limitation Of Connection Time

1. Time-Dependent Access Control

Policy: All multi-user computer systems must employ positive user identification systems to control access to both information and programs that are restricted by time of day and day of the week.

Commentary: The default access control found on many systems is based on various types of access to information or application programs. Organizations wishing to bolster this control environment, can mandate additional restrictions based on time and day as mentioned in this policy. The policy's intent is to require more than simple access controls, normally based on user IDs and passwords. More than the ordinary user IDs and passwords need not mean smart cards, biometrics, or some of the more expensive technologies. In addition to time dependent access controls, another example of a readily-available and low-cost way to augment user IDs and passwords is through terminal-ID codes or network addresses. Each organization should base the specific positive user identification control measures it uses on a risk assessment. Recent studies of hacker activity show that they are most active at night, just the time that systems are sparsely staffed, if they are staffed at all. Given so many people are working odd hours these days, this policy may be restricted to only those applications handling sensitive or valuable data, such as wire transfer systems. This policy is most relevant to organizations that have established official hours of operation. The globalization that goes along with Internet commerce and organizational intranets may require that this policy be reworded to reflect local time zones. This policy is relevant to batch jobs and interactive sessions.

Related Policies: "Privilege Restriction — Need To Know."

Audience: Management and technical staff

Security Environments: Medium and high

9.06 Application Access Control

9.06.01 Information Access Restriction

1. Customer Service Passwords

Policy: The fixed passwords used to verify a customer's identity over the telephone must never be displayed by Company X information systems.

Commentary: This policy limits the number of internal Company X workers who have access to customer service passwords. These passwords are often different from logon passwords. If these customer service passwords were to be known by internal workers, these workers could masquerade as the involved customers, and engage in fraud, privacy invasions, and other abuses. For example, the wire transfer departments at many banks utilize customer service passwords that authorize the disclosure of confidential customer information and that authorize the transfer of funds between accounts. This policy describes an easy-to-implement approach where the system only provides a "correct" or "not correct" response to a password typed in by a customer service representative. This approach prevents well-meaning customer service representatives from providing unauthorized hints, or from deciding that the provided passwords are close enough to system resident passwords, then proceeding with sensitive transactions or disclosures. Hints can be officially supported as part of the software, should management decide to do so. This policy is in keeping with the notion that only the customer or user should know his or her password.

Related Policies: "Concealing Customer Account Numbers" and "Compromising Security Mechanisms For Customers."

Audience: Technical staff

Security Environments: Medium and high

2. Secret User IDs Or Passwords

Policy: Developers must not build or deploy secret user IDs or passwords that have special privileges, and that are not clearly described in the generally available system documentation.

Commentary: This policy is directed to an act that has been committed by many programmers. This act involves the definition of special user IDs or passwords that nobody knows about. Although relatively easy to code, and difficult for others to discover, these access mechanisms circumvent the organization's systems development life cycle controls. These access mechanisms also circumvent the end-user organization's standard request for privilege process and subsequent management authorization process. These mechanisms can give the programmers access to powerful functionality, even if these programmers no longer work for the employer. Because they are fixed in the code, these access mechanisms cannot be readily removed or disabled when a developer leaves the employment of a software vendor, even if they do become generally known. Likewise, hackers can exploit these same user IDs or passwords. Another reason to outlaw such user IDs and passwords is that they give one or more individual developers control over the security of software when that control should have been transferred to the user organization when software was licensed, rented, or sold. The reference to system documentation is intended to be a deterrent. If developers would be embarrassed to have a special access mechanism described in the documentation, then it probably should not be in the system at all.

Related Policies: "Circumventing Access Controls," "Access Paths In Production Software," and "Physical Access Of Terminated Workers."

Audience: Technical staff

Security Environments: All

3. Computer System Access Controls

Policy: All computer-resident information that is sensitive, critical, or valuable must have system access controls to ensure that it is not improperly disclosed, modified, deleted, or rendered unavailable.

Commentary: This policy requires that only the information that needs it will be protected with access control systems. Ideally, security measures are designed in a consistent manner, such that information is properly protected wherever it travels, whoever handles it, whatever technology is employed, and whatever form it takes. This policy mandates the use of access controls to support that notion. The policy assumes that a data classification system has been adopted. The words "sensitive," "critical," and "valuable" need to be specifically defined by management before this policy can be practically applied. It is also a good idea to define "system access controls." Although many personal computer operating systems do not include access controls, most multi-user operating systems and network operating systems do include the type of access controls required by this policy. For those systems lacking native software to support access control, supplementary software packages will be required. This policy is also relevant to client-server systems, mobile computing systems, and personal digital assistants. Very small remote systems, such as alphanumeric pagers, may not be able to support the desired access control, in which case the organization must decide whether it will accept the risk, or prohibit the handling of such information on these systems.

Related Policies: "Four-Category Data Classification," "Business Applications Security Functionality," and "Systems Architecture For Logging Activities."

Audience: Technical staff

Security Environments: All

4. Adult Material Access

Policy: Prior to providing access to any material that the general public would consider inappropriate for children, all Company X systems must employ an age verification access control system approved by Information Security management.

Commentary: This policy informs technical staff about the circumstances where a special type of access control system is required. This access control system is not the usual type, which could for example involve dynamic or fixed passwords, but one that verifies a user's age. This could involve simply clicking on a button stating that a user affirms that they are at least a certain age. This could also involve collection of a legitimate credit card number, which could be confirmed online. The ability to provide a legitimate driver's license number can also be used as a mechanism to verify age. The policy deliberately avoids reference to a specific technical solution. This policy is prompted by the exploding use of the Internet, and the access to adult material that children are accessing over the Internet. The existence of this policy can serve as evidence of management's intention to restrict access to certain materials to adults only, and to be in compliance with local laws.

Related Policies: "Children's Personal Information Collection" and "Storing Mixed Classified Information."

Audience: Technical staff

Security Environments: All

5. Separation Of Activities And Data

Policy: Management must define user privileges such that ordinary users cannot gain access to, or otherwise interfere with, either the individual activities or the private data of other users.

Commentary: This policy prevents system managers from establishing the access controls on multi-user systems so that users can damage the files of other users, look at the work of other users, or otherwise exceed the privileges they need in order to do their own work. Much of this type of damage is often unintentional, as might be wrought by a program written by one user that alters the data belonging to another user. Implicitly this policy prohibits sharing of a single user ID and the use of passwords that are known and used by several people. The policy assumes separate logical workspaces for each user, and is worded in such a manner that it is fully consistent with computing environments such as groupware systems, knowledge management systems, data warehouses, or certain virtual reality systems. Nothing in this policy prohibits the use of shared resources as are commonly found on a local area network, including public directories for storing shared files.

Related Policies: "Privilege Restriction — Need To Know" and "Separation Of Duties."

Audience: Management and technical staff

Security Environments: All

6. User Access Capabilities

Policy: Users must not read, modify, delete, or copy a file belonging to another user without obtaining permission from the Owner of the file.

Commentary: This policy defines appropriate boundaries around the files maintained by personal computer (PC) users, who often have no file access controls whatsoever. No mention of PCs was made in the policy because the policy could conceivably also apply to larger systems. For larger systems, whenever access controls are deficient, or when an inconsistency in the existing access controls has been discovered, this policy would apply. The policy makes reference to information Owners, which ideally would make decisions about access to certain types of information. Nonetheless, for many types of information, the Owner is by default the user on whose PC the information resides. Some organizations may wish to change this policy so that it refers to the user of a system as a surrogate for the Owner of a file. The word "file" could also be generalized to be an "information collection."

Related Policies: "Malfunctioning Access Control."

Audience: End users

Security Environments: All

7. Default User Privileges

Policy: Without specific written approval from management, administrators must not grant any privileges, beyond electronic mail and word processing, to any user.

Commentary: This policy establishes a group of system privileges that all authorized users will be given so that they may communicate with other users and get their jobs done, beyond which special permission is required. The basic set of privileges might for example be given to all employees when they join the organization. When their duties have been sufficiently defined, they will need to make specific requests for more privileges. These privilege requests are generally handled with special forms, which can be delivered by electronic mail or electronic forms. The idea behind this policy can be extended to include the establishment of default privileges by job title and default privileges by department. Other privileges can be added to this default list of privileges. For example, Internet web surfing and spreadsheet programs could be added.

Related Policies: "Privilege Restriction — Need To Know."

Audience: Management and technical staff

Security Environments: All

8. System Capabilities And Commands

Policy: End users must be presented with only the system capabilities and commands that they have privileges to perform.

Commentary: This policy limits the end-user choices to those options for which privileges have been granted. This makes system usage simpler and more direct, and also increases security. If users do not know that they cannot do something they will be less likely to request those privileges. The policy may trigger a marginal reduction in access control administration costs. This policy also prevents curious users from attempting to employ capabilities and commands for which they lack

training or authorization. The policy makes it very clear which privileges are authorized and which are not, and may help administrators and systems designers make appropriate decisions about access control. This policy also diagnoses user problem. If a certain option is not shown, this means that privileges have not yet been granted. This policy will be applicable only to software developed in-house. The software developed by third parties generally is not modifiable to make it comply with this policy.

Related Policies: "Special System Privileges," "Single Sign-On," and "Privilege Restriction — Need To Know."

Audience: Technical staff

Security Environments: All

9. Production Business Information Privileges

Policy: System privileges permitting the modification of production Company X business information must be restricted to production applications.

Commentary: Users must not be able to modify production data unless such modification is through well-defined and previously-approved production software. For example, employees should not be able to modify payroll amounts due unless this is done through a prescribed process including the access controls built into the payroll application system. Only when this process is followed can logging, data input validation, and other controls be consistently applied. Ordinary users should not be permitted to use text editors, programming debuggers, and other powerful system tools to modify production information directly. There will always be an occasional need for certain staff, such as a select few systems programmers, to be able to modify production data directly. This should be severely restricted, supervised, logged, and periodically reviewed. Many personal computer and local area network commercial operating systems make this policy hard to implement, although this is clearly an emerging trend. The policy might be implemented by the removal of certain utility programs like compilers and text editors. This is standard practice on Internet commerce servers.

Related Policies: "Operating System Command Access" and "Modification Of Production Business Information."

Audience: Technical staff

Security Environments: Medium and high

10. Database Updates

Policy: Updates to production databases must be made only through established channels that have been approved by management.

Commentary: This policy prevents staff members from causing operational problems that could interrupt or otherwise interfere with production processing. This policy prohibits the use of utilities, which can circumvent database access controls, and which go directly to a database to modify the data contained therein. It provides the basis for disciplinary action should systems programming, systems administration, or computer operations staff commit such abusive acts. Perhaps the most effective way to implement this policy is to encrypt production files such as a database.

Related Policies: "Modification Of Production Business Information" and "Background Push Software Updates."

Audience: Technical staff

Security Environments: All

11. Multi-User Production Applications

Policy: All production business applications supporting multiple users must be secured by an access control system approved by Information Security management.

Commentary: It is possible with some access control systems to establish a list of applications to which access controls do not apply. This is undesirable because it permits an exception that may not be consistent with other access controls, and may not be as well secured or logged as other access controls. This policy, directed primarily to system administrators, states that all business applications must be controlled using standard and approved access control systems. The policy also applies to smaller systems. It is on departmental servers and other small systems that applications without adequate access control often exist. This policy also prompts the reader to ask what types of access control systems are approved by Information Security management. This answer is generally provided on a list of standard products and approved vendors.

Related Policies: "Business Production Information Updates."

Audience: Technical staff

Security Environments: All

12. Systems Log And Audit Trail Disclosure

Policy: Systems logs or application audit trails must not be disclosed to any person outside the team of individuals who ordinarily view such information to perform their jobs or investigate information security incidents.

Commentary: This policy prevents system logs and application audit trails from being disclosed to persons who do not have a legitimate need to know such information. System administrators or others may think that the requesting party has authorization or a legitimate reason to view such information, when in fact they do not. Hackers, industrial spies, and others may use social engineering to convince system administrators and other technical staff that they have a legitimate reason for access to this type of information. Likewise, departmental managers may claim that they are doing their own investigation of a worker's performance. To prevent these types of abuses, this policy requires the person who would disclose the log or audit trail to contact Information Security management.

Related Policies: "Access To Logs" and "Information Security Investigations."

Audience: Technical staff

Security Environments: All

13. Production Application Information Access

Policy: Business application software development staff must not be permitted to access production information, with the exception of the production information relevant to the particular application software on which they are currently working.

Commentary: This policy limits each developer's access to production information such that access is granted only for that production information required to support his or her development work. For example, if a developer is working on a new accounts receivable system, he or she does not need access to accounts payable production information. The policy requires management to implement access controls at a level of detail that they may not have previously specified. They may have given all developers access to all production information. This policy supports the principle of separation of duties. Although perhaps more difficult to achieve in the client-server, local area network, personal computer, and related small systems environments, this policy is not restricted to large scale systems.

Related Policies: "Privilege Restriction — Need To Know," "Separation Of Duties," and "Developer Access To Production Business Information."

Audience: Technical staff

Security Environments: All

14. Third-Party Confidential And Proprietary Information

Policy: Unless specified otherwise by contract, all confidential or proprietary information that has been entrusted to Company X by a third party must be protected as though it was Company X confidential information.

Commentary: In many cases the people handling third-party information do not have access to the contracts that define agreed-upon procedures for handling information entrusted to Company X. An expedient way to overcome this lack of information is to use the internal data classification scheme at the recipient organization to designate how the information should be protected. This policy by default assigns a classification of confidential to all such information. The policy could be modified to require that an internal Company X information Owner or sponsor be assigned, who then is required to assign a data classification label consistent with an internal data classification scheme. As a general strategy, it is advisable for all such information sharing agreements to employ existing information security classifications and procedures. One variation to this policy would require that third-party information include a notice designating the information's true Owner.

Related Policies: "Four-Category Data Classification."

Audience: Management and technical staff

Security Environments: All

15. Personal Information Access

Policy: All identifying information about customers such as credit card numbers, credit references, and social security numbers, must be accessible only to those Company X personnel who need such access in order to perform their jobs.

Commentary: This policy makes it clear that financial and personal information about customers must only be used by those people who have a genuine need for this information. This is desirable because it is the general availability of this information that often makes identity

theft so easy to commit. This policy is deliberately silent about the mechanisms used to restrict access. This gives local management significant flexibility to choose the controls best suited to meet the objective defined in the policy. The policy could be extended to employees and other groups of people for whom the organization keeps records. The policy could additionally be useful for public relations as an indication of the organization's proactive position.

Related Policies: "Disposal Of Payment Information."

Audience: Management and technical staff

Security Environments: All

16. Data Warehouse Access

Policy: Access to the data warehouse must be restricted to Company X top and middle management.

Commentary: Access to a data warehouse should be restricted only to top and middle management or some other select group of authorized workers such as strategic planners. An alternative approach would be to make it accessible only through an intermediary, such as a research assistant, who could also make an assessment of the requestor's genuine need for the requested information. While inefficient, this intermediary approach to implementing the policy has the advantage that it will be consistently applied. This policy should be distributed only to system administrators and others who grant system privileges. This policy can be adapted for use in a variety of information collections including very large databases.

Related Policies: "Information Collection Restrictions" and "Multiple Classification Labeling"

Audience: Technical staff

Security Environments: All

17. Secondary Dissemination Of Secret Information

Policy: Secret information must be disclosed only after the information Owner's explicit authorization has been obtained, and any individual who has been granted access to secret information must not disclose it to any other person.

Commentary: This policy prevents people who are in receipt of secret information from passing it to others when they do not have permission from the information Owner. People in receipt of secret information do not inherit the right to disseminate it further. Because this notion is contrary to common practice, there is often need for a specific policy. This policy assumes the term "information Owner" has been previously defined. The word "secret" could be replaced by "sensitive" or a set of specific sensitive information classifications used by the organization. The policy assumes that the term "secret" has already been defined.

Related Policies: "Information Ownership," "Four-Category Data Classification," "Confidentiality Agreements," and "Sensitive Information Handling."

Audience: All

Security Environments: All

18. Sensitive Or Valuable Information Access

Policy: Access to Company X sensitive or valuable information must be provided only after express management authorization has been obtained.

Commentary: This policy restricts access to Company X sensitive and valuable data, not permitting people to gain access unless they have obtained explicit management approval. The policy furthermore discourages workers from sharing such information with other workers or outsiders in the absence of management approval. The policy is a general high-level policy under which various more-detailed policies related to access control could be added. Rather than simply using the term "management authorization" the policy could refer to the "information Owner authorization." Instead of "sensitive," the terms "secret," "confidential," and "private" could be used here. Although this policy can be used without an in-house data classification system, it is most effective when the words "sensitive" and "valuable" have been defined in another policy.

Related Policies: "Four-Category Data Classification" and "Privilege Restriction — Need To Know."

Audience: All

Security Environments: All

19. Secret Information Access

Policy: Access to secret information must be granted only to specific individuals, not groups of individuals.

Commentary: This policy requires that management make person-by-person decisions when granting access to the most sensitive types of information. If access is granted to groups of individuals, inevitably there will be greater access than is necessary. Likewise, if access is granted to a group, it will be much more difficult to establish accountability. When deciding to grant access to sensitive information, management should consider the individual's tenure with the organization, his or her current responsibilities, any disciplinary problems, potential conflicts of interest, the degree of loyalty to the organization, and related matters. This policy supports the practice of having one user ID for each individual. This policy could be expanded to all types of sensitive information. The policy assumes that the word "secret" has been defined in another policy.

Related Policies: "Privilege Restriction — Need To Know," "Unique User ID And Password Required," "Four-Category Data Classification," and "Sensitive Or Valuable Information Access."

Audience: All

Security Environments: All

9.06.02 Sensitive System Isolation

1. Critical Application Servers

Policy: Unless technical considerations indicate that it would be excessively costly, critical production servers must be dedicated purpose machines, running only a single application.

Commentary: This policy isolates critical applications so that they have their own servers. This will reduce the chances that these servers will crash due to conflicts and incompatibilities between various software packages. There are often asynchronous combinations of system

events that will cause operating systems to crash. For example, one application may have a programming error that causes a buffer overflow. If that application had its own server, only that machine would crash. But if it were hosted on a shared server, then all the applications on that machine will crash. So this policy is intended to increase the uptime and reliability of servers, to simplify system administration, to facilitate system performance monitoring, and to keep the number of ways that a server could be compromised to a minimum.

Related Policies: "Computer System Dispersion" and "Firewall Computers."

Audience: Technical staff

Security Environments: Medium and high

2. Secret Information System Isolation

Policy: Company X computer systems containing secret information must not be connected to any network or any other computer.

Commentary: This policy prevents the unauthorized disclosure of particularly sensitive information. Knowing that network access controls are somewhat unreliable, some organizations choose to prohibit all network connections, lest the information somehow be improperly disclosed. This conservative policy can often be replaced by a policy requiring strong encryption when the secret information not in use. Some organizations may prohibit any other applications on the involved computer, effectively making it a dedicated computer. In the wake of the rush to interconnect virtually every system within organizations, some managers may wish to keep some high-security systems off the network, particularly the Internet. This need not cause major problems in terms of getting the work done. Whenever there is a need to transfer data from a high security system to a lower security system, floppy disks or some other storage media can be used rather than a network.

Related Policies: "System Interconnection" and "Secret Information On Web."

Audience: Technical staff

Security Environments: High

9.07 Monitoring System Access And Use

9.07.01 Event Logging

1. Sensitive Application Systems Logs

Policy: All production application systems that handle sensitive Company X information must generate logs that capture every addition, modification, and deletion to such sensitive information.

Commentary: This policy offers the ability to account for all changes to sensitive information like personnel records, strategic plans, and design specifications. For example, the payroll database in most organizations should have an associated log that shows who updated the payroll amounts and when. This type of information will be very helpful when attempting to investigate and correct problems like errors and defalcations. This policy indicates which applications should have associated logs or audit trails. The log data elements will need to be determined on a case-by-case basis. The scope of the policy could be readily expanded to include sensitive, critical, and valuable Company X information. In some instances, the operating system, application system, or database management system will be able to capture sufficient log information.

Related Policies: "Four-Category Data Classification"

Audience: Management and technical staff

Security Environments: All

2. Production Application System Log Contents

Policy: All computer systems running Company X production application systems must include logs that record, at a minimum, user session activity including user IDs, logon date and time, logoff date and time, and applications invoked, changes to critical application system files, additions and changes to the privileges of users, and system start-ups and shut-downs.

Commentary: This policy provides a collection of log data that can be available on every internal system running a production application. Not only will this information assist with problem resolution efforts and system restore operations, it will also be invaluable to system penetration attack investigations and fraud investigations. By standardizing on a minimum logging requirement, an organization can assist system administrators with decisions about how to configure a system. A policy like this can also lay the foundation for an integrated multi-machine intrusion detection system.

Related Policies: "Logging Security-Relevant Events"and "Sensitive Application Systems Logs."

Audience: Technical staff

Security Environments: All

3. Logging Security-Relevant Events

Policy: Computer systems handling sensitive, valuable, or critical information must securely log all significant security relevant events including, but not limited to, password guessing attempts, attempts to use privileges that are not authorized, modifications to production application software, and to system software.

Commentary: This policy specifies which computer systems must have system logs reflecting security relevant events. It is particularly appropriate for personal computers, workstations, local area network servers, client-server systems, and similar small systems that often lack adequate logs. It may be necessary to further specify what constitutes a security relevant event in the policy. Another way to handle this is to indicate that Information Security management will determine exactly what constitutes a security relevant event. The policy only requires logs for systems handling sensitive, valuable, or critical information. Because it makes reference to sensitive, valuable, or critical information, this policy implicitly relies on a data classification policy.

Related Policies: "Four-Category Data Classification."

Audience: Technical staff

Security Environments: All

4. Logging Logon Attempts

Policy: Whether successful or not, all user initiated logon attempts to connect with Company X production information systems must be logged.

Commentary: This policy creates a comprehensive set of operating system logs across all internal production information systems that can be used for investigative or administrative purposes. Logs are also a very important input to computer intrusion detection systems, which can automatically alert technical staff that an attack is underway. A string of incorrect logons will be evidence of a password guessing attack or a user who needs additional training. These system logs will show the user ID, the time and date, the port that the user employed, and whether the logon was successful. This policy is restricted to production information systems so that system logs will not be necessary on desktop machines and other computers that are not critical to the business.

Related Policies: "Production Application System Log Contents" and "Clock Synchronization."

Audience: Technical staff

Security Environments: All

5. User-Initiated Security Event Logs

Policy: One or more logs tracing security relevant activities to specific users must be securely maintained for a reasonable period of time.

Commentary: This policy specifies that all user-initiated security-relevant activities must be logged and retained for an adequate period. This information will be helpful to those people in security administration, computer operations, and internal auditing. The information also serves as a deterrent to abusive acts, and important information for the Help Desk to use when investigating a problem. The policy makes reference to security relevant activities like user changes to file access privileges or user changes to a secret password. If the policy was only distributed to management and technical people, the policy could include a specific definition of security relevant activities. It may be appropriate to keep the term "security relevant activities" ambiguous so that local systems management can interpret it in light of their own situations. Local systems managers may determine that both applications and systems activities are security relevant, or they may alternatively determine that only systems activities are security relevant.

Related Policies: "Consent For Questionable System Actions."

Audience: All

Security Environments: All

6. Private Information Access Logs

Policy: The identity of every user who accesses private information resident on Company X information systems must be logged.

Commentary: This policy clarifies the types of information that must be recorded in logs or audit trails. This type of information would generally be captured in an application system audit trail, rather than a system log. This policy is useful in any organization where privacy is an issue. Such a policy would also be useful in cases of identity fraud, or in any investigation attempting to identify how certain private information got into the hands of unauthorized persons.

Related Policies: "Personal Record Handling" and "Sensitive Application Systems Logs."

Audience: Technical staff

Security Environments: Medium and high

7. Retention Period Of Logs

Policy: Computerized logs containing security relevant events must be retained for at least three months, during which time they must be secured such that they cannot be modified, and such that they can be read only by authorized persons.

Commentary: This policy specifies the retention period for logs and the need for secure storage of logs. The policy can be expanded to define explicitly what events are deemed as security relevant. There is nothing special about three months. The retention period will vary by industry and jurisdiction and the information involved. Internal legal counsel and records management staff should be consulted about the appropriate time period to retain such records. The retention period for business transactions will generally be much longer than the retention period for logs of security relevant events.

Related Policies: "Access Control System Records" and "Access Control Privilege Log Retention."

Audience: Management and technical staff

Security Environments: All

8. Removal Of Logs From Internet-Accessible Computers

Policy: If they are resident on Internet-accessible computers, system logs and application logs must be moved at least daily to other machines that are not directly Internet-accessible.

Commentary: This policy safeguards the integrity of logs. If logs are kept for a prolonged period on Internet-accessible machines, then the chances that hackers and other unauthorized parties have modified them is significantly increased. The need to protect logs is greatly magnified if the logs contain payment information such as credit card numbers, or if the logs contain private information such as customer telephone numbers. Daily transfer to a more secure machine could simply mean uploading the logs to a machine behind another firewall. It may mean putting the logs on tape and storing them off-line. Rather than the process described in this policy, a more secure option is to refrain from keeping any logs on Internet-accessible machines. This might involve transfer of logging information on a real-time event-by-event basis to another machine that is behind another firewall.

Related Policies: "Customer Log Information," "Log Deactivation, Modification, Or Deletion," and "Access Control Privilege Log Retention."

Audience: Technical staff

Security Environments: All

9. Access Control Privilege Log Retention

Policy: Computerized records reflecting the access privileges of each user of Company X multi-user systems and networks must be securely maintained for a reasonable period of time.

Commentary: As part of an investigation of a computer crime, management may wish to determine who could have performed certain actions on a system or network. This policy specifies that logs about user access control privileges be captured and maintained for a certain period of time. Some organizations will want to explicitly state a log retention period, such as three months, in the policy. Some other organizations will want to leave the retention period open so that local management may determine it. In this policy, reference was made to multi-user systems because the identity of the perpetrator of an abusive act is much less of an issue with a personal computer or workstation. Likewise, these smaller systems are much less likely to have any sort of log reflecting user privileges. The policy could be expanded to include these smaller systems if desired. Simple deletion of the phrase "multi-user" may be sufficient. The policy, as written, is relevant to both voice and data communication systems.

Related Policies: "Granting System Privileges."

Audience: Technical staff

Security Environments: All

10. Systems Architecture For Logging Activities

Policy: Application or database management system software must keep logs of user activities and statistics related to these activities that will permit them to be identified and issue alarms reflecting suspicious business events.

Commentary: Consider a company that issues a credit card and that keeps a record of the number of transactions on each card per week. If this statistic far exceeds historical baseline statistics, it could indicate that the card has been stolen and is being used to make fraudulent purchases. This policy specifies where certain types of logs are to be maintained, whether in a computer operating system, network operating system, access control software, database management system software, or application software. This policy indicates that business events, such as the amount of charges made to a credit card, should be captured in logs maintained by an application or database management system. The organization can specify where other types of information, such as changes in user privileges, should be recorded as well. This policy is a technical systems design instruction, and is often part of information security architecture. Many organizations now are developing a plan, or architecture, specifying where critical controls such as logging will be supported.

Related Policies: "Computer System Access Controls."

Audience: Technical staff

Security Environments: All

11. Computer System Audit Logs

Policy: Logs of computer security-relevant events must provide sufficient data to support comprehensive audits on the effectiveness of and compliance with security measures.

Commentary: External auditors may not be able to rely on an organization's financial records if there is insufficient evidence that the controls are working as they should be. If this is the case, it means the external auditors will have to perform other tests of the records to verify their correctness, perhaps incurring significant additional auditing fees. Similarly, without sufficient logging information, internal auditors may not be able to do their jobs, which may make management uneasy about systems security. This policy ensures that logs provide sufficient information to permit both internal and external audits to proceed without excessive costs. Effective logs can also be helpful with resolution of operational problems, such as determining the cause of a system crash. This policy is additionally helpful because it can prompt management to consider exactly what types of data should be recorded in logs. Some organizations may wish to expand this policy to include the data needed for legal actions or staff disciplinary actions.

Related Policies: "Information System Control Reviews — Internal."

Audience: Management and technical staff

Security Environments: All

12. Remotely-Mirrored Logs

Policy: All Company X production information systems that are accessible by any external network must employ remotely mirrored system logs.

Commentary: This policy requires a certain design that is popular with Internet merchants. This secure systems design involves remote recording of system logs on another machine, ideally a machine with a different type of operating system. The use of a different operating system means that an intruder will have additional difficulty breaking into the remote logging system. This difficulty will impose a delay that should be enough for an intrusion detection system to alert authorities to the intruder's presence. The policy is based on the assumption that one of the first things that an intruder does when he or she compromises a machine is to turn-off, modify, or erase the systems log. These actions can conceal an intruder's trail, but if the systems log is stored on another machine, tampering with it will be much more difficult. For the very highest level of security, remote logs can be encrypted to prevent unauthorized disclosure and undetected modification, and also stored in a write-only fashion to prevent any modification.

Related Policies: "Critical Application Logs" and "Log Deactivation, Modification, Or Deletion."

Audience: Technical staff

Security Environments: Medium and high

13. System Log Rotation and Archival

Policy: A formal log rotation and archival process must be employed for all network periphery security systems and all multi-user production servers.

Commentary: This policy is for system administrators to establish and follow a formalized process for system log rotation and archival. In some organizations, system administrators do not think about logs until they exceed their disk quota. Log files that are too large are difficult to handle, to move from machine to machine, and to search for specific events. Having reasonably-sized log files that are rotated to separate storage media improves these activities.

Related Policies: "Multiple Backup Copies."

Audience: Technical staff

Security Environments: All

14. User Awareness Of Logging And Security Violations

Policy: Users must be clearly informed about the actions that constitute security violations and that such violations will be logged.

Commentary: This policy requires that all users be clearly informed about the actions that constitute security violations. To discourage users from engaging in these actions, they should be told that their activities will be logged. Disciplinary action will be very difficult if users have not been told about, and do not clearly understand what is expected of them. If the policy is to be distributed to users, the policy may additionally include words indicating that "violations will subject users to disciplinary actions up to and including termination and prosecution." An advisable explanation that accompanies this policy could give specific examples of security violations. Typically these violations would include attempts to compromise controls through password guessing, changing system access controls, masquerading as another user, and other actions such as crashing the system.

Related Policies: "Systems Monitoring Tools."

Audience: Technical staff

Security Environments: All

9.07.02 Monitoring System Use

1. Privileged User ID Activity Logging

Policy: All user ID creation, deletion, and privilege change activity performed by system administrators and others with privileged user IDs must be securely logged and reflected in periodic management reports.

Commentary: This policy specifies which activities associated with privileged user IDs need to be logged and reflected in periodic management reports. Management is sometimes unclear about this, and as a result, insufficient logs and management reports are generated. In the absence of specific instructions, system administrators and others are likely to turn-off the logs and management reports to free disk space. One variation of this policy would involve addition of another sentence requiring system Owners, information Owners, or others responsible for the involved systems to review these privileged user ID activity management reports. The words "securely logged" imply that system administrators and other privileged users cannot readily modify or delete log entries.

Related Policies: "Privileged System Command Accountability And Traceability" and "Override Facility Logs."

Audience: Technical staff

Security Environments: All

2. Production Change Reconstructability

Policy: All user activities affecting production information must be reconstructible from logs.

Commentary: This policy ensures that all errors, fraudulent changes, and other improper modifications to production information can be expediently detected and corrected. For example, in the event that a system crash damages a production database, such logs will be instrumental in reconstructing the database from a prior copy. In this case, database snapshots showing before-and-after images could be used. In this policy the emphasis is on being able to reconstruct data, and preserve or enhance its integrity.

Related Policies: "User-Initiated Security Event Logs," "Non-Production Business Transactions," "Record Change Orders," and "Integrity Controls Failure Notification."

Audience: All

Security Environments: All

3. Privileged User ID Keystroke Logs

Policy: All activity with privileged user IDs on Company X production systems must be recorded with keystroke logs.

Commentary: This policy requires that intensive logging be turned-on for privileged user IDs on production systems. Every key pressed by these privileged users will go into a log so that all actions can be precisely reconstructed. This policy is a deterrent against abuse of the capabilities that go along with privileged user IDs. The policy also mandates extensive logging that could be most useful when investigating a computer crime, prosecuting a computer crime, or just trying to determine what went wrong. There is a more intense type of log and that involves not only keystrokes but also mouse clicks. In the very highest security environments, both types of information could be recorded for privileged user IDs. Keystroke logging is applicable only to privileged user IDs due to disk space limitations, but in very high security environments such as a bank's wire transfer room, it could be extended to all user IDs on production machines. This policy assumes that the keystroke log cannot be readily disabled by privileged user IDs. This might be achieved by having the logging software run on a different computer system than the one it monitors.

Related Policies: "System Logon Banner" and "Sensitive Application Systems Logs."

Audience: Technical staff

Security Environments: Medium and high

4. Privileged System Command Accountability And Traceability

Policy: All privileged commands issued by computer system operators must be traceable to specific individuals through the use of comprehensive logs.

Commentary: This policy is particularly relevant to servers, minicomputers, and mainframes, where more than one operator could initiate certain commands. The intention of the policy is to maintain accountability and traceability for all privileged system commands that were issued. The policy is not intended for small systems such as personal computers, for which specific operators are not usually designated. In those environments needing high security, the policy could be applied to small systems or systems containing particularly sensitive, valuable, or critical information. This policy instructs system management to keep records of all commands and an indication of who issued them. This policy and the controls used to implement it serve as a deterrent to abusive acts. Such logs also provide information that can be useful for disciplinary actions or legal proceedings. Most importantly, the logs of privileged system commands can be an important tool in both the resolution and understanding of system problems. Beyond computer system operators, the policy could also be expanded to include other types of people who typically have special privileges, such as information security administrators, internal auditors, systems programmers, and local area network administrators. The definition of "privileged system commands" can be included in the policy or left for local system management to determine.

Related Policies: "Operating System Command Access" and "Privileged User ID Activity Logging."

Audience: Management and technical staff

Security Environments: All

5. Password Logging

Policy: Unencrypted passwords must not be recorded in system logs.

Commentary: This policy prevents passwords from being revealed to computer operators, system administrators, and others who do not have authorization to view user passwords. If these technical people were to view user passwords it would be a violation of a fundamental approach to the design of fixed password systems. Specifically, in order to get accountability for a user ID and a related password, only the involved user must know his or her own password. If logs record passwords, then the technical staff who reviews the logs would discover the passwords of other users, and with this information could impersonate the other users. This policy prohibits even the logging of incorrect passwords, as this may permit anyone reviewing the log to use guessing techniques to determine the correct password. Recording of passwords with encryption is, however, permissible and may be warranted in high security environments. Encrypted passwords can be decrypted by a restricted group of security specialists in order to gain additional information that might help with an investigation.

Related Policies: "Logon Information" and "Computer Operator Log Review."

Audience: Technical staff

Security Environments: All

6. System Log Modification Controls

Policy: All Company X production information systems must employ cryptographic checksums to protect system logs.

Commentary: This policy ensures that unauthorized modification or deletion of system logs will be immediately evident. One of the first things that hackers and other intruders do when they gain system access is to disable the system log. While the controls dictated by this policy will not detect that a log has been turned off, they will highlight the fact that a log has been tampered with, and hopefully this will be used as input to an intrusion detection system. Such cryptographic checksums are available in the form of commercial and shareware software. These checksum methods involve a serial dependency of data such that modifying only one bit will cause an immediate alarm. Because cryptography is involved, this policy introduces the need for a key management process. Just because a cryptographic checksum is used to detect modification and deletion does not mean that the entire log needs to be encrypted. Using an encryption process only for a log checksum has less impact on system performance. A digital signature or hash total applied to the log as a whole could be used in place of a cryptographic checksum to achieve much the same result.

Related Policies: "Encryption Key Management Systems," "Intrusion Detection Systems," and "Log Deactivation, Modification, Or Deletion."

Audience: Technical staff

Security Environments: Medium and high

7. Log Deactivation, Modification, Or Deletion

Policy: Mechanisms to detect and record significant computer security events must be resistant to attempts to deactivate, modify, or delete the logging software and logs.

Commentary: The effectiveness of logs is dependent on the mechanisms used to protect the integrity of the logs and the mechanisms used to generate the logs. If a systems programmer were able to turn a log on and off, this would permit him or her to perform an act that did not appear in the log. This policy informs technical staff that proper access controls must be in place to protect both logs and the mechanisms used to generate logs. Some organizations may wish to add additional verbiage to this policy indicating that all changes to the logging system must themselves be logged. Readers may wish to consider a variety of mechanisms to protect logs including operating system based access controls, encryption, digital signatures, hash totals, and file authentication codes. In some instances logs are also kept on separate machines that use a different operating system.

Related Policies: "Backup Media Encryption."

Audience: Technical staff

Security Environments: All

8. Production System Storage Media

Policy: Production systems connected to the Internet must store all system logs on storage media that cannot be modified once created.

Commentary: This policy prevents modification to system logs. Write-once-read-many times (WORM) storage media can be used to irreversibly record what happened on a production computer. This approach does not record what happened if the logging facilities were deactivated, but the fact that the logging facilities were deactivated would appear in a log. This policy is a recommended way to generate reliable logs that could then be admissible in a court of law.

Related Policies: "Modification Of Production Business Information," "Critical Backup Files," and "Critical Information Backups."

Audience: Technical staff

Security Environments: All

9. System Log Protection

Policy: All Company X production computer system logs must be protected with digital signatures and log entry sequence numbers, and must also be automatically monitored for sudden decreases in size, failures of digital signatures, and gaps in log entry sequence.

Commentary: This policy requires that production systems be augmented with control measures that will detect tampering with system logs. One of the first things that intruders do when they gain unauthorized access to a system is to turn-off, delete, or modify the system log. This policy ensures that production machine logging systems detect these activities, then promptly notify those who are in a position to remove the intruder from the involved system. Many operating systems do not include code to perform the functions defined in the policy, and that most often additional software will be required. The controls defined in this policy assume that an intrusion detection system or a network management system is in place. If an organization categorizes its machines by security needs, the words "production computer system" in the policy could be replaced with or augmented by the words "infrastructure servers and network periphery servers."

Related Policies: "Production Input Transactions" and "Remotely-Mirrored Logs."

Audience: Technical staff

Security Environments: High

10. Access To Logs

Policy: All system and application logs must be secure and access provided only to those with a need to know.

Commentary: This policy limits access to logs, both application and system, to only those persons who have a genuine need to have such access. Access by unauthorized persons can reveal user IDs, transaction specifics, and other information that may be instrumental in fraud, sabotage, industrial espionage, and other abuses. In some instances passwords, particularly incorrectly typed passwords, may also appear in logs although this practice is not advisable. The policy could make specific mention of encryption, although this is not necessary. If logs are encrypted, they will be exceedingly difficult for unauthorized people to view or modify in a coherent way. In terms of off-site storage, encryption is the only truly effective way to prevent unauthorized access. This policy requires that an effective method of access control is in place.

Related Policies: "Log Deactivation, Modification, Or Deletion."

Audience: Technical staff

Security Environments: All

11. System Log Review

Policy: Computer operations or information security staff must review records reflecting security relevant events on multi-user machines in a periodic and timely manner.

Commentary: This policy requires that computer operations or information security staff promptly review logs. This review process can be greatly facilitated if the logs produce exception reports indicating items of a suspicious nature in need of follow-up. To ask a person to go through a log reflecting all system events on a busy multi-user system is impractical. Prompt review of logs might, for example, be important if there was a hacker who was attempting to guess passwords through a dial-up line. If the logs were never reviewed, and if there were no other mechanism to notify someone who could respond, the organization may never have become aware of the attacks. If the attacks were not stopped, or at least discouraged by telling the hacker that he was being closely monitored, the hacker may be encouraged to continue. Likewise, the chronological window for taking remedial action closes quickly unless corrective steps are promptly initiated. In some environments, such as electronic funds transfer systems, the window in which

adjustments must be made is very small. In these environments, the time frame for log review also may be included in the policy. The policy could be expanded to include application logs, in which case user management or information Owners or sponsors may be involved in the review process. Because they filter logs, tools such as intrusion detection systems increasingly reduce the need for human review of logs. However, someone must review the results from these systems, then take prompt action.

Related Policies: "Computer Operator Log Review" and "Internal Record Change Reviews."

Audience: Technical staff

Security Environments: All

12. Monitoring Internet Activity

Policy: Management must not monitor worker Internet traffic unless it receives a complaint, in which case existing monitoring systems will be enabled without prior notice to workers.

Commentary: This policy informs workers that management is able to watch what they do, but does not generally engage in surveillance. The policy is less restrictive than most because a complaint could come from anywhere. The types of monitoring systems are not stated in the policy and this is intended to deter abusive activity. The policy emphasizes trust based on worker's judgment. The policy assumes a homogeneous audience of users, who would generally agree on what is morally and ethically defensible behavior and what is not. This may not work in especially diverse working environments. The use of this policy does not reduce the need to tell workers about specific actions that should not be performed with Company X information systems.

Related Policies: "Internet Usage Logs" and "Electronic Mail Message Monitoring."

Audience: End users

Security Environments: All

13. Systems Monitoring Tools

Policy: Tools for the monitoring or observation of computer user activities must not be used unless the involved users are notified that their work may be monitored or observed, unless the tools are being used for investigations of suspected criminal activity.

Commentary: Remote monitoring programs may be useful for diagnosing problems that end users may be experiencing, but can also be used to secretly watch their activities in real-time. There is great resistance to the notion of monitoring systems about which the subject knows nothing. This policy assures employees that they know of all monitoring systems. The policy does not require that subjects be told at the specific time they are monitored. It only says that they must be told that they may be monitored. For example, a manager may listen in on a telemarketer's conversation with a potential customer at any time, as long as the telemarketer has been notified that this might happen. The exception, involving criminal investigations, is appropriate because management in most instances will not want to reveal to the suspect that an investigation is in process. To do so would risk the suspect's escape or destruction of evidence. Some organizations may wish to replace the words "computer user" with "worker."

Related Policies: "Surreptitious Collection Of Private Information," "Electronic Monitoring Areas," and "User Awareness Of Logging And Security Violations."

Audience: All

Security Environments: All

14. User Monitoring Notification And Logging

Policy: Whenever a user's computer or network account is monitored for investigative or disciplinary purposes, the involved user's manager must be promptly informed of this activity, and all of the monitoring must be logged.

Commentary: This policy assures Company X workers that the use of monitoring tools is not abused by requiring notification of the user's manager, and also by logging the activity. If the policy does not provide sufficient control over monitoring facilities, Company X may wish to require the user's manager to authorize the secret monitoring before it begins. Organizations that wish to provide more assurance to users may require notification of Human Resources management or a corporate ethics representative.

Related Policies: "Electronic Performance Monitoring Notification" and "Systems Monitoring Tools."

Audience: Technical staff

Security Environments: All

15. Internet Usage Logs

Policy: Department managers must receive, review, and approve reports of web sites visited, files downloaded, and related information exchanges over the Internet for their department's business activities.

Commentary: This policy notifies users that their Internet activities are logged, and that a department manager determines whether this usage is appropriate. The policy encourages users to follow existing policies, notably a policy regarding personal use. The policy is desirable because it assigns responsibility for disciplinary measures to the department manager and not to a central information security group or Information management. Realistically, only departmental managers will know what type of activity is consistent with local business objectives. This policy is a more flexible and potentially more economical alternative to blocking certain web sites.

Related Policies: "User Monitoring Notification And Logging" and "Personal Use Of Internet."

Audience: End users

Security Environments: All

16. Internet Customer Usage Profiles

Policy: Company X must not capture key words, mouse clicks, or any other indications of customer system usage or usage profiles beyond those needed to prepare billing statements.

Commentary: This policy generates trust, which should lead to additional traffic over the Internet. This policy assures customers that there is no activity log being kept and that this information will not be used to compromise their privacy. Although it is most appropriate for service providers, this policy can be adapted for use by any organization offering a product or service through the Internet.

Related Policies: "Transaction Log Destruction," "Information Gathered By Internet," and "Customer Activity Log Disclosure."

Audience: End users

Security Environments: All

17. Performance Monitoring

Policy: The performance of Company X workers must not be monitored by computers unless the monitoring is performed on a group basis.

Commentary: Computer monitoring of workers is much more likely to be accepted and effective when done on a group, rather than individual basis. The policy does not interfere with management's personal observations about the performance of specific employees, such as attendance. This policy permits monitoring but in a manner that is most likely to foster both teamwork and worker acceptance.

Related Policies: "Monitoring Or Recording Telephone Conversations."

Audience: Management and technical staff

Security Environments: All

18. Monitoring And Recording Activity

Policy: Information about user activities must be collected anonymously, unless the information is being collected for authorized law enforcement purposes.

Commentary: This policy permits system monitoring and logging while ensuring that the privacy of users is maintained. The policy is applicable to web sites where users are concerned that their activities are being recorded. These sites might include those that post information about which people have strong opinions. The policy notably includes specific exemptions for law enforcement purposes, and may also prevent hackers from thinking that a privacy policy is in some way a shield against tracing their activities. The policy does not prevent the tracking of a specific user's mouse movements or typed material, only the attachment of an identity to that recorded information.

Related Policies: "Performance Monitoring" and "Personal Information For Business Functioning."

Audience: End users

Security Environments: All

19. Electronic Performance Monitoring Notification

Policy: If it applies to them, prospective employees, contractors, and consultants must be notified in writing during their initial job interview that their work may be electronically monitored, the type of information that will be gathered, how this information will be used, existing standards of production, and production expectations for the individual involved.

Commentary: This policy prevents worker complaints about performance monitoring because the employees were informed when they interviewed for their new positions. Without a notice about monitoring systems, workers may complain that they were mislead about the nature of the jobs they now hold. This policy requires management to disclose the existence of monitoring systems before a prospective worker accepts a job offer. Special forms acknowledging the receipt of this information also may be used to create a paper trail showing that workers were made aware of monitoring systems.

Related Policies: "Monitoring Or Recording Telephone Conversations" and "Prospective Employee Information."

Audience: Management

Security Environments: All

20. Electronic Mail Message Monitoring

Policy: Messages sent over Company X internal electronic mail systems may be read by Company X management and system administrators.

Commentary: This policy makes it clear that management and technical staff may read worker electronic mail messages. This is a "may" rather than a "must" policy. To avoid legal problems, an organization that monitors electronic mail should make every effort to inform its workers that it does such monitoring. If notified in advance, workers are then able to change their usage patterns to reflect the fact that they may be monitored. This resulting behavior change is fully consistent with a policy indicating the organization's systems must be used for business purposes only.

Related Policies: "Non-Business Use Of Organization Information," "Examination Of Data Stored On Systems," "Electronic Mail Message Monitoring," and "Electronic Mail Privacy."

Audience: All

Security Environments: All

21. Override Facility Logs

Policy: Whenever system controls have been overridden, a log must be generated and promptly reviewed for changes made and the privileged commands that were used.

Commentary: This policy specifies when control override logs must be generated, reviewed, and what management must determine when reviewing the logs. Use of exception reports will reduce the time taken to perform the review. If there is no log reflecting usage of control override facilities, privileged users will be tempted to abuse these facilities. Intrusion detection systems in some cases can perform this log review automatically.

Related Policies: "Control Override Facilities" and "Control Override Usage."

Audience: Management and technical staff

Security Environments: All

22. Information Gathered By Internet

Policy: Whenever Company X gathers information about people who visit its web site, the users must be notified of this monitoring process, given an opportunity to specify how this information will be used, and notified to whom it will be disclosed.

Commentary: Web sites have the ability to gather many types of information about individuals who have visited their site. The information now available includes the screens an individual has examined, how long they examined these screens, and where they clicked the cursor. Internet electronic mail addresses also may be gathered without a user's knowledge. Tools are available that permit the user to see what messages an individual has posted to Usenet. With marketers eager to get a definitive picture of Internet web site activity, there is considerable pressure to utilize this newly-available data. This policy avoids a privacy backlash, that might lead to bad press for the organization that established or owns the web site.

Related Policies: "Customer Information Privacy" and "Private Data System Opt Out."

Audience: Technical staff

Security Environments: All

9.07.03 Clock Synchronization

1. Clock Synchronization

Policy: All multi-user computers connected to the Company X internal network must always have the current time accurately reflected in their internal clocks.

Commentary: Having synchronized clocks will assist system problem diagnosis and resolution, particularly for client-server and other systems involving interdependent hardware. This policy will also help with reliable event logging, automatic software updates, database replication, automatic encryption key changes, and other security-related activities. This policy permits investigators to reliably trace the actions of hackers or other unauthorized intruders on the network. If clocks are not synchronized and accurate, then investigations may be hampered. The evidence uncovered will most likely be unreliable, and therefore unusable as the reason for disciplinary action or prosecution. Accurate internal clocks are furthermore important because some access controls depend on this information, such as mechanisms that permit users to run privileged commands only during business hours. All clocks should be set to local standard time, and should be promptly changed to reflect periodic shifts that are made throughout the year. Whenever there has been a system crash, a power outage, an operating system upgrade, or some other event that might affect the clock, the clock should be promptly reset. Computer clocks often drift with time, so they should be periodically synchronized. The policy could be extended to all network-connected computer systems, although it is most important for multi-user systems.

Related Policies: "Log Deactivation, Modification, Or Deletion."

Audience: Technical staff

Security Environments: All

9.08 Mobile Computing

9.08.01 Mobile Computing

1. Small Portable Computer Usage

Policy: Personal digital assistants, handheld computers, and smart phones must not be used for Company X business information unless they have been configured with the necessary controls and approved for such use by Information Security management.

Commentary: The devices in this policy are convenient and useful, but they may expose Company X information to unauthorized disclosure. Users may opt for ease-of-use over security, and this policy prevents that decision. The policy acknowledges that these devices are often lacking adequate security measures. Most of these and other small systems have been used simply as sophisticated calendars and address books. But widespread use of now-available wireless capabilities will radically change the way these small computers are used. Encrypted communications for these wireless transmissions are available, but many users may not choose to use this feature. This policy ensures that these new devices are adequately secured for use with business information. While an employer may not have jurisdiction over an individual's personal property, it does have the right to assert boundaries to its own information.

Related Policies: "Cordless Or Cellular Telephones."

Audience: End users

Security Environments: Medium and high

2. Sensitive Information On Small Computers

Policy: The security mechanisms available on personal digital assistants, handheld computers, smart phones, and similar small portable computers must not be used with sensitive Company X information.

Commentary: This policy prohibits the use of small portable computers for sensitive Company X information to prevent this sensitive information from unauthorized disclosure. This might happen simply by the theft or loss of one of these devices. This might also happen because a user does not know how to properly operate security mechanisms on one of these small computers. The policy assumes that the term "sensitive information" has already been defined through a data classification scheme. If this is not the case, then the policy could be modified to prohibit these small

computers from handling any Company X information, although that may adversely degrade worker productivity.

Related Policies: "Password-Based Boot Protection," "Secret Information On Transportable Computers," and "Lending Computers Containing Sensitive Information."

Audience: End users

Security Environments: Medium and high

3. Secret Information On Transportable Computers

Policy: Workers possessing a portable, laptop, notebook, handheld, or other transportable device containing confidential Company X information must not leave these items unattended at any time unless the information is encrypted.

Commentary: This policy prevents secret information from falling into the hands of unauthorized persons. It has become a standard industrial espionage technique for spies to steal the transportable personal computers of executives. Encryption of the data held on the hard drive is the only definitive way to prevent the disclosure that goes along with such a theft. Ideally, everything on the hard drive would be encrypted and the user would have to provide a password to gain access to the data. A number of low cost products on the market support this policy. The large number of very small computers available makes this policy appropriate. Nonetheless, for the very smallest systems such as handhelds, there may be no commercially-available encryption systems. Until such products are available, it may be necessary to keep secret information off these systems. The word "secret" in the policy could be replaced by "sensitive" or a set of data classification terms used by the organization. This policy assumes the term "secret" has already been defined.

Related Policies: "Four-Category Data Classification," "Removing Hardcopy Sensitive Information," "Transportable Computers On Airplanes," and "Backup Media Encryption."

Audience: All

Security Environments: Medium and high

4. Portable Computer Usage

Policy: Until requirements for the secure operation of portable computers have been issued, workers must not use these systems to process any Company X information classified as confidential or secret.

Commentary: This policy issues a policy immediately, even if an organization has not had time to perform a risk assessment or otherwise seriously consider what it should be doing when it comes to mobile computing, telecommuting, and related security issues. This policy assumes that a data classification system has been adopted. If this is not the case, the policy can be modified so that it prohibits use of these machines with any Company X data that has not been publicly released. Exceptions may be provided for address books, telephone number lists, and schedule books resident on these machines. The policy is notable because it is an immediate way to control the usage of these machines. After management has clarified requirements for portable system security, then this policy can be replaced with more specific security instructions.

Related Policies: "Sensitive Information On Small Computers" and "Small Portable Computer Usage."

Audience: End users

Security Environments: Medium and high

5. Transportable Computers With Sensitive Information

Policy: All portables, laptops, notebooks, and other transportable computers containing sensitive Company X information must consistently employ both hard disk encryption for all files and boot protection.

Commentary: This policy protects the sensitive information stored on transportable computers. These machines are often stolen, lost, or otherwise unaccounted for. Unfortunately, when this happens, the information stored on the hard disk drives in these machines is also unaccounted for. While the cost of the hardware and software packages is often significant, this most often is much less than the cost of the information stored on these machines. The only reliable method to protect this information when the machines are unattended is to encrypt information on the hard disk drive. This policy requires that all files be encrypted when stored on the hard drive. Background encryption of all files makes the encrypt and decrypt process a system function rather than something that the user must invoke. This approach also imposes a performance penalty. This policy goes further by requiring that a

password be provided at the time the machine is turned on. In many instances the two controls mentioned in this policy will need to be acquired as separate hardware or software systems.

Related Policies: "Secret Information On Transportable Computers."

Audience: All

Security Environments: Medium and high

6. Transportable Computers On Airplanes

Policy: When traveling by air with a portable, laptop, notebook, or other transportable computers containing sensitive Company X information, workers must not check these computers in airline luggage systems.

Commentary: This policy prevents the theft or loss of transportable computers containing sensitive information. Numerous thefts from airline passenger luggage make it dangerous to check a computer with luggage even if it is packed. Many bags are misdirected or lost when entrusted to the airlines. Keeping the machine in the user's possession is a less risky approach. This policy is unnecessary if all user information on the computer's hard drive and accompanying storage media is encrypted. But even with encryption the financial impact of replacing the hardware could be significant. Some organizations may want to augment the policy to permit an exception to this approach whenever such encryption processes are being used.

Related Policies: "Secret Information On Transportable Computers."

Audience: All

Security Environments: All

7. Sensitive Information On Personal Computers

Policy: If sensitive information is to be stored on the hard disk drive or other internal components of a personal computer, it must be protected by either a password access control package or encryption.

Commentary: This policy is intended to concisely delineate special procedures for handling sensitive information with personal computers (PCs). Because PCs are often not adequately physically secured, unauthorized persons may be able to gain physical access to them, and thereby to the sensitive information contained thereon. This policy assumes that the term "sensitive" has been previously defined in other policy-related documents. The term "sensitive" could be replaced with "confidential" or similar words. The words "or other internal components" were used to recognize that non-volatile flash memory and other internal PC memory subsystems may hold sensitive information, yet properly speaking, not be an internal hard drive. This policy is relevant to portables, handheld computers, laptops, and other transportable machines, not just desktop machines. Organizations also may investigate special disk and other storage media labels such as those that incorporate bar codes.

Related Policies: "Information Life Cycle Labeling," "Comprehensive Classification Labeling," and "Sensitive Information Storage."

Audience: All

Security Environments: Medium and high

8. Lending Computers Containing Sensitive Information

Policy: A personal computer, handheld computer, transportable computer, personal digital assistant, smart phone, or any other computer used for business activities that contains sensitive information must not be lent to anyone.

Commentary: This policy prohibits workers from lending their personal machine to others. A variety of controls, such as personal computer fixed password-based boot controls and encryption measures are set up for a specific individual, given that individual's present job duties and their need to know. Permitting another person to access that machine, would permit the other person to circumvent these controls. To permit others to use a personal computer also jeopardizes the veracity of logs, and other mechanisms that monitor user behavior. Personal computers need to be considered as unique and specifically assigned to a certain individual, just as is the case with user IDs. The word "sensitive" will need to be defined elsewhere.

Related Policies: "Unique User ID And Password Required" and "Password Sharing."

Audience: End users

Security Environments: Medium and high

9. Organization Property At Alternative Work Sites

Policy: At alternative work sites, reasonable precautions must be taken to protect Company X hardware, software, and information from theft, damage, and misuse.

Commentary: This policy notifies telecommuters and others working with Company X information systems at locations other than a central office that the same security measures apply no matter where they are located. Information should be protected in a manner consistent with its value, sensitivity, and criticality. Protective measures should apply no matter where the information is located, what form it takes, and what technology is used to handle it. For example, if sensitive information is being handled, it should be encrypted when in storage, no matter if a computer is in the main office or at an alternative work site. This policy permits an organization to avoid having to specify a new set of control requirements for off-site information handling.

Related Policies: "Protection Of Information," "Removal Of Sensitive Information," and "Downloading Sensitive Information."

Audience: End users and technical staff

Security Environments: All

10. Information Stored In Organization Portable Computers

Policy: The information stored in Company X portable computer equipment is Company X property, can be inspected or used in any manner at any time by Company X and, like the equipment, it must be returned to Company X at the time workers are no longer employed by Company X.

Commentary: This policy prevents confusion about ownership regarding the information stored in portable computers. Because these computers travel with workers, they are considered by some to be personal property. This policy overcomes that perspective by stating that these devices are provided to perform specific duties and that the devices should be used primarily for business purposes. After reading this policy users of these devices will know that they should not store any private information on the devices, because an auditor from Company X can examine its contents at any time. This policy extends the boundary between organizational property and personal worker property because the technology has permitted new types of distributed computing. Assuming that another policy on this topic was not also issued, if a worker employs his or her own equipment, then an employer has no rights to the information contained therein.

Related Policies: "Sensitive Information On Personal Computers" and "Information Retention At Employment Termination."

Audience: End users

Security Environments: All

11. Possession Of Portable Computers

Policy: Workers must keep Company X portable computers in their possession at all times unless they have been deposited in a secure location such as a locked closet or a hotel safe.

Commentary: This policy limits the loss of portable computers due to theft, and the loss of the information that may be stored on such computers. As long as a computer is in an employee's possession it is unlikely to be stolen. If it is left in an unattended office or in some other relatively public place, it may be gone when the user returns. This policy says nothing about encryption or access control systems, both of which are important for portables, but can be addressed in other policies.

Related Policies: "Transportable Computers With Sensitive Information," "Secret Information On Transportable Computers," and "Dynamic Password Tokens."

Audience: End users

Security Environments: All

9.08.02 Teleworking

1. Telecommuting Data Entry Operators

Policy: All Company X data entry operators must employ thin clients as configured by Information Systems management and download the software for their work at the beginning of each business day.

Commentary: This policy reflects a relatively high-security environment where data entry operators can use their machines for no activity other than Company X business. Because the machines are thin clients, they do not have a hard drive and cannot permanently store the software they execute. With this approach, each completed transaction must be submitted to a Company X server, which is where

12. Mobile Computer Alternatives

Policy: When away from Company X offices, mobile computer users must utilize either encryption software to protect the sensitive information when in storage or employ some technique to physically secure the media on which the sensitive information resides.

Commentary: This policy specifies how mobile computer users should protect Company X sensitive information when away from the office. The policy specifies alternatives that involve concealment of the information without removing it from the machine or physically securing the information. Special attention is necessary for mobile computers because they are more likely to be stolen. With this policy, theft of the computer itself while the worker was away from it would not result in the unauthorized disclosure of sensitive information. This policy assumes that the worker knows what is and what is not sensitive information. If this distinction has not been made, the organization could require at least one of these approaches for all Company X information resident on a mobile computer.

Related Policies: "Telecommuting Equipment," "Traveling With Secret Information," and "Public Exposure Of Sensitive Information."

Audience: End users

Security Environments: Medium and high

business data is stored. If peripheral devices like a floppy drive are locked out, this approach prevents telecommuters from electronically taking business information that is the property of Company X. The configuration must have a fast modem or other type of connection because the software can be quite large, and may otherwise take a long time to download. Also, this configuration assumes that a relatively reliable network connection is available. Otherwise, telecommuter work may be seriously impeded when communications interruptions occur. This approach is restrictive, and is not appropriate for general office telecommuters. This approach permits Company X to change the software daily, if it needs to, and to ensure that all client machines were updated at the same time. A change control mechanism on the thin client can be used to prevent any changes in the operating system or other software.

Related Policies: "Diskless Workstations," "Downloading Software," and "Downloading Sensitive Information."

Audience: Technical staff

Security Environments: Medium and high

2. Telecommuting Equipment

Policy: Employees working on Company X business at alternative work sites must use Company X-provided computer and network equipment, unless other equipment has been approved by the Help Desk as compatible with Company X information systems and controls.

Commentary: This policy ensures that telecommuting workers do not use information systems that could cause malfunctions or damage to Company X systems or information, or provide insufficient protection for Company X information. The latter might, for example, occur if telecommuting equipment was not able to encrypt sensitive information stored on a computer at an employee's home. A burglary could then lead to unauthorized disclosure of this sensitive information. Many organizations have a checklist of standard information systems equipment issued to telecommuters. This list can include a modem, a special high-speed phone line, a pager, an answering machine, a fax machine, a copier, a printer, and a personal computer. The list could include software and documentation such as standard application programs and standard utilities. Organizations may wish to issue a separate policy stating that Company X is not responsible for loss, damage, or wear-and-tear of employee-owned equipment used for Company X business. It also may be desirable to state that such employee-owned equipment may continue to be used for personal activities provided Company X information is not jeopardized. These policies should be supplemented by words defining terms like "alternative work site" and "telecommuter."

Related Policies: "Security Requirements For Telecommuters," "Transportable Computers With Sensitive Information," and "Lockable Metal Furniture."

Audience: End users and technical staff

Security Environments: All

3. Telecommuter Working Environments

Policy: To retain the privilege of doing off-site work, all telecommuters must structure their remote working environment so that it is in compliance with Company X policies and standards.

Commentary: This policy is intended to inform telecommuters that being a telecommuter is a privilege, not a right, and as such this privilege may be revoked if the workers do not follow Company X policies and standards. The policy specifically avoids dictating the specifics of remote working environments, because these can change. The security specifics typically include keeping equipment and other materials in a locked room, and regular use of a surge protector, a hard disk drive password-based access control system, a paper shredder, and a virus-screening program. There will be other specifics not related to security typically dealing with human resource issues, like accounting for time worked.

Related Policies: "Reauthorization Of User Access Privileges" and "Secret Information On Transportable Computers."

Audience: End users

Security Environments: All

4. Security Requirements For Telecommuters

Policy: Before a telecommuting arrangement can begin, the worker's manager must be satisfied that an alternative work site is appropriate for the Company X work performed by the involved worker.

Commentary: Discussions about alternative work sites have become more prevalent in the last few years. Whenever these arrangements are being considered it is important to consider what happens to Company X physical assets and information assets. This policy is intended to give management broad latitude to decide who will be permitted to telecommute, and under what circumstances. Many organizations have adopted a checklist that, among other things, lists the security requirements for telecommuting. These generally include tools such as hard disk encryption packages, locking file cabinets, and paper shredders. Some organizations take it one step further, requiring telecommuters to sign a statement where they promise to follow specific rules for securing off-site information. The policy could be augmented with definitions clarifying terms such as "alternative work site" and "telecommuter."

Related Policies: "Property Passes," "Current Virus Software," and "Lockable Metal Furniture."

Audience: All

Security Environments: All

5. Telecommuter Information Security Procedures

Policy: Telecommuters must follow all remote system security policies and procedures including, but not limited to, compliance with software license agreements, performance of regular backups, and use of shredders to dispose of sensitive paper-resident information.

Commentary: This policy makes telecommuters aware of the procedures they must perform on a day-to-day basis. Some organizations may need a more detailed description of the security requirements associated with telecommuting, in which case the policy could be augmented with a separate memo. Organizations may want to augment this precaution list with other considerations, such as returning the organization's equipment at the time that the working relationship ends. If an organization is going to permit its sensitive information to be used in remote locations that cannot be easily supervised, it is reasonable for it to insist that security precautions be observed. Because telecommuting introduces new risks, a stringent and documented policy dealing with telecommuters may be appropriate in those instances where no similar policy exists for workers who come into the office every day. This policy may be appropriate for workers who are not telecommuters, but who nonetheless take organizational information to their home or on business trips.

Related Policies: "Third-Party Agreements" and "Compliance Agreement."

Audience: End users

Security Environments: All

6. Inspections Of Telecommuter Environments

Policy: Company X must maintain the right to conduct inspections of telecommuter offices with one or more days advance notice.

Commentary: This policy informs telecommuters that Company X representatives may conduct inspections of their home offices. This will ensure that telecommuters observe both safety and security policies and procedures. In return for permitting employees to telecommute, Company X can receive the right to conduct inspections of its property kept in the houses of telecommuters. By conducting inspections, Company X management is carrying out its duty to protect Company X assets. A separate policy is generally not needed to notify computer users that auditors will examine the controls in the organization's office. It is only because the home is generally the domain of the employee that such a right to inspect must be clearly communicated or negotiated. An inspection is often conducted as soon as workers have set up their offices. Thereafter, annual or on-demand inspections may be sufficient. The policy permits multiple follow-up inspections to correct deficiencies that were detected during prior visits. Some organizations may not wish to give advance warning.

Related Policies: "Information System Control Reviews — Internal."

Audience: End users

Security Environments: All

7. Lockable Metal Furniture

Policy: All workers who must keep sensitive Company X information at their homes in order to do their work must receive lockable furniture for the proper storage of this information.

Commentary: This policy ensures that telecommuters and other staff who work in their homes have the proper furniture to securely store sensitive Company X information. If a worker already has suitable furniture, then Company X need not provide it. If furniture was provided, ownership of the furniture remains with Company X. Labels on the furniture should probably note this, and a memo to the employee clarifying ownership is also appropriate. To make this policy more selective, the word "sensitive" could be replaced with "secret." This policy assumes the word "sensitive" has been defined elsewhere. With an increasing number of people working in their cars or trucks, this policy could be expanded to include transportation vehicles. The policy could also be expanded to include other security tools needed to work at home, such as encryption programs for a personal computer or workstation.

Related Policies: "Four-Category Data Classification," "Telecommuting Equipment," "Security Of Sensitive Information," "Security Requirements For Telecommuters," and "Removal Of Sensitive Information."

Audience: Management

Security Environments: Medium and high

10 SYSTEMS DEVELOPMENT AND MAINTENANCE

10.01 Security Requirements Of Systems

10.01.01 Security Requirements Analysis And Specification

1. Security Requirements Identification

Policy: Before a new system is developed or acquired, management of the user department must have clearly specified the relevant security requirements.

Commentary: This policy requires that user department management consider security requirements early in the systems development life cycle (SDLC). If a formal SDLC exists, then the policy could be expanded to make reference to specific milestones in the process where the consideration of security should occur. This policy makes it clear that it is the user department management or perhaps the information Owner who is responsible for incorporating relevant controls into a new system. The involved user department management can, and should, enlist the consulting assistance of Information Security management. The scope of the policy could be expanded to include significantly modified systems, not just new systems. What constitutes a significant upgrade or modification will need to be defined.

Related Policies: "Security In The Systems Development Life Cycle" and "Specifications For Software Developed In-House."

Audience: Management

Security Environments: All

2. In-House Systems Development Proposals

Policy: The proposal for every in-house information systems development project with a proposed budget over $100,000 must be copied to Information Security management at the same time that it is distributed to top management for review and approval.

Commentary: This policy ensures that Information Security management is included in the discussion when management is considering major development projects. In some organizations, Information Security is brought into the conversation only when a project has been completed, or before it goes into production. Independent studies indicate that it is 10 times more costly to add controls to a business application after it goes into production rather than before. This policy ensures that Information Security is involved in every

major project related to information systems. A proposal also will identify the involved members of the management team, and Information Security can contact these people directly when necessary. There is nothing special about the monetary amount mentioned in the policy. This could just have easily been some other figure.

Related Policies: "New Technology Evaluation" and "Security Impact Statements."

Audience: Technical staff

Security Environments: All

3. Embedding Security In Systems

Policy: In-house systems developers must embed security in the systems they build or enhance in every instance where a commercially-available, reasonably-priced, and generally accepted solution exists.

Commentary: This policy saves money and makes its systems easier to use. Studies show that organizations adding controls after a business application goes into production will pay 10 times more than those organizations who built-in security during the development process. This policy will require a higher up-front expenditure, but will reduce the cost of information security over the long run. Using packaged security solutions provided by third parties reduces long-run costs. Whenever possible, information security should be automated and removed from the user's domain. For example, users should not be required to back up their own data resident on a desktop machine. Instead, an automatic backup process to a server can be employed over a local area network. This policy attempts to remove security from the domain of user department management. This policy assumes that no information security architecture has been published and endorsed by management. If this architecture exists, developers should subscribe to the requirements found there.

Related Policies: "Security Control Usability" and "Security Requirements Identification."

Audience: Technical staff

Security Environments: All

4. Specifications For Software Developed In-House

Policy: All software developed by in-house staff intended to process sensitive, valuable, or critical information, must have a written formal specification that is part of an agreement between the involved information Owner and the system developer, and drafted and approved prior to the time when programming efforts begin.

Commentary: Formal specifications define the functionality on which users, developers, auditors, and other parties can rely. Formal specifications should also clearly specify the control measures to be incorporated into software. This policy is intended to ensure that the information Owner has specified what will be delivered in advance of the time when development efforts get underway. This policy is deliberately aimed at countering the problem where developers begin work before the nature of the intended system is clarified. Nothing in this policy prevents the use of prototyping as a mechanism for the refinement of requirements, for the testing of new ideas, or for the solicitation of user feedback. A specification can be modified as work proceeds, as users better understand what they need, and as business requirements change. This policy requires only an advance specification. Some organizations may wish to be more specific about what goes into the specification. In most instances, what goes into an acceptable specification would be defined elsewhere, such as in systems development documentation. Because the specification deals with information of interest to Information Security management, some organizations may wish to add approval by Information Security management to the approval by the information Owner. This policy is particularly relevant to those environments in which end users are doing their own programming, such as client-server computing, intranets, local area networks, and personal computers, because these new programmers may not be familiar with traditional systems development approaches.

Related Policies: "Information Security Impact Analysis."

Audience: Management and technical staff

Security Environments: All

5. Application Coding Principles

Policy: Secure coding principles and practices specified and updated by Information Security management must be used for all software developed or maintained in-house.

Commentary: This policy ensures that developers observe secure coding principles and practices when they write computer code. A review of the historical vulnerabilities indicates that the same programming problems occur repeatedly. For example, buffer overflows are simple to prevent, but when programmers do not adequately protect against them, security can be, and often is compromised. These secure coding principles and practices encompass a variety of considerations that should be integrated into the standard systems development life cycle. These considerations include risk assessment, documentation, and testing. An exception to this policy may be provided for scripts embedded in spreadsheet files, in word processing documents, and in user-maintained databases.

Related Policies: "Specifications For Software Developed In-House" and "Security Requirements Identification."

Audience: Technical staff

Security Environments: All

6. Mature Development Tools And Techniques

Policy: All in-house software development projects must use mature development tools and techniques.

Commentary: The use of new or untried tools and techniques, such as new compilers, increases the risks associated with development projects and the results produced. For example, developers may not be aware of security problems with new tools or techniques, and may inadvertently permit the results of these problems to be incorporated into production systems. Mature tools and techniques often have the bugs and problems corrected, whereas new tools and techniques often do not. Mature tools are often offered by vendors who have been in business for a long while and are therefore more likely to be financially stable. This policy eliminates the problems that new tools and techniques could bring. This policy also involves a trade-off. For competitive or other reasons, management may want to use new tools and techniques. Because the definition of mature is not provided in the policy, there is some latitude for management to investigate new tools and techniques, whether they seem to do the job management wants, and if they have received good reviews in the media or from other customers, at which point they can be declared mature.

Related Policies: "Operating System Versions" and "External Network Interfaces."

Audience: Management and technical staff

Security Environments: All

7. Higher-Level Programming Languages

Policy: All in-house system development projects involving over $100,000 of effort must be programmed in an approved higher-level language, unless Information Systems management permission is obtained.

Commentary: This policy ensures that development staff consistently uses higher-level languages. The organization may specify which languages are permitted in the policy. This is important when end users do their own programming outside the purview of Information Systems. By limiting the nature and types of permissible languages, this policy ensures the maintainability and controllability of end-user programming efforts, particularly for client-server environments, local area networks, intranets, and personal computers. Modules for security procedures such as encryption would be pre-defined objects that could be incorporated into business applications through an object-oriented programming environment. Information Systems should set the standard for the higher-level language to be employed, and should handle exceptions. There is nothing special about the monetary amount mentioned in the policy. This could just have easily been some other figure.

Related Policies: "End-User Application Programs."

Audience: All

Security Environments: All

8. Re-Usability Of Software

Policy: All in-house development projects, with a budget over $100,000, must have as a secondary goal the development of reliable modular software that can be entered into a shared software repository.

Commentary: The development and use of standard shared modules not only reduces costs, but it also reduces risk of errors and the risk of inadvertent security exposures. This policy ensures that all major in-house software development effort produce code that can be reused in the future. Some organizations may want to add certain documentation requirements to this policy such that other developers will be able to understand what the original developers actually did. Other prerequisites for insertion into a software repository also may be specified in this policy. The policy could also include some words urging developers to use modules stored in a repository whenever relevant. This policy encourages developers to think about breaking their code into logically distinct modules so that some of these same modules can be entered into a repository. This type of policy is becoming increasingly important as computer-aided software engineering tools and object oriented programming environments become more widely used. There is nothing special about the monetary amount mentioned in the policy. This could just have easily been some other figure.

Related Policies: "Software Migration."

Audience: Technical staff

Security Environments: All

9. Security In The Systems Development Life Cycle

Policy: For all business application systems, systems designers and developers must consider security from the beginning of the systems design process through conversion to a production system.

Commentary: While consideration early in the development process is desirable because it is considerably more efficient and effective, this should not be the end of the control selection process. Typically the systems development life cycle will involve several points where security is formally included in the process. Hand-rendered signatures, or perhaps digital signatures, indicating the adequacy of security work may be required at these points. This policy requires the technical staff to consider security as a formal part of the systems development life cycle (SDLC). This policy assumes that an enforced SDLC exists. This may not be the case in the personal computer, workstation, client-server, intranet, and local area network computing environments.

Related Policies: "Specifications For Software Developed In-House," "Business Application Change Control Process," and "Systems Development Conventions."

Audience: Technical staff

Security Environments: All

10. Reliance On Common Mechanisms For Controls

Policy: Cost-justified, information security controls must be selected and designed such that reliance on a common mechanism is minimized.

Commentary: If a common mechanism is used by many controls, its failure or unavailability will have a serious effect on overall security. For example, if a single node on a network was the sole provider of gateway-style access control services, then the unavailability of this one node might mean that the whole network is unavailable. This policy instructs systems designers and other technical staff to avoid such vulnerable designs. At the very least, the policy requires that systems designers raise the question of reliance on a common mechanism. Some readers may wish to include in the policy a definition of common mechanism. One definition could be "a systems component that provides security services to a variety of other systems." This policy is often in opposition to other systems design objectives like simplicity and cost. Part of the information security specialist's job is to achieve a workable balance between such competing objectives. The scope of the policy could readily be expanded to include all systems components and not just controls.

Related Policies: "Independent Security Systems," "Control Implementations Standard," and "Human Intervention In Computer-Assisted Processes."

Audience: Technical staff

Security Environments: All

11. Business Applications Security Functionality

Policy: Whenever feasible and cost-effective, system developers must rely on system services for security functionality rather than incorporating such functionality into applications.

Commentary: This policy ensures that internal system developers employ standard security functionality, such as the logon process associated with operating systems. If developers write their own versions, these routines are likely to be inadequately tested, documented, and supported in the future. By insisting that all developers use system services, a consistent level of security can be maintained on a cross-application basis. Improvements to the security of the system services will be easier to integrate with applications. Numerous proprietary security routines built into applications may prevent an organization from moving to the latest release of an operating system, or at the very least prove administratively unmanageable. There will be certain functions that cannot be achieved with system services, and these are best done at the application level. For example, a routine that performs input error checking is generally done at the application level. This policy works best if there is a formal review and approval process associated with development efforts, in which case deviations from this policy can be identified. The policy also works better if the organization has a set of approved security software routines that have been tested, documented, and made generally-available to developers.

Related Policies: "Computer System Access Controls" and "Business Application Change Control Process."

Audience: Technical staff

Security Environments: All

12. Purchasing Information Security Solutions

Policy: Company X must purchase commercially-available information security solutions rather than build the solutions in-house, unless the cost-effectiveness of an in-house solution has been clearly analyzed, documented, and approved by Information Security management.

Commentary: This policy saves money and permits its personnel to address business problems rather than information security systems development problems. Commercially available solutions are generally much cheaper than in-house solutions. Commercial solutions generally are more extensively tested than in-house systems, more extensively documented than in-house solutions, more likely to be modified in response to the most recent threats, and more likely to provide superior security. However, in certain instances, no commercial products meet unique in-house needs, and in these cases it is necessary to develop in-house solutions. Even in these cases, it is often possible to put together an in-house solution that incorporates several commercial products. Some may wish to extend this policy to apply to all information systems solutions.

Related Policies: "Industry-Specific Information Security Standards," "Hardware And Software Procurement," and "Emergency And Disaster Support Requirements."

Audience: Management and technical staff

Security Environments: All

13. Minimum Information System Controls

Policy: At the very least, all Company X information systems must include the standard controls found in other organizations facing similar circumstances.

Commentary: This policy refers to the legal notion of the "standard of due care." The standard of due care defines the minimum acceptable set of controls that an organization would be expected to have, given its industry, its location, the nature of its business, and other aspects of its situation. This policy is intended to keep the organization out of trouble because not having standard of due care controls subjects the organization's management to accusations of negligence, breach of fiduciary duty and computer professional malpractice. The policy requires that management must address the unique risks faced by the organization, implicitly requiring a risk assessment.

Related Policies: "Production System Risk Assessments," "Control Implementations Standard," and "Information System Control Reviews — Independent."

Audience: Management and technical staff

Security Environments: All

14. Use Of Evaluated Products

Policy: An officially-evaluated information systems security product must be used rather than a product that has not been evaluated.

Commentary: This policy informs systems designers that management requires products that have been evaluated by a credible testing source. Evaluated products have been documented and tested according to a predefined set of security objectives. A grade indicating the level of security provided by the product has been issued to these products by the evaluating agency. Evaluated products will be more secure than those that have not been evaluated. The policy is written so that management can deal with security as a secondary consideration. All other functional requirements must be met before security will affect the decision. If management does not wish to downplay security to this extent, then it may wish to change the policy. The policy assumes the evaluation entity's objectives will closely match the organization's security objectives. If this is not so, then this policy may not be appropriate.

Related Policies: "Industry-Specific Information Security Standards."

Audience: Technical staff

Security Environments: Medium and high

10.02 Security In Application Systems

10.02.01 Input Data Validation

1. Production Input Transactions

Policy: Each input transaction submitted to a production computer system must be assigned a unique sequence number or identifier.

Commentary: This policy properly accounts for all input transactions, and facilitates the reconciliation of input transactions should there be a problem, or even suspicion of a problem. The existence of a serial number permits computer input data to be linked in a chronological way to source documents. It also ensures that no transactions were duplicated and that no transactions were lost. To reduce its impact and cost, this policy may be limited to certain critical applications or other important activities. The policy assumes that the organization has already defined the terms "transaction" and "production" in a clear and unambiguous way.

Related Policies: "Business Source Document Retention," "Physical Access Of Terminated Workers," and "Non-Production Business Transactions."

Audience: Technical staff

Security Environments: All

2. Input Data Validation And Rejected Item Handling

Policy: All transactions to be input to a multi-user production computer system must be subjected to reasonableness checks, edit checks, or validation checks, and transactions that fail such checks must either be rejected with a notification of the rejection sent to the submitter, corrected and resubmitted, or suspended pending further investigation.

Commentary: This policy requires that management properly validate all data submitted to multi-user computer systems. Validation means subjecting the data to tests to show that it has been properly formatted, defined, or typed. For example, an accounts payable program should reject an entry in the amount field that includes an alphabetic character. Input should be subjected to such tests before it ever gets an opportunity to be posted to production databases, master files, or other organizational books and records. If this validation is not performed, then eradicating an error passed from system to system becomes difficult and expensive. This policy attempts to detect and correct problems with data integrity at the earliest possible time. Beyond errors and omissions, the policy provided here also indirectly protects against fraud, embezzlement, sabotage, and related intentional acts. One increasingly popular and potentially quite powerful way to implement this policy is through an active data dictionary. In this case, the data dictionary would be called upon for production processing by various application systems to determine what input data validation routines to execute. Data definitions and tests are defined only once even though they apply to a number of different applications. Specific examples of problems that should fail data validation checks include out-of-range values, invalid characters in data fields, missing or incomplete data, and unauthorized or inconsistent control data. This policy may be modified to require correction of the problem within a certain period of time.

Related Policies: "Rejected Input Transactions" and "Suspense File Resolution Timings."

Audience: Technical staff

Security Environments: All

3. Double-Keying Large Transactions

Policy: All keyboard-based production computer input processes involving amounts over $1,000 that will initiate a transaction must include entry of the amount twice.

Commentary: This policy prevents problems due to typing errors. The policy would, for example, require a wire transfer data entry clerk to enter all amount fields over $1,000 twice. This policy would require that the whole process pertaining to that transaction be double-keyed. For example, the beneficiary bank account number would need to be entered twice. Although it provides less effective data integrity checking, it may be sufficient in some environments for

a computer to simply come back with a request for a confirmation. Because it is more effective, the actual entry of the amount twice is a preferred approach. The scope of this policy can be narrowed to only certain critical fields, such as the spelling of a beneficiary's name for a check over $1,000. The entry of amounts over $1,000 into a spreadsheet or some other application that does not generate a transaction will not be within the scope of this policy. For added protection, the policy can be expanded to require that the second entry involve another individual. This policy assumes that the word "production" has been defined elsewhere. The presence of this word exempts many single-user situations such as work on a personal computer where informal analysis is not directly connected with a production application. There is nothing special about the monetary amount mentioned in the policy. This could just have easily been some other figure.

Related Policies: "Error Investigation" and "Errors And Record Manipulations."

Audience: Technical staff

Security Environments: All

4. Transaction Originator

Policy: Transactions affecting sensitive, critical, or valuable information must be initiated only by source documents or computerized messages in which the originating individual or system is clearly identified.

Commentary: The ability to trace transactions back to the originating individual or system is critical for auditing, forensics, problem resolution, and other efforts. This policy requires that an audit trail exist for all transactions affecting sensitive, critical, or valuable information. Some organizations may wish to go beyond an indication of the source. This can be achieved through digital signatures, message authentication codes, encryption, and hand-rendered signatures. The policy assumes that the terms "sensitive, critical, or valuable" have already been defined elsewhere.

Related Policies: "Production System Input Transaction Authorization," "Four-Category Data Classification," "Five-Category Application Criticality Classification Scheme," and "Signatures In Electronic Mail."

Audience: Technical staff

Security Environments: All

10.02.02 Control Of Internal Processing

1. Modification Of Production Business Information

Policy: Privileges must be established such that system users are not able to modify production data in an unrestricted manner.

Commentary: This policy ensures that unauthorized changes to production data are not being made. This policy indicates there must be certain well-controlled paths by which production data is altered, and that the data should not be altered unless these paths are employed. For example, a database should only be modified if the associated database management system (DBMS) is employed. In this example, there are certain controls built into the DBMS, such as privilege restrictions, while there are less likely to be controls built into a general-purpose program that enables users to modify files of various formats.

Related Policies: "Production Business Information Privileges" and "Separation Of Duties."

Audience: Technical staff

Security Environments: All

2. Software Failure To Properly Operate

Policy: Whenever software developed in-house fails to produce the expected results, it must always provide either an error message or some other indication of failure, one or both of which must be presented to the user.

Commentary: It is dangerous for software to be producing erroneous results, particularly when users may be unwittingly relying on these results for their business activities. For example, if a program could not accept new input data, it might automatically use the last input data provided to it. This difference in input data might be undetectable to the user. Without specific notice of the problem, the user may go on to make erroneous decisions based on inaccurate information. This policy ensures that users are always made aware that in-house software is failing to operate as intended. This policy also partially compensates for the fact that many users accept computer-generated reports without further thought, assuming reports to be correct. Externally-provided software generally includes failure

notification features, although this policy could be extended to include external software. If this change to the policy were made, then the policy would be used for software acquisition decisions. This policy also implicitly requires that in-house developers incorporate reasonableness checks in the software they build. This is the only way they know whether the software produced the expected results.

Related Policies: "Software Feedback To User" and "Preventive Maintenance."

Audience: Technical staff

Security Environments: All

3. Software Feedback To User

Policy: Whenever software developed in-house receives input from a user, feedback must be provided indicating whether the request was performed.

Commentary: Confusion can result when users think that they have instructed a system to perform a certain action, when in fact they have not. For example, when using an automated teller machine, a customer may think that he or she requested the system to transfer a certain sum from his money-market savings account to his checking account. Instead he or she may have hit the wrong button, thereby indicating that the money should be transferred from a regular savings account. If the customer does not have a regular savings account, then the automated teller machine may simply ignore his input. If the automated teller machine does not respond with an error message, the customer may assume the transfer has been made. This policy requires that systems designers always provide users with error messages indicating that the system did not perform their request if this is the situation. The policy also requires a confirmation when input is acceptable. The policy could apply to all software, although having internal staff make modifications or patches, to software packages written by third parties is often too difficult.

Related Policies: "Software Failure To Properly Operate."

Audience: Technical staff

Security Environments: All

4. System Interruption For Safety

Policy: Robots and other computerized machinery must be programmed so that the current activity immediately stops if the activity is harming or is likely to harm a human.

Commentary: This policy is applicable to process control systems, computerized conveyor belts, manufacturing assembly lines, and similar computerized systems. The intention of the policy is that designers be required to consider the circumstances when the system might jeopardize human safety. The policy could be expanded to include immediate notice to the operator of a dangerous condition. Such a policy also may be useful when demonstrating that the system was designed with human safety in mind. This might be useful when defending against a lawsuit alleging negligence. Such a policy may also help with management and employee relations because it demonstrates a concern for worker safety.

Related Policies: "Duress Passwords" and "Human Intervention In Computer-Assisted Processes."

Audience: Management and technical staff

Security Environments: All

5. Tracing Errors And Security Problems To Developers

Policy: All complaints about software errors, omissions, and security problems that are attributable to software developed in-house must be traced back to the designers, programmers, and other development staff involved.

Commentary: This policy encourages development staff to take security seriously at the time that they design a new or enhanced software system. These technical staff members are sometimes under great pressure to deliver something that works reasonably well according to unrealistic deadlines. In order to meet these deadlines, they often ignore security, and their choices in this matter are often supported by project management staff. This policy fosters a sense of accountability for the problems that may be encountered in the future. If development staff members know they will be held responsible for future problems, they will bring a new level of professionalism and concern to the security-related work that they perform. This policy will also illuminate those places where the systems development process breaks down and needs repairing. Notice

that the words "development staff" do not refer to employees alone. These words include contractors, consultants, and temporaries.

Related Policies: "Projects Involving Human Safety Issues" and "Transaction Originator."

Audience: Technical staff

Security Environments: All

6. Changes To Sensitive, Critical, Or Valuable Information

Policy: Transactions affecting sensitive, critical, or valuable information must be processed only if the originating individual or system is authorized to submit such transactions.

Commentary: This policy requires that management establish and maintain an adequate access control system such that only authorized users can modify sensitive, critical, or valuable information. The most frequently encountered way to do this is with fixed passwords, although dynamic passwords are rapidly becoming the norm for dial-up and Internet-connected computers. Authorization checking also may be performed by smart cards, digital signatures on electronic mail messages, message authentication code comparisons for wire transfer instructions, and digital certificates. The policy assumes that the terms "sensitive, critical, or valuable" have already been defined elsewhere.

Related Policies: "Dial-Up User Authentication," "Four-Category Data Classification," "Five-Category Application Criticality Classification Scheme," and "Operating System User Authentication."

Audience: Technical staff

Security Environments: All

7. Control Validation

Policy: Prior to use in decisions involving over $100,000, all financial data critical to the decision at hand must be crosschecked through control totals, record counts, or similar controls.

Commentary: This policy ensures that data used for important decisions is reliable, complete, and adequately documented. The policy requires supporting data to be validated with standard control measures. This policy is particularly relevant to personal computers, workstations, and other small computers such as client-server systems because such controls are so often missing in these informal computing environments. For example, a user may have mistyped when entering data into a spreadsheet, and this may not be revealed unless controls such as those referenced in the policy are employed. The notion of "criticality" may also need to be defined for this policy to be fully understood. There is nothing special about the monetary amount mentioned in the policy. This could just have easily been some other figure, and should be based in part on the degree of risk that the organization is willing to accept.

Related Policies: "Five-Category Application Criticality Classification Scheme," "Information Cross-Validation," and "Computer Analyses Review."

Audience: All

Security Environments: All

8. Rejected Input Transactions

Policy: All rejected input transactions must be placed in a suspense file and listed in exception reports until they are successfully resubmitted for processing or otherwise resolved.

Commentary: This policy specifies a standard method for handling rejected transactions so that all transactions will be promptly processed. A suspense file is a holding area into which rejected items are placed. Suspense files should be resolved daily and items that are not resolved should be subjected to additional management scrutiny. Special management attention should be placed on the prompt resolution of the reasons why certain transactions were rejected. If this is not done, suspense files can be used to perpetrate fraud and other unauthorized acts. It may be desirable to expand the policy to require periodic purging of suspense files.

Related Policies: "Suspense File Resolution Timings" and "Rejected Or Suspended Input Validation."

Audience: Technical staff

Security Environments: All

9. Suspense File Resolution Timings

Policy: All input transactions that are held in suspense status pending further investigation must either be resubmitted or otherwise handled within 10 business days of their original entry.

Commentary: This policy ensures that all rejected items are promptly resolved. If this is not done, fraud and other unauthorized acts may result. The time period would typically be much briefer for a bank, while it may be longer for a government agency. In some cases special permission may be required to keep an item in a suspense file longer than the specified number of days.

Related Policies: "Rejected Input Transactions" and "Rejected Or Suspended Input Validation."

Audience: Technical staff

Security Environments: All

10. Concealing Customer Account Numbers

Policy: The account numbers appearing on computer-generated receipts provided to customers must be partially-concealed or truncated.

Commentary: This policy prevents unauthorized parties from using the information printed on discarded or lost receipts to commit a fraud. At the same time, if account information is partially provided, customers will be able to determine which of their accounts was involved in the transaction. This policy meets the objectives of both fraud prevention and good customer service. One of the most prevalent examples of this involves receipts for automated teller machine transactions. On these receipts, a credit card cash advance number may have certain account digits obscured. For credit card receipts, the expiration date may deliberately be obscured. This policy is not relevant to transactions where the receipt is a source document for subsequent computer input. For example, the policy is not suitable for credit card sales drafts done manually because the entire number will be needed to complete the transaction or to subsequently reference the transaction. But the policy is suitable for transactions that have already been recorded inside an information system, or that have already been completed. The partial-concealment mentioned here can be achieved by masking part of the account number with other characters such as an "X."

Related Policies: "Customer Activity Log Disclosure," "Secondary Dissemination Of Secret Information," and "Delivery Of Secret Information."

Audience: Technical staff

Security Environments: All

11. Providing Purchase Receipt

Policy: A sign indicating "customers who are not offered a receipt will be given their purchase for free" must be prominently displayed on every cash register.

Commentary: This policy prevents cashiers from secretly taking money from cash registers. This control requires that every transaction be entered into a cash register. If cashiers are permitted to accept cash for transactions, but not ring them up on the register, they can easily keep the cash without being caught. This policy requires that the cash collected by a cashier on their shift must match the amount tallied by the cash register. The provision of free goods makes the customer motivated to become a part of the internal control system. The prominent display of a sign describing this arrangement is necessary if the customer is going to be notified of their role in the internal control system. A similar division of responsibilities can be applied to other situations where there is a risk of theft of cash, checks, bonds, or other forms of money. Another important reason to issue receipts to customers involves the provision of an authoritative source record that they can check against their monthly statements, to ensure that accounting and other activities have been performed accurately and promptly.

Related Policies: "Separation Of Duties" and "Concealing Customer Account Numbers."

Audience: End users

Security Environments: All

12. Credit Card Number Usage

Policy: Credit card numbers must not be used for customer identification or any other purpose other than processing payments for goods or services.

Commentary: The more that credit card numbers are used for other purposes besides payment processing, the more likely they are to appear in readable form in places where they will not be adequately protected. This may lead to fraud, identity theft, and other abuses. In some retail establishments, credit cards are used as identification, for example to cash a check. Clerks at these retail establishments may even write down a credit card number on a check, which then exposes it to every person who handles the clearing of the check and related check-handling accounting activities. This policy also sets the tone for fraud and identity theft prevention, and may be useful when showing that the organization took diligent steps to protect credit card numbers from unauthorized use.

Related Policies: "Payment Data Encryption" and "Bank Account Numbers."

Audience: End users

Security Environments: All

13. Designing Information Security Controls

Policy: When designing information security controls, workers must use large margins of error and large time horizons.

Commentary: This policy reinforces that information security systems design must incorporate significant margins of error and long time horizons. This policy acknowledges that systems built today are likely to be used a decade from now, maybe much further in the future. The policy also provides for unexpected developments, such as new mathematical techniques that make the analysis easier and faster. Such an unexpected development could mean that existing encryption systems are now readily compromised even though they could not be readily compromised in the recent past. This policy is not just relevant to encryption key length. It also applies to fixed password length, random number generator seed length, and other security parameters. This policy directly addresses the tendency to minimize costs, which if used as the primary decision factor, in many instances will lead to information security systems that are obsolete or weak within a short period of time.

Related Policies: "Errors And Record Manipulations" and "Reliance On Common Mechanisms For Controls."

Audience: Technical staff

Security Environments: All

14. Human Intervention In Computer-Assisted Processes

Policy: All computer-assisted processes must involve human intervention prior to initiating any action that could result in human life-threatening or human safety-threatening events.

Commentary: This policy prevents systems designers from turning over important decisions to computers. For example, triggers for some missile systems require two authorized people to simultaneously initiate them. They cannot be initiated by a computer acting without human intervention. The reference to "life-threatening" and "safety-threatening" situations could be expanded to include significant financial decisions, and decisions that could significantly impact other areas. No mention is made of expert systems, neural networks, artificial intelligence, or other specific technology.

Related Policies: "Reliance On Common Mechanisms For Controls" and "System Interruption For Safety."

Audience: Technical staff

Security Environments: All

15. Errors And Record Manipulations

Policy: Company X computer systems must be built so that no single person can make an error or manipulate the records without such events being detected by some other person during the routine execution of that other person's duties.

Commentary: This policy is a detection-oriented expression of the principle of separation of duties. Rather than focusing on preventing problems, it takes a less stringent approach requiring only that errors and manipulations readily be discovered. This approach may involve fewer controls or less costly controls than the more stringent preventative approach, and therefore may be attractive to small businesses. In the long run, total costs will generally be higher than they would be with a preventative approach.

Related Policies: "Separation Of Duties," "Double-Keying Large Transactions," and "Error Investigation."

Audience: Management and technical staff

Security Environments: All

16. Temporary Files And Storage

Policy: Temporary files, and temporary storage locations within the memory of general-purpose computers, must be overwritten when the programmed process that created them completes its work.

Commentary: This policy ensures that sensitive information such as passwords and encryption keys are not inadvertently disclosed to unauthorized parties. Sensitive information is often written to a temporary file or to a temporary memory location in order to complete an application. This policy instructs programmers and system designers that this information must be overwritten before the programmed process completes. It is not sufficient to simply erase or delete this information because in many computers, these commands simply delete the reference to the data, but they do not obliterate the information itself. This means that the information is available to people who may scavenge around the system. Use of disk repair utilities for example will reveal information that has been erased or deleted, but is available on the involved hard disk. Repeated overwriting processes also are advisable because it is with this repetition that residual recorded data can be overcome.

Related Policies: "Powering Down Computers," "Certificate Of Destruction Of Storage Media," and "Password Generation Materials."

Audience: Technical staff

Security Environments: High

10.02.03 Message Authentication

1. Production System Input Transaction Authorization

Policy: Methods must be in place to ensure that all input to production computer systems that has been submitted for processing has been properly authorized.

Commentary: This policy preserves the integrity of Company X books or records. If unauthorized transactions are posted to the books or records, all of the books or records become of questionable value. This policy also prevents fraud, embezzlement, sabotage, and a number of other abusive acts that could be perpetrated by people who had information system access but who

did not have proper authorization. Authorization could take the form of source document signature verification, digital signatures for electronic mail messages and message authentication codes for wire transfers. One of the most common ways to indicate authorization is to use a secret password.

Related Policies: "Production Transaction Authorization," "Production Changes" and "Transaction Originator."

Audience: Technical staff

Security Environments: All

2. Rejected Or Suspended Input Validation

Policy: Input transactions that are corrected for resubmission, or that are suspended and later approved for resubmission, must be subjected to the same validation procedures that original input transactions receive.

Commentary: This policy requires the uniform application of controls to all input transactions. If the same validation procedures are not used for items that have been rejected or suspended, then a security vulnerability exists. This is because the people handling the items could reject or suspend an item, modify it, and resubmit it. If the same validation checks were not used, the modified item could by-pass important control measures. Beyond fraud and embezzlement, this vulner-ability could also lead to a degradation in information integrity. This policy is consistent with standard testing procedures for software that require all tests to be performed again if there has been a change to the underlying code. Such testing procedures recognize the complexity of the computing environment, and the fact that humans fail to see the consequences associated with minor changes.

Related Policies: "Software Testing" and "Rejected Input Transactions."

Audience: Technical staff

Security Environments: All

10.02.04 Output Data Validation

1. Output Data Controls

Policy: Controls and procedures must be established to validate all sensitive or critical information processed by Company X application systems.

Commentary: This policy ensures that all output data from Company X processing systems has been validated by an effective and routine process. While systems are typically validated, verified and tested, there is no assurance that the information processed therein is correct. For example, processes should be implemented that execute plausibility checks or reconcile control counts. There should also be procedures established that define the responsibilities of those involved in the output validation process. Policies for each of these processes may be documented to ensure that they are given the appropriate level of attention and are routinely reviewed by examination authorities.

Related Policies: "Input Data Validation And Rejected Item Handling" and "Rejected Or Suspended Input Validation."

Audience: All

Security Environments: All

2. Internal Record Change Reviews

Policy: Management must review or establish mechanisms for suitably-qualified and responsible people to review the reasonableness and accuracy of all changes to internal records.

Commentary: This policy requires that all updates to Company X records be reviewed by management or a properly-authorized delegate of management. Often this policy will be so much a part of the organizational culture at publicly-traded companies that it is superfluous. This is because securities laws have most stringent requirements for such review activities. For smaller companies, non-profit organizations, and government agencies the policy may be warranted. Reasonableness checks are generally done through ratio analysis, reconciliation, and similar procedures. Accuracy checks are done through physical inventories and similar review steps.

Related Policies: "System Log Review."

Audience: Management

Security Environments: All

10.03 Cryptographic Controls

10.03.01 Policy On The Use Of Cryptographic Controls

1. Digital Signature And File Encryption Software Versions

Policy: Users must retain backup copies of all versions of the software used to render digital signatures and used to encrypt files.

Commentary: This policy ensures that users understand that they must retain reliable copies of all software used to generate or check digital signatures, or used to encrypt or decrypt files. To do otherwise risks the possibility that a user may not be able to prove that he or she signed a file, and this may damage his or her position in a court case, in arbitration proceedings, or a mediation process. To do otherwise also risks the possibility that a user will not be able to recover a previously encrypted file. This may seem like a difficult task if users are individually maintaining a software archive. Ideally this would be done centrally by a system administrator who is also handling the automated software distribution associated with new versions of this same software.

Related Policies: "Private Digital Signature Key Lifetime" and "System Log Modification Controls."

Audience: End users and technical staff

Security Environments: Medium and high

10.03.02 Encryption

1. Encryption Process Approval — Systems

Policy: Encryption processes must not be used for Company X information unless the processes are approved by Information Security management.

Commentary: This policy prevents users from damaging or destroying Company X information because they do not have the expertise or knowledge required to use encryption facilities properly. Only after Information Security management is satisfied that adequate controls exist to recover the involved information, should it approve the use of encryption. One of the best controls for encryption is to have management override keys, that permit management to decrypt information even if the key has been lost, misplaced, or intentionally withheld. These are also called "key escrow" or "key recovery" facilities. One of the major risks that an organization faces when it permits its staff to use encryption is that important information will be encrypted, then the key will be ransomed by the staff. The policy is also intended to ensure that only approved algorithms, modes of operation, and other implementation aspects of encryption processes meet in-house standards. If all users were free to go their own directions, the resulting activity would interfere with the secure communication of confidential or private information. In some jurisdictions, encryption is illegal, or the key may need to be disclosed to government agencies. To ensure that users are not inadvertently breaking the law, Information Security management should be involved in decisions to use encryption.

Related Policies: "International Trade Armaments."

Audience: End users

Security Environments: All

2. Encryption Process Approval — Users

Policy: Users must not employ encryption, digital signatures, or digital certificates for any Company X business activity or business information without the written authorization of their department manager, the completion of proper training and having their systems configured by authorized personnel.

Commentary: This policy is intended to prevent staff members from getting into trouble by encrypting a file, losing the key, and deleting the readable version. The policy requires all those who would use these processes to get management approval, then get trained, and lastly get their systems properly configured. This policy prevents the use of these new tools until the need has been established and other prerequisites have been addressed. Without this approach, the chances are great that users will download encryption process software from the Internet and try to do it themselves. This policy also permits the deletion from hard drives of encryption software that was discovered with auto discovery software routines. This can all be performed automatically, and can ensure that users are not using these tools. This will ensure that critical data is not maliciously encrypted and kept from those who need it.

Related Policies: "Encryption Process Approval — Systems."

Audience: End users

Security Environments: All

3. Encryption Utilities Passwords And Keys

Policy: Workers must never employ encryption utilities requiring a user to input a password or encryption key.

Commentary: This policy attempts to keep information perpetually available for business activities. The policy states that management does not want to run the risk that the password or key entered by a user is lost, forgotten, or deliberately withheld. This policy permits auto discovery software to be used to detect the existence of encryption utilities. If a personal computer software change management system is used, an encryption utility can even be erased from a user's hard drive through remote commands initiated by a system administrator. Many word processing packages now include encryption features. Some organizations may wish to disable these features. It is desirable that users not be able to exclusively control organizational data. This policy attempts to prevent such a dangerous situation. The policy does not prevent the use of user-transparent encryption facilities that are embedded in networks. Those businesses with particularly sensitive data will need user-controlled encryption utilities. For them, key escrow systems managed by an employer will be a preferred option to this policy.

Related Policies: "Encryption Process Approval — Systems."

Audience: End users

Security Environments: Low

4. Standard Encryption Algorithm And Implementation

Policy: If encryption is used, government-approved standard algorithms and standard implementations must be employed.

Commentary: This policy requires all systems within an organization employ the same encryption algorithm and the same encryption system implementation. This policy will help ensure interoperability that will lower costs and facilitate secure business communications. This policy will also ensure compliance with local government laws and regulations, and may permit encryption to be used in situations where it would otherwise be illegal. For example, international network encrypted traffic may be illegal according to a certain country's laws, but these laws may be relaxed if government standard algorithms and implementations are used, and if certain approval processes are followed.

Related Policies: "Hardware And Software Procurement."

Audience: Technical staff

Security Environments: Medium and high

5. Publicly-Evaluated Encryption Algorithms

Policy: Every general-purpose encryption algorithm used to protect Company X production information and information systems must be publicly disclosed and must have been evaluated by cryptography experts.

Commentary: This policy prevents organizations from getting into trouble because they created insecure encryption systems or they bought a weak proprietary algorithm from a vendor. Cryptography is very complex and it is difficult to do it right. This policy ensures that experts are involved in the cryptographic design work, whereas a variety of others can be involved in the implementation of the systems these experts develop. This means that organizations will purchase modules that have been written by encryption vendors. Some people argue against this policy saying that confidentiality will make cracking the system more difficult. But nothing prevents an organization from using open algorithms while not disclosing which algorithms are employed. This approach provides the assurance that the algorithm has been evaluated and is strong, but at the same time because the implementation is kept confidential, increases the effort required to break the system. The words "general purpose" were added to the policy to exempt encryption algorithms that are built into security systems.

Related Policies: "Standard Encryption Algorithm And Implementation."

Audience: Technical staff

Security Environments: All

6. Encryption System Initialization

Policy: Whenever an encryption system to be used for Company X production information systems is being initialized, installed, enabled, or reset, a computer audit specialist must be present.

Commentary: While many things can be done to limit the damage that a someone can do to an organization's systems, management trusts its technical staff to follow established procedures. This is especially important when loading encryption keys into Internet commerce servers and other production information systems on which the organization will place great reliance. The policy is intended to provide management with some additional assurance that the process has been completed correctly, reliably, and securely. The presence of an auditor will have a sobering effect on all who are there, and may be important should there later be some allegations of negligence on management's part. The focus is on system set-up because that is the time of greatest vulnerability. After an encryption system has been established, keys can be automatically changed with less risk. This policy assumes that an automated key management process will be used. If this is not the case, then the presence of an auditor may be advisable for each key change process. The presence of an auditor also may be useful for marketing and public relations purposes, helping to establish a higher level of trust in the involved information system.

Related Policies: "Implementing Multi-User Systems" and "Information System Control Reviews — Internal."

Audience: Technical staff

Security Environments: Medium and high

7. Deletion Of Source Data After Encryption

Policy: Whenever encryption is used, workers must not delete the sole readable version of data unless they have demonstrated that the encryption process is able to reestablish a readable version of the data.

Commentary: This policy prevents all copies of sensitive data from being lost. Without checking that an encryption process works, an encryption system malfunction could mean that the only copy of data is lost forever. Some organizations prefer the term "cleartext" instead of "readable." A substitution in the policy can easily be made. Some organizations may wish to specify how to demonstrate that an encryption process works.

Related Policies: "General Purpose Encryption Systems."

Audience: End users and technical staff

Security Environments: Medium and high

8. Compression And Encryption Of Secret Data

Policy: If secret information is to be stored on a multi-user computer system, it must be compressed, then encrypted using an approved encryption algorithm.

Commentary: By compressing data, a good deal of the redundancy in natural languages is eliminated. This makes the job of analysis considerably more difficult, which protects the confidentiality of the data. By compressing, then encrypting, the strength of the encryption process is enhanced. This policy requires systems designers, programmers, and other technical people to implement data compression with encryption, and to specify the sequence in which these processes are to be applied to data. Compression can be linked with encryption so that the two processes occur simultaneously, in a manner transparent to the end user. "Approved encryption algorithms" will be defined by each organization issuing a policy such as this. The need for external approval and endorsement, such as by government agencies, might also be added to this policy.

Related Policies: "Encryption Process Approval — Systems."

Audience: Technical staff

Security Environments: Medium and high

9. Encryption Process Hardware Modules

Policy: All encryption related processes must be performed in tamper-resistant hardware modules.

Commentary: Tamper-resistant modules will automatically erase sensitive data, such as encryption keys and initialization vectors, which are held in memory when the modules are opened or tampered with. Such modules are also shielded to prevent the keys and other security-relevant data from being revealed through electro-magnetic emanations. This policy requires that all encryption processes be implemented using special equipment that will increase the security of encryption processes. Such modules remove the keys from manual handling, reducing the chances that unauthorized persons will obtain them. In some environments this policy will be difficult or prohibitively costly. For example, if the encryption process is expected to change frequently then each new change will require new hardware. In some cases, "tamper resistant modules" are called "security modules." Beyond encryption, tamper-resistant modules are also appropriate for a number of other security processes such as message authentication code calculations, encryption key generation, and pseudo-random number password generation.

Related Policies: "Encryption Key Disclosure — Controls," "Electromagnetic Radiation Protection," and "Encryption Key Disclosure — Approval."

Audience: Technical staff

Security Environments: Medium and high

10. Encrypted Message Protection

Policy: All content sent over the Company X internal data network must be encrypted, accompanied by diversionary messages and be padded with extraneous information to conceal the length of the actual messages being sent.

Commentary: This policy prevents third parties from determining who is sending messages to whom, when they are doing it, and how long the messages are. Although such messages may be encrypted, the discovery of this information about network traffic can reveal things that the parties involved never intended to reveal. For example, if a small organization is known to be in financial trouble and looking for a larger organization to buy it, and if a wiretap is placed on the Internet, then a third party might notice that there are many messages of significant length being exchanged between a large company and this same small company. From this information, the third party might deduce that the larger company was in the process of negotiating a purchase of the smaller company. These considerations are also of great concern to military agencies. Information about who is sending messages to whom, when, and how long the messages are could be used to signal an upcoming maneuver. For these reasons, organizations that are very security conscious might wish to consider

this policy. The costs of a network to support this policy are quite high and justifiable only when the risks are also quite high.

Related Policies: "Concealing Information Transmission" and "Privacy Of Correspondent Contact Information."

Audience: Technical staff

Security Environments: High

11. Anonymous FTP Server Information

Policy: All user-provided files that have not been explicitly approved for public release by Marketing management, and that are resident on the Company X anonymous FTP server, must be encrypted using Company X standard software.

Commentary: This policy informs the user community that they must not leave readable files on an anonymous file transfer protocol (FTP) server unless these files have been approved for public release. A few organizations have employees who have developed a dangerous habit of leaving readable files on an anonymous FTP server so that the files can be picked up by business partners, customers, and others external to the organization. This exposes these same files to unauthorized access by other people who happen to visit that same server. It is relatively easy to write a script to periodically erase all files on the anonymous FTP web server that are not encrypted with an in-house standard encryption package. This is an automatic enforcement process for this policy. This policy also permits an organization to abandon the security practice where user IDs and fixed passwords were shared by both inside and outside parties, thereby permitting the outside parties to gain access to files placed on a web server. Another desirable aspect of encrypting these files is that unauthorized modifications will be immediately evident. Without encryption for this purpose, digital signatures may be required to quickly spot unauthorized changes.

Related Policies: "Secret Data Transmission."

Audience: End users and technical staff

Security Environments: All

10.03.03 Digital Signatures

1. Java Program Execution

Policy: Workers must not execute Java applications downloaded from the Internet unless the application is from a known and trusted source and the digital signature has been checked and no problem has been discovered.

Commentary: This approach to running Java applications, also known as applets, on desktop machines is intended to prevent viruses, Trojan horses, and other malicious code from being executed on Company X computers. The policy assumes that users can distinguish between those circumstances where a digital signature has been checked and no error message is presented to the user, and those circumstances where the digital signature checking mechanism has been turned off. The policy assumes a technically aware audience, and an audience that is motivated to perform this extra chore. For a less technically sophisticated audience, many organizations will want to simply block the inbound passage of applets at a firewall. The scope of this policy could be expanded to include all active content.

Related Policies: "Disabling Java."

Audience: End users

Security Environments: All

2. Internet Web And Commerce Sites

Policy: A current digital certificate is required for every Internet server handling Company X business to which customers, prospects, and others may connect.

Commentary: This policy prevents third parties from establishing Internet systems that masquerade as Company X systems. Digital certificates are like passports because they definitively authenticate the identity of either individuals or computers. Digital certificates include certain encryption related information that permits a remote third party to check that they have reached a genuine Company X system. This usage of digital certificates does not require that remote third parties have digital certificates, or that they even check the digital certificate that is posted by Company X on its Internet systems. This usage is relatively inexpensive and provides one of the basic control mechanisms necessary for Internet commerce activities. The word "current" in the policy is necessary because third-party certificate authorities issue digital certificates for brief periods of time, which means that they need to be periodically renewed.

Related Policies: "Encryption Process Approval — Users," "Positive Identification For System Usage," and "Personal Identifiers On Publicly-Accessible Locations."

Audience: End users

Security Environments: All

10.03.04 Non-Repudiation Services

1. General Purpose Encryption Systems

Policy: All general-purpose encryption processes running on Company X information systems must include key escrow functions.

Commentary: This policy requires encryption systems used for regular business activities to employ a system with key escrow. Key escrow permits management, or some other trusted party, to circumvent the encryption process when needed. This secure escrow process is needed to protect the special key that permits the encryption process to be broken. This may be required in the event of emergencies, staff unavailability, or criminal investigations. Without key escrow features, management runs a risk that staff will use the power that encryption provides for unintended purposes. For example, staff could use encryption to conceal illegal activities. The policy does not address encryption processes embedded in information systems. It deals with general purpose, not special purpose encryption systems like those that handle message authentication codes, digital signatures, and password encryption. The policy could be changed to exclude encryption for communications systems. Key escrow is needed for stored data accessed through word processing packages and stand-alone encryption utilities.

Related Policies: "Automated Encryption Key Management" and "Deletion Of Source Data After Encryption."

Audience: Technical staff

Security Environments: All

10.03.05 Key Management

1. Encryption Key Disclosure — Approval

Policy: Encryption keys must not be revealed to consultants, contractors, or other third parties unless the approval of a senior vice president is obtained.

Commentary: This policy informs workers that encryption keys should be protected with the most stringent security measures. This is why most information technology shops will encrypt keys if these encryption keys are kept in a file or in other locations that might be accessible by unauthorized persons. This means that encryption keys should not be stored in main memory on a multi-user machine unless they are encrypted. A separate encryption device called a "security module" should be used. Key loading modules and other devices should be used to prevent any individual from gaining access to an encryption key.

Related Policies: "Encryption Key Management Systems" and "Suspected Password Disclosure."

Audience: Technical staff

Security Environments: Medium and high

2. Encryption Key Management Systems

Policy: Company X encryption systems must be designed such that no single person has full knowledge of any single encryption key.

Commentary: This policy prevents any individual from gaining access to a full encryption key. If any one individual held a full encryption key, then this individual could, depending on the encryption set-up, decrypt other keys or decrypt sensitive information. This could lead to fraud, sabotage, privacy invasion and other problems. By breaking keys into components such activities are then not possible without collusion. Breaking keys into components usually involves creating two bit strings, that when combined yield a production encryption key. This entire process is often automated through hardware. The techniques described in this policy can be also applied to passwords, initialization vectors, pseudo-random number generator seeds, and other parameters used in security-related processes.

Related Policies: "Separation Of Duties" and "Password Generation Algorithms."

Audience: Technical staff

Security Environments: Medium and high

3. Management Responsibility Delegation

Policy: Key management responsibility must be delegated only to a party who has passed a background check, passed an operational security audit, and signed a confidentiality agreement.

Commentary: This policy keeps middle management from delegating key management responsibility to outsourcing organizations, service bureaus, business partners, and other external organizations that may not handle keys in as secure a manner as they should. A policy like this can also be used to specify the internal staff who may take on key management duties. The policy describes a process for ensuring that the receiving entity meets Company X criteria for a trusted party. Organizations must precisely define with whom they will share sensitive key information. After this, they must decide how to screen people and organizations so that only trusted parties receive key information. It is the second step that is reflected in this policy. In this policy, the three criteria for determining trustworthiness could be modified to include other considerations, such as being registered with a governmental agency. As another option, they could also be well-known certificate authorities that are being recognized as the keepers of the keys for Internet commerce activities. The three criteria mentioned in the policy can be restated as personal character and historical records, current operating practices, and legal obligations. This policy could be generalized to include other security responsibilities on a shared network, such as user ID issuance and password management.

Related Policies: "Granting System Privileges" and "Information Ownership Delegation."

Audience: Management and technical staff

Security Environments: Medium and high

4. Digital Certificate Validity Period

Policy: The validity period for digital certificates issued by Company X must never be longer than one year.

Commentary: This policy limits the damage that might be done if the private keys associated with a digital certificate were to fall into the hands of an unauthorized person, and if the authorized person did not inform the certificate authority (CA). The CA is the issuing organization, which in this case is Company X. A digital certificate is like a passport for the use of the Internet, and digital certificates will form a critical part of the future public key infrastructure. By limiting a certificate's life to one year, the continuation of any associated unauthorized usage will be stopped. The shorter the period of validity for a digital certificate, the greater the level of security. The same is true of encryption keys. The more frequently they are changed, the greater the security of the associated security system. The danger of a compromise of the private keys associated with a digital certificate is lessened by the existence of, and periodic distribution of, a certificate revocation list (CRL). A CRL will inform correspondents that a digital certificate is no longer valid. The CA must have received notice that a certificate has been compromised, or it assumes it continues to be valid. An entry in a CRL can be removed after the digital certificate expires. The size of a CRL will be kept within manageable bounds by the existence of automatic digital certificate expirations.

Related Policies: "Encryption Key Secrecy" and "Encryption Key Life."

Audience: Technical staff

Security Environments: Medium and high

5. Digital Certificate Root Key Protection

Policy: Root keys for digital certificate hierarchies must be protected with rigorous physical security, dual control, split key components, and separation of duties.

Commentary: Many organizations are acting as their own certificate authority, issuing their own digital certificates. Because crypto processes such as digital signatures and certificates critically depend on these root keys, it is imperative that the root keys be kept with the utmost security. This policy is intended to specify four specific security mechanisms that must be employed in all cases. Rigorous physical security generally means storing sensitive information in safes, requiring badges for physical access to equipment, or keeping logs of who had access to equipment, using closed circuit television. Dual control refers to the use of no less than two people to perform critical acts such as generating root keys. Split key components are the result of mathematical transformations that conceal keys. Separation of duties refers to the use of different people to perform different activities, such that each checks on the work of others.

Related Policies: "Management Responsibility Delegation" and "Internet Web And Commerce Sites."

Audience: Technical staff

Security Environments: All

6. Data And Encryption Key Transmission

Policy: If encryption is used, and if keys are transmitted to a remote party in a readable form, then the information protected with encryption must be transmitted over a different communication channel than the keys used to govern the encryption process.

Commentary: This policy prevents a wiretapper from obtaining readable versions of both the keys and the sensitive data. If the wiretapper had broken the encryption process, then he would have all the information needed for breaking new transmissions. Sending the keys over a separate communication channel raises the level of effort. An example would be to send the keys by courier and not on a computer network linking the communicating parties. This policy assumes the use of a traditional symmetric encryption algorithm where the encryption key is the same as the decryption key. The policy is not needed if asymmetric algorithms are used where the encryption key is different from the decryption key. The key management protocols on the Internet are using the latter type of algorithm. This policy is not necessary if only standard Internet protocols are being employed for a network.

Related Policies: "Separation Of Duties," "Encryption Key Storage Media," and "Encryption Key Management Systems."

Audience: Technical staff

Security Environments: High

7. Automated Encryption Key Management

Policy: Whenever such facilities are commercially available, Company X must employ automated key management processes.

Commentary: This policy saves Company X money and time, and obtains the most effective security system available. For some encryption systems, there are no applicable commercially-available key management systems. But recent commercial offerings include a number of strong key management systems. Automation reduces the probability of accidental key disclosure to unauthorized persons. Some organizations may wish to put the word "standard" into the policy to ensure interoperability with other key management systems.

Related Policies: "Key Management Responsibility" and "Encryption Key Management Systems."

Audience: Technical staff

Security Environments: Medium and high

8. Encryption Key Life

Policy: Keys used for encrypting Company X data must be changed at least every 90 days.

Commentary: This policy requires periodic changes in encryption keys. Changing the keys will increase the security of an encryption system. If an adversary is able to derive a particular encryption key through analysis, he or she must start from the beginning whenever the key is changed. Because they are concerned about the strength of some algorithms' limited key length, some organizations require that keys be changed for every transmission. Another option is to use triple-encryption, a process that uses two keys for a single encryption process. To further increase the level of required effort for adversaries, some organizations may also wish to change initialization vectors on a periodic basis.

Related Policies: "Encryption Key Expiration" and "Required Password Changes."

Audience: Technical staff

Security Environments: Medium and high

9. Encryption Key Expiration

Policy: All encryption keys must have a stated life and must be changed on or before the stated expiration date.

Commentary: This policy clarifies that the people handling keys must assign an expiration date to all keys. Unless a one-time pad cipher is being used, it is not acceptable to use keys that do not have an expiration date. One-time ciphers are inefficient, costly, and rarely used outside military or diplomatic circles. Because such keys are used only once, they do not need an expiration date or stated life. All other systems use the same key repeatedly. After a certain time, the security provided by these other encryption systems becomes degraded. The key needs to be changed to bolster the security of the encryption process. An encryption system where each session or transaction has its own key will provide higher security than if the same key is used for months. From a conceptual standpoint, a stated life for an encryption key is related to, and is somewhat similar to, sensitivity classification labels for ordinary data.

Related Policies: "Encryption Key Life" and "Information Life Cycle Labeling."

Audience: Technical staff

Security Environments: Medium and high

10. Encryption Key Generation

Policy: Whenever encryption is used, the keys employed must be generated by means that are not practically discernible by an adversary, and that will yield keys that are difficult-to-guess.

Commentary: The intention of this process is to ensure that encryption systems provide all the security they are meant to provide. If encryption keys are easily guessed, then the security provided by encryption systems may be easily compromised. For example, if users choose their own encryption keys, a guessibility-related screening process is recommended. This policy is a derivative of a policy regarding weak keys. Certain weak keys make DES analysis easier and these keys must be avoided. Often the key generation process is part of an automated key management process, in which case this policy will not be necessary.

Related Policies: "Automated Encryption Key Management," "User-Chosen Encryption Key Length," and "Seed For System-Generated Passwords."

Audience: Technical staff

Security Environments: Medium and high

11. User-Chosen Encryption Key Length

Policy: Whenever user-chosen encryption keys are employed, the encryption system must prevent users from employing keys made-up of less than 10 characters.

Commentary: This policy ensures that an encryption system provides the security it was meant to provide. If encryption keys are easily guessed, an encryption system can be readily compromised. There is nothing special about 10 characters. For very high-security environments the number may need to be higher, while for low- to medium-security environments the number may be slightly lower. Other screening mechanisms for user-chosen encryption keys may be warranted. For example, some algorithms have several weak keys that permit the encryption process to be easily defeated. These weak keys should not be permitted.

Related Policies: "Encryption Key Generation" and "Minimum Password Length."

Audience: Technical staff

Security Environments: Medium and high

12. Key Generation Materials

Policy: Whenever encryption is used, materials to develop encryption keys and hardcopy versions of keys must be kept locked-up when not in use.

Commentary: Key generation materials include data encryption keys, keys that encrypt other keys, also known as master keys, initialization vectors, pseudo-random number generator seeds, and other parameters used to control or initialize encryption processes. This policy prevents the parameters used to construct encryption keys from falling into the wrong hands, then being used to construct or intelligently-guess encryption keys. As soon as possible after their use, these keying materials should be destroyed according to approved procedures for most sensitive information. The need for this policy may be partially overcome through the use of automated key management systems.

Related Policies: "Key Generation Material Destruction" and "Automated Encryption Key Management."

Audience: Technical staff

Security Environments: Medium and high

13. Plaintext Encryption Master Keys

Policy: Plain text master keys must be either manually handled through dual control with split knowledge or they may be stored in tamper-proof modules.

Commentary: This policy specifies the permissible ways to protect the most sensitive type of encryption keys. Master keys are used to encrypt all other keys, or at least encrypt keys that encrypt other keys. If a master key is revealed, an entire encryption system can quickly be compromised. Significant efforts are needed to prevent these keys from falling into the wrong hands. When in readable form, master keys must be segmented. Each component will not reveal the original master key. They may be stored in hardware modules that will automatically erase the keys if someone tampers with the module. These modules are sometimes called "security modules."

Related Policies: "Key Generation Materials" and "Encryption Key Management Systems."

Audience: Technical staff

Security Environments: Medium and high

14. Key Generation Material Destruction

Policy: All supplies used for the generation, distribution, and storage of keys must be protected from disclosure to unauthorized persons and when they are no longer needed, they must be destroyed by pulping, shredding, burning, or other approved methods.

Commentary: This policy prevents unauthorized parties from obtaining access to the information used to generate, distribute, or store encryption keys. This could include carbon copies and printer ribbons. This might permit these parties to obtain copies of the keys, which would permit them to obtain the sensitive information protected with encryption. The policy also makes workers aware that these materials are sensitive and that they should be handled with care.

Related Policies: "Key Generation Materials," "Hardcopy Disposal," and "Sensitive Information Materials."

Audience: Technical staff

Security Environments: Medium and high

15. Key Exchange Material Destruction

Policy: Custodians of key exchange material must destroy this material according to approved procedures within a reasonable time, not to exceed 10 business days, following the successful verification of a key exchange process.

Commentary: The intent of this policy is to clearly specify when Custodians of keying materials must destroy the keying materials they have received. The smaller the amount of time that these materials exist outside the system, and the fewer the number of people that have them, the more secure the encryption process will be. Multi-organizational networking environments are particularly in need of this policy. While the key management process is increasingly being automated, there are many encryption systems where manual key loaders and other technology require human involvement. It is for those manual situations that this policy was intended.

Related Policies: "Intermediate Products Containing Sensitive Information" and "Sensitive Information Materials."

Audience: Technical staff

Security Environments: Medium and high

16. Encryption Key Secrecy

Policy: The secrecy of any encryption key used for confidentiality purposes must be maintained until all of the protected information is no longer considered confidential.

Commentary: This policy provides systems designers and systems operators with a basic security principle for key management systems. The policy cautions them not to disclose encryption keys until all of the information protected with these keys is no longer considered confidential. From a practical standpoint, in many cases this time frame will be longer than an individual's lifetime. The secrecy of a key is assured if the key has been destroyed through authorized processes. For example, if confidential data was sent over the Internet in encrypted form some time ago, the key could be destroyed even though the information is considered confidential. This policy communicates the great emphasis that must be placed on the continued secrecy of keys, a message that is often unknown to, or ignored by encryption system users. The life a key is the time period in which it is employed.

Related Policies: "Encryption Key Life" and "Encryption Key Expiration."

Audience: End users and technical staff

Security Environments: Medium and high

17. Private Digital Signature Key Lifetime

Policy: Private digital signature keys must be kept confidential and accessible for at least the number of years that they might be used in a legal challenge.

Commentary: This policy informs users how long they must keep their private keys used for digital signatures. The exact number of years will vary by jurisdiction, and so was not stated in the policy. For a multi-national company, this policy could be accompanied by a table showing the requirements of different countries, or the maximum number of years could be placed into the policy itself. The policy could be expanded to include the need for a data integrity measure, such as a checksum to assure that the digital signature key has not been corrupted. Some organizations may want to destroy private keys after they are no longer in use, thereafter relying on public keys to prove the authenticity of a message. This is possible with Internet-based public key systems where the private key differs from the public keys. On the other hand, those organizations that wish to retain the private keys for legal challenges would use this policy. This policy applies to any type of organiza-

tion using traditional symmetric key encryption systems. Digital signatures are special encryption processes that prove a specific party generated a message and that unauthorized parties have not modified this message. Private digital signature keys must be kept secret, while public digital signature keys are widely available and are not generally kept secret.

Related Policies: "Digital Signature And User Authentication Keys" and "Java Program Execution."

Audience: End users

Security Environments: All

18. Private Key Backups

Policy: Users must not permit automatic backup systems to make a copy of the readable version of their private key used for digital signatures and digital certificates.

Commentary: This policy preserves the confidentiality of private encryption keys used for both digital signatures and digital certificates. These private keys should be kept under the control of the specific user to whom they pertain. If users simply store the readable version of their private keys on personal computer hard disks, then automatic backup systems can transfer these private keys to backup storage media where unauthorized parties can find them. This policy does not prevent a user from making a backup on a floppy disk, then locking this backup in a safe.

Related Policies: "Digital Signature And User Authentication Keys" and "Digital Certificate Root Key Protection."

Audience: End users

Security Environments: All

19. Encryption Key Duplication

Policy: Encryption keys used to conceal backup data must themselves be backed-up and must be stored with security measures comparable to or more stringent than measures applied to the involved backed-up data.

Commentary: This policy ensures that information systems staff has taken the necessary steps to securely back up encryption keys used to protect backup data media. If the keys were not adequately backed-up, then data recovery efforts may be severely hampered or even prevented. Financial institutions, credit bureaus, research labs, and other organizations that store backups at an off-site location often employ encryption of backup media. This policy indicates that the keys should be protected in a manner at least as secure as the protected data. This is because physical security at an off-site location may be easily compromised, in which case the encryption process is the only significant control preventing the disclosure of the backed-up data.

Related Policies: "Digital Signature And User Authentication Keys" and "Encryption Key Storage Media."

Audience: Technical staff

Security Environments: Medium and high

20. Encryption Key Disclosure — Controls

Policy: Encryption keys must be prevented from unauthorized disclosure through technical controls such as encryption under a separate key and use of tamper-resistant hardware.

Commentary: This policy specifies that measures must always be taken to prevent the unauthorized disclosure of encryption keys. If encryption keys are disclosed, the security of encryption systems is in most instances defeated. Tamper resistant hardware prevents people from opening encryption devices to recover the encryption keys stored inside. Also called "security modules," such hardware will automatically erase the keys contained inside if the module has been opened. This hardware is also shielded so that electromagnetic emanations do not reveal the keys stored inside. In terms of encrypting encryption keys, rather than using only one master key to encrypt other keys, many organizations use a hierarchy of master keys. This can get quite complicated and this complexity presents another reason why it is desirable to automate key management processes.

Related Policies: "Automated Encryption Key Management" and "Encryption Process Hardware Modules."

Audience: Technical staff

Security Environments: Medium and high

21. Digital Certificate Private Key Security

Policy: The private key associated with each worker at Company X must be protected against unauthorized disclosure when not in use by utilizing techniques beyond just physical security.

Commentary: This policy informs users that they must protect their private keys against unauthorized disclosure and subsequent fraudulent usage. If an unprotected private key was discovered, it could be used in an unauthorized manner. Just as cardholders are told not to leave their credit cards unsecured, this policy informs that private key holders must take certain precautions in order to maintain the security of the encryption processes that depend on their private keys.

Related Policies: "Private Digital Signature Key Lifetime."

Audience: End users

Security Environments: All

22. Encryption And Digital Signature Key Storage

Policy: Keys employed by end users for encryption and digital signatures must always be stored in a tamper-resistant hardware device.

Commentary: This policy prevents unauthorized people from gaining access to encryption keys or digital signature keys. If these people were able to gain such access they could examine confidential information that they were not meant to see, masquerade as though they were people who they were not, and initiate transactions that they are not authorized to initiate. Storage in a smart card is generally accepted as the safest way to proceed, but it is more costly and more complex to administer. Perhaps the most problematic aspect about using smart cards is installing readers on personal computers. Finding staff with the necessary expertise to set-up and administer smart card systems is also difficult. A personal identification number or a fixed password can be used to enable a smart card. This means that someone who steals a smart card, or who finds a lost smart card, cannot use it for unauthorized purposes. If these keys are stored on the desktop, users must be sure to encrypt them with strong passwords.

Related Policies: "Encryption Process Hardware Modules" and "Sensitive Information On Personal Computers."

Audience: Technical staff

Security Environments: Medium and high

23. Private Encryption Key Transmission

Policy: If private encryption keys are transmitted over communication lines, they must be encrypted with a stronger algorithm than is used to encrypt other sensitive data protected by encryption.

Commentary: This policy prevents users from inadvertently sending readable private encryption keys over communication systems. If this is done, then the encryption process may be easily circumvented. This policy is applicable to both the new public key encryption systems or the more traditional symmetric encryption systems. Whatever the underlying technology, private keys must never be sent in unencrypted form.

Related Policies: "Data And Encryption Key Transmission."

Audience: Technical staff

Security Environments: Medium and high

24. Public Key Changes

Policy: If a public encryption key has been posted on a web server or in another publicly accessible location, all regular correspondents must be notified whenever there is a change in this public key.

Commentary: This policy is relevant only to those organizations that use public key encryption systems. This policy recognizes that some encryption systems permit a user to post their public key in a public spot. This permits electronic mail and other transmissions to be easily encrypted, and it also permits digital signatures to be easily checked. With this approach, there is a possibility that an imposter can pose as a legitimate user and post another public key in the legitimate user's public location. Until detected, this imposter may then be able to spoof correspondents into communicating with him or her rather than the legitimate user. This policy prevents such abuse, or at least significantly reduces the time period when this abuse could take place. The messages that notify correspondents of future changes in a public key can be signed with a current and not-yet-expired private key. This will assure correspondents that they have received a message from the legitimate user and not an imposter.

Related Policies: "Private Encryption Key Transmission."

Audience: All

Security Environments: Medium and high

25. Compromised Keys

Policy: Encryption keys that have been compromised, or revealed to third parties under a key escrow arrangement, must immediately be revoked retroactively to the last known time when the keys were safe.

Commentary: This policy supports the resilience of key management systems. This policy supports the rapid notification of other participants in a key management system, then later the prompt issuance of new and trusted keys. If keys that had been revealed to third parties were to be revoked only back to the point when this revelation is known to have occurred, then there might have been earlier compromises that had not yet come to the attention of the key holder or the authority managing the keys. The continued support of transactions and messages executed and sent when there could have been undisclosed key compromises sets the stage for unrevealed fraud. A compromised key is instead revoked all the way back to the point when the key was known to be safe. This point often coincides with a previous key change.

Related Policies: "General Purpose Encryption Systems" and "Encryption Utilities Passwords And Keys."

Audience: Technical staff

Security Environments: Medium and high

26. Encryption Key Storage Media

Policy: If encryption is used to protect sensitive data resident on computer storage media, the encryption keys and related encryption keying materials used in the encryption process must not be stored anywhere on this storage media in unencrypted form.

Commentary: This policy prevents an analyst from taking advantage of the fact that the keying materials are stored on the same data storage media as encrypted data. If these materials are stored together, then the associated encryption process is easily circumvented. Several commercial encryption packages use this approach. Use of hidden files or hidden directories for the unencrypted storage of these keying materials is not acceptable.

Related Policies: "Data And Encryption Key Transmission."

Audience: Technical staff

Security Environments: Medium and high

27. Key Recovery Operation Controls

Policy: Two authorized Company X staff members must be present whenever keys are recovered from an encryption key archive and all such operations must be securely logged.

Commentary: This policy prevents a single staff member from using the key recovery system. If a single person were to recover keys, then that same person could conceivably masquerade as though he or she was somebody else, signing messages with digital signatures, and examining confidential files that he or she was not authorized to see. This policy requires the use of dual control, which says that to get a higher level of security, you must have two trusted individuals both present before a sensitive operation is performed.

Related Policies: "Encryption Utilities Passwords And Keys" and "General Purpose Encryption Systems."

Audience: Technical staff

Security Environments: Medium and high

28. Backup Encryption Keys

Policy: If a Company X worker is going to employ encryption for production business information processing activities, the worker must securely deposit backup copies of all keys with Information Security department management.

Commentary: This policy makes up for deficiencies in many encryption software packages. The policy permits an organization to enjoy the benefits of key escrow, even though the encryption package they are using includes no key escrow functionality. The objective of key escrow is to be able to read the protected data, even if the relevant encryption key is lost or stolen. Key escrow mechanisms can employ a separate key that permits encrypted data to be decrypted, even when the original encryption key is unavailable. Under this policy, backup copies of keys are deposited with a trusted third party, in this case an in-house information security specialist. This policy may be considered to be intrusive by some users. The policy is not intrusive because it pertains only to production information, not to personal details.

Related Policies: "Workstation Key Locks" and "Encryption Utilities Passwords And Keys."

Audience: End users

Security Environments: Medium and high

29. Digital Signature And User Authentication Keys

Policy: Keys used for digital signatures, digital certificates, and user authentication must never be included in a key escrow arrangement.

Commentary: This policy is intended to ensure that users cannot readily repudiate their encryption keys, also called non-repudiation. Repudiation would wreak havoc with legal proceedings that rely on digital signatures or other security mechanisms based on encryption keys. In general, digital signatures and a number of other control measures assume that only the involved user has control over a key or password. But key escrow is an arrangement whereby encryption keys can be shared with certain parties.

Related Policies: "General Purpose Encryption Systems."

Audience: Technical staff

Security Environments: All

30. Encryption And Digital Signature Key Separation

Policy: If both encryption and digital signatures are used, separate keys must be used for each of these two control measures.

Commentary: This policy prevents an adversary who gains possession of one key from compromising both encryption and digital signature systems. If separate keys are used, the amount of effort required to defeat a system is increased, assuming that both encryption and digital signatures must be compromised in order to compromise the entire system. With separate keys, both the complexity and the cost of security systems also is increased. Digital signatures are short addendums added to messages or files to reflect the result of an encryption process applied to them. Digital signatures are used to show that messages or files come from an authorized source and that they have not been tampered with. Digital signatures also are known as message authentication codes.

Related Policies: "Encryption Key Storage Media" and "Data And Encryption Key Transmission."

Audience: Technical staff

Security Environments: Medium and high

31. Key Management Responsibility

Policy: Whenever encryption is used to protect sensitive data, the relevant Owner of the data must explicitly assign responsibility for encryption key management.

Commentary: When encryption is employed, responsibility for protecting sensitive data has been changed to responsibility for protecting encryption keys. The protection activity is needed, even though the quantity of information that needs to be protected shrinks dramatically. Having the Owners of the involved data explicitly assign key management responsibilities is important. This policy requires Owners to explicitly make such an assignment. This policy assumes that encryption is handled on an organizationally-decentralized basis, rather than centrally by Information Technology or Information Security management.

Related Policies: "Information Ownership" and "Automated Encryption Key Management."

Audience: Management and technical staff

Security Environments: Medium and high

10.04 Security Of System Files

10.04.01 Control Of Operation Software

1. Business Application System Testing

Policy: All application systems developed in-house must go through three cycles of testing where all errors are discovered and corrected before these same application systems can be placed into production operation.

Commentary: This policy ensures that business application systems in production are reliable and reasonably free of serious bugs, errors, out-of-specification features, and other problems. The traditional approach to systems development calls for a testing cycle, efforts to fix the problems encountered, a regression test, then a launch of the application into production. The trouble with this traditional approach is that the bug fixes and other changes made after the testing cycle introduce new bugs and other problems. These new bugs and other problems may not be discovered by the regression test, and the schedule did not permit them to be fixed. This policy adopts a more rigorous approach that replaces the long initial testing cycle at the very end of the development process with three smaller cycles. This policy will often increase the time and money required to develop an application, but it will also lower the long run costs.

Related Policies: "Developer Access To Production Business Information" and "Systems Development Conventions."

Audience: Technical staff

Security Environments: Medium and high

2. Software Migration

Policy: Application and systems development staff must not have the ability to move any software into the production environment.

Commentary: This policy is intended to prevent developers from prematurely moving their own application systems into production. They might, for example, do this to avoid comprehensive testing that would reveal inadequate control measures. They might also want to move their own systems into production quickly to avoid other scrutiny that might reveal unauthorized code. The objective described in this policy may be difficult to achieve if there are very few people in an organization, or if personal computers or workstations are to run the production versions of these applications. Too few personnel will require certain compromises in terms of the separation of duties, while use of small systems like client-server systems or local area networks will often prevent the rigorous separation of development and production.

Related Policies: "Separation Of Duties."

Audience: Technical staff

Security Environments: All

10.04.02 Protection Of System Test Data

1. Software Testing Information

Policy: Unless written permission is obtained from Information Security management, all software testing for systems designed to handle private information must be accomplished with production information that no longer contains specific details that might be valuable, critical, sensitive, or private.

Commentary: An information sanitization process obscures certain information without significantly modifying the characteristics relevant to testing. For example, the actual first and last names of individuals in a human resources database might be mixed up such that they no longer reflect any specific persons. In this manner the actual field lengths required, the number of records in the database, and other statistics remain the same for testing purposes. This policy prevents unauthorized disclosure of testing information to persons such as in-house programmers and contractors. This policy is appropriate for third-party packages and software developed in-house. The policy is particularly relevant to those environments in which end users are doing their own programming. Most organizations will want to specify how to sanitize data. Rather than mentioning valuable, critical, sensitive or private information, the policy can make reference to certain data classifications used within Company X.

Related Policies: "Four-Category Data Classification," "Third-Party Private Information Disclosure," and "Developer Access To Production Business Information."

Audience: Management and technical staff

Security Environments: Medium and high

2. Developer Access To Production Business Information

Policy: Where access to production business information is required so that new or modified business application systems may be developed or tested, only "read" and "copy" access must be granted on production machines for the duration of the testing and related development efforts, and must be promptly revoked upon the successful completion of these efforts.

Commentary: This policy specifies the times when access to production business data on production machines will be granted to testing personnel such as quality assurance experts. The policy also strictly limits the type of access they will have. After they have read or copied production data over to a test system, they can update and delete as much as they need to on the test machine. The policy enforces a clear distinction between production and development environments. The policy is also intended to specify the type of access privileges that developers will be given. The policy defines access privileges for an area where excessive privileges are sometimes commonplace. Without such a policy and associated control measures, it will be difficult to establish a clear separation between production and development computing environments. The policy also prevents and discourages developer manipulation of production data. The policy assumes that production users are different people than those doing the development and testing. Although not specifically addressed by this policy, the development personnel should also be different from the testing personnel.

Related Policies: "Privilege Restriction — Need To Know," "Production Application Information Access," and "Software Testing Information."

Audience: Technical staff

Security Environments: All

10.04.03 Access Control To Program Source Library

1. Technical Staff Privileges

Policy: Computer operations staff must not be given any access to production data, production programs, or the operating system beyond that which they need to perform their jobs.

Commentary: This policy is a specific example of separation of duties, as reflected by a typical mainframe shop. Because adequate separation of duties related access control mechanisms may not be available, the policy may not be practical for smaller systems such as personal computers or workstations. As the Internet continues to permit extranets and other automated business partnerships, the policy will become increasingly applicable to the small systems environment. The intention of the policy is to clearly indicate that computer operations staff should not be given universal access to production data, production programs, and the operating system. Because this control is so often ignored in data processing shops, a specific policy may be required to clarify exactly what should be done.

Related Policies: "Privilege Restriction — Need To Know" and "Separation Of Duties."

Audience: Management and technical staff

Security Environments: All

2. Production Programs And Information Access

Policy: Access controls must be configured such that production programs and information systems software support personnel are not granted access privileges except for problem resolution, application development personnel are not granted privileges to update systems software, or be granted access to the master copy of production information except for problem resolution and computer operations personnel are restricted from modifying systems software, application software, and production information.

Commentary: This policy defines the classic and frequently-encountered separation of duties for staff working in the computer operations, systems software support, and application development areas. The policy is intended to prevent people working in any one of these three areas from abusing their privileges, and causing damage to programs or information thereby. There are two exceptions written into the policy that permit otherwise denied access in order to resolve a serious problem. Under these circumstances, it is advisable to turn-on more extensive logging, then later have a manager or supervisor review the work of those with the additional privileges. This policy cannot be implemented unless some form of access control system has been installed on the production computer systems at the organization adopting the policy. These access control systems are generally not found on personal computers, but can instead be found on larger multi-user systems. This policy does not cover a change control process for the development of, testing of, and movement into production of application programs.

Related Policies: "Operating System Command Access" and "Production Business Information Privileges."

Audience: Management and technical staff

Security Environments: All

10.05 Security In Development And Support Processes

10.05.01 Change Control Procedures

1. Software And Information Testing

Policy: Prior to distributing any software or information in computerized form to third parties, Company X workers must have subjected the software or information to appropriate testing, including comprehensive scanning to identify the presence of computer viruses.

Commentary: This policy avoids liability for bugs in software or for spreading a virus. Although many organizations do not consider themselves to be publishers, this policy may be relevant if they distribute software or information in any electronic form. For example, a freight company may provide its customers with a program on a floppy disk, permitting customers to determine the shipping charges and number of days to deliver a package to a certain location. This company should subject this software to the tests described in this policy. The policy could be expanded to mention the title of the person, or the department, that determines what tests should be applied.

Related Policies: "Software Testing."

Audience: Management and technical staff

Security Environments: All

2. Program Resource Consumption

Policy: Computer users must not run or write any computer program or process that is likely to consume significant system resources or otherwise interfere with Company X business activities.

Commentary: This policy prohibits software that may damage the ability of Company X to promptly process business transactions. Computer worms would be prohibited by this policy. Internet-based games can consume a great deal of bandwidth on internal networks, and are banned by this policy. Often excessive system usage is a good indicator of a virus or some other unauthorized program or process. Some computer operators will terminate jobs that consume inordinate amounts of resources, and this policy will provide them with the management authorization to do so. The word "process" was included in the policy in addition to the word "program" to include things like macros, shell scripts and command files, which may not be considered computer programs. If users are prohibited from writing or running such programs or processes, then management can take disciplinary action. In addition to discouraging the experimentation with viruses, worms, and similar software, this policy is a deterrent to manipulating production business systems just to determine what would happen.

Related Policies: "Excessive Resource Consumption," "User Processes, Sessions, And Files," and "Sending Unsolicited Electronic Mail."

Audience: End users and technical staff

Security Environments: All

3. Systems Development Conventions

Policy: Management must ensure that all software development and software maintenance activities performed by in-house staff subscribe to Company X policies, standards, procedures, and other systems development conventions.

Commentary: This policy instructs both local and centralized management to ensure that all software development activities performed by in-house staff are in compliance with standard systems development conventions. The growing popularity of end-user programming makes this policy increasingly important because end users often construct and alter production application systems without proper testing or documentation. This makes this policy particularly important for small system environments such as client-server systems, local area networks, and personal computers. Even if end-user programming is prohibited, or simply not performed, there is a need for a policy like this to ensure that local departmental management consistently observes Company X systems development conventions.

The policy assumes that such systems development conventions have already been specified. The word "production" may be added to the policy to limit its applicability. If this is done, it would permit the unmanaged development of non-production software, but once that software was moved into production, it should be required to comply with these conventions. A definition of what "software development" entails also may be necessary. This could include development of new databases, new expert systems, and synchronized scripted updates between multiple files in a client-server network.

Related Policies: "End-User Application Programs," "Security In The Systems Development Life Cycle," and "Centralized Information Security."

Audience: All

Security Environments: All

4. Access Paths In Production Software

Policy: Prior to moving software that has been developed in-house to production status, programmers and other technical staff must remove all special access paths and system privileges.

Commentary: This policy informs programmers and other system developers that they must eliminate all pathways that could be used to compromise security. Although programmers may only want to save themselves time at some point in the future, by leaving such unauthorized pathways in production systems, they also create pathways that can be exploited by unauthorized parties. The policy also implicitly requires all special access paths to be disclosed in documentation. This policy is particularly relevant to those environments in which end users are doing their own programming, including client-server computing, local area networks, intranets, and personal computers because these new programmers may not be familiar with traditional systems development approaches.

Related Policies: "Compromising Security Mechanisms For Customers" and "Circumventing Access Controls."

Audience: Technical staff

Security Environments: All

5. Systems Functionality

Policy: With the exception of emergency fixes, only those functions described in an approved system design document must be included in a production computer or communications system that has been developed in-house.

Commentary: Undocumented functions may pose grave security risks. For example, an undocumented mechanism to permit the original programmer to circumvent access controls, if retained in the production version of an application, may be exploited by an unauthorized user. This policy ensures that all functionality is documented and approved. In this context, "system" could be an entire computer or communications system, system programs, or application programs. This policy also may be used to discipline or terminate a programmer who built undocumented functionality into a system. This policy becomes more important as users develop their own client-server systems, local area network systems, departmental systems, intranets, and systems tying together personal computers.

Related Policies: "Access Paths In Production Software."

Audience: Management and technical staff

Security Environments: All

6. Projects Involving Human Safety Issues

Policy: All in-house software projects that involve human safety risks must have a computer development project manager's signature on the testing approval forms prior to being used for production business purposes.

Commentary: This policy makes an individual accountable for the inclusion of appropriate safety-related control measures. Some organizations may wish to specify what is meant by the term "human safety risks," while others may keep it vague to widen its applicability to unforeseen future circumstances. If an organization chooses to get specific about this term, they may wish to make reference to repetitive motion and other ergonomic matters, not just severe personal injury that could be inflicted in a certain moment.

Related Policies: "Production System Controls," "System Interruption For Safety," and "Duress Passwords."

Audience: Management and technical staff

Security Environments: Medium and high

7. System Problem Notification

Policy: Systems designers and developers are individually responsible for notifying project management about any problems that might be caused by the applications they are building or modifying.

Commentary: This policy makes systems designers and developers personally responsible for notifying management about potential problems associated with the systems they are developing or enhancing. In many organizations, these more technical staff members do not say anything about serious issues such as fraud and privacy violation. Management may then put a system into production operation, and only later discover these previously-known problems. Computer technology is often so far different from what people are used to, that they have trouble imagining how the new technology will operate once placed into production. The more people who think about potential problems before a system goes into production operation, the more likely these problems are to be discovered and corrected before serious losses are incurred.

Related Policies: "Security Contact Information" and "Reporting System Vulnerabilities."

Audience: Technical staff

Security Environments: All

8. Change Control Procedure

Policy: All computer and communications systems used for production processing at Company X must employ a formal change control procedure to authorize all significant changes to software, hardware, communications networks, and related procedures.

Commentary: This policy stabilizes the production processing environment by controlling all changes made to it. A formal change control process will help to ensure that only authorized changes are made, that they are made at the approved time, and that they are made in the approved manner. This should increase the percentage of time the system is available for processing business transactions. Such change control processes are also a useful way to require the preparation of documentation, which will be important for problem resolution and contingency planning purposes. An explicit definition of "production processing" may be an important supplement to this policy. This policy is relevant to voice communications systems such as voice mail and private branch exchanges, and data communications systems like intranets. Software license management software and hardware inventory systems can be used to provide such change control for small systems like client-server, local area networks, and personal computers.

Related Policies: "Production Changes" and "Security In The Systems Development Life Cycle."

Audience: Technical staff

Security Environments: All

9. Security Considerations For Production System Changes

Policy: Every non-emergency change to production systems must be shown to be consistent with the information security architecture and approved by management as part of the formal change control process.

Commentary: This policy ensures that both computer operations staff and systems administration staff install only the hardware and software that is consistent with an information security architecture document. The policy states that production systems may only be changed in a manner that is compliant with an information security architecture. The policy establishes the importance of an information security architecture and specifies some of the circumstances when it must be referenced. Because the policy applies to the end of the systems development and testing process, it implies that systems developers and designers have already considered the architecture. A separate process is required if the changes are for an emergency situation. Prior to adopting a policy like this, the organization should write, then obtain management approval for an architecture.

Related Policies: "Loading External Programs" and "Internet Business Arrangements."

Audience: Management and technical staff

Security Environments: Medium and high

10. Production Operation Access Controls

Policy: All user-level and administrative-level access controls required by Company X information security policies must be established and enabled before production information systems can be placed into operation.

Commentary: This policy prevents technical staff from placing a system into production operation without having defined access controls at a reasonable level. Sometimes systems are placed in production but access controls have not been turned-on, or if they are turned on, they are not defined at a secure level. For example, in many cases, fixed password access controls are defined, but group user IDs are employed. Unless individual user IDs are employed, logs will not show which user took what actions, and separation of duties will be difficult to enforce. The policy assumes that access control policies are previously or simultaneously established.

Related Policies: "Remote System Access Controls" and "Computer System Access Controls."

Audience: Technical staff

Security Environments: Medium and high

11. Unnecessary Software

Policy: Software features that could be used to compromise security, and that are clearly unnecessary in the Company X computing environment, must be disabled at the time when software is installed on multi-user systems.

Commentary: This policy prevents unnecessary but enabled features from being used by hackers and others intent on compromising systems security. Software packages often have far more features than most organizations need. While this may attract buyers for the software, it also frequently provides additional vulnerabilities that can be exploited by unauthorized users. This policy could be expanded to apply to software on single-user systems, in which case the words "on multi-user systems" would be removed. Nothing in the policy prevents disabled features from being enabled later, should circumstances require. Ideally users would be prevented from re-enabling these features through access control mechanisms or other security measures.

Related Policies: "Disabling Java," "Access Paths In Production Software," and "Privilege Restriction — Need To Know."

Audience: Technical staff

Security Environments: All

12. Production Systems Change Documentation

Policy: Documentation reflecting the nature, approval and performance of all significant changes to production computer and communications systems at Company X must be prepared within a week from the time that a change took place.

Commentary: The purpose of this policy is to require technical workers to adhere to a deadline for the preparation of documentation. If there is no definitive deadline, many of these people will keep postponing the preparation of documentation for extended periods of time. If this happens, there is a high likelihood that the technical people involved will have left the organization, transferred to another position, or simply forgotten much about the change. Not having current documentation is also a hindrance to resolving day-to-day problems, training new people, and contingency planning and disaster recovery efforts. Giving technical people a week to prepare documentation keeps it current, and also permits them to make emergency changes without having to document these changes. Some organizations may find this policy too lenient. They may want to have full documentation prepared prior to a change, with the exception of emergency fixes. Others may want to state that documentation should be prepared in advance of a change. While some organizations may find it too rigid, it is also possible to prevent software from moving into a production processing environment unless documentation has been prepared.

Related Policies: "Training And Operating Documentation" and "Production Operating System Changes."

Audience: Technical staff

Security Environments: All

13. Training And Operating Documentation

Policy: Business application systems in development or undergoing significant modification must not be moved into a production processing environment without having adequate training materials and operating documentation.

Commentary: Undocumented systems or systems operating by untrained people are very difficult to control. Significant losses can occur when operators are not sufficiently trained. Embezzlers and others intent on committing computer crimes frequently take advantage of the confusion surrounding a newly-introduced or improperly-documented system. This policy is intended to require that adequate training and operating documentation be prepared, and approved, before a system is formally moved to production status. Although generally more difficult to implement due to less sophisticated security tools, this policy is applicable to small systems such as those involving client-server systems, local area networks, and personal computers.

Related Policies: "Information User Responsibilities," "Production Systems Change Documentation," and "Production Systems Documentation."

Audience: Management and technical staff

Security Environments: All

14. Externally-Provided Software Testing

Policy: Executable programs provided by external entities must be tested in accordance with Company standards and must also be properly documented before installation on any Company X production system.

Commentary: This policy is intended to prevent unauthorized code from damaging Company X systems, software, and data. It is common for hackers to modify programs that are placed on electronic bulletin boards, Internet web pages, and similar public places. This policy applies only to production systems, not the majority of personal computers and local area networks. The word "production" will need to have been defined previously. A testing process accompanied by a testing documentation preparation process will both need to be prepared for this policy to work as intended. Although public-domain software is the most significant risk here, it is also good practice to test and examine code received from trusted vendors. This policy is intended for Information Systems department staff, rather than end users.

Related Policies: "Software Testing" and "Software Scanning."

Audience: Technical staff

Security Environments: Medium and high

15. Software Review And Recompilation

Policy: Fully-tested software modules must be independently reviewed and recompiled before being moved to production libraries.

Commentary: Beyond the early detection and correction of errors and omissions, this policy prevents the incorporation of unauthorized code into production software. The policy also has an element of the separation of duties in that the reviewer must not be the same person as the tester. The policy could be further expanded to require that the tester not be the same person as the developer. These separation of duties controls are generally possible only in large organizations that have available staff to perform different jobs. Another purpose of this policy is to ensure that the executable version of a program is identical to the program's source code. This policy is relevant to client-server systems, local area networks, personal computers, and other small systems although it will generally be more difficult to implement. Another benefit of this policy is that it requires the preparation of adequate documentation for loading the new system. Without it another person cannot install the new software. The term "compilation" can be modified to suit the terminology used at the organization.

Related Policies: "Separation Of Duties."

Audience: Technical staff

Security Environments: All

16. Business Application Change Control Process

Policy: A formal change control process must be used to ensure that all business application software that is migrated into production is authorized by Information Systems management and user organization management.

Commentary: This policy requires a formal and written change control process for the development of production business applications. The benefits of a formal change control process include more current documentation, greater system stability, and a more structured systems environment that is more easily controlled and managed. This policy addresses the requirement for a change control process, not the privileges used to support such a process. A definition of "business application software" considered to be production may also accompany this policy. The change control process described in this policy may be extended to packaged software and other parts of data processing operations. Any additional explanatory words for this policy should reflect only the essential components of a formal change control process. This is because there are many methodologies and because Information Systems departments often change methodologies. This policy

may be used in those circumstances where the organization is not yet ready to extend change control to other information systems areas such as hardware and communications. The words "user organization management" can in some organizations be replaced with words "application Owner."

Related Policies: "Software Migration" and "End-User System Development."

Audience: Technical staff

Security Environments: All

17. Production Software Package Change Approvals

Policy: Modifications to vendor-provided application software must be made only after obtaining written permission from Information Systems management and follow the change control procedures used for application software developed in-house.

Commentary: This policy requires changes to third-party packaged software to follow the same change control process used for software developed in-house. Such modifications could jeopardize compatibility with subsequent versions of the software, cause the vendor to deny additional support for the software, or cause the vendor to justifiably renounce any responsibility for the software's behavior. Such changes may also cause the software to perform in an unauthorized, less secure, or undesired fashion. A version of this policy may be appropriate for users of personal computers, workstations, local area networks, and client-server systems. Selection of certain parameters during either the installation process or the user-customization process does not constitute a modification of the software itself.

Related Policies: "Business Application Change Control Process" and "New Or Enhanced Service."

Audience: End users and technical staff

Security Environments: All

18. Software Maintenance

Policy: All permanent changes to production software must be made using source code.

Commentary: Maintenance of source code is considerably easier than maintenance of object code. Changes to object code are more likely to lead to the introduction of new problems. It is also desirable to have a compiler or interpreter check the validity of new code prior to its execution. This cannot be done if changes are made directly in object code. This policy requires that developers make changes in production software at the source rather than at the object level. This policy is also desirable because it implicitly requires that documentation to be prepared for the source code.

Related Policies: "Software Escrow."

Audience: Technical staff

Security Environments: All

19. Change Control Documentation

Policy: Production application change control documentation must be maintained that indicates what changed and how, who made the changes, who tested the changes, who authorized the changes, who migrated the changes into production and permit any and all prior versions of production applications to be readily recreated.

Commentary: This policy is intended to outline a change control process and related documentation. It is not intended to stand on its own but is instead intended to be supported with procedural change control documentation. A significant separation of duties is embedded in the policy in that separate people are making changes, testing changes, migrating changes, and approving changes. This policy will assist auditors and computer crime investigators in their efforts to determine how applications changed over time. The policy assists contingency planning because it states that prior versions of applications must be available, should there be a need to rollback to these prior versions.

Related Policies: "Software Escrow" and "Production Systems Change Documentation."

Audience: Technical staff

Security Environments: All

20. Production Information System Change Implementation

Policy: All changes must be communicated to affected parties at least two weeks prior to the change, and the implementation of all non-emergency changes must be held until the first weekend of each month.

Commentary: The policy does not permit frequent and unannounced changes, both of which can cause many problems for users. This policy is most relevant to those organizations that provide services to others such as common carriers, Internet service providers and application service providers. It can also be used for large multi-user systems or internal networks where there are varieties of users who wish to know about upcoming changes. Organizations adopting this policy should also have well-developed contingency plans to handle problems with new changes. The reason why changes are held until the first weekend is that accounting for the prior month will be completed, and demand for services will be low. This stipulation will need to be modified depending on the issuing organization's industry and accounting cycles.

Related Policies: "Business Application Change Control Process" and "Security Fixes."

Audience: Technical staff

Security Environments: High

21. Software Features And Functions Documentation

Policy: All features and functions of software released to the public must be fully revealed in the documentation provided to users.

Commentary: This policy prevents programmers and others involved in the systems development process from incorporating features or functions that are not fully revealed to users or internal management. To avoid loss of customer confidence and allegations of bad intent, all features and functions should be revealed in the documentation. Users do not need to be able to change or disable these functions or features. They just need to know that they exist. This policy is only relevant for software distributed to outsiders. If software is only for internal use, then this policy may not be necessary.

Related Policies: "Access Paths In Production Software" and "Circumventing Access Controls."

Audience: Technical staff

Security Environments: All

10.05.02 Technical Review Of Operating System Changes

1. Operating System Configuration

Policy: Company X technical staff must configure production servers with those operating systems that permit unwanted or unneeded functionality to be completely removed.

Commentary: This policy expresses a preference for operating systems where unwanted or unneeded software modules can be removed and deleted. This is quite different from operating systems where such removal is very difficult, if possible at all. About the best system administrators can do with some operating systems is turn certain features and functions off. The problem is that hackers, industrial spies, disgruntled employees, and other unauthorized users can sometimes turn these functions back on. Turning-on disabled or dormant functionality is a lot easier than reconfiguring the operating system, then rebooting.

Related Policies: "Disabling Critical Security Components" and "Firewall Configuration."

Audience: Technical staff

Security Environments: Medium and high

2. Software Patches, Bug Fixes, and Upgrades

Policy: All Company X networked production systems must have an adequately-staffed process for expediently and regularly reviewing and installing all newly released systems software patches, bug fixes, and upgrades.

Commentary: This policy ensures that an organization's networks and systems are not penetrated by hackers, industrial spies, terrorists, and other unwelcome users. If software, especially software running on those systems at the periphery of an internal network, is not the latest version, in many cases there are bugs or security problems that these intruders can exploit. If a serious vulnerability has been publicly announced, then the software should be updated immediately. This is especially of concern because shareware vulnerability identification software is now available, and intruders typically use this software to identify systems that have not yet posted the latest updates to their systems.

Related Policies: "Personal Computer Software Upgrades," "Software Versions," and "Systems Interfacing External Networks."

Audience: Technical staff

Security Environments: All

10.05.03 Restrictions On Changes To Software Packages

1. Vendor-Provided Systems Software Installation

Policy: Prior to being installed, new or different versions of the operating system and related systems software for multi-user production computers must go through the established change control process.

Commentary: It is not a certainty that vendor provided software will benefit all user organizations. In some cases, existing applications will fail when newer systems software is installed. In other cases, memory or disk space constraints will cause problems when systems software is updated. This policy prevents computer operations personnel from installing systems software unless the software has been approved by management

through the change control process. The policy also prevents systems programmers and others from testing new software on production systems, causing possible data corruption, system crashes, and related problems. This policy could easily be expanded to include applications provided by external vendors. The policy could also be expanded to include single-user production systems, but in most instances single-user systems do not have effective change control systems.

Related Policies: "Business Application Change Control Process" and "Production Changes."

Audience: Technical staff

Security Environments: All

2. Third-Party Vendor Access To Packaged Software

Policy: Every third-party software package that Company X uses for production information systems purposes must be free of deactivation mechanisms that could be triggered by the vendor without Company X consent.

Commentary: This policy prevents Company X from being in a position where it is dependent on a third party for critical software, but the third party then turns-off this software to compel Company X to perform some action. This type of functionality has been incorporated into a number of software packages, but it has proven to be very disruptive to the user organization. As a result, it has been disparagingly discussed in information systems publications. The mechanism can be implemented by a variety of techniques including a computerized timer, an execution counter, or remote access on and off switch. The policy could be reinforced by adding these words: "Every written contract with a third-party software vendor must include an assurance that no vendor-controlled deactivation functionality exists." While smaller organizations will have trouble getting words such as this written into a contract, larger customers will have the power to make changes to a vendor's standard licensing contract. This policy is not applicable to outsourced information services, such as those provided by an application service provider.

Related Policies: "Unnecessary Software" and "Back-Off Procedures."

Audience: Technical staff

Security Environments: All

10.05.04 Covert Channels And Trojan Code

1. Use Of Software Tools And Languages

Policy: Company X system designers and developers must not use software tools and languages that have unproven security attributes when they build web sites, extranets, or any other system having an interface to external parties, unless advance approval of Information Security management has been obtained.

Commentary: This policy encourages systems designers and developers to consider which software tools and languages are proven to be secure. The delineation between proven to be secure and not proven to be secure is not quantitative or logically irrefutable. It must instead be the result of consultation with Information Security management. The policy is restricted to external interfaces, where hackers or industrial spies could enter, and does not apply to internal systems.

Related Policies: "Mature Development Tools And Techniques" and "External Network Interfaces."

Audience: Technical staff

Security Environments: All

2. Software Integrity Statements

Policy: If procurement of third-party software is being considered, management must obtain a written integrity statement from the involved vendor that provides assurances that the software does not contain undocumented features, does not contain hidden mechanisms that could be used to compromise the software's security, and will not require the modification or abandonment of controls found in the affected operating system.

Commentary: This policy gets written assurance from external providers of software that the software performs as represented, and that the software does not include other mechanisms that might be used to circumvent security. This written assurance can be later used in a court of law if it is shown that the vendor's software contained malicious code. The process of requesting and obtaining an integrity statement notifies the vendor that the purchasing organization is serious about security, and that it intends the vendor to bear responsibility for the integrity of their product. Some sites may wish to expand the policy to include a requirement that the vendor fix any major security problems that the purchasing organization discovers, perhaps within a certain period of time. Although the policy is written for application systems, the same policy can be readily applied to systems software.

Related Policies: "Compromising Security Mechanisms For Customers."

Audience: Technical staff

Security Environments: Medium and high

10.05.05 Outsourced Software Development

1. Third-Party Software Development

Policy: Third parties who develop software for Company X must be bound by a contract that includes, but is not limited to, clear and distinct definition of licensing arrangements, quality and accuracy expectations, escrow arrangements, auditing procedures, and testing requirements.

Commentary: This policy ensures that all software developed for Company X by any third party is completed according to the terms and conditions stipulated by contract. This will hold the third party to the expectation levels of Company X with respect to the functionality and quality of the software. It will also bind the third party to delivering a product that is free of any malicious code. Should any aspect of the software not meet the Company X standards or expectations, the binding nature of a signed agreement will provide Company the necessary legal leverage in resolving any disputes.

Related Policies: "Outsourcing Contract Approvals," "Information Transfer To Third Parties," "Production Systems and Software Tools," and "Software Integrity Statements."

Audience: Management and technical staff

Security Environments: All

11   BUSINESS CONTINUITY MANAGEMENT

11.01 Aspects Of Business Continuity Management

11.01.01 Business Continuity Management Process

1. Emergency And Disaster Support Requirements

Policy: All subsidiaries, divisions, departments, and other Company X organizational units that require support by the Information Systems department on a priority basis in the event of an emergency or a disaster must implement hardware, software, policies, and related procedures consistent with Company X standards.

Commentary: Non-standard systems make the preparation of, and maintenance of, a contingency plan very difficult. This is because prepared contingency planning material cannot be used, and relevant in-house expertise is less likely to be available. This policy notifies organizational units that Information Systems management cannot support them to the same extent that they support organizational units that comply with in-house standards. The policy is considered by some to be an exceptionally effective tool for forcing organizational units to comply with information technology standards. The policy is helpful with efforts to re-centralize information security. Information security has become distributed at many organizations, and in some cases is less effective.

Related Policies: "Computer System Dispersion" and "Centralized Information Security."

Audience: Technical staff

Security Environments: All

2. Contingency Plan Accessibility

Policy: Business and information systems contingency plans must be continuously accessible over the Internet through at least two separate Internet addresses that are supported by different Internet service providers.

Commentary: This policy ensures that the most recent version of the recovery plans will continue to be available, no matter what happens to the offices, computers, networks, and other facilities at Company X. If, for example, the headquarters building of Company X was destroyed, the most current contingency plan would be readily available to any authorized person who had a computer with an Internet connection. Data replication software can also be used to ensure that the computers of authorized personnel have the latest version of these plans stored on the hard drive. This can be achieved each time one of these remote computers logs on. If the contingency plans have been updated, then the latest version of the plans will be automatically downloaded through data replication software. A standard file format can be used to save the plans so that they can be viewed on virtually any computer.

Related Policies: "Computer Emergency Response Team."

Audience: Technical staff

Security Environments: All

11.01.02 Business Contingency And Impact Analysis

1. Multi-User Application Criticality Rating

Policy: In conjunction with the information Owners, Information Systems management must periodically prepare or revise an assessment of the degree of criticality of all production multi-user computer applications.

Commentary: The process whereby criticality ratings are assigned to applications is a necessary precursor to writing an effective contingency plan. With this dependency in mind, this policy requires Information Systems management or Information Security management to periodically prepare or revise a list of critical applications. As business systems change, so will the criticality of these systems. Likewise, some applications will be retired, others will be introduced, some will become more important, and others will become less important. As a result of these and other changes, contingency plans should be periodically updated. This policy acknowledges that user department management will indicate that their systems are critical when they are not. To receive a reasonable and consistent view across an organization it is often necessary to have a centralized authority perform this ranking. This policy clarifies that both Information Systems management and information Owners are responsible for an annual report showing application criticality. This policy assumes the word "production" has been defined clearly in other documents. The policy also assumes the existence of another policy that defines the word "critical."

Related Policies: "Five-Category Application Criticality Classification Scheme," "Information Security Plans," and "Information Resource Classification."

Audience: Technical staff

Security Environments: All

2. Five-Category Application Criticality Classification Scheme

Policy: All production computer applications must be placed into one of five criticality classifications, each with separate handling requirements: highly critical, critical, priority, required, and deferrable.

Commentary: This policy specifies standard criticality categories to be used throughout an organization. Once standardization is achieved, then the applications can be ranked, and the most critical ones can receive special contingency planning attention. The number of criticality categories will vary from organization to organization, as will the meanings of the terms like "priority." Generally, each of these terms will have a time period during which the application must be recovered. For example, "highly critical" applications could be those that must be recovered within 15 minutes. Information could be rated according to criticality, but because information is so often processed by many different applications, it is frequently easier just to focus on applications when preparing a contingency plan.

Related Policies: "Four-Category Data Classification," "Multi-User Application Criticality Rating," and "Essential Information And Software."

Audience: Technical staff

Security Environments: All

3. Business Impact Analysis

Policy: After the annual organization-wide risk assessment has been completed, Information Security management or its designee must perform a business impact analysis that will specify the maximum period that Company X can go without critical information processing services, the time period in which management must decide whether to move to an alternative processing site, and the minimum acceptable production information systems recovery configuration.

Commentary: The purpose of this policy is to require the performance of not only an annual risk assessment or risk assessment, but also to require an annual business impact analysis (BIA). A BIA is very important for contingency planning purposes because it specifies the different consequences of various types of system downtime or system unavailability. A BIA will also measure these consequences over time. Only when management has this information will it be able to make grounded and logical decisions about moving to a back-up site. A designee for Information Security management could be an outsourcing organization or a contingency planning consulting organization.

Related Policies: "New Technology Evaluation" and "Production System Risk Assessments."

Audience: Technical staff

Security Environments: Medium and high

11.01.03 Writing And Implementing Contingency Plans

1. Information Resource Classification

Policy: Computer Operations management must establish and use a logical framework for classifying all information resources by recovery priority that will permit the most critical information resources to be recovered first.

Commentary: This policy specifies which organizational unit is responsible for defining the categories and overall framework for prioritizing information resources. This will permit various contingency plans to be more readily coordinated, merged, and prioritized. The words "Computer Operations" could just as easily be changed to "Information Security" or some other organizational group. The framework could include categories like "mission critical must be recovered within one hour," "critical must be recovered within eight hours," and "all others must be recovered within 48 hours."

Related Policies: "Multi-User Application Criticality Rating."

Audience: Technical staff

Security Environments: All

2. Preparation And Maintenance Of Business Contingency Plans

Policy: Management must prepare, periodically update, and regularly test a business recovery plan that specifies how alternative facilities will be provided so workers can continue operations in the event of a business interruption.

Commentary: A business contingency plan deals with facilities and other business matters besides computers and communications systems. A computer and communications contingency plan is considerably narrower in scope. This policy is intended to supplement the policy dealing with disaster recovery plans because the business facilities will be necessary if the organization is going to remain operational. The workers who create business contingency plans are often not the same as those who are responsible for systems contingency planning. For example, physical security specialists may create business contingency plans, while information systems technicians may be focusing on system contingency planning. Nonetheless, a policy requiring business contingency planning is advisable, especially where subsidiaries and other decentralized management structures prevail.

Related Policies: "Computer Disaster Recovery Plans."

Audience: Management and technical staff

Security Environments: All

11.01.04 Business Continuity Planning Framework

1. Business And Computer Continuity Planning

Policy: A standard organization-wide process for developing and maintaining both business contingency plans and computer contingency plans must be documented and maintained by Information Systems management.

Commentary: This policy requires that a formal process exist for the preparation of both business contingency plans and computer contingency plans. To cover a wider variety of systems, the policy could be changed to reference "computer and communication system contingency plans" rather than simply "computer contingency plans." The planning process itself ordinarily would involve areas such as: identification and prioritization of critical business processes, identification of the risks facing the organization, assessment of the potential impacts of various types of emergencies and disasters, identifying and assigning responsibility for handling emergencies and disasters, documentation of procedures and processes, education of staff, and periodic testing of plans. The policy could be expanded to include mention of such specific activities. An Information Security group may define the standard process mentioned in the policy, although

Information Technology, Risk Management, Insurance, Security, Operations Planning, or other departments may also do this.

Related Policies: "Information Resource Classification" and "Exceptions To Policies."

Audience: Management and technical staff

Security Environments: All

2. Business Restoration Employee Expectations

Policy: Employees are expected to be present, and to assist to the best of their abilities, with the restoration of normal business activity after an emergency or a disaster disrupts Company X business activity.

Commentary: This policy is intended to inform employees that they are expected to participate in the restoration of normal business operations, including the reestablishment of computer and communications services. Some organizations place a policy like this in their employee handbook to ensure that there is no misunderstanding about what is expected during these stressful times. In the event of a disaster, some employees may wish to volunteer with various relief organizations. This policy informs them that they must attend to the affairs of Company X. Other employees may claim that it is not their job to assist with business recovery. This policy eliminates disputes on that point. It is unreasonable to expect that employees will view their job as more important than their family or personal assets, so the policy could be expanded to acknowledge the need to ascertain the safety of family and personal assets. This policy deals only with employees. Contrac-tors, temporaries, and consultants are not expected to assist in the same fashion because they do not have the same type of relationship with Company X.

Related Policies: "Computer Emergency Response Team."

Audience: End users

Security Environments: All

11.01.05 Testing, Maintaining, And Re-Assessing Business Continuity Plans

1. Reversion To Manual Procedures

Policy: If Company X critical business activities could reasonably be performed with manual procedures rather than computers, a manual computer contingency plan must be developed, tested, periodically updated, and integrated into computer and communication system contingency plans.

Commentary: This policy instructs management to look at the support of critical business activities through manual procedures. Sometimes people get locked into a way of looking at things, in this case thinking about business activities as always computer-supported. This policy requires management to look at the manual performance of ordinary business activities. For example, an automobile rental desk at an airport may have trouble working without computer support, but they can probably operate on a manual basis. In this case, clerks at the rental desk could have manual procedures to follow if the computer were down. These procedures might also require that price lists and other information be printed out every so often so that the hardcopy can be referenced when the computer system is down. Some organizations may wish to expand this policy to require the consideration of certain topics in a manual procedures contingency plan. Manual business procedures also can be the early steps in a business recovery plan. When this is the case, a contingency plan could cover the specific information that users must record manually, what business activities can be performed, and what restrictions apply.

Related Policies: "Computer Disaster Recovery Plans."

Audience: Technical staff

Security Environments: All

2. Off-Site Personnel Rotation

Policy: The workers who participate in off-site recovery operations with Company X information systems must be rotated regularly so that at all times at least two people will have the technical knowledge needed to perform each essential recovery task.

Commentary: This policy lets those managing off-site recovery activities know that they must include a job rotation process along with the work that they do. Sometimes job rotation is not considered, leaving the organization critically dependent on a select few technical people. If these few people were to be suddenly no longer available, then recovery operations would be very difficult, time-consuming, and expensive. Studies have revealed that 40% of small business do not open their doors after a disaster such as a tornado, an earthquake, or a flood. This is in large measure because adequate documentation and adequate cross-training have not been completed. If cross training and job rotation are required, this will also strongly encourage the development of current recovery documentation. This policy requires those involved with recovery planning to designate certain tasks as essential.

Related Policies: "Key Technical Jobs" and "Job Rotation."

Audience: Technical staff

Security Environments: All

3. Business Interruption Support Levels

Policy: Each year, user department management and Information Technology management must agree and document the support levels that will be provided in the event of a disaster or emergency.

Commentary: This policy establishes the type of technical and administrative support that will be provided in the event of a disaster or emergency. For example, departments with applications that are not highly critical, will not be restored at the same time as those of other departments. This policy protects Information Technology management or whoever is preparing a contingency plan because it documents the appropriate support levels. If these support requirements are in writing, users know they cannot blame Information Technology for certain problems about which they had been given notice, and they will be encouraged to pay more attention to contingency planning. Early in the development of a contingency plan, a policy like this may also foster the performance of a risk assessment to determine the impact of a disaster or an emergency. The policy could be expanded to require these support levels to be reviewed annually. This is recommended if there are many changes made to information systems. Because of independence in the decision-making process, this policy is especially important for those organizations dependent on client-server systems, local area networks, and other distributed computing systems.

Related Policies: "Emergency And Disaster Support Requirements," "Five-Category Application Criticality Classification Scheme," and "Preventive Maintenance."

Audience: Management and technical staff

Security Environments: All

4. Contingency Plan Testing

Policy: Computer and communication system contingency plans must be routinely tested and followed up with a brief report to top management detailing the results.

Commentary: This policy requires the periodic testing of contingency plans. Confidence in the ability to recover after a disaster or an emergency comes only from regular testing. Computer and contingency planning personnel can change, so periodic testing is necessary to ensure that previously-developed recovery strategies and procedures are relevant. The requirement of a report to top management keeps top management informed about contingency planning, requires the work to be documented, and encourages testing and adjustments to

the contingency plan. If an organization does not yet have a contingency plan, then the policy does not apply. Some organizations may want the policy to be more stringent, in which case a time frame for testing can be specified. Testing at regular intervals rather than at random moments is recommended, although it is somewhat less realistic. It is important to require those who performed the test to report deficiencies, even if these people do not yet have the resources or management permission to make the necessary repairs or adjustments.

Related Policies: "Computer Disaster Recovery Plans."

Audience: Management and technical staff

Security Environments: All

5. Telephone Number Testing

Policy: Each calendar quarter, Information Security staff must test and revise a call tree indicating every available telephone number for every worker involved in information-systems-related contingency planning, and disaster and emergency response.

Commentary: This policy requires the periodic testing and update of a call tree. A call tree lists telephone numbers including pager numbers, cell phone numbers, voice mail numbers, home phone numbers, and names, and sometimes, areas of responsibility. Because workers change jobs, residences, and phone numbers, it is important to ensure that a call tree contains current information. When a disaster or emergency takes place, this is no time to be calling directory assistance and trying to convince the operator that an unlisted number should in fact be disclosed. A call tree in many cases will be part of the computer emergency response team (CERT) documentation, but it is nonetheless necessary even if an organization does not have a CERT. This call tree includes those who do the planning, not just those charged with handling a response. This means that all involved personnel can be contacted when necessary.

Related Policies: "Contact Information" and "Computer-Related Access Numbers."

Audience: Technical staff

Security Environments: All

6. Contingency Planning And Systems Recovery Roles

Policy: The roles and responsibilities for both information systems contingency planning and information systems recovery must be reviewed and updated annually by Information Security management.

Commentary: This policy assigns responsibility for reviewing and updating information systems contingency planning roles and responsibilities. Sometimes these roles and responsibilities take the form of job descriptions and computer emergency response team procedural documentation, but they could show up in a wide variety of other documents. In some organizations, responsibility for reviewing and updating these roles and responsibilities is not clearly assigned, and because contingency planning and system recovery are both multi-departmental and multi-functional in nature, this work may not be properly completed.

Related Policies: "Information Security Management Committee" and "Back-Up Security Administrators."

Audience: Technical staff

Security Environments: All

12 COMPLIANCE

12.01 Compliance With Legal Requirements

12.01.01 Identification Of Applicable Legislation

1. Regulations And Requirements

Policy: All relevant statutory, regulatory, and contractual requirements must be defined and documented for each Company X information system.

Commentary: This policy ensures that all Company X information systems comply with all relevant legal, regulatory or contractual requirements. More and more regulations are being adopted that require specific application of information security controls. Some of these include prohibitions on the disclosure of customer account information, standards to protect security and confidentiality, and annual customer notification of privacy. This policy will require that the development of all information systems thoroughly consider, implement and document all relevant requirements.

Related Policies: "Software Copyright Notices."

Audience: Management and technical staff

Security Environments: All

12.01.02 Intellectual Property Rights

1. Software Development Source

Policy: Software that supports production business applications must be either developed in-house, or obtained from a known and reliable third-party vendor.

Commentary: This policy prevents workers from downloading free software over the Internet, some of which may contain malicious code. The policy also prevents computing environments from being built with technology that may not be regularly updated, that may not be robust, and that may not be supported by a solvent business. Free software also can create incompatibilities and unexpected results in an otherwise stable computing environment. This is another reason to be staunch in a prohibition against free software. While there are some good free software packages available over the Internet, each of these packages should be completely evaluated before they are permitted to be used on production machines. The evaluation would typically determine that good documentation is available, decent training is available, on-demand technical support is available, updates are regularly provided, and the vendor has a financially stable business. This policy can be implemented with a change control software package on a personal computer, which can prevent end users from making any changes to the software running on their personal computers unless initiated by approved administrators.

Related Policies: "Externally-Provided Software Testing."

Audience: End users and technical staff

Security Environments: All

2. Production Systems and Software Tools

Policy: Company X production information systems must run only those software tools that have been developed by legitimate and trusted vendors, professional associations, trade groups, or government agencies.

Commentary: This policy ensures that Company X uses only legitimate software from vendors who have been shown to be reliable and trustworthy. If an organization does not care what software is loaded and run on production systems, malicious code could be introduced to damage the system. This policy prevents an organization from being misled by third parties offering software, especially shareware or freeware, when these third parties are seeking a way to get onto the organization's systems. The policy is intended to prevent system administrators and others from simply downloading what appears to be useful software from the Internet, only later discovering that it has malicious code embedded therein. This policy does not address those situations in which a software package from an approved vendor includes code inserted by an unauthorized party.

Related Policies: "Externally-Provided Software Testing" and "Software Development Source."

Audience: Technical staff

Security Environments: All

3. Software Escrow

Policy: If third-party software is to be used for critical business activity, the vendor must either license source code to Company X or the vendor must provide accessibility to the source code through an escrow agreement with a third party.

Commentary: Under certain contractually-defined conditions, software escrow permits a purchasing organization to gain access to previously-restricted source code if the vendor does not satisfy its contractual terms or goes out of business. This policy is applicable to a wide variety of business relationships with a third-party software vendor including software leasing, rental, and purchase. This policy also may be appropriate in those cases where an application service provider or some other type of outsourcing organization is employed. In this policy, the words "application software" used for a "critical business activity" are deliberately ambiguous so that they will apply to a wide variety of software. For very large organizations, the scope of the policy could be expanded to include systems software but that is quite rare. For a definition of the word "critical," this policy assumes the existence of an approved data classification policy.

Related Policies: "Five-Category Application Criticality Classification Scheme," "Software Distributed To Third Parties," and "Software Maintenance."

Audience: Technical staff

Security Environments: Medium and high

4. Software In Escrow Verification

Policy: For each major release of software critical to Company X business and held in third-party escrow facilities an independent third party must verify that all necessary software and documentation have been received by the escrow agent.

Commentary: This policy ensures that existing software escrow arrangements provide the appropriate protection. If an independent auditor or some other third party does not verify that all necessary materials are on deposit at the escrow agent's premises, then Company X may be in trouble should the software vendor go out of business, discontinue a product, refuse to fix a major bug, or otherwise be in violation of an agreement they worked out with Company X. The existence of this policy ideally is communicated to both the software vendor and the escrow agent prior to establishing a software escrow arrangement. The policy will encourage both of them to strictly follow the terms and conditions of the contract. Instead of this policy, some organizations may feel comfortable with reports from the escrow agent indicating what has been received. Other organizations, such as the ones who adopt a policy like this, will want to have independent third party verify the materials that have been deposited at the escrow agent's premises. The escrow agent may not permit the user organization employees to gain access to the escrowed materials. This rule may require the use of a third party for auditing work.

Related Policies: "Software Escrow."

Audience: Technical staff

Security Environments: All

5. Information Attribution

Policy: Company X workers must always give proper credit to the source of information used for Company X purposes.

Commentary: This policy assists management in understanding the source of and reliability of information presented to it for review. The policy additionally alerts management to the existence of rights to the information that may have been ignored by a worker when preparing a report, or developing a new product. This behavior reduces the frequency of allegations that Company X improperly appropriated certain information. This policy also fosters an attitude respectful of intellectual property rights, which may be important when it comes to discouraging unauthorized software copying and other intellectual-property abuses. This policy additionally fosters responsible use of the Internet and electronic bulletin boards in that employees will be less likely to post information after eliminating reference to a source.

Related Policies: "Intellectual Property Labeling" and "Identity Misrepresentation."

Audience: All

Security Environments: All

6. Intellectual Property Labeling

Policy: All users who submit information for which they do not possess the copyright or any other right to the public area on the Company X web site or electronic bulletin board system must clearly indicate the source of the information.

Commentary: This policy clarifies the attribution of rights to information in what may otherwise be an ambiguous situation. It also clearly assigns responsibility for specifying ownership rights to the information submitted to a public area. The policy conveys the right of the web site operator or bulletin board system (BBS) operator to use posted information for marketing and other reasons without the need to get additional approval or pay royalties. Rather than being relevant just to web pages and BBSs, this policy is appropriate to any multi-organizational system such as commercial online services.

Related Policies: "Information Attribution" and "Labeling Management Decision Data."

Audience: All

Security Environments: All

7. Software Copyright Notices

Policy: All computer programs and program documentation owned by Company X must include appropriate copyright notices.

Commentary: Although in some jurisdictions no such explicit notice is required for copyrights to be enforceable, the existence of a notice has a deterrent effect. Other jurisdictions may require explicit notices. The places where copyright notices should appear can also be specified in the policy. For example, notices could occur on screen displays, source code listings, object code listings, or user manuals. The policy also may be expanded to include the wording needed in the particular jurisdiction. In some cases, the words "Electronic Archival Rights Reserved By Company X" also may be needed to restrict unauthorized inclusion of the material in online databases.

Related Policies: "Intellectual Property Rights."

Audience: Technical staff

Security Environments: All

8. Multiple Copies Of Information

Policy: Workers must not make multiple copies of material from any publications unless permission from the copyright Owner is obtained or this is both reasonable and customary.

Commentary: This policy prevents copyright problems before they evolve into a formal complaint. It is intended to communicate the meaning of the legal term "fair use," which permits copies to be made without compensating the copyright Owner. Some organizations may wish to expand the policy given here to include permissible single copies for personal use. The policy could also be expanded to instruct workers how to get permission before generating copies beyond the number that would generally be considered fair use. The policy deliberately does not mention a particular technology, so the copies could just as easily be made with a personal computer as they could by a duplicating machine.

Related Policies: "Intellectual Property Rights."

Audience: End users and technical staff

Security Environments: All

9. Software Licensing Agreement Reviews

Policy: The agreements for all computer programs licensed from third parties must be periodically reviewed.

Commentary: This policy will indicate that an organization is concerned about compliance with software license agreements, should Company X ever be taken to court for unauthorized copying. Checking compliance with license agreements is increasingly automated, for example on local area networks with inventory programs. These programs automatically survey the hardware and software in each personal computer (PC) or workstation connected to a network. The existence of a policy like this may also serve as a deterrent to users who may be tempted to make unauthorized copies. Some organizations may wish to restrict this policy to PCs and workstations, the small-scale systems environment in which most unauthorized copying takes place.

Related Policies: "Authorized Copies Of Software."

Audience: Management and technical staff

Security Environments: All

10. Software License Evidence

Policy: Whenever bundled systems are being procured, the source must provide written evidence of the software licenses conveyed.

Commentary: This policy is primarily intended for purchasing and procurement departments, although it is also relevant to any staff member who purchases computer and communications systems. Sources of bundled systems, such as original equipment manufacturers and value added resellers, in some instances make unauthorized copies of software. In the process, they violate copyright licenses. There are an increasing number of cases on record where personal computer systems are sold with software on the hard drive but the software is not properly licensed. To prevent recipient organizations from being responsible for copyright license violations, recipients should obtain written evidence that the licenses are legitimate. Because there may be disputes about what was said at the time of purchase, verbal assurances from the vendor are not sufficient.

Related Policies: "Software Copyright Notices" and "Software Licensing Agreement Reviews."

Audience: Technical staff

Security Environments: All

11. Authorized Copies Of Software

Policy: Management must make appropriate arrangements with all software vendors for additional licensed copies, if and when additional copies are needed for business activities.

Commentary: This policy ensures that management places orders for additional copies of needed software, rather than simply making unauthorized copies. Workers often claim they were required to make additional unauthorized copies because management did not provide them with the needed number of authorized copies. This policy prevents that claim from being the excuse for illegal software copying. This policy may be helpful in demonstrating that Company X intended to comply with its software licensing agreements.

Related Policies: "Software Licensing Agreement Reviews."

Audience: All

Security Environments: All

12. Making Copies Of Software

Policy: Third-party software in the possession of Company X must not be copied unless such copying is consistent with relevant license agreements and either management has previously approved of such copying, or copies are being made for contingency planning purposes.

Commentary: This policy is particularly relevant to personal computers, workstations, local area network servers, client-server systems, and other small-scale systems. This is because the small-scale systems environment is where most unauthorized copying takes place. This policy informs users that all copying must be consistent with license agreements. The policy also notifies users that copying may not be permitted, even if it is consistent with a license agreement, unless management permission is obtained or unless the copying is for contingency planning purposes.

Related Policies: "Master Copies Of Software."

Audience: End users and technical staff

Security Environments: All

13. Unauthorized Copyrighted Information And Software

Policy: Third-party copyrighted information or software that Company X does not have specific approval to store or use must not be stored on Company X systems or networks and must be removed by system administrators unless authorization from the rightful Owner can be provided by the involved users.

Commentary: Workers at some organizations are downloading copyrighted material from the Internet, electronic bulletin boards, online database services, and other public sources. In many instances, the copying is unauthorized and a violation of copyright laws. This policy is intended to inform users that they must not store these materials on Company X systems or networks. The policy is a good way to reinforce management's intent to uphold the copyrights of others. The policy implies that system administrators, internal auditors, and perhaps others have the right to browse through the file directories of users to identify unauthorized information and software. In some instances, the word "periodically" may be added to the policy, in which case there will be a regular user directory examination process. The effectiveness of this examination process may be easily thwarted by users employing encryption utilities, and for this and perhaps other reasons, Company X may wish to ban the use of encryption.

Related Policies: "Inappropriate Public Postings" and "Removing Offensive Material."

Audience: End users

Security Environments: All

14. Default Copyright Protection

Policy: Workers must investigate intellectual property rights for all material they discover on the Internet before using it for any other purpose.

Commentary: This policy prevents Company X workers from violating the intellectual property rights of other parties. By reminding users about copyrights, Company X also may be able to at least partially protect itself against damages associated with the illegal acts of its workers. This policy is not restricted to data and may help make a case that Company X does not in any way encourage or support unauthorized software copying.

Related Policies: "Unauthorized Copyrighted Information And Software" and "Unauthorized Software And Data Copies."

Audience: End users

Security Environments: All

15. Software Duplication

Policy: Users must not copy software provided by Company X to any storage media, transfer such software to another computer, or disclose such software to outside parties without written permission from Information Technology management.

Commentary: This policy ensures that users do not change the configuration of their systems or make any copies, transfers, or disclosures that might violate software vendors' licenses. The policy may be useful when it comes to controlling the distribution of proprietary software developed in-house. Commercial software is available that will permit this policy to be enforced automatically, in which case there will be no need for a written policy. But until software like this is generally used, a policy may be necessary. This policy does not interfere with normal business activities as long as adequate technical support is provided. When users must perform their own technical support, this policy will be problematic. This policy works best when users have a pre-installed software configuration that meets their needs, and when they have been given a separate policy about only using software that has been adopted as a standard.

Related Policies: "Software Copyright Notices" and "Critical Backup Files."

Audience: End users

Security Environments: All

16. Unauthorized Software And Data Copies

Policy: All users of Company X systems or the Internet must not make unauthorized copies of software or any copyrighted material that is not legally considered fair use without the permission of either the author or publisher.

Commentary: This policy is intended to clearly assign responsibility and legal culpability for unauthorized copying of both software and data. Because it is not feasible for management to supervise every act performed by workers, workers who make unauthorized copies are informed that they shoulder the risk of penalties. This policy is noteworthy in that it goes beyond the ordinary prohibition against making unauthorized copies of software, it specifically makes reference to making unauthorized copies of material taken from the Internet. A common example involves the graphics used on Internet home pages. Many users steal such graphics and use them elsewhere without obtaining the Owner's permission. It may not be possible for management to completely transfer blame for unauthorized copying. Discussion with internal legal counsel is highly advised before issuance of a policy such as this.

Related Policies: "Master Copies Of Software" and "Software Licensing Agreement Reviews."

Audience: End users

Security Environments: All

17. Unauthorized Copyrighted Material

Policy: Workers must not participate in any manner and at any time in the distribution, transfer, or exchange of illegal copies of any copyrighted material.

Commentary: This policy informs workers that Company X does not tolerate any illegal activity involving unauthorized duplication of copyrighted material. The policy is motivated by Internet sites that provide free but illegal copies of software, books, music, and other material, and that migrate rapidly across Internet sites in order to avoid detection or prosecution. The policy is also motivated by the sites that distribute the serial numbers needed to activate software that is not copy-protected. Visiting, contributing to, or taking copies from any of these and other related sites are all prohibited by the policy. The organization adopting this policy clarifies that it does not encourage a worker's involvement with these sites. This will show that the organization should not be held responsible for any damages sustained by third parties, even if the information systems of the policy-issuing organization were used by the involved worker.

Related Policies: "Software Duplication" and "Publicly-Modifiable Directories."

Audience: End users

Security Environments: All

18. Copyrighted Electronic Books

Policy: All electronic books or other text-based copyrighted works published by Company X on the Internet or on any other publicly-accessible networked system must be in bit-mapped form.

Commentary: This policy reflects the reluctance of publishers to post their copyrighted materials to the Internet. Many publishers legitimately fear that such publication would promptly lead to massive unauthorized copying and as a result their rights to the work would be irretrievably lost. To be able to post their work, or at least a part of it for marketing purposes, publishers have used bit-mapped versions. The intent of this approach is to thwart piracy, or misappropriation of copyrighted material, and it does make piracy a whole lot more difficult. This approach unfortunately means that the value of the posted material is also degraded because key word searches and other automated functions are unavailable. This policy will be superseded by encryption systems that will control the purchasing and distribution of copyrighted information on the Internet.

Related Policies: "Internet Monitoring For Information Use" and "Unauthorized Copyrighted Material."

Audience: Technical staff

Security Environments: All

19. Internet Monitoring For Information Use

Policy: The Legal department must monitor the Internet on at least a monthly basis for the unauthorized use of Company X trademarks, service marks, brand names, or copyrighted materials owned by Company X.

Commentary: This policy assigns a function that involves scanning the Internet on a regular basis to ensure that the organization's legal rights have not been infringed. Beyond trademark infringement and copyright infringement, this effort could include efforts to detect defamatory statements against the organization. The work could be performed by other departments, but the Legal department must follow-up with the other parties involved. Third-party services that perform this function can use special software to perform much of this work automatically. Certain public domain software can scan the Web looking for copyrighted materials including graphics. Search engines can be used to find occurrences of company names, trademarks, and service marks. Some organizations may also wish to see who is linking to their site. Organizations must take steps to protect their legal rights, or in some jurisdictions they may lose these legal rights.

Related Policies: "Electronic Mail Message Monitoring" and "Content Monitoring Responsibility."

Audience: Management

Security Environments: All

20. Use Of Third-Party Trademarks

Policy: Company X web and commerce sites must not use any other organization's trademarks or service marks anywhere unless the usage reflects the actual attributes of Company X products or services, and advance permission has been obtained from Company X corporate legal counsel.

Commentary: This policy prevents legal problems, bad publicity, and strained relations with competitors, business partners, or suppliers. The use of another organization's trademark or service mark can be perceived to be a device to deceptively bring people into one's own web site through search engines. This policy acknowledges the rights of third-party organizations to their own trademarks and service marks and takes a conservative position with respect to the use of these character strings. Beyond the avoidance of litigation, this policy may also help maintain good relations with prospective customers because complaints are minimized.

Related Policies: "Intellectual Property" and "Unofficial Web Pages."

Audience: Technical staff

Security Environments: All

21. Third-Party Confidentiality Agreements

Policy: Workers must not sign confidentiality agreements provided by third parties without the advance authorization of Company X legal counsel designated to handle intellectual property matters.

Commentary: In an effort to expedite discussions with suppliers, customers, and potential strategic partners, workers may sign third-party confidentiality agreements without thinking about it. They may thereby obligate their organization to pay royalties, should the organization later market a similar product or service. They may also cause their employer to be accused of stealing ideas, when the same ideas were already known by their employer. Similarly, by signing a confidentiality agreement, they may legally prohibit their organization from introducing a similar product or service. To avoid these and other unfortunate and detrimental outcomes, this policy requires all confidentiality agreements to be routed through internal legal counsel or designated external legal counsel.

Related Policies: "Non-Disclosure Agreements — Third Party."

Audience: End users

Security Environments: All

22. Review Of Trade Secrets And Copyrights

Policy: The Legal department, working in conjunction with Information Security management, must perform an annual intellectual property and information protection law review that includes the development of an inventory of the legal issues surrounding Company X

information, an assessment of the efficiency and effectiveness of the controls that address these issues, and a list of recommended changes for subsequent review and discussion by the Information Security management committee.

Commentary: This policy requires the Legal department and the Information Security department to pay attention to the legal issues associated with information security. These issues include trademark and service mark infringement, patent infringement, copyright violation, and privacy violation. Legal and regulatory requirements in many instances will dictate information systems requirements. In many organizations the legal and regulatory issues have not yet been adequately explored. These organizations are then at a great disadvantage because sometimes they are operating without adequate external guidance or assistance. This policy shifts the ordinary way of dealing with these legal matters from a reactionary approach to a proactive approach. It is necessary to make a clear distinction between this type of a legal and regulatory analysis and an information security risk assessment. Although some of the same topics may be addressed in each type of project, the two projects involve different methodologies, different specialists, and separate topics. Nothing in this policy is meant to imply that an outside consultant or some other third-party assistance cannot be used for this specialized work.

Related Policies: "Organization-Wide Information Security Risk Assessment" and "Declaration Of A Trade Secret."

Audience: Management

Security Environments: Medium and high

12.01.03 Safeguarding Of Organizational Records

1. Customer Log Information

Policy: The individuals maintaining logs reflecting the activities of computer users or those served by computers, must delete information that identifies users or persons served as soon as the Company X relationship with these individuals has been completed.

Commentary: This policy preserves the privacy of an individual user or person served with computers. If Company X no longer has a need for the information contained in the log, then this information must be promptly deleted. For example, a library would delete the identity of the borrower of a book as soon as the

book is returned and found to be in good condition. The words "as soon as" may be too immediate for some organizations. They may wish to substitute the words "within 30 days from the time when." This policy does not restrict Company X from keeping statistics about business activity. It only restricts the keeping of information permitting this activity to be traced to individuals. A library could keep statistics about which books are most frequently borrowed without the need for details about the specific customers who borrowed these books. The word "customer" in the title may need to be modified to suit the organization. Common alternatives include "client," "patient," and "user." This policy may need to be modified to reflect the fact that certain logs will need to be retained until such time as payments have been received, accounts have been balanced, or the security of a computer system has been shown to be acceptable. For example, computer user activity logs may need to be kept for three months. A time period like this may be necessary for management to be satisfied that there were no computer crimes, system crashes, or other incidents for which the logs might be of assistance.

Related Policies: "Customer Activity Log Disclosure."

Audience: Management and technical staff

Security Environments: All

2. Personal Information Retention

Policy: Personal information held in Company X information systems must be deleted when the information is both no longer needed to conduct business, and when it is no longer needed to meet legal or regulatory requirements.

Commentary: This policy deletes personal or private information soon after it becomes unnecessary, preventing further use for unauthorized purposes. This policy also prevents additional disclosures that could violate the privacy of the individuals described in the records. The policy is deliberately vague about the meaning of the words "no longer needed." If Company X wanted to retain an individual's address and phone number for future notices about product upgrades or enhancements, that would be a business purpose, and therefore permissible under this policy. This policy also has a secondary intention and that is to keep business records to a minimum to thereby assist in their economical and orderly management. The policy also reduces historical records that might be the target of discovery legal proceedings that find incriminating information that could be used by an opposing party in a lawsuit.

Related Policies: "Customer Log Information" and "Information Retention Period."

Audience: End users

Security Environments: All

3. Transaction Log Destruction

Policy: Company X must destroy the transaction log entry after a transaction has been completed and after the period in which a refund might be provided has elapsed.

Commentary: This policy routinely destroys the information that could be used to compromise the privacy of customers. This policy is suitable not only for internal consumption, but also for public release. The policy acknowledges that the archival storage of transaction logs introduces serious threats to individual privacy. Opposition from marketing management may occur when adopting this policy. Marketing specialists will claim that they need transaction log information for a data warehouse, for data mining, and for the generation of customer profiles in order to provide better service. This policy is likely to be adopted only by conscientious organizations who truly believe in safeguarding the privacy of customers, and who understand how transaction profiles can be serious privacy risks. Nothing in this policy prevents an organization from gathering statistics about which products are selling well, or when these products are bought because all such information could be provided on a general statistical basis. Some accounting information must be maintained for tax and financial reporting purposes. This information can link to a particular credit card number or some other payment information rather than to customer name, social security number, or some other personal identifiers.

Related Policies: "Electronic Mail Message Destruction" and "Private And Identification Information Linkage."

Audience: End users and technical staff

Security Environments: All

4. Sensitive Information Retention

Policy: A retention period must be assigned to all sensitive information.

Commentary: This policy encourages disposal of sensitive information when it is no longer needed. This reduces the chances of it falling into the hands of unauthorized persons. The information may be classified as sensitive at the time it is destroyed. Simple disposal is generally not appropriate for sensitive information. A separate policy should specify destruction methods. This policy facilitates disposal of the information at the proper time, which will reduce storage costs. The policy can be modified to include words that claim that, in the absence of a specific date for disposal, a date when a decision about the date of disposal will be made may be used. If this option is provided, then a contact name and phone number may be needed. This policy assumes the existence of a policy that defines the term "sensitive."

Related Policies: "Hardcopy Disposal," "Four-Category Data Classification," "Information Retention Period," and "Archival Storage Retention Schedule."

Audience: All

Security Environments: Medium and high

5. Vital Record Identification

Policy: Department managers must identify and maintain a current list of the vital records that their department needs to restore operations following a disaster.

Commentary: This policy is intended to clearly assign responsibility for the identification and maintenance of a list of vital records, sometimes called essential records. The fact that department managers must prepare and maintain the list requires them to think about the information that their department absolutely needs. This list can be used for contingency planning and backup procedure purposes. Some organizations may want to define vital records more explicitly. They could, for example, mention the information needed to conduct ordinary business transactions, recreate the Company X financial and legal position, and preserve the rights of the company and its staff and customers. A definition of a disaster also may be appropriate. In some organizations, a worksheet is distributed by the contingency planning staff. This worksheet asks questions to help department managers identify vital records and the appropriate frequency of backups for this information. This policy would generally be distributed only to department managers.

Related Policies: "Copies Of Sensitive, Critical, Or Valuable Information" and "Business Source Document Retention."

Audience: Management

Security Environments: All

6. Vital Record Storage

Policy: Vital business records must be kept in locked, fireproof safes whenever they are not being used for business purposes.

Commentary: The intention of this policy is not only to ensure that the organization specifically designates some records as vital business records, but also to ensure that they protect these records against fire. Sometimes these records take the form of business contracts, minutes of board of directors meetings, filings with various government agencies, and tax returns. These are often in paper form because they include hand-rendered signatures. Fire is one of the most common causes of damage to paper records, and this policy ensures that the vital business records will continue to be available even if an office burns to the ground. Some organizations may wish to specify what type of fireproof safe is to be used for this purpose. Keeping these records on-site permits an additional level of physical access control to be employed. For example, the safes could be located in a locked closet.

Related Policies: "Vital Record Identification" and "Destruction Of Information."

Audience: Management

Security Environments: Medium and high

7. Information Retention Period

Policy: Information that is not specifically listed on the Information Retention Schedule must be retained only for as long as necessary.

Commentary: This policy specifies the retention periods for various types of information. Information is broken into those types listed on an information retention schedule, and those types not listed on the schedule. For example, financial, tax, and medical information will be listed on a schedule, while information about inventory on hand for certain products will not. Often the Legal department prepares a schedule based on local laws and regulations. One attractive aspect of the approach of this policy is that information types listed on the schedule can change, whereas the words in the policy remain the same. This policy recognizes that the retention of information beyond the time when it is needed slows down information retrieval processes, and may also subject Company X to legal problems. This policy could be modified so the reader is referred to the Records Management department or departmental management in the event that there is doubt about the proper retention period. The policy could be expanded to permit extended retention of information in the event that legal proceedings may require it, if outside approval is needed for disposal or destruction, or if the information might help with the collection of a past-due account receivable.

Related Policies: "Archival Storage Retention Schedule" and "Sensitive Information Retention."

Audience: All

Security Environments: All

8. Archival Storage Retention Schedule

Policy: All financial accounting, tax accounting, and legal records must be retained for a period of at least seven years and all other records must be retained for a period of at least five years.

Commentary: This policy definitively specifies the minimum time frames that certain types of records must be retained. After these time periods, the records can be discarded without legal violation. Some organizations may want to add a sentence to this policy requiring the destruction of such records after the retention period has run out. Destruction will prevent these records from being used by opponents in a legal discovery process. The policy may also specify time frames for information in certain forms, such as electronic mail messages, rather than just for information types. Legal counsel should be consulted to determine the appropriate time periods for the local jurisdiction, industry, and existing contracts. This policy uses broad information categories in the policy itself to describe different retention requirements. The emphasis in this policy is on making sure that information is retained at the very least for the specified period of time.

Related Policies: "Information Retention Period," "Data Retention Schedule," "Hardcopy Disposal," and "Electronic Mail Message Handling."

Audience: All

Security Environments: All

9. Data Retention Schedule

Policy: All Company X information must be securely retained according to a schedule published by the Legal department.

Commentary: The intention of this policy is only to define who sets the retention periods for information. Generally it will be the Legal department, but it also may be a Records Management department or an Information Security department. Some organizations may want to expand on the words "securely retained" so as to clarify where and how the information should be stored. These storage requirements could for example vary based on data sensitivity, criticality, and value.

Related Policies: "Archival Storage Retention Schedule" and "Information Retention Period."

Audience: Management and technical staff

Security Environments: All

10. Business Source Document Retention

Policy: Business source documents and original electronic input files must be retained until the related transactions have been completed, a management review of the records incorporating these transactions has been performed, and a period in which the transactions may be disputed has passed.

Commentary: The intention behind this policy is to ensure that paper or electronic source documents are not destroyed prematurely. An example of a source document is the application form that people complete when they are seeking a job at a company. Certain information from the application form frequently gets entered into a computer system, at which point the application form becomes a source document. Because many organizations do not put all information appearing on a source document into a computer, and because this process often involves errors, it is important to retain the source document until the transaction is complete. Management may not have enough information about a candidate to make an employment decision. They may then go back to the source document or application to gather additional data. Management review is necessary to ensure that the transaction was completed in accordance with management's intentions. This requirement permits the source documents to be used for audits, for example to reconcile the accounting records. The policy requires the time period for a dispute to have elapsed, so that the source document can be discarded without problems.

Related Policies: "Information Retention Period," "Business Source Document Retention Period," and "Archival Storage Retention Schedule."

Audience: Management and technical staff

Security Environments: All

11. Business Source Document Retention Period

Policy: Business source documents containing input data must be retained for at least 90 days beyond the date when this information was entered into the Company X computer system.

Commentary: This policy preserves original information that may be important should there be computer problems or data entry errors. The retained source documents also may be useful for quality control or auditing purposes. There is nothing special about the 90-day retention period. The retention period will vary based on industry practice, the nature of the information involved, local laws and regulations, and other considerations. Legal counsel should be consulted on this point. It gives operations management a standard that they can use to determine when source documents may be destroyed, preferably by shredding or by some other secure means.

Related Policies: "Business Source Document Retention" and "Archival Storage Retention Schedule."

Audience: Management and technical staff

Security Environments: All

12. Application Transaction Data Retention

Policy: All application transaction data must be maintained in a protected state until the full backup of all related production master files has been completed.

Commentary: This policy specifies an absolute minimum time period for the retention of transaction or input data. Beyond that time period, the Owner can specify additional retention requirements, and these may include off-site storage. The reason for the absolute minimum retention period is so that the application transaction data can be used as a reference if the related application program crashes or otherwise experiences some trouble and the input data must be resubmitted. The policy is deliberately silent with respect to the ways to ensure that the application transaction data will be protected. The specific ways to do this should be determined by the information Owner, preferably with advice from an in-house information security specialist. The words "transaction data" in some environments can be replaced with the words "source records."

Related Policies: "Business Source Document Retention Period" and "Pre-Processing Backup."

Audience: Technical staff

Security Environments: All

13. Destruction Of Information

Policy: All Company X information must be destroyed or disposed of when no longer needed.

Commentary: This policy keeps business records and files to a minimum and thereby eliminates unneeded records. This process is sometimes referred to as purging. The process can help eliminate information that could be used against the organization, and that might be disclosed during a legal discovery process. An important addition to this policy may be a data dictionary. A data dictionary may be used to define what types of data exist within an organization, where this data exists, how old the data is, and what controls apply to the data.

Related Policies: "Personal Information For Business Functioning," "Archival Storage Retention Schedule," "Archival Storage Directory," "Time-Sensitive Information," and "Hardcopy Disposal."

Audience: Management and technical staff

Security Environments: All

14. Record Destruction

Policy: Workers must not destroy or dispose of potentially important Company X records or information without specific advance management approval.

Commentary: This policy informs workers that they must not destroy or dispose of potentially important information unless prior management approval has been received. This policy should be supported with other guidance listing the time periods for which different types of information must be kept. This is often referred to as a data retention schedule. This policy indirectly holds management responsible for the destruction of records and information. This is desirable as a way to ensure management oversight of this important area. The policy is also a way to avoid problems where records are destroyed, then management disclaims any knowledge of the activities described in the records. Restricting the persons authorized to perform the destruction of records and information is another way to address the problem handled by this policy.

Related Policies: "Information Destruction Personnel."

Audience: All

Security Environments: All

15. Record Destruction Schedule

Policy: Workers must not destroy Company X records unless these records appear on a list of records authorized for destruction, or can be destroyed according to instructions appearing in the Company X Records Retention and Disposition Schedule.

Commentary: This policy informs workers that they may not destroy Company X records unless specifically authorized to do so by written documents. Without such specific instructions, workers may destroy records to obscure unauthorized acts, or innocently destroy records that later prove to be useful. Some organizations may wish to expand the exceptions mentioned in the policy to include verbal authorization by the organizational archivist or information Owner. The authorized destruction list typically includes rough drafts that have not been circulated, copies made for short-term use, reference material, outdated publications, superseded backup copies, and blank forms.

Related Policies: "Sensitive Information Destruction Procedures."

Audience: End users

Security Environments: All

16. Data Destruction Moratorium

Policy: Whenever an electronic discovery request is received by Company X, all organized and periodic electronic data destruction activities must immediately be placed on hold until the Legal department determines whether these destruction activities jeopardize sought-after data.

Commentary: This policy notifies system administrators, data archivists, and computer operators that they must be ready to stop normal data destruction processes immediately if and when they receive notice from the Legal department. The discovery process involves an opposing party in a lawsuit requesting certain internal records in the possession of the defendant. If the defendant negligently permits a data destruction process to proceed after a discovery notice has been received, the organization may suffer legal sanctions, and the defendant's position in the case may be damaged. The policy could be expanded to include other types of legal requests for information such as a subpoena. The existence of a policy such as this is an indication that

Company X intends to fully comply with legal requirements. Some organizations may wish to go beyond the requirements of this policy, including the establishment of a formal process for the immediate notification of all internal parties who engage in organized and periodic data destruction activities. An end user deleting files from his or her hard drive to free-up disk space is not intended to be an organized and periodic data destruction process, and therefore does not fall within the purview of this policy. The end user should, however, be personally notified if their personal computer might contain sought-after information.

Related Policies: "Personal Information Retention" and "Electronic Mail Message Destruction."

Audience: Technical staff

Security Environments: All

17. Sensitive Information Retention For Destruction

Policy: Workers must not discard sensitive information in publicly-accessible trash containers and must retain sensitive information until it can be shredded or destroyed with approved methods.

Commentary: Workers may simply throw away sensitive information. Without thinking, they may discard sensitive documents that can be scavenged by industrial spies, hackers, and other interested parties. This policy requires workers to retain sensitive information until they can dispose of it properly. Nowhere in the policy is hardcopy paper mentioned. The policy is applicable to floppy disks and other ways to capture sensitive information. To make the policy more readily understood by readers, some may wish to specifically mention different ways that sensitive information can be recorded. This policy recognizes that many workers are on the road, away from the office where shredders, degaussers, and related information destruction equipment may be located. The policy is equally applicable to mobile workers as it is to telecommuters.

Related Policies: "Security Requirements For Telecommuters" and "Hardcopy Disposal."

Audience: End users

Security Environments: All

18. Security Violation And Problem Information Retention

Policy: Information describing all reported information security problems and violations must be retained for a period of three years.

Commentary: This policy informs management that certain important information security-related information must not be destroyed. The information referred to in the policy is helpful when performing risk assessments, planning information security projects, and developing budgets. It also may be useful for prosecution or disciplinary actions. The policy applies to computer logs and internal correspondence, and notes from secret investigations. Management may want to quickly destroy certain information for fear that it will be used to discredit them. Some organizations may want to forgo this policy because they may want the flexibility to destroy certain information for fear that parties opposing the organization in a lawsuit could gain access to the information, and thereby achieve an advantage in court. This concern can be dealt with by adding words such as "unless approved in advance by corporate counsel." In support of the notion that information describing information security problems is valuable, certain government regulations now require the reporting of information security problems to government regulators. The scope of the policy could be changed to deal with all security problems and violations, not just those related to information security.

Related Policies: "Violation And Problem Analysis" and "External Violation Reporting."

Audience: Management and technical staff

Security Environments: All

12.01.04 Data Protection And Privacy Of Personal Information

1. Private Personal Effects And Communications

Policy: Workers must not bring personal effects to Company X premises or use Company X systems for private communications without understanding that these may be searched or randomly monitored.

Commentary: This policy notifies workers that they are taking a risk if they bring private personal effects to work or if they have private personal communications while they are at work. The policy clearly defines the workplace as a public space rather than a private space. The policy is notably friendly in that it tells workers how to maintain their privacy, all the while reinforcing the fact that Company X information systems should be used only for business purposes, and the fact that Company X information systems may be monitored. The policy implicitly acknowledges that there will be some personal use of Company X information systems. The policy can be used as a defense against worker allegations that they have been spied upon unjustly or unlawfully.

Related Policies: "Immediate Terminations."

Audience: End users

Security Environments: All

2. Pretext Personal Data Collection

Policy: Company X must not at any time gather personal information using misrepresentations or pretext statements about its right to receive such information.

Commentary: This policy assures customers and prospects that Company X does not engage in an unethical and, in some jurisdictions illegal practice. This practice involves making allegations about an entity's right to receive certain personal information when these statements are in fact false. For example, a private investigator may tell a bank that he or she is an employer and that he or she is considering hiring a certain person. The private investigator may then ask whether the individual has bounced checks, been late with payments, or otherwise managed their account poorly. Thinking that the requestor has a right to this information, the bank may reveal this information. The statements made by the investigator would then be pretext requests. The policy presented here is intended to assure those reading a privacy statement that the adopting organization does not engage in this type of behavior as a way to circumvent privacy policies, regulations, or legislation. The policy addresses only actions taken in an effort to obtain personal information. It does not address blocking the requests of others. This is because in most cases the organization possessing the private information is not going to conduct an investigation into the background of the requestor. If the request seems reasonable, the information will be provided.

Related Policies: "Use Of Investigators."

Audience: End users

Security Environments: All

3. Privacy Rights Waiver

Policy: Company X must retain the right to release private and confidential information to outside parties in order to collect outstanding bills or to otherwise compel performance with contractual terms and conditions.

Commentary: This policy clarifies to outside parties who may have provided Company X with personal information, and to internal workers, that there are some limitations to the privacy rights that the organization has published. For example, Company X may need to go to court to require a customer to pay their bill, but the process of finding the facts in court will necessitate the release of personal information. Company X does not want to restrict its own ability to collect bills, requiring the necessity of a policy like this if other privacy assurances have been adopted. Those concerned about abuse of this right might consider inclusion of words in the policy that describe a process by which the legitimacy of a claim is verified prior to public release of personal information.

Related Policies: "Exceptions To Policies" and "Information Retention Period."

Audience: End users

Security Environments: All

4. Disclosures Of Private Information

Policy: Private information records must be disclosed only to those personnel who are actively engaged in a professional relationship with the individual or when the individual provides written authorization.

Commentary: This policy clarifies when the disclosure of private information is permissible even though the individual involved has not expressly given consent. For example, if a patient in a hospital is in a coma, and is therefore unable to give consent, this policy will permit doctors not previously associated with the patient to view the patient's records and to assist with treatment.

While this policy is found in the health care industry, it could be adapted to suit other industries as well. A telephone company could use it to define who obtains access to customer calling patterns. The policy is desirable because it minimizes the paperwork associated with the consent process, but at the same time establishes a minimum privacy protection level. The policy is also desirable because it permits the organization to disclose private data in order to safeguard the welfare of other parties.

Related Policies: "Blocking Private Information Disclosures" and "Personal Record Usage."

Audience: End users

Security Environments: All

5. Collection Of Private Information

Policy: Company X workers and information systems must not collect private information unless this effort has been approved in advance by corporate legal counsel.

Commentary: The purpose of this policy is to keep the issuing organization out of trouble when it comes to collecting private information. It is better to never have collected the information than to worry about protecting it, using it only for approved purposes, and releasing it only to authorized recipients. This approach is particularly well-suited to Internet commerce businesses that operate in many different countries. Rather than having to keep track of all the relevant laws about private information handling, this policy makes it possible to safely ignore many of the issues. Many businesses do not require personal information for their activities, and for them the most economical and most expedient way to address privacy issues is to simply forbid the collection of such data. The policy does not prohibit the collection of any private data forever. It is possible to collect race data, for example, if a government agency required the compilation of an anti-discrimination report.

Related Policies: "Prospective Employee Information" and "Message Content Restrictions."

Audience: End users

Security Environments: Low

6. Personal Information For Business Functioning

Policy: Company X must collect, process, store, and disseminate only that information that is necessary for the proper functioning of its business.

Commentary: This policy can be expanded to prohibit the collection of information about employee personal activities performed after hours that do not affect business matters. This policy preserves the privacy rights of employees, customers, and others who may have some contact with the organization. This policy simplifies the information systems by keeping the amount of information retained by Company X to a minimum. The scope of this policy is broader than just privacy matters. It pertains to all information. The policy does not provide detailed guidance about determining whether certain information is necessary. This is a deliberate omission because both the decision process and the information to which it pertains may change dramatically over time. An organizational data dictionary also may be an important supplement to this policy.

Related Policies: "Asset Inventory — Information" and "Destruction Of Information."

Audience: All

Security Environments: All

7. Freedom Of Speech Information

Policy: Company X must not collect information about worker expressions of freedom of speech.

Commentary: This policy can be expanded to prohibit the collection of information about employee personal activities performed after hours that do not affect business matters. If management collects such free speech and expression information, it may result in workers being afraid to express themselves lest management judge it adversely. This policy builds employee trust for his or her employer because it shows the employer respects and wants to support employee rights like privacy. The term "worker" found in the policy could be substituted with appropriate distinctions such as "employee," "temporary," or "contractor."

Related Policies: "Right To Free Speech."

Audience: Management and technical staff

Security Environments: All

8. Private Information Collection Approval

Policy: Before Company X workers collect private information about workers, customers, or other people, the need for such information must be documented and approved by Human Resources management.

Commentary: This policy is intended to limit the collection of private information. This will reduce the need for special controls to protect newly-collected private information. This policy also indirectly prevents Company X management from keeping secret databases about employees, or from establishing covert performance monitoring systems. While originally intended for government use, this policy is equally applicable to private sector organizations that want to control the cost of information security.

Related Policies: "Performance Monitoring Information" and "Database Indexes Containing Private Information."

Audience: Management

Security Environments: All

9. Private Data Collection

Policy: The collection of private data by Company X workers must be performed by lawful means, and only for a purpose related to the activities of Company X.

Commentary: This policy makes it look like an organization is doing something about privacy, when it is not. This policy is a public relations ploy rather than a substantial control that actually improves the privacy of individuals. The policy holds the issuing organization to nothing substantive that it would not otherwise be required to achieve. The policy provides a means to terminate employees who deviate from these limits, but the employees probably could have been terminated for other reasons. This policy is included here because it is fairly common, and so that it can be compared to other policies that have some substance. This policy is not included in this book because it is recommended.

Related Policies: "Private Information Collection Approval" and "Personal Information For Business Functioning."

Audience: End users

Security Environments: All

10. Surreptitious Collection Of Private Information

Policy: Company X computer and communications systems must not collect private data from customers or potential customers without having obtained their clear and unambiguous consent.

Commentary: This policy improves the Company X public image and customer loyalty. By prohibiting clandestine private data gathering, customers and potential customers are given more confidence that they know all about the private information handling practices at Company X. An example involves automatic number identification (ANI) or caller-ID. ANI captures telephone callers' phone numbers without the potential customers' or existing customers' consent. Some organizations then use this information for follow-up telemarketing calls. Some organizations may also sell these numbers to other organizations without the consent of the callers. This policy prohibits the collection of ANI information in the absence of the callers' consent. This policy is a manifestation of a more general idea that people should be the Owners of the information that portrays them.

Related Policies: "Systems Monitoring Tools," "Electronic Monitoring Areas," "Use Of Telephone Conference Or Recording Technology," and "Collection Of Private Information."

Audience: Management and technical staff

Security Environments: All

11. Private Information Collection Consent

Policy: Company X must obtain written consent from customers before it records any information about them in a computerized information system.

Commentary: This policy takes a pro-privacy position, not permitting information about customers to even be entered into a computer system unless these customers have specifically given written consent. This policy prohibits targeted marketing campaigns, such as direct mail campaigns or telemarketing calls to specific types of people. Some organizations will consider these restrictions on their marketing activities to be unacceptable, and they should not adopt this policy unless they are compelled to do so by law. The policy permits paper records until such time as this customer permission has been obtained. If the adopting organization is a health care organization, it should replace the word "customer" with the word "patient."

Related Policies: "Private Information Collection Approval" and "Collection Of Private Information."

Audience: Technical staff

Security Environments: Medium and high

12. Information Collection Notice

Policy: In every instance where personally-identifiable information is collected, an explicit and understandable notice must be provided at the time and place the information is collected.

Commentary: This policy is intended to clarify when and where a notice about information collection should be provided. The policy places the greatest emphasis on collection of personally-identifiable information, such as an electronic mail address, and requires all web locations where such collection is being performed to be marked irrespective of user knowledge or participation in the collection process. If electronic mail addresses were collected automatically from user web browsers when users visited a web site, this fact would need to be disclosed. Of lesser concern is information that is not personally-identifiable. Because this latter type of information is not associated with any particular person, the potential for abuse is considerably less, and this fact is reflected in the lack of need for a notice. Some organizations may wish to mention an exception where private information may be collected secretly, such as investigation of a suspected crime or an allegedly abusive activity.

Related Policies: "Monitoring And Recording Activity" and "Customer Anonymity."

Audience: Technical staff

Security Environments: All

13. Children's Personal Information Collection

Policy: Personal information about children must not be collected by any Company X information system without obtaining clear and unambiguous consent from the child's parents or guardians.

Commentary: This policy notifies technical staff that they must not gather personal information from children unless parental or guardian consent is obtained. Just how this consent is to be obtained is deliberately not stated in this policy. Ideally, this consent would be through an electronic mail message signed by a parent with a digital signature that was verifiable through a digital certificate. This can be rather time consuming, so something more expedient will in most instances be involved. For example, the provision of a valid credit card number is often deemed sufficient evidence that one is an adult. This policy is motivated by the increasing use of the Internet to gather personal information about people, notably children. Children sometimes do not have the sophistication to protect their own privacy, so their parents or guardians must perform this role. The policy is not specific to the Internet, because such information might be gathered by other means, for example through the telephone. The policy also establishes that Company X is conscientious. This policy could, in slightly modified form, be posted on a web site. The policy deliberately refrains from stating how the information is gathered. It might be explicitly solicited through user data entry and a web form, or it might be automatically gathered through user activity logging software.

Related Policies: "Adult Material Access" and "Private Data System Approval."

Audience: Technical staff

Security Environments: All

14. Personal Information Distribution

Policy: Access to any collection of personal information about potential customers and others with whom Company X has a business relationship must be strictly controlled on a need-to-know basis, and unless consent is obtained, the information must not be sold, exchanged, or distributed to any third party.

Commentary: This policy permits certain information to be gathered for business purposes, and preserves the individual's privacy by not permitting it to be distributed to third parties. Prohibition against unapproved distribution to third parties is a way to ensure that the information will not be used in a manner that is unintended by the individual. The policy permits the information to be used for internal purposes, including purposes other than those originally intended. This would, for example, permit data mining where new relationships are discovered between various types of customer data. The policy does not require the individual to agree in advance about the collection of the information. This policy may be an acceptable compromise for some businesses. Other businesses may believe that this policy grants the individual additional rights to

data about them. These businesses will want to exchange mailing lists and other collections of personal information without contacting their customers. Some organizations may wish to specify the need for consent when dealing with certain types of information, but no need for consent when dealing with other types of information. The policy does not imply that personal information distribution required by law must go through the consent process. Some organizations may wish to specify this in the policy.

Related Policies: "Surreptitious Collection Of Private Information."

Audience: Management and technical staff

Security Environments: All

15. Customer Information Collection

Policy: Company X computer-supported procedures must not require the provision of customer personal information that is unnecessary for the completion of a transaction, or unnecessary for the provision of products or services.

Commentary: The policy is intended to simplify transactions and permit customers to decide not to provide certain personal information. A notice that the provision of certain personal information is optional may be added to certain paper forms, or be provided over the phone when collecting personal information. Some organizations may wish to mention the need for this notice in the policy. For example, a customer sending in a product warranty registration card can simply choose not to answer a question about his or her income. The registration process will proceed without this information. This policy says nothing about requesting certain personal information, it only says that this information will never be required. Market research and other efforts to understand customers will not be hindered. The policy does not interfere with the collection of necessary personal information, such as the collection of a social security number for the completion of certain income tax documents.

Related Policies: "Private Information Collection Approval."

Audience: Management and technical staff

Security Environments: All

16. Private Information Collection Methods

Policy: Company X must employ the least intrusive methods available to gather private information about its customers, prospects, employees, and others associated with its organization.

Commentary: This policy is intended to assure customers, prospects, employees, and others that the issuing organization is deliberately trying to respect their privacy, and deliberately attempting to keep the burden of data gathering to a minimum. A statement such as this could be useful for marketing purposes, offering another reason to do business with the issuing organization. This policy assumes that the issuing organization has integrated customer records rather than isolated customer databases that serve various purposes.

Related Policies: "Surreptitious Collection Of Private Information" and "Customer Information Collection."

Audience: End users

Security Environments: All

17. Biometric Information Collection

Policy: Personal biometric information may not be captured by any Company X information systems unless the individual described has been previously notified of and has consented to the capture.

Commentary: This policy prevents surreptitious collection of personal biometric information that could later be used to perpetrate a fraud or violate the privacy of the individual described by the information. A fraud could take place if the information was incorporated into a driver's license or some other counterfeit identification badge. Privacy violation could take place if biometric information were used to masquerade as the individual in order to obtain information that would otherwise be restricted. Covert collection of biometric information might also be a serious publicity problem if it later was revealed that such information was being collected without the knowledge or consent of individuals. This policy assumes that strong mechanisms to protect such biometric information are in place. This policy could be modified to specifically recognize an exception involving the investigation of alleged criminal activity. This exception was not written into the suggested policy because the data capturing process is most often performed by law enforcement staff, not Company X staff or information systems.

Related Policies: "Private Information Collection Approval" and "Positive Identification For System Usage."

Audience: Technical staff

Security Environments: Medium and high

18. Biometric Information Transfer

Policy: Workers must not provide personal biometric information to third parties unless compelled to do so by law.

Commentary: This policy assures individuals who use biometric systems that their personal biometric data will not be released to third parties. This should be of particular concern to every person who is registered in a biometric system because such personal data could be used to commit identity theft. For example, fingerprint data could be used to perform an online identification process, and if a thief had another person's data he or she could masquerade as that other person. Biometric data could also be used for purposes other than those to which the user agreed when he or she enrolled in the biometric system. This policy assures those who are considering enrolling in a biometric system that there are no ulterior motives. The organization gathering this special type of personal data could use it in new ways, but the risk of unauthorized uses is markedly reduced if the information is not shared with third parties.

Related Policies: "Biometric Information Collection."

Audience: End users

Security Environments: Medium and high

19. Privacy Expectations And Information Stored On Organization Systems

Policy: Company X management must notify all computer system users that at any time and without prior notice that Company X may examine archived electronic mail, personal file directories, hard disk drive files, and other information stored on Company X information systems.

Commentary: This policy informs computer users that the information they store, transmit, or otherwise process through Company X information systems is subject to management review. This will encourage them to use such information systems for business purposes only. It will also help to deter unethical or illegal activities. The policy is particularly pro-monitoring rather than pro-privacy, but at least establishes worker expectations.

Related Policies: "Electronic Mail Privacy," "Backup Information Review," and "Personal File Privacy."

Audience: End users

Security Environments: All

20. Employee Off-the-Job Behavior

Policy: Management must not pry into the lives of employees or otherwise seek to manage off-the-job behavior unless it impairs the ability of the employee to perform regular job assignments, or unless it affects the reputation of Company X in a significant way.

Commentary: The intention of the policy is to restrict management from prying into the lives of employees. Certain events, such as an employee's stay in the hospital and the circumstances surrounding this stay should be discussed with the employee's manager. Romantic liaisons between coworkers also can be discussed because this could affect employee performance. The policy is written in such a general way that a wide latitude for interpretation is provided. The policy can also be used to discourage behavior that may lead to sexual harassment or privacy invasion lawsuits.

Related Policies: "Intellectual Property Rights" and "Prospective Employee Information."

Audience: Management

Security Environments: All

21. Secret Systems

Policy: With the exception of criminal investigations, there must be no system of personnel records at Company X whose very existence is kept secret from the individuals described therein.

Commentary: This policy prohibits secret databases that may be maintained by supervisors or others as a way to persecute, harass, intimidate, or otherwise control employees. The policy builds worker trust that they definitely know of all systems being used to judge their performance and promotion prospects. The intention of the policy is also to ensure that all systems containing personnel information are known by not only the individuals but also by the information security staff. If the information security staff knows about the existence of such systems, it will be better able to ensure

that these systems incorporate appropriate control measures. The policy is also desirable because it requires the disclosure of all personal information, which could then be included in a data dictionary or data directory. This would assist with efforts to standardize, categorize, and rationalize the different types of information across an organization. An exception for criminal investigations is necessary because it would be counterproductive to inform an alleged perpetrator that an investigation is in progress.

Related Policies: "Asset Inventory — Information" and "Systems Monitoring Tools."

Audience: All

Security Environments: All

22. Access To Personal Information

Policy: Upon written request, every individual must be granted access to the Company X records that contain personal information pertaining to the individual's life or condition.

Commentary: Many businesses provide employees with the right to periodically view the information contained in their file. This policy gives the individuals the right to know the information that has been used in decisions about them. Knowledge of this information then permits the individuals to object to or correct inaccuracies or misleading statements appearing in the record. Nothing in this policy requires the organization to disclose details that do not relate to that same individual. These details may be obscured before disclosure of the record to the individual. Nothing in the policy prevents a thorough review of the record by management prior to release to ensure that only information directly applicable to the individual is released. Some organizations permit employees to insert a brief statement in their personal record if management has received a complaint about an inaccuracy or a misleading piece of information, but has decided not to change the information appearing in the individual's record. This policy can indirectly be an information integrity policy.

Related Policies: "Employee Explanatory Statement," "Incorrect Personal Information," "Employee File Examination," "Personnel Record Distributions," and "Personnel File Access."

Audience: End users and management

Security Environments: All

23. Third-Party Private Information Disclosure

Policy: Disclosure of private information about Company X workers to third parties must not occur unless required by law, or unless permitted by clear and explicit consent of the worker.

Commentary: This policy prevents invasion of privacy, defamation of character, libel, and slander lawsuits. The intention of the policy is to ensure that third parties are not given access to private information about workers. The only exceptions are when specifically required by law, as would be the case if a subpoena were tendered, or when the individual expressly authorized the transfer, as would be the case if the information were to be used by a prospective employer doing a background check. For this reason, without further authorization from the worker, many employers disclose only the fact that an individual worked or works at the organization, the most recent place of work, the dates of employment, and perhaps an indication whether the employee would be rehired. Some organizations disclose just a subset of these types of information. Examples of the types of information to be withheld should accompany the explanation of this policy. For example, the reason for termination is not generally provided because this could lead to a defamation lawsuit. This policy implies that creditors, attorneys, private detective agencies, and others desiring non-job-related information do not receive it without the worker's consent.

Related Policies: "Reason For Termination Disclosure" and "Disclosure Of Information To Law Enforcement."

Audience: End users and management

Security Environments: All

24. Transferring Private Data

Policy: Company X must release private data only to third-party organizations that commit in writing to maintain the information with an adequate level of protection, as determined by Information Security management.

Commentary: This policy prevents disclosure to those third-party organizations that will not promise to adequately protect private information. The disclosures addressed by this policy are those chosen by the organization possessing the data, not those chosen by the individual described by the data. This policy reflects common practice where lists are sold for one-time use, the exact use is specified in advance, and further usage is not permitted. While these contracts for list rental also help protect the disclosing organization's rights to the data, they preserve the privacy of the involved individuals because each usage remains defined and limited. Because the specific requirements may change over time and by jurisdiction, the policy identifies Information Security management to be the judge whether a particular release can proceed.

Related Policies: "Third-Party Access Terms And Conditions" and "Information Dissemination."

Audience: End users

Security Environments: All

25. Private Information Disclosure Records — Details

Policy: Company X workers who release private information to third parties must keep records of all such disclosures including what information was disclosed, to whom it was disclosed, and the date of such disclosure.

Commentary: This policy protects the organization against unjustified accusations of privacy invasion. Certain individuals may accuse an organization of releasing personal information about them. Without records such as those described in the policy, the organization would have a difficult time claiming that it did not release the information. In addition, the policy is intended to support individuals in their efforts to investigate and prosecute identity theft. With these disclosure records, a list of initial suspects can be developed. These records can be used by individuals who are correcting errors that have been propagated across multiple databases or multiple organizations.

Related Policies: "Use Of Personal Information For New Purposes," "Customer Information Recipient Disclosure," and "Customer Notification Of Record Requests."

Audience: End users

Security Environments: All

26. International Transfer Of Private Information

Policy: Transfers of private information to another country, no matter what technology is employed, must not take place unless prior approval of Information Security management has been obtained when the individual is, was, or will be located in the destination country, or when the individual has specifically requested such a transfer.

Commentary: This policy prevents private data from being transferred from highly-regulated jurisdictions into less-regulated jurisdictions. Without impediments to this information flow, business would tend to make such a transfer to lower costs and perhaps to thwart the intention of the privacy laws and regulations. This policy prevents the development of locations where business can do what they please without the constraints of laws and regulations. When an organization adopts this policy, it shows that it is serious about privacy and intends to prevent the movement of private data from defeating the protections provided by law.

Related Policies: "Transferring Private Data" and "Chain Of Trust Agreements."

Audience: Management and technical staff

Security Environments: All

27. Blocking Private Information Disclosures

Policy: Individuals must be given advance notice that their personal data held by Company X has been requested by a third party, unless compelled to release the data by clear and authoritative law or regulation, and a reasonable period of several weeks must be provided for an individual to block this disclosure.

Commentary: This policy prevents future disputes where an individual complains that Company X should have obtained their permission before releasing certain personal data. This policy is expedient, but provides some privacy protection. The implementation of this policy may require a "return receipt required" which indicates that the party did receive the notice about the disclosure. The policy provides flexibility for other uses of the information such as cross marketing of other products and services assuming these offerings are sold by the same organization. This policy establishes the individual as the one in control of personal information. The policy applies to a wide variety of personal information including computer-resident address books and appointment calendars, and to personal information, such as medical records.

Related Policies: "Consent For Questionable System Actions."

Audience: Technical staff

Security Environments: All

28. Disclosure Of Worker Contact Information

Policy: Company X must not disclose the names, titles, phone numbers, locations, or other contact information of its workers unless required for business purposes, required by law, or when the involved persons have previously clearly consented to the disclosure.

Commentary: This policy protects the privacy of workers. A potential side effect of this policy is that business operation will be more difficult for clients, customers, and others who have a legitimate need for this information. Many telemarketers call organizations asking for the name of the individual in a particular position, such as the director of Marketing, then ask to be put through to him or her. The director of Marketing is then subjected to a sales pitch that he or she does not want to hear. This policy would prevent these calls. To ensure that the organization does not lose important information, receptionists and telephone operators can request solicitors to send the material by mail addressed to "Director of Marketing" or whatever other position they are targeting. This policy does not address private information such as worker salary, only contact information. In general it is advisable that receptionists, telephone operators, security guards, and other people who have significant public contact be given specific instructions about the internal information that they are permitted to release.

Related Policies: "Third-Party Private Information Disclosure."

Audience: End users and management

Security Environments: All

29. Reason For Termination Disclosure

Policy: The reason for termination of workers must not be disclosed to third parties unless the prior approval of a Company X senior manager has been obtained or if the disclosure is required by law.

Commentary: This policy, beyond preserving the privacy of the involved employee, prevents libel, slander, defamation of character, and related lawsuits. Some organizations may wish to disclose this additional intention in the policy wording, while others may wish not to mention it explicitly. In some jurisdictions, the former employer may be held negligent if the reason for termination is criminal behavior and the former employee goes on to repeat this behavior at his or her next employer. This situation can be added to the policy as another permissible exception. The scope of this policy can be narrowed to relate to anyone who does not have a need to know. Other workers who did not ordinarily have any business interaction with a departed employee would not be given this information. This narrower scope further lessens the risks of libel, slander, defamation of character, and related lawsuits.

Related Policies: "Third-Party Private Information Disclosure" and "Change Of Status Disclosure."

Audience: End users and management

Security Environments: All

30. Change Of Status Disclosure

Policy: Detailed worker change of status information is strictly confidential, and must not be disclosed to anyone except those people who have a legitimate need to know.

Commentary: This policy prevents people in Human Resources management and others who are privy to worker change of status information from disclosing it to people who do not need this information. While the fact that there was a change of status would typically be communicated to receptionists, building guards, security management staff, and information security administrators, the reasons for this change should not be communicated to these people. If the information is disclosed to people who do not have a need to know, then the individual involved may allege character defamation or privacy invasion. This could lead to a lawsuit or vengeful acts.

Related Policies: "Reason For Termination Disclosure."

Audience: Management

Security Environments: All

31. Access To Disclosures Of Private Data Records

Policy: Workers must be given access to records reflecting the disclosure of their own private information to third parties and must be given sufficient information to permit them to contact such third parties to correct errors or supply additional information.

Commentary: Workers should have an opportunity to provide their own interpretation of events, should that interpretation differ from the interpretation found in Company X records. This policy permits workers to correct what they may consider to be inaccurate or misleading information when Company X elects to take

no action to correct their records. The policy could be modified to state that workers will be given this information only in those cases where Company X decides not to alter a private record in the manner requested by the involved workers.

Related Policies: "Private Information Disclosure Records — Maintenance."

Audience: Management and technical staff

Security Environments: All

32. Worker Performance Information

Policy: Individual worker performance information must not be made available to others who do not have a legitimate business-related need to know.

Commentary: This policy is intended to prevent workers from feeling humiliated, harassed, or harried because their performance has been posted in a public place. In many instances, coworkers will have a general idea of a worker's performance, and the availability of this information will come as no surprise to them. This policy does not interfere with management's right to discipline or terminate the employee based on poor performance. The policy may help foster positive employee opinions about the intention of management and the extent to which the organization cares about employee welfare. This policy may also help an organization avoid trouble related to privacy laws and regulations.

Related Policies: "Privilege Restriction — Need To Know."

Audience: End users and management

Security Environments: All

33. Personal File Privacy

Policy: Personal files on Company X computers and in Company X worker desks must be handled to ensure that other workers, including managers and system administrators, cannot read such personal files, unless the action is part of a formal investigation initiated by Security management, or an effort to dispose of or reassign files after a worker has left Company X.

Commentary: This policy clarifies privacy expectations about the personal files of workers. This policy requires that the files of workers are not to be read by other workers, including managers and system administrators.

The policy can be modified to make specific mention of electronic mail, personal computer and workstation files.

Related Policies: "Examination Of Data Stored On Systems" and "Electronic Mail Privacy."

Audience: All

Security Environments: Low and medium

34. Private Information Disclosure Records — Maintenance

Policy: Every disclosure of private information to third parties must be recorded and these records must be maintained for at least five years.

Commentary: This policy shows exactly what information has been disclosed to which third parties, and that the disclosures have been in keeping with law, organizational policies, and general business practices. Keeping a log of disclosures will also be important when notifying information recipients of errors found in a private record. Credit bureaus keep a record of all third parties to whom they have disclosed details of an individual's debts and payment history. If an error in a record is detected, the credit bureaus are then in a position to immediately notify the recipients about the corrected information.

Related Policies: "Third-Party Private Information Disclosure" and "Access To Disclosures Of Private Data Records."

Audience: Management and technical staff

Security Environments: All

35. Customer Information Privacy

Policy: Information that can be directly linked to a specific customer must only be released to third parties if the customer has provided prior written consent, or if Company X is legally required to disclose the information.

Commentary: This policy restricts the unauthorized dissemination of information about an organization's customers. The policy is relevant to those organizations that provide some personal product or service, such as medical insurance or psychological counseling. It also may be relevant to airlines, supermarkets, and other organizations that track customer purchasing patterns. The policy may interfere with certain database matching initiatives across organizations, but these are unpopular with the public and widely considered be a violation of privacy. Some organizations go further than having an in-house policy of this nature. They include a different version of the policy in the materials distributed to customers. Several insurance companies, for example, explicitly inform customers about their policies regarding disclosures to third-party organizations. Some people claim these types of customer communications improve the organization's public image and help bring in new business.

Related Policies: "Customer Record Statistical Information."

Audience: Management and technical staff

Security Environments: All

36. Sharing Private Information

Policy: Company X must not disclose specific information about customer accounts, transactions, or relationships to unaffiliated third parties for their independent use, unless the disclosure of information is to a reputable information reporting agency, the disclosure is related to a customer's request to perform a certain action, the customer requests the disclosure, the disclosure is required or permitted by law, or the customer has been informed about the possibility of such a disclosure for marketing or similar purposes, and has been given an opportunity to decline.

Commentary: This policy is meant to constitute a privacy policy for customers, which in some jurisdictions may be required by law. The policy is instead intended to give the issuing organization wide latitude to do basically whatever it wishes. For example, the issuing organization can affiliate itself with another organization, perhaps in a joint venture, and this then would permit private data to be exchanged without prior notice to the involved customers. Likewise, if the organization wanted to sell private information to third parties, it would simply give customers a notice to this effect, and if any customers objected, it would remove their data from the database to be shared with a third party. Because this policy is primarily meaningless, it is not recommend.

Related Policies: "Customer Information Privacy" and "Disclosure Of Customer Information."

Audience: End users

Security Environments: All

37. Disclosure Of Private Information To Outsourcing Organizations

Policy: Company X must not sell, rent, or otherwise transfer customer information to third parties in any manner unless the third parties sign a confidentiality agreement prohibiting them from further dissemination of this information and prohibiting them from using this information for unauthorized purposes.

Commentary: This policy assures customers that their private data will be kept confidential, while providing an organization with flexibility to share private data with outside parties without customer consent. For example, the policy permits organizations to share summaries of customer information with third-party market research organizations, data mining consultants, and strategic planning consultants. The policy permits organizations to outsource any and all of their internal functions without customer notification or consent. A merger or acquisition could in some cases be considered to be an outsourcing of services. Legal advice is recommended. The policy permits disclosure of customer information to government agencies for tax collection, discrimination law enforcement, and related purposes.

Related Policies: "Customer Information Privacy."

Audience: End users

Security Environments: All

38. Disclosure Of Customer Information

Policy: Company X must not disclose information about its customers to external parties without explicit written permission.

Commentary: This policy gives customers assurance that they can safely do business with Company X. A policy like this is useful for an organization where even knowing that a customer does business with them may be embarrassing. The policy is intended to be provided on a web site or in a brochure, not just distributed to in-house workers. If compelled to disclose customer information as required by law, this information will be disclosed. This is considered by some to be obvious, and therefore not requiring reiteration in the policy itself. This policy also prevents trademark disputes where a customer says that a particular business is inappropriately using its name to lure people to its web sites.

Related Policies: "Customer Information Privacy."

Audience: End users

Security Environments: Medium and high

39. Disclosure Of Personal Data

Policy: Personal information including, but not limited to, aggregated information, summarized information, anonymous information, individual case studies, or specific identifiable information about individuals, gathered by Company X must not be sold, rented, transferred, given, or otherwise conveyed to third parties.

Commentary: This policy communicates that the organization's privacy policy is absolute, and it will not be compromised. This policy states that Company X will not erode the privacy of its customers, its workers, or other people about whom it keeps personal information. The policy illustrates that management has a higher-level understanding of what is happening in the area of privacy.

Related Policies: "Monitoring And Recording Activity" and "Information Collection Notice."

Audience: End users

Security Environments: Medium and high

40. Customer Information Recipient Disclosure

Policy: When requested in writing, Company X must promptly disclose the name, address, and telephone number of all third parties receiving private information about any customer or individual.

Commentary: This policy permits a customer or individual to determine who has received his or her private information. The individual does not have the right to object to this initial disclosure, just to determine after the fact who received the information. Rather than providing a high level of privacy protection and individual control over private data, this policy provides accountability among those who are in possession of the information. The policy is also useful for those situations where identity fraud is being investigated. If identity fraud has occurred, in most cases the individual must take on the task of informing all involved parties that someone else has been using his or her name and credit without authorization. This policy assumes that records of disclosures to third parties are being maintained.

Related Policies: "Private Information Disclosure Records — Details" and "Personal Information Access."

Audience: Technical staff

Security Environments: All

41. Customer Notification Of Record Requests

Policy: Company X must not release customer records to third parties unless a customer requests it, or unless compelled to do so by law or regulation, and only after giving the customer two weeks advance notice prior to the release.

Commentary: This policy is intended to tighten the privacy policy observed by many organizations where they do not release personal customer records to third parties. The policy may prevent third parties from using a lawsuit as a mechanism to gain access to personal records that would otherwise be kept in confidence. The policy can be used to assist customers in their defense of their own privacy. The actual cost to the organization is that related to the administrative activity regarding notices sent in those instances where a subpoena is received. All legal costs associated with the challenge of a request for records are borne by the customer. The two-week period is arbitrary, and could be lengthened as long as the organization holding the records is not likely to be held in contempt of court for delaying the release of such records.

Related Policies: "Release Of Organization Information" and "Personal Customer Information."

Audience: Technical staff

Security Environments: All

42. Privacy Policy Application

Policy: All customer information must be protected according to the privacy policy in effect at the time the information is collected unless consent to act otherwise has been provided by the customer.

Commentary: This policy informs the policy reader that Company X considers its privacy policy to be similar to a legal contract. This contractual perspective relies on the fact that customers provide information under certain stated terms and conditions, and they expect the recipient organization to follow its stated policy. Under this policy, Company X cannot simply change its policy, then use customer information gathered under the previous policy for purposes that are not permitted under the previous policy. This policy imposes additional overhead on the issuing organization because it must now use mechanisms to time-and-date stamp information from customers. It could create special identifiers reflecting the privacy policy applicable to a certain customer record. Different mailing lists and different processing routines also may be required in order to handle two or more sets of customers in ways consistent with different privacy policies. This policy reflects a trend in the Internet-posted privacy policy area. Government regulators are increasingly holding organizations to the words appearing in their privacy policies, proceeding as though these same policies were legal contracts.

Related Policies: "Personal Data Uses After Merger Or Acquisition" and "Private Data System Approval."

Audience: End users

Security Environments: All

43. Privacy Of Correspondent Contact Information

Policy: The electronic mail addresses and telephone numbers of correspondents with all users of Company X communication systems must not be released to third parties unless Company X is compelled to do so by law or regulation.

Commentary: While some members of the general public believe that both the phone numbers and the electronic mail addresses of correspondents are confidential, this information sometimes can be shared by a telephone company or another communication system provider without the consent of the involved users. The policy assures users that information revealing correspondents will remain private. The policy assumes that the organization already has a policy about the privacy of the content of these communications. The policy is an attempt to prevent communications system information from being used by any third parties. This policy is intended to be adopted by a provider of information systems services, such as an Internet service provider or a telephone company.

Related Policies: "Personal Customer Information" and "Private Information Disclosure Records — Maintenance."

Audience: Technical staff

Security Environments: Medium and high

44. Customer Anonymity

Policy: Company X must provide elective mechanisms for customers who wish to remain anonymous when using Company X systems.

Commentary: The intention of this policy is give customers a clear picture of what is meant by anonymous user IDs, anonymous remailers, anonymous electronic cash, and similar anonymous mechanisms. This policy is intended primarily for organizations offering computer and communications services to the public, although the same ideas apply to intranet discussion groups, and automated internal suggestion boxes.

Related Policies: "Anonymous User IDs" and "Customer Information Privacy."

Audience: End users and management

Security Environments: All

45. Famous Customer Identifications

Policy: Workers must not publicly acknowledge the identity of famous customers when in their presence, must refrain from talking about famous customers with anyone else other than Company X workers, and must not reveal the identity of a famous customer unless conducting a legitimate business activity.

Commentary: This policy preserves the privacy of famous customers, and to make them feel comfortable doing business with Company X. The policy prohibits gossip and unnecessary conversation that may lead to slander or defamation charges. This policy is also consistent with the security notion of maintaining a low profile.

Related Policies: "Monitoring And Recording Activity" and "Anonymous User IDs."

Audience: End users

Security Environments: All

46. Customer Record Statistical Information

Policy: Statistical information derived from customer records must not be disclosed to parties outside Company X unless the specific customers involved cannot be identified by the information.

Commentary: This policy prevents workers from distributing reports to outsiders that might inadvertently reveal the identity of, or information about customers. This policy is relevant to the preparation of annual reports, government forms, and all other reporting mechanisms. The word "statistical" could be replaced with "numerical." The idea behind this policy is that customer information should be aggregated or summarized so much that its disclosure does not

damage the privacy of customers. If aggregated information cannot be changed to conceal the identity of customers, then the information should not be disclosed. The organization may wish to change the policy to include at least one level of management approval prior to disclosure of such statistical information because the determination that specific customers cannot be identified may be a complex and time-consuming task.

Related Policies: "Customer Information Privacy" and "Information Collection Restrictions."

Audience: Management and technical staff

Security Environments: All

47. Customer Activity Log Disclosure

Policy: Logs reflecting the activities of computer users or those served by computers must not be disclosed to third parties unless Company X is compelled to do so by court order, law, or regulation, or in receipt of written approval from the involved individuals.

Commentary: This policy protects the privacy of those individuals whose activities appear in logs. The policy covers library-provided literature searches, videotape rental histories, bank transaction records, supermarket frequent-buyer records, and other information collections. Common computer user activity logs are also covered. Some organizations may wish to restrict the scope of this policy by making reference to specific types of logs.

Related Policies: "Privilege Restriction — Need To Know" and "Customer Log Information."

Audience: Management and technical staff

Security Environments: All

48. Employee Observance Of Privacy

Policy: Workers must not consent to a violation of Company X privacy or waive the Company X right to privacy unless senior management permission is obtained.

Commentary: This policy partially defines an organizational right to privacy. The intention is to inform employees that such a right exists, that they are not to waive it without prior management permission, and that they are required to defend it. A policy such as this may be important when it comes to protecting confidential information potentially useful to an opposing party in a court of law. The notion of privacy for an organization rather than an individual is different and may be unfamiliar to some people. To compensate for this unfamiliarity, some organizations may wish to further specify the ways in which Company X rights to privacy actually exist. For example, employees must not enter into legal contracts where they agree to disclose Company X confidential information unless management approval is obtained. Similarly, the requirement for a search warrant can be overcome if the parties involved agree to a police search. Employees must not provide such agreement in the absence of top management approval. Consultation with internal legal counsel is advisable on all policies such as this.

Related Policies: "Third-Party Confidentiality Agreements" and "Disclosure Of Information To Law Enforcement."

Audience: End users and management

Security Environments: All

49. Consent For Questionable System Actions

Policy: When in doubt about performing any particular computer-assisted action, Company X workers must inform those whom the action will affect by providing a description of the action they propose to take, the intention behind the action, and the potential impacts that it may have on the recipients of the communication, and obtain consent from those who are affected or the permission of a vice president.

Commentary: This policy is meant to prevent workers from performing some computer-related act that workers have reason to believe may harm other people. For example, a recent product launch would have facilitated direct mail advertising by a wide variety of organizations, at considerably lower prices, and would have included personal information about many individuals. Concerned about privacy violations, over 30,000 individuals objected to being included in the database, and the project was abandoned. For some organizations, the policy may be too vague as stated here, and may need specific examples such as those dealing with privacy violation.

Related Policies: "Information Security Responsibility"

Audience: Management and technical staff

Security Environments: All

50. Individual Record Access Authorization

Policy: Patients must not be permitted to view their own medical records without the prior authorization of the health care provider who generated these records.

Commentary: This policy recognizes the privacy and professional courtesy rights of health care providers as more important than a patient's right to know information about his or her own medical condition. Many jurisdictions have laws specifically regulating a patient's access to his or her health information. A conflict between the objectives of the patient and the health care provider can exist. For example, a patient may want to know his or her health status, yet the doctor may not wish to reveal this information, thinking this will worsen the condition. A doctor may also want to restrict access to patient records for fear that these records will provide evidence for malpractice lawsuits. Some laws grant a right to access records about one's own medical condition, but this right does not always apply to all types of patients. The policy title was deliberately generalized beyond the health care industry to show that the notion of record creator rights is applicable to other areas besides health care.

Related Policies: "Personnel File Access."

Audience: End users

Security Environments: All

51. Disclosure Of Intended Uses Of Personal Information

Policy: Before a customer places an order or otherwise discloses personal information, all Company X representatives must inform the customer of the ways that this personal information will be used.

Commentary: This policy ensures that all personal information gathered is obtained fairly, without misleading the consumers. This policy eliminates any ambiguity about the nature of the relationship between a consumer and an organization about to be established. Most consumers will have no objection, but those who do object can be placed in a special category. Because discussion about such a policy could jeopardize a sale, many organizations will deal with these matters after a sale has been completed. Others will take a more passive role, choosing to include a notice about uses of personal information in advertisements or brochures. Organizations that, as a matter of principle, do not resell mailing addresses or other personal information, may find that this policy provides them with a competitive advantage.

Related Policies: "Private Data System Opt Out."

Audience: End users and management

Security Environments: All

52. Personnel File Access

Policy: Employees must be permitted to both examine and make one copy of the information appearing in their personnel file.

Commentary: To simply permit employees to look at their personnel files severely restricts their ability to rectify errors. This policy permits employees to gather the information they need, then take it home, to an attorney, or to some other third party. To permit employees to have a copy also permits them to better prepare letters and other requests for changes in their file. This policy provides a mechanism to increase the integrity of information. It is consistent with the ethic that employees should have control over information about them. A positive side effect of this policy is that it discourages the insertion of inaccurate information into personnel files. At the same time the existence of this policy may encourage unauthorized secret files that contain information that workers are not intended to see. The policy could be expanded so as to apply to all workers including contractors, consultants, and temporaries.

Related Policies: "Access To Personal Information," "Secret Systems," and "Personnel Record Distributions."

Audience: End users and management

Security Environments: All

53. Employee File Examination

Policy: All employees wishing to examine their personnel file must submit a written request to Human Resources management, and review their files at appointed times, during business hours, and in the presence of a Human Resources representative.

Commentary: This policy is intended to prevent management from maintaining inappropriate information in personnel files. The policy requires that a formal request be filed. This gives management an opportunity to remove off-color references or inappropriate material. The removal of this material can help prevent discrimination or harassment lawsuits. The policy creates a controlled environment where questions about the record can be handled immediately by Human Resources management. This immediate problem

resolution may help prevent grievances, unnecessary gossip, and unwarranted lawsuits. The presence of this representative also means that copying and removal of material in the file can be prevented. Limits on the number of times a record can be examined can also be established, although these limits in most cases are not required.

Related Policies: "Personnel Record Distributions" and "Individual Record Access Authorization."

Audience: End users

Security Environments: All

54. Employee Explanatory Statement

Policy: If employees object to the accuracy, relevance, or completeness of information appearing in their personnel file, they must be given an opportunity to add a supplementary statement.

Commentary: This policy permits employees to tell their side of a particular matter described in their personnel files. If the organization chooses not to make requested adjustments to a personnel file in response to an employee's complaint, then this right to insert a statement may be applicable. The employee may not file a formal complaint about the information in the file, but they may wish to add some explanation because the record may be misleading without the supplementary information. The addition of a supplementary statement may be a one-time privilege, or it may be used repeatedly for each contested piece of information. The policy also may be used for individuals other than employees. There is deliberately no requirement that incorrect information be removed or changed under this policy.

Related Policies: "Access To Personal Information."

Audience: All

Security Environments: All

55. Incorrect Personal Information

Policy: Whenever Company X receives notice that certain personal information held in its records is incorrect, it must promptly modify the information, or else append to the record an indication that this information is disputed and alleged to be incorrect.

Commentary: This policy ensures that records containing personal information are current and correct. If errors in personal records are not promptly corrected, the individuals described therein may suffer serious harm. For example, if a credit bureau did not correct, or label as incorrect, certain false bankruptcy information, then the person described in the record would be likely to suffer personal harm. This policy does not require a change to a record if Company X personnel are unsure of the accuracy of the corrected information. This is where a label indicating the existence of a dispute is appropriate. This policy assumes that a related policy has already granted the individuals described in personal records a right or opportunity to examine information appearing in Company X records. While this policy reflects good practice in the database management area, it is useful to put it in writing to give the people described in the records additional assurance that personal information about them will be treated with both respect and proper care.

Related Policies: "Access To Personal Information" and "Customer Information Recipient Disclosure."

Audience: Management and technical staff

Security Environments: All

56. Personal Record Integrity

Policy: Management must make reasonable efforts to ensure that all personal information maintained by Company X is accurate, timely, relevant, and complete.

Commentary: This policy requires management to maintain records containing personal information. With this policy, management is required to make corrections if the organization has been informed about inaccuracies in a record by the person described therein. This is important for those organizations that use personal information as part of their regular business, rather than organizations that use personal information in the course of their own internal Human Resources management activities. This is a good general policy on which other policies may rely. It is also appropriate for a brief policy statement. Some organizations may wish to add a description of the words "personal information" or simply provide examples. Personal information includes personnel information, but can be a more broadly defined category. Customer personal information would fall within the purview of this policy, while technically it is not personnel information. In this policy, the word "private" might be used instead of "personal."

Related Policies: "Error Investigation" and "Employee Contact Information."

Audience: Management and technical staff

Security Environments: All

57. Personal Record Handling

Policy: Documented procedures for handling personal information must be established, consistently followed, and regularly updated.

Commentary: This policy requires that operational groups that handle private data clearly conceptualize, document, and faithfully follow established procedures. The existence of these procedures will ensure consistent and secure handling of private data and also give internal auditors a reference point for their examinations. Should there be a publicly-revealed problem or a court case, these same procedures can also be used to demonstrate that management took prudent steps to protect this private data. Such procedures will typically deal with the routine and non-routine receipt of private data, the manipulation and processing of this data, the storage and retention of the data, the dissemination and transmission of this data, and the disposal and destruction of this data.

Related Policies: "Computer Operator Log Review" and "Intrusion Response Procedures."

Audience: Management and technical staff

Security Environments: All

58. Personal Record Usage

Policy: Management must make reasonable efforts to ensure that all personal information is used only as intended, and that precautions preventing misuse are effective and appropriate.

Commentary: This policy requires management to ensure that Company X does not use certain information for purposes other than those originally intended. The policy also will ensure that this information is not passed along to third parties without the knowledge or consent of the person who originally created or provided it. This is a good overall policy on which other policies may rely. It is also appropriate for a brief policy statement. Personal information includes personnel information, but can be a more broadly defined category. Customer personal information would fall within the purview of this policy, even though it is not personnel information. In this policy, the word "private" might be used instead of "personal."

Related Policies: "Unacceptable Use Of Computer And Communication Systems."

Audience: Management and technical staff

Security Environments: All

59. Private Information Access Logging

Policy: For every production system containing information labeled as "private," access controls must be established such that every access to private information initiated by a user is logged, identifying the individual whose information was accessed, the user requesting access, and the time and date.

Commentary: This policy ensures that a sufficient audit trail exists such that it can later be determined who accessed what private information and when. The policy is pro-privacy and often requires the development of custom software. This is because few database management systems or access control software packages provide such fine granularity in their logging systems. This policy provides a rigorous approach to privacy protection. This policy assumes that a data classification system has been adopted, and that the word "private" has some generally understood meaning within the organization. The words "initiated by a user" are important because they exempt software that may access private information as part of an automated system maintenance process.

Related Policies: "Sensitive Application Systems Logs," "Systems Architecture For Logging Activities," and "Transaction Originator."

Audience: Technical staff

Security Environments: Medium and high

60. Use Of Personal Information For New Purposes

Policy: Personal information about employees, consultants, or contractors, that has been gathered for one purpose, may not be used for another purpose without the clear and unambiguous consent of the parties to whom this information pertains.

Commentary: The intent of this policy is to stop the misuse of personal information for purposes other than those originally intended. If a citizen of a national government disclosed certain information on his tax return so that the government could carry out tax laws, this policy would prohibit the information on his tax return from being used for any other purposes. This policy reduces the flexibility that management may otherwise employ the information in whatever way it wishes. The existence of this policy may encourage individuals to disclose information that they would not otherwise reveal. This is a widely-subscribed-to privacy policy, but in spite of general public support of the idea,

many businesses and government agencies find the policy too restrictive. In this policy, the word "private" might be used instead of "personal."

Related Policies: "Personal Telephone Usage" and "Non-Business Use Of Organization Information."

Audience: All

Security Environments: All

61. Anonymous Information Linking

Policy: Company X information systems and staff must not link anonymous information with personally-identifiable information unless the involved individuals have given their consent.

Commentary: This policy addresses a serious problem associated primarily with Internet business activities. Certain personal information that is anonymous is often gathered unbeknownst to the involved users. This information may then be linked with personally-identifiable information, such as a customer buying patterns, to form a more revealing picture of individual behavior or activities. This policy prohibits this linkage in an effort to preserve the privacy of the individuals involved. By adopting this policy, an organization can assure users that it is genuinely concerned about privacy. This policy is suitable for posting on a web site. The words in the policy are stringent. A less-restrictive version could replace the words about giving consent with words about robust notice.

Related Policies: "Use Of Personal Information For New Purposes," "Private Information Links," and "Personal Record Usage."

Audience: End users and technical staff

Security Environments: All

62. Personal Customer Information

Policy: All customer records containing personal information that are in the possession of Company X must be used only for purposes directly related to Company X business, and disclosed to outside parties only with the customer's permission or if Company X has received either a subpoena or court order.

Commentary: This policy prohibits secondary uses of personal or private information about customers. This policy also prohibits the sale, rental, exchange, or any other method for conveying personal information to other organizations that might use it to solicit business from Company X customers. The term "in the possession of Company X" is used because Company X will have trouble exercising control over customer records that are not in Company X possession, although this may be possible if possession is held by outsourcing organizations. The policy could specifically identify the types of information that cannot be disclosed externally. The policy could be changed to incorporate an exception whenever the receiving party is an authorized government agency.

Related Policies: "Customer Contact Information Usage."

Audience: All

Security Environments: All

63. Customer Access To Personal Information

Policy: Customers must be given the opportunity to obtain confirmation from Company X that personal information about them is kept on Company X systems, and an explanation of the nature of this information.

Commentary: This policy informs customers and internal workers that customers are legitimately to receive certain types of internal Company X information. The policy does not release the information itself, it only releases metadata, which is information about customer information. There will generally be fewer disputes about metadata than there will be about the specific information. Regulations in some industries, such as the consumer credit reporting industry, will require that specific personal information be divulged, not just metadata. This policy is pro-consumer, yet it requires very little of the organization adopting it.

Related Policies: "Customer Information Collection" and "Personal Information For Business Functioning."

Audience: End users

Security Environments: All

64. Customer Contact Information Usage

Policy: Contact information gathered about customers or potential customers must be used only for internal Company X purposes.

Commentary: This policy guarantees that customer contact information will go no further than the organization that needs it in order to provide a product or service. This type of policy is particularly appropriate for those organizations providing a product or service about which the customer might be embarrassed or self-conscious. The existence of a policy like this may also generate additional business for these organizations because some people may have refrained from becoming customers lest their name and contact information are placed on a list. The most prevalent concern involves the sale or swap of customer phone and address data, leading to unwanted mail and telephone solicitations. This policy is intended to be distributed to customers and potential customers.

Related Policies: "Personal Customer Information" and "Disclosure Of Private Information To Outsourcing Organizations."

Audience: Management and technical staff

Security Environments: All

65. Embedded Personal Information

Policy: Company X information systems must not employ secret serial numbers, secret personal identification numbers, or any other secret mechanisms that might reveal the identity of, or activities of customers.

Commentary: This policy responds to the recent use of secret identifying numbers in some commercial personal computer applications. Using these numbers, it is possible to trace a file back to its originator. Users were not told about these numbers, and may have compromised their privacy unknowingly when they posted files to the Internet or some other public forum. This policy gains additional business for electronic commerce systems by assuring customers that they will not be misled when conducting a transaction, only later to discover that there were some secret mechanisms used to compromise their privacy. This policy advances the cause of privacy, but at the expense of criminal investigations. The policy is intended to be posted to a web site, an electronic bulletin board, or some other public place. For Internet commerce environments, specific mention can be made of cookies, the mechanism that inconspicuously identifies customers.

Related Policies: "Private And Identification Information Linkage" and "Cookies For Automatic Log On."

Audience: End users

Security Environments: All

66. Personal Identifiers On Publicly-Accessible Locations

Policy: No personal identifiers except public encryption keys and digital certificates, must appear on any publicly-accessible location managed by or controlled by Company X including web pages, Internet commerce sites, product manuals, or magazine advertisements.

Commentary: This policy preserves the privacy of both customers and employees. If personal identifiers are not available, then the activities of these individuals cannot be traced back to them. This policy also prevents identity theft. If personal identifiers, telephone numbers, credit card numbers, electronic mail addresses, and other identifiers do not appear in publicly-accessible places, they cannot be stolen and used. The policy does not prevent the organization from posting personal identifiers in restricted locations. This could for example be a list of soon-to-be-shipped orders posted to the Internet. A customer could see only his or her own order by providing a user ID. In some cases, the word "real" could be added to the very beginning of the policy to distinguish between real and fictitious personal identifiers.

Related Policies: "Embedded Personal Information" and "Internet Identity."

Audience: End users and technical staff

Security Environments: All

67. Account Number Intelligence

Policy: Company X must not use externally-meaningful identifiers as its own internal customer account numbers.

Commentary: This policy prevents identity theft. Because it is convenient, many organizations use personal identifiers on their monthly statements. This usage of personal identifiers invites abuse by third parties who may come in contact with the number when they go through the trash or otherwise receive copies of customer statements. These identifiers now need to be safeguarded as confidential information. This policy will demonstrate that Company X is genuinely trying to help prevent the increasingly common abuse known as identity fraud.

Related Policies: "Computer Support Identification Codes" and "Personal Information Access."

Audience: Technical staff

Security Environments: All

68. Private And Identification Information Linkage

Policy: A link between personally-identifying information and private data must be maintained no longer than is necessary to carry out the purpose for which the data was originally gathered.

Commentary: This policy prevents archival medical records, customer activity databases, or some other information containing personal identifiers from inadvertently violating the privacy of the subjects. Used most often for research, this policy permits background information to be gathered and analyzed, but then the link to personal identifiers is deleted. This can take the form of a personal contact file and a research data file for each individual. Serial numbers or pointers that cross-reference each other connect the files. When the data gathering is complete, the cross-reference information is deleted. At this point, all information is available, but the individual's privacy is assured. Beyond research, the policy also may be appropriate for certain commercial activities. For example a chain of bookstores that provides a frequent buyer program could create a contact file that it could use for solicitations and customer service, while it also maintained a separate anonymous market research file containing all the purchases made but no contact information.

Related Policies: "Private Information Links," "Anonymous User IDs," and "Incident Reporting."

Audience: Technical staff

Security Environments: Medium and high

69. Private Information Links

Policy: Information systems must not support any links between private information and other types of information related to the same individual without written approval from Information Security management.

Commentary: To assure the privacy of individuals, this policy limits the number of people who have access to personal information. In the health care industry, this policy prohibits the establishment of links between health care information and other types of information such as financial data and employment data. This would, for example, prevent staff in a hospital's billing department from seeing the specifics of the treatment given to a patient. There is a potentially adverse side effect of this policy. It may discourage the establishment of a customer information file (CIF) that describes all of the different relationships maintained with a particular individual. CIFs and similar databases are common in the banking industry, and are also used elsewhere to permit customer service staff to respond to an individual in an intelligent manner with current information. The approval required will permit an organization to have both a CIF or similar database and also a privacy policy such as this. The word "link" is deliberately vague so that it applies to a corporate data dictionary, an intranet, or a database matching effort.

Related Policies: "Private And Identification Information Linkage" and "Anonymous Information Linking."

Audience: Technical staff

Security Environments: All

70. Private Data System Opt Out

Policy: Prior to the implementation of any new or substantially modified information system that handles private data, the affected individuals must be given an opportunity to choose whether they wish to participate in the new system.

Commentary: This policy gives the people who are described by the private data involved an opportunity to not participate in a new system. This will require the system provider to be proactive, contacting the individuals, and explaining the new system. One example involves database matching, the linking of two previously connected databases to illuminate new information. This is why the policy requires obtaining permission prior to implementation. After implementation the privacy of the involved individuals may already be violated. Some may say that individuals should be excluded by default and be given the right to opt in. This policy, which permits individuals to opt out, is more in keeping with standard pro-business practices.

Related Policies: "Private Data System Approval," "Customers Opt-Out Of Direct Mail," and "Disclosure Of Intended Uses Of Personal Information."

Audience: Management and technical staff

Security Environments: All

71. Privacy Policy Reminder

Policy: All Company X customers must be sent annually a copy of the Company X official privacy policy and instructions informing customers how they can opt out of Company X data sharing activities.

Commentary: This policy specifies a minimum frequency for the submission of a revised privacy policy to all customers. It is also to ensure that customers get regular reminders about the ways that they can restrict the usage of information about them. The words "data-sharing activities" in the policy refer to the ways that Company X shares customer information with other organizations. If customers tell Company X they do not want to be part of these data sharing activities, they may decline participation or opt out. The method used for the transmission of a copy of the privacy policy is deliberately not stated because it could be an insert into an envelope containing an invoice, a printed message on a statement, an electronic mail message, or some other communication method.

Related Policies: "Customers Opt-Out Of Direct Mail" and "Privacy Policy Change Notification."

Audience: Management and technical staff

Security Environments: All

72. Private Data System Approval

Policy: To be included in any Company X system that handles private data, the affected individuals must specifically elect to participate in the system.

Commentary: This policy prevents management from establishing systems where private data is stored against the wishes of the individuals described on the system. This approach eliminates many privacy issues, but may also eliminate some business opportunities. Some organizations may wish to set up a policy such as this only for certain types of data rather than all private data. No mention is made of system implementation because individuals would not be described in such a system if they had not specifically elected to be. The system could be initially implemented with no personal data stored in it. This policy is a pro-consumer, rather than a pro-business policy. It would be to a business' advantage to adopt this policy if the contemplated system or business activity involved extremely private matters.

Related Policies: "Private Data System Opt Out."

Audience: Management and technical staff

Security Environments: All

73. Individual Control Of Personal Data Usage

Policy: If an individual or customer elects to revoke the permission that they gave Company X to use their personal data, Company X must promptly update its records and ensure that their wishes are observed.

Commentary: This policy assures customers that they can change their mind at any time about the permission that they gave to Company X to use or share their personal data. Many organizations treat this permission process as though it is an annual window to change an individual's status, if he or she so desires, while others treat this process as a one-time event that takes place when the relationship with the individual is established. This policy recognizes it as a continuously open window permitting the individual to change his or her mind at any time. If permission has already been given to share personal data with third parties, this sharing cannot realistically be reversed. One advisable addition to this policy would be to add a statement assuring customers that there will be no fee or charge associated with this change in their status. Also advisable are clear instructions on how to submit such a notification to Company X personnel.

Related Policies: "Privacy Policy Application" and "Private Data System Opt Out."

Audience: End users

Security Environments: All

74. Location-Specific Information Usage

Policy: Company X will not use information related to the precise location of its customers or workers with wireless devices or permit other commercial organizations to use this information, for marketing purposes unless specific authorization has been given by each individual.

Commentary: This policy controls the use of information resulting from the use of location-specific systems. These new functions are opportunities for impromptu marketing. As written, the policy is actually quite lenient and permissive. In most cases, users will want to create a profile indicating what they are interested in, so an opt-in approach is necessary. Using these new location-related functions without obtaining user permission in advance could create a public relations problem. The policy is deliberately silent about sharing this data with government agencies because the laws and prevailing norms about this have yet to be determined. This policy projects a positive image for an organization, but at the same time it requires very little of the organization adopting it in order to remain in compliance. This policy would in most cases be adopted by a service provider such as an Internet service provider or an application service provider, but in some cases it may be adopted by other types of organizations that support wireless communications.

Related Policies: "Personal Customer Information" and "Small Portable Computer Usage."

Audience: End users

Security Environments: Medium and high

75. Database Removal Of Individuals

Policy: If an individual requests to be removed from a Company X internal customer or prospect database, workers must immediately remove the individual from the database.

Commentary: This policy ensures that Company X workers understand that they cannot delay responding to requests to be removed from a regular mail mailing list, an electronic mail mailing list, a telephone calling list, or some other marketing-oriented list. If employees take their time with this task, the list is likely to be used for yet another mass mailing, electronic mail broadcast, or telephone campaign, and the individual's request not met. This can cause great trouble for customer service representatives, and may result in complaints to top management or legal action. This policy makes reference to a Company X owned database and not lists purchased or rented from third parties. Company X has no obligation to notify third parties who provide lists for one-time use. This policy prevents unwanted electronic mail messages, regular mail, and telephone solicitations. This policy will help Company X maintain compliance with many privacy laws. From an operational standpoint, it is desirable to keep a record of the deleted individuals, perhaps in an archival database, just in case there is a dispute, a mistake, or an unauthorized request for deletion. The action described in the policy is sometimes referred to as "unsubscribing from a mailing list," but this term is not used in the suggested policy because most of the time individuals never initially subscribed.

Related Policies: "Electronic Marketing Material Source" and "Customer Log Information."

Audience: End users

Security Environments: All

76. Deletion Of Customer Or Prospect Information

Policy: When customers or prospects request that information about them be deleted from Company X records, Company X must promptly comply except that Company X must retain the portions of its transaction records that are needed by government authorities, or that may be needed to show compliance with laws and regulations.

Commentary: The intention of this privacy policy is to demonstrate that the organization is concerned about privacy and is willing to take immediate action if so requested by customers or prospects. Deletion of customer or prospect personal information will prevent these people from being contacted again by the organization, will prevent the information from being passed to third parties, and will prevent the information from being used for unauthorized purposes. Some transaction information must be kept in order to make proper reports to government authorities, to detect fraud, and other legitimate business purposes.

Related Policies: "Personal Information Retention" and "Private And Identification Information Linkage."

Audience: End users

Security Environments: All

77. Blocking Private Data Usage

Policy: Company X workers must diligently observe the unconditional right of individuals to block data about them from being used for marketing purposes, to block the sale of such data to third parties, and to have such data permanently erased from direct marketing lists.

Commentary: This policy gives the individuals described in a database or some other collection of data the right to block the storage, usage, and distribution of that data. The policy applies to direct mail marketing activities, but could be expanded into other areas like telemarketing. The policy focuses on direct mail because that is one of the major areas where consumers feel their privacy is most violated. If an individual requests any one of the three actions mentioned in the policy, Company X workers must follow through with their request in a conscientious manner. Problems with the follow through may be encountered if this information

has already been distributed to third parties. Some organizations may wish to include mention of procedures to be followed if this third-party dissemination has already taken place. Underlying this policy is the idea that individuals are the Owners of their private information.

Related Policies: "Logging Movement Of Secret Documents" and "Distribution Of Marketing Materials."

Audience: All

Security Environments: All

78. Sharing Personal Information

Policy: Company X must not sell, rent, trade, lend, or otherwise transfer any personal information of customers or prospects to any other organization including, but not limited to, affiliates, subsidiaries, sister companies, holding companies, parent companies, and strategic partners.

Commentary: This policy addresses a loophole in many privacy laws and privacy policies. This loophole permits organizations with a privacy policy to say that they do not transfer private information to outside organizations, but they never explicitly define the term "outside organization." Instead, they declare many organizations to be part of their organizational structure. This permits them to share the private information in ways that customers and prospects did not originally intend and never explicitly agreed upon. For example, some banks have shared private information with insurance companies when they both have the same holding company. This policy prevents such abuses, and lets the public know that the organization has no intention of engaging in these deceptive practices. An exception for a transfer of personal information to an outsourcing organization may need to be added to this policy. In this case some additional assurances about confidentiality agreements and appropriate controls also may be added to the policy.

Related Policies: "Personal Data Transfer" and "Chain Of Trust Agreements."

Audience: End users

Security Environments: All

79. Transfer Of Customer Information

Policy: If Company X may go out of business, merge, be acquired, or otherwise change the legal form of its organizational structure, and as a result, Company X may need to share some or all of its customer information with another entity all customers must be promptly notified.

Commentary: This policy permits an organization to have great flexibility in the way it conducts its business, and not have certain business opportunities declared out of the question because a restrictive privacy policy has been previously adopted. The policy implicitly acknowledges that information systems service providers often go through changes in business form. The policy is decidedly pro-business and provides very little in terms of protection for the customer. The protection that this policy provides could be bolstered if another sentence were to be added to the end of the policy, such as "If customers object to this transfer, their information will not be transferred or otherwise used by the other entity." The policy does not permit the organization to sell customer information as a separate and distinct asset, whether the sale is in the midst of a bankruptcy action or otherwise. Only if similar products or services continue to be provided would such a sale of a customer list be permissible.

Related Policies: "Personal Data Uses After Merger Or Acquisition."

Audience: End users

Security Environments: All

80. Personal Data Transfer

Policy: Company X must not share the personal data about its customers with any other organization other than Company X subsidiaries, outsourcing organizations, and strategic business partners unless Company X experiences a bankruptcy, a merger, or an acquisition.

Commentary: This policy protects the issuing organization and provides little privacy protection. The policy is not presented as a good example of a privacy policy. This policy is based on the policies of a number of large online businesses that exempt themselves from protecting personal data in the event of bankruptcy or buyout. While an organization in some jurisdictions may legally adopt a policy like this, it should have sufficient public relations support to defend itself against allegations that it is a bad corporate citizen,

deliberately violating the rights of customers, and unwilling to take a stand on privacy matters. A backup policy that is more stringent should also be approved and available, so that a new and more rigorous policy can be issued quickly when and if such allegations are made against the organization.

Related Policies: "Transfer Of Customer Information" and "Blocking Private Data Usage."

Audience: End users

Security Environments: All

81. Personal Data Uses After Merger Or Acquisition

Policy: If Company X or any of its personal information collections are sold, merged, acquired, or otherwise transferred to another organization, such personal information may not be used for new and unanticipated purposes unless the involved individuals approve these new uses.

Commentary: This policy is intended to provide customers and prospects with additional assurance that their personal information will not be used for new and different purposes that they did not approve simply because the Custodian of their data happens to have been merged, been acquired, gone bankrupt, or in some other way changed the nature of its business. This policy not only addresses changes in the ownership of the personal information Custodian, but it also considers the outright sale of the personal information to another entity. The policy informs customers and prospects that such a sale or transfer might take place, and it assures them that new uses will not occur as a result of this change unless their explicit consent is obtained. This policy assumes that the uses of the personal or private data are explained elsewhere in a policy statement. This policy deliberately restricts the activities of internal Marketing management that wishes to utilize the latest technology to learn about customers and prospects. Anticipated internal uses should be mentioned in the policy that could be posted to a web site or Internet commerce site.

Related Policies: "Privacy Policy Application" and "Private Data System Approval."

Audience: End users and technical staff

Security Environments: All

82. Business Structure Changes And Transfer Of Private Data

Policy: Company X must not transfer customer private data to third parties no matter what business changes the organization experiences.

Commentary: This policy responds to Internet commerce customers who are concerned that their private information may be sold to a third party in order to satisfy unpaid obligations of the business. This would be a violation of the privacy policy unless the policy specifically mentioned business changes such as bankruptcy. This policy is necessary because the practice of transferring customer private data as part of a merger or acquisition is common in the business world. The policy blocks such transfers, and eliminates any uncertainty that might later lead to a legal dispute. Some organizations attempt to avoid their prior commitments to privacy, stating that the name of the organization will be transferred along with the list, so technically they are not selling to a third party. But claims such as this give the Internet business community a bad name with privacy advocates. The policy described here can help restore some of this lost confidence.

Related Policies: "Personal Data Uses After Merger Or Acquisition."

Audience: End users

Security Environments: All

83. Database Indexes Containing Private Information

Policy: Company X must annually update an index to all in-house databases and files containing private information, and make this index available to workers and third parties described in these databases and files.

Commentary: This policy ensures that the people who are described are aware of all private computerized records about them. This knowledge will permit individuals to check the records for accuracy, and to oversee the proper distribution of this private information. If individuals do not know that such information exists and where it is kept, they cannot object or otherwise exercise their rights regarding information about them. An index of all databases containing private information is also useful from an information security management standpoint, because it can be used to ensure that private information is consistently receiving the protection it needs. It would, for example, be helpful when determining whether information is protected in a manner commensurate with its sensitivity no matter where it resides, no matter who has access to it, no matter what form it takes, no matter what technology is used to handle it, and no matter what purpose it serves.

Related Policies: "Private Information Collection Approval" and "Asset Inventory — Information."

Audience: Management

Security Environments: All

84. Employee Access Production Information Type List

Policy: Information Technology management must create and annually update a complete list of the types of production information maintained by Company X, make this list available to all employees, and inform employees which types of information are available for their inspection.

Commentary: The purpose of this policy is to reveal the types of information in the possession of the organization, and to inform employees what types of personal information the organization keeps about them. The policy is supportive of privacy in that it requires that all employees be informed why they cannot access certain types of data, if that is the case. While this policy may seem difficult to implement, it does not require much beyond the establishment and maintenance of an organization-wide data dictionary. The requirements are not as burdensome as they may seem because this data dictionary is restricted to production information types. The benefits of the policy are mostly in the area of public relations and employee morale improvement. The policy will also help with information systems management activities such as database and application system planning.

Related Policies: "Private Information Collection Approval" and "Corporate Data Dictionary."

Audience: Management

Security Environments: All

85. Refusal To Provide Unnecessary Information

Policy: No benefit provided by Company X must be denied to any person if they refuse to provide unnecessary private information with all disputes about the definition of "necessary private information" resolved by Company X legal counsel.

Commentary: This policy prevents workers, customers, and others from suffering because they choose to withhold private information that is not required. For example, if a supermarket asked for information about marital status, then check cashing and other services of the supermarket should not be withheld because marital status information is not provided. Products or services may be withheld if the information that has not been provided is necessary.

Related Policies: "Malfunctioning Access Control," "Grievance Resolution," and "Prospective Employee Credit Checks."

Audience: Management

Security Environments: All

86. Encryption Of Private Electronic Mail

Policy: Unencrypted information that has been labeled private must never be transmitted through electronic mail.

Commentary: This policy prevents private information from being intercepted by unauthorized parties. The encryption described in the policy could be provided by the user or it could be a part of the electronic mail system itself. The user is required to ensure that encryption is used before he or she sends private information. The policy assumes that a data classification system that defines the label "private" has already been adopted. This is a recommended policy because Internet electronic mail is not a secure method of transmitting any information.

Related Policies: "Faxing Secret Information — Encryption" and "Secret Information In Electronic Mail."

Audience: End users

Security Environments: All

87. Privacy Policy Change Notification

Policy: Company X staff members must take reasonable steps to promptly notify all affected individuals whenever there has been a material change in documented privacy policies.

Commentary: This policy ensures that workers take steps to promptly notify affected individuals whenever there has been a significant change in a privacy policy. For example, a restriction of previously-promised privacy rights would warrant such a notice. Such a notification could, for example, be easily achieved by posting a few words on the home page at web site. This policy is intended to provide evidence that management attempted to notify all affected individuals when it changed its privacy policy. Realistically, not all individuals will be accessible due to changes of address, unlisted phone numbers, inaccurate electronic mail addresses, and other problems. Reflecting difficulties associated with notifying the affected individuals, the policy uses the words "reasonable steps." The policy requires notice after the change has taken place and permits these affected individuals to change their relationship with the involved organization, should they wish to do so in response to the policy change. The policy permits the notified individuals to then accept or reject a new service, perhaps through the Internet with a form that can handle this process automatically.

Related Policies: "Personal Data Gathering Points And Privacy" and "Systems Monitoring Tools."

Audience: Management

Security Environments: All

88. Privacy Policy Differences Summary

Policy: When Company X changes the privacy policy, all who are affected must be notified and provided with a summary of all changes and their anticipated impact.

Commentary: This policy builds user confidence about doing business with an Internet merchant. Customers and prospects want to know what their interaction with an organization is going to be like in the future. This policy reduces fears about future abuse of private data collected by an Internet merchant. The policy indicates that the issuer of the policy will provide a summary of differences. This makes life much easier for users because they do not have to read the entire policy again, then try to determine what has changed. This policy is in distinct opposition to the privacy unfriendly practices of some online merchants who expect the reader to look at their privacy policy periodically to determine, on their own, if the policy has been changed, and if it has, how it has changed. The latter approach puts an unreasonable burden on the user.

Related Policies: "Privacy Policy Relevance" and "Privacy Policy Change Notification."

Audience: End users

Security Environments: All

89. Privacy Policy Relevance

Policy: Company X must ensure that its privacy policy is complete, that there are no exceptions to the policy that are not included and that the policy pertains to all interactions with customers, no matter what communications channel, no matter what involved department within Company X, and no matter what topic the interaction covers.

Commentary: This policy may appear to be unnecessary. However, the latest privacy abuses by Internet merchants indicate otherwise. Some health care organizations have posted a privacy policy for their web site that indicates they will not share personal health information with third parties. They also have chat rooms or other facilities that have another policy saying that "anything a participant transmits or posts can be used for any purpose." Some visitors to the site may have read the web site policy but may not have carefully read the policy that pertains to the chat rooms or other facilities. Privacy policy is already a very complex area, and these Internet merchant maneuvers only confuse participants and give the industry a bad reputation. This policy informs policy readers that there is only one policy, and that they do not have to locate and read separate policies for different types of interactions with Company X.

Related Policies: "Customer Access To Personal Information."

Audience: End users

Security Environments: All

90. Personal Data Gathering Points And Privacy

Policy: All points where personal data is gathered for use in Company X information systems must include a copy of the Company X privacy policy approved by Information Security management.

Commentary: The purpose of this policy is to require that prospects and customers be consistently informed about the Company X privacy policy. This policy indicates that at every point where personal data is gathered, there must be a statement about privacy. Not all of these copies of the privacy policy will need to be comprehensive. The information can instead be tailored to the nature of the information being collected. This policy prevents disputes that occur by different departments saying different things about privacy. This policy assumes that a corporate privacy policy has been developed and published. The policy also assumes that workers know what personal data is.

Related Policies: "Systems Monitoring Tools" and "Prospective Employee Credit Checks."

Audience: Technical staff

Security Environments: All

91. Identity Of Private Information Collector

Policy: Both the collecting organization's legal name and current contact information must be disclosed at each point where private information is collected.

Commentary: This policy prevents the collection of private information by third parties unbeknownst to a user. Certain marketing organizations now collect mouse movement information from web surfers, but the entity collecting this information and the contact particulars for this entity are regularly not disclosed. To not disclose the third party's name, and to not provide contact information, to many people seems to be dishonest and reprehensible. The fact that the information is being collected should also be disclosed. This policy will help instruct web site and commerce site designers about the disclosures they must make. If some of these designers believe that the disclosures mandated by this policy will jeopardize their private information collection activities, then the propriety of the collection activities needs further examination. The word "private" may also need a definition at the organization adopting this policy. For example, if click stream data were anonymous, it generally would not be considered to be private, even though it describes activities of certain people.

Related Policies: "Information Collection Notice" and "Surreptitious Collection Of Private Information."

Audience: Technical staff

Security Environments: All

92. Private Information Requirement Explanation

Policy: Whenever private information is requested by Company X information systems or workers, the full and complete reasons for collecting this information must also be disclosed.

Commentary: This policy gives the individual disclosing private data sufficient information on which to base a disclosure decision. For example, someone applying for government welfare payments may be required to provide information about their income, their financial resources, and their personal property. Without this information, the government may refuse to provide welfare, and this fact may be disclosed to the individual at the point of information collection. This policy limits the things that the collecting organization can do with the private information because the purposes for collection were disclosed at the time that the information was provided. Some organizations may wish to delete the words "full and complete" from the policy, in order to give themselves an opportunity to use the information for other purposes in the future. The removal of these words is discouraged because subsequent use for undisclosed purposes is likely to place the organization in an awkward public relations and customer relations situation.

Related Policies: "Employee Explanatory Statement" and "User Awareness Of Logging And Security Violations."

Audience: Technical staff

Security Environments: All

93. Distribution Of Privacy Policies

Policy: All internal Company X privacy policies that a prospect or a customer may need to know must be publicly posted or otherwise periodically distributed to these same people.

Commentary: This policy gets internal management thinking about what prospects and customers need to know about the privacy of data in the possession of Company X. Whatever these policies may be, they must be communicated to these people so that these people can appropriately manage information about themselves. This policy is recommended because it requires internal management to regularly adjust its privacy policies in line with changes in the matters that prospects and customers need to know. For example, as identity theft becomes more of an issue in the years ahead, these same people will need to know more about how to protect themselves and what the adopting organization is doing to help prevent identity theft. This would typically involve periodic revisions to the posted privacy policy. The way that many financial institutions implement this policy is to include paper inserts with their monthly bills once or twice a year. Posting privacy policies to web sites and other public locations is also advisable.

Related Policies: "Privacy Policy Change Notification" and "Personal Data Gathering Points And Privacy."

Audience: Management and technical staff

Security Environments: All

94. Examination Of Private User Files

Policy: Whenever private user files are examined to handle emergencies or other business needs by authorized system administrators, the involved user must be promptly notified, unless an investigation of alleged abusive or criminal acts is underway.

Commentary: This policy is intended to inform users that their files may be examined and copied by a system administrator in the course of normal business activities. Some organizations may also wish to require that administrators get management permission prior to examining private user files. An alternative and more expedient way to handle the management approval issue is to require administrators to notify management after the fact. Some organizations may wish to limit the notification part of policy to internal users. Notification to outsiders may cause problems. This policy provides a weak assurance of privacy because it states administrators will only look at user files for legitimate business needs.

Related Policies: "Sensitive Or Valuable Information Access," "Granting Access To Organization Information," and "Electronic Mail Privacy."

Audience: End users and technical staff

Security Environments: All

95. Personal Information Changes

Policy: Before any personal information in Company X production systems is altered based on a customer request, the correct prior information must be provided by the customer.

Commentary: This policy requires that customer service representatives confirm the prior version of personal information before these representatives make any changes to production information system databases. If a customer at the other end of an Internet connection or a phone line is not able to provide the correct prior version, chances are that he or she is not the authorized person to request the change. This is a weak control that needs to be used in conjunction with other security measures such as a customer specific password, or some other mechanism to verify the identity of the person submitting a change request. Some organizations permit customer service representatives to give hints that will prompt the customer to provide the correct prior information, even though this minimizes the effectiveness of the control.

Related Policies: "Customer Service Passwords" and "Computer Support Identification Codes."

Audience: Technical staff

Security Environments: All

12.01.05 Prevention Of Misuse Of Information Processing Facilities

1. Games On Organization Computer Systems

Policy: Games may not be stored or used on any Company X computer systems.

Commentary: This policy states that games must not be used on Company X systems. Games are often downloaded from web sites and bulletin boards, and may be infected with computer viruses or Trojan horses. Likewise, games may distract employees from their assigned duties. Games may additionally set an inappropriately playful and informal atmosphere that some organizations see as unbusinesslike. Because games are often duplicated and distributed illegally, games may also inadvertently subject an organization to liability for unauthorized software copying. Because most games reside on personal computers, workstations, and other small systems, this policy is particularly relevant to the small systems environment. Some organizations will want to expand the scope of the policy to include public domain software. Public domain software is also likely to contain viruses, Trojan horses, and other undesirable and unauthorized functionality. This policy may be enforced through automated software license managers that prevent execution of software that has not been approved by management.

Related Policies: "Personal Use Of Computer And Communications Systems" and "Making Copies Of Software."

Audience: All

Security Environments: All

2. Personal Use Of Computer And Communications Systems

Policy: Company X computer and communications systems must be used for business purposes only, unless special permission of a department manager has been obtained.

Commentary: This policy provides guidance regarding personal use of computer and communication systems. Without such notice, an employee could, for example, be covertly running his or her own computer service bureau, supporting betting pools, playing computer games, or making excessive long-distance personal phone calls. When confronted about such activity, they may say that they understood it was permissible, or that it was a fringe benefit. As a variation on the standard approach described in this policy, some organizations permit personal use if it is strictly personal. With this variation, if the use is to support another business, such as selling insurance as a second job, then such use is prohibited. Other organizations permit personal usage during off-peak hours or during staff non-working hours. Whatever philosophy the organization adopts, it is wise to provide a precise definition of the term "personal use." This definition needs to address situations such as computer programming homework assignments for a course taken at a local university, that is intended to augment the skills used on this employee's regular job. This policy applies to in-house staff rather than those who subscribe to a Internet service provider operation, or run an outsourcing computer center. The person to provide approval is a department manager, perhaps a vice president instead of an information Owner because this policy relates to an employee's use of systems rather than information. Unless special monitoring software is used, this policy may be difficult to police because mobile phones, portable computers, and related equipment is often used in the field away from management's eyes. That is not to say that the policy should be abandoned. In fact the policy may become increasingly important as a way for an organization to prevent liability for unauthorized activity performed with its systems.

Related Policies: "Non-Business Use Of Organization Information," "Personal Telephone Usage," "Electronic Mail System Usages," "Personal Use Of Internet," and "Games On Organization Computer Systems."

Audience: All

Security Environments: All

3. Incidental Personal Use Of Computer Communications Systems

Policy: Company X computer and communication systems must be used only for business purposes unless the use does not consume more than a trivial amount of resources that could otherwise be used for business purposes, does not interfere with worker productivity, and does not preempt any business activity.

Commentary: This policy defines personal use of business information systems such as telephone systems, electronic mail systems, and Internet access dial-up systems. This policy describes prevailing practice at many organizations in a truthful way. This policy should be compared with many existing personal use policies that are excessively rigid. For example, some policies prohibit a worker from making a personal call to a baby-sitter to arrange a time to pick up a child. This could be counterproductive when the worker needs to make new arrangements so that he or she can stay overtime. The restrictions mentioned in this policy about incidental use permit personal usage as long as the stated conditions are met. This approach makes employees responsible for policing personal use rather than management.

Related Policies: "Personal Use Of Computer And Communications Systems," "Personal Telephone Usage," and "Games On Organization Computer Systems."

Audience: All

Security Environments: All

4. Reasonable Personal Use Of Computer And Communications Systems

Policy: Reasonable personal use of Company X computer and communications systems must be consistent with conventional standards of ethical and polite conduct.

Commentary: This policy clarifies what constitutes acceptable personal use of Company X information systems. The policy is deliberately flexible in nature, and it need not be adjusted much, if at all, because conventional standards of ethical and polite conduct change. For example, the transmission of unrestrained and heated insults is becoming less of a problem on the Internet and this change is a reflection of an evolving standard of conduct. The word "reasonable" was used to permit management to have confidential talks with workers about their personal usage of system resources, which then hopefully will encourage these workers to spend more time on business matters and less time on personal matters. This policy works best if supplemented with controls that measure or block certain types of personal use. For example, a firewall can be used to block specific sites on the Web.

Related Policies: "Personal Use Of Computer And Communications Systems" and "Incidental Personal Use Of Computer Communications Systems."

Audience: End users and management

Security Environments: All

5. User Access To Internet

Policy: Users who access the Internet with Company X facilities must be informed that they do so at their own risk, and that Company X is not responsible for material viewed, downloaded, or received by users through the Internet.

Commentary: This policy informs users that they are likely to encounter offensive material on the Internet, and that Company X has not screened the Internet for them. Even when various software filters are used to block objectionable web sites and screen out undesirable electronic mail messages, some objectionable material will inevitably get through. These filters are never perfect, and in part because the Internet is changing so rapidly, the filters can never realistically be configured to block everything. The policy informs users that this objectionable material is out there, and that they should not hold Company X responsible for protecting them from this material. With this policy, allegations that Company X created a hostile workplace or fostered an unacceptable working environment can be avoided.

Related Policies: "Non-Business Web Sites," "Internet Traffic Control," and "Outbound Internet Communications."

Audience: End users

Security Environments: All

6. Classifying Acceptable Internet Use

Policy: Internet usage must be classified as red, which is prohibited at all times, yellow, which is permissible only if departmental managers approve, or green, permissible at any time.

Commentary: This policy is intended to succinctly describe what is and what is not permissible when it comes to Internet usage with Company X facilities. For example, the red group could include release of internal Company X information, downloading software or copyrighted material, downloading offensive material, for-profit personal use of Company X resources, issuing threats, making sexually harassing remarks, or bothering other users. The yellow group may include personal Internet shopping, surfing to stay on top of personal interests, and personal financial management. The green group might include buying products and services for Company X, business-related electronic mail, professional development, research for Company X and research for academic courses. This approach is flexible because additional behaviors can easily be added to any of the three categories. This policy offers an uncommon amount of flexibility because the yellow category is left to the discretion of local management.

Related Policies: "Network Security Zones" and "Large Internet Downloads."

Audience: End users

Security Environments: All

7. Unacceptable Use Of Computer And Communication Systems

Policy: Subscribers to Company X computing and communications services must not use these facilities for soliciting business, selling products, or otherwise engaging in commercial activities other than those expressly permitted by Company X management.

Commentary: This policy strictly limits the authorized uses of the computer and communications services provided by Company X. This policy applies to those who pay to use Company X facilities. This policy is relevant to an electronic bulletin board, a computer service bureau, a value added network, an Internet service provider, an Internet information content provider, and similar organizations. Many organizations are uneasy about the establishment of value-added products and services on top of their basic computer and communications services, and at the very least require that such value-added products and services be approved in advance. Some organizations may want to add a clause to this policy that prohibits charitable, political, religious, and other activities that are not directly business-related. Some organizations may find this policy especially helpful when denying future services to a user or subscriber.

Related Policies: "Personal Use Of Computer And Communications Systems" and "Electronic Mail System Usages."

Audience: All

Security Environments: All

8. Personal Use Of Internet

Policy: Company X information systems must not be used to access the Internet for personal purposes.

Commentary: This policy about Internet access makes it clear that workers must not be using Company X facilities to access the Internet. Nothing in the policy prohibits workers from cruising the Internet on their own time, using their own systems. A policy such as this is often adopted by management out of frustration with the inordinate amount of time that workers spend on the Internet. It is primarily a productivity-enhancement policy. The policy also reduces the incidence of unauthorized representations of Company X on the Internet. This is achieved by clearly separating work-related and personal uses of the Internet. This policy may be viewed as too strict for some organizations. Other options include personal use of the Internet only after explicit management approval, or use only in response to an approved business purpose. Some organizations may wish to give examples of prohibited personal use. These may include operating an outside business, searching for jobs outside Company X, sending chain letters, and soliciting contributions for religious or political causes.

Related Policies: "Unacceptable Use Of Computer And Communication Systems," "Personal Use Of Computer And Communications Systems," and "Personal Telephone Usage."

Audience: End users

Security Environments: All

9. Personal Use Of Organization Internet Facilities

Policy: All workers who access the Internet for personal reasons using Company X Internet facilities must limit this activity to their personal time.

Commentary: The purpose of this policy is to ensure employees know that they should not be accessing the Internet for personal reasons during work hours. Some managers are concerned that the availability of Internet access will distract workers from their regular duties. This policy permits users to take advantage of Company X facilities for personal purposes, but makes it clear when such use must take place. The organization should also consider deployment of a number of monitoring products that permit management to determine the nature of Internet usage and the times when this usage is occurring, then to determine whether this usage is consistent with in-house policy. This policy recognizes that, at many organizations, personal Internet use is already recognized as a fringe benefit. The policy assumes that personal use will help workers become more proficient with Internet, and that this will indirectly assist with business uses of the Internet. Those organizations wanting to take a stricter approach may forbid all personal Internet use during business hours.

Related Policies: "Personal User IDs — Responsibility" and "Personal Use Of Computer And Communications Systems."

Audience: End users

Security Environments: All

10. Personal Internet Access Time

Policy: Worker access to the Internet for personal reasons while using Company X Internet facilities must occur only after normal business hours.

Commentary: This policy sets a time after which it is permissible for staff to access the Internet. The existence of such a time makes it clear that during working hours, workers should be using information systems only for business purposes. The existence of such a cut-off time makes it much easier for automated log analysis routines to determine whether inappropriate Internet surfing is taking place during working hours. The policy not only reduces network bandwidth requirements during the day, but it also promotes productivity. To formally permit the usage of Company X information systems for personal purposes is also realistic and most likely will be appreciated by the involved workers. This policy will work poorly at an organization that supports flextime.

Related Policies: "Personal Use Of Computer And Communications Systems" and "Personal Use Of Internet."

Audience: End users

Security Environments: All

11. Personal Use Restrictions

Policy: Incidental personal use of Company X computer and communication systems must be restricted to an hour or less per month, and must not include creation or distribution of chain letters, exchanging information that might be considered indecent, receipt or forwarding of jokes, moonlighting or searching for another job, participation in gambling activities, or engagement in political or charitable activities.

Commentary: This policy is intended to make it clear exactly what is expected in terms of personal use. A specific time limit on personal use is coupled with a list of prohibited activities to clarify expectations. Such a policy can be especially useful when disciplinary actions are taken in response to certain unauthorized usage. Some organizations may wish to extend the list of prohibited activities to include issuance of solicitations or advertisements, and receiving messages from electronic mailing lists that are not related to Company X business. There is nothing special about the one hour period mentioned in the policy. This could just have easily been some other period of time.

Related Policies: "Personal Use Of Internet."

Audience: End users

Security Environments: All

12. User IDs Employed In Abusive Activity

Policy: All system privileges for a user ID shown to be engaged in abusive or criminal activity must be immediately revoked.

Commentary: This policy prevents further abuse or criminal activity. While this policy makes it difficult for staff to trace and log further activity on the involved user ID, it has the merits of immediately taking action in order to minimize losses. The policy clearly puts the priority on loss minimization, not on gathering sufficient evidence to prosecute. Most organizations would agree with this prioritization because they do not want the publicity associated with a court case. This policy permits a scripted response to be programmed in response to conclusions reached by an intrusion detection system (IDS) or operating system logging software. If an operating system logging routine reveals that someone is abusing a particular user ID, for example by attempting to guess passwords, then the user ID's privileges can be immediately disabled. This automated response can be fully scripted with an IDS so that much more complicated attacks can be noticed and immediately acted upon. One such example is a hacker's attempt to exploit certain known vulnerabilities inherent in operating system software. The response dictated by the policy can also be manual. Some organizations may wish to exempt system administrator user IDs from this policy, because shutting down privileges for these user IDs may lock certain authorized persons off the system.

Related Policies: "Access Privileges Termination" and "Password Reset After Lockout."

Audience: Technical staff

Security Environments: All

13. Systems Security Testing Tools

Policy: Company X workers must not acquire, possess, trade, or use hardware or software tools that could be employed to evaluate or compromise information systems security, unless specifically authorized by Information Security management.

Commentary: Because these tools can be and often are used to circumvent controls, their possession and use should be severely restricted. Possession and use should be permitted only for those who have a need for such powerful tools, such as information technology auditors and penetration attack team members. While these tools are readily available on the open market, on the Internet, and on electronic bulletin boards, Company X users should not be in possession of them. For the same reason, users should not have a database that contains working serial numbers needed to operate stolen software. There is a potential problem with this policy. It could prohibit use of powerful system utilities. In some cases these utilities can be used to circumvent control mechanisms, such as certain password-based access control systems for personal computers. To ensure that users do not confuse these common utilities with the programs deliberately intended to break security, adjectives like "unauthorized" could precede each type of tool mentioned in the policy. Another way to handle this distinction is through the use of a list of organization-approved hardware and software. Additional explanatory text can clarify this distinction, as the needs of the policy-reading audience require. Some users may claim that they never intended to use such tools, that they only acquired them to learn about computers. This policy removes the whole question of the user's intent from the discussion. If users have the tools, they may be disciplined or terminated.

Related Policies: "Testing Information System Controls," "Disclosure Of Information System Vulnerabilities," and "System Security Status Tools."

Audience: End users and technical staff

Security Environments: All

14. Non-Business Use Of Organization Information

Policy: Use of Company X information for any purpose that is specifically designated by management must be approved by written permission from the designated Owner of the information.

Commentary: This policy provides clear guidance regarding the use of Company X internal information resources for purposes other than ordinary business activities. It is advisable to attach an explanation to this policy providing examples of both acceptable and unacceptable business purposes. This explanation can also provide a variety of other scenarios that are prohibited. If an employee has a question about a certain use of Company X information, this policy implies that he or she should ask before using the information. The policy also should result in staff being more conscious about using internal information for a purpose other than the originally intended purpose. Requests to clarify certain uses of information will require management to define appropriate use. Over time, the existence of the approval process may tend to discourage questionable practices that could create problems. This policy eliminates those circumstances where an employee says that they did not know that it was not acceptable to use internal information for non-business purposes. Lack of employee notice has been effectively used as a defense in various legal proceedings.

Related Policies: "Personal Use Of Computer And Communications Systems," "Use Of Information," and "Electronic Mail System Usages."

Audience: All

Security Environments: All

15. Examination Of Data Stored On Systems

Policy: Company X management must reserve the right to examine all information stored in or transmitted by its computer and communications systems, and must inform all workers that they should have no expectation of privacy associated with the information they store in or send through these systems.

Commentary: While management can choose to provide employees with the same privacy rights that they would enjoy when using a common carrier such as the telephone company, most employers are adopting a policy such as the one shown here. Whatever position management chooses to follow, it is important that the privacy status of employee-generated data on Company X systems be clearly specified. If employees know that management may examine such data, they will be more likely to refrain from using Company X systems for non-business activities. Employee expectations should also be clarified to avoid litigation, employee grievances, and morale problems.

Related Policies: "Intellectual Property Rights," "Electronic Mail Message Monitoring," and "Personal File Privacy."

Audience: All

Security Environments: All

16. Electronic Monitoring Areas

Policy: Workers must be informed that they may be subject to electronic monitoring in areas where there is no reasonable expectation of privacy while on Company X premises in order to support the measurement of worker performance and to protect worker personal property, worker safety, and Company X property.

Commentary: This policy informs workers that they are subject to electronic monitoring. This negates any objection that they may later make stating that their privacy was invaded without their knowledge. The policy clearly states the areas where worker privacy will be honored. Some organizations may wish to drop the phrase, "where there is no reasonable expectation of privacy" in order to not disclose where they may perform illegal activities without being noticed. The policy establishes an understanding about the areas where electronic monitoring may and may not be used.

Related Policies: "Electronic Mail Message Monitoring" and "Surreptitious Collection Of Private Information."

Audience: End users

Security Environments: All

17. Discussions Using Computer and Communication Facilities

Policy: Company X internal computer and communication systems must not be used as an open forum to discuss Company X organizational changes or business policy matters.

Commentary: This policy permits management to censor certain uses of internal computer and communication systems and, if necessary, to discipline the individuals using these systems for unauthorized activity. This would, for example, be important when personnel changes were being performed. For employee morale reasons, open discussion of such matters should not be found on these internal systems. An announcement describing the appointment of a new manager or staff member would be permissible under the policy as it is written because this does not involve "discussion." It is free and open exchange about the referenced topics that many organizations find threatening and therefore wish to prohibit. The list of topics referenced may be expanded to include new products, strategic planning, product pricing, customer relations, and related considerations. This policy makes it clear that the named systems are not an appropriate place to address such matters.

Related Policies: "Right To Free Speech" and "Personal Use Of Internet."

Audience: End users

Security Environments: All

12.01.06 Regulation Of Cryptographic Controls

1. International Trade Armaments

Policy: Users must not distribute, directly or indirectly, encryption software or any other munitions of war as defined in any international trade in armaments regulations.

Commentary: This policy reduces the liability risk faced by the provider of network services or similar facilities. Another intention of this policy relates to training and awareness. The policy gives users an opportunity to acknowledge that they will not distribute encryption software or other items considered to be munitions of war. Although these regulations are widely considered to be antiquated and of questionable value, and although they are increasingly coming under attack as constraints to the expansion of the software industry and Internet businesses, the regulations are in effect. Some organizations require users to acknowledge that they will comply with these regulations before they are given access to organizational facilities. Sometimes this is done for physical entrance to offices. This policy would be shown at the time that a new user is given an overview of available network services. Another way to handle this type of acknowledgement is to have users sign a piece of paper stating that they will not knowingly export, directly or indirectly, any technical data, product, or software to any restricted country, without having obtained government permission. If an illegal distribution of munitions of war does take place, this policy may be helpful in reducing fines or other penalties to the organization issuing the policy.

Related Policies: "Faxing Sensitive Information — Unencrypted."

Audience: End users

Security Environments: Medium and high

12.01.07 Collection Of Evidence

1. Computer Crime Or Abuse Evidence

Policy: All information related to a suspected computer crime of abuse including, but not limited to, the current system configuration and backup copies of all potentially involved files, must be immediately captured and securely stored off-line until official custody is given to another authorized person or the chief legal counsel determines that Company X will no longer need the information.

Commentary: This policy is intended to inform systems management staff that certain information must be captured and securely stored until needed by internal auditors, corporate counsel, security administrators, and others. The policy permits evidence to be captured and properly secured, in order to be admissible in court. If the evidence remained on the involved computer for a certain period, there is a possibility that unauthorized parties could have modified it. If the evidence could have been modified, it will not be considered admissible evidence. The process of capturing information should take place even if there is only a suspected problem. It is better to have this information, then dispose of it when not needed, than to not have the information for prosecution. The policy ensures that a snapshot of the current state of systems and files is preserved for later use.

Related Policies: "Privileged System Command Accountability And Traceability."

Audience: Technical staff

Security Environments: All

2. Sources Of Digital Evidence

Policy: For every production computer system, the Information Security department must identify the sources of digital evidence that reasonably could be expected to be used in a court case and implement a standardized capture, retention, and destruction process comparable to that used for vital records.

Commentary: This policy establishes a formal process to identify sources of digital evidence before a security incident takes place. With this proactive approach, system administrators and other staff members can take steps to properly handle any digital evidence. For example, potential digital evidence needs to go through a chain of custody process, whereas what was perceived to be system logs from production systems would usually not go though such a process. If the process was not being observed from the time when this information was originally recorded, such log files may not be admissible in court as evidence. This depends on the rules of evidence within the affected jurisdiction. This policy fosters a new consciousness about the potential value of system logs, application audit trails, database transaction logs, and other records. This policy also ensures that information that is potentially important for forensic investigations is being properly captured.

Related Policies: "Logging Logon Attempts" and "Electronic Mail Archival."

Audience: Technical staff

Security Environments: Medium and high

3. Disclosure Of Information To Law Enforcement

Policy: Users must consent to permit all information they store on Company X systems to be divulged to law enforcement at the discretion of Company X management.

Commentary: This policy informs users that they should not have an expectation of privacy with respect to Company X systems. It also notifies users that no search warrant will be necessary before law enforcement agents gain access to information that they store on Company X systems. Management may wish to reveal certain information to law enforcement. This could be appropriate if management discovered the use of its computing facilities to conduct some illegal activity. This policy manages user expectations, ensuring that users understand they do not have normal privacy protections applicable to public communications carriers like the phone company.

Related Policies: "Examination Of Data Stored On Systems," "Third-Party Private Information Disclosure," and "Electronic Mail Message Monitoring."

Audience: All

Security Environments: All

4. Performance Monitoring Information

Policy: Management must not use computers to automatically collect information about the performance of workers unless the involved workers have collectively agreed that such information realistically reflects their job-related performance.

Commentary: Union contracts may dictate that a collective decision be made prior to the installation of such performance monitoring systems. Regardless of the presence of a union, from a personnel relations

standpoint, it is advisable for employees to be aware of any decision to collect and use such data. This policy prevents management from installing and using performance monitoring technology unless it is discussed with employees and acknowledged as relevant. The policy does not interfere with certain information systems security tools such as those that permit a computer operator to surreptitiously examine the information displayed on a remote user's screen. These tools are used by help desk personnel to resolve problems, and by information security staff to perform investigations.

Related Policies: "Private Information Collection Approval" and "Use Of Telephone Conference Or Recording Technology."

Audience: All

Security Environments: All

5. Monitoring Permission

Policy: Company X must not monitor the communications of an employee without obtaining the employee's permission, unless advance permission is likely to change any specific behavior.

Commentary: This policy assures employees that they are not being monitored without their knowledge. Some organizations will want to augment this policy with further exceptions necessary to properly manage the involved information systems. This can include processes to recover from a virus infestation or to gather evidence of unauthorized systems penetrations. This policy covers only employees and not to temporaries, consultants, contractors, strategic business partners, or other third parties. If these other categories of individuals should be covered, then the word "workers" can be used.

Related Policies: "Electronic Mail Message Monitoring."

Audience: End users

Security Environments: All

6. Blanket Monitoring Employee Communications

Policy: Company X must not engage in blanket monitoring of employee communications unless a legitimate business need exists that cannot be satisfied by other means, the involved employee is unavailable and timing is critical to a business activity, there is reasonable cause to suspect criminal activity or policy violation, or monitoring is required by law, regulation, or third-party agreement.

Commentary: This policy informs employees that their communications may be monitored under certain circumstances. The policy also assures employees that a blanket monitoring process does not exist, and the right to monitor will be used judiciously and only when a legitimate business need exists. This policy covers only employees and not temporaries, consultants, contractors, strategic business partners, or other third parties. A legitimate business need can cover a variety of technical problems such as recovery from a virus infestation.

Related Policies: "Privacy Expectations And Information Stored On Organization Systems."

Audience: End users

Security Environments: All

7. Monitoring Or Recording Telephone Conversations

Policy: Company X worker telephone conversations must not be monitored or recorded unless a clearly audible beeping tone accompanies the monitoring.

Commentary: A provision permitting unannounced monitoring to prevent or investigate illegal activities may be added to this policy as an exception. In keeping with certain wiretapping statutes, this policy requires that the parties to a conversation be informed that a third party is listening or recording the conversation. The policy requires that non-private telephone conversations be clearly understood as such by both parties. The policy also requires that employees who are recording their own conversations with third parties inform the third parties about the recording activity.

Related Policies: "Performance Monitoring."

Audience: All

Security Environments: All

8. Internal Investigations Information Confidentiality

Policy: All investigations of alleged criminal or abusive conduct must be kept strictly confidential to preserve the reputation of the suspected party until charges are formalized or disciplinary action taken.

Commentary: Beyond the objective stated in the policy, this policy reduces the probability that Company X will be subject to a lawsuit alleging defamation of character. The intention of the policy is to clearly define the point when it becomes permissible to disclose information about employee investigations. One desirable aspect of this policy is that investigations that do not result in either prosecution or disciplinary action will never be disclosed. If the employee and the employee's coworkers never knew about the investigation, then the employee can remain in good standing with a good reputation. If the employee heard about an investigation in process that later turned out to be inappropriate, he or she may become disgruntled or soon leave the organization. If coworkers learn of an investigation that does not materialize, then the reputation of the accused has been needlessly degraded.

Related Policies: "Four-Category Data Classification," "Computer Crime Investigation," and "Worker Transfers."

Audience: Management

Security Environments: All

9. Law Enforcement Inquiries

Policy: Company X workers must not reveal any internal Company X information through any communications mechanism unless they have established the authenticity of the individual's identity and the legitimacy of the inquiry.

Commentary: This policy prevents social engineering where attackers pose as members of the law enforcement community. This is a common occurrence and such a masquerade or spoof can be successful. If a hacker posing as a government agent is able to get information about an organization's information system configurations, its previous intrusion problems, and the relevant decision-making managers, this can be of great use in a subsequent attack. The policy indicates that not everybody who alleges they are a member of the law enforcement community is in fact such a member. The specific ways to establish the requestor's identity and the ways to establish the legitimacy of an inquiry are deliberately not stated because they will vary based on jurisdiction and also the type of inquiry. In many instances, a confirming telephone call can be made to the director of the involved law enforcement agency to validate the identity of the person who is making inquires. ID badges can be examined if the contact is made in person. A warrant, a subpoena, or some other legal document may establish the legitimacy of an inquiry.

Related Policies: "Information Disclosure By Telephone" and "Requests For Organization Information."

Audience: End users

Security Environments: All

10. Legal Proceeding Participation

Policy: Any Company X worker called by a subpoena or in any other manner called to appear or testify before a judicial board or government agency must immediately notify the chief legal counsel in writing about the call.

Commentary: This policy alerts the Legal department about a call to testify before the appearance actually takes place. The Legal department may then take evasive action such as filing a motion to postpone the appearance or filing a formal objection. They may provide counsel to the person who will appear so that damage to Company X can be minimized. This policy is a specific instance of an overall objective to control the outflow of confidential information about the internal operations or historical activities of an organization.

Related Policies: "Violation Of Law" and "Electronic Mail Message Handling."

Audience: End users

Security Environments: All

11. Providing Information In Legal Proceedings

Policy: Workers must not provide any Company X records, or any copies thereof, to third parties outside of Company X or to government officials, whether in answer to a subpoena or otherwise, and must not testify to facts coming to their knowledge while performing in their official Company X capacities, unless the prior permission of the chief legal counsel has been obtained.

Commentary: This policy prevents workers from simply handing over internal documents or offering internal information, with the false understanding that

they were compelled to do so as required by law. Such requests for information can be initiated by an opposing party's legal counsel, and they may not be required. To disclose such information may furthermore damage the Company X position in a lawsuit that may be currently in court, or potentially in court sometime in the future.

Related Policies: "Legal Action Information" and "Data Destruction Moratorium."

Audience: End users

Security Environments: All

12. Criminal Justice Community Contact

Policy: Technical information systems staff must not contact the police or other members of the criminal justice community about any information systems problems unless they have received permission of the director of the Legal department.

Commentary: This policy limits reporting of information security problems to the criminal justice community. These technical staff members may be mistaken about a problem, may be overly-stressed, or may be holding a grudge against management. Reporting a problem to the criminal justice community may also lead to public relations problems that the organization may prefer to avoid altogether. Criminal justice agencies often have minimums before they will even open a case. The director of the Legal department can help technical staff determine whether to file a report, even if the alleged event did actually happen and there is plenty of good evidence. Rather than going through the director of the Legal department, technical staff members may be directed to get the approval of Information Security management. This policy assumes that the organization does not have a fully-developed computer emergency response team with documented procedures and in-depth training. If these exist, this policy will typically be covered in that documentation.

Related Policies: "Violation And Problem Reporting Interference" and "Employee Observance Of Privacy."

Audience: Technical staff

Security Environments: All

13. Investigation Status Reports

Policy: The status of information security investigations must be communicated to management only by the lead investigator or the management representative of the investigation team.

Commentary: This policy stops inaccurate and unnecessarily alarming reports from being passed to management. After an intrusion or some other information security problem, a number of people may act as though they know something about the incident, when in fact they have not been directly involved. This can lead to staff confusion, internal political problems, and excessive costs. This policy defines one for the transmission of information about the status of an investigation. The documentation of this limited pathway in the form of a policy also ensures that members of the management team do not react to, or take inappropriate action based on, the comments of people who do not know what is going on. This policy also ensures that specific details about the investigation are disclosed only to those persons who have a need to know. This will lower the chances of slander, libel, defamation of character, and other legal problems.

Related Policies: "Violation And Problem Analysis" and "Information Security Compliance Checking."

Audience: Technical staff

Security Environments: All

14. Computer Crime Investigation Information

Policy: All evidence, ideas, and hypotheses about computer crimes experienced by Company X, including possible attack methods and perpetrator intentions, must be communicated to internal legal counsel and treated as restricted and legally privileged information.

Commentary: The purpose of this policy is to severely restrict who has access to information about computer crimes suffered by Company X. This can prevent Company X from suffering negative publicity, declining stock prices, and other adverse effects that may result from inappropriate disclosures. When information is legally privileged, it is also protected from certain types of legal information gathering, such as discovery. The policy may help keep computer crime information in the hands of a restricted few managers and technical staff at the organization even though a lawsuit is underway. This policy also emphasizes that computer crime information is very sensitive and should be distributed only to those who have a need for the information. The policy reduces the chances that spokespersons for Company X will offer unsubstantiated theories about perpetrator intentions or attack methods to the media, which may expose Company X to slander or libel allegations. The word "internal" could be deleted from the policy if the organization uses only external legal counsel.

Related Policies: "Disclosure Of Computer System Attacks" and "Centralized Problem Reporting."

Audience: Management and technical staff

Security Environments: All

15. Forensic Analysis Process

Policy: Every analysis or investigation using data storage media that contains information that might at some point become important evidence to a computer crime or computer abuse trial, must be performed with a copy rather than the original version.

Commentary: This policy prevents changing the original copy of important evidence. If the original is changed in any way, then the opposing party in a court case can allege that other changes have also been made. Investigators typically employ specialized software that can make a full copy of an entire hard drive, including erased files, fragments from updated files, portions of erased electronic mail messages, and deleted contents of an Internet browser cache. The policy applies to other data storage media including floppy disks and magnetic-optical cartridges. Certain data storage media such as CD-ROMs cannot be changed without special equipment. Even in these cases it is wise to use a copy to avoid any allegations of evidence tampering. The original data media should also be locked up and a documented chain of custody should be established.

Related Policies: "Electronic Mail Message Destruction" and "Computer Crime Or Abuse Evidence."

Audience: Technical staff

Security Environments: All

16. Information Security Investigations

Policy: All Company X internal investigations of information security incidents, violations, and problems, must be conducted by trained staff authorized by Information Security management.

Commentary: This policy prevents system administrators, department managers, and others from conducting their own information security investigations. Not only can privacy laws and policies be violated, but also important evidence may be destroyed or improperly handled. The policy indicates that such work is a highly-technical matter that must be left to specialists. This policy is consistent with the emergence of computer forensics. This policy, while seemingly innocuous, can be very useful to an information security specialist from an internal political standpoint. The specific training required is deliberately not stated in the policy because the technical staff available for the work, and the specific nature of the work, will vary from investigation to investigation.

Related Policies: "Examination Of Private User Files" and "Unauthorized Access Problems."

Audience: Technical staff

Security Environments: All

17. Information Security Investigation Teams

Policy: Any person who is a personal friend or acquaintance of a suspect in an investigation must not participate on an information security incident investigation team.

Commentary: This policy prevents conflicts of interest, such as personal loyalties, from getting in the way of investigations. Those members of an investigation team who know the suspects may deliberately ignore evidence, deliberately misinterpret evidence, destroy evidence, misrepresent the status of the investigation, or in some other way unduly interfere with the investigation. This policy assumes the use of internal investigators, and works best when applied to a large organization. In a small organization, it will be difficult to find people who have the requisite technical skills to perform investigations, and who do not personally know the suspects. In a small organization, it may be appropriate to use external consultants for investigations in order to get reliable results. Small organizations may wish to add a sentence to the policy that addresses the use of outsiders for this purpose.

Related Policies: "Information Security Investigations" and "Intrusion Investigations Details."

Audience: Technical staff

Security Environments: All

18. Internal Investigations And Official Inquiries

Policy: All Company X workers must testify or otherwise respond to questions associated with internal investigations when directed to do so by the chief legal counsel.

Commentary: This policy is intended to inform workers that their support and cooperation is expected in all internal investigations and official inquiries. The policy is meant to emphasize the expectation that such support and cooperation is part of their jobs. The policy prevents the attempts of some workers to protect other workers against disciplinary measures or termination. Workers could always claim that they chose to remain silent about the topic being investigated or inquired about. This will then most likely lead to disciplinary measures, which could include termination. This policy does not violate the law in some jurisdictions regarding the right to remain silent if their testimony might tend to incriminate them. Such investigations are in most cases not held in a court of law, so the right to remain silent does not generally apply.

Related Policies: "Legal Proceeding Participation" and "Investigation Status Reports."

Audience: End users

Security Environments: All

19. Intrusion Investigations Details

Policy: Details about current investigations of information system intrusions must not be sent through electronic mail and files that describe a current investigation must not be stored on potentially compromised systems or anywhere on a related network where they could be reasonably expected to be viewed by intruders.

Commentary: This policy prevents attackers from researching how they are being investigated, and taking steps to evade those people who seek to drive them out of the involved systems. Attackers can and have performed such counter-surveillance, such as intercepting electronic mail messages of specific users such as system administrators. If hackers have investigation details at their disposal, not only are they likely to destroy evidence, but also they are likely to take evasive action that will only postpone the time before they are barred from once again entering the organization's information systems. If the investigation information is encrypted, then in some cases it can safely be sent through electronic mail or stored in places where attackers may find it. But it is generally advisable to keep such information off the affected systems. This is because the information must be decrypted at some point in order to be used, and at this point it might be viewed by intruders. Also, if one of the investigators makes a mistake, and fails to encrypt the information, it may then be accessible by one of the intruders.

Related Policies: "Violation And Problem Reporting" and "Computer Crime Or Abuse Evidence."

Audience: Technical staff

Security Environments: All

12.02 Reviews Of Security Policy And Technical Compliance

12.02.01 Compliance With Security Policy

1. Dial-Up Compliance

Policy: Dial-up connections to internal systems and networks must be reviewed by the department making the installation and any deviation from published internal standards must be approved in advance by Information Security management.

Commentary: In addition to controlling unauthorized dial-up access, This policy reduces the work required by Information Security management. This policy transfers responsibility for checking compliance with internal standards to local department management. Dial-up connections have become so common that they are often best managed on a local basis. In the era of decentralized and distributed computing, local management is often the only management branch in position to exercise control over changes made to systems. This policy assumes that internal standards defining how to establish secure connections already exist. The existence of such standards will also significantly reduce the amount of dial-up approval work required by Information Security management. Because dial-up lines are often used by hackers and other unauthorized parties to gain network access, this policy responds to one of the most common vulnerabilities in small systems.

Related Policies: "Dial-Up Connections" and "Third-Party Remote Access."

Audience: End users and technical staff

Security Environments: All

2. Worker Termination Responsibility

Policy: In the event that an employee, consultant, or contractor is terminating his or her relationship with Company X, the worker's immediate manager must ensure that all property in the custody of the worker is returned before the worker leaves Company X, notify all administrators handling the computer and communications accounts used by the worker as soon as the termination is known, and terminate all other work-related privileges of the individual at the time that the termination takes place.

Commentary: The purpose of this policy is to inform specific management that they must take certain systems-related actions at the time that a worker leaves an organization. These actions should be taken even if a consultant's or a contractor's project has ended. Disgruntled employees who have been terminated for cause can do significant information-systems-related damage. Of particular concern are those employees who have computer or communication system access and who are in a significant position of trust. For these trusted employees, some organizations may wish to develop a separate policy with more stringent requirements such as immediate escort out the building at the time of termination. Early preparation for specific terminations is advisable, including consultations with internal legal counsel and Human Resources management.

Related Policies: "Return Of Property At Employment Termination."

Audience: Management

Security Environments: All

3. Divisional Plans For Information Security Compliance

Policy: Management within each Company X division must prepare an annual plan for bringing its computer and communications systems into compliance with published policies and standards.

Commentary: This policy requires middle management to prepare specific written plans reflecting the ways that they will improve information security. For organizations that are just beginning to get serious about information security, a policy such as this may help to communicate to middle management that they must pay attention to information security. By requiring middle management to prepare plans and periodic reports reflecting progress on these plans, this policy can be an important way to get management to comply. This policy ensures that distributed systems management will adequately address information security. It is of particular use in those organizations heavily dependent upon local area networks, departmental systems, personal computers, client-server systems, and similar equipment. The reference to "division" could be replaced with "department," "unit," "subsidiary," or some other organizational grouping.

Related Policies: "Information Security Plans."

Audience: Management

Security Environments: All

4. Control Implementations Standard

Policy: Management must implement information system controls in a manner that is consistent with generally-accepted business practice and that is consistent with the criticality, value, and sensitivity of the information being processed.

Commentary: This policy informs management that they must implement controls that are consistent with what a court of law would consider to be "due diligence." This policy will reduce management liability for inadequate controls because it specifically acknowledges the need for such controls, although the controls themselves may not yet have been put into place. If an organization does take this action, it runs the risk of being accused of negligence, breach of fiduciary duty, failing to use the security measures found in other organizations in the same business, failing to exercise the due care expected from a computer professional, or failure to act after an actual notice such as a compromise of security. The existence of a published policy has been an important factor in a number of court cases.

Reflecting the fact that each organization has its own unique needs, this policy indicates that the controls should be customized to the business environment found at the organization.

Related Policies: "Correcting Business Records," "Protection Of Information," "Variances From Generally-Accepted Control Practices," "Information System Control Reviews — Independent," and "Industry-Specific Information Security Standards."

Audience: Management and technical staff

Security Environments: All

5. Variances From Generally-Accepted Control Practices

Policy: Management must reveal variances from generally accepted information system control practices, and also are responsible for promptly initiating corrective action.

Commentary: This policy informs management to note variances from the standard of due care, and take steps to correct these variances. In this sense, the word variances refers not only to those situations where standard of due care controls are absent, but also to those circumstances where the organization is not in compliance with previously-specified or previously-implemented controls. In most organizations, internal auditors are delegated the job of investigating these matters. Sometimes this is the job responsibility of external auditors or special consultants. Management is ultimately responsible for being aware of and implementing appropriate internal controls.

Related Policies: "Control Implementations Standard" and "Industry-Specific Information Security Standards."

Audience: Management

Security Environments: All

6. System Risk Assessments

Policy: Each organizational unit within Company X that manages its own computers or networks must annually perform a security-related risk assessment of these systems, then certify that adequate security measures have been implemented.

Commentary: This policy delegates responsibility for performing regular risk assessments to the distributed organizational units such as departments, divisions, or subsidiaries that manage local information systems. This policy states that information security is also a line management responsibility, not just the responsibility of a centralized information security group. While annual risk assessments are required by each unit managing information systems, a centralized information security group, an information technology audit group, or an independent consulting organization should periodically perform independent risk assessments of these same information systems. A centralized information security group should also perform risk assessments of centrally-managed resources like a wide area network. While some may believe that this introduces a conflict of interest, distributed units are not the only groups

evaluating the security of distributed systems. Having distributed groups evaluate their own security is only one step in responsibly managing security. Distributed groups cannot effectively or efficiently manage information security if they do not understand what the risks are. This policy can be supported by a guideline for performing risk assessments that could be issued by a centralized information security unit.

Related Policies: "Exceptions To Policies" and "Organization-Wide Information Security Risk Assessment."

Audience: Management and technical staff

Security Environments: Medium and high

12.02.02 Technical Compliance Checking

1. Production Backup Audits

Policy: Internal Audit management must perform an annual review and random tests of production computer system backup processes.

Commentary: This policy encourages system administrators and computer operators to pay attention to the important area of computerized information backup. The existence of this policy emphasizes the importance of diligently attending to backup every day of the year. These technical staff members know that every time a backup is performed they are creating extensive computer-readable records of their backup efforts. This policy also applies to end users, should they be in charge of making backups for production systems. Production systems generally do not run on desktop or portable machines over which end users have control, and therefore this policy would not impact the end-user community.

Related Policies: "Backup Review" and "Web And Commerce Site File Archives."

Audience: Technical staff

Security Environments: All

2. Information Systems Security Risk Assessments

Policy: Information systems security risk assessments for critical information systems and critical production applications must be performed at least once every two

years, and all major enhancements, upgrades, conversions, and related changes associated with these systems or applications must be preceded by a risk assessment as defined in the Information Security manual.

Commentary: This policy requires staff to perform risk assessments before major changes are made to critical information systems or critical production applications. This policy assumes that the organization has already prioritized its information systems based on their criticality to the organization. The policy also assumes that a methodology for performing risk assessments has been defined in another internal document such as an Information Security Manual. The exact methodology for the risk assessment is deliberately not specified in the policy. This permits the methodology to evolve over time without the need to change this policy. The type of risk assessment will in many cases also vary based on circumstances. For example, if a risk assessment was performed on an application six months ago, then only an abbreviated update to the prior assessment may be required. But if no risk assessment has ever been performed, then a full-scale risk assessment may be required.

Related Policies: "Five-Category Application Criticality Classification Scheme" and "Information Security Plans."

Audience: Technical staff

Security Environments: All

3. Organization-Wide Information Security Risk Assessment

Policy: Each year, Information Security management must conduct, or manage an independent party who conducts, an organization-wide risk assessment, with the report resulting from this project including a detailed description of the information security risks currently facing the organization, and specific recommendations for preventing or mitigating these risks.

Commentary: This policy requires Information Security management to annually identify important threats, recent developments, and next steps. Information security is a complex field, and it is important for those working in the field to periodically reprioritize what they are doing. Without this policy, information security resources are likely to be spent on efforts that do not have much impact. Some information security efforts are narrowly focused on viruses, contingency planning, and system access control, while there is a great deal more to information security that desperately needs attention. An annual risk assessment will identify these additional tasks. No two organizations are alike, and the steps that will need to be taken need to be customized for each organization. In order to perform this customization process, or even plan for it, a risk assessment must be performed. A risk assessment is also a very important reference document when preparing policies, standards, procedures, architectures, and other organizational infrastructure material. The policy deliberately avoids specifying the method for a risk assessment because it should change over time to give a better understanding of the true situation.

Related Policies: "Violation And Problem Analysis" and "Production System Risk Assessments."

Audience: Management

Security Environments: All

12.03 System Audit Considerations

12.03.01 System Audit Controls

1. Information Integrity Attributes

Policy: To the extent feasible, management must be periodically notified about the accuracy, timeliness, relevance, and other information integrity attributes that describe the information they use for decision making.

Commentary: This policy achieves full disclosure of the nature of the information used for decision-making. Management needs to know the extent to which they can rely on the information they receive. This information about integrity assists management when making decisions about information reliability and, how likely it is that their decisions will be accurate. Explanatory text can be developed to accompany this policy. Such text can give specific ways to measure information integrity. For example, the time period between data capture and processed information presentation can be provided. Analysis of the integrity attributes of information is often performed by database administrators, data modelers, systems architects, and others working to standardize data on a cross-application and cross-platform basis. Information security specialists should be involved, although this work is not typically included in their job function.

Related Policies: "Nature And Location Of Organization Information" and "Incomplete Or Obsolete Information."

Audience: Management and technical staff

Security Environments: All

2. Information System Control Reviews — Internal

Policy: Internal Audit must periodically review the adequacy of information system controls and compliance with such controls.

Commentary: This policy states the information-security-related responsibilities of Internal Audit. In some organizations, Internal Audit does not have sufficient expertise to do this job, so they ignore information security. This policy notifies Internal Audit that they should be trained so that they can perform this job, hire an information technology auditor, or else retain an outsider to assist with this work. Instead of Internal Audit, Information Security management could perform these security reviews. The important objective here is the clear assignment of responsibility. The policy could be modified to reflect the fact that often Internal Audit checks on the adequacy of information security, rather than performing detailed technical work.

Related Policies: "Computer System Audit Logs" and "Production System Risk Assessments."

Audience: Management

Security Environments: All

3. Information Security Compliance Checking

Policy: Internal Audit must periodically perform compliance checking related to information security policies, standards, and procedures.

Commentary: This policy states that Internal Audit, not Information Security management, should perform compliance checking. If Information Security management were to do this, it would be a conflict of interest. It is not desirable for people who designed, installed, and administered a system to also audit themselves. While Information Security management may install and run tools that can help enforce policies, standards, and procedures, the responsibility of compliance checking should be assigned to Internal Audit.

Related Policies: "Information System Control Reviews — Internal."

Audience: Management and technical staff

Security Environments: All

12.03.02 Protection Of System Audit Trails

1. System Penetration Software Source Code

Policy: Programming source code and its related technical analyses used to compromise security must be disclosed only to those persons with a demonstrable need to know.

Commentary: This policy prevents unauthorized persons from using this information to compromise systems security. Many computer criminals use previously-written material to achieve new objectives. For example, many of the viruses currently infecting systems are simply derivatives of older viruses. The analysis of such system penetration routines is also sensitive because it can be used by the system attackers to learn about what works and what does not. Such analysis can be considered to be a list of needed system enhancements for the next generation of system attack software. Also of concern is an organization's liability for disclosing sensitive vulnerability information.

Related Policies: "Disclosure Of Information System Vulnerabilities," "Compromising Security Mechanisms For Customers," and "Presentation Of Public Image."

Audience: Management and technical staff

Security Environments: All

2. Vulnerability Identification

Policy: All systems directly connected to the Internet must be subjected to an automated risk assessment performed through vulnerability identification software at least once a month.

Commentary: The purpose of this policy is to ensure that Company X knows what vulnerabilities a hacker could exploit to break into its systems. Armed with this information, Company X staff can make appropriate adjustments, such as install the latest version of certain systems software. If the staff does not know what the vulnerabilities are, then taking the appropriate next steps will be impossible. This policy supports the conclusion reached by various statistical studies that it is less expensive to prevent or recover from problems than it is to correct them. Vulnerability identification software is especially important for Internet-connected systems because these systems are exposed to much more severe attacks than any other systems.

Related Policies: "Intrusion Detection Systems," "Vendor Default Passwords," and "Computer Crime Or Abuse Evidence."

Audience: Technical staff

Security Environments: All

Chapter 4   SAMPLE HIGH-LEVEL INFORMATION SECURITY POLICY

Role Of Information And Information Systems—Company X is critically dependent on information and information systems. If important information were disclosed to inappropriate persons, the company could suffer serious losses or go out of business. The good reputation that Company X enjoys is also directly linked with the way that it manages both information and information systems. For example, if private customer information were to be publicly disclosed, the organization's reputation would be harmed. For these and other important business reasons, executive management working in conjunction with the board of directors has initiated and continues to support an information security effort. One part of that effort is definition of these information security policies.

Team Effort—To be effective, information security must be a team effort involving the participation and support of every Company X worker who deals with information and information systems. In recognition of the need for teamwork, this policy statement clarifies the responsibilities of users and the steps they must take to help protect Company X information and information systems. This document describes ways to prevent and respond to a variety of threats to information and information systems including unauthorized access, disclosure, duplication, modification, appropriation, destruction, loss, misuse, and denial of use.

Involved Persons—Every worker at Company X must comply with the information security policies found in this and related information security documents. Workers who deliberately violate this and other information security policy statements will be subject to disciplinary action up to and including termination.

Involved Systems—This policy applies to all computer and network systems owned by or administered by Company X. This policy applies to all operating systems, computer sizes, and application systems. The policy covers only information handled by computers and networks. Although this document includes mention of other manifestations of information such as voice and paper, it does not directly address the security of information in these forms. For information about the protection of information in paper form, see the Information Classification Policy [a link to intranet page for that document can be inserted here].

Primary Departments Working On Information Security—Guidance, direction, and authority for information security activities are centralized for all Company X organizational units in the Information Security department [insert an intranet link to the Information Security mission statement]. Information Security is responsible for establishing and maintaining organization-wide information security policies, standards, guidelines, and procedures. Compliance checking to ensure that organizational units are operating in a manner consistent with these requirements is the responsibility of the Information Technology Audit unit within the Internal Audit department [insert a link to the Internal Audit mission statement]. Investigations of system intrusions and other information security incidents are the responsibility of the Physical Security department [insert a intranet link to the Industrial Security mission statement]. Disciplinary matters resulting from violations of information security requirements are handled by local managers working in conjunction with the Human Resources department [insert an intranet link to the Human Resources mission statement].

Three Categories Of Responsibilities—To coordinate a team effort, Company X has established three categories, at least one of which applies to each worker. These categories are Owner, Custodian, and User. These categories define general responsibilities with respect to information security. More detailed information about these responsibilities can be found in the information ownership policy [insert a link to that document].

Owner Responsibilities—Information Owners are the department managers, members of the top management team, or their delegates within Company X who bear responsibility for the acquisition, development, and maintenance of production applications that process Company X information. Production applications are computer programs that regularly provide reports in support of decision making and other business activities. All production application system information must have a designated Owner. For each type of information, Owners designate the relevant sensitivity classification, designate the appropriate level of criticality, define which users will be granted access, and approve requests for various ways in which the information will be utilized.

Custodian Responsibilities—Custodians are in physical or logical possession of either Company X information or information that has been entrusted to Company X. While Information Technology department staff members clearly are Custodians, local system administrators are also Custodians. Whenever information is maintained only on a personal computer, the User is also a Custodian. Each type of production application system information must have one or more designated Custodians. Custodians are responsible for safeguarding the information, including implementing access control systems to prevent inappropriate disclosure, and making backups so that critical information will not be lost. Custodians are also required to implement, operate, and maintain the security measures defined by information Owners.

User Responsibilities—Users are responsible for familiarizing themselves with and complying with all Company X policies, procedures, and standards dealing with information security. Questions about the appropriate handling of a specific type of information should be directed to either the Custodian or the Owner of the involved information.

Consistent Information Handling—Company X information, and information that has been entrusted to Company X, must be protected in a manner commensurate with its sensitivity and criticality. Security measures must be employed regardless of the media on which information is stored, the systems that process it, or the methods by which it is moved. Information must be protected in a manner that is consistent with it classification, no matter what its stage in the life cycle from origination to destruction.

Information Classification Designations—Company X has adopted an information classification system that categorizes information into four groupings. All information under Company X control, whether generated internally or externally, falls into one of these categories: Secret, Confidential, Internal Use Only, or Public. All workers must familiarize themselves with the definitions for these categories and the steps that must be taken to protect the information falling into each of these categories. Details can be found in the Information Classification Policy [insert a link here]. For purposes of this policy, "sensitive information" is information that falls into either the Secret or Confidential categories.

Information Classification Labelling—If information is sensitive, from the time it is created until the time it is destroyed or declassified, it must be labeled with an appropriate information classification designation. Such markings must appear on all manifestations of the information. The vast majority of Company X information falls into the Internal Use Only category. For this reason, it is not necessary to apply a label to Internal Use Only information. Information without a label is therefore by default classified as Internal Use Only. Further instructions about labelling sensitive information can be found in the Information Classification Policy [insert a link here].

Need to Know—Access to information in the possession of, or under the control of Company X must be provided based on the need to know. Information must be disclosed only to people who have a legitimate business need for the information. At the same time, workers must not withhold access to information when the Owner of the information instructs that it be shared. To implement the need-to-know concept, Company X has adopted an access request and Owner approval process. Workers must not attempt to access sensitive information unless the relevant Owner has granted them access rights. When a worker changes job duties, including termination, transfer, promotion and leave of absence, his or her supervisor must immediately notify the Information Security department [insert a link with another screen showing details on this notification process]. The privileges granted to all workers must be periodically reviewed by information Owners and Custodians to ensure that only those with a current need to know presently have access.

User IDs And Passwords—To implement the need-to-know process, Company X requires that each worker accessing multi-user information systems have a unique user ID and a private password. These user IDs must be employed to restrict system privileges based on job duties, project responsibilities, and other business activities. Each worker is personally responsible for the usage of his or her user ID and password.

Anonymous User IDs—With the exception of electronic bulletin boards, Internet sites, intranet sites, and other systems where all regular users are intended to be anonymous, users are prohibited from logging into any Company X system or network anonymously. Anonymous access might, for example, involve use of "guest" user IDs. When users employ system commands that permit them to change active user IDs to gain certain privileges, they must have initially logged on employing user IDs that clearly indicated their identities.

Difficult-to-Guess Passwords—Users must choose passwords that are difficult to guess. This means that passwords must not be related to one's job or personal life. For example, a car license plate number, a spouse's name, or fragments of an address must not be used. This also means passwords must not be a word found in the dictionary or some other part of speech. For example, proper names, places, technical terms, and slang must not be used.

Easily Remembered Passwords—Users can choose easily-remembered passwords that are at the same time difficult for unauthorized parties to guess if they:

- String several words together.

- Shift a word up, down, left, or right one row on the keyboard.

- Bump characters in a word a certain number of letters up or down the alphabet.

- Transform a regular word according to a specific method, such as making every other letter a number reflecting its position in the word.

- Combine punctuation or numbers with a regular word.

- Create acronyms from words in a song, poem, or another known sequence of words.

- Deliberately misspell a word.

- Combine several preferences like hours of sleep desired and favorite colors.

Repeated Password Patterns—Users must not construct passwords with a basic sequence of characters that is then partially changed based on the date or some other predictable factor. Users must not construct passwords that are identical or substantially similar to passwords they have previously employed.

Password Constraints—Passwords must be at least 10 characters long. Passwords must be changed every 90 days or at more frequent intervals. Whenever a worker suspects that a password has become known to another person, that password must immediately be changed.

Password Storage—Passwords must not be stored in readable form in batch files, automatic logon scripts, software macros, terminal function keys, in computers without access control systems, or in other locations where unauthorized persons might discover them. Passwords must not be written down in some readily-decipherable form and left in a place where unauthorized persons might discover them.

Sharing Passwords—If workers need to share computer-resident data, they must use electronic mail, groupware databases, public directories on local area network servers, manual floppy disk exchange, and

other mechanisms. Although user IDs are shared for electronic mail and other purposes, passwords must never be shared with or revealed to others. System administrators and other technical information systems staff must never ask a worker to reveal their personal password. The only time when a password should be known by another is when it is issued. These temporary passwords must be changed the first time that the authorized user accesses the system. If a user believes that his or her user ID and password are being used by someone else, the user must immediately notify the system administrator for the information system.

Compliance Statement—All workers who wish to use Company X multi-user computer systems must sign a compliance statement prior to being issued a user ID [insert a link to the statement]. Where users already have user IDs, such signatures must be obtained prior to receiving annually-renewed user IDs. A signature on this compliance statement indicates the involved user understands and agrees to adhere to Company X policies and procedures related to computers and networks, including the instructions contained in this policy.

Release Of Information To Third Parties—Unless it has specifically been designated as public, all Company X internal information must be protected from disclosure to third parties. Third parties may be given access to Company X internal information only when a demonstrable need to know exists, when a Company X non-disclosure agreement [insert a link to a copy of the agreement] has been signed, and when such a disclosure has been expressly authorized by the relevant Company X information Owner [insert a link to a corporate data dictionary with a list of Owners and the types of information they manage]. If sensitive information is lost, is disclosed to unauthorized parties, or is suspected of being lost or disclosed to unauthorized parties, the information Owner and the Information Security department must be notified immediately [insert a link to a separate screen with telephone numbers and additional instructions for this notification process].

Third-Party Requests For Company X Information—Unless a worker has been authorized by the information Owner to make public disclosures, all requests for information about Company X and its business must be referred to the Public Relations department. Such requests include questionnaires, surveys, and newspaper interviews. This policy does not apply to sales and marketing information about Company X products and services, nor does it pertain to customer technical support calls. If a worker is to receive sensitive information from third parties on behalf of Company X, this receipt must be preceded by the third-party signature on a Company X release form [insert a link to form]. For further details on this topic, consult the External Party Information Disclosure Policy [insert a link]. Additional relevant information can be found in the External Communications Security Policy [insert a link].

Physical Security to Control Information Access—Access to every office, computer machine room, and other Company X work area containing sensitive information must be physically restricted to those people with a need to know. When not in use, sensitive information must always be protected from unauthorized disclosure. When left in an unattended room, sensitive information in paper form must be locked away in appropriate containers. If a Custodian of such information believes he or she will be away for less than 30 minutes, information in paper form may be left on a desk or in some other readily observed spot only if all doors and windows to the unattended room are closed and locked. During non-working hours, workers in areas containing sensitive information must lock-up all information. Unless information is in active use by authorized people, desks must be clear and clean during non-working hours to prevent unauthorized access to information. Workers must position their computer screens such that unauthorized people cannot look over their shoulder and see the sensitive information displayed.

Internal Network Connections—All Company X computers that store sensitive information, and that are permanently or intermittently connected to internal computer networks must have a password-based access control system approved by the Information Security department. Regardless of the network connections, all stand-alone computers handling sensitive information must also employ an approved password-based access control system [insert a link to approved information security products list and procurement details on how to order them]. Users working with all other types of computers must employ the screen saver passwords that are provided with operating systems, so that after a period of no activity the screen will go blank until the correct password is again entered. Multi-user systems throughout Company X must employ automatic log off systems that automatically terminate a user's session after a defined period of inactivity.

External Network Connections—All in-bound session connections to Company X computers from external networks must be protected with an approved dynamic password access control system [insert a link to approved information security products list]. Dynamic passwords are different each time they are used, and

therefore cannot be replayed to gain unauthorized access. Users with personal computers connected to external networks are prohibited from leaving unattended modems turned-on while data communications software is enabled, unless an authorized dynamic password system has been previously installed. When using Company X computers, Company X workers must not establish connections with external networks including Internet service providers unless these connections have been approved by the Information Security department. For further information on this process, see the External Communications Security Policy [insert a link].

Network Changes—With the exception of emergency situations, all changes to Company X computer networks must be documented in a work order request, and approved in advance by the Information Technology department. All emergency changes to Company X networks must be made only by persons who are authorized by the Information Technology department. This process prevents unexpected changes from inadvertently leading to denial of service, unauthorized disclosure of information, and other problems. This process applies not only to workers but also to vendor personnel.

Telecommuting—At management's discretion, certain qualified workers can do some of their work at home. Permission to telecommute must be granted by each worker's immediate supervisor based on a checklist of relevant factors [insert link to the checklist, which may be a subsidiary intranet page under the Human Resources department's main intranet page]. Continued permission to telecommute is partially dependent on continued compliance with a number of information security policies and standards. For further information on these requirements, see the Telecommuting Policy [insert a link]. Periodic checking of electronic mail while on the road or from home is not considered telecommuting, but does require that workers follow many of the same security precautions.

Internet Access—Workers are provided with Internet access to perform their job duties, but this access may be terminated at any time at the discretion of a worker's supervisor. Internet access is monitored to ensure that workers are not visiting sites unrelated to their jobs, and also to ensure that they continue to be in compliance with security policies. Workers must take special care to ensure that they do not represent Company X on Internet discussion groups and in other public forums, unless they have previously received top management authorization to act in this capacity. All information received from the Internet should be considered to be suspect until confirmed by reliable sources. Workers must not place Company X material on any publicly-accessible computer system such as the Internet unless the posting has been approved by both the information Owner and the director of the Information Technology department. The establishment of Internet pages is separately handled by an approval process involving the external communications committee [insert a link to the Public Relations department]. Users are prohibited from establishing any electronic commerce arrangements over the Internet unless Information Technology and the Information Security department have evaluated and approved of such arrangements. Sensitive information, including passwords and credit card numbers, must not be sent across the Internet unless this information is in encrypted form. These and related considerations are discussed in greater detail in the Internet Communications Policy [insert a link].

Electronic Mail—Every Company X worker who uses computers in the course of their regular job duties will be granted an Internet electronic mail address and related privileges. All Company X business communications sent by electronic mail must be sent and received using this company electronic mail address. A personal Internet service provider electronic mail account or any other electronic mail address must not be used for Company X business unless a worker obtains management approval. When transmitting messages to groups of people outside Company X, workers must always use either the blind carbon copy facility or the distribution list facility. Unsolicited electronic mail transmissions to prospects and customers are prohibited. Emotional outbursts sent through electronic mail and overloading the electronic mail account of someone through a deluge of messages are forbidden. All business electronic mail communications must be proofread before they are sent, and professional and businesslike in both tone and appearance. Electronic mail is a public communication method much like a postcard. All Company X workers must refrain from sending credit card numbers, passwords, or other sensitive information that might be intercepted. All Company X staff must additionally employ a standard electronic mail signature that includes their full name, job title, business address, and business telephone number. Users should not store important messages in their electronic mail inbox. Additional details can be found in the Electronic Mail Security Policy [insert a link].

Computer Virus Screening—All personal computer users must keep the current versions of approved virus screening software enabled on their computers [insert a link to list of approved information security products]. Users must not abort automatic software processes that update virus signatures. Virus screening software must be used to scan all software and data files coming from either third parties or other Company X groups. This scanning must take place before new data files are opened and before new software is executed. Workers must not bypass or turn off the scanning processes that could prevent the transmission of computer viruses.

Computer Virus Eradication—If workers suspect infection by a computer virus, they must immediately stop using the involved computer and call the help desk [insert a link to the help desk page]. Floppy disks and other magnetic storage media used with the infected computer must not be used with any other computer until the virus has been successfully eradicated. The infected computer must also be immediately isolated from internal networks. Users must not attempt to eradicate viruses themselves. Qualified Company X staff or consultants must complete this task in a manner that minimizes both data destruction and system downtime.

Clean Backups—All personal computer software must be copied prior to its initial usage, and such copies must be stored in a secure location such as a locked file cabinet. These master copies must not be used for ordinary business activities, but must be reserved for recovery from computer virus infections, hard disk crashes, and other computer problems.

Software Sources—Company X computers and networks must not run software that comes from sources other than other Company X departments, knowledgeable and trusted user groups, well-known systems security authorities, or established computer, network, or commercial software vendors. Software downloaded from electronic bulletin boards, shareware, public domain software, and other software from untrusted sources must not be used unless it has been subjected to a rigorous testing regimen approved by the Information Security department [insert a link to a page describing this process and who to contact].

Written Specifications for Owners—All software developed by in-house staff, intended to process critical or sensitive Company X information, must have a formal written specification. This specification must include discussion of security risks and controls including access control systems and contingency plans. The specification must be part of an agreement between the information Owner and the system developer. Macros in spreadsheets and word processing documents are not considered software in this paragraph.

Security Sign-Off Required—Before being used for production processing, new or substantially changed application systems must have received written approval from the Information Security department for the controls to be employed. This requirement applies to personal computers just as it does to larger systems [insert a link to form requesting Information Security department review and sign-off].

Formal Change Control—All computer and communications systems used for production processing must employ a documented change control process that is used to ensure that only authorized changes are made. This change control procedure must be used for all significant changes to production system software, hardware, communications links, and procedures. This policy applies to personal computers running production systems and larger multi-user systems. For further information on this topic, see the Software Development And Change Control Policy [insert a link].

Systems Development Conventions—All production software development and software maintenance activities performed by in-house staff must adhere to Information Technology department policies, standards, procedures, and other systems development conventions. These conventions include the proper testing, training, and documentation. For further information on this topic, see the Software Development And Change Control Policy [insert a link].

Adequate Licenses—Company X management must make appropriate arrangements with software vendors for additional licensed copies, if and when additional copies are needed for business activities. All software must be purchased through the Procurement department [insert a link to list of approved software products for the desktop and a link to the Procurement department's purchase request form].

Unauthorized Copying—Users must not copy software provided by Company X to any storage media, transfer such software to another computer, or disclose such software to outside parties without advance permission from their supervisor. Ordinary backup copies are an authorized exception to this policy.

Backup Responsibility—Personal computer users must regularly back up the information on their personal computers, or ensure that someone else is doing this for them. For multi-user computer and communication systems, a system administrator is responsible for making periodic backups. If requested, the Information Technology department must install, or provide technical assistance for the installation of backup

hardware and software [insert a link to list of approved security products]. All backups containing critical or sensitive information must be stored at an approved off-site location with either physical access controls or encryption. A contingency plan must be prepared for all applications that handle critical production information. It is the responsibility of the information Owner to ensure that this plan is adequately developed, regularly updated, and periodically tested.

Theft Protection—All Company X computer and network equipment must be physically secured with anti-theft devices if located in an open office. Local area network servers and other multi-user systems must be placed in locked cabinets, locked closets, or locked computer rooms. Portable computers must be secured with locking cables, placed in locking cabinets, or secured by other locking systems when in an open office environment but not in active use. Computer and network gear may not be removed from Company X offices unless the involved person has obtained a property pass from the building manager. Pagers and cellular phones are not subject to these requirements.

External Disclosure Of Security Information—Information about security measures for Company X computer and network systems is confidential and must not be released to people who are not authorized users of the involved systems unless approved by the director of Information Security. For example, publishing modem phone numbers or other system access information in directories is prohibited. Public disclosure of electronic mail addresses is permissible.

Rights To Material Developed—While performing services for Company X, workers must grant to Company X exclusive rights to patents, copyrights, inventions, or other intellectual property they originate or develop. All programs and documentation generated by, or provided by workers for the benefit of Company X are the property of Company X. Company X asserts the legal ownership of the contents of all information systems under its control. Company X reserves the right to access and use this information at its discretion.

Right To Search And Monitor—Company X management reserves the right to monitor, inspect, or search at any time all Company X information systems. This examination may take place with or without the consent, presence, or knowledge the involved workers. The information systems subject to such examination include, but are not limited to, electronic mail system files, personal computer hard drive files, voice mail files, printer spool files, fax machine output, desk drawers, and storage areas. All searches of this nature must be conducted after the approval of the Legal and Security departments has been obtained. Because Company X computers and networks are provided for business purposes only, workers must have no expectation of privacy associated with the information they store in or send through these information systems. Company X management retains the right to remove from its information systems any material it views as offensive or potentially illegal. For further information on this topic, see the Information Privacy Policy [insert a link].

Personal Use—Company X information systems are intended to be used for business purposes only. Incidental personal use is permissible if the use does not consume more than a trivial amount of resources that could otherwise be used for business purposes, does not interfere with worker productivity, and does not preempt any business activity. Permissible incidental use of an electronic mail system would, for example, involve sending a message to schedule a luncheon. Personal use that does not fall into these three categories requires the advance permission of a department manager. Games that are shipped with computer operating systems can be played during scheduled breaks or lunch as long as this activity does not interfere with either worker productivity or intention. Games that take the form of separate software packages are prohibited. Use of Company X information systems for chain letters, charitable solicitations, political campaign material, religious work, transmission of objectionable material, or any other non-business use is prohibited.

Unbecoming Conduct—Company X management reserves the right to revoke the system privileges of any user at any time. Conduct that interferes with the normal and proper operation of Company X informa-

tion systems, which adversely affects the ability of others to use these information systems, or that is harmful or offensive to others is not permitted.

Security Compromise Tools—Unless specifically authorized by the Information Security department, Company X workers must not acquire, possess, trade, or use hardware or software tools that could be employed to evaluate or compromise information systems security. Examples of such tools include those that defeat software copy protection, discover secret passwords, identify security vulnerabilities, or decrypt encrypted files. Without this type of approval, workers are prohibited from using any hardware or software that monitors the traffic on a network or the activity on a computer.

Prohibited Activities—Users must not test, or attempt to compromise computer or communication system security measures unless specifically approved in advance and in writing by the director of the Internal Audit department. Incidents involving unapproved system hacking, password guessing, file decryption, bootleg software copying, or similar unauthorized attempts to compromise security measures may be unlawful, and will be considered serious violations of Company X internal policy. Short-cuts bypassing systems security measures, and pranks and practical jokes involving the compromise of systems security measures are absolutely prohibited.

Mandatory Reporting—All suspected policy violations, system intrusions, virus infestations, and other conditions that might jeopardize Company X information or Company X information systems must be immediately reported to the Information Security department (voice mail with pager alert XXX-XXX-XXXX) [insert a link with computer emergency response team intranet web page]. Messages may be left anonymously in this voice mail box.

Chapter 5   SAMPLE DETAILED INFORMATION SECURITY POLICY

Executive Summary

Everyone recognizes that the highway system and motor vehicles are essential to commerce. But people are only recently coming to appreciate how information systems made up of computers and networks are another infrastructure essential to commerce. In recognition of the critical role that information systems play in Company X business activities, this policy defines the rules of the road and other requirements necessary for the secure and reliable operation of the Company X information systems infrastructure.

Just as every driver has a role to play in the orderly and safe operation of the transportation infrastructure, so too are there information security roles and duties for every worker at Company X. For example, it is a driver's duty to report accidents, and it is a worker's duty to report information security problems. Just as car manufacturers are required to provide safety belts with vehicles, system designers at Company X are required to include necessary security measures such as user access restrictions based on the need to know.

This policy also defines baseline control measures that everyone at Company X is expected to be familiar with and to consistently follow. Sometimes called standard of due care controls, these security measures are the minimum required to prevent a variety of different problems including: fraud and embezzlement, industrial espionage, sabotage, errors and omissions, and system unavailability. These policies also define the minimum controls necessary to prevent legal problems such as allegations of negligence, breach of fiduciary duty, or privacy violation. This policy document details both reasonable and practical ways for all of us at Company X to prevent unnecessary losses.

Company X critically depends on continued customer confidence. This confidence has been gradually increased and is the result of many years of dedicated effort on the part of Company X workers. While it is slow to grow, this confidence can be rapidly lost due to problems such as hacker intrusions causing system outages. The trust that customers have in Company X is a competitive advantage that must be nurtured and grown with efforts such as this information security initiative.

Introduction

Critical Business Function—Information and information systems are necessary for the performance of just about every essential activity at Company X. If there were to be a serious security problem with this information or these information systems, Company X could suffer serious consequences including lost customers, reduced revenues, and degraded reputation. As a result, information security now must be a critical part of the Company X business environment.

Supporting Business Objectives—This information security requirements document has been prepared to ensure that Company X is able to support further growth of the business, and ensure a consistently high level of customer, supplier, employee, and business-partner service. This document is also intended to support the organization's reputation for high-integrity and high-quality business dealings. Because prevention of security problems is considerably less expensive than correction and recovery, this document will help reduce costs in the long run.

Consistent Compliance Essential—A single unauthorized exception to security measures can jeopardize other users, the entire organization, and even outside organizations such as business partners. The interconnected nature of information systems requires that all workers observe a minimum level of security. This document defines that minimum level of due care. In some cases, these requirements will conflict with other objectives such as improved efficiency and minimized costs. Top management has examined these trade-offs and has decided that the minimum requirements defined in this document are appropriate for all workers at Company X. As a condition of continued employment, all workers, employees, contractors, consultants, and temporaries, must consistently observe the requirements set forth in this document.

Team Effort Required—The tools available in the information security field are relatively unsophisticated. Many of the needed tasks cannot be achieved with products now on the market. This means that users at Company X must step in and play an important role in the information security area. Now that information and information systems are distributed to the office desktop, and are used in remote locations, the worker's role has become an essential part of information security. Information security is no longer the exclusive domain of the Information Systems department. Information security is now a team effort requiring the participation of every worker who comes into contact with Company X information or information systems.

Information Security Responsibilities

Information Owners—Middle-level managers in user departments must be designated as the Owners of all types of information used for regular business activities. Each type of "production system information" must have an Owner. When information Owners are not clearly implied by organizational design, the chief information officer will make the designation. Information Owners do not legally own the information. They are instead members of the Company X management team who make decisions on behalf of the organization. Information Owners or their delegates must make the following decisions and perform the following activities:

- Approve information-oriented access control privileges for specific job profiles.

- Approve information-oriented access control requests that do not fall within the scope of existing job profiles.

- Select a data retention period for their information, relying on advice from the Legal department.

- Designate an original source for information from which all management reports will be derived.

- Select special controls needed to protect information, such as additional input validation checks or more frequent backup procedures.

- Define acceptable limits on the quality of their information, such as accuracy, timeliness, and time from capture to usage.

- Approve all new and different uses of their information.

- Approve all new or substantially-enhanced application systems that use their information before these systems are moved into production operational status.

- Review reports about system intrusions and other events that are relevant to their information.

- Review and correct reports that indicate the current production uses of their information.

- Review and correct reports that indicate the job profiles that currently have access to their information.

- Select a sensitivity classification category relevant to their information, and review this classification every five years for possible downgrading.

- Select a criticality category relevant to their information so that appropriate contingency planning can be performed.

Information Owners must designate a back-up person to act if they are absent or unavailable. Owners may not delegate ownership responsibilities to third-party organizations such as outsourcing organizations, or to any individual who is not a full-time Company X employee. When both the Owner and the back-up Owner are unavailable, immediate Owner decisions may be made by the department manager who ordinarily handles the information.

Worker's Manager—Owners do not approve ordinary access control requests. Instead, a worker's immediate manager must approve a request for system access based on existing job profiles. If a job profile does not exist, it is the manager's responsibility to create the profile, obtain the approval of relevant Owners, and inform the Information Security department. When a worker leaves Company X, it is the responsibility of the worker's immediate manager to promptly inform the Information Security department that the privileges associated with the worker's user ID must be revoked. User IDs are specific to individuals, and must not be reassigned to, or used by, others. Shortly after separation from Company X, a worker's manager is additionally responsible for reassigning the involved duties and files to other workers.

Information Custodians—Custodians are in physical or logical possession of information and information systems. Like Owners, Custodians are specifically designated for different types of information. In many cases, a manager in the Information Systems department will act as the Custodian. If a Custodian is not clear, based on existing information systems operational arrangements, then the chief information officer will designate a Custodian. Custodians follow the instructions of Owners, operate systems on behalf of Owners, but also serve users authorized by Owners. Custodians must define the technical options, such as information criticality categories, and permit Owners to select the appropriate option for their information. Custodians also define information systems architectures and provide technical consulting assistance to Owners so that information systems can be built and run to best meet business objectives. If requested, Custodians additionally provide reports to Owners about information system operations and information security problems. Custodians are responsible for safeguarding the information in their possession, including implementing access control systems to prevent inappropriate disclosure, and developing, documenting, and testing information systems contingency plans.

Information Users—Users are not specifically designated, but are broadly defined as any worker with access to internal information or internal information systems. Users are required to follow all security requirements defined by Owners, implemented by Custodians, or established by the Information Security department. Users must familiarize themselves with, and act in accordance with, all Company X information security requirements. Users also must participate in information security training and awareness efforts. Users must request access from their immediate manager, and report all suspicious activity and security problems. For more information about information users, see "Reporting Problems" on page 473.

Information Security Department—The Information Security department is the central point of contact for all information security matters at Company X. Acting as internal technical consultants, it is this department's responsibility to create workable information security compromises that take into consideration the needs of users, Custodians, Owners, and selected third parties. Reflecting these compromises, this department defines information security standards, procedures, policies, and other requirements applicable to the entire organization. Information Security must handle all access control administration activities, monitor the security of Company X information systems, and provide information security training and awareness programs to Company X workers. The department is responsible for periodically providing management with reports about the current state of information security at Company X. While information systems contingency planning is the responsibility of information Custodians, the Information Security department must provide technical consulting assistance related to emergency response procedures and disaster recovery. The Information Security department is also responsible for organizing a computer emergency response team to promptly respond to virus infections, hacker break ins, system outages, and similar information security problems.

Internal Audit Department—The Company X Internal Audit department periodically performs compliance checks to ensure that all parties are performing their assigned duties, and to ensure that other information security requirements are being consistently observed. Internal Audit acts as the eyes and ears of top management at Company X, ensuring that internal controls, including those related to information security, are consistent with both top management expectations and organizational goals.

Information Sensitivity Classification

Reasons For Classification—To assist in the appropriate handling of information, a sensitivity classification hierarchy must be used throughout Company X. This hierarchy provides a shorthand way of referring to sensitivity, and can be used to simplify information security decisions and minimize information security costs. One important intention of a sensitivity classification system is to provide consistent handling of the information, no matter what form it takes, where it goes, or who possesses it. For this reason, it is important to maintain the labels reflecting sensitivity classification categories. Company X uses four sensitivity classification categories:

> **Public**—This information has been specifically approved for public release by Public Relations department or Marketing department managers. Unauthorized disclosure of this information will not cause problems for Company X, its customers, or its business partners. Examples are marketing brochures and material posted to the Company X web page. Disclosure of Company X information to the public requires the existence of this label, the specific permission of the information Owner, or long-standing practice of publicly distributing this information.

> **Internal Use Only**—This information is intended for use within Company X, and in some cases within affiliated organizations, such as Company X business partners. Unauthorized disclosure of this information to outsiders may be against laws and regulations, or may cause problems for Company X, its customers, or its business partners. This type of information is already widely distributed within Company X, or it could be so distributed within the organization without advance permission from the information Owner. Examples are the Company X telephone book and most internal electronic mail messages.

Confidential—This information is private or otherwise sensitive in nature and must be restricted to those with a legitimate business need for access. Unauthorized disclosure of this information to people without a business need for access may be against laws and regulations, or may cause significant problems for Company X, its customers, or its business partners. Decisions about the provision of access to this information must be cleared through the information Owner. Examples are customer transaction account information and worker performance evaluation records.

Secret—This information is the most private or otherwise sensitive, and must be monitored and controlled at all times. Unauthorized disclosure of this information to people without a business need for access may be against laws and regulations, or may cause severe problems for Company X, its customers, or its business partners. Decisions about the provision of access to this information must be cleared through the information Owner. Examples are merger and acquisition plans and legal information protected by attorney-client privilege.

Default Category—If information is not marked with one of these categories, it will default into the Internal Use Only category. If information falls into the Internal Use Only category, it is not necessary to apply a sensitivity label. Information that falls into the Confidential or Secret categories is designated Sensitive.

Labeling—The Owner or creator of information must designate an appropriate label, and the user or recipient of this information must consistently maintain an assigned label. Labels for sensitive information must be used in the subject field of electronic mail messages or paper memos. Labels for sensitive information must appear on the outside of floppy disks, magnetic tape reels, CD-ROMs, audiocassettes, and other storage media. If a storage volume such as a floppy disk contains information with multiple classifications, the most sensitive category should appear on the outside label. Likewise, when creating a collection of information from sources with various classifications, the collection must be classified at the highest sensitivity level of the source information.

Handling Instructions—All users must observe the requirements for handling information based on its sensitivity. For more information on these definitions, see Chapter 17, "Sample Data Classification Quick Reference Table." Owners may designate additional controls to further restrict access to, or to further protect their information.

Access Control

Access Philosophy—Access to Public and Internal Use Only information is not restricted with access controls that discriminate by specific user. For example, Public information is available at the Company X web site, and Internal Use Only information is available on the Company X intranet. Access to Confidential or Secret information must be granted only when a legitimate business need has been demonstrated and access has been approved in advance by the information Owner. Access to special hardware and software must be restricted based on business need.

Access Approval Process—A worker's manager must initiate the access control approval process, and the privileges granted remain in effect until the worker's job changes or the worker leaves Company X. If either of these two events occur, the manager must notify the Information Security department immediately. All non-employees, contractors, consultants, temporaries, and outsourcing organizations must also go through a similar access control request and authorization process initiated by the project manager. The privileges of these non-employees must be immediately revoked by the Information Security department when the project is complete, or when the non-employees stop working with Company X. The relevant project manager must review the need for the continuing privileges of non-employees every three months.

Default Facilities—By default, all users must be granted basic information systems services such as electronic mail and word processing facilities. These basic facilities will vary by job title and be determined jointly by Information Security and the Information Systems department. All other system capabilities must be provided through job profiles or by special request directed to the Owner of the involved information. The existence of certain access privileges does not, in and of itself, mean that an individual is authorized to use these privileges. If users have any questions about access control privileges, they must direct these questions to the Information Security department.

Departures From Company X—When a user leaves Company X, all system privileges and access to Company X information must cease immediately. For example, departed users must not be permitted to continue to maintain an electronic mail account with Company X. At this point, all Company X information disclosed to users must be returned or destroyed. For example, customer contact lists must remain with Company X. All work done by users for Company X is Company X property, and it too must remain with

Company X when users depart. For example, a computer program written by a member of the Information Systems department while employed by Company X is Company X property and must remain with Company X.

Unique User IDs—Each user must be assigned their own unique user ID. This user ID follows an individual as they move through the organization. It must be permanently decommissioned when a user leaves Company X. Re-use of user IDs is not permitted. Every Company X user ID and related password is intended for the exclusive use of a specific individual. While user IDs can be shared in electronic mail messages and in other places, passwords must never be shared with anyone. Information systems technicians have all the privileges they need to do their job, and must never obtain a user's password. User IDs are linked to specific people, and are not associated with computer terminals, departments, or job titles. With the exception of Internet pages, intranet pages, and other places where anonymous interaction is both generally understood and expected, anonymous and guest user IDs are not permitted unless approved in advance by the Information Security department.

Privilege Deactivation—After a period of no activity defined in minutes by the Information Security department, online sessions with multi-user machines must be terminated automatically. Users must be sure to log-off from multi-user computers when they leave their desks for any more than a few minutes. Dormant user IDs on multi-user computers that have no any activity for a period defined in weeks by the Information Security department must have their privileges automatically revoked and the related files archived. Users who return from an extended vacation or a leave of absence must have their manager contact Information Security to reestablish their privileges.

User Authentication—All production information system user IDs must have a linked password or a stronger mechanism such as a dynamic password token, to ensure that only the authorized user is able to utilize the user ID. Users are responsible for all activity that takes place with their user ID and password or other authentication mechanism. A user must change their password immediately if they suspect that it has been discovered or used by another person. Users must notify Information Security if other access control mechanisms are broken or if they suspect that these mechanisms have been compromised.

Fixed Password Management

Choosing Passwords—Users must choose difficult-to-guess passwords. Fixed passwords must not be found in the dictionary and must not be a reflection of the user's personal life. All fixed passwords must be at least 10 characters, and this minimum length must be enforced automatically where systems support it. Users must choose fixed passwords that include both alphabetic and numeric characters.

Changing Passwords—User-chosen fixed passwords must not be reused or recycled. Where systems support it, fixed passwords must be required to change every 60 days and passwords must be changed the first time they are used. If a user suspects that somebody else may know his or her password, the password must be changed immediately. The Information Systems department's Help Desk will not reset user passwords unless a user is identified.

Protecting Passwords—Users must not share a fixed password with anyone, including managers and co-workers. Users must employ authorized mechanisms to share information such as local server shared directories, electronic mail, intranet pages, or floppy disks. Users must not store fixed passwords in any computer files, such as logon scripts or computer programs, unless the passwords have been encrypted with authorized encryption software. Passwords must not be written down unless a transformation process has concealed them, or they are physically secured, such as placed in a locked file cabinet. All fixed passwords set by default by the hardware or software vendor must be changed before the involved system can be used for Company X business activities.

Privacy

Expectations Of Privacy—Users must have no expectation of privacy when using information systems at Company X. To manage systems and enforce security, Company X may log, review, and otherwise utilize any information stored on or passing through its systems. Company X may capture user activity such as telephone numbers dialed and web sites visited.

Collecting Information—Company X does not collect information that is unnecessary for business purposes. Company X does not collect information from third parties such as customers unless these parties are notified about the collection activities before they occur.

Third-Party Information Privacy—A wide variety of third parties have entrusted their information to Company X for business purposes, and all workers at Company X must do their best to safeguard the privacy and security of this information. Customer account data is Confidential and access must be strictly limited based on business need for such access. Customer account information must not be distributed to third parties without advance authorization by the customer. Exceptions will be made in the case of customer incapacitation or death.

Third-Party Disclosures

Preauthorization For Public Statements—All workers who will be delivering speeches, writing papers, or otherwise disclosing information about Company X or its business must obtain preauthorization from the Public Relations department. Only designated individuals are authorized to be spokespersons for Company X. Unless a worker is one of these designated spokespersons, all inquires from the media must be directed to Public Relations.

Company X Non-Disclosure Agreements—Whenever communications with third parties necessitate the release of sensitive Company X information, a standard non-disclosure agreement (NDA) must be signed by the third party. Information released to these third parties must be limited to the topics directly related to the involved project or business relationship, and the disclosure must be approved in advance by the involved information Owner.

Third-Party Non-Disclosure Agreements—In some instances, before discussions can be commenced, third parties must require that workers at Company X sign their non-disclosure agreements (NDAs). Recipients of third-party NDAs must forward these agreements to the Legal department. Third-party NDAs must be signed only by members of the Company X Legal department.

Acceptable Use Of The Internet

Not A Fringe Benefit—Internet access beyond electronic mail must be provided only if necessary to perform a worker's job. If a user needs additional access to Internet facilities, a request must be directed to the user's manager, who must contact Information Security.

Information Reliability—All information acquired from the Internet must be considered suspect until confirmed by separate information from another source. Users must not rely on the alleged identity of a corespondent through the Internet unless the identity of this person is confirmed through methods approved by the Information Security department such as digital certificates or digital signatures.

Posting Information To Discussing Groups—Users must not post to public discussion groups, chat rooms, or other public forums on the Internet unless they have been preauthorized by the Public Relations department to make this type of representation on behalf of Company X. Management reserves the right to remove any Internet posting by a worker at Company X that it deems inappropriate and potentially damaging to the organization's reputation.

Downloading Software—Users must not download software from the Internet unless specifically authorized to do so by the Information Systems or Information Security department. Users may download data files from the Internet, but must check these files for viruses before executing them. Depending on the file, decompression or decryption may need to be performed before downloading.

Sending Security Parameters—Users must not send any sensitive parameters such as credit card numbers, telephone calling card numbers, fixed passwords, or customer account numbers through the Internet unless the connection is encrypted. Users must not include sensitive parameters in electronic mail messages sent through the Internet unless these messages are encrypted with software approved by the Information Security department. It is not sufficient for a user to employ a virtual private network (VPN) to connect with Company X computers, even though the result is that the communications link between a remote computer and Company X computers is encrypted. Use of a VPN permits an electronic mail message sent to an outside party to travel over unencrypted links. Security parameters must not be sent through electronic mail to outside parties unless end-to-end encryption is employed.

International Transfer Of Data—The movement of private information such as human resources records across international borders in some countries is illegal. Before transferring any private information across a border, users must check with the Information Security department to ensure that laws are not violated.

Setting Up Extra Services—Subscription to real-time automatic information distribution services on the Internet must be approved by the Information Systems department. Subscription to electronic mail distribution lists is permissible without this approval. The establishment of any network connection with a third party is forbidden unless the Information Security department has approved the controls associated with this connection. Users must not establish web pages, electronic bulletin boards, or other mechanisms that provide public access to information about Company X without the advance approval of both Information Security and the Public Relations department. The establishment of electronic data interchange and other electronic business system arrangements is prohibited unless approved by both Information Security and Information Systems department.

User Anonymity—Users must not misrepresent, obscure, suppress, or replace their own or another user's identity on the Internet or on any other Company X information system. In all instances, the user name, electronic mail address, organizational affiliation, and related contact information must reflect the actual originator of a message or posting. The use of anonymous re-mailers or other identity-hiding mechanisms is forbidden. The use of web browsers, anonymous FTP log ons, and other methods established with the expectation that users do not need to identify themselves is permissible.

False Security Reports—All users in receipt of information about system vulnerabilities must forward this information to the Information Security department, which will determine what action is appropriate. Users must not redistribute system vulnerability information.

Establishing Network Connections

Company X computers or networks may be connected to third-party computers or networks only after the Information Security department has determined that the combined systems will be in compliance with Company X security requirements. Real-time connections between two or more in-house Company X computer systems must not be established unless Information Security has determined that such connections will not jeopardize information security. Connections of internal Company X computers to the Company X internal network do not require such permissions, unless the involved systems store sensitive information. Connections to the Internet through Company X firewalls do not require such permissions.

Workers must not connect their own computers with Company X computers or networks without prior authorization from their department head. Personally-owned systems must not be used to process any Company X information unless the systems have been approved for use by Information Security.

Workers and vendors working for Company X must not make arrangements for, or actually complete, the installation of voice or data lines with any carrier unless they have obtained written approval from the director of the Telecommunications department.

All connections between Company X internal networks and the Internet or any other publicly-accessible computer network must include an approved firewall or related access control system. The privileges permitted through this firewall or related access control system must be based on business needs and must be defined in an access control standard issued by the Information Systems Security department [a link to that document must be inserted here].

Dial-Up Access

With the exception of portable computers and telecommuting computers, the use of modems directly attached to, or integrated into, personal computers to establish communications sessions with Company X computers or networks is prohibited. All dial-up connections with Company X computers and networks must be routed through a modem pool that includes an extended user authentication security system approved by the Information Security department.

Third-Party Access

Before third-party users are permitted to reach Company X internal systems through real-time computer connections, specific written approval of the Information Security department manager must be obtained. These third parties include information providers such as outsourcing organizations, business partners, contractors, and consultants working on special projects.

Third-party information system vendors must be given only in-bound connection privileges when the applicable system manager determines that they have a legitimate business need. These privileges must be enabled only for the time period required to accomplish previously-defined and approved tasks. Third-party vendor access that will last longer than one day must be approved by the Information Security department.

Unless the relevant information Owner has approved in advance, workers must not place anything other than Company X public information in a directory, on a server, or in any other location where unknown parties could readily access it.

As a condition of gaining access to the Company X computer network, every third party must secure its own connected systems in a manner consistent with Company X requirements. Company X must reserve the right to audit the security measures in effect on third party-connected systems without prior warning. Company X also must reserve the right to immediately terminate network connections with all third-party systems not meeting such requirements.

Encryption

Default Protection Not Provided—Company X networks and the Internet and other public networks are not protected from wiretapping by default. In all but a few rare instances, if information is to be protected, then the user must take specific action to enable encryption facilities. Users who employ cellular or mobile phones must not discuss Confidential or Secret information unless they have taken steps to encrypt the call. Video conferences must not involve discussion of sensitive information unless encryption facilities are known to be enabled.

When To Use Encryption—Whenever Confidential or Secret information is sent over a public computer network like the Internet, encryption methods authorized by the Information Security department must be used to protect it. Whenever Secret information is stored in a computer, this storage must be achieved with similar authorized encryption methods. For more information about these circumstances, see Chapter 17, "Sample Data Classification Quick Reference Table."

Key Selection—Many encryption routines require that the user provide a seed or a key as input. Users must protect these security parameters from unauthorized disclosure, just as they would protect passwords from unauthorized disclosure. Rules for choosing strong seeds or keys must follow all rules for choosing strong passwords.

Electronic Mail

Sharing And Forwarding—Electronic mail accounts, like user IDs, are for specific individuals and must not be shared. If a user goes on vacation or is otherwise unable to check their mail for extended periods, mail can be forwarded to another Company X worker. Notices can be established that will automatically inform correspondents that the recipient will not be responding for a certain period of time. Upon departure from Company X, a user's electronic mail account must be terminated. No forwarding of electronic mail to addresses outside Company X is permitted. If an electronic mail message contains sensitive information, users must not forward it to another recipient unless the other recipient is known to be authorized to view the information, or the originator approves the forwarding. Broadcast electronic mail message facilities must not be employed unless department manager approval is obtained, but the use of selected distribution lists is both advisable and permissible without such approval.

Default Protection—Users must be careful about the inclusion of sensitive information in electronic mail messages that are not protected by encryption. Users must employ encryption facilities approved by the Information Security department.

Message Recording—Users are responsible for saving important messages that might be needed at a future date. Electronic mail systems must not be used for message storage. Users must move important messages from electronic mail systems into other storage places such as word processing documents.

Contents Of Messages—Users must not use profanity, obscenities, or derogatory remarks in any electronic mail messages discussing employees, customers, competitors, or others involved with Company X business. Such remarks may create legal problems such as trade libel and defamation of character. Special caution is warranted because backup and archival copies of electronic mail made by third parties may actually be more permanent and more readily accessible than traditional paper communications.

Harassing Or Offensive Messages—Company X information systems must not be used for the exercise of a user's right to free speech. Sexual, ethnic, and racial harassment, including unwanted telephone calls, electronic mail, and internal mail, is strictly prohibited. Users must to respond directly to the originator of offensive electronic mail messages, telephone calls, or other communications. If the originator does not promptly stop sending offensive messages, workers must report the communications to their manager and the Human Resources department.

Printing, Copying and Fax Transmission

Destruction Of Waste Copies—If a printer, copier, or fax machine jams or malfunctions when printing Confidential or Secret information, the involved users must not leave the machine until all copies of the sensitive information are removed or are no longer legible. All paper copies of sensitive information must be disposed of by shredding or other methods approved by the Information Security department.

Faxing Precautions—Sensitive materials must not be faxed unless an authorized staff member is on-hand at the time of transmission to properly handle the materials at the receiving site, the fax is sent to a locked room to which only authorized workers have access, or a password-protected fax mailbox is used to restrict release to an authorized recipient. Sensitive information must not be faxed through untrusted intermediaries such as hotel staff or rented mailbox service staff. Secret information may be faxed only if the connection is protected with encryption systems approved by the Information Security department. The receipt of sensitive information by fax must be confirmed promptly. All faxes must employ a standard cover page that includes language approved by the Company X Legal department. Third-party signatures on contracts, purchase orders, and similar legal documents sent by fax must always be followed-up with an exchange of paper originals.

Printer Precautions—When printing sensitive information, the user must be present at the printer at the time of printing to prevent the information from being revealed to unauthorized parties, or direct the output to a printer inside an area where only authorized workers are permitted to go.

Copy Machine Precautions—Unless permission from the copyright Owner is obtained, making multiple copies of material from magazines, journals, newsletters, and other publications is forbidden unless this is both reasonable and customary. For more information about copying software and other materials, see "Intellectual Property Rights" on page 473.

Repair Services—The repair of fax machines, printers, and copy machines must be performed only by third-party vendors who have signed a Company X non-disclosure agreement.

Mobile Computing And Work At Home

Approval For Remote Access—Remote access to Company X computers must be granted only to those users who have a demonstrable business need for such access. Permission to access Company X computers remotely is granted by and annually reviewed by a user's manager. All remote users must attend a special class before remote access privileges are granted or annually renewed. Company X reserves the right to conduct surprise audits of users with remote access privileges. These surprise audits could include visits to remote sites and a review of the contents of a computer used to access Company X systems.

Location Independence—All security requirements apply at remote locations, although they may be implemented in different ways. For example, paper-based Confidential or Secret information must be locked up when not in active use. In Company X offices, a file cabinet might be used, but on the road, a locking briefcase might be employed.

Access Control Packages—All portable and remote computers that are under the control of Company X workers and that are used to process Company X business information must be protected with an access control package approved by the Information Security department. These access control packages must prevent unauthorized use of the machines and unauthorized access to Company X information. These access control packages must prevent virus infections and other types of damage from malicious software.

Handling Of Sensitive Information—Sensitive (Confidential or Secret) information must not leave Company X offices. If it is necessary to remove computer-readable sensitive information from Company X offices, this information must be protected with encryption facilities approved by Information Security. If sensitive information is transmitted over public computer networks such as the Internet, this transmission must take place with encryption facilities approved by Information Security. All portable and remote systems storing sensitive Company X information must also employ hard disk encryption systems.

Authentication Of Remote Users—Remote access to Company X computers and networks requires that all users be definitively authenticated with dynamic passwords or other identification systems approved by the Information Security department. All remote users must connect to Company X computers and internal networks through authorized communications systems such as firewalls and modem pools. Inbound connection to Company X computers or networks through an office desktop modem is prohibited unless specific approval has been obtained from Information Security. Outbound connection to third-party networks including the Internet is permissible through office desktop modems or other types of modems. Leaving personal- computer-linked modems in auto-answer mode is prohibited unless a remote user identification system approved by Information Security has been installed.

Theft Of Equipment—If information systems equipment used to handle Company X information is not stored in a locked area, users must employ anti-theft equipment approved by the Information Security department. Users must not store passwords, user IDs, or any other access information in portable or remote systems. Dynamic password tokens or other access control mechanisms employed for remote access must not be stored in the same case as portable computers.

Remote Office Security—Before approval for working at home or telecommuting is granted, a user's manager must review the security environment of the proposed working environment. If the user works with sensitive information, a shredder must be employed or issued by Company X. If sensitive information will be stored in paper form, locking furniture or a safe must be available or provided by Company X. Users must ensure that their files will be remotely backed-up over the network, or that they will have appropriate remote systems to perform their own backups.

Travel Considerations—Users must be careful not to discuss sensitive information when in public places like hotel lobbies, restaurants, and elevators. Viewing sensitive information on a computer screen or hardcopy report is prohibited when a user is in a public place such as seated on an airplane. Users must be careful not to provide sensitive information in voice mail messages or alphanumeric pager messages.

Viruses, Malicious Software, And Change Control

Virus Checking Required—Virus-checking systems approved by the Information Security department must be in place on all personal computers with operating systems susceptible to viruses, on all firewalls with external network connections, and on all electronic mail servers. All files coming from external sources must be checked before execution or usage. If encryption or data compression has been used, these processes must be

reversed before the virus-checking process takes place. Users must not turn off or disable virus-checking systems.

If A Virus Is Detected—If users obtain virus alerts, they must immediately disconnect from all networks and cease further use of the affected computer, and call the Information Systems help desk for technical assistance. Users must not remove viruses on their own. If users believe they may have been the victim of other malicious software, they must immediately call the help desk to minimize the damage. User possession or development of viruses or other malicious software is prohibited.

Change Control—Users must not install new or upgraded operating systems or application software on personal computers or other machines used to process Company X information. Systems used to process Company X information may be owned by Company X, but have been specifically recognized as systems used for regular business activities. This approach permits Company X to perform automatic software distribution, automatic software license management, automated remote backup, and related functions on a centralized and coordinated basis. While change control will be maintained through the above-mentioned access control packages, users can, however, change the preferences on software packages, such as the fonts for a word processing package.

Personal Use Of Information Systems

Personal Use—All user activity is subject to logging and subsequent analysis. Users must not perform any activity on Company X information systems that could damage the reputation of Company X. Unbecoming conduct could lead to disciplinary action including revocation of access control privileges. Incidental personal use of Company X information systems including the telephone is permissible as long as the usage does not interfere with job performance, does not deny other users access to the system resources, and does not incur significant costs. Personal use of Company X information, such as a mailing list, requires the advance approval of the relevant information Owner. Use of software licensed to Company X on a personal computer owned by a user is not authorized unless the system has been designated a system that is used to process Company X information.

Testing Prohibition—Users must not test or attempt to compromise any information security mechanism unless specifically authorized to do so by the Information Security department. Users must not possess software or other tools that are designed to compromise information security.

Intellectual Property Rights

Legal Ownership—With the exception of material clearly owned by third parties, Company X is the legal Owner of all business information stored on or passing through in its systems. Unless the chief information officer has signed a specific written agreement, all business-related information developed while a user is employed by Company X is Company X property.

Making Copies Of Software—Users must not make copies of or use software unless they know that the copies are in keeping with the vendor's license to Company X. If a system that is used to process Company X information has been set up by the Information Systems department, users can rely on the fact that all software on this system is licensed and authorized. Questions about licensing must be directed to Information Systems, which maintains documentation reflecting software licenses throughout Company X. Making regular backups of software for contingency planning purposes is permissible. Information Systems must remove all software that is not authorized on systems that are used to process Company X information.

Labeling—In addition to maintaining the labels mentioned in "Information Sensitivity Classification" on page 465, users must maintain information about source, date, and usage restrictions for all information provided by third parties. These labels will be important for management decision-making purposes, and will demonstrate that Company X observed appropriate copyright and other intellectual property laws. Users must assume that all materials on the Internet are copyrighted unless specific notice states otherwise.

Systems Development

Production System Definition—Information systems that have been designated production systems have special security requirements. A production system is a system that is regularly used to process information critical to Company X business. Although a production system may be physically situated anywhere, the production system designation is assigned by the Information Systems department Computer Operations manager.

Special Production System Requirements—All software developed in-house that runs on production systems must be developed according to the Information Systems department's systems development method-ology (SDM). This methodology must ensure that the software will be adequately documented and tested before it is used for critical Company X information. The SDM also must ensure that production systems include adequate control measures. Production systems also must have designated Owners and Custodians for the critical information they process. Information Security must perform periodic risk assessments of production systems to determine whether the controls employed are adequate. All production systems must have an access control system to restrict who can access the system and restrict the privileges available to these users. A designated access control administrator who is not a regular user on the system must be assigned for all production systems.

Separation Between Production, Development, And Test Systems—Where resources permit, there must be a separation between the production, development, and test environments. Where these distinctions have been established, development and test staff must not be permitted to have access to production systems. All production software testing must proceed with sanitized information where Confidential or Secret information is replaced with dummy data. All security fixes provided by software vendors must go through the systems development methodology testing process, and must be promptly installed. Application programmers must not be given access to production information. A formal and documented change control process must be used to restrict and approve changes to production systems. All application program-based access paths other than the approved user access paths must be deleted or disabled before software is moved into production.

User Programming—Users must not write production computer programs unless specifically authorized by the chief information officer. The construction of spreadsheet formulas, automatic execution scripts that are run when a system is booted, or databases is not considered programming for purposes of this document. Both users and programmers must be careful never to embed user IDs, readable passwords, encryption keys, or other security parameters in any file.

Reporting Problems

What To Report—All workers must promptly report to the Information Security department any loss of, or severe damage to, their hardware or software. Workers must report all suspected compromises to Company X information systems. All serious information security vulnerabilities known to exist must be reported. All instances of suspected disclosure of Confidential or Secret information also must be reported.

How To Report—An unattended voice mail hotline with a pager alert has been established to handle information security problem reports. Callers to the hotline can leave messages on this line anonymously. Reports must not be sent by electronic mail unless the message is encrypted with software authorized by the Information Security department. All reports must be investigated before any action is taken. Workers may also use this hotline with a question about information security.

Non-Compliance Situations

Risk Acceptance—Non-compliance with these and other information security requirements can result in disciplinary action up to and including termination. In rare cases, a business case for non-compliance can be established. In all such cases, the non-compliance situation must be approved in advance through a risk acceptance process. This process requires a risk acceptance memo signed by a department manager and approved by the Information Security, Information Systems, and Internal Audit departments. Further details on the risk acceptance process can be obtained through Internal Audit.

Further Information—Questions about this document should be directed to Information Security department manager. Further policy information can be found in the Human Resources Manual [an intranet link to that document could be inserted here].

Chapter 6   SAMPLE TELECOMMUTING AND MOBILE COMPUTER SECURITY POLICY

MANAGEMENT ISSUES

Telecommuting Privileges—Working at home or alternative site work arrangements, both known as telecommuting, are a management option, not a universal employee fringe benefit. Permission to telecommute is granted by an employee's manager. Before a telecommuting arrangement can begin, this manager must be satisfied that the job can be effectively performed off-site, that the worker has the personality and work habits suitable for telecommuting, and that an alternative work site is appropriate for the Company X tasks performed by the involved worker. Work site considerations include physical and information security for Company X property and a low-distraction work environment. Management also must be satisfied that the ways to measure worker performance are both clearly specified and realistic, and that the methods to stay in touch with other workers are adequate. A worksheet or checklist for making these approval decisions is available from the Help Desk [an intranet link to this checklist can be inserted here].

Periodic Privilege Reevaluation—The system privileges granted to all users, including the privilege to telecommute and to remotely access Company X systems, must be reevaluated by management every six months. Consistent compliance with the policies described in this document and related policies is an important factor in management's decision regarding the continuation of a telecommuting arrangement. Related policies include, but are not limited to, compliance with software license agreements and reporting suspected computer virus infections. Many related policies are not reiterated here because they appear in other Company X documents [a link to table of contents for the information security policies intranet site can be inserted here]. This document is restricted to security matters relevant to telecommuters and mobile computer users.

Work Site Inspections—Company X maintains the right to conduct physical inspections of telecommuter offices without advance notice. Company X also maintains the right to examine the contents of any computer that contains or is thought to contain Company X internal information, including computers that have been purchased by employees, contractors, consultants, temporaries, and others. Company X additionally retains the right to remotely inspect the contents of and configuration of computers used by telecommuters, through remote systems administration tools.

Consistent Security—Company X information must at all times be protected in a manner commensurate with its sensitivity and criticality. The precautions described in this policy apply regardless of the storage media on which information is recorded, the locations where the information is stored, the systems used to process the information, the individuals who have access to the information, or the processes by which the information is handled. This means that workers must protect information in a similar manner no matter whether they are in a Company X office, a hotel room, or at a home office.

Required Training—Company X workers must complete an approved remote systems access training course, and pass the online examination associated with this course, prior to being granted privileges to use dial-up, in-bound Internet telnet, or any other Company X remote access data communications system [a link to the intranet site that permits them to sign up for and download this computer based training course can be inserted here].

Intellectual Property Rights—Intellectual property developed or conceived of while a worker is attending to Company X business at an alternative work site is the exclusive property of Company X. Such intellectual property includes patent, copyright, trademark, and all other intellectual property rights as manifested in memos, plans, strategies, products, computer programs, documentation, and other Company X materials.

Reporting Loss or Damage—Workers at remote working locations must promptly report to their manager any damage to or loss of Company X computer hardware, software, or sensitive information that has been entrusted to their care [a link to the Help Desk intranet trouble ticket system can be inserted here].

ACCESS CONTROL

Encryption And Boot Protection—All computers used for telecommuting, and portables, laptops, notebooks, and other transportable computers containing sensitive (Confidential or Secret) Company X information must consistently employ both hard disk encryption for all data files and boot protection through a password. These two essential controls must be provided through software or hardware systems approved by the Information Security department [a link to list of approved information security products can be inserted here]. Personal digital assistants, handheld computers, and smart phones must not be used to handle Company X sensitive information unless they have been configured with the necessary controls, such as encryption and boot protection, and approved for such use by the Informa-

tion Systems department. Exceptions will be made for calendars, address books, and stored connection information such as telephone numbers.

Sharing Access Devices and Systems—Telecommuters must not share dynamic password token cards, smart cards, fixed passwords, or any other access devices or parameters with anyone without prior approval from the Information Security department. This means that a remote computer used for Company X business must be used exclusively by the telecommuter. Family members, friends, and others must not be permitted to use this machine. Telecommuters must never lend to others a handheld computer, a personal digital assistant, a smart phone, or any other computer that stores information about Company X business activities.

BACKUP AND MEDIA STORAGE

Backup—Telecommuters are responsible for ensuring that their remote systems are backed up on a periodic basis, either automatically through the network or remotely with tape drives or similar equipment. If network backup is not available or feasible, Company X will provide telecommuters with local backup equipment. If backups are made locally, telecommuting workers must store copies of these same backups at a secure location away from the remote working site at least every two weeks. If these backups contain sensitive information, the backups must be encrypted using software approved by the Information Security department [a link to list of approved information security products can be inserted here].

Sensitive Media Marking and Storage—When sensitive information is written to a floppy disk, magnetic tape, CD-RW or other storage media, the media must be

externally marked with the highest relevant sensitivity classification. Unless encrypted, when not in use, this media must be stored in heavy locked furniture. Smart cards and tamper-resistant security modules are an exception to this rule.

Automatic Device Synchronization—Systems that automatically exchange data between devices, such as the file synchronization mechanism used with a personal digital assistant and a personal computer, must not be enabled unless the systems have been evaluated and approved by the Information Security department.

Setting Date and Time—Telecommuting workers must diligently keep their remote computers' internal clocks synchronized to the actual date and time.

COMMUNICATIONS LINKS

Establishing Dial-Up Facilities—Workers must not leave their personal computers unattended with a modem turned on and communications software enabled unless they have installed an access control system approved by the Information Security department [an intranet link to approved information security products list can be inserted here]. Workers must not establish any communications systems that ordinarily accept in-coming dial-up calls unless these systems have been approved by an Information Security manager [a link to the External Communications Security Policy can be inserted here].

Inbound Dial-Up to Company X Networks—All in-bound dial-up lines connected to Company X internal networks and networked computer systems must pass through an additional access control point, such as a firewall, modem pool, telecommunications front end, or similar system, before users are permitted to reach an operating system-based computer logon screen asking for a user ID and fixed password. This additional access point must employ dynamic passwords or another extended user authentication technology approved by the Information Security department [a link to list of approved information security products can be inserted here].

Establishing Internet Connections—Workers must not establish firewalls, routers, communications servers, or any other facilities on their remote computer systems that handle Company X business if these facilities permit telnet or any other type of real-time inbound remote access through the Internet. Outbound connections from a remote system through the Internet, terminating at a Company X networked computer system, are permissible as long as these connections are secured by a virtual private network software package, as defined in the External Communications Security Policy [a link can be inserted here].

Other Connections—Other than dial-up and Internet connections, workers must not establish any other interface between a remote computer used for Company X business activities and another network, such as value-added networks, unless prior approval of the Information Security department has been obtained in writing. This means that workers are prohibited from establishing their own personal accounts with Internet service providers and using these accounts for Company X business. Instead, all Company X business Internet electronic mail and Internet surfing must be accomplished through a Company X-managed firewall with Company X approved electronic mail software [a link to that part of the External Communications Security Policy can be inserted here].

DSL Lines And Cable Modem Lines—Digital subscriber lines, cable modem lines, and other high-speed lines must not be used for any Company X business communications unless a firewall and an approved virtual private network is employed. Telecommuters must contact the Help Desk for assistance in the establishment of these facilities before making any arrangements with third-party vendors.

Radio Networks—Workers transmitting sensitive Company X information must not employ radio networks, such as cellular modems, unless these network channels are encrypted. The use of digital communications protocols rather than traditional analog communications protocols does not qualify as encryption.

Telephone Discussions—Workers must take steps to avoid discussing sensitive information when on the telephone. If discussion of such information is absolutely required, workers must use guarded terms and refrain from mentioning sensitive details beyond those needed to get the job done. Secret information must not be discussed on speakerphones unless all participating parties acknowledge that no unauthorized persons are in close proximity such that they might overhear the conversation. Unless an encryption system approved by the Information Security department is used, secret Company X information must never be discussed on cordless or cellular telephones.

Message Machines—Unless the receiving message machine or voice mail system is known to be password protected, workers must refrain from leaving messages containing sensitive information on these recording systems. Unless their message machine or voice mail system is password protected, telecommuting workers must record an outgoing message informing callers that their incoming message recording system is not secure and is not suitable for sensitive information.

SYSTEM MANAGEMENT

Company X-Provided Machines—Employees working on Company X business at alternative work sites must use Company X-provided computer and network equipment. An exception will be made only if other equipment has been approved by the Help Desk as compatible with Company X information systems and controls.

Access Control System—Telecommuters must not use a remote computer for Company X business activities unless this same computer runs an access control system approved by the Information Security department [a link to list of approved products can be inserted here].

Telecommuting Systems—Workers attending to Company X business at alternative work sites must use only Company X-provided computer software, hardware, and network equipment. An exception will be made only if other systems have been approved by the Information Systems department as compatible with Company X information systems and controls. Workers should not bring personally-owned computers into Company X offices to process or otherwise handle Company X information without prior approval from the Information Systems department.

Changes to Configurations And Software—On Company X-supplied computer hardware, workers must not change the operating system configuration or install new software. If such changes are required, they must be performed by Help Desk personnel with remote system maintenance software. Changing the font defaults for a word processing program, or otherwise altering the templates provided with an application, is permissible without Help Desk assistance or advance approval.

Changes to Hardware—Computer equipment supplied by Company X must not be altered or added to in any way without prior knowledge and authorization from the Help Desk.

Downloading Software—Without prior authorization, workers must not download software from dial-up electronic bulletin board systems, the Internet, or other systems outside Company X onto computers used to handle Company X data.

Ownership Versus Possession—If Company X supplied a telecommuter with software, hardware, furniture, information or other materials to perform Company X business remotely, the title to, and all rights and interests to these items will remain with Company X. In such instances, telecommuter possession does not convey ownership or any implication of ownership. All such items must be promptly returned to Company X when a telecommuter separates from Company X, or when so requested by the telecommuter's manager.

Liability For Company X Property—If Company X supplied a telecommuter with software, hardware, furniture, information or other materials to perform Company X business remotely, Company X assumes all risks of loss or damage to these items unless such loss or damage occurs due to the telecommuter's negligence. Company X expressly disclaims any responsibility for loss or damage to persons or property caused by, or arising out of the usage of such items.

Electromagnetic Interference—In some cases, use of computers or other electronic devices will generate electromagnetic interference that will affect televisions, radios, or other machines. If a telecommuting system set-up to perform Company X business generates such interference, its use must be terminated immediately until such time as the specific nature of and a solution for the problem has been identified. The Company X Help Desk will assist telecommuters with this process [a link to Help Desk intranet page can be inserted here].

TRAVEL CONSIDERATIONS

Removal Of Information—Sensitive (Confidential or Secret) information may not be removed from Company X premises unless the information's Owner has approved in advance. This policy includes sensitive information stored on portable computer hard disks, floppy disks, CD-ROMs, magnetic tape cartridges, and paper memos. An exception is made for authorized off-site backups that are in encrypted form [a link to Information Classification Policy can be inserted here].

Traveling with Secret Information—Unless specific approval from a local department manager has been granted, workers must avoid traveling on public transportation when in the possession of Secret Company X information.

Foreign Transport—Whenever Secret information is carried by a Company X worker into a foreign country, the information must either be stored in some inaccessible form, such as an encrypted floppy disk, or must remain in the worker's possession at all times. Company X workers must not take Secret Company X information into another country unless the permission has been obtained from Physical Security management.

Public Exposure—Sensitive Company X information must not be read, discussed, or otherwise exposed in restaurants, on airplanes, on trains, or in other public places where unauthorized people might discover it.

Checked Luggage—Workers in the possession of portable, laptop, notebook, palmtop, handheld, smart phones, personal digital assistants, and other transportable computers containing sensitive Company X information must not check these computers in airline luggage systems. These computers must remain in the possession of the traveler as hand luggage.

Securing Hardcopy Sensitive Information—Whenever a hardcopy version of Secret information is removed from Company X premises, it must either be stored in a safe, locking furniture, or some other heavy container with a lock, or carried in a locked briefcase when not in use. Such information must not be left in an unattended motor vehicle, hotel room, or external office, even if this vehicle or room is locked.

Faxing Sensitive Information—If secret information is sent by fax, the recipient must have been notified of the time when it will be transmitted, and also have agreed that an authorized person will be present at the destination machine when the material is sent. An exception will be made if the area surrounding the fax machine is physically restricted such that persons who are not authorized to see the material being faxed may not enter. This means that sensitive Company X information must not be faxed through a hotel desk or other untrusted third parties. Another exception will be made in those instances in which the destination fax machine is password protected and authorized parties are the only ones who have access to the involved password.

PHYSICAL SECURITY

Similarity In Approaches—At alternative work sites, reasonable precautions must be taken to protect Company X hardware, software, and information from theft, damage, and misuse.

Provision Of Secure Containers—Workers who must keep Secret or Confidential Company X information at their homes in order to do their work must have safes or lockable heavy furniture for the proper storage of this information. If these workers do not have such furniture or safes, Company X will loan these items to the telecommuting workers.

Shredders—Telecommuters must have or be provided with a shredder to appropriately dispose of printed versions of sensitive information. Shredders that make strips of paper are not acceptable for the disposal of Company X sensitive material. Acceptable shredders

make confetti or other small particles. All sensitive Company X paper-resident information plus any information containing financial account numbers, like credit card numbers, must be shredded. Intermediate work products containing sensitive information, such as carbon copies, photocopies, photographic negatives, or paper memo drafts, must also be shredded. Telecommuting workers on the road must not throw away Company X sensitive information in hotel wastebaskets or other publicly-accessible trash containers. Sensitive information must be retained until it can be shredded, or destroyed with other approved methods.

Property Passes—Portable computers, cellular phones, personal digital assistants, modems, and related information systems equipment belonging to Company X must not leave Company X offices unless accompanied by an approved property pass. Property passes must be obtained when bringing personally-owned equipment into Company X offices. Office computer equipment owned by Company X, and situated at a remote work site, must not be relocated without the prior approval of a telecommuter's manager. An exception will be provided for equipment with an approved property pass form.

Moving Residence Location—If a telecommuting worker has an intention to move his or her residence or off-site work location to another site, the worker must notify his or her manager and get approval prior to the move. The worker also must follow Information Security department instructions associated with telecommuter residence moves. The new location must meet all the current telecommuter site requirements [a link to telecommuter checklist can be inserted here].

Screen Positioning—The display screens for all systems used to handle Company X sensitive information must be positioned such that they cannot be readily viewed by unauthorized persons through a window, over a shoulder, or by similar means.

Logging-Out—After a worker has completed a remote session with Company X computers, the worker must log off and then hang up, rather than only hanging up. Workers using remote communications facilities must wait until they receive a confirmation of their log off command from the remotely connected Company X machine before they leave the computer they are using.

Chapter 7 SAMPLE EXTERNAL COMMUNICATIONS SECURITY POLICY

Policy Objectives and Scope—This policy describes the security requirements for remote information systems connections to Company X internal computers and networks. It covers a wide variety of technologies including cellular phone connections, dial-up modem links, value-added networks, and Internet value-added networks. Every individual worker or organization making these and other types of automated remote connections to Company X internal computers and networks must follow the rules described here.

External Connections Require Approval—Access to Company X internal networks from remote locations including worker homes, hotel rooms, and customer offices must, in all instances, be approved in advance by the involved worker's immediate manager. Such remote access is not a universal fringe benefit, and may be revoked at any time for cause including unsatisfactory performance and non-compliance with security policies. Further details about this approval process can be found within the Telecommuting Security Policy [insert a link to intranet site where this document exists].

Third-Party Access to Company X Internal Networks—In strictly controlled situations, Company X permits third parties to access Company X internal networks and connected computer systems. Both the Owner of the information to which the third party will be given access and the project manager in charge of the third-party work must agree in writing to such access before it will be established. The decision-making process for granting such access includes consideration of the controls on the systems to be connected, the third-party security policies, whether a non-disclosure agreement has been signed, and the results of a background check. System privileges for these third parties must be strictly limited to the system facilities and information needed to achieve predefined business objectives. These access privileges must be reviewed every six months by the relevant project manager to determine whether they need to be continued.

Third-Party Vendor Access—Third-party vendors who have sold Company X hardware, software, or communication services are not automatically granted repeated access to Company X internal computers or networks. They must go either through the approval process described in the previous paragraph, or go through a separate remote access for systems maintenance process administered by the Information Security department [insert an intranet link to contact information for the department]. A system administrator may enable temporary remote access privileges for vendors without going through either of these approval processes. This temporary access must be granted only for the time period required to accomplish approved tasks, one day or less. This temporary access must be provided by positive identification of the vendor personnel before the connection is established, and logging of all activity while the connection exists.

Third-Party Compliance Statement—All third parties wanting to remotely access Company X internal computers or networks must sign a compliance statement prior to being issued a user ID. If a certain third party already has a user ID, a signature must be obtained prior to receiving a renewed user ID. This renewal process takes place every six months. A signature on this compliance statement indicates that the user understands and agrees to adhere to Company X policies and procedures related to computers and networks. Company X retains the right to periodically audit third parties who have access to Company X computers and networks to ensure compliance with this and other policies and requirements.

Responsibility for User IDs—All workers including third parties are responsible for the activity performed with their personal user IDs, despite whether these user IDs are connecting through external network facilities. User IDs must never be shared with associates, friends, family members, or others. User IDs must not be utilized by anyone but the individuals to whom they have been issued. Workers are forbidden from performing any activity with user IDs belonging to other individuals with the exception of authorized anonymous user IDs such as "guest."

Default to Denial—If a Company X computer or network access control system is not functioning properly, it must default to denial of privileges to users. If access control systems are malfunctioning, the systems they support must remain unavailable until such time as the problem has been rectified.

Dynamic Passwords—All network connections initiated from a location outside an official Company X office, and connecting to a Company X internal network, must employ dynamic password systems approved by Information Security. Dynamic passwords are passwords that change each time a new session is established. Store-and-forward network connections, such as those used for electronic mail and Internet news services, need not employ dynamic passwords.

Outbound Connections—Computer network connections initiated from inside an official Company X office, and connecting to an external network or computer, do not need to employ dynamic passwords. These connections must be routed through dial-up modem pools, Internet firewalls, and other systems expressly established to provide secure network access.

Modems on Desktop Systems—Modems inside Company X offices or connected to office desktop personal computers (PCs) are not permitted. Home-based, mobile, or telecommuting PCs are an exception to this rule. Connections to remote computers and networks must be routed through modem pools or the Company X Internet firewall. Unless a dynamic password system is installed, workers with home-based, mobile, or telecommuting PCs must not leave modems in auto-answer mode, with communications software enabled, such that dial-up calls could be received.

Encrypted Links—Whenever a computer network connection is established between a Company X computer and another computer at a location outside an official Company X office, and whenever this connection transmits or is likely to transmit either Confidential or Secret information, the link must be encrypted. Such encryption must be accomplished only with systems approved by the Information Security department [Insert an intranet link to approved products list issued by Information Security]. These systems include virtual private networks that incorporate not only encryption but also user authentication mechanisms.

Using Radio Technology for Data—Portable phones using radio technology and cellular phones must not be used for data transmissions containing Company X Secret or Confidential information unless the connection is encrypted. Other broadcast networking technologies, such radio-based local area networks, must not be used for these types of Company X information unless the link is encrypted. Such links may be used for electronic mail as long as involved users understand that the transmissions must not contain readable Secret or Confidential information. Workers must not discuss Confidential or Secret matters on cordless or cellular phones employing a regular voice connection, unless this connection has been encrypted with technology approved by the Information Security department [insert an intranet link to approved products list]. Phones using digital transmission rather than traditional analog transmission protocols are not considered to be encrypted for purposes of this policy.

Privilege Access Controls—All computers permanently or intermittently connected to either external networks or Company X networks must operate with privilege access controls approved by the Information Security department [insert an intranet link to approved products list]. Multi-user systems must employ user IDs unique to each user, and user privilege restriction mechanisms including directory and file access permissions. Network-connected single-user systems must employ approved hardware or software mechanisms that control system booting and that includes a time-out-after-no-activity screen saver.

Changing Initial Passwords—All vendor-supplied default passwords or other alternative access mechanisms must be changed before any computer or communications system is used for any Company X business activity. This policy applies to passwords associated with user IDs, and passwords associated with system administrators and other privileged user IDs.

Shared File Systems—The establishment of a connection between any external computer or network and a Company X internal computer or network must not involve the use of shared file systems. An exception will be made if the Information Security department approves the configuration prior to usage.

Required Virus Checking Programs—Current virus-checking programs approved by the Information Security department [insert an intranet link to approved products list] must be continuously enabled on all web servers, local area network servers, mail servers, firewalls, and networked personal computers. An exception will be made in those cases where the operating system is not generally subject to viruses.

Eradicating Viruses—Workers must not attempt to eradicate them without expert assistance. If workers suspect infection by a virus, or if virus detection software indicates an infection, workers must immediately stop using the involved computer, physically disconnect the machine from all networks, and call the corporate help desk [insert their telephone number or a link to their intranet page]. If the suspected virus appears to be damaging information or software, workers must turn off the computer immediately.

Decompress Before Running Virus Software—All externally-supplied, computer-readable files must be decompressed prior to being subjected to an approved virus-checking process. This applies to encrypted files.

Unpatched Or Virus-Infested Systems—Workers who have not installed the required software patches on their remote computers or whose systems are virus-infested must be disconnected from the Company X network until they have reestablished a secure computing environment. In order to regularly check the status of remotely-connected systems, Company X must use remote administration software that examines stored files, system configurations, and software installed. Workers making connection to a Company X network must agree to such remote monitoring.

Downloading Software—Workers must not download software from dial-up electronic bulletin board systems, the Internet, or other systems outside Company X. An exception is made for system administrators and other authorized technical personnel downloading patches and updated software packages. An exception is provided for external network automated software distribution systems such as those that distribute the latest virus-checking software and have been approved by Information Security [insert an intranet link to approved products list issued by Information Security].

Downloading Content and Assigning Labels—With the exception of general business correspondence and copyrighted software, all externally-provided information that is not clearly in the public domain must receive a Company X information classification system label. The Company X worker who receives this information is responsible for assigning an appropriate classification label on behalf of the external party. When assigning a classification label, this worker must preserve copyright notices, author credits, guidelines for interpretation, and information about restricted dissemination. Further details can be found in the Data Classification System Policy [insert an intranet link to that document].

Reliance on Downloaded Content—All information acquired from the Internet and other external networks must be considered suspect until confirmed by separate information from another source.

Time-Out After No Activity—All information systems accepting remote connections from public networks such as the dial-up phone network or the Internet must include a time-out mechanism. This mechanism must terminate all sessions without activity for a period of 30 minutes or less. All user IDs registered to networks or computers with external access facilities must be automatically suspended after 30 days of inactivity.

Failure to Establish a Connection—All Company X computers with interfaces to external networks must temporarily terminate the connection or time out the user ID for at least 10 minutes following a sequence of several unsuccessful attempts to log on. Repeated unsuccessful attempts to establish a connection using a privileged user ID must not result in revocation.

No Trespassing Banners—Where systems software permits, logon banners must be used on all Company X networks and computers that are directly accessible through external networks. These banners must employ standard no trespassing warning notices adopted by the Information Security department. These banners must refrain from disclosing the fact that Company X systems have been reached, the nature of the information available on these systems, and the specific systems software running on these computers. Web servers, telephone voice response units, and other systems that are designed to respond to anonymous users do not need to have such banners.

Anonymous Interaction—With the exception of web servers, electronic bulletin boards, or other systems where all regular users are anonymous, users must not log on to any Company X system or network anonymously. If users employ systems facilities that permit them to change their active user ID to gain certain privileges, they must have initially logged on employing a user ID that clearly indicates their identity.

Logs for Externally Connected Systems—All Company X computers and networks that interface to external networks must keep system logs that indicate the identity and activity performed by each user who accesses these systems. These logs must indicate time of day, date, user ID employed, any privileges utilized, and other details associated with all connections. System administrators must review summaries of these logs. System administrators must employ automated intrusion detection systems approved by the Information Security department to immediately inform them of suspicious activity [insert a link to intranet page with list of approved information security products].

Flow Control for Externally Connected Systems—All Company X networks that are connected to external networks must employ flow control mechanisms to restrict the machines to which users can connect based on the need for such access. Flow control can be implemented through internal firewalls, routers, gateways, front-ends, and other network components.

Browsing—With the exception of the Company X intranet, workers must not browse Company X systems or networks. For example, curious searching for interesting files and programs in the directories of other users is prohibited. Steps taken to legitimately locate information needed to perform one's job are not considered browsing. This statement on browsing does not apply to external networks such as the Internet.

Gaining Unauthorized Access—Workers using Company X computer networks must not gain unauthorized access to any information system or network to which they have not been expressly granted access. Workers using Company X computer networks are prohibited from damaging, disrupting, or interfering with the operations of multi-user information systems to which they are connected. Workers must not capture or otherwise be in possession of passwords, encryption keys, or any other access control mechanisms that have not been expressly assigned to them. Workers are prohibited from possessing or using software tools that could provide unauthorized access to system resources.

Changes to Company X Networks—Changes to Company X internal networks include loading new software, changing network addresses, reconfiguring routers, and adding dial-up lines. With the exception of emergency situations, all changes to Company X computer networks must be documented in a work order request [insert an intranet link to that form here], and must be approved in advance by the Information Technology department. Emergency changes to Company X networks must only be made by persons who are authorized by Information Technology.

Establishing System Connections—Workers must not establish or make arrangements for the establishment of electronic bulletin boards, local area networks, modem connections to existing local area networks, or other multi-user systems for communicating information without the specific approval of the director of the Information Technology department. New types of real-time connections between two or more in-house computer systems must not be established unless such approval has been obtained.

Installation of Communications Lines—Workers and vendors must not make arrangements for, or actually complete the installation of voice or data lines with any carrier, if they have not obtained approval from the director of the Information Systems department [insert an intranet link to a form for this].

Subscription to External Networks—Workers must not establish connections with Internet service providers (ISPs) or other external networks for the transmission of Company X data unless the director of the Information Security department has approved this arrangement. For further information about ISPs, see the Internet Security Policy [Insert an intranet link here].

Establishing New Business Networks—Unless the director of Information Technology and the chief legal counsel have approved, workers must not use the Internet or any other external network to establish new or different business channels. These channels include electronic data interchange arrangements, electronic malls with online shopping, online database services, and acceptance of credit cards through the Internet.

Participation in External Networks—Participation in external networks as a provider of services that external parties rely on is expressly prohibited unless the Company X chief legal counsel has identified the legal risks involved, and the director of the Information Technology department has expressly accepted these and other risks associated with the proposal.

Disclosure of Systems Information—The internal addresses, configurations, and related system design information for Company X computers and networks is confidential and must not be released to third parties who do not have a demonstrable need to know such information. The security measures employed to protect Company X computers and networks is confidential and must be similarly protected.

Related Information—For additional information on a related topic, see the policies entitled Telecommuting Security Policy [insert an intranet link here], and External Party Information Disclosure Policy [insert an intranet link here].

Approved By: [insert approving executive's name]

Approved On: DD/MM/YY

Effective Date: DD/MM/YY

Version Number: XX

Chapter 8   SAMPLE PERSONAL COMPUTER SECURITY POLICY

DOCUMENT OVERVIEW

Objectives And Scope—A large portion of Company X business is conducted with personal computers, including Macintoshes, UNIX workstations, portable computers, handheld computers, personal digital assistants, and similar computers dedicated to a single user's activity. Protection of personal computers and the information handled by these systems is an essential part of doing business at Company X. To this end, this policy provides information security instructions applicable to all workers who use Company X personal computers. All personal computer users are expected to comply with this policy as a condition of continued employment. This policy applies whether personal computers are standalone or connected to a network such as a local area network or the intranet. For related information, see Chapter 6, "Sample Telecommuting and Mobile Computer Security Policy" and Chapter 12, "Sample Intranet Security Policy."

BUSINESS USE ONLY

Business Use Only—In general, Company X computer and communication systems are intended to be used for business purposes only. Incidental personal use is nonetheless permissible if the use does not consume more than a trivial amount of resources that could otherwise be used for business purposes, does not interfere with worker productivity, does not preempt any business activity, and does not cause distress, legal problems, or morale problems for other workers. Permissible incidental use of a personal computer would, for example, involve responding to an electronic mail message about a luncheon, purchasing a gift online, and paying bills through the Internet. Offensive material that might cast Company X in a bad light, including sexist, racist, violent, or other content, is strictly forbidden from all Company X personal computers.

CONFIGURATION CONTROL

Changes To Application Software—Company X has a standard list of permissible software packages that users can run on their personal computers [a link to an intranet-posted personal computer configuration standard could be provided here]. Workers must not install other software packages on personal computers without obtaining advance permission from the Personal Computer group in the Information Systems department. Workers must not permit automatic software installation routines to be run on Company X personal computers unless these routines have been approved by the Personal Computer group. Unless separate arrangements are made with the Personal Computer group, upgrades to authorized software will be downloaded to personal computers automatically. Unapproved software may be removed without advance notice to the involved worker.

Changes To Operating System Configurations—On Company X-supplied computer hardware, workers must not change operating system configurations, upgrade existing operating systems, or install new operating systems. If such changes are required, they must be performed by corporate help desk personnel, in person or with remote system maintenance software.

Changes To Hardware—Computer equipment supplied by Company X must not be altered or added to in any way without the prior knowledge of and authorization from the Personal Computer group within the Information Systems department.

ACCESS CONTROL

Access Control Package—All Company X personal computers must run an access control package approved by the Information Security department [a link to list of approved products could be inserted here]. Typically these packages require a fixed password at the time a personal computer is booted and again after a certain period of no activity. Users must set the time frame for this period of no activity, at which point the contents of the screen are obscured, to 15 minutes or less. If sensitive information resides on a personal computer, the screen must immediately be protected with this access control package, or the machine turned off, whenever a worker leaves the location where the personal computer is in use.

Choice Of Passwords—The user-chosen passwords employed by access control software packages, and the keys employed by encryption packages, must be at least 10 characters in length. These passwords and keys must be difficult to guess. Words in a dictionary, derivatives of user IDs, and common character sequences such as "123456" must not be employed. Personal details such as spouse's name, license plate, social security number, and birthday must not be used unless accompanied by additional unrelated characters. User-chosen passwords and keys must not be any part of speech including, proper names, geographical locations, common acronyms, and slang.

Storage Of Passwords—Workers must maintain exclusive control of their personal passwords. They must not share them with others at any time. Passwords must not be stored in readable form in batch files, automatic logon scripts, software macros, terminal function keys, in computers without access controls, or in any other locations where unauthorized persons might discover them.

Encryption Of Secret Information—All computerized secret information must be encrypted when not in active use, for example, when not manipulated by software or viewed by an authorized user. The use of physical security measures such as safes, locking furniture, and locking office doors is recommended as a supplementary measure to protect secret information.

Logging Of Events Related To Secret Information—Personal computers handling secret information must securely log all significant computer security relevant events. Examples of computer security relevant events include password guessing attempts, attempts to use privileges that have not been authorized, modifications to production application software, and modifications to system software.

VIRUSES

Virus Program Installed—All personal computers must continuously run the current version of virus detection package approved by the Information Security department [a link to list of approved products can be inserted here]. The current version of this virus package must be automatically downloaded to each personal computer when the machine is connected to the Company X internal network. Workers must not abort this download process. At a minimum, this package must execute whenever external storage media is supplied.

Decompression Before Checking—Externally-supplied floppy disks, CD-ROMs, and other removable storage media must not be used unless they have been checked for viruses. Attachments to electronic mail must not be executed or opened unless they have been checked for viruses. Externally-supplied, computer-readable files, software programs, databases, word processing documents, and spreadsheets must be decompressed

prior to being subjected to an approved virus-checking process. If the files have been encrypted, they must be decrypted before running a virus-checking program.

Eradicating Viruses—Workers must not attempt to eradicate a virus without expert assistance. If workers suspect infection by a virus, they must immediately stop using the involved computer, physically disconnect from all networks, and call the Information Systems department Help Desk [a telephone number could be inserted here]. If the suspected virus appears to be damaging information or software, workers must immediately turn off the personal computer.

Playing With Viruses—Users must not intentionally write, compile, copy, propagate, execute, or attempt to introduce any computer code designed to self-replicate, damage, or otherwise hinder the performance of any Company X computer system.

BACKUP

Archival Copies—All personal computer software that is not standard Company X software must be copied prior to its initial usage, and such copies must be stored in a safe and secure location. These master copies, perhaps the media issued by the vendor, must not be used for ordinary business activities, but must be reserved for recovery from virus infections, hard disk crashes, and other computer problems. Documentation about the licenses for such software must be retained to get technical support, qualify for upgrade discounts, and verify the legal validity of the licenses.

Periodic Backup—All sensitive, valuable, or critical information resident on Company X computer systems must be periodically backed up. Such backup processes must be performed at least weekly. Unless automatic backup systems are known to be operational, all end users are responsible for making at least one current backup copy of sensitive, critical, or valuable files. These separate backup copies should be made each time that a significant number of changes are saved. User-generated backups must be periodically stored off-site in a physically secure location. Selected files from backups must be periodically restored to demonstrate the effectiveness of every backup process. Department managers must verify that proper backups are being made on all personal computers used for production business activities. Help Desk technical support is available for those workers that are having difficulty specifying, configuring, or otherwise establishing backup systems.

Reporting Software Purchases—All user department purchases of personal computer software that have not been handled through the Purchasing department must promptly be reported to the Information Systems department Help Desk.

Copyright Protection—Making unauthorized copies of licensed and copyrighted software, even if for "evaluation" purposes, is forbidden. Company X permits reproduction of copyrighted materials only to the extent legally considered fair use or with the permission of the author or Owner. If workers have any questions about the relevance of copyright laws, they must contact corporate legal counsel. Unless they receive information to the contrary, workers must assume that software and other materials are copyrighted.

DESTRUCTION

Deletion of Old Information—Workers must delete information from their personal computers if it is clearly no longer needed or potentially useful. Prior to deleting any Company X information, workers should consult the Document Retention Schedule prepared by corporate legal counsel [an intranet link could be inserted here]. Use of an erase feature is not sufficient for sensitive information because the information may be recoverable. Sensitive information should be deleted by an overwrite program approved by the Information Security department [a link to a list of approved products could be inserted here].

Destruction Of Information—Prior to disposal, defective or damaged floppy disks containing sensitive information must be destroyed using scissors or other methods approved by the Information Security department. Other storage media containing sensitive information must be disposed of in the locked destruction bins found in Company X offices. All hardcopy containing sensitive information must be disposed of in these bins or through an approved paper shredder.

DOCUMENTATION

Documentation For Production Systems—Every user who develops or implements software or hardware to be used for Company X production business activities must document the system in advance of its deployment. The documentation must be written so that the system may be run by persons unacquainted with it. Such documentation must be prepared even when standard software, such as a spreadsheet program, is employed.

Production System Development Conventions—All workers who are creating or upgrading production Company X applications that run on a personal computer must adhere to the Information Systems department's abbreviated systems development requirements. These abbreviated requirements have been specifically prepared for personal computers and require much less effort than the requirements for multi-user systems. These requirements include a risk assessment, a quick check to ensure that the involved production system is in compliance with existing technical standards, and the use of standardized file names.

Contingency Plans—When a personal computer is used as a critical part of any production business application, it must have a documented and tested contingency plan. Contingency plans must be prepared in accordance with the guidelines issued by the Information Security department [an intranet link could be inserted here].

Consistent Classification Marking—If information is sensitive, from the time when it is created until it is destroyed or declassified, it must be labeled with an appropriate data classification designation. Such markings must appear on hardcopy versions of the information, and the labels for storage media containing this information. Further information about data classification and marking can be found in the Data Classification Policy [an intranet link could be inserted here].

NETWORKING

Modems—Modems inside or attached to Company X office desktop personal computers are not permitted. Mobile and telecommuting personal computers are an exception to this rule. Communications software must always employ a password with at least 10 characters that has been constructed according to the rules found elsewhere in this document. When in Company X offices, users needing to make outbound connections with remote computers must route their connections through modem pools or the Internet firewall.

Internet—As a matter of policy, inbound Internet connections to Company X personal computers is forbidden unless these connections employ an approved virtual private network (VPN) software package approved by the Information Security department. These VPN systems must employ both user authentication features with at least fixed passwords and data interception prevention features, such as encryption.

Downloading Sensitive Information—Sensitive Company X information may be downloaded from a multi-user system to a personal computer only if a clear business need exists, adequate controls to protect the information are currently installed on the involved personal computer, and advance permission from the information Owner has been obtained. This policy is not intended to cover electronic mail or memos, but does apply to databases, master files, and other information stored on mainframes, minicomputers, servers, and other multi-user machines. This applies regardless of the media on which information is stored, the locations where the information is stored, the systems technology used to process the information, the people who handle it, or the processes by which information is handled.

Installation Of Communications Lines—Workers and vendors must not make arrangements for, or actually complete the installation of voice or data lines with any carrier, if they have not obtained approval from the director of the Information Systems department.

Establishing Networks—Workers must not establish electronic bulletin boards, local area networks, modem connections to existing internal networks, Internet commerce systems, or other multi-user systems for communicating information without the specific approval of the Information Security department.

Automatic Device Synchronization—Systems that automatically exchange data between devices, such as a personal digital assistant and a personal computer, must not be enabled unless the systems have been evaluated and approved by the Information Security department.

PHYSICAL SECURITY

Equipment Theft—All office desktop personal computers except portables must be physically secured to desks with approved devices such as locking wires or plates that bolt the equipment to furniture. All personal computer equipment must be marked with invisible identification information that clearly indicates it is Company X property. Periodic physical inventories must be completed to track the movement of personal computers and related equipment.

Donation Or Sale Of Equipment—Before personal computer equipment or storage media that has been used for Company X business is provided to any third party, the equipment or media must be physically inspected by the Information Security department to determine that all sensitive information has been removed. This policy does not apply when a non-disclosure agreement has been signed by the third party.

Lending Personal Computers To Others—Workers must never lend a Company X personal computer containing sensitive information to another person unless that other person has received prior authorization from the Owner if the sensitive information to access such information.

Custodians For Equipment—The primary user of a personal computer is considered a Custodian for the equipment. If the equipment has been damaged, lost, stolen, borrowed, or is otherwise unavailable for normal business activities, a Custodian must promptly inform the involved department manager. With the exception of portable machines, personal computer equipment must not be moved or relocated without the knowledge and approval of the involved department manager.

Use Of Personal Equipment—Workers must not bring their own computers, computer peripherals, or computer software into Company X facilities without prior authorization from their department head. Workers must not use their own personal computers for production Company X business unless these systems have been evaluated and approved by the Information Security department. Writing memos or reports is not considered production Company X business for purposes of this policy.

Property Pass—Personal computers, portable computers, typewriters, and related information systems equipment must not leave Company X offices unless accompanied by a property pass signed by a department manager. Equipment owned by workers and brought into Company X offices also must have a property pass. Guards in the lobby of all Company X buildings must check the contents of briefcases, suitcases, handbags, and other luggage to ensure that all equipment leaving Company X offices has an approved property pass. Remote sensing devices must be installed at selected locations to trigger an alarm if certain Company X computer related devices are removed from Company X offices.

Positioning Display Screens—The display screens for all personal computers used to handle sensitive or valuable data must be positioned such that the information cannot be readily viewed through a window, by persons walking in a hallway, or by persons waiting in reception and related areas. Care must also be taken to position keyboards so that unauthorized persons cannot readily see workers enter passwords, encryption keys, and other security-related parameters.

Locking Sensitive Information—When not being used by authorized workers, or when not clearly visible in an area where authorized persons are working, all hardcopy sensitive information must be locked in file cabinets, desks, safes, or other furniture. When not being used, or when not in a clearly visible and attended area, all computer storage media containing sensitive information must be locked in similar enclosures.

Environmental Considerations—All personal computers in Company X offices must use surge suppressors. Those personal computers running production applications must also have uninterruptible power systems approved by the Information Security department.

Static Discharges And Electromagnetic Fields—If weather or building conditions pose a significant risk of static electricity discharge, personal computers must be outfitted with static protection equipment that has been approved by the Information Systems department. Magnetic storage media such as floppy disks and magnetic tapes must be kept at least several inches away from electric fields, such as those generated by magnets and a telephone when it rings.

Smoking, Eating and Drinking—Workers must not to smoke, eat, or drink when using personal computers.

MANAGEMENT

Rights To Programs Developed—Without a specific written exception, all computer programs and documentation generated by, or provided by workers for the benefit of Company X are the property of Company X. All other material developed by Company X workers using personal computers is considered the property of Company X. This material includes patents, copyrights, and trademarks.

Browsing—Workers must not browse through Company X computer systems or networks. Steps taken by workers to legitimately locate information needed to perform their job are not considered browsing. Use of the Company X intranet is not considered browsing.

Tools To Compromise Systems Security—Unless specifically authorized by the Information Security department, Company X workers must not acquire, possess, trade, or use hardware or software tools that could be employed to evaluate or compromise information systems security. Examples of such tools include those that defeat software copy protection, discover secret passwords, identify security vulnerabilities, or decrypt encrypted files.

Reporting Problems—Users must promptly report all information security alerts, warnings, and suspected vulnerabilities to the Information Systems Help Desk. Users must not use Company X systems to forward such information to other users, whether the other users are internal or external to Company X.

Additional Information—Every department must have a designated information security liaison that should be the reader's first stop in a search for more information. If this liaison cannot answer a question or provide a satisfactory resolution to a problem, the next step is to call the corporate Information Security department at XXX-XXX-XXXX.

Approved By: [insert approving executive's name]

Approval Date: DD/MM/YY

Effective Date: DD/MM/YY

Version Number: XX

Chapter 9   SAMPLE ELECTRONIC MAIL POLICY

Company Property—As a productivity enhancement tool, Company X encourages the business use of electronic communications systems, notably the Internet, telephone, pager, voice mail, electronic mail, and fax. Unless third parties have clearly noted copyrights or some other rights on the messages handled by these electronic communications systems, all messages generated on or handled by Company X electronic communications systems are considered to be the property of Company X.

Authorized Usage—Company X electronic communications systems generally must be used for business activities only. Incidental personal use is permissible as long as it does not consume more than a trivial amount of system resources, does not interfere with worker productivity, and does not preempt any business activity. Company X electronic communication systems must not be used for charitable fund raising campaigns, political advocacy efforts, religious efforts, private business activities, or personal amusement and entertainment. News feeds, electronic mail mailing lists, push data updates, and other mechanisms for receiving information over the Internet must be restricted to material that is clearly related to both Company X business and the duties of the receiving workers. Workers are reminded that the use of corporate information system resources must never create the appearance or the reality of inappropriate use.

Default Privileges—Electronic communication systems must be established and maintained such that only the privileges necessary to perform a job are granted to a worker. For example, when a worker's relationship with Company X comes to an end, all of the worker's privileges on Company X electronic communications systems also must cease. With the exception of emergencies and regular system maintenance notices, broadcast facilities must be used only after the permission of a department manager has been obtained.

User Separation—These facilities must be implemented where electronic communications systems provide the ability to separate the activities of different users. For example, electronic mail systems must employ personal user IDs and associated passwords. Unless a computerized fax mailbox system is employed, fax machines that do not generally have separate mailboxes for different recipients, so such user separation is not required. If

Company X has established user separation, workers must not employ the user ID or the identifier of any other user.

User Accountability—Regardless of the circumstances, individual passwords must never be shared or revealed to anyone else besides the authorized user. Information Technology department staff must never ask users to reveal their passwords. If users need to share computer resident data, they should utilize message forwarding facilities, public directories on local area network servers, groupware databases, and other authorized information-sharing mechanisms. To prevent unauthorized parties from obtaining access to electronic communications, users must choose passwords that are difficult to guess. For example, users must not choose a dictionary word, personal history detail, name, or reflection of work activities.

User Identity—Misrepresenting, obscuring, suppressing, or replacing another user's identity on an electronic communications system is forbidden. The user name, electronic mail address, organizational affiliation, and related information included with electronic messages or postings must reflect the actual originator of the messages or postings. With the exception of hot lines that are intended to be anonymous, workers must not send anonymous electronic communications. At a minimum, all workers must provide their name and phone number in all electronic communications. Electronic mail signatures indicating job title, company affiliation, address, and other particulars are strongly recommended for all electronic mail messages. Digital certificates are also recommended for electronic mail.

Use Only Company X Electronic Mail Systems—Unless permission from the Information Security manager has been obtained, workers must not use their personal electronic mail accounts with an Internet service provider or any other third party for any Company X business messages. Workers must not use the electronic mail features found in web browsers for any Company X business communications. They must employ authorized Company X electronic mail software.

Use Of Encryption Programs—Workers are reminded that Company X electronic communications systems are not encrypted by default. If sensitive information such as Confidential or Secret must be sent by electronic communication systems, an encryption process approved by the Information Security department must be employed. These encryption systems must protect the sensitive information from end to end. They must not involve decryption of the message content before the message reaches its intended final destination. Mobile computers, notebook computers, portable computers, personal digital assistants, and similar computers that store Company X sensitive information must consistently employ file encryption to protect this sensitive information when it is stored inside these same computers, and when it is stored on accompanying data storage media. Users of these types of computers who are recipients of sensitive information sent by electronic mail must delete this information from their systems if they do not have encryption software that can properly protect it. Workers must not use encryption for any production electronic communications system unless a backup key or a key escrow system has been established with the cooperation of Information Security.

Labeling Electronic Mail Messages—All electronic mail messages containing sensitive information must include the appropriate classification in the header. This label will remind recipients that the information must not be disseminated further or be used for unintended purposes without the proper authorization.

Respecting Intellectual Property Rights—Although the Internet is an informal communications environment, the laws for copyrights, patents, and trademarks apply. Workers using Company X electronic mail systems must repost or reproduce material only after obtaining permission from the source, quote material from other sources only if these other sources are properly identified, and reveal internal Company X information on the Internet only if the information has been officially approved for public release. All information acquired from the Internet must be considered suspect until confirmed by another source.

Respecting Privacy Rights—Except as otherwise specifically approved by the Information Security manager, workers must not intercept or disclose, or assist in intercepting or disclosing, electronic communications. Company X is committed to respecting the rights of its workers, including their reasonable expectation of privacy. Company X also is responsible for operating, maintaining, and protecting its electronic communications networks. To accomplish these objectives, it is occasionally necessary to intercept or disclose, or assist in intercepting or disclosing, electronic communications. To meet these objectives, Company X may employ content monitoring systems, message logging systems, and other electronic system management tools. By making use of Company X systems, users consent to permit all information they store on Company X systems to be divulged to law enforcement at the discretion of Company X management.

No Guaranteed Message Privacy—Company X cannot guarantee that electronic communications will be private. Workers must be aware that electronic communications can, depending on the technology, be forwarded, intercepted, printed, and stored by others. Electronic communications can be accessed by people other than the intended recipients in accordance with this policy. Because messages can be stored in backups, electronic communications actually may be retrievable when a traditional paper letter would have been discarded or destroyed. Workers must be careful about the topics covered in Company X electronic communications, and must not send a message discussing anything that they would not be comfortable reading about on the front page of their local newspaper.

Contents Of Messages—Workers must not use profanity, obscenities, or derogatory remarks in electronic mail messages discussing employees, customers, competitors, or others. Such remarks may create legal problems such as trade libel and defamation of character. Workers must concentrate on business matters in Company X electronic communications. As a matter of standard business practice, all Company X electronic communications must be consistent with conventional standards of ethical and polite conduct.

Statistical Data—Consistent with generally-accepted business practice, Company X collects statistical data about its electronic communication systems. Using such information, technical support personnel monitor the use of electronic communications to ensure the ongoing availability, reliability, and security of these systems. Company X employs computer systems that analyze these types of statistical information to detect unauthorized usage, toll fraud, denial of service attacks, and other problems.

Incidental Disclosure—Technical support personnel must not review the content of an individual worker's communications out of personal curiosity or at the request of individuals who have not gone through proper approval channels. Advance approval by the Information Security manager is required for all such monitoring.

Addendum On Outbound Electronic Mail—A footer prepared by the Legal department must be automatically appended to all outbound electronic mail originating from Company X computers. This footer must make reference to the possibility that the message may contain confidential information, that it is for the use of the named recipients only, that the message has been logged for archival purposes, that the message may be reviewed by parties at Company X other than those named in the message header, and that the message does not necessarily constitute an official representation of Company X.

Handling Attachments—When sending an attachment to a third party, workers must attempt to use rich text format or simple text files whenever possible. Workers must encourage third parties to send them files in these same formats whenever reasonable and practical. All other attachment files must be scanned with an authorized virus detection software package before opening or execution. In some cases, attachments must be decrypted or decompressed before a virus scan takes place. Workers must be suspicious about unexpected electronic mail attachments received from third parties, even if the third party is known and trusted.

Message Forwarding—Electronic communications users must exercise caution when forwarding messages. Company X sensitive information such as Confidential or Secret must not be forwarded to any party outside Company X without the prior approval of a local department manager. Blanket forwarding of messages to parties outside Company X is prohibited unless the prior permission of the Information Security manager has been obtained. Messages sent by outside parties must not be forwarded to other third parties unless the sender clearly intended this and such forwarding is necessary to accomplish an customary business objective. In all other cases, forwarding of messages sent by outsiders to other third parties can be done only if the sender expressly agrees to this forwarding.

Handling Alerts About Security—Users must promptly report all information security alerts, warnings, and reported vulnerabilities to the Information Security department. Information Security is the only organizational unit authorized to determine appropriate action in response to such notices. Users must not utilize Company X systems to forward these notices to other users, whether the other users are internal or external to Company X. Users must promptly report all suspected security vulnerabilities or problems that they notice to Information Security [an intranet link to a form for reporting problems could be inserted here].

Public Representations—No media advertisement, Internet home page, electronic bulletin board posting, electronic mail message, voice mail message, or any other public representation about Company X may be issued unless it has been approved by the Marketing or Public Relations departments. Company X, as a matter of policy, does not send unsolicited electronic mail, nor does it issue unsolicited fax advertising. Nobody outside Company X may be placed on an electronic mail distribution list without indicating their intention to be included on the list through an opt-in process. If Company X workers are bothered by an excessive amount of unwanted messages from a particular organization or electronic mail address, they must not respond directly to the sender. Recipients must forward samples of the messages to the system administrator in charge of the electronic mail system for resolution. Workers must not send large number of messages in order to overload a server or user's electronic mailbox in retaliation for any perceived issue.

User Backup—If an electronic mail message contains information relevant to the completion of a business transaction, contains potentially important reference information, or has value as evidence of a Company X management decision, it must be retained for future reference. Users must regularly move important information from electronic mail message files to word processing documents, databases, and other files. Electronic mail inboxes must not be used for the archival storage of important information.

Archival Storage—All official Company X electronic mail messages, including those containing a formal management approval, authorization, delegation, or handing over of responsibility, or similar transactions, must be copied to the Archival Records department. All legal contracts, financial statements, public advertisements, help wanted notices, tax returns, and related communications must be sent to Archival Records.

Purging Electronic Messages—Messages no longer needed for business purposes must be periodically purged by users from their personal electronic message storage areas. After six months of electronic mail messages are stored on Company X mail servers, they must be automatically deleted by systems administration staff.

Harassing Or Offensive Materials—Company X computer and communications systems are not intended to be used for, and must not be used for the exercise of the workers' right to free speech. These systems must not be used as an open forum to discuss Company X organizational changes or business policy matters. Sexual, ethnic, and racial harassment, including unwanted telephone calls, electronic mail, and internal mail, is strictly prohibited. Workers who receive offensive unsolicited material from outside sources must not forward or redistribute it to either internal or external parties, unless this forwarding or redistribution is to the Company X Human Resources department in order to assist with the investigation of a complaint.

Responding Directly To The Sender—Workers must respond directly to the originator of offensive electronic mail messages, telephone calls, or other electronic communications. If the originator does not promptly stop sending offensive messages, workers must report the communications to their manager and the Human Resources department. Company X retains the right to remove from its information systems any material it views as offensive or potentially illegal.

Use At Your Own Risk—Workers access the Internet with Company X facilities at their own risk. Company X is not responsible for material viewed, downloaded, or received by users through the Internet. Electronic mail systems may deliver unsolicited messages that contain offensive content.

Establishing Electronic Business Systems—Although Company X implements electronic data interchange (EDI), Internet commerce, and other electronic business systems with third parties, all contracts must be formed by paper documents prior to purchasing or selling through electronic systems. EDI, electronic mail, and similar binding business messages must be releases against blanket orders, such as a blanket purchase order. All electronic commerce systems must be approved by the chief information officer, the Information Security manager, and the chief legal counsel prior to usage.

Paper Confirmation For Contracts—All contracts formed through electronic offer and acceptance messages must be formalized and confirmed through paper documents within two weeks of acceptance. Workers must not employ scanned versions of hand-rendered signatures to give the impression that an electronic mail message or other electronic communications were signed by the sender.

Approved By: [insert approving executive's name]

Approved Date: DD/MM/YY

Effective Date: DD/MM/YY

Version Number: XX

Document Reference Number: XXXX-XXXX

Chapter 10 SAMPLE COMPUTER NETWORK SECURITY POLICY

PURPOSE

The purpose of this policy is to establish management direction, procedural requirements, and technical guidance to ensure the appropriate protection of Company X information handled by computer networks.

SCOPE

This policy applies to all employees, contractors, consultants, temporaries, volunteers, and other workers at Company X, including those workers affiliated with third parties who access Company X computer networks. Throughout this policy, the word "worker" will be used to collectively refer to all such individuals. The policy also applies to all computer and data communication systems owned by or administered by Company X.

GENERAL POLICY

All information traveling over Company X computer networks that has not been specifically identified as the property of other parties will be treated as though it is a Company X corporate asset. It is the policy of Company X to prohibit unauthorized access, disclosure, duplication, modification, diversion, destruction, loss, misuse, or theft of this information. In addition, it is the policy of Company X to protect information belonging to third parties that have been entrusted to Company X in a manner consistent with its sensitivity and in accordance with all applicable agreements.

RESPONSIBILITIES

An information security management committee will be composed of middle-level managers or their delegates from each Company X major division and subsidiary, and the director of Information Technology, the director of Security, and the chief Company X attorney responsible for intellectual property. At quarterly and ad hoc meetings, this committee will periodically review the status of Company X computer and network security, review and monitor remedial work related to computer and network security incidents, authorize and later judge the results of major projects dealing with computer and network security, approve new or modified information security policies, standards, guidelines, and procedures, and perform other high-level information security management activities.

The Information Security manager is responsible for establishing, maintaining, implementing, administering, and interpreting organization-wide information systems security policies, standards, guidelines, and procedures. This manager also is responsible for activities related to this policy. While responsibility for information systems security on a day-to-day basis is every worker's duty, specific guidance, direction, and authority for information systems security is centralized for all of Company X and its subsidiaries in the Information Security department. This department will perform information systems risk assessments, prepare information systems security action plans, evaluate information security products, and perform other activities necessary to assure a secure information systems environment.

The Physical Security manager is responsible for conducting investigations into any alleged computer or network security compromises, incidents, or problems. All compromises or potential compromises must be immediately reported to the Physical Security manager.

System administrators are responsible for acting as local information systems security coordinators. These individuals are responsible for establishing appropriate user privileges, monitoring access control logs, and performing similar security actions for the systems they administer. They also are responsible for reporting all suspicious computer and network-security-related activities to the Physical Security manager. System administrators also implement the requirements of this and other information systems security policies, standards, guidelines, and procedures. If information security is not handled by another department or group, each Company X department must designate an individual to serve as a system administrator.

Departmental managers are responsible for ensuring that appropriate computer and communication system security measures are observed in their areas. Besides allocating sufficient resources and staff time to meet the requirements of these policies, departmental managers are responsible for ensuring that all users are aware of Company X policies related to computer and communication system security.

Users are responsible for complying with this and all other Company X policies defining computer and network security measures. Users also are responsible for bringing all known information security vulnerabilities and violations that they notice to the attention of the Physical Security manager.

SYSTEM ACCESS CONTROL

End-User Passwords

Users must choose fixed passwords that are difficult to guess. This means that passwords must not be related to a user's job or personal life. For example, a car license plate number, a spouse's name, or fragments of an address must not be used. This also means passwords must not be a word found in the dictionary or some other part of speech. For example, proper names, places, technical terms, and slang must not be used. Where this type of systems software is available, users must be prevented from selecting easily-guessed passwords.

Users can choose easily-remembered passwords that are difficult for unauthorized parties to guess if they:

- String together several words into a pass phrase.

- Shift a word up, down, left, or right one row on the keyboard.

- Bump characters in a word a certain number of letters up or down the alphabet.

- Transform a regular word according to a specific method, such as making every other letter a number reflecting its position in the word.

- Combine punctuation or numbers with a regular word.

- Create acronyms from words in a song, a poem, or another known sequence of words.

- Deliberately misspell a word.

- Combine a number of personal facts like birth dates and favorite colors.

Users must not construct passwords that are identical or similar to passwords they have previously employed. Where systems software facilities are available, users must be prevented from reusing previous passwords.

Users must not construct passwords using a basic sequence of characters that is then partially changed based on the date or some other predictable factor. For example, users must not employ passwords like "X34JAN" in January and "X34FEB" in February.

Passwords must not be stored in readable form in batch files, automatic logon scripts, software macros, terminal function keys, in data communications software, in web browsers, on hard drives, or in other locations where unauthorized persons might discover them.

Passwords must not be written down and left in a place where unauthorized persons might discover them. Aside from initial password assignment and password-reset situations, if there is reason to believe that a password has been disclosed to someone other than the authorized user, the password must be changed immediately.

Passwords must never be shared or revealed to anyone else besides the authorized user. If users need to share computer resident data, they should use electronic mail, public directories on local area network servers, and other mechanisms. This policy does not prevent the use of default passwords, typically used for new user ID assignment or password reset situations, which are then immediately changed when the user next logs onto the involved system. All passwords must be immediately changed if they are suspected of being disclosed or known to have been disclosed to anyone other than the authorized user.

Password System Set-Up

All computers permanently or intermittently connected to Company X networks must have password access controls. If the computers contain Confidential or Secret information, an extended user authentication system approved by the Information Security department must be used. At the very least, multi-user systems must employ user IDs and passwords unique to each user, and user privilege restriction mechanisms with privileges based on an individual's need to know. Network-connected, single-user systems must employ hardware or software controls approved by Information Security that prevent unauthorized access including a screen blanker triggered by a certain period of no keyboard activity.

Unless an extended user authentication system is involved, computer and communication system access control must be achieved through fixed passwords that are unique to each individual user. Access control to files, applications, databases, computers, networks, and other system resources through shared passwords or group passwords is prohibited.

Wherever systems software permits, the display and printing of fixed passwords must be masked, suppressed, or otherwise obscured such that unauthorized parties will not be able to observe or subsequently recover them.

Wherever systems software permits, the initial fixed passwords issued to a new user by a security administrator must be valid only for the user's first online session. At that time, the user must be required to choose another password. This same process applies to the resetting of passwords in the event that a user forgets a password.

All vendor-supplied default fixed passwords must be changed before any computer or communications system is used for production Company X business. This policy applies to passwords associated with end-user user IDs and passwords associated with privileged user IDs.

Where systems software permits, the number of consecutive attempts to enter an incorrect password must be strictly limited. After three unsuccessful attempts to enter a password, the involved user ID must be suspended until reset by a system administrator or temporarily disabled for no less than three minutes. If dial-up connections are involved, the session must be disconnected. If DSL, ISDN, cable modem, or other constant connections are employed, a time-out period must be initiated.

Whenever system security has been compromised or if there is a reason to believe that it has been compromised, the involved system administrator must immediately change all involved privileged user passwords and require every end-user password on the involved system to be changed at the time of the next log on. If systems software does not provide the latter capability, a broadcast message must be sent to all users telling them to change their passwords immediately.

Whenever system security has been compromised or if there is a reason to believe that it has been compromised, a trusted version of the operating system and all security-related software must be reloaded from trusted storage media such as CD-ROMs, magnetic tapes, or original source-code floppy disks. The involved system then must be rebooted. All changes to user privileges taking effect since the time of suspected system compromise must be reviewed immediately by the system administrator for unauthorized modifications.

Logon and Logoff Process

All users must be positively identified prior to being able to use any Company X multi-user computer or communications system resources. Positive identification for internal Company X networks involves a user ID and fixed password, both of which are unique to an individual user, or an extended user authentication system.

Positive identification for all Internet and dial-up lines involves the use of hand-held tokens, cryptographic challenge and response protocols, or other approved extended user authentication techniques. The combination of a user ID and fixed password does not provide sufficient security for Internet or dial-up connections to Company X systems or networks. Modems attached to network-connected workstations located in Company X offices are forbidden unless they have an extended user authentication system approved by the Information Security department. Modems connected to isolated computers, such as portable computers and home computers, are permissible, as long as an approved personal computer firewall is installed, and the related communications software is not left in an enabled state such that it could receive incoming calls.

Where systems software permits, every logon banner on multi-user computers must include a special notice. This notice must state the system is for the use of authorized users only, by continuing to use the system, the user represents that he or she is an authorized user, the user acknowledges that all system usage is logged, and the user understands that violations of Company X information security policies and other requirements may trigger disciplinary action up to and including termination, and civil or criminal prosecution.

The logon process for network-connected Company X computer systems must simply ask the user to log on, providing prompts as needed. Specific information about the organization managing the computer, the computer operating system, the network configuration, or other internal matters must not be provided until a user has successfully provided both a valid user ID and a valid password.

If there has been no activity on a computer terminal, workstation, or personal computer for a certain period of time, the system must automatically blank the screen and suspend the session. Re-establishment of the session must take place only after the user has provided a valid password. The recommended period of time is 15 minutes. An exception to this policy will be made in those cases where the immediate area surrounding a system is physically secured by locked doors, secured-room badge readers, or similar technology.

With the exception of electronic bulletin boards or other systems where all regular users are anonymous, users are prohibited from logging into any Company X system or network anonymously, for example, by using guest user IDs. If users employ systems facilities that permit them to change the active user ID to gain certain privileges, they must have initially logged on employing a user ID that clearly indicates their identity.

System Privileges

Limiting System Access

The computer and communications system privileges of all users, systems, and independently-operating programs such as agents, must be restricted based on the need to know. This means that privileges must not be extended unless a legitimate business-oriented need for such privileges exists.

Default user file permissions must not automatically permit anyone on the system to read, write, execute or delete a file. Although users may reset permissions on a file-by-file basis, such permissive default file permissions are prohibited. Default file permissions granted to limited groups of people who have a genuine need to know are permitted.

Users with personal computers are responsible for administering a screen saver program securing access to their machine's hard disk drive, and setting passwords for all applications and systems software that provide the capability.

Company X computer and communications systems must restrict access to the computers that users can reach over Company X networks. These restrictions can be implemented through routers, gateways, firewalls, and other network components. These restrictions must be used to, for example, control the ability of a user to log on to a certain computer then move from that computer to another.

Process For Granting System Privileges

Requests for new user IDs and changed privileges must be in writing and approved by the user's manager before a system administrator fulfills these requests. Documents reflecting these requests must be retained for a period of at least one year.

Individuals who are not Company X employees must not be granted a user ID or be given privileges to use Company X computers or networks unless the written approval of a department head has been obtained.

Privileges granted to users who are not Company X employees must be granted for periods of 90 days or less. As needed, users who are not Company X employees must have their privileges reauthorized by the sponsoring department head every 90 days.

Special privileges, such as the default ability to write to the files of other users, must be restricted to those responsible for systems administration or systems security. An exception to this policy can be made if a department head has approved the exception in writing. Configuration changes, operating system changes, and related activities that require system privileges must be performed by system administrators, not end users.

Third-party vendors must not be given Internet or dial-up privileges to Company X computers or networks unless the system administrator determines that they have a legitimate business need. These privileges must be enabled only for the time period required to accomplish the approved tasks, such as remote maintenance. If a perpetual or long-term connection is required, then the connection must be established by approved extended user authentication methods.

All users wishing to use Company X internal networks, or multi-user systems that are connected to Company X internal networks, must sign a compliance statement prior to being issued a user ID. If a certain user already has a user ID, a signature must be obtained prior to receiving a renewed user ID. The latter process must be performed periodically.

Establishment Of Access Paths

Changes to Company X internal networks include loading new software, changing network addresses, reconfiguring routers, and adding dial-up lines. With the exception of emergency situations, all changes to Company X computer networks must be documented in a work order request and approved in advance by Information Technology except as delegated by

Process for Revoking System Access

All user IDs must have the associated privileges revoked after a certain period of inactivity not exceeding 30 days.

If a computer or communication system access control subsystem is not functioning properly, it must default to denial of privileges to users. If access control subsystems are malfunctioning, the systems must remain unavailable until such time as the problem has been rectified.

Users must not test or attempt to compromise computer or communication system security measures unless specifically approved in advance and in writing by the Information Security manager. Incidents involving unapproved system hacking, password guessing, file decryption, bootleg software copying, or similar unauthorized attempts to compromise security measures may be unlawful, and will be considered serious violations of Company X policy. Customer requests that Company X security mechanisms be compromised must not be satisfied unless the Information Security manager approves in advance or Company X is compelled to comply by law. Short-cuts bypassing systems security measures, pranks, and practical jokes involving the compromise of systems security measures are absolutely prohibited.

The privileges granted to users must be reevaluated by management every six months. In response to feedback from, system administrators must promptly revoke all privileges no longer needed by users.

Management must report all significant changes in worker duties or employment status promptly to the system administrators responsible for user IDs associated with the involved persons. For all terminations, the Human Resources department also must issue a notice of status change to all system administrators who might be responsible for a system on which the involved worker might have a user ID.

Information Technology. Emergency changes to networks must be made by persons who are authorized by Information Technology. This process prevents unexpected changes from leading to denial of service, unauthorized disclosure of information, and other problems. This process applies not only to workers, but also to vendor personnel.

Workers must not establish electronic bulletin boards, local area networks, FTP servers, web servers, modem connections to existing local area networks, or other multi-user systems for communicating information without the specific approval of the Information Security manager. New types of real-time connections between two or more in-house computer systems must not be established unless such approval is obtained.

Participation in external networks as a provider of services that external parties rely on is prohibited unless Company X legal counsel has identified the legal risks involved and the director of Information Technology has expressly accepted these and other risks associated with the proposal.

All Company X computers that connect to an internal or external network must employ password-based access controls or an extended user authentication system. Multi-user computers must employ software that restricts access to the files of each user, logs the activities of each user, and has special privileges granted to a system administrator. Single-user systems must employ access control software approved by the Information Security department that includes boot control and an automatic screen blanker that is invoked after a certain period of no input activity. Portable computers and home computers that contain Company X information are also covered by this policy, as are network devices such as firewalls, gateways, routers, and bridges.

All inter-processor commands from non-Company X locations are prohibited unless a user or process has properly logged on. Examples of such commands include remotely-initiated requests for a list of users currently logged on and a remote procedure call.

Users initiating sessions through dial-up lines connected to Company X internal networks or multi-user computer systems must pass through an additional access control point or firewall before users employing these lines can reach a logon banner. Unless approved in advance by the director of Information Security, dial-up connections that do not go through approved firewalls in order to reach Company X internal-network connected systems are prohibited. This policy applies to Internet inbound calls and electronic data interchange.

Remote maintenance ports for Company X computer and communication systems must be disabled until the time they are needed by the vendor. These ports must be disabled immediately after use. Dial-up connections can be established with vendors through outbound calls initiated by Company X workers. No firewall access control is needed for either type of connection.

Portable phones using radio technology and cellular phones must not be used for data transmissions containing Company X confidential or secret information unless the connection is encrypted. Other broadcast networking technologies, such radio-based local area networks, must not be used for these types of Company X information unless the link is encrypted. Such links may be used for electronic mail as long as users understand that confidential or secret information must not be transmitted using this technology.

COMPUTER VIRUSES, WORMS, AND TROJAN HORSES

Users must keep approved and current virus-screening software enabled on their computers. This software must be used to scan all software coming from third parties or other Company X departments and must take place before the new software is executed. Users must not bypass scanning processes that could stop the transmission of computer viruses.

Users are responsible for eradicating viruses from all personal computer systems under their control whenever viruses have been detected using software installed by Company X staff. As soon as a virus is detected, the involved user must immediately call the Information Security department to assure that no further infection takes place and that any experts needed to eradicate the virus are promptly engaged [the telephone number could be inserted here].

All personal computer software must be copied prior to its initial usage, and such copies must be stored in a safe place. These master copies must not be used for ordinary business activities, but must be reserved for recovery from computer virus infections, hard disk crashes, and other computer problems. These master copies also must be stored in a secure location.

Company X computers and networks must not run software that comes from sources other than business partners, knowledgeable and trusted user groups, well-known systems security authorities, computer or network vendors, or commercial software vendors. Software downloaded from electronic bulletin boards, shareware, public domain software, and other software from untrusted sources must not be used unless it has been subjected to a rigorous testing regimen approved by the Information Security manager.

DATA AND PROGRAM BACKUP

Personal computer users are responsible for backing up the information on their machines. For multi-user computer and communication systems, a system administrator is responsible for making periodic backups. If requested, the Information Technology department will install or provide technical assistance for the installation of backup hardware or software.

All sensitive information such as Confidential or Secret, valuable, or critical, resident on Company X computer systems and networks must be periodically backed up. User department managers must define which information and which machines are to be backed up, the frequency of backup, and the method of backup based on the following guidelines:

- If the system supports more than one individual and contains data that is critical to day-to-day operations within Company X, then a backup is required daily.

- If the system is used to support job-related functions and contains key data critical to the day-to-day operations of that job, then a backup is required weekly.

- If the system is primarily used as a personal productivity tool and contains no data that would be classified as job or departmental in nature, then a backup is at the discretion of the individual user.

Nothing in the time frames for periodic backup mentioned immediately above restricts the generation of more frequent backups, as will occasionally be required for operational and business reasons.

Company X requires the use of at least three sets of backup storage media to be used in rotation. For multi-user machines, whenever systems software permits, backups must be performed without end-user involvement, over an internal network and during the off hours.

Storage of backup media is the responsibility of the personal computer user or multi-user machine system administrator involved in the backup process. Media must be stored in fireproof safes, at a separate location at least several city blocks away from the system being backed up.

Unless the type of information is specifically listed on the Company X Information Retention Schedule, available from the Legal department, information must be retained for as long as necessary but for no longer. Information listed on the Information Retention Schedule must be retained for the period specified. Other information must be destroyed when no longer needed, which is generally within two years.

Department managers who define the backup schedule are also responsible for preparing and periodically updating user department contingency plans to restore service for all production applications, despite whether internal network services are required for the support of these applications. The Information Technology department is responsible for preparing and periodically updating network service contingency plans. The Internal Audit department is responsible for the periodic review of these same contingency plans, including the review of tests performed to validate the contingency plans.

All Company X Confidential or Secret information stored on backup computer media must be encrypted using approved encrypting methods.

ENCRYPTION

When Company X Confidential or Secret information is transmitted over any communication network, it must be sent in encrypted form. Whenever Company X source code, or source code that has been entrusted to Company X by a business partner, is to be sent over a network, it too must be in encrypted form. Specific definitions of the words "Confidential" and "Secret" can be found in the Data Classification Policy [an intranet link to that policy can be inserted here].

Whenever Confidential or Secret information is not being actively used, it must be stored in encrypted form. This means that when this information is stored or transported in computer-readable storage media, it must be in encrypted form.

Encryption of information in storage or in transit must be achieved through commercially-available products approved by the Information Security department.

Whenever encryption is used, workers must not delete the sole readable version of the information unless they have demonstrated that the decryption process is able to reestablish a readable version of the information.

Encryption keys used for Company X information are always classified as Confidential or Secret information. Access to such keys must be limited only to those who have a need to know. Unless the approval of the Information Security manager is obtained, encryption keys must not be revealed to consultants, contractors, temporaries, or other third parties. Encryption keys always must be encrypted when sent over a network.

Whenever such facilities are commercially available, Company X must employ automated rather than manual encryption key management processes for the protection of information on Company X networks.

PORTABLE COMPUTERS

Workers in the possession of portable, laptop, notebook, handheld, and other transportable computers containing Confidential or Secret Company X information must not leave these computers unattended at any time unless the information is stored in encrypted form.

Workers in the possession of transportable computers containing unencrypted Confidential or Secret Company X information must not check these computers in airline luggage systems or with hotel porters. These computers must remain in the possession of the traveler as hand luggage.

Whenever Confidential or Secret information is written to a floppy disk, magnetic tape, smart card, or other storage media, the storage media must be suitably marked with the highest relevant sensitivity classification. When not in use, this media must be stored in a locked safe, locked furniture, or a similarly secured location. Further information can be found in the Telecommuting Information Security Policy [an intranet link can be inserted here].

REMOTE PRINTING

Printers must not be left unattended if Confidential or Secret information is being printed or soon will be printed. The persons attending the printer must be authorized to examine the information being printed.

Unattended printing is permitted if the area surrounding the printer is physically protected such that persons who are not authorized to see the material being printed may not enter.

PRIVACY

Unless contractual agreements dictate otherwise, messages sent over Company X computer and communications systems are the property of Company X. Management reserves the right to examine all data stored in or transmitted by these systems. Because Company X computer and communication systems must be used for business purposes only, workers must have no expectation of privacy associated with the information they store in or send through these systems.

When providing computer-networking services, Company X does not provide default message protection services such as encryption. No responsibility is assumed for the disclosure of information sent over Company X networks, and no assurances are made about the privacy of information handled by Company X internal networks. In those instances where session encryption or other special controls are required, it is the user's responsibility to ensure that adequate security precautions have been taken. Nothing in this paragraph must be construed to imply that Company X policy does not support the controls dictated by agreements with third parties, such as organizations that have entrusted Company X with confidential information.

LOGS AND OTHER SYSTEMS SECURITY TOOLS

Every multi-user computer or communications system must include sufficient automated tools to assist the system administrator in verifying a system's security status. These tools must include mechanisms for the recording, detection, and correction of commonly-encountered security problems.

Whenever cost justifiable, automated tools for handling common security problems must be used on Company X computers and networks. For example, software that automatically checks personal computer software licenses through a local area network must be used on a regular basis.

To the extent that systems software permits, computer and communications systems handling sensitive, valuable, or critical Company X information must securely log all significant security relevant events. Examples of security relevant events include users switching user IDs during an online session, attempts to guess passwords, attempts to use privileges that have not been authorized, modifications to production application software, modifications to system software, changes to user privileges, and changes to logging system configurations.

Logs containing computer or communications system security relevant events must be retained for at least three months. During this period, logs must be secured such that they cannot be modified, and such that only authorized persons can read them.

Certain information must be captured whenever it is suspected that computer or network related crime or abuse has taken place. The relevant information must be securely stored offline until such time as it is determined that Company X will not pursue legal action or otherwise use the information. The information to be immediately collected includes the system logs, application audit trails, other indications of the current system states, and copies of all potentially involved files.

Records reflecting security relevant events must be periodically reviewed in a timely manner by computer operations staff, information security staff, or systems administration staff.

Users must be informed of the specific acts that constitute computer and network security violations. Users must also be informed that such violations will be logged.

Although system administrators are not required to promptly load the most recent version of operating systems, they are required to promptly apply all security patches to the operating system that have been released by knowledgeable and trusted user groups, well-known systems security authorities, or the operating system vendor. Only those systems security tools supplied by these sources or by commercial software organizations may be used on Company X computers and networks.

HANDLING NETWORK SECURITY INFORMATION

From time to time, the director of Information Security will designate individuals to audit compliance with this and other computer and network security policies. At the same time, every worker must promptly report any suspected network security problem, including intrusions and out-of-compliance situations, to the Physical Security manager.

Provided that no intent to damage Company X systems existed, if workers report a computer virus infestation immediately after it is noticed, even if their negligence was a contributing factor, no disciplinary action will be taken.

All network or systems software malfunctions must be reported immediately to the Information Technology department or the involved external information system service provider.

Information about security measures for Company X computer and communication systems is confidential and must not be released to people who are not authorized users of the involved systems unless the permission of the Information Security manager has been obtained. For example, publishing modem phone numbers or other system access information in directories is prohibited. Release of Internet electronic mail addresses is permissible.

PHYSICAL SECURITY OF COMPUTER AND COMMUNICATIONS GEAR

All Company X network equipment must be physically secured with anti-theft devices if located in an open office environment. Additional physical access control also may be used for these devices. For example, local area network servers must be placed in locked cabinets, locked closets, or locked computer rooms. Computer equipment located in sales service offices must additionally be secured with anti-theft devices.

Access to systems development staff offices, telephone wiring closets, computer machine rooms, network switching rooms, and other work areas containing Confidential or Secret information must be physically restricted. Management responsible for the staff working in these areas must consult the Information Security department to determine the appropriate access control method.

All workers who must keep Confidential or Secret Company X information at their homes in order to do their work must receive lockable furniture for the proper storage of this information. At the time of separation from Company X, both the furniture and the information stored therein must be returned immediately.

Confidential or Secret information must not be downloaded to remote locations, such as sales offices, unless proper physical security and encryption facilities are installed and faithfully observed.

EXCEPTIONS

The Information Security manager acknowledges that under rare circumstances, certain workers will need to employ systems that are not compliant with these policies. All such instances must be approved in writing and in advance by the Information Security manager.

VIOLATIONS

Company X workers who willingly and deliberately violate this policy will be subject to disciplinary action up to and including termination.

GLOSSARY

Access control: A system to restrict the activities of users and processes based on the need to know.

Agents: A new type of software that performs special tasks on behalf of a user, such as searching multiple databases for designated information.

Algorithm: A mathematical process for performing a certain calculation. In the information security field, it is generally used to refer to the process for performing encryption.

Badge reader: A device that reads worker identity badges and interconnects with a physical access control system that may control locked doors.

Booting: The process of initializing a computer system from a turned-off or powered-down state.

Bridge: A device that interconnects networks or that otherwise permits networking circuits to be connected.

Compliance statement: A document used to obtain a promise from a computer user that such user will abide by system policies and procedures.

Confidential information: A sensitivity designation for information, the disclosure of which is expected to damage Company X or its business affiliates.

Critical information: Any information essential to Company X business activities, the destruction, modification, or unavailability of which would cause serious disruption to Company X business.

Cryptographic challenge and response: A process for identifying computer users involving the issuance of a random challenge to a remote workstation, which is then transformed using an encryption process and a response is returned to the connected computer system.

Default file permission: Access control file privileges, read, write, execute, and delete, granted to computer users without further involvement of either a security administrator or users.

Default password: An initial password issued when a new user ID is created, or an initial password provided by a computer vendor when hardware or software is delivered.

Dynamic password: A password that changes each time a user logs on to a computer system.

Encryption key: A secret password or bit string used to control the algorithm governing an encryption process.

Encryption: A process involving data coding to achieve confidentiality, anonymity, time stamping, and other security objectives.

End User: A user who employs computers to support Company X business activities, who is acting as the source or destination of information flowing through a computer system.

Extended user authentication technique: Any of various processes used to bolster the user identification process typically achieved by user IDs and fixed passwords, such as hand-held tokens and dynamic passwords.

Firewall: A logical barrier stopping computer users or processes from going beyond a certain point in a network unless these users or processes have passed some security check, such as providing a password.

Front-end processor (FEP): A small computer used to handle communications interfacing for another computer.

Gateway: A computer system used to link networks that can restrict the flow of information and that employ some access control method.

Hand-held token: A commercial dynamic password system that employs a smart card to generate one-time passwords that are different for each session.

Information retention schedule: A formal listing of the types of information that must be retained for archival purposes and the time frames that these types of information must be kept.

Isolated computer: A computer that is not connected to a network or any other computer. For example, a stand-alone personal computer.

Logon banner: The initial message presented to a user when he or she makes connection with a computer.

Logon script: A set of stored commands that can log a user onto a computer automatically.

Master copies of software: Copies of software that are retained in an archive and that are not used for normal business activities.

Multi-user computer system: Any computer that can support more than one user simultaneously.

Password guessing attack: A computerized or manual process whereby various possible passwords are provided to a computer in an effort to gain unauthorized access.

Password reset: The assignment of a temporary password when a user forgets or loses his or her password.

Password-based access control: Software that relies on passwords as the primary mechanism to control system privileges.

Password: Any secret string of characters used to positively identify a computer user or process.

Positive identification: The process of definitively establishing the identity of a computer user.

Privilege: An authorized ability to perform a certain action on a computer, such as read a specific computer file.

Privileged user ID: A user ID that has been granted the ability to perform special activities, such as shut down a multi-user system.

Router: A device that interconnects networks using different layers of the Open Systems Interconnection (OSI) Reference Model.

Screen blanker or **screen saver:** A computer program that automatically blanks the screen of a computer monitor or screen after a certain period of inactivity.

Secret information: Particularly sensitive information, the disclosure of which is expected to severely damage Company X or its business affiliates.

Security patch: A software program used to remedy a security or other problem, commonly applied to operating systems, database management systems, and other systems software.

Sensitive information: Any information, the disclosure of which could damage Company X or its business associates.

Shared password: A password known by or used by more than one individual.

Software macro: A computer program containing a set of procedural commands to achieve a certain result.

Special system privilege: Access system privileges permitting the involved user or process to perform activities that are not normally granted to other users.

Suspending a user ID: The process of revoking the privileges associated with a user ID.

System administrator: A designated individual who has special privileges on a multi-user computer system, and who looks after security and other administrative matters.

Terminal function keys: Special keys on a keyboard that can be defined to perform certain activities such as save a file.

User IDs: Also known as accounts, these are character strings that uniquely identify computer users or computer processes.

Valuable information: Information of significant financial value to Company X or another party.

Verify security status: The process by which controls are shown to be both properly installed and properly operating.

Virus screening software: Commercially-available software that searches for certain bit patterns or other evidence of computer virus infection.

Chapter 11 SAMPLE INTERNET SECURITY POLICY FOR USERS

INTRODUCTION

Opportunities and Risks—The wide array of new resources, services, and inter-connectivity available through the Internet all introduce new business opportunities, and new security and privacy risks. In response to the risks, this policy describes the Company X official policy regarding Internet security.

Applicability—This policy applies to all workers, employees, contractors, consultants, temporaries, and volunteers, who use the Internet with Company X computing or networking resources. The policy applies to all those who use the Internet and represent themselves as being connected in some way with Company X. All of these Internet users are expected to be familiar with and fully comply with this policy. Questions about the policy should be directed to the reader's departmental Information Security coordinator or the corporate Information Security manager. Violations of this policy can lead to revocation of system privileges or additional disciplinary action up to and including termination.

Prior Management Approval—Access to the Internet, aside from electronic mail, will be provided to only those workers who have a legitimate business need for such access. The ability to access the Internet and engage in other Internet activities is not a fringe benefit to which all workers are entitled. If a worker does not have sufficient Internet access, but needs access for a particular project, he or she can use the special shared systems found in the corporate library. In order to receive Internet access privileges, all workers must complete the Company X computer-based training information security course then pass the accompanying test.

INFORMATION INTEGRITY

Information Reliability—All information acquired from the Internet must be considered suspect until confirmed by separate information from another source. Before using free Internet-supplied information for business decision-making purposes, workers must corroborate the information by consulting other sources.

Virus Checking—All non-text files downloaded from non-Company X sources through the Internet must be screened with current virus detection software prior to being used. Whenever an external provider of the software is not trusted, downloaded software must be tested on a stand-alone, non-production machine that has been recently backed up. Downloaded files must be decrypted and decompressed before being screened for viruses. The use of digital signatures to verify that a file has not been altered by unauthorized parties is recommended, but this does not assure freedom from viruses, Trojan horses, and other problems.

Software Downloading—Company X has implemented an automatic software distribution system to install the latest release of licensed software on Company X computers. A separate system is used to automatically trace all software resident on these same systems. As discussed in the Personal Computer Security Policy, workers must not install software on their Company X-supplied computers, whether the software was downloaded from the Internet or procured elsewhere.

Push Technology—Automatic updating of software or information on Company X computers through background push Internet technology is prohibited unless the involved vendor's system has been tested and approved by the Internet group within the Information Systems department.

Spoofing Users—Before workers release any internal Company X information, enter into any contracts, or order any products through public networks, the identity of the individuals and organizations contacted must be confirmed. Identity confirmation is ideally performed through digital signatures or digital certificates, but in cases where these are not available, other means such as letters of credit, third-party references, and telephone conversations may be used.

User Anonymity—Misrepresenting, obscuring, suppressing, or replacing a user's identity on the Internet or any Company X electronic communications system is forbidden. The user name, electronic mail address, organizational affiliation, and related information included with messages or postings must reflect the actual originator of the messages or postings. If users have a need to employ remailers or other anonymous facilities, they must do so on their own time, with their own information systems and Internet service provider accounts. Use of anonymous FTP logons, anonymous UUCP logons, HTTP or web browsing, and other access methods established with the expectation that users would be anonymous are permissible.

Electronic Mail Attachments—Workers must not open electronic mail attachments unless they were expected from a trusted sender. When they are expected from a known and trusted sender, attachments must be scanned with a virus package prior to being opened.

Web Page Changes—Workers must not establish new Internet pages dealing with Company X business, or make modifications to existing web pages dealing with Company X business, unless they have obtained the approval of the Internet management committee. Modifications include the addition of links to other sites, updating the information displayed, and altering the graphic layout of a page. This committee must ensure that all posted material has a consistent and polished appearance, is aligned with business goals, and is protected with adequate security measures.

Web Page Archives—Every version of the Company X Internet site and commerce site files must be securely archived in two physically separated locations. The Internet management committee will designate a web master who will keep this archive and provide copies of historical pages on demand.

INFORMATION CONFIDENTIALITY

Information Exchange—Company X software, documentation, and all other types of internal information must not be sold or otherwise transferred to any non-Company X party for any purposes other than business purposes expressly authorized by management. Exchanges of software or data between Company X and any third party must not proceed unless a written agreement has been signed. Such an agreement must specify the terms of the exchange, and the ways that the software or data is to be handled and protected. Regular business practices, such as shipment of a product in response to a customer purchase order, need not involve such a specific agreement since the terms and conditions are implied.

Posting Materials—Workers must not post unencrypted Company X material on any publicly-accessible Internet computer that supports anonymous FTP or similar publicly-accessible services, unless the posting of these materials has been approved by the director of Public Relations. Company X internal information must not be placed in any computer unless the persons who have access to that computer have a legitimate business need to know the involved information.

Message Interception—Company X secret, proprietary, or private information must not be sent over the Internet unless it has been encrypted by approved methods. Unless specifically known to be in the public domain, source code must always be encrypted before being sent over the Internet. For the same reasons, Internet telephone services must not be used for Company X business unless the connection is known to be encrypted.

Security Parameters—Unless a connection is known to be encrypted, credit card numbers, telephone calling card numbers, fixed logon passwords, and other security parameters that can be used to gain access to goods or services, must not be sent over the Internet in readable form. Encryption processes are permissible if they are approved by the corporate Information Security manager.

PUBLIC REPRESENTATIONS

External Representations—Workers may indicate their affiliation with Company X in mailing lists, chat sessions, and other offerings on the Internet. This may be done by explicitly adding certain words, or it may be implied, for example through an electronic mail address. In either case, whenever workers provide an affiliation, unless they have been expressly designated as a spokesperson of Company X, they also must clearly indicate the opinions expressed are their own, and not necessarily those of Company X. If an affiliation with Company X is provided, political advocacy statements and product or service endorsements also are prohibited unless they have been previously cleared by the director of Public Relations. With the exception of ordinary marketing and customer service activities, all representations on behalf of Company X must be cleared by the director of Public Relations.

Appropriate Behavior—Whenever any affiliation with Company X is included with an Internet message or posting, written attacks are strictly prohibited. Workers must not make threats against another user or organization over the Internet. All Internet messages intended to harass, annoy, or alarm another person are similarly prohibited.

Removal Of Postings—Those messages sent to Internet discussion groups, electronic bulletin boards, or other public forums, that include an implied or explicit affiliation with Company X, may be removed if management deems them to be inconsistent with Company X business interests or existing company policy. Messages in this category include political statements, religious statements, cursing or other foul language, and statements viewed as harassing others based on race,

creed, color, age, sex, physical handicap, or sexual orientation. The decision to remove electronic mail must be made by the corporate Information Security manager or the director of Human Resources. When practical and feasible, individuals responsible for the message will be informed of the decision and given the opportunity to remove the message themselves.

Disclosing Internal Information—Workers must not publicly disclose internal Company X information through the Internet that may adversely affect the Company X stock price, customer relations, or public image unless the approval of the director of Public Relations or a member of the top management team has been obtained. Such information includes business prospects, products now in research and development, product performance analyses, product release dates, and internal information systems problems. Responses to specific customer electronic mail messages are exempted from this policy.

Inadvertent Disclosure—Care must be taken to properly structure comments and questions posted to mailing lists, public news groups, Usenet, and related public postings on the Internet. Before posting any material, workers must consider whether the posting could put Company X at a significant competitive disadvantage or whether the material could cause public relations problems. Workers should keep in mind that several separate pieces of information can be pieced together by a competitor to form a picture revealing confidential information that then could be used against Company X. Workers must never post on the Internet the specific computer or network products employed by Company X.

INTELLECTUAL PROPERTY RIGHTS

Copyrights—When at work, or when Company X computing or networking resources are employed, copying of software in a manner that is not consistent with the vendor's license is strictly forbidden. Off-hours participation in pirate software bulletin boards and similar activities represent a conflict of interest with Company X work, and are therefore prohibited. The reproduction, forwarding, or in any other way republishing or redistribution of words, graphics, or other copyrighted materials must be done only with the permission of the author or Owner. Workers must assume that all materials on the Internet are copyrighted unless specific notice states otherwise. When informa-

tion from the Internet is integrated into internal reports or used for other purposes, all material must include labels such as "copyright, all rights reserved" and specifics about the source of the information.

Publicly-Writable Directories—All publicly-writable directories on Company X Internet-connected computers must be reviewed and cleared each evening. Workers using Company X computers must not be involved in any way with the exchange of pirated software, purloined passwords, stolen credit card numbers, and inappropriate written or graphic material.

ACCESS CONTROL

Inbound User Authentication—All users wishing to establish a real-time connection with Company X internal computers through the Internet must employ a virtual private network (VPN) product approved by the Information Security department that can encrypt all traffic exchanged. These VPN products also must authenticate remote users at a firewall before permitting access to the Company X internal network. This authentication process must be achieved through a dynamic password system approved by the corporate Information Security manager. Examples of approved technology include hand-held smart cards with dynamic passwords and user-transparent challenge and response systems. Designated public systems do not need user authentication processes because anonymous interactions are expected.

Remote Machine Security—Workers who have not installed required software patches or upgrades, or whose systems are virus-infested must be disconnected automatically from the Company X network until they have reestablished a secure computing environment. The computers used by all workers employing VPN technology must be remotely scanned automatically to determine that the software is current and that the system has been properly secured.

Restriction Of Third-Party Access—Inbound Internet access privileges must not be granted to third-party vendors, contractors, consultants, temporaries, outsourcing organization personnel or other third parties unless the relevant system manager determines that these individuals have a legitimate business need for such access. These privileges must be enabled only for specific individuals and only for the time period required to accomplish approved tasks.

Browser User Authentication—Workers must not save fixed passwords in their web browsers or electronic mail clients. These fixed passwords must be provided each time that a browser or electronic mail client is invoked. Browser passwords may be saved if a boot password must be provided each time the computer is powered up, and if a screen saver password must be provided each time the system is inactive for a specified period of time. Company X computer users must refuse all offers by

software to place a cookie on their computer so that they can automatically log on the next time that they visit a particular Internet site. Cookies that serve other purposes are permissible.

Data Aggregators—Workers must not provide their Internet user IDs and passwords to data aggregators, data summarization and formatting services, or any other third parties.

Internet Service Providers—With the exception of telecommuters and mobile computer users, workers must not employ Internet service provider accounts and dial-up lines to access the Internet with Company X computers. All Internet activity must pass through Company X firewalls so that access controls and related security mechanisms can be applied. Users must employ their Company X electronic mail address for Internet electronic mail. Use of a personal electronic mail address for this purpose is prohibited.

Establishing Network Connections—Unless the prior approval of the manager of Telecommunications Services has been obtained, workers must not establish Internet or other external network connections that could permit non-Company X users to gain access to Company X systems and information. These connections include the establishment of multi-computer file systems, Internet pages, Internet commerce systems, and FTP servers.

Establishing New Business Channels—Unless the vice president of Information Systems, the vice president of Marketing, and the chief legal counsel have approved in advance, workers must not use new or existing Internet connections to establish new business channels. These channels include electronic data interchange arrangements, electronic malls with online shopping, and online database services.

Conducting Business Over The Internet—Unless advance approval of the Purchasing department has been obtained, Company X workers must not purchase any goods or services through the Internet if these goods or services are offered by a business based in, or operating out of, a foreign country.

PERSONAL USE

Personal Use—Workers who have been granted Internet access who wish to explore the Internet for personal purposes must do so on personal rather than company time. Games, news groups, and other non-business activities must be performed on personal, not company time. Use of Company X computing resources for these personal purposes is permissible as long as the incremental cost of the usage is negligible, no Company X business activity is preempted by the personal use, and the usage is not likely to cause either a hostile working environment or a poor behavioral example. Workers must not employ the Internet or other internal information systems in such a way that the productivity of other workers is eroded. Examples of this include chain letters and broadcast charitable solicitations. Company X computing resources must not be resold to other parties or used for any personal business purposes such as running a consulting business on off-hours.

Offensive Web Sites—Company X is not responsible for the content that workers may encounter when they use the Internet. When and if users make a connection with web sites containing objectionable content, they must promptly move to another site or terminate their session. Workers using Company X computers who discover they have connected with a web site that contains sexually explicit, racist, sexist, violent, or other potentially offensive material must immediately disconnect from that site.

Blocking Sites and Content Types—The ability to connect with a specific web site does not in itself imply that users of Company X systems are permitted to visit that site. Company X may, at its discretion, restrict or block the downloading of certain file types that are likely to cause network service degradation. These file types include graphic and music files.

PRIVACY EXPECTATIONS

No Default Protection—Workers using Company X information systems or the Internet must realize that their communications are not automatically protected from viewing by third parties. Unless encryption is used, workers must not send information over the Internet if they consider it to be confidential or private.

Management Review—At any time and without prior notice, Company X management reserves the right to examine electronic mail messages, files on personal computers, web browser cache files, web browser bookmarks, logs of web sites visited, computer system configurations, and other information stored on or passing through Company X computers.

Logging—Company X routinely logs the web sites visited, files downloaded, time spent on the Internet, and related information. Department managers receive reports of such information and use it to determine what types of Internet usage are appropriate for their department's business activities.

Junk Electronic Mail—Users must not use Company X computer systems for the transmission of unsolicited bulk electronic mail advertisements or commercial messages that are likely to trigger complaints from the recipients. These prohibited messages include a wide variety of unsolicited promotions and solicitations such as chain letters, pyramid schemes, and direct marketing pitches. When workers receive unwanted and unsolicited electronic mail, they must refrain from responding directly to the sender. They must forward the message to the electronic mail administrator at Company X who then can take steps to prevent further transmissions.

REPORTING SECURITY PROBLEMS

Notification Process—If sensitive Company X information is lost, disclosed to unauthorized parties, or suspected of either, the Information Security manager must be notified immediately. If any unauthorized use of Company X information systems has or is suspected of taking place, the corporate Information Security manager must be notified immediately. Whenever passwords or other system access control mechanisms are lost, stolen, or disclosed, or are suspected of being lost, stolen, or disclosed, the corporate Information Security manager must be notified immediately. All unusual systems behavior, such as missing files, frequent system crashes, and misrouted messages must be immediately reported to the help desk. The specifics of security problems must not be discussed widely but should instead be shared on a need-to-know basis.

False Security Reports—Workers in receipt of information about system vulnerabilities must forward it to the corporate Information Security manager, who then will determine what if any action is appropriate. Workers must not personally redistribute system vulnerability information to other users.

Testing Controls—Workers must not test or probe security mechanisms at either Company X or other Internet sites unless they have obtained written permission from the corporate Information Security manager. The possession or the usage of tools for detecting information system vulnerabilities, or tools for compromising information security mechanisms, are prohibited without the advance permission of the corporate Information Security manager.

Chapter 12 Sample Intranet Security Policy

Business Use Only—The Company X intranet is intended to facilitate more efficient and more effective ways for Company X staff to communicate and conduct business. Like other Company X information systems, because it is intended for business purposes, personal use is permitted only if the approval of a department manager has been obtained.

Respecting Intellectual Property Rights—Although the intranet is an informal internal communications environment, the laws for copyrights, patents, and trademarks apply. Workers may post material to the intranet only after using the following steps:

- If material to be posted originates outside Company X, written permission from the source must be obtained, and the source must be given adequate credit.

- If copyright infringement, confidential information disclosure, libel, defamation of character, or other possible legal issues could be involved, Company X legal counsel must approve the posting.

- Workers must independently confirm the material's accuracy, timeliness, and relevance to Company X business.

- All user-developed web pages must be tested for security and operational problems by a web master according to an approved process issued by the Information Security department.

Prohibited Content—Company X secret information must not reside on either Internet or intranet servers.

Content Control—Company X computer and communications systems are not intended for, and must not be used for the exercise of the participants' right to free speech. These systems, including the intranet, must not be used as an open forum to discuss Company X organizational changes, business policy matters, or similar topics. Company X management has the right to censor, delete, or amend any information posted to Company X computers and networks, including the intranet.

Approvals For Postings—Before any information is posted to the Company X intranet, the department manager in charge of the relevant intranet page and the Owner of the involved information, or creator of the information if the Owner has not yet been designated, must approve. In some cases, these two approvals may come from the same person. A formal change control procedure must be used for all changes to the content posted to the Company X intranet, and this procedure must include documentation reflecting management approvals and archival storage of all prior versions of posted material. Whenever push data or push software transfers through the Internet will used for the Company X intranet, this transfer arrangement must go through the same formal change control process prior to cutover.

Classification For Postings—The content posted to the Company X intranet must be classified as either Public or Internal Use Only. Confidential or Secret information must never be posted to the intranet. Staff in the Information Security department must review all postings to the Company X intranet quarterly to confirm that none of these postings contain Confidential or Secret information.

Legal Ownership Of Material Posted—Unless approved in advance by the director of the Information Technology department, and explicitly noted on the intranet page, all content posted to the Company X intranet is the property of Company X.

Designated Information Owner—All content posted to the Company X intranet must have a designated Owner. Contact information for this Owner must be clearly indicated on the page where the content appears.

Production Systems—All intranet servers are considered production systems and must comply with all the production system requirements specified in the Systems Development Methodology. These requirements include the formal assignment of responsibilities, adequate training for staff working on the production system, at least two trained staff members who are trained and technically competent to manage the system, regular backups, and periodic upgrades of software.

Third-Party Access—All third-party access to Company X internal computer systems that are not clearly public, such as the intranet, must be approved in advance by the Information Security manager.

Restricted Dissemination—The Company X intranet is for the exclusive use of authorized persons and all information contained therein may be disseminated only to authorized persons. Workers must not forward information appearing on the intranet to third parties without going through the appropriate internal channels, such as Marketing, Human Resources, or Public Relations.

Relevant Standards And Resources—All Company X intranet pages must conform to layout standards, navigation standards, legal wording standards, and similar requirements specified by the intranet management committee. All personnel developing intranet sites must consistently observe the intranet style guide and use the resources found in the intranet implementation repository.

Connections To Production Systems—The intranet must not be used to provide real-time connections to any Company X production information system that has extended user authentication access controls, which is anything beyond a fixed password and a user ID, unless the approval of the Information Security department manager has been obtained.

Connecting Systems To The Intranet—Before any computer system, network segment, or network access mechanism, such as a modem, may be connected to the Company X intranet, it must be deemed to have met the necessary security criteria established by the Information Security manager. These criteria include, but are not limited to, no connection to the Internet that is not guarded by an acceptable firewall, an acceptable user authentication system, an acceptable user privilege control system, an established change control process, a clearly-written definition of system management responsibilities, and adequate operational documentation.

Server Approval—Before they are connected to the internal network, the network services manager in the Information Technology department must preauthorize all Company X intranet servers. This authorization process includes assuring that authorized software, such as virus detection software, has been installed properly. This process assures that all active content applets have been adequately tested. This process also assures that compatible hardware and network protocols are being used.

Establishing Internet Links—Links that transfer a user's session from a Company X intranet site to the web site of any outside entity are not permitted unless the approval of the Information Security department manager has been obtained. Whenever these links are established, they must clearly notify the user that they are leaving the intranet and entering the Internet.

Chapter 13 SAMPLE PRIVACY POLICY — STRINGENT

OVERVIEW AND APPLICABILITY

Company X supports the right to privacy, including the rights of individuals to control the dissemination and use of personal data that describes them, their personal choices, or life experiences. Company X supports domestic and international laws and regulations that seek to protect the privacy rights of such individuals.

This policy applies to all Company X employees, contractors, temporaries, and consultants, and other workers. All of these people are expected to be familiar with and fully in compliance with these policies. Workers who are not in compliance are subject to disciplinary action up to and including termination.

This policy also applies to outsourcing organizations that perform information-processing services on behalf of Company X. Use of outsourcing organizations to process personal data must always include a contractual commitment to consistently observe these policies and related Company X procedures and standards as specified by the Information Security department. All outsourcing organizations handling personal data provided by Company X must periodically issue certificates of compliance with this policy, and permit Company X to initiate independent audits to determine compliance with this policy.

DEFINITIONS

Personal data—Any information relating to an individual. Such data includes name, address, telephone number, address, social security number, driver's license number, and personal business transaction details. For example, such a person could be a purchaser of Company X products. The following policies do not apply to statistical reports or other collections of information in which specific natural persons are not identifiable.

Processing of personal data or "processing"—Any operation or set of operations performed on personal data, whether by automatic means, such as collection, recording, organization, storage, adaptation or alteration, retrieval, consultation, use, disclosure by transmission, dissemination or otherwise making available, combination, blocking, erasure or destruction.

Owner—The Company X manager or executive, who determines the purposes for processing personal data, and who makes decisions about the security mechanisms to be used to protect such personal data.

Custodian—The Company X manager, or third-party organization manager if processing is outsourced, who processes personal data according to the instructions provided by the Owner.

Third party—Any person, partnership, corporation, public authority, government agency, or any other entity other than the individual, Owner, Custodian, and the persons who, under the direct authority of the Owner or the Custodian, are authorized to process the data.

Recipient—The person, public authority, government agency, or any other entity to whom personal data is disclosed, even if the recipient is a third party.

Consent—Any freely-given informed indication of his or her wishes by which the individual signifies his or her agreement to have his or her personal data processed, which may include disclosure.

No distinction between data, information, knowledge, or wisdom is made in this policy.

SPECIFIC REQUIREMENTS

1   All personal data must be processed fairly and lawfully, according to the laws and regulations of all jurisdictions where Company X does business.

2   Personal data must be collected for purposes communicated to the individual and not further processed in a way incompatible with those purposes. Further processing of such data for historical, statistical or other business purposes is not incompatible with the original purpose provided the further processing includes adequate additional controls protecting the rights of the individual.

3   The amount of personal data collected must be adequate, relevant, and not excessive in relation to the purposes for which they are collected or for which they are further processed.

4   Personal data must be accurate and complete, and where necessary, kept up to date. Every reasonable step must be taken to ensure that personal data that is inaccurate or incomplete, keeping in mind the purposes for which it was collected or for which it is further processed, are definitively erased or corrected.

5   Individuals must be given an opportunity to examine, and issue complaints about, inaccuracies and incompletions in records containing their personal data. Investigations of complaints must be performed promptly, and must be answered with a letter informing the involved individuals about the courses of action that Company X will take. Any resulting erasures or corrections must be performed promptly and at no cost to the individuals. Reasonable steps to prevent reoccurrence of the same inaccuracies or incompletions must also be taken, for instance by adding an explanatory paragraph in the subject's file. An exception to the requirements stated in this paragraph is permitted for personal data in management succession planning records, criminal activity investigation records, and other legitimate business activities where disclosure to the individual would be highly likely to jeopardize the project underway.

6   Personal data must not be kept in a form that permits identification of individuals for any longer than is necessary for the purposes for which the data was collected or for which it is further processed. For example, this can be implemented with linked separate files respectively containing identification information and related sensitive information.

Owners of personal data are responsible for ensuring that items in the preceding points are complied with.

7   Personal data may be processed only if:

— The individual has given his or her consent unambiguously.

— Processing is necessary for the performance of a contract to which the individual is party, such as completing an order for goods.

— Processing is required to respond to a request made by the individual.

— Processing is necessary for compliance with a legal obligation to which the Owner is subject.

— Processing is necessary in order to protect the vital interests of the individual.

— Processing is necessary to explore or provide new business products or services that may be of use to the Owner, as long as these new products or services do not override the fundamental rights or freedoms of the individual.

8   Processing personal data revealing racial or ethnic origin, political opinions, religious or philosophical beliefs, trade-union membership, criminal offenses, health, or sex life is prohibited unless:

— The individual has provided explicit consent to such processing.

— Processing is necessary for the purposes of carrying out the obligations and specific rights of the Owner in the field of employment law.

— Processing is necessary to protect the vital interests of the individual or of another person where the individual is physically or legally incapable of giving his or her consent.

Custodians of personal data are responsible for ensuring that items in the preceding two points are complied with.

INFORMATION TO BE GIVEN TO THE INDIVIDUAL

The Owner or his or her representative must provide individuals with the following information:

- The identity of the Custodian and of his or her representative, if any.

- The purposes of the processing for which the data is intended.

- The policies related to handling personal data, including material changes to these policies that have gone into effect since the personal data was collected.

- Any further information such as:

  — The recipients or categories of recipients of the data.

  — Whether replies to the questions are obligatory or voluntary, and the possible consequences of the failure to reply.

  — The existence of the right of access to and the right to correct the data concerning the individual.

Where personal data has not been obtained directly from the individual, the Owner or his or her representative must notify the individual at the time when personal data will be processed. If a disclosure to a third party is anticipated, the individual must be notified no later than the time when the data is disclosed. The Owner must provide the individual with at least the following information, except where the individual already knows it:

- The identity of the Custodian and the Custodian's representative, if any.

- The purposes of the processing.

- Any further information such as:

  — The categories of data concerned.

  — The recipients or categories of recipients.

  — The existence of the right of access to and the right to correct information concerning the individual.

Upon request, the Owner or his or her representative must provide all individuals with a brief written summary of the subject's rights to learn about, get copies of, lodge objections to, and correct personal data. Trained personnel who can explain an individual's rights must be available to subjects by telephone.

If Company X changes its privacy policy, an attempt to notify all individuals must be promptly initiated. As a part of this notification, Company X must provide individuals with a summary of the words that have changed and what these changes mean. Individuals also must be given an opportunity to be removed from Company X records.

INDIVIDUAL'S RIGHT OF ACCESS TO DATA

Every individual has the right to obtain the following from the Custodian:

1 Without undue constraint at reasonable intervals and without excessive delay or expense:

  — Confirmation as to whether data relating to him or her is processed and information at least as to the purposes of the processing, the categories of data concerned, and the recipients or categories of recipients to whom the data is disclosed.

  — Details as to the source of information about the individual, if such information is recorded.

  — Communication of the personal data to the subject in an intelligible form.

  — Knowledge of the logic involved in any automatic processing of data concerning him or her at least in the case of the automated decisions affecting the individual.

2 When appropriate, an indication that his or her personal data has been corrected, erased, or blocked because it was incomplete or inaccurate.

3 Notification to third parties to whom the data has been disclosed of any correction, erasure, or blocking carried out in compliance with the prior paragraph, unless this proves impossible or involves a unreasonable effort or expense.

INDIVIDUAL'S RIGHT TO OBJECT

Individuals may object, free of charge, to the processing of personal data that the Owner anticipates will be processed for the purposes of direct marketing. Owners must provide prompt processing mechanisms that permit individuals who objected to be removed from direct marketing lists.

Individuals must be informed before personal data is disclosed for the first time to third parties or used on their behalf for the purposes of direct marketing. Individuals must be expressly offered the right to object free of charge to such disclosures or uses. Owners must provide processing mechanisms that permit individuals who objected to block such a disclosure.

DISCLOSURE OF PERSONAL DATA TO THIRD PARTIES

Company X may provide third parties with personal data processed on its systems for generally accepted business purposes such as court orders, subpoenas, employment verification, governmental licensing, underwriting, and other reasons. All recipients of such information must definitively identify themselves, certify in writing the legal and customary purposes for which the information is sought and certify that the personal data will be used for no other purposes.

All disclosures to government agencies and other third parties must be preceded by written or other notice sent to the individual. A blanket, one-time approval of such disclosures is sufficient. Sufficient time must be provided between the receipt of such notice to the individual and the actual disclosure to the third party to permit the individual to object, should he or she so elect.

PROCESSING CONFIDENTIALITY AND SECURITY

The Owner must implement appropriate technical and organizational measures to protect personal data against accidental or unlawful destruction, accidental loss, unauthorized alteration, and unauthorized disclosure or access. These measures must be consistent with the standards and procedures issued by the Information Security department.

Transfers of private information to another country, no matter what technology is employed, must not take place unless prior approval of the Information Security manager has been obtained. An exception is made in those cases where the individual is, was, or will be located in the destination country, or when the individual has specifically requested such a transfer.

Company X information systems or staff must not link anonymous information about individual behavior or activities with personally-identifiable information unless the involved individuals have given their consent. For example, such a linkage could tie Internet shopping purchase information with web browsing logs.

The Owner or his or her designated representative must prepare a documented risk assessment to determine the privacy implications of all significantly new or different uses of personal data. Such a risk assessment must be completed before these uses take place, and must include all steps in the proposed processing, including access, storage, transmission, and destruction. Such a risk assessment must include not only consideration of the risks, but also the security measures to be employed such as access controls, encryption, logs, data retention schedules, and data destruction procedures.

When building, testing, enhancing, and maintaining processing systems, developers must not use actual personal data. Instead, they must use fictional or sanitized personal data that preserves the essential characteristics of the data, but that does not relate to identifiable individuals. In emergency situations where processing with actual personal data is required, use of such information is permitted under strict security procedures defined by Information Security.

All user access to processing systems and networks containing personal data must be logged so that every recent access to personal data can be traced to a specific user. Custodians of these systems and networks are responsible for the routine monitoring of such logs and the follow-up on potential security-relevant events.

When not in use, personal data must be stored in encrypted form if held in a computer or network, or in locked or similarly secured containers if held in paper, microfiche, or other non-computerized form. When sent over public computer networks such as the Internet, personal data must be protected by encryption. Procedures and standards issued by Information Security provide additional details on these topics.

When they are no longer needed, all copies of personal data, including those on backup tapes, must be irreversibly destroyed according to standards and procedures defined by the Information Security department. A document describing the personal data destroyed and the reasons for such destruction must be prepared for each destruction process, and promptly submitted to the relevant Owner. Permission to destroy personal data may be granted by only the Owner, and only if all legal retention requirements and related business purposes have been met.

The use of cookies, web bugs, images, and other techniques to covertly gather information about individuals who use the Internet is incompatible with this policy. Whenever Company X gathers information about individuals, these same subjects must have agreed upon the collection effort in advance. For this same reason, Company X does not deposit cookie files on individual hard drives or does not perform any other covert recording of the Internet activity in which individuals have engaged.

Company X streamlines and expedites all of its computerized business interactions with individuals, but at the same time to be forthright and clear about its privacy policies. To support these objectives and to encourage individuals to use Internet commerce sites and other computerized business systems, Company X adopts and supports all generally-accepted standards for web content rating, web site privacy protection, and Internet commerce security, including third-party seals of approval.

Company X does not use externally-meaningful identifiers as its own internal individual account numbers. For example, to prevent identity theft, Company X customer account numbers must never be equivalent to social security numbers, driver's license numbers, or any other identifier that might be used in an unauthorized fashion by a third party.

Monitoring Of Internal Activities

In general terms, Company X does not engage in blanket monitoring of internal communications. It does, however, reserve the right at any time to monitor, access, retrieve, read, or disclose internal communications when a legitimate business need exists that cannot be satisfied by other means, the involved individual is unavailable and timing is critical to a business activity, there is reasonable cause to suspect criminal activity or policy violation, or monitoring is required by law, regulation, or third-party agreement.

At any time, Company X may log web sites visited, files downloaded, and related information exchanges over the Internet. Company X may record the numbers dialed for telephone calls placed through its telephone systems. Department managers may receive reports detailing the usage of these and other internal information systems, and are responsible for determining that such usage is both reasonable and business-related.

All files and messages stored on Company X processing systems are routinely backed up to tape, disk, and other storage media. This means that information stored on Company X information processing systems, even if a worker has specifically deleted it, is often recoverable and may be examined at a later date by system administrators and others designated by management.

At any time and without prior notice, Company X management reserves the right to examine archived electronic mail, personal computer file directories, hard disk drive files, and other information stored on Company X information processing systems. This information may include personal data. Such examinations are typically performed to assure compliance with internal policies, support the performance of internal investigations, and assist with the management of Company X information processing systems.

Chapter 14 SAMPLE PRIVACY POLICY — LENIENT

COMPANY INTENTIONS AND MANAGEMENT RESPONSIBILITIES

Intentions And Objectives—In the course if its business, it is necessary for Company X to record, store, process, transmit, and otherwise handle private information about individuals. Company X takes these activities seriously and provides fair, secure, and fully-legal systems for the appropriate handling of this private information. All such activities at Company X are intended to be consistent with both generally accepted privacy ethics and standard business practices.

Management Responsibilities—Management must take reasonable efforts to ensure that all private information maintained by Company X is accurate, timely, relevant, and complete. Management also must make reasonable efforts to ensure that all private information is used only as intended, and that precautions preventing misuse are both effective and appropriate. Management is respon-

sible for establishing appropriate controls to ensure that private information is disclosed only to those who have a legitimate business need for such access. Management must establish and maintain sufficient controls to ensure that all Company X information is free from a significant risk of undetected alteration.

Data Classification Labels—Management, specifically information Owners, must consistently apply a standard data classification label indicating that information is private. For example, this label must appear on computer screens when private information is displayed, and it must also be stamped on hardcopy versions of private information. This label must follow private information no matter what form it takes, what technology is used to handle it, who handles the information, and where the information resides.

DISCLOSURE OF PRIVATE INFORMATION

Revealing Information About Policies and Procedures—As a general rule, information security policies and procedures should be revealed only to Company X workers and selected outsiders, such as auditors, who have a legitimate business need for this information. A notable exception involves the policies that deal with private information about individuals. All involved individuals have a right to receive an officially-approved statement of Company X policies and procedures regarding the handling of information about them. In addition, Company X must disclose the existence of systems containing private information and the ways that this information is used. With the exception of criminal and policy-violation investiga-

tions, there must be no system of personnel records within Company X whose very existence is kept secret from the people described therein.

Handling Private Information Requests—All requests for private information coming from a person or organization outside Company X must be forwarded to the Company X chief legal counsel. All requests for private information that fall outside normal business procedures and that come from a Company X insider must be forwarded to the director of the Human Resources department. These managers will decide whether the requests will be granted.

APPROPRIATE HANDLING OF PRIVATE INFORMATION

Collect Only Necessary Information—In general, Company X may collect, process, store, transmit, and disseminate only that private information that is necessary for the proper functioning of its business. For example, Company X management must not collect

information about worker activities during non-work hours unless these activities are highly likely to influence the involved worker's performance, or unless they could adversely affect the reputation of Company X.

Destruction Of Private Information—When private information is no longer needed, it must be destroyed by shredding, or by other destruction methods approved by the Information Security department. Destruction of private information resident on computer disks and other magnetic media must be accomplished with an overwriting process. A simple erase process is not sufficient. To assure the proper destruction of private or confidential information, disposal of computers with embedded hard disk drives or other data storage systems must proceed according to procedures issued by Information Security.

Removal Of Private Information—Private or confidential information must not be removed from Company X offices. Permission to take such information offsite may be granted by a departmental manager provided the involved worker has completed the information security segment of telecommuter training, and passed the associated test. Signed third-party non-disclosure agreements may additionally be required when private information is removed from Company X offices.

Private information must not be moved to another country unless the permission of the manager of the Information Security department is obtained.

Preventing Inadvertent Disclosure on Screens—The display screens for all personal computers, workstations, and dumb terminals used to process sensitive or valuable data, including private information, must be positioned such that they cannot be readily viewed through a window, by persons walking by a hallway, or by persons waiting in reception and related areas.

Preventing Inadvertent Disclosure By Hardcopy—Whenever a worker is handling private information, if a person who is not authorized to view that information enters the immediate area, steps to conceal the information must promptly be taken. If the information is in physical form, the information can be covered with other material. If the information is displayed on a computer screen, the worker can invoke a screen saver or log off.

PRIVATE INFORMATION ON COMPUTER AND COMMUNICATION SYSTEMS

Expectation Of Privacy—All messages sent over Company X internal computer and communications systems are the property of Company X. Management reserves the right to examine all information transmitted through these systems. Examination of such information may take place without prior warning to the parties sending or receiving such information. Because the Company X computer and communications systems must be used for business purposes only, workers must have no expectation of privacy associated with the information they store in or send through these systems.

Examination Of Stored Information—At any time and without prior notice, Company X management reserves the right to examine archived electronic mail, private file directories, hard disk drive files, and other information stored on Company X information systems. Such examinations are typically performed to assure compliance with internal policies, support the performance of internal investigations, and assist with the management of Company X information systems.

Manager Involvement In Monitoring—Whenever a worker's computer or communications user ID is monitored for investigative or disciplinary purposes, the involved worker's manager must be informed of this

activity promptly. All worker monitoring must itself be logged for subsequent management review and possible use in disciplinary or legal actions.

Department Manager Activity Review—Company X routinely logs web sites visited, files downloaded, and related information exchanges over the Internet. Company X records the numbers dialed for telephone calls placed by each worker. Department managers routinely receive reports detailing the usage of these and other internal information systems, and are responsible for determining that such usage is both reasonable and business-related.

Changing Information Resident on Systems—Management reserves the right to delete, summarize, or edit any information posted to Company X computers or communication systems. These facilities are privately-owned business systems, and not public forums, and as such do not provide free-speech guarantees.

Routine Usage of Backup Systems—All files and messages stored on Company X systems are routinely copied to tape, disk, and other storage media. This means that information stored on Company X information systems, even if a worker has specifically deleted it, is often recoverable and may be examined at a later date by system administrators and others designated by management.

Remote Computer Monitoring—Company X routinely scans the personal computers connected to its networks. These scans ensure that remote computers are operating only with approved and licensed software, are free from viruses and worms, and have been used only for approved business purposes.

Encryption Of Electronic Mail—Workers must consider electronic mail to be the computerized equivalent of a postcard. Unless material sent by electronic mail is encrypted, workers must refrain from sending credit card numbers, passwords, research and development information, medical histories, computer programming source code, and other private or confidential information through electronic mail.

Links Between Separate Types Of Private Data—Without advance consent from the manager of the Information Security department, Company X information systems must not be configured to support new links between private information and other types of information related to the same individual.

Testing With Sanitized Data—Unless written permission is obtained from the Information Security department manager, all software testing for systems designed to handle private data must be accomplished exclusively with production information that no longer contains specific details that might be valuable, critical, or sensitive.

ACTIVITY MONITORING

Physical Security Systems—Workers may be subject to electronic monitoring of their activities while on Company X premises. This monitoring is used to measure worker performance and to protect worker private property, worker safety, and Company X property. In areas where there is a reasonable expectation of privacy, such as bathrooms, dressing rooms, and locker rooms, no electronic monitoring will be performed.

Personal Effects and Private Communications—All personal effects brought to Company X premises are subject to search at any time without advance notice. Workers wishing to keep certain aspects of their personal life private must not bring related personal effects to Company X premises. To keep these matters private, workers must not communicate about such matters using Company X telephones, electronic mail systems, or other communications systems that may be monitored and which are intended to be used for business purposes only.

Use Of Informants—From time to time, Company X uses informants who may be placed in various internal positions and who may appear to be the same as any other worker. Management has no obligation to notify workers about the presence of, or nature of the work performed by, such informants.

Pretext Requests—Company X believes that all business activities must be conducted in a forthright and honest manner. However, in certain circumstances authorized by the director of Physical Security, the organization may utilize investigators who pose as other persons in order to test customer service, test security policies, or investigate alleged wrongdoing.

HANDLING PERSONNEL INFORMATION

Access to Own Personnel File—Upon written request, every worker must be given access to his or her own personnel file. Employees must be permitted to both examine and make one copy of the information appearing in their personnel file. If employees object to the accuracy, relevance, or completeness of information appearing in their personnel file, each year they may add a supplementary statement of up to 200 words.

Disclosure To Third Parties—Disclosure of private information about Company X workers to third parties must not take place unless required by law or permitted by explicit consent of the worker. Company X must not disclose the names, titles, phone numbers, locations, or other contact particulars of its workers unless required for business purposes. Exceptions will be made when such a disclosure is required by law or when the involved persons have previously consented to the disclosure. The reason for termination of workers must not be disclosed to third parties. Two permissible exceptions are the prior approval of a Company X senior manager or if the disclosure is required by law. Every disclosure of private information to third parties must be recorded by the Human Resources department and these records must be maintained for at least five years.

Summary Of Disclosures—If they request it, workers must be provided with a summary of all disclosures of their private information to third parties. In addition, workers must be given sufficient information to permit them to contact such third parties to rectify errors or supply additional explanatory information.

Change Of Status Information—Detailed worker change of status information is strictly confidential, and must not be disclosed to anyone except those people who have a genuine need to know. Detailed change of status information includes the reasons for terminations, retirements, resignations, leaves of absence, leaves of absence pending the results of an investigation, inter-departmental transfers, relocations, and changes to consultant or contractor status.

PRIVATE INFORMATION FROM JOB SEEKERS

Gathering Unnecessary Information—Private information about a prospective employee may not be gathered unless it is both necessary to make an employment decision and also relevant to the job. This policy addresses marital status, family planning objectives, off-hours activities, political affiliations, performance on previous jobs, previous employers, credit history, education, and other personal details.

Credit And Background Checks—Whenever a credit report will be examined or a background check will be performed, prospective workers must provide a written release indicating their approval of the process. These

prospective workers must be given an opportunity to withdraw their application for employment or contract work if they choose not to disclose such private information to Company X.

Permissible Tests—Candidates for a job with Company X must not be subjected to drug tests, AIDS tests, psychological tests, or other tests that may illuminate the candidates' lifestyle, political associations, or religious preferences. An exception may be made if this information is clearly needed to determine a candidate's suitability for a certain position.

PRIVATE INFORMATION ABOUT CUSTOMERS

Consent For Collection Required—The collection of private information on prospects, customers, and others with whom Company X does business, is customary and expected. However, Company X workers must not collect private information from prospects or customers without having obtained their knowledge and consent.

Consent For Uses Required—Before a customer places an order or otherwise discloses private information, all Company X representatives must inform the customer about the ways that this private information will be used, and the third parties, if any, to whom the information will be disclosed.

Collection Of Unnecessary Information—Company X workers or information systems must never require the provision of prospect or customer private information that is unnecessary for the provision of information, for the completion of a transaction, or for the delivery of products or services. No product or service provided by Company X may be denied to any person if they refuse

to provide unnecessary private information. All disputes about necessary private information will be resolved by the Company X chief legal counsel.

Opting Out From Unsolicited Contacts—Company X customers must be given an opportunity to inform Company X that they do not wish to be contacted through unsolicited direct mail, telemarketing, and related promotions. Company X staff must faithfully observe and act on these customer requests. Company X workers must diligently observe the unconditional right of individuals to block data about them from being included in mailing lists or calling lists, block the sale of data about them to third parties, and to have data about them erased from direct marketing lists.

Sharing Of Customer Information—Company X does not disclose specific information about customer accounts, transactions, or relationships to unaffiliated third parties for their independent use, except under certain circumstances. These circumstances are limited to the disclosure of information to a reputable information reporting agency such as a credit bureau, when performing its own due diligence related to a customer's request to perform a certain action such as extend the amount of an existing line of credit, those circumstances when the customer requests the disclosure, the disclosure is required by or permitted by law, or the customer has been informed about the possibility of such a disclosure for marketing or similar purposes, and has been given an opportunity to decline.

Change Of Business Structure—Should Company X go out of business, merge, be acquired, or otherwise change the legal form of its organizational structure, Company X may need to share some or all of its customer information with another entity in order to continue to provide products and services. If such a change and associated information transfer takes place, customers must be promptly notified.

Use Of Outsourcing Organizations—Company X may outsource some or all of its information handling activities, and it may be necessary to transfer prospect and customer information to third parties to perform work under an outsourcing agreement. In all such cases, the third parties involved must sign a confidentiality agreement prohibiting them from further dissemination of this information and prohibiting them from using this information for unauthorized purposes.

Approved By: [insert approving executive's name]

Approved Date: DD/MM/YY

Effective Date: DD/MM/YY

Version Number: XX

Policy Number: XX-XXXX

Chapter 15 SAMPLE WEB PRIVACY POLICY

Objectives—Company X has created this security and privacy statement in order to document and communicate its commitment to doing business with the highest ethical standards and appropriate internal controls.

Explicit Information Gathering—You can examine our entire web site without providing any information whatsoever. Our web site's request-for-more-information form requires users to give us contact information. This information is used to provide information to those who inquire about our products and services, to ship orders, to bill orders, and to handle related business matters. This information is also used to get in touch with customers when necessary. From time to time, the information gathered through this site will be used to notify you about products and services that we think will be of interest to you.

Covert Information Gathering—Our site does not covertly capture information regarding the specific activities of any particular user. We do not have any arrangements with any other sites to track or monitor user activities on the Web. Our site does, however, produce reports that permit us to view your activity on our site in anonymous or aggregated form. We do not use cookies, web bugs, or any other active content mechanism to capture or maintain information about users without their prior consent. The only personal information that we capture has been specifically submitted to us through the request-for-more-information form. We do not store any persistent information on your computer.

Precautions For Children—Company X does not attempt to collect personal information from children. If a child sends personal information to us, and this information can be identified as originating from a child, the information will be deleted. We cannot always determine which information originates with a user that is a child. We do not maintain databases about children.

Information Usage—When you disclose personal information to us, that is where it stays. The only exception involves disclosure to the government according to normal business practice, for instance for the collection of taxes, and according to the orders of a court, for example responding to a subpoena or search warrant. We do not sell, rent, trade, lend, or otherwise transfer such personal information to affiliates, subsidiaries, sister companies, holding companies, parent companies, strategic partners, or any other organization.

Links to Other Sites—This site contains a number of links to other sites. Company X is not responsible for the security or privacy practices of these sites, the products or services offered by these sites, or the content appearing at these sites. Company X does not endorse any of the products or services marketed at these other sites.

Security Measures—Our site is protected with a variety of security measures such as change control procedures, passwords, and physical access controls. We also employ a variety of other mechanisms to ensure that data you provide is not lost, misused, or altered inappropriately. These controls include data confidentiality policies and regular database backups.

Contacting Us—With respect to this web site, there are two options regarding your personal information. If you wish to contact us about our products or services, then you need to disclose your contact information so that we can service your request, or if you do not wish to contact us about our products or services, we will have gathered

If you wish to remove your name and related information from our database, we will promptly take action to comply with your request. We are pleased to process address error correction notices and address change requests through any of the following channels:

- Sending electronic mail to [insert electronic mail address]

- Sending regular mail to [insert physical address]

- Calling [insert telephone number] during regular business hours [time zone]

- Faxing [insert fax number] any time of day or night

If you have any questions about this security and privacy statement, the practices of this site, or your dealings with our company, you can contact us using any of the above communications channels.

Chapter 16 SAMPLE DATA CLASSIFICATION POLICY

INTRODUCTION AND OVERVIEW

Worker Responsibility—Every worker who has access to Company X information or information systems has an important information security role in the organization. For example, each one of these workers is personally responsible for the protection of information that has been entrusted to their care. All workers who come into contact with sensitive Company X internal information are expected to familiarize themselves with this data classification policy and to consistently use these same ideas in their daily Company X business activities. Sensitive information is either Confidential or Secret information, and both are defined later in this document. Although this policy provides overall guidance, to achieve consistent information protection, workers are expected to apply and extend these concepts to fit the needs of day-to-day operations. This document provides a conceptual model for classifying information based on its sensitivity, and an overview of the required approaches to protect information based on these same sensitivity classifications.

Addresses Major Risks—The Company X data classification system, as defined in this document, is based on the concept of need to know. This term means that information is not disclosed to any person who does not have a legitimate and demonstrable business need to receive the information. This concept, when combined with the policies defined in this document, will protect Company X information from unauthorized disclosure, use, modification, and deletion.

Consistent Approach Required—A single lapse in information security can have significant long-term consequences. Consistent use of this data classification system is essential if sensitive information is to be adequately protected. Without the consistent use of this data classification system, Company X unduly risks loss of customer relationships, loss of public confidence, internal operational disruption, excessive costs, and competitive disadvantage. This policy consistently protects sensitive information no matter what form it takes, what technology is used to process it, who handles it, where the information may be located, and in what stage of its life cycle the information may be.

Applicable Information—This data classification policy is applicable to all information in the possession or under the control of Company X. For example, Confidential information entrusted to Company X by customers, business partners, suppliers, and other third parties must be protected with this data classification policy. Workers are expected to protect third-party information with the same care that they protect Company X information. No distinctions between the words "data," "information," "knowledge," and "wisdom" are made for purposes of this policy.

Trade Secrets—One special type of sensitive information is called a Trade Secret. Trade Secrets are a type of proprietary information that gives Company X competitive advantage in some manner. This document covers Trade Secrets, all of which need to be separately designated. Trade Secrets must be identified as such prior to being disclosed to any worker. By default, all Trade Secrets are classified as Secret information. The Company X chief legal counsel is the only person authorized to designate any Company X information as a Trade Secret.

ACCESS CONTROL

Need to Know—Every one of the policy requirements set forth in this document are based on the concept of need to know. If a worker is unclear how the requirements set forth in this policy should be applied to any particular circumstance, he or she must conservatively apply the need to know concept. That is to say that information must be disclosed only to those people who have a legitimate business need for the information. This principle applies to private employee information such as medical histories, just as it applies to proprietary corporate information such as plans for a new product.

System Access Controls—Access to all Company X sensitive computer-resident information must be protected by access controls to ensure that it is not improperly disclosed, modified, deleted, or rendered unavailable. Traditional access control systems employ user IDs and fixed passwords, but these are currently being phased out in favor of more secure technologies such as dynamic passwords and biometrics. Whatever technology is employed, access must be controlled for each individual based on that individual's need to know. The notion of the need to know includes not only viewing information, but other privileges such as modifying information or using information to complete a transaction. Company X access control systems must log which users accessed what sensitive data, and the time and date of each such access.

Access Granting Decisions—Access to Company X sensitive information must be provided only after the written authorization of the information Owner has been obtained. Custodians of the involved information must refer all requests for access to the relevant Owners or their delegates. Standard templates of system privileges are defined for all job titles, and Owners approve these privileges in advance. Special needs for other access privileges will be dealt with on a request-by-request basis.

CLASSIFICATION LABELS

Owners And Production Information—All production information types possessed by or used by a particular organizational unit within Company X must have a designated Owner. Production information is information routinely used to accomplish business objectives. Examples include payroll summaries, shipping schedules, and managerial cost accounting reports. Information Owners are responsible for assigning appropriate sensitivity classifications as defined below. Owners do not legally own the information entrusted to their care. They are instead designated members of the Company X management team who act as stewards, and who supervise the ways in which certain types of information are used and protected [a hotlink to the data ownership policy could go here].

SECRET—This classification label applies to the most sensitive business information that is intended for use strictly within Company X. Its unauthorized disclosure could seriously and adversely impact Company X, its customers, its business partners, and its suppliers. Examples include merger and acquisition documents, corporate level strategic plans, litigation strategy memos, reports on breakthrough new product research, and Trade Secrets such as certain computer programs.

CONFIDENTIAL—This classification label applies to less-sensitive business information that is intended for use within Company X. Its unauthorized disclosure could adversely impact Company X or its customers, suppliers, business partners, or employees. Information that some people would consider to be private is included in this classification. Examples include employee performance evaluations, customer transaction data, strategic alliance agreements, unpublished internally-generated market research, computer passwords, identity token personal identification numbers, and internal audit reports.

FOR INTERNAL USE ONLY—This classification label applies to all other information that does not clearly fit into the previous two classifications. While its unauthorized disclosure is against policy, it is not expected to seriously or adversely impact Company X or its employees, suppliers, business partners, or its customers. Examples include the Company X telephone directory, dial-up computer access numbers, new employee training materials, and internal policy manuals.

PUBLIC—This classification applies to information that has been approved by Company X management for release to the public. By definition, there is no such thing as unauthorized disclosure of this information and it may be disseminated without potential harm. Examples include product and service brochures, advertisements, job opening announcements, and press releases.

Other Labels—Company X department or division-specific data classification labels are permissible, but must be consistent with and supplemental to the Company X data classification system. These supplementary labels might for example include the use of words like "Private" or "Financial."

Owners And Access Decisions—Owners must make decisions about who will be permitted to gain access to information, and the uses to which this information will be put. Owners must take steps to ensure that appropriate controls are utilized in the storage, handling, distribution, and regular usage of information. Readers of this policy can quickly determine the appropriate Owner by consulting the Information Security department's page on the Company X intranet [a link to that page could be placed here].

LABELING

Consistent Classification Labeling—If information is sensitive, from the time it is created until the time it is destroyed or declassified, it must be labeled with an appropriate data classification designation. Such markings must appear on all manifestations of the information, such as hard copies, floppy disks, and CD-ROMs. Workers must not remove or change data classification system labels for sensitive information unless the permission of the Owner has been obtained.

What Gets Labeled—The vast majority of Company X information falls into the Internal Use Only category. For this reason, it is not necessary to apply a label to Internal Use Only information. Information without a label is by default classified as Internal Use Only.

Labels Believed To Be Incorrect—If the recipient of Company X internal information believes that the data classification label accompanying this information is incorrect, the recipient must protect the information in a manner consistent with the more stringent of the two possible classification labels. Before using this information or distributing it to any other party, such a recipient must check with the information Owner to ensure that the label currently applied to the information is correct.

Information Collections—Workers who create or update a collection of information are responsible for choosing an appropriate data classification label for the new collection. This label must be consistent with the decisions made by the relevant Owners and generally should be the most restricted classification level found in the collection. For example, if a new database is being created, and if it contains Internal Use Only and Confidential information, then the entire database must be classified as Confidential. Other examples of such collections include an internally-generated competitive intelligence report, management decision background reports, and access-controlled intranet pages. At the time that it is being compiled, every worker creating a new collection of this nature must notify the involved information Owner about the creation of their new collection.

Storage Media—If information recorded on computer storage media with a higher sensitivity classification is moved to media with a lower sensitivity classification, then the media with the lower sensitivity classification must be upgraded so that its classification reflects the highest sensitivity classification. For example, if information labeled Secret were to be placed on a floppy disk containing information with no label, then the floppy disk must immediately be reclassified as Secret. If information with several different data classification levels is resident on a single computer, then the system controls must reflect the requirements associated with most restrictive data classification level. In general, because it increases handling costs and operational complexity, commingling information with different sensitivity classifications is discouraged.

Labels For Externally-Supplied Information—With the exception of general business correspondence and copyrighted software, all externally-provided information that is not clearly in the public domain must receive a Company X data classification system label. The Company X worker who receives this information is responsible for assigning an appropriate classification on behalf of the external party. When assigning a Company X classification label, this staff member must preserve copyright notices, author credits, guidelines for interpretation, and information about restricted dissemination.

Labeling Hardcopy—All printed, handwritten, or other paper manifestations of sensitive information must have a clearly-evident sensitivity label on the upper right hand corner of each page. If bound, all paper manifestations of sensitive information must have an appropriate sensitivity label on the front cover, the title page, and the rear cover. The cover sheet for faxes containing sensitive information must contain the appropriate classification label. Microfiche and microfilm also must contain labels if they contain sensitive information.

Labeling Computer Storage Media—All CD-ROMs, floppy disks, and other computer storage media containing sensitive information must be externally labeled with the appropriate sensitivity classification. Unless it would adversely affect the operation of an application program, computer files containing sensitive information must also clearly indicate the relevant classification label in the first two data lines.

Other Displays—If information is sensitive, all instances in which it is displayed on a screen or otherwise presented to a computer user must involve an indication of the information's sensitivity classification. Teleconferences and telephone conference calls where sensitive information will be discussed must be preceded by a statement about the sensitivity of the information involved. Teleconferences and telephone calls where sensitive information is discussed must be preceded by a determination that all parties to the discussion are authorized to receive the sensitive information. Persons other than those specifically invited must not attend meetings where sensitive information will be discussed.

Additional Public Information Labels—Unless it is unquestionably already public information, all Company X information with a Public label must also be labeled "Approved For Public Release" along with the date when the Owner declared the information Public.

Dictation Machines And Tape Recorders—To reduce the chance of unauthorized disclosure, in general, workers must not record sensitive information with dictation machines, tape recorders, telephone answering machines, or similar devices. If the use of these devices is an operational necessity, the proper sensitivity classification must be specified at the beginning and end of each segment of sensitive information. In this case, the recording media must also be marked with the most stringent data classification found on the media. In addition, the media must be protected in accordance with the most stringent classification found on the media, and erased as soon as possible.

THIRD-PARTY INTERACTIONS

Third Parties And The Need To Know—Unless it has been specifically designated as Public, all Company X internal information must be protected from disclosure to third parties. Third parties may be given access to Company X internal information only when a demonstrable need to know exists, and when such a disclosure has been expressly authorized by the relevant Company X information Owner. Contractors, consultants, temporaries, volunteers and every other type of individual or entity that is not a Company X employee, is by definition a third party for purposes of this policy.

Disclosures To Third Parties And Non-Disclosure Agreements—The disclosure of sensitive information to consultants, contractors, temporaries, or any other third parties must be preceded by the receipt of a signed Company X non-disclosure agreement. Disclosures of Company X sensitive information to these third parties must be accompanied by a running log indicating exactly what type of information was provided. This log will be important when the time arrives to recover these materials or obtain a letter certifying destruction of the materials at the end of a contract.

Disclosures From Third Parties And Non-Disclosure Agreements—Workers must not sign non-disclosure agreements provided by third parties without the authorization of Company X legal counsel designated to handle intellectual property matters. These forms may contain terms and conditions that unduly restrict the future business directions of Company X.

Third-Party Requests For Company X Information—Unless a worker has been authorized by the information Owner to make public disclosures, all requests for information about Company X and its business must be referred to Public Relations. Such requests include questionnaires, surveys, and newspaper interviews. This policy does not apply to sales and marketing information about Company X products and services, nor does it pertain to customer support calls.

Prior Review—Every speech, presentation, technical paper, book, or other communication to be delivered to the public must have been approved for release by the involved employee's immediate manager. This policy applies if the employee will represent Company X or discuss Company X affairs, or if the communication is based on information obtained in the course of performing Company X job duties. If new products, research results, corporate strategies, customer information, or marketing approaches are to be divulged, prior approval of the director of Research and Development and the director of the Legal department also must be obtained.

Owner Notification—If sensitive information is lost, is disclosed to unauthorized parties, or is suspected of being lost or disclosed to unauthorized parties, the information Owner and the manager of the Information Security department must be notified immediately.

SHIPPING AND HANDLING

Making Copies—Making additional photocopies or printing extra copies of sensitive information must not take place without the advance permission of the information Owner. Workers must be aware that selected Company X photocopy machines and fax machines keep logs of the information copied or faxed.

Unattended Printing—Printers must not be left unattended if sensitive information is being printed or soon will be printed. The persons attending the printer must be authorized to examine the printed information. Unattended printing of sensitive information is permitted only if physical access controls are used to prevent unauthorized persons from entering the area by the printer and viewing the material being printed.

Use Of Outside Services—Prior to sending any sensitive information to a third party for copying, printing, formatting, or other handling, the third party must sign a Company X non-disclosure agreement.

Page Numbering—All sensitive Company X information manifested in paper form must indicate both the current and the last page, for example, "Page X of Y."

Backup Storage Media—All sensitive information recorded on backup computer media and stored outside Company X offices must be in encrypted form. If an encryption system with key escrow is not used for this purpose, all keys used to make these backup copies must be promptly provided to the Information Security department shortly after their initial use.

Envelopes—If sensitive information is to be sent through internal mail, external mail, or by courier, it must be enclosed in two envelopes or containers. The outside envelope or container must not indicate the classification or the nature of the information contained therein. The inside sealed and opaque envelope or container must be labeled with the appropriate classification label. Envelopes containing sensitive information must be addressed to a specific person, and must contain sufficient return address information. All sensitive Company X information sent through these delivery systems must require a signature by an authorized party at the destination.

Delivery Of Computer Output—Sensitive computer system output must be personally delivered to the designated recipients. Such output must not be delivered to an unattended desk, placed in an uncontrolled computer output receptacle, or left out in the open in an unoccupied office. It may be made available to only the designated recipients through password-protected fax mailboxes, departmental or personal computer output lockers, or other physical security methods.

Removal From Offices—Sensitive Company X information must not be removed from Company X premises unless there has been prior approval from the information's Owner. This policy includes portable computers with hard disks, floppy disks, hard-copy output, and paper memos. An exception is made for authorized offsite backups.

Locked Containers In The Office—Sensitive information in hardcopy form must be secured when not actively in use, even if it is within a building to which access is controlled. If not encrypted, all sensitive information must be locked in safes, heavy furniture, or other containers approved by the Information Security department. Unattended sensitive information found lying on a desk after business hours, or sensitive information that is otherwise readily accessible to passers-by after hours, may be confiscated and later claimed in person from the Information Security department.

Locked Containers Off-Site—Whenever a hardcopy version of sensitive information is removed from Company X premises, it must be carried in a locked briefcase or container when not in use. Such information must not be left in an unattended motor vehicle, hotel room, office, or some other location, even if the vehicle or room is locked.

Oral Warnings—If Confidential information is released orally in a meeting, seminar, lecture, or related presentation, the speaker must communicate the sensitivity of the information. The speaker must remind the audience to use discretion when disclosing it to others. Visual aids such as projector slides and overhead transparencies must include the appropriate data classification labels.

Cellular And Cordless Phones—Unless an encrypted link has been established, workers must never discuss sensitive information over cellular or cordless phones. For the same reason, radio local area networks must not be used to transmit sensitive information unless an encryption process approved by the Information Security department is consistently employed. Computer links established over cellular phones or other airwave broadcast systems must not include the transfer of sensitive information unless the link is known to be encrypted. Internet telephone facilities must not be employed to discuss sensitive Company X information unless the link is encrypted [a link to the Internet acceptable use policy could go here].

DECLASSIFICATION AND DOWNGRADING

Dates For Reclassification—If known, the date that Secret or Confidential information will no longer be sensitive or declassified must be indicated on all Company X sensitive information. This will assist those in possession of the information with its proper handling, even if these people have not been in recent communication with the information's Owner. Those workers in possession of sensitive information that was slated to be declassified on a date that has come and gone, but is not known definitively to have been declassified, must check with the information Owner before they disclose the information to any third parties.

Classification Extensions—The designated information Owner may, at any time prior to scheduled declassification or downgrading, extend the period that information is to remain at its current classification level. To achieve this, the Owner must change the declassification or downgrading date appearing on the original document, notify all known recipients and Custodians, initiate a cost-effective search for additional recipients, and notify the Company X archives Custodian. Owners must not to specify a date for declassification or downgrading unless they are relatively sure that the date will not be changed.

Notifications—The designated information Owner may, at any time, declassify or downgrade the classification of information entrusted to his or her care. To achieve this, the Owner must change the classification label appearing on the original document, notify all known recipients and Custodians, and notify the Company X archives Custodian.

Schedule For Review—To determine whether sensitive information may be declassified or downgraded, at least once annually, information Owners must review the sensitivity classifications assigned to information for which they are responsible. From the standpoint of sensitivity, information must be declassified or downgraded as soon as practical. Owners must follow the guidelines for declassification and downgrading as specified in the information ownership policy [a link to that policy could be placed here].

No Unauthorized Downgrading—Workers must not move information classified at a certain sensitivity level to a less sensitive level unless this action is a formal part of a declassification or downgrading process approved by the Owner.

DESTRUCTION AND DISPOSAL

Destruction And Disposal—All Company X information must be destroyed or disposed of when no longer needed for business purposes. To support this policy, information Owners must review the continued value and usefulness of information on a periodic basis.

Owners also must review the data retention schedule issued by the Legal department to determine the minimum legal periods that information must be retained [an intranet link to the data retention schedule could be placed here].

Destruction And Locked Boxes—All sensitive information no longer being used or no longer needed must be placed in designated locked metal boxes until such time as authorized Company X personnel or a bonded destruction service picks it up. If no locked disposal boxes are in the immediate vicinity, sensitive information in hardcopy form must be either shredded or incinerated, while sensitive information in all other forms must be delivered to the Physical Security department for secure destruction. The shredders used for this purpose must create confetti or other similar small particles. Strip-cut shredders must not be used for this purpose. Erasing or reformatting magnetic media such as floppy disks is not an acceptable data destruction method. The use of overwriting programs approved by the Information Security department is permissible as a way to destroy sensitive information on magnetic storage media such as floppy disks. Only after these programs have been used can storage media containing sensitive information be reused, trashed, recycled, or donated to charity.

Destruction Approval—Workers must not destroy or dispose of potentially important Company X records or information without specific advance management approval. Unauthorized destruction or disposal of Company X records or information will subject the worker to disciplinary action including termination and prosecution. Records and information must be retained if they are likely to be needed in the future, regulation or statute requires their retention, or they are likely to be needed for the investigation or prosecution of unauthorized, illegal, or abusive acts. Any questions about data destruction must be referred to the information Owner or the Owner's delegate.

Permissible Destruction—Workers may destroy Company X records when approval has been granted by verbal instructions from the Owner or the Owner's delegate, an Information Security department or Archive department memo detailing the type of records that may be destroyed and when, or the records retention and disposition schedule issued by the Legal department. Destruction is defined as any action that prevents the recovery of information from the storage medium on which it is recorded.

Intermediate Products—All materials used in the handling of sensitive information, which could be analyzed to deduce sensitive information, must be destroyed in a manner similar to that required for sensitive information. This policy covers typewriter ribbons, carbon paper sheets, mimeograph stencil masters, photographic negatives, aborted computer hardcopy output, and unacceptable photocopies.

Photocopies—All waste copies of Secret information that are generated in the course of copying, printing, or other sensitive information handling must be destroyed according to the instructions found in this policy. If a copy machine jams or malfunctions when workers are making copies of Secret information, the involved workers must not leave the machine until all copies of the information are removed from the machine or destroyed beyond recognition.

Equipment Disposal Or Servicing—Before computer or communications equipment is sent to a vendor for trade, servicing, or disposal, all Company X sensitive information must be destroyed or concealed according to methods approved by the Information Security department. Internal hard drives and other computer storage media may not be donated to charity, disposed of in the trash, or otherwise recycled unless they have been subjected to overwriting processes approved by the Information Security department.

PHYSICAL SECURITY

Office Access—Access to every office, computer room, and work area containing sensitive information must be physically restricted. Management responsible for the staff working in these areas must consult the Physical Security department to determine the appropriate access control method.

Locked When Not In Use—When not in use, sensitive information must be protected from unauthorized disclosure. When left in an unattended room, such information must be locked in appropriate containers. If a Custodian of such information believes he or she will be away for less than 30 minutes, the information may be left on a desk or in some other readily-observed spot only if all doors and windows to the unattended room are closed and locked.

Unauthorized Screen Viewing—The screens on computers used to handle sensitive information must be positioned such that unauthorized persons cannot readily look over the shoulder of the person using the workstation. Screens should be positioned such that sensitive information cannot be seen through windows or skylights using binoculars or telescopes.

SPECIAL CONSIDERATIONS FOR SECRET INFORMATION

Background Checks—All workers who will have access to Secret information must have passed a standardized background check performed by the Human Resources department. Access to Secret information must not be provided before this background check is completed.

Storage On Personal Computers—If Secret information is going to be stored on a personal computer, portable computer, personal digital assistant, or any other single-user system, the system must support and continuously run an access control package approved by the Information Security department. When these users are not currently accessing or otherwise actively using the Secret information on such a machine, they must not leave the machine without logging off, invoking a screen saver, or otherwise restricting access to the Secret information.

Numbering Document Copies—All copies of Secret documents must be individually numbered with a sequence number to ensure that the persons responsible for the documents and the location of the documents can both be readily tracked. Hardcopy manifestations of Secret information must include the words "Do Not Copy Without Explicit Permission From The Information Owner."

Secret Information Logs—When Secret information is involved, the Owner or delegate of the Owner must keep a log reflecting the number of copies made, the location of copies, the names of recipients, the addresses of recipients, and any persons viewing the copies. This log must be maintained as long as such information retains a Secret sensitivity classification. This log also must be classified as Secret. All production application systems that handle Secret Company X information must generate logs that show every addition, modification, and deletion to such Secret information.

Removal From Offices—Secret Company X information must not leave Company X offices unless the approval of the Information Security manager has been obtained.

Couriers—Secret information in hardcopy form must be sent by trusted courier or registered mail. Other methods such as regular mail are prohibited. All deliveries of Secret information must be conducted such that the intended recipient personally acknowledges that the information has been received. Delivery of Secret information to intermediaries such as receptionists is prohibited.

Transportation With Computers—Workers in the possession of portable, laptop, notebook, handheld, personal digital assistant, and other transportable computers containing Secret Company X information must not leave these computers unattended at any time unless the Secret information has been encrypted. If Secret data is to be transported in computer-readable storage media, it must be in encrypted form.

Viewing In Public—Workers must avoid traveling on public transportation when in the possession of Secret information. Secret information must not be read, discussed, or otherwise exposed on airplanes, or in restaurants, elevators, restrooms, or other public places. Company X workers must not take Secret Company X information into another country unless permission has been obtained from the Physical Security manager.

Storage—Computerized Secret information must be encrypted when not in active use. All systems used for the processing of Secret information must be powered down immediately after processing is completed, or have these temporary storage locations overwritten with programs approved by the Information Security department.

Transmission Over Networks—If Company X Secret data is to be transmitted over any communication network, it must be sent only in encrypted form. Such networks include internal electronic mail systems, the Internet, and dial-up lines. All such transmissions must use a virtual public network or similar software as approved by the Information Security department.

Transfer To Another Computer—Before any Secret information may be transferred from one computer to another, the person making the transfer must ensure that access controls on the destination computer are commensurate with access controls on the originating computer. If comparable security cannot be provided with the destination system's access controls, then the information must not be transferred.

Fax Transmission—Secret information must not be sent to an unattended fax machine unless the destination machine is in a locked room for which only people authorized to receive the information possess the keys. Transmission to a fax server that uses passwords to control access to received faxes is a permissible exception to this policy. All fax transmissions containing Secret data must also employ an encrypted link.

Speaker Phones—Secret information must not be discussed on speakerphones unless all participating parties acknowledge that no unauthorized persons are in close proximity such that they might overhear the conversation. Workers must refrain from leaving messages containing Secret information on answering machines or voice mail systems.

Telephone Conversations—Workers must take steps to avoid discussing sensitive information when on the telephone. If discussion of such information is absolutely required, workers must use guarded terms and refrain from mentioning sensitive details beyond those needed to get the job done.

Approved By: [insert approval executive's name]

Approval Date: DD/MM/YY

Effective Date: DD/MM/YY

Version Number: XX

Responsible Department: [insert responsible department name]

Chapter 17 SAMPLE DATA CLASSIFICATION QUICK REFERENCE TABLE

Table 17-1: HIGHLY RESTRICTED Classification Table

Action	Requirement
Storage on Fixed Media	Encrypted
Storage on Exchangeable Media	Encrypted
Copying	Permission of Owner Required
Faxing	Encrypted Link plus Password Protected Recipient Mailbox or Attended Receipt
Sending By Public Network	Encrypted
Disposal	Shredding or Secure Disposal Boxes
Release to Third Parties	Owner Approval and Non-Disclosure Agreement
Electronic Media Labeling Required	External and Internal Labels
Hardcopy Labeling Required	Each Page if Loose Sheets
	Front and Back Covers, and Title Page if Bound
Internal and External Mail Packaging	Address to Specific Person but Label Only on the Inside Envelope
Granting Access Rights	Owner Only
Tracking Process by Log	Recipients, Copies Made, Locations, Addresses, Those Who Viewed, and Destruction

Table 17-2: CONFIDENTIAL Classification Table

Action	Requirement
Storage on Fixed Media	Encrypted or Physical Access Control
Storage on Exchangeable Media	Encrypted
Copying	Permission of Owner Advised
Faxing	Password Protected Recipient Mailbox or Attended Receipt
Sending By Public Network	Encrypted
Disposal	Shredding or Secure Disposal Boxes
Release to Third Parties	Owner Approval and Non-Disclosure Agreement
Electronic Media Labeling Required	External and Internal Labels
Hardcopy Labeling Required	Each Page if Loose Sheets
	Front and Back Covers, and Title Page if Bound
Internal and External Mail Packaging	Address to Specific Person but Label Only on the Inside Envelope
Granting Access Rights	Owner Only
Tracking Process by Log	Not Required

Table 17-3: INTERNAL USE ONLY Classification Table

Action	Requirement
Storage on Fixed Media	Encryption Optional
Storage on Exchangeable Media	Encryption Optional
Copying	No Restrictions
Faxing	No Restrictions
Sending By Public Network	Encryption Optional
Disposal	Ordinary Trash Can
Release to Third Parties	Non-Disclosure Agreement
Electronic Media Labeling Required	No Label Required
Hardcopy Labeling Required	No Label Required
Internal and External Mail Packaging	Only One Envelope with No Markings
Granting Access Rights	Local Manager
Tracking Process by Log	Not Advised

Table 17-4: PUBLIC Classification Table

Action	Requirement
Storage on Fixed Media	Encryption Not Advisable
Storage on Exchangeable Media	Encryption Not Advisable
Copying	No Restrictions
Faxing	No Restrictions
Sending By Public Network	Encryption Not Advisable
Disposal	Ordinary Trash Can
Release to Third Parties	No Restrictions
Electronic Media Labeling Required	Release Date plus Classification
Hardcopy Labeling Required	Release Date plus Classification
Internal and External Mail Packaging	Only One Envelope with No Markings
Granting Access Rights	No Restrictions
Tracking Process by Log	Not Advised

Chapter 18 SAMPLE EXTERNAL PARTY INFORMATION DISCLOSURE POLICY

DETERMINING IF DISCLOSURE IS APPROPRIATE

Duty To Take Special Care—To the extent required to perform their job duties, workers are given access to Company X sensitive internal information. Proper protection of this information is essential if the interests of not only Company X, but also customers and business partners, are to be preserved. These interests include maintenance of competitive advantage, trade secret protection, and preservation of personal privacy. As indicated in the non-disclosure agreement signed by all workers, special care must be taken to prevent disclosure of sensitive internal information to unauthorized third parties.

Sources Of Additional Information—While this policy describes the considerations that workers should bear in mind before, during, and after disclosure to third parties, it cannot specifically address every possible situation. Questions about the disclosure of specific information must be directed to the relevant information Owner [insert a link to the corporate data dictionary that indicates who is the Owner for various types of information]. Additionally, workers are expected to extend these policies to fit the specific circumstances they face, to use their professional judgement, and ask the Information Security department for guidance in those instances where the appropriate handling of sensitive information is unclear.

Two Types Of Information—For the purpose of this policy, there are basically two types of information. The first type of information has been approved for release to a specific group such as customers, an organization such as a regulatory agency, or an individual such as a contractor. Information that has been specifically designated as Public also falls into this first category. If the party requesting information falls within the limits of the approved group of recipients, or if the Public label has been applied, then no Owner approval is required. The second type of information has not yet been approved for release to a specific group, organization, or individual. This policy discusses the specific requirements for dealing with the second category. Additional guidance may be found in the Information Classification Policy [insert an intranet link to that policy].

Third Parties And The Need To Know—Unless it has specifically been designated as Public, all Company X internal information must be protected from unauthorized disclosure to third parties. Third parties may be given access to Company X internal information only when a demonstrable need to know exists, and when such a disclosure has been expressly authorized by the relevant Company X information Owner.

Non-Disclosure Agreements—The disclosure of sensitive information to consultants, contractors, temporaries, volunteers, outsourcing organization staff, and other third parties must be preceded by the receipt of a signed non-disclosure agreement (NDA). When an NDA pertains to an organization, to be valid, an officer of the recipient organization must sign the NDA. Workers must not sign NDAs provided by third parties without the advance authorization of Company X legal counsel designated to handle intellectual property matters.

Disclosing Information Belonging To Third Parties—Company X workers must not disclose third-party information to other third parties unless the third party providing the information or the legal Owner of the information has provided advance approval of the disclosure. Even when this disclosure has been approved in advance, the receiving party must sign a non-disclosure agreement.

Third-Party Requests For Company X Information—Unless a worker has been authorized by the information Owner to make disclosures, all requests for information about Company X and its business must be referred to the Public Relations department [insert an intranet link to that department's page]. Such requests include questionnaires, surveys, and newspaper interviews. This policy does not apply to sales and marketing information about Company X products and services, nor does it pertain to customer requests for information that has been approved for release to customers.

Prior Review—Every speech, presentation, technical paper, book, or other communication to be delivered to the public must be approved for release by the involved employee's immediate manager. This policy applies if the employee will represent Company X or discuss Company X affairs, or if the communication is based on information obtained in the course of performing Company X duties. If new products, research results, corporate strategies, customer information, or marketing approaches are to be divulged, approval of the director of Research and Development and the director of the Legal department must be obtained.

Releasing Information About Internal Events—Specific information about Company X internal events, including new products and services, staff promotions, reorganizations, and information system problems, must not be released to third parties, including members of the news media, without specific authorization from the Public Relations department.

Discussions In Public Forums—Care must be taken to properly structure comments and questions posted to electronic bulletin boards, mailing lists, online news groups, and related forums on public networks like the Internet. Care must be taken when wording requests for proposals and help wanted advertisements so that strategic directions, new products, and other sensitive information are not indirectly divulged. If a worker is part of a project team developing an unannounced new product or service, a research and development effort, or related confidential Company X matters, all related postings must be cleared with one's manager prior to being posted to any public network. Workers must be careful not to reveal specifics about Company X internal systems through public postings.

RESOLVING PROBLEMS WITH DISCLOSURE PROCESSES

Unassigned Owner—If the Company X internal information being considered for disclosure to a third party does not have a designated Owner, then the disclosure decision must be made by the Company X Information Security manager. Before referring such decisions to the Information Security manager, those workers handling a request for disclosure must consult the corporate data dictionary to determine whether an Owner has been assigned [insert a link to the corporate data dictionary here, which indicates the Owners for certain types of information]. Workers also can ask the designated information Custodian to identify the Owner.

Unmarked Information—If the information being considered for disclosure to third parties is not marked with an appropriate information classification, workers must assume that the information is Company X Internal Use Only information, and not approved for public release. Information marked Public does not require Owner approval prior to release to third parties.

Marking Preservation—The worker disclosing Company X internal information to third parties must preserve markings indicating author, date, version number, usage restrictions, and other details that might be useful in determining the approved usage, currency, accuracy, and relevance of the information. An exception may be made, with Owner approval, in those cases where such markings would reveal Company X information that should not be disclosed to the third party.

Disclaimers—It is the information Owner's responsibility to ensure that when controversial, frequently changing, highly uncertain, or potentially-damaging information is released to third parties that it contain the appropriate legal disclaimers. Such disclaimers, generally provided by the Company X Legal department, include words that limit Company X liability, define the information's intended uses, and inform recipients of potential problems associated with the information.

Naming—The terminology used to refer to information released to the third parties must be consistent with the terminology employed in the Company X corporate data dictionary. Exceptions are permissible in those cases where specialized technical terms would not be readily understandable to a third party, or where use of such terms would reveal information that Company X does not wish to disclose. If there is any difference between the terminology used within Company X and the terminology used within the information disclosed to a third party, this difference must be approved in advance by the designated Owner.

REQUIRED DISCLOSURE RECORDS

Disclosure Records—The worker releasing the information to the third party must maintain records reflecting the sensitive Company X internal information that has been distributed to third parties. Such records must indicate the types of information disclosed, the receiving third party's name and contact information, and the date of release. Even though a confidentiality agreement may have been signed, and although management has approved third-party access to certain information, it is the responsibility of the worker releasing the information to keep records reflecting the information disclosed.

Recovery Or Destruction—All copies of Secret information provided to third parties must be returned to the worker within Company X who provided it. All such copies must be destroyed and a certificate of destruction sent to the worker within Company X who provided it. Such recovery or destruction must occur within a month of the time when the information ceases to be useful for the intended purposes. The Company X worker who provided the information is responsible for recovering the information or obtaining a certificate of destruction. This Company X worker must note the recovery or destruction of the information in his or her records reflecting disclosures.

Reporting Improper Disclosures—If sensitive information has been inappropriately disclosed, or is believed to have been inappropriately disclosed, the circumstances must be reported immediately to the relevant information Owner. If an Owner has not been assigned for the information, the Legal department must be informed immediately. It is the Owner's responsibility to determine whether the disclosure or suspected disclosure must be reported to third parties such as government banking regulators, criminal justice system personnel, customers, and others. If no Owner has been assigned, this decision is the Legal department's responsibility.

PREPARING INFORMATION FOR DISCLOSURE

Using The Best Information—Authorized disclosures of Company X internal information must be performed with the most current, accurate, timely, and relevant information available. The worker disclosing the information must be aware of and extract the information from the system of record, or the definitive master copy of such information within Company X. If the worker involved is not aware of the system of record, the corporate data dictionary can provide this information [an intranet link to the data dictionary could be inserted here].

Updates To Previously Disclosed Information—Owners must have correct information that has been made public, or that has been disclosed to certain third parties, if subsequent events have made this information misleading or materially incorrect. Timely and prompt correction of the previously disclosed information is especially important in those instances where the public or a third party is likely to rely on the information in its decision-making processes. This requirement does not apply if the disclosure took place a year or more in the past, and the information is unlikely to be in use.

Designated Source For Public Disclosures—Information generated by Company X and released to the public must be accompanied by the name of a designated staff member acting as the single recognized official source and point of contact. All updates and corrections to this information that are released to the public must flow through this official source.

Phased Disclosure Of Controversial Information—Unless prevented from doing so by court order, controversial and sensitive Company X information must be released to the public in installments.

Chapter 19 SAMPLE INFORMATION OWNERSHIP POLICY

New Centrality Of Information—Information is no longer simply something that supports the provision of a product or service. Information has become a product that Company X now offers. Information has become a critical and integral part of other products and services that Company X provides. The new centrality of information necessitates the establishment of new roles and responsibilities to properly manage and protect it. To this end, this policy defines the information security roles and responsibilities of Owners, Custodians, and users. Information security can no longer be a concern of technical specialists alone. A large team of individuals must address it. This team is made up of every Company X worker who comes into contact with Company X information or information systems.

Policy Scope And Applicability—This policy applies to the handling of all Company X production information, regardless of the origin of this information. Production information is information routinely used to perform important business activities or routinely used to support management decision making. This policy applies despite what information handling technology is used, where the information resides, how the information is employed to meet business needs, and which users have access to the information. This policy applies regardless of geographical region, to all Company X units, all subsidiaries and other companies controlled by Company X, and all third parties performing business on behalf of Company X or these other entitles.

Roles And Responsibilities Of Owners—Information Owners are senior business unit managers with the authority for acquiring, creating, and maintaining information and information systems within their assigned area of control. Owners are responsible for categorizing the information for which they have been designated an Owner using the classifications defined in the Data Classification Policy [a link to that document through the intranet can be inserted here]. To assist with contingency planning efforts, Owners also are responsible for categorizing information, or specific application systems, according to a criticality scale defined by the Information Security department [a link to a separate intranet page dealing with contingency planning matters can be inserted here]. Owners are responsible for authorizing user access to information based on the need to know [a link to that specific policy in an overall information security policy document can be inserted here]. Designated information Owners are responsible for establishing and updating specific written policies regarding the categories of people who will be granted permission to access information. As needed, these policies must specify limitations on the use of this information by those to whom access has been granted. The Information Security department will provide Owners with training, reference material, and consulting assistance so that they may appropriately make these and related decisions and distinctions. Owners also must make decisions about the permissible uses of information including relevant business rules. Owners are responsible for choosing appropriate information systems, and relevant controls for information handled by these systems, consistent with policies and standards issued by the Information Security department [an intranet link to these policies can be inserted here]. For example, Owners must define the validation rules used to verify the correctness and acceptability of input data. These validation rules and other controls for protecting information must be formally approved in writing by the relevant Owner before major modifications can be made to production application systems. Owners must understand the uses and risks associated with the information for which they are accountable. This means that they are responsible for the consequences associated with improper disclosure, insufficient maintenance, inaccurate classification labeling, and other security-related control deficiencies pertaining to the information for which they are the designated Owner.

Roles And Responsibilities Of Custodians—Information Custodians are individuals, often staff within the Information Systems department or local department system administrators, in physical or logical possession of information from Owners. Custodians are charged with the provision of information systems services consistent with the instructions of Owners, including information security measures such as encryption. Using physical and logical access control systems, Custodians must protect the information in their possession from unauthorized distribution, access, alteration, destruction, or usage. Custodians also are responsible for providing and administering general controls such as backup and recovery systems consistent with the policies and standards issued by the Information Security department. Custodians are responsible for establishing, monitoring, and operating information systems in a manner consistent with policies and standards issued by the Information Security department [a link to those policies could be inserted here]. Custodians must provide Owners with regular reports about the resources consumed on their behalf, often through a charge-back system, and reports indicating user activities. Custodians must not change the production information in their possession unless they have received explicit and temporary permission from either the Owner or an authorized user.

Roles And Responsibilities Of Users—Information users are individuals who have been granted explicit authorization to access, modify, delete, or utilize information by the relevant Owner. Users must use the information only for the purposes specifically approved by the Owner. Users are not permitted to make additional copies of, or otherwise reproduce or disseminate sensitive information unless the Owner has expressly agreed. Users also must comply with all security measures defined by the Owner, implemented by the Custodian, or defined by the Information Security department. Users must additionally refrain from disclosing information in their possession, unless it has been designated as Public, without obtaining permission from the Owner [a link to external disclosure policy could be inserted here]. Users must report to the Information Security department all situations where they believe an information security vulnerability or violation may exist [a link to the help desk trouble ticket system or another reporting mechanism could be inserted here]. Local management also must provide users with sufficient time to receive periodic information security training, and users are required to attend such training on a periodic basis. Users of personal computers have special responsibilities, for example relating to backups and virus screening, that are defined in the Personal Computer Security Policy [an intranet link to that document could be inserted here].

Multiple Roles And Responsibilities—It is likely that certain individuals will act in multiple capacities with respect to certain types of information. For example, an employee may be the creator of a new type of production information that is stored in a desktop personal computer. In this case, the worker must, at least temporarily, act in the capacity of Owner, Custodian, and user. To achieve a more secure operating environment, separate individuals must perform the roles of Owner, Custodian, and user wherever production information has more than one user. Creators of new

types of production information must promptly inform the Information Systems Architecture group within the Information Technology department so that appropriate roles and responsibilities may be established and maintained.

Designating Owners—If there are several potential information Owners, the chief information officer must assign ownership responsibility to the senior manager of the business unit that makes the greatest use of the information. When acting in his or her capacity of Owner, this individual must take into consideration the needs and interests of other stakeholders who rely upon or have an interest in the information. With the exception of operational computer and network information, managers in the Information Systems department must not be Owners for any information. An Owner's roles and responsibilities may be delegated to any full-time manager in the Owner's business unit. An Owner's roles and responsibilities may not be assigned or delegated to contractors, consultants, or individuals at outsourcing organizations or external service bureaus.

Designating Custodians—Management must specifically assign responsibility for the control measures protecting every major production type of information [a link to a corporate data dictionary that defines these types of information could be inserted here]. Owners are responsible for identifying all those individuals who are in possession of the information for which they are the designated Owner. These individuals by default become Custodians. Although special care must be taken to clearly specify security-related roles and responsibilities when outsiders are involved, it is permissible for Custodians to be contractors, consultants, or individuals at outsourcing organizations or external service bureaus.

Designating Users—Users may be employees, temporaries, contractors, consultants, or third parties with whom special arrangements, such as non-disclosure agreements, have been made [a link to a non-disclosure form could be inserted here]. All users must be known to and authorized by Owners. The security-relevant activities of all users must be tracked and logged by Custodians. Users must always be specific individuals. Users must not be defined as departments, project teams, or other groups.

Changes In Status—The individuals who play the roles of information Owners, Custodians, and users will change on a regular basis. It is the responsibility of the local manager of all individuals to promptly report status changes to the corporate Human Resources department. As soon as they are known, status changes must be reflected in the corporate Human Resources database immediately. These changes in worker status will be automatically communicated to the Information Security department and local system administrators. Custodians must maintain access control systems so that previously-provided user privileges are no longer provided whenever there has been a user status change. When a Custodian has a change in status, it is the responsibility of the Owner to promptly assign a new Custodian, and to assist the new Custodian with the assumption of tasks previously performed by the former Custodian, including necessary training. When an Owner has a change in status, it is the chief information officer's responsibility to promptly designate a new Owner [Owners could be listed on the corporate data dictionary page that is accessible through the intranet and a link to that page could be provided here].

Handling Of Information Following Status Changes—Users who change their status must leave all production information with their immediate manager. Soon after a user has a change of status, both computer-resident files and paper files must be reviewed by the user's immediate manager to determine who should be given possession of the files, or the appropriate methods to be used for file disposal or destruction. The manager must promptly reassign the user's duties and specifically delegate responsibility for information formerly in the user's possession. It is this manager's responsibility to train the new user so that the new user is able to fully perform the tasks previously performed by the former user. It is this manager's responsibility that the new user become acquainted with the relationships that the previous user had with both insiders and outsiders, and become acquainted with all pending transactions and incomplete projects handled by the previous user.

Periodic Privilege List Review—Each calendar quarter, the Information Security department must provide Owners with a list of users who are authorized to access the information for which the Owners are responsible. Within 10 business days after the receipt of such a list, Owners must return to the Information Security department their approval of all current permissions given to the users of the information for which they are the designated Owner, and any corrections or deletions that may be necessary.

Externally-Supplied Information—In the course of normal business activities, Company X often takes possession of third-party sensitive information. Whenever a non-disclosure agreement (NDA) has been signed, an internal Company X Owner must be assigned for information so received [a link to an online NDA form could be inserted here]. The manager of the business unit utilizing the information is ordinarily designated as the Owner. The Owner must promptly report the existence of this third-party information to the Information Architecture group within the Information Technology department for inclusion in the corporate data dictionary [a link for a form to report such information could be inserted here]. This third-party information must be labelled with the appropriate data classification category and treated as though it was Company X internal information with the same classification [a link to a data classification policy could be inserted here]. The roles and responsibilities for Custodians and users are also relevant to externally-supplied information.

Corporate Data Dictionary—To assist with the management of information, the Information Systems department must compile and annually update a corporation-wide data dictionary and other high-level descriptions of the major Company X information assets found in production systems. It is the responsibility of the chief information officer to ensure that this data dictionary includes a current indication of the Owners for all major Company X production information assets. It is the responsibility of all Owners to know the identity of the Custodians and users for the information types that have been entrusted to their care.

Supporting Role Of Information Architecture Group—Although not directly involved with Owners, Custodians, and users in day-to-day information handling activities, the Information Architecture group in the Information Technology department is responsible for developing and maintaining an enterprise information architecture. The Information Architecture group is also responsible for the creation and maintenance of a corporate data dictionary, including appropriate definitions for various types of production information. The Information Architecture group is furthermore responsible for building a database that tracks the people playing the roles of Owner and Custodian. Working in conjunction with the Information Security department, the Information Architecture group is additionally responsible for fostering the efficient and appropriately-secured sharing of Company X production information.

System of Record—Each Owner must designate a system of record that will serve as the most authoritative copy of the information under his or her care. Updates to this information must be made to the system of record before or at the same time that updates are made to other systems containing this information. It is the Owner's responsibility to ensure that all production copies of the information for which he or she is the designated Owner are maintained with appropriate controls to ensure a reasonable degree of information accuracy, timeliness, and integrity.

Risk Acceptance Process—In rare circumstances, exceptions to information security policies and standards will be permitted if the information Owner, the director of the Information Security department, and the chief information officer have all signed a properly completed risk acceptance form. In the absence of such management approval reflected on a risk acceptance form, all Owners, Custodians, and users must consistently observe relevant Company X information security policies and standards.

Notifications Of Loss Or Disclosure—If sensitive information is lost, disclosed to unauthorized parties, or suspected of being lost or disclosed to unauthorized parties, its Owner and the director of the Information Security department must be notified immediately.

Approved By: [insert approving executive's name]

Approved Date: DD/MM/YY

Effective Date: DD/MM/YY

Version Number: XX

Chapter 20 SAMPLE FIREWALL POLICY

Policy Objective And Scope—Firewalls are an essential component of the Company X information systems security infrastructure. Firewalls are defined as security systems that control and restrict network connectivity and network services. Firewalls establish a control point where access controls may be enforced. Connectivity defines which computer systems are permitted to exchange information. A service is sometimes called an application, and it refers to the way for information to flow through a firewall. Examples of services include file transfer protocol (FTP) and web browsing (HTTP). This policy defines the essential rules regarding the management and maintenance of firewalls at Company X and it applies to all firewalls owned, rented, leased, or otherwise controlled by Company X workers.

Playing The Role Of Firewalls—In some instances, systems such as routers, air gaps, telecommunications front ends, or gateways may be functioning as though they are firewalls when they are not formally known as firewalls. All Company X systems playing the role of firewalls, whether they are formally called firewalls, must be managed according to the rules defined in this policy. In some instances this will require that these systems be upgraded so that they support the minimum functionality defined in this policy.

Policy Applicability—All firewalls on Company X networks, whether managed by employees or by third parties, must follow this policy. Departures from this policy will be permitted only if approved in advance and in writing by the Information Security manager.

Required Documentation—Prior to the deployment of every Company X firewall, a diagram of permissible paths with a justification for each, and a description of permissible services accompanied by a justification for each, must be submitted to the Information Security manager. Permission to enable such paths and services will be granted by the Information Security manager only when these paths or services are necessary for important business reasons, and sufficient security measures will be consistently employed. The conformance of actual firewall deployments to the documentation provided will be periodically checked by the Internal Audit department. Any changes to paths or services must go through this same process as described below.

Default To Denial—Every connectivity path and service that is not specifically permitted by this policy and supporting documents issued by the Information Security department must be blocked by Company X firewalls. The list of currently approved paths and services must be documented and distributed to all system administrators with a need to know by the Information Security department. An inventory of all access paths into and out of Company X internal networks must be maintained by the Information Security department.

Connections Between Machines—Real-time connections between two or more Company X computer systems must not be established or enabled unless the Information Security department has determined that such connections will not unduly jeopardize information security. In many cases, firewalls or similar intermediate systems must be employed. This requirement applies no matter what the technology employed, including wireless connections, microwave links, cable modems, integrated services digital network lines, and digital subscriber line connections. Any connection between an in-house Company X production system and any external computer system, or any external computer network or service provider, must be approved in advance by the Information Security department.

Regular Testing—Because firewalls provide such an important control measure for Company X networks, their strength and proper configuration must be tested on a regular basis. Where vendor software supports it, this testing must include the use of software agents that automatically check to determine whether firewalls remain configured and running in a manner that is consistent with both Company X security policies and the Company X Information Security Architecture group. This testing process must include consideration of defined configuration parameters, enabled services, permitted connectivity paths, current administrative practices, and adequacy of the deployed security measures. These tests must include the regular execution of vulnerability identification software and the regular performance of penetration tests. These tests must be performed by technically proficient persons, either in the Internal Audit department. or working for a third-party contractor. Those responsible for either the administration or management of the involved firewalls must not perform these tests.

Logs—All changes to firewall configuration parameters, enabled services, and permitted connectivity paths must be logged. All suspicious activity that might be an indication of either unauthorized usage or an attempt to compromise security measures also must be logged. The integrity of these logs must be protected with checksums, digital signatures, encryption, or similar measures. These logs must be promptly removed from the recording systems and stored in a physically protected container for at least six months after the time they were recorded. These logs must be reviewed periodically to ensure that the firewalls are operating in a secure manner.

Intrusion Detection—All Company X firewalls must include intrusion detection systems approved by the Information Security department. Each of these intrusion detection systems must be configured according to the specifications defined by the Information Security department. Among other potential problems, these intrusion detection systems must detect unauthorized modifications to firewall system files, and detect denial of service attacks in progress. Such intrusion detection systems must also immediately notify by pager the technical staff that is in a position to take corrective action. All technical staff working on firewalls must be provided with remote access systems and privileges so that they can immediately respond to these incidents even when they are physically removed from the firewall.

Contingency Planning—Technical staff working on firewalls must prepare and obtain Information Security department approval for contingency plans that address the actions to be taken in the event of various problems including system compromise, system malfunction, system crash, system overload, and Internet service provider unavailability. These contingency plans must be kept current to reflect changes in the Company X information systems environment. These plans must be periodically tested to ensure that they will be effective in restoring a secure and reliable networking environment.

External Connections—All in-bound real-time Internet connections to Company X internal networks or multi-user computer systems must pass through a firewall before users can reach a logon banner. Aside from personal computers that access the Internet on an outbound single-user session-by-session dial-up basis, no Company X computer system may be attached to the Internet unless it is protected by a firewall. The computer systems requiring firewall protection include web servers, electronic commerce servers, and mail servers. All personal computers with digital subscriber line or cable modem connectivity must employ a firewall

approved by the Information Security department. Wherever a firewall supports it, logon screens must have a notice indicating that the system may be accessed only by authorized users, users who log on represent that they are authorized to do so, unauthorized system usage or abuse is subject to disciplinary action including criminal prosecution, and system usage will be monitored and logged.

Extended User Authentication—Inbound traffic, with the exception of Internet electronic mail, regular news distributions, and push broadcasts previously approved by the Information Security department, that accesses Company X networks through a firewall must in all instances involve extended user authentication measures approved by the Information Security department. Examples of approved extended user authentication systems include dynamic passwords and digital certificates.

Virtual Private Networks—To prevent unauthorized disclosure of sensitive and valuable information, all inbound traffic, with the exception of Internet mail, approved news services, and push broadcasts, that accesses Company X networks must be encrypted with the products approved by the Information Security department [a link to approved products list could be inserted here]. These connections are often called virtual private networks (VPNs). The VPNs permissible on Company X networks combine extended user authentication functionality with communications encryption functionality [a link to intranet page with approved information security products list could be inserted here].

Firewall Access Mechanisms—All Company X firewalls must have unique passwords or other access control mechanisms. The same password or access control code must not be used on more than one firewall. Whenever supported by the involved firewall vendor, those who administer Company X firewalls must have their identity validated through extended user authentication mechanisms. In certain high security environments designated by the Information Security manager, such as the Company X Internet commerce site, remote access for firewall administrators is prohibited. All firewall administration activities must take place in person and on site.

Firewall Access Privileges—Privileges to modify the functionality, connectivity, and services supported by firewalls must be restricted to a few technically-trained individuals with a business need for these same privileges. Unless permission from the Information Security manager has been obtained, these privileges must be granted only to individuals who are full-time permanent employees of Company X, and not to temporaries, contractors, consultants, or outsourcing personnel. All firewalls must have at least two staff members who are adequately trained to make changes, as circumstances require. Such training includes periodic refresher training course or conference attendance to permit these staff members to stay current with the latest developments in firewall technology and firewall operations. Care must be taken to schedule out-of-town vacations so that at least one of these firewall administration staff members is readily available at all times.

Secured Subnets—Portions of the Company X internal network that contain sensitive or valuable information, such as the computers used by the Human Resources department, must employ a secured subnet. Access to this and other subnets must be restricted with firewalls and other access control measures. Based on periodic risk assessments, the Information Security department will define the secured subnets required in the Information Security Architecture.

Demilitarized Zones—All Internet commerce servers including payment servers, database servers, and web servers must be protected by firewalls, and be located within a demilitarized zone (DMZ), a subnet that is protected from the Internet by one or more firewalls. An internal network, such as an intranet, is also protected from the DMZ subnet by one or more firewalls.

Network Management Systems—Firewalls must be configured so that they are visible to internal network management systems. Firewalls also must be configured so that they permit the use of remote automatic auditing tools to be used by authorized Company X staff members. Unless deliberately intended as a test, such automatic auditing tools must not trigger a response sequence through firewall-connected intrusion detection systems.

Disclosure Of Internal Network Information—The internal system addresses, configurations, products deployed, and related system design information for Company X networked computer systems must be restricted such that both systems and users outside the Company X internal network cannot access this information.

Secure Backup—Current offline back-up copies of firewall configuration files, connectivity permission files, firewall systems administration procedural documentation files, and related files must be kept close to the firewall at all times. A permissible alternative to offline copies involves online encrypted versions of these same files. Where systems software permits it, the automatic reestablishment of approved copies of these systems files must proceed whenever an unauthorized modification to these files has been detected.

Virus Screening and Content Screening—Virus screening software approved by the Information Security department must be installed and enabled on all Company X firewalls. Because the files passing through a firewall may be encrypted or compressed, firewall-based virus detection systems may not detect all virus-infected files. For this reason, virus-screening software is also required at all Company X mail servers, departmental servers, and desktop personal computers. Both content screening software and software that blocks users from accessing certain non-business web sites must also be enabled on all Company X firewalls.

Firewall Dedicated Functionality—Firewalls must run on dedicated machines that perform no other services, such as acting as a mail server. Sensitive or critical Company X information must never be stored on a firewall. Such information may be held in buffers as it passes through a firewall. Firewalls must have only the bare minimum of operating systems software resident and enabled on them. Where the supporting operating system permits it, all unnecessary and unused systems software must be removed from firewalls. Company X does not permit its internal information to be resident on or processed by any firewall, server, or other computer that is shared with another organization at an outsourcing facility. Outsourcing organization-provided shared routers, hubs, modems, and other network components are permissible.

Firewall Change Control—Because they support critical Company X information systems activities, firewalls are considered to be production systems. The Information Security manager must approve all changes to the software provided by vendors, excluding vendor-provided upgrades and patches, in advance. The same documentation that is required for changes on production systems must also be prepared for firewall changes.

Posting Updates—Company X firewalls must be running the latest release of software to repel these attacks. Where available from the involved vendor, all Company X firewalls must subscribe to software maintenance and software update services. Unless approved in advance by the Information Security manager, staff members responsible for managing firewalls must install and run these updates within two business days of receipt.

Monitoring Vulnerabilities—Company X staff members responsible for managing firewalls must subscribe the Computer Emergency Response Team advisories and other relevant sources providing current information about firewall vulnerabilities. Any vulnerability that appears to affect Company X networks and systems must promptly be brought to the attention of the Information Security department.

Standard Products—Unless advance written approval is obtained from the Information Security manager, only those firewalls appearing on the list of approved vendors and products may be deployed with Company X networks [insert a link to that list of approved products]. All firewall interfaces and features deployed, such as virus screening, must be consistent with the Information Security Architecture issued by the Information Security department.

Firewall Physical Security—All Company X firewalls must be located in locked rooms accessible only to those who perform authorized firewall management and maintenance tasks approved by the Information Technology department management. The placement of firewalls in an open area within a general purpose data processing center is prohibited, although placement within separately locked rooms or areas, which themselves are within a general data processing center is acceptable. These rooms must be equipped with alarms and an automated log of all persons who gain entry to the room.

Approved By: [insert approving executive's name]

Approval Date: DD/MM/YY

Effective Date: DD/MM/YY

Version Number: XX

Appendix A   LIST OF INFORMATION SECURITY POLICY REFERENCES

This list of recommended supplementary references may be consulted when writing original policies or maintaining existing policies.

Access to and Use and Disclosure of Electronic Mail on Company Computer Systems: A Tool Kit for Formulating Your Company's Policy. Electronic Messaging Association, Arlington, VA. 1996.

Checklist of Responsible Information-Handling Practices. Privacy Rights Clearing House, University of San Diego, Center for Public Interest Law, Fact Sheet #12, January 1995.

Cobb, Steven. *NCSA Firewall Policy Guide.* National Computer Security Association, Carlisle, PA. 1996. www.ncsa.com

Code of Practice for Information Security Management. British Standards Institution, Department of Trade and Industry. British Government. London, England. 1995 (second edition). Also known as BS 7799.

Corby, Michael, and Robert E. Johnston. "Intranet Security Guidelines: How To Protect The Enterprise As Your Intranet Grows," *Computer Security Journal*, vol. XIV, no. 4, 1998.

Datapolicy: Information Security in Nordic Countries. Nordic Council of Ministers, Kobenhavn, Denmark. 1993.

Draft United Nations Manual on Computer Related Crime. Canadian Department of Justice, Ottawa, Canada. September 1992.

Fair Information Practices Checklist. Direct Marketing Association, New York, NY. 1992.

Fair Information Practices Manual. Direct Marketing Association, New York, NY. 1994.

Gilbert, Gregory A. "How to Develop a Computer Security Policy," *Datapro Reports on Information Security.* McGraw-Hill. January 1989.

Gritzalis, Dimitris. "A Baseline Security Policy For Distributed Healthcare Information Systems," *Computers & Security.* vol. 16, no. 8, pp. 709-719. 1997.

Guidelines for Establishing Information Security Policies at Organizations Using Computer-based Patient Record Systems, February 1995. Computer-based Patient Record Institute Inc., 1000 E. Woodfield Road, Suite 102, Schaumburg, IL 60173 USA. Tel. 708-706-6746.

Guidelines for Information Security Education Programs at Organizations Using Computer-based Patient Record Systems, June 1995. Computer-based Patient Record Institute Inc., 1000 E. Woodfield Road, Suite 102, Schaumburg, IL 60173 USA. Tel. 708-706-6746.

Guidelines on Safeguards for Online Medical Records, 1996. American Health Information Management Association, 919 N. Michigan Ave., Suite 1400, Chicago, IL 60611-1683 USA. Tel. 312-787-2672.

Internet Usage and Security Template. On Technology Corporation. Cambridge, MA. 1997. www.on.com

Lindup, Kenneth. "A New Model for Information Security Policies," *Computers & Security.* vol. 14, pp. 691-695. 1995.

Overbeek, Paul, Wim Sipman, and Leon Strous. *Handbook of Information Security Standards.* 1994. Kluver Academic Publishers. Dordrect, The Netherlands Fax 078-334911.

Ozier, Will. *Generally-Accepted System Security Principles (GSSP).* Exposure Draft 2.0. Information Systems Security Association. Chicago, IL. November 1995. www.ibm.com/security/ wpconsul.htm

Page, Stephen B. *Establishing A System Of Policies And Procedures.* Page Publishing. Westerville, Ohio. 1998.

Ruthberg, Zella G. and Harold F. Tipton. *Handbook of Information Security Management.* Auerbach Publishers. Boston, MA. 2000.

Schweitzer, James. "Classifying Information for Security," *DataPro Reports On Information Security.* IS15-250-101. January 1989.

Wood, Charles Cresson. "Establishing Internal Technical Systems Security Standards," *Computers & Security* (UK). pp. 193-200. Elsevier. Oxford, England. August 1986.

Wood, Charles Cresson. *Information Security Roles & Responsibilities Made Easy*. PentaSafe Security Technologies, Inc. Houston, Texas. 2001.

Wood, Charles Cresson. "Principles of Secure Information Systems Design," *Computers & Security* (UK). vol. 9, no. 1, pp. 13-24. Elsevier. Oxford, England. February 1990.

Wright, Benjamin. *The Law of Electronic Commerce: EDI, Fax, and E-Mail—Technology, Proof, and Liability*. Little, Brown and Company. Boston, MA. 1991.

Appendix B LIST OF INFORMATION SECURITY PERIODICALS

2600: The Hacker Quarterly—An underground hacker how-to newsletter and magazine. P.O. Box 752, Middle Island, NY 11953-0752 USA; phone (631) 751-2600; fax (631) 474-2677; www.2600.com and 2600@well.sf.ca.us

Cipher: Newsletter of the Technical Committee on Security & Privacy—A newsletter of engineering research-oriented articles. Institute of Electrical and Electronics Engineers (IEEE) Computer Society, Code 5540, Naval Research Laboratory, Washington, DC 20375-5337 USA; phone (202) 404-7931; fax (202) 404-7942; www.ieee-security.org/cipher.html and cipher@issl.iastate.edu

Computer Fraud & Security—A newsletter that deals with the latest computer crime cases and practical management tips. Elsevier Science, 655 Avenue of the Americas, New York, NY 10010-5107 USA; phone +1-212-633-3730; fax +1-212-633-3680; www.elsevier.com and usinfo-f@elsevier.com

Computer Law & Security Report—A legalistic analysis of recent high-tech problems and what to do about them, intended for lawyers and information security specialists. Elsevier Science, 655 Avenue of the Americas, New York, NY 10010-5107 USA; phone +1-212-633-3730; fax +1-212-633-3680; www.elsevier.com and usinfo-f@elsevier.com

Computer Professionals For Social Responsibility Newsletter—An ethics-oriented review of recent developments related to information security, particularly privacy and freedom issues. Computer Professionals For Social Responsibility; PO Box 717, Palo Alto, CA 94302-0717 USA; phone (650) 322-3778; fax (650) 322-4748; www.cpsr.org and djlin@quark.cpsr.org

Computers & Security—An international information security research journal that deals with innovative developments in the information security field and focuses on recent research. Elsevier Science, 655 Avenue of the Americas, New York, NY 10010-5107 USA; phone +1-212-633-3730; fax +1-212-633-3680; www.elsevier.com and usinfo-f@elsevier.com

Computer Security Alert—A newsletter that provides practical hands-on advice and experience from other information security practitioners working in the trenches. Computer Security Institute (Division of CMP), 600 Harrison St., San Francisco, CA 94107 USA; phone (415) 947-6320, fax (415) 947-6023; www.gocsi.com and csi@cmp.com

Computer Security Journal—A journal that provides case studies and articles by experienced practitioners. Computer Security Institute, 600 Harrison St., San Francisco, CA 94107 USA; phone (415) 947-6320; fax (415) 947-6023; www.gocsi.com; csi@cmp.com

Contingency Planning & Management—A periodical that deals with management issues associated with information systems and other types of contingency planning. Witter Publishing Company, 84 Park Ave., Flemington, NJ 08822 USA; phone (908) 788-0343; fax (908) 788-3782; www.contingencyplanning.com and cpmmagazine@witterpublishing.com

Cyber Security Advisor—A newsletter that deals with the highlights of new developments in the information security field. Advisor Media (division of Aspen Publishers), 7201 McKinney Circle, Frederick, MD 21704 USA; phone (858) 278-5600; www.cybersecurityadvisor.com

Cybertek—A survival and technological magazine combined with computer anti-security (archival material only). Cybertek Magazine, PO Box 64, Brewster, NY 10509 USA; www3.l0pht.com/~oblivion//cybertek/cybertek.html

Disaster Recovery Journal: The Journal Dedicated to Corporate Disaster Recovery Planning—A journal for those responsible for managing, preparing, or supervising contingency planning (information-systems related and otherwise). Systems Support, Inc., PO Box 510110, St. Louis, MO 63151 USA; phone (314) 894-0276; fax (314) 894-7474; www.drj.com and drj@drj.com

E-Business Advisor—A periodical that deals with strategies and tools for Internet commerce. Advisor Media, 5675 Ruffin Road, Suite 200, San Diego, CA 92123 USA; phone (858) 278-5600; fax (858) 278-0300; www.advisor.com and order@advisor.com

EDPACS: The EDP Audit, Control & Security Newsletter—A newsletter that covers a wide variety of computer-security-related topics. CRC Press LLC, 2000

NW Corporate Blvd., Boca Raton, FL 33431 USA; phone (800) 272-7737 or (561) 994-0555; fax (800) 374-3401; www.crcpress.com

Emergency Preparedness Digest—A magazine that deals with contingency planning issues, many computer related. Emergency Preparedness Canada—Communications Directorate, 122 Bank Street, 2nd Floor, Ottawa, Ontario K1A 0W6 Canada; phone (613) 991-7077; fax (613) 996-0995; www.epc-pcc.gc.ca and opscen@ocipep-bpiepc.gc.ca

Emergency Preparedness News—A newsletter devoted to various contingency planning matters including crisis management. Business Publishers, 8737 Colesville Rd., Ste. 1100, Silver Spring, MD 20910-9973 USA; phone (800) 274-6737 or (301)589-5103; fax (301) 587-4530; www.bpinews.com and stet@bpinews.com

FISSEA News and Views—A newsletter that highlights information security training developments relevant to government agencies. Federal Information Systems Security Educators' Association, c/o US Department of Commerce, National Institute of Standards & Technology, 100 Bureau Drive, Mail Stop 8930, Gaithersburg, MD 20899-8930 USA; http://csrc.nist.gov/ organizations/fissea.html and fisseamembership@nist.gov; phone (301) 975-2489; fax (301) 948-0279

Fraud Intelligence—A newsletter about Internet fraud scams, fraud prevention technology, and investigation techniques. Informa Professional Publishers, Sheepen Place, Colchester, Essex CO3 3LP United Kingdom; phone +44 (0) 1206 772223; fax +44 (0) 1206 772771; www.informafinance.com/fi and informa.asia@informa.com

Frontline Solutions—A magazine that deals with bar codes, fingerprint recognition, eye blood vessel recognition, and related technologies. Advanstar Communications, Inc., 7500 Old Oak Blvd., Cleveland, OH 44130 USA; phone (440) 891-2766; fax (218) 723-9533; www.advanstar.com

Hack-Tic—A Dutch magazine that deals with computer hacking that can be accessed only through the web site. www.hacktic.nl

Information Executive—A newsletter that deals with a variety of technology topics including information security. Association of Information Technology Professionals (AITP), 315 South Northwest Highway, Suite 200, Park Ridge, IL 60068-4278 USA; phone (800) 224-9371 x226 or (847) 825-8124; fax (847) 825-1693; www.aitp.org/publications/contents.html

Information Management & Computer Security—A journal that deals with current developments in information systems control. MCB University Press Ltd., 60/62 Toller Lane, Bradford BD8 9BY, West Yorkshire, England; phone +44 (0) 1274 777700; fax +44 (0) 1274 785200; www.emeraldinsight.com/imcs.htm and feedback@emeraldinsight.com

Information Security Bulletin—A magazine that covers a wide variety of current technical and management topics. Chi Publishing Ltd.; 26 Bunkers Hill, Lincoln LN2 4QP England; phone +44 (0) 1522-858280; fax +44 (0) 1522-858280; www.chi-publishing.com or isb@chi-publishing.com

Information Security Technical Report—A journal that deals with the technical details of how to implement information security products. Elsevier Science, 655 Avenue of the Americas, New York, NY 10010-5107 USA; phone (212) 633-3730; fax (212) 633-3680; www.elsevier.com and usinfo-f@elsevier.com

Information Security—A magazine that deals with all areas of information security management. TruSecure, 1200 Walnut Bottom Road, Carlisle, PA 17013 USA; phone (888) 627-2281 or (717) 258-1816 or (781) 255-0200; fax (781) 255-0215; www.trusecure.com/html/tspub/index.shtml or info@trusecure.com

Information Systems Auditor—A magazine that deals with all aspects of information systems auditing in a concise manner. International Newsletters, PO Box 133, Witney, Oxon OX8 6ZH England; phone +44 (0) 1993 824130, fax +44 (0) 1993 824150; www.intnews.com; sales@intnews.com

Information Systems Security—A magazine that management-oriented advice about information security matters. CRC Press, 2000 Corporate Blvd. NW, Boca Raton, FL 33431 USA; phone (800) 272-7737; fax (800) 374-3401; www.crcpress.com or orders@crcpress.com

Inside Fraud Bulletin—A bulletin that deals with high-tech and low-tech investigator oriented news and articles. Maxima Partnering Limited, Hillend House, Nutley, East Sussex TN22 3HB, England; phone +44 (0) 1825 712868 or +44 (0) 1825 712069; fax +44 (0) 1825 712026; www.insidefraud.com; ifbulletin@maxima-group.com

Intelligence Online—A newsletter that deals with industrial espionage-related information security. Indigo Publications Group, 142 rue Montmarte,

F-75002 Paris, France; phone +33 1 44 88 26 10; fax +33 1 44 88 26 15; www.indigo-net.com and indigo@indigo-net.com

Information Systems Control Journal—A professional association journal that deals with EDP auditing or computer auditing. Information Systems Audit and Control Association (ISACA), 135 South LaSalle, Dept. 1055, Chicago IL 60674-1055 USA; phone (847) 253-1545; fax (847) 253-1443; www.isaca.org/jrnlhome.htm

Journal of Computer Security—A journal that deals with research and development topics associated with secure information systems. IOS Press, Nieuwe Hemweg 6B, 1013 BG Amsterdam, The Netherlands; phone +31 20 688 3355; fax +31 20 620 3419; www.iospress.nl and market@iospress.nl

Law Enforcement Product News—A magazine that deals with new products and services for the law enforcement, physical security, and corrections industries, and includes coverage of some information security products. General Communications, 100 Garfield St., Suite 300, Denver, CO 80206-5550 USA; phone (303) 322-6400; fax (303) 322-0627; www.law-enforcement.com

Managerial Auditing Journal—A journal on how the expanded role of the internal auditor is being accomplished, including ways to help rather than criticize management. MCB University Press, Limited, 60/62 Toller Lane, Bradford BD8 9BY England; phone +44 (0) 1274 777700; fax +44 (0) 1274 785200; www.mcb.co.uk/maj.htm; feedback@emeraldinsight.com

Manufacturing and Logistics IT—A newsletter that deals with the latest developments in IT security on a world-wide basis, giving special emphasis to Internet commerce supply chain security. IBC Ltd., Latimer House, 189 High Street, Potters Bar, Herts EN6 5DA England; phone +44 (0) 1707 664200; fax +44 (0) 1707 664800; www.ibcpub.com

Operations Management—A newsletter that deals with the legal and security issues associated with an Internet presence. Institutional Investor Inc., 488 Madison Ave., New York, NY 10022 USA; phone (212) 224-3800; fax (212) 224-3689; www.operationsmanagement.com or customerservice@iinews.com

Password—A magazine for information security specialists that deals with certification of professionals, standards, policies and related issues. Information

Systems Security Association (ISSA), 7044 S. 13th Street, Oak Creek, WI 53154 USA; phone (414) 768-8000, fax (414) 768-8001; www.issa-intl.org

Technical Security Branch—A newsletter that deals with information security management issues. Technical Security Branch, Technical Operations Directorate, Royal Canadian Mounted Police, 1426 St. Joseph Blvd., Gloucester, Ontario, K1A OR2 Canada; phone (613) 993-8235; fax (613) 993-7060; www.rcmp-grc.gc.ca/tsb/pubs/index_e.htm; brian.feagan@rcmp-grc.gc.ca

Risk & Continuity—A journal aimed at top management in large enterprises covering all aspects of contingency planning including information systems. Chi Publishing Ltd.; 26 Bunkers Hill, Lincoln LN2 4QP England; phone +44 (0) 1522-858280; fax +44 (0) 1522-858280; www.chi-publishing.com or subs@chi-publishing.com

Risk Management Magazine—A management-oriented publication on risk management. Risk Management Society Publishing, Inc., 655 Third Ave., New York, NY 10017 USA; phone (212) 286-9292; fax (212) 922-0716; www.rims.org and www.rmmag.com

SC Magazine—A magazine that deals with the latest product developments and reviews of these same products. West Coast Publishing, 161 Worchester Road, Suite 201, Framingham, MA 01701 USA; phone (508) 879-9792; fax (508) 879-2755; www.scmagazine.com

Security Magazine—A magazine that deals with information security and often additional information security articles. Business News Publishing, PO Box 941724, Plano, TX 95094 USA; phone (972) 509-0113; fax (972) 509-0764; www.securitymagazine.com

Security Insider Report—A newsletter that deals with information security developments. Infowar.com and Interpact, Inc., 3030 N. Rocky Drive West #240, Tampa, FL 33607 USA; phone (813) 288-1955; fax (813) 288-1985; www.infowar.com/chezwinn/sir/sir_home.html-ssi

Security Law—A newsletter that deals with court cases, some of which are information security related. Strafford Publications, 590 Dutch Valley Rd., NE, Atlanta, GA 30324-0729 USA; phone (404) 881-1141; fax (404) 881-0074; www.straffordpub.com

Security Management—A magazine that deals with a wide variety of security topics including frequent coverage of information security. American Society for

Industrial Security, 1625 Prince St., Alexandria, VA 22314-2818 USA; phone (703) 519-6200; fax (703) 519-6299; www.asisonline.org; asis@asisonline.com

Security Technology News—A newsletter that deals with biometrics, patents, and other data protection topics in addition to a variety of physical security topics. BCC Publications, 25 Van Zant St., Norwalk, CT 06855-4266 USA; phone (203) 853-4266; fax (203) 853-0348; www.bccresearch.com

Security Watch—A newsletter that deals with physical security issues, but that includes information security articles. Bureau of Business Practice, 125 Eugene O'Neill Drive, Suite 103, New London, CT 06320 USA; phone (800) 876-9105 toll-free or (860) 442-4365 international; fax (800)437-3150 toll-free; www.bbpnews.com; customer.service@ aspenpubl.com

Telecom & Data Network Security—A newsletter that deals with protecting public branch exchanges from toll fraud and "telabuse." Telecommunications Reports International, 1333 H St., NW, Suite 100 East, Washington, DC 20005-4707 USA; phone (800) 822-6338 or (202) 312-6100; fax (202) 312-6065; www.tr.com/newsletters/tns/ index.htm; customerservice@tr.com

Topical Issues on White Collar Crime—A white paper that deals with forensic and investigative nature of computer crime. Association of Certified Fraud Examiners, The Gregor Building, 716 West Ave., Austin, Texas 78701 USA; phone (800) 245-3321 or (512) 478-9070, fax (512) 478-9297; www.cfenet.com; info@cfenet.com

Appendix C LIST OF PROFESSIONAL ASSOCIATIONS AND RELATED ORGANIZATIONS

GENERIC

American National Standards Institute (ANSI), 25 West 43rd St., New York, NY 10036 USA. Tel. 212-642-4900 or 212-764-3274. Fax 212-398-0023. www.ansi.org. An organization that wrote standards on various information security issues such as encryption.

American Society for Industrial Security (ASIS), 1625 Prince St., Alexandria, VA 22314 USA. Tel. 703-519-6200. Fax 703-519-6299. www.asisonline.org. A physical security-oriented professional society that frequently addresses computer security issues in conferences and publications.

Association for Computing Machinery (ACM) Special Interest Group on Security, Auditability, and Control (SIGSAC), One Astor Plaza, 1515 Broadway, 17th floor, New York, NY 10036 USA. Tel. 800-342-6626 or 212-626-0500. Fax 212-944-1318. www.acm.org. A professional association that issues publications and a newsletter about information security.

Association of Contingency Planners (ACP), 7044 S. 13th Street, Oak Creek, WI 53154 USA. Tel. 414-768-8000 ext. 116. www.acp-international.com. The largest contingency planning organization within the information security area.

Association of Information Technology Professionals, (AITP), 315 South Northwest Highway, Suite 200, Park Ridge, IL 60068-4278. Tel. 800-224-9371 or 847-825-8124. Fax 847-825-1693. www.aitp.org and tina_turnbull@aitp.org. A management-oriented computer professional association that hosts conferences dealing with security and has a special interest group that addresses security issues.

Association For Information Management Professionals, 4200 Somerset Dr., Suite 215, Prairie Village, KS 66208 USA. Tel. 800-422-2762 or 913-341-3808. Fax 913-341-3742. www.arma.org or hq@arma.org. An organization that deals primarily with paper-resident information.

Computer Emergency Response Team (CERT), Software Engineering Institute, Carnegie Mellon University, Pittsburgh, PA 15213-3890 USA. Tel. 412-268-7090. Fax 412-268-6989. www.cert.org or cert@cert.org. An organization that monitors loss experience on the Internet and prepares special reports about vulnerabilities.

Computer Professional for Social Responsibility (CPSR), P.O. Box 717, Palo Alto, CA 94302 USA. Tel. 650-322-3778. Fax 650-322-4748. www.cpsr.org. An organization that focuses on privacy violation, ethics, and related information security issues.

Computer Security Institute (CSI), 600 Harrison St., San Francisco, CA 94107 USA. Tel. 415-947-6320. Fax 415-947-6023. www.gocsi.com or csi@cmp.com. An organization that hosts information security conferences including one of the largest information security conferences in the world, and markets an information security technical journal, related books, and a monthly newsletter.

Data Interchange Standards Association, Inc. (DISA), 333 John Carlyle St., Suite 600, Alexandria, VA 22314-5743 USA. Tel. 703-548-7005. Fax 703-548-5738. www.disa.org. An organization that handles data formatting and communications standardization issues that include security matters.

Electronic Funds Transfer Association, 950 Herndon Parkway, Suite 390, Herndon, VA 20170 USA. Tel. 703-435-9800. Fax 703-435-7157. www.efta.org. An organization that handles financial services issues including the security of electronic payments.

Electronic Industries Alliance, 2500 Wilson Blvd., Arlington, VA 22201-3834 USA. Tel. 703-907-7794. Fax 703-907-7501. www.eia.org. An alliance of many other professional associations and companies such as the Solid State And Semiconductor Technology Association, the Government Electronics and Information Technology Association, and the Consumer Electronics Association, involved with computer industry lobbying on issues such as privacy.

Electronic Messaging Association, The Open Group, 44 Montgomery St., Suite 960, San Francisco, CA 94104-4704 USA. Tel. 415-374-8280. Fax 415-374-8293. www.ema.org. A vendor-oriented technology-neutral consortium that worked on standards for electronic mail security.

Electronic Privacy Information Center (EPIC), 1718 Connecticut Ave., NW, Suite 200, Washington, DC 20009 USA. Tel. 202-483-1140. Fax 202-483-1248. www.epic.org and info@epic.org. An organization that publishes a number of influential reports about privacy.

Federal Information Systems Security Educator's Association (FISSEA), Department of Commerce, National Institute of Standards and Technology, Bldg. 820, Rm. 426, Gaithersburg, MD 20899 USA. Tel. 301-975-3883. Fax 301-948-2067. csrc.nist.gov/organizations/fissea.html. An organization that sponsors an annual conference and coordinates activities for information security educators in government.

Information Systems Audit & Control Association (ISACA), 135 South LaSalle, Dept. 1055, Chicago IL 60674-1055 USA. Tel. 847-253-1545. Fax 847-253-1443. www.isaca.org. The largest and oldest professional society directly related to information security that issues several publications on standards and a monthly magazine.

Information Systems Security Association (ISSA), 7044 S. 13th Street, Oak Creek, WI 53154 USA. Tel. 414-768-8000. Fax 414-768-8001. www.issa.org. An information security practitioner-oriented professional society that hosts annual conferences with MIS Training and provides a newsletter.

Institute of Electrical and Electronics Engineers (IEEE), 1828 L St., NW, Suite 1202, Washington, DC 20036-5104 USA. Tel. 202-785-0017. Fax 202-752-4929. www.ieee.org. An organization that hosts conferences on information security, participates in standards activities, issues a cryptography newsletter, and publishes books related to information security.

Institute of Internal Auditors (IIA), 249 Maitland Ave., Altamonte Springs, FL 32701-4201 USA. Tel. 407-830-7600. Fax 407-831-5171. www.theiia.org or iia@theiia.org. An organization that offers a financial internal auditor viewpoint and has special interest group that deals with information security.

International Federation for Information Processing (IFIP), Hofstraße 3, A-2361 Laxenburg, Austria; Tel. +43 2236 73616. Fax +43 2236 73616 9. www.ifip.or.at or ifip@ifip.or.at. An organization that provides a variety of technical conferences dealing with computer topics, including conferences on information security.

International Information System Security Certification Consortium (ISC2), Certification office: PO Box 1117, Dunedin, FL 34697 USA. Tel. 888-333-4458 or 727-738-8657. Fax 727-738-8522. Operations office: 860 Worcester Rd., Suite 101, Framingham, MA 01701 USA. Tel. 508-875-8400. Fax 508-875-8450. www.isc2.org. An organization that administers tests for the Certified Information Systems Security Professional (CISSP) examination.

International Standards Organization (ISO), Brussels, Belgium, c/o American National Standards Institute (ANSI), 25 West 43rd St., New York, NY 10036 USA. Tel. 212-642-4900. Fax 212-398-0023. www.ansi.org or ansionline@ansi.org. An organization that develops international standards on information security, notably ISO 17799, which deals with information security management.

MIS Training Institute, 498 Concord St., Framingham, MA 01702-2357 USA. Tel. 508-879-7999. Fax 508-872-1153. www.misti.com. An organization that provides a variety of audit-related information security conferences and training seminars.

National Computer Security Center (NCSC), 9800 Savage Road, Fort Meade, MD 20755-6765 USA. Tel. 800-688-6115 or 410-854-4371. Fax 410-854-4375. www.nsa.gov or radium.ansc.mil. A government agency associated with the Department of Defense and provides evaluations of information security products, guidelines for configuring certain products.

Security Industry Association, 635 Slaters Lane, Suite 110, Alexandria, VA 22314-1177 USA. Tel. 703-683-2075. Fax 703-683-2469. www.siaonline.org. An association of equipment manufacturers and other vendors in the physical security industry that deals with information security issues, develops technical standards, and engages in lobbying to obtain certain legislative results.

Society of Competitive Intelligence Professionals, 1700 Diagonal Rd., Suite 600, Alexandria, VA 22314 USA. Tel. 703-739-0696. Fax 703-739-2524. www.scip.org and info@scip.org. An organization that deals with ethical competitive intelligence gathering and industrial espionage prevention.

Software and Information Industry Association, 1090 Vermont Ave., 6th Floor, NW, Washington, DC 20005 USA. Tel. 202-289-7442. Fax 202-289-7097. www.siia.net. An organization that addresses privacy and related information security issues in its studies and Congressional testimony.

The World Institute for Security Enhancement (WISE), PO Box 4646, Miami Lakes, FL 33014 USA. Tel. 305-825-0088. Fax 305-556-9639. www.worldinstitute.org and securitytraining@pobox.com. An organization that provides education and interdisciplinary research on safety and security issues, including information security.

BY INDUSTRY

American Bankers Association, 1120 Connecticut Ave. NW, Washington, DC 20036 USA. Tel. 202-663-5000. Fax 202-663-7543. www.aba.com. An organization that prepares and promulgates standards specific to the commercial banking industry.

American Institute of Certified Public Accountants, 1211 Avenue of the Americas, New York, NY 10036 USA. Tel. 212-596-6200. Fax 212-596-6213. www.aicpa.org. An organization that prepares guidelines for auditors working on information security matters and publishes a magazine that deals with information security issues.

Bank Administration Institute, One North Franklin, Suite 1000, Chicago, IL 60606-3421 USA. Tel. 312-683-2464. Fax 312-683-2373. www.bai.org and info@bai.org. An organization that publishes a newsletter that deals with information security issues.

Canadian Institute of Chartered Accountants, 277 Wellington Street West, Toronto ON M5V 3H2, Canada. Tel. 416-977-3222. Fax 416-977-8585. www.cica.ca. An organization that has developed and published several information security-related standards.

Information Technology Industry Council (ITIC), 1250 Eye St., NW, Suite 200, Washington, DC 20005 USA. Tel. 202-737-8888. Fax 202-638-4922. www.itic.org. A computer industry consortium that is involved with lobbying and standards activities associated with information security.

International Association for Healthcare Security and Safety, P.O. Box 637, Lombard, IL 60148 USA. Tel. 888-353-0990 or 630-871-9936. Fax 630-871-9938. www.iahss.org or nancy@iahss.org. An organization that deals with security and safety issues such as patient privacy and provides educational material.

International Association of Financial Crimes Investigators, 385 Bel Marin Keys, Suite H, Novato, CA 94949 USA. Tel. 415-884-6600. Fax 415-884-6605. www.iafci.org. An association of specialists in credit card fraud, that now deals with a wide variety of financial transaction frauds.

BY MARKET SEGMENT

Cisco, c/o Advanced Network Information, 3567 Benton St., Suite 248, Santa Clara, CA 95051 USA. Tel. 408-241-1314. Fax 707-371-4967. www.ani-training.com or www.cisco.com. An organization that hosts several users groups for those involved in the technical side of the data communications area, and provides information security training courses including certifications.

Computer Associates, World Headquarters, One Computer Associates Plaza, Islandia, NY 11749 USA. Tel. 631-342-6049. Fax 516-342-8179. www.cai.com. An organization that hosts user groups for the top IBM mainframe access control packages.

International Biometric Association, 1444 I Street NW, Suite 700, Washington, DC 20005-6542 USA. Tel. 202-712-9049. Fax 202-216-9646. www.tibs.org or ibs@bostromdc.com. An association of vendors of biometric equipment and systems.

Microsoft Corporation, One Microsoft Way, Redmond, WA 98052-6399 USA. Tel. 425-882-8080. www.microsoft.com. An organization that provides user groups for customers, and certifications for information security professionals.

Redsiren Technologies, I4 Division (International Information Integrity Institute), 650 Smithfield St., Pittsburgh, PA 15222 USA. Tel. 253-952-0365. Fax 253-952-0365. www.i4online.com. An organization that provides subscription services for large organizations and focuses on practical administration aspects of information security.

SHARE (IBM users group), 401 N. Michigan Ave. Suite 2400, Chicago, IL 60611 USA. Tel. 888-574-2735 or 312-321-5160. Fax 312-644-6363. www.share.org. An organization that has prepared security requirements and published papers on information security.

Appendix D   LIST OF SUGGESTED AWARENESS-RAISING METHODS

The following topics are not organized by priority, but are grouped by the type of communication involved. Consider this list to be a menu from which appropriate activities may be selected. Do not select just one or two of the following methods, but 10 or 20 of them. Repetition of information security policy ideas is essential. Repetition impresses users and other audiences with the importance that management places on information security.

IN PERSON

- Provide special classroom-style training courses at convenient locations every year or so for users, system administrators, remote site information security coordinators, new hires, and other audiences identified in a needs analysis.

- Bring in guest speakers who have expertise in information security to talk to staff at organization-wide lunch meetings, departmental staff meetings, and other internal gatherings.

- Deliver policy ideas and other material at new employee orientation meetings.

- Send influential information systems staff to off-site information security conferences.

- Hold video conferences where people from various sites discuss information security.

- Stage vulnerability demonstrations such as tiger-team or penetration attacks.

- Set up a special demonstration computer and provide staff with a demonstration of what happens when a virulent virus attacks a personal computer.

- Conduct information security risk assessments, especially when interviewing and other methods are used to engage staff in the process.

- Have the Legal department conduct an intellectual property inventory and an associated risk assessment.

- Give small prizes such as free lunches to exemplary staff that observe policies and procedures.

- Give traffic warnings reflecting policy violations.

- Conduct internal information technology audits, checking the extent to which compliance exists.

- Bring in an outside consultant to conduct an external information technology audit looking at compliance.

- Initiate an unauthorized software duplication inventory project where personal computers are checked for illegal software.

- Install a software license management system that checks that all software in use is legitimately licensed and have discussions with people who have unauthorized software.

- Integrate information security training content with other face-to-face computer training materials, such as a course for telecommuters that is required before they telecommute.

- Require that staff take an online quiz proving that they read the information security policy, and only if they receive a passing score will they be given the system privileges that they requested.

- Require that staff take and pass a brief quiz immediately after they log on to the system, before they are permitted to accomplish anything else. Be careful about adverse productivity implications.

- Establish and promote the existence of an information security management committee.

- Establish a committee of system administrators and other first-line staff who must deal with information security.

- Host quarterly luncheons for system administrators from various sites to discuss security.

- Start disciplining staff for violations of information security policies, and let others know the reasons why disciplinary actions were used.

- Initiate strategic planning, new product development, and other initiatives that see information and information systems as a key to future competitive advantage.

- Prevent the use of new and desired system services, such as Internet access, until certain security projects like a firewall, have been completed.

- Prevent new business application software from being moved into production until adequate controls have been installed. Talk to management about the issues.

- Institute a new or more serious change control approval process, such as the prohibition against the establishment of new phone lines without getting the information security manager's approval. Talk to management about the issues.

- Declare an amnesty day for information security violators who wish to obtain technical or other assistance so that they now may be in compliance.

- Test the backups being made by departmental system administrators and discuss with department managers the adequacy of these backups.

- Adopt an annual Information Security Day on which special educational materials are presented and special events take place. Coordinate with national Computer Security Day, if possible.

- Initiate a high-profile investigation into an information security breach and engage a number of staff members in the investigation.

- Schedule top management briefings to address the strategic issues regarding changes in corporate culture to support information security.

- Conduct an internal survey of mid- and lower-level managers asking them what they think should be done to improve information security, thereby getting them to think about something that they probably do not think about much.

- Conduct a survey of customers, suppliers, and other third parties asking them what they think should be done to improve the security of computerized business activities.

- Conduct a gap analysis whereby existing information security training and awareness materials are compared to a set of messages that management wants to communicate, and prepare a management proposal to upgrade the materials.

IN WRITING

- Add information security questions to written performance reviews. A simple "Yes" or "No" may be sufficient in many organizations.

- Require a signature on a personal responsibility statement that indicates that employees consider compliance with policies to be a condition of continued employment.

- Require a signature on a form verifying that a worker has received a copy of, read, and understood the information security manual.

- Require all employees to annually sign a statement saying they have read and understood the Information Security Policy manual.

- Require users to sign a security compliance statement before they get user IDs.

- Write security articles for in-house newspapers, newsletters, and magazines.

- Periodically issue written policy statements, procedures, and technical standards.

- Issue pamphlets or brochures to end users describing a code of conduct.

- Publish a self-paced learning booklet that steps people through the basics of information security.

- Ghostwrite memos from top management reminding the staff about security.

- Distribute copies of relevant clippings from newspapers and technical magazines.

- Hang posters and signs around the office to remind people about information security.

- Print stickers and decals and place them in those locations where people will look, such as on the photocopy machine and fax machine.

- Make up special labels for disks, tape reels, and similar media, indicating sensitivity, handling instructions, and ownership.

- Post security notices on bulletin boards.

- Insert security notices in paycheck and air flight ticket envelopes.

- Integrate security ideas with systems development process documentation.

- Issue information security responsibility organizational design memos that clarify areas of confusing responsibility.

- Write expanded job descriptions for system administrators and others such that information security is explicitly included.

- Write expanded mission statements for various departments so that information security is explicitly recognized as a part of their charter.

- Prepare an information security architecture document or otherwise integrate security into the organization's technology plans.

- Issue an information security manual containing policies, contact persons, and a list of approved in-house products.

- Create checklists that discuss how to implement an information security policy.

- Write detailed backup instructions and insist that staff comply with them.

- Develop and test a contingency plan to deal with information system emergencies and disasters.

- Require that information security risk acceptance forms be signed by all managers who are in charge of units that are not in compliance and that do not intend in the near future to come into compliance.

- Prepare non-disclosure agreements and educate staff when they should be used.

- Prepare non-compete agreements and educate staff when they should be used.

- Prepare notices to be given to all people who come into contact with trade secrets, notifying them that certain information is a trade secret and must be handled according to special rules or policies.

- Prepare reports about recent information security incidents along with recommendations for control improvements that are generally distributed only to people with a need to know.

- Prepare a summary of information security laws and regulations relevant to the organization.

ON SYSTEMS

- Add security instructions to application program and system utility help screens.

- Purchase computer-based training software that runs on personal computers and requires staff to go through it. This should automatically report back to an information security officer's personal computer just how many workers have completed the training, ideally with time and date stamps, and digital signatures to create evidence that could be admissible in court, demonstrating that the worker read the policy.

- Establish online quizzes or questionnaires that determine how well staff understands information security policy material, perhaps providing prizes, or at least entries into a drawing for prizes, for those who get perfect scores.

- Before users gain access to certain applications or systems facilities, require them to go through a brief online training program.

- Prepare a personal computer security utility software disk including encryption routines, a

password access control utility, a disk scrub utility, and a self-assessment questionnaire.

- Employ written or automated questionnaires to gauge the self-assessed level of compliance.

- Use special vulnerability identification software to check security parameters, alerting security staff that problems exist. These problems could include incorrectly-installed operating systems and easily-guessed passwords.

- Install intrusion detection software to monitor break-in attempts to internal systems and use these reports as evidence of the need for greater funding.

- Set-up an in-house intranet server and post all information security documentation including forms to that server.

- Post a frequently-asked question list on the intranet, giving people answers to common information security questions, hopefully reducing the time that Information Security department staff spends answering these questions.

- Set-up key word search mechanisms on the Information Security department intranet server, so that people can quickly locate material of interest.

- Set-up job title filters for information security documentation and integrate these filters with an intranet to permit people to see only the documentation they need to see for their job title.

- Establish web site-blocking software at the firewall to control what sites staff visit and issue a memo explaining the new system.

- Install content monitoring software that looks at the material flowing through the firewall, and let staff know their communications are monitored.

- Require that all portable personal computers used for Company X business employ an access control software package including a boot password and screen blanker.

- Adopt a commercial encryption product as an in-house standard and internally publicize the ways that this will assist the organization with a move toward implementing public key infrastructure.

- Establish logging systems that detect security violations, and create a formal process for notifying users and their managers as needed.

- Change the logon banner to prohibit electronic trespassing, state that the system facilities are for business use only, and that all user activity is subject to monitoring.

- Place a notice on logon screens, at a firewall or dial-up modem pool, that says users should proceed no further unless they have reviewed and understand the information security policy.

- Establish a screen that appears after users log on that changes each time they log on, summarizes an information security policy, and requires users to click an OK button before proceeding.

- Require users to click a button indicating their agreement to comply with all information security polices at the time they log on to Company X information systems or networks.

- Change the initial invocation banners for specific applications, including electronic mail, to provide application-specific security policies or other security instructions.

- Install regularly changing on-screen reminders, such as those that display at log on.

- Use software agents that remind staff to perform certain security activities such as regularly backup their systems.

- Give system administrators the Computer Emergency Response Team electronic mail address and have them receive notices about vulnerabilities.

ON OTHER THINGS

- Write information security messages on coffee mugs, mouse pads, glass coasters, envelope openers, and other objects that are given to staff.

- Summarize security messages on note pads that are freely distributed to internal staff.

- Write information security messages on T-shirts and sweat shirts and give these to staff who have been supportive of information security efforts.

- Prepare videotapes that can be distributed to all remote locations, most often splicing material from previously-prepared videos.

- Establish a hot line with a message machine where information security problems can be reported, perhaps anonymously.

- Cycle awareness materials on kiosks with built-in personal computers, or on closed-circuit televisions in staff-only areas like a lunchroom.

- Provide messages on the organization's in-house television station.

- Write security messages on air fresheners that staff hang from their vehicle's rear-view mirror.

Appendix E   EXTERNAL NETWORK INTERFACE SECURITY POLICY HARMONIZATION

Many information systems specialists are confused when they have been instructed by management to connect their own organization's internal network with the internal network of another organization. The other organization could be a supplier, major customer, subcontractor, government agency, or outsourcing organization. These connections could, for example, be established through an extranet, third-party electronic data interchange network, or third-party business-to-business Web intermediary.

Whoever the third party or parties may be, and whatever the nature of the business arrangement, it is critical that the participants in this new network agree on certain fundamental security policies. If these security policies are incompatible, then there is a possibility that inadequate security at one organization could lead to security incidents at another organization. For example, suppose one organization employed group user IDs and had a serious argument with a particular worker, who then became disgruntled. This worker could go on to disrupt the network, but the system logs could not pinpoint exactly who was causing the trouble. Because a connection has been enabled to an outside organization, that outside organization's network-connected systems could be damaged by the disgruntled worker.

To assist with the harmonization of security policies for organizations seeking to establish a network connection, this chapter provides a list of essential policy points. These points may be used by management when negotiating the arrangement. If that did not happen, they can at least be used by technical staff when implementing the arrangement that has already been negotiated. In some cases, a review of this list will indicate that the arrangement should be renegotiated before systems reflecting this arrangement are implemented.

The intention of harmonizing security policies is to establish a baseline or a standard of due care to which all parties to the arrangement must follow. This baseline must define the minimum information security requirements that must be maintained in order to participate in the networking arrangement. Not being willing or able to meet these requirements should be sufficient justification for exclusion or expulsion from the multi-organizational networking arrangement.

The information security topic areas below are accompanied by the section number in *Information Security Policies Made Easy* where details about the topic may be found. The following list assumes that the connection to an outside organization is accomplished through the Internet. If the connection is by dial-up lines, see "9.04.03 User Authentication For External Connections" on page 308.

ACCESS CONTROL CONSIDERATIONS

User IDs reflecting individual users rather than groups of people, see "9.02.01 User Registration" on page 280.

Length of fixed passwords employed and construction rules, see "9.05.04 Password Management System" on page 319.

Required password changes after a certain time period has elapsed, see "9.05.04 Password Management System" on page 319.

Required password changes for all newly-assigned or reset passwords, see "9.02.03 User Password Management" on page 290.

Extended user authentication systems like one-time passwords, see "9.04.03 User Authentication For External Connections" on page 308.

Cookies to authenticate the usage of a specific computer used to logon, see "9.05.04 Password Management System" on page 319.

Encrypted or digital signature-protected cookies to prevent spoofing, see "9.05.04 Password Management System" on page 319.

Anonymity of users prevented through logon processes, see "9.02.01 User Registration" on page 280.

Assigned privileges of users based on the need to know, see "9.02.02 Privilege Management" on page 287.

Removal of access privileges as soon as an authorized worker departs, see "9.02.01 User Registration" on page 280.

Dormant user IDs automatically have privileges revoked, see "9.02.01 User Registration" on page 280.

Session time out after no activity for a designated period, see "9.05.07 Terminal Time-Out" on page 331.

Use of single sign-on systems or other gateways for users, see "9.05.03 User Identification And Authentication" on page 317.

Types of firewalls, routers, and other flow control systems, see "8.05.01 Network Controls" on page 183.

Use of demilitarized zones as a buffer against attackers, see "8.05.01 Network Controls" on page 183.

ENCRYPTION AND PUBLIC KEY INFRASTRUCTURE CONSIDERATIONS

Encryption process employed for sensitive transmitted data, see "8.06.03 Information Handling Procedures" on page 201.

Encryption key management process used to automatically handle keys, "10.03.05 Key Management" on page 372.

Use of hardware or software for provision of encryption, "10.03.02 Encryption" on page 367.

Digital certificates as a mechanism to identify users, "10.03.03 Digital Signatures" on page 371.

Digital certificates as a mechanism to identity servers, "10.03.03 Digital Signatures" on page 371.

Digital certificates to restrict privileges of specific users, "10.03.03 Digital Signatures" on page 371.

Background checking for issuance of digital certificates, "10.03.03 Digital Signatures" on page 371.

Cross-certification of certificate authorities to support digital certificates, "10.03.05 Key Management" on page 372.

Certificate revocation lists and other procedures for disabling users, see "10.03.05 Key Management" on page 372.

Electronic wallets to protect digital certificates and other information, see "10.03.05 Key Management" on page 372.

Digital signatures to assure absence of changes to certain data, see "10.03.05 Key Management" on page 372.

Digital signatures to assure that data originated with certain parties, see "10.03.05 Key Management" on page 372.

CHANGE CONTROL AND CONTINGENCY PLANNING CONSIDERATIONS

Virus detection and eradication software and procedures, see "8.03.01 Controls Against Malicious Software" on page 168.

Change control approval process for all modifications to the network, see "10.05.01 Change Control Procedures" on page 382.

Rapid installation of patches from firewall and operating system vendors, "10.05.02 Technical Review Of Operating System Changes" on page 389.

Testing of new software prior to use in production network environment, see "10.04.01 Control Of Operation Software" on page 380.

Computer emergency response team to mobilize against attacks, see "8.01.03 Incident Management Procedures" on page 156.

Contingency plan to deal with disasters or other significant events, see "11.01.03 Writing And Implementing Contingency Plans" on page 393.

Intrusion detection systems to notify technicians about break-ins, see "8.05.01 Network Controls" on page 183.

Physical security measures for all data centers connected to network, see "7.01.03 Securing Offices, Rooms, And Facilities" on page 133.

Uninterruptible power systems prevent downtime when power fails, see "7.02.02 Power Supplies" on page 142.

NETWORK MANAGEMENT CONSIDERATIONS

Management observation of information sent over the network—privacy, see "12.01.04 Data Protection And Privacy Of Personal Information" on page 410.

Timestamps and date-stamps to validate that certain activity occurred, see "9.07.01 Event Logging" on page 338.

Network time synchronization sources and procedures, "9.07.03 Clock Synchronization" on page 348.

Logs and audit trails recorded on servers and client machines, see "9.07.01 Event Logging" on page 338.

Network management systems and visibility of specific machines, see "8.05.01 Network Controls" on page 183.

Appendix F CHECKLIST OF STEPS IN POLICY DEVELOPMENT PROCESS

This checklist is intended to provide a quick overview of the major steps associated with the development, refinement, and approval of an internal information security policy document. For a more detailed description of the necessary development, refinement, and approval steps, see Chapter 2, "Instructions." For a list of steps to complete after a policy document has been produced, see Appendix I, "Suggested Next Steps." Many of the following steps can be pursued simultaneously or in an order different than the following:

1 Perform a risk assessment or information technology audit to determine your organization's unique information security needs. These needs must be addressed in a policy document.

2 Clarify what the word "policy" means within your organization so that you are not preparing a "standard," "procedure," or some other related material.

3 Ensure that roles and responsibilities related to information security are clarified, including responsibility for issuing and maintaining policies.

4 Convince management that it is advisable to have documented information security policies.

5 Identify the top management staff who will be approving the final information security document and all influential reviewers.

6 Collect and read all existing internal information security awareness material and make a list of the included bottom-line messages.

7 Conduct a brief internal survey to gather ideas that stakeholders believe should be included in a new or updated information security policy.

8 Examine other policies issued by your organization such as those from Human Resources management, to identify prevailing format, style, tone, length, and cross-references. The goal is to produce information that conforms with previous efforts.

9 Identify the audience to receive information security policy materials and determine whether they will each get a separate document or a separate page on an intranet site.

10 Determine the extent to which the audience is literate, computer knowledgeable, and receptive to security messages. This includes understanding the corporate culture surrounding information security.

11 Decide whether some other awareness efforts must take place before information security policies are issued. For example, one effort might show that information itself has become a critical factor of production.

12 Using ideas from the risk assessment, prepare a list of absolutely essential policy messages that must be communicated. Consult the policy statements as well the as sample policies found in this book.

13 If there is more than one audience, match the audiences with the bottom-line messages to be communicated through a coverage matrix. For more information, see Chapter 2, "Instructions."

14 Determine how the policy material will be disseminated, noting the constraints and implications of each medium of communication. An intranet site is recommended, but the appendix dealing with awareness methods provides many other alternatives.

15 Review the compliance checking process, disciplinary process, and enforcement process to ensure that they all can work smoothly with the new policy document.

16 Determine whether the number of messages is too large to be handled all at one time, and if so, identify different categories of material that will be issued at different times.

17 Have an outline of topics to be included in the first document reviewed by several stakeholders. An information security management committee is the ideal review board.

18 Based on comments from the stakeholders, revise the initial outline and prepare a first draft, extracting policies as needed from this book.

19 Have the first draft document reviewed by the stakeholders for initial reactions, presentation suggestions, and implementation ideas.

20 Revise the draft in response to comments from stakeholders. Expect this step to repeat several times.

21 Request top management approval on the policy. Changes may be necessary, in which case this step may repeat several times.

22 Prepare extracts of the policy document for selected purposes. For example, for a form signed by users receiving new or renewed user IDs and passwords.

23 Develop an awareness plan that uses the policy document as a source of ideas and requirements.

24 Create a working papers memo indicating the disposition of all comments received from reviewers, even if no changes were made.

25 Write a memo about the project, what you learned, and what needs to be fixed so that the next version of the policy document can be prepared more efficiently, better received by the readers, and more responsive to the unique circumstances facing your organization.

26 Prepare a list of next steps that will be required to implement the requirements specified in the policy document. This can include the development of an information security architecture, manual procedures documents, and technical information security standards, and acquisition of new products, hiring new technical staff, and other matters.

Appendix G OVERVIEW OF POLICY DEVELOPMENT PROCESS TASKS

Figure G-1: Overview Of Policy Development Process

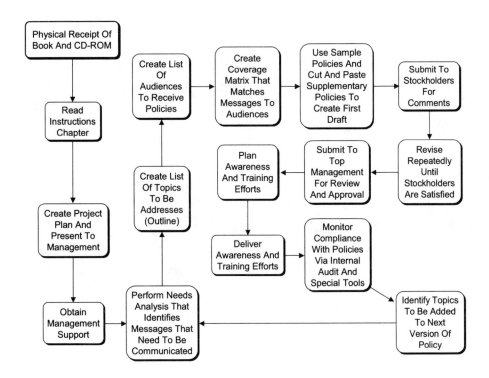

Appendix H REAL WORLD PROBLEM CASES CAUSED BY MISSING POLICIES

GOVERNMENT AGENCY

A clerk spent a great deal of time surfing the Internet while on the job. Because there was no policy specifying what constituted excessive personal use, management could not discipline this employee. Then management discovered that the clerk had downloaded a significant amount of pornography. Using this as justification, management fired him. The clerk appealed the termina- tion with the Civil Service Board, claiming that he could not be fired because he had never been told that he could not download pornography. After a Civil Service hearing, the board ordered him to be reinstated with back pay. This situation could have been avoided if the employer had a clear and current policy dealing with personal use of information systems.

LAW FIRMS

The manager of data processing took a job with a competing law firm. Because his former employer had nobody who could do the job that he did, they kept him on as a part-time contractor. For months, this sophisti- cated technician performed a wide variety of systems management tasks for his former employer. In order to do these tasks he needed full privileges on the former employer's network. One day a partner at the former employer learned that the manager's new employer was opposing them in a high-visibility lawsuit. The partners at the manager's former employer started asking some questions, such as could the former data processing manager gain access to any file on the network and perhaps the legal strategies for this case. The answer was yes, but nobody knew whether the manager had exploited these capabilities because no data access logs were being kept. This situation could have been avoided if the former employer had commonly-encountered policies about conflicts of interest, system access privileges, and keeping logs.

OIL COMPANY

An oil company computer technician compiled a list of jokes about sex. Proud of his list, he broadcasted this list on the Internet, appending his electronic mail address to the end, just in case the recipients happened to have heard any new ones. Management was able to have the posting deleted from several discussion groups, but was not able to control copies that had already been made. Around the same time this technician had printed a copy of his list, and when distracted by something else, had left it in the hopper of a departmental printer. Women in the department objected that they had been subjected to sex jokes through electronic mail that they did not want to hear. They pointed to the Internet postings and the printer output as examples. The pending sexual harass- ment lawsuit was settled for an undisclosed sum. A policy about permissible use of the Internet, and a policy about representations made with the company name over the Internet were noticeably lacking.

LOCAL NEWSPAPER

A local newspaper had no policy requiring the termina- tion of user ID and password privileges after an employee had left. A reporter left the newspaper, and shortly thereafter, the newspaper had trouble because a competing local newspaper consistently picked-up on their exclusive investigative reporting stories. A review of the system logs revealed that the departed reporter had been consistently dialing-up his former employer's computer to get ideas for stories to use at his new employer. This access could have been avoided if the newspaper had adopted a policy about turning off access privileges when workers are terminated.

MIDWEST MANUFACTURING COMPANY

A virus hoax sent by electronic mail through the Internet indicated that if people receive a message with the heading "Join the Crew" they should not read it. The hoax went on to state that this electronic mail message would erase a hard drive if ever it should be displayed. Thinking that they were doing others a favor, 10% of the staff at a large manufacturing company broadcasted the hoax to all the people they knew. Because no policy defined how they should handle these warnings, they flooded the company's internal networks with electronic mail and caused a great deal of unnecessary technical staff time to be wasted. A policy requiring all reported information security vulnerabilities to be forwarded to the Information Security department could have avoided this loss of worker productivity.

WEST COAST MANUFACTURING COMPANY

Because it had no policy requiring employee private data to be encrypted when held in storage, a large manufacturing company found itself facing a public relations problem. A burglar made off with a computer disk containing detailed personal details and bank account information on more than 20,000 current and former employees. The press speculated that this could be used to facilitate identity theft, including application for credit cards in the names of other people. The event precipitated a massive notification process including recommendations on changes to bank account numbers.

MAJOR ONLINE SERVICE COMPANY

A Navy enlisted man registered with an Internet online service company and filled out a profile form on which he indicated that he was gay. An employee at the service company, after an inquiry from the Navy, shared this profile information with the Navy's "top brass." Based on this information, the enlisted man was given a dishonorable discharge. The enlisted man sued the Navy for violating its own policy, and won an honorable discharge with retirement benefits as a result. The online service company publicly stated that its employee had violated the "privacy policy," but this policy had been violated on multiple occasions in the past, including top management's publicly-stated intention to sell customer home telephone numbers to telephone marketers. At least the service organization now admits that it has a policy. Training associated with policies is absolutely essential if these policies are going to be faithfully observed.

Appendix I   Suggested Next Steps

There are many paths available after an information security policy has been approved. The following list of suggested next steps provides some answers, but it is not intended to provide a comprehensive list of all possible next steps. Each of these suggested next steps are commonly-encountered, although not all the items will apply to all organizations. These suggestions should be used as a starting point when creating an information security policy implementation project plan. The suggestions are organized in a rough chronological order, and may be addressed individually. A better alternative would be to pursue several of these steps at the same time in order to make significant progress.

There will typically be many other projects that are initiated as a result of preparing an information security policy document. For example, a policy preparation effort may have illuminated the fact that an existing information security requirement is obsolete. A specific example might involve callback technology for dial-in access to an organization's networks. If this requirement is widely subscribed to within the organization, an effort to adopt a more current alternative may be yet another project to add to a project plan. Continuing with this specific example, dynamic password tokens could be used instead of callback systems.

Post Polices To Intranet Or Equivalent—The new document should be placed on the Company X intranet, and links to related documents should be added. Multiple indexes should be prepared so that users can quickly locate material of interest. A key word search facility should be added. Other electronic bulletin board equivalents, such as a Human Resources kiosk, could include the document. For more information about where to post policies, see Appendix D, "List Of Suggested Awareness-Raising Methods."

Develop A Self-Assessment Questionnaire—The essential requirements found in the new information security policy document should be extracted and reformatted in the form of a questionnaire. Internal Audit then should issue the questionnaire to department managers. Responses to the questionnaire will highlight those areas where departments are out of compliance and where additional control enhancements are needed. Based on the results of the survey, remedial projects can be proposed. The questionnaire can be used as part of a regular compliance-checking internal audit process. For more information about obtaining compliance, see "Handling Non-Compliance" on page 28.

Develop Revised user ID Issuance Form—A form is used at many organizations as a way to document management approval prior to the issuance of a user ID. For more information about this topic, see "User ID Forms" on page 285. A summary of the critical ideas in the new information security policy document should be included as part of this form along with words such as "the user mentioned below has read and agrees to abide by Company X information security policies as a condition of their continued use of Company X information systems." All new or reissued user IDs should then be enabled only after the form is signed.

Develop Agreement To Comply With Information Security Policies Form—A legal document reflecting an agreement by employees to comply with information security policies should be drafted, edited, and later approved by management. This form should be signed by all workers, or at the very least by all newly hired or retained workers. An awareness program should be initiated to publicize the existence of the new policy document and to get signed forms. For an example of this agreement and further information about complying with policies, see Appendix J, "Agreement To Comply With Information Security Policies."

Develop Tests To Determine If Workers Understand Policies—A set of tests or quizzes can be developed to determine if workers understand the essential points covered in an information security policy document. These tests and quizzes can be used to determine what additional training and awareness material needs to be developed and delivered. The tests and quizzes also can be used as gateways to certain privileges. For example, only after a worker passes a test or a quiz will telecommuting privileges be enabled. For more information about this topic, see "Policy Quiz" on page 105.

Assign Information Security Coordinators—Many centralized Information Security departments are understaffed and cannot handle all the information security jobs that need to be done. To assist in the implementation of the controls described in the new policy document, decentralized information security coordinators should be assigned. System administrators, systems managers, network managers, and other technical staff often serve in this part-time capacity. Coordinators serve as a local liaison with the central information security group, interpreting policies for a department or division. For more information about the role of an information security coordinator, see "Information Security Liaisons" on page 41.

Train Information Security Coordinators—Before the information security coordinators can be expected to do substantive work, they should receive a training course. A half-day course should be developed to acquaint them with the requirements defined in the new information security policy document, existing organizational resources, and the best ways to deal with a variety of problems such as power failures, hacker intrusions, and computer virus infections. A handbook for local information security coordinators is also recommended. For more information about the sources of information that could be included in these trainings, see Appendix B, "List Of Information Security Periodicals."

Prepare And Deliver A Basic Information Security Training Course—A brief training course should be prepared and presented to all employees at Company X. The policy document can be the primary source of ideas for a training and awareness course. A variety of other material, such as the corporate code of conduct, should also be drawn upon when preparing this course. After this course has been presented several times, it can be revamped, then recorded by videotape or computer based training software. In some instances, separate audiences may need different training courses. Possible audiences include new hires going through orientation, current employees in need of additional training, system administrators, network administrators, and others likely to be designated as information security coordinators, and systems analysts, application programmers, systems related project managers, systems quality assurance staff, and other technical staff who will not be serving in an information security coordinator capacity. For more information about preparing a training course, see "Intended Target Audience" on page 25.

Develop Application Specific Information Security Policies—Certain highly-sensitive applications will need additional application-specific policies and procedures. Now that the new information security policy document has been prepared, more detailed policies and related requirements for high-risk application systems should be developed. Certain computing environments, not just applications, such as Internet electronic commerce, may warrant more detailed policies and procedures. The conceptual hierarchy described below can be used to describe the linkage between these application specific documents and the new information security policy. For more information about detailed and specific policies, see "Policy Objectives And Scope" on page 26.

Develop A Conceptual Hierarchy Of Information Security Requirements—The information security area is complex, and this complexity shows up in various documents that define information security requirements. In many organizations, these include standards, guidelines, policies, procedures, and architectures. A general information security policy document should be at the top of a conceptual hierarchy, with application-related information security policy documents falling underneath. Standards, guidelines, procedures, and other documents should be controlled by the general organization-wide information security policy statement. A conceptual hierarchy should indicates when certain documents apply, which documents take precedence when a conflict exists, and which documents are current or outdated. This conceptual hierarchy will be useful for training and awareness purposes, and can be posted to the Company X information security intranet page. For more information on creating a hierarchy, see "Information Security Policies" on page 3.

Assign Information Ownership And Custodianship—Management ownership of specific types of information should be assigned according to the requirements defined in the new information security document. After ownership roles have been assigned, Custodianship roles should come next. In many instances, these efforts will be a natural transition to the

Establish An Information Security Management Committee—To supervise the various information security initiatives now underway, a committee should be formed with middle-level managers from each of the major divisions at Company X. This committee will ensure that current and proposed information security activities are consistent with business objectives. The committee will serve as a sounding board for proposals, prior to presenting these same proposals to top management. The committee ordinarily would meet once a quarter, and would not provide any technical assistance to the Information Security department. For more information about committees, see "Information Security Management Committee" on page 35. A mission statement and related details about such a committee can also be found in the book *Information Security Roles and Responsibilities Made Easy.*

Develop An Information Security Architecture Document—Even though the basic rules for information security are specified in a policy document, in most cases there is a need to put together a grand vision for designing secure systems. The larger an organization, the more the need for a document such as this. Complexity is much more of a problem in these organizations. An architecture should specify the controls that will be used now and in the near future, and provide a plan for the migration to controls to be adopted in the near future. Some organizations also use an architecture document as a place to specify certain approved information security products and vendors. An architecture deals with system interfaces, technical standards, and other more technical considerations than a policy document. For more information about an information security architecture, see "Systems Architecture For Logging Activities" on page 340.

Information Security Policies Made Easy

Appendix J   AGREEMENT TO COMPLY WITH INFORMATION SECURITY POLICIES

A signed paper copy of this form must be submitted with all requests for authorization of a new user ID, authorization of a change in privileges associated with an existing user ID, or periodic reauthorization of an existing user ID. Company X management will not accept modifications to the terms and conditions of this agreement.

_____

User's Printed Name

_____

User's Department

_____

User's Telephone Number

_____

User's Physical Address and Mail Location

I, the user, agree to take all reasonable precautions to assure that Company X internal information, or information that has been entrusted to Company X by third parties such as customers, will not be disclosed to unauthorized persons. At the end of my employment or contract with Company X, I agree to return to Company X all information to which I have had access as a result of my position with Company X. I understand that I am not authorized to use this information for my own purposes, nor am I at liberty to provide this information to third parties without the express written consent of the internal Company X manager who is the designated information Owner.

I have access to a copy of the Company X Information Security Policies Manual, I have read and understand the manual, and I understand how it impacts my job. As a condition of continued employment at Company X, I agree to abide by the policies and other requirements found in that manual. I understand that non-compliance will be cause for disciplinary action up to and including system privilege revocation, dismissal from Company X, and perhaps criminal and/or civil penalties.

I agree to choose a difficult-to-guess password as described in the Company X Information Security Policies Manual, I agree not to share this password with any other person, and I agree not to write this password down unless it has been transformed in an unrecognizable way.

I also agree to promptly report all violations or suspected violations of information security policies to the director of the Information Security department (at XXX-XX-XXXX).

_____

User's Printed Name

Appendix K IDENTIFY TOKEN RESPONSIBILITY STATEMENT

By signing this form, I acknowledge receipt of a dynamic password identity token (hereafter called a "token"). I understand that this token provides access to Company X information systems and restricted information stored thereon. I understand that the access privileges that go with this token may, at any time, be revoked by Company X management if they believe that I have not acted in a manner consistent with the Information Security Policy Statement, or if my employment with Company X for any reason is discontinued or suspended. I have read and understood the material contained in the Information Security Policy Statement and I agree to adhere to these rules whenever using Company X information and information systems.

I understand that this token is exclusively for my personal use in the performance of Company X business, and I promise that I will not share it or the system privileges that it provides with any other person. I agree not to write or store the token's activating personal identification number on anything that is stored anywhere near the token.

I agree that I will immediately report to the Information Security department the fact that my token has been lost or stolen, or that I suspect that it has been lost or stolen. I agree to surrender the token at the time that I discontinue my work for Company X. At such a point in time, I additionally agree to surrender to Company X staff all other Company X information and computer and communications equipment provided to me in order to perform my job.

_____

Employee's Signature and Date

_____

Employee's Printed Name and Employee Number

Appendix L   MANAGEMENT RISK ACCEPTANCE MEMO

WHEN TO USE THIS FORM

This form must be employed when:

- an information system, a communications system, or an organizational unit is known to be out of compliance with Company X information security policies or standards, and

- the responsible manager does not intend to come into full compliance within a three-month period.

If this out-of-compliance situation is to continue, the brief risk assessment regarding the out of compliance situation must be updated annually, the approvals must be obtained annually, and this form must be signed by the responsible manager annually. Each year the responsible manager must return a signed copy of this form to the manager of the Information Security who will keep it on file.

RISK ACCEPTANCE MEMO

__ Regarding Company X policy or standard no.:

_____

__ Dealing with the topic of:

_____

_____

I understand that compliance with Company X information security policies and standards is expected for all organizational units, information systems, and communication systems. I have read the above-named policy or standard and I believe that the control(s) described therein should not be required for the following:

__ organizational unit

__ information system

__ communication system

> (circle the relevant choice among the above options and describe below):

_____

_____

I furthermore understand that a control deficiency in one network-connected system can jeopardize other information systems because erroneous data may be inherited, or because a conduit for a intruder to enter Company X systems may be created. I also understand that non-compliance in this instance may adversely affect the morale or willingness of staff associated with other systems to comply with information security policies and standards.

I understand that an exception to information security policies and standards is appropriate only when it would:

__ adversely affect the accomplishment of Company X business, or

__ cause a major adverse financial impact that would not be offset by the reduced risk occasioned by compliance. I believe that an exception to this policy or standard is warranted because:

_____

_____

I have prepared, or have had a staff member reporting to me prepare, a written assessment of the risks associated with being out of compliance with the above-mentioned policy or standard. This risk assessment has been reviewed and approved by the manager of the Information Systems Security department and the manager of Internal Audit.

I accept personal responsibility for this situation to be out of compliance with information security policies and/or standards. Personal responsibility does not mean that I am financially responsible for losses that may take place as a result of this out of compliance situation. Personal responsibility does mean that my job performance evaluation, my salary and bonus, and my continued employment status at Company X can be jeopardized or damaged if a major loss takes place because this out of compliance situation existed.

I also understand that this exception will expire one year from the date the approvals are obtained.

_____

Signature of Responsible Manager

_____

Printed Name of Responsible Manager

_____

Date Signed

Appendix M TWO-PAGE SIMPLE NON-DISCLOSURE AGREEMENT

This confidentiality agreement is entered into as of _____ (date), by and between Company X, and _____ (recipient organization name), which together with its subsidiaries and affiliates, shall individually and collectively be referred to hereinafter as the "Recipient."

Company X and Recipient hereby agree as follows:

1. Company X created and is the Owner and developer of an idea for a new product (hereinafter referred to as the "System"). By disclosing this information, Company X grants Recipient no license or right, by implication or otherwise, to use this information for any purpose other than the specific business purposes of Company X as found in written agreement(s) to be separately negotiated.

2. Recipient acknowledges that the System and all related documentation, including but not limited to descriptions of the System or its component parts, all product mock-ups, product prototypes, product samples, product technical specifications, product input data, product-related know-how, product-related new and different ideas, product technology, all or any of which may be derived from any of the foregoing (all of which, individually and collectively, shall hereinafter be referred to as the "Proprietary Information") are valuable, confidential, and proprietary to Company X.

3. Company X and Recipient wish to discuss mutually beneficial business arrangements and relationships that in some way concern, or are related to the System. Recipient acknowledges that disclosure of this information constitutes consideration for this agreement because it wishes to pursue the opportunity of business dealings with Company X. Recipient agrees not to use Proprietary Information for its own use or for any other purpose except to evaluate whether it desires to enter into a business relationship with Company X, or as necessary, to carry on such a relationship. Recipient furthermore agrees to manage all of its workers who come into contact with Proprietary Information such that the obligations and duties described in this agreement will be strictly enforced.

4. Recipient agrees to hold the Proprietary Information in strict confidence. Recipient furthermore agrees not to reproduce, transcribe, or disclose the Proprietary Information to third parties without prior written approval of Company X. Recipient also agrees not to make, have made, use, distribute or sell for its own purposes or for any purpose other than on behalf of Company X, any product incorporating Proprietary Information. Recipient furthermore agrees to promptly return all copies, renderings, transformations, and derivatives of such information to Company X at the termination of its discussions or work dealing with the System.

5. The obligations imposed by this Agreement shall not apply to any information that is:

    __ Rightfully received from a third party without accompanying use of disclosure restrictions, and can be documented as such.

    __ Independently developed without access to Proprietary Information.

    __ Publicly available through no wrongful act of the Recipient.

    __ Already known to Recipient as evidenced by third-party documentation bearing a date prior to the date of Proprietary Information disclosure.

    __ Approved for release in writing by an authorized representative of Company X.

6. This agreement supersedes and replaces all existing agreements, written or otherwise, entered into between Recipient and Company X dealing with the subject matter discussed herein.

7. Recipient agrees that, in the event of a breach of this non-disclosure agreement, that Company X shall be entitled to an injunction to enforce the terms and conditions of this agreement, and to protect its Proprietary Information. Recipient additionally agrees that this shall not preclude Company X for pursuing further actions or remedies at law or in equity, for any breach or threatened breach of the terms of this agreement, including but not limited to the recovery of damages.

8. If any one or more of the terms of this agreement shall for any reason be held to be invalid, illegal, or unenforceable in any other respect, these problems shall not affect the overall intention of the agreement, nor shall it affect the degree to which the other terms remain binding, nor shall it interfere with the enforcement of or the duty to comply with the other terms found in this agreement. This agreement is governed by the laws of [insert relevant jurisdiction].

9. The terms of this agreement will be in effect for five years from the time that the Recipient receives information from Company X. Each time that Company X provides new confidential information to Recipient, the period when this information must be held confidential will then continue for five years from that time. Termination of the proposed or actual working relationship between Recipient and Company X in no way invalidates the binding nature of this agreement or the period when it remains in effect.

10. The person signing below for Recipient represents that he or she is an authorized representative and/or corporate officer of the Recipient organization.

_____

Recipient Signing Officer and Date

_____

Printed Name of Signing Officer

_____

Company X Officer and Date

Appendix N INDEX OF NEW POLICIES

The following policies have been added to *Information Security Policies Made Easy* since the last version. This list is intended for those licensees who have a copy of the previous version and who wish to update their existing policy statements focusing only on the new policies.

Table N-1: New Policies

Policy Number	Policy Title
4.01.03.03	"Management Security Approach"
4.01.03.04	"Risk Assessments"
4.01.03.08	"Information Systems Change Approval"
4.01.03.19	"Default Information Ownership"
4.01.04.01	"New Technology Control"
4.01.06.01	"Information Security Products Disclosure"
4.01.06.02	"Public Disclosure Of Business Information"
4.02.01.02	"Temporary Worker Privileges"
4.02.01.04	"Consultant Note Taking"
4.02.02.04	"Information Handling At Contract Termination"
4.02.02.05	"Circumventing Privacy Policy With Third Parties"
4.02.02.07	"Vendor Relationship Disclosure"
4.02.02.13	"Security Measures At Third-Party Organizations"
4.02.02.14	"Third-Party Security Policy"
4.03.01.01	"Independent Control Reports"
4.03.01.02	"Application Service Provider Software"
4.03.01.03	"Alternate Processing Provider"

Table N-1: New Policies (Continued)

Policy Number	Policy Title
4.03.01.05	"Outsourced Production Systems Back-Out Plans"
4.03.01.06	"Shared Outsourcer Firewalls And Servers"
4.03.01.07	"Accessibility To Outsourced Information"
4.03.01.08	"Access Control Decisions"
4.03.01.10	"Outsourcing Organization Financial Statements"
4.03.01.11	"Production Processing Outsourced To Foreign Companies"
5.02.01.04	"Closed Two-Category Data Classification"
5.02.01.05	"Open Two-Category Data Classification"
5.02.01.08	"Incorrect Data Classification Labels"
5.02.01.21	"Declassification Of Secret Archives"
5.02.01.22	"Essential Information And Software"
5.02.02.01	"File Grouping Data Retention"
5.02.02.03	"Computer System Names"
5.02.02.33	"Releasing Declassified Information"
6.01.02.12	"Polygraph Tests"
6.01.02.17	"Non-Employee Background Checks"
6.01.02.19	"Former Hackers And Reformed Criminals"
6.01.04.04	"Internal Informants"
6.01.04.05	"Competitive Intelligence"
6.02.01.01	"Policy Quiz"
6.03.01.06	"Information Security Pranks"

Table N-1: New Policies (Continued)

Policy Number	Policy Title
6.03.01.10	"Incident Reporting Severity"
6.03.01.12	"Violation And Problem Reporting Alternatives"
6.03.01.15	"Violation And Problem Reporting Identity"
6.03.01.19	"Reporting Security Breaches To Third Parties"
6.03.01.21	"Reporting Questionable Events"
6.03.01.23	"Contacting Law Enforcement"
6.03.02.04	"Security Weaknesses And Vulnerability Discussion"
6.03.02.05	"Reporting Security Vulnerabilities"
6.03.03.02	"Vulnerability Disclosure"
6.03.05.05	"Duress Terminations"
7.01.01.02	"Physical Security Plan"
7.01.02.07	"Man-Trap Entrances"
7.02.01.07	"Backup Data Center Infrastructure"
7.02.03.01	"Power And Telecommunications Cables"
7.02.04.04	"Retaining Hardware and Software"
7.02.05.01	"Off-Site Equipment Usage Approval"
7.03.01.03	"Information Handling On Off Shifts"
7.03.02.02	"Shoplifting Tags"
8.01.01.03	"Production Application Documentation"
8.01.05.02	"Separation Of Information Technology Duties"
8.01.06.01	"Contractor Risks And Expectations"

Table N-1: New Policies (Continued)

Policy Number	Policy Title
8.02.02.01	"System Configuration"
8.02.02.03	"New Technology Evaluation"
8.03.01.01	"Systems Network Access"
8.03.01.17	"Scanning Backup Files For Viruses"
8.03.01.23	"Downloading Software Using The Internet"
8.04.01.05	"On-Site Backup Files"
8.04.01.22	"Paper Forms Stored Off Site"
8.05.01.04	"Scanning Remote Connections"
8.05.01.05	"Internet Traffic Control"
8.05.01.11	"Integrity Assessment Tools"
8.05.01.16	"Host-Based Intrusion Detection Systems"
8.05.01.18	"Internet Firewall Administrator Access"
8.05.01.44	"Wireless Networks"
8.05.01.45	"Wireless Network Gateways"
8.06.03.09	"Master Copy Of Critical Production Data"
8.07.01.05	"Online Contracts By Exchange Of Paper And Signatures"
8.07.02.01	"Third-Party Delivery Of Secret Information"
8.07.03.01	"Interrogation Of Cookie Files"
8.07.03.02	"Content Rating And Privacy Protection"
8.07.03.04	"Placing Prospects and Customers On Mailing Lists"
8.07.03.07	"Confirming Customer-Initiated Changes"

Table N-1: New Policies (Continued)

Policy Number	Policy Title
8.07.03.21	"Dormant Credit Card Numbers"
8.07.04.13	"Customer Electronic Mail Encryption"
8.07.04.24	"Electronic Mail Scanning And Footers"
8.07.04.25	"Outbound Electronic Mail Footers"
8.07.04.28	"Sales Department Electronic Mail"
8.07.04.35	"Unexpected Electronic Mail Attachments"
8.07.05.13	"Faxing Confidential Information — Speed Dial"
8.07.05.40	"Personal Internet Service Provider Accounts"
8.07.05.43	"Mobile Code Execution"
8.07.06.07	"Public Access Workstations"
8.07.06.11	"Messages From Criminals Or Terrorists"
8.07.06.14	"Internet Discussion Groups"
8.07.06.26	"Internet Computer Security Queries"
8.07.06.45	"Internet Web Site Content Changes"
8.07.06.46	"Web Page Defacement"
8.07.06.47	"Customer Financial Information Storage"
8.07.06.48	"Internet Domain Name"
8.07.06.49	"Internet Server Command Response"
8.07.06.50	"Web Site HTML"
8.07.06.52	"Secret Information On Intranet"
8.07.07.01	"Recording Of Internet Communications"

Table N-1: New Policies (Continued)

Policy Number	Policy Title
9.01.01.08	"Centralized Access Control Database"
9.01.01.09	"Command Line Interpreter Software"
9.01.01.18	"Legal Action Information"
9.01.01.26	"Information Disclosure Approval"
9.01.01.30	"Creating Security Tools"
9.02.01.02	"Non-Anonymous User IDs"
9.02.01.12	"System Access Request Authorization"
9.03.01.15	"Third-Party Password Usage"
9.04.01.05	"Internal Network Access"
9.04.01.09	"Blocking Access To Non-Business Sites"
9.04.01.10	"Large Internet Downloads"
9.04.03.01	"Remote Access Passwords"
9.04.03.02	"Two-Factor User Authentication"
9.04.05.01	"Diagnostic Port Access"
9.05.01.01	"Physical Terminal Security"
9.04.08.01	"Network Security Zones"
9.04.09.01	"Personal Computer and Workstation Firewalls"
9.05.03.02	"Portable Identification Credentials"
9.05.04.03	"Network-Connected Computer Passwords"
9.05.04.04	"Role-Based Password Length"
9.05.04.19	"Access Control Information In Cookies"

Table N-1: New Policies (Continued)

Policy Number	Policy Title
9.06.01.12	"Systems Log And Audit Trail Disclosure"
9.06.02.01	"Critical Application Servers"
9.07.01.06	"Private Information Access Logs"
9.07.02.12	"Monitoring Internet Activity"
9.08.01.04	"Portable Computer Usage"
10.01.01.02	"In-House Systems Development Proposals"
10.01.01.05	"Application Coding Principles"
10.02.02.16	"Temporary Files And Storage"
10.02.04.01	"Output Data Controls"
10.03.01.01	"Digital Signature And File Encryption Software Versions"
10.03.02.10	"Encrypted Message Protection"
10.03.05.04	"Digital Certificate Validity Period"
10.03.05.22	"Encryption And Digital Signature Key Storage"
10.03.05.27	"Key Recovery Operation Controls"
10.04.01.01	"Business Application System Testing"
10.04.03.02	"Production Programs And Information Access"
10.05.01.19	"Change Control Documentation"
10.05.02.01	"Operating System Configuration"
10.05.02.02	"Software Patches, Bug Fixes, and Upgrades"
10.05.05.01	"Third-Party Software Development"
11.01.01.02	"Contingency Plan Accessibility"

Table N-1: New Policies (Continued)

Policy Number	Policy Title
11.01.02.03	"Business Impact Analysis"
11.01.05.02	"Off-Site Personnel Rotation"
11.01.05.05	"Telephone Number Testing"
11.01.05.06	"Contingency Planning And Systems Recovery Roles"
12.01.01.01	"Regulations And Requirements"
12.01.02.02	"Production Systems and Software Tools"
12.01.02.18	"Copyrighted Electronic Books"
12.01.03.06	"Vital Record Storage"
12.01.03.12	"Application Transaction Data Retention"
12.01.04.01	"Private Personal Effects And Communications"
12.01.04.02	"Pretext Personal Data Collection"
12.01.04.11	"Private Information Collection Consent"
12.01.04.36	"Sharing Private Information"
12.01.04.37	"Disclosure Of Private Information To Outsourcing Organizations"
12.01.04.39	"Disclosure Of Personal Data"
12.01.04.59	"Private Information Access Logging"
12.01.04.67	"Account Number Intelligence"
12.01.04.71	"Privacy Policy Reminder"
12.01.04.73	"Individual Control Of Personal Data Usage"
12.01.04.74	"Location-Specific Information Usage"
12.01.04.76	"Deletion Of Customer Or Prospect Information"

Table N-1: New Policies (Continued)

Policy Number	Policy Title
12.01.04.78	"Sharing Personal Information"
12.01.04.79	"Transfer Of Customer Information"
12.01.04.80	"Personal Data Transfer"
12.01.04.84	"Employee Access Production Information Type List"
12.01.04.86	"Encryption Of Private Electronic Mail"
12.01.04.93	"Distribution Of Privacy Policies"
12.01.05.05	"User Access To Internet"
12.01.05.06	"Classifying Acceptable Internet Use"
12.01.05.10	"Personal Internet Access Time"
12.01.05.12	"User IDs Employed In Abusive Activity"
12.01.07.02	"Sources Of Digital Evidence"
12.01.07.09	"Law Enforcement Inquiries"
12.01.07.10	"Legal Proceeding Participation"
12.01.07.11	"Providing Information In Legal Proceedings"
12.01.07.12	"Criminal Justice Community Contact"
12.01.07.13	"Investigation Status Reports"
12.01.07.15	"Forensic Analysis Process"
12.01.07.16	"Information Security Investigations"
12.01.07.17	"Information Security Investigation Teams"
12.01.07.18	"Internal Investigations And Official Inquiries"
12.01.07.19	"Intrusion Investigations Details"

Appendix O INDEX OF POLICY TITLE CONVERSION

Most of the *Information Security Policies Made Easy* policy titles have been modified from the previous version. The following list contains the title of the policy in ISPME version 8, along with the title as presented in this version of the book. Each of the policies are listed below in the order in which they appeared in version 8.

Table O-1: Index of Policy Title Conversion

Previous Policy Number	ISPME v8 Title	Current Policy Number	ISPME v9 Title
1	Minimum Password Length	9.05.04.01	"Minimum Password Length"
2	Minimum Password Length ConstrainedBy System Limitations	9.05.04.02	"Minimum Password Length Constraint"
3	Difficult-To-Guess Passwords Required	9.03.01.01	"Password Structure"
4	Cyclical Passwords Prohibited	9.03.01.02	"Cyclical Passwords"
5	User-Chosen Passwords Must Not Be Reused	9.05.04.05	"Password Reuse"
6	Passwords Must Contain Both Alphabetic And Non-Alphabetic Characters	9.05.04.06	"Password Characters"
7	Passwords Must Contain Both Upper And Lower Case Characters	9.05.04.07	"Password Case"
8	Seed For System-Generated Passwords	9.05.04.09	"Seed For System-Generated Passwords"
9	Pronounceable System-Generated Passwords	9.05.04.10	"System-Generated Passwords"
10	Storage Of System-Generated Passwords	9.05.04.11	"System-Generated Password Issuance And Storage"
11	Zeroization Of Password Generation Materials	9.05.04.12	"Password Generation Materials"
12	Protection Of Password Generation Algorithms	9.05.04.13	"Password Generation Algorithms"
13	Previous Password History File	9.05.04.08	"Password History"
14	Anonymous User IDs	9.02.01.01	"Anonymous User IDs"
15	Display And Printing Of Passwords	9.05.04.14	"Password Display And Printing"

Table O-1: Index of Policy Title Conversion (Continued)

Previous Policy Number	ISPME v8 Title	Current Policy Number	ISPME v9 Title
16	User-Chosen Passwords Must Be Entered Twice If Masked When Entered	9.05.04.15	"Masking Password Changes"
17	Periodic Forced Password Changes	9.05.04.16	"Required Password Changes"
18	Password Change Interval Synchronization Across Platforms	9.05.04.17	"Password Change Interval Synchronization"
19	Assignment Of Expired Passwords	9.02.03.01	"Initial Passwords"
20	Initial Passwords Transmitted To Remote Users By Authorized Means	9.02.03.02	"Initial Password Transmission"
21	Limit On Consecutive Unsuccessful Attempts To Enter A Password	9.05.02.01	"Password Attempts"
22	Single Sign-On Process	9.05.03.01	"Single Sign-On"
23	All Workstations Must Have Password-Based Boot Protection	9.05.02.02	"Password-Based Boot Protection"
24	Passwords Never In Readable Form When Outside Workstations	9.05.04.18	"Passwords In Readable Form"
25	Customer Service Fixed Passwords Not Displayed By Company X Systems	9.06.01.01	"Customer Service Passwords"
26	Fixed Password Changes Confirmed By Regular Mail To Detect Abuse	9.02.03.03	"Fixed Password Change Confirmation"
27	Protection Of Passwords Sent Through The Mail	9.02.03.04	"Sending Passwords By Mail"
28	Reregistration Required For All Users Forgetting Fixed Passwords	9.02.03.05	"Forgetting Fixed Passwords"
29	Password Guessing Lockout Requires Help Desk Password Reset	9.02.03.06	"Password Reset After Lockout"
30	Storage Of Passwords In Readable Form	9.03.01.03	"Storage Of Passwords In Readable Form"
31	Encryption Of Passwords	9.05.04.20	"Password Encryption"

Table O-1: Index of Policy Title Conversion (Continued)

Previous Policy Number	ISPME v8 Title	Current Policy Number	ISPME v9 Title
32	Incorporation Of Passwords Into Software	9.02.03.07	"Passwords Into Software"
33	Prevention Of Password Retrieval	9.05.04.21	"Password Retrieval"
34	Reliance On Operating System User Authentication Process	9.05.03.03	"Operating System User Authentication"
35	Special Privileges Associated With Secret User IDs Or Passwords Prohibited	9.06.01.02	"Secret User IDs Or Passwords"
36	System Access Control With Individualized Passwords (Not Lockwords)	9.05.04.22	"System Access Control Passwords"
37	Unique Passwords For Each Internal Network Device	9.04.07.01	"Internal Network Device Passwords"
38	Use Of Duress Passwords	9.05.06.01	"Duress Passwords"
39	Changing Vendor Default Passwords	9.05.04.23	"Vendor Default Passwords"
40	Requirement For Different Passwords On Different Systems	9.03.01.04	"Passwords On Different Systems"
41	Permission To Use Same Password On Different Systems	9.03.01.05	"Passwords On Different Systems — Permission"
42	Suspected Disclosure Forces Password Changes	9.03.01.06	"Suspected Password Disclosure"
43	Password Changes After Compromise Of A Multi-User Computer System	9.05.04.24	"Security Changes After System Compromise"
44	Writing Passwords Down And Leaving Where Others Could Discover	9.03.01.07	"Public Password Disclosure"
45	Passwords Must Never Be Written Down Near Related Access Devices	9.03.01.08	"Password Proximity To Access Devices"
46	No Fixed Passwords Stored In Dial-Up Programs Or Internet Browsers	9.03.01.09	"Passwords In Communications Software"
47	User Controlled Machines Must Not Employ Cookies For Automatic Log-In	9.03.01.10	"Cookies For Automatic Log On"

Table O-1: Index of Policy Title Conversion (Continued)

Previous Policy Number	ISPME v8 Title	Current Policy Number	ISPME v9 Title
48	Dynamic Password Tokens Must Not Be Stored In Portable Cases	9.03.01.11	"Dynamic Password Tokens"
49	Personal Identification Numbers (PINs) Constructed Using Password Rules	9.03.01.12	"Personal Identification Numbers"
50	Writing Passwords Down Using Secrecy Techniques	9.03.01.13	"Writing Down Passwords"
51	Password Sharing Prohibition	9.03.01.14	"Password Sharing"
52	Users Responsible For All Activities Involving Personal User IDs	9.03.01.16	"Personal User IDs — Responsibility"
53	Forced Change Of All Passwords After System Compromise	9.02.03.08	"Password Changes After System Compromise"
54	Forced Change Of All Passwords After Supervisor Account Compromise	9.02.03.09	"Password Changes After Privileged User ID Compromise"
55	In-Person Proof Of Identity To Obtain A Password	9.02.03.10	"In-Person Password Authentication"
56	When And How Passwords May Be Disclosed By Security Administrators	9.02.03.11	"Disclosure Of Passwords"
57	Positive Identification Required For System Usage	9.02.03.12	"Positive Identification For System Usage"
58	Access Controls For Remote Systems Connecting To Production Systems	9.04.03.03	"Remote System Access Controls"
59	User ID And Password Required For Computer-Connected Network Access	9.04.03.04	"Computer-Connected Network Access"
60	Unique User ID And Password Required	9.02.01.03	"Unique User ID And Password Required"
61	Disclosure Of Incorrect Log-In Information	9.05.02.03	"Logon Information"
62	Prohibition Against Any Feedback In Response To Incorrect Log-In	9.05.02.04	"Incorrect Logon Feedback"
63	Security Notice In System Log-in Banner	9.05.02.05	"System Logon Banner"

Table O-1: Index of Policy Title Conversion (Continued)

Previous Policy Number	ISPME v8 Title	Current Policy Number	ISPME v9 Title
64	Disclosure Of Information In System Log-In Banner	9.05.02.06	"Logon Banner Information"
65	Network Log-In Banner Wording Required	9.05.02.07	"Network Logon Banner"
66	Notice Of Last Log-In Time And Date	9.05.02.08	"Last Logon Time And Date"
67	Limitation On Number Of Daily Log-Ins Prevents Unauthorized Use	9.05.02.09	"Daily Logon Limitation"
68	Prohibition Of Multiple Simultaneous On-Line Sessions	9.05.03.04	"Multiple Simultaneous Sessions"
69	Automatic Log-Off Process	9.05.07.01	"Automatic Log Off"
70	Leaving Sensitive Systems Without Logging-Off	9.03.02.01	"Unattended Active Sessions"
71	Logging-Off Personal Computers Connected To Networks	9.03.02.02	"Unattended Network Systems"
72	Games May Not Be Stored Or Used On Company X Computer Systems	12.01.05.01	"Games On Organization Computer Systems"
73	Personal Use Of Computer And Communications Systems	12.01.05.02	"Personal Use Of Computer And Communications Systems"
74	Incidental Personal Use Of Business Systems Permissible	12.01.05.03	"Incidental Personal Use Of Computer Communications Systems"
75	Reasonable Personal Use Consistent With Conventional Ethical Standards	12.01.05.04	"Reasonable Personal Use Of Computer And Communications Systems"
76	Prohibition Against Non-Approved System Uses	12.01.05.07	"Unacceptable Use Of Computer And Communication Systems"
77	Internet Use For Personal Purposes Prohibited	12.01.05.08	"Personal Use Of Internet"
78	Personal Use Of Company X Internet Facilities Only On Personal Time	12.01.05.09	"Personal Use Of Organization Internet Facilities"
79	Personal Use Time Limit And Prohibited Activities	12.01.05.11	"Personal Use Restrictions"

Table O-1: Index of Policy Title Conversion (Continued)

Previous Policy Number	ISPME v8 Title	Current Policy Number	ISPME v9 Title
80	Permissible Uses Of Company X Information	3.01.01.02	"Use Of Information"
81	Granting User IDs To Outsiders	4.02.01.01	"Third-Party User IDs"
82	Third Party Access To Company X Systems Requires Signed Contract	4.02.02.01	"Third-Party Access Terms And Conditions"
83	When Established, Outsider User IDs Must Have Defined Expiration Date	9.02.01.04	"Non-Employee User ID Expiration"
84	Information Systems Access Privileges Terminate When Workers Leave	9.02.01.05	"Access Privileges Termination"
85	Time Limits For User IDs And File Retention Period After Expiration	9.02.01.06	"User ID Expiration"
86	Disclaimer Of Responsibility For Damage To Data And Programs	3.01.01.04	"Data And Program Damage Disclaimers"
87	Gaining Unauthorized Access Via Company X Information Systems	9.01.01.01	"Hacking Activities"
88	Where To Use Computer System Access Controls	9.06.01.03	"Computer System Access Controls"
89	Personal Digital Assistant Use For Corporate Business Information	9.08.01.01	"Small Portable Computer Usage"
90	No Sensitive Information On Personal Digital Assistants, Handhelds, Etc.	9.08.01.02	"Sensitive Information On Small Computers"
91	All Software Must Be Regulated By Access Control Systems Software	9.01.01.02	"Regulating Software"
92	Systems Requiring Password-Based Access Control Package	9.01.01.03	"Password-Based Access Control"
93	Privilege Restriction Based On The Need-To-Know	9.02.02.01	"Privilege Restriction — Need To Know"
94	Privilege Restriction Based On The Need-To-Withhold	9.02.02.02	"Privilege Restriction — Need To Withhold"

Table O-1: Index of Policy Title Conversion (Continued)

Previous Policy Number	ISPME v8 Title	Current Policy Number	ISPME v9 Title
95	Specific Information Access Policies Must Be Prepared	4.01.03.24	"Information Access Policies"
96	Information Ownership Must Be Assigned	4.01.03.01	"Information Ownership"
97	No Read Up Permissions To Access Sensitive Information	9.01.01.04	"Read Access Sensitive Information"
98	No Write Down Permissions To Access Sensitive Information	9.01.01.05	"Write Access Sensitive Information"
99	Age Verification Required Prior To Adult Material Access	9.06.01.04	"Adult Material Access"
100	User-To-User Separation Of Activities And Data	9.06.01.05	"Separation Of Activities And Data"
101	Default File Permissions For Networked Systems	9.01.01.06	"Default File Permissions"
102	Existence Of User Access Capabilities Does Not Imply Usage Permission	9.06.01.06	"User Access Capabilities"
103	User IDs Must Each Uniquely Identify A Single User	9.02.01.07	"Unique User IDs"
104	Generic User IDs Based On Job Function Prohibited	9.02.01.08	"Generic User IDs"
105	Re-Use Of Unique User IDs Prohibited	9.02.01.09	"Re-Use Of User IDs"
106	Naming Standard For A Single User ID Used On All Platforms	9.02.01.10	"User ID Naming Standard"
107	Separate User IDs For Internet Connected & Internal Network Systems	9.02.01.11	"Multiple User IDs"
108	Exclusive Personal Use Of Access Codes Such As User IDs & Credit Cards	9.03.01.17	"Access Code Sharing"
109.	Positive Identification Required For Initiation of Computer Transactions	9.05.03.05	"Computer Transaction Initiations"
110	Support For Special Privileged Type Of Users	9.02.0203	"Special Privileged Users"

Table O-1: Index of Policy Title Conversion (Continued)

Previous Policy Number	ISPME v8 Title	Current Policy Number	ISPME v9 Title
111	Restriction Of Special System Privileges	9.02.02.04	"Special System Privileges"
112	Restricted Remote Administration Of Internet-Connected Computers	9.04.03.05	"Remote Administration"
113	Limited Number Of Privileged User IDs	9.02.02.05	"Number Of Privileged User IDs"
114	Two User IDs Required For All Systems Administrators	9.02.02.06	"System Administrator User IDs"
115	Logging And Reporting On Privileged User ID Activity	9.07.02.01	"Privileged User ID Activity Logging"
116	Default User Privileges And Need for Explicit Written Approvals	9.06.01.07.	"Default User Privileges"
117	Approvals Required For User ID Creation And Privilege Assignment	9.02.02.07	"User ID And Privilege Approval"
118	Restriction Of Third Party Dial-In & Inbound Internet Privileges	4.02.01.03	"Third-Party Remote Access"
119	Time Dependent Access Control	9.05.08.01	"Time-Dependent Access Control"
120	Dormant User IDs And Automatic Privilege Revocations	9.02.01.13	"Dormant User ID Privileges"
121	Default To Denial Of Access Control Privileges	9.01.01.07	"Malfunctioning Access Control"
122	Trusted Host Relationships Must Not Be Established Without Permission	8.05.01.01	"Trusted Host Relationships"
123	Unbecoming Conduct And The Revocation Of Access Privileges	3.01.01.09	"Revocation Of Access Privileges"
124	End-User Access To Operating System Commands	9.02.02.08	"Operating System Command Access"
125	Limiting End-User Knowledge Of System Capabilities And Commands	9.06.01.08	"System Capabilities And Commands"
126	Termination Of User Processes Or Sessions And Removal Of User Files	8.01.01.01	"User Processes, Sessions, And Files"

Table O-1: Index of Policy Title Conversion (Continued)

Previous Policy Number	ISPME v8 Title	Current Policy Number	ISPME v9 Title
127	Prohibition Against Testing Information System Controls	9.03.01.18	"Testing Information System Controls"
128	Prohibition Against Exploiting Systems Security Vulnerabilities	9.03.01.19	"Exploiting Systems Security Vulnerabilities"
129	Recipient Screening For Distribution Of Powerful Security Tools	9.05.05.01	"Security Tool Screening"
130	Removal Of Vulnerability Identification Software When Not In Use	9.05.05.02	"Vulnerability Identification Software"
131	Limitation Of Functionality For Powerful Information Systems Tools	9.05.05.03	"Powerful Information Systems Tools"
132	Privileges For Modification Of Production Business Information	9.06.01.09.	"Production Business Information Privileges"
133	Controlled Process For Modification Of Production Business Information	10.02.02.01	"Modification Of Production Business Information"
134	Business Production Information Updates By Non-Production Staff	9.02.02.09.	"Business Production Information Updates"
135	Database Updates Must Be Made Only Through Established Channels	9.06.01.10	"Database Updates"
136	Access Control Required For All Multi-User Production Applications	9.06.01.11	"Multi-User Production Applications"
137	Technical Staff Privileges And Production System Change Control	10.04.03.01	"Technical Staff Privileges"
138	Signed Forms Required For Issuance Of User ID	9.02.01.14	"User ID Forms"
139	Multi-Platform Systems Parameter Naming Conventions	5.02.02.02	"Naming Conventions"
140	Administrative Security Management For All Networked Computers	8.05.01.02	"Security Configuration"
141	Tools For Determining Security Status of System	9.05.05.04	"System Security Status Tools"

Table O-1: Index of Policy Title Conversion (Continued)

Previous Policy Number	ISPME v8 Title	Current Policy Number	ISPME v9 Title
142	Periodic Review And Reauthorization Of User Access Privileges	9.02.04.01	"Reauthorization Of User Access Privileges"
143	Human Resources Sends Worker Status Changes To System Administrators	4.01.03.02	"Worker Status Changes"
144	Reporting Changes In User Duties To Systems Security Administration	9.02.01.15	"Reporting Employee Changes"
145	Users Must Inform Systems Administration About Status Changes	9.02.01.16	"User Status Changes"
146	Maintenance Of Master User ID And Privilege Database	9.02.02.10	"Master User ID Database"
147	Transfer Of Information Custodian Duties After Employee Terminations	9.02.01.17	"Custodian Responsibility Transfer"
148	Schedule For Deletion Of Files Following Worker Termination	9.02.01.18	"Deletion Of Terminated Worker Files"
149	Logs Required On Application Systems Handling Sensitive Information	9.07.01.01	"Sensitive Application Systems Logs"
150	Keystroke Logs Required For All Production System Privileged User IDs	9.07.02.03	"Privileged User ID Keystroke Logs"
151	Inclusion Of Security Relevant Events In System Logs	9.07.01.03	"Logging Security-Relevant Events"
152	Computer System Logs Must Support Audits	9.07.01.11	"Computer System Audit Logs"
153	Accountability And Traceability For All Privileged System Commands	9.07.02.04	"Privileged System Command Accountability And Traceability"
154	Contents Of Logs For Systems Running Production Applications	9.07.01.02	"Production Application System Log Contents"
155	All Attempted System Log-Ins, Successful Or Not, Must Be Logged	9.07.01.04	"Logging Logon Attempts"
156	Log-In Passwords Must Not Be Logged Unless In Encrypted Form	9.07.02.05	"Password Logging"

Table O-1: Index of Policy Title Conversion (Continued)

Previous Policy Number	ISPME v8 Title	Current Policy Number	ISPME v9 Title
157	Required Retention Period Of Logs	9.07.01.07	"Retention Period Of Logs"
158	Daily Removal Of Logs From Internet-Accessible Computers	9.07.01.08	"Removal Of Logs From Internet-Accessible Computers"
159	Logs Of User-Initiated Security Relevant Activities	9.07.01.05	"User-Initiated Security Event Logs"
160	Retention Of Access Control Privilege Logs	9.07.01.09.	"Access Control Privilege Log Retention"
161	Reconstructability Of Changes To Production Information	9.07.02.02	"Production Change Reconstructability"
162	Cryptographic Checksums To Detect Modifications Of System Logs	9.07.02.06	"System Log Modification Controls"
163	Information To Capture When Computer Crime Or Abuse Is Suspected	12.01.07.01	"Computer Crime Or Abuse Evidence"
164	Logs Required For Rapid Resumption Of Production System Activities	8.01.01.02	"Critical Application Logs"
165	Systems Architecture For Logging Activities	9.07.01.10	"Systems Architecture For Logging Activities"
166	Clock Synchronization For Accurate Logging Of Events On Network	9.07.03.01	"Clock Synchronization"
167	Logs Of All Inbound And Outbound Faxes	8.07.05.01	"Fax Logs"
168	Resistance Of Logs Against Deactivation, Modification, Or Deletion	9.07.02.07	"Log Deactivation, Modification, Or Deletion"
169	Writing Logs To WORM Storage Media Prevents Alteration	9.07.02.08	"Production System Storage Media"
170	Externally Accessible Systems Must Employ Remotely Mirrored Logs	9.07.01.12	"Remotely-Mirrored Logs"
171	Digital Signatures & Sequence Numbers Required For System Logs	9.07.02.09	"System Log Protection"

Table O-1: Index of Policy Title Conversion (Continued)

Previous Policy Number	ISPME v8 Title	Current Policy Number	ISPME v9 Title
172	System Log Rotation & Archive Process For High Security Systems	9.07.01.13	"System Log Rotation and Archival"
173	Persons Authorized To View Logs	9.07.02.10	"Access To Logs"
174	Regular And Prompt Review Of System Logs	9.07.02.11	"System Log Review"
175	Notification Of Users About Logging Of Security Violations	9.07.01.14	"User Awareness Of Logging And Security Violations"
176	Users Must Not Attempt To Eradicate Computer Viruses	8.03.01.02	"Eradicating Computer Viruses"
177	Virus Eradication Requires Support Of Systems Administrator	8.03.01.03	"Virus Eradication By System Administrators"
178	Prohibition Against Down-Loading Software From Third Party Systems	8.03.01.04	"Downloading Software"
179	Testing For Viruses Prior To Use On Company X Systems	8.03.01.05	"Software Scanning"
180	Testing For Viruses On A Stand-Alone Non-Production Machine	8.03.01.06	"Virus Test System"
181	All Outbound Software And Executable Files Must Be Virus Free	8.03.01.07	"Outbound Software And Executables"
182	Virus Checking At Firewalls, Servers, And Desktop Machines	8.03.01.08	"Virus Software Installation"
183	At Least Two Virus Screening Software Packages Must Be Employed	8.03.01.09	"Multiple Virus-Screening Packages"
184	Virus Checking Decal Required For All Externally-Supplied Floppy Disks	8.03.01.10	"Virus Certification Decal"
185	Required Process For Checking Software Down-Loaded From Internet	8.03.01.11	"Scanning Downloaded Software"
186	System Integrity Checking Programs Required For Personal Computers	8.03.01.12	"System Integrity Checking"

Table O-1: Index of Policy Title Conversion (Continued)

Previous Policy Number	ISPME v8 Title	Current Policy Number	ISPME v9 Title
187	Approved Virus Checking Programs Required On PCs And LAN Servers	8.03.01.13	"Virus-Checking Programs"
188	Current Virus Software Required For Certain Worker-Owned Computers	8.03.01.14	"Current Virus Software"
189	Material Must Be Decrypted Before Checking For Viruses	8.03.01.15	"Decrypting Files For Virus Checking"
19	Write Protection For Software On Micros And Workstations	8.03.01.16	"Software Write Protection"
191	Initial Backup Copies Of Microcomputer Software	8.04.01.01	"Master Copies Of Software"
192	Testing Of Software And Information Prior To Third Party Distribution	10.05.01.01	"Software And Information Testing"
193	Prohibition Against Programs Consuming Excessive System Resources	10.05.01.02	"Program Resource Consumption"
194	All User Involvement With Computer Viruses Prohibited	8.03.01.18	"Involvement With Computer Viruses"
195	Security Requirements Identification Prior To Development/Acquisition	10.01.01.01	"Security Requirements Identification"
196	Developers Embed Security In Systems If Commercial Solution Exists	10.01.01.03	"Embedding Security In Systems"
197	Compliance With Organizational Systems Development Conventions	10.05.01.03	"Systems Development Conventions"
198	Software Testing With Sanitized Rather Than Production Information	10.04.02.01	"Software Testing Information"
199	Software Developed In-House--Notice Of Failure To Properly Operate	10.02.02.02	"Software Failure To Properly Operate"
200	Software Developed In-House--Notice When No Action Taken	10.02.02.03	"Software Feedback To User"
201	Formal Specifications Required For Software Developed In-House	10.01.01.04	"Specifications For Software Developed In-House"

Table O-1: Index of Policy Title Conversion (Continued)

Previous Policy Number	ISPME v8 Title	Current Policy Number	ISPME v9 Title
202	Removal Of All Unauthorized Access Paths In Production Software	10.05.01.04	"Access Paths In Production Software"
203	Use Of Mature Development Tools And Techniques	10.01.01.06	"Mature Development Tools And Techniques"
204	Use Of Software Tools & Languages With Unproven Security Attributes	10.05.04.01	"Use Of Software Tools And Languages"
205	Use Of Higher Level Programming Languages	10.01.01.07	"Higher-Level Programming Languages"
206	Re-Usability Of Software Developed In-House	10.01.01.08	"Re-Usability Of Software"
207	Naming Convention For Production Files	5.02.02.04	"File Naming Convention"
208	Special Labelling For All Non-Production Business Transactions	5.02.02.05	"Non-Production Business Transactions"
209	Documentation Required For All Production Business Systems	8.02.02.02	"Production Systems Documentation"
210	Permissible Functionality Of Systems Developed In-House	10.05.01.05	"Systems Functionality"
211	Immediate System Interruption If Human Beings Are Jeopardized	10.02.02.04	"System Interruption For Safety"
212	Restricted Use Of Diagnostic Test Hardware And Software	9.05.05.05	"Diagnostic Hardware And Software"
213	Systems Utilities Resident On Production System Storage Media	9.05.05.06	"Storage Of Systems Utilities"
214	Restricted And Monitored Use Of Systems Software Utilities	9.05.05.07	"Systems Software Utility Usage"
215	External Network Interfaces Must Be Approved By Information Security	8.05.01.03	"External Network Interfaces"
216	Access To Production Business Information For System Testing	10.04.02.02	"Developer Access To Production Business Information"

Table O-1: Index of Policy Title Conversion (Continued)

Previous Policy Number	ISPME v8 Title	Current Policy Number	ISPME v9 Title
217	Separation Between Production And Development Environments	8.01.05.01	"Production And Development Separation"
218	Separation Between Programming And Testing Environments	8.01.05.03	"Separation Of Programming And Testing"
219	Development Staff Access To Production Application Information	9.06.01.13	"Production Application Information Access"
220	System Developers Must Not Perform Formal Testing	8.01.05.04	"Software Testing"
221	Special Sign-Off Required For Projects Involving Human Safety Issues.	10.05.01.06	"Projects Involving Human Safety Issues"
222	Designers & Developers Must Notify Management Of Potential Problems	10.05.01.07	"System Problem Notification"
223	Complaints Regarding Errors & Security Problems Traced To Developers	10.02.02.05	"Tracing Errors And Security Problems To Developers"
224	Formal Change Control Procedure Required For All Production Systems	10.05.01.08	"Change Control Procedure"
225	Production System Changes Must Be Consistent With Security Architecture	10.05.01.09	"Security Considerations For Production System Changes"
226	User Installation Of Software On Personal Computers Is Prohibited	8.03.01.19.	"User Installation Of Software"
227	Users Prohibited From Upgrading Software For Personal Computers	8.07.05.02	"Personal Computer Software Upgrades"
228	Access Controls Defined Prior To Cut-Over To Production Operation	10.05.01.10	"Production Operation Access Controls"
229	Disabling Privileged User IDs Prior To Operating System Installation	8.01.02.01	"Vendor-Supplied Privileged User IDs"
230	Disabling Unnecessary Software Features At Installation Time	10.05.01.11	"Unnecessary Software"
231	Removal Of Unnecessary Systems Software At Installation Time	8.01.02.02	"Removal Of Software"

Table O-1: Index of Policy Title Conversion (Continued)

Previous Policy Number	ISPME v8 Title	Current Policy Number	ISPME v9 Title
232	When To Prepare Production Systems Change Documentation	10.05.01.12	"Production Systems Change Documentation"
233	Training & Operating Documentation Required For Production Systems	10.05.01.13	"Training And Operating Documentation"
234	Loading External Programs Onto Network-Connected Computers	8.03.01.20	"Loading External Programs"
235	Use Of Push Background Updates For Software Requires Approval	8.03.01.21	"Background Push Software Updates"
236	Testing Externally-Provided Software Prior To Use	10.05.01.14	"Externally-Provided Software Testing"
237	Free Software May Not Be Used For Production Applications	12.01.02.01	"Software Development Source"
238	Automatic Detection Of End-User Application Programs	8.07.05.03	"End-User Application Programs"
239	Critical Business Logic Must Not Reside On Desktop Computers	8.07.05.04	"Critical Business Logic"
240	Control Over Movement Of Software From Development To Production	10.04.01.02	"Software Migration"
241	Vendor Provided Systems Software Must Go Through Change Control	10.05.03.01	"Vendor-Provided Systems Software Installation"
242	Review And Recompilation Required Before Movement To Production	10.05.01.15	"Software Review And Recompilation"
243	Formal Change Control Process Required For Business Applications	10.05.01.16	"Business Application Change Control Process"
244	Separate Approval Required For Production System Controls	8.02.02.04	"Production System Controls"
245	Approvals Required For Production Multi-User Applications	8.02.02.05	"Production Application Acceptance"
246	Approval For End-User Production System Development Efforts	8.02.02.06	"End-User System Development"

Table O-1: Index of Policy Title Conversion (Continued)

Previous Policy Number	ISPME v8 Title	Current Policy Number	ISPME v9 Title
247	Approval Required For Changes To Production Operating Systems	8.01.02.03	"Production Operating System Changes"
248	Periodic Review Of Production Operating System Changes	8.01.02.04	"Production Operating System Change Reviews"
249	Prohibition Against Trap Doors To Circumvent Access Controls	9.01.01.10	"Circumventing Access Controls"
250	Prompt Implementation Of Security Problem Fix Software, Scripts, Etc.	8.01.03.01	"Security Fixes"
251	Systems Software & Applications Software At Most Recent Stable Levels	8.01.02.05	"Software Versions"
252	Special Approval Required For Production Software Package Changes	10.05.01.17	"Production Software Package Change Approvals"
253	Software Maintenance With Source Rather Than Object Code	10.05.01.18	"Software Maintenance"
254	Timing Of Changes To Company X Production Information Systems	10.05.01.20	"Production Information System Change Implementation"
255	Rapid Roll-Back To Prior Versions Of Production Software	8.01.02.06	"Back-Off Procedures"
256	Production Software Conversion Contingency Plans	8.02.02.07	"Software Conversion Contingency Plans"
257	When Information Security Impact Statements Are Required	8.02.02.08	"Information Security Impact Analysis"
258	Security Impact Statements For New Or Modified Business Applications	8.02.02.09	"Security Impact Statements"
259	Vendor-Provided Written Integrity Statements	10.05.04.02	"Software Integrity Statements"
260	Packaged Software And Unilateral Deactivation By Third Party Vendor	10.05.03.02	"Third-Party Vendor Access To Packaged Software"
261	Escrow For Software Used In Critical Business Activities	12.01.02.03	"Software Escrow"

Table O-1: Index of Policy Title Conversion (Continued)

Previous Policy Number	ISPME v8 Title	Current Policy Number	ISPME v9 Title
262	Software In Escrow Must Be Verified By Independent Third Party	12.01.02.04	"Software In Escrow Verification"
263	Form Of Company X Software Distributed To Third Parties	8.07.01.01	"Software Distributed To Third Parties"
264	Third Party Agreements On Usage Of Company X Software	8.07.01.02	"Third-Party Software Agreements"
265	Release Of Systems Documentation To Third Parties	8.06.04.01	"Systems Documentation Release"
266	Software Features & Functions Must Be Fully Revealed In Documentation	10.05.01.21	"Software Features And Functions Documentation"
267	Access To Company X Letterhead, Check Stock, And Other Forms	8.06.03.01	"Access To Forms"
268	Smoking, Eating And Drinking In The Computer Machine Room	7.02.01.01	"Smoking, Eating, And Drinking"
269	Production Computer Systems Must Be Physically Located In Data Center	7.02.01.02	"Production Computer System Location"
270	Computer Operator Logs Required For Multi-User Production Systems	8.04.02.01	"Computer Operator Logs"
271	Computer Operator Logs Must Be Periodically Reviewed	8.04.02.02	"Computer Operator Log Review"
272	Information As An Important Company X Asset	3.01.01.03	"Information Handling, Access, And Usage"
273	Assignment Of Patent, Copyright, And Other Intellectual Property Rights	6.01.04.01	"Intellectual Property Rights"
274	Property Rights To Computer Programs And Documentation	6.01.03.01	"Property Rights"
275	Legal Ownership Of Information Systems Files And Messages	5.02.01.01	"File And Message Ownership"
276	Recovery Of Computer-Related Property Belonging To Company X	6.01.04.02	"Recovery Of Organization Property"

Table O-1: Index of Policy Title Conversion (Continued)

Previous Policy Number	ISPME v8 Title	Current Policy Number	ISPME v9 Title
277	Attribution Of Sources For Information	12.01.02.05	"Information Attribution"
278	Labelling For Paternity Rights To Intellectual Property	12.01.02.06	"Intellectual Property Labeling"
279	Copyright Notices On Computer Programs And Documentation	12.01.02.07	"Software Copyright Notices"
280	Workers May Make Multiple Copies Only If Reasonable And Customary	12.01.02.08	"Multiple Copies Of Information"
281	Periodic Review Of Software Licensing Agreements	12.01.02.09	"Software Licensing Agreement Reviews"
282	Systems Acquisition And Evidence Of Software Licenses	12.01.02.10	"Software License Evidence"
283	Registration Of Information Systems Products With Vendors	7.02.04.01	"Information Systems Products"
284	Ordering Authorized Copies Of Software Needed For Business Activities	12.01.02.11	"Authorized Copies Of Software"
285	When Making Additional Copies Of Software Is Permissible	12.01.02.12	"Making Copies Of Software"
286	Removal Of Unauthorized Copyrighted Information And Software	12.01.02.13	"Unauthorized Copyrighted Information And Software"
287	Default Copyright Protection For Information Posted To Internet	12.01.02.14	"Default Copyright Protection"
288	Copying, Transferring, Or Disclosing Software Prohibited	12.01.02.15	"Software Duplication"
289	Responsibility For Making Unauthorized Software And Data Copies	12.01.02.16	"Unauthorized Software And Data Copies"
290	Tools Used To Break Systems Security Prohibited	12.01.05.13	"Systems Security Testing Tools"
291	Participation In Pirated Software Bulletin Boards & Related Internet Sites	12.01.02.17	"Unauthorized Copyrighted Material"

Table O-1: Index of Policy Title Conversion (Continued)

Previous Policy Number	ISPME v8 Title	Current Policy Number	ISPME v9 Title
292	Handling Of Third Party Confidential And Proprietary Information	9.06.01.14	"Third-Party Confidential And Proprietary Information"
293	Use Of Company X Information For Non-Business Purposes	12.01.05.14	"Non-Business Use Of Organization Information"
294	Transfer Of Company X Information To Third Parties	4.02.02.02	"Information Transfer To Third Parties"
295	Software Or Data Exchanges With Third Parties Require Agreements	8.07.01.03	"Software And Data Exchange Agreements"
296	Designation Of Software And Systems As Competitive Information	5.01.01.01	"Software And System Classification"
297	Monitoring Internet For Use Of Trademark And Copyrighted Materials	12.01.02.19	"Internet Monitoring For Information Use"
298	Internet Use Of Other Organization's Trademarks And Service Marks	12.01.02.20	"Use Of Third-Party Trademarks"
299	Prohibition Against Any Third Party Use Of Company X's Name	4.02.02.03	"Third-Party Use Of Organization Name"
300	Every Public Written Use Of Company X's Name Requires Approval	8.07.06.01	"Use Of Organization Name"
301	Loss Of Critical Knowledge And Employees Flying On Same Airplane	6.01.04.03	"Employees Traveling Together"
302	Right Of Management To Examine Data Stored On Company X Systems	12.01.05.15	"Examination Of Data Stored On Systems"
303	Pretext Requests Used To Test Both Customer Service And Security Policies	4.01.07.01	"Use Of Investigators"
304	Areas Where Electronic Monitoring Of Workers May Be Used	12.01.05.16	"Electronic Monitoring Areas"
305	Disclosure Of Information On Company X Systems To Law Enforcement	12.01.07.03	"Disclosure Of Information To Law Enforcement"
306	Privacy Rights Waived When Collecting Bills Or Enforcing Contracts	12.01.04.03	"Privacy Rights Waiver"

Table O-1: Index of Policy Title Conversion (Continued)

Previous Policy Number	ISPME v8 Title	Current Policy Number	ISPME v9 Title
307	Disclosures Of Private Information Without Data Subject Consent	12.01.04.04	"Disclosures Of Private Information"
308	Affected Individuals Notified About Material Changes In Privacy Policy	12.01.04.87	"Privacy Policy Change Notification"
309	Privacy Policy Changes Require Posting Of Clear Differences Summary	12.01.04.88	"Privacy Policy Differences Summary"
310	Privacy Policy Pertains To All Types Of Interactions With Customers	12.01.04.89	"Privacy Policy Relevance"
311	Permissible Information To Collect From Prospective Employees	6.01.02.01	"Prospective Employee Information"
312	Collection Of Private Information Banned Except By Permission	12.01.04.05	"Collection Of Private Information"
313	Personal Information Necessary For Proper Functioning Of Business	12.01.04.06	"Personal Information For Business Functioning"
314	Collecting Information About Expressions Of First Amendment Rights	12.01.04.07	"Freedom Of Speech Information"
315	Need To Collect Private Information Must First Be Justified	12.01.04.08	"Private Information Collection Approval"
316	Private Data Collection Only If Lawful And Necessary	12.01.04.09	"Private Data Collection"
317	Surreptitious Collection Of Customer Private Data Prohibited	12.01.04.10	"Surreptitious Collection Of Private Information"
318	Personally-Identifiable Information Collection Requires Robust Notice	12.01.04.12	"Information Collection Notice"
319	Children's Personal Information Gathering Needs Parental Consent	12.01.04.13	"Children's Personal Information Collection"
320	Personal Information Collection Permissible But Distribution Prohibited	12.01.04.14	"Personal Information Distribution"
321	Permissible Information To Collect From Customers	12.01.04.15	"Customer Information Collection"

Table O-1: Index of Policy Title Conversion (Continued)

Previous Policy Number	ISPME v8 Title	Current Policy Number	ISPME v9 Title
322	Least Intrusive Methods Available To Gather Private Information	12.01.04.16	"Private Information Collection Methods"
323	Involuntary Capture Of Personal Biometric Information Prohibited	12.01.04.17	"Biometric Information Collection"
324	Prohibited Transfer Of Personal Biometric Data To Third Parties	12.01.04.18	"Biometric Information Transfer"
325	Personal Data Gathering Points And Corporate Privacy Policy Posting	12.01.04.90	"Personal Data Gathering Points And Privacy"
326	Name Of Organization Collecting Private Information Must Be Disclosed	12.01.04.91	"Identity Of Private Information Collector"
327	Full Explanation Why Private Information Is Required	12.01.04.92	"Private Information Requirement Explanation"
328	Performance Monitoring Information And Relevance To The Job	12.01.07.04	"Performance Monitoring Information"
329	Privacy Expectations And Information Stored On Company X Systems	12.01.04.19	"Privacy Expectations And Information Stored On Organization Systems"
330	Employee Permission Required Before Monitoring Is Used	12.01.07.05	"Monitoring Permission"
331	No Blanket Monitoring Of Employee Communications	12.01.07.06	"Blanket Monitoring Employee Communications"
332	Management Attention To Employee Off-the-Job Behavior	12.01.04.20	"Employee Off-the-Job Behavior"
333	Notifying Subjects Of Existing Monitoring Systems	9.07.02.13	"Systems Monitoring Tools"
334	All User Monitoring Reported To User's Manager And Logged	9.07.02.14	"User Monitoring Notification And Logging"
335	Managers Receive Logs And Determine Appropriate Internet Usage	9.07.02.15	"Internet Usage Logs"
336	No Internet Customer Usage Profiles Will Be Compiled	9.07.02.16	"Internet Customer Usage Profiles"

Table O-1: Index of Policy Title Conversion (Continued)

Previous Policy Number	ISPME v8 Title	Current Policy Number	ISPME v9 Title
337	Monitoring Or Recording Telephone Conversations	12.01.07.07	"Monitoring Or Recording Telephone Conversations"
338	Group Monitoring Rather Than Individual Monitoring	9.07.02.17	"Performance Monitoring"
339	Monitoring And Recording Activity In An Anonymous Fashion	9.07.02.18	"Monitoring And Recording Activity"
340	Timing Of Notification About Electronic Performance Monitoring	9.07.02.19	"Electronic Performance Monitoring Notification"
341	Existence Of Secret Systems Containing Personnel Records	12.01.04.21	"Secret Systems"
342	Guaranteed Access To Personal Information Held In Company X Records	12.01.04.22	"Access To Personal Information"
343	Periodic Distribution Of Employee Personnel Records	6.01.04.06	"Personnel Record Distributions"
344	Prospective Employees Given Opportunity To Decline Credit Checks	6.01.02.02	"Prospective Employee Credit Checks"
345	Disclosure Of Private Information To Third Parties	12.01.04.23	"Third-Party Private Information Disclosure"
346	Transfer Of Private Data Only To Organizations With Sufficient Controls	12.01.04.24	"Transferring Private Data"
347	Keeping Records Of All Third Parties Receiving Private Information	12.01.04.25	"Private Information Disclosure Records — Details"
348	Transfer Of Private Information To Other Countries Requires Approval	12.01.04.26	"International Transfer Of Private Information"
349	Subjects Given Opportunity To Block Private Information Disclosures	12.01.04.27	"Blocking Private Information Disclosures"
350	Disclosure Of Worker Names, Titles, And Other Contact Particulars	12.01.04.28	"Disclosure Of Worker Contact Information"
351	Disclosure Of Reason For Termination Of An Employee	12.01.04.29	"Reason For Termination Disclosure"

Table O-1: Index of Policy Title Conversion (Continued)

Previous Policy Number	ISPME v8 Title	Current Policy Number	ISPME v9 Title
352	Disclosure Of Worker Change Of Status Information	12.01.04.30	"Change Of Status Disclosure"
353	Granting Workers Access To Disclosures Of Private Data Records	12.01.04.31	"Access To Disclosures Of Private Data Records"
354	Privacy Of Individual Worker Performance Information	12.01.04.32	"Worker Performance Information"
355	Confidentiality Of Internal Investigations Information	12.01.07.08	"Internal Investigations Information Confidentiality"
356	Mandatory Disclosure Of Worker Health And Safety Information	6.01.04.07	"Health And Safety Information"
357	Use Of Tests To Determine Lifestyle, Political, & Religious Information	6.01.02.03	"Prospective Employee Lifestyle Information"
358	Privacy Of Personal Files Stored On Computers And In Desks	12.01.04.33	"Personal File Privacy"
359	Keeping Records Of Private Information Disclosed To Third Parties	12.01.04.34	"Private Information Disclosure Records — Maintenance"
360	Protection Of The Privacy Of Customer Information	12.01.04.35	"Customer Information Privacy"
361	Disclosure Of Customer Information Including Customer Identity	12.01.04.38	"Disclosure Of Customer Information"
362	Customer Right To Know Third Parties Receiving His Or Her Data	12.01.04.40	"Customer Information Recipient Disclosure"
363	Customer Objection Opportunity For Subpoena Record Requests	12.01.04.41	"Customer Notification Of Record Requests"
364	Privacy Policy Considered Contract Made At Time Information Provided	12.01.04.42	"Privacy Policy Application"
365	Privacy Of Correspondent Email Addresses And Telephone Numbers	12.01.04.43	"Privacy Of Correspondent Contact Information"
366	Telephone Disclosures Require Positive Caller Identification	8.07.07.02	"Information Disclosure By Telephone"

Table O-1: Index of Policy Title Conversion (Continued)

Previous Policy Number	ISPME v8 Title	Current Policy Number	ISPME v9 Title
367	No Discussions Of Private Information In Public Places	8.07.07.03	"Discussions In Public Places"
368	Customer Requests For Anonymity On Company X Systems	12.01.04.44	"Customer Anonymity"
369	Public Acknowledgement Of Or Reference To Famous Customers	12.01.04.45	"Famous Customer Identifications"
370	Distribution Of Statistical Information About Customer Records	12.01.04.46	"Customer Record Statistical Information"
371	Disclosure Of Computer Logs Reflecting Customer Activities	12.01.04.47	"Customer Activity Log Disclosure"
372	Deletion Of Log Information About Customer Activities	12.01.03.01	"Customer Log Information"
373	Monitoring Of Electronic Mail Messages	9.07.02.20	"Electronic Mail Message Monitoring"
374	Worker Rights To Read Third Party Electronic Mail Messages	8.07.04.01	"Third-Party Electronic Mail Message Review"
375	Employee Observance Of Company X's Right To Privacy	12.01.04.48	"Employee Observance Of Privacy"
376	Informed Consent Required For Questionable System Actions	12.01.04.49	"Consent For Questionable System Actions"
377	Record Creators Decide Whether Record Subjects May View Records	12.01.04.50	"Individual Record Access Authorization"
378	Disclosure Of Intended Uses Of Personal Information Prior To Collection	12.01.04.51	"Disclosure Of Intended Uses Of Personal Information"
379	Customers Given Opportunity To Decide To Receive Direct Mail	8.07.07.04	"Customers Opt-Out Of Direct Mail"
380	Placement Of Internet Advertising Only With Firms Valuing Privacy	8.07.06.02	"Internet Advertising"
381	Making Copies Of Information Appearing In One's Personnel File	12.01.04.52	"Personnel File Access"

Table O-1: Index of Policy Title Conversion (Continued)

Previous Policy Number	ISPME v8 Title	Current Policy Number	ISPME v9 Title
382	Conditions Under Which Employees May Examine Their Files	12.01.04.53	"Employee File Examination"
383	Employee Right To Add Explanatory Statement To Personnel File	12.01.04.54	"Employee Explanatory Statement"
384	Allegedly Incorrect Information To Be Corrected Or Labeled As Disputed	12.01.04.55	"Incorrect Personal Information"
385	Required Efforts To Ensure Integrity Of All Personal Records	12.01.04.56	"Personal Record Integrity"
386	Documented Procedures Required For Personal Record Handling Activities	12.01.04.57	"Personal Record Handling"
387	Required Efforts To Ensure Personal Records Are Used Only As Intended	12.01.04.58	"Personal Record Usage"
388	Use Of Personal Information For New Purposes	12.01.04.60	"Use Of Personal Information For New Purposes"
389	Linking Anonymous Information With Personally-Identifiable Information	12.01.04.61	"Anonymous Information Linking"
390	Use And Disclosure Of Personal Information About Customers	12.01.04.62	"Personal Customer Information"
391	Customer's Right-To-Know Nature Of Personal Information	12.01.04.63	"Customer Access To Personal Information"
392	Resale Or Subsequent Dissemination Of Customer Contact Information	12.01.04.64	"Customer Contact Information Usage"
393	Distribution Of Unsolicited Company X Marketing Materials	8.06.03.02	"Distribution Of Marketing Materials"
394	Major Systems Changes And Privacy Impact Review Committee	8.02.02.10	"Privacy Impact Reviews"
395	Source And Purpose Of Cookies And Web Bugs Must Be Revealed	8.07.06.03	"Internet Cookies And Web Bugs"
396	Compelling Need Required Prior To Usage Of Cookies Or Web Bugs	8.05.01.06	"Cookies And Web Bugs"

Table O-1: Index of Policy Title Conversion (Continued)

Previous Policy Number	ISPME v8 Title	Current Policy Number	ISPME v9 Title
397	No Embedded Secret Personal Identifiers Or Serial Numbers	12.01.04.65	"Embedded Personal Information"
398	Personal Identifiers Must Not Appear On Publicly-Accessible Locations	12.01.04.66	"Personal Identifiers On Publicly-Accessible Locations"
399	Severing Link Between Identifying Information And Research Data	12.01.04.68	"Private And Identification Information Linkage"
400	No Links Between Private Information And Other Information Types	12.01.04.69	"Private Information Links"
401	Retaining Personal Information Only As Long As Needed For Business	12.01.03.02	"Personal Information Retention"
402	Routine Destruction Of Transaction Logs Prevents Profile Compilation	12.01.03.03	"Transaction Log Destruction"
403	Subjects Given Opportunity To Opt-Out Of Private Data Systems	12.01.04.70	"Private Data System Opt Out"
404	All Marketing Communications Must Provide An Opt-Out Opportunity	8.07.03.03	"Marketing Communication Opt-Out Provision"
405	Subjects Must Opt-In To Be Included In Systems Handling Private Data	12.01.04.72	"Private Data System Approval"
406	Immediate Action For Individuals Requesting Database Removal	12.01.04.75	"Database Removal Of Individuals"
407	Subjects May Block Their Private Data From Being Used	12.01.04.77	"Blocking Private Data Usage"
408	Subjects Must Approve New Personal Data Uses After Merger/Acquisition	12.01.04.81	"Personal Data Uses After Merger Or Acquisition"
409	Business Structure Changes Do Not Permit Transfer Of Private Data	12.01.04.82	"Business Structure Changes And Transfer Of Private Data"
410	Maintenance Of Index To Databases Containing Private Information	12.01.04.83	"Database Indexes Containing Private Information"
411	Denial Of Benefits Due To Refusal To Provide Unnecessary Information	12.01.04.85	"Refusal To Provide Unnecessary Information"

Table O-1: Index of Policy Title Conversion (Continued)

Previous Policy Number	ISPME v8 Title	Current Policy Number	ISPME v9 Title
412	Confidentiality Agreements Required For All Company X Workers	6.01.03.02	"Non-Disclosure Agreements — Organization"
413	Chain Of Trust Agreements Required For Private & Sensitive Information	4.02.02.06	"Chain Of Trust Agreements"
414	Confidentiality Agreements Required For Office Machine Repair Staff	4.02.01.05	"Machine Repair Staff Confidentiality Agreements"
415	Changes In Employment Require Review Of Confidentiality Agreements	6.01.03.03	"Changes In Employment"
416	Default Restrictions On Dissemination Of Company X Information	4.02.01.06	"Information Dissemination"
417	Notification Of Suspected Loss Or Disclosure Of Sensitive Information	6.03.01.01	"Loss Or Disclosure Of Sensitive Information"
418	Revealing Information Systems Technical Details To Job Applicants	6.01.02.04	"Revealing Information To Prospective Employees"
419	Disclosure Of Information System Control Specifics To Third Parties	8.06.03.03	"Disclosure Of Information System Controls"
420	Material Financial Information Disclosures To Selected Parties	8.07.07.05	"Financial Information Disclosure"
421	Disclosure Of Information About Information System Vulnerabilities	6.03.01.02	"Disclosure Of Information System Vulnerabilities"
422	Vulnerability Information Detail Level In Press Releases Must Be Low	6.03.01.03	"Public Releases Of Vulnerability Information"
423	Disclosure Of System Vulnerability Exploitation And Victim Data	6.03.01.04	"System Vulnerability Exploitation And Victim Data"
424	Disclosure Of System Penetration Software Source Code And Analysis	12.03.02.01	"System Penetration Software Source Code"
425	Security Mechanisms Must Not Be Compromised for Customers	9.01.01.11	"Compromising Security Mechanisms For Customers"
426	Presentation Of Low-Profile And Secure Image	8.07.06.04	"Presentation Of Public Image"

Table O-1: Index of Policy Title Conversion (Continued)

Previous Policy Number	ISPME v8 Title	Current Policy Number	ISPME v9 Title
427	Information Access Control Systems And The Mosaic Theory	9.01.01.12	"Information Collection Restrictions"
428	Limitations On Third Party Collection Of Pricing Information	4.02.02.08	"Third-Party Collection Of Pricing Information"
429	Identity Theft Prevention By Restricting Access To Personal Information	9.06.01.15	"Personal Information Access"
430	Data Warehouse Access Restricted To Top And Middle Management	9.06.01.16	"Data Warehouse Access"
431	Dithering To Conceal True Nature Of Signal	8.05.01.07	"Concealing Information Transmission"
432	Right To Block, Conceal, Deny, Or Discontinue Service At Any Time	9.04.01.01	"Discontinuing Service"
433	Information With Multiple Sensitivity Classifications On Single System	5.02.01.13	"Multiple Sensitivity Classifications Computer Systems"
434	Choosing Computer Storage Media Data Classifications	5.02.01.14	"Storage Media Data Classifications"
435	Four Category Data Classification Scheme	5.02.01.02	"Four-Category Data Classification"
436	Three Category Data Classification Scheme	5.02.01.03	"Three-Category Data Classification"
437	Descriptive Prefixes For Data Classification Categories	5.02.01.06	"Data Classification Category Prefixes"
438	Trade Secrets Specifically Identified Prior To Disclosure	5.02.02.06	"Trade Secret Disclosure"
439	Company X Trade Secrets Must Be Named & Described On Intranet Page	8.07.06.05	"Trade Secrets On Intranet"
440	Chief Legal Counsel Is Sole Person To Declare Information A Trade Secret	5.02.01.07	"Declaration Of A Trade Secret"
441	Limited Data Classification System Labelling Requirements	5.02.02.07	"Data Classification Labeling"

Table O-1: Index of Policy Title Conversion (Continued)

Previous Policy Number	ISPME v8 Title	Current Policy Number	ISPME v9 Title
442	Information Treated As Secret Whenever Sensitivity Label Unknown	5.02.02.08	"Unknown Sensitivity Label"
443	Department Specific Data Classification Labels Permissible	5.02.02.09	"Department-Specific Classification Labels"
444	Responsibility For Assigning Data Classification System Labels	5.02.01.09	"Assigning Data Classification Labels"
445	Responsibility For Labelling Externally-Provided Information	5.02.02.10	"Externally-Provided Information Labeling"
446	Creator Must Select Data Classification Label For New Files & Messages	5.02.02.11	"Classification Labels For New Information"
447	Comprehensive Data Classification System Labelling Requirements	5.02.02.12	"Comprehensive Classification Labeling"
448	Location On The Page Of Hardcopy Sensitivity Labels	5.02.02.13	"Hardcopy Sensitivity Labels"
449	Bound Hardcopy Material And Sensitivity Labels	5.02.02.14	"Labeling Bound Hardcopy Material"
450	Labelling And Presentation Of Sensitive Information To Computer Users	5.02.02.15	"Presentation Of Sensitive Information"
451	Use Of Labels Throughout Sensitive Information's Life Cycle	5.02.02.16	"Information Life Cycle Labeling"
452	Maintaining, Propagating, And Reestablishing Data Classification Labels	5.02.02.17	"Maintaining Classification Labels"
453	Labels For Collections Of Information With Various Sensitivities	5.02.01.10	"Multiple Classification Labeling"
454	New Label After Storage Media Exposure To Secret Data Or Applications	5.02.01.11	"Media Exposure To Secret Data"
455	User-Generated Classification Labels Do Not Bind Company X	5.02.01.12	"User-Generated Classification Labels"
456	Permission Required When Making Copies Of Sensitive Information	5.02.02.18	"Copying Sensitive Information"

Table O-1: Index of Policy Title Conversion (Continued)

Previous Policy Number	ISPME v8 Title	Current Policy Number	ISPME v9 Title
457	Tracking Copies Of Sensitive Information	5.02.02.19	"Tracking Sensitive Information"
458	Destruction Of Intermediate Products Containing Sensitive Information	5.02.02.20	"Intermediate Products Containing Sensitive Information"
459	Destruction Of Waste Copies Of Sensitive Information	5.02.02.21	"Waste Copies Of Sensitive Information"
460	Attended Operation Required When Printing Sensitive Information	5.02.02.22	"Printing Sensitive Information"
461	Page Numbering and Accountability for Sensitive Information	5.02.02.23	"Accountability for Sensitive Information"
462	Third Party Non-Disclosure Agreements And Sensitive Information	4.02.01.07	"Non-Disclosure Agreements — Third Party"
463	Disclosure Of Third Party Information In Possession Of Company X	9.01.01.13	"Disclosure Of Third-Party Information"
464	Private And Confidential Information Sent By Internal Or External Mail	8.07.05.05	"Sending Private And Confidential Information"
465	Secret Information Sent By Internal Or External Mail	8.07.07.06	"Sending Secret Information"
466	Two Envelopes Required For Sensitive Information Sent By Mail	8.07.07.07	"Sending Sensitive Information"
467	Permissible Methods For Transmitting Secret Hardcopy Information	8.07.07.08	"Transmitting Secret Hardcopy Information"
468	Special Paper Preventing Copying Of Sensitive Documents	5.02.02.24	"Preventing Copies Of Sensitive Documents"
469	Secret Information May Only Be Printed On Paper Indicating Originals	5.02.02.25	"Printing Secret Information"
470	Delivery Of Sensitive Computer Output To Intended Recipients	5.02.02.26	"Delivering Sensitive Computer Output"
471	Delivery Via Courier Of Sensitive Hardcopy Information	5.02.02.27	"Using Couriers"

Table O-1: Index of Policy Title Conversion (Continued)

Previous Policy Number	ISPME v8 Title	Current Policy Number	ISPME v9 Title
472	Acknowledgement Required For Deliveries Of Secret Information	5.02.02.28	"Delivery Of Secret Information"
473	Immediate Written Acknowledgment Of Receipt For Secret Information	5.02.02.29	"Receipt Of Secret Information"
474	Log Book Reflecting Movement Of Secret Documents	5.02.02.30	"Logging Movement Of Secret Documents"
475	Sequence Numbers For Secret Documents	5.02.02.31	"Secret Document Sequence Numbers"
476	Those With Custody Of Sensitive Information Must Restrict Access	5.02.02.32	"Securing Sensitive Information"
477	Prior Notice And Attended Operation For Sensitive Information Faxing	8.07.05.06	"Faxing Sensitive Information — Notification"
478	Faxing Sensitive Information Requires Human Presence	8.07.05.07	"Faxing Sensitive Information — Human Presence"
479	Faxing Sensitive Information Via Untrusted Third Parties	8.07.05.08	"Faxing Sensitive Information — Intermediaries"
480	Cover Sheet Receipt Confirmation Before Faxing Sensitive Information	8.07.05.09	"Faxing Sensitive Information — Cover Sheet"
481	When Faxing Sensitive Information Is Permissible	8.07.05.10	"Faxing Sensitive Information — Unencrypted"
482	Destination Physical Security For Sensitive Information Faxing	8.07.05.11	"Faxing Sensitive Information — Physical Security"
483	Encryption Required For Sending Secret Information By Fax	8.07.05.12	"Faxing Secret Information — Encryption"
484	Password Required For Sending Secret Information By Fax	8.07.05.14	"Faxing Secret Information — Passwords"
485	Fax Cover Sheet Must Contain Restricted Dissemination Notice	8.07.05.15	"Fax Cover Sheet Notice"
486	Binding Signatures Must Be Sent By Traditional Paper Means	8.07.07.09	"Binding Signatures"

Table O-1: Index of Policy Title Conversion (Continued)

Previous Policy Number	ISPME v8 Title	Current Policy Number	ISPME v9 Title
487	Discussion Of Secret Information And Use Of Speaker Phones	8.07.05.16	"Secret Information On Speaker Phones"
488	Guarded Terms For Telephone Discussions Of Sensitive Information	8.07.07.10	"Telephone Discussions Of Sensitive Information"
489	Use Of Cordless Or Cellular Telephones For Secret Discussions	8.07.07.11	"Cordless Or Cellular Telephones"
490	Secret Discussions On Wireless Microphones And Radio Networks	8.07.07.12	"Wireless Transmissions Of Secret Information"
491	Internet Telephone Facilities May Not Be Used For Secret Discussions	8.07.06.06	"Internet Telephone Facilities"
492	Secondary Dissemination Of Secret Information	9.06.01.17	"Secondary Dissemination Of Secret Information"
493	Travelling On Public Transportation With Secret Information	8.07.02.02	"Traveling With Secret Information"
494	Exposure Of Sensitive Information In Public Places	8.07.07.13	"Public Exposure Of Sensitive Information"
495	Secret Information Discussions In Company X Administrative Areas	8.07.07.14	"Discussions In Administrative Areas"
496	Storing Secret Information On Transportable Computers	9.08.01.03	"Secret Information On Transportable Computers"
497	Controls For Transportable Computers With Sensitive Information	9.08.01.05	"Transportable Computers With Sensitive Information"
498	Transportable Computers Must Be Hand Luggage on Airplanes	9.08.01.06	"Transportable Computers On Airplanes"
499	Taking Secret Information Into A Foreign Country	8.07.02.03	"International Transport Of Secret Information — Security"
500	Permission Required To Take Secret Information Into Foreign Country	8.07.02.04	"International Transport Of Secret Information — Authorization"
501	Floppy Disk Input/Output Encryption Drivers Prevent Disclosure	8.06.01.01	"Floppy Disks"

Table O-1: Index of Policy Title Conversion (Continued)

Previous Policy Number	ISPME v8 Title	Current Policy Number	ISPME v9 Title
502	Removal Of Sensitive Information From Company X Premises	8.06.03.04	"Removal Of Sensitive Information"
503	Secret Information Must Not Leave Company X Offices In Any Form	8.06.03.05	"Secret Information Leaving Offices"
504	Log for Sensitive Information Removed From Company X Premises	8.06.03.06	"Sensitive Information Removal Log"
505	Handling Hardcopy Sensitive Information Off Company X Premises	8.07.02.05	"Removing Hardcopy Sensitive Information"
506	Transfer Of Sensitive Information To Third Parties On Computer Media	8.07.02.06	"Transfer Of Sensitive Information"
507	Certificate Of Destruction Rather Than Return Of Storage Media	8.07.01.04	"Certificate Of Destruction Of Storage Media"
508	Confidentiality Of Company X Computer Related Documentation	8.06.04.02	"Documentation Confidentiality"
509	Secret Information Sent By Electronic Mail	8.07.04.02	"Secret Information In Electronic Mail"
510	Diskless Workstations Must Be Used By R&D Department Workers	8.07.05.17	"Diskless Workstations"
511	Information Systems Unsuitable For Time-Sensitive Information	8.07.05.18	"Time-Sensitive Information"
512	Use Of Hard-Disk Drives For Storage Of Sensitive Information	8.07.05.19	"Storage Of Sensitive Information"
513	Commingling Of Sensitive And Non-Sensitive Information	8.06.01.02	"Storing Mixed Classified Information"
514	Clean Desks And Working Areas	7.03.01.01	"Clean Desks — Non-Working Hours"
515	Traditional Clean Desk Policy	7.03.01.02	"Clean Desks — Active Use"
516	Securing Sensitive Information In Unattended Rooms	7.03.01.04	"Unattended Rooms"

Table O-1: Index of Policy Title Conversion (Continued)

Previous Policy Number	ISPME v8 Title	Current Policy Number	ISPME v9 Title
517	Storage Of Sensitive Information On Personal Computers	9.08.01.07	"Sensitive Information On Personal Computers"
518	Storage Of Sensitive Information When Not In Use	7.03.01.05	"Sensitive Information Storage"
519	Retention Period Required For All Sensitive Information	12.01.03.04	"Sensitive Information Retention"
520	Date For Declassification Must Be Specified If Known	5.02.01.15	"Declassification Date"
521	Accelerated Declassification And Downgrading Of Sensitive Information	5.02.01.16	"Accelerated Information Declassification"
522	Extension Of Declassification Or Downgrading Date	5.02.01.17	"Declassification Extension"
523	Automatic Schedule For Downgrading Company X Information	5.02.01.18	"Declassification Schedule"
524	Annual Declassification Review For Sensitive Information	5.02.01.19	"Annual Declassification Review"
525	Declassification Of Sensitive Information Required As Soon As Practical	5.02.01.20	"Declassification Of Sensitive Information"
526	Sensitive Information Destruction/Concealment Before Servicing Done	5.02.02.34	"Sensitive Information Storage Media"
527	Release Of Computer Storage Media Prior To Degaussing/Zeroizing	8.06.03.07	"Release Of Computer Storage Media"
528	Destruction Of Sensitive Information On Computer Storage Media	8.06.02.01	"Sensitive Information Destruction"
529	Zeroization Required For Erasure Of Sensitive Information	8.06.01.03	"Erasure of Sensitive Information"
530	Approved Methods For Hardcopy Sensitive Information Disposal	8.06.02.02	"Hardcopy Disposal"
531	Strip Shredders Must Not Be Used For Destruction Of Sensitive Information	8.06.02.03	"Strip Shredders"

Table O-1: Index of Policy Title Conversion (Continued)

Previous Policy Number	ISPME v8 Title	Current Policy Number	ISPME v9 Title
532	Areas Containing Sensitive Information Must Have Shredders	8.06.03.08	"Areas Containing Sensitive Information"
533	Use Of Secure Containers For All But Secret Information Disposal	8.06.02.04	"Secure Information Containers"
534	Security Staff Must Follow Information Destruction Instructions	8.06.02.05	"Information Destruction Instructions"
535	Sensitive Information Destruction Must Follow Specified Procedures	8.06.02.06	"Sensitive Information Destruction Procedures"
536	Persons Authorized To Destroy Sensitive Company X Information	8.06.02.07	"Information Destruction Personnel"
537	Use Of Metal Boxes To Hold Sensitive Information To Be Destroyed	8.06.02.08	"Sensitive Information Destruction Boxes"
538	Destruction Of Materials Used In Handling Sensitive Information	8.06.02.09	"Sensitive Information Materials"
539	Approval Required Before Access To Sensitive Or Valuable Information	9.06.01.18	"Sensitive Or Valuable Information Access"
540	Access To Secret Information Granted On Individual (Not Group) Basis	9.06.01.19	"Secret Information Access"
541	Granting System Privileges By Chain Of Authority Delegation	9.02.02.11	"Granting System Privileges"
542	Confidentiality Agreements And Disclosures Of Sensitive Information	4.02.01.08	"Confidentiality Agreements"
543	Specific Handling Instructions For Recipients Of Sensitive Information	4.02.02.09	"Sensitive Information Handling"
544	Requests For Company X Information Referred To Public Relations	9.01.01.14	"Requests For Organization Information"
545	Prohibition Against Disclosing Customer Projects, Strategies, Etc.	9.01.01.15	"Disclosing Customer Business Information"
546	Marketing Information Must Never Be Shared With Competitors	9.01.01.16	"Sharing Marketing Information"

Table O-1: Index of Policy Title Conversion (Continued)

Previous Policy Number	ISPME v8 Title	Current Policy Number	ISPME v9 Title
547	Information Released To The Public Must Have Single Official Source	9.01.01.17	"Information Released To The Public — Contact Name"
548	Approval Required Prior To Release Of Company X Information	9.01.01.19	"Release Of Organization Information"
549	Public Representations About Future Earnings Or New Product Prospects	9.01.01.20	"Future Earnings Or Products"
550	Waiting Period Prior To External Disclosure Of Requested Information	9.01.01.21	"External Information Requests"
551	Phased Public Release Of Controversial Sensitive Information	9.01.01.22	"Controversial Sensitive Information"
552	Approval For Help Wanted Ads And Disclosure Of Sensitive Material	9.01.01.23	"Help Wanted Advertising"
553	Established Procedure For Review Of Information Released To Public	9.01.01.24	"Information Released To The Public — Authorization"
554	Prior Review For Speeches, Presentations, Technical Papers, Etc.	9.01.01.25	"Public Communications"
555	Conditions For Acceptance Of Third Party Sensitive Information	4.02.02.10	"Receiving Third-Party Information"
556	Signing Third Party Confidentiality Agreements Without Approval	12.01.02.21	"Third-Party Confidentiality Agreements"
557	Sensitive Information Access For Temporaries And Consultants	4.02.01.09	"Temporary Worker And Consultant Access"
558	Workers Have Right To Know All Workplace Hazards	6.01.04.08	"Workplace Hazards"
559.	Nature Of Labels On Hazardous Products And Services	5.02.02.35	"Labeling Hazardous Products And Services"
560	Refrain From Pressuring Employees Who Worked At Competitors	6.01.03.04	"Confidentiality Agreements At Previous Employers"
561	Disclosure Of Privacy Related Information Security Policies & Procedures	6.02.01.02	"Privacy-Related Policies and Procedures"

Table O-1: Index of Policy Title Conversion (Continued)

Previous Policy Number	ISPME v8 Title	Current Policy Number	ISPME v9 Title
562	Uninvited Attendees At Meetings Covering Secret Information	8.07.07.15	"Meeting Attendees"
563	Third Party Visitor Meetings In Enclosed Conference Rooms	8.07.07.16	"Meetings With Third Parties"
564	Oral Disclosure Of Confidential Information In Meetings	8.07.07.17	"Confidential Information In Meetings"
565	Black Boards And White Boards Must Be Erased After Meetings	8.07.07.18	"Erasable Surfaces"
566	Erasure Of Sensitive Information On Black Boards And White Boards	8.07.07.19	"Erasure Of Erasable Surfaces"
567	Nature And Location Of Company X Information Is Confidential	9.01.01.27	"Nature And Location Of Organization Information"
568	Information Security Policies & Procedures Are For Internal Use Only	3.01.01.11	"Use Of Information Security Policies And Procedures"
569	Location Of Data Processing Centers Considered Confidential	7.02.01.03	"Computer Center Address"
570	Browsing On Company X Systems And Networks Prohibited	9.01.01.28	"Browsing Systems"
571	Authorized Systems Administrator Examination Of Private User Files	12.01.04.94	"Examination Of Private User Files"
572	Power Down Required For Systems Processing Sensitive Information	7.03.01.06	"Powering Down Computers"
573	Covering Sensitive Information When Interrupted At Work	7.03.01.07	"Covering Sensitive Information"
574	Never Lend Computers Containing Sensitive Information To Others	9.08.01.08	"Lending Computers Containing Sensitive Information"
575	Locking File Cabinets Must Be Provided To And Used By All Workers	7.03.01.08	"Locking File Cabinets"
576	Prohibited Trading Dates For Employee Stock Transactions	6.01.04.09	"Employee Stock Transactions"

Table O-1: Index of Policy Title Conversion (Continued)

Previous Policy Number	ISPME v8 Title	Current Policy Number	ISPME v9 Title
577	Dictation Machines And Tape Recorders For Sensitive Information	8.07.05.20	"Recording Sensitive Information"
578	Periodic Sweeps For Bugging, Interception, And Recording Equipment	7.01.03.01	"Periodic Sweeps For Surveillance Equipment"
579	Specific Quantitative Goal For System Availability	8.01.01.04	"System Availability"
580	Limitation Of User Abilities To Delay Or Interrupt Service	8.07.05.21	"Excessive Resource Consumption"
581	Establishment And Use Of Control Override Facilities	9.05.05.08	"Control Override Facilities"
582	Management Definition Of Circumstances For Use Of Control Overrides	9.05.05.09	"Control Override Usage"
583	Generation And Review Of Logs Showing Use Of Override Facilities	9.07.02.21	"Override Facility Logs"
584	Computing Environment Supporting Equipment Required	7.02.01.04	"Computer Center Environmental Controls"
585	Power Conditioning Equipment Required For All Microcomputers	7.02.02.01	"Power Conditioning Equipment"
586	Static Electricity Protection Equipment And Local Conditions	7.02.01.05	"Static Electricity Protection"
587	Dispersion Of Computer And Communication Systems	7.02.01.06	"Computer System Dispersion"
588	Web And Commerce Servers Must Not Store Critical Information	8.07.03.05	"Web And Commerce Server Storage"
589	Avoidance Of Communication Network Central Point Of Failure	8.05.01.08	"Network Central Point Of Failure"
590	Diverse Long Distance Network Routing Required	8.05.01.09	"Multiple Carriers"
591	Compliance With Standards Required For Emergency/Disaster Support	11.01.01.01	"Emergency And Disaster Support Requirements"

Table O-1: Index of Policy Title Conversion (Continued)

Previous Policy Number	ISPME v8 Title	Current Policy Number	ISPME v9 Title
592	Framework For Segmenting Information Resources By Recovery Priority	11.01.03.01	"Information Resource Classification"
593	Annual Criticality Rating For Multi-User Applications	11.01.02.01	"Multi-User Application Criticality Rating"
594	Five Category Application Criticality Classification Scheme	11.01.02.02	"Five-Category Application Criticality Classification Scheme"
595	Preparation And Maintenance Of Computer Emergency Response Plans	8.01.03.02	"Computer Emergency Response Plans"
596	Continuous Computer Center Staffing For Prompt Problem Resolution	7.01.04.01	"Computer Center Staffing"
597	Organization/Maintenance Of Computer Emergency Response Team	8.01.03.03	"Computer Emergency Response Team"
598	Regular Simulated Incidents To Test Computer Emergency Response Team	8.01.03.04	"Testing the Computer Emergency Response Team"
599	Required Actions Following Suspected System Intrusion	8.01.03.05	"Suspected System Intrusions"
600	Operations Staff Must Have Documented Intrusion Response Procedure	8.01.03.06	"Intrusion Response Procedures"
601	Regular Monitoring Of Information Security Vulnerability Advisories	8.01.03.07	"Vulnerability Advisories"
602	Information Security Alert System	8.01.03.08	"Information Security Alert System"
603	Users Must Not Distribute Information About System Vulnerabilities	6.03.02.01	"Reporting System Vulnerabilities"
604	Users Must Notify Help Desk About All Production System Problems	6.03.01.05	"Production System Problems"
605	Notify Management Of Conditions That May Disrupt Work	6.03.02.02	"Disruptive Conditions"
606	Expected Employee Assistance During Business Restoration	11.01.04.02	"Business Restoration Employee Expectations"

Table O-1: Index of Policy Title Conversion (Continued)

Previous Policy Number	ISPME v8 Title	Current Policy Number	ISPME v9 Title
607	Inventory Of Key Technical Jobs And Individuals Who Fill Them	8.01.01.06	"Key Technical Jobs"
608	Cross Training For Staff In Critical Technical Jobs	8.01.01.07	"Cross Training"
609	Preparation And Maintenance Of Computer Disaster Recovery Plans	8.01.01.05	"Computer Disaster Recovery Plans"
610	Preparation And Maintenance Of Business Contingency Plans	11.01.03.02	"Preparation And Maintenance Of Business Contingency Plans"
611	Business And Computer Continuity Planning Process	11.01.04.01	"Business And Computer Continuity Planning"
612	Reversion To Manual Procedures Where Cost-Effectively Possible	11.01.05.01	"Reversion To Manual Procedures"
613	Annual Inventory Of Information Systems Hardware, Software, Etc.	5.01.01.02	"Asset Inventory — Technology"
614	Equipment Custodians Must Control Inventory With Serial Numbers	5.01.01.03	"Controlling Inventory"
615	Annual Determination Level Of Disaster/Emergency Support Levels	11.01.05.03	"Business Interruption Support Levels"
616	Computer And Communications System Contingency Plan Testing	11.01.05.04	"Contingency Plan Testing"
617	Preventive Maintenance On Computer And Communication Systems	7.02.04.02	"Preventive Maintenance"
618	Information Systems Equipment Maintenance Requirements	7.02.04.03	"Equipment Maintenance"
619	Internet Domain Name Registration Payments Must Be Confirmed	8.05.01.10	"Internet Domain Name Registration"
620	Contact Numbers For Information Systems Department Staff	8.01.01.08	"Contact Information"
621	Access Control For End-User File Restoration Processes	9.05.05.10	"File Restoration Access Control"

Table O-1: Index of Policy Title Conversion (Continued)

Previous Policy Number	ISPME v8 Title	Current Policy Number	ISPME v9 Title
622	What Data To Backup And Minimum Backup Frequency	8.04.01.02	"Data Backups"
623	Periodic And Supplementary Backups Required For Portable Computers	8.07.05.22	"Portable Computer Backups"
624	Do Not Use Hard Drives On Public Access Computers For Backup	8.04.01.03	"Backup Media"
625	Encrypting Backup Media Stored Off-Site	8.04.01.04	"Backup Media Encryption"
626	Two Copies Of Sensitive, Critical, Or Valuable Information	8.07.05.23	"Copies Of Sensitive, Critical, Or Valuable Information"
627	Two Copies Of Critical Company X Records Stored Off-Site	8.04.01.06	"Multiple Backup Copies"
628	Management Review Of End-User Backup Process	8.07.05.24	"Backup Review"
629	Specification Of Backup Process And Frequency	8.04.01.07	"Backup Process"
630	Automatic Backup To Local Area Network Server	8.04.01.08	"Automatic Backups"
631	Users Notified That All Data Is Routinely Backed-Up	8.04.01.09	"Backup Information Review"
632	Make At Least One Copy of Critical Backed-Up Files Prior To Use	8.04.01.10	"Critical Backup Files"
633	Production Batch Processing Only If Pre-Processing Backup Is Complete	8.04.01.11	"Pre-Processing Backup"
634	Annual Audits To Determine Whether Production Backup Is Performed	12.02.02.01	"Production Backup Audits"
635	Off-Site Storage Of Backup Media	8.04.01.12	"Backup Media Storage"
636	Backup Media Stored In Separate Fire Zones From Originating Machine	8.04.01.13	"Backup Media Fire Zone"
637	Backup Media Storage Rooms, Vaults, & Cabinets Must Be Kept Locked	8.04.01.14	"Backup Media Storage Units"

Table O-1: Index of Policy Title Conversion (Continued)

Previous Policy Number	ISPME v8 Title	Current Policy Number	ISPME v9 Title
638	Archival Storage Of Every Version Of Internet Web & Commerce Sites	8.04.01.15	"Web And Commerce Site File Archives"
639	Quarterly Archival Backups Required For All Critical Information	8.04.01.16	"Critical Information Backups"
640	Department Managers Must Identify Vital Records	12.01.03.05	"Vital Record Identification"
641	Directory Of Information Held In Archival Storage	8.04.01.17	"Archival Storage Directory"
642	Acceptable Archival Storage Data Media	8.04.01.18	"Archival Storage Media"
643	Regular Testing Of Archival Storage Data Media	8.04.01.19	"Archival Storage Media Testing"
644	Regular Testing Of Used Data Media Employed For Archival Storage	8.04.01.20	"Archival Storage Media Quality"
645	Preservation Of Data Held In Archival Storage	8.04.01.21	"Archival Storage Preservation"
646	Minimum Information Retention Period	12.01.03.07	"Information Retention Period"
647	Definition Of Archival Storage Data Retention Schedule	12.01.03.08	"Archival Storage Retention Schedule"
648	Responsibility For Archival Storage Data Retention Schedule	12.01.03.09	"Data Retention Schedule"
649	Business Source Document Data Retention Requirements	12.01.03.10	"Business Source Document Retention"
650	Business Source Document Data Retention Period	12.01.03.11	"Business Source Document Retention Period"
651	Regular Purging Of Information Which Is No Longer Needed	12.01.03.13	"Destruction Of Information"
652	Procedure For Release Of Used Equipment And Media To Third Parties	7.02.06.01	"Used Component Release"
653	Information Destruction And Information Systems Equipment Disposal	7.02.06.02	"Information And Equipment Disposal"

Table O-1: Index of Policy Title Conversion (Continued)

Previous Policy Number	ISPME v8 Title	Current Policy Number	ISPME v9 Title
654	Destruction Of Records Or Information Requires Management Approval	12.01.03.14	"Record Destruction"
655	Record Destruction Prohibited Unless Authorized By List Or Schedule	12.01.03.15	"Record Destruction Schedule"
656	Data Destruction Process Placed On Hold In Response To Discovery	12.01.03.16	"Data Destruction Moratorium"
657	Management Must Be Notified Of Information Integrity Attributes	12.03.01.01	"Information Integrity Attributes"
658	Management Notification Of Information Integrity Controls Failure	6.03.03.01	"Integrity Controls Failure Notification"
659	Calculation Recipients Must Receive Information To Verify Correctness	8.07.03.06	"Account Calculation Verification"
660	Nature Of Information Modifications Must Be Disclosed	8.06.03.10	"Disclosure Of Information Modifications"
661	Source And Date Labels Required For Major Decision Input	5.02.02.36	"Labeling Management Decision Data"
662	Suppression Or Labelling Of Incomplete Or Obsolete Information	5.02.02.37	"Incomplete Or Obsolete Information"
663	Production Input Transactions Must Have Sequence Numbers	10.02.03.01	"Production System Input Transaction Authorization"
664	Authorization Required For All Production System Input Transactions	10.02.03.02	"Rejected Or Suspended Input Validation"
665	Changes To Sensitive, Critical, Or Valuable Information	10.02.02.06	"Changes To Sensitive, Critical, Or Valuable Information"
666	Input Data Validation And Rejected Item Handling	10.02.01.02	"Input Data Validation And Rejected Item Handling"
667	Email & Regular Mail Address Change Confirmed Via Previous Address	8.07.05.25	"Address Change Confirmation"
668	Double Keying Required For All Amounts Over $1,000.	10.02.01.03	"Double-Keying Large Transactions"

Table O-1: Index of Policy Title Conversion (Continued)

Previous Policy Number	ISPME v8 Title	Current Policy Number	ISPME v9 Title
669	Line Numbering Required For Critical Free-Form Text Messages	8.07.05.26	"Critical Message Line Numbering"
670	Originator Of Transactions Must Be Clearly Identified	10.02.01.04	"Transaction Originator"
671	Data Warehouse Input Requires Source, Classification, And Other Labels	5.02.01.23	"Data Warehouse Input Labels"
672	Official Documents Prepared By Hand Must Exclusively Use Ink	5.02.02.38	"Official Manually-Prepared Documents"
673	Review For Important Computer Analyses Done By Individuals	8.01.04.04	"Computer Analyses Review"
674	Controls For Data Used To Arrive At Decisions Involving $100,000.	10.02.02.07	"Control Validation"
675	Acceptable Risk Of Undetected Information Alteration	4.01.01.01	"Undetected Information Alteration"
676	Altered Photographs Must Be So Labeled	5.02.02.39	"Altered Photographs"
677	Handling Of Rejected Input Transactions Via Suspense Files	10.02.02.08	"Rejected Input Transactions"
678	Time For Problem Resolution Of Items In Suspense Files	10.02.02.09	"Suspense File Resolution Timings"
679	Input Validation Procedures For Rejected Or Suspended Input	10.02.02.08	"Rejected Input Transactions"
680	Personal Information Changed Only After Correct Prior Values Provided	12.01.04.95	"Personal Information Changes"
681	Authorization For Changes To Production Data And Programs	8.01.01.09	"Production Changes"
682	All Production Transactions Must Be Authorized By Management	8.01.01.10	"Production Transaction Authorization"
683	Review Reasonableness And Accuracy Of Changes To Internal Records	10.02.04.02	"Internal Record Change Reviews"

Table O-1: Index of Policy Title Conversion (Continued)

Previous Policy Number	ISPME v8 Title	Current Policy Number	ISPME v9 Title
684	Required Actions After Errors In Records Are Detected	8.07.03.08	"Error Investigation"
685	Standard Control Procedures For Correcting Business Records	8.01.01.11	"Correcting Business Records"
686	Cellular Phones Must Not Be Used Anywhere In Data Center	7.01.04.02	"Cellular Telephone Usage"
687	Truthful Representations By Company X Employees	8.07.07.20	"Organization Representations"
688	Misrepresentation Of Identity On Electronic Communication Systems	8.07.06.08	"Identity Misrepresentation"
689	Consistent Way Of Representing Employee Contact Information	8.06.03.11	"Employee Contact Information"
690	Need For Cross-Validation Of Important Information	8.07.06.09	"Information Cross-Validation"
691	All Public Representations Must Be Cleared Through Public Relations	8.07.07.21	"Public Representation Approval"
692	Right To Free Speech Does Not Apply To Company X Systems	8.07.05.27	"Right To Free Speech"
693	Right To Censor Data On Organizational Systems	8.07.05.28	"Data Censoring"
694	New Information Types Must Be Reflected In Corporate Data Dictionary	5.01.01.04	"Corporate Data Dictionary"
695	Right To Remove Offensive Material Without Warning	8.07.05.29	"Removing Offensive Material"
696	No Responsibility For Monitoring Content Of Information Systems	8.07.05.30	"Content Monitoring Responsibility"
697	Prohibited Uses Of Company X Computer & Communication Facilities	12.01.05.17	"Discussions Using Computer and Communication Facilities"
698	Disclaimer Of Responsibility Or Liability For Message Contents	8.07.06.10	"Message Disclaimer"

Table O-1: Index of Policy Title Conversion (Continued)

Previous Policy Number	ISPME v8 Title	Current Policy Number	ISPME v9 Title
699	Comments On Systems Do Not Necessarily Reflect Company X Positions	8.07.06.12	"Public Comments On Electronic Systems"
700	Warnings Required If Recipients Might Be Offended Or Upset	8.07.07.22	"Potentially-Offensive Communications"
701	All Information Posted To Internet Must Have Standard Content Labels	8.07.06.13	"Internet Content Labels"
702	Network Message Protection Services Not Provided	8.05.01.12	"Network Message Protection Services"
703	Prohibition Against Sexual, Ethnic, And Racial Harassment	6.01.04.10	"Sexual, Ethnic, And Racial Harassment"
704	Restricted Behavior For Outbound Internet Communications	8.07.06.15	"Outbound Internet Communications"
705	Internal Network Addresses Must Not Be Publicly Released	8.05.01.13	"Internal Network Addresses"
706	Access Control Packages Required For Computers On The Network	9.04.01.02	"Network Computer Access Control"
707	Access Control Packages For Network-Connected Computers	9.04.02.01	"Network-Connected Computers Access Control"
708	Large Networks Must Be Divided Into Separate Domains	8.05.01.14	"Network Domains"
709	Internet Connected Machines Must Have Intrusion Detection Systems	8.05.01.16	"Intrusion Detection Systems"
710	Permissible Internet Access Without Firewalls	9.04.07.02	"Internet Access Without Firewalls"
711	All Internet Web Servers Must Be Firewall Protected	9.04.09.01	"Web Server Firewalls"
712	Internet Commerce Servers Must Be In Demilitarized Zone (DMZ)	8.05.01.19	"Internet Commerce Server Firewalls"
713	Public Servers On Internet Must Be Placed On Separate Subnets	8.05.01.20	"Public Internet Servers"

Table O-1: Index of Policy Title Conversion (Continued)

Previous Policy Number	ISPME v8 Title	Current Policy Number	ISPME v9 Title
714	Internet Commerce Servers Must Use Digital Certificates & Encryption	8.07.03.09	"Internet Commerce Server Security"
715	Dial-Up Connections Must Always Utilize Firewalls	8.05.01.21	"Dial-Up Connections"
716	Real-Time External Network Connections Require Firewalls	8.05.01.22	"Real-Time External Network Connections"
717	Firewalls Must Be Configured So All Services Are Denied Unless Approved	8.05.01.23	"Firewall Configuration"
718	Firewalls Must Run On Dedicated Computers	8.05.01.24	"Firewall Computers"
719	Firewall Configuration Change Requires Information Security Approval	8.05.01.25	"Firewall Configuration Changes"
720	Internet Connections Require Approved Firewalls	8.05.01.26	"Internet Connections"
721	Trusted Host Relationships Prohibited For Internet Connected Machines	8.05.01.27	"Shared Directory Systems"
722	Direct Network Connections With Outside Organizations (Tunnels)	8.05.01.28	"Network Connections with Outside Organizations"
723	Inter-Processor Commands From Outside Locations Prohibited	9.04.03.06	"Inter-Processor Commands"
724	Isolate Systems Containing Secret Information From Network	9.06.02.02	"Secret Information System Isolation"
725	Customers Must Specifically Agree To Receive New/Enhanced Service	8.07.03.10	"New Or Enhanced Service"
726	Prior Approval Required For All Communication Line Changes	8.05.01.29	"Communication Line Changes"
727	Prior Approval Required For Set-Up Of Multi-User Systems	8.02.01.01	"Implementing Multi-User Systems"
728	Prior Approval Required For In-House System Interconnection	8.02.01.02	"System Interconnection"
729	Separate Subnet Required For Walk-Up Network Connections	9.04.06.01	"Walk-Up Network Connections"

Table O-1: Index of Policy Title Conversion (Continued)

Previous Policy Number	ISPME v8 Title	Current Policy Number	ISPME v9 Title
730	Unattended Active Network Ports In Public Areas Prohibited	9.04.07.03	"Public Access To Active Network Ports"
731	Network Ports In Vacant Offices Must Be Promptly Disabled	9.04.07.04	"Network Ports In Vacant Offices"
732	Configuration To Prevent/Detect Unauthorized Network Connections	8.05.01.30	"Network Connection Configuration"
733	Criteria For Connecting Company X Networks To Third Party Networks	9.04.02.02	"Connecting Third-Party Networks"
734	Security Requirements For Network-Connected Third Party Systems	4.02.02.11	"Network-Connected Third-Party Systems"
735	Approval Required For Internet Connection Establishment	9.04.01.03	"Internet Connection Approval"
736	Security Criteria A Prerequisite For Intranet Connection	8.05.01.31	"Intranet Connection Security Criteria"
737	Inventory Of Connections To External Networks	8.05.01.32	"External Network Connection Inventory"
738	Standards Of Common Carriers Do Not Apply	9.04.01.04	"Standards Of Common Carriers"
739	Participation In Public Networks As Service Provider	8.05.01.33	"Providing Public Network Services"
740	Formation Of Binding Contracts Via Electronic Systems	8.07.03.11	"Binding Contracts By Electronic Systems"
741	Conducting Business Over The Internet With Foreign Companies	8.07.03.12	"International Internet Business Transactions"
742	Trading Partner Agreement Prior To Use Of Computerized Networks	8.07.03.13	"Trading Partner Network Agreement"
743	Only Designated Employees May Form Contracts Via Email	8.07.03.14	"Electronic Mail Contracts"
744	Criteria For Accepting And Acting On Computerized Transactions	8.07.03.15	"Accepting Computerized Transactions"

Table O-1: Index of Policy Title Conversion (Continued)

Previous Policy Number	ISPME v8 Title	Current Policy Number	ISPME v9 Title
745	Multiple Communication Channels For Electronic Offers & Acceptances	8.07.03.16	"Electronic Offers And Acceptances"
746	Internet Customers Must Specifically Agree To Terms & Conditions	8.07.06.16	"Internet Terms And Conditions"
747	Encryption Processes Must Not Be Used Unless Previously Approved	10.03.02.01	"Encryption Process Approval — Systems"
748	Use Of Any Encryption Process Requires Prior Written Approval	10.03.02.02	"Encryption Process Approval — Users"
749	Encryption Utilities With User-Provided Passwords Or Keys Prohibited	10.03.02.03	"Encryption Utilities Passwords And Keys"
750	Compliance With International Trade In Armaments Regulations	12.01.06.01	"International Trade Armaments"
751	Secret Data Sent Over Networks Must Be Encrypted	8.06.03.12	"Secret Data Transmission"
752	Transportation Of Secret Data In Computer-Readable Storage Media	8.06.03.13	"Transportation Of Secret Data"
753	Secret Information Must Be Encrypted When Not In Active Use	8.06.03.14	"Secret Information Encryption"
754	Data Stored On Hard Disk Drives Must Be Encrypted	8.06.03.15	"Disk Storage Encryption"
755	Government Standard Encryption Algorithm & Implementation	10.03.02.04	"Standard Encryption Algorithm And Implementation"
756	Deployed Encryption Algorithms Must Be Publicly Evaluated (Open)	10.03.02.05	"Publicly-Evaluated Encryption Algorithms"
757	Disclosure Of Encryption Keys Requires Special Approval	10.03.05.01	"Encryption Key Disclosure — Approval"
758	Encryption Key Management Systems And Separation Of Duties	10.03.05.02	"Encryption Key Management Systems"
759	Initialization Of Encryption Systems Requires Auditor Presence	10.03.02.06	"Encryption System Initialization"

Table O-1: Index of Policy Title Conversion (Continued)

Previous Policy Number	ISPME v8 Title	Current Policy Number	ISPME v9 Title
760	Conditions For Delegation Of Key Management Responsibility	10.03.05.03	"Management Responsibility Delegation"
761	Protection Of Digital Certificate Root Keys At Certificate Authorities	10.03.05.05	"Digital Certificate Root Key Protection"
762	Separate Communication Channel For Data And Encryption Keys	10.03.05.06	"Data And Encryption Key Transmission"
763	Automated Encryption Key Management Systems Preferred	10.03.05.07	"Automated Encryption Key Management"
764	Maximum Life Of Encryption Keys	10.03.05.08	"Encryption Key Life"
765	Stated Life For All Encryption Keys	10.03.05.09	"Encryption Key Expiration"
766	Process For Generating Encryption Keys	10.03.05.10	"Encryption Key Generation"
767	Minimum Length For User-Chosen Encryption Keys	10.03.05.11	"User-Chosen Encryption Key Length"
768	Protection For Encryption Key Generation Materials	10.03.05.12	"Key Generation Materials"
769	Protection For Plaintext Encryption Master Keys	10.03.05.13	"Plaintext Encryption Master Keys"
770	Destruction Of Encryption Key Generation Materials	10.03.05.14	"Key Generation Material Destruction"
771	Time Frame For Destruction Of Key Exchange Material	10.03.05.15	"Key Exchange Material Destruction"
772	Time Period For Protection Of Encryption Keys Used For Confidentiality	10.03.05.16	"Encryption Key Secrecy"
773	Time Period For Protection Of Private Digital Signature Keys	10.03.05.17	"Private Digital Signature Key Lifetime"
774	Never Automatically Backup Private Key Used For Digital Certificates	10.03.05.18	"Private Key Backups"
775	Duplication Of Encryption Keys For Data That Has Been Backed-Up	10.03.05.19	"Encryption Key Duplication"

Table O-1: Index of Policy Title Conversion (Continued)

Previous Policy Number	ISPME v8 Title	Current Policy Number	ISPME v9 Title
776	Prevention Of Unauthorized Disclosure Of Encryption Keys	10.03.05.20	"Encryption Key Disclosure — Controls"
777	Private Key For Digital Certificates Must Be Encrypted Or In Smart Card	10.03.05.21	"Digital Certificate Private Key Security"
778	Transmission Of Cleartext Private Encryption Keys Prohibited	10.03.05.23	"Private Encryption Key Transmission"
779	Notifying Correspondents About Changes In Public Keys	10.03.05.24	"Public Key Changes"
780	Compromised Keys Revoked Back To Last Time Known To Be Safe	10.03.05.25	"Compromised Keys"
781	Storing Encryption Keys On Same Media As Protected Data Prohibited	10.03.05.26	"Encryption Key Storage Media"
782	Backup Encryption Keys Provided To Information Security Officer	10.03.05.28	"Backup Encryption Keys"
783	General Purpose Encryption Systems Must Include Key Escrow	10.03.04.01	"General Purpose Encryption Systems"
784	Digital Signature And User Authentication Keys Must Not Be Escrowed	10.03.05.30	"Digital Signature And User Authentication Keys"
785	Separate Keys For Encryption And Digital Signatures	10.03.05.31	"Encryption And Digital Signature Key Separation"
786	Explicit Assignment Of Encryption Key Management Functions	10.03.05.32	"Key Management Responsibility"
787	Deletion Of Readable Data After Encrypted Version Has Been Made	10.03.02.07	"Deletion Of Source Data After Encryption"
788	Compression And Encryption Of Sensitive Data To Be Held In Storage	10.03.02.08	"Compression And Encryption Of Secret Data"
789	Tamper Resistant Hardware Modules For Encryption Processes	10.03.02.09	"Encryption Process Hardware Modules"
790	Insertion Of Computer-Related Contact Numbers In Directories	8.05.01.34	"Computer-Related Access Numbers"

Table O-1: Index of Policy Title Conversion (Continued)

Previous Policy Number	ISPME v8 Title	Current Policy Number	ISPME v9 Title
791	Periodic Changes In Computer Communications Line Numbers	8.05.01.35	"Dial-Up Number Changes"
792	Extended User Authentication Systems Required For Dial-Up Lines	9.04.03.07	"Dial-Up User Authentication"
793	Dial-Out User Identity Must Be Authenticated Before Session Established	8.05.01.36	"Dial-Out Connections"
794	Use Of Cable Modems For Business Communications	8.05.01.37	"Cable Modems"
795	Modems On Workstations Connected To Internal Networks	9.04.02.03	"Workstation Modems"
796	Direct Dial Connections Prohibited Unless Modem Pool Is Used	9.04.02.04	"Direct Dial Connections"
797	Registry Of All Modem Lines And Related Advance Approval Process	9.04.02.05	"Modem Line Registry"
798	Approval Required For Systems Accepting In-Coming Dial-Up Calls	9.04.04.01	"Systems Accepting In-Coming Dial-Up Calls"
799	Prohibition Against Personal Computer Modems In Autoanswer Mode	9.04.02.06	"Auto-Answer Modems"
800	In-Coming Dial-Up Calls Must Not Be Answered Until Fourth Ring	8.05.01.38	"Dial-Up Calls Modem Configuration"
801	Department Management Responsible For Dial-Up Compliance	12.02.01.01	"Dial-Up Compliance"
802	Maximum Permissible Password Attempts For Dial-Up Users	9.04.03.08	"Dial-Up Password Attempts"
803	Process For Down-Loading Software From An Internet Mirror Site	8.03.01.22	"Downloading Internet Mirror Site Software"
804	Controls Needed For Down-Loading Sensitive Company X Information	8.06.03.16	"Downloading Sensitive Information"
805	Down-Loading Sensitive Information Prohibited Without Permission	8.06.03.17	"Downloading Sensitive Information Approval"

Table O-1: Index of Policy Title Conversion (Continued)

Previous Policy Number	ISPME v8 Title	Current Policy Number	ISPME v9 Title
806	Automatic Device Synchronization Allowed Only With Permission	8.07.05.31	"Device Synchronization"
807	Collect And Third-Party Bill-To Calls Prohibited On Voicemail Lines	8.07.05.32	"Collect And Third-Party Bill-To Calls"
808	Disable Area Code 9.00 Calls On All Company X PBXs	8.07.05.33	"Information Service Calls"
809	PBX Defined Calling Areas Must Be Restricted	8.07.05.34	"Calling Areas"
810	Workers Must Not Return Area Code 9.00 or Similar Calls	8.06.03.18	"Returning Long-Distance Calls"
811	Unusual Phone Operation Requests Must Be Denied And Reported	8.06.03.19	"Unusual Phone Operation Requests"
812	Leaving Sensitive Information On Answering Machines	8.07.07.23	"Sensitive Information On Answering Machines"
813	Voicemail Passwords Not Subject To Password Construction Standards	9.03.01.20	"Voice Mail Password Construction"
814	Heard Voicemail Messages Deleted After One Month In Storage	8.07.05.35	"Voice Mail Message Storage"
815	Placement Of Telephone Credit Card Calls Through PBX Systems	8.07.05.36	"Credit Card Calls"
816	Use Of Credit Cards On Public Pay Phones	8.07.07.24	"Use Of Credit Cards"
817	PBX - DISA Features Require Fraud Detection Facilities	8.07.05.37	"Direct Inward System Access Implementation"
818	Telephone Book Contains Restricted Information	4.02.01.10	"Telephone Books"
819	Two-Party Consent For All Speaker Phone Use Or Tape Recording	8.07.07.25	"Use Of Telephone Conference Or Recording Technology"
820	Special Permission Required To Record Video-Conferencing Sessions	8.07.07.26	"Recording Video Conferences"
821	Use Of Telephones For Personal Purposes	8.06.03.20	"Personal Telephone Usage"

Table O-1: Index of Policy Title Conversion (Continued)

Previous Policy Number	ISPME v8 Title	Current Policy Number	ISPME v9 Title
822	Reimbursement For Personal Telephone Calls	8.06.03.21	"Long-Distance Personal Telephone Calls"
823	Maintaining Accurate Records To Prevent Unwanted Telemarketing	8.07.03.17	"Telemarketing Records"
824	Orders To Change Internal Records Placed Via Phone	8.07.05.38	"Record Change Orders"
825	Conference Bridge Activated Only When Needed	8.07.05.39	"Conference Bridge Activation"
826	Computer Support Identification Codes	9.05.03.06	"Computer Support Identification Codes"
827	Using An Electronic Mail Account Assigned To Another Individual	9.03.01.21	"Unique Electronic Mail Accounts"
828	Using Electronic Mail Addresses Other Than Official Addresses	8.07.04.03	"Electronic Mail Addresses"
829	Sender Contact Information Must Be Included In Electronic Mail	8.07.04.04	"Sender Contact Information"
830	Clearly Identified Source For Electronic Mail Marketing Material	8.07.04.05	"Electronic Marketing Material Source"
831	Forwarding Electronic Mail To An External Network Address	8.07.04.06	"Forwarding Electronic Mail Externally"
832	Forwarding Externally Provided Electronic Mail Messages	8.07.04.07	"Inappropriate Electronic Mail Messages"
833	Recording And Retention Of Electronic Mail	8.07.04.08	"Electronic Mail Message Handling"
834	User Retention Of Electronic Mail Messages For Future Reference	8.07.04.09	"Retention Of Electronic Mail Messages"
835	Users Must Not Employ Electronic Mail Systems As A Database	8.07.04.10	"Electronic Mail Message Storage"
836	Periodic Destruction Of Archived Electronic Mail Messages	8.07.04.11	"Electronic Mail Message Destruction"

Table O-1: Index of Policy Title Conversion (Continued)

Previous Policy Number	ISPME v8 Title	Current Policy Number	ISPME v9 Title
837	Privacy Expectations And Electronic Mail	8.07.04.12	"Electronic Mail Privacy"
838	Treat Electronic Mail As Public Communications	8.07.04.14	"Electronic Mail Encryption"
839	Authorization To Read Electronic Mail Messages Of Other Workers	8.07.04.15	"Electronic Mail Message Monitoring Approval"
840	Modifying Electronic Mail Message Contents Or Header Prohibited	8.07.04.16	"Electronic Mail Modification"
841	Profane, Obscene Or Derogatory Remarks In Electronic Mail Messages	8.07.04.17	"Electronic Mail Message Contents"
842	Message Content Restrictions For Company X Information Systems	8.07.04.18	"Message Content Restrictions"
843	Notification Of Content Monitoring For Electronic Mail Transmissions	8.07.04.19.	"Electronic Mail Content Monitoring"
844	Reporting Offensive Electronic Mail Messages To Originator And HR	6.03.01.07	"Offensive Electronic Mail Messages"
845	Sending Unsolicited Personal Email Messages After Request To Stop	8.07.04.20	"Unsolicited Personal Electronic Mail Messages"
846	Prohibition Against Unsolicited Bulk Email Advertisements (SPAM)	8.07.04.21	"Bulk Electronic Mail"
847	Forwarding Is Appropriate Response To Junk Email (SPAM)	8.07.04.22	"Responding To Unsolicited Electronic Mail"
848	Sending Large Quantities Of Unsolicited Email (Mail Bombing)	8.07.04.23	"Sending Unsolicited Electronic Mail"
849	Electronic Mail Messages Are Company Records	8.07.04.26	"Electronic Mail Message Monitoring"
850	All Electronic Mail Archived And Subject To Supervisory Review	8.07.04.27	"Electronic Mail Archival And Review"
851	Forwarding Copies Of Official Electronic Mail To Archival Records	8.07.04.29	"Electronic Mail Archival"
852	Personal Use Of Electronic Mail Systems	8.07.04.30	"Electronic Mail System Usages"

Table O-1: Index of Policy Title Conversion (Continued)

Previous Policy Number	ISPME v8 Title	Current Policy Number	ISPME v9 Title
853	Authorization To Issue Broadcasts On Electronic Mail And Voice Mail	8.07.05.41	"Electronic Mail And Voice Mail Broadcasts"
854	Authorization To Issue Electronic Mail Or Voice Mail To Groups	8.07.05.42	"Voice Mail To Groups"
855	Placement On Electronic Mail Distribution List Requires Opt-In	8.07.04.31	"Electronic Mail Distributions"
856	Prohibition Against Use Of Scanned Hand-Rendered Signatures	8.07.04.32	"Signatures In Electronic Mail"
857	Prohibition Against Opening Attachments Unless They Were Expected	8.07.04.33	"Electronic Mail Attachments"
858	Inbound Attachments To Internet Electronic Mail Prohibited	8.07.04.34	"In-bound Electronic Mail Attachments"
859	Browser Electronic Mail Capabilities Must Not Be Used For Business	8.07.06.17	"Browser Electronic Mail Capabilities"
860	Telecommuting Data Entry Operators Must Employ Thin Clients	9.08.02.01	"Telecommuting Data Entry Operators"
861	Permissible Equipment For Telecommuting	9.08.02.02	"Telecommuting Equipment"
862	Alteration/Expansion Of Computers Provided By Company X	7.02.04.05	"Computer Modifications"
863	Reporting Of Damage To Company X Off-Site Systems	6.03.01.08	"Off-Site Systems Damage And Loss"
864	Protection Of Company X Property At Alternative Work Sites	9.08.01.09	"Organization Property At Alternative Work Sites"
865	Rights To Intellectual Property Developed Off-Site	6.01.04.11	"Intellectual Property Developed Off-Site"
866	Information Stored In Portable Computers Owned By Company X	9.08.01.10	"Information Stored In Organization Portable Computers"
867	Telecommuters And Structured Working Environments	9.08.02.03	"Telecommuter Working Environments"

Table O-1: Index of Policy Title Conversion (Continued)

Previous Policy Number	ISPME v8 Title	Current Policy Number	ISPME v9 Title
868	Use Of Computer Systems Belonging To Workers On Company Property	7.02.01.08	"Personally-Owned Computer Systems"
869	Security Requirements For Work At Home Arrangements	9.08.02.04	"Security Requirements For Telecommuters"
870	Sensitive Information Retention For Destruction Via Approved Method	12.01.03.17	"Sensitive Information Retention For Destruction"
871	Telecommuter Remote System Information Security Procedures	9.08.02.05	"Telecommuter Information Security Procedures"
872	Right To Conduct Inspections Of Telecommuter Environments	9.08.02.06	"Inspections Of Telecommuter Environments"
873	Training Course Required Prior To Use Of Remote Access Systems	6.02.01.03	"Remote Access Training"
874	Workers Must Keep Portable Computers In Their Possession Or Locked	9.08.01.11	"Possession Of Portable Computers"
875	Mobile Computer Alternatives For Protecting Company X Information	9.08.01.12	"Mobile Computer Alternatives"
876	Access To Internet Requires Completion Of Training Course	6.02.01.04	"Internet Training"
877	Internet Privileges Reserved For Those With A Business Need	9.04.01.06	"Internet Access Privileges"
878	Workers Who Do Not Perform Research Denied Internet Web Access	9.04.01.07	"Internet Access Restriction"
879	Expiration Of User IDs On Internet Accessible Computers	9.02.01.19	"User ID Expiration"
880	Company X Blocks Certain Non-Business Internet Web Sites	9.04.01.08	"Non-Business Web Sites"
881	News Feeds From Internet For Company X Related Topics	8.07.06.18	"Internet News Sources"
882	Extended User Authentication Required For In-Bound Internet Users	9.04.03.09	"In-Bound Internet Access"

Table O-1: Index of Policy Title Conversion (Continued)

Previous Policy Number	ISPME v8 Title	Current Policy Number	ISPME v9 Title
883	Telnet Connections With Fixed Passwords Over Internet Prohibited	8.05.01.38	"Telnet Connection Passwords"
884	Updating Company X Information Through The Internet	8.07.06.19	"Internet Information Modifications"
885	Disabling Java Within Internet Web Browsers	9.04.07.05	"Disabling Java"
886	Java Program Execution Prohibited Unless Digital Signature Validated	10.03.03.01	"Java Program Execution"
887	Firewalls Screen Out All Active Content (Java, Active X, Etc.)	8.05.01.40	"Active Content Screening"
888	Internet Access With Company X Computers Must Go Through Firewall	8.05.01.41	"Internet Access"
889	Disclaimer Must Accompany All Internet Personal Messages	8.07.06.20	"Personal Internet Message Disclaimers"
890	Internet Representations Including Company X Affiliation	8.07.06.21	"Internet Representations Including Affiliation"
891	Internet Discussion Group And Chat Room Participation Forbidden	8.07.04.36	"Public Electronic Forums"
892	Internet Representations About Company X Products & Services	8.07.06.22	"Internet Product And Service Representations"
893	Disclosure Of Personal Contact Information In Public Internet Forums	8.07.06.23	"Internet Disclosure Of Contact Information"
894	Political Advocacy Statements And Product/Service Endorsements	8.07.06.24	"Political Advocacy And Product Or Service Endorsements"
895	Internet Discussion Group Participation And Release Of Trade Secrets	8.07.06.25	"Internet Trade Secret Releases"
896	Validating The Identity Of External Parties On The Internet	8.07.01.06	"Identity Validation Of External Parties"
897	Digital Certificate For All Company X Internet Web And Commerce Sites	10.03.03.02	"Internet Web And Commerce Sites"

Table O-1: Index of Policy Title Conversion (Continued)

Previous Policy Number	ISPME v8 Title	Current Policy Number	ISPME v9 Title
898	Workers Must Not Conceal Their Identity When Using The Internet	9.04.01.11	"Internet Identity"
899	Respecting The Intellectual Property Rights Of Others On The Internet	9.04.01.12	"Intellectual Property"
900	Sending Software And Other Sensitive Information Over The Internet	8.07.06.27	"Internet Transmission Of Sensitive Information"
901	Removal Of Inappropriate Electronic Postings To Public Forums	8.07.06.28	"Inappropriate Public Postings"
902	Search Engines To Detect Misleading Web Sites With Similar Names	8.07.06.29	"Web Sites With Similar Names"
903	Posting Company X Material On The Internet	8.07.06.30	"Internet Posting Of Material"
904	Establishing New Business Arrangements Via Internet	8.07.06.31	"Internet Business Arrangements"
905	Production In-House Systems May Not Be Directly Internet Connected	8.05.01.42	"Direct Internet Connections"
906	Publicly-Writable Directories On Company X Computers Cleared Nightly	8.05.01.43	"Publicly-Modifiable Directories"
907	Encryption For Files Left On Anonymous FTP Servers	10.03.02.11	"Anonymous FTP Server Information"
908	Encryption Of All Payment Information On Internet-Accessible Machines	8.07.03.18	"Payment Information Encryption"
909	Avoid Tipping-Off Competition Through Public Network Postings	8.07.06.32	"Public Network Postings"
910	Handling Software And Files Down-Loaded From Internet	8.03.01.24	"Downloaded Information"
911	Transferring Files Down-Loaded From Internet To Another Computer	8.07.06.33	"Transferring Downloaded Files"
912	Reliability Of Information Down-Loaded from Internet	8.07.06.34	"Internet Information Reliability"

Table O-1: Index of Policy Title Conversion (Continued)

Previous Policy Number	ISPME v8 Title	Current Policy Number	ISPME v9 Title
913	Exchanges Of Information Over The Internet	8.06.03.22	"Internet Information Exchange"
914	Up-Loading Software To Other Machines Via The Internet	8.07.06.35	"Uploading Software"
915	User Control Over Information Gathered Via Internet Web Site	9.07.02.22	"Information Gathered By Internet"
916	Acceptance Of Unsolicited Ideas Through The Internet	8.07.06.36	"Unsolicited Internet Information"
917	Production Systems Must Not Rely On Free Internet Information	8.07.06.37	"Internet Information In Production Systems"
918	Unofficial Web Pages Permitted Only By Contract	8.07.06.38	"Unofficial Web Pages"
919	Responsibility For Content Posted To Personal Web Pages	8.07.06.39	"Personal Web Pages"
920	Company X Internet Web Page Management Committee	8.07.06.40	"Internet Web Page Management Committee"
921	Internet Web Page Design Requirements	8.07.06.41	"Internet Web Page Design"
922	Management Approval Required For Internet Hot-Link Establishment	8.07.06.42	"Internet Hot-Link Establishments"
923	Internet Hot-Links Must Be Accompanied By Legal Disclaimer	8.07.06.43	"Internet Hot-Link Disclaimer"
924	Daily Review Of Contents And Hot-Links For Company X Web Page	8.07.06.44	"Internet Web Page Review"
925	Owner/Department Manager Permission Required For Intranet Postings	8.07.05.44	"Intranet Postings"
926	All Content Posted To Intranet Is Owned By Company X	8.07.05.45	"Intranet Content Ownership"
927	User Checking Of Information Before Posting To The Intranet	8.07.05.46	"Intranet Information Validation"
928	Staging Area For New/Changed Intranet Content Review And Testing	8.07.05.47	"Intranet Content Review And Testing"

Table O-1: Index of Policy Title Conversion (Continued)

Previous Policy Number	ISPME v8 Title	Current Policy Number	ISPME v9 Title
929	Cleansing Process For Downloaded Internet Content Moved To Intranet	8.07.05.48	"Internet Content Moved To Intranet"
930	Intranet Sites Must Not Use Unapproved Active Content	8.07.05.49	"Active Content On Intranet Sites"
931	Webmaster Review Of Intranet Web Pages Prior To Posting	8.07.05.50	"Intranet Web Page Review"
932	All Information Posted On Intranet Pages Must Have Designated Owner	8.07.05.51	"Intranet Information Owner"
933	All Intranet Pages Must Include Information Owner Digital Signatures	8.07.05.52	"Information Owner Digital Signatures"
934	Secret Information Must Not Be Placed On Internet Or Intranet Systems	8.07.06.51	"Secret Information On Web"
935	Intranet Reviewed Quarterly To Confirm Sensitive Data Not Posted	8.07.05.53	"Intranet Data Review"
936	Intranet Server Establishment Requires Information Systems Approval	8.07.05.54	"Intranet Server Approval"
937	Real-Time Connections To Company X Production Systems Via Intranet	8.07.05.55	"Access To Production Systems By Intranet"
938	Approval Required For Access To Internal Systems By Third Parties	4.02.01.11	"Third-Party Access To Internal Systems"
939	Forwarding Information On Company X Intranet To Third Parties	8.07.05.56	"Forwarding Intranet Information"
940	Direct Transfer To Internet Sites Not Permitted From Intranet	8.07.05.57	"Transfer To Internet From Intranet"
941	Intranet Site Developers Must Use Company X Style Guide	8.07.05.58	"Intranet Style Guide"
942	Concealing Account Numbers On Customer Receipts	10.02.02.10	"Concealing Customer Account Numbers"
943	Receipt Must Be Provided For Every Purchase Or The Purchase Is Free	10.02.02.11	"Providing Purchase Receipt"

Table O-1: Index of Policy Title Conversion (Continued)

Previous Policy Number	ISPME v8 Title	Current Policy Number	ISPME v9 Title
944	Payment Information Never Provided In Its Entirety To Customers	8.07.03.19	"Payment Information Confirmation"
945	Disclosure Of Bank Account Numbers	8.06.03.23	"Bank Account Numbers"
946	Shredding Of Credit Card Receipts And Other Payment Information	5.02.02.40	"Disposal Of Payment Information"
947	Encrypt Credit Card Numbers & Other Payment Data When Not Used	8.07.03.20	"Payment Data Encryption"
948	Credit Card Numbers Must Be Used Only For Payment Processing	10.02.02.12	"Credit Card Number Usage"
949	New Account Opening Requires Robust Identity Authentication	9.02.01.20	"New Account Authentication"
950	Any Demonstrated Fraud Forces Immediate Financial Account Closure	8.07.03.22	"Accounts Involved With Fraud"
951	Alternative Communications Channel Confirmation For Transactions	8.07.03.23	"Confirmation Channel"
952	Daily Balancing And Reconciliation Of Accounting Records	8.07.03.24	"Account Balancing And Reconciliation"
953	Receipt Must Be Confirmed Before Payment Token Will Be Activated	8.07.03.25	"Payment Token Activation"
954	All New Workers Must Receive Information Security Policy Pamphlet	6.02.01.05	"Information Security Policy Pamphlet"
955	Information Security Training Required For All Information Workers	6.02.01.06	"Information Security Training"
956	Information Security Training Only After Workers Pass Other Training	6.02.01.07	"Basic Training"
957	Information Security Policy Change Notices Distributed To All Workers	6.02.01.08	"Information Security Policy Changes"
958	Information Security Department Responsible For Related Training	6.02.01.09.	"Training Responsibility"

Table O-1: Index of Policy Title Conversion (Continued)

Previous Policy Number	ISPME v8 Title	Current Policy Number	ISPME v9 Title
959	Information Security Training Time Required	6.02.01.10	"Training Time"
960	Work According To Information Security Policies & Procedures	6.02.01.11	"Work Agreement"
961	Attendance At Information Security Class Mandatory	6.02.01.12	"Information Security Class"
962	Information Security Training Course Prior To Gaining System Access	6.02.01.13	"Computer Access Training"
963	Required Compliance With Corporate Code Of Conduct	6.01.04.12	"Corporate Code Of Conduct"
964	Signed Acknowledgement For Understanding The Code Of Conduct	6.01.04.13	"Code Of Conduct Acknowledgement"
965	Required User Training For Production Systems	6.02.01.14	"Production Systems Training"
966	Required Reporting of Information Security Incidents	6.03.01.09	"Incident Reporting"
967	Computer Crime Investigation Information Is Legally Privileged	12.01.07.14	"Computer Crime Investigation Information"
968	Issuance Of Cease And Desist Messages To Attackers	8.01.03.10	"Messages To Attackers"
969	Inclusion Of Information Security Contact Information On Web Site	8.07.06.53	"Security Contact Information"
970	Internal Reporting Of Information Security Violations & Problems	6.03.01.11	"Violation And Problem Reporting"
971	Centralized Reporting Of Information Security Problems	6.03.02.03	"Centralized Problem Reporting"
972	Interference With Reporting Of Information Security Problems	6.03.01.13	"Violation And Problem Reporting Interference"
973	Protection Of Workers Who Report Information Security Problems	6.03.01.14	"Violation And Problem Reporting Protection"

Table O-1: Index of Policy Title Conversion (Continued)

Previous Policy Number	ISPME v8 Title	Current Policy Number	ISPME v9 Title
974	External Reporting Of Information Security Violations	6.03.01.16	"External Violation Reporting"
975	Reporting Problems To Investors & Government Regulatory Authorities	6.03.01.17	"Violation And Problem Reporting To Authorities"
976	Public And Governmental Disclosure Of Computer System Attacks	6.03.01.18	"Disclosure Of Computer System Attacks"
977	Immediate Reporting Of Suspected Computer Virus Infestation	6.03.03.03	"Reporting A Suspected Virus"
978	Required Reporting Of Software Malfunctions	6.03.03.04	"Reporting Of Software Malfunctions"
979	Reporting Unauthorized Data Changes & Questionable System Use	6.03.01.20	"Reporting Unauthorized Activity"
980	Required Investigation Following Computer Crimes	6.03.01.24	"Computer Crime Investigation"
981	When To Seek Assistance With Unauthorized Access Problems	8.01.03.09.	"Unauthorized Access Problems"
982	Retention Of Information Security Violation & Problem Information	12.01.03.18	"Security Violation And Problem Information Retention"
983	Annual Analysis Of Information Security Violations & Problems	6.03.04.01	"Violation And Problem Analysis"
984	Problem Reporting And Management Process	8.04.03.01	"Problem Reporting"
985	Systems Designers & Developers Must Inform Management Of Problems	6.03.01.22	"Reporting Design Problems"
986	Reliance On New Information Systems Security Products	9.01.01.29	"Security Product Maturity"
987	Ease-Of-Use Required For Computer & Communications Security	9.01.01.31	"Security Control Usability"
988	Required User Acceptance Of Information Security Measures	8.02.02.11	"User Acceptance Of Information Security Measures"

Table O-1: Index of Policy Title Conversion (Continued)

Previous Policy Number	ISPME v8 Title	Current Policy Number	ISPME v9 Title
989	Incorporation Of Security Into Systems Development Life Cycle	10.01.01.09	"Security In The Systems Development Life Cycle"
990	Hardware/Software Procurement Via Standard Purchasing Channels	5.01.01.05	"Hardware And Software Procurement"
991	Consistent Protection Of Information Regardless Of Manifestation	3.01.01.01	"Protection Of Information"
992	Every Information System Privilege Not Specifically Allowed Is Forbidden	9.01.01.32	"Information System Privilege Usage"
993	Minimization Of Reliance On Common Mechanism For Controls	10.01.01.10	"Reliance On Common Mechanisms For Controls"
994	Independent Security Systems For Each Computer System	9.01.01.33	"Independent Security Systems"
995	Dedicated Computers & Networks For High-Security/High-Reliability	9.04.06.02	"High-Security And High-Reliability Computers And Networks"
996	Designing Controls With Large Margins Of Error	10.02.02.13	"Designing Information Security Controls"
997	Use Of Most Current Computer Operating System Versions	8.01.02.07	"Operating System Versions"
998	Latest Software Release On Systems Interfacing External Networks	8.05.01.46	"Systems Interfacing External Networks"
999	Network Security Measures Must Not Be Backwards Compatible	8.05.01.47	"Network Security Measures"
1000	Keeping Security Functionality Out Of Business Applications	10.01.01.11	"Business Applications Security Functionality"
1001	Systems Must Be Configured & Customized According To Templates	8.02.02.12	"Systems Configuration Templates"
1002	Risk Assessments Required For Production Information Systems	4.01.05.01	"Production System Risk Assessments"
1003	When To Perform An Information Systems Security Risk Assessment	12.02.02.02	"Information Systems Security Risk Assessments"

Table O-1: Index of Policy Title Conversion (Continued)

Previous Policy Number	ISPME v8 Title	Current Policy Number	ISPME v9 Title
1004	Vulnerability Identification Software For Internet-Connected Systems	12.03.02.02	"Vulnerability Identification"
1005	Purchase Rather Than Build Information Security Solutions	10.01.01.12	"Purchasing Information Security Solutions"
1006	Best-Of-Breed Solutions For Critical Information Security Functions	4.01.03.05	"Security Products And Services"
1007	Compliance With Industry Specific Information Security Standards	3.01.01.10	"Industry-Specific Information Security Standards"
1008	Legal Framework For Information Security Policies	3.01.01.05	"Legal Conflicts"
1009	Risk Acceptance Process And Permissible Exceptions To Policies	3.01.01.09	"Exceptions To Policies"
1010	Non-Enforcement Of Any Policy Does Not Constitute Consent	3.01.01.07	"Policy Non-Enforcement"
1011	Minimum Information System Controls Dictated By Standard Practice	10.01.01.13	"Minimum Information System Controls"
1012	Response Required For Every Significant Information Security Risk	4.01.02.01	"Significant Information Security Risks"
1013	Approval Before Disabling Critical Components Of Security Infrastructure	4.01.04.02	"Disabling Critical Security Components"
1014	Adequate Information Security Insurance Coverage Must Be Maintained	4.01.02.02	"Insurance Coverage"
1015	Allocation Of Sufficient Resources To Address Information Security	4.01.03.06	"Information Security Resources"
1016	Information Security Is Overhead, Not A Charge-Back Item	4.01.03.07	"Budgeting For Information Security"
1017	Security Measures Must Be Enforceable Prior To Installation	3.01.02.01	"Security Controls Enforceability"
1018	Whenever They Are Available, Use Of Evaluated Products Required	10.01.01.14	"Use Of Evaluated Products"

Table O-1: Index of Policy Title Conversion (Continued)

Previous Policy Number	ISPME v8 Title	Current Policy Number	ISPME v9 Title
1019	Agreements With Third Parties Which Handle Company X Information	4.02.02.12	"Third-Party Agreements"
1020	Outsourced Hosting Arrangements Require Backup Plan And Testing	4.03.01.04	"Service Provider Contingency Plans"
1021	External Firms Gathering Company X Information Must Make It Available	4.02.02.15	"Externally-Gathered Information"
1022	Security Responsibilities For Real-Time Connections With Third Parties	4.02.01.12	"Third-Party Security Responsibilities"
1023	Clear Definition Of Third Party Information Security Responsibilities	4.02.02.16	"Third-Party Information Security Responsibilities"
1024	Termination Of Outsourcing Contracts For Security Violations	4.03.01.09.	"Outsourcing Contract Approvals"
1025	Financial Condition Of Critical Vendors Reviewed Annually	4.02.01.13	"Critical Vendor Financial Review"
1026	Avoid Actual And Apparent Conflict of Interest	6.01.04.14	"Conflicts of Interest"
1027	Researchers Must Disclose Sponsors And All Potential Conflicts	8.07.06.54	"Public Research"
1028	Workers May Not Have Romantic Relationships With Competitor Staff	6.01.04.15	"Personal Relationships With Competition"
1029	Disciplinary Measures For Information Security Non-Compliance	6.03.05.01	"Consequences Of Non-Compliance"
1030	Disciplinary Measures For Various Information Security Violations	6.03.05.02	"Consequences Of Violations"
1031	Unauthorized Information Disclosure And Loss Of Stock Options	6.03.05.03	"Loss Of Stock Options"
1032	Security Violations Requiring Instant Terminations	6.03.05.04	"Immediate Terminations"
1033	Notification And Handling Of Employees Leaving For A Competitor	6.01.04.16	"Employees Leaving For A Competitor"

Table O-1: Index of Policy Title Conversion (Continued)

Previous Policy Number	ISPME v8 Title	Current Policy Number	ISPME v9 Title
1034	Immediate Notification Of Employees Regarding Worker Terminations	6.01.04.17	"Notification Of Worker Terminations"
1035	Informing Relevant Contractors And Vendors Of Worker Terminations	6.01.04.18	"Notification To Third Parties Of Worker Terminations"
1036	Handling Involuntary Terminations Of Computer Workers	6.01.04.19	"Involuntary Terminations"
1037	Security Guard Escort For Workers Who Are Involuntarily Terminated	6.01.04.20	"Escorting Involuntarily Terminated Workers"
1038	Removal Of Information Upon Termination Of Employment	6.01.04.21	"Information Retention At Employment Termination"
1039	Return Of Information By Contractors, Consultants, And Temporaries	4.02.02.17	"Information Return By Contract Personnel"
1040	Return Of Company X Property At Time Of Separation From Company X	6.01.04.22	"Return Of Property At Employment Termination"
1041	Responsibility For Taking Action In Response To Worker Terminations	12.02.01.02	"Worker Termination Responsibility"
1042	Those Involuntarily Terminated Not To Be Re-Hired Or Retained	6.01.02.05	"Rehiring Involuntarily Terminated Workers"
1043	Probationary Period For New, Re-Hired, Or Retained Again Workers	6.01.02.06	"Probationary Period For New Workers"
1044	Leave Without Pay Required During Extended Investigations	6.03.01.25	"Extended Investigations"
1045	Annual Signature On Agreement To Comply With Security Policies	6.02.01.15	"Compliance Agreement"
1046	When To Prosecute Or Seek Restitution	3.01.01.08	"Violation Of Law"
1047	Human Intervention Required For Important Decisions	10.02.02.14	"Human Intervention In Computer-Assisted Processes"
1048	Reliance On A Single Person For Important Systems Expertise	8.01.01.12	"Systems Expertise"

Table O-1: Index of Policy Title Conversion (Continued)

Previous Policy Number	ISPME v8 Title	Current Policy Number	ISPME v9 Title
1049	Five Consecutive Days Of Vacation Required Each Year	6.01.04.23	"Consecutive Vacation Days"
1050	Second Job Impact On Objectivity And Competition With Employer	6.01.04.24	"Second Jobs"
1051	Second Jobs Must Be Disclosed At Initial Interview Or When Taken	6.01.04.25	"Disclosure Of Second Jobs"
1052	Periodic Job Rotation For Computer-Related Workers	8.01.04.01	"Job Rotation"
1053	Bonding Of Persons In Computer-Related Position Of Trust	6.01.02.07	"Bonding Workers"
1054	Staff Qualifications For Working On Most Sensitive Company X Projects	6.01.02.08	"Working On Sensitive Projects"
1055	Workers In Positions Of Trust Must Not Also Be Company X Customers	6.01.04.26	"Workers As Customers"
1056	Duty To Report Status Changes Affecting Eligibility For Certain Position	6.01.04.27	"Reporting Status Changes"
1057	Transfer Of Certain Workers To Positions With Less Exposure	6.01.04.28	"Worker Transfers"
1058	Use Of Convicted Felons And A Safe Work Place	6.01.02.09	"Convicted Felons"
1059	Use Of Convicted Felons In Computer-Related Positions Of Trust	6.01.02.10	"Computer-Related Positions Of Trust"
1060	Background Checks For Computer-Related Positions Of Trust	6.01.02.11	"Background Checks"
1061	Staff Must Pass Background Check Before Accessing Private Information	6.01.02.13	"Accessing Private Information"
1062	Sensitive Product Information Access Requires Background Check	6.01.02.14	"Sensitive Product Information"
1063	Fingerprinting For Employees With Access To Sensitive Information	6.01.02.15	"Fingerprinting Employees"

Table O-1: Index of Policy Title Conversion (Continued)

Previous Policy Number	ISPME v8 Title	Current Policy Number	ISPME v9 Title
1064	Honesty And Emotional Stability Tests For Computer-Related Workers	6.01.02.16	"Honesty And Emotional Stability Tests"
1065	Foreign Nationals Prohibited From Working On Information Systems	6.01.02.18	"Foreign Nationals"
1066	Significant Unexplained Increases In Wealth Must Be Investigated	6.01.02.20	"Significant Increases In Wealth"
1067	Adequate Grievance Resolution Procedures	6.01.04.29	"Grievance Resolution"
1068	Free Confidential Counselling Services For Workers	6.01.04.30	"Confidential Counseling"
1069	Drug-Free And Alcohol-Free Work Place	6.01.04.31	"Drugs And Alcohol"
1070	Agreements Not To Compete Required For Employees	6.01.03.05	"Non-Compete Agreements"
1071	Technical Information Systems Staff Training & Continuing Education	6.02.01.16	"Technical Training And Continuing Education"
1072	Information Security Management Committee	4.01.01.02	"Information Security Management Committee"
1073	Information Ownership And Management's Responsibilities	5.01.01.06	"Information Ownership"
1074	Divisional Plans For Information Security Compliance	12.02.01.03	"Divisional Plans For Information Security Compliance"
1075	Assignment Of Responsibility For Information Asset Controls	5.01.01.07	"Information Asset Control"
1076	Control Implementations Consistent With Standard Of Due Care	12.02.01.04	"Control Implementations Standard"
1077	Handling Variances From Generally Accepted Control Practices	12.02.01.05	"Variances From Generally-Accepted Control Practices"
1078	Information Security Is Every Worker's Duty	6.02.01.17	"Information Security Responsibility"

Table O-1: Index of Policy Title Conversion (Continued)

Previous Policy Number	ISPME v8 Title	Current Policy Number	ISPME v9 Title
1079	Centralized Responsibility For Information Security	4.01.03.09	"Centralized Information Security"
1080	Overview Of Tasks Performed By Information Security Department	4.01.03.10	"Information Security Department Responsibilities"
1081	Specific Tasks Performed By The Information Security Department	4.01.03.11	"Information Security Department Tasks"
1082	Information Security Department Mission Supports Company X Goals	4.01.03.12	"Information Security Department Mission"
1083	Authority To Create Information Security Standards And Procedures	4.01.03.13	"Information Security Standards And Procedures"
1084	Annual Information Security Planning Process Required	4.01.03.14	"Information Security Plans"
1085	Annual Organization-Wide Information Security Risk Assessment	12.02.02.03	"Organization-Wide Information Security Risk Assessment"
1086	Risk Assessments Performed By Organizational Units Managing Systems	12.02.01.06	"System Risk Assessments"
1087	Current Information Security Manual Required	4.01.03.15	"Information Security Manual"
1088	Involvement Of In-House Information Security Department	8.01.03.11	"Information Security Problem Resolution"
1089	Prompt Review Of Invoices For Computer & Communications Services	8.01.01.13	"Computer and Communication Service Invoices"
1090	Who Must Comply With Information Security Requirements	4.02.02.18	"Information Security Compliance"
1091	Designated Security Administrator For All Multi-User Systems	5.01.01.08	"Designated Security Administrator"
1092	Backup Security Administrator Must Be Designated And Trained	5.01.01.09	"Back-Up Security Administrators"
1093	Each Department Must Have An Information Security Liaison	4.01.03.16	"Information Security Liaisons"

Table O-1: Index of Policy Title Conversion (Continued)

Previous Policy Number	ISPME v8 Title	Current Policy Number	ISPME v9 Title
1094	Annual Review Of Trade Secrets, Copyrights, Etc. By Legal Department	12.01.02.22	"Review Of Trade Secrets And Copyrights"
1095	Internal Audit Review Of Information System Controls	12.03.01.02	"Information System Control Reviews — Internal"
1096	Internal Audit Performs Information Security Compliance Checking	12.03.01.03	"Information Security Compliance Checking"
1097	Periodic Independent Review Of Information System Controls	4.01.07.02	"Information System Control Reviews — Independent"
1098	Information Security Responsibilities In Job Descriptions	6.01.01.01	"Job Descriptions"
1099	Information Security Considered In Employee Performance Evaluations	6.01.01.02	"Performance Evaluations"
1100	Separation Of Duties And Control Over Company X Assets	8.01.04.02	"Separation Of Duties"
1101	Building Systems So That Errors And Manipulations Come To Light	10.02.02.15	"Errors And Record Manipulations"
1102	Specific Instructions Regarding Separation Of Duties	8.01.04.03	"Separation Of Duty Instructions"
1103	Incident Management Responsibilities	8.01.03.12	"Incident Management Responsibilities"
1104	High-Level Inventory Of Information Assets	5.01.01.10	"Asset Inventory — Information"
1105	Criteria For Assigning Information Ownership	4.01.03.17	"Assigning Information Ownership"
1106	Information Systems Department Must Not Be Owner Of Information	4.01.03.18	"Information Systems Department Ownership Responsibility"
1107	Designated Custodian Required For All Major Information Types	4.01.03.20	"Information Custodian"
1108	Security Responsibilities Of Information Custodians	4.01.03.21	"Information Custodian Responsibilities"

Table O-1: Index of Policy Title Conversion (Continued)

Previous Policy Number	ISPME v8 Title	Current Policy Number	ISPME v9 Title
1109	Security Responsibilities Of Information Users	4.01.03.22	"Information User Responsibilities"
1110	Process For Granting Access To Company X Information	9.01.01.34	"Granting Access To Organization Information"
1111	Restricted Delegation Of Information Owner Duties	4.01.03.23	"Information Ownership Delegation"
1112	Physical Access Control For Areas Containing Sensitive Information	7.01.02.01	"Physical Access Control To Sensitive Information"
1113	When Personal Offices Are Not In Use, The Doors Must Be Locked	7.01.02.02	"Locking Personal Offices"
1114	Multi-User Computer Or Communications Systems In Locked Rooms	7.01.03.02	"Securing Computer Or Communications Systems"
1115	Guards Or Receptionists For Areas Containing Sensitive Information	7.01.01.01	"Third-Party Physical Access"
1116	Badges Must Be Worn In Visible Places When In Company X Premises	7.01.02.03	"Identification Badges"
1117	Temporary Badges For Workers Who Have Forgotten Their Badges	7.01.02.04	"Temporary Badges"
1118	Reporting Lost/Stolen Identification Badges And System Access Tokens	6.03.01.26	"Missing Access Devices"
1119	Each Individual Must Have Their Badge Read At Every Controlled Door	7.01.02.05	"Badge-Controlled Access"
1120	No 'Piggybacking' Through Controlled Doors Permitted	7.01.02.06	"Badge Access Sharing"
1121	Propped-Open Doors To Computer Center Requires Presence Of A Guard	7.01.03.03	"Securing Propped-Open Computer Center Doors"
1122	Testing Physical Access Controls Forbidden	7.01.02.08	"Unauthorized Physical Access Attempts"
1123	Working Alone In Restricted Areas Forbidden	7.01.04.03	"Working In Restricted Areas"

Table O-1: Index of Policy Title Conversion (Continued)

Previous Policy Number	ISPME v8 Title	Current Policy Number	ISPME v9 Title
1124	Working In Restricted Areas Only During Official Business Hours	7.01.04.04	"Restricted Area Working Hours"
1125	Physical Security Or Encryption Required For All Sensitive Information	8.06.03.24	"Security Of Sensitive Information"
1126	Property Pass For Removal Of All Computer And Communications Gear	7.03.02.01	"Property Passes"
1127	Computer Storage Media Must Have A Pass When Leaving Premises	7.03.02.03	"Media Removal"
1128	Workers Must Show Contents Of Luggage When Leaving Premises	7.01.02.09	"Bag Inspection"
1129	Provision Of Lockable Metal Furniture To Staff Working At Home	9.08.02.07	"Lockable Metal Furniture"
1130	Maintaining Building Access Control System Records	7.01.02.10	"Access Control System Records"
1131	Changing Physical Access Control Codes On Worker Termination	7.01.02.11	"Physical Access Of Terminated Workers"
1132	Access Rights To Restricted Areas Must Be Revoked On Termination	7.01.02.12	"Terminated Worker Access To Restricted Areas"
1133	Maintenance Of List Showing Those Permitted To Grant Physical Access	7.01.02.13	"Physical Access Grantor List"
1134	Periodic Identification Badge Reports Issued To Department Heads	7.01.02.14	"Identification Badge Reports"
1135	Identification And Sign-In Process Required For All Visitors	7.01.02.15	"Visitor Identification"
1136	Escorts Required For All Visitors	7.01.02.16	"Escorting Visitors"
1137	Escorts Required For All Visitors Outside Normal Business Hours	7.01.02.17	"Escorts Required For All After-Hour Visitors"
1138	Third Party Supervision In Areas Containing Sensitive Information	7.01.02.18	"Third-Party Supervision"

Table O-1: Index of Policy Title Conversion (Continued)

Previous Policy Number	ISPME v8 Title	Current Policy Number	ISPME v9 Title
1139	Individuals Without Identification Badges Must Be Challenged	7.01.02.19	"Individuals Without Identification Badges"
1140	Removal Of Badges After Leaving Company X Facilities	6.01.04.32	"Removing Identification Badges"
1141	Handling Badges When Workers Are Away From Company X Facilities	6.01.04.33	"Securing Identification Badges"
1142	Unescorted Visitors In Restricted Areas Must Be Challenged	7.01.02.20	"Unescorted Visitors"
1143	No Visitors Allowed In Data Center Or Information Systems Department	7.01.02.21	"Data Center And Information Systems Department Visitors"
1144	All Workstations Must Use Metal Keys To Control Access	7.02.01.09	"Workstation Key Locks"
1145	Computer And Communications Equipment Rack Doors Must Be Locked	7.02.01.10	"Equipment Rack Doors"
1146	Internet Commerce & Financial Systems Must Be Physically Isolated	7.02.01.11	"Internet Commerce and Financial Systems"
1147	Equipment Isolation Between Company X And Third Party Systems	7.02.01.12	"Equipment Isolation"
1148	Physical Security Measures For Computers & Communications Systems	7.01.02.22	"Access To Computers and Communications Systems"
1149	Critical Or Sensitive Activities Permitted Only In Physically Secure Areas	7.01.02.23	"Securing Critical Or Sensitive Information Handling Activities"
1150	Computer Center Is A Closed Shop	7.01.02.24	"Computer Center Access"
1151	Computer Center Authorized Staff Access List Reviewed Quarterly	7.01.02.25	"Computer Center Staff Access"
1152	Centralization Of All Critical Voice And Data Networking Devices	8.05.01.48	"Critical Voice and Data Networking Devices"
1153	Restricted Access To Magnetic Tape, Disk, And Documentation Libraries	7.01.02.26	"Access To Media Libraries"

Table O-1: Index of Policy Title Conversion (Continued)

Previous Policy Number	ISPME v8 Title	Current Policy Number	ISPME v9 Title
1154	Vacated Equipment Areas Must Be Locked And Periodically Checked	7.01.04.05	"Vacated Equipment Areas"
1155	Locked Communications Equipment Areas And Escorted Access	7.01.04.06	"Communications Equipment Areas"
1156	Public Tours Of Computer Facilities Prohibited	7.01.02.27	"Computer Facility Tours"
1157	Cameras Plus Audio Or Video Recording Equipment Prohibited	7.01.04.07	"Audio Or Video Recording Equipment"
1158	Printers, Copiers, & Fax Machines Banned From Secret Information Areas	7.01.03.04	"Equipment In Secret Information Areas"
1159	Location Of New Computer Or Communications Centers	7.02.01.13	"Computer Center Locations"
1160	Redundant Supplies For Public Utility Resources	7.02.02.02	"Redundant Utility Suppliers"
1161	Adequate Construction For Computer Or Communications Centers	7.02.01.14	"Computer Center Construction"
1162	Computer And Communications Facility Location Within A Building	7.01.01.03	"Computer And Communications Facility Location"
1163	Computer Equipment Locations Must Have Water Damage Precautions	7.02.01.15	"Water Damage Precautions"
1164	Intermediate Holding Area Required To Restrict Computer Room Access	7.01.05.01	"Computer Room Deliveries"
1165	No Signs Indicating Location Of Computer Or Communications Center	7.01.03.05	"Computer And Communications Center Signs"
1166	Computer Center Fire Resistance And Self-Closing Openings	7.01.01.04	"Computer Facility Fire Resistance"
1167	Computer Facilities And Doors Resistant To Forcible Entry	7.01.01.05	"Computer Facility Door Strength"
1168	Computer Facilities And Automatically Closing Doors	7.01.01.06	"Computer Facility Door Closing"

Table O-1: Index of Policy Title Conversion (Continued)

Previous Policy Number	ISPME v8 Title	Current Policy Number	ISPME v9 Title
1169	Secondary Computer Center Doors Must Have Alarmed Crash Bars	7.01.01.07	"Secondary Computer Center Doors"
1170	Computer-Assisted Equipment Tracking	5.01.01.11	"Equipment Tracking"
1171	Marking Information Systems Equipment With Identification Codes	5.01.01.12	"Equipment Identification Codes"
1172	Moving Microcomputer Equipment Without Approval Prohibited	8.07.05.59	"Moving Office Computer Equipment"
1173	Fire, Water, And Physical Intrusion Alarms Trigger Immediate Action	7.02.01.16	"Computer Center Alarms"
1174	Positioning Of Computer Display Screens With Respect To Windows	8.07.05.60	"Positioning Computer Display Screens"
1175	Electromagnetic Radiation (Emanation) Protection For Secret Systems	8.07.05.61	"Electromagnetic Radiation Protection"

ABOUT THE AUTHOR

Based in the San Francisco Bay Area, Charles Cresson Wood is an independent information security consultant, researcher, and author. As part of his consulting work, he prepares and reviews standards, architectures, policies, codes of conduct, procedures, budgets, action plans, mission statements, job descriptions, and other parts of an organizational infrastructure to support information security. He also performs risk assessments and designs custom information security solutions.

Working in the field full-time since 1979, he has been a computer security management consultant at SRI International (formerly Stanford Research Institute) and lead data communications security consultant at the Bank of America. He has done information security consulting work with over 120 organizations, many of them Fortune 500 companies. His consulting projects have taken him to Australia, Austria, Belgium, Brazil, Canada, England, Finland, France, Holland, Ireland, Italy, Japan, Norway, Portugal, Saudi Arabia, South Africa, and Sweden.

Mr. Wood has delivered over 125 information security presentations at various conferences; he has also been a keynote speaker at several of these same conferences. He has been quoted as an expert in publications such as Business Week, Computerworld, Information Week, LA Times, PC Week, The Wall Street Journal, and Time. In 1996 he received the Lifetime Achievement Award from the Computer Security Institute (San Francisco) for "sincere dedication to the computer security profession."

Mr. Wood is the Senior North American Editor for the technical journals Computers & Security and Computer Fraud and Security Bulletin. For the last six years he has written a monthly information security policies column for Computer Security Alert. He has published over 225 technical articles and five other books dealing with information security. His best selling book is entitled *Information Security Policies Made Easy*. Mr. Wood's work has been or is now being translated into a number of foreign languages including Brazilian Portuguese, Finnish, French, Japanese, Hebrew, Portuguese, Spanish, and Swedish.

Mr. Wood holds an MBA in financial information systems and a BSE in accounting, both from the Wharton School at the University of Pennsylvania. He also holds an MSE degree in computer science from the Moore School of Engineering at the same University (birthplace of the ENIAC, the world's first general purpose electronic computer). In addition to passing the Certified Public Accountant (CPA) exam, he is a Certified Information Systems Auditor (CISA), and a Certified Information Systems Security Professional (CISSP).

Other Books By Charles Cresson Wood

Information Security Roles and Responsibilities Made Easy (PentaSafe, Houston, Texas, USA, 2001)

Best Practices In Internet Commerce Security (PentaSafe, Houston, Texas, USA, 1998)

How to Handle Internet Electronic Commerce Security: Risks, Controls and Product Guide (PentaSafe, Houston, Texas, USA, 1996)

Effective Information Security Management (Elsevier Science Publishers, Oxford, England, 1991)

Computer Security: A Comprehensive Controls Checklist (John Wiley and Sons, New York, New York, USA 1987)

Information Security Policies Made Easy

Index

A

about policies, 3
abuse
  activity, 442
  evidence, 444
accelerated declassification, 71
acceptance
  computerized transaction, 216
  electronic, 216
  information security, 167
  production application, 165
access
  adult material, 333
  badge
    controlled, 127
    sharing, 127
  capability, 333
  code sharing, 300
  communication system, 132
  computer, 132
    center
      all, 132
      staff, 132
    number, 193
    training, 108
  consultant, 48
  contingency plan, 392
  control
    circumventing, 273
    cookies, 325
    database, 272
    decisions, 59
    file restoration, 330
    malfunction, 272
    network-connected computers, 305
    production operation, 385
    remote system, 308
    retaining privilege logs, 340
    system
      protection, 332
      records, 128
    time dependent, 331
  data warehouse, 336
  form, 201
  in-bound Internet, 310

information
  configuration, 382
  consistency, 31
  outsourced, 59
  secret, 337
  sensitive, 337
  valuable, 337
internal network, 303
Internet
  administrator, 188
  firewall, 195
  privileges, 304
  restriction, 304
  user, 439
logs
  authorization, 345
  private information, 339
media library, 133
missing device, 118
network ports, 312
non-firewall, 312
organization information, 280
password-based control, 270
paths, 383
personal information
  authorization, 336
  written request, 416
physical
  grantor list, 129
  sensitive information, 126
  terminated worker, 129
  third party, 124
  unauthorized, 128
private
  data records, 419
  information, 90
privilege
  revocation, 33
  termination, 282
problem, 159
production
  business information, 381
  systems, 244
  type list, 434

remote
   password, 308
   third party, 47
   training, 105
  restricted area, 129
  system
   implementation, 239
   network, 168
   third party, 49
  temporary worker, 48
  third party
   risks, 46
   software, 390
   terms, 50
account
  authentication, 287
  balancing, 219
  fraud, 218
  Internet service provider, 240
  number
   bank, 207
   concealing, 363
   intelligence, 429
  reconciliation, 219
  verifying calculations, 213
accountability, 80
acknowledging conduct code, 98
activating conference bridge, 240
active content
  intranet sites, 243
  screening, 195
activity
  coordination, 8
  hacking, 270
  separation, 333
  unauthorized reporting, 116
adapting policies, 8
address
  computer center, 138
  confirming changes, 236
  electronic mail, 220
  internal network, 187
administrative area discussion, 266
administrator
  firewall access, 188
  remote, 309
  security
   backup, 64
   designated, 63
adult material, 333
advertising
  help wanted, 277
  Internet, 246

advice
  information security, 44
  need, 30
advisories, 158
affiliation, 252
agreement
  compliance, 109
  confidentiality
   previous employer, 94
   restrictions, 48
  data exchange, 209
  licensing, 400
  non-compete, 94
  non-disclosure, 93
  software
   third party, 208
   written, 209
  third party, 54
  trading partner network, 215
  trust, 52
  work, 108
alarm, 142
alcohol, 104
alert system, 158
algorithms
  public evaluation, 368
  standard, 368
altered
  photographs, 85
  undetected, 35
alternative
  processing provider, 57
  reporting
   problem, 114
   violation, 114
  work sites, 351
analysis
  computer review, 161
  impact
   business, 393
   information security, 166
  problem, 122
  violation, 122
annual declassification review, 72
anonymous
  customer, 422
  FTP server, 370
  information linking, 427
  user IDs, 280
answering machines, 268

application
  coding principles, 356
  critical log, 150
  end-user programs, 230
  privacy policy, 422
  production
    acceptance, 165
    documentation, 150
  security functionality, 358
  service provider software, 57
  transaction data retention, 408
approval
  downloading, 205
  information disclosure, 277
  intranet server, 244
  monitoring electronic mail messages, 223
  private data system, 430
  process, 15
  production
    software, 387
    system change, 155
  public representation, 268
archive
  declassifying secrets, 73
  electronic mail messages
    management, 227
    review, 226
  file
    commerce site, 180
    web site, 180
  storage
    directory, 180
    media
      period, 181
      quality, 181
      testing, 181
    preservation, 182
    retention schedule, 407
area
  contents, 203
  equipment
    communication, 136
    vacated, 136
  restricted
    terminated worker access, 129
    working
      hours, 135
      single, 135
arrangements, 255
assessment
  risk, 37
  tool, 186

asset
  control, 63
  inventory
    information, 64
    technology, 61
assign
  information ownership, 41
  labels, 68
attachments
  inbound, 228
  scanning, 228
  unexpected, 229
attack
  disclosure, 116
  message, 159
attempting access, 128
attendees, 266
attribution information, 399
audience, 25
audio recording equipment, 136
audit trail, 335
authentication
  password, 293
  two-factor user, 308
author, 681
authorization
  information
    processing, 43
    transportation, 211
  problem, 115
  production transaction, 153
  requesting system access, 284
  software copies, 401
  violation, 115
automatic
  answer modems, 307
  backup, 178
  encryption key management, 373
  enforcement, 17
  log off, 331
  log on, 298
availability, 151
avoiding liability, 6

B

background
  check
    employee, 90
    non-employee, 92
    push software update, 174
back-off procedure, 156
back-out plans, 58

backup
    audits, 452
    automatic, 178
    critical
        file, 178
        information, 180
    data
        center, 139
        monthly, 176
    encryption key, 379
    file, 173
    information review, 178
    media
        encryption, 176
        fire zone, 179
        location, 176
        storage
            protection, 179
            units, 180
    multiple copies, 177
    on-site file, 177
    portable computer, 235
    pre-processing, 179
    private key, 376
    process, 177
    review, 236
    security administrator, 64
badge
    access
        control, 127
        sharing, 127
    identification
        removing, 104
        report, 129
        securing, 104
        wearing, 126
        without, 131
    temporary, 127
bag inspection, 128
balancing trade-offs, 29
bank account number, 207
basic training, 106
behavior, 416
binding
    contract, 215
    signature, 265

biometric information
    collection, 415
    transfer, 415
blanket monitoring, 445
blocking
    access, 304
    private
        data use, 432
        information, 418
bonding workers, 88
boot protection, 315
bound hardcopy labels, 78
breaching security, 116
broadcast
    electronic mail, 240
    voice mail, 240
browser capability, 251
browsing systems, 278
budgeting, 38
bug
    fixes, 389
    web, 185
bulk electronic mail, 225
business
    application
        change control, 387
        security functionality, 358
        system testing, 380
    arrangements, 255
    correcting records, 153
    critical logic, 230
    impact analysis, 393
    information
        disclosure
            customer, 274
            public, 45
        modification, 361
        updates, 289
    interruption support levels, 395
    plan
        contingency, 394
        continuity, 394
    restoration expectation, 394
    source document retention
        period, 407
        requirements, 407
    structure changes, 434
    transaction

C

cable
    modem, 194
    power, 143
    security, 143
    telecommunications, 143
calling area, 238
capability, 334
capacity planning, 163
carriers, 186
category classification
    five category, 393
    four category, 65
    prefixes, 67
    three category, 66
    two category
        closed, 67
        open, 67
cellular telephone
    secret information, 265
    use, 135
censoring data, 237
center
    access
        all, 132
        staff, 132
    address, 138
    alarm, 142
    construction, 141
    environmental control, 138
    location, 141
    sign, 134
    staffing, 135
    visitors, 131
central
    access control database, 272
    information security, 39
    point failure, 185
    problem reporting, 119
CERT
    organization, 157
    testing, 157
certificate
    storage media destruction, 209
    virus decal, 171
change
    control
        business application, 387
        documentation, 388
        procedure, 384

customer initiated, 213
dial-up number, 193
employment, 94
firewall, 190
information
    critical, 362
    security policy, 107
    sensitive, 362
    systems, 38
    valuable, 362
internal records, 366
notification, 435
password
    system, 293
    user ID, 293
production
    operating system
        approval, 155
        considerations, 385
        documentation, 386
        review, 155
    program, 152
    software package, 387
public key, 378
status
    disclosure, 419
    reporting, 103
    workers, 37
channel
    confirmation, 218
    incident reporting, 112
check
    background
        non-employee, 92
        worker, 90
    system integrity, 171
    virus program, 172
child information collection, 413
circumventing
    access controls, 273
    privacy policy, 52
classes, 108
classification
    category prefixes, 67
    five category, 393
    four category, 65
    guidelines, 65
    information
        resource, 393
        storage, 198
    Internet use, 440

labels
  assigning, 68
  comprehensive, 77
  department, 76
  incorrect, 68
  maintaining, 78
  multiple, 69
  new, 77
  use, 75
  user generated, 69
  sensitivity, 70
  software, 61
  storage media data, 70
  system, 61
  three category, 66
  two category
    closed, 67
    open, 67
clean desk
  active use, 146
  non-working hours, 146
clock synchronization, 348
closing door, 125
code
  conduct
    acknowledgement, 98
    corporate, 98
  equipment identification, 65
coding principles, 356
collect calls, 238
collecting information
  biometric, 415
  notice, 413
  private
    approval, 411
    consent, 413
command
  line interpreter software, 272
  response, 260
  system, 334
comments, 250
commerce
  server
    firewall, 188
    security, 214
    storage, 213
  site
    file archive, 180
    Internet, 371
  system, 140

common
  carriers, 303
  mechanisms, 358
communication
  center
    location, 124
    sign, 134
  equipment, 136
  Internet recording, 262
  line change, 191
  marketing opt-out provision, 212
  offensive, 268
  outbound, 251
  private, 410
  public, 277
  service invoice, 154
  system
    access, 132
    securing, 133
competition
  former employees, 99
  intelligence, 96
  personal relationships, 99
compliance
  agreement, 109
  information security, 56
component release, 145
comprehensive labels, 77
compressing secret data, 369
compromise
  key encryption, 378
  security mechanisms, 273
computer
  access
    authorization, 132
    number, 193
    training, 108
  analysis review, 161
  assisted processes, 364
  center
    access
      all, 132
      staff, 132
    address, 138
    alarm, 142
    construction, 141
    door, 125
    environmental control, 138
    location, 141
    sign, 134
    staffing, 135
  continuity plans, 394

crime
   evidence, 444
   investigation
      communication, 448
      process, 118
delivery, 137
disaster recovery plan, 151
emergency response
   plan, 157
   team
      organization, 157
      testing, 157
eradicating virus, 168
facility
   door
      closing, 125
      securing, 134
      strength, 125
   fire resistance, 125
   location, 124
   tour, 133
firewall, 190
games, 438
mobile, 352
modification, 144
network, 305
operator log
   contents, 182
   review, 182
output, 81
powering down, 147
production system location, 137
related position, 89
security, 254
service invoice, 154
storage media release, 203
support identification codes, 319
system
   access controls, 332
   attack, 116
   audit logs, 341
   classification, 70
   dispersion, 139
   names, 74
   personal ownership, 139
   securing, 133
transactions, 319
use, 349
virus, 173
computerized transaction, 216
concealing
   account numbers, 363
   information transmission, 185

condition
   disruptive, 119
   employment, 95
   equipment, 142
   Internet, 251
conduct
   acknowledgement, 98
   corporate, 98
conference bridge activation, 240
confidential
   agreement
      disclosure, 48
      repair staff, 47
      third party, 404
   counseling, 103
   documentation, 208
   information
      meetings, 267
      sending, 230
   previous employer, 94
   speed dial, 232
configuration
   firewall
      authorization, 190
      rules, 190
   network connection, 192
   operating system, 389
   security, 183
   system
      requirements, 164
      template, 167
confirmation
   address change, 236
   channel, 218
   customer-initiated change, 213
   payment information, 217
conflicts
   interest, 98
   legal, 32
connection
   configuration, 192
   dial out, 194
   dial up, 189
   direct
      dial, 306
      Internet, 195
   Internet, 190
   intranet security criteria, 192
   network
      external
         inventory, 192
         real time, 189

outside, 191
   third party, 306
  scanning remote, 184
  Telnet password, 195
consecutive vacation days, 101
consent, 424
consequence
  non-compliance, 122
  violation, 122
consistent security, 8
construction, 141
consultant
  access, 48
  notes, 47
consumption, 235
contact
  information
    employee, 204
    security, 262
    sender, 220
    travel, 152
  Internet disclosure, 253
  law enforcement, 117
  worker, 418
container, 199
content
  electronic mail messages, 224
  Internet web site changes, 260
  labels, 250
  message, 224
  monitoring
    electronic mail messages, 224
    responsibility, 237
  ownership, 242
  rating, 212
  review, 242
  testing, 242
contingency plan
  accessibility, 392
  review, 397
  service provider, 58
  software conversion, 166
  testing, 396
continuing education, 109
continuity plan, 394
contract
  approvals, 59
  electronic
    mail, 216
    system, 215
  online, 209

security requirements
  outsourcing, 56
  third party, 50
  termination, 51
contractor
  expectation, 163
  risk, 163
control
  access system record, 128
  common mechanisms, 358
  computer center, 138
  decisions, 59
  downloading sensitive information, 205
  encryption key recovery, 379
  enforceability, 34
  implementation, 451
  information
    asset, 63
    security, 364
    system
      disclosure, 201
      minimum, 359
  Internet traffic, 184
  inventory, 61
  operational change, 154
  output data, 366
  override
    facilities, 329
    use, 330
  practices, 451
  production
    operation, 385
    system, 165
  security usability, 279
  validation, 362
controlled access, 127
controversial sensitive information, 276
conventional naming
  file, 75
  overall, 74
converting software contingency plans, 166
convicted felons, 89
cookies
  access control, 325
  authorization, 185
  automatic logon, 298
  file interrogation, 212
  Internet, 247
cooperation, 45
coordinating
  activities, 8
  information security, 36

copies
  authorized software, 401
  documents, 81
  information
    critical, 235
    sensitive
      permission, 79
      users, 235
      waste, 80
    valuable, 235
  multiple backups, 177
  preventing, 81
  software, 401
  unauthorized
    data, 402
    software, 402
copyright
  electronic books, 403
  information, 401
  notices, 400
  protection, 402
  review, 404
  software, 401
  unauthorized material, 402
cordless telephone, 265
corporate
  conduct code, 98
  data dictionary, 62
correcting business records, 153
correspondent content, 422
counseling, 103
couriers, 82
cover sheet
  fax notice, 233
  faxing sensitive information, 231
coverage matrix, 11
covering sensitive information, 147
creating security tools, 279
credentials, 681
credit
  card
    calls, 239
    number
      dormant, 218
      use, 364
    use, 269
  check, 87
crime
  computer
    abuse, 444
    investigation, 448
  investigation, 118

criminal
  justice contact, 447
  messages, 249
  reformed, 92
critical
  application
    log, 150
    servers, 337
  backup file, 178
  business logic, 230
  information
    backup, 180
    changes, 362
    copies, 235
    securing, 132
  message line numbering, 236
  networking device
    data, 197
    voice, 197
  production data, 203
criticality rating, 392
cross-training, 152
cross-validation, 249
current virus software, 172
custodian
  destination, 42
  responsibilities, 42
  transfer, 286
customer
  activity log, 423
  anonymity, 422
  compromising security mechanisms, 273
  concealing account numbers, 363
  confirm change, 213
  direct mail, 263
  electronic mail encryption, 222
  identifications, 423
  information
    collection, 414
    contact use, 428
    deletion, 432
    disclosure
      business, 274
      statistics, 421
    financial, 260
    personal
      access, 428
      use, 427
    privacy, 420
    recipient disclosure, 421
    transfer, 433
  log, 404
  mailing list, 213

record
    requests, 422
    statistics, 423
    service passwords, 332
    worker, 102
customization
    need, 29
    specifics, 25
cyclical passwords, 295

D

daily logon limitation, 317
damage
    off-site system, 112
    water, 141
data
    backup, 176
    censoring, 237
    center
        infrastructure, 139
        visitor, 131
    classification
        category prefixes, 67
        five category, 393
        four category, 65
        labels
            assigning, 68
            incorrect, 68
            use, 75
        three category, 66
        two category
            closed, 67
            open, 67
    critical
        networking device, 197
        production, 203
    destruction moratorium, 409
    dictionary, 62
    disclaimer, 32
    exchange agreement, 209
    labels
        decision management, 84
        input, 73
    payment encryption, 217
    personal use, 433
    private, 417
    retention
        application transactions, 408
        file grouping, 74
        schedule, 407
    review, 244

secret
    media exposure, 69
    transportation, 204
separation, 333
storage media, 70
system approval, 430
transfer, 433
transmission
    channels, 373
    secret, 204
unauthorized copies, 402
victim, 111
warehouse access, 336
database
    centralized access control, 272
    indexes, 434
    removing individuals, 431
    updates, 335
    user ID, 290
deactivating logs, 344
decision data, 84
declaring trade secrets, 68
declassification
    accelerated, 71
    annual review, 72
    date, 70
    extension, 71
    information
        releasing, 83
        sensitive, 72
    schedule, 71
    secret archives, 73
decrypting files, 173
defacing web pages, 260
default
    copyright protection, 402
    file permissions, 271
    information ownership, 42
    user privileges, 334
defining framework, 10
delegating responsibility, 372
delete
    information
        customer, 432
        prospect, 432
    logs, 344
    source data, 369
    terminated worker files, 286
delivery
    computer
        output, 81
        room, 137

secret information
  acknowledgement, 82
  third party, 210
department classification labels, 76
design
  critical system decisions, 15
  information security controls, 364
  Internet web pages, 258
  reporting problems, 117
designated security administrator, 63
destruction
  box, 200
  data moratorium, 409
  electronic mail messages, 222
  information
    instruction, 199
    necessary, 408
    personnel, 200
    sensitive
      methods, 198
      procedure, 200
  record, 408
  schedule, 409
  storage media certificate, 209
  transaction log, 405
detection
  approval, 187
  host based, 188
developer
  access, 381
  security problems, 362
  tracing errors, 362
development
  conventions, 383
  end-user system, 165
  policies, 9
  process, 5
  proposals, 355
  security life cycle, 357
  separation, 161
  software, 398
  techniques, 356
  third-party software, 391
  time, 18
  tools, 356
device
  access, 118
  synchronization, 238
diagnostic
  hardware, 328
  port access, 311
  software, 328

dial up
  compliance, 450
  connection, 189
  modem configuration, 194
  number change, 193
  password attempts, 310
  user authentication, 309
dial-out connection, 194
dictionary, 62
digital
  certificate
    private key security, 377
    root key protection, 373
    validity period, 372
  evidence, 444
  signature
    information owner, 243
    key
      escrow, 379
      lifetime, 376
      separation, 379
      storage, 377
    software, 367
direct
  dial connections, 306
  Internet connection, 195
  inward system access, 239
  mail, 263
directory
  archive file, 180
  publicly modified, 196
  shared system, 191
disabling
  critical security components, 44
  Java, 313
disaster
  computer recovery plan, 151
  support requirements, 392
disclaimer
  Internet
    hot link, 259
    personal message, 252
  message, 249
disclosure
  approval, 277
  computer system attack, 116
  encryption key
    approval, 372
    controls, 377
  information
    business, 45
    contact, 253

customer
  business, 274
  statistics, 421
  financial, 264
  modification, 203
  personal, 424
  private
    authorization, 411
    outsourcing, 421
  security products, 45
  sensitive, 110
  system
    controls, 201
    vulnerability, 110
  telephone, 263
  third party, 274
  worker contact, 418
  law enforcement, 445
  passwords
    action, 296
    requirements, 293
  personal data, 421
  second jobs, 102
  status, 419
  termination, 418
  trade secret, 75
  vulnerability, 121
discontinuing service, 302
discussion
  administrative area, 266
  groups, 250
  public places, 263
  security weakness, 120
  vulnerability, 120
disk storage encryption, 205
diskless workstations, 234
dispersion, 139
disposal
  equipment, 145
  information
    hardcopy, 199
    payment, 85
    responsibility, 145
disruptive condition, 119
disseminating information
  secret, 336
  third party, 48
distribution
  electronic mail messages, 227
  marketing material, 201
  personnel record, 96
  privacy policies, 437
  software, 208
divisional plans, 451

documentation
  change control, 388
  confidentiality, 208
  information security policies, 31
  official, 85
  operating, 386
  production
    application, 150
    system, 164
  retention
    period, 407
    requirements, 407
  secret, 83
  sensitive, 81
  sequence numbers, 83
  software
    features, 388
    functions, 388
  system, 207
  training, 386
domain
  name
    Internet, 260
    registration, 186
  network, 187
door
  closing, 125
  computer center
    secondary, 125
    securing, 134
  equipment rack, 140
  strength, 125
dormant
  credit card numbers, 218
  user ID privileges, 284
double-keying large transactions, 360
download
  information, 175
  Internet
    large files, 305
    mirror site software, 175
  scanning, 171
  sensitive information
    approval, 205
    controls, 205
  software
    Internet, 175
    prevention, 169
  transferring files, 256
drinking, 137
drugs, 104
duplicating
  encryption keys, 376
  software, 402

duress
   passwords, 330
   termination, 123
duty
   information technology separation, 162
   reporting
      problem, 113
      violation, 113
   separation
      information, 160
      instruction, 161
dynamic password tokens, 298

E

eating, 137
education
   continuing, 109
   information security, 105
electromagnetic radiation protection, 246
electronic
   acceptance, 216
   books, 403
   forums, 229
   mail
      address, 220
      archiving, 226
      attachments
         approval, 228
         inbound, 228
         unexpected, 229
      broadcast, 240
      browser capability, 251
      bulk, 225
      content monitoring, 224
      contract, 216
      distribution, 227
      encryption
         customer messages, 222
         private, 435
      footers, 225
      forwarding, 221
      message
         approval, 223
         archival, 227
         contents, 224
         destruction, 222
         footers, 226
         handling, 221
         inappropriate, 221
         modification, 223
         monitoring, 226
         offensive, 112
         purpose, 347
         response, 225
         retention, 221
         review, 226
         secret information, 220
         sending, 225
         storage, 222
         third party, 219
         unsolicited, 224
      privacy, 222
      sales department, 227
      scanning, 225
      system use, 227
      unique accounts, 301
   marketing material source, 220
   monitoring areas, 443
   notification, 347
   offer, 216
   static protection, 138
   system
      binding contract, 215
      public comment, 250
electronic mail signatures, 228
embedded
   personal information, 428
   security, 355
emergency
   requirements, 392
   response
      plan, 157
      team
         organization, 157
         testing, 157
emotional stability test, 91
employee
   access, 434
   behavior, 416
   changes, 285
   competitor, 99
   contact, 204
   credit check, 87
   explanatory statement, 425
   file examination, 425
   fingerprinting, 91
   information, 86
   lifestyle, 87
   privacy, 423
   revealing information, 87
   stock transactions, 97
   termination
      information retention, 101
      returning property, 101
   travel, 95

employment
    change, 94
    condition, 95
    confidentiality agreements, 94
    term, 95
encryption
    algorithms
        publicly evaluated, 368
        standard, 368
    backup media, 176
    disk storage, 205
    electronic mail
        customer, 222
        private, 435
    faxing secret information, 232
    file, 367
    general purpose systems, 371
    hardware, 369
    implementation, 368
    key
        backup, 379
        compromised, 378
        disclosure
            approval, 372
            controls, 377
        duplication, 376
        expiration, 374
        generation, 374
        length, 374
        life, 374
        management
            automated, 373
            systems, 372
        master, 375
        materials
            destruction, 375
            exchange, 375
            security, 375
        private transmission, 378
        recovery operation controls, 379
        secrecy, 376
        separation, 379
        storage
            device, 377
            media, 378
        transmission, 373
        utilities, 368
    message protection, 370
    passwords
        storage, 325
        utilities, 368

payment
    data, 217
    information, 217
    process approval
        systems, 367
        users, 367
    secret
        data, 369
        information, 204
    system initialization, 369
end user
    application programs, 230
    system development, 165
endorsement
    product, 253
    service, 253
enforcement
    automating, 17
    process, 15
enhanced service, 214
entrance, 127
environmental control, 138
equipment
    area
        communication, 136
        vacated, 136
    disposal, 145
    identification codes, 65
    isolation, 140
    maintenance, 144
    moving, 245
    off-site use approval, 145
    power conditioning, 142
    protection, 137
    rack door, 140
    recording
        audio, 136
        video, 136
    secret information, 134
    siting, 137
    surveillance, 133
    tracking, 64
eradicating viruses
    computer, 168
    system administrator, 168
erasable surfaces
    erasing, 267
    existence, 267
erasing
    erasable surfaces, 267
    sensitive information, 198

error
  investigation, 214
  manipulations, 365
  tracing, 362
escorting
  visitors
    after hours, 130
    work hours, 130
  workers, 100
escrow
  third-party software, 399
  verification, 399
essential
  information, 73
  software, 73
establishing policies, 7
ethnic harassment, 97
evaluation
  information security policies, 34
  performance, 86
  products, 359
  technology, 164
events
  logs, 339
  reporting, 117
evidence
  abuse, 444
  digital, 444
examination
  private user files, 437
  stored data, 443
exceptions, 32
excessive resource consumption, 235
exchanging Internet information, 207
executables, 170
executing mobile code, 241
expectations
  business restoration, 394
  contractor, 163
expiration
  encryption keys, 374
  user IDs
    Internet-accessible computers, 286
    non-employee, 281
    user, 282
explanatory statement, 425
exploitation
  security, 300
  system vulnerability, 111
exposing secret data, 69
extended investigation, 118

external
  electronic mail forwarding, 221
  information
    gathered, 55
    labels, 76
    requests, 276
  loading program, 174
  network
    connection
      inventory, 192
      real time, 189
    interface, 184
    system, 196
  software testing, 386
  validating party identification, 210
  violation reporting, 115

F

facility
  door closing, 125
  door strength, 125
  fire resistance, 125
  location, 124
  personal use, 441
  tour, 133
failure
  integrity control notification, 120
  network central point, 185
  software, 361
famous customer identifications, 423
faxing
  cover sheet notice, 233
  information
    confidential, 232
    secret
      encrypted, 232
      passwords, 233
    sensitive
      cover sheet, 231
      human presence, 231
      intermediaries, 231
      notification, 231
      physical security, 232
      unencrypted, 232
  logs, 229
feature documentation, 388
feedback
  incorrect, 315
  software, 361
felons, 89

file
  access, 425
  archive
    commerce site, 180
    web site, 180
  backups
    critical, 178
    on site, 177
    scanning, 173
  cabinet, 148
  cookie interrogation, 212
  encryption, 367
  examination, 425
  grouping data retention, 74
  naming convention, 75
  ownership, 65
  permissions, 271
  personal privacy, 419
  restoration access control, 330
  temporary, 365
  transferring downloads, 256
  user, 150
financial
  information
    disclosure, 264
    storage, 260
  statements, 60
  system, 140
  vendor review, 50
fingerprinting, 91
fire
  backup media, 179
  facility resistance, 125
firewall
  administrator access, 188
  computer
    dedicated, 190
    personal, 188
  configuration
    approval, 190
    change, 190
  server
    Internet commerce, 188
    web, 314
  shared, 58
  workstation, 188
five-category data classification, 393
fixed passwords, 291
floppy disks, 197
footers, 225

foreign
  companies, 60
  nationals, 92
forensic analysis, 448
forgotten passwords, 292
former hacker, 92
forms
  access, 201
  user ID, 285
forwarding
  electronic mail, 221
  intranet information, 244
four-category data classification, 65
framework, 10
fraud, 218
free speech, 236
FTP, 370
function documentation, 388
functionality
  business applications, 358
  systems, 384
future earnings, 276

G

games, 438
gateway wireless network, 196
gathering
  information
    external, 55
    Internet, 348
  reference materials, 9
generating
  encryption keys
    materials
      destruction, 375
      security, 375
    standards, 374
  passwords
    algorithms, 323
    materials, 323
generic user IDs, 283
granting
  access, 280
  system privileges, 290
grantor list, 129
grievance resolution, 103
group
  data retention, 74
  Internet discussion, 250
  voice mail, 241

H

hacker
  activities, 270
  former, 92
handling
  electronic mail messages, 221
  information
    off shift, 146
    protection, 31
    sensitive, 53
  rejected items, 359
harassment
  ethnic, 97
  racial, 97
  sexual, 97
hardcopy
  disposal, 199
  information
    secret, 265
    sensitive, 211
  labels
    bound materials, 78
    sensitivity, 77
hardware
  diagnostic, 328
  encryption, 369
  procurement, 62
  retention, 144
hazardous
  products, 84
  services, 84
  workplace, 97
health information, 97
help wanted advertising, 277
high reliability
  computers, 311
  networks, 311
high security
  computers, 311
  networks, 311
higher-level programming languages, 357
honesty test, 91
host relationship, 183
host-based intrusion detection system, 188
hot link
  disclaimer, 259
  establishments, 259
HTML, 261
human
  intervention, 364
  presence, 231
  safety issues, 384

I

identification
  badge
    removing, 104
    report, 129
    securing, 104
    wearing, 126
    without, 131
  credentials, 317
  equipment codes, 65
  security requirements, 355
  software, 327
  visitor, 130
  vital record, 406
  vulnerability, 454
identity
  misrepresentation, 249
  private information, 436
  reporting
    problem, 115
    violation, 115
  validation, 210
image, 247
immediate termination, 123
impact
  analysis, 393
  information security analysis, 166
  review, 167
  security statement, 166
implementation
  direct inward system access, 239
  encryption, 368
  multi-user system, 163
important policies, 5
in house
  software specifications, 356
  systems development proposals, 355
inappropriate
  electronic mail message, 221
  public postings, 254
inbound
  electronic mail attachments, 228
  Internet access, 310
incident
  learning, 122
  management responsibility, 160
  reporting
    channel, 112
    severity, 113
incidental computer use, 439
incomplete information, 85

incorrect
  data classification labels, 68
  logon feedback, 315
  personal information, 425
increasing wealth, 93
independent
  control reports, 56
  security systems, 280
indexes, 434
individual
  control personal data use, 431
  record access authorization, 424
industry-specific information security, 33
informants, 96
information
  access
    configuration, 382
    policies, 43
    production application, 335
    protection, 31
  alteration, 35
  asset
    control, 63
    inventory, 64
  attribution, 399
  backup review, 178
  biometric
    collection, 415
    transfer, 415
  business production updates, 289
  changes, 438
  collection
    notice, 413
    restrictions, 273
  confidential
    meetings, 267
    third party, 336
  contact
    Intranet disclosure, 253
    travel, 152
  critical
    backups, 180
    copies, 235
    securing, 132
  cross-validation, 249
  custodian
    destination, 42
    responsibilities, 42
  customer
    collection, 414
    disclosure, 421
    privacy, 420

declassification
  accelerated, 71
  releasing, 83
destruction
  instruction, 199
  personnel, 200
  requirements, 408
disclosure
  approval, 277
  customer business, 274
  telephone, 263
  third party, 274
disposal, 145
dissemination, 48
distribution, 414
download, 175
employee
  contact, 204
  prospective, 86
essential, 73
external requests, 276
faxing
  confidential, 232
  secret
    encrypted, 232
    passwords, 233
  sensitive
    cover sheet, 231
    human presence, 231
    intermediaries, 231
    notification, 231
    physical security, 232
    unencrypted, 232
financial disclosure, 264
freedom, 412
handling
  contract termination, 51
  off shift, 146
  protection, 31
health, 97
incomplete, 85
integrity attributes, 453
Internet exchange, 207
intranet
  forwarding, 244
  owner, 243
  validation, 242
labeling, 74
labels
  classification, 77
  external, 76
  life cycle, 78

legal action, 275
linking, 427
location, 278
logon, 315
modification
    disclosure, 203
    Internet, 252
    production business, 361
multiple copies, 400
nature, 278
obsolete, 85
organization
    access, 280
    release, 275
ownership, 41
    authority, 36
    delegation, 43
    digital signature, 243
    responsibility, 62
payment
    confirmation, 217
    disposal, 85
    encryption, 217
personal
    access, 416
    business functioning, 412
    customer, 427
    purpose, 427
    retention, 405
private
    access
        background check, 90
        logging, 427
    collection
        approval, 412
        consent, 413
        process, 411
        surreptitious, 413
    disclosure
        authorization, 411
        third party, 417
    links
        approval, 429
        purpose, 429
    sharing, 420
processing, 43
production system, 257
proprietary, 336
protection, 31
public release
    contact name, 275
    review, 277

release, 277
reliability, 256
requests, 274
resource classification, 393
retention
    period, 406
    terminated employee, 101
return, 56
safety, 97
secret
    access, 337
    delivering, 82
    dissemination, 336
    electronic mail, 220
    encryption, 204
    equipment, 134
    international transport
        authorization, 211
        security, 211
    intranet, 261
    printing, 81
    removal, 202
    sending, 264
    speaker phones, 233
    system isolation, 338
    third-party delivery, 210
    transmitting, 265
    transportable computers, 349
    web, 261
    wireless transmission, 266
secure container, 199
security
    alert system, 158
    budget, 38
    centralized, 39
    class, 108
    compliance
        checking, 454
        responsibility, 56
    contacts, 262
    controls, 364
    coordination, 36
    education, 105
    impact analysis, 166
    industry specific, 33
    investigations, 449
    liaison, 41
    management
        committee, 35
        forum, 35
    manual, 40
    measures, 167
    mission, 39
    plans, 40

problem resolution, 159
procedures, 40
product disclosure, 45
resources, 38
responsibilities, 39
risk
  assessment, 453
  significant, 36
standards, 40
tasks, 39
sender contact, 220
sending
  confidential, 230
  private, 230
sensitive
  access
    authorization, 337
    physical, 126
    read, 271
    write, 271
  accountability, 80
  answering machines, 268
  area content, 203
  controversial, 276
  copies, 235
  copying, 79
  covering, 147
  declassification, 72
  destruction
    box, 200
    methods, 198
    procedure, 200
  disclosure, 110
  downloading
    approval, 205
    controls, 205
  erase, 198
  loss, 110
  material, 200
  personal computers, 350
  presenting, 78
  printing, 80
  product
    access, 91
    intermediate, 79
  public exposure, 266
  removal
    hardcopy, 211
    log, 202
    premises, 202
  retention, 405
  securing
    authorization, 83
    location, 132

  security, 207
  sending, 264
  small computers, 349
  storage
    locked, 147
    media, 84
    review, 234
  telephone discussion, 265
  tracking, 79
  transmission, 254
  transportable computers, 350
  waste, 80
separating duties, 160
service calls, 238
sharing, 275
storage
  customer financials, 260
  mixed classified, 198
  portable computers, 351
system
  assessments, 452
  change
    approval, 38
    implementation, 388
  control
    disclosure, 201
    independent reviews, 46
    internal, 453
    minimum, 359
    testing, 300
  department visitor, 131
  ownership, 41
  privilege use, 279
  product, 143
  tools, 328
  vulnerability disclosure, 110
technology, 162
testing, 382
time sensitive, 234
transfer
  sensitive, 211
  third party, 51
transmission, 185
unauthorized, 401
unnecessary, 435
unsolicited, 257
use
  consistency, 31
  location specific, 431
  purpose, 31
user responsibility, 42

Information Security Policies Made Easy

valuable
  access, 337
  copies, 235
vulnerability, 111
information security
policies
  about, 3
  adapting, 8
  advice, 30
  change, 107
  controls, 4
  customization
    need, 29
    specifics, 25
  developing
    iterative, 22
    steps, 9
    time, 18
  disclaimers, 29
  document, 31
  establishing, 7
  evaluation, 34
  framework, 10
  guidelines, 3
  importance, 5
  length, 21
  matrix
    coverage, 11
    sample, 13
  non-compliance, 28
  number, 19
  objectives
    motivational, 26
    operational, 27
  organization, 26
  pamphlet, 106
  procedures, 4
  review
    independent, 45
    internal, 34
  scope, 27
  searching, 25
  servers, 17
  standards, 3
  topic order, 24
  using, 25
pranks, 112
responsibility, 110
solutions, 358
training, 106
infrastructure, 139
initial password
  issuance, 290
  transmission, 290

initializing encryption, 369
in-person password authentication, 293
input
  data
    validation, 359
    warehouse labels, 73
  transactions
    authorization, 365
    production, 359
    rejecting, 363
inspection, 128
installing software
  systems, 389
  user, 174
instruction
  book use, 3
  information destruction, 199
  separating duties, 161
insurance coverage, 36
integrity
  assessment tool, 186
  checking system, 171
  control failure notification, 120
  statements, 390
intellectual property
  labeling, 400
  off-site development, 98
  permission, 305
  right, 95
intelligence, 96
interconnection system, 163
interface external network
  approval, 184
  system, 196
interference reporting
  problem, 114
  violation, 114
intermediary, 231
intermediate products, 79
internal
  informant, 96
  investigations
    confidentiality, 446
    response, 449
  network
    access, 303
    address, 187
    device passwords, 312
  record change reviews, 366
international
  Internet business transaction, 215
  trade armaments, 444
  transferring private information, 417
  transporting secret information

authorization, 211
  security, 211
Internet
  access
    computers, 340
    firewall, 195
    non-firewall, 312
    privileges, 304
    restriction, 304
    user, 439
  activity monitoring, 345
  advertising, 246
  affiliation, 252
  business arrangements, 255
  commerce
    server firewall, 188
    sites, 371
    system, 140
  computer security query, 254
  conditions, 251
  connection
    approval, 303
    firewall, 190
  contact information disclosure, 253
  content
    labels, 250
    move, 242
  cookies, 247
  customer use profiles, 346
  direct connection, 195
  discussion groups, 250
  domain name
    change control, 260
    registration, 186
  download
    large files, 305
    mirror site software, 175
    software, 175
  financial system, 140
  firewall administrator access, 188
  gathering information, 348
  hot link
    disclaimer, 259
    establishments, 259
  identity, 305
  in-bound access, 310
  information
    exchange, 207
    modification, 252
    reliability, 256

  international business transaction, 215
  material posting, 255
  monitoring, 403
  news source, 251
  outbound communications, 251
  personal
    access time, 441
    message disclaimer, 252
    use, 440
  production system information, 257
  recording communications, 262
  representation
    products, 253
    services, 253
  server
    command response, 260
    public, 189
    security commerce, 214
  service provider
    contingency plan, 58
    personal accounts, 240
  telephone facilities, 248
  terms, 251
  trade secret releases, 254
  traffic control, 184
  training, 106
  transfer, 245
  unsolicited information, 257
  use
    classification, 440
    logs, 346
  web
    bugs, 247
    page
      design, 258
      management committee, 258
      review, 259
    site
      content changes, 260
      digital certificate, 371
inter-processor commands, 309
interrogating cookie files, 212
interrupting business, 395
intranet
  active content, 243
  connection security criteria, 192
  content
    ownership, 242
    review, 242
    testing, 242
  data review, 244
  information
    forwarding, 244
    owner, 243

secret, 261
  validation, 242
posting, 241
production system access, 244
server approval, 244
style guide, 245
trade secrets, 248
transfer, 245
web page review, 243
introduction, 1
intrusion
  detection system approval, 187
  host-based detection, 188
  investigations, 449
  response procedure, 158
  suspected system, 157
inventory
  asset
    information, 64
    technology, 61
  controlling, 61
  external network connection, 192
investigation
  computer crime, 118
  confidentiality, 446
  error, 214
  extended, 118
  intrusion, 449
  response, 449
  status reports, 448
  teams, 449
investigators, 45
invoice
  communication, 154
  computer, 154
involuntary termination
  escorting worker, 100
  relieving duty, 100
involving computer viruses, 173
isolation equipment, 140

J

Java
  disabling, 313
  program execution, 371
job
  description, 86
  key technical, 151
  rotation, 160
  second
    disclosure, 102
    permission, 102

K

key
  destruction
    exchange material, 375
    generation material, 375
  digital signature
    escrow, 379
    lifetime, 376
    separation, 379
    storage, 377
  encryption
    approval, 372
    automated, 373
    backup, 379
    compromised, 378
    controls, 377
    duplication, 376
    expiration, 374
    generation, 374
    length, 374
    life, 374
    management, 372
    master, 375
    recovery, 379
    secrecy, 376
    separation, 379
    storage
      device, 377
      media, 378
    transmission
      channels, 373
      private, 378
    utilities, 368
  generation material security, 375
  management responsibility, 380
  private
    backups, 376
    digital certificate, 377
  public changes, 378
  root protection, 373
  technical job, 151
  user authentication, 379
  workstation, 139

L

labels
  classification
    comprehensive, 77
    department, 76
    maintaining, 78
    multiple, 69
    user generated, 69

content, 250
data
  classification
    assigning, 68
    incorrect, 68
    use, 75
  management, 84
  hardcopy bound, 78
  hazardous
    products, 84
    services, 84
  information
    external, 76
    life cycle, 78
  input data warehouse, 73
  intellectual property, 400
  sensitivity
    hardcopy, 77
    unknown, 76
languages
  high level, 357
  software, 390
last logon
  date, 317
  time, 317
law
  enforcement
    contacting, 117
    disclosure, 445
    inquiries, 446
  violation, 33
learning incident, 122
legal
  action, 275
  conflicts, 32
  proceedings
    information, 447
    participation, 447
lending computers, 351
length
  encryption keys, 374
  policies, 21
liability avoidance, 6
liaison, 41
library media access, 133
licensing
  agreement reviews, 400
  evidence, 401
life
  cycle
    labels, 78
    systems development, 357
  encryption keys, 374
  style, 87

line
  change, 191
  numbering, 236
linking private information
  approval, 429
  purpose, 429
listing grantors, 129
loading external programs, 174
location
  backup media, 176
  computer center, 141
  facility
    communication, 124
    computer, 124
  information use, 431
  production computer system, 137
lock
  file cabinet, 148
  metal furniture, 354
  personal office, 126
  workstation, 139
logging off automatically, 331
logic, 230
logon
  attempts, 339
  banner
    information, 316
    network, 316
    system, 316
  information feedback, 315
logs
  access, 345
  activities, 340
  archiving, 341
  audit, 341
  computer operator
    contents, 182
    review, 182
  critical application, 150
  customer, 404
  deactivation, 344
  deletion, 344
  destruction, 405
  fax, 229
  Internet
    accessible computers, 340
    use, 346
  keystroke, 342
  modification, 344
  movement, 83
  override, 348
  password, 343

privilege
    access control, 340
    user ID activity, 342
protection, 344
remotely mirrored, 341
removing sensitive information, 202
retention period, 340
rotation, 341
security-relevant events, 339
system review, 345
long-distance telephone call
    personal, 206
    returning, 206
loss
    off-site system, 112
    sensitive information, 110
    stock option, 123

M

mailing list
    customer, 213
    prospect, 213
maintenance
    business contingency plans, 394
    classification labels, 78
    equipment, 144
    preventive, 143
    software, 387
malfunction
    access control, 272
    reporting, 121
management
    committee
        information security, 35
        Internet web pages, 258
    data labels, 84
    encryption key, 372
    information security forum, 35
    responsibility
        delegate, 372
        incident, 160
        key, 380
    security approach, 37
    support, 6
man-trap entrance, 127
manual
    information security, 40
    prepared documents, 85
    procedures, 395

marketing
    communication opt-out provision, 212
    electronic source, 220
    information sharing, 275
    material distribution, 201
masking password changes, 324
master
    copy
        critical production data, 203
        software, 176
    encryption keys, 375
material
    marketing, 220
    sensitive information, 200
matrix
    preparing, 11
    sample, 13
mature development
    techniques, 356
    tools, 356
measures
    information security, 167
    network security, 197
mechanisms, 358
media
    archive storage
        period, 181
        quality, 181
        testing, 181
    backup
        encryption, 176
        fire zone, 179
        location, 176
        storage
            protection, 179
            units, 180
    computer storage release, 203
    data storage classification, 70
    encryption key, 378
    exposing secret data, 69
    library access, 133
    removal, 149
    storage
        classification, 70
        destruction certificate, 209
        production system, 344
        sensitive information, 84
meetings
    attendees, 266
    confidential information, 267
    third party, 267

message
attacker, 159
content restriction, 224
criminal, 249
disclaimer
personal, 252
web sites, 249
electronic mail
contents, 224
destruction, 222
handling, 221
inappropriate, 221
offensive, 112
retention, 221
storage, 222
unsolicited, 224
encryption, 370
monitoring, 347
ownership, 65
protection, 186
terrorist, 249
voice mail storage, 239
migrating software, 380
minimum
information system controls, 359
password length
constraint, 320
designation, 319
mirror site, 175
misrepresentation, 249
missing access device, 118
mission, 39
mobile
code execution, 241
computers, 352
modem
auto answer, 307
cable, 194
configuring dial-up, 194
line registry, 307
workstation, 306
modification
computer, 144
electronic mail messages, 223
information
disclosure, 203
Internet, 252
production business, 361
logs, 344
monitoring
activity, 347
areas, 443
blanketing employee communications, 445
content

electronic mail messages, 224
responsibility, 237
electronic mail messages
approval, 223
purpose, 226
review, 347
information, 445
Internet
activity, 345
information use, 403
performance, 347
permission, 445
telephone conversations, 446
monitoring tools, 345
moving
Internet content, 242
office computer equipment, 245
secret documents, 83
multiple
carrier, 186
classification
labels, 69
sensitivity, 70
copies
backup, 177
information, 400
simultaneous sessions, 318
user IDs, 284
virus screening package, 171
multi-user
application criticality rating, 392
production applications, 335
system implementation, 163

N

naming
computer systems, 74
convention
consistency, 74
files, 75
user IDs, 283
web sites, 255
need to know, 287
need to withhold, 287
network
access, 309
agreement, 215
computer access control, 302
connection
computers, 305
configuration, 192
inventory, 192
outside organization, 191

walk up, 311
domain, 187
external interface, 184
failure, 185
internal address, 187
logon banner, 316
message protection service, 186
passwords, 320
ports
    public access, 312
    unattended, 313
postings, 256
public service, 193
security measures, 197
system
    access, 168
    third party, 54
    unattended, 302
third party, 306
wireless
    configuration, 196
    gateways, 196
new
    account authentication, 287
    information classification labels, 77
    service, 214
    technology control, 43
news source, 251
non-anonymous user IDs, 281
non-business
    information use, 442
    web site, 304
non-compete agreement, 94
non-compliance
    consequence, 122
    handling, 28
non-disclosure agreement
    organization, 93
    third party, 48
non-employee
    background check, 92
    user ID expiration, 281
non-enforcement, 32
non-production business transaction, 75
note taking, 47
notice fax cover sheet, 233
notification
    electronic, 347
    faxing sensitive information, 231
    integrity control failure, 120
    record requests, 422
    worker termination
        internal, 99
        third party, 100

number
    bank account, 207
    change, 193
    computer access, 193
    concealing customer accounts, 363
    credit card use, 364
    intelligence, 429
    policies, 19
    telephone testing, 396

O

objectives
    motivational, 26
    operational, 27
obsolete information, 85
offensive
    communications, 268
    electronic mail message, 112
    material removal, 237
office
    computer equipment, 245
    locking, 126
official documents, 85
off-shift information handling, 146
off-site
    equipment use approval, 145
    intellectual property development, 98
    paper storage, 182
    personnel rotation, 395
    system
        damage, 112
        loss, 112
online contract, 209
on-site backup file, 177
open two-category data classification, 67
operating
    documentation, 386
    procedures, 150
    system
        command access, 289
        configuration, 389
        production change
            approval, 155
            review, 155
        user authentication, 318
        version, 156
operational
    change control, 154
    objectives, 27
operator computer log
    contents, 182
    review, 182
opt-out provision, 212

orders, 240
organization
    cooperation, 45
    information
        release, 275
        request, 274
    name
        third party, 51
        use, 246
    non-disclosure agreement, 93
    policies, 26
    representations, 268
organizational information, 278
outbound
    electronic mail message footers, 226
    executable, 170
    Internet communications, 251
    software, 170
output
    data controls, 366
    sensitive, 81
outside network connection, 191
outsource
    contract approvals, 59
    financial statements, 60
    information access, 59
    production systems, 58
    security requirements, 56
override facility logs, 348
ownership
    content, 242
    file, 65
    information
        authority, 36
        intranet, 243
        responsibility, 62
    message, 65
    responsibility, 41

P

paper storage, 182
partner network agreement, 215
passes, 148
password
    access
        control, 270
        device proximity, 297
    attempts
        dial up, 310
        suspension, 314

authentication, 293
boot protection, 315
case, 321
change
    compromise
        system, 293
        user ID, 293
    confirmation, 291
    masking, 324
    required, 324
characters, 321
communication software, 297
customer service, 332
cyclical, 295
disclosure
    action, 296
    public, 297
    requirements, 293
display, 323
duress, 330
encryption
    storage, 325
    utilities, 368
faxing, 233
forgotten, 292
generation
    algorithm, 323
    materials, 323
history, 321
initial
    issuance, 290
    transmission, 290
internal network device, 312
interval synchronization, 324
length
    constraint, 320
    designation, 319
    role based, 320
logs, 343
network-connected computers, 320
permission, 296
printing, 323
readable, 325
reset, 292
retrieval, 326
re-use, 321
secret, 332
sending, 291
sharing, 299
software, 292
storage, 296
structure, 295

Information Security Policies Made Easy

system
  access control, 326
  different, 296
  generated
    issuance, 322
    pronounceable, 322
    seed, 322
    storage, 322
  Telnet connection, 195
  third party, 299
  tokens, 298
  vendor default, 326
  voice mail, 301
  writing down, 299
patches, 389
paths, 383
payment
  data encryption, 217
  information
    confirmation, 217
    disposal, 85
    encryption, 217
  token activation, 219
performance
  evaluation, 86
  monitoring
    group, 347
    information, 445
periodic surveillance sweep, 133
permissions, 271
personal
  computer
    firewall, 188
    sensitive information, 350
    software upgrades, 229
  data
    collection, 410
    disclosure, 421
    points, 436
    privacy, 436
    transfer, 433
    use, 433
  effects, 410
  file privacy, 419
  identification numbers, 298
  identifiers, 429
  information
    access
      authorization, 336
      written request, 416
    business functioning, 412
    changes, 438
    children, 413
    customer, 427
    disclosure, 424
    distribution, 414
    embedded, 428
    incorrect, 425
    purpose, 427
    retention, 405
    sharing, 432
  Internet
    access time, 441
    message disclaimer, 252
    service provider accounts, 240
    use, 440
  locking office, 126
  record
    handling, 426
    integrity, 426
    use, 426
  relationship competition, 99
  telephone
    long-distance call, 206
    use, 206
  time, 441
  use
    communications, 438
    computer, 438
    restrictions, 441
  user IDs, 299
  web pages, 258
personally-owned computer system, 139
personnel
  file access, 425
  information destruction, 200
  record distribution, 96
  rotation, 395
photographs, 85
physical
  access
    grantor list, 129
    sensitive information, 126
    terminated worker, 129
    third party, 124
    unauthorized, 128
  security
    faxing, 232
    plan, 124
  terminal security, 314
plaintext, 375
plan
  computer
    disaster recovery, 151
    emergency response, 157

contingency
  review, 397
    software conversion, 166
  information security, 40
policies
  about, 3
  adapting, 8
  advice, 30
  controls, 4
  coverage matrix, 11
  customization
    need, 29
    specifics, 25
  developing
    steps, 9
    time, 18
  disclaimers, 29
  document, 31
  establishing, 7
  evaluation, 34
  exceptions, 32
  framework, 10
  guidelines, 3
  importance, 5
  information security
    change, 107
    pamphlet, 106
  iterative development, 22
  length, 21
  non-compliance, 28
  non-enforcement, 32
  number, 19
  objectives
    motivational, 26
    operational, 27
  organization, 26
  privacy
    application, 422
    differences, 435
    related, 105
    relevance, 436
    reminder, 430
  procedures, 4
  quiz, 105
  review
    independent, 45
    internal, 34
  sample matrix, 13
  scope, 27
  searching, 25
  servers, 17
  standards, 3
  topic order, 24
  use, 33

political advocacy, 253
polygraph test, 90
portable
  computer
    backups, 235
    possession, 352
    storage, 351
    use
      approval, 349
      classified information, 350
  identification credentials, 317
ports, 313
position
  computer display screens, 245
  trust, 89
positive identification, 294
posting
  inappropriate, 254
  Internet, 255
  intranet, 241
  network, 256
power
  cable, 143
  conditioning equipment, 142
  supply, 142
powering down computers, 147
pranks, 112
prefixes, 67
premises, 202
preparing business contingency plans, 394
pre-processing backup, 179
presenting sensitive information, 78
preserving archives, 182
pretext personal data collection, 410
preventing copies, 81
preventive maintenance, 143
pricing, 53
printing information
  secret, 81
  sensitive, 80
privacy
  employee observance, 423
  expectations, 415
  impact review, 167
  information correspondent content, 422
  personal data, 436
  policy
    application, 422
    change notification, 435
    circumventing, 52
    distribution, 437
    relevance, 436
    reminder, 430
    summary, 435

Information Security Policies Made Easy

protection, 212
related
  policy, 105
  procedure, 105
rights waiver, 411
private
communications, 410
data, 417
  collection, 412
  system
    approval, 430
    opt out, 430
  use, 432
electronic mail, 222
examination, 437
information
  access
    background, 90
    logging, 427
    logs, 339
  collection
    approval, 412
    consent, 413
    methods, 415
    process, 411
    surreptitious, 413
  disclosure
    authorization, 411
    private, 418
    record details, 417
    record maintenance, 420
  identity, 436
  links
    approval, 429
    purpose, 429
  outsourcing disclosure, 421
  requirement explanation, 437
  sending, 230
  sharing, 420
key
  backups, 376
  digital
    certificate, 377
    signature, 376
  encryption transmission, 378
personal effects, 410
privilege
approval, 289
logs, 340
production business information, 334
restriction
  need to know, 287
  need to withhold, 287

revoking access, 33
system command
  accountability, 343
  traceability, 343
temporary worker, 46
termination, 282
use, 279
user ID
  activity logging, 342
  dormant, 284
  keystroke logs, 342
  limited, 288
  vendor supplied, 154
probationary period, 88
problem
analysis, 122
design reporting, 117
information
  retention, 410
  security resolution, 159
notification, 384
production system, 111
reporting
  alternative, 114
  authority, 115
  centralized, 119
  duty, 113
  formal, 183
  identity, 115
  interference, 114
  protection, 114
security, 362
unauthorized access, 159
procedure
back-off, 156
documented operating, 150
information security, 40
intrusion response, 158
manual, 395
privacy-related, 105
sensitive information destruction, 200
use, 33
process
backup, 177
computer assisted, 364
development, 5
encryption
  systems, 367
  users, 367
user, 150
procurement
hardware, 62
software, 62

product
  endorsement, 253
  evaluation, 359
  hazardous labels, 84
  information
    sensitive
      background check, 91
      intermediate, 79
    system, 143
  Internet representation, 253
  maturity, 278
  security, 37
  selection, 5
production
  application
    acceptance, 165
    documentation, 150
    information access, 335
    multi-user, 335
    system log contents, 338
  backup audits, 452
  business information
    access, 381
    modification, 361
    privileges, 334
  change
    program, 152
    reconstructability, 342
  computer system location, 137
  information
    change implementation, 388
    updates, 289
  input transactions, 359
  operating system change
    approval, 155
    review, 155
  operation access control, 385
  processing, 60
  programs, 382
  separation, 161
  software
    access paths, 383
    changes approvals, 387
  system
    change
      considerations, 385
      documentation, 386
    controls, 165
    documentation, 164
    input transaction authorization, 365
    Internet information, 257
    intranet access, 244
    problem, 111
    risk assessment, 44

    specific, 398
    storage media, 344
    training, 109
  transaction authorization, 153
program
  damage disclaimer, 32
  end-user applications, 230
  execution, 371
  loading, 174
  production, 382
  resource consumption, 382
  virus checking, 172
programming
  high-level languages, 357
  separation, 162
projects
  human safety issues, 384
  sensitive, 89
property
  intellectual
    developed off-site, 98
    rights, 95
  labels, 400
  pass, 148
  return, 101
  right, 93
proposals, 355
prospect mailing list, 213
prospective employee
  credit check, 87
  information
    necessity, 86
    reveal, 87
  lifestyle, 87
protection
  default copyright, 402
  digital certificate, 373
  electromagnetic radiation, 246
  encryption, 370
  equipment, 137
  information, 31
  network message, 186
  privacy, 212
  reporting
    problem, 114
    violation, 114
  software write, 173
  static electricity, 138
  trade secrets, 6
  water damage, 141
providing
  public network service, 193
  purchase receipts, 364
  unnecessary information, 435

public
    access
        active network ports, 312
        workstations, 248
    comments, 250
    communications, 277
    disclosure, 45
    discussions, 263
    electronic forums, 229
    image, 247
    inappropriate postings, 254
    information
        authorization, 277
        release, 275
    Internet server, 189
    key changes, 378
    network
        postings, 256
        providing service, 193
    password disclosure, 297
    releasing vulnerability information, 111
    representation approval, 268
    research, 262
    sensitive information exposure, 266
publicly-modifiable directory, 196
purchase
    information security solutions, 358
    receipts, 364

Q

quality archive storage media, 181
questionable
    events, 117
    system actions, 424
quiz, 105

R

racial harassment, 97
rack doors, 140
rating content, 212
read access, 271
readable passwords, 325
real-time external network connection, 189
reasonable personal use
    communications, 439
    computers, 439
reauthorizing user access privileges, 294
receipt
    information, 82
    purchase, 364
    secret information, 82
receiving third party information, 53
recompiling software, 386

reconciliation account, 219
record
    access authorization, 424
    change orders, 240
    correction, 153
    destruction
        approval, 408
        schedule, 409
    handling, 426
    identification, 406
    integrity, 426
    manipulations, 365
    personnel distribution, 96
    storage, 406
    system, 128
    telemarketing, 216
    use, 426
recording
    activity, 347
    equipment
        audio, 136
        video, 136
    Internet communication, 262
    sensitive information, 234
    technology, 269
    video conferences, 269
recovery
    computer disaster plan, 151
    encryption key, 379
redundant utility supplier, 142
reference materials, 9
reformed criminals, 92
registering Internet domain names, 186
regulation
    software, 270
    system, 398
rehiring involuntarily terminated workers, 88
rejected
    input
        transactions, 363
        validation, 366
    item handling, 359
related
    policies, 105
    procedures, 105
relationship
    competition, 99
    trusted host, 183
release
    computer storage media, 203
    information
        declassified, 83
        organization, 275
        public, 275

system documentation, 207
trade secrets, 254
used component, 145
relevant privacy policies, 436
reliable Internet information, 256
reminders, 430
remote
  access
    passwords, 308
    training, 105
  administration, 309
  connection scans, 184
  mirrored logs, 341
  system access controls, 308
remove
  identification badges, 104
  individuals, 431
  information
    secret, 202
    sensitive
      hardcopy, 211
      log, 202
      premises, 202
  media, 149
  offensive material, 237
  software, 154
repair staff confidentiality agreements, 47
report
  design problems, 117
  employee changes, 285
  identification badge, 129
  incident
    channel, 112
    severity, 113
  problem
    alternative, 114
    authority, 115
    centralized, 119
    duty, 113
    identity, 115
    interference, 114
    process, 183
    protection, 114
  questionable events, 117
  security
    third party, 116
    vulnerability, 120
  software malfunctions, 121
  status changes, 103
  system vulnerability, 119
  unauthorized activity, 116
  violation
    alternative, 114
    authority, 115

duty, 113
  external, 115
  identity, 115
  interference, 114
  protection, 114
viruses, 121
representation
  approval, 268
  Internet
    product, 253
    service, 253
  organization, 268
request
  information
    external, 276
    organization, 274
  unusual telephone operation, 206
requirements
  disaster support, 392
  emergency, 392
  password
    access, 281
    changes, 324
  security, 355
  system, 398
  user IDs, 281
research, 262
reset password, 292
resisting fire, 125
resolution
  grievance, 103
  information security problem, 159
  timings, 363
resource
  consumption
    excessive, 235
    program, 382
  information security, 38
response
  computer emergency
    plan, 157
    team
      organization, 157
      testing, 157
  procedure, 158
  unsolicited electronic mail messages, 225
responsibility
  content monitoring, 237
  custodian, 286
  delegating, 372
  incident management, 160
  information security
    tasks, 39
    workers, 110

key management, 380
third-party security, 50
training, 107
restoring
employee expectations, 394
files, 330
restricted area
terminated worker access, 129
working
hours, 135
single, 135
restrictions
information collection, 273
message content, 224
personal use, 441
retention
electronic mail messages, 221
file grouping, 74
hardware, 144
information
period, 406
personal, 405
sensitive, 409
terminated employee, 101
period, 340
schedule, 407
software, 144
retrieving passwords, 326
return
long-distance call, 206
property, 101
re-use
passwords, 321
software, 357
user IDs, 283
revealing information, 87
reversion, 395
review
annual declassification, 72
backup, 236
computer analysis, 161
copyrights, 404
electronic mail message
authority, 226
third-party, 219
independent, 45
information
backup, 178
security enforcement, 34
internal record changes, 366
Internet web pages, 259

intranet
content, 242
web pages, 243
privacy impact, 167
process, 15
production operating system change, 155
software, 386
trade secrets, 404
revoking access privileges, 33
right
free speech, 236
property
agreements, 93
intellectual, 95
waiver, 411
risk
assessment
production, 44
system, 451
third party, 37
contractor, 163
identifying, 46
significant, 36
room
deliveries, 137
unattended, 147
rotation
job, 160
personnel, 395

S

safety
information, 97
interruption, 362
issues, 384
sales department electronic mail, 227
sample matrix, 13
scanning
downloaded software, 171
electronic mail messages, 225
remote connection, 184
software, 169
virus, 173
schedule
archival storage, 407
data retention, 407
declassification, 71
scope, 27
screening active content, 195
searching, 25
second job
disclosure, 102
permission, 102

secondary computer center door, 125
secret
  archive declassification, 73
  data
    media exposure, 69
    transmission, 204
    transportation, 204
  disclosure, 75
  document
    logging movement, 83
    sequence numbers, 83
  faxing
    encrypted, 232
    passwords, 233
  information
    access, 337
    compression, 369
    delivering, 82
    dissemination, 336
    electronic mail, 220
    encryption, 204, 369
    equipment, 134
    international transport
      authorization, 211
      security, 211
    intranet, 261
    printing, 81
    receipt, 82
    removal, 202
    sending, 264
    speaker phones, 233
    system isolation, 338
    third-party delivery, 210
    transmitting, 265
    transportable computers, 349
    travel, 210
    web, 261
    wireless, 266
  passwords, 332
  systems, 416
  trade, 68
  user IDs, 332
secure
  communications, 133
  computer
    facility doors, 134
    system, 133
  identification badges, 104
  information
    containers, 199
    critical, 132
    sensitive
      activities, 132
      authorization, 83

security
  administrator
    backup, 64
    designated, 63
  breach, 116
  cabling, 143
  classes, 108
  compromising, 273
  configuration, 183
  considerations, 385
  consistent, 8
  contact information, 262
  control
    design, 364
    enforceability, 34
    usability, 279
  creating tools, 279
  digital certificate private key, 377
  embedded, 355
  fix, 156
  functionality, 358
  impact statement, 166
  independent systems, 280
  information
    alert system, 158
    impact analysis, 166
    problem resolution, 159
    user acceptance, 167
  Internet
    commerce server, 214
    computer query, 254
  intranet connection criteria, 192
  measures
    network, 197
    third party, 54
  physical terminal, 314
  plan, 124
  policy, 55
  problems, 362
  product maturity, 278
  products, 37
  requirements
    identification, 355
    outsourcing contracts, 56
    third-party contracts, 50
  secret information transport, 211
  sensitive information, 207
  services, 37
  solutions, 358
  system
    compromise, 327
    development life cycle, 357
    status tools, 328

Information Security Policies Made Easy

testing tools, 442
third-party responsibility, 50
tool screening, 327
violation retention, 410
vulnerability reporting, 120
weaknesses, 120
sender contact information, 220
sending
information
confidential, 230
private, 230
secret, 264
sensitive, 264
passwords, 291
unsolicited electronic mail messages, 225
sensitive
application system logs, 338
document copies, 81
fax
cover sheet, 231
intermediaries, 231
notification, 231
physical security, 232
presence, 231
unencrypted, 232
information
access, 337
accountability, 80
answering machines, 268
area content, 203
changes, 362
controversial, 276
copies, 235
copying, 79
covering, 147
declassification, 72
destruction
box, 200
methods, 198
destruction procedure, 200
disclosure, 110
downloading
approval, 205
controls, 205
erase, 198
handling, 53
hardcopy removal, 211
lending, 351
loss, 110
material, 200
personal computers, 350
physical access, 126
presenting, 78
printing, 80

product
background check, 91
intermediate, 79
public exposure, 266
read access, 271
recording, 234
removal
log, 202
premises, 202
retention
assignment, 405
destruction, 409
securing
activities, 132
authorization, 83
security, 207
sending, 264
small computers, 349
storage, 234
locked, 147
media, 84
telephone discussions, 265
tracking, 79
transfer, 211
transmission, 254
transportable computers, 350
waste, 80
write access, 271
output, 81
projects, 89
sensitivity
label
hardcopy, 77
unknown, 76
separation
activities, 333
data, 333
development, 161
duty
information, 160
instruction, 161
information technology duties, 162
production, 161
programming, 162
testing, 162
sequence numbers, 83
server
anonymous, 370
commerce
firewall, 188
storage, 213
Internet
command response, 260
commerce security, 214

intranet approval, 244
public Internet, 189
web storage, 213
service
  communication invoice, 154
  computer invoice, 154
  endorsement, 253
  enhanced, 214
  hazardous labels, 84
  Internet representation, 253
  network message protection, 186
  new, 214
  providing public network, 193
  security, 37
sessions, 150
severity, 113
sexual harassment, 97
shared
  badge access, 127
  directory systems, 191
  firewalls, 58
  information
    marketing, 275
    personal, 432
    private, 420
  passwords, 299
  servers, 58
shoplifting tag, 148
shredder, 199
sign
  communication center, 134
  computer center, 134
signature
  binding, 265
  electronic mail, 228
simultaneous sessions, 318
single sign-on, 317
siting equipment, 137
smoking, 137
software
  access paths, 383
  agreement, 209
    third party, 208
  authorized copies, 401
  big fixes, 389
  change approvals, 387
  classification, 61
  command line interpreter, 272
  conversion contingency plans, 166
  copies, 401
  copyright notices, 400
  current virus, 172
  development source, 398

diagnostic, 328
digital signatures, 367
distribution, 208
documentation
  features, 388
  functions, 388
downloading
  Internet
    end users, 175
    mirror site, 175
  prevention, 169
duplication, 402
escrow
  third party, 399
  verification, 399
essential, 73
failure, 361
feedback, 361
file encryption, 367
installation
  vendor provided, 389
  virus, 170
integrity statements, 390
languages, 390
licensing
  agreement reviews, 400
  evidence, 401
maintenance, 387
malfunction reports, 121
master copy, 176
migration, 380
outbound, 170
passwords, 292
patches, 389
procurement, 62
recompilation, 386
removing, 154
retention, 144
re-use, 357
review, 386
scanning
  approval, 169
  download, 171
specifications, 356
system utilities, 329
testing
  external, 386
  information, 381
  responsibility, 162
  verification, 382
third party
  access, 390
  development, 391

tools
    approval, 390
    specific, 398
unauthorized
    copies, 402
    copyright, 401
unnecessary, 385
update background push, 174
upgrades
    personal computers, 229
    process, 389
uploading, 256
user installation, 174
version, 155
write protection, 173
software regulation, 270
solutions, 358
source
    data deletion, 369
    document retention
        period, 407
        requirements, 407
    electronic marketing material, 220
speaker phones, 233
special
    privileged users, 288
    system privileges, 288
specifications, 356
speed dial, 232
staff privileges, 381
staffing computer centers, 135
standards, 40
statements, 166
static electricity protection, 138
status
    changes
        reporting, 103
        users, 285
        workers, 37
    disclosure, 419
    report investigations, 448
stock
    employee transactions, 97
    option loss, 123
storage
    archive
        directory, 180
        media
            period, 181
            quality, 181
            testing, 181
        preservation, 182

backup media
    protection, 179
    units, 180
commerce server, 213
computer media release, 203
customer financial information, 260
data examination, 443
digital signature key, 377
disk encryption, 205
electronic mail messages, 222
encryption key
    device, 377
    media, 378
information
    mixed classified, 198
    sensitive, 147
media
    data classifications, 70
    destruction certificate, 209
    information, 84
off site, 182
passwords, 296
production system, 344
retention schedule, 407
system utilities, 329
temporary, 365
vital records, 406
web server, 213
strength, 125
strip shredder, 199
structure
    changes, 434
    passwords, 295
style guide, 245
summary, 435
supervision, 131
supply
    power, 142
    redundant utilities, 142
support, 6
surface erasing
    existence, 267
    use, 267
surreptitious information collecting, 413
surveillance sweeps, 133
suspected system intrusion, 157
suspended input validation, 366
suspense file, 363
synchronization
    clocks, 348
    devices, 238

system
  access
    control passwords, 326
    request authorization, 284
  administrator
    eradicating virus, 168
    user IDs, 288
  architecture, 340
  assessments, 452
  attack disclosure, 116
  availability, 151
  browsing, 278
  capabilities, 334
  classification, 61
  commands, 334
  communications, 133
  computer
    dispersion, 139
    names, 74
    personally owned, 139
  configuration
    requirements, 164
    template, 167
  design, 15
  development
    conventions, 383
    end user, 165
    life cycle, 357
    proposals, 355
  direct inward access implementation, 239
  documentation release, 207
  electronic mail, 227
  embedded security, 355
  encryption process approval, 367
  expertise, 153
  financial, 140
  functionality, 384
  host-based intrusion detection, 188
  implementation, 163
  in-coming dial-up calls, 310
  independent security, 280
  information
    control disclosure, 201
    department visitor, 131
    product, 143
  integrity checking, 171
  interconnection, 163
  interface, 196
  Internet commerce, 140
  interruption, 362
  intrusion detection approval, 187
  log

    archives, 341
    disclosure, 335
    modification controls, 343
    protection, 344
    review, 345
    rotation, 341
  logon banner, 316
  monitoring tools, 345
  network access, 168
  off-site
    damage, 112
    loss, 112
  operating version, 156
  penetration, 454
  private data opt out, 430
  privilege
    granting, 290
    special, 288
    use, 279
  problem notification, 384
  production
    computer location, 137
    controls, 165
    documentation, 164
    problem, 111
    specific, 398
    training, 109
  record, 128
  recovery, 397
  risk assessments, 451
  securing computers, 133
  security tools
    status, 328
    testing, 442
  shared directory, 191
  software
    installation, 389
    utility use, 329
  suspected intrusion, 157
  testing, 380
  utility storage, 329
  virus test, 170
  vulnerability
    exploitation, 111
    reporting, 119
system-generated passwords
  issuance, 322
  pronounceable, 322
  seed, 322
  storage, 322

T

target audience, 25
tasks, 39
team
  organization, 157
  testing, 157
technical
  key job, 151
  staff privileges, 381
  training, 109
technology
  asset inventory, 61
  evaluation, 164
  separating information, 162
telecommunications
  cable, 143
  data entry operators, 352
  environment inspection, 354
  equipment, 353
  information security procedures, 354
  security requirements, 353
  working environment, 353
telemarketing record, 216
telephone
  books, 49
  calls
    collect, 238
    credit card, 239
    information service, 238
    third-party bill-to, 238
  cellular, 265
  conference use, 269
  conversation monitoring, 446
  cordless, 265
  facilities, 248
  information disclosure, 263
  number testing, 396
  personal
    long-distance call, 206
    use, 206
  sensitive information discussion, 265
  unusual request, 206
Telnet connection password, 195
template, 167
temporary
  badge, 127
  files, 365
  storage, 365
  worker
    access, 48
    privileges, 46

termination
  access privileges, 282
  disclosure, 418
  duress, 123
  employee information retention, 101
  immediate, 123
  involuntary
    escort, 100
    rehiring, 88
    relieving duty, 100
  property return, 101
  responsibility, 450
  worker
    access
      physical, 129
      restricted area, 129
    files, 286
    notification
      internal, 99
      third party, 100
terrorist messages, 249
testing
  archive storage media, 181
  contingency plan, 396
  emotional stability, 91
  honesty, 91
  information
    system controls, 300
    verification, 382
  intranet content, 242
  polygraph, 90
  separation, 162
  software
    external, 386
    information, 381
    responsibility, 162
    verification, 382
  system, 380
  telephone number, 396
  virus system, 170
third party
  access
    internal systems, 49
    physical, 124
    remote, 47
    terms, 50
  agreements
    confidentiality, 404
    controls, 54
    non-disclosure, 48
  bill-to calls, 238
  contracts, 50
  electronic mail message review, 219
  information

confidential, 336
disclosure, 274
private, 417
proprietary, 336
receiving, 53
secret, 210
transfer, 51
meetings, 267
networks, 306
organization name, 51
password use, 299
pricing, 53
responsibility, 55
security
breach reporting, 116
measures, 54
policy, 55
responsibility, 50
software
access, 390
agreement, 208
development, 391
distribution, 208
supervision, 131
systems, 54
trademarks, 403
user IDs, 46
three-category data classification, 66
time
dependent access control, 331
sensitive information, 234
training, 107
token activation, 219
tools
information system, 328
integrity assessment, 186
mature development, 356
monitoring, 345
security, 279
software
approval, 390
specific, 398
topic order, 24
touring computer facility, 133
tracing errors, 362
tracking
equipment, 64
sensitive information, 79
trade armaments, 444
trade secret
declaration, 68
disclosure, 75
Internet release, 254

intranet, 248
protecting, 6
review, 404
trademarks, 403
trade-offs, 29
trading partner network agreement, 215
traffic control, 184
training
basic, 106
computer access, 108
cross, 152
documentation, 386
information security, 106
Internet, 106
production system, 109
remote access, 105
responsibility, 107
technical, 109
time, 107
transaction
business, 75
computerized, 216
double keying, 360
initiations, 319
international Internet business, 215
log destruction, 405
originator, 360
production
authorization, 153
input, 359
rejecting input, 363
stock, 97
transfer
biometric information, 415
downloaded files, 256
information
customer, 433
private, 417
sensitive, 211
third party, 51
Internet, 245
intranet, 245
private data, 417
worker, 103
transmission
data, 373
encryption key
channels, 373
private, 378
information
concealed, 185
hardcopy, 265
secret, 204
sensitive, 254

transportable computers
   information
      secret, 349
      sensitive, 350
   travel, 350
transporting secret data, 204
trap entrance, 127
travel
   employee, 95
   secret information, 210
trust
   agreements, 52
   position, 89
trusted host relationship, 183
two-category data classification
   closed, 67
   open, 67
two-factor user authentication, 308
type list, 434

U

unacceptable use, 440
unattended
   network systems, 302
   room, 147
unauthorized
   access problem, 159
   activity, 116
   copies
      data, 402
      software, 402
   copyrighted
      information, 401
      material, 402
      software, 401
   physical access, 128
undetected information alteration, 35
unencrypted faxing, 232
unescorted visitor, 131
unexpected electronic mail attachments, 229
unique
   electronic mail accounts, 301
   user ID
      required, 281
      system, 282
unknown sensitivity label, 76
unnecessary
   information, 435
   software, 385
unofficial web pages, 257

unsolicited
   electronic mail
      messages, 224
      response, 225
      sending, 225
   Internet information, 257
unusual telephone operation request, 206
update
   background push software, 174
   databases, 335
upgrades
   process, 389
   software, 229
uploading software, 256
usability, 279
use
   cellular telephone, 135
   couriers, 82
   credit card
      numbers, 364
      physical, 269
   information
      consistency, 31
      purpose, 31
   investigators, 45
   off-site equipment, 145
   organization name, 246
   policies, 25
   portable computers, 350
   recording technology, 269
   telephone
      conference, 269
      personal, 206
used component release, 145
user
   acceptance, 167
   access
      capability, 333
      privileges, 294
   authentication
      dial up, 309
      key, 379
      operating system, 318
      two factor, 308
   awareness, 342
   encryption process approval, 367
   file, 150
   generated classification labels, 69
   initiated security event logs, 339
   installing software, 174

monitoring
  logging, 346
  notification, 346
privileged, 288
privileges, 334
process, 150
session, 150
status changes, 285
user ID
  anonymous, 280
  approval, 289
  database, 290
  expiration
    Internet-accessible computers, 286
    non-employee, 281
    user, 282
  forms, 285
  generic, 283
  logging, 342
  multiple, 284
  naming convention, 283
  non-anonymous, 281
  personal, 299
  privileged
    limited, 288
    vendor supplied, 154
  privileges, 284
  re-use, 283
  secret, 332
  system administrator, 288
  third party, 46
  unique, 282
utility supplier, 142

V

vacated equipment area, 136
vacation, 101
validation
  controls, 362
  external party identification, 210
  input data, 359
  intranet information, 242
  rejected, 366
  suspended, 366
valuable information
  access, 337
  changes, 362
  copies, 235
vendor
  default passwords, 326
  financial review, 50
  privileged user ID, 154
  relationship disclosure, 52

verification
  account calculation, 213
  software escrow, 399
version
  operating system, 156
  software, 155
victim data, 111
video recording
  conferences, 269
  equipment, 136
violation
  analysis, 122
  consequence, 122
  law, 33
  logging, 342
  report, 115
  reporting
    alternative, 114
    authority, 115
    duty, 113
    identity, 115
    interference, 114
    protection, 114
  security, 342
virus
  certification decal, 171
  checking
    decrypting file, 173
    program, 172
  computer involvement, 173
  current software, 172
  eradication
    computer, 168
    system administrator, 168
  multiple screening package, 171
  scanning backup file, 173
  software installation, 170
  suspected, 121
  test system, 170
visitor
  data center, 131
  escorting
    after hours, 130
    work hours, 130
  identification, 130
  information system department, 131
  unescorted, 131
vital record
  identification, 406
  storage, 406

voice
  critical networking device, 197
  mail
    broadcast, 240
    group, 241
    message storage, 239
    password construction, 301
vulnerability
  advisory, 158
  disclosure, 121
  discussion, 120
  identification
    assessment, 454
    software, 327
  information
    public release, 111
    system disclosure, 110
  security reporting, 120
  system
    exploitation, 111
    reporting, 119

W

waiver, 411
walk-up network connections, 311
warehouse input labels, 73
waste copies, 80
water damage protection, 141
weaknesses, 120
wealth increase, 93
web
  bugs
    approval, 185
    Internet, 247
  page
    defacement, 260
    Internet design, 258
    intranet review, 243
    management committee, 258
    personal, 258
    review, 259
    unofficial, 257
  secret information, 261
  server
    firewalls, 314
    storage, 213

site
  content changes, 260
  file archive, 180
  HTML, 261
  Internet, 371
  similar names, 255
wireless
  network
    configuration, 196
    gateway, 196
  transmitting secret information, 266
Wood, Charles Cresson, 681
work
  agreement, 108
  restricted area
    hours, 135
    single, 135
  sites, 351
worker
  background checks, 90
  bonding, 88
  customer, 102
  performance, 419
  polygraph test, 90
  probationary period, 88
  status changes, 37
  terminated, 286
  termination
    notification
      internal, 99
      third party, 100
    physical access, 129
    rehiring, 88
    responsibility, 450
    restricted areas, 129
  transfer, 103
workplace hazard, 97
workstation
  diskless, 234
  firewall, 188
  key lock, 139
  modems, 306
  public access, 248
write
  access, 271
  software protection, 173
writing down passwords, 299